Contents

HOW TO USE THIS BOOK

Doing psychology consists of three skills: describing what you know, applying your knowledge and analysing/evaluating this knowledge. This applies to all students – AS students and A level students.

From page 387 onwards we give you an overview of practice questions, which will help you to see why we have designed our spreads as they are.

Describing what you know

Assessment objective 1 (AO1)
is concerned with your ability to report detailed descriptions of psychological knowledge and demonstrate your understanding of this knowledge.

On most spreads in this book we have presented all the AO1 material on the left-hand side.

We have divided the text up with subheadings to help you organise your understanding. Each heading should act as a cue for material to recall and matches the material in the summary at the end of each chapter.

Applying your knowledge

Assessment objective 2 (AO2)
is concerned with being able to apply your psychological knowledge.

It is a really good way to assess whether you do understand psychological knowledge.

On every spread we usually have two or three '**Apply it**' questions which give you a chance to practise this AO2 skill of application in relation to both concepts and research methods.

Research methods topics are covered in Chapter 3 but we have given you a chance to apply them throughout the book.

Analysing and evaluating

Assessment objective 3 (AO3)
is concerned with your ability to evaluate the concepts and studies you have learned about.

On most spreads in this book we have presented the AO3 material on the right-hand side.

Generally we have focused on three criticisms, each one clearly elaborated to demonstrate the skill of evaluation.

Three criticisms is sufficient for *reasonable* performance. For *excellent* performance you may need to add the **evaluation extra**. It is better to do three that are well elaborated than five that are mediocre. It is best to do five that are elaborated.

What is an 'assessment objective'?

It is something that is used to assess your ability.

You can demonstrate what you know by describing it but there is more to knowledge than that. There is the further skill of being able to use your knowledge in new situations (applying your knowledge). And a further skill is to be able to judge the value of your knowledge (evaluation).

All three of these skills are part of your studies.

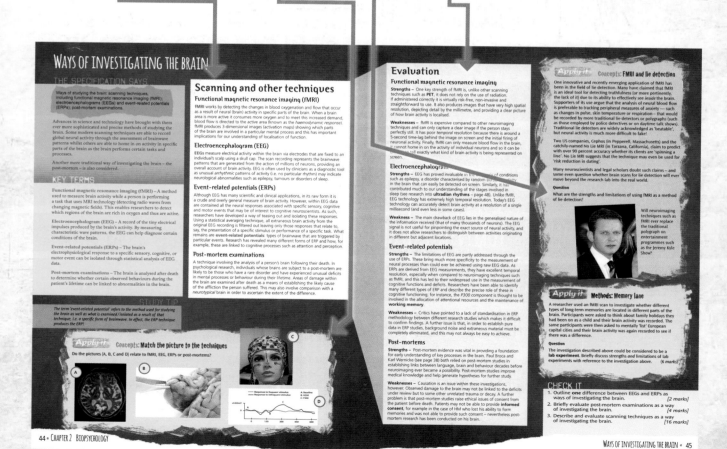

AQA
PSYCHOLOGY
FOR A LEVEL
YEAR 2

Cara Flanagan
Dave Berry
Matt Jarvis
Rob Liddle

Illuminate
Publishing

QA4

Published in 2016 by Illuminate Publishing Ltd,
P.O. Box 1160, Cheltenham, Gloucestershire GL50 9RW

Orders: Please visit www.illuminatepublishing.com
or email sales@illuminatepublishing.com

British Library Cataloguing in Publication Data

A catalogue record for this book is available from the
British Library

ISBN 978-1-908682-41-3

Printed in the UK by Cambrian Printers, Aberystwyth

07.17

The publisher's policy is to use papers that are natural,
renewable and recyclable products made from
wood grown in sustainable forests. The logging and
manufacturing processes are expected to conform to the
environmental regulations of the country of origin.

Every effort has been made to contact copyright holders
of material produced in this book. If notifed, the publisher
will be pleased to rectify any errors or omissions at the
earliest opportunity.

Editor: Geoff Tuttle

Design and layout: Nigel Harriss

Approval message from AQA

This textbook has been approved by AQA for use with
our qualification. This means that we have checked that it
broadly covers the specification and we are satisfied with
the overall quality. Full details of our approval process can
be found on our website.

We approve textbooks because we know how important
it is for teachers and students to have the right resources
to support their teaching and learning. However, the
publisher is ultimately responsible for the editorial control
and quality of this book.

Please note that when teaching the Psychology A level
course (7181; 7182), you must refer to AQA's specification
as your definitive source of information. While this book
has been written to match the specification, it cannot
provide complete coverage of every aspect of the course.

A wide range of other useful resources can be found on the
relevant subject pages of our website: www.aqa.org.uk.

A LEVEL COURSE:

A level

- There are three papers.
- Each paper is 2 hours and 96 marks in total.
- Each paper is worth 33.3% of the final A level mark.

Paper 1 Introductory Topics in Psychology

Each section is worth 24 marks. All questions are compulsory.
Section A: Social influence
Section B: Memory
Section C: Attachment
Section D: Psychopathology

Paper 2 Psychology in Context

*Sections A and B are worth 24 marks, C is worth 48 marks. All
questions are compulsory.*
Section A: Approaches in psychology
Section B: Biopsychology
Section C: Research methods

Paper 3 Issues and Options in Psychology

*Each section is worth 24 marks. Section A is compulsory,
Sections B, C and D contain three topics each and students
select one from each section.*
Section A: Issues and Debates in Psychology
Section B: Relationships, Gender or Cognition and
Development
Section C: Schizophrenia, Eating Behaviour or Stress
Section D: Aggression, Forensic Psychology or Addiction

The topics highlighted in red are covered in our Year 1 book.

Research methods Also covered in the Year 1 book is the AS content for research
methods.

Note that a minimum of 25% of the overall assessment will assess skills in relation to
research methods.

Extra features on each spread

What the specification says

The spread begins (top left) with an excerpt from the specification showing you what is covered on the spread. There is also a brief analysis of what the specification entry means.

Definition of specification terms

The specification terms are explained, mirroring what you might be expected to know if you were asked to explain the terms. These key terms are emboldened in blue in the text.

Other important words are emboldened in the text and explained in the **glossary**, which forms part of the index.

Study tips

This book has been written by very experienced teachers and subject experts. When there is room they give you some of their top tips about the skills necessary to develop your understanding of psychology. They may also include pointers about typical misunderstandings.

Check it

A sample of practice questions to help you focus on how you will be using the material on the spread.

The final question is an extended writing question. A level students need to answer 16-mark questions. Extended writing skills are discussed on pages 396–397.

Student digital book

A digital version of this student book is also available if your school has access to our Digital Book Bundle of student and teacher resources. You can view this digital version via a tablet or computer at school, home or on the bus – wherever it suits you.

There are extra features in the student digital book that support your studies. For every spread in this book there are:

- **Lifelines**: Very straightforward, easy-to-digest key descriptive points for the spread topic.
- **Extensions**: Extra information, studies or activities to challenge and stretch you further.
- **Web links** to YouTube videos or other sites.
- **Answers** to the Apply it and Evaluation extra questions in this book (invaluable!).
- **Quizzes**: Interactive, self-marking quizzes that help to check and reinforce your understanding of a topic.
- **Practice questions**: Extra questions to help you practise your skills.

Need a lifeline? The SDB is your answer.

Extra features in each chapter

Chapter introduction

Each chapter begins with discussion points that might help you start thinking about the topic.

Chapter summary

Each chapter ends with a useful spread summarising the key points from each spread.

These summaries should help you revise. Look at each key point and see what you can remember. Look back at the spread to remind yourself. Each time you do this you should remember more.

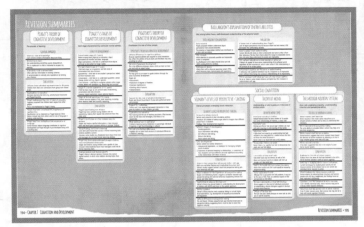

Practical corner

Questions on research methods account for a minimum of 25% of the assessment, therefore you should devote a lot of time to understanding how psychologists conduct research. There is no better way to do this than being a researcher yourself. We offer some ideas for research activities and provide additional opportunities to practise mathematical skills.

Practice questions, answers and feedback

Learning how to produce effective question answers is a SKILL. On this spread in each chapter we look at some typical student answers to practice questions. The comments provided indicate what is good and bad in each answer.

Multiple-choice questions (MCQs)

Here's a chance to test your new-found knowledge. Questions on each spread in the chapter, with answers at the bottom right of each spread. Keep trying until you get 100%.

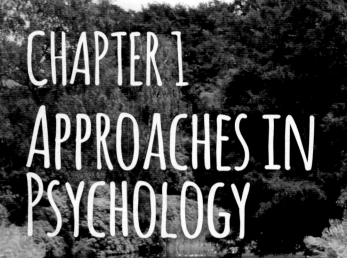

CHAPTER 1
APPROACHES IN PSYCHOLOGY

If you were a painter . . .	. . . how would you describe this picture?
	What features or aspects would be of most interest to you?
If you were a geographer . . .	. . . how would you describe this picture?
If you were a historian . . .	. . . how would you describe this picture?
If you were a mathematician . . .	. . . how would you describe this picture?
If you were a bee . . .	. . . how would you describe this picture?
You are a psychologist . . .	How would you describe this picture?

Just as this picture could be described in different ways by different people (or insects!), so different psychologists approach the study of human beings in different ways.

In this chapter, we explore some of the key approaches in psychology and their suggestions as to how we should best investigate and understand human behaviour and experience.

First, however, we chart the origins of psychology, from its early beginnings, through to the present day.

Chapter contents

ORIGINS OF PSYCHOLOGY

Origins of psychology: Wundt, introspection and the emergence of psychology as a science.

The idea of psychology as a distinct branch of study in its own right is generally dated at around 1880 when the first experimental lab was established.

That said, the philosophical roots of psychology stretch back much earlier than this. We shall consider these early roots as well as chart the emergence of psychology as a scientific discipline.

KEY TERMS

Psychology – The scientific study of the human mind and its functions, especially those functions affecting behaviour in a given context.

Science – A means of acquiring knowledge through systematic and objective investigation. The aim is to discover general laws.

Introspection – A systematic method used to study the mind by breaking up conscious awareness into basic structures of thoughts, images and sensations.

Psychology's early philosophical roots

René Descartes (1596–1650)

Descartes, a French philosopher, suggested that the mind and body are independent from each other – a philosophical stance that came to be known as **Cartesian dualism**. Although this view has since been challenged, it suggested that the mind could be an object of study in its own right. Descartes demonstrated his own existence with the famous quote 'I think therefore I am'.

John Locke (1632–1704)

Locke proposed **empiricism**, the idea that all experience can be obtained through the senses, and that human beings inherit neither knowledge nor instincts. This view would later form the basis of the **behaviourist approach** that the world can be understood by investigating external events that are observed and measured.

Charles Darwin (1809–1882)

Central to Darwin's **evolutionary theory** is the notion that all human and animal behaviour has changed over successive generations, so that the individuals with stronger, more **adaptive** genes survive and reproduce, and the individuals with weaker genes do not survive and reproduce. Thus, these weaker genes are 'weeded out' (**survival of the fittest**).

The assumption that many human behaviours, such as social behaviour, have evolved due to their adaptive value is deeply rooted in many areas of psychology, especially the **biological approach**.

Wundt and introspection

Wundt's lab

The first ever lab dedicated to psychological enquiry was opened by Wilhelm Wundt in Leipzig, Germany in 1879. The objective Wundt set himself was to document and describe the nature of human consciousness. This pioneering method came to be known as **introspection**, and involved Wundt and his co-workers recording their own conscious thoughts, with the aim of breaking these down into their constituent parts. Isolating the structure of consciousness in this way is called **structuralism**.

Controlled methods

This early attempt to investigate the mind might be regarded by many as naïve, but some of the methods and techniques Wundt and his co-workers used would nevertheless be recognised as 'scientific' today. All introspections were recorded under strictly controlled conditions using the same stimulus every time (such as a ticking metronome). The same **standardised instructions** were issued to all participants, and this allowed procedures to be repeated (**replicated**) every single time. Thus, Wundt's work was significant in that it marked the separation of the modern *scientific* psychology from its broader philosophical roots.

What we're gonna do right now is go back...back in time

1900s
Sigmund Freud publishes *The interpretation of dreams*, and the **psychodynamic approach** is established. Freud emphasised the influence of the unconscious mind on behaviour, alongside development of his person-centred therapy: **psychoanalysis**. He argued that physical problems could be explained in terms of conflicts within the mind.

1879
Wilhelm Wundt opens the first experimental psychology lab in Germany, and psychology emerges as a distinct discipline in its own right.

17th century – 19th century
Psychology is a branch of the broader discipline of philosophy. If psychology has a definition during this time it is best understood as **experimental philosophy**.

The emergence of psychology as a science

Watson and the early behaviourists

By the beginning of the 20th century, the scientific status and value of introspection was being questioned by many, most notably the behaviourist John B. Watson (1913). Watson's main problem with introspection was that it produced data that was subjective, in that it varied greatly from person to person, so it became very difficult to establish general principles. Watson was also highly critical of introspection's focus on 'private' mental processes and proposed that a truly scientific psychology should restrict itself only to studying phenomena that could be observed and measured. Thus, the behaviourist approach was born, and with it the emergence of psychology as a science.

Scientific approach

Watson (1913), and later Skinner (1953), brought the language, rigour and methods of the natural sciences into psychology. The behaviourist focus on the scientific processes involved in learning, alongside the use of carefully controlled **lab experiments**, would go on to dominate the discipline for the next five decades.

The legacy of behaviourism can still be observed today. Many modern psychologists continue to rely on the **experimental method** as part of their research and practices. However, the scope of this research has broadened considerably since the behaviourists first studied learning in the lab. Following the cognitive revolution of the 1960s, the study of mental processes is now seen as a legitimate and highly scientific area within psychology. Although mental processes remain 'private', cognitive psychologists are able to make inferences about how these work on the basis of lab tests.

The biological approach also makes use of experimental data. Researchers within this area have taken advantage of recent advances in technology to investigate physiological processes as they happen, including live activity in the brain using sophisticated **scanning** techniques such as **fMRI** and **EEG**. Suffice to say that, even though the scientific method is still a major cornerstone of psychology, it has come a long way since its early beginnings.

1913
John B. Watson writes *Psychology as the Behaviourist views it* and with **BF Skinner**'s later contributions establishes the **behaviourist approach**. The psychodynamic and behaviourist approaches dominate psychology for the next fifty years.

1950s
Carl Rogers and **Abraham Maslow** develop the **humanistic approach** – the so-called 'third force' in psychology, rejecting the views favoured by behaviourism and the psychodynamic approach that human behaviour was not determined by the individual. Humanistic psychologists emphasise the importance of self-determination and free will.

1960s
The cognitive revolution came with the introduction of the digital computer. This gave psychologists a metaphor for the operations of the human mind. The **cognitive approach** reintroduces the study of mental processes to psychology but in a much more scientific way than Wundt's earlier investigations.

1960s
Around the time of the cognitive revolution, **Albert Bandura** proposes the **social learning theory**. This approach draws attention to the role of cognitive factors in learning, providing a bridge between the newly established cognitive approach and traditional behaviourism.

1980s onwards
The **biological approach** begins to establish itself as the dominant scientific perspective in psychology. This is due to advances in technology that have led to increased understanding of the brain and the biological processes.

Eve of the 21st century
Towards the end of the last century, **cognitive neuroscience** emerges as a distinct discipline bringing together the cognitive and biological approaches. Cognitive neuroscience is built on the earlier computer models and investigates how biological structures influence mental states.

onwards

René Descartes, he thinks therefore he is.

CHECK IT

1. Explain what Wundt meant by *introspection*. [3 marks]
2. Define what is meant by the term *psychology*. [2 marks]
3. Briefly explain the emergence of psychology as a science. [4 marks]

THE LEARNING APPROACH: BEHAVIOURISM

The behaviourist approach including classical conditioning and Pavlov's research, operant conditioning, types of reinforcement and Skinner's research.

The behaviourist approach emerged at the beginning of the 20th century and became the dominant approach in psychology for half of that century.

It is also credited as being the driving force in the development of psychology as a scientific discipline.

KEY TERMS

Behaviourist approach – A way of explaining behaviour in terms of what is observable and in terms of learning.

Classical conditioning – Learning by association. Occurs when two stimuli are repeatedly paired together – an unconditioned (unlearned) stimulus (UCS) and a new 'neutral' stimulus. The neutral stimulus eventually produces the same response that was first produced by the unlearned stimulus alone.

Operant conditioning – A form of learning in which behaviour is shaped and maintained by its consequences. Possible consequences of behaviour include positive reinforcement, negative reinforcement or punishment.

Reinforcement – A consequence of behaviour that increases the likelihood of that behaviour being repeated. Can be positive or negative.

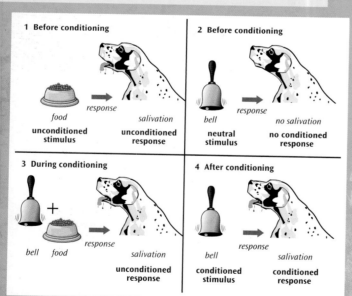

1 **Before conditioning**
food → response → salivation
unconditioned stimulus / unconditioned response

2 **Before conditioning**
bell → response → no salivation
neutral stimulus / no conditioned response

3 **During conditioning**
bell + food → response → salivation
unconditioned response

4 **After conditioning**
bell → response → salivation
conditioned stimulus / conditioned response

> *Often, students have difficulty explaining the distinction between negative reinforcement and punishment. Remember that negative reinforcement increases the likelihood of a behaviour being repeated (because it avoids an unpleasant consequence). In contrast, punishment decreases the likelihood of a behaviour being repeated (because of its unpleasant consequence).*

STUDY TIP

The behaviourist approach

Assumptions

The **behaviourist approach** is only interested in studying behaviour that can be observed and measured. It is not concerned with investigating mental processes of the mind. Early behaviourists such as John B. Watson (1913) rejected **introspection** as it involved too many concepts that were vague and difficult to measure. As a result, behaviourists tried to maintain more control and objectivity within their research and relied on **lab experiments** as the best way to achieve this.

Following Darwin, behaviourists suggested that the basic processes that govern learning are the same in all species. This meant that in behaviourist research, animals could replace humans as experimental subjects. Behaviourists identified two important forms of learning: **classical conditioning** and **operant conditioning**.

Classical conditioning – Pavlov's research

Classical conditioning is learning through *association* and was first demonstrated by Ivan Pavlov. Pavlov revealed that dogs could be conditioned to salivate to the sound of a bell if that sound was repeatedly presented at the same time as they were given food. Gradually, Pavlov's dogs learned to associate the sound of the bell (a stimulus) with the food (another stimulus) and would produce the salivation response every time they heard the sound.

Thus, Pavlov was able to show how a **neutral stimulus**, in this case a bell, can come to elicit a new learned response (**conditioned response**) through association (see diagram below left).

Operant conditioning – Skinner's research

BF Skinner (1953) suggested that learning is an active process whereby humans and animals operate on their environment. In operant conditioning there are three types of consequences of behaviour:

- **Positive reinforcement** is receiving a reward when a certain behaviour is performed; for example, praise from a teacher for answering a question correctly in class.
- **Negative reinforcement** occurs when an animal (or human) avoids something unpleasant. When a student hands in an essay so as not to be told off, the avoidance of something unpleasant is the negative reinforcement. Similarly, a rat may learn through negative reinforcement that pressing a lever leads to avoidance of an electric shock (below).
- **Punishment** is an unpleasant consequence of behaviour, for example being shouted at by the teacher for talking during a lesson. (Finding a way to avoid that would be negative reinforcement.)

Positive and negative reinforcement increase the likelihood that behaviour will be repeated. Punishment decreases the likelihood that behaviour will be repeated.

Apply it   Concepts: The Skinner Box

(A) Skinner conducted experiments with rats, and sometimes pigeons, in specially designed cages called *Skinner Boxes*. Every time the rat activated a lever (or pecked a disc in the case of the pigeon) within the box it was rewarded with a food pellet. After many repetitions the animal would continue to perform the behaviour.

(B) Skinner also showed how rats and pigeons could be conditioned to perform the same behaviour to avoid an unpleasant stimulus, for example an electric shock.

Questions

1. Which aspect of operant conditioning does paragraph A illustrate?
2. Which aspect of operant conditioning does paragraph B illustrate?

Evaluation

Scientific credibility

Behaviourism was able to bring the language and methods of the natural sciences into psychology by focusing on the measurement of observable behaviour within highly controlled lab settings. By emphasising the importance of scientific processes such as objectivity and **replication**, behaviourism was influential in the development of psychology as a scientific discipline, giving it greater credibility and status.

Real-life application

The principles of conditioning have been applied to a broad range of real-world behaviours and problems. For instance, operant conditioning is the basis of **token economy systems** that have been used successfully in institutions, such as prisons and psychiatric hospitals. These work by rewarding appropriate behaviour with tokens that can then be exchanged for privileges. For an example of how classical conditioning has been applied to the treatment of **phobias**, see Year 1 book page 144.

Treatments such as these have the advantage of requiring less effort from a patient because the patient doesn't have to think about their problem (as they do in 'talking therapies'). Such therapies are also suitable for patients who lack insight.

Mechanistic view of behaviour

From a behaviourist perspective, animals (including humans) are seen as *passive* and machine-like responders to the environment, with little or no conscious insight into their behaviour. Other approaches in psychology, such as the **social learning theory** and the **cognitive approach**, have emphasised the importance of mental events during learning.

These processes, which mediate between stimulus and response, suggest that people may play a much more *active* role in their own learning. This means that learning theory may apply less to human than to animal behavour.

Evaluation eXtra

Environmental determinism

The behaviourist approach sees all behaviour as determined by past experiences that have been conditioned. Skinner suggested that everything we do is the sum total of our reinforcement history. This ignores any possible influence that **free will** may have on behaviour. Skinner suggested that any sense of free will is simply an illusion. When something happens we impose a sense of having made the decision but, according to Skinner, our past conditioning history determined the outcome.

Consider: *How much of our behaviour do you think is determined by the environment and how much is the result of our own free will?*

Ethical and practical issues in animal experiments

Although experimental procedures such as the *Skinner Box* enabled behaviourists to maintain a high degree of control over their experimental 'subjects', many critics have questioned the ethics of conducting such investigations. The animals involved were exposed to stressful and aversive conditions, which may also have affected how they reacted to the experimental situation.

Consider: *Does what we learn from experimental studies such as the Skinner Box justify the way in which the animals were treated?*

Apply it

Concepts: Behaviourism and gambling

Skinner discovered that if an animal was rewarded every time it activated the lever or pecked the disc, the conditioned behaviour would quickly die out (become **extinct**) as the animal was *satiated* (full of food pellets!).

It was revealed that a **variable ratio** schedule would prolong the behaviour and was most resistant to extinction. Here, reinforcement is given after an unpredictable (variable) number of responses are produced, for example, every 10, 15, 12, etc., times the lever is pressed.

This has been applied to a number of forms of human behaviour, including gambling addiction.

Question

Explain how addiction to gambling could be explained by the principles above.

How could the urge to shoot zombies in a video game be explained by operant conditioning?

Apply it   Concepts: Behaviourism and gaming

David Wong (2008) has used Skinnerian principles to explain addiction to video games in his article *5 creepy ways video games are trying to get you addicted*. His argument is that the video game environment is a form of Skinner Box providing reinforcement contingencies and rewards that are dependent upon certain behaviours (killing zombies, shooting aliens, successful completion of the level, etc).

The use of the lever or joystick in many video games, it is argued, is analogous to the behaviour exhibited by the rat in the Skinner Box, and the success and addictive nature of many early video games, such as Pac-Man, is explained by the fact that the central character navigates its way around the screen literally munching on food pellets!

Question

How could video game addiction be explained using behaviourist principles?

CHECK IT

1. Explain **one** assumption of the behaviourist approach. [3 marks]
2. Outline **two** types of reinforcement as suggested by the behaviourist approach. [4 marks]
3. Outline and evaluate the behaviourist approach in psychology. [16 marks]

THE SPECIFICATION SAYS...

Social learning theory including imitation, identification, modelling, vicarious reinforcement, the role of mediational processes and Bandura's research.

Albert Bandura proposed social learning theory as a development of the behaviourist approach. He argued that classical and operant conditioning could not account for all human learning – there are important mental processes that mediate between stimulus and response.

KEY TERMS

Social learning theory – A way of explaining behaviour that includes both direct and indirect reinforcement, combining learning theory with the role of cognitive factors.

Imitation – Copying the behaviour of others.

Identification – When an observer associates themselves with a role model and wants to be like the role model.

Modelling – From the observer's perspective, modelling is imitating the behaviour of a role model. From the role model's perspective, modelling is the precise demonstration of a specific behaviour that may be imitated by an observer.

Vicarious reinforcement – Reinforcement which is not directly experienced but occurs through observing someone else being reinforced for a behaviour. This is a key factor in imitation.

Mediational processes – Cognitive factors (i.e. thinking) that influence learning and come between stimulus and response.

A child may want to imitate the dribbling skills of Lionel Messi (pictured), but may lack the necessary ability required to reproduce the behaviour.

Social learning theory

Assumptions

Albert Bandura agreed with the **behaviourists** that much of our behaviour is learned from experience. However, his **social learning theory (SLT)** proposed a different way in which people learn: through observation and **imitation** of others within a social context, thus *social* learning. SLT suggested that learning occurs directly, through classical and operant conditioning, but also *indirectly*.

Vicarious reinforcement

For indirect learning to take place an individual observes the behaviour of others. The learner may imitate this behaviour but, in general, imitation only occurs if the behaviour is seen to be rewarded (reinforced) rather than punished, i.e. **vicarious reinforcement** occurs (see box below). Thus, the learner observes a behaviour but most importantly observes the consequences of a behaviour.

The role of mediational processes

SLT is often described as the 'bridge' between traditional **learning theory** (previous spread) and the **cognitive approach** (next spread) because it focuses on how mental (cognitive) factors are involved in learning. These mental factors mediate (i.e. intervene) in the learning process to determine whether a new response is acquired. Four mental or **mediational processes** in learning were identified by Bandura:

1. *Attention* – the extent to which we notice certain behaviours.
2. *Retention* – how well the behaviour is remembered.
3. *Motor reproduction* – the ability of the observer to perform the behaviour.
4. *Motivation* – the will to perform the behaviour, which is often determined by whether the behaviour was rewarded or punished.

The first two of these relate to the *learning* of behaviour and the last two to the *performance* of behaviour. Unlike traditional behaviourism, the learning and performance of behaviour need not occur together. Observed behaviours may be stored by the observer and reproduced at a later time.

Identification

People (especially children) are much more likely to imitate the behaviour of people with whom they *identify*, called **role models**. This process is called **modelling**. A person becomes a role model if they are seen to possess similar characteristics to the observer and/or are attractive and have high status. Role models may not necessarily be physically present in the environment, and this has important implications for the influence of the media on behaviour (see facing page).

Apply it **Concepts: Do children imitate what they see?**

(A) Bandura *et al.* (1961) recorded the behaviour of young children who watched an adult behave in an aggressive way towards a Bobo doll (see right). The adult hit the doll with a hammer and shouted abuse at it.

When these children were later observed playing with various toys, including a Bobo doll, they behaved much more aggressively towards the doll and the other toys than those who had observed a non-aggressive adult.

Question: *Which aspect of SLT does study A illustrate?*

(B) Bandura and Walters (1963) showed videos to children where an adult behaved aggressively towards the Bobo doll. One group of children saw the adult praised for their behaviour (being told 'Well done'). A second group saw the adult punished for their aggression towards the doll, by being told off. The third group (**control group**) saw the aggression without any consequence.

When given their own Bobo doll to play with, the first group showed much more aggression, followed by the third group, and then the second.

Question: *Which aspect of SLT does study B illustrate?*

Evaluation

The importance of cognitive factors in learning

Neither classical nor operant conditioning can offer an adequate account of learning on their own. Humans and many animals store information about the behaviour of others and use this to make judgements about when it is appropriate to perform certain actions. As Bandura observed:

'Learning would be exceedingly laborious, not to mention hazardous, if people had to rely solely on the effects of their own actions to inform them what to do. From observing others one forms an idea of how new behaviours are performed, and on later occasions this coded information serves as a guide to action' (Bandura 1977).

As such, SLT provides a more comprehensive explanation of human learning by recognising the role of mediational processes.

Over-reliance on evidence from lab studies

Many of Bandura's ideas were developed through observation of young children's behaviour in **lab** settings. Lab studies are often criticised for their contrived nature where participants may respond to **demand characteristics**. It has been suggested, in relation to the Bobo doll research (bottom of facing page) that, because the main purpose of the doll is to strike it, the children were simply behaving in a way that they thought was expected.

Thus the research may tell us little about how children actually learn aggression in everyday life.

Underestimates the influence of biological factors

Bandura makes little reference to the impact of biological factors on social learning. One consistent finding in the Bobo doll experiments was that boys were often more aggressive than girls regardless of the specifics of the experimental situation. This may be explained by **hormonal** factors, such as differences in levels of **testosterone**, a hormone that is present in greater quantities in boys than girls and which is linked to increased aggressive behaviour.

This means that this important influence on behaviour is not accounted for in SLT.

Evaluation eXtra

Explains cultural differences in behaviour

Social learning theory has the advantage of being able to explain cultural differences in behaviour. Social learning principles can account for how children learn from other individuals around them, as well as through the media, and this can explain how cultural norms are transmitted through particular societies. This has proved useful in understanding a range of behaviours, such as how children come to understand their gender role.

Consider: *How could the learning of gender-appropriate behaviour be explained by social learning theory? Why would the biological approach have difficulty accounting for cultural differences in gender behaviour?*

Less determinist than the behaviourist approach

Bandura emphasised **reciprocal determinism**, in the sense that we are not merely influenced by our external environment, but we also exert an influence *upon it*, through the behaviours we choose to perform. This element of choice suggests that there is some **free will** in the way we behave.

Consider: *Why is this a less determinist position than that suggested by the behaviourist approach? In what way is this preferable?*

Apply it Concepts: **Video nasties**

Bandura's Bobo doll experiments have implications for the media – are children, and indeed some adults, influenced by the violence and aggression they see on television, in movies and video games?

This debate was brought into sharp focus in 1990 following the death of James Bulger, a toddler from Liverpool murdered by two ten-year-old boys. At the time it was argued by many UK newspapers that the child killers were inspired by the horror film *Child's Play 3*, and there were many calls for rules and censorship on such 'video nasties' to be tightened.

However, many researchers dispute the link between the media and real-life violence. For example, Guy Cumberbatch (2001) argues that supposed 'video nasties', of the type cited in the Bulger case, are much more likely to frighten children than to make them frightening (aggressive) towards others. He argues that isolated incidents such as these are better explained by other factors such as social deprivation, child abuse and early exposure to violence in the home.

Questions

1. Using social learning principles explain why media (such as violent videos) may potentially have a negative impact on children's behaviour.
2. How might the media vicariously reinforce violence and aggression?

Stanley Kubrick withdrew his controversial 1971 film *A Clockwork Orange* from British cinemas after a series of 'copycat' incidents based on scenes from the film.

STUDY TIP

If you need to evaluate social learning theory you might, for example, use the Bobo doll studies (or other studies) to illustrate key points. However, you should keep descriptions of the procedures and findings within these studies to a minimum and instead make it clear how the implications/ conclusions from these studies support (or contradict) key SLT concepts.

CHECK IT

1. Outline what is meant by the term *identification* in relation to the social learning theory approach. [2 marks]
2. Explain **one** limitation of the social learning theory approach. [3 marks]
3. Outline and evaluate the social learning theory approach. Refer to the behaviourist approach as part of your evaluation. [16 marks]

THE COGNITIVE APPROACH

The cognitive approach developed in the 1960s as a response to the behaviourists' failure to acknowledge mental processes. The development of the first computers gave cognitive psychologists a metaphor for describing mental processes.

KEY TERMS

Cognitive approach – The term 'cognitive' has come to mean 'mental processes', so this approach is focused on how our mental processes (e.g. thoughts, perceptions, attention) affect behaviour.

Internal mental processes – 'Private' operations of the mind such as perception and attention that mediate between stimulus and response.

Schema – A mental framework of beliefs and expectations that influence cognitive processing. They are developed from experience.

Inference – The process whereby cognitive psychologists draw conclusions about the way mental processes operate on the basis of observed behaviour.

Cognitive neuroscience – The scientific study of biological structures that underpin cognitive processes.

Misperceived song lyrics

Did Celine Dion really sing 'The hot dogs go on' on the 1997 Titanic movie soundtrack? A case of schema distorting our interpretations of sensory information, leading to perceptual errors.

The cognitive approach

Assumptions

In direct contrast to the **behaviourist approach**, the **cognitive approach** argues that **internal mental processes** can, and should, be studied scientifically. As a result, the cognitive approach has investigated those areas of human behaviour that were neglected by behaviourists, such as memory, perception and thinking. These processes are 'private' and cannot be observed, so cognitive psychologists study them *indirectly* by making **inferences** about what is going on inside people's minds on the basis of their behaviour.

Theoretical and computer models

One way to study internal processes is through the use of **theoretical models**. One important theoretical model is the **information processing approach**, which suggests that information flows through the cognitive system in a sequence of stages that include input, storage and retrieval, as in the **multi-store model** (see Year 1 book page 48).

The cognitive approach also uses **computer models**, where the mind is compared to a computer (the 'computer analogy') by suggesting that there are similarities in the way information is processed. These models use the concepts of a central processing unit (the brain), the concept of **coding** (to turn information into a useable format) and the use of 'stores' to hold information. Such computational models of the mind have proved useful in the development of 'thinking machines' or **artificial intelligence**.

The role of schema

Cognitive processing can often be affected by a person's beliefs or expectations, often referred to as **schema**. Schema are 'packages' of ideas and information developed through experience. They act as a mental framework for the interpretation of incoming information received by the cognitive system; for example, you have a schema for a chair – something with legs that you can sit on. That's a package of information learned through experience that helps you to respond to the object appropriately.

Babies are born with simple motor schema for innate behaviours such as sucking and grasping. For example, the grasping schema consists of moving a hand towards an object and shaping the hand around the object in co-ordination with visual input. (This is discussed on page 178.)

As we get older, our schema become more detailed and sophisticated. Adults have developed mental representations for everything from the concept of psychology to a schema for what happens in a restaurant or what a typical zombie looks like.

Schema enable us to process lots of information quickly and this is useful as a sort of mental short-cut that prevents us from being overwhelmed by environmental stimuli. However, schema may also distort our interpretations of sensory information, leading to perceptual errors (see examples on facing page).

The emergence of cognitive neuroscience

Cognitive neuroscience is the scientific study of the influence of brain structures on mental processes. Mapping brain areas to specific cognitive functions has a long history in psychology. As early as the 1860s Paul Broca had identified how damage to an area of the **frontal lobe** (which came to be known as **Broca's Area**) could permanently impair speech production.

It is only in the last twenty years, however, with advances in brain imaging techniques such as **fMRI** and **PET** scans, that scientists have been able to systematically observe and describe the **neurological** basis of mental processes. For example, in research involving tasks that required the use of **episodic** and **semantic memory**, Tulving *et al.* (see Year 1 book page 51) were able to show how these different types of **long-term memory** may be located on opposite sides of the **prefrontal cortex**. As well as this, the system in overall charge of **working memory** – the **central executive** – is thought to reside in a similar area (see the 1997 study by Braver *et al.* in Year 1 book, page 53).

Scanning techniques have also proved useful in establishing the neurological basis of some mental disorders. In the Year 1 book (page 150) the link between the **parahippocampal gyrus** and **OCD** is discussed. It appears to play a role in processing unpleasant emotions.

The focus of cognitive neuroscience has expanded recently to include the use of computer-generated models that are designed to 'read' the brain. This has led to the development of mind mapping techniques known as 'brain fingerprinting'. One possible future application of this could be to analyse the brain wave patterns of eyewitnesses to determine whether they are lying in court!

Evaluation

Scientific and objective methods

The cognitive approach has always employed highly controlled and rigorous methods of study in order to enable researchers to *infer* cognitive processes at work. This has involved the use of **lab experiments** to produce reliable, objective data. In addition, the emergence of cognitive neuroscience has enabled the two fields of biology and cognitive psychology to come together.

This means that the study of the mind has established a credible scientific basis.

Machine reductionism

Although there are similarities between the human mind and the operations of a computer (inputs and outputs, storage systems, the use of a central processor), the computer analogy has been criticised by many. Such **machine reductionism** ignores the influence of human emotion and motivation on the cognitive system, and how this may affect our ability to process information.

For instance, research has found that human memory may be affected by emotional factors, such as the influence of anxiety on eyewitnesses (see Year 1 book page 60).

Application to everyday life

As we have seen, cognitive psychologists are only able to infer mental processes from the behaviour they observe in their research. As a consequence, cognitive psychology occasionally suffers from being too abstract and theoretical in nature.

Similarly, experimental studies of mental processes are often carried out using artificial stimuli (such as tests of memory involving word lists) that may not represent everyday memory experience.

Therefore research on cognitive processes may lack **external validity**.

Evaluation eXtra

Real-life application

The cognitive approach is probably the dominant approach in psychology today and has been applied to a wide range of practical and theoretical contexts. For example, cognitive psychology has made an important contribution in the field of artificial intelligence (AI) and the development of 'thinking machines' (robots), exciting advances that may revolutionise how we live in the future.

Consider: *How has cognitive psychology been applied to the treatment of depression? In what way has cognitive psychology improved the reliability of eyewitness testimony?*

Less determinist than other approaches

The cognitive approach is founded on **soft determinism** – it recognises that our cognitive system can only operate within the limits of what we know, but that we are free to think before responding to a stimulus. This is a more reasonable 'interactionist' (middle-ground) position than the hard determinism suggested by some other approaches.

Consider: *Explain how this is more flexible than the hard determinism of the behaviourist approach.*

CHECK IT

1. Outline the emergence of cognitive neuroscience. **[4 marks]**
2. Briefly explain how theoretical models are used in cognitive psychology to make inferences about mental processes. **[4 marks]**
3. Describe the cognitive approach in psychology. Evaluate the research methods used by cognitive psychologists. **[16 marks]**

Concepts: The influence of schema on perception

1. Read the following paragraph:

The Pschyology of Zombeis

Evrey gneneration gtes the mosnter it deserevs as the reprsenetaiton of its depeest faers. Tdoay's zombeis, who are usulaly infetced in thier thuosands, repersent our modren faer of contaiguos disesaes, uncnotrolled medcial techonolgoy and socail colalpse. Zombeis are lniked, in our cutlure, with daeth and we probalby evolved to aviod daed and disesaed bodeis to aviod infcetoin', accrodnig to Lynn Alden, a profsesor of pschyology at the Univesrity of Britsih Colmobia. 'But its one thnig to aviod a corspe that ins't movnig and qiute anotehr wehn tehy strat chasnig you!'

Question:

Explain the role of schema in helping you make sense of the information above.

2. In contrast, many people misread the following sentences.

Question:

Explain the role of schema in the misperception of the sentences above.

3. Bugelski and Alampay (1962) – the rat-man

Two groups of participants were shown a sequence of pictures, either a number of different faces or a number of different animals. They were then shown the ambiguous figure the 'rat-man' (below).

Participants who saw a sequence of faces were more likely to perceive the figure as a man, whereas participants who saw a sequence of animals were more likely to perceive the figure as a rat.

Question:

Explain how the influence of schema may account for this.

Apply it   Methods: Problem solving

A cognitive psychologist carried out an experiment into the effects of other people on problem solving. An **independent groups design** was used. In Condition A, 15 children were given 30 problems each to solve in two hours. The children completed the task in the same room and were allowed to talk to each other. In Condition B, a different group of 15 children were given the same problems and the same time to solve them but worked in silence.

The number of problems solved in Condition A was 204; the number of problems solved in Condition B was 324.

Questions

1. What percentage of the total number of problems solved were solved in Condition B? (*2 marks*)
2. Calculate the **mean** number of problems solved in Condition A and Condition B. (*2 marks*)
3. Sketch a suitable graphical display to represent the **mean** number of problems solved in Condition A and Condition B. (*3 marks*)
4. Explain *one* conclusion that can be drawn from the mean number of problems solved in Condition A and Condition B. (*2 marks*)

THE BIOLOGICAL APPROACH

The biological approach: the influence of genes, biological structures and neurochemistry on behaviour. Genotype and phenotype, genetic basis of behaviour, evolution and behaviour.

The biological approach predates psychology but in recent years has gained prominence due to advances in technology such as the development of brain scanning techniques and increased understanding of the genetic basis of behaviour.

KEY TERMS

Biological approach – A perspective that emphasises the importance of physical processes in the body such as genetic inheritance and neural function.

Genes – They make up chromosomes and consist of DNA which codes the physical features of an organism (such as eye colour, height) and psychological features (such as mental disorder, intelligence). Genes are transmitted from parents to offspring, i.e. inherited.

Biological structure – An arrangement or organisation of parts to form an organ, system or living thing.

Neurochemistry – Relating to chemicals in the brain that regulate psychological functioning.

Genotype – The particular set of genes that a person possesses.

Phenotype – The characteristics of an individual determined by both genes *and* the environment.

Evolution – The changes in inherited characteristics in a biological population over successive generations.

The biological approach

Assumptions

The **biological approach** suggests that everything psychological is at first biological, so to fully understand human behaviour, we must look to **biological structures** and processes within the body, such as **genes**, **neurochemistry** and the **nervous system**. An understanding of brain structure and function can explain our thoughts and behaviour. From a biological perspective, the mind lives in the brain – meaning that all thoughts, feelings and behaviour ultimately have a physical basis. This is in contrast to, say, the **cognitive approach** that sees mental processes of the mind as being separate from the physical brain.

The genetic basis of behaviour

Behaviour geneticists study whether behavioural characteristics, such as intelligence, personality, mental disorder, etc., are inherited in the same way as physical characteristics such as height and eye colour. **Twin studies** are used to determine the likelihood that certain traits have a genetic basis by comparing the **concordance rates** between pairs of twins; that is, the extent to which both twins share the same characteristic.

If identical (**monozygotic**) twins are found to have higher concordance rates than non-identical (**dizygotic**) twins – for musical ability, schizophrenia, love of romantic films or whatever – this would suggest a genetic basis. This is because MZ twins share 100% of each other's **genes**, whilst DZ twins share about 50% (the same as any siblings).

Genotype and phenotype

A person's **genotype** is their actual genetic make-up, whereas **phenotype** is the way that genes are expressed through physical, behavioural and psychological characteristics. The expression of a genotype is inevitably influenced by environmental factors. For instance, identical adult twins usually look slightly different because one has exercised more or one has dyed their hair and so on. So, despite having the same genes, the way identical twins' genes are expressed (the phenotype) is different – see also the example of **PKU** (opposite). This illustrates what many biological psychologists would accept, that much of human behaviour depends upon an interaction between inherited factors (nature) and the environment (nurture).

Evolution and behaviour

The **evolution** of animals and plants is a fact. In the 19th century, Charles Darwin proposed a theory to explain this fact – the theory of **natural selection**. The main principle of this theory is that any genetically determined behaviour that enhances an individual's survival (and reproduction) will continue in future generations, i.e. be naturally selected. This happens in a similar way to a farmer deciding which animals to use for breeding – the farmer *selects* the ones who possess desirable characteristics. For example, if one of a farmer's cows has a high milk yield the farmer chooses this cow for further breeding so his stock of cows become progressively better milk producers.

In nature this selection takes place 'naturally' – no one 'decides', the selection occurs simply because some traits give the possessor certain advantages. The possessor is more likely to survive, reproduce and pass on these traits. If the individual survives but does not reproduce, the traits do not remain in the gene pool.

Apply it — Concepts: Giraffes, long necks and Bowlby

When considering the long neck of the giraffe, the evolutionary argument (put forward by Darwin himself) is that its extra height gives the giraffe an advantage in obtaining food that would not be available to shorter-necked rivals. This is an example of how an animal has **adapted** *physically* in response to its environment. However, what psychologists are really interested in is the evolution of *behaviour*. Some examples of behaviours that are seen in humans and animals are:

Memory – human memory evolved because it provided advantages.

Attachment – Bowlby argued that attachment to a primary caregiver is adaptive.

Mental disorder – there is evidence that some mental disorders, such as **OCD**, have a genetic basis. Some psychologists argue, therefore, that these genes must have some adaptive advantage.

Question

In each of the above examples, can you suggest what the adaptive advantages might be?

Evaluation

Scientific methods of investigation

In order to investigate the genetic and biological basis of behaviour, the biological approach makes use of a range of precise and highly scientific methods. These include scanning techniques, such as **fMRIs** and **EEGs**, family and **twin studies**, and drug trials. With advances in technology, it is possible to accurately measure biological and neural processes in ways that are not open to bias.

This means that the biological approach is based on reliable data.

Real-life application

Increased understanding of biochemical processes in the brain has led to the development of **psychoactive drugs** that treat serious mental illnesses, such as **depression**. Although these drugs are not effective for all patients, they have revolutionised treatment for many.

This is a strength of the biological approach because it means that sufferers are able to manage their condition and live a relatively normal life, rather than remain in hospital.

Causal conclusions

The biological approach offers explanations for mental illness in terms of the action of **neurotransmitters** in the brain. The evidence for this relationship comes from studies that show a particular drug reduces symptoms of a mental disorder and thus it is assumed that the neurochemical in the drug *causes* the disorder. This is a bit like assuming that the cause of a headache is lack of paracetamol simply because taking paracetamol is effective in relieving symptoms of a headache. Discovering an association between two factors does not mean that one is a cause.

This is a limitation because the biological approach is claiming to have discovered causes where only an association exists.

Evaluation eXtra

Determinist view of behaviour

The biological approach is **determinist** in the sense that it sees human behaviour as governed by internal, biological causes over which we have no control. This has implications for the legal system and wider society. One of the rules of law is that offenders are seen as legally and morally responsible for their actions. The discovery of a 'criminal gene', if there was such a thing, may complicate this principle.

Consider: *If scientists discovered a 'criminal gene' that made someone more likely to offend, and carriers could use this as a defence in court, what would be the implications for society and the legal system?*

Cannot separate nature and nurture

Identical twins, non-identical twins and members of the same family all have genetic similarities. Therefore, the biological approach argues, any similarities in the way that they look or behave must be genetic. However, there is an important **confounding variable**. They are also exposed to similar environmental conditions. This means that findings could just as easily be interpreted as supporting **nurture** rather than **nature**. This approach also has difficulty accounting for the fact that, in research studies, DZ twins often show higher concordance rates than pairs of ordinary siblings (as in the 'Apply it' example above right). This is likely to be explained by the influence of nurture as DZs and ordinary siblings both have about 50% (on average) genes in common.

Consider: *What are the implications of this for genetic explanations of behaviour?*

 **Methods: Twin study**

In a study of depression, a researcher investigated the genetic basis of the disorder. One way to do this is to compare concordance rates for identical twins (monozygotic) who have exactly the same genes with non-identical (dizygotic) twins who share about 50% of the same genes. Both kinds of twins grow up in similar environments. Concordance rates express the likelihood that a trait present in one twin is also found in the other twin.

The following mean concordance rates found by the researcher were:

Monozygotic (MZ) twins – 49%

Dizygotic (DZ) twins – 17%

Ordinary siblings – 9%

Questions

1. Is this a **lab**, **field**, **natural** or **quasi-experiment**? Explain your choice. (*2 marks*)

2. What type of **experimental design** has been used? Explain your answer. (*2 marks*)

3. Identify the **independent** and **dependent variables** within this experiment. (*2 marks*)

4. Explain what the findings above tell us about the genetic basis of depression. Refer to all **three** findings in your answer. (*3 marks*)

 **Concepts: PKU**

Phenylketonuria (PKU) is a rare genetic disorder that can be detected in babies using a heel prick test. If left unchecked, PKU causes severe learning difficulties in those who carry the genotype. If detected early enough, however, the child can be placed on a restricted diet and will develop normally without any complications.

Questions

1. Explain how PKU illustrates the relationship between genotype and phenotype.

2. Do some further research yourself and identify another genetic condition that illustrates the relationship between genotype and phenotype.

STUDY TIP

If writing an essay on the biological approach, make sure you do not include too much description of biological structures and processes. An essay should be a concise overview of the approach itself.

IDEA FOR YOU

Why not look back over the four approaches you have studied and try comparing them. Draw up a table showing the ways in which they are similar and the ways in which they are different.

CHECK IT

1. Using an example, explain what is meant by 'evolution of behaviour'. [3 marks]

2. Using an example, distinguish between *genotype* and *phenotype*. [3 marks]

3. Discuss the contribution of the biological approach to our understanding of human behaviour. [16 marks]

THE PSYCHODYNAMIC APPROACH

The psychodynamic approach: the role of the unconscious, the structure of personality that is Id, Ego and Superego, defence mechanisms including repression, denial and displacement, psychosexual stages.

The psychodynamic approach is most closely associated with the work of Sigmund Freud (though several post-Freudians were influenced by and expanded upon many of Freud's ideas).

KEY TERMS

Psychodynamic approach – A perspective that describes the different forces (dynamics), most of which are unconscious, that operate on the mind and direct human behaviour and experience.

The unconscious – The part of the mind that we are unaware of but which continues to direct much of our behaviour.

Id – Entirely unconscious, the id is made up of selfish aggressive instincts that demand immediate gratification.

Ego – The 'reality check' that balances the conflicting demands of the id and the superego.

Superego – The moralistic part of our personality which represents the ideal self: how we ought to be.

Defence mechanisms – Unconscious strategies that the ego uses to manage the conflict between the id and the superego.

Psychosexual stages – According to Freud, five developmental stages that all children pass through. At most stages there is a specific conflict, the outcome of which determines future development.

Psychosexual stages

Stage	Description	Consequence of unresolved conflict
Oral 0–1 years	Focus of pleasure is the mouth, mother's breast is the object of desire.	Oral fixation – smoking, biting nails, sarcastic, critical.
Anal 1–3 years	Focus of pleasure is the anus. Child gains pleasure from withholding and expelling faeces.	Anal retentive – perfectionist, obsessive. Anal expulsive – thoughtless, messy.
Phallic 3–5 years	Focus of pleasure is the genital area. Child experiences the Oedipus or Electra complex (see facing page).	Phallic personality – narcissistic, reckless, possibly homosexual.
Latency	Earlier conflicts are repressed.	
Genital	Sexual desires become conscious alongside the onset of puberty.	Difficulty forming heterosexual relationships.

The psychodynamic approach

The role of the unconscious

Freud suggested that the part of our mind that we know about and are aware of – the *conscious* mind – is merely the 'tip of the iceberg'. Most of our mind is made up of the **unconscious**: a vast storehouse of biological drives and instincts that has a significant influence on our behaviour and personality. The unconscious also contains threatening and disturbing memories that have been **repressed**, or locked away and forgotten. These can be accessed during dreams or through 'slips of the tongue' (what Freud referred to as **parapraxes**). An example of such a slip is calling a female teacher 'mum' instead of 'miss'.

Just bubbling under the surface of our conscious mind is the **preconscious** which contains thoughts and memories which are not currently in conscious awareness but we can access if desired'.

The structure of personality

Freud described personality as 'tripartite', composed of three parts:

- The **id** is the primitive part of our personality. It operates on the **pleasure principle** – the id gets what it wants. It is a seething mass of unconscious drives and instincts. Only the id is present at birth (Freud described babies as being 'bundles of id'). Throughout life the id is entirely selfish and demands instant gratification of its needs.
- The **ego** works on the **reality principle** and is the mediator between the other two parts of the personality. The ego develops around the age of two years and its role is to reduce the conflict between the demands of the id and the superego. It manages this by employing a number of **defence mechanisms** (see below).
- The **superego** is formed at the end of the **phallic stage**, around the age of five. It is our internalised sense of right and wrong. Based on the **morality principle** it represents the moral standards of the child's same-sex parent and punishes the ego for wrongdoing (through guilt).

Psychosexual stages

Freud claimed that child development occurred in five stages, see table below left. Each stage (apart from *latency*) is marked by a different conflict that the child must resolve in order to progress successfully to the next stage. Any psychosexual conflict that is unresolved leads to **fixation** where the child becomes 'stuck' and carries certain behaviours and conflicts associated with that stage through to adult life.

Apply it   Concepts: Defence mechanisms

The ego has a difficult job balancing the conflicting demands of the id and the superego but it does have help in the form of defence mechanisms. These are unconscious and ensure that the ego is able to prevent us from being overwhelmed by temporary threats or traumas. However, they often involve some form of distortion of reality and as a long-term solution they are regarded as psychologically unhealthy and undesirable.

Three defence mechanisms are listed in the table below with their definitions.

Repression	Forcing a distressing memory out of the conscious mind.
Denial	Refusing to acknowledge some aspect of reality.
Displacement	Transferring feelings from true source of distressing emotion onto a substitute target.

Question

Three examples of defence mechanisms in action are given below. Match each example to one defence mechanism listed in the table above.

A. Continuing to turn up for work even though you have been sacked.

B. An individual forgetting the trauma of their favourite pet dying.

C. Slamming the door after a row with your girlfriend.

Evaluation

Explanatory power

Although Freud's theory is controversial in many ways, and occasionally bizarre, it has nevertheless had a huge influence on psychology and Western contemporary thought. Alongside **behaviourism**, the psychodynamic approach remained the dominant force in psychology for the first half of the 20th century and has been used to explain a wide range of phenomena including personality development, abnormal behaviour, moral development and gender. The approach is also significant in drawing attention to the connection between experiences in childhood, such as our relationship with our parents, and later development (see research into the effects of early attachment patterns on adulthood and adolescence – page 92 in the Year 1 book).

The case study method

Freud's theory was based on the intensive study of single individuals who were often in therapy (see the case of Little Hans – right – and other Freudian case studies such as *Dora* and *Rat-man*). Although Freud's observations were detailed and carefully recorded, critics have suggested that it is not possible to make such universal claims about human nature based on studies of such a small number of individuals who were psychologically abnormal. Furthermore, Freud's interpretations were highly subjective; it is unlikely, in the case of Little Hans for instance, that any other researcher would have drawn the same conclusions. In comparison with the other approaches we have come across in this chapter, Freud's methods lack scientific rigour.

Untestable concepts

The philosopher of science Karl Popper argued that the psychodynamic approach does not meet the scientific criterion of **falsification**, in the sense that it is not open to empirical testing (and the possibility of being disproved). Many of Freud's concepts (such as the id and the Oedipus complex) are said to occur at an unconscious level, making them difficult, if not impossible, to test. According to Popper this affords psychodynamic theory the status of *pseudoscience* ('fake' science) rather than real science.

Evaluation eXtra

Practical application

Alongside the theoretical basis of the psychodynamic approach, Freud also brought to the world a new form of therapy: **psychoanalysis**. Employing a range of techniques designed to access the unconscious, such as hypnosis and dream analysis, psychoanalysis is the forerunner to many modern-day psychotherapies that have since been established. Although Freudian therapists have claimed success with many patients suffering from mild **neuroses**, psychoanalysis has been criticised as inappropriate, even harmful, for people suffering more serious mental disorders (such as **schizophrenia**).

Consider: *Why do you think psychoanalysis might not be effective with serious mental disorders?*

Psychic determinism

Freud believed, in relation to human behaviour, that there was no such thing as an 'accident'. Even something as apparently random as a 'slip of the tongue' (such as mistakenly describing your partner's new outfit as 'fattening' rather than 'flattering') is driven by unconscious forces and has deep symbolic meaning (though the meaning's pretty obvious in the case of the 'fattening' example!). The psychodynamic approach explains all behaviour – even accidents – as determined by unconscious conflicts that are rooted in childhood such that any **free will** we may think we have is an illusion.

Consider: *How does this psychic determinism compare with other approaches we have come across?*

Apply it Concepts:

The Oedipus complex and the case study of Little Hans

In the **phallic stage**, little boys develop incestuous feelings towards their mother and a murderous hatred for their rival in love – their father (the **Oedipus complex**). Fearing that their father will castrate them, boys repress their feelings for their mother and identify with their father, taking on his gender role and moral values.

Girls of the same age experience **penis envy**: they desire their father – as the penis is the primary love object – and hate their mother (the **Electra complex**). Although Freud was less clear on the process in girls, they are thought to give up the desire for their father over time and replace this with a desire for a baby (identifying with their mother in the process).

Freud supported his concept of the Oedipus complex with his case study of Little Hans. Hans was a five-year-old boy who developed a **phobia** of horses after seeing one collapse in the street. Freud suggested that Hans' phobia was a form of displacement in which his repressed fear of his father was transferred (displaced) onto horses. Thus, horses were merely a symbolic representation of Hans' real unconscious fear: the fear of castration experienced during the Oedipus complex.

Questions

1. Is the Little Hans case study good evidence for the Oedipus conflict? Explain your answer.

2. Is this a scientific way of investigating phobias? Explain your answer.

3. How might a behaviourist explain Hans' phobia of horses?

Apply it

Concepts:

Id, ego and superego

What would the ID, EGO and SUPEREGO suggest you do in the following situations?

1. You have missed lunch and are walking past a cake shop.

2. You are just leaving work and your boss asks you to stay an extra hour.

3. You are sat on a bus and notice someone has left a wallet full of £50 notes.

4. You are driving home and another car pulls out in front of you nearly causing a collision.

CHECK IT

1. Using an example, explain the *role of the unconscious*. [3 marks]

2. Identify **one** Freudian defence mechanism and explain how it would affect behaviour. [3 marks]

3. Discuss the psychodynamic approach. Refer to at least **two** other approaches in psychology in your answer. [16 marks]

HUMANISTIC PSYCHOLOGY

Humanistic psychology: free will, self-actualisation
and Maslow's hierarchy of needs, focus on the self,
congruence, the role of conditions of worth.
The influence on counselling psychology.

Humanistic psychology emerged in the United States in
the 1950s largely as a result of the work of Carl Rogers and
Abraham Maslow. It became known as the 'third force' in
psychology – alongside behaviourist and psychodynamic
approaches – and represented a challenge to both. Rogers
felt that Freud had dealt with the 'sick half' of psychology,
so the humanistic approach concerned itself with
explanations of 'healthy' growth in individuals.

KEY TERMS

Humanistic psychology – An approach to understanding
behaviour that emphasises the importance of subjective
experience and each person's capacity for self-
determination.

Free will – The notion that humans can make choices and
are not determined by biological or external forces.

Self-actualisation – The desire to grow psychologically
and fulfil one's full potential – becoming what you are
capable of.

Hierarchy of needs – A five-levelled hierarchical sequence
in which basic needs (such as hunger) must be satisfied
before higher psychological needs (such as esteem and self-
actualisation) can be achieved.

Self – The ideas and values that characterise 'I' and 'me'
and includes perception and valuing of 'what I am' and
'what I can do'.

Congruence – The aim of Rogerian therapy; when the self-
concept and ideal self are seen to broadly accord or match.

Conditions of worth – When a parent places limits or
boundaries on their love of their children; for instance, a
parent saying to a child, 'I will only love you if...you study
medicine' or '...if you split up with that boy'.

Humanistic psychology

Free will

All the approaches we have considered so far are **determinist** to some degree in
their suggestion that our behaviour is entirely, or at least partly, shaped by forces over
which we have no control. Even the **cognitive approach**, which claims we are free
to choose our own thoughts, would still argue that such choice is constrained by the
limits of our cognitive system. Humanistic psychology is quite different in this respect,
claiming that human beings are essentially *self-determining* and have **free will**. This
does not mean that people are not affected by external or internal influences but we
are *active agents* who have the ability to determine our own development.

For this reason, humanistic psychologists such as Rogers and Maslow, reject
scientific models that attempt to establish general principles of human behaviour. As
active agents we are all unique, and psychology should concern itself with the study
of subjective experience rather than general laws. This is often referred to as a *person-
centred approach* in psychology.

Self-actualisation

Every person has an **innate** tendency to achieve their full potential – to become
the best they can possibly be. **Self-actualisation** represents the uppermost level
of Maslow's **hierarchy of needs** (see below). All four lower levels of the hierarchy
('deficiency needs') must be met before the individual can work towards self-
actualisation (a 'growth need') and fulfil their potential. Humanistic psychologists
regard *personal growth* as an essential part of what it is to be human. Personal
growth is concerned with developing and changing as a person to become fulfilled,
satisfied and goal-orientated. Not everyone will manage this, however, and there
are important psychological barriers that may prevent a person from reaching their
potential.

The self, congruence and conditions of worth

Rogers argued that for personal growth to be achieved an individual's concept of **self**
(the way they see themselves) must be broadly equivalent to, or have **congruence**
with, their **ideal self** (the person they want to be). If too big a gap exists between the
two 'selves' the person will experience a state of incongruence and self-actualisation
will not be possible due to the negative feelings of self-worth that arise from
incongruence.

In order to reduce the gap between the self-concept and the ideal self, Rogers
developed **client-centred therapy** (see facing page) to help people cope with the
problems of everyday living. Rogers claimed that many of the issues we experience
as adults, such as worthlessness and low **self-esteem**, have their roots in childhood
and can often be explained by a lack of **unconditional positive regard** (or lack
of *unconditional love*) from our parents. A parent who sets boundaries or limits on
their love for their child (**conditions of worth**) by claiming '*I will only love you if...*'
is storing up psychological problems for that child in the future. Thus, Rogers saw
one of his roles as an effective therapist as being able to provide his clients with the
unconditional positive regard that they had failed to receive as children.

Maslow's hierarchy of zombie needs

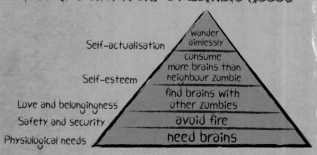

Although it might be possible to apply the hierarchy of needs
to zombies, Maslow argued that the need for self-actualisation
is uniquely human.

Apply it   Concepts: Maslow's hierarchy of needs

Maslow's main interest was in what motivates people. In order to achieve our
primary goal of self-actualisation, a number of other deficiency needs must first
be met. The first of these is physiological. Imagine you wanted to produce the
best psychology essay you had ever written; this would be very difficult if you
were hungry or tired.

Moving up the hierarchy, the next deficiency need is safety and security followed
by love and belongingness and then self-esteem. A person is only able to
progress through the hierarchy once the current need in the sequence has been
met.

Maslow characterised life as a series of peak experiences: moments of great
achievement, ecstasy or elation when all deficiency needs are satisfied. He also
identified and researched a number of self-actualisers: people who, for whatever
reason, were fulfilled in life and had used their abilities to the fullest.

Question

Can you think of any people, in the **media** or who you know, who could be
described as self-actualisers? Explain your choices in each case.

Evaluation

Not reductionist

Humanists reject any attempt to break up behaviour and experience into smaller components. Behaviourists explain human and animal learning in terms of simple stimulus-response connections; Freud described the whole of personality as a conflict between three things: id, ego and superego; biological psychologists reduce behaviour to its basic physiological processes and supporters of the cognitive approach see human beings as little more than information processing 'machines'. In contrast, humanistic psychologists advocate **holism**, the idea that subjective experience can only be understood by considering the whole person. This approach may have more **validity** than its alternatives by considering meaningful human behaviour within its real-life context.

Limited application

Unlike some of the other approaches we have come across, humanistic psychology has relatively little real-world application. It is true that Rogerian therapy has revolutionised **counselling** techniques (see right), and Maslow's hierarchy of needs has been used to explain motivation (see facing page), particularly in the workplace. However, it remains the case that the approach has had limited impact within the discipline of psychology as a whole. This may in part be due to humanistic psychology lacking a sound evidence-base (see below) and also due to the fact that the approach has been described, not as a comprehensive theory, but as a loose set of rather abstract concepts.

Positive approach

Humanistic psychologists have been praised for 'bringing the person back into psychology' and promoting a positive image of the human condition. Freud saw human beings as slaves to their past and claimed all of us existed somewhere between 'common unhappiness and absolute despair'. Humanistic psychology offers a refreshing and optimistic alternative; it sees all people as basically good, free to work towards the achievement of their potential and in control of their lives.

Evaluation eXtra

Untestable concepts

Humanistic psychology does include a number of vague ideas that are abstract and difficult to test. Concepts such as 'self-actualisation' and 'congruence' may be useful therapeutic tools but would prove problematic to assess under experimental conditions. Rogers did attempt to introduce more rigour into his work by developing the **Q-sort** – an objective measure of progress in therapy. Nevertheless, as would be expected of an approach that describes itself as anti-scientific, humanistic psychology is short on **empirical** evidence to support its claims.

Consider: *What would a behaviourist's view of humanistic psychology be?*

Cultural bias

Many of the ideas that are central to humanistic psychology, such as individual freedom, autonomy and personal growth, would be much more readily associated with **individualist** cultures in the Western world such as the United States. **Collectivist** cultures such as India, which emphasise the needs of the group, community and interdependence, may not identify so easily with the ideals and values of humanistic psychology. Therefore, it is possible that this approach would not travel well and is a product of the cultural context within which it was developed.

Consider: *Look back at the other approaches in this chapter. Is there evidence of culture bias in any of the theories or ideas suggested?*

Apply it

Concepts: Counselling psychology

Rogers' client-centred (or latterly, *person-centred*) therapy is an important form of modern-day psychotherapy. Rogers referred to those in therapy as 'clients' rather than 'patients' as he saw the individual as the expert on their own condition. Thus, therapy is non-directive, and the client is encouraged towards the discovery of their own solutions within a therapeutic atmosphere that is warm, supportive and non-judgemental.

For Rogers, an effective therapist should provide the client with three things: genuineness, empathy and unconditional positive regard. The aim of Rogerian therapy is to increase the person's feelings of self-worth, reduce the level of incongruence between the self-concept and the ideal self, and help the person become a more fully functioning person.

Rogers' work transformed psychotherapy and introduced a variety of counselling techniques. In the UK and the US, similar counselling skills are practised, not only in clinical settings, but throughout education, health, social work and industry.

Client-centred therapy has been praised as a forward-looking and effective approach that focuses on present problems rather than dwelling on the past. However, much like **psychoanalysis** (see previous spread), it is best applied to the treatment of 'mild' psychological conditions, such as anxiety and low self-worth.

Question

Why would Rogers' therapy be less effective in treating more serious mental disorders such as schizophrenia?

Apply it

Concepts: Joyce: teacher or dancer?

Joyce is a successful teacher and is well-liked by her colleagues. However, Joyce has always dreamed of becoming a ballroom dancer. She spends much of her free time with her partner practising elaborate lifts, and can often be seen twirling around the classroom during break times.

Joyce is considering leaving teaching and becoming a professional dancer. Her colleagues have described Joyce's plans as 'ridiculous', and her parents, who are very proud of the fact that their daughter is a teacher, have told Joyce they will not speak to her again if she does. Joyce is beginning to feel sad and miserable.

Question

Referring to features of humanistic psychology, explain how Joyce's situation may affect her personal growth.

CHECK IT

1. Explain what humanistic psychologists mean by *conditions of worth*. Give an example. **[3 marks]**
2. Outline and briefly evaluate the influence of humanistic psychology on counselling. **[5 marks]**
3. Outline assumptions of humanistic psychology. Discuss how humanistic psychology is different from other approaches within psychology. **[16 marks]**

Comparison of approaches

Comparison of approaches

In this chapter, we have considered six of the major psychological approaches. Here, we outline some of the areas of agreement, disagreement, contention and overlap between these different ways of viewing and explaining human behaviour. Our discussion is organised around five themes: views on development, nature versus nurture, reductionism, determinism, explanation and treatment of abnormal/atypical behaviour.

We also revisit the different research methods associated with each approach before finally, assessing the benefits (and otherwise) of adopting an eclectic approach which aims to combine elements from different approaches.

Concepts: Let's be friends: areas of overlap and agreement between approaches

Although there are many significant differences between the theories and assumptions within each approach, there are some areas of overlap and ways in which approaches complement each other.

You may recall how the social learning theory approach was described as a 'bridge' between the behaviourist and cognitive approaches because it emphasised the importance of learning from the environment as well as the role of mediating cognitive factors.

The fusion of cognitive and biological approaches has led to the development of cognitive neuroscience – a sophisticated field that links mental states to biological structures.

The psychodynamic approach shares much in common with the biological approach as both see biological drives and instincts as crucial determinants of human development.

Finally, humanistic and psychodynamic approaches can both be reasonably described as person-centred in the way that they place subjective experience at the centre of their research.

These are just some of the ways in which psychological approaches overlap.

Question

Select two or three approaches. Draw Venn diagrams (see example on right) to show the ways in which these approaches overlap and intersect. Use this page and the rest of the chapter to draw out the features and assumptions that different approaches have in common.

Views on development

In terms of child development, the **psychodynamic approach** presents the most coherent theory of development, tying its concepts and processes to specific (psychosexual) stages that are determined by age. That said, Freud saw very little further development once the child enters the genital stage in the teen years.

Stage theories within the **cognitive approach** have contributed to our understanding of child development. For example, as part of their intellectual development, children form increasingly complex concepts (**schema**) as they get older.

Maturation is an important principle within the **biological approach** whereby genetically determined changes in a child's physiological status influence psychological and behavioural characteristics.

Humanistic psychologists see the development of the **self** as ongoing throughout life; a child's relationship with its parents is seen as a key determinant of psychological health.

Finally, the **behaviourist approach** and **social learning theory** do not offer coherent stage theories of development but instead see the processes that underpin learning as continuous, occurring at any age.

Nature versus nurture

The debate about whether human behaviour is more influenced by **innate** biological factors (**nature**) or by the environment and experience (**nurture**) has a long history in psychology. The biological approach and the two learning approaches are furthest apart in this respect. Behaviourists characterised babies as 'blank slates' at birth and suggest that all behaviour comes about through learned associations, **reinforcement** contingencies or, in the case of social learning theory, observation and imitation. In contrast, the biological approach argues from a position that 'anatomy is destiny' and behaviour is the result of a **genetic** blueprint that we inherit from our parents.

Other approaches are less easy to categorise. Although Freud thought that much of our behaviour was driven by biological drives and instincts, he also saw relationships with parents as playing a fundamental role in future development. Similarly, humanistic psychologists regard parents, friends and wider society as having a critical impact on the person's **self-concept**. Finally, although cognitive psychologists would recognise that many of our information processing abilities and schema are innate, they would also point to the fact that these are constantly refined through experience.

Reductionism

Reductionism refers to the belief that human behaviour can be most effectively explained by breaking it down into constituent parts. The opposing view is **holism**, that phenomena are best understood by looking at the interplay and interaction of many different factors.

Behaviourism is reductionist in the sense that it breaks up complex behaviour into stimulus-response units for ease of testing in the **lab**. Also reductionist is the biological approach in the way that it explains human behaviour and psychological states at the level of the gene or **neuron**. The psychodynamic approach reduces much of our behaviour to the influence of sexual drives and biological instincts, although Freud's argument that personality is a dynamic interaction between the three parts of the personality is often viewed as a more holistic explanation. The cognitive approach has been accused of **machine reductionism** by presenting people as information processing systems and ignoring the influence of emotion on behaviour. Like behaviourists, social learning theorists reduce complex learning to a handful of key processes (imitation, modelling, etc.) though they do at least place emphasis on cognitive factors that mediate learning, and how these interact with external influences.

Finally, and quite distinct from other approaches, is humanistic psychology, which formulates a holistic approach to understanding human behaviour. This involves investigating all aspects of the individual, including the effects of interaction with others and wider society.

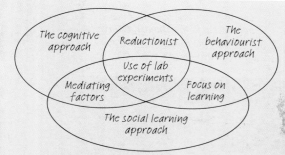

An example of a Venn diagram.

Determinism

Determinism is often confused with reductionism but is quite distinct from it – though many determinist explanations are also reductionist. Determinism proposes that all behaviour has an internal or external cause and is thus predictable.

As we have seen, the behaviourist approach sees all behaviour as environmentally determined by external influences that we are unable to control. The biological approach advocates a form of **genetic determinism** in its assumption that much of our behaviour is directed by innate influences. **Psychic determinism** is a key feature of the psychodynamic approach insofar as we cannot know the **unconscious** forces that drive our behaviour, and that these are simply rationalised by our conscious minds.

The positions described above are known as **hard determinism**; the next two approaches take a 'softer' view. The cognitive approach suggests that we are the 'choosers' of our own thoughts and behaviours, yet these choices can only operate within the limits of what we know and have experienced. Social learning theorists, like Bandura, put forward the notion of **reciprocal determinism** – the idea that as well as being influenced by our environment, we also exert some influence upon it through the behaviours we choose to perform. Only humanistic psychology stands alone in its assertion that human beings have **free will** and operate as active agents who determine their own development.

Explanation and treatment of abnormal/atypical behaviour

The behaviourist model sees abnormality as arising from maladaptive or faulty learning in the sense that inappropriate or destructive patterns of behaviour have been reinforced. **Behaviour therapies**, such as **systematic desensitisation**, which take a symptom-based approach have been applied successfully to the treatment of **phobias**.

Social learning theory has had relatively little application to treatment, but the principles of **modelling** and **observational learning** have been used to explain how negative behaviours such as aggression may be learned through the influence of dysfunctional **role models**.

Freud saw anxiety disorders as emerging from unconscious conflict, childhood trauma and the overuse of **defence mechanisms**. **Psychoanalysis** has had some success as a therapy but it is not appropriate for everyone because it requires a considerable input from the patient in terms of time and also ability to talk about and reflect on emotions.

Much more effective and applicable is cognitive therapy (especially when combined with behaviour therapy as **CBT**) in the treatment, for example, of **depression**. It aims to identify and eradicate faulty thinking which is assumed to be the root cause of maladaptive behaviour.

Also effective is humanistic therapy (or **counselling**) based on Rogers' philosophy that closing the gap between the self-concept and the ideal self will stimulate personal growth.

Finally, the biological approach, many would claim, has revolutionised the treatment of mental disorders through the development of **drug therapy** which regulates chemical imbalances in the brain.

To what extent is our behaviour dictated by forces beyond our control?

Apply it — Concepts: The eclectic approach

As was mentioned at the beginning of the chapter, many modern psychologists take a multidisciplinary approach to the study of human behaviour. Eclecticism in psychology refers to the combining of several approaches, methods and/or theoretical perspectives in order to provide a more comprehensive account of human behaviour.

Such an ethos has proved fruitful in the field of mental illness. Combining treatment options from several different perspectives – such as drugs, cognitive therapy and family therapy – has led to more effective outcomes for schizophrenic patients and lower relapse rates (e.g. Stein and Test 1980).

Many topic areas in psychology have also benefitted from 'interactionist' theories that combine different levels of explanation. The **diathesis-stress model** in psychiatry accounts for the fact that many mental disorders are a complex interaction of biological predisposition and environmental triggers. Similarly, the **biosocial approach** rejects the traditional distinction between nature and nurture by explaining how basic biological differences are reinforced by the environment during gender development, for instance.

Question

Although there are obvious advantages associated with eclecticism in psychology, what issues/problems might such an approach present?

Apply it

Concepts: Idiographic and nomothetic approaches

The six approaches are also divided in terms of whether they are attempting to establish general laws by studying large groups of people (**nomothetic approach**) or whether they are aiming to understand what makes individuals unique (**idiographic approach**). The former generally involves the use of the **experimental method** whereas the latter tends to be more concerned with in-depth **qualitative methods** such as **case studies** and **unstructured interviews**.

Broadly speaking, the more scientific approaches – behaviourist, social learning theory, cognitive and biological – subscribe to the experimental method. That said, the biological and cognitive approaches often draw upon data derived from case studies, especially those involving individuals who suffer from unusual abnormalities or deficits (as in the case of HM in memory described in the Year 1 book on page 51). The person-centred approaches – psychodynamic and humanistic – are idiographic in that they exclusively favour the case study method, usually carried out within clinical settings.

Question

What are the strengths and limitations of adopting:

(i) An idiographic approach to human behaviour?

(ii) A nomothetic approach to human behaviour?

STUDY TIP

You might enhance your understanding of the information on this spread by drawing a table with the five themes across the top and the six approaches down the side. Then summarise the information on this spread in relation to each approach.

CHECK IT

1. Outline **one** way in which the behaviourist approach and social learning theory approach overlap. *[2 marks]*

2. Explain **two** differences between the cognitive approach and humanistic psychology. *[6 marks]*

3. Outline and compare any **two** approaches in psychology. *[16 marks]*

Knowledge and understanding of ... research methods, practical research skills and maths skills. These should be developed through ... ethical practical research activities.

This means that you should conduct practical investigations wherever possible. Here, we suggest an idea for an experiment that you might conduct related to the biological approach, as well as a demonstration of electrical transmission in the nervous system. There is also a naturalistic observation linked to your knowledge of learning approaches.

Ethics check

Ethics were discussed in the Year 1 book. We suggest strongly that you complete this checklist before collecting data.

1. Do participants know participation is voluntary?
2. Do participants know what to expect?
3. Do participants know they can withdraw at any time?
4. Are individuals' results anonymous?
5. Have I minimised the risk of distress to participants?
6. Have I avoided asking sensitive questions?
7. Will I avoid bringing my school/teacher/psychology into disrepute?
8. Have I considered all other ethical issues?
9. Has my teacher approved this?

Table of results for an experiment on the effects of arousal

Condition A: Time in seconds to cross out e's without an audience

Condition B: Time in seconds to cross out e's with an audience

Participant	Condition A	Condition B
1	56	52
2	63	64
3	60	48
4	72	71
5	57	46
6	62	64
7	70	53
8	81	83
9	50	54
10	66	56
Totals		
Standard deviation	8.9573	11.4450

Practical idea 1: The effect of arousal on performance

Evidence suggests that performing in front of an audience causes physiological arousal (activation of the **autonomic nervous** system) and the release of **adrenaline**. This can improve performance on a simple task (or one we are very good at), which explains why athletes usually break records competing in front of an audience rather than in training. On unfamiliar or difficult tasks, however, people tend to become stressed (or over-aroused) leading to more errors and poorer performance.

The aim of this study is to see whether the physiological arousal caused by an audience affects performance on a simple task. This is a **laboratory experiment**.

The practical bit

Materials and basic design

The task participants will complete is straightforward – crossing out the letter 'e' from a passage of text as quickly as possible. The text needs to be long enough to keep participants occupied for a reasonable period of time, but not so long that they are there all day! There are a number of ways to assess the dependent variable. Probably the easiest way is simply to time how long participants take to complete the task. (You could also take into account any mistakes made, e.g. letter e's that they missed.)

All participants should complete the task alone and then with an audience of about three or four people. As this is a **repeated measures** design, the order of conditions should be **counterbalanced**.

Keep control

This only thing that should affect the **dependent variable** in this experiment (time taken to complete the task) is the **independent variable** (whether an audience is present or not). All other possible **extraneous variables** should be kept constant. For this reason, there should be strict **standardisation** of procedures for all participants. You should write a **briefing** statement, **standardised instructions** (for both conditions of the experiment) and a **debriefing**. These should take account of all relevant **ethical issues** (see left) and participants should be treated with respect.

It might be wise to inform participants at the beginning that they will be placed in a situation where their performance on a task will be observed by others, as some participants may be reluctant to continue. However, revealing the full aim of the investigation may be best left to the end as this could have some influence on how participants approach the tasks.

Which hypothesis?

On the face of it this looks a simple task, and evidence suggests that the arousing effects of an audience lead to improved performance when a task is easy. However, for some people, the distracting effects of the audience may lead to 'over-arousal' and poorer performance as a result, e.g. **Yerkes–Dodson Law**. For this reason, we would recommend writing a **non-directional hypothesis** for this study.

Sampling

You will need to consider a suitable **sampling technique** for this study and you need to think about what would make an appropriate sample size.

Analysing your data

Finally, you should present your results in the form of tables and graphs so that the effect of arousal on performance of a task can be clearly seen. You could also use the **sign test** (covered in the Year 1 book) to analyse the data.

Apply it — Methods: The maths bit 1

1. In the table on the left, what percentage of participants improved their performance with an audience? (*1 mark*)
2. Using the data in this table, calculate the **mean** time it took to cross out letter e's in Condition A and B. (*1 mark*)
3. Explain *one* strength and *one* limitation of the mean as a **measure of central tendency**. (*2 marks + 2 marks*)
4. Sketch a suitable graph to represent the mean values calculated in question 2. (*3 marks*)
5. Give each **standard deviation** in the table on the left to one decimal place. (*1 mark*)
6. What do the standard deviations tell us about the spread of data in each condition of the experiment? (*2 marks*)

Practical idea 2: Gender differences in adult–child play

The aim of this study is to see if there is a difference in the way that adults interact with their children depending on the child's gender.

Following learning theory, are gender differences in children's play reinforced by the ways in which adults interact with children?

This is a **quasi-experiment** because gender is the independent variable. **Observational techniques** are used to collect data.

The practical bit

We have chosen a **naturalistic observation** as the most suitable method to collect data. It may be possible to simply ask parents or guardians, via a **questionnaire** or **interview**, what forms of play they prefer to engage in with their children but there may be a **social desirability bias** as parents may not want to appear gender-stereotypical in their answers (or look as if they don't play with their children at all!). Similarly, if parents know they are being observed within a controlled environment – as in a **lab** observation – they may change their normal behaviour due to the **demand characteristics** of the situation. Therefore, this study will take the form of a **covert observation** in a natural environment, in this case, a local park.

Is it ethical?

Covert observations are ethical as long they involve *public* behaviour that would be happening anyway in the absence of the researcher. If it is not obvious that you are recording behaviour then there is no need to ask for **consent** or **debrief** your participants on this occasion.

Designing your observation

Perhaps you will simply record the type of play that the adults and children are engaged in, for instance, 'playing football' or 'hide and seek'. Alternatively, you might want to categorise adult–child interaction as, say, 'active' or 'passive', in which case you will need a list of **behavioural categories** that specify the difference between the two. For instance, 'active play' may involve running around whereas 'passive play' may involve sitting and talking. Once these categories are drawn up, you can then record the frequency with which they occur.

You also need to determine the **sampling method** for the observation. Will you record the number of times behaviour occurs (**event sampling**) or record the behaviour of participants at specific time intervals (**time** sampling)? This may also affect *how* behaviour is recorded, that is, through written description or the use of a tally chart.

Will you work alone or with someone else?

Observations conducted by a single researcher may introduce **bias** so it might be a good idea to work with a partner. To this end, you might wish to conduct a **pilot study**, for instance of a family member or friend playing with their children, so you can assess the **reliability** of your observations with your co-researcher.

Whatever you decide, you will need to present your results in the form of tables and graphs to give an instant picture of the gender differences in play.

Try it – The speed of electrical transmission

Stand in a line with a bunch of your friends (or classmates) all holding hands. The person on one end of the line needs a stopwatch and the person on the other end of the line should hold a bicycle horn (the squeezy kind).

On the count of three the person with the watch should start the timer and squeeze the hand of the person next to them. That person then squeezes the hand of the person next to them, and so on. When the person holding the horn's hand is squeezed they should sound the horn and the timer is stopped. Bear in mind that you might need to practise a couple of times to get it right!

Do the same but this time hold the hand of the person on your left and touch the shoulder of the person on your right. Does the time from start to end change?

Now for the maths bit...

Measure the span from tip of right hand to tip of left for all the people in the group and calculate the total distance the signal travelled. Divide the distance travelled by the time the signal travelled to determine the speed in metres per second.

Scientists have estimated that the speed of electrical transmission across a large **myelinated axon** is around 200 metres per second.

How did you compare? Have another go and see if you can beat your time (but chances are you're unlikely to catch the electrical impulse!).

The maths bit

Overall, at least 10% of the marks in assessments for Psychology will require the use of mathematical skills and at least 25% in total will involve research methods.

Don't avoid it!

Apply it

Methods: The maths bit 2

1. Using the data in the table on the right, calculate the total number of times active play was observed in adult–boy pairs and in adult–girl pairs. Do the same for passive play. (*2 marks*)

2. Draw a **bar chart** to show the difference in active play and passive play for adult–girl pairs and adult–boy pairs. (*3 marks*)

3. Explain *one* conclusion that can be drawn from the bar chart you have drawn. (*2 marks*)

4. Identify the type of data in the table on the right. Explain *one* limitation of using this type of data. (*1 mark + 2 marks*)

The data collected for frequency of active and passive play between adult–girl pairs and adult–boy pairs.

	Type of play					
	Active play			Passive play		
	Running	Shouting	Physical contact	Sitting	Talking	No physical contact
Adult–boy pair	11	8	5	3	2	3
Adult–girl pair	4	3	5	5	6	3

REVISION SUMMARIES

ORIGINS OF PSYCHOLOGY

We're going to go back in time.

WUNDT AND INTROSPECTION

Wundt's lab
First psychology lab in Leipzig, introduced structuralism.

Controlled methods
Standardised instructions made the procedures replicable.

Early philosophical roots
Descartes, Locke, Darwin.

THE EMERGENCE OF PSYCHOLOGY AS A SCIENCE

Watson and the early behavourists
Rejection of introspection.

Scientific approach
Behaviourism, the cognitive revolution, the biological approach, cognitive neuroscience.

THE LEARNING APPROACH: BEHAVIOURISM

All behaviour is learning through association or reinforcement.

THE BEHAVIOURIST APPROACH

Assumptions
Observable.
Basic processes same in all species.

Classical conditioning – Pavlov
Association of NS with UCS to produce new CS and CR.

Operant conditioning – Skinner
Reinforcement (positive and negative).
Punishment.

EVALUATION

Scientific credibility
Objectivity and replication helped create psychology as a science.

Real-life application
Token economy used in prisons.
Focus on here and now, e.g. treating phobias.

Mechanistic
Humans are passive responders, mental events not included.

Evaluation extra
Environmental determinism.
Ethical and practical issues in animal experiments.

THE LEARNING APPROACH: SOCIAL LEARNING THEORY

All behaviour is learned from observing other people in social context.

THE SOCIAL LEARNING APPROACH

Assumptions
Observable.
Basic processes same in all species.

Vicarious reinforcement
Observation leads to imitation if behaviour is vicariously reinforced (Bobo doll experiment).

Mediational processes
Attention, retention, motivation, reproduction.

Identification
More likely to imitate role models you identify with.

EVALUATION

Cognitive factors in learning
More comprehensive account of learning.

Evidence from lab studies
Demand characteristics and low validity.

Underestimates influence of biology
Aggression involves hormonal factors, e.g. testosterone.

Evaluation extra
Explains cultural differences.
Less determinist than behaviourism (reciprocal determinism).

THE COGNITIVE APPROACH

The study of internal mental processes.

THE COGNITIVE APPROACH

Assumptions
Internal mental processes can be studied through inference.

Theoretical and computer models
Information processing approach.
Mind is likened to a computer and applied to artificial intelligence.

The role of schema
Beliefs and expectation affect thoughts and behaviour.
Innate or learned.
Mental short-cut, leads to perceptual errors.

The emergence of cognitive neuro-science
Biological structures link to mental states, e.g. Broca.
Brain imaging (e.g. fMRI) used to read the brain.

EVALUATION

Scientific and objective methods
Lab experiments to produce reliable, objective data.
Credible basis.

Machine reductionism
Ignores the influence of emotion.
For example anxiety and EWT.

Application to everyday life
Abstract and overly theoretical.
Artificial stimuli.

Evaluation extra
Real-world application, such as AI.
Less determinist than other approaches.

THE BIOLOGICAL APPROACH

Everything psychological is at first biological.

THE BIOLOGICAL APPROACH

Assumptions
Biological processes: genes, neurochemistry and the nervous system.

Genetic basis of behaviour
Twin and family studies.

Genotype and phenotype
Interaction between nature and nurture.

Evolution and behaviour
Natural selection of genes based on survival value and, ultimately, reproductive success.

EVALUATION

Scientific methods
Precise techniques, such as scanning techniques, family studies, drug trials.

Real-life application
Psychotherapeutic drugs.

Causal conclusions
Drugs may only be associated with symptom reduction, not causes.

Evaluation extra
Determinist.
Cannot separate nature and nurture.

THE PSYCHODYNAMIC APPROACH

Behaviour is determined by unconscious forces that we cannot control.

THE PSYCHODYNAMIC APPROACH

Role of the unconscious
The conscious mind is the 'tip of the iceberg'.

Structure of the personality: id, ego and superego
In constant conflict, ego protected by defence mechanisms (e.g. repression, denial, displacement).

Psychosexual stages
Five stages, a different conflict at each stage.

EVALUATION

Explanatory power
Huge influence on psychology and Western thought.

Case study method
Unique and abnormal cases, lacks scientific rigour.

Untestable concepts
Much of the theory is unfalsifiable and untestable, thus pseudoscientific.

Evaluation extra
Practical application in psychoanalysis.
Psychic determinism denies our free will.

HUMANISTIC PSYCHOLOGY

Emerged as the third force in psychology.

HUMANISTIC PSYCHOLOGY

Free will
People are active agents who are self-determining.

Self-actualisation
Everyone has an innate tendency to want to reach their potential.

The self, congruence and conditions of worth
Personal growth requires congruence between self and ideal self.

Hierarchy of needs
Maslow identified physiological deficiency needs to be satisfied before safety and self-actualisation.

EVALUATION

Not reductionist
Humanism places importance on the whole person.

Limited application
Not a comprehensive theory but a loose set of concepts.

Positive approach
Optimistic approach that sees people as basically good.

Evaluation extra
Untestable concepts.
Cultural bias (individualist).
Vague ideas that are abstract and difficult to test so the approach lacks evidence.

PRACTICE QUESTIONS, ANSWERS AND FEEDBACK

Question 1   Explain what Wundt meant by 'introspection'. *(2 marks)*

Morticia's answer   This is a method that was used by Wundt to investigate the way people thought.

Morticia's answer is too vague.

Luke's answer   It means to look inwards, specifically to look inside a person's head to understand what they are thinking and the way their mind works. It's a way to access conscious thinking.

Luke's answer is somewhat better but there remains little reference to what Wundt did or how he did it.

Vladimir's answer   Wundt opened the first lab dedicated to the study of psychology. He wanted to investigate human behaviour and consciousness and used introspection to do this.

Again, a disappointing answer. Vladimir's reference to the first psychology lab does not help define the term and the word 'consciousness' is irrelevant.

Question 2   Using an example, distinguish between genotype and phenotype. *(3 marks)*

Morticia's answer   Genotypes are your genes which determine things like eye colour and many aspects of behaviour. Phenotype is what you actually see in terms of what people are like.

The phenotype explanation is too vague to be of any value. The genotype definition is marginally better.

Luke's answer   You are born with a set of genes, called your genotype. However, these are expressed through the environment so the outcome is your phenotype which is your genes plus the environment. A good example is PKU, a genetic disorder which can cause learning difficulties unless baby's diet is adjusted (their environment). This adjustment of the environment leads to the baby's phenotype.

Luke's definitions are supported by the example that clearly communicates the distinction between the two terms.

Vladimir's answer   Identical twins are a good example of phenotype because they have exactly the same genotype but not necessarily the same phenotype. Their phenotype is affected by their experiences (environment) which may be different.

Vladimir almost communicates what is meant by 'phenotype' in the last sentence but more explanation is required. The only solid comment is the example of identical twins.

Question 3   Outline **one** assumption of humanistic psychology. *(3 marks)*

Morticia's answer   One assumption of the humanistic approach is that people have free will. Free will means an individual can choose what they do, as opposed to determinism where people's behaviour is caused by outside forces. Other approaches like the behaviourist approach support determinism whereas the humanistic approach supports free will.

Morticia's answer includes relevant description of the concept of free will, mostly made clear by the contrast with determinism. The point about the behaviourist approach does not really add anything to the answer.

Luke's answer   Humanistic psychology is quite different to the other approaches because it has the assumption that people have free will, and suggests that people can be self-determining. They are the agent of their own behaviour and can over-ride external or internal causes if they wish to.

Luke's answer is well explained. He focuses entirely on the key concept and provides sufficient detail.

Vladimir's answer   Humanistic psychologists believe that people have free will and that it is important to have free will for healthy psychological development (self-actualisation). We are each responsible for our decisions. However this may apply more to Western individualist cultures than collectivist cultures where group needs are more important than personal growth and decision-making.

Vladimir's answer provides a brief outline of free will but the link to healthy psychological development is not made explicit and doesn't really help the explanation of the assumption. Finally, the evaluation point at the end – though accurate – would be best reserved for another, more discursive question. .

Question 4   A research report claimed that people who believe in aliens are 17 times more likely to claim that they have seen a UFO compared to people who do not.

Explain what cognitive psychologists mean by the term schema. Refer to the information above in your answer. *(4 marks)*

Morticia's answer   Schema are packages of ideas that generate expectations. They are part of the way we think. Cognitive psychologists use them to explain thinking. People see UFOs because they believe in aliens and therefore are more likely to report them.

Morticia gives a brief but accurate definition of schema supported by a similarly brief link to the stem, so neither component amounts to more than a partial answer.

Luke's answer   Schema are used by cognitive psychologists to describe how people think about the world and their experiences. This would explain UFOs because if you don't believe in them you wouldn't see them. This is an example of schemas because it shows how people are thinking and it is affected by their schema.

Luke's definition of schema offered here is not strong, though the link to the stem is partially successful.

Vladimir's answer   In the example the schema would be the belief that some people have that aliens do exist. Such schema are a mental framework for thinking about certain types of things such as UFOs as well as aliens. Having this belief leads to expectations and makes such people more likely to actually interpret something they see as a UFO. Schema may speed up information processing or may make our cognitive system prone to error (the UFO may not be there).

There is reference within Vladimir's answer to 'mental framework', 'expectations' and to the idea that schema may speed up or distort processing, all of which show clear understanding of the concept. The application is also thorough and well embedded in the answer.

On this spread we look at some typical student answers to questions. The comments provided indicate what is good and bad in each answer. Learning how to produce effective question answers is a SKILL. Read pages 387–397 for guidance.

Question 5 Describe and evaluate the behaviourist approach in psychology. As part of your answer you should refer to the research methods used by behaviourist psychologists. *(16 marks)*

Morticia's answer

Behaviourists take the view that the only thing that psychologists should concern themselves with is observable behaviour. Behaviourists are also focused on learning. They believe that all behaviour can be explained through learning – the experiences you have after you have been born.

Learning may involve classical conditioning or operant conditioning. In the case of classical conditioning, first described by the Russian Pavlov, learning begins with a basic stimulus–response link. An unconditioned stimulus causes an unconditioned response. If a neutral stimulus becomes associated with the unconditioned stimulus it eventually predicts the unconditioned response, then it has become a conditioned stimulus producing a conditioned response. Pavlov demonstrated this with dogs and salivation. The dogs eventually salivated when they heard a bell because that became associated with the arrival of food.

Operant conditioning is about operating on your environment. An animal operates on its environment and this has consequences. If these consequences are rewarding then this reinforces the behaviour that brought about the reward and it will be repeated. A behaviour might lead an animal to avoid a negative experience and this is also reinforcing (negative reinforcement), so the behaviour is likely to be repeated. Punishment decreases the likelihood that behaviour will be repeated.

One criticism of behaviourist ideas is that they present a rather mechanistic view of behaviour. They leave out the thought and emotion that influences human behaviour and, to some extent, animal behaviour. People take a much more active role in their behaviour rather than the passive control suggested by conditioning.

One strength of the approach is that it is very scientific with lots of very controlled studies of animals where there are few extraneous variables so the conclusions are firm. On the other hand there is the question of whether such very controlled artificial research with non-human animals really can be applied to human behaviour in the real world.

Another strength of the behaviourist approach is that it has been applied usefully. For example, token economy systems are used in prisons where rewards are used to shape prisoner behaviour.

(340 words)

Morticia's answer is well written. The first paragraph is clear enough and followed by accurate, detailed accounts of the two forms of learning. Her descriptive content demonstrates knowledge, accuracy, clarity and organisation as well as use of specialist terminology.

There are relevant strengths and a limitation here too. Some of these – such as the point about being a mechanistic explanation – might have been supported by reference to alternative approaches. This is not a requirement of the question but is just plain good analysis. On the other hand there is reference to the research methods used by behaviourists, so this satisfies that aspect of the question. Morticia could have offered more commentary/analysis in relation to the use of lab studies.

Overall the answer is light on evaluation, which is especially important for A level. In order to produce good answers students must give special focus to evaluation and evaluation skills.

Vladimir's answer

The behaviourist approach is to explain all behaviour in terms of classical and operant conditioning, i.e. learning.

The first demonstration of classical conditioning was by Pavlov. He was investigating salivation in dogs and noticed that they could be trained to salivate to the sound of a bell. He demonstrated this process in a controlled lab conditions. If a bell was rung repeatedly at the same time as food was presented, the animal learned to associate the bell with food and eventually salivated to the bell alone.

Operant conditioning was demonstrated by Skinner with rats and pigeons in a cage called a Skinner Box. If the animal pressed a lever a food pellet appeared. This reinforced the lever press behaviour so that the animal repeated it more and more. Rats (and pigeons) could also be conditioned to avoid a stimulus such as an electric shock.

Both kinds of learning involve no thought. New connections are formed in the brain but behaviourists are not interested in what goes on in the brain – they just focused on how new behavioural links are formed, i.e. learned. They proposed that everything can be learned in this way.

Behaviourists suggest that humans are made of the same building blocks as animals and therefore the same laws apply. So all human behaviour too is learned and it is a passive process. Your behaviour is conditioned by things outside you. Of course this suggests that we have no free will yet most people do feel they have a sense of their own will. Skinner would argue that this is just an illusion of having made a decision.

The assumption that the same laws apply is challenged because animals are different from humans because human behaviour is more influenced by thinking and emotion. The basis of behaviourism is on research with animals which enables high control but such studies may not generalise to humans or even to some other animals.

(321 words)

Vladimir also describes the two forms of learning but with slightly less sophistication than in the answer above.

Besides this initial description there is further descriptive detail. He makes points related to the focus on observable behaviour and the link between human and animal learning though these are not always clearly expressed.

Evaluation/analysis is present but it is not the main focus of the essay. There is some analytic reference to free will (or lack of it), the qualitative difference between humans and animals, and a very brief comment on the limitations of animal studies at the end.

Overall, not as strong on evaluation as the previous answer and an overly descriptive answer. The evaluation content is partly effective whereas the description is mostly clear and organised and specialist terminology has been used.

MULTIPLE-CHOICE QUESTIONS

Origins of psychology

1. From earliest to most recent, which of the following is the correct chronological order of when the following psychological approaches were first established?

(a) Social learning theory : humanistic : behaviourist : cognitive neuroscience

(b) Cognitive neuroscience : social learning theory : behaviourist : humanistic

(c) Humanistic : behaviourist : cognitive neuroscience : social learning theory

(d) Behaviourist : humanistic : social learning theory : cognitive neuroscience

2. Which of the following is a criticism that Watson made of introspection?

(a) It can't be replicated.

(b) It doesn't deal with experience.

(c) It produces objective data.

(d) It is unscientific.

3. Who suggested that the mind and the body (brain) were separate and independent of one another?

(a) Darwin.

(b) Wundt.

(c) Descartes.

(d) Locke.

4. Who suggested that humans inherit neither knowledge nor instincts?

(a) Darwin.

(b) Wundt.

(c) Descartes.

(d) Locke.

The learning approach: behaviourism

1. Which is a basic assumption of the behaviourist approach?

(a) Learning processes in animals cannot be generalised to humans.

(b) The main influence on behaviour is your genes.

(c) Learning is influenced by private mental processes.

(d) Learning should be studied scientifically in a laboratory.

2. Pavlov identified the following steps in classical conditioning:
Bell (before learning) – food – salivation (before learning) – bell (after learning).
Which is the correct sequence of terms for the features listed above?

(a) Unconditioned response – neutral stimulus – unconditioned stimulus – conditioned stimulus

(b) Neutral stimulus – unconditioned response – conditioned stimulus – unconditioned response

(c) Unconditioned stimulus – conditioned stimulus – unconditioned response – neutral stimulus

(d) Neutral stimulus – unconditioned stimulus – unconditioned response – conditioned stimulus

3. Complete this sentence: Operant conditioning is best described as . . .

(a) A form of learning in which behaviour is shaped and maintained by its consequences.

(b) A form of learning in which a stimulus is associated with a response.

(c) A form of learning in which an observer imitates the behaviour of a role model.

(d) A form of learning in which new behaviour is produced that avoids an unpleasant consequence.

4. A Behaviourist researcher carried out a lab experiment. He put a rat in a specially designed box. Every time a light came on, the rat would receive an electric shock to its feet. However, over time, the rat learned that if it pressed a lever when the light came on, it would not receive the shock.

What aspect of operant conditioning is the Behaviourist researcher investigating?

(a) Partial reinforcement.

(b) Positive reinforcement.

(c) Negative reinforcement.

(d) Punishment.

The learning approach: social learning

1. Which one of the following statements about Bandura's Bobo doll experiments is false?

(a) Children were more likely to imitate aggression that was rewarded (reinforced).

(b) Children who saw the model punished were more likely to imitate aggression than children who saw no consequences.

(c) The experiments have been used to support the idea that children may be influenced by what they see in the media.

(d) The experiments support the idea that learning can often occur indirectly.

2. Which of the following is not a mediational process in the social learning approach?

(a) Motivation.

(b) Attention.

(c) Retention.

(d) Application.

3. The idea that human beings influence their environment as well as being influenced by it, best describes:

(a) Hard determinism.

(b) Environmental determinism.

(c) Soft determinism.

(d) Reciprocal determinism.

4. Which statement about the social learning theory approach is false?

(a) Learning and performance always occur together.

(b) Attention and retention are more likely to be involved in the learning than performance of behaviour.

(c) Motor reproduction and motivation are more likely to be involved in the performance than learning of behaviour.

(d) Role models that children identify with need not be real but may be symbolic.

The cognitive approach

1. Which statement about the role of schema is false?

(a) They allow us to make mental short cuts.

(b) They may lead to perceptual errors.

(c) They are not present at birth.

(d) They act as a mental framework of interpretation.

2. A cognitive psychologist gave students simple word lists to learn under lab conditions. The students were able to recall an average of seven words within their short-term memory (STM). The psychologist concluded that the capacity of STM is seven items. This is a good example of . . .

(a) Inference.

(b) Interference.

(c) Implication.

(d) Illustration.

3. The cognitive approach is a good example of . . .

(a) Internal determinism.

(b) External determinism.

(c) Hard determinism.

(d) Soft determinism.

4. Which statement about cognitive neuroscience is false?

(a) It was first identified in the 1970s as an emergent discipline.

(b) It investigates how biological structures influence mental processes.

(c) It brings together the fields of cognitive psychology, anatomy and neurophysiology.

(d) It makes use of advances in brain imaging technology such as fMRI.

The biological approach

1. Which of the following formulas is true?

(a) Genotype + phenotype = environment.

(b) Phenotype + environment = genotype.

(c) Genotype + environment = phenotype.

(d) Genotype – phenotype = environment.

2. The biological approach is an example of . . .

(a) Internal and soft determinism.

(b) Internal and hard determinism.

(c) External and soft determinism.

(d) External and hard determinism.

3. The fact DZ twins tend to show higher concordance rates than ordinary siblings suggests . . .

(a) The importance of hereditary/genetic factors in development.

(b) The importance of environmental factors in development.

(c) That DZ twins are more genetically similar than ordinary siblings.

(d) That ordinary siblings may be raised in a more similar way than DZ twins.

4. Which of the following is *not* an assumption of the biological approach?

(a) The brain and the mind are distinct and separate.

(b) Psychological characteristics may be genetically determined in the same way that physical characteristics are.

(c) An imbalance in neurochemical levels may explain mental illness.

(d) Human behaviour has adapted to the environment through natural selection.

The psychodynamic approach

1. Which of the following is *not* a term used by Freud in relation to the structure of the mind?

(a) Conscious.

(b) Preconscious.

(c) Subconscious.

(d) Unconscious.

2. In which stage does the Oedipus complex take place?

(a) Oral.

(b) Anal.

(c) Phallic.

(d) Genital.

3. Which of the following is 'transferring feelings from the true source of distressing emotion onto a substitute object'?

(a) Displacement.

(b) Denial.

(c) Repression.

(d) Regression.

4. Freud's theory is most associated with . . .

(a) Environmental determinism.

(b) Biological determinism.

(c) Reciprocal determinism.

(d) Psychic determinism.

Humanistic psychology

1. When it first emerged, humanistic psychology came to be known as:

(a) The first force.

(b) The second force.

(c) The third force.

(d) May the force be with you.

2. When there is a mismatch between the self-concept and the ideal self, this is referred to as . . .

(a) Self-actualisation.

(b) Conditions of worth.

(c) Congruence.

(d) Incongruence.

3. According to Rogers, an effective therapist should provide the client with three things. Which of the following is *not* one of these?

(a) Being empathic.

(b) Being judgemental.

(c) Being genuine.

(d) Unconditional positive regard.

4. Which of the following is a 'growth need' in Maslow's hierarchy?

(a) Self-actualisation.

(b) Love and belongingness.

(c) Safety and security.

(d) Physiological.

MCQ answers

Origins of psychology 1d, 2d, 3c, 4d
The behaviourist approach 1d, 2d, 3a, 4c
The social learning theory approach 1b, 2d, 3d, 4a
The cognitive approach 1c, 2a, 3d, 4a
The biological approach 1c, 2b, 3b, 4a
The psychodynamic approach 1c, 2c, 3a, 4d
Humanistic psychology 1c, 2d, 3b, 4a

CHAPTER 2
BIOPSYCHOLOGY

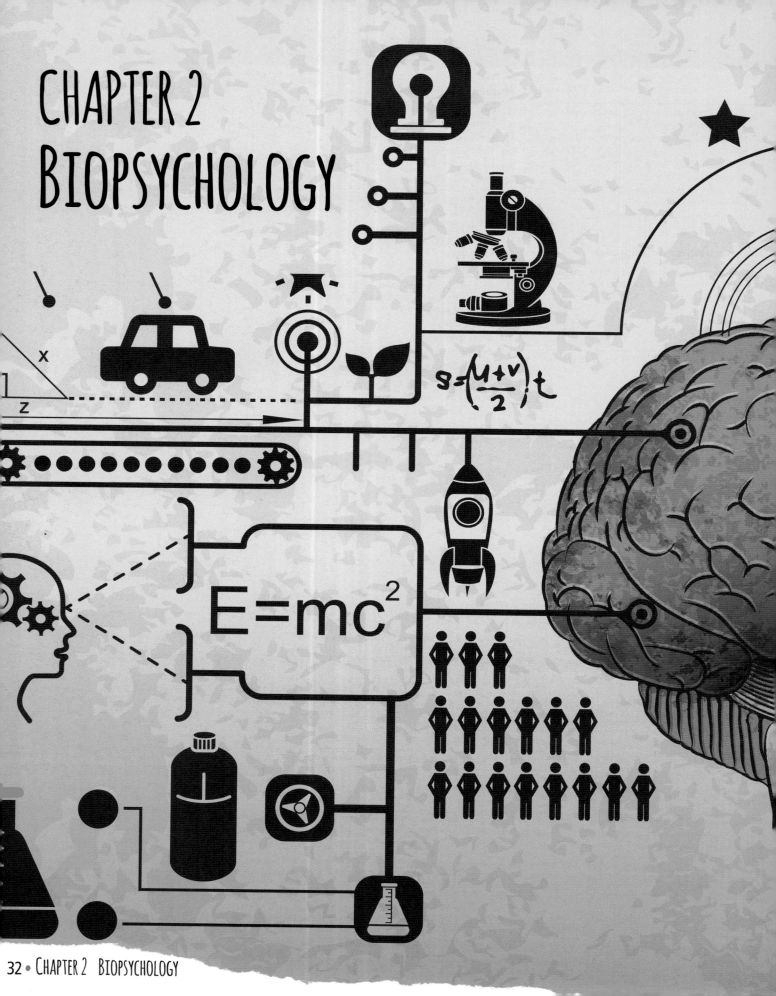

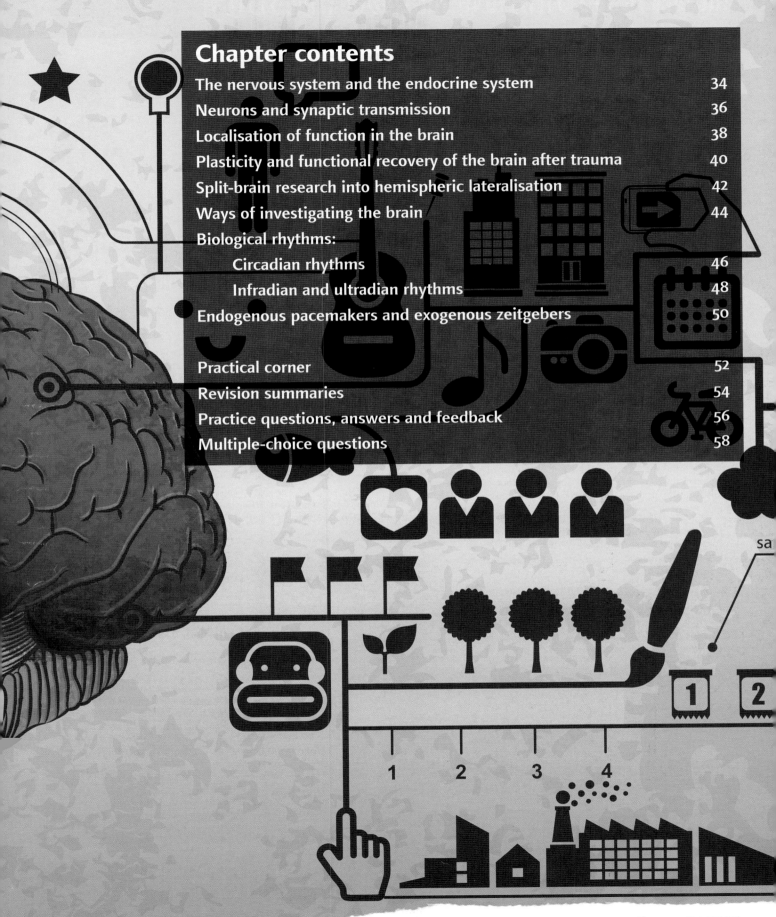

Chapter contents

THE NERVOUS SYSTEM AND THE ENDOCRINE SYSTEM

This spread and the following spread were presented in the AS/Year 1 book because the content forms part of the AS specification.

For A level these two spreads are included in the stand-alone topic 'Biopsychology' – on Paper 2 there is one section devoted to Biopsychology. At AS Biopsychology is examined as part of approaches.

THE SPECIFICATION SAYS...

The divisions of the nervous system: central and peripheral (somatic and autonomic).

The function of the endocrine system: glands and hormones.

The fight or flight response and the role of adrenaline.

Humans, like animals, have two major physiological systems that regulate behaviour in response to the environment. These are the nervous system and the endocrine system.

KEY TERMS

Nervous system – Consists of the central nervous system and the peripheral nervous system.

Central nervous system (CNS) – Consists of the brain and the spinal cord and is the origin of all complex commands and decisions.

Peripheral nervous system (PNS) – Sends information to the central nervous system (CNS) from the outside world, and transmits messages *from* the CNS to muscles and glands in the body.

Somatic nervous system – Transmits information from receptor cells in the sense organs to the central nervous system (CNS). It also receives information from the CNS that directs muscles to act.

Autonomic nervous system (ANS) – Transmits information to and from internal bodily organs. It is 'autonomic' as the system operates involuntarily (i.e. it is automatic). It has two main divisions: the *sympathetic* and *parasympathetic* nervous systems.

The nervous system

The **nervous system** is a specialised network of cells in the human body and is our primary internal communication system. It has two main functions:

- To collect, process and respond to information in the environment.
- To co-ordinate the working of different organs and cells in the body.

It is divided into two sub-systems:

- **Central nervous system** (**CNS**)
- **Peripheral nervous system** (**PNS**).

The central nervous system

The CNS is made up of the brain and the spinal cord.

- The brain is the centre of all conscious awareness. The brain's outer layer, the **cerebral cortex**, is highly developed in humans and is what distinguishes our higher mental functions from those of animals. Only a few living creatures – sponges, sea squirts, jellyfish and some Manchester United fans – do not have a brain. The brain is divided into two **hemispheres**.
- The **spinal cord** is an extension of the brain. It is responsible for reflex actions such as pulling your hand away from a hot plate.

It passes messages to and from the brain and connects nerves to the PNS.

The peripheral nervous system

The PNS transmits messages, via millions of **neurons** (nerve cells), to and from the central nervous system. The peripheral nervous system is further sub-divided into the:

- **Autonomic nervous system** (**ANS**) governs vital functions in the body such as breathing, heart rate, digestion, sexual arousal and stress responses.
- **Somatic nervous system** (**SNS**) controls muscle movement and receives information from sensory receptors.

Human Nervous System

- Peripheral Nervous System
  - Autonomic Nervous System
    - Sympathetic Nervous System
    - Parasympathetic Nervous System
  - Somatic Nervous System
- Central Nervous System
  - Brain
  - Spinal Cord

The major sub-divisions of the human nervous system.

Apply it

Concepts: A frightening experience

Jim Bob was telling his friend Sue Ellen about his recent frightening experience.

'I was walking home by myself in the dark. Suddenly, I heard a shuffling noise behind me and the faint smell of rotting flesh. I realised it was coming closer. I saw a bus at the bus stop and decided to run. I could hear the footsteps getting closer. I don't think I've ever moved so quickly. I leapt on the bus – shaking, sweating and my heart was beating fast. I turned to see an empty street as the bus pulled away from the stop. Had I imagined it?'

Question

Outline the role of the central nervous system **and** autonomic nervous system in behaviour. Refer to Jim Bob's experience in your answer.

The endocrine system

Glands and hormones

The **endocrine system** works alongside the nervous system to control vital functions in the body. The endocrine system acts much more slowly than the nervous system but has very widespread and powerful effects. Various **glands** in the body, such as the **thyroid gland**, produce **hormones**. Hormones are secreted into the bloodstream and affect any cell in the body that has a receptor for that particular hormone.

Most hormones affect cells in several organs or throughout the entire body, leading to many diverse and powerful responses. For example, the thyroid gland produces the hormone **thyroxine**. This hormone affects cells in the heart (increases heart rate). It also affects cells throughout the body increasing metabolic rates (the chemical processes taking place in the cells). This in turn affects growth rates.

The main glands of the endocrine system are shown in the diagram on the right. The major endocrine gland is the **pituitary gland**, located in the brain. It is often called the 'master gland' because it controls the release of hormones from all the other endocrine glands in the body.

Endocrine and ANS working together: Fight or flight

Often the endocrine system and the autonomic nervous system work in parallel with one another, for instance during a stressful event. When a stressor is perceived (your friend jumps out to frighten you or you think about your upcoming exams) the first thing that happens is a part of the brain called the hypothalamus triggers activity in the sympathetic branch of the autonomic nervous system. The ANS changes from its normal resting state (the **parasympathetic state**) to the physiologically aroused, **sympathetic state** (try it – think of having to learn all this for your exams).The stress hormone **adrenaline** is released from the adrenal medulla (a part of the adrenal gland) into the bloodstream. Adrenaline triggers physiological changes in the body (e.g. increased heart rate) which creates the physiological arousal necessary for the **fight or flight** response. All of this happens in an instant as soon as the threat is detected – an acute response – and is an automatic reaction in the body. The physiological changes associated with this sympathetic response are listed in the table below right. These changes explain why stress, panic, or even excitement, is often experienced as a 'sick' feeling ('butterflies' in your stomach – does that describe what you were feeling?).

Finally, once the threat has passed, the parasympathetic nervous system returns the body to its resting state. The parasympathetic branch of the ANS works in opposition to the sympathetic nervous system – its actions are *antagonistic* to the sympathetic system. The parasympathetic system acts as a 'brake' and reduces the activities of the body that were increased by the actions of the sympathetic branch. This is sometimes referred to as the *rest and digest* response.

The main endocrine glands in the human body.

Adrenals
Pancreas
Ovaries (female)
Testes (male)

KEY TERMS

Endocrine system – One of the body's major information systems that instructs glands to release hormones directly into the bloodstream. These hormones are carried towards target organs in the body.

Gland – An organ in the body that synthesises substances such as hormones.

Hormones – Chemical substances that circulate in the bloodstream and only affect target organs. They are produced in large quantities but disappear quickly. Their effects are very powerful.

Fight or flight response – The way an animal responds when stressed. The body becomes physiologically aroused in readiness to fight an aggressor or, in some cases, flee.

Adrenaline – A hormone produced by the adrenal glands which is part of the human body's immediate stress response system. Adrenaline has a strong effect on the cells of the cardiovascular system – stimulating the heart rate, contracting blood vessels and dilating air passages.

Apply it — Methods: Stress and illness

Research has shown that people who get ill have often experienced major stressful life events in the previous few months and years, such as getting married, divorce, death of a loved one, etc. A researcher investigated this relationship between illness and life events. She gave 150 participants a questionnaire in which they had to indicate the number of major life events (from a list of 20) they had experienced over the past three years. This was compared to the number of days off work through illness the participants had had over the same period.

The researcher found a **positive correlation** between the two co-variables.

1. In the context of the investigation above, what is meant by 'a positive correlation between the two co-variables'? (*2 marks*) (See page 63)

2. Suggest a suitable graphical display that the researcher could have used to show the relationship between the two co-variables. (*1 mark*)

3. Explain *one* advantage of **correlational studies**. Refer to the investigation above in your answer. (*2 marks*)

4. Explain the difference between correlations and experiments. (*3 marks*)

Biological changes associated with the sympathetic and parasympathetic response.

Sympathetic state	Parasympathetic state
Increases heart rate	Decreases heart rate
Increases breathing rate	Decreases breathing rate
Dilates pupils	Constricts pupils
Inhibits digestion	Stimulates digestion
Inhibits saliva production	Stimulates saliva production
Contracts rectum	Relaxes rectum

CHECK IT

1. Name and briefly outline **two** divisions of the human nervous system. [4 marks]

2. Identify and describe **two** glands of the endocrine system. [2 marks + 2 marks]

3. Briefly outline **two** hormones and explain the function of each of these. [2 marks + 2 marks]

4. Using an example, explain what is meant by the fight or flight response. [3 marks]

The structure and function of sensory, relay and motor neurons.

The process of synaptic transmission including reference to neurotransmitters, excitation and inhibition.

On the previous spread we considered the major biological structures and systems. Now we will delve a little deeper and, in so doing, get a good deal smaller! We will investigate how the nervous system transmits signals for communication via the billions of nerve cells (neurons) it houses.

We will also consider how these nerve cells communicate with each other, through electrical and chemical messages, within the body and the brain.

KEY TERMS

Neuron – The basic building blocks of the nervous system, neurons are nerve cells that process and transmit messages through electrical and chemical signals.

Sensory neurons – These carry messages from the PNS (peripheral nervous system) to the CNS (central nervous system). They have long dendrites and short axons.

Relay neurons – These connect the sensory neurons to the motor or other relay neurons. They have short dendrites and short axons.

Motor neurons – These connect the CNS (central nervous system) to effectors such as muscles and glands. They have short dendrites and long axons.

Apply it

Concepts: Function of neurons

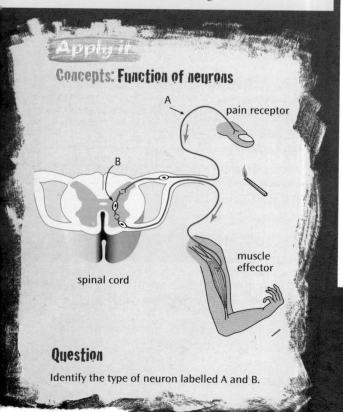

Question

Identify the type of neuron labelled A and B.

The structure and function of neurons

There are 100 billion **neurons** (nerve cells) in the human nervous system, 80% of which are located in the brain. By transmitting signals *electrically* and *chemically*, these neurons provide the nervous system with its primary means of communication.

Types of neuron

There are three types of neurons: **motor neurons**, **sensory neurons** and **relay neurons**. The features of each are summarised in the key terms on the left and illustrated in the diagram below.

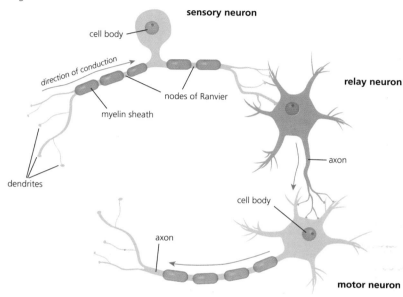

The structure of a neuron

Neurons vary in size from less than a millimetre to up to a metre long, but all share the same basic structure.

The **cell body** (or soma) includes a **nucleus**, which contains the genetic material of the cell. Branch-like structures called **dendrites** protrude from the cell body. These carry nerve impulses from neighbouring neurons towards the cell body.

The **axon** carries the impulses away from the cell body down the length of the neuron. The axon is covered in a fatty layer of **myelin sheath** that protects the axon and speeds up electrical transmission of the impulse.

If the myelin sheath was continuous this would have the reverse effect and slow down the electrical impulse. Thus, the myelin sheath is segmented by gaps called **nodes of Ranvier**. These speed up the transmission of the impulse by forcing it to 'jump' across the gaps along the axon.

Finally, at the end of the axon are **terminal buttons** that communicate with the next neuron in the chain across a gap known as the synapse (see facing page).

Electric transmission – the firing of a neuron

When a neuron is in a resting state the inside of the cell is negatively charged compared to the outside. When a neuron is activated by a stimulus, the inside of the cell becomes positively charged for a split second causing an **action potential** to occur. This creates an electrical impulse that travels down the axon towards the end of the neuron.

Synaptic transmission

Chemical transmission – synapses

Neurons communicate with each other within groups known as **neural networks**. Each neuron is separated from the next by a **synapse**. The synapse includes the space between them (called the synaptic cleft) as well as the presynaptic terminal and postsynaptic receptor site. Signals *within* neurons are transmitted electrically; however, signals *between* neurons are transmitted chemically by **synaptic transmission**.

When the electrical impulse reaches the end of the neuron (the **presynaptic terminal**) it triggers the release of **neurotransmitter** from tiny sacs called **synaptic vesicles**.

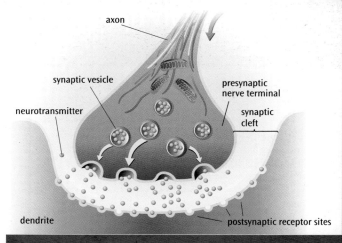

Neurotransmitter

Neurotransmitters are chemicals that diffuse across the synapse to the next neuron in the chain.

Once the neurotransmitter crosses the gap, it is taken up by the **postsynaptic receptor sites** – in other words, the dendrites of the next neuron. Here, the chemical message is converted back into an electrical impulse and the process of transmission begins again in this other neuron.

Several dozen types of neurotransmitter have been identified in the brain (as well as in the spinal cord and some **glands**). Each neurotransmitter has its own specific molecular structure that fits perfectly into a post-synaptic receptor site, similar to a lock and a key. Neurotransmitters also have specialist functions. For instance, **acetylcholine** (ACh) is found at each point where a motor neuron meets a muscle, and upon its release, it will cause muscles to contract.

Excitation and inhibition

Neurotransmitters have either an **excitatory** or **inhibitory** effect on the neighbouring neuron. For instance, the neurotransmitter **serotonin** causes inhibition in the receiving neuron, resulting in the neuron becoming more negatively charged and less likely to fire. In contrast, **adrenaline** (an element of the stress response which is both a **hormone** and a neurotransmitter) causes excitation of the postsynaptic neuron by increasing its positive charge and making it more likely to fire.

Summation

The question of whether a postsynaptic neuron does fire is decided by the process of **summation**. The excitatory and inhibitory influences are summed: if the net effect on the postsynaptic neuron is inhibitory then the postsynaptic neuron is less likely to fire; if the net effect is excitatory it is more likely to fire - and, momentarily, the inside of the postsynaptic neuron becomes positively charged. Once the electrical impulse is created, it travels down the neuron.

Therefore the action potential of the postsynaptic neuron is only triggered if the sum of the excitatory and inhibitory signals at any one time reaches the threshold.

KEY TERMS

Synaptic transmission – The process by which neighbouring neurons communicate with each other by sending chemical messages across the gap (the synaptic cleft) that separates them.

Neurotransmitter – Brain chemicals released from synaptic vesicles that relay signals across the synapse from one neuron to another. Neurotransmitters can be broadly divided into those that perform an excitatory function and those that perform an inhibitory function.

Excitation – When a neurotransmitter, such as adrenaline, increases the positive charge of the postsynaptic neuron. This *increases* the likelihood that the neuron will fire and pass on the electrical impulse.

Inhibition – When a neurotransmitter, such as serotonin, makes the charge of the postsynaptic neuron more negative. This *decreases* the likelihood that the neuron will fire and pass on the electrical impulse.

Apply it Concepts: The reflex arc

Fill in the gaps using the terms provided in the box.

Missing words:
relay neuron
CNS (central nervous system),
sensory neuron
PNS (peripheral nervous system)
motor neuron
effector

The knee-jerk reflex is an example of a reflex arc:

A stimulus, such as a hammer, hits the knee. This is detected by sense organs in the _____, which convey a message along a _____,

The message reaches the _____, where it connects with a _____, This then transfers the message to a _____, This then carries the message to an _____, such as a muscle, which causes the muscle to contract and, hence, causes the knee to move or jerk.

Apply it Concepts: Psychoactive drugs

Increased understanding of the mode of action of neurotransmitters in the brain has led to the development of **psychoactive drugs** to treat mental disorders. For instance, depression has been linked to a lack of serotonin, which is thought to play an important role in stabilising mood.

A category of drugs known as **SSRIs** (selective serotonin reuptake inhibitors) such as *Prozac*, slow down the reuptake of serotonin after it has crossed the synapse, ensuring it stays active for longer in the brain.

Question

Use your knowledge of synaptic transmission to explain what is happening at the synapse.

CHECK IT

1. Briefly explain the process of synaptic transmission.
[4 marks]

2. With reference to neurotransmitters, explain what is meant by both *excitation* and *inhibition*. [4 marks]

3. Distinguish between a sensory neuron and a relay neuron. [2 marks]

Localisation of function in the brain: motor, somatosensory, visual, auditory and language centres; Broca's and Wernicke's areas.

The human brain is surely one of the most complex and fascinating of all biological systems. On this spread, we discuss the idea that different functions of the brain are *localised* in specific areas as well as taking a whistle-stop tour through some of the key parts of the brain.

KEY TERMS

Localisation of function – The theory that different areas of the brain are responsible for different behaviours, processes or activities.

Motor area – A region of the frontal lobe involved in regulating movement.

Somatosensory area – An area of the parietal lobe that processes sensory information such as touch.

Visual area – A part of the occipital lobe that receives and processes visual information.

Auditory area – Located in the temporal lobe and concerned with the analysis of speech-based information.

Broca's area – An area of the frontal lobe of the brain in the left hemisphere (in most people) responsible for speech production.

Wernicke's area – An area of the temporal lobe (encircling the auditory cortex) in the left hemisphere (in most people) responsible for language comprehension.

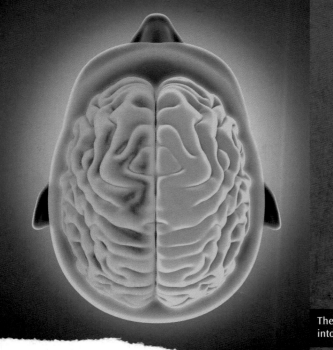

The brain – like the Earth – is divided into two distinct hemispheres.

Localisation of function in the brain

Localisation versus holistic theory

During the 19th century, scientists such as Paul Broca and Karl Wernicke discovered that specific areas of the brain are associated with particular physical and psychological functions. Before these investigations (and before the case of Phineas Gage – see facing page), scientists generally supported the holistic theory of the brain – that *all* parts of the brain were involved in the processing of thought and action.

In contrast, Broca and Wernicke argued for localisation of function (sometimes referred to as *cortical specialisation*). This is the idea that different parts of the brain perform different tasks and are involved with different parts of the body. It follows then, that if a certain area of the brain becomes damaged through illness or injury, the function associated with that area will also be affected.

Hemispheres of the brain and the cerebral cortex

The brain is divided into two symmetrical halves called left and right hemispheres. Some of our physical and psychological functions are controlled or dominated by a particular hemisphere – this is called lateralisation (see next spread). As a general rule, activity on the left-hand side of the body is controlled by the right hemisphere and activity on the right-hand side of the body by the left hemisphere. The outer layer of both hemispheres is the **cerebral cortex** (or 'cortex') like a tea cosy covering the inner parts of the brain. This 'tea-cosy' is about 3 mm thick and is what separates us from other animals because the human cortex is much more developed. The cortex appears grey due to the location of cell bodies (hence the phrase 'grey matter' to describe the surface appearance of the brain).

The motor, somatosensory, visual and auditory centres

The cortex of both hemispheres is sub-divided into four lobes which are named after the bones beneath which they lie: the frontal lobe, the parietal lobe, the occipital lobe and the temporal lobe (see diagram on facing page). Each lobe is associated with different functions.

At the back of the frontal lobe (in both hemispheres) is the **motor area** which controls voluntary movement in the opposite side of the body. Damage to this area of the brain may result in a loss of control over fine movements.

At the front of both parietal lobes is the **somatosensory area** which is separated from the motor area by a 'valley' called the *central sulcus*. The somatosensory area is where sensory information from the skin (e.g. related to touch, heat, pressure, etc.) is represented. The amount of somatosensory area devoted to a particular body part denotes its sensitivity, for instance, receptors for our face and hands occupy over half of the somatosensory area.

In the occipital lobe at the back of the brain is the **visual area** (or visual cortex). Each eye sends information from the right visual field to the left visual cortex and from the left visual field to the right visual cortex. This means that damage to the left hemisphere, for example, can produce blindness in part of the right visual field of both eyes.

Finally, the temporal lobes house the **auditory area**, which analyses speech-based information. Damage may produce partial hearing loss; the more extensive the damage, the more extensive the loss. In addition, damage to a specific area of the temporal lobe – Wernicke's area (discussed below) – may affect the ability to comprehend language.

The language area of the brain

Unlike the areas above which are found in both hemispheres, language is restricted to the left side of the brain in most people. In the 1880s, Paul Broca, a surgeon, identified a small area in the left frontal lobe responsible for speech production. Damage to **Broca's area** causes Broca's aphasia which is characterised by speech that is slow, laborious and lacking in fluency (as seen in a number of Broca's patients like 'Tan' – so-called because that was the only word he could say).

Around the same time as Broca, Karl Wernicke was describing patients who had no problem producing language but severe difficulties understanding it, such that the speech they produced was fluent but meaningless. Wernicke identified a region (**Wernicke's area**) in the left temporal lobe as being responsible for language comprehension which would result in *Wernicke's aphasia* when damaged. Patients who have Wernicke's aphasia will often produce nonsense words (*neologisms*) as part of the content of their speech.

Evaluation

Brain scan evidence of localisation

There is a wealth of evidence providing support for the idea that many neurological functions are localised, particularly in relation to language and memory. For instance, Petersen *et al.* (1988) used **brain scans** to demonstrate how Wernicke's area was active during a listening task and Broca's area was active during a reading task, suggesting that these areas of the brain have different functions.

Similarly, a study of long-term memory by Tulving *et al.* (1994) revealed that **semantic** and **episodic memories** reside in different parts of the prefrontal cortex. There now exists a number of highly sophisticated and objective methods for measuring activity in the brain (see page 44) which provide sound scientific evidence of localisation of brain function.

Neurosurgical evidence

The practice of surgically removing or destroying areas of the brain to control aspects of behaviour developed in the 1950s. Early attempts, such as those pioneered by Walter Freeman who developed the **lobotomy**, were brutal and imprecise and typically involved severing connections in the **frontal lobe** in an attempt to control aggressive behaviour.

Controversially, neurosurgery is still used today, albeit sparingly, in extreme cases of **obsessive-compulsive disorder** and **depression**. For example, Dougherty *et al.* (2002) reported on 44 OCD patients who had undergone a *cingulotomy* – a neurosurgical procedure that involves lesioning of the cingulate gyrus. At post-surgical follow-up after 32 weeks, a third had met the criteria for successful response to the surgery and 14 percent for partial response. The success of procedures like this strongly suggests that symptoms and behaviours associated with serious mental disorders are localised.

Case study evidence

Unique cases of neurological damage support localisation theory such as the case of Phineas Gage (see right).

Evaluation eXtra

Lashley's research	Plasticity

Lashley's research

The work of Karl Lashley (1950) suggests that higher cognitive functions, such as the processes involved in learning, are not localised but distributed in a more holistic way in the brain. Lashley removed areas of the cortex (between 10 and 50%) in rats that were learning a maze. No area was proven to be more important than any other area in terms of the rats' ability to learn the maze. The process of learning appeared to require *every part* of the cortex, rather than being confined to a particular area. This seems to suggest that learning is too complex to be localised and requires the involvement of the whole of the brain.

Consider: *Lashley's work was conducted using animals (rats). Explain why this means we should be cautious in drawing conclusions related to human learning.*

Plasticity

A further and compelling argument against localisation of function is the notion of *cortical remapping* or **plasticity** (see next spread). When the brain has become damaged, say through illness or accident, and a particular function has been compromised or lost, the rest of the brain appears able to reorganise itself in an attempt to recover the lost function. Lashley described this as the *law of equipotentiality* whereby surviving brain circuits 'chip in' so the same neurological action can be achieved. Although this does not happen every time, there are several documented cases of stroke victims being able to recover those abilities that were seemingly lost as a result of the illness.

Consider: *Explain how the apparent plasticity of the brain lends support to holistic, rather than localisation, theory.*

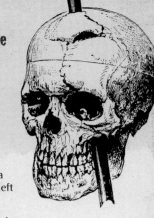

Apply it **Concepts:**

The curious case of Phineas Gage

Whilst working on the railroad in 1848, 25-year-old Phineas Gage was preparing to blast a section of rock with explosives to create a new railway line. During the process, Gage dropped his tamping iron onto the rock causing the explosive to ignite. The explosion hurled the metre-length pole through Gage's left cheek, passing behind his left eye, and exiting his skull from the top of his head taking a portion of his brain with it – most of his left frontal lobe.

Incredibly, Gage survived but the damage to his brain had left a mark on his personality – by all accounts he had turned from someone who was calm and reserved to someone who was quick-tempered, rude and 'no longer Gage'.

Gage is seen as a landmark case in science as the change in his temperament following the accident suggests that the frontal lobe may be responsible for regulating mood.

Questions

1. Does the case of Phineas Gage support localisation theory or holistic theory? Why?
2. Why is it difficult to draw general conclusions from the case of Gage?

Apply it **Concepts: Label the brain**

Use the information on the facing page to help you label the areas of the brain.

Labels:

Auditory area
Broca's area
Motor area
Somatosensory area
Visual area
Wernicke's area

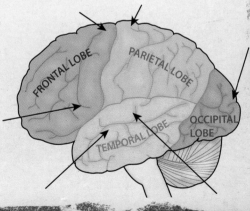

CHECK IT

1. Using an example, explain what is meant *localisation of function*. [3 marks]
2. Describe **one** study in which localisation of brain function was investigated. Include details of what the psychologists did and what was found. [3 marks]
3. State the location in the brain of each of the following:
   (i) The motor area
   (ii) The visual area
   (iii) The auditory area. [3 marks]
4. Discuss the extent to which brain functions are localised. Refer to evidence in your answer. [16 marks]

THE SPECIFICATION SAYS...

Plasticity and functional recovery of the brain after trauma.

Neural plasticity is the apparent ability of the brain to change and adapt its structures and processes as a result of experience and new learning. This links directly to the notion of functional recovery – the way that certain abilities of the brain may be moved or redistributed rather than lost following damage or trauma to the brain.

KEY TERMS

Plasticity – (also referred to as *neuroplasticity* or *cortical remapping*) This describes the brain's tendency to change and adapt (functionally and physically) as a result of experience and new learning.

Functional recovery – A form of plasticity. Following damage through trauma, the brain's ability to redistribute or transfer functions usually performed by a damaged area(s) to other, undamaged area(s).

'You wouldn't believe the size of my mid-posterior hippocampus, mate.' A London cabbie talks brain plasticity.

Apply it

Methods: Brainy cab drivers

A researcher compared the hippocampal volume of taxi drivers (who drive different routes every day) with bus drivers (who follow the same routes every day). The researcher used an **unrelated *t*-test** to analyse the data and a **significant** difference was found at the 0.05 level.

Questions

1. Explain *two* reasons why the unrelated *t*-test was an appropriate choice for this investigation. *(4 marks)* (See page 70)

2. With reference to this investigation, explain what is meant by the phrase 'a significant difference was found at the 0.05 level'. *(2 marks)* (See page 72)

Plasticity and functional recovery of the brain after trauma

Brain plasticity

The brain would appear to be 'plastic' (not literally – it's a metaphor!) in the sense that it has the ability to change throughout life. During infancy, the brain experiences a rapid growth in the number of **synaptic** connections it has, peaking at approximately 15,000 at age 2–3 years (Gopnick *et al.* 1999). This equates to about twice as many as there are in the adult brain. As we age, rarely used connections are deleted and frequently used connections are strengthened – a process known as *synaptic pruning*.

It was originally thought that such changes were restricted to the developing brain within childhood, and that the adult brain, having moved beyond a critical period, would remain fixed and static in terms of function and structure. However, more recent research suggests that at any time in life existing neural connections can change, or new neural connections can be formed, as a result of learning and experience (**plasticity**).

Research into plasticity

Eleanor Maguire *et al.* (2000) studied the brains of London taxi drivers and found significantly more volume of grey matter in the posterior **hippocampus** than in a matched control group. This part of the brain is associated with the development of spatial and navigational skills in humans and other animals. As part of their training, London cabbies must take a complex test called 'The Knowledge', which assesses their recall of the city streets and possible routes. It appears that the result of this learning experience is to alter the structure of the taxi drivers' brains. It is also noteworthy that the longer they had been in the job, the more pronounced was the structural difference (a **positive correlation**).

A similar finding was observed by Draganski *et al.* (2006) who imaged the brains of medical students three months before and after their final exams. Learning-induced changes were seen to have occurred in the posterior hippocampus and the parietal cortex presumably as a result of the exam. Finally, Mechelli *et al.* (2004) also found a larger parietal cortex in the brains of people who were bilingual compared to matched monolingual controls.

Functional recovery of the brain after trauma

Following physical injury, or other forms of trauma such as the experience of a stroke, unaffected areas of the brain are often able to adapt and compensate for those areas that are damaged. The **functional recovery** that may occur in the brain after trauma is another example of neural plasticity. Healthy brain areas may take over the functions of those areas that are damaged, destroyed or even missing. Neuroscientists suggest that this process can occur quickly after trauma (spontaneous recovery) and then slow down after several weeks or months. At this point the individual may require rehabilitative therapy to further their recovery (see facing page).

What happens in the brain during recovery?

The brain is able to rewire and reorganise itself by forming new synaptic connections close to the area of damage (a bit like avoiding roadworks on the way to school by finding a different route). Secondary neural pathways that would not typically be used to carry out certain functions are activated or 'unmasked' to enable functioning to continue, often in the same way as before (Doidge 2007). This process is supported by a number of structural changes in the brain including:

* *Axonal sprouting*: The growth of new nerve endings which connect with other undamaged nerve cells to form new neuronal pathways.

* *Reformation of blood vessels*.

* *Recruitment of homologous* (similar) *areas* on the opposite side of the brain to perform specific tasks. An example would be if Broca's area was damaged on the left side of the brain, the right-sided equivalent would carry out its functions. After a period of time, functionality may then shift back to the left side.

STUDY TIP

Functional recovery after trauma is one dramatic example of how the brain is plastic and has the ability to adapt to changing circumstances. For this reason, if you are discussing brain plasticity, it would be acceptable to use material on 'functional recovery after trauma' within the answer.

Evaluation

Practical application

Understanding the processes involved in plasticity has contributed to the field of *neurorehabilitation*. Following illness or injury to the brain, spontaneous recovery tends to slow down after a number of weeks so forms of physical therapy may be required to maintain improvements in functioning. Techniques may include movement therapy and electrical stimulation of the brain to counter the deficits in motor and/or cognitive functioning that may be experienced following a stroke, for instance. This shows that, although the brain may have the capacity to 'fix itself' to a point, this process requires further intervention if it is to be completely successful.

Negative plasticity

The brain's ability to rewire itself can sometimes have maladaptive behavioural consequences. Prolonged drug use, for instance, has been shown to result in poorer cognitive functioning as well as an increased risk of dementia later in life (Medina *et al.* 2007). Also, 60–80% of amputees have been known to develop *phantom limb syndrome* – the continued experience of sensations in the missing limb as if it were still there. These sensations are usually unpleasant, painful and are thought to be due to cortical reorganisation in the **somatosensory cortex** that occurs as a result of limb loss (Ramachandran and Hirstein 1998).

Age and plasticity

Functional plasticity tends to reduce with age. The brain has a greater propensity for reorganisation in childhood as it is constantly adapting to new experiences and learning.

That said, Ladina Bezzola *et al.* (2012) demonstrated how 40 hours of golf training produced changes in the neural representation of movement in participants aged 40–60. Using **fMRI**, the researchers observed reduced **motor cortex** activity in the novice golfers compared to a **control group**, suggesting more efficient neural representations after training. This shows that neural plasticity does continue throughout the lifespan.

Evaluation eXtra

Support from animal studies

Early evidence of neuroplasticity and functional recovery was derived from animal studies. A pioneering study by David Hubel and Torsten Wiesel (1963) involved sewing one eye of a kitten shut and analysing the brain's cortical responses. It was found that the area of the **visual cortex** associated with the shut eye was not idle (as had been predicted) but continued to process information from the open eye.

Consider: *Early studies such as this paved the way for modern research into neuroplasticity and functional recovery. Does what we learn from early studies such as these justify the procedures that were used which caused permanent damage to the animals? Conduct a cost-benefits analysis and decide.*

The concept of cognitive reserve

Evidence suggests that a person's educational attainment may influence how well the brain functionally adapts after injury. Eric Schneider *et al.* (2014) discovered that the more time brain injury patients had spent in education – which was taken as an indication of their 'cognitive reserve' – the greater their chances of a disability-free recovery (DFR). Two-fifths of patients studied who achieved DFR had more than 16 years' education compared to about 10% of patients who had less than 12 years' education.

Consider: *What other factors may influence how well a person recovers from a brain injury?*

Apply it — Concepts: Meditation and mindfulness

A number of recent neuroscientific studies have examined the effects of prolonged periods of meditation on the brain. Some of these studies have more specifically explored the concept of *mindfulness* – an ancient Buddhist practice defined as 'an intentional and non-judgemental focus on one's own emotions, thoughts and sensations occurring in the present moment' (www.anniegurton.com, 2015).

As well being linked to reduced everyday tension and stress, meditation and mindfulness may alter the structure and function of the brain. Lazar *et al.* (2005), using **MRI scans**, demonstrated how experienced meditators had a thicker cortex than non-meditators, particularly in areas related to attention and sensory processing. Individuals who took part in an 8-week Mindfulness-Based Stress Reduction course showed an increase in grey matter in the left hippocampus, a part of the brain strongly associated with learning and memory (Holzel *et al.* 2011). Finally, Tang *et al.* (2012) found that four weeks of meditation resulted in an increase in white matter in the *anterior cingulate cortex*, a part of the brain that contributes to self-regulation and control (a key aspect of meditational practice).

Question

Can you think of examples of other everyday behaviours that could alter the structure and/or function of the brain?

Apply it — Methods: The case of Gabby Giffords

Gabby Giffords is a former US Democratic politician who survived an assassination attempt in 2011 when she was shot in the head from point blank range. Doctors placed Giffords into a waking coma such was the critical nature of her condition. Within months, however, she had made staggering progress. With the aid of physical rehabilitation, Giffords was able to walk under supervision with perfect control of her left arm and leg, and able to write with her left hand. She could read, understand and speak in short phrases. Doctors suggested that Giffords' progress would place her in the top 5% of people recovering from serious brain injury – a remarkable example of the brain's ability to heal itself.

Question

With reference to the example of Gabby Giffords above, briefly discuss strengths and limitations of the case study approach. (6 marks)

CHECK IT

1. Define what is meant by *plasticity* in the brain. [3 marks]
2. Briefly outline research into functional recovery of the brain after injury. [5 marks]
3. Discuss research into plasticity of the brain including functional recovery. [16 marks]

SPLIT-BRAIN RESEARCH INTO HEMISPHERIC LATERALISATION

> Hemispheric lateralisation; split-brain research

Neuroscientists are interested in whether certain activities and behaviours are controlled or dominated by one hemisphere rather than the other (known as lateralisation – as distinct from localisation). Broadly speaking, the right hemisphere controls activity on the left side of the body and vice versa. Here, we discuss this question with the help of some ground-breaking experiments involving so-called split-brain patients.

KEY TERMS

Hemispheric lateralisation – The idea that the two halves (hemispheres) of the brain are *functionally different* and that certain mental processes and behaviours are mainly controlled by one hemisphere rather than the other, as in the example of language (which is localised as well as lateralised).

Split-brain research – A series of studies which began in the 1960s (and are still ongoing) involving epileptic patients who had experienced a surgical separation of the hemispheres of the brain. This allowed researchers to investigate the extent to which brain function is lateralised.

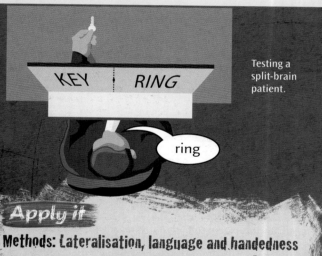

KEY | RING

ring

Testing a split-brain patient.

Apply it

Methods: Lateralisation, language and handedness

An investigation of 400 right-handed people revealed that 380 of them had left-hemisphere dominance for language, i.e. language was lateralised on the left. This reflects the trend in the general population.

Questions

1. What percentage of right-handed people in the investigation above were left hemisphere dominant for language? (*1 mark*)

2. Express your answer to question 1 as a fraction. (*1 mark*)

In left-handed people the situation was more complex. In a further study there were 400 left-handed people tested. In 80 cases language was located on the right hemisphere, and for a further 80, language functions were arranged *bilaterally*, that is, across both hemispheres.

3. What percentage of left-handed people's language functions were arranged bilaterally? (*1 mark*)

4. How might the results of Sperry's studies have been different if some of his patients were left-handed? (*3 marks*)

Split-brain research

Hemispheric lateralisation

As we have already seen, the ability to produce and understand language, for most people, is controlled by the left hemisphere. This suggests that for the majority of us, language is subject to **hemispheric lateralisation**. In other words, the specialised areas associated with language are found in one of the brain's hemispheres rather than both. The question of whether other neural processes may be organised in this way was investigated in a series of ingenious experiments conducted by Roger Sperry and his colleagues (known as **split-brain research**) for which Sperry was awarded the Nobel Prize in 1981.

Split-brain studies

Sperry's (1968) studies involved a unique group of individuals, all of whom had undergone the same surgical procedure – an operation called a *commissurotomy* – in which the *corpus callosum* and other tissues which connect the two hemispheres were cut down the middle in order to separate the two hemispheres and control frequent and severe epileptic seizures. This meant that for these split-brain patients the main communication line between the two hemispheres was removed. This allowed Sperry and his colleagues to see the extent to which the two hemispheres were specialised for certain functions, and whether the hemispheres performed tasks independently of one another.

Procedure

Sperry devised a general procedure (see picture, left) in which an image or word could be projected to a patient's right visual field (processed by the left hemisphere) and the same, or different, image could be projected to the left visual field (processed by the right hemisphere). In the 'normal' brain, the corpus callosum would immediately share the information between both hemispheres giving a complete picture of the visual world. However, presenting the image to one hemisphere of a split-brain patient meant that the information could not be conveyed from that hemisphere to the other.

Key findings

Describing what you see When a picture of an object was shown to a patient's right visual field, the patient could easily describe what was seen. If, however, the same object was shown to the left visual field, the patient could not describe what was seen, and typically reported that there was nothing there. You may recall that for most people (and this was true of all of Sperry's patients) language is processed in the left hemisphere. Thus, the patient's inability to describe objects in the left visual field (processed in the right hemisphere) was because of the lack of language centres in the right hemisphere! In the normal brain, messages from the right hemisphere would be relayed to the language centres in the left hemisphere.

Recognition by touch Although patients could not attach verbal labels to objects projected in the left visual field, they were able to select a matching object from a grab-bag of different objects using their left hand (linked to right hemisphere). The objects were placed behind a screen so as not to be seen (see picture). The left hand was also able to select an object that was most closely associated with an object presented to the left visual field (for instance, an ashtray was selected in response to a picture of a cigarette). In each case the patient was not able to verbally identify what they had seen but could nevertheless 'understand' what the object was using the right hemisphere and select the corresponding object accordingly.

Composite words If two words were presented simultaneously, one on either side of the visual field (for example, a 'key' on the left and 'ring' on the right as in the picture), the patient would select a key with their left hand (the left visual field goes to right hemisphere linked to left hand) and say the word 'ring'. The superiority of the right hemisphere in terms of drawing tasks is illustrated in the 'Apply-it' on drawing abilities on the facing page.

Matching faces The right hemisphere also appeared dominant in terms of recognising faces. When asked to match a face from a series of other faces, the picture processed by the right hemisphere (left visual field) was consistently selected, whilst the picture presented to the left hemisphere was consistently ignored. When a composite picture made up of two different halves of a face was presented – one half to each hemisphere – the left hemisphere dominated in terms of verbal description whereas the right hemisphere dominated in terms of selecting a matching picture.

Evaluation

Demonstrated lateralised brain functions

Sperry's (and later Michael Gazzaniga's) pioneering work into the split-brain phenomenon has produced an impressive and sizeable body of research findings, the main conclusion of which appears to be that the left hemisphere is more geared towards analytic and verbal tasks whilst the right is more adept at performing spatial tasks and music. The right hemisphere can only produce rudimentary words and phrases but contributes emotional and holistic content to language.

Research suggests that the left hemisphere is the *analyser* whilst the right hemisphere is the *synthesiser* – a key contribution to our understanding of brain processes.

Strengths of the methodology

The experiments involving split-brain patients made use of highly specialised and **standardised procedures**. Sperry's method of presenting visual information to one hemispheric field at a time was quite ingenious. Typically, participants would be asked to stare at a given point, the 'fixation point'. The image projected would be flashed up for one-tenth of a second, meaning the split-brain patient would not have time to move their eye across the image and so spread the information across both sides of the visual field, and subsequently, both sides of the brain. This allowed Sperry to vary aspects of the basic procedure and ensured that only one hemisphere was receiving information at a time. Thus he developed a very useful and well-controlled procedure.

Theoretical basis

Sperry's work prompted a theoretical and philosophical debate about the degree of communication between the two hemispheres in everyday functioning and the nature of consciousness. Some theorists, for example Roland Pucetti (1977), have suggested that the two hemispheres are so functionally different that they represent a form of *duality* in the brain – that in effect we are all *two minds* (and that this is a situation that is only *emphasised* rather than created in the split-brain patient).

In contrast, other researchers have argued that, far from working in isolation, the two hemispheres form a highly integrated system and are both involved in most everyday tasks.

Evaluation eXtra

Issues with generalisation

As fascinating as the findings from these studies are, many researchers have urged caution in their widespread acceptance, as split-brain patients constitute such an unusual sample of people. There were only 11 who took part in all variations of the basic procedure, all of whom had a history of epileptic seizures. It has been argued that this may have caused unique changes in the brain that may have influenced the findings. It is also the case that some participants had experienced more disconnection of the two hemispheres as part of their surgical procedure than others. Finally, the **control group** Sperry used, made up of 11 people with no history of epilepsy, may have been inappropriate.

Consider: *Who may have made a better control group and why?*

Differences in function may be overstated

One (perhaps unfortunate) legacy of Sperry's work is a growing body of pop-psychological literature that overemphasises and oversimplifies the functional distinction between the left and right hemispheres. Although the 'verbal' and 'non-verbal' labels can, on occasion, be usefully applied to summarise the differences between the two hemispheres, modern neuroscientists would contend that the actual distinction is less clear-cut and much more messy than this. In the normal brain the two hemispheres are in constant communication when performing everyday tasks, and many of the behaviours typically associated with one hemisphere can be effectively performed by the other when the situation requires it.

Consider: *This is an example of plasticity in the brain. Explain some further examples of brain plasticity.*

Apply it

Concepts: The drawing abilities of the left and right hemispheres

What the right hemisphere lacks in linguistic skill, it partly makes up for in terms of its superior drawing abilities. This has been shown in tests with split-brain patients. A picture is flashed to either their right or left visual field. As you can see in the drawings below, the left hand continually outperformed the right hand in such tests despite the fact that, for all the patients, the right hand was their preferred hand.

Question

Using your knowledge of split-brain studies, explain why this shows that the right hemisphere is dominant for drawing skill.

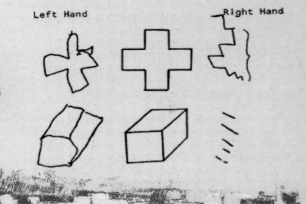

Apply it

Concepts: Kim Peek – a natural split-brain

Kim Peek was not one of Sperry's patients but was the inspiration for the 1988 Oscar-winning movie *Rain Man*, the story of a very high functioning autistic savant. However, Peek's exceptional abilities, depicted in the film, were not attributable to **autism**. Rather, Peek was born with severe brain damage including a total absence of a corpus callosum. This meant that unlike Sperry's participants, Peek's split-brain was due to natural causes.

Although socially awkward with a low IQ of 87, Peek's powers of memory were prodigious. He had word-for-word recall of over 12,000 books. He could read two pages in around ten seconds, employing his split-brain to simultaneously read one page with his right eye and one page with his left. He knew phone books by heart, and could say what day of the week a particular date fell on going back decades. His party trick was to tell strangers the names of people who used to live next door to them years ago.

Question

It is likely that Peek had fully-developed (*bilateral*) language centres in both hemispheres of his brain which may explain some of his extraordinary abilities. How does this make him different from Sperry's patients?

CHECK IT

1. Outline **one** research procedure used to investigate split-brain patients.   *[3 marks]*
2. Briefly evaluate research using split-brain patients to investigate hemispheric lateralisation.   *[4 marks]*
3. Discuss split-brain research. Refer to examples of such research in your answer.   *[16 marks]*

Ways of studying the brain: scanning techniques, including functional magnetic resonance imaging (fMRI); electroencephalograms (EEGs) and event-related potentials (ERPs); post-mortem examinations.

Advances in science and technology have brought with them ever more sophisticated and precise methods of studying the brain. Some modern scanning techniques are able to record global neural activity through the assessment of brainwave patterns whilst others are able to home in on activity in specific parts of the brain as the brain performs certain tasks and processes.

Another more traditional way of investigating the brain – the post-mortem – is also considered.

KEY TERMS

Functional magnetic resonance imaging (fMRI) – A method used to measure brain activity while a person is performing a task that uses MRI technology (detecting radio waves from changing magnetic fields). This enables researchers to detect which regions of the brain are rich in oxygen and thus are active.

Electroencephalogram (EEG) – A record of the tiny electrical impulses produced by the brain's activity. By measuring characteristic wave patterns, the EEG can help diagnose certain conditions of the brain.

Event-related potentials (ERPs) – The brain's electrophysiological response to a specific sensory, cognitive, or motor event can be isolated through statistical analysis of EEG data.

Post-mortem examinations – The brain is analysed after death to determine whether certain observed behaviours during the patient's lifetime can be linked to abnormalities in the brain.

Scanning and other techniques

Functional magnetic resonance imaging (fMRI)

fMRI works by detecting the changes in blood oxygenation and flow that occur as a result of neural (brain) activity in specific parts of the brain. When a brain area is more active it consumes more oxygen and to meet this increased demand, blood flow is directed to the active area (known as the *haemodynamic response*). fMRI produces 3-dimensional images (activation maps) showing which parts of the brain are involved in a particular mental process and this has important implications for our understanding of localisation of function.

Electroencephalogram (EEG)

EEGs measure electrical activity within the brain via electrodes that are fixed to an individual's scalp using a skull cap. The scan recording represents the brainwave patterns that are generated from the action of millions of neurons, providing an overall account of brain activity. EEG is often used by clinicians as a diagnostic tool as unusual *arrhythmic* patterns of activity (i.e. no particular rhythm) may indicate neurological abnormalities such as epilepsy, tumours or disorders of sleep.

Event-related potentials (ERPs)

Although EEG has many scientific and clinical applications, in its raw form it is a crude and overly general measure of brain activity. However, within EEG data are contained all the neural responses associated with specific sensory, cognitive and motor events that may be of interest to cognitive neuroscientists. As such, researchers have developed a way of teasing out and isolating these responses. Using a statistical averaging technique, all extraneous brain activity from the original EEG recording is filtered out leaving only those responses that relate to, say, the presentation of a specific stimulus or performance of a specific task. What remains are **event-related potentials**: types of brainwave that are triggered by particular events. Research has revealed many different forms of ERP and how, for example, these are linked to cognitive processes such as attention and perception.

Post-mortem examinations

A technique involving the analysis of a person's brain following their death. In psychological research, individuals whose brains are subject to a post-mortem are likely to be those who have a rare disorder and have experienced unusual deficits in mental processes or behaviour during their lifetime. Areas of damage within the brain are examined after death as a means of establishing the likely cause of the affliction the person suffered. This may also involve comparison with a *neurotypical* brain in order to ascertain the extent of the difference.

Apply it **Concepts: Match the picture to the techniques**

Do the pictures (A, B, C and D) relate to fMRI, EEG, ERPs or post-mortems?

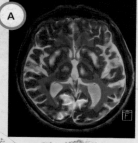

A

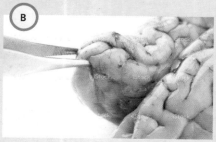

B

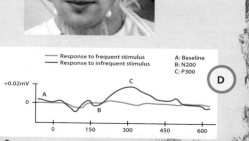

C

Response to frequent stimulus
Response to infrequent stimulus

A: Baseline
B: N200
C: P300

+0.02mV

A

C

0

B

0   150   300   450   600

D

Evaluation

Functional magnetic resonance imaging

Strengths – One key strength of fMRI is, unlike other scanning techniques such as **PET**, it does not rely on the use of radiation. If administered correctly it is virtually risk-free, non-invasive and straightforward to use. It also produces images that have very high spatial resolution, depicting detail by the millimetre, and providing a clear picture of how brain activity is localised.

Weaknesses – fMRI is expensive compared to other neuroimaging techniques and can only capture a clear image if the person stays perfectly still. It has poor *temporal* resolution because there is around a 5-second time-lag behind the image on screen and the initial firing of neuronal activity. Finally, fMRI can only measure blood flow in the brain, it cannot home in on the activity of individual neurons and so it can be difficult to tell exactly what kind of brain activity is being represented on screen.

Electroencephalogram

Strengths – EEG has proved invaluable in the diagnosis of conditions such as epilepsy, a disorder characterised by random bursts of activity in the brain that can easily be detected on screen. Similarly, it has contributed much to our understanding of the stages involved in sleep (see research into **ultradian rhythms** – page 48). Unlike fMRI, EEG technology has extremely high temporal resolution. Today's EEG technology can accurately detect brain activity at a resolution of a single millisecond (and even less in some cases).

Weakness – The main drawback of EEG lies in the generalised nature of the information received (that of many thousands of neurons). The EEG signal is not useful for pinpointing the exact source of neural activity, and it does not allow researchers to distinguish between activities originating in different but adjacent locations.

Event-related potentials

Strengths – The limitations of EEG are partly addressed through the use of ERPs. These bring much more specificity to the measurement of neural processes than could ever be achieved using raw EEG data. As ERPs are derived from EEG measurements, they have excellent temporal resolution, especially when compared to neuroimaging techniques such as fMRI, and this has led to their widespread use in the measurement of cognitive functions and deficits. Researchers have been able to identify many different types of ERP and describe the precise role of these in cognitive functioning; for instance, the *P300 component* is thought to be involved in the allocation of attentional resources and the maintenance of **working memory**.

Weaknesses – Critics have pointed to a lack of standardisation in ERP methodology between different research studies which makes it difficult to confirm findings. A further issue is that, in order to establish pure data in ERP studies, background noise and extraneous material must be completely eliminated, and this may not always be easy to achieve.

Post-mortems

Strengths – Post-mortem evidence was vital in providing a foundation for early understanding of key processes in the brain. Paul Broca and Karl Wernicke (see page 38) both relied on post-mortem studies in establishing links between language, brain and behaviour decades before neuroimaging ever became a possibility. Post-mortem studies improve medical knowledge and help generate hypotheses for further study.

Weaknesses – Causation is an issue within these investigations, however. Observed damage to the brain may not be linked to the deficits under review but to some other unrelated trauma or decay. A further problem is that post-mortem studies raise ethical issues of consent from the patient before death. Patients may not be able to provide **informed consent**, for example in the case of HM who lost his ability to form memories and was not able to provide such consent – nevertheless post-mortem research has been conducted on his brain.

Apply it — Concepts: FMRI and lie detection

One innovative and recently emerging application of fMRI has been in the field of lie detection. Many have claimed that fMRI is an ideal tool for detecting truthfulness (or more pertinently, the lack of it) due to its ability to effectively see *inside* the brain. Supporters of its use argue that the analysis of neural blood flow is preferable to tracking peripheral measures of anxiety — such as changes in pulse, skin temperature or respiration – that would be recorded by more traditional lie detectors or polygraphs (such as those employed by police detectives or on daytime talk shows). Traditional lie detectors are widely acknowledged as 'beatable,' but neural activity is much more difficult to fake!

Two US companies, Cephos (in Pepperell, Massachusetts) and the catchily-named No Lie MRI (in Tarzana, California), claim to predict with over 90 percent accuracy whether its clients are 'spinning a line'. No Lie MRI suggests that the technique may even be used for 'risk reduction in dating'.

Many neuroscientists and legal scholars doubt such claims – and some even question whether brain scans for lie detection will ever move beyond the research lab into the real world.

Question

What are the strengths and limitations of using fMRI as a method of lie detection?

Will neuroimaging techniques such as fMRI ever replace the traditional polygraph on entertainment programmes such as the Jeremy Kyle Show?

Apply it — Methods: Memory lane

A researcher used an fMRI scan to investigate whether different types of long-term memories are located in different parts of the brain. Participants were asked to think about family holidays they had been on as a child and their brain activity was recorded. The same participants were then asked to mentally 'list' European capital cities and their brain activity was again recorded to see if there was a difference.

Question

The investigation described above could be considered to be a **lab experiment**. Briefly discuss strengths *and* limitations of lab experiments with reference to the investigation above.   *(6 marks)*

CHECK IT

1. Outline **one** difference between EEGs and ERPs as ways of investigating the brain.   *[2 marks]*
2. Briefly evaluate post-mortem examinations as a way of investigating the brain.   *[4 marks]*
3. Describe and evaluate scanning techniques as a way of investigating the brain.   *[16 marks]*

Biological rhythms: circadian rhythms.

A biological rhythm is a change in body processes or behaviour in response to cyclical changes within the environment. For instance, most of us show a distinct pattern of going to sleep when it's dark and waking up when it's light. This is an example of a circadian rhythm – a specific type of bodily rhythm that occurs across a 24-hour period.

KEY TERMS

Biological rhythms – Distinct patterns of changes in body activity that conform to cyclical time periods. Biological rhythms are influenced by internal body clocks (endogenous pacemakers) as well as external changes to the environment (exogenous zeitgebers).

Circadian rhythm – A type of biological rhythm, subject to a 24-hour cycle, which regulates a number of body processes such as the sleep/wake cycle and changes in core body temperature.

Michel Siffre – the man, the cave, the beard.

Apply it

Concepts: Core body temperature

Core body temperature varies by around two degrees centigrade during the course of a day. It is at its lowest around 4 in the morning (36°C) and peaks around 6 in the evening at 38°C. Evidence suggests that body temperature may have an effect on our mental abilities: the warmer we are (internally), the better our cognitive performance.

Folkard *et al.* (1977) demonstrated how children who had stories read to them at 3pm showed superior recall and comprehension after a week compared to children who heard the same stories at 9am. Similarly, Gupta (1991) found improved performance on IQ tests when participants were assessed at 7pm as opposed to 2pm and 9am.

Question

Given the results of these studies, when would be a good time of day to take your psychology exam?

Circadian rhythms

Biological rhythms

All living organisms – plants, animals and people – are subject to **biological rhythms** and these exert an important influence on the way in which body systems behave. All biological rhythms are governed by two things: the body's internal biological 'clocks', which are called **endogenous pacemakers** and external changes in the environment known as **exogenous zeitgebers** (see page 50). Some of these rhythms occur many times during the day (**ultradian rhythms**). Others take longer than a day to complete (**infradian rhythms**) and in some cases much longer (circannual rhythms).

Our focus on this spread is on **circadian rhythms** – those rhythms that last for around 24 hours (circa meaning 'about' and *diem* meaning 'day'). Two examples of circadian rhythms are the sleep/wake cycle and core body temperature (see Apply it, below).

The sleep/wake cycle

The fact that we feel drowsy when it's night-time and alert during the day demonstrates the effect of daylight – an important exogenous zeitgeber – on our sleep/wake cycle. However, what if the biological clock was 'left to its own devices' without the influence of external stimuli such as light (what researchers refer to as 'free-running')? If we had no idea whether it was night or day would we still fall asleep and wake up at regular times? Several studies have tried to answer this question.

Siffre's cave study

Michel Siffre (pronounce '*Seef*') is a self-styled caveman who has spent several extended periods underground to study the effects on his own biological rhythms. Deprived of exposure to natural light and sound, but with access to adequate food and drink, Siffre re-surfaced in mid-September 1962 after two months in the caves of the Southern Alps believing it to be mid-August! A decade later he performed a similar feat but this time for six months in a Texan cave.

In each case, his 'free-running' biological rhythm settled down to one that was just beyond the usual 24 hours (around 25 hours) though he did continue to fall asleep and wake up on a regular schedule.

Other research

Similar results were recorded by Jürgen Aschoff and Rütger Wever (1976) who convinced a group of participants to spend four weeks in a WWII bunker deprived of natural light. All but one of the participants (whose sleep/wake cycle extended to 29 hours) displayed a circadian rhythm between 24 and 25 hours. Both Siffre's experience and the bunker study suggest that the 'natural' sleep/wake cycle may be slightly longer than 24 hours but that it is entrained by exogenous zeitgebers associated with our 24-hour day (such as the number of daylight hours, typical meal-times, etc.).

Despite this, we should not overestimate the influence of environmental cues on our internal biological clock. Simon Folkard *et al.* (1985) studied a group of 12 people who agreed to live in a dark cave for 3 weeks, retiring to bed when the clock said 11.45pm and rising when it said 7.45am. Over the course of the study, the researchers gradually speeded up the clock (unbeknown to the participants) so an apparent 24-hour day eventually lasted only 22 hours! It was revealed that only one of the participants was able to comfortably adjust to the new regime. This would suggest the existence of a strong free-running circadian rhythm that cannot easily be overridden by changes in the external environment.

STUDY TIP

Remember, when asked about 'research', within this or any other section, you can refer to both theories/explanations and/or research studies as part of your answer. So writing about 'research into circadian rhythms' you could include details of specific studies (such as Siffre's case study) as well as broader explanations of the effects of such rhythms.

Evaluation

Practical application to shift work

Knowledge of circadian rhythms has given researchers a better understanding of the adverse consequences that can occur as a result of their disruption (known as *desynchronisation*). For instance, night workers engaged in **shift work** experience a period of reduced concentration around 6 in the morning (a *circadian trough*) meaning mistakes and accidents are more likely (Boivin *et al.* 1996). Research has also suggested a relationship between shift work and poor health: shift workers are three times more likely to develop heart disease (Knutsson 2003) which may in part due to the stress of adjusting to different sleep/wake patterns and the lack of poor quality sleep during the day.

Thus, research into the sleep/wake cycle may have economic implications in terms of how best to manage worker productivity.

Practical application to drug treatments

Circadian rhythms co-ordinate a number of the body's basic processes such as heart rate, digestion and hormone levels. This in turn has an effect on *pharmacokinetics*, that is, the action of drugs on the body and how well they are absorbed and distributed. Research into circadian rhythms has revealed that there are certain peak times during the day or night when drugs are likely to be at their most effective. This has led to the development of guidelines to do with the timing of drug dosing for a whole range of medications including anticancer, cardiovascular, respiratory, anti-ulcer and anti-epileptic drugs (Baraldo 2008).

Use of case studies and small samples

Studies of the sleep/wake cycle tend to involve small groups of participants, as in the experiment by Aschoff and Wever, or studies of single individuals, as in the case of Siffre. The people involved may not be representative of the wider population and this limits the extent to which meaningful **generalisations** can be made. In his most recent cave experience in 1999, Siffre observed, at the age of 60, that his internal clock ticked much more slowly than when he was a young man. This illustrates the fact that, even when the same person is involved, there are factors that vary which may prevent general conclusions being drawn.

Evaluation eXtra

Poor control in studies

Although participants in the studies on the facing page were deprived of natural light, they still had access to artificial light. For instance, Siffre turned on a lamp every time he woke up which remained on until he went to bed. It was assumed by him and others that artificial light, unlike daylight, would have no effect on the free-running biological rhythm. However, in tests, Charles Czeisler *et al.* (1999) were able to adjust participants' circadian rhythms from 22 to 28 hours using dim lighting. As such, the use of a light may be analogous to participants taking a drug that resets their biological clock.

Consider: *Explain why the use of artificial light in the cave and bunker studies may act as a* **confounding variable**.

Individual differences

One further issue which complicates the generalisation of findings from studies of the sleep/wake cycle is that individual cycles can vary, in some cases from 13 to 65 hours (Czeisler *et al.* 1999). In addition, a study by Jeanne Duffy *et al.* (2001) revealed that some people display a natural preference for going to bed early and rising early (known as 'larks') whereas some people prefer to do the opposite ('owls'). There are also age differences in sleep/wake patterns (see the Apply-it above right).

Consider: *Why are these individual differences (and the use of case studies mentioned above) a problem for research into the sleep/wake cycle?*

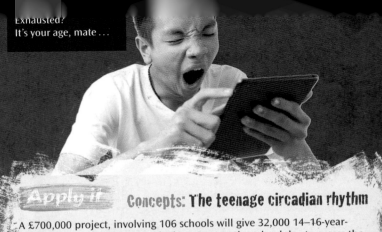

Exhausted? It's your age, mate …

Apply it — Concepts: The teenage circadian rhythm

A £700,000 project, involving 106 schools will give 32,000 14–16-year-olds the chance of a lie-in and a later start to the school day to assess the impact on their educational achievement.

According to neuroscientists, teenagers' circadian rhythms typically begin two hours after those of adults, so current school start times mean they wake up too early and are trying to focus when their body still needs sleep. It also means, at bed time, they tend not to be as tired as they should be.

A **pilot study** was run at Monkseaton High School in North Tyneside in 2010. Dr Paul Kelley, who now works as a research associate at Oxford University's Sleep and Circadian Neuroscience Institute, which is leading the new project, was headteacher at the time. After a decade of researching all the available evidence, he decided to put the start of the school day back to 10am over a two-year period.

'There were very positive outcomes, both academic and in terms of health', said Kelley. 'Academic results went up, illness down and the atmosphere in school changed. The students were much nicer to each other, it was bliss.'

Question

What evidence is there that the sleep/wake cycle may vary due to individual differences?

Apply it — Methods: Meta-analysis

A researcher conducted a **meta-analysis** of studies that investigated the length of the sleep/wake cycle. As a result of the meta-analysis, the researcher concluded that the average length of the sleep/wake cycle is between 24 and 25 hours.

Questions

1. Explain what is meant by a meta-analysis. Refer to this investigation in your answer. (*2 marks*)
2. Outline *one* strength and *one* limitation of conducting a meta-analysis. Refer to this investigation in your answer. (*4 marks*)
3. Briefly discuss the implications of psychological research for the economy. Refer to this investigation in your answer. (*4 marks*)
4. The studies of the sleep/wake cycle the researcher analysed were from a number of neuroscience journals and had all been through a process of **peer review**. Outline and briefly discuss the role of peer review in psychological research. (*8 marks*)

CHECK IT

1. With reference to an example, define what is meant by a *circadian rhythm*. [3 marks]
2. Describe **one** study that investigated a circadian rhythm. [4 marks]
3. Discuss research into circadian rhythms. Refer to evidence in your answer. [16 marks]

> Biological rhythms: infradian and ultradian rhythms.

Infradian rhythms are those that take longer than 24 hours to complete. Here, we discuss two examples of these – the menstrual cycle and seasonal affective disorder (SAD).

Also featured on this spread are the stages of sleep (more commonly referred to as the *sleep cycle*). The sleep cycle is an example of an ultradian rhythm: biological rhythms that take less than 24 hours to complete and may often occur more than once over the course of a day.

KEY TERMS

Infradian rhythm – A type of biological rhythm with a frequency of less than one cycle in 24 hours, such as menstruation and seasonal affective disorder.

Ultradian rhythm – A type of biological rhythm with a frequency of more that one cycle in 24 hours, such as the stages of sleep.

Sleep stages

Stage 1
Theta waves
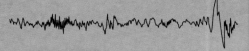

Stage 2
Light sleep

Stages 3 & 4
Delta waves

REM sleep
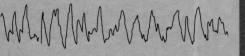

The different patterns of brainwave activity during sleep.

Apply it   Concepts: EEGs and sleep

It is the case that not all dreams occur during REM sleep. Hypnogogic dreams occur during stages 1 and 2, shortly after drifting off to sleep, and are those in which we may experience the feeling of being out of control or that we are falling. These dreams are significant for the fact that we often wake with a jolt (a *hypnic twitch*) when we are sure we are about to hit the ground!

Question
Brainwave activity during sleep is measured in sleep labs using an EEG. What are the strengths and limitations of EEGs in the context of this research?

Infradian rhythms

The menstrual cycle

The female menstrual cycle, an example of an **infradian rhythm**, is governed by monthly changes in hormone levels which regulate ovulation. The cycle refers to the time between the first day of a woman's period, when the womb lining is shed, to the day before her next period. The typical cycle takes approximately 28 days to complete (though anywhere between 24 and 35 days is generally considered normal). During each cycle, rising levels of the hormone oestrogen cause the ovary to develop an egg and release it (ovulation). After ovulation, the hormone progesterone helps the womb lining to grow thicker, readying the body for pregnancy. If pregnancy does not occur, the egg is absorbed into the body, the womb lining comes away and leaves the body (the menstrual flow).

Research study

Although the menstrual cycle is an **endogenous** system, evidence suggests that it may be influenced by **exogenous** factors, such as the cycles of other women. A study by Kathleen Stern and Martha McClintock (1998) demonstrated how menstrual cycles may synchronise as a result of the influence of female pheromones.

McClintock involved 29 women with a history of irregular periods. Samples of **pheromones** were gathered from 9 of the women at different stages of their menstrual cycles, via a cotton pad placed in their armpit. The pads were worn for at least 8 hours to ensure that pheromones were picked up. The pads were treated with alcohol and frozen, to be rubbed on the upper lip of the other participants. On day one, pads from the start of the menstrual cycle were applied to all 20 women, on day two they were all given a pad from the second day of the cycle, and so on. McClintock found that 68% of women experienced changes to their cycle which brought them closer to the cycle of their 'odour donor'.

Seasonal affective disorder (SAD)

SAD is a depressive disorder which has a seasonal pattern of onset, and is described and diagnosed as a mental disorder in **DSM-5**. As with other forms of **depression**, the main symptoms of SAD are persistent low mood alongside a general lack of activity and interest in life. SAD is often referred to as the *winter blues* as the symptoms are triggered during the winter months when the number of daylight hours becomes shorter. SAD is a particular type of infradian rhythm called a *circannual rhythm* as it is subject to a yearly cycle. However, it can also be classed as a **circadian rhythm** as the experience of SAD may be due to the disruption of the sleep/wake cycle and this can be attributed to prolonged periods of daily darkness during winter.

Psychologists have hypothesised that the **hormone melatonin** is implicated in the cause of SAD. During the night, the pineal gland (see next spread) secretes melatonin until dawn when there is an increase in light. During winter, the lack of light in the morning means this secretion process continues for longer. This is thought to have a knock-on effect on the production of **serotonin** in the brain – a chemical that has been linked to the onset of depressive symptoms.

Ultradian rhythms

One of the most intensively researched **ultradian rhythms** is the stages of sleep – the sleep cycle. Psychologists have identified five distinct stages of sleep that altogether span approximately 90-minutes – a cycle that continues throughout the course of the night. Each of these stages is characterised by a different level of brainwave activity which can be monitored using an **EEG** (see page 44).

Stages 1 and 2 of the 'sleep escalator', as it is sometimes known, are light sleep where the person may be easily woken. At the beginning of sleep, brainwave patterns start to become slower and more rhythmic (*alpha waves*), becoming even slower as sleep becomes deeper (*theta waves*).

Stages 3 and 4 involve *delta waves* which are slower still and have a greater amplitude than earlier wave patterns. This is deep sleep or **slow wave sleep** and it is difficult to rouse someone at this point.

In stage 5, REM sleep, the body is paralysed yet brain activity speeds up significantly in a manner that resembles the awake brain. REM stands for *rapid eye movement* to denote the fast, jerky activity of the eyes under the eyelids at this point. Research has suggested that REM activity during sleep is highly correlated with the experience of dreaming.

Evaluation

Practical activity on page 52

Evolutionary basis of the menstrual cycle

Menstrual synchrony, of the kind observed in the McClintock study, is thought by many to have an evolutionary value. For our ancestors it may have been advantageous for females to menstruate together and therefore fall pregnant around the same time. This would mean that new-borns could be cared for collectively within a social group increasing the chances of the offspring's survival.

The **validity** of the evolutionary perspective has been questioned by some: Jeffrey Schank (2004) has argued that if there were too many females cycling together within a social group, this would produce competition for the highest quality males (and thereby lowering the fitness of any potential offspring). From this point of view, the *avoidance* of synchrony would appear to be most adaptive evolutionary strategy and therefore naturally selected.

Methodological limitations in synchronisation studies

Criticisms have been made of early synchronisation studies and the methods employed. Commentators argue that there are many factors that may effect change in a woman's menstrual cycle, including stress, changes in diet, exercise, etc., that might act as **confounding variables**. This means that any supposed pattern of synchronisation, as seen in the studies by McClintock and others, is no more than would have been expected to occur by chance. In addition, research typically involves small samples of women and relies on participants self-reporting the onset of their own cycle. Perhaps more critically, other studies (e.g. by Trevathan *et al.* 1993) failed to find any evidence of menstrual synchrony in all-female samples.

Evidence supports the idea of distinct stages in sleep

A landmark study by William Dement and Nathaniel Kleitman (1957) monitored the sleep patterns of nine adult participants in a sleep lab. Brainwave activity was recorded on an EEG and the researchers controlled for the effects of caffeine and alcohol. REM activity during sleep was highly **correlated** with the experience of dreaming, brain activity varied according to how vivid dreams were, and participants woken during dreaming reported very accurate recall of their dreams.

Replications of this investigation have noted similar findings, though the small size of the original sample has been criticised by some. Nevertheless, this study suggests that REM (dream) sleep is an important component of the ultradian sleep cycle.

Evaluation eXtra

Animal studies

Much of the knowledge of the effects of pheromones on behaviour is derived from animal studies. The role of pheromones in animal sexual selection is well-documented. For instance, the fact that sea urchins release pheromones into the surrounding water so other urchins in the colony will eject their sex cells simultaneously. In contrast, evidence for the effects in human behaviour remains speculative and inconclusive (and this includes the, so far unproven, idea that transmission of pheromones between humans may act as an aphrodisiac!).

Consider: *What are the issues with applying the findings from animal studies to human behaviour in pheromone research – and psychology generally?*

Practical application – SAD

One of the most effective treatments for SAD is phototherapy. This is a lightbox that simulates very strong light in the morning and evening. It is thought to reset melatonin levels in people with SAD. This relieves symptoms in up to 60% of sufferers (Eastman *et al.* 1998). However, the same study recorded a **placebo** effect of 30% using a 'sham negative-ion generator' (participants were told it was another form of treatment). This casts doubt on the chemical influence of phototherapy.

Consider: *What is the 'placebo effect'? Explain why this is a problem in treatment studies particularly.*

According to Ericsson et al. and the basic rest activity cycle, the key to world class violin playing is having a break every 90 minutes.
Now, that, I can do …

Apply it

Concepts:

The Basic Rest-Activity Cycle

Much evidence from EEG recordings suggests the existence of the 90-minute cycle during sleep (see facing page). However, Kleitman (1969) also suggested that a similar 90-minute rhythm cycle continues during waking hours. He called this the *Basic Rest–Activity Cycle* (or BRAC for short) which is characterised by a period of alertness followed by a spell of physiological fatigue. This occurs across a 90-minute cycle which then recurs during the course of the day.

Anecdotal evidence supports the existence of BRAC such as the frequent observation that students find it difficult to concentrate for periods longer than 90 minutes at a time. Similarly, most people will require a (coffee) break in order to divide up their working morning and also their afternoon.

In a widely cited study of prodigious violinists, Ericsson *et al.* (1993) found that the best performers tended to practise for three sessions during the course of the day, each session lasted no more than 90 minutes, and there was a break between each in order to 'recharge'.

Question

Explain what type of rhythm BRAC is. Justify your answer.

Apply it   Methods: SAD

In a study, patients suffering from *seasonal affective disorder* (SAD) were divided into two different groups:

Group 1 received phototherapy treatment.
Group 2 received no treatment.

The progress of the two groups was studied for the same length of time during the winter period. At the end of the study, all patients were required to complete a **questionnaire** which assessed their mood and the difference in mood scores between the two groups was calculated.

Question

1. Explain the purpose of Group 2 in the investigation above.
(3 marks)

2. Which **statistical test** would be most appropriate to analyse the difference in mood scores between Group 1 and Group 2 in the investigation above? Justify your answer. (4 marks) (See page 70)

CHECK IT

1. With reference to an example, define what is meant by an *ultradian rhythm*.   [3 marks]

2. Describe **one** study that investigated an infradian rhythm.   [4 marks]

3. Discuss research into infradian and/or ultradian rhythms.   [16 marks]

THE SPECIFICATION SAYS...

The effect of endogenous pacemakers and exogenous zeitgebers on the sleep/wake cycle.

Biological rhythms are influenced by two things: internal body clocks (endogenous pacemakers) and external cues in the environment (exogenous zeitgebers).

As with nature and nurture in psychology, it is very difficult to separate the relative influence of pacemakers and zeitgebers as they are so closely linked. However, we shall attempt to examine the effect of each on one type of circadian rhythm: the sleep/wake cycle.

KEY TERMS

Endogenous pacemakers – Internal body clocks that regulate many of our biological rhythms, such as the influence of the suprachiasmatic nucleus (SCN) on the sleep/wake cycle.

Exogenous zeitgebers – External cues that may affect or *entrain* our biological rhythms, such as the influence of light on the sleep/wake cycle.

Sleep/wake cycle – A daily cycle of biological activity based on a 24-hour period (circadian rhythm) that is influenced by regular variations in the environment, such as the alternation of night and day.

If you're a fan of chipmunks, the DeCoursey study (above right) is probably best avoided.

Apply it — Concepts: Use of studies

You shouldn't be short of studies to illustrate the effects of endogenous pacemakers and exogenous zeitgebers. As well as the studies presented on this spread, you can also discuss those in relation to circadian and infradian rhythms featured on previous spreads.

Question

Explain how the following studies could be used to support the influence of endogenous pacemakers *and* exogenous zeitgebers:

- Siffre
- Aschoff and Wever
- Stern and McClintock

Endogenous pacemakers and the sleep/wake cycle

The suprachiasmatic nucleus (SCN)

The *suprachiasmatic nucleus* (SCN) is a tiny bundle of nerve cells located in the **hypothalamus** in each hemisphere of the brain. It is one of the primary **endogenous pacemakers** in mammalian species (including humans) and is influential in maintaining **circadian rhythms** such as the **sleep/wake cycle**. Nerve fibres connected to the eye cross in an area called the *optic chiasm* on their way to the **visual area** of the **cerebral cortex**. The SCN lies just above the optic chiasm (thus 'supra', which means 'above'). It receives information about light directly from this structure. This continues even when our eyes are closed, enabling the biological clock to adjust to changing patterns of daylight whilst we are asleep.

Animal studies and the SCN

The influence of the SCN has been demonstrated in studies involving animals. Patricia DeCoursey *et al.* (2000) destroyed the SCN connections in the brains of 30 chipmunks who were then returned to their natural habitat and observed for 80 days. The sleep/wake cycle of the chipmunks disappeared and by the end of the study a **significant** proportion of them had been killed by predators (presumably because they were awake and vulnerable to attack when they should have been asleep).

In another study, Martin Ralph *et al.* (1990) bred 'mutant' hamsters with a 20-hour sleep/wake cycle. When SCN cells from the foetal tissue of mutant hamsters were transplanted into the brains of normal hamsters, the cycles of the second group defaulted to 20 hours.

Both of these studies emphasise the role of the SCN in establishing and maintaining the circadian sleep/wake cycle.

The pineal gland and melatonin

The SCN passes the information on day length and light that it receives to the *pineal gland* (a pea-like structure in the brain just behind the hypothalamus). During the night, the pineal gland increases production of **melatonin** – a chemical that induces sleep and is inhibited during periods of wakefulness. Melatonin has also been suggested as a causal factor in **seasonal affective disorder** (see previous spread).

Exogenous zeitgebers and the sleep/wake cycle

The German word *zeitgeber* means 'time giver'. **Exogenous zeitgebers** are external factors in the environment that reset our biological clocks through a process known as *entrainment*. We have seen that, in the absence of external cues, the free running biological clock that controls the sleep/wake cycle continues to 'tick' in a distinct cyclical pattern (as in the Siffre study – see page 46). Thus, sleeping and wakefulness would seem to be determined by an interaction of internal and external factors.

Light

Light is a key zeitgeber in humans. It can reset the body's main endogenous pacemaker, the SCN, and thus plays a role in the maintenance of the sleep/wake cycle. Light also has an indirect influence on key processes in the body that control such functions as **hormone** secretion and blood circulation.

In an innovative study, Scott Campbell and Patricia Murphy (1998) demonstrated that light may be detected by skin receptor sites on the body even when the same information is not received by the eyes. Fifteen participants were woken at various times and a light pad was shone on the back of their knees. The researchers managed to produce a deviation in the participants' usual sleep/wake cycle of up to 3 hours in some cases! This suggests that light is a powerful exogenous zeitgeber that need not necessarily rely on the eyes to exert its influence on the brain.

Social cues

As every parent knows, infants are seldom on the same sleep/wake cycle as the rest of the family. In human infants, the initial sleep/wake cycle is pretty much random. At about 6 weeks of age, the circadian rhythms begin and by about 16 weeks, most babies are entrained. The schedules imposed by parents are likely to be a key influence here, including adult-determined mealtimes and bedtimes. Research also suggests that adapting to local times for eating and sleeping (rather than responding to ones own feelings of hunger and fatigue), is an effective way of entraining circadian rhythms and beating jet lag when travelling long distances.

It's probably reasonable to assume that this man has some difficulty adjusting to his sleep/wake cycle.

Evaluation

Beyond the master clock

Research has revealed there are numerous circadian rhythms in many organs and cells of the body. These are called *peripheral oscillators*, and are found in the adrenal gland, oesophagus, lungs, liver, pancreas, spleen, thymus and skin. Although these peripheral clocks are highly influenced by the actions of the SCN, they can act independently. Francesca Damiola *et al.* (2000) demonstrated how changing feeding patterns in mice could alter the circadian rhythms of cells in the liver by up to 12 hours, whilst leaving the rhythm of the SCN unaffected. This suggests that there may be many other complex influences on the sleep/wake cycle, aside from the master clock (the SCN).

Ethics in animal studies

On previous spreads we have made reference to the problems involved in **generalising** findings of the sleep/wake cycle from animal studies to humans. A more disturbing issue, however, particularly in relation to the DeCoursey *et al.* study, is the ethics involved in such research. The animals were exposed to considerable harm, and subsequent risk, when they were returned to their natural habitat. Whether what we learn from investigations such as these justifies the aversive procedures involved is a matter of debate.

Influence of exogenous zeitgebers may be overstated

Laughton Miles *et al.* (1977) recount the story of a young man, blind from birth, with a circadian rhythm of 24.9 hours. Despite exposure to social cues, his sleep/wake cycle could not be adjusted, and consequently, he had to take sedatives at night and stimulants in the morning to keep pace with the 24-hour world. Similarly, studies of individuals who live in Arctic regions (where the sun does not set during the summer months) show normal sleep patterns despite the prolonged exposure to light. Both these examples suggest that there are occasions when exogenous zeitgebers may have little bearing on our internal rhythm.

Evaluation eXtra

Methodological issues in studies

The findings from the Campbell and Murphy study have yet to be **replicated**. Other psychologists have been critical of the manner in which the study was conducted and have suggested that there may have been some limited light exposure to the participants' eyes – a major **confounding variable**. Also, isolating one exogenous zeitgeber (light) in this way does not give us insight into the many other zeitgebers that influence the sleep/wake cycle, and the extent to which these may interact.

Consider: *As well as light and social cues, what other exogenous zeitgebers may affect the sleep/ wake cycle?*

Interactionist system

Only in exceptional circumstances are endogenous pacemakers free-running and unaffected by the influence of exogenous zeitgebers. Total isolation studies, such as Siffre's cave study, are extremely rare and could be judged as lacking **validity** for this reason. In real-life, pacemakers and zeitgebers interact, and it may make little sense to separate the two for the purpose of research.

Consider: *Explain how endogenous pacemakers and exogenous zeitgebers interact in the context of the sleep/wake cycle.*

Apply it **Methods: Delayed sleep-phase disorder**

Delayed sleep-phase disorder (DSPD) is a circadian rhythm sleep disorder affecting the timing of sleep, peak period of alertness, the core body temperature rhythm, hormonal and other daily rhythms. People with DSPD generally fall asleep some hours after midnight and have difficulty waking up in the morning. Patients can sleep well and have a normal need for sleep. However, they find it very difficult to wake up in time for a typical school or work day.

Twenty patients who suffered from DPSD were involved in an investigation. Researchers randomly allocated the 20 patients into two groups: Group A (the treatment group) and Group B (the control group).

Group A were given a course of drugs that increased melatonin production for six weeks at bed-time (around 11pm). Group B were given a **placebo** for the same period of time. At the end of the six-week period, all the participants were assessed on a number of **self-report** measures. These examined their performance at work, their attention levels during the day and their relationship with their families.

Questions

1. Suggest an appropriate **hypothesis** for the investigation above. (*2 marks*)
2. Identify the **experimental design** in the investigation above. (*1 mark*)
3. Explain *one* strength and *one* limitation of the experimental design you have identified in question 2. (*4 marks*)
4. Explain *one* way in which participants may have been **randomly allocated** to one of the two groups. (*2 marks*)
5. Explain *one* limitation with the use of self-report measures described above. (*3 marks*)

Apply it **Concepts: Jet lag**

On page 47, we noted the unpleasant and potentially dangerous effects of shift work on the body's biological clock. **Jet lag** is another important form of desynchronisation that can disrupt the sleep/wake cycle, causing sleeplessness, irritability and nausea, as the body struggles to adapt to changing time zones.

Question

Using research into endogenous pacemakers, what advice would you give would-be travellers on how best to minimise the negative effects of jet lag?

CHECK IT

1. With reference to an example, define what is meant by an *endogenous pacemaker*. [3 marks]
2. Describe **one** study that investigated the effect of an exogenous zeitgeber on the sleep/wake cycle. [4 marks]
3. Discuss the effect of endogenous pacemakers and exogenous zeitgebers on the sleep/wake cycle. [16 marks]

THE SPECIFICATION SAYS...

Knowledge and understanding of ... research methods, practical research skills and maths skills. These should be developed through ... ethical practical research activities.

This means you should conduct practical activities wherever possible. On this spread one activity is a correlational analysis to determine whether there is a relationship between the amount of exercise people do and the circadian rhythm of sleep. The other is also correlation, this time to see whether there is a relationship between how fast someone can run and their index finger to ring finger ratio.. Confused? Read on ...

Ethics check

We suggest strongly that you complete this checklist before starting:

1. Do participants know participation is voluntary?
2. Do participants know what to expect?
3. Do participants know they can withdraw at any time?
4. Are individuals' results anonymous?
5. Have I minimised the risk of distress to participants?
6. Have I avoided asking sensitive questions?
7. Will I avoid bringing my school/teacher/psychology into disrepute?
8. Have I considered all other ethical issues?
9. Has my teacher approved this?

Practical idea 1:
The effects of exercise on sleep

The **aim** of this study is to explore whether there is a relationship between the amount of exercise done in a day and the sleep/wake cycle.

More specifically we are interested in whether there is a positive correlation between the number of hours exercise people do and the number of hours sleep they have over the course of a week.

The practical bit

It might be possible to test the relationship between levels of exercise and sleep patterns experimentally but this would involve depriving some participants of one or the other in order to manipulate the **independent variable**. So, we must rule out **experiments** for ethical reasons. An **observation** is a possibility too but participants would quickly become irritated by the constant presence of the researcher waiting patiently for them to break into a trot, and their nightly appearance at the end of the bed may well prove distracting! For practical and ethical reasons then, we would recommend that participants keep a record of how much exercise they do, as well as how much sleep they have, over a weekly period.

Recording data for each co-variable

As part of their involvement within the study, participants will be required to keep a simple diary of the number of hours they sleep and exercise over a weekly period. This may be more complicated than it sounds, though. The definition of what counts as 'exercise' may vary greatly from person to person. For some, lifting the remote control may constitute a rare feat of physical prowess. Whereas for others, a six-mile jog to the shops may barely draw a bead of sweat.

'Number of hours sleep' may also not be as self-evident as it sounds. Does this include a twenty-minute power nap before dinner at the end of a school day? Or the ten minutes that someone lost consciousness during an A level history video? For these reasons, it would be wise for you as a researcher to fully **operationalise** the **co-variables** in this study for the benefit of participants. This will involve drawing up a detailed list of what you define as 'exercise' and 'sleep' so participants can make accurate recordings at the end of each day.

Ethical issues

This study should be ethically acceptable as long as it is conducted well, but there are some issues to be aware of. Participants' data should remain **confidential**, not least because some may not want their data made public or shared with others. Some participants may be reluctant to report their data for reasons of, say, embarrassment so must be reminded that they have the **right to withdraw** their participation at any point. Participants may also need reassurance that the data they provide is 'normal' and so any **debrief** that is offered at the end of the study should be carefully worded.

Analysing your data

You will want to be able to display your results so that the relationship between the number of hours exercise and the number of hours sleep can be clearly seen. You should also use **inferential statistics**.

Methods: The maths bit 1

1. In Table 1, what percentage of participants slept for less than 50 hours in the week they recorded data? (*2 marks*)
2. What percentage of participants exercised for more than 15 hours in the week they recorded data? (*2 marks*)
3. Which graphical display would be most suitable to show the relationship between number of hours sleep and number of hours exercise in Table 1? Explain your answer. (*2 marks*)
4. Sketch a suitable graphical display to show the relationship between number of hours sleep and number of hours exercise in Table 1. (*4 marks*)
5. Referring to Table 1, and the display you have drawn for Q4, explain the relationship between number of hours sleep and number of hours exercise. (*2 marks*)
6. Explain why, from this investigation, it is not possible to conclude that there is a causal relationship between exercise and sleep. (*3 marks*)

Table 1

Ppt	Total hours sleep in a week	Total hours exercise in a week
1	56	17
2	63	21
3	58	10
4	42	5
5	34	2
6	70	23
7	54	11
8	60	17
9	50	14
10	49	8

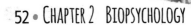

Practical idea 2:
Digit ratio and running speed

The aim of this study is to see if there is a correlation between a person's index finger (2nd digit – 2D) and their ring finger (4th digit – 4D) ratio and how fast they can run.

In other words, is 2D:4D ratio related to sporting performance – specifically the time it takes someone to run 100 metres? This is based on a study by Manning *et al.* (2001) who found that high 2D:4D ratio in males was associated with reduced performance in sport.

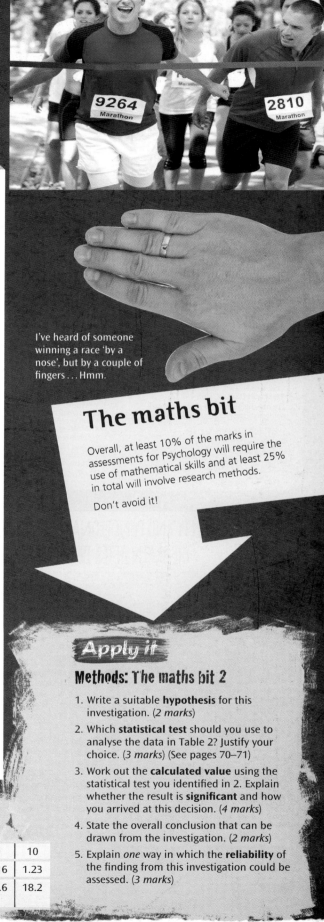

The practical bit

'Digit ratio' is the ratio of the lengths of different fingers measured from the midpoint of the bottom crease (where the finger joins the hand) to the tip of the finger. It has been suggested by a number of researchers that the ratio of the 2nd 'index finger' (the one you use for pointing) and the 4th 'ring finger' is affected by exposure to **androgens**, e.g. **testosterone,** whilst in the womb, with *lower* 2D:4D ratios pointing (no pun intended) to *higher* prenatal androgen exposure. Researchers investigating 2D:4D have linked digit ratio to a wide range of behaviours including ADHD, schizophrenia, depression, alcohol dependency and video game addiction.

Why running speed?

Clearly, none of the behaviours listed above are suitable territory for a study investigation. However, a study by Manning *et al.* (2001) found that superior *sporting ability* in male participants was correlated with *low* index finger to ring finger ratio (a **negative correlation**). This is based on the theory that high testosterone (low 2D:4D ratio) may lead to the development of attributes that are useful in the sporting arena – including competitiveness and a general 'will to win'.

Manning *et al.*'s study focused on football ability in males, in particular professional footballers who had represented their country. It's probably a safe bet to assume that you don't know that many professional footballers (and even fewer that have reached international standard), so your task is to examine the relationship between 2D:4D ratio and how fast your male *and* female friends can run 100 metres.

Measuring the 2D:4D ratio

The 2D:4D ratio is calculated by dividing the length of the index finger of the right hand by the length of the ring finger of the right hand. A longer index finger will result in a ratio higher than 1, while a longer ring finger will result in a ratio of less than 1. It is likely that the lower 2D:4D ratios will be those of the male participants in your study – but not necessarily. There are wide individual differences in digit ratio and these may vary within and between the genders. Once you have measured and recorded 2D:4D ratios for all of your participants, you are ready to start the race.

Run participants, run...

One thing we should have mentioned is how many participants you'll need. One of the co-variables will be determined by performance in a sprint – with everyone running at the same time – a cast of thousands is not really appropriate. It would be OK to organise a series of races if you manage to recruit quite a lot of participants but individual time trials are not an option. The point is that participants must be given the opportunity to show how competitive they are by running against each other, rather than on their own 'against the clock'.

You'll need a bit of a help

Despite your best efforts, it will be difficult to **replicate** Olympic-style running conditions in your 100m race, and without access to sophisticated recording equipment, you're going to have to rely on a little help from your (non-participant) friends. Make sure you have enough people present on race day to ensure everybody's time is reasonably accurately recorded.

I've heard of someone winning a race 'by a nose', but by a couple of fingers... Hmm.

The maths bit

Overall, at least 10% of the marks in assessments for Psychology will require the use of mathematical skills and at least 25% in total will involve research methods.

Don't avoid it!

Apply it

Methods: The maths bit 2

1. Write a suitable **hypothesis** for this investigation. (*2 marks*)

2. Which **statistical test** should you use to analyse the data in Table 2? Justify your choice. (*3 marks*) (See pages 70–71)

3. Work out the **calculated value** using the statistical test you identified in 2. Explain whether the result is **significant** and how you arrived at this decision. (*4 marks*)

4. State the overall conclusion that can be drawn from the investigation. (*2 marks*)

5. Explain *one* way in which the **reliability** of the finding from this investigation could be assessed. (*3 marks*)

Table 2 shows example data collected for participants' 2D:4D ratio and the time taken to run 100 metres.

Participant	1	2	3	4	5	6	7	8	9	10
2D:4D ratio	0.82	0.85	0.91	0.88	0.98	1.01	0.99	1.12	1.16	1.23
Time taken to run 100 metres (sec)	11.6	12.1	13.6	12.9	13.6	13.9	14.4	14.0	15.6	18.2

Revision summaries

The nervous system and the endocrine system

A major physiological system that regulates behaviour.

The nervous system

Central nervous system
Brain and the spinal cord.

Peripheral nervous system
Autonomic nervous system (sympathetic and parasympathetic).
Somatic nervous system (body).

The endocrine system

Glands and hormones
Hormones distributed in bloodstream.
Pituitary is the master gland.

Fight or flight
Sympathetic arousal: pituitary → ACTH → adrenal gland → adrenaline.

Neurons and synaptic transmission

Another major physiological system that regulates behaviour.

Structure and function of neurons

Types of neuron
Motor, sensory and relay neurons.

Structure of a neuron
Cell body contains nucleus, has dendrites.
Axon covered in myelin sheath divided by nodes of Ranvier.

Electrical transmission
Positive charge leads to action potential.

Synaptic transmission

Synapse
Terminal buttons at synapse, presynaptic vesicles release neurotransmitter.

Neurotransmitters
Postsynaptic receptor site receives neurotransmitters from dendrites of adjoining neuron.
Specialist functions, e.g. acetylcholine for muscle contraction.

Excitation or inhibition
Adrenaline is excitatory, serotonin is inhibitory.

Psychotherapeutic drugs
SSRIs increase serotonin activity.

Localisation of function in the brain

Different behaviours are controlled by specific areas of the brain.

Localisation of function in the brain

Localisation versus holistic theory
Are brain functions in specific areas or across the whole brain?

Hemispheres of the brain and the cerebral cortex
Each hemisphere controls the opposite side of the body.
Cortex is outer layer of the brain.

Motor, somatosensory, visual and auditory centres
Each of the four lobes of the brain (frontal, parietal, occipital and temporal lobes) is linked to different functions.

Language centre in the brain
Broca's related to production, Wernicke's related to understanding.

Evaluation

Brain scan evidence of localisation
Peterson et al. showed Broca and Wernicke areas active.

Neurosurgical evidence
Dougherty et al.: One third of OCD patients responded to cingulotomy, supports localisation.

Case study evidence
Phineas Gage: Personality change.

Lashley's research
Rats' maze learning unaffected by removeal of cortical material.

Plasticity
The law of equipotentiality (Lashley).

Plasticity and functional recovery of the brain after trauma

The brain's ability to change and adapt permits recovery from trauma.

Plasticity and functional recovery of the brain after trauma

Brain plasticity
Research suggests that neural connections can change or new connections can be formed.

Research into plasticity
Maguire et al.: Hippocampus in taxi drivers changes structure after learning the Knowledge.
Draganski et al.: Changes in hippocampus and the parietal cortex before and after exams.

Functional recovery of the brain after trauma
Healthy brain areas take over functions of damaged areas.

What happens in the brain during recovery?
Axonal sprouting.
Reforming of blood vessels.
Recruitment of homologous brain areas.

Evaluation

Practical application
Neurorehabilitation required to maintain improvement because spontaneous recovery slows down.

Negative plasticity
Drug use may cause neural changes (Medina et al.).
Phantom limb syndrome due to reorganisation in somatosensory cortex (Ramachandran).

Age and plasticity
Plasticity reduces with age, though Bezzola et al. showed how golf training caused neural changes in over 40s.

Support from animal studies
Hubel and Wiesel: Pioneering research into kittens' cortical response, caused permanent damage.

The concept of cognitive reserve
Schneider et al.: The more time spent in education, the greater the brain's capacity to heal.

Split-brain research into hemispheric lateralisation

Right and left hemisphere not connected.

Split-brain research

Hemispheric lateralisation
Left hemisphere has different functions (e.g. language).

Split-brain studies
Corpus callosum cut to prevent electrical signals crossing between hemispheres.

Procedure
Images presented to one hemisphere at a time.

Key findings
Can't describe an object in left visual field.
Can recognise with left hand.
Composite words: Write 'key' with left hand, say 'ring'.
Right hemisphere better at recognising faces.

Evaluation

Demonstrated lateralised brain functions
The left hemisphere analyses, the right hemisphere synthesises.

Strengths of the methodology
Standardised and controlled procedures to control input into each hemisphere.

Theoretical basis
Puvetti: Two minds = duality in the brain.
In reality it is an integrated system.

Issues with generalisation
Small unrepresentative sample, with no control group.

Differences in function may be overstated
Distinction between hemispheres is messier than the research suggests.

WAYS OF INVESTIGATING THE BRAIN

Measuring brain activity and structure.

SCANNING AND OTHER TECHNIQUES

fMRI
Detects changes in blood flow to show active areas.

EEG
Measures brainwave patterns via electrodes.

ERP
Types of brainwave triggered by particular events that can be extracted from EEG recordings.

Post-mortems
Deficits during life correlated with brain damage after death.

EVALUATION

fMRI
+ Risk-free and high spatial resolution.
– Poor temporal resolution.

EEG
+ Good for diagnosing illness, and high temporal resolution.
– Overly general.

ERP
+ Precise measurement of cognitive functions.
– Lack of standardised method.

Post-mortem
+ Early pioneering research.
– Causation an issue, consent is difficult.

BIOLOGICAL RHYTHMS:

CIRCADIAN RHYTHMS

A bodily rhythm that takes about 24 hours to complete.

BIOLOGICAL RHYTHMS

Biological rhythms
Controlled by internal body clocks (endogenous pacemakers) and external cues (exogenous zeitgebers).

The sleep/wake cycle
Determines sleepiness, but does free-running cycle continue in the absence of daylight?

Siffre's cave study
His free-running rhythm extended slightly to 25 hours when deprived of daylight.

Other research
Studies by Aschoff and Wever (bunker) and Folkard *et al.* (cave) showed longer and shorter rhythms

Core body temperature
Associated with improved variations in cognitive performance.

EVALUATION

Practical application to shift work
Mistakes made when rhythms desynchronised (Boivin *et al.*) and poor health (Knutsson).
Thus economic implications of research.

Practical application
Pharmacokinetics applies understanding of circadian rhythms to improve drug effectiveness (Baraldo).

Use of case studies and small samples
Lack generalisability, e.g. Siffre was over 60 and small samples.

Poor control in studies
Dim artificial light may have reset the body clock (Czeisler *et al.*).

Individual differences
Sleep cycles vary between 13 and 65 hours in some cases (Czeisler *et al.*) and larks/owls (Duffy *et al.*).

INFRADIAN AND ULTRADIAN RHYTHMS

Infradian – more that 24 hours; ultradian – less than 24 hours.

INFRADIAN RHYTHMS

The menstrual cycle
Oestrogen regulates ovulation, progesterone readies body for pregnancy (endogenous factors).

Research study
Stern and McClintock: Evidence that menstrual cycles may synchronise through pheromones (exogenous factors).

Seasonal affective disorder
Form of depression triggered in the winter months and regulated by melatonin, a circannual rhythm.

Other research
Studies by Aschoff and Wever (bunker) and Folkard *et al.* (cave) showed longer and shorter rhythms

ULTRADIAN RHYTHMS:

Stages of sleep
5 stages that occur in a 90-minute cycle:
Stages 1 and 2: Alpha and theta waves.
Stages 3 and 4: Deep sleep, delta waves.
Stage 5: REM sleep.

EVALUATION

Evolutionary basis of the menstrual cycle
Synchronisation may have an adaptive function because newborns cared for collectively. However, this would also produce competition for the fittest males.

Methodological issues in synchronisation studies
Many confounding factors not controlled, e.g. stress, diet. Small samples.

Evidence supports the idea of distinct stages in sleep
Deement and Kleitman (1957) using EEGs showed how REM (dream) sleep is an important part of the sleep cycle.

Animal studies
Role of pheromones in human behaviour is unclear.

Practical application
Phototherapy for SAD, effective in 60% (Eastman *et al.*).

ENDOGENOUS PACEMAKERS AND EXOGENOUS ZEITGEBERS

Rhythms are affected by body clocks and external cues

EXOGENOUS ZEITGEBERS AND THE SLEEP-WAKE CYCLE

Exogenous zeitgebers
Entrain free-running rhythms.

Light
Campbell and Murphy – shone light pad on back of knees.

Social cues
Babies' rhythms are entrained by bedtimes and mealtimes.

ENDOGENOUS PACEMAKERS AND THE SLEEP-WAKE CYCLE

The SCN
Receives info about light directly.

Animal studies and the SCN
DeCoursey *et al.*: Sleep–wake cycle disappeared when SCN destroyed.
Ralph *et al.*: Mutant hamsters with 20-hour sleep cycle.

The pineal gland and melatonin
The SCN passes info to the pineal gland that controls melatonin.

EVALUATION

Beyond the master clock
Peripheral oscillators are found in many areas of the body. Damiola *et al.* showed how these can act independently of the SCN.

Ethics in animal studies
DeCoursey *et al.* study harmed animals, is this ethically justifiable?

Influence of zeitgebers may be overstated
Zeitgebers may have little bearing on our internal rhythm, e.g. blind man (Miles *et al.*).

Methodological issues in studies
Light pad study findings not replicated and isolating one zeitgeber may be unrealistic.

Interactionist system
Attempts to separate pacemakers and zeitgebers may not reflect real-life.

Question 1 Using an example, explain what is meant by localisation of function. *(2 marks)*

Morticia's answer Localisation of function means that the parts of the brain all have a specific function such as the language area of the brain.	Morticia has provided a brief response to both parts of the question.
Luke's answer A localised function is where different areas of the brain are responsible for different behaviours or processes. One example of this is the visual area of the brain, which is in the occipital lobe and has the specific function of processing information from the eyes. If this area is damaged then no other part of the brain takes over.	Luke's definition is clear and precise, and the example is well explained.
Vladimir's answer Areas of the brain have specific functions, for example the left side of the brain controls the right side of the body and is also related to language.	Similar to Morticia's answer: the definition lacks detail, as does the example and so limited credit overall.

Question 2 A researcher conducted a meta-analysis of studies that investigated the length of the sleep-wake cycle. The researcher concluded that the average length of the sleep-wake cycle is between 24 and 25 hours.

What is meant by a meta-analysis? Refer to the investigation above in your answer. *(2 marks)*

Morticia's answer This is a study where the results from a number of other studies are analysed, for example in this case the researcher is looking at a number of studies that have investigated sleep.	There is a brief definition of meta-analysis and reference to the question stem. However, the main aim of meta-analysis (to produce an overall conclusion) is not present.
Luke's answer A researcher may combine a number of different studies as has been done here. The studies are all related to the same topic – in this case it is the length of the sleep-wake cycle. Then the researcher produces an overall conclusion.	Luke has included the key element not present in Morticia's answer.
Vladimir's answer Meta-analysis is the process of combining results from a number of studies on a particular topic (such as the sleep-wake cycle) to provide an overall view.	Vladimir's answer is similar to Luke's and the notion of 'an overall view' is sufficient.

Question 3 Briefly discuss the implications of psychological research for the economy. Refer to the investigation in question 2 in your answer. *(4 marks)*

Morticia's answer Research on the sleep-wake cycle has implications for the economy because it is used to inform practices on shift work. One study by Boivin et al. found that found that mistakes are more likely to happen early in the morning for nightshift workers. Sleep-wake research also has implications for drug treatments because it matters what time of day certain drugs are given for them to be most effective. Many other areas of psychological research have implications for the economy such as research related to attachment and memory and mental illness. In all of these areas the government can save a lot of money by following advice given by psychologists about the things that cause certain negative behaviours. The research costs a lot to fund but it saves billions and that is why psychological research is good for the economy.	This answer starts well though the link to shift workers' errors and the implications for the economy could be made more specific. The reference to drug treatment does not add anything substantial to the answer, as again the implications for the economy are not explained. The last paragraph also adds little to the answer. Morticia would have been better advised to select one example from the list offered and link this clearly to the economy.
Luke's answer Research such as on the sleep-wake cycle can be applied to improving shift work to avoid expensive accidents. Psychological research has shown that people working at night lose concentration and make mistakes, which can be very costly for the government – both economically and also just in terms of a personal cost. Furthermore, research shows that shift work is related to poor health outcomes, which costs the national economy money. Therefore, if psychologists can recommend ways to reduce the health issues, it will benefit the economy.	Notice how Luke's answer makes a clear link to economic gains and losses in the context of shift work which Morticia's response failed to do. There are two clear issues discussed here: the increased likelihood of mistakes and the negative impact on workers' health, which are clearly linked to the economy.
Vladimir's answer Psychological research can provide great benefits to our economy. For example, work on sleep and circadian rhythms is important and so is research on mental illness. Mental illness costs us billions of pounds every year and is going to get worse because of increasing dementia. If psychologists can find ways to reduce cases of dementia or cheap treatments to help people with dementia, that's our only way of avoiding bigger and bigger taxes.	The link to sleep and circadian rhythms in Vladimir's answer is poorly realised and the economic implication is not discussed. The material on dementia is better in this respect though the reference to 'bigger and bigger taxes' is a little vague.

CHAPTER 2 BIOPSYCHOLOGY

Question 4   Discuss research using split-brain patients to investigate hemispheric lateralisation. *(16 marks)*

Morticia's answer Lateralisation is not the same as localisation but they can be easily confused. Localisation refers to the fact that specific areas of the brain have specific functions, whereas lateralisation refers to the fact that the two parts of the brain control different things, in other words they have different functions.

The left half of the brain controls the right side of the body such as the right hand or right leg. The eyes are a bit different because each eye is divided into a left and right visual field and the left side of the brain processes the left visual field. The right side of the brain process the right visual field coming from both eyes.

This was shown in a study by Roger Sperry. He used people who had their brains cut in half – called split-brain patients. The operation was done because they suffered from severe epilepsy and one way to treat this is to cut the connections between the two parts of the brain to stop the electrical signals going back and forth. This means that patients weren't deliberately harmed just for this operation which would have been unethical.

Sperry tested his patients a lot using quite a clever method so they could see images on a screen but couldn't see what their hands were doing. This meant he could show images on the left part of the screen which are then processed by the left hemisphere. If the patients were then asked to select the same object they couldn't because the left hemisphere doesn't control the left hand.

Another test that he used was to ask people to say what they saw on the screen. They could only do this if the object was on the left side of the screen because that is linked to the left side of the brain where speech is located. Words were flashed for a very brief time otherwise people could move their heads and then both halves of the brain would see the words.

To evaluate this research we can think about ethics. It was unethical because the operation was done anyway. It was a good study because it involved real patients and the tasks were everyday tasks which could show what they could and couldn't do. However, there are issues with generalising because the patients may have brain damage from their epilepsy. Also the control group should have had epilepsy as well rather than being normal.

(403 words)

These definitions are not really necessary for a question that focuses on 'research'.

Again, this second paragraph is not addressing 'research' and there is also an error – the left side of the brain does not process the left visual field.

In paragraph 3 the answer begins to focus on evidence but unfortunately, although the description contains some accurate detail, it is muddled.

Again, another error in paragraph 4 – objects projected on the right, not the left, would be named as this information is processed by the left hemisphere.

The first two evaluative points in the final paragraph are not relevant. The last two are but could have been developed more.

Luke's answer In the 1960s, Roger Sperry conducted research using split-brain patients to reveal how the brain is lateralised, i.e. how the two hemispheres perform different functions. Split-brain patients undergo an operation (to treat severe epileptic seizures) where the corpus callosum and other structures which connect the two hemispheres are severed. This means that functionally the person has two separate brains.

Sperry was thus able to demonstrate that speech was controlled in the left hemispheres and the right visual field was connected to the left hemisphere (and vice versa). He did this by briefly exposing images on a screen to the left and right visual fields. Patients could say what they saw in the right visual field but not the left visual field.

He also demonstrated this using touch. The patient's hands were placed under the screen and the patient couldn't see objects that could be touched. A patient could select an item with his right hand that was displayed to the left but not right visual field. This shows that the right hand is connected to the left hemisphere.

This research was very important in establishing how the brain is lateralised and led to a Nobel prize for Sperry. The research also suggested that the left side of the brain is more an analyser and the right hemisphere is a synthesiser.

However, this rather simplistic idea of left- and right-brained behaviour has been criticised as not representing brain function accurately. More recent research has shown that the brain is more plastic than once thought and each hemisphere can take on some of the functions of the other if required. In addition, in 'real' life the two hemispheres work together.

His research was very well designed and objective and controlled, which meant the abilities of patients could be demonstrated. The key feature was ensuring that information was only received by one hemisphere, which was achieved using the short exposure time.

One of the implications of the research is the question of whether we actually have two minds, each of which is functionally different, or whether the two hemispheres normally work in unison and therefore we do have one mind.

One limitation of this research is that the participants had experienced severe epilepsy. This may have caused brain damage, which might influence the connections in their brain. Therefore we may not justifiably generalise the findings to the brains of normal individuals. Sperry did have a control group of normal individuals but it might have been better to have a control group of epileptics who didn't have a split-brain in order to see whether the differences were due to the split brain.

(432 words)

Right from the beginning Luke's answer appears to be much more concentrated than Morticia's. The description of lateralisation is relevant here in the context of Sperry's research.

Paragraphs 2 and 3 provide accurate descriptive detail and a brief conclusion that could be developed.

In paragraph 4 the points are brief and could be further discussed, particularly the latter point.

Paragraph 5 contains a very clear, fully elaborated discussion point, and the following paragraph is a relevant methodological critique.

The answer ends with a well-made philosophical point and some detailed discussion.

The nervous system and the endocrine system

1. Which division of the nervous system is divided into sympathetic and parasympathetic branches?
(a) The central nervous system.
(b) The peripheral nervous system.
(c) The somatic nervous system.
(d) The autonomic nervous system.

2. Which describes the somatic nervous system?
(a) Maintains homeostasis by regulating body temperature, heartbeat, etc.
(b) Made up of the brain and the spinal cord.
(c) Controls muscle movement.
(d) Passes messages to and from the brain and connects nerves to the PNS.

3. The master endocrine gland is the ...
(a) Adrenal gland.
(b) Pituitary gland.
(c) Thyroid gland.
(d) Hypothalamus.

4. Which is *not* an action of the parasympathetic branch of the ANS?
(a) Inhibits digestion.
(b) Contracts pupil.
(c) Stimulates saliva production.
(d) Decreases heart rate.

Neurons and synaptic transmission

1. Which of the following carries messages from the PNS to the CNS?
(a) Sensory neuron.
(b) Motor neuron.
(c) Relay neuron.
(d) Synaptic neuron.

2. Which is *not* part of the basic structure of a neuron?
(a) Cell body.
(b) Axon.
(c) Effector.
(d) Dendrite.

3. Which of the following does *not* occur as part of the process of synaptic transmission?
(a) The neuron is in a resting state.
(b) An electrical impulse triggers the release of neurotransmitter.
(c) Neurotransmitter diffuses across the synaptic gap.
(d) The chemical message is converted back into an electrical impulse.

4. The following describes what process? 'When a neuron is activated by a stimulus, the inside of the cell becomes positively charged for a split second. This creates an electrical impulse that travels down the axon towards the end of the neuron.'
(a) Synaptic transmission.
(b) Inhibitory response.
(c) Pre-synaptic terminal.
(d) Action potential.

Localisation of function

1. The theory that all parts of the brain are involved in the processing of thought and action is called ...
(a) Holistic theory.
(b) Localisation theory.
(c) Plasticity.
(d) Law of equipotentiality.

2. Broca's area is located in the ...
(a) Left parietal lobe.
(b) Right occipital lobe.
(c) Left frontal lobe.
(d) Left temporal lobe.

3. Damage to which area of the brain may result in a loss of control of fine movements?
(a) The somatosensory area.
(b) The motor area.
(c) The auditory area.
(d) Wernicke's area.

4. Most of the damage to Phineas Gage's brain was sustained in the ...
(a) Frontal lobe.
(b) Parietal lobe.
(c) Temporal lobe.
(d) Occipital lobe.

Plasticity and functional recovery in the brain

1. The deleting of rarely used connections in the brain is known as ...
(a) Synaptic priming.
(b) Synaptic pluming.
(c) Synaptic pruning.
(d) Synaptic planning.

2. In the Maguire *et al.* study of London taxi drivers which area was seen to have undergone learning-induced changes?
(a) Posterior hippocampus.
(b) Anterior hypothalamus.
(c) Interior gyrus.
(d) Bacteria epiglottis.

3. Which of the following refers to the activation of secondary neural pathways to carry out new functions?
(a) Revealing.
(b) Unmasking.
(c) Unearthing.
(d) Renewing.

4. The Bezzola *et al.* study saw 40 hours of training produce changes in neural representations of movement within which sport?
(a) Snooker.
(b) Chess.
(c) Golf.
(d) Darts.

Split-brain research into hemispheric lateralisation

1. The fact that language is controlled by the left hemisphere in most people is known as ...
(a) Lateralisation.
(b) Aphasia.
(c) Holism.
(d) Plasticity.

2. If an object was shown to the left visual field of one of Sperry's patients, they would report ...
(a) That they had seen the object.
(b) That there was nothing there.
(c) That they saw two objects.
(d) That they saw a different object.

3. Which of the following is specialised in the right hemisphere in most people?
(a) Musical ability.
(b) Analytic tasks.
(c) Verbal ability.
(d) Right hand.

4. Roger Sperry was awarded the Nobel Prize in which year?
(a) 1961
(b) 1971
(c) 1981
(d) 1991

Ways of investigating the brain

1. A method of detecting changes in blood oxygenation and flow that occur as a result of neural activity best describes what?
(a) fMRI.
(b) EEG.
(c) ERP.
(d) Post-mortem.

2. Which of the following is most likely to measure 'global' (whole) brain activity rather than specific areas of activity/damage?
(a) fMRI.
(b) EEG.
(c) ERP.
(d) Post-mortem.

3. Which of the following uses a statistical averaging technique to remove extraneous scan data?
(a) fMRI.
(b) EEG.
(c) ERP.
(d) Post-mortem.

4. Which of the following describes a post-mortem examination?
(a) Removal of the frontal lobe.
(b) Microscopic removal of brain cells.
(c) Cutting the brain down the middle to separate hemispheres.
(d) Examining a brain after death.

Circadian rhythms

1. Which of the following is an example of the circadian rhythm?
(a) The menstrual cycle.
(b) Seasonal affective disorder.
(c) The sleep/wake cycle.
(d) The stages of sleep.

2. In Siffre's cave study and Aschoff and Wever's bunker study the biological clock is not influenced by exogenous zeitgebers (such as light). Within these studies, the biological clock is described as . . .
(a) Free-wheeling.
(b) Free-trading.
(c) Free-flowing.
(d) Free-running.

3. Core body temperature varies by approximately how many degrees over a 24-hour period?
(a) 1 degree C.
(b) 2 degrees C.
(c) 3 degrees C.
(d) 5 degrees C.

4. Research into circadian rhythms has contributed to our understanding of chronotherapeutics. What is chronotherapeutics?
(a) The study of the timing of drug dosing.
(b) The study of how circadian and infradian rhythms interact.
(c) The study of how endogenous pacemakers are detected by skin receptors.
(d) The study of the effects of disruption of circadian rhythms (including shift work and jet lag).

Infradian rhythms

1. The Stern and McClintock study investigated the influence of which chemicals?
(a) Hormones.
(b) Pheromones.
(c) Phonemes.
(d) Garden gnomes.

2. Rapid eye movement (REM) occurs in which phase of the sleep cycle?
(a) Stages 1 and 2.
(b) Stages 3 and 4.
(c) Stage 5.
(d) It is not part of the sleep cycle.

3. Melatonin is secreted by the . . .
(a) Adrenal gland.
(b) Thyroid gland.
(c) Pituitary gland.
(d) Pineal gland.

4. Which pattern of brainwave activity is not a feature of the sleep cycle?
(a) Alpha waves.
(b) Beta waves.
(c) Delta waves.
(d) Theta waves.

Endogenous pacemakers and exogenous zeitgebers

1. The SCN is located within which part of the brain?
(a) Hypothalamus.
(b) Hippocampus.
(c) Amygdala.
(d) Corpus callosum.

2. The mutant hamsters in the Ralph *et al.* study were bred to have circadian rhythms of how long?
(a) 28 days.
(b) 28 hours.
(c) 24 hours.
(d) 20 hours.

3. Campbell and Murphy's participants had light shone . . .
(a) On the back of their necks.
(b) On the soles of their feet.
(c) On the backs of their knees.
(d) Up their noses.

4. DSPD stands for?
(a) Deep sleep phase disease.
(b) Dream sequence placement detector.
(c) Dedicated serotonin producing drug.
(d) Delayed sleep phase disorder.

MCQ answers

The nervous system and the endocrine system 1d, 2c, 3b, 4a
Neurons and synaptic transmission 1a, 2c, 3a, 4d
Localisation of function in the brain 1a, 2c, 3b, 4a
Plasticity and functional recovery of the brain after trauma 1c, 2a, 3b, 4c
Split-brain research into hemispheric lateralisation 1a, 2b, 3a, 4c
Ways of investigating the brain 1a, 2b, 3c, 4d
Biological rhythms: circadian rhythms 1c, 2d, 3b, 4a
Biological rhythms: infradian and ultradian rhythms 1b, 2c, 3d, 4b
Endogenous pacemakers and exogenous zeitgebers 1a, 2d, 3c, 4d

CHAPTER 3
RESEARCH METHODS

The 50–50–90 rule: Anytime you have a 50–50 chance of getting something right, there's a 90% probability you'll get it wrong.

Andy Rooney (US author and commentator)

Chapter contents

What is the probability that you will throw a six?

What is the probability it will rain next week?

What are the chances that you'll win the National Lottery next week?

What is the probability that the things psychologists discover are 'true'?

Is scientific 'proof' of something even possible?

The answers to these questions (and more) in the next few pages. Probably.

RESEARCH METHODS RECAP

Students should demonstrate knowledge and understanding of the following research methods, scientific processes and techniques of data handling and analysis, be familiar with their use and be aware of their strengths and limitations.

Welcome back to Research Methods! Included on this spread is a summary of the Research Methods content that you need to know by the end of A level.

On the right is a recap of what you have already covered in Year 1. Below is a breakdown of the content for this year that is A level only.

KEY TERM

Research methods – The processes by which information or data is collected usually for the purpose of testing a hypothesis and/or a theory.

The methods bit

Overall, at least 25% of the marks in assessments for Psychology will be based on assessment of research methods. Although 50% of Paper 2 at A level will assess Research Methods, it could also be assessed in any other topic on any other paper!

Research methods – still to come...

A level only

(You can use this to tick off topics as you complete them.)

Case studies. Content analysis and coding. Thematic analysis. ☐

Reliability across all methods of investigation. Ways of assessing reliability: test–retest and inter-observer; improving reliability. ☐

Types of validity across all methods of investigation: face validity, concurrent validity, ecological validity and temporal validity; assessment of validity; improving validity. ☐

Factors affecting the choice of statistical test, including level of measurement and experimental design. ☐

When to use the following tests: Spearman's rho, Pearson's r, Wilcoxon, Mann–Whitney, related t-test, unrelated t-test and Chi-Squared test. ☐

Analysis and interpretation of correlation, including correlation coefficients. ☐

Probability and significance: use of statistical tables and critical values in interpretation of significance; Type I and Type II errors. ☐

Reporting psychological investigations: sections of a scientific report: abstract, introduction, method, results, discussion and referencing. ☐

Features of science: objectivity and the empirical method; replicability and falsifiability; theory construction and hypothesis testing; paradigms and paradigm shifts. ☐

Research methods – the story so far...

AS and Year 1 Specification content

Tick off what you already know and would feel confident answering questions on in the exam. Revisit concepts if necessary.

Aims: stating aims, the differences between aims and hypotheses. ☐

Hypotheses: directional and non-directional. Variables and control. ☐

Types of experiment, laboratory and field experiments; natural and quasi-experiments. Experimental designs: repeated measures, independent groups, matched pairs. ☐

Sampling: the difference between population and sample; sampling techniques including: random, systematic, stratified, opportunity and volunteer; implications of sampling techniques, including bias and generalisation. ☐

Ethics, including the role of the British Psychological Society's code of ethics; ethical issues in the design and conduct of psychological studies; dealing with ethical issues in research. ☐

Observational techniques. Types of observation: naturalistic and controlled observation; covert and overt observation; participant and non-participant observation. Observational design: behavioural categories, event sampling, time sampling. ☐

Self-report techniques. Questionnaires; interviews, structured and unstructured. Questionnaire construction, including use of open and closed questions; design of interviews. ☐

Correlations. Analysis of the relationship between co-variables. The difference between correlations and experiments. Positive, negative and zero correlations. ☐

Quantitative and qualitative data; the distinction between qualitative and quantitative data collection techniques. Primary and secondary data, including meta-analysis. ☐

Descriptive statistics: measures of central tendency: mean, median, mode; calculation of mean, median and mode; measures of dispersion: range and standard deviation; calculation of range. ☐

Mathematical content – calculation of percentages, converting a percentage to a decimal, converting a decimal to a fraction, using ratios, mathematical symbols, probability, significant figures. ☐

Introduction to statistical testing: the sign test. ☐

Presentation and display of quantitative data: graphs, tables, scattergrams, bar charts, histograms. Distributions: normal and skewed distributions; characteristics of normal and skewed distributions. ☐

Pilot studies and the aims of piloting. ☐

The role of peer review in the scientific process. ☐

The implications of psychological research for the economy. ☐

At the end of each chapter in this book (including this one) you will find suggestions for practical investigations. You should carry out as many of these as you can to support your understanding of research methods.

CORRELATIONS

THE SPECIFICATION SAYS...

Analysis and interpretation of correlation, including correlation coefficients.

Correlation is not new to you – you learned about it in Year 1 of the course; the analysis and interpretation of correlation coefficients is. All correlations can be represented by a number somewhere between −1 and +1. What this number means is explained here.

KEY TERMS

Correlation – A mathematical technique in which a researcher investigates an association between two variables, called co-variables.

Correlation coefficient – A number between −1 and +1 that represents the direction and strength of a relationship between co-variables.

Apply it Methods:
Interpretation of correlation coefficients

Questions

1. What sort of relationship is suggested by the following coefficients? *(5 marks)*
   (i) −.40
   (ii) +.90
   (iii) +.13
   (iv) −.76
   (v) 0

2. What are the strengths and limitations of using correlations in psychological research? *(6 marks)*

Apply Now

Look out for the
Apply it Methods
features in every chapter (like the one above!) so you can test your Research Methods skills...

Analysis and interpretation of correlations

Correlations and correlation coefficients

The term **correlation** refers to a mathematical technique which measures the relationship/association between two continuous variables (properly called **co-variables**). Such relationships are plotted on a **scattergram** where each axis represents one of the variables investigated. We shall also see, later in this chapter, how correlations/associations may be analysed using **statistical tests**.

You will study two statistical tests of correlation (see pages 78–79) each of which, when calculated, produces a numerical value somewhere between −1 and +1 known as the **correlation coefficient**. This value tells us the *strength* and *direction* of the relationship between the two variables.

Working out what a coefficient means

As can be seen on the picture below, a value of +1 represents a *perfect* **positive correlation**, and a value of −1, a *perfect* **negative correlation**.

The closer the coefficient is to +1 or −1, the *stronger* the relationship between the co-variables is; the closer to zero, the *weaker* the relationship is.

However, it should be noted that coefficients that appear to indicate weak correlations can still be **statistically significant** – it depends on the size of the data set.

Scattergrams showing various correlation coefficients

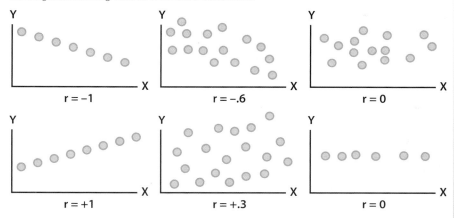

The letter 'r' stands for correlation coefficient.

Descriptive and inferential statistics

At A level you need to be aware of the difference between **descriptive statistics** and **inferential statistics**. Descriptive statistics refers to things like graphs, tables and summary statistics (such as measures of central tendency and measures of dispersion). These are used to identify trends and analyse sets of data.

Inferential statistics refers to the use of **statistical tests** which tell psychologists whether the differences or relationships they have found are statistically significant or not. This helps decide which **hypothesis** to accept and which to reject. A **correlation coefficient** is calculated using a statistical test and, as such, is an inferential statistic.

CHECK IT

1. Explain what is meant by the term *correlation coefficient*.
   [2 marks]

2. Sketch a graph to represent a negative correlation between 'number of people in a room' and 'amount of personal space'.
   [2 marks]

3. Using an example, explain what is meant by the term *correlation*.
   [2 marks]

CASE STUDIES AND CONTENT ANALYSIS

Case studies. Content analysis and coding. Thematic analysis.

We look at two ways of investigating human behaviour not considered in Year 1: case studies and content analysis.

Case studies allow a detailed insight into a single individual, group or institution. It is a method often favoured by researchers who adopt an idiographic approach to the study of human behaviour.

We came across types of observational research in Year 1. Content analysis is a form of observation which analyses the communication that people produce. Anything from a single email or text to a series of films or television programmes may be an appropriate object of study.

KEY TERMS

Case studies – An in-depth investigation, description and analysis of a single individual, group, institution or event.

Content analysis – A research technique that enables the indirect study of behaviour by examining communications that people produce, for example, in texts, emails, TV, film and other media.

Coding – The stage of a content analysis in which the communication to be studied is analysed by identifying each instance of the chosen categories (which may be words, sentences, phrases, etc.).

Thematic analysis – An inductive and qualitative approach to analysis that involves identifying implicit or explicit ideas within the data. Themes will often emerge once the data has been coded.

Apply it

Concepts: Gynotikolobomassophobia

Patient X is a *gynotikolobomassophobic* – he has a morbid fear of women's ear lobes. His fear is so extreme that Patient X finds it impossible to talk to women in social situations (unless their ears are covered) and spends much of his time alone in his home.

A psychologist carrying out a case study of Patient X has conducted detailed interviews with him about his childhood. Patient X has also been encouraged to keep a diary as a record of his everyday experiences. The psychologist has concluded that Patient X's phobia may have been the result of childhood trauma.

Questions

1. What are the main features of a case study? Refer to Patient X as part of your answer.
2. Briefly discuss the strengths and limitations of the case study approach. Again, refer to Patient X as part of your discussion.
3. What ethical issues are associated with the case study approach?

Case studies

To study a 'case' in psychology is to provide a detailed and in-depth analysis of an individual, group, institution or event. **Case studies** often involve analysis of *unusual* individuals or events, such as a person with a rare disorder or the sequence of events that led to the 2011 London riots (see below). However, case studies may also concentrate on more 'typical' cases, such as an elderly person's recollections of their childhood.

Conducting a case study usually – though not exclusively – involves the production of **qualitative data**. Researchers will construct a **case history** of the individual concerned, perhaps using interviews, observations, questionnaires, or a combination of all of these. It is even possible that the person may be subject to experimental or psychological testing to assess what they are (or are not) capable of, and this may produce **quantitative data**.

Case studies tend to take place over a long period of time (**longitudinal**) and may involve gathering additional data from family and friends of the individual as well as the person themselves.

Content analysis

Content analysis is a type of observational research in which people are studied *indirectly* via the communications they have produced. The forms of communication that may be subject to content analysis are wide-ranging and may include spoken interaction (such as a conversation or speech/presentation), written forms (such as texts or emails) or broader examples from the media (such as books, magazines, TV programmes or films). The aim is to summarise and describe this communication in a systematic way so overall conclusions can be drawn.

Coding and quantitative data

Coding is the initial stage of content analysis. Some data sets to be analysed may be extremely large (such as the transcripts of several dozen lengthy interviews) and so there is a need to *categorise* this information into meaningful units. This may involve simply counting up the number of times a particular word or phrase appears in the text to produce a form of quantitative data. For instance, newspaper reports may be analysed for the number of times derogatory terms for the mentally ill are used, such as 'crazy' or 'mad'. Another example would be TV adverts which may be examined to see how often men and women are depicted in 'professional roles' (at work) or 'familial roles' (at home) (which is similar to a study carried out by Furnham and Farragher (2000) – see page 164 for more details).

Thematic analysis and qualitative data

Content analysis may also involve generating qualitative data, one example of which is **thematic analysis**. The process of coding and the identification of themes are closely linked insofar as themes may only emerge once data has been coded. A *theme* in content analysis refers to any idea, explicit or implicit, that is *recurrent* – in other words, which keeps 'cropping up' as part of the communication being studied. These are likely to be more descriptive than the coding units described above. For instance, the mentally ill may be represented in newspapers as 'a threat to the wellbeing of our children' or as 'a drain on the resources of the NHS'. Such themes may then be developed into broader categories, such as 'control', 'stereotyping' or 'treatment' of the mentally ill.

Once the researcher is satisfied that the themes they have developed cover most aspects of the data they are analysing, they may collect a new set of data to test the **validity** of the themes and categories. Assuming these explain the new data adequately, the researcher will write up the final report, typically using direct quotes from the data to illustrate each theme.

A scene from the London riots in 2011. Psychologists were interested in this one-off event and what it could tell us about so-called 'mob' behaviour.

Evaluation

Strengths

Case studies are able to offer rich, detailed insights that may shed light on very unusual and atypical forms of behaviour. This may be preferred to the more 'superficial' forms of data that might be collected from, say, an experiment or questionnaire.

As well as this, case studies may contribute to our understanding of 'normal' functioning. For example, the case of HM was significant as it demonstrated 'normal' memory processing – the existence of separate stores in STM and LTM.

Case studies may generate hypotheses for future study and one solitary, contradictory instance may lead to the revision of an entire theory – 'the single pebble that starts an avalanche'.

Limitations

Generalisation of findings is obviously an issue when dealing with such small sample sizes. Furthermore, the information that makes it into the final report is based on the subjective selection and interpretation of the researcher. Add to this the fact that personal accounts from the participants and their family and friends may be prone to inaccuracy and memory decay, especially if childhood stories are being told. This means that the evidence from case studies begins to look more than a little low in validity.

Evaluation

Strengths

Content analysis is useful in that it can circumnavigate (a posh word for 'get around') many of the **ethical issues** normally associated with psychological research. Much of the material that an analyst might want to study, such as TV adverts, films, personal ads in the newspaper or on the Internet, etc., may already exist within the public domain. Thus there are no issues with obtaining permission, for example. Communication of a more 'dubious' and sensitive nature, such as a conversation by text, still has the benefit of being high in **external validity**, provided the 'authors' consent to its use.

We have also seen that content analysis is flexible in the sense that it may produce both qualitative and quantitative data depending on the aims of the research.

Limitations

People tend to be studied *indirectly* as part of content analysis so the communication they produce is usually analysed *outside* of the context within which it occurred. There is a danger (similar to case studies above) that the researcher may attribute opinions and motivations to the speaker or writer that were not intended originally.

To be fair, many modern analysts are clear about how their own biases and preconceptions influence the research process, and often make reference to these as part of their final report (see the idea of **reflexivity** on page 95). However, content analysis may still suffer from a lack of objectivity, especially when more descriptive forms of thematic analysis are employed.

Apply it — Methods:
Analysing driving behaviour

A researcher was interested to know whether there is a gender difference in driving behaviour and decided to conduct a **content analysis** of film clips of male and female drivers.

Question

Explain how the researcher might have carried out content analysis to analyse the film clips of driver behaviour. (*4 marks*)

Apply it — Concepts: Toilet humour

Several studies in psychology have involved qualitative analysis of the content of *latrinalia* – that is, the graffiti often seen scribbled on toilet walls.

A more recent study by Matthews *et al.* (2012) involved the analysis of 1,200 instances of graffiti gathered from toilet walls in US bars. Graffiti was coded according to a number of distinct categories: *sexual references, socio-political (religion, politics, race, etc.), entertainment (music, TV), physical presence (the writing of one's name for instance), love/romance* and *scatological (for example, reference to defecation)*. Graffiti was also classified in terms of whether it was *interactive* (a response to other graffiti) or *independent* (a stand-alone comment).

Matthews *et al.* found that males composed significantly more sexual and physical presence graffiti, whilst females authored more romantic and interactive graffiti.

Question

Explain how this investigation illustrates some of the strengths and limitations of content analysis.

Bathroom banter … but how might a content analysis of toilet wall graffiti be conducted?

Apply it

Methods:
How to conduct a content analysis

Content analysis, like any observational research, involves design decisions about the following:

- *Sampling method* – how material should be sampled, e.g. **time sampling** or **event sampling**.

- *Recording data* – should data be transcribed or recorded, for instance, using video? Should data be collected by an individual researcher or within a team? (See the next spread for a discussion of the importance of **inter-rater reliability** when conducting content analysis.)

- *Analysing and representing data* – how should material be categorised or coded in order to summarise it? Should the number of times something is mentioned be calculated (quantitative analysis) or described using themes (qualitative analysis)?

Question

Explain how, in designing their study of latrinalia, Matthews *et al.* might have addressed each of the design decisions outlined above. (*6 marks*)

CHECK IT

1. Briefly evaluate the use of case studies in psychology. [*5 marks*]
2. Explain **one** limitation of using content analysis with research data. [*3 marks*]
3. Explain the processes involved in content analysis with reference to coding and thematic analysis. [*4 marks*]

RELIABILITY

Practical activity on page 84

THE SPECIFICATION SAYS...

> Reliability across all methods of investigation. Ways of assessing reliability: test–retest and inter-observer; improving reliability.

In everyday life, when we describe someone (or some*thing*) as 'reliable', we mean that they are *dependable*; that we know to expect the same level of behaviour from them every single time. A reliable individual, for instance, is always punctual and never late or always late and never punctual. A reliable car is one that rarely breaks down and maintains the same level of performance over time.

Psychology's version of reliability is pretty similar: to what extent are the tests, scales, surveys, observations or experiments that psychologists use consistent – in the sense that their measurements of behaviour are the same (or at least similar) every single time they are used.

KEY TERMS

Reliability – Refers to how consistent the findings from an investigation or measuring device are. A measuring device is said to be reliable if it produces consistent results every time it is used.

Test–retest reliability – A method of assessing the reliability of a questionnaire or psychological test by assessing the same person on two separate occasions. This shows to what extent the test (or other measure) produces the same answers i.e. is consistent or reliable.

Inter-observer reliability – The extent to which there is agreement between two or more observers involved in observations of a behaviour. This is measured by correlating the observations of two or more observers. A general rule is that if (total number of agreements) / (total number of observations) > +.80, the data have high inter-observer reliability.

Reliability: it ain't great unless it's . . .

+.8

Statisticians don't write correlations with a leading zero and in reality they always write it as two decimal places but +.80 kinda spoils the rhyme!

Reliability

Reliability is a measure of *consistency*. In general terms, if a particular measurement can be repeated then that measurement is described as being reliable.

A ruler should find the same measurement for a particular object (let's say a chair) every time that object is measured – unless the ruler is broken or, in the words of Phoebe Buffay (*Friends*, Season 5, Episode 3), 'all the rulers are wrong'. If there is a change in the measurement over time, then we would attribute that change to the object rather than the ruler (someone may have sat on the chair and squashed it).

Similarly, if a test or measure in psychology assessed some 'thing' on a particular day (let's say intelligence), then we would expect the same result on a different day, unless the 'thing' itself had changed. Maybe we tested a different person with a different IQ or the same person's IQ went up a little (or possibly down after watching *Friends* . . .).

Unlike rulers, psychologists tend not to measure concrete things, like length or height, but are more interested in abstract concepts such as attitudes, aggression, memory and IQ. Can researchers have the same confidence in their **psychological tests**, **observations** and **questionnaires** as most of us—apart from Phoebe that is—have in a ruler?

Ways of assessing reliability

Test–retest

Psychologists have devised ways of assessing whether their measuring tools are reliable. The most straightforward way of checking reliability is the **test–retest** method. This simply involves administering the same test or questionnaire to the same person (or people) on different occasions. If the test or questionnaire is reliable then the results obtained should be the same, or at least very similar, each time they are administered. Note that this method is most commonly used with questionnaires and psychological tests (such as IQ tests) but can also be applied to **interviews**.

There must be sufficient time between test and retest to ensure, say, that the participant/respondent cannot recall their answers to the questions to a survey but not so long that their attitudes, opinions or abilities may have changed. In the case of a questionnaire or test, the two sets of scores would be **correlated** to make sure they are similar (see below). If the correlation turns out to be **significant** (and positive) then the reliability of the measuring instrument is assumed to be good..

Inter-observer reliability

The phrase '*beauty is in the eye of the beholder*' suggests that everyone has their own unique way of seeing the world. This issue is relevant to **observational research** as one researcher's interpretation of events may differ widely from someone else's – introducing **subjectivity**, **bias** and unreliability into the data collection process.

The recommendation is that would-be observers should not 'go it alone' but instead conduct their observations in teams of at least two. However, **inter-observer reliability** must be established. This may involve a small-scale trial run (a **pilot study**) of the observation in order to check that observers are applying **behavioural categories** in the same way, or it may be reported at the end of a study to show that the data collected was reliable. Observers obviously need to watch the same event, or sequence of events, but record their data independently. As with the test–retest method, the data collected by the two observers should be correlated to assess its reliability. Note that similar methods would apply to other forms of observation, such as **content analysis** (though this would be referred to as **inter-rater reliability**) as well as **interviews** if they are to be conducted by different people (known as **inter-interviewer reliability** – which is a bit of a mouthful).

Apply it **Concepts: The correlation 'test'**

When assessing test–retest reliability or inter-observer reliability two sets of data will be correlated to see whether they match. The degree of correlation can be measured statistically using a **statistical test** of correlation such as **Spearman's rho** (see page 78).

Once the test has been performed on the two sets of data, a **correlation coefficient** will be calculated. The value of the coefficient must be +.80 or above for data to be judged reliable. Any figure lower than this and researchers must 'go back to the drawing board' so to speak and redesign their test or questionnaire – or reassess their observational categories.

Question

What would a correlation coefficient of +.95 between the data of two observers suggest?

Improving reliability

Questionnaires

As we have seen, the reliability of questionnaires over time should be measured using the test–retest method. Comparing two sets of data should produce a correlation that exceeds +.80 (see facing page). A questionnaire that produces low test–retest reliability may require some of the items to be 'deselected' or rewritten. For example, if some questions are complex or ambiguous, they may be interpreted differently by the same person on different occasions. One solution might be to replace some of the open questions (where there may be more room for (mis)interpretation) with closed, fixed choice alternatives which may be less ambiguous.

Interviews

For interviews, probably the best way of ensuring reliability is to use the same interviewer each time. If this is not possible or practical, all interviewers must be properly trained so, for example, one particular interviewer is not asking questions that are too **leading** or ambiguous. This is more easily avoided in **structured interviews** where the interviewer's behaviour is more controlled by the fixed questions. Interviews that are unstructured and more 'free-flowing' are less likely to be reliable.

Experiments

Lab experiments are often described as being 'reliable' because the researcher can exert strict control over many aspects of the procedure, such as the instructions that participants receive and the conditions within which they are tested. Certainly such control is often more achievable in a lab than in the field. This is more about precise **replication** of a particular *method* though rather than demonstrating the reliability of a *finding*. That said, one thing that may affect the reliability of a finding is if participants were tested under slightly different conditions each time they were tested.

Observations

The reliability of observations can be improved by making sure that behavioural categories have been properly **operationalised**, and that they are measurable and self-evident (for instance, the category 'pushing' is much less open to interpretation than 'aggression'). Categories should not overlap ('hugging' and 'cuddling' for instance) and all possible behaviours should be covered on the checklist.

If categories are not operationalised well, or are overlapping or absent, different observers have to make their own judgements of what to record where and may well end up with differing and inconsistent records.

 **Concepts:**

Inter-observer reliability amongst *Friends*

Two psychology students decided to see whether they could establish inter-observer reliability between themselves. They watched five episodes of *Friends* and recorded the different types of 'humour' within the programme. Before the study, they agreed on five observational categories of humour: sarcastic, slapstick, sexual/relationship-based, play on words and teasing.

Questions

1. Invent some data for their observations and put the data in a table. (*3 marks*)
2. The students compared their data and found a correlation coefficient of +.64, what does this indicate in terms of for the reliability of the two students' data? (*2 marks*)
3. What should the students do next to improve the reliability of their observation? (*4 marks*)

Concepts: Personality testing

Personality tests in psychology take several forms and are often used in forensic settings to support clinical diagnosis (see the *Eysenck Personality Inventory (EPI)* on page 330). A more controversial measure of personality is the *Rorschach 'inkblot' test*. People are presented with a series of ambiguous inkblot images and are required to 'say what they see' in the pictures. The aim is to reveal the respondent's unconscious motivations and wishes as interpreted by the researcher or therapist. One criticism of the inkblot method is that one 'scorer' may not necessarily produce the same interpretation as another.

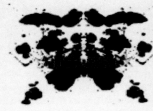

Questions

1. The inkblot-test has been criticised by many as an 'unreliable' measure of personality. Why do you think this is?
2. Explain *one* way of assessing the reliability of the Rorschach inkblot-test.

Q: What's the same as half an apple pie?

A: The other half!

Hilarious. But with halves of apple pie at least, we can assume reliability.

Methods: Ghostly goings on – Part 1

A psychologist wanted to investigate the extent to which people believe in ghosts and devised a questionnaire as a way of assessing this. There were 20 items on the questionnaire in total.

Questions

1. Outline *one* way in which the psychologist could have assessed the **reliability** of the questionnaire. (*3 marks*)

Following the questionnaire, the psychologist selected a sample of 10 respondents who had completed the questionnaire and then observed their behaviour overnight in a house that was supposedly haunted. Working alongside another observer, the psychologist recorded evidence of a fear reaction to a number of stimuli including a creaking door, a gust of wind and a squeaky floorboard.

Questions

2. State *three* behavioural categories that could be used to measure the variable 'fear'. (*3 marks*)
3. Explain *one* way in which the researchers could have assessed the reliability of their observations. (*3 marks*)

CHECK IT

1. Outline what is meant by *reliability* in psychological research. [2 marks]
2. Explain **two** ways of assessing reliability. [6 marks]
3. Explain ways of improving reliability. [5 marks]

THE SPECIFICATION SAYS...

Types of validity across all methods of investigation: face validity, concurrent validity, ecological validity and temporal validity. Assessment of validity. Improving validity.

Consistency within psychological research is one thing – but it is not the *only* thing. Demonstrating the same (or similar) findings on a number of different occasions is all very well – but what if the thing we are demonstrating each time turns out to be meaningless? Or not what we thought we were demonstrating? This is the issue of validity in psychological research – whether a study, investigation or investigative tool is a legitimate or genuine measure.

KEY TERMS

Validity – The extent to which an observed effect is genuine – does it measure what is was supposed to measure, and can it be generalised beyond the research setting within which it was found?

Face validity – A basic form of validity in which a measure is scrutinised to determine whether it appears to measure what it is supposed to measure – for instance, does a test of anxiety look like it measures anxiety?

Concurrent validity – The extent to which a psychological measure relates to an existing similar measure.

Ecological validity – The extent to which findings from a research study can be generalised to other settings and siutations. A form of external validity.

Temporal validity – The extent to which findings from a research study can be generalised to other historical times and eras. A form of external validity.

Whilst measuring your head produces a **reliable** result – in that it is the same (or similar) every time – as a measure of intelligence it is not **valid**.

Validity

Introducing validity

Validity refers to whether a **psychological test**, **observation**, **experiment**, etc., produces a result that is legitimate. In other words, whether the observed effect is genuine and represents what is actually 'out there' in the real world. This includes whether the researcher has managed to measure what they intended to measure (**internal validity**). It also refers the extent to which findings can be generalised beyond the research setting in which they were found (**external validity**).

It is possible for studies and measures to produce **reliable** data that is not valid. For instance, a broken set of scales may give a consistent reading of someone's weight which is always 7lbs more than their actual weight. In this example, the scales are reliable but the weight that is reported is not 'true' so the measurement lacks validity. In psychology, a test that claims to measure intelligence (or IQ) may not measure something 'true' about intelligence – it may simply measure a person's familiarity with IQ tests!

Internal validity

Internal validity refers to whether the effects observed in an experiment are due to the manipulation of the **independent variable** and not some other factor. One major threat to the internal validity of a study is if participants respond to **demand characteristics** and act in a way that they think is expected. For example, some commentators have questioned the internal validity of Milgram's obedience study claiming that participants were 'playing along' with the experimental situation and did not really believe they were administering shocks, i.e. they responded to the *demands* of the situation.

External validity

Meanwhile, external validity relates more to factors outside of the investigation, such as generalising to other settings, other populations of people and other eras.

Ecological validity

Ecological validity concerns generalising findings from one setting to other settings – most particular to 'everyday life' as that is what psychologists are interested in studying.

The concept of ecological validity is often misunderstood because students think it is about the naturalness of a study – a more natural setting should mean the findings from the study can be generalised to everyday life (high ecological validity). A lab is an artificial setting and therefore results of lab research should have low ecological validity because people don't behave naturally in a lab.

However, this isn't quite true. If the task that is used to measure the **dependent variable** in an experiment is not 'like everyday life' (i.e. low **mundane realism**) this can lower ecological validity. For example, a researcher might give people a list of words to remember to assess memory and could do this in a shopping mall – this would be a field study. However, in this case the *setting* doesn't make the findings more 'realistic'. The fact that we are using a word list makes the findings of the study lack ecological validity.

This means we must look at all sorts of aspects of the research set up in order to decide whether findings can be generalised beyond the particular research setting.

Temporal validity

Temporal validity is the issue of whether findings from a particular study, or concepts within a particular theory, hold true over time. Critics have suggested that high rates of conformity within the original Asch experiments were a product of a particularly conformist era in recent American history (the 1950s). Some of Freud's concepts, such as the idea that females experience **penis envy**, are deemed to be outdated, sexist and a reflection of the patriarchal Victorian society within which he lived.

Ecological validity versus mundane realism

*We have seen how the debate about whether findings from lab studies have ecological validity is often oversimplified. Both Asch's and Milgram's studies might be said to have high ecological validity as they were describing processes that often occur in everyday life (conformity and obedience). However, the tasks that participants had to complete within these studies (comparing line lengths and administering electric shocks) were not things people would normally be asked to do. Better to say then that the studies had low **mundane realism** as the experimental set-up did not mirror everyday life.*

Assessment of validity

Practical activity on page 84

One basic form of validity is **face validity**, whether a test, scale or measure appears 'on the face of it' to measure what it is supposed to measure. This can be determined by simply 'eyeballing' the measuring instrument or by passing it to an expert to check.

The **concurrent validity** of a particular test or scale is demonstrated when the results obtained are very close to, or match, those obtained on another recognised and well-established test. A new intelligence test, for instance, may be administered to a group of participants and the IQ scores they achieve may be compared with their performance on a well-established test (such as the *Stanford-Binet test*). Close agreement between the two sets of data would indicate that the new test has high concurrent validity – and close agreement is indicated if the correlation between the two sets of scores exceeds +.80.

Improving validity

Experimental research

In **experimental** research, validity is improved in many ways. For example, using a **control group** means that a researcher is better able to assess whether changes in the dependent variable were due to the effect of the **independent variable** (see Lombroso's research on page 326 for how the lack of a control group may affect validity). For instance, in a study looking at the effectiveness of a therapy, a control group who did not receive therapy means that the researcher can have greater confidence that improvement was due to effects of the therapy rather than, say, the passage of time.

Experimenters may also **standardise** procedures to minimise the impact of **participant reactivity** and **investigator effects** on the validity of the outcome. The use of **single-blind** and **double-blind procedures** is designed to achieve the same aim. You may remember that in a single-blind procedure participants are not made aware of the aims of a study until they have taken part (to reduce the effect of **demand characteristics** on their behaviour). In a double-blind study, a third party conducts the investigation without knowing its main purpose (which reduces both demand characteristics and investigator effects and thus improves validity).

Questionnaires

Many **questionnaires** and **psychological tests** incorporate a **lie scale** within the questions in order to assess the consistency of a respondent's response and to control for the effects of **social desirability bias**. Validity may be further enhanced by assuring respondents that all data submitted will remain **anonymous**.

Observations

Observational research may produce findings that have high ecological validity as there may be minimal intervention by the researcher. This is especially the case if the observer remains undetected, as in **covert observations**, meaning that the behaviour of those observed is likely to be natural and authentic.

In addition, **behavioural categories** that are too broad, overlapping or ambiguous may have a negative impact on the validity of the data collected.

Qualitative methods

Qualitative methods of research are usually thought of as having higher ecological validity than more **quantitative**, less interpretative methods of research. This is because the depth and detail associated with **case studies** and **interviews**, for instance, is better able to reflect the participant's reality.

However, the researcher may still have to demonstrate the **interpretive validity** of their conclusions. This is the extent to which the researcher's interpretation of events matches those of their participants. This can be demonstrated through such things as the *coherence* of the researcher's reporting and the inclusion of *direct quotes* from participants within the report. Validity is further enhanced through **triangulation** – the use of a number of different sources as evidence, for example, data compiled through interviews with friends and family, personal diaries, observations, etc.

Apply it · Methods: Ghostly goings on – Part 2

A psychologist wanted to investigate the extent to which people believe in ghosts and devised a questionnaire as a way of assessing this. There were 20 questions in total.

Questions

1. Explain what is meant by validity. Refer to the investigation above in your answer. (*3 marks*)
2. Explain *two* ways in which the psychologist could have improved the validity of the investigation above. (*4 marks*)

Apply it · Concepts: Threats to validity

The following are threats to validity that we came across as part of Research Methods in Year 1 – though some will apply to particular forms of research more than others.

Identify each from the definitions below:

1. Any variable, other than the IV, that may have an effect on the DV if it is not controlled. These are essentially nuisance variables that do not vary systematically with the IV.
2. Any variable, other than the IV, that may have affected the DV so we cannot be sure of the true source of changes to the DV. They vary systematically with the IV.
3. Any cue from the researcher or the research situation that may be interpreted by participants as revealing the true purpose of the investigation.
4. Any effect of the researcher's behaviour (conscious or unconscious) on the research outcome. This may include everything from the design of the study to the selection of, and interaction with, participants.
5. A question which, because of the way it is phrased, suggests a certain answer that may influence the response of the participant.

Did you get what you were aiming for? One of the concerns for psychologists trying to improve the validity of their research studies is that their expectations may influence the behaviour of their participants.

When assessing concurrent validity, the **correlation coefficient** between the two sets of scores must exceed +.80. Now where have we seen that before …? It ain't great unless … **+.8**

CHECK IT

1. Outline what is meant by *concurrent validity* in psychological research. [2 marks]
2. Distinguish between ecological validity and temporal validity as types of validity. [6 marks]
3. Explain **two** ways of assessing validity. [6 marks]
4. Explain ways of improving validity. [5 marks]

CHOOSING A STATISTICAL TEST

THE SPECIFICATION SAYS...

Factors affecting the choice of statistical test, including level of measurement and experimental design. When to use the following tests: Spearman's rho, Pearson's r, Wilcoxon, Mann–Whitney, related t-test, unrelated t-test and Chi-Squared test.

Quantitative (numerical) data can be summarised using descriptive statistics which include measures of central tendency, measures of dispersion, graphs and charts.

Although these are useful, they do not tell us whether the differences or correlations psychologists find are statistically significant (explained on the next spread), this is the job of statistical tests.

KEY TERMS

Levels of measurement – Quantitative data can be classified into types or levels of measurement, such as nominal, ordinal and interval.

Statistical tests – Used in psychology to determine whether a significant difference or correlation exists (and consequently, whether the null hypothesis should be rejected or retained).

Chi-Squared – A test for an association (difference or correlation) between two variables or conditions. Data should be nominal level using an unrelated (independent) design.

Mann–Whitney – A test for a significant difference between two sets of scores. Data should be at least ordinal level using an unrelated design (independent groups).

Pearson's r – A parametric test for correlation when data is at interval level.

Related t-test – A parametric test for difference between two sets of scores. Data must be interval with a related design, i.e. repeated measures or matched pairs.

Sign test – A statistical test used to analyse the difference in scores between related items (e.g. the same participant tested twice). Data should be nominal or better.

Spearman's rho – A test for correlation when data is at least ordinal level.

Unrelated t-test – A parametric test for difference between two sets of scores. Data must be interval with an unrelated design, i.e. independent groups.

Wilcoxon – A test for a significant difference between two sets of scores. Data should be at least ordinal level using a related design (repeated measures).

Choosing a statistical test

Statistical testing

In Year 1 you had a brief introduction to the concept of **statistical testing** using the example of the **sign test**. You will recall that a statistical test is used to determine whether a difference or an association found in a particular investigation is statistically **significant** – that is, more than could have occurred by **chance**. The outcome of this has implications for whether we accept or reject the **null hypothesis** – but we shall return to this shortly. For now, we need to consider which statistical test is used under what circumstances. There are three factors used to decide this:

1. Whether a researcher is looking for a *difference* or **correlation**.
2. In the case of a difference, what **experimental design** is being used.
3. The **level of measurement**.

These criteria are summarised in the table below.

1. Difference or correlation?

The first thing to consider when deciding which statistical test to use relates to the aim or purpose of the investigation – namely, is the researcher looking for a difference or correlation. This should be obvious from the wording of the **hypothesis**. In this context, 'correlation' can include *correlational analyses* as well as investigations that are looking for an *association* (see the **Chi-Squared** test on page 80).

2. Experimental design

You will also remember from Year 1 studies that there are three types of experimental design: **independent groups**, **repeated measures** and **matched pairs**. The last two of these are referred to as **related designs**. In a repeated measures design, the same participants are used in all conditions of the experiment. In a matched pairs design, participants in each condition are not the same but have been 'matched' on some variable that is important for the investigation which makes them 'related'. For this reason, both designs are classed as *related*.

As participants in each condition of an independent groups design are different, this design is **unrelated**. Thus, the researcher chooses from two alternatives here: *related* or *unrelated*.

Note that if the investigation is looking for a correlation, rather than a difference, then question 2 doesn't matter.

Choosing a statistical test

	Test of Difference		Test of association or correlation
	Unrelated design	Related design	
Nominal data	Chi-Squared	**Sign test**	Chi-Squared
Ordinal data	**Mann–Whitney**	**Wilcoxon**	**Spearman's rho**
Interval data	**Unrelated t-test**	**Related t-test**	**Pearson's r**

Note that Chi-Squared is a test of both difference and association/correlation. Data items must be unrelated.

Also note that the three tests on the blue background are parametric tests (the two forms of t-test and Pearson's r).

You will need to learn the table above so you know which test to use under what circumstances. If you are learning the table exactly as it looks here, the following mnemonic might help you remember the sequence of the tests (the first letter in each of the words in the sentence corresponds to the first letter of the stats test):

Carrots **S**hould **C**ome

Mashed **W**ith **S**wede

Under **R**oast **P**otatoes

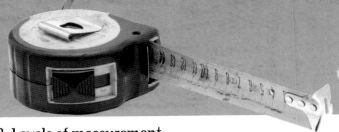

3. Levels of measurement

Quantitative data can be divided into different **levels of measurement** and this is the third factor influencing the choice of statistical test. There are three levels of measurement: **nominal**, **ordinal** and **interval**.

Nominal data Data is represented in the form of categories – hence nominal data is sometimes referred to as **categorical data**. For example, you can count how many boys and girls in your Year group – male and female are the categories and you take a count of how many in each group.

Nominal data is **discrete** in that one item can only appear in one of the categories. For example, if you asked people to name their favourite football team their vote only appears in one category.

Ordinal data is ordered in some way. An example of ordinal data would be asking everyone in your class to rate how much they like psychology on a scale of 1 to 10 where 1 is 'do not like psychology at all' and 10 is 'absolutely love psychology'.

Ordinal data does not have equal intervals between each unit (unlike in interval data, below). For instance, in our example it would not make sense to say that someone who rated psychology an 8 enjoys it twice as much as someone who gave it a 4 .

Ordinal data also lacks precision because it is based on subjective opinion rather than objective measures. In our example, what constitutes a '4' or an '8' for the people doing the rating may be quite different. In the case of an IQ test the questions are derived from a view of what constitutes intelligence rather than any universal measurement. Questionnaires, psychological tests and so on do not measure something 'real' (i.e. they are not observable physical entities whereas, for example, reaction times and height are 'real'). Questionnaires etc. measure psychological constructs.

For these reasons, ordinal data is sometimes referred to as 'unsafe' data because it lacks precision. Due to its unsafe nature, ordinal data is not used as part of statistical testing. Instead, raw scores are converted to ranks (i.e. 1st, 2nd, 3rd, etc) and it is the ranks – not the scores – that are used in the calculation (see pages 74–75 and 78 for tests using ordinal data).

Interval data In contrast to ordinal data above, interval data is based on numerical scales that include units of equal, precisely defined size. In this sense it is 'better' than ordinal data because more detail is preserved (and ordinal is 'better' than nominal level).

Think of the kinds of things you would use to take measurements with in maths or other sciences, such as a stopwatch, a thermometer or weighing scales. These are public scales of measurement that produce data based on accepted units of measurement (time, temperature, weight). So, for instance, if we recorded how long it took each of our students to complete a written recall test in psychology, we would have collected interval data. Interval data is the most precise and sophisticated form of data in psychology and is a necessary criterion for the use of parametric tests (see right).

Table showing levels of measurement and their relation to the appropriate measures of central tendency and measures of dispersion.

Level of measurement	Measure of central tendency	Measure of dispersion
Nominal	Mode	n/a
Ordinal	Median	Range
Interval	Mean	Standard deviation

Note that the range and standard deviation cannot be calculated on nominal data as such data is in the form of frequencies. It is not appropriate to use the mean or the standard deviation for ordinal data as the intervals between the units of measurement are not of equal size.

Apply it Concepts: **Which level of measurement?**

Identify whether the following would produce data at the nominal, ordinal or interval level.

1. Time taken to sort cards into categories.
2. Peoples' choice of the *Sun*, *The Times* or the *Guardian*.
3. Participants' sense of self-worth, estimated on a scale of 1–10.
4. Judges in a dancing competition giving marks for style and presentation.
5. Participants' reaction to aversive stimuli measured using a heart rate monitor.
6. A set of medical records classifying patients as either chronic, acute or 'not yet classified'.

STUDY TIPS

Some of the data produced in psychology is quite difficult to classify. For example, should we treat 'number of words recalled' in a memory test as interval or ordinal data?

Strictly speaking, this would only be interval data if the words are all of equal difficulty (so the units of measurement are all equivalent). This would be very difficult to achieve as some words will always be more memorable than others! For this reason, it is probably 'safer' to treat number of words recalled as ordinal data and rank the set of scores accordingly.

But you should always provide your reasoning when deciding which level of measurement is appropriate.

Apply it Concepts: **Parametric tests**

The related *t*-test, unrelated *t*-test and Pearson's r are collectively known as **parametric tests**. Parametric tests are more powerful and robust than other tests. If a researcher is able to use a parametric test they will do so, as these tests may be able to detect significance within some data sets that non-parametric tests cannot.

There are three criteria that must be met in order to use a parametric test:

1. Data must be **interval level** – parametric tests use the actual scores rather than ranked data.
2. The data should be drawn from a population which would be expected to show a **normal distribution** for the variable being measured. Variables that would produce a **skewed distribution** are not appropriate for parametric tests.
3. There should be *homogeneity of variance* – the set of scores in each condition should have similar dispersion or spread. One way of determining variance is by comparing the standard deviations in each condition; if they are similar, a parametric test may be used. In a related design it is generally assumed that the two groups of scores have a similar spread.

Question

If a researcher compared two related sets of data and was looking to see if they were different, why would it be preferable to use a related *t*-test instead of a Wilcoxon?

CHECK IT

1. Identify and explain the difference between **two** levels of measurement in psychological research.
   [4 marks]
2. Identify **three** factors that influence the choice of statistical test.
   [3 marks]
3. Explain **two** factors that would be required for use of an unrelated *t*-test.
   [4 marks]

Probability and significance: use of statistical tables and critical values in interpretation of significance; Type I and Type II errors.

All statistical tests end with a number – the calculated value. This number is crucial in determining whether the researcher has found a result that is statistically significant, and consequently, whether they should accept the alternative or null hypothesis.

To understand how statistical tests work requires an understanding of the related concepts of probability and significance.

KEY TERMS

Probability – A measure of the likelihood that a particular event will occur where 0 indicates statistical impossibility and 1 statistical certainty.

Significance – A statistical term that tells us how sure we are that a difference or correlation exists. A 'significant' result means that the researcher can reject the null hypothesis.

Critical value – When testing a hypothesis, the numerical boundary or cut-off point between acceptance and rejection of the null hypothesis.

Type I error – The incorrect rejection of a true null hypothesis (a false positive).

Type II error – The failure to reject a false null hypothesis (a false negative).

Probability and significance

The null hypothesis

Researchers begin their investigations by writing a **hypothesis**. This may be **directional** or **non-directional** depending how confident the researcher is in the outcome of the investigation. Here is a an example of a hypothesis (you may remember it from the Year 1 book):

After drinking 300ml of SpeedUpp, participants say more words in the next five minutes than participants who drink 300ml of water.

This is sometimes referred to as an **alternative hypothesis** (or H_1 for short) because it is alternative to the **null hypothesis** (H_0). The null hypothesis states there is 'no difference' between the conditions:

There is no difference in the number of words spoken in five minutes between participants who drink 300ml of SpeedUpp and participants who drink 300ml of water.

The **statistical test** determines which hypothesis is 'true' and thus whether we accept or reject the null hypothesis.

Levels of significance and probability

Actually, 'true' is probably the wrong word. Statistical tests work on the basis of **probability** rather than certainty. All statistical tests employ a **significance level –** the point at which the researcher can claim to have discovered a significant difference or correlation within the data. In other words, the point at which the researcher can reject the null hypothesis and accept the alternative hypothesis.

*The usual level of **significance** in psychology is 0.05 (or 5%).*

This is properly written as $p \leq 0.05$ (where p stands for probability).

This means the probability that the observed effect (the result) occurred by chance is equal to or less than 5%. In effect, this means that even when a researcher claims to have found a significant difference/correlation, there is still up to 5% probability that the observed effect occurred by chance – that it was a 'fluke'.

Psychologists can never be 100% certain about a particular result as they have not tested all members of the population under all possible circumstances! For this reason, psychologists have settled upon a conventional level of probability where they are prepared to accept that results may have occurred by chance – this is the 5% level.

People often refer to probability and chance in everyday life. We might surmise that the chance of rain is around '50/50', that our favourite football team has a 'good chance' of winning on Saturday or that we have 'no chance' of winning the National Lottery (the actual statistical probability is about 1 in 14 million).

In psychological research, the 5% significance level ensures that, in the case of a significant result, there is equal to or less than 5% probability that the result occurred by chance. However, in these circumstances, it is not correct to state that we can be '95% certain that the result did not occur by chance'. If you think about it, the phrase '95% certain' is a contradiction in terms – we can only ever be 100% certain of anything – and statistical testing deals with probabilities not certainties!

What is the probability of two people in a football match sharing the same birthday? There are 23 people on the pitch (including the referee). The chance that any two people will have the same birthday is 1 in 365. If all 23 people shook hands with each other, there would be 253 handshakes. This equates to the number of pairs of people who could potentially share the same birthday. 253/365 = 0.69. The probability of two people in a football match sharing the same birthday is 69% i.e. well over half. Most people are surprised by how high this is!

Apply it   Concepts: Drug testing

A researcher is testing the effectiveness of a new drug that relieves the symptoms of anxiety disorder – *Anxocalm*. The researcher is comparing two groups of people who suffer from anxiety: one group will complete a course of Anxocalm and the other group will be given a **placebo**. There is a possibility that the drug may cause mild side effects in those who take it (such as a headache and nausea). For this reason, the researcher can only test the drug once on human participants.

The researcher has decided to use the 1% level when testing for significance.

Question

Explain why the researcher has decided to use the 1% level of significance on this occasion.

Use of statistical tables

The critical value

Once a statistical test has been calculated, the result is a *number* – the **calculated value** (or observed value). To check for statistical significance, the calculated value must be compared with a **critical value** – a number that tells us whether or not we can reject the null hypothesis and accept the alternative hypothesis.

Each statistical test has its own **table of critical values,** developed by statisticians. These tables look like very complicated bingo cards (see example on the next spread). For some statistical tests, the calculated value must be equal to or greater than the critical value; for other tests, the calculated value must be equal to or less than the critical value (see the 'Rule of R' below).

Using tables of critical values

How does the researcher know which critical value to use? There are three criteria:

- **One-tailed** or **two-tailed test**? You use a one-tailed test if your hypothesis was directional and a two-tailed test for a non-directional hypothesis. Probability levels *double* when two-tailed tests are being used as they are a more *conservative* prediction.
- The number of participants in the study. This usually appears as the *N* value on the table. For some tests **degrees of freedom (df)** are calculated instead.
- The **level of significance** (or *p* value). As discussed, the 0.05 level of significance is the standard level in psychological research.

Lower levels of significance

Occasionally, a more stringent level of significance may be used (such as 0.01) in studies where they may be a *human cost* – such as drug trials – or 'one-off' studies that could not, for practical reasons, be repeated in future. In all research, if there is a *large* difference between the calculated and critical values – in the preferred direction – the researcher will check more stringent levels, as the *lower* the p value is, the more statistically significant the result.

Type I and Type II errors

Due to the fact that researchers can never be 100% certain that they have found statistical significance, it is possible (*usually up to 5% possible*) that the wrong hypothesis may be accepted.

A **Type I error** is when the null hypothesis is rejected and the alternative hypothesis is accepted when it should have been the other way round because, in reality, the null hypothesis is 'true'. This is often referred to as an optimistic error or false positive as the researcher claims to have found a significant difference or correlation when one does not exist.

A **Type II error** is the reverse of the above: when the null hypothesis is accepted but it should have been the alternative hypothesis because, in reality, the alternative hypothesis is true. This is a pessimistic error or 'false negative'.

We are more likely to make a Type I error if the significance level is too lenient (too high) e.g. 0.1 or 10% rather than 5%. A Type II error is more likely if the significance level is too stringent (too low) e.g. 0.01 or 1%, as potentially significant values may be missed. Psychologists favour the 5% level of significance as it best balances the risk of making a Type I or Type II error.

Apply it   **Concepts: Pregnancy tests**

Pregnancy tests are not 100% reliable so women who suspect they are pregnant are advised to take more than one test in order to make sure.

Question

If the result says you are not pregnant – in what way could this be a Type II error?

STUDY TIP

If you are testing a directional hypothesis you may find that your calculated value is significant – but there is a further issue. Are your results in the direction you predicted? If they are not, then you must accept the null hypothesis even though the calculated value is significant. Before you ask – you can't just change the original hypothesis!

In fact, in such cases this should be obvious when looking at the data and a researcher would not carry out any statistical testing.

STUDY TIP

As suggested above, it is okay to check more stringent levels of significance as long as the critical value at the 5% level has been checked first to establish significance. However, higher levels of significance, such as 10% should be disregarded. At these levels, the null hypothesis cannot be rejected – though the hypothesis may be worth pursuing and refining the methodology.

Apply it   **Concepts: The rule of R**

Some statistical tests require the calculated value to be *equal to or more than* the critical value for statistical significance; for other tests, the calculated value must be *equal to or less than* the critical value.

The *rule of R* can help with this. Those statistical tests with a letter 'R' in their name are those where the calculated value must be equal to or *more* than the critical value (note that there is also an 'r' in 'more' which is a further clue!)

Questions

1. List the statistical tests with a letter R in their name.
2. List the statistical tests without a letter R.

CHECK IT

1. Distinguish between a type I and type II error in psychological research. *[3 marks]*
2. Define what is meant by the *critical value* in statistical testing. *[2 marks]*
3. What is the accepted level of significance in psychological research? *[1 mark]*

THE SPECIFICATION SAYS...

> Students should be familiar with the use of inferential tests.

An 'inferential test' is another term for a statistical test. In Year 1 of the course you learned to use a statistical test of difference – the sign test. This spread includes two further statistical tests that are used to determine whether two samples are significantly different: Mann–Whitney and Wilcoxon. In each case a worked example is given so you can understand how the test is calculated and how significance is determined.

Note that, in an independent groups design, the numbers of participants in each group may be different as is the case here – Group A has 10 participants and group B has 8 participants.

Table 3 Critical values of U for a two-tailed test, $p \leq 0.05$

N_A	2	3	4	5	6	7	8	9	10
N_B									
2							0	0	0
3			0	1	1	2	2	3
4		0	1	2	3	4	4	5
5	0	1	2	3	5	6	7	8
6	1	2	3	5	6	8	10	11
7	1	3	5	6	8	10	12	14
8	0	2	4	6	8	10	13	15	17
9	0	2	4	7	10	12	15	17	20
10	0	3	5	8	11	14	17	20	23
11	0	3	6	9	13	16	19	23	26
12	1	4	7	11	14	18	22	26	29
13	1	4	8	12	16	20	24	28	33
14	1	5	9	13	17	22	26	31	36

Calculated value of U must be EQUAL TO or LESS THAN the critical value in this table for significance to be shown.

Apply it

Methods: What does it all mean ...

The investigation described on the right found a significant difference at $p \leq 0.05$.

1. Explain what is meant by the phrase 'a significant difference was found at $p \leq 0.05$'. (*2 marks*)
2. What conclusion can be drawn from the investigation described? (*2 marks*)

Mann–Whitney: A worked example

Why Mann–Whitney?

In this worked example we are looking for a difference between two groups of employers based on their rating of whether a candidate (who had suffered from **schizophrenia**) was suitable for a job interview. There are two **independent groups** of employers, which means the design is unrelated. Finally, the level of measurement is **ordinal** as data is based on scores on an 'unsafe' scale (subjective ratings of interview suitability) which are converted to ranks for the purposes of the test.

The aim ...

A study of the effects of labelling in schizophrenia was conducted to see if there is a difference in someone's perceived 'employability' based on whether they had been diagnosed with schizophrenia in the past. Eighteen employers were shown an application form and ask to rate the candidate in terms of how likely they would be called for an interview, on a scale of 1–20 (where 1 = definitely would not be interviewed and 20 = definitely would be interviewed).

All employers saw the same application form, the only difference was that for employers in Group A the form included the phrase 'recovering schizophrenic'. For employers in Group B, that phrase was absent from the form.

The hypotheses ...

Alternative hypothesis: *There is a difference in ratings for 'suitability for an interview' based on whether a job applicant is described as having been diagnosed with schizophrenia (Group A) or not (Group B).* (**non-directional, two-tailed**)

Null hypothesis: *There is no difference in ratings for 'suitability for an interview' based on whether a job applicant is described as having been diagnosed with schizophrenia (Group A) or not (Group B).*

Step 1: The table of ranks ...

To rank the ratings you need to consider the data from both Groups A and B at the same time (data is given in the table below). The lowest number has a rank of 1. In the case where two data items are the same you add up the rank they would get and give the mean for those ranks. For example the rating of 12 appears four times in the table at rank position 7, 8, 9 and 10 therefore they all are given the rank of 8.5.

Where there are a lot of multiple ranks it may help to use a frequency table (see Table 1).

Calculate the sum of the ranks for Group A (R_A) and for Group B (R_B) (see Table 2).

Table 1 Frequency table

Rating	Frequency	Rank
8	I	1
9	I	2
10	II	3 and 4
11	II	5 and 6
12	IIII	7, 8, 9 and 10
13	I	11
14	I	12
15	II	13 and 14
16	I	15
17	II	16 and 17
18	I	18

Table 2 Calculations table

Group A participant number	Suitability for interview rating	Rank	Group B participant number	Suitability for interview rating	Rank
1	12	8.5	11	16	15
2	10	3.5	12	12	8.5
3	13	11	13	14	12
4	8	1	14	15	13.5
5	12	8.5	15	18	18
6	10	3.5	16	17	16.5
7	11	5.5	17	11	5.5
8	15	13.5	18	17	16.5
9	9	2			
10	12	8.5			
		$R_A = 65.5$			$R_B = 105.5$

Step 2: Working out the value of U ...

Calculate the smaller value of U, which in this case will be Group A (the value of U is now called U_A and the number of participants in group A is referred to as N_A).

$U = U_A = R_A - [N_A (N_A + 1)] / 2 = 65.5 - [10 \times (10 + 1)] / 2 = 10.5$

Step 3: The calculated and critical values ...

The **calculated value** of U is **10.5**

The **critical value** (in Table 3) of U for a two-tailed test at the 0.05 level where $N_A = 10$ and $N_B = 8$ is 17 (see table of critical values, above left).

As the calculated value of U is less than the critical value the result is **significant** ($p \leq 0.05$) and we can reject the null hypothesis and accept the alternative hypothesis: *There is a difference in ratings for 'suitability for an interview' based on whether a job applicant is described as having been diagnosed with schizophrenia (Group A) or not (Group B)* ($p \leq 0.05$).

Wilcoxon: A worked example

Henry Wilcoxon, who brought us the Wilcoxon test (not surprisingly). On a motorbike (perhaps surprisingly).

Practical activity on page 85

Why Wilcoxon?

In this worked example we are looking for a difference in anger scores before and after using an **anger management** programme. This is a **repeated measures** design (i.e. related) as the same participants are assessed before and after receiving treatment. The data is **ordinal** as anger scores are based on a subjective 'unsafe' **self-report questionnaire**.

The aim...

An investigation in forensic psychology was conducted to assess the effectiveness of a new anger management programme. Twenty teenagers serving time in a young offenders institute for violent crime were involved in the study. At the beginning of the investigation, all the offenders completed a questionnaire to measure their level of anger. This gave each offender an anger score out of 50. The offenders then completed eight intensive sessions of anger management. Following the treatment, the offenders completed the same anger questionnaire. The two sets of scores – before and after treatment – were compared to see if there was a difference.

The hypotheses...

Alternative hypothesis: *There is a difference in young offenders' scores on an anger questionnaire before and after treatment.* (**non-directional, two-tailed**).

Null hypothesis: *There is no difference in young offenders' scores on an anger questionnaire before and after treatment.*

Step 1: Calculate a difference and rank the difference...

This time ranking is done on the difference between the two sets of data. When ranking, the signs are ignored.

If the difference is zero the data is not included in the ranking, as below.

Table 4 Calculations table

Participant	Anger score before treatment	Anger score after treatment	Difference	Rank of difference
1	39	30	+9	7.5
2	42	44	-2	1
3	28	25	+3	3
4	35	32	+3	3
5	32	32	-	-
6	40	30	+10	9
7	50	44	+6	6
8	46	50	-4	5
9	29	20	+9	7.5
10	44	29	+15	10
11	25	28	-3	3
12	38	38	-	-

Step 2: Working out the value of T

The **calculated value** of T is the sum of the less frequent sign. The less frequent sign is *minus*, so the sum of the ranks is 1 + 5 + 3.

T = 9

Step 3: The calculated and critical values...

The **calculated value** of T is 9.

The **critical value** of T for a two-tailed test at the 0.05 level when N = 10 is 8 (see table of critical values, above right).

As the calculated value of T is more than the critical value of T the result is not significant ($p \leq 0.05$) and we must accept the null hypothesis: *There is no difference in young offenders' scores on an anger questionnaire before and after treatment* ($p > 0.05$).

We reject the alternative hypothesis at $p \leq 0.05$ (i.e. less than a 5% probability that the results are due to chance) and therefore accept the null hypothesis at $p > 0.05$ (i.e. there was more than a 5% probability the results are due to chance).

Table 5 Critical values of T

Level of significance for a one-tailed test	0.05	0.025	0.01
Level of significance for a two-tailed test	0.10	0.05	0.02
N = 5	0		
6	2	0	
7	3	2	0
8	5	3	1
9	8	5	3
10	11	8	5
11	13	10	7
12	17	13	9
13	21	17	12
14	25	21	15
15	30	25	19

Calculated value of T must be EQUAL TO or LESS THAN the critical value in this table for significance to be shown.

Apply it

Methods: Using the critical value table

In a similar investigation, a **matched pairs design** was used to assess the effectiveness of the anger management programme. 20 offenders were matched on anger score at the beginning of the investigation and one from each pair was allocated either to the treatment condition (eight sessions of anger management) or the control condition (no treatment). Anger scores were assessed at the end of the investigation.

The calculated value of T was 6. The hypothesis was non-directional. Note that, in a matched pairs design, the N value is based on the number of pairs (10).

Questions

1. Is the result significant? Explain your answer. (*3 marks*)

2. What conclusion can be drawn from this study? (*2 marks*)

CHECK IT

A researcher was interested to know whether there was a gender difference in 'enjoyment rating' of A level Psychology students.

1. Which statistical test would be used to analyse the data? Justify your choice. *[4 marks]*

2. When would a researcher decide to use a Wilcoxon test? Refer to **three** factors in your answer. *[3 marks]*

> Students should be familiar with the use of inferential tests.

There are two other difference tests that can be used when data is interval level instead of the less powerful non-parametric Mann–Whitney and Wilcoxon tests. These are the two tests of difference, the unrelated and related *t*-test.

Table 2 Critical values of t

Level of significance for a one-tailed test	0.05	0.025
Level of significance for a two-tailed test	0.10	0.05
df= 1	6.314	12.706
2	2.920	4.303
3	2.353	3.182
4	2.132	2.776
5	2.015	2.571
6	1.943	2.447
7	1.895	2.365
8	1.860	2.306
9	1.833	2.262
10	1.812	2.228
11	1.796	2.201
12	1.782	2.179
13	1.771	2.160
14	1.761	2.145
15	1.753	2.131
16	1.746	2.120
17	1.740	2.110
18	1.734	2.101
19	1.729	2.093
20	1.725	2.086
21	1.721	2.080
22	1.717	2.074
23	1.714	2.069
24	1.711	2.064
25	1.708	2.060
26	1.706	2.056
27	1.703	2.052
28	1.701	2.048
29	1.699	2.045
30	1.697	2.042
40	1.684	2.021
60	1.671	2.000
120	1.658	1.980

Calculated value of *t* must be EQUAL TO or MORE THAN the critical value in this table for significance to be shown.

Apply it

Methods: Increasing sample size

Question

If the same investigation was repeated with 61 boys and 61 girls, and the same calculated value was achieved, would the result be significant? Explain your answer. (*3 marks*)

Unrelated *t*-test: A worked example

Why the unrelated *t*-test?

The **unrelated *t*-test** is a test of difference between two sets of data. It is used with interval level data only. When an **independent groups design** is used, the test selected is the unrelated *t*-test.

In this worked example, we are looking for a difference in the time taken to complete a jigsaw puzzle between boys and girls. The type of design is independent groups (unrelated) because one group were girls and the other group were boys. The level of measurement is **interval** as time taken to complete a jigsaw puzzle is measured on a 'safe' scale (a scale of public measurement) made up of equal units. It is assumed that the participants are drawn from a **normally distributed sample** within the population and there is **homogeneity of variance** as the standard deviations in both groups are similar.

The aim...

An investigation of **gender** looked into whether there was a difference in visuo-spatial ability between boys and girls. Ten girls and ten boys took part in the test which involved completing a simple jigsaw puzzle in the shortest time possible. All participants completed the same puzzle and the time it took for each of them was recorded and compared.

The hypotheses...

Alternative hypothesis: *There is a difference in the time taken by males and females to complete a jigsaw puzzle.* (**non-directional, two-tailed**)

Null hypothesis: *There is no difference in the time taken by males and females to complete a jigsaw puzzle.*

Step 1: The table of data...

In Table 1 below various calculations need to be made for the Group A and B scores:

- Calculate the sum of the scores for Group A (ΣX_A). (X_A refers to scores in group A.)
- Repeat for Group B (ΣX_B).
- Square each value in Group A (X_A^2).
- Repeat for Group B (X_B^2).

Σ means 'sum of'. See completed table (below).

Table 1 Calculations table

Group A male participants	Time taken (sec) X_A	X_A^2	Group B female participants	Time taken (sec) X_B	X_B^2
1	64	4096	1	52	2704
2	56	3136	2	59	3481
3	89	7921	3	90	8100
4	55	3025	4	112	12544
5	79	6241	5	84	7056
6	102	10404	6	73	5329
7	80	6400	7	79	6241
8	69	4761	8	64	4096
9	69	4761	9	49	2401
10	80	6400	10	90	8100
	$\Sigma X_A = 743$	$\Sigma X_A^2 = 57145$		$\Sigma X_B = 752$	$\Sigma X_B^2 = 60052$

Step 2: Working out the value of t...

$$t = \frac{(\overline{X}_A - \overline{X}_B)}{\sqrt{\left(\frac{S_A + S_B}{N_A + N_B - 2}\right) \times \left(\frac{N_A + N_B}{N_A N_B}\right)}}$$

$\overline{X}$ stands for the mean.

N_A and N_B are the numbers of scores in group A and B.

Where: $S_A = \Sigma X_A^2 - (\Sigma X_A)^2 / N_A$
$S_B = \Sigma X_B^2 - (\Sigma X_B)^2 / N_B$

$S_A = 57145 - 55204.9 = 1940.1$
$S_B = 60052 - 56550.4 = 3501.6$

$$t = \frac{(74.3 - 75.2)}{\sqrt{\left(\frac{1940.1 + 3501.6}{10 + 10 - 2}\right) \times \left(\frac{10 + 10}{100}\right)}} = -0.116$$

Step 3: The calculated and critical values...

The **calculated value** of t = −0.116 (note that t is a negative value because the mean for group B was larger than group A, when checking the critical values table ignore the negative sign).

The **critical value** (in Table 2) for a two-tailed test at the 0.05 level where $df = N_A + N_B - 2 = 18$, is 2.101.

As the calculated value (ignoring the sign) is less than the critical value ($p \leq 0.05$) the result is not significant and we must accept the null hypothesis: *There is no difference between males and females in the time taken to complete a jigsaw puzzle* ($p > 0.05$).

Related *t*-test: A worked example

Practical activity on page 85

Why the related *t*-test?

When a **repeated design** is used the test selected is the **related *t*-test**.

Here, we are looking for a difference in the average heart rate before and after treatment (**CBT**). The type of design is **repeated measures** (related) because the same participants were tested twice. The level of measurement is interval as measurements of heart rate (beats per minute, bpm) are based on a 'safe' scale (a scale of public measurement) made up of equal units. Let us assume for the purpose of this test that participants were drawn from a **normally distributed sample** within the population and **homogeneity of variance** is assumed as this is a related design.

The aim...

In a study of **addiction,** researchers investigated the effects of CBT on the physiological arousal of gamblers. Ten participants who were categorised as 'persistent gamblers' were given a six-week course of CBT to change their gambling behaviour. Before treatment, all of the participants played on a fruit machine for 20 minutes whilst their heart rate activity was monitored as a measure of physiological arousal. Following treatment, the same participants played on the same game for the same length of time and their heart rate activity was monitored.

The hypotheses...

Alternative hypothesis; *There is a reduction in heart rate activity when comparing heart rate before and after cognitive behaviour therapy.* **(directional, one-tailed)**

Null hypothesis: *There is no difference in heart rate activity comparing heart rate before and after cognitive behaviour therapy.*

Step 1: The table of data...

In the Table 3 below, various calculations need to be made for condition A and B: Calculate the difference between the two sets of scores (d). See completed Table 3.

- Calculate the difference (d) between scores for condition A and condition B.
- Square each difference (d²).
- Add up the values in the d column to give the sum of d (Σd).
- Add up the values in the d² column to give the sum of d² (Σd²).

Table 3 Calculations table

Participant	Condition A Heart rate (bpm) before treatment	Condition B Heart rate (bpm) after treatment	Difference (d)	d²
1	84	80	4	16
2	71	70	1	1
3	52	55	−3	9
4	66	58	8	64
5	58	58	0	0
6	77	70	7	49
7	63	61	2	4
8	81	75	6	36
9	71	74	−3	9
10	70	61	9	81
			Σd = 31	Σd² = 269

Step 2: Working out the value of t...

$$t = \sqrt{\dfrac{\Sigma d^2 - \dfrac{(\Sigma d)^2}{N}}{N(N-1)}} \quad t = \sqrt{\dfrac{269 - \dfrac{31/10}{961}}{10(10-1)}} \quad t = \sqrt{\dfrac{3.1}{\dfrac{172.9}{90}}} \quad t = \dfrac{3.1}{1.386} \quad = 2.236$$

Step 3: The calculated and critical values...

The **calculated value** of t is 2.236

The **critical value** of t (in Table 2 on the facing page) for a one-tailed test at the 0.05 level where *df* is N − 1 = 9, is 1.833

As the calculated value of t is greater than the critical value ($p > 0.05$) the result is significant and we can reject the null hypothesis and conclude: *There is a reduction in heart rate activity comparing heart rate before and after cognitive behaviour therapy* ($p > 0.05$).

Andrea appeared to have misunderstood the suggestion from her psychology teacher that she should carry out a *t*-test.

Apply it

Methods: *t*-tests and taxi drivers

Read the Maguire *et al*. taxi driver study on page 40. A different researcher wanted to assess whether there was a *change* in taxi drivers' hippocampal volume as a result of taking 'The Knowledge' test. They analysed the hippocampal volume of 30 trainee London cabbies before they began studying for the test. After all the drivers had completed their training and taken 'The Knowledge' test, the researchers took the same measurement again.

Questions

1. Write a directional hypothesis for the investigation described above. (*2 marks*)
2. Which of the two *t*-tests should be used to analyse the data? Justify your answer. (*2 marks*)

The researcher analysed the data. The calculated value of t was 1.526.

3. Is the result significant? Explain your answer. (*3 marks*)
4. What conclusion can be drawn from this study? (*2 marks*)

CHECK IT

A researcher wanted to know whether A level PE students could throw a ball further than A level Geography students.

1. Which statistical test would be used to analyse the data? Justify your choice. [*4 marks*]
2. When would a researcher decide to use a related *t*-test? Refer to **three** factors in your answer. [*3 marks*]

Practical activiti for both tests o pages 84 and 8

THE SPECIFICATION SAYS...

> Students should be familiar with the use of inferential tests.

And the statistical (inferential) tests keep on coming.... Both of the tests featured here – Spearman's rho and Pearson's r – are looking for a correlation between co-variables rather than a difference between sets of scores.

Spearman's can be used with *ordinal* or *interval* data. Pearson's test can only be used if the data are *interval*.

Table 2 Critical values of rho

Level of significance for a one-tailed test		0.05	0.025
Level of significance for a two-tailed test		0.10	0.05
N =	1	1.000	
	5	.900	1.000
	6	.829	.886
	7	.714	.786
	8	.643	.738
	9	.600	.700
	10	.564	.648
	11	.536	.618
	12	.503	.587
	13	.484	.560
	14	.464	.538
	15	.443	.521
	16	.429	.503
	17	.414	.485
	18	.401	.472
	19	.391	.460
	20	.380	.447
	25	.337	.398
	30	.306	.362

Calculated value of rho must be EQUAL TO or MORE THAN the critical value in this table for significance to be shown.

Apply it
Methods: Substituting and estimating values

A similar investigation with the same hypothesis was conducted with 21 couples. The sum of the difference between the ranks squared (Σd^2) was calculated to be 1000.

Questions

1. Substitute the correct values into the formula on the right to calculate rho. (*2 marks*)
2. Estimate the value of rho based on the values in the formula for Q1. (*1 mark*)
3. Calculate the actual value of rho based on the values in the formula for Q1. Show your calculations. (*3 marks*)
4. Explain whether or not the calculated value of rho in Q3 is significant. (*2 marks*)
5. What conclusion can be drawn from your answer to Q4? (*2 marks*)

Spearman's rho: A worked example

Why Spearman's rho?

Spearman's is a test of **correlation** between two sets of values. The test is selected when one or both of the variables are **ordinal level** (though it can be used with interval data). The type of design is not an issue here as the investigation is correlational rather than experimental.

In this worked example, we are looking for a **positive correlation** between the attractiveness ratings given to each member of the couples. The level of measurement is ordinal as data is based on scores on an 'unsafe' scale (subjective ratings of attractiveness) which are converted to ranks for the purposes of the test.

The aim...

A study of relationships was conducted to investigate the **matching hypothesis** (Walster *et al.* 1966, see page 122) which proposes that couples in a long-term relationship tend to be similar in terms of physical attractiveness. Twelve couples were selected for the study. Each partner had their photograph taken and these photographs were placed in a random order so it was not obvious who was in a relationship with whom.

The 24 photographs were then given to 20 participants (who had never met any of the couples before). The participants were asked to rate the person in each photograph – out of 20 – in terms of their physical attractiveness. The median attractiveness rating for each photograph was calculated to see if there was a **significant** correlation between pairs in a couple.

The hypotheses...

Alternative hypothesis: *There is a positive correlation between ratings of physical attractiveness given to two partners in a relationship.* (**directional, one-tailed**)

Null hypothesis: *There is no correlation between ratings of physical attractiveness given to two partners in a relationship.*

Step 1: The table of ranks...

Rank each set of scores separately in each group/condition (in this case, for each partner in the couple) from lowest to highest. As before, if two or more scores share the same ranks, find the **mean** of their total ranks.

Step 2: Calculate the difference...

Find the difference between each pair of ranks and square the difference (as shown in the table below). Finally add the differences up, Σ means 'sum of'.

Table 1 Calculations table

Median physical attractiveness rating for female (out of 20)	Rank for female partner	Median physical attractiveness rating for male (out of 20)	Rank for male partner	Difference between ranks (d)	d^2
12.5	8	11	2.5	5.5	30.25
16	10	12	4.5	5.5	30.25
13	9	13	6.5	2.5	6.25
8.5	2	14.5	9	–7	49
12	7	15	10.5	–3.5	12.25
10	4.5	7	1	3.5	12.25
11.5	6	13.5	8	–2	4
7	1	15	10.5	–9.5	90.25
9	3	11	2.5	0.5	0.25
17	11	18.5	12	–1	1
18	12	12	4.5	7.5	56.25
10	4.5	13	6.5	–2	4
				$\Sigma d^2 =$	296

Step 3: Working out the value of rho...

$$\text{rho} = 1 - \frac{6\Sigma d^2}{N(N^2-1)} \quad = 1 - \frac{6 \times 296}{12(144-1)} \quad = 1 - \frac{1776}{1716} \quad = -.035$$

Step 4: The calculated and critical values...

The **calculated value** of rho is –.035

The **critical value** of rho (in Table 2) for a one-tailed test at the 0.05 level where N = 12 is .503

As the calculated value of rho (ignoring the sign) is less than the critical value ($p \leq 0.05$) the result is not significant and we must accept the null hypothesis: *There is no correlation between ratings of physical attractiveness given to two partners in a relationship* ($p \leq 0.05$).

In addition the result is actually in the wrong direction (negative rather than positive) and so the hypothesis would not be accepted even if the calculated value was sufficiently large.

Pearson's r: A worked example

Why Pearson's?

Pearson's is a test of correlation between two sets of values. This test is selected when the data are **interval level**. The type of design is not an issue here as the investigation is correlational rather than experimental.

In this worked example, we are looking for a positive correlation between the length of time (in days) spent using biofeedback and the reduction in resting heart rate (measured in beats per minute, bpm). The level of measurement is interval as data is based on 'safe' mathematical (public measurement) scales. The investigation meets the criteria for a **parametric test**.

The aim ...

An investigation into **stress** was carried out to see if there is a relationship between the length of time using **biofeedback** (see page 274) and resting heart rate (bpm). Ten participants suffering from chronic stress who had all been using biofeedback for varying lengths of time were selected for the study.

The researchers hypothesised that those who had been using the technique for the longest would have experienced the biggest reduction in their resting heart rate. Medical records were checked so that the participants' baseline heart rate (before using biofeedback) could be compared with their present heart rate to work out the reduction. This reduction was correlated with the length of time (in days) that they had been using biofeedback.

The hypotheses ...

Alternative hypothesis: *There is a positive correlation between the number of days participants have been using biofeedback and the reduction in their resting heart rate (bpm).* (**directional, one-tailed**)

Null hypothesis: *There is no correlation between the number of days participants have been using biofeedback and the reduction in their resting heart rate.*

Step 1: The table of data ...

In the Table 3 various calculations need to be made for the x and y scores:
- Calculate the sum of the scores for x (Σx) and y (Σy).
- Square each x value and each y value. Calculate Σx^2 and Σy^2.
- Multiply x and y for each participant. Add these values together = $\Sigma(xy)$.

Table 3 Calculations table

Participant	Days spent using biofeedback (x)	x^2	Reduction in heart rate (y)	y^2	xy
1	4	16	2	4	8
2	7	49	2	4	14
3	15	225	4	16	60
4	22	484	6	36	132
5	23	529	5	25	115
6	32	1024	5	25	160
7	44	1936	2	4	88
8	51	2601	8	64	408
9	62	3844	7	49	434
10	80	6400	8	64	640
	$\Sigma x = 340$	$\Sigma x^2 = 17108$	$\Sigma y = 49$	$\Sigma y^2 = 291$	$\Sigma(xy) = 2059$

Step 2: Working out the value of r ...

$$r = \frac{N(\Sigma xy) - (\Sigma x)(\Sigma y)}{\sqrt{[N\Sigma x^2 - (\Sigma x)^2][N\Sigma y^2 - (\Sigma y)^2]}}$$

$$r = \frac{10(2059) - (340)(49)}{\sqrt{(171080 - 115600)(2910 - 2401)}} = \frac{3930}{5314} = .740$$

Step 3: The calculated and critical values ...

The **calculated value** of r is .740

The **critical value** of r (in Table 4) for a one-tailed test at the 0.05 level where $df = N - 2 = 8$, is .549.

As the calculated value of r is more than the critical value the result is significant at the 0.05 level and we can reject the null hypothesis and accept the alternative hypothesis: *There is a positive correlation in the number of days participants have been using biofeedback and the reduction in their resting heart rate ($p \leq 0.05$).*

Table 4 Critical values of r

Level of significance for a one-tailed test	0.05	0.025
Level of significance for a two-tailed test	0.10	0.05
df = 2	.9000	.9500
3	.805	.878
4	.729	.811
5	.669	.754
6	.621	.707
7	.582	.666
8	.549	.632
9	.521	.602
10	.497	.576
11	.476	.553
12	.475	.532
13	.441	.514
14	.426	.497
15	.412	.482
16	.400	.468
17	.389	.456
18	.378	.444
19	.369	.433
20	.360	.423
25	.323	.381
30	.296	.349
35	.275	.325
40	.257	.304
45	.243	.288
50	.231	.273
60	.211	.250
70	.195	.232
80	.183	.217
90	.173	.205
100	.164	.195

Calculated value of r must be EQUAL TO or MORE THAN the critical value in this table for significance to be shown.

Apply it

Methods: Using the critical value table

A researcher was interested to know if there was a positive correlation between heat and aggression. The researcher made a note of the average temperature in his local town on various days throughout the year. He also recorded the number of violent incidents that were reported in the local newspapers on those days.

The researcher used a Pearson's test to analyse his data. The calculated value of r was 0.281. Data for daily temperature and number of violent incidents was recorded for 52 days throughout the year.

Questions

1. Is the result significant? Explain your answer. (*3 marks*)

2. What conclusion can be drawn from this study? (*2 marks*)

CHECK IT

1. When would a researcher decide to use a Spearman's rho test? Refer to **two** factors in your answer. [*2 marks*]

2. When would a researcher decide to use a Pearson's r test? Refer to **two** factors in your answer. [*2 marks*]

Practical activity on page 85

THE SPECIFICATION SAYS

> Students should be familiar with the use of inferential tests.

There is one final statistical (inferential) test that you have to study, the Chi-Squared test, which can be used for differences or association.

The key feature of Chi-Squared is that each data item is not listed separately but, instead, a frequency count is given. Usually the data are entered in 4 cells (a 2 x 2 table), but 6 cells or 9 cells etc. can be used and then the contingency table is called 3 x 2 or 3 x 3 respectively. The first number identifies the number of rows and the second number is the number of columns.

The data in each cell must be independent – imagine that each data item is one person, each person can only be placed in one cell of the contingency table (Table 1) below right.

Table 3 Critical values of χ^2

Level of significance for a one-tailed test	0.10	0.05	0.025	0.01
Level of significance for a two-tailed test	0.20	0.10	0.05	0.02
df = 1	1.64	2.71	3.84	5.41
2	3.22	4.60	5.99	7.82
3	4.66	6.25	7.82	9.84
4	5.99	7.78	9.49	11.67

Calculated value of χ^2 must be EQUAL TO or MORE THAN the critical value in this table for significance at the level shown.

Apply it

Methods: Calculating Chi

A researcher wanted to see whether there was an association between age and voting preference in the General Election. One hundred voters were classified as either young (under 25) or old (over 60). Of the 50 'young' voters, 42 voted for the Pro-Zombie Party and 8 for the Anti-Zombie Party. Of the 50 'old' voters, 32 voted for the Anti-Zombie Party and 18 voted for the Pro-Zombie Party.

Questions

1. Construct a 2 × 2 contingency table for the data above. (3 marks)
2. Calculate the value of χ^2 for the data above. (3 marks)
3. Explain whether the value of χ^2 you calculated in Q2 is significant. (2 marks)
4. Suggest one conclusion that could be drawn from your answer to Q3. (2 marks)

Chi-Squared

Why Chi?

Chi-Squared is a test of *difference* or *association*. The data are **nominal** and recorded as a frequency count of the categories.

In this worked example, we are looking for a difference in the ability to **decentre** in children aged 5 and children aged 8. There are two **independent groups** of children which means the design is **unrelated**. Finally, the level of measurement is nominal as data is collected in the form of frequencies in two categories: ability to decentre or not.

The aim...

A study of **cognitive development** was conducted to see if there was a difference in children's ability to decentre (see the world from the perspective of another) depending on their age. A group of 5-year-olds and 8-year-olds were given the **three mountains task** (see page 180) to see whether they could choose a card that corresponded to a doll's view rather than their own.

The hypotheses...

Alternative hypothesis: *More 8-year-olds than 5-year-olds are able to select a card that represents a perspective different from their own.* (**directional, one-tailed**)

Null hypothesis: *There is no difference between the number of 5-year-olds and 8-year-olds who can select a card that represents a perspective different from their own.*

Step 1: A 2 × 2 contingency table...

Draw a 2 × 2 contingency table showing the *observed frequencies* (i.e. the data that was collected) in each cell and calculate the totals for each row, each column and the overall total.

Table 1 Contingency table

	5-year-olds	8-year-olds	Totals
Decentre	6 (cell **A**)	28 (cell **B**)	34
Could not decentre	27 (cell **C**)	9 (cell **D**)	36
Totals	33	37	70

Step 2: The table of expected frequencies...

Expected frequencies (E) are now calculated for each of the four cells in the 2 × 2 table. An expected frequency is the frequency that would be expected if there was no difference between the two groups *(if the age of the child had no effect on their ability to decentre)*. The expected frequency is calculated for each cell by multiplying the total for the row by the total for the column divided by the grand total of 70 (taking the data from Table 1).

This calculation is done as shown below, taking the data from Table 1.

O = observed frequencies from the table in Step 1.

Table 2 Calculations table

	E	E–O	(E–O)²	(E–O)² / E
Cell A	34 × 33 / 70 = 16	6 – 16 = –10	100	6.3
Cell B	34 × 37 / 70 = 18	28 – 18 = 10	100	5.6
Cell C	36 × 33 / 70 = 17	27 – 17 = 10	100	5.9
Cell D	36 × 37 / 70 = 19	9 – 19 = –10	100	5.3

Answers have been rounded to the nearest whole number, except in the final column where they are rounded to one decimal place. This has been done to save space, normally you should work to two or even three decimal places.

Step 3: Working out the value of χ^2...

Add up the values in the final column.

The **calculated value of χ^2 is 23.1.**

Step 4: The calculated and critical values...

To find the **critical value**, calculate the **degrees of freedom** (df) by multiplying *(rows – 1) × (columns – 1)* = 1. ('Rows' and 'columns' refers to the contingency table.)

The critical value of χ^2 (in Table 3) for a one-tailed test at the 0.05 level, where df =1, is 2.71.

As the calculated value of χ^2 is more than the critical value ($p \leq 0.05$) we can reject the null hypothesis and accept the alternative hypothesis: *There is a difference in the number of 5-year-olds and 8-year-olds who can select a card that represents a perspective different from their own ($p \leq 0.05$).*

REPORTING PSYCHOLOGICAL INVESTIGATIONS

When psychologists come to write up their research for publication in journal articles, they use a conventional format. On this half-spread we describe each of the sections that make up a scientific report.

KEY TERMS

Abstract – The key details of the research report.

Introduction – A look at past research (theory and/or studies) on a similar topic. Includes the aims and hypothesis.

Method – A description of what the researcher(s) did, including design, sample, apparatus/materials, procedure, ethics.

Results – A description of what the researcher(s) found, including descriptive and inferential statistics.

Discussion – A consideration of what the results of a research study tell us in terms of psychological theory.

References – List of sources that are referred to or quoted in the article, e.g. journal articles, books or websites, and their full details.

STUDY TIPS

Try it! There is no formal requirement to complete coursework for A level Psychology as there used to be. However, we would definitely recommend that you carry out as many practical investigations as you can. This will give you vital understanding of issues involved in the design of studies, as well as the techniques involved in collecting, summarising and analysing data, and will be of great help to you when it comes to tackling Research Methods questions.

Why not write up one of your investigations in the conventional report format described here? Use one of the practical activities suggested in this book or make up your own (having checked with your teacher that what you propose to do is ethical of course!).

CHECK IT

1. When would a researcher decide to use a Chi-Squared test? Refer to **three** factors in your answer. *[3 marks]*
2. Briefly outline what information psychologists should include within an abstract when reporting psychological investigations. *[3 marks]*
3. Identify and outline **two** sections of a scientific report. *[6 marks]*
4. List **four** sub-sections that should be included within the method section of a psychological report. *[4 marks]*

Sections of a scientific report

Abstract

The first section in a journal article is a short summary/**abstract** (150–200 words in length) that includes all the major elements: the aims and hypotheses, method/procedure, results and conclusions. When researching a particular topic, psychologists will often read lots of abstracts in order to identify those investigations that are worthy of further examination.

Introduction

The **introduction** is a literature review of the general area of investigation detailing relevant theories, concepts and studies that are related to the current study. The research review should follow a logical progression – beginning broadly and gradually becoming more specific until the **aims** and **hypotheses** are presented.

Method

Split into several sub-sections, the **method** should include sufficient detail so that other researchers are able to precisely **replicate** the study if they wish:

- *Design* – The design is clearly stated, e.g. independent groups, naturalistic observation, etc., and reasons/justification given for the choice.
- *Sample* – Information related to the people involved in the study: how many there were, biographical/demographic information (as long as this does not compromise anonymity) and the **sampling method** and **target population**.
- *Apparatus/materials* – Detail of any assessment instruments used and other relevant materials.
- *Procedure* – A 'recipe-style' list of everything that happened in the investigation from beginning to end. This includes a verbatim record of everything that was said to participants: **briefing**, **standardised instructions** and **debriefing**.
- *Ethics* – An explanation of how these were addressed within the study.

Results

The **results** section should summarise the key findings from the investigation. This is likely to feature **descriptive statistics** such as tables, graphs and charts, measures of central tendency and measures of dispersion.

Inferential statistics should include reference to the choice of **statistical test**, **calculated** and **critical values**, the **level of significance** and the final outcome, i.e. which hypothesis was rejected and which retained.

Any **raw data** that was collected and any calculations appear in an appendix rather than the main body of the report.

If the researcher has used **qualitative methods** of research, the results/findings are likely to involve analysis of themes and/or categories.

Discussion

There are several key elements in the **discussion** section. The researcher will summarise the results/findings in verbal, rather than statistical, form. These should be discussed in the context of the evidence presented in the introduction and other research that may be considered relevant.

The researcher should be mindful of the limitations of the present investigation and discuss these as part of this section. This may include reference to aspects of the method, or the sample for instance, and some suggestions of how these limitations might be addressed in a future study.

Finally, the wider implications of the research are considered. This may include real-world applications of what has been discovered and what contribution the investigation has made to the existing knowledge-base within the field.

Referencing

Full details of any source material that the researcher drew upon or cited in the report. **Referencing** may include journal articles, books, websites, etc. Here's an example of a reference from a journal article that appears in the Biopsychology section of this book:

Gupta, S. (1991). Effects of time of day and personality on intelligence test scores. *Personality and Individual Differences, 12(11)*. 1227–1231.

Book references take the following format: author(s), date, title of book (in italics), place of publication, publisher. For example:

Flanagan, C. and Berry, D. (2016). *A level Psychology*. Cheltenham: Illuminate Publishing.

Note how the name of the journal and title of the book appear in italics as does the journal volume and issue number (12 and 11 respectively). For a journal article the last information is the page number(s). See more examples of formal academic referencing at the back of this book (page 386).

FEATURES OF SCIENCE

Features of science: objectivity and the empirical method; replicability and falsifiability; theory construction and hypothesis testing; paradigms and paradigm shifts.

What makes *science* scientific? And is psychology a science? On this spread we attempt to tackle both of these questions by first describing the key features and assumptions of scientific enquiry. We will then consider to what extent psychology as a social scientific discipline rather than a 'natural' science meets these criteria.

KEY TERMS

Paradigm – A set of shared assumptions and agreed methods within a scientific discipline.

Paradigm shift – The result of a scientific revolution: a significant change in the dominant unifying theory within a scientific discipline.

Objectivity – When all sources of personal bias are minimised so as not to distort or influence the research process.

The empirical method – Scientific approaches that are based on the gathering of evidence through direct observation and experience.

Replicability – The extent to which scientific procedures and findings can be repeated by other researchers.

Falsifiability – The principle that a theory cannot be considered scientific unless it admits the possibility of being proved untrue (false).

STUDY TIP

A word about hypotheses.

*We have distinguished between the **null hypothesis** and the **alternative hypothesis** (which might be **one-tailed** or **two-tailed** depending on the aim of the research). An alternative hypothesis might also – alternatively(!) – be referred to as a research **hypothesis**. If a researcher is using an experiment to investigate the hypothesis, the research hypothesis may be referred to as an **experimental hypothesis**. Or if the method of research is a correlation, the research hypothesis is a **correlational hypothesis**. Phew! That was probably a bit more than a word...*

Features of science

Paradigms and paradigm shifts

The philosopher Thomas Kuhn (1962) suggested that what distinguishes scientific disciplines from non-scientific disciplines is a shared set of assumptions and methods – a **paradigm**. Kuhn suggested that social sciences (including psychology) lack a universally accepted paradigm and are probably best seen as 'pre-science' as distinct from natural sciences such as biology or physics. Natural sciences are characterised by having a number of principles at their core such as the theory of evolution in biology, or the standard model of the universe in physics. Psychology, on the other hand, is marked by too much internal disagreement and has too many conflicting approaches to qualify as a science and therefore is a pre-science (this view of psychology has been challenged – see below).

According to Kuhn, progress within an established science occurs when there is a scientific revolution. A handful of researchers begin to question the accepted paradigm, this critique begins to gather popularity and pace, and eventually a **paradigm shift** occurs when there is too much contradictory evidence to ignore. Kuhn cited the change from a Newtonian paradigm in physics towards Einstein's theory of relativity as an example of a paradigm shift.

Theory construction and hypothesis testing

Science tests theories – but what is a **theory**? A theory is a set of general laws or principles that have the ability to explain particular events or behaviours. *Theory construction* occurs through gathering evidence via direct observation (see the **empirical method** on the facing page). For instance, I may have a 'hunch' that **short-term memory** has a limited capacity based on the observation that people struggle to remember much when they are 'bombarded' with information. A series of **experiments** reveals that the average short-term memory span is around 7 (give or take 2) items of information. Let's call this *Berry's Law* . . . OK fine, someone else got there first – but this is a good example of a theory as it proposes a simple and economical principle which appears to reflect reality. It provides understanding by explaining regularities in behaviour.

It should also be possible to make clear and precise predictions on the basis of the theory. This is the role of hypothesis testing. An essential component of a theory is that it can be scientifically tested. Theories should suggest a number of possible hypotheses – for instance, *Berry's Law* (see – it's catching on . . .) suggests that people will remember 7-digit postcodes more effectively than 14-digit mobile phone numbers. A hypothesis like this can then be tested using systematic and objective methods to determine whether it will be supported or refuted. In the case of the former, the theory will be strengthened; in the case of the latter, the theory may need to be revised or revisited. The process of deriving new hypotheses from an existing theory is known as deduction.

Apply it · Concepts: Does psychology have a paradigm?

Kuhn's argument was that psychology's lack of an accepted paradigm means it is yet to achieve the status of normal science, and is instead, pre-science. Certainly there are a number of theoretical perspectives in psychology that have suggested quite different ideas and ways of investigating the human subject.

However, not all commentators agree with Kuhn's conception of psychology as pre-scientific. For instance, the vast majority of researchers would accept a definition of psychology as *the study of mind and behaviour* suggesting there is broad agreement. Similarly, it could be argued that psychology has already progressed through several paradigm shifts from Wundt's early **structuralism** to the dominant **cognitive neuroscience** model of today.

Finally, several researchers (including Feyerabend 1975) have suggested that Kuhn's conception of 'proper' science as orderly and paradigmatic is flawed – and that most sciences are in fact characterised by internal conflict, dispute and a refusal to accept new ideas in the face of evidence.

Questions

1. Choose *two* approaches in psychology and explain how the main assumptions and methods of enquiry within these two approaches differ.

2. Use your knowledge of the historical development of psychology to explain how the discipline may have experienced several paradigm shifts.

Falsifiability

Another philosopher of science whose work appeared around the same time as Thomas Kuhn was Karl Popper (1934) who argued that the key criterion of a scientific theory is its **falsifiability**. Genuine scientific theories, Popper suggested, should hold themselves up for **hypothesis** testing and the possibility of being proven *false*. He believed that even when a scientific principle had been successfully and repeatedly tested, it was not necessarily true. Instead it had simply not been proven false – yet! This became known as the *theory of falsification*. Popper drew a clear line between good science, in which theories are constantly challenged, and what he called 'pseudosciences' which couldn't be falsified.

Those theories that survive most attempts to falsify them become the strongest – not because they are necessarily true – but because, despite the best efforts of researchers, they have not been proved false. This is why psychologists avoid using phrases such as '*this proves*' in favour of '*this supports*' or '*this seems to suggest*' – and why, as we have seen, an alternative hypothesis must always be accompanied by a **null hypothesis**.

Replicability

An important element of Popper's **hypothetico-deductive method** (described above) is **replicability**. If a scientific theory is to be 'trusted', the findings from it must be shown to be repeatable across a number of different contexts and circumstances.

Replication has an important role in determining the **validity** of a finding. We have already discussed the role of **replication** in determining the **reliability** of the *method* used in a study (see pages 66–69). Replication is also used to assess the validity of a *finding*; by repeating a study, as Popper suggests, over a number of *different* contexts and circumstances then we can see the extent to which the findings can be **generalised**. In order for replicability to become possible, it is vital that psychologists report their investigations with as much precision and rigour as possible, so other researchers can seek to *verify* their work and verify the findings they have established.

Objectivity and the empirical method

Scientific researchers must strive to maintain **objectivity** as part of their investigations. In other words, they must keep a 'critical distance' during research. They must not allow their personal opinions or biases to 'discolour' the data they collect or influence the behaviour of the participants they are studying. As a general rule, those methods in psychology that are associated with the greatest level of **control** – such as **lab experiments** – tend to be the most objective.

Objectivity is the basis of the **empirical method**. The word *empiricism* is derived from the Greek for 'experience' and empirical methods emphasise the importance of data collection based on direct, sensory experience. The **experimental method** and the **observational method** are good examples of the empirical method in psychology. Early empiricists such as John Locke saw knowledge as determined only by experience and sensory perception. Thus, a theory cannot claim to be scientific unless it has been empirically tested and verified.

'It is a capital mistake to theorise before you have all the evidence. It biases the judgment.'

Sherlock Holmes, *A Study in Scarlet*

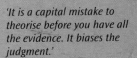

Apply it — Concepts:

Psychology as a science: the case against ...

Although many psychologists try to maintain objectivity within their research, some of the methods that psychologists use are **subjective**, non-standardised and unscientific.

Science is based on the assumption that it is possible to produce universal laws that can be generalised across time and space. However, this may not be possible in psychology: samples of participants in studies are rarely representative and conclusions drawn may often be influenced by cultural and social norms.

Much of the subject matter in psychology cannot be directly observed and must be based on **inference** rather than objective measurement.

Questions

1. Provide an example of subjective methods in psychology, with reference to specific studies.
2. Even when more objective methods are used, explain why objectivity may be much harder to achieve in psychology than in other sciences, e.g. physics, chemistry.
3. Why might replicability be harder to achieve in psychology than other sciences?
4. Explain which psychological approaches this most applies to and why.
5. Explain why many findings gained from experimental research may lack **ecological validity** and/or **temporal validity**. Give some examples.
6. Explain why the issue of inference is a criticism that may be levelled at the **cognitive approach**.

Apply it

Concepts: Psychology as a science: the case for ...

Scientific psychology lifts everyday understanding of human behaviour above the level of commonsense. Critics of psychology may claim it amounts to little more than commonsense, but many key findings in psychology are counter-intuitive and not what a commonsense view would predict.

By adopting a scientific model of enquiry, psychology gives itself greater credibility by being placed on equal footing with other, more established sciences (despite Kuhn's suggestion that psychology is just a pre-science).

The scientific approach in psychology has provided many practical applications that have improved people's lives and challenged/modified dysfunctional behaviour.

Questions

1. As an example of counter-intuitive findings, explain why Milgram's findings were not what most people would have predicted.
2. List at least *two* of the practical applications of psychology and examine their effectiveness.

CHECK IT

1. Outline what is meant by *replicability* and *falsifiability* in psychological research. **[4 marks]**
2. Outline what is meant by the following terms in scientific research: (i) paradigm (ii) paradigm shift. **[4 marks]**
3. Briefly discuss the importance of theory construction and hypothesis testing in scientific research. **[6 marks]**
4. Briefly discuss arguments for and against the idea that psychology is a science. **[10 marks]**

> Knowledge and understanding of ... research methods, practical research skills and maths skills. These should be developed through ... ethical practical research activities.

This means that you should conduct practical investigations throughout all topics. Here, we suggest some ways in which you might put your research methods skills into practice. Firstly, in the development of an IQ test which you should then assess in terms of its reliability and validity. Secondly, it's over to you for the ideas – and ways to generate data for all those fascinating statistical tests!

Ethics check

We suggest strongly that you complete this checklist before starting:

1. Do participants know participation is voluntary?
2. Do participants know what to expect?
3. Do participants know they can withdraw at any time?
4. Are individuals' results anonymous?
5. Have I minimised the risk of distress to participants?
6. Have I avoided asking sensitive questions?
7. Will I avoid bringing my school/teacher/psychology into disrepute?
8. Have I considered all other ethical issues?
9. Has my teacher approved this?

Apply it — Methods: The maths bit

Imagine you recorded the scores for the first time your participants sat the IQ test and compared these with the scores for the second time participants sat the test. **Spearman's rho** was used to work out the relationship between the two sets of scores and a correlation coefficient of +.91 was found.

Questions

1. Explain why Spearman's rho was used to analyse the relationship between the two sets of scores. (*4 marks*)

2. Explain what is meant by the term **correlation coefficient**. (*2 marks*)

3. Explain what a correlation coefficient of +.91 means in this context. (*3 marks*)

Imagine you also got the same participants to complete an established IQ test and compared these scores with the scores on the first test. Again, Spearman's rho was used to analyse the relationship and the correlation coefficient was +.57.

4. Explain what a correlation coefficient of +.57 means in this context. (*3 marks*)

5. Explain what type of **validity** is being tested in the example above. Justify your answer. (*2 marks*)

6. Outline *one* other way in which you could have assessed the validity of the IQ test. (*3 marks*)

Practical idea 1: Assessing reliability and validity of an IQ test.

On pages 66–69 we talked about the importance psychologists place on designing measuring instruments that are reliable (consistent) and valid (true). Now it's your chance to develop a test of intelligence (IQ) and establish whether it has **test–retest reliability** and **concurrent validity**.

The aim of this study is to develop a simple form of IQ test and assess whether it is reliable and valid.

The practical bit

There are many ways of testing intelligence – exams (you'll be familiar with them), puzzles, problem-solving exercises and **IQ** tests (IQ stands for *intelligence quotient*). Your first task is to develop a simple IQ test.

Designing the test

There are many different types of IQ test. Typically most 'traditional' forms of the test contain questions (items) that assess skills of mathematics, verbal reasoning, spatial awareness and comprehension. In order to get a 'feel' for the kind of IQ test you want to design, it would be worth having a look at a few examples online (be aware though that not all tests are free and some will charge for the results if you take the test). A good free online test can be found at the following link: www.iqtestcc.co.uk

If you feel that some of the questions you've seen may be a little difficult to design, you might want to go a different way. Your IQ test could check respondents' general knowledge – of world history, geography, current affairs, literature, etc.

Alternatively, your test could be based on one specific area, such as world football, cinema, pop music or basket weaving. The actual content of the test is not all that important, just so long as there are a decent number of questions (say, around 30–40), and some are easier and some more difficult than others.

Assessing reliability

Once you're reasonably happy with the content of your IQ test (and you've had it checked by a teacher) you are ready to assess its reliability. On page 66 we discussed the concept of test–retest reliability. Reliable measuring instruments should produce the same (or similar) results if they are used again with the same sample of people. In order to assess this, you're going to have to find some willing participants to take the test—*twice*. Between 10 and 20 people should do the trick, but really it's the more the merrier. You need to leave a reasonable period of time between the two tests, maybe a couple of weeks, to reduce the possibility that participants will remember most of the questions (and more importantly, the answers!) Details on how to analyse the two sets of scores are included below.

Assessing validity

On page 69 we introduced the idea of concurrent validity. One way of assessing validity is to compare the scores produced on your test with the scores produced on an established test that measures the same variable (intelligence). So you're going to need to find a famous IQ test – or, you could just follow this link to the *Stanford–Binet test*, a widely recognised and well established test: www.stanfordbinet.net/

The same participants who completed your test above are also required to complete the *Stanford–Binet test*. Make sure you record all the sets of scores.

Statistical analysis

Your final task is to perform two statistical analyses. The first is to determine the **correlation** between the scores produced on the IQ test the first time the participants take it and the scores produced the second time they take it. This will assess test–retest reliability.

The second analysis is to calculate the correlation between the scores on the IQ test (the first time participants take it) and their scores on the Stanford-Binet-test. This will assess concurrent validity.

Spearman's rho

Both of the calculations above require you to use **Spearman's rho**. You will need to remind yourself of the steps involved in this test (page 78) in order to work out the **correlation coefficient** in each case. Finally, remember that in order to establish reliability and validity your correlation coefficients need to exceed .80 (*it ain't great unless it's .8 . . .*).

Practical idea 2: Devising practical ideas for research

The aim of this half spread is to encourage you to develop plans for practical ideas for research.

See if you can come up with one practical idea for each of the **statistical tests** described on pages 74–80.

Plan some investigations – on your own or with some mates (coffee optional ...)

The introductory bit

By this stage, you should have experience of designing and carrying out practical investigations on your own or in a small group. Your task on this page is to design a further *seven* investigations (some of which you may want to carry out) to generate data for *all* of the statistical tests you have come across in this chapter. This is no mean feat and will require many of the research methods skills you have developed – as well as some careful thought ...

An investigation for Chi-Squared

Chi-Squared is the most flexible of the statistical tests and can be used to test for an *association* (relationship) or a *difference*. The level of measurement is **nominal** so data needs to be represented in the form of categories. You might want to analyse some difference between the sexes as the number of male and female students (in your year group for instance) can easily be counted and recorded. Is there a difference between the number of male and female students who do and do not study psychology, for instance? Remember, you'll need to construct a **contingency table** (a 2 × 2 table) of the relevant data so you are able to calculate the difference/association you are looking for.

An investigation for Mann–Whitney

This test of difference requires **ordinal data** and **independent groups**. For this reason, it is a good test for comparing the opinions or ratings given by two different groups. Is someone's enjoyment of their A level programme influenced by whether they study psychology or not? Alternatively, **Mann–Whitney** is appropriate for measuring the difference in performance of groups on a non-interval scale test. Would Year 13s outperform Year 12s on the IQ test you devised on the left?

An investigation for Wilcoxon

The same criteria for Mann–Whitney apply to **Wilcoxon** except data is drawn from *related* rather than unrelated samples. If participants were *matched pairs* in the investigations above, Wilcoxon would be suitable because that is a **related design**. Alternatively participants could be asked to give a rating for something *before* and *after* they are given new information. Do students' ratings of their perceived ability in psychology change after they are told that everyone in last year's class got an A grade? (Ed – this may or may not be true of course!)

Investigations for Spearman's and Pearson's

Both of these are tests of **correlation** so there is no **experimental design** to consider here. The distinction between the two types of test is the **level of measurement**. If you are looking for a correlation between **co-variables** where at least one of these is based on data at an ordinal level – such as whether the number of friends a student has is related to their level of self-esteem – it's **Spearman's**. If both sets of data are **interval level** then it's the **parametric** equivalent, **Pearson's** (for example, whether time taken to complete a jigsaw puzzle is related to age).

Investigations for the *t*-tests

Both forms of *t*-test analyse the difference between two sets of scores and require interval data for their use. The distinction between the **related** and **unrelated** *t*-test hinges on the type of experimental design. If this is independent groups, then the unrelated *t*-test is used – for instance, investigating whether A level PE students can throw a tennis ball further than non-PE students. In the case of matched pairs or repeated measures designs, the related *t*-test is used. For example, investigating whether the presence of an audience affects how far students throw a tennis ball.

Parametric versus non-parametric assumptions

Remember that the two *t*-tests and Pearson's are parametric tests and certain assumptions must be met for their use. You must be sure that the data you are using is interval data. Generally speaking, if data has been recorded using some specialist mathematical measuring device (such as a tape measure in the example above) it is likely to be interval data – but check with your teacher if you are unsure. Using students from your school is likely to ensure that your sample is drawn from a **normally distributed population**. Finally, if you are using a related design, **homogeneity of variance** is assumed. If your design is unrelated, you will need to work out the **standard deviations** for each condition to make sure they are *similar* (see page 71 for a discussion of parametric criteria).

Stats test checklist

Make sure you ...

- Write an **operationalised alternative** and **null hypothesis** at the beginning of the investigation (you'll need to accept one and reject the other at the end).

- Decide on a **directional** or **non-directional hypothesis** (and, consequently, a **one-tailed** or a **two-tailed test**) (See page 73).

- Design a well-controlled and ethical investigation – check this with your teacher if you intend to carry it out.

- Choose the correct statistical test.

- Select the correct **critical value** using an appropriate **level of significance** (usually 5%).

You won't have to calculate any of the statistical tests on the left in the exam but you might want to work out a couple just for – er – fun. (Also, it will help your understanding of maths and statistics in general.)

The maths bit

In the Year 1 book we gave a list of the mathematical skills you will be expected to demonstrate.

Overall, at least 10% of the marks in assessments for Psychology will require the use of mathematical skills and at least a further 15% will be related to research methods.

Revision summaries

Correlations

Revisiting the analysis of co-variables.

Analysis and interpretation of correlations

Correlations and correlation coefficients
Relationship between two continuous co-variables.
Correlation coefficient represents strength and direction of relationship.

Working out what a coefficient means
The closer the coefficient is to −1 or +1, the stronger the relationship.

Case studies and content analysis

Two forms of research method.

Case studies

Case studies
Detailed analysis of an unusual individual or event, e.g. the London riots.

Characteristics
Tend to produce qualitative data, and be longitudinal.

Evaluation

Strengths
Insight into unusual cases, e.g. HM may provide understanding of normal functioning.
Generate hypotheses for future studies.

Limitations
Generalisation is a problem and conclusions based on subjective interpretation of the researcher.

Content analysis

Content analysis
A form of observation in which communication is studied indirectly.

Coding and quantitative data
Data must be categorised into meaningful units (and then analysed by counting words, etc).

Thematic analysis and qualitative data
Recurrent ideas that keep 'cropping up' in the communication are described.

Evaluation

Strengths
Fewer ethical issues and high external validity.

Limitations
Information may be studied out of context and descriptive forms of analysis may be less objective.

Reliability

A measure of consistency.

Reliability

Introducing reliability
Psychologists tend not to measure concrete things so reliability is difficult to establish.

Test–retest
The same test is administered to the same person (or group) on different occasions and results compared.

Inter-observer reliability
Observers should compare data in a pilot study or at end of actual study to make sure behavioural categories are consistently applied.

Improving reliability

Questionnaires
If a questionnaire has low test–retest reliability, some items may need to be changed to closed questions as these may be less ambiguous.

Interviews
Should avoid questions that are leading or ambiguous and ensure interviewers are trained.

Experiments
Standardisation of procedures will minimise extraneous variables.

Observations
Behavioural categories should be properly operationalised and not overlap.

Types of validity

A measure of 'truth'.

Validity

Introducing validity
Whether a test, scale, etc, produces a legitimate result which represents behaviour in the real world.

Internal and external validity
Whether something measures what it was designed to measure, and whether findings can be generalised.

Ecological validity
The extent to which findings can be generalised from one setting to other settings.
Mundane realism of task may affect ecological validity.

Temporal validity
Do findings from a study hold true over time?

Assessment of validity

Face and concurrent validity
Does a test measure what it is supposed to 'on the face of it'?
Do results match with a previously established test?

Improving validity

Experimental research
Use of a control group.
Standardised procedures.
Single-blind and double-blind trials.

Questionnaires
Use of lie scales and anonymity to reduce social desirability.

Observations
Findings may be more authentic in covert observations.

Qualitative methods
Depth and detail may increase validity but further enhanced through triangulation.

Choosing a statistical test

Statistical tests tell us whether results are significant.

Choosing a statistical test

Statistical testing
Determine whether we can accept or reject the null hypothesis.

Difference or correlation
Correlation includes tests of association (Chi-Squared).

Experimental design
Related (repeated measures or matched pairs) or unrelated (independent groups).

Parametric tests
Interval level data, normal distribution and homogeneity of variance.

Levels of measurement

Nominal data
Data represented in the form of categories, e.g. counting how many boys and girls in a year group – boys and girls are discrete categories.

Ordinal data
'Unsafe' data which can be placed in rank order, e.g. rating your liking of psychology on a scale of 1–10.

Interval data
Based on numerical and public scales of measurement with units of equal size, e.g. length, temperature.

PROBABILITY AND SIGNIFICANCE

Psychological research works on probabilities rather than certainties.

PROBABILITY AND SIGNIFICANCE

The null hypothesis
The null hypothesis states no difference between conditions. Statistical tests determine whether this should be accepted or rejected.

Levels of significance and probability
The significance level is the point at which the researcher can accept the alternative hypothesis (usually 5% in psychology).

USE OF STATISTICAL TABLES

Calculated and critical values
The calculated value must be compared with a critical value to determine significance.

Using tables of critical values
Is the test one-tailed or two-tailed?
What is the N value?
Which level of significance?

Lower levels of significance
A more stringent level, e.g. 1%, should be used when research has a human cost or the study is a one-off.

TYPE I AND TYPE II ERRORS

Type I error
The incorrect rejection of a true null hypothesis.

Type II error
The incorrect acceptance of a false null hypothesis.

DIFFERENT STATISTICAL TESTS

Formula for determining significance.

TESTS OF DIFFERENCE

Mann–Whitney
Test of difference between two sets of data.
Unrelated design.
Data at least ordinal level.

Wilcoxon
Test of difference between two sets of data.
Related design.
Data at least ordinal level.

PARAMETRIC TESTS OF DIFFERENCE

Unrelated *t*-test
Test of difference between two sets of data.
Unrelated design.
Data at interval level.
Data drawn from normally distributed sample population and homogeneity of variance.
Homogeneity of variance.

Related *t*-test
Test of difference between two sets of data.
Related design.
Data at interval level.
Data drawn from normally distributed sample population and homogeneity of variance.
Homogeneity of variance.

TESTS OF CORRELATION

Spearman's
Test of correlation between co-variables.
Data at least ordinal level.

Pearson's
Test of correlation between co-variables.
Data at interval level.
Data drawn from a normally distributed population and homogeneity of variance.

TEST OF DIFFERENCE/ASSOCIATION

Chi-Squared
Test of difference between two sets of data or association between co-variables.
Data is independent.
Nominal data.

RULE OF R

Rule of R
Tests with a letter 'R' in their name are those where the calculated value must be equal to or more than the critical value.

FEATURES OF SCIENCE

What makes science scientific?

Paradigms and paradigm shifts
Scientific subjects have a shared set of assumptions and a scientific revolution occurs when there is a paradigm shift.

Theory construction and hypothesis testing
Theory construction occurs through gathering evidence from direct observation.
Researchers can produce clear and precise hypotheses to test the validity of the theory.

Falsifiability
Scientific theories should hold themselves up for hypothesis testing and the possibility of being proved false.

Replicability
If a scientific theory is to be 'trusted' (i.e. valid), its findings must be shown to be repeatable across time and context.
The methods used should also be repeatable, i.e. reliable.

Objectivity and the empirical method
Scientists must minimise all sources of personal bias and gather evidence through direct observation and experience.

REPORTING PSYCHOLOGICAL INVESTIGATIONS

Psychologists use a conventional format when presenting their research.

Abstract
A short summary of the different elements in the report.

Introduction
Literature review including aim and hypothesis.

Method
Includes design, sample, apparatus/materials, procedure, ethics.

Results
Descriptive and inferential statistics.

Discussion
Analysis of results, limitations and wider implications.

References
List of sources (journal articles, books, web sources).

PRACTICE QUESTIONS, ANSWERS AND FEEDBACK

Question 1   A call centre company is conducting research to see whether the type of music customers listen to whilst they are on hold affects how long they will remain on hold. The first 200 customers who phoned the call centre on a Monday morning were told they had to be transferred to another department and were placed on hold (in reality, they were not being transferred, they were simply being placed on hold and the time it took each customer to put the phone down was recorded).

During the time on hold, 100 customers were played classical music, and the other 100 customers were played pop music. The difference in average time spent listening to classical music and pop music on hold before putting the phone down was analysed.

(a)   Write a suitable non-directional hypothesis for the investigation above. *(2 marks)*

Morticia's answer The hypothesis would be 'There is a difference between the customers who listened to classical music and the customers who listed to pop music'.	A difference in what? The DV is not made clear.
Luke's answer The customers who heard classical music listen longer on hold than the customers who heard pop music.	Unfortunately, a directional hypothesis is offered by Luke.
Vladimir's answer The kind of music that is played affects how long people stay on hold.	Both variables are stated and the hypothesis is non-directional.

(b)   Which sampling technique was used to recruit participants in the investigation? Explain your answer. *(2 marks)*

Morticia's answer The researcher used an opportunity sample because it was just the most convenient people.	'Most convenient people' is an odd phrase but just sufficient.
Luke's answer Opportunity sample. They were the most willing and available.	Participants were not given the option to be 'willing', but still a sufficient answer.
Vladimir's answer Volunteer sample because they were willing to take part.	Vladimir's answer has no relevance.

(c)   Outline **one** limitation of the sampling technique you have identified in (b). *(2 marks)*

Morticia's answer Using an opportunity sample is not always the most representative.	A limitation is stated but more detail is required.
Luke's answer This sample may be biased because it is a narrow sample of people who happened to be at home to answer their phones.	A more thorough answer but the link to the stem is inaccurate.
Vladimir's answer Volunteers may be more willing than people generally which makes them unrepresentative.	Vladimir has fully addressed a limitation of the sampling method he identified earlier.

(d)   Which statistical test could have been used to analyse the difference in average time spent on hold in the investigation in question 1? Justify your answer. *(3 marks)*

Morticia's answer It would be a t-test for unrelated samples. This is because the study is independent groups and the data are interval.	Morticia has produced a strong answer, though it is good practice to link the answer more clearly to the stem (as in Vladimir's excellent answer below).
Luke's answer It would be a Mann–Whitney test because there are two groups of participants and we can't be sure that parametric criteria are satisfied.	Luke's answer lacks key elements – the type of design is not named, nor is the fact that a difference is being tested for.
Vladimir's answer Unrelated t-test because there were two groups of participants (those who heard classical or heard pop), we are looking for a difference between the groups, the data are interval (number of seconds) and parametric criteria would be satisfied.	Vladimir has got it right.

(e)   After the results had been analysed, a significant difference was found at the 0.05 level. Explain what this means in relation to the investigation above. *(3 marks)*

Morticia's answer It means that there is a 5% chance that the results were due to chance.	Morticia's answer is the only one here that contains relevant material. The other two answers are too vague. None of the answers refers to which hypothesis would be retained and which rejected, and what this would mean in the context of the investigation.
Luke's answer 0.05 is the same as 5% which is the level of certainty we have that there was a difference.	
Vladimir's answer The difference was 5% certain.	

On this spread we look at some typical student answers to questions. The comments provided indicate what is good and bad in each answer. Learning how to produce effective question answers is a SKILL. Read pages 387–397 for guidance.

As soon as customers put the phone down in the investigation described on the facing page, they were called back and debriefed.

(f) Write a debriefing statement that could have been read out to customers who were played pop music whilst on hold in this investigation. (*4 marks*)

Morticia's answer I am ringing you to say that the phone call you just received was part of a research study run by Littletown University. We played music for each participant – with classical or pop – to see how long they would stay on the phone. If you'd like to know the final results of the study I can send them to you. Do you have any questions?	The aim is clearly stated in Morticia's debrief and the reference to any questions and knowledge of the final results is appropriate. She could perhaps have asked if the data could still be used.
Luke's answer Hello, my name is Luke. I am ringing to tell you that the phone call you just received was part of a psychological study where we were investigating whether people were more willing to stay on hold if they listened to classical or pop music. We hope you were not distressed by the experience. Thank you for your time.	The aim of the investigation is clearly stated but Luke should have asked for permission to use the data. The reference to 'distress' is rather vague and unnecessary.
Vladimir's answer This is a follow up call to the one you just received to tell you that it was part of a psychological study. We hope it didn't upset you in any way or take up too much of your time. If you have any complaints or would like to withdraw your data then let us know now. Otherwise thank you and I'll be in touch again to tell you the results if you wish.	A good appreciation of relevant ethical issues in Vladimir's debrief. However, this answer needs more detailed reference to the aim of the study and relevant conditions.

Customers were asked if they would complete a structured interview about their experience of call centres. Those who agreed were called back and the interview was conducted over the phone.

(g) Briefly discuss **one** limitation of a structured interview. (*3 marks*)

Morticia's answer A structured interview does not give the interviewer any opportunity to ask questions arising from the conversation during the phone interview.	Morticia's and Vladimir's answers are briefly stated and require further elaboration – perhaps through contrast with unstructured interviews.
Luke's answer One limitation of a structured interview is that the interviewer can't stray from the listed questions, for example to explain the question. In this interview they might want to ask some different questions than were on the list. That said, the data from structured interviews is much easier to analyse as it is more focused than that produced in unstructured interviews.	Luke's answer is much better for this reason. It also includes relevant counterargument which can be used as effective elaboration in a 'briefly discuss' question.
Vladimir's answer It lacks the flexibility of an unstructured interview.	

(h) Explain how the reliability and validity of the interview could have been assessed. (*5 marks*)

Morticia's answer The reliability could be assessed by asking the same interviewer to repeat the interview a second time with the same people and compare the answers to see if they were consistent. Validity could be checked in terms of face validity to see if the questions looked like they were assessing thoughts and feelings about call centres.	Morticia's answer is detailed and accurate. The ways of assessing reliability and validity are well explained and relevant to the investigation.
Luke's answer For reliability you could use test–retest and repeat the interviews a second time. For validity you could use concurrent validity and compare with another interview.	Luke's answer is less successful. Two relevant methods are named but the description of these lack key details.
Vladimir's answer One way to assess reliability is using the test–retest method where the same test (or questions) are given a second time to the same person. Validity could be ecological validity. The ecological validity is good because these were people just answering their phones in everyday life.	Vladimir's first point is relevant – though generic – but the material in the latter half of the question is not really 'assessing validity'.

Multiple-Choice Questions

Correlations

1. All correlation coefficients fall somewhere between . . .
(a) −1 and +1.
(b) 0 and 1.
(c) +1 and 0.
(d) −10 and +10.

2. As the number of people in a room increases, personal space decreases is an example of a . . .
(a) Positive correlation.
(b) Negative correlation.
(c) Zero correlation.
(d) Curvilinear relationship.

3. As the daily temperature goes down, people's mood rating decreases is an example of a . . .
(a) Positive correlation.
(b) Negative correlation.
(c) Zero correlation.
(d) Curvilinear relationship.

4. Correlations are plotted on a . . .
(a) Bar chart.
(b) Histogram.
(c) Line graph.
(d) Scattergram.

Case studies and content analysis

1. Case studies tend to take place over a long period of time. This is referred to as . . .
(a) Longitudinal research.
(b) Timescale research.
(c) Hexagonal research.
(d) Temporal research.

2. Which of the following is a strength of case studies?
(a) The final report is not based on the subjective interpretation of the researcher.
(b) Construct validity.
(c) Generalisation of findings is usually possible with small sample sizes.
(d) Study of unusual cases may contribute to our understanding of normal functioning.

3. Categorising information into meaningful units is known as . . .
(a) Filing.
(b) Magnifying.
(c) Separating.
(d) Coding.

4. Recognising the part that one's own biases play in the research process is called . . .
(a) Reflexivity.
(b) Rigidity.
(c) Reactivity.
(d) Reliability.

Reliability

1. Reliability is a measure of . . .
(a) Complexity.
(b) Conformity.
(c) Consistency.
(d) Clarity.

2. If two or more observers are collecting data they must first establish . . .
(a) Construct validity.
(b) Test–retest reliability.
(c) Inter-observer reliability.
(d) External reliability.

3. If participants are given the same questionnaire twice, for test–retest reliability the correlation must exceed . . .
(a) .70
(b) .80
(c) .90
(d) 1.00

4. Reliability is most often achieved in which type of interview?
(a) Structured.
(b) Unstructured.
(c) Semi-structured.
(d) Television.

Validity

1. Which of the following does *not* describe validity?
(a) Whether a test is legitimate.
(b) Whether a test is genuine.
(c) Whether a finding can be generalised.
(d) Whether a test is consistent.

2. 'The extent to which findings from a research study can be generalised to other times' is a definition of . . .
(a) Concurrent validity.
(b) Temporal validity.
(c) Face validity.
(d) Internal validity.

3. 'The extent to which a psychological measure relates to an existing similar measure' is a definition of . . .
(a) Concurrent validity.
(b) Temporal validity.
(c) Face validity.
(d) Internal validity.

4. Validity can be improved through the use of a number of different sources as evidence. This is referred to as . . .
(a) Reticulation.
(b) The square peg principle.
(c) Circle theory.
(d) Triangulation.

Choosing a statistical test

1. Which of the following is *not* one of the criteria when deciding on a statistical test?
(a) Whether the hypothesis is directional or non-directional.
(b) The level of measurement.
(c) Whether the researcher is looking for a difference or relationship.
(d) The experimental design.

2. Which of the following tests would be used when looking for a correlation with interval level data?
(a) Mann–Whitney.
(b) Chi-Squared.
(c) Pearson's.
(d) Spearman's.

3. Which of the following tests would be used with nominal data?
(a) Related *t*-test.
(b) Wilcoxon.
(c) Sign test.
(d) Unrelated *t*-test.

4. Which of the following is *not* one of the three criteria required for use of a parametric test?
(a) Data at interval level.
(b) A test of relationship rather than difference.
(c) Data must be drawn from a normally distributed population.
(d) Homogeneity of variance.

Probability and significance

1. A probability of 1 would indicate . . .
(a) Statistical certainty.
(b) Statistical impossibility.
(c) Statistical significance.
(d) Statistical likelihood.

2. Which of the following is associated with a Type II error?
(a) An optimistic error.
(b) Incorrect rejection of the null hypothesis.
(c) Incorrect acceptance of the alternative hypothesis.
(d) Made more likely when the significance level is set too low.

3. The usual level of significance in psychological research is . . .
(a) 1%
(b) 5%
(c) 10%
(d) 50%

4. Which of the following is *not* required when consulting a critical value table?
(a) Knowing the level of measurement.
(b) Knowing whether the test is one-tailed or two-tailed.
(c) Knowing the N value/degrees of freedom.
(d) Knowing the level of significance.

Tests of difference: Mann–Whitney and Wilcoxon

1. Mann–Whitney would be used when the researcher has used . . .
(a) An independent groups design.
(b) A repeated measures design.
(c) A matched pairs design.
(d) A quasi-experiment.

2. Wilcoxon would be used when the researcher has used . . .
(a) An independent groups design.
(b) Stratified sampling.
(c) A matched pairs design.
(d) A quasi-experiment.

3. Mann–Whitney and Wilcoxon are used when . . .
(a) The data are interval.
(b) The data are nominal.
(c) The data are ratio.
(d) The data are ordinal or interval.

4. Which test would be used to analyse differences on an attitude questionnaire between males and females?
(a) Mann–Whitney.
(b) Wilcoxon.
(c) Neither of the above.
(d) Either of the above.

Parametric tests of difference: Unrelated and related *t*-test

1. Why are parametric tests superior to non-parametric tests?
(a) They use the actual data collected rather than ranks.
(b) They are more powerful and robust than other tests.
(c) They are more likely to detect significance in data sets.
(d) All of the above.

2. An unrelated *t*-test would be used when the researcher has used . . .
(a) An independent groups design.
(b) A repeated measures design.
(c) A matched pairs design.
(d) A quasi-experiment.

3. *t*-tests are used when . . .
(a) The data are interval.
(b) The data are nominal.
(c) The data are ordinal.
(d) The data are independent.

4. Which test would be used to analyse an association between gender and smoking behaviour?
(a) Wilcoxon.
(b) Related *t*-test.
(c) Neither of the above.
(d) Either of the above.

Tests of correlation: Spearman's and Pearson's

1. Spearman's would be used when . . .
(a) The data are at least interval.
(b) The data are at least nominal.
(c) The data are at least ratio.
(d) The data are at least ordinal.

2. Pearson's would be used when . . .
(a) The data are at least interval.
(b) The data are at least nominal.
(c) The data are at least ordinal.
(d) There is no data.

3. Spearman's and Pearson's are both used to analyse . . .
(a) A correlation.
(b) A difference.
(c) Dispersion.
(d) Central tendency.

4. Which test would be used to analyse the relationship between temperature and heart rate?
(a) Mann–Whitney.
(b) Pearson's.
(c) Neither of the above.
(d) Either of the above.

Tests of association: Chi-Squared and Reporting psychological investigations

1. Chi-Squared is used when . . .
(a) The data are interval.
(b) The data are nominal.
(c) The data are ratio.
(d) The data are ordinal.

2. Observed frequencies are recorded in a . . .
(a) Consistency table.
(b) Continuity table.
(c) Contingency table.
(d) Constancy table.

3. Which of these is defined as a 150–200 word summary of the major elements of a scientific report?
(a) The abstract.
(b) The design.
(c) The discussion.
(d) The references.

4. Which of the following would *not* appear in the method section of a scientific report?
(a) Sample.
(b) Procedure.
(c) Discussion.
(d) Apparatus/materials.

Features of science

1. Kuhn referred to a shared set of assumptions and methods as a . . .
(a) Parametric.
(b) Parapax.
(c) Paradigm.
(d) Parasite.

2. Popper argued that scientific progress occurs through a process of . . .
(a) Ramification.
(b) Amplification.
(c) Falsification.
(d) Materialisation.

3. When all sources of personal bias are minimised so as not to influence the research process.
(a) Replicability.
(b) Generalisability.
(c) Falsifiability.
(d) Objectivity.

4. 'Collecting data through direct sensory experiece' refers to . . .
(a) Existentialism.
(b) Essentialism.
(c) Eclecticism.
(d) Empiricism.

MCQ answers

Correlations 1a, 2b, 3a, 4d
Case studies and content analysis 1a, 2d, 3d, 4a
Reliability 1c, 2c, 3b, 4a
Validity 1d, 2b, 3a, 4d
Choosing a statistical test 1a, 2c, 3c, 4b
Probability and significance 1a, 2d, 3b, 4a
Tests of difference: Mann Whitney and Wilcoxon 1a, 2c, 3d, 4a
Parametric tests of difference: Unrelated and related *t*-test 1d, 2a, 3a, 4c
Tests of correlation: Spearman's and Pearson's 1d, 2a, 3a, 4b
Test of association: Chi-Squared and Reporting psychological investigations 1b, 2c, 3a, 4c
Features of science 1c, 2c, 3d, 4d

CHAPTER 4
ISSUES AND DEBATES

Chapter contents

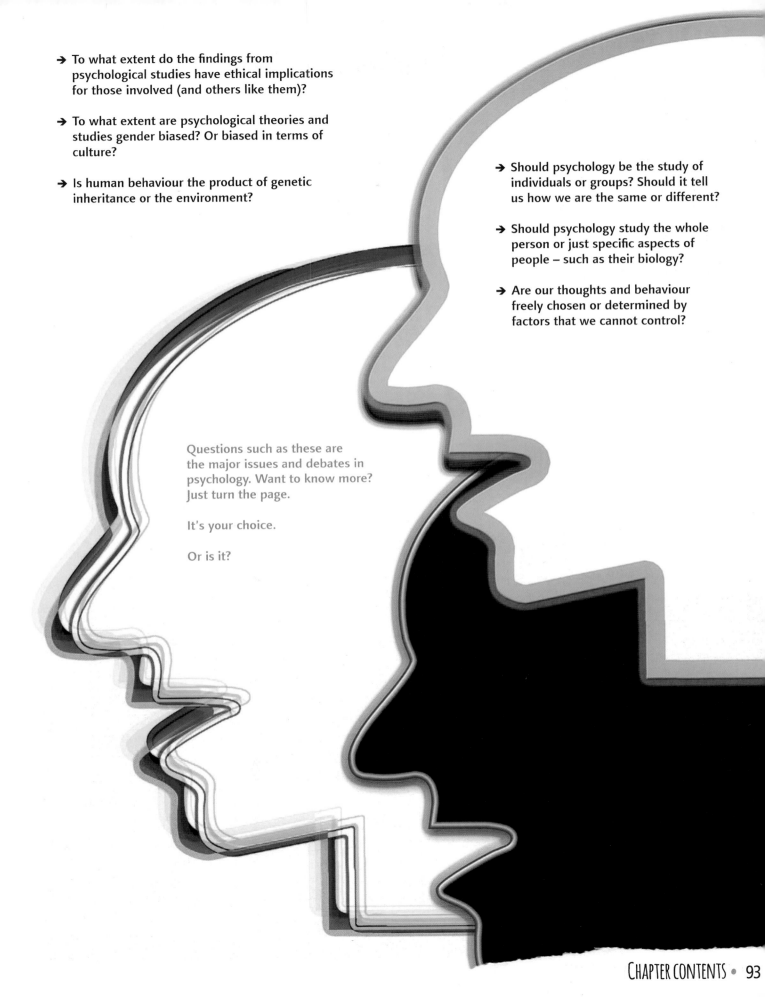

→ To what extent do the findings from psychological studies have ethical implications for those involved (and others like them)?

→ To what extent are psychological theories and studies gender biased? Or biased in terms of culture?

→ Is human behaviour the product of genetic inheritance or the environment?

→ Should psychology be the study of individuals or groups? Should it tell us how we are the same or different?

→ Should psychology study the whole person or just specific aspects of people – such as their biology?

→ Are our thoughts and behaviour freely chosen or determined by factors that we cannot control?

Questions such as these are the major issues and debates in psychology. Want to know more? Just turn the page.

It's your choice.

Or is it?

Gender and culture in Psychology – universality and bias. Gender bias including androcentrism and alpha and beta bias.

'The representation of the world, like the world itself, is the work of men; they describe it from their own point of view, which they confuse with the truth' – Simone De Beauvoir (1949).

Does this apply to psychology? Historically, psychology has been a male-dominated discipline and the charge is that many of its major theories and explanations reflect this. Worse – it may be that male bias is so endemic within the research practices of psychology that if the female voice has been heard at all, it has been minimised, marginalised or judged as 'abnormal' against the male standard. Here we explore forms of gender bias within psychology, claims of sexism within theory and research, and ask whether modern psychology is in a position to correct this.

KEY TERMS

Universality – Any underlying characteristic of human beings that is capable of being applied to all, despite differences of experience and upbringing. Gender bias and culture bias threaten the universality of findings in psychology.

Gender bias – When considering human behaviour, bias is a tendency to treat one individual or group in a different way from others. In the context of gender bias, psychological research or theory may offer a view that does not justifiably represent the experience and behaviour of men or women (usually women).

Androcentrism – Male-centred; when 'normal' behaviour is judged according to a male standard (meaning that female behaviour is often judged to be 'abnormal' or 'deficient' by comparison).

Alpha bias – Psychological theories that suggest there are real and enduring differences between men and women. These may enhance or undervalue members of either sex, but typically undervalue females.

Beta bias – Theories that ignore or minimise differences between the sexes.

The work of Sigmund Freud – an example of gender bias in psychology?

Gender bias

Universality and bias

First and foremost, psychologists are *people* who – just like the rest of us – possess beliefs and values that have been influenced by the social and historical context within which they live. Thus, bias may be an inevitable aspect of the research process. This is despite the arguments psychologists might make to have discovered 'facts' about human behaviour that are 'objective' and 'value-free'. It also undermines psychology's claims to **universality** – that conclusions drawn can be applied to everyone, anywhere, regardless of time or culture. We shall explore two particular forms of bias within psychology: **gender bias** and **cultural bias**. On this spread we look at gender bias and its widespread influence on mainstream psychology.

Gender bias

Alpha bias within psychological research is that which exaggerates or overestimates differences between the sexes. Such differences are typically presented as real and enduring; fixed and inevitable. Although these differences may occasionally heighten the value of women, they are more likely to *devalue* females in relation to their male counterparts.

An example of alpha bias is the **sociobiological theory** of relationship formation (for example Wilson 1975), which explains human sexual attraction and behaviour through the principle of 'survival efficiency'. It is in the male's interest to try to impregnate as many women as possible to increase the chances of his **genes** being passed on to the next generation. For the female, the best chance of preserving her genes is to ensure the healthy survival of the relatively few offspring she is able to produce in her lifetime. The central premise of sociobiological theory is that sexual promiscuity in males is genetically determined whilst females who engage in the same behaviour are regarded as going against their 'nature' – an exaggeration of the difference between the sexes (alpha bias). This is also an example of an **essentialist** argument in psychology (see facing page).

In contrast, **beta bias** ignores, minimises or underestimates differences between men and women. This often occurs when female participants are not included as part of the research process and then it is assumed that research findings apply equally to both sexes. The beta bias within Kohlberg's theory of moral development is described on the right (see Apply-it on the facing page). Another astounding example of beta bias is the **fight or flight response** (page 254). Early research into fight or flight was based exclusively on male animals (preferred for research because female hormones fluctuate) and was assumed to be a universal response to a threatening situation. More recently, Shelley Taylor *et al.* (2000) have suggested that female biology has evolved to inhibit the fight or flight response, shifting attention towards caring for offspring (tending) and forming defensive networks with other females (befriending) (see page 276).

Androcentrism

One possible consequence of beta bias is **androcentrism**. If our understanding of what counts as 'normal' behaviour is being drawn from research that involves all-male samples, then any behaviour that deviates from this standard is likely to be judged as 'abnormal', 'inferior' or 'deficient' by comparison. At best, this leads to female behaviour being misunderstood, and at worst, pathologised – that is, taken as a sign of psychological instability or disorder.

For example, many feminist commentators have objected to the diagnostic category *premenstrual syndrome* (PMS) on the grounds that it stereotypes and trivialises female experience. Critics claim that PMS is a *social construction* which medicalises female emotions, especially anger, by explaining these in hormonal terms. Male anger, on the other hand, is often seen as a rational response to external pressures (Brescoll and Uhlman 2008).

Apply it   Concepts: Freudian theory

In Freudian theory, because a girl does not experience **castration anxiety** in the **phallic stage** of psychosexual development, she is not under the same pressure as a boy to form an identification with the same-sex parent. This has implications for the development of the female **superego**. The girl forms a *weaker* superego than her male counterpart and therefore the sense of morality she acquires is *inferior* to that of the male (see discussion on page 160).

Freud saw femininity as an expression of failed masculinity. His central concept of **penis envy** means that women are defined psychologically by the fact that they are not men! In addition, he sought to explain female 'vanity' as a **defence mechanism**: women wish to make up for their sexual inferiority to men by focusing on their 'physical charms'.

Unsurprisingly, critics have dismissed the 'phallocentrism' in Freud's theory. Among them was the neo-Freudian Karen Horney (1926) who argued that Freud overlooked the fact that men are more likely to harbour jealousy of women's ability to conceive and bear children ('womb envy').

Question

Which of the biases described on this spread could Freud's theory be accused of and why?

Evaluation

Implications of gender bias

Gender-biased research may create misleading assumptions about female behaviour, fail to challenge negative stereotypes and validate discriminatory practices. It may provide a scientific 'justification' to deny women opportunities within the workplace or in wider society (see example of PMS on facing page). In any domain in which men set the standard of normalcy, as Carol Tavris (1993) puts it, 'it becomes normal for women to feel abnormal'.

Thus, gender bias in research is not just a methodological problem but may have damaging consequences which affect the lives and prospects of real women (for instance, the statistic that females are around twice as likely to be diagnosed with depression than men).

Sexism within the research process

A lack of women appointed at senior research level means that female concerns may not be reflected in the research questions asked. Male researchers are more likely to have their work published and studies which find evidence of gender differences are more likely to appear in journal articles than those that do not. Also, the **laboratory experiment** – seen as the cornerstone of 'scientific' enquiry in psychology – may further disadvantage women. Female participants are placed in an inequitable relationship with a (usually male) researcher who has the power to label them unreasonable, irrational and unable to complete complex tasks (Nicolson 1995).

This means that psychology may be guilty of supporting a form of institutional sexism that creates bias in theory and research (Denmark *et al.* 1988).

Reflexivity

Many modern researchers are beginning to recognise the effect their own values and assumptions have on the nature of their work. Rather than seeing such bias as a problem that may threaten the objective status of their work, they embrace it as a crucial and critical aspect of the research process in general. For instance, in their study of the lack of women in executive positions in accountancy firms, Claire Dambrin and Caroline Lambert (2008) include reflection on how their gender-related experiences influence their reading of events.

Such *reflexivity* is an important development in psychology and may lead to greater awareness of the role of personal biases in shaping research in the future.

Evaluation eXtra

Essentialism

Many of the gender differences reported by psychologists over the years are based on an *essentialist* perspective: that the gender difference in question is inevitable (essential) and 'fixed' in nature. Valerie Walkerdine (1990) reports how, in the 1930s, 'scientific' research revealed how intellectual activity – such as attending university – would shrivel a woman's ovaries and harm her chances of giving birth! Such essentialist accounts in psychology are often politically motivated arguments disguised as biological 'facts'. This often creates a 'double-standard' in the way that the same behaviour is viewed from a male and female perspective.

Consider: *Explain how the sociobiological theory could be accused of a double-standard in the way it presents male and female behaviour.*

Feminist psychology

Feminist commentators such as Judith Worrell (1992) have put forward a number of criteria that should be adhered to in order to avoid gender bias in research. Women should be studied within meaningful real-life contexts, and genuinely *participate* in research, rather than being the *objects of study*. Diversity *within* groups of women should be examined, rather than comparisons made *between* women and men. Finally, there should be greater emphasis placed on *collaborative* research methods that collect **qualitative**, as opposed to numerical, data.

Consider: *Explain how this way of 'doing' research may be preferable (and less gender biased) than the laboratory-based research described above.*

Apply it **Concepts:**

Moral development – Kohlberg versus Gilligan

Another psychologist who has come under fire for gender bias is Lawrence Kohlberg. Kohlberg (1973) proposed a stage theory of moral development based entirely on the **longitudinal** study of a sample of American men. Kohlberg's research was based on male-orientated principles – though he argued such principles were *universal* and represented the moral reasoning of both males and females.

Question

1. Which form of gender bias was Kohlberg guilty of? Explain your answer.

In her 1981 book *In a Different Voice*, Carol Gilligan attacked Kohlberg for the absence of female participants within his research. Her argument was that whilst male morality is based on abstract principles (such as the importance of justice), female morality is more influenced by an ethic of care and responsibility to others. Gilligan argued that the natural female tendency towards care would place women at a *lower* and *less mature* level of moral reasoning in Kohlberg's model. Through her own research with female participants she sought to demonstrate how female morality, whilst being different from that of men, is no less mature or sophisticated.

Question

2. Ironically, Gilligan has also been accused of gender bias within her own research. Can you explain why?

Research in the 1930s suggested that the intellectual development of females would harm their chances of falling pregnant – an 'essentialist' (as well as inaccurate) argument.

Apply it **Methods:** Social influence research

A psychologist conducted a **content analysis** of 20 studies in social psychology from the 1960s and 70s and concluded that the majority of these showed clear evidence of alpha bias.

Questions

1. Explain how the psychologist may have carried out this content analysis. Refer to **coding** *and/or* **thematic analysis** in your answer. (6 marks) (See page 64)
2. Are the results an example of **primary** or **secondary data**? Explain your answer. (3 marks)

CHECK IT

1. Outline what is meant by *universality* and *bias* in psychological research. **[6 marks]**
2. Describe **one** example of psychological research that demonstrates *alpha bias*. **[4 marks]**
3. Describe **one** example of psychological research that demonstrates *beta bias*. **[4 marks]**
4. Discuss gender bias in psychological research. Refer to examples of alpha bias **and** beta bias in your answer. **[16 marks]**

The charge is that psychological research has often ignored differences between cultures and developed theories almost entirely based on the study of one culture alone – the United States.

KEY TERMS

Cultural bias – Refers to a tendency to ignore cultural differences and interpret all phenomena through the 'lens' of one's own culture.

Ethnocentrism – Judging other cultures by the standards and values of one's own culture. In its extreme form it is the belief in the superiority of one's own culture which may lead to prejudice and discrimination towards other cultures.

Cultural relativism – The idea that norms and values, as well as ethics and moral standards, can only be meaningful and understood within specific social and cultural contexts.

STUDY TIP

Cultural difference versus cultural bias. Don't confuse the two. We would expect to observe basic cultural differences in behaviour from society to society, culture to culture, as different norms and values influence the way people think and behave in different places (such as the difference in cultural levels of conformity – see right).

The argument, however, is that psychology, in some areas of research particularly, has ignored or misinterpreted differences between cultures and imposed an understanding based on the study of one culture alone – cultural bias.

Only 5 minutes to go! But would the idea of testing intelligence against the clock be regarded as peculiar in other cultures?

Cultural bias

In 1992, 64% of the world's 56,000 psychology researchers were American. In Baron and Byrne's 1991 textbook on social psychology, 94% of the studies cited were conducted in North America. Statistics such as these would suggest that, as well as being a male-dominated discipline (see previous spread), psychology is mainly the study of white American males. Despite having restricted their enquiries to particular parts of the world, many psychologists routinely claim to have discovered 'facts' about human behaviour that are 'universal'.

Universality and bias (revisited)

To what extent do the theories, models and concepts considered in this book represent universal human behaviour? Many argue that although psychology may claim to have unearthed 'truths' that say something about people all over the world, in reality, findings from studies only apply to the particular groups of people who were studied.

Critics argue that mainstream psychology has generally ignored culture as an important influence on human behaviour, and by doing so, has mistakenly assumed that findings derived from studies carried out in Western culture can be straightforwardly applied all over the world. For example, classic social influence studies of **conformity** (Asch) and **obedience** (Milgram), originally conducted with US participants, revealed very different results when they were replicated in other parts of the world, for example Kilham and Mann (1974).

If the 'norm' or 'standard' for a particular behaviour is judged only from the standpoint of one particular culture, then any cultural *differences* in behaviour – that depart or deviate from this standard – will inevitably be seen as 'abnormal', 'inferior' or 'unusual'. This is **cultural bias**.

Ethnocentrism

Ethnocentrism refers to a particular form of cultural bias and is a belief in the superiority of one's own cultural group. In psychological research this may be communicated through a view that any behaviours which do not conform to the (usually Western) model are somehow deficient, unsophisticated or underdeveloped.

Mary Ainsworth's **Strange Situation** (1970) is an example of this, criticised as reflecting only the norms and values of American culture. Ainsworth identified the key defining variable of **attachment** type as the child's experience of anxiety on separation. She suggested that 'ideal' (or **secure**) attachment was characterised by the infant showing moderate amounts of distress when left alone by the mother-figure. However, this led to misinterpretation of child-rearing practices in other countries which were seen to deviate from the American 'norm' – for instance, German mothers were seen as cold and rejecting rather than encouraging independence in their children. Thus, the Strange Situation was revealed as an inappropriate measure of attachment type for non-US children.

Cultural relativism

Ainsworth's research is one example of an **imposed etic** in psychology. In assuming that the US-based model of classifying attachment was the norm, Ainsworth imposed her own cultural understanding upon the rest of the world.

John Berry (1969) has drawn a distinction between *etic* and *emic* approaches in the study of human behaviour. An etic approach looks at behaviour from *outside* of a given culture and attempts to describe those behaviours that are universal. An emic approach functions from within or *inside* certain cultures and identifies behaviours that are *specific* to that culture. Ainsworth's research is an example of an imposed etic – she studied behaviour within a single culture (America) and then assumed her ideal attachment type could be applied universally.

Berry argues that psychology has often been guilty of imposing an etic approach – arguing that theories, models, concepts, etc., are universal, when they actually came about through emic research within a single culture. The suggestion is that psychologists should be much more mindful of the **cultural relativism** of their research – that the 'things' they discover may only make sense from the perspective of the culture within which they were discovered – and being able to recognise this is one way of avoiding cultural bias in research.

Apply it — Concepts: Intelligence testing – a Western invention!

Richard Brislin (1976) illustrates the concepts of ethnocentrism and imposed etic using the example of intelligence tests. Demonstrations of intelligence in Western culture often involve completing tasks 'against the clock' such as in timed assessments like exams (remember them?!). However, Brislin asks about the **validity** of this notion of 'mental quickness' in relation to intelligence. The Baganda people of Uganda characterise intelligence as slow, careful and deliberate thought (Wober 1974). They might view 'speed of thought' as thoughtlessness or rashness.

Question

Explain why culturally biased intelligence tests may lead to racial stereotyping and discrimination of particular groups in society.

Evaluation

Individualism and collectivism

Often in the past, when psychologists have made reference to 'culture' they have done so within the context of the individualist-collectivist distinction. **Individualist culture** is associated with Western countries (like the US) who are thought to value personal freedom and independence. **Collectivist cultures** such as India and China are said to place more emphasis on interdependence and the needs of the group. However, critics have suggested, in this age of global communication and increased *interconnectedness*, that such a 'lazy' and simplistic distinction between cultures no longer applies.

Yohtaro Takano and Eiko Osaka (1999) found that 14 out of 15 studies that compared the USA and Japan found no evidence of the traditional distinction between individualism and collectivism. This could perhaps suggest that cultural bias in research is less of an issue than it once was.

Cultural relativism versus universality

Berry's concept of imposed etic (see facing page) is a useful reminder to psychologists of the culturally specific nature of their work. However, it should not be assumed that *all* psychology is culturally relative and that there is no such thing as universal human behaviour. Research (e.g. Ekman 1989) suggests that basic facial expressions for emotions (such as happiness or disgust) are the same all over the human and animal world. Critiques of Ainsworth's Strange Situation should not obscure the fact that some features of human attachment – such as imitation and **interactional synchrony** – are universal.

A full understanding of human behaviour requires the study of both universals and variation among individuals and groups.

Unfamiliarity with research tradition

When conducting research in Western culture the participants' familiarity with the general aims and objectives of scientific enquiry is assumed. However, the same knowledge and 'faith' in scientific testing may not extend to cultures that do not have the same historical experience of research.

For this reason, **demand characteristics** (always an issue within any investigation) may be exaggerated when working with members of the local population (Bond and Smith 1996) – and this may have an adverse effect on the validity of the research.

Evaluation eXtra

Operationalisation of variables

One other issue with conducting research in different cultures is that the variables under review may not be experienced in the same way by all participants. For instance, the *behavioural* expression (as opposed to the *facial* expression described above) of emotions such as 'aggression' may give rise to quite different behaviours within an indigenous population than they would in the West. In China, the invasion of personal space is seen as normal, whereas in the West this may be seen as threatening or confrontational. Issues like these may affect interactions between the researcher and participants, or between Western and non-Western participants, in cross-cultural studies.

Consider: *Can you think of other examples of possible variables in research that may not 'travel well'? Explain why this is an issue when conducting cross-cultural research.*

Challenging 'implicit' assumptions

One of the great benefits of conducting cross-cultural research is that it may challenge our typically Western ways of thinking and viewing the world. Being able to see that some of the knowledge and concepts we take for granted are not shared by other people around the world may promote a greater sensitivity to individual difference and cultural relativism in the future. This not only counters the charge of 'scientific racism' that has been made against some psychological theories in the past (see page 107), but also means that the conclusions psychologists draw are likely to have more **validity** if they include recognition of the role of culture in bringing them about.

Consider: *Experienced cross-cultural researchers recommend the inclusion of at least one member of the local population within the research team. Why do you think this is?*

This man's mental confusion might be diagnosed as *brain fag* in West Africa.

Apply it   Concepts:

Cultural bias in diagnosis of mental disorder

A 1995 study by Cochrane and Sashidharan revealed the alarming statistic that African-Caribbean immigrants are seven times more likely to be diagnosed with a mental illness! This finding and others like it have led many to question the **validity** of **DSM** and **ICD** (the diagnostic manuals of mental illness used in the US and Europe respectively) for diagnosing individuals who are born outside of the dominant culture. To counter this, DSM-4 included in its appendix a list of 25 **culture-bound syndromes** (CBSs) – groups of symptoms classified as treatable illnesses in certain cultures that are not recognised as such in the West.

These include *brain fag* (difficulty concentrating, remembering and thinking – West Africa) and *koro* (the belief that the penis is retracting into the body – China). The very existence of CBSs suggests that DSM and ICD were ethnocentric and that 'mental illness' is not a universally agreed concept. Indeed, it has been argued that eating disorders, such as **anorexia**, should be considered CBSs as they are much more prevalent in the Western world and virtually absent in many other cultures.

Question

In the latest revision of DSM (DSM-5) the list of CBSs has been replaced with guidance for clinicians on how people from ethnic minorities may present symptoms differently. Why do you think the CBS list was removed from DSM-5?

Apply it   Methods: Professor Emic

Professor Emic wants to conduct cross-cultural research with the Mashco-Piro tribe of Peru – a community that has had very limited contact with the wider world. The Professor is keen to investigate levels of conformity among the Mashco-Piro and intends to replicate the Asch line matching study (in our Year 1 book) with some of the members of the community.

Question

Discuss some of the potential methodological issues of **replicating** the Asch study with the Mashco-Piro. (*6 marks*)

CHECK IT

1. Outline what is meant by *cultural bias* in psychology.   [3 marks]
2. Describe **one** example of *ethnocentrism* in psychology.   [4 marks]
3. Discuss cultural bias in psychology. Refer to examples of research in your answer.   [16 marks]

Free will and determinism: hard determinism and soft determinism; biological, environmental and psychic determinism. The scientific emphasis on causal explanations.

Coming to this debate for the first time students are often puzzled by the idea of determinism: that our thoughts and behaviour are influenced by forces beyond our control. Our everyday experience would seem to suggest that what we do and think is a matter of choice and within our conscious control (free will). Surely what you are wearing today, what you have eaten, and your decision to pick up this book were all choices you freely made!

Despite this, most psychologists accept the role of determinism in behaviour to some degree – though, as we shall see, there is disagreement surrounding the exact form this determinism might take.

KEY TERMS

Free will – The notion that humans can make choices and are not determined by biological or external forces.

Determinism – The view that an individual's behaviour is shaped or controlled by internal or external forces rather than an individual's will to do something.

Hard determinism – Implies that free will is not possible as our behaviour is always caused by internal or external events beyond our control.

Soft determinism – All events, including human behaviour, have causes, but behaviour can also be determined by our conscious choices in the absence of coercion. In contrast with hard determinism.

Biological determinism – The belief that behaviour is caused by biological (genetic, hormonal, evolutionary) influences that we cannot control.

Environmental determinism – The belief that behaviour is caused by features of the environment (such as systems of reward and punishment) that we cannot control.

Psychic determinism – The belief that behaviour is caused by unconscious conflicts that we cannot control.

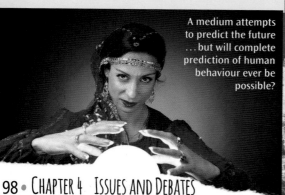

A medium attempts to predict the future …but will complete prediction of human behaviour ever be possible?

Free will and determinism

Free will

The notion of **free will** suggests that as human beings we are essentially self-determining and free to choose our thoughts and actions. A belief in free will does not deny that there may be biological and environmental forces that exert some influence on our behaviour, but nevertheless implies that we are able to reject these forces as the masters (or mistresses) of our own destiny. This is a view of human behaviour that is advocated by the **humanistic approach** (see Apply-it, facing page).

Determinism

In contrast **determinism** proposes that free will has no place in explaining behaviour, though there are hard and soft versions.

Hard determinism, sometimes referred to as *fatalism*, suggests that all human behaviour has a cause, and, in principle, it should be possible to identify and describe these causes. Such a position is compatible with the aims of **science** – to uncover the causal laws that govern thought and action (see below) – and always assumes that everything we think and do is dictated by internal or external forces that we cannot control. For some, however, this is too extreme a position.

Soft determinism The philosopher William James (1890) was the first to put forward the notion of soft determinism – a position that later became an important feature of the **cognitive approach**. Whilst acknowledging that all human action has a cause, soft determinists also suggest some *room* for *manoeuvre* in that people have conscious mental control over the way they behave. James thought that whilst it may be the job of scientists to explain the many determining forces that act upon us, this does not detract from the freedom we have to make rational conscious choices in everyday situations.

Biological, environmental and psychic determinism

Biological determinism The **biological approach** emphasises the role of biological determinism in behaviour. There is no doubt that many of our physiological and neurological (brain) processes are not under our conscious control – such as the influence of the **autonomic nervous system** during periods of stress and anxiety (see page 254). In addition, lots of behaviours and characteristics, such as mental disorders, are thought to have a **genetic basis** (see page 204), and research has demonstrated the effect of **hormones** – such as the role of **testosterone** in aggressive behaviour (see page 290). Modern biopsychologists would also recognise the mediating influence of the environment on our biological structures (see the **nature–nurture debate** – next spread) but this simply means we are 'doubly-determined' in ways that we cannot control.

Environmental determinism BF Skinner famously described free will as 'an illusion' and argued that all behaviour is the result of **conditioning**. Our experience of 'choice' is merely the sum total of **reinforcement** contingencies that have acted upon us throughout our lives. Although we might think we are acting independently, our behaviour has been shaped by environmental events, as well as *agents of socialisation* – parents, teachers, institutions, etc.

Psychic determinism Sigmund Freud, like Skinner, agreed that free will is an 'illusion' but placed much more emphasis on the influence of biological drives and instincts than the Behaviourists. His particular brand of determinism sees human behaviour as determined and directed by unconscious conflicts, repressed in childhood. There is no such thing as an accident, according to Freud, and even something as seemingly random and innocuous as a 'slip of the tongue' can be explained by the underlying authority of the unconscious.

The scientific emphasis on causal explanations

One of the basic principles of science is that every event in the universe has a cause and that causes can be explained using general laws. Knowledge of causes and the formulation of laws are important as they allow scientists to predict and control events in the future. For instance, in chemistry, it can be demonstrated how adding *X chemical* to *Y chemical* will result in *Z reaction* within the controlled environment of a test tube.

Hence, in psychology, the **laboratory experiment** enables researchers to simulate the conditions of the test tube and remove all other **extraneous variables** in an attempt to precisely control and predict human behaviour.

Apply it **Methods: The scientific approach**

In its search for causal laws, scientific psychology adopts a determinist approach to the study of human behaviour.

Questions

1. Explain why science is determinist. Refer to the features of science in your answer. *(8 marks)* (See page 82)

2. Explain why the idea of free will would seem to be incompatible with the aims of science. *(4 marks)*

Evaluation

Practical activity on page 108

Determinism – the case for …

As discussed, determinism is consistent with the aims of science. The notion that human behaviour is orderly and obeys laws places psychology on equal footing with other more established sciences. In addition, the value of such research is that the prediction and control of human behaviour has led to the development of treatments, therapies and behavioural interventions that have benefitted many – for instance, psychotherapeutic drug treatment in controlling and managing **schizophrenia**.

Indeed, the experience of mental disorders like schizophrenia (see page 202) where sufferers experience a total loss of control over their thoughts and behaviour casts doubt on the concept of free will (no-one would 'choose' to have schizophrenia). At least in terms of mental illness then, behaviour would appear to be determined.

…and the case against

The hard determinist stance – that individual choice is not the cause of behaviour – is not consistent with the way in which our legal system operates. In a court of law, offenders are held morally accountable for their actions (see right).

Also, despite its scientific credentials, determinism as an approach is **unfalsifiable**. It is based on the idea that causes of behaviour will always exist, even though they may not yet have been found. As a basic principle, this is impossible to prove wrong! This suggests that the determinist approach to human behaviour may not be as scientific as it first appears.

Free will – the case for …

Everyday experience 'gives the impression' that we are constantly exercising free will through the choices we make on any given day. This gives **face validity** to the concept of free will – it makes cognitive sense.

Also, research suggests that people who have an internal **locus of control**, believing that they have a high degree of influence over events and their own behaviour, tend to be more mentally healthy. A study by Roberts et al. (2000) demonstrated that adolescents with a strong belief in fatalism – that their lives were 'decided' by events outside of their control – were at significantly greater risk of developing **depression**.

This suggests that, even if we do not have free will, the fact that we think we do may have a positive impact on mind and behaviour.

…the case against

Neurological studies of decision making have revealed evidence against free will – and slightly disturbing evidence at that! Studies by Benjamin Libet (1985), and more recently Chun Siong Soon et al. (2008), have demonstrated that the brain activity that determines the outcome of simple choices may predate our knowledge of having made such a choice. The researchers found that the activity related to whether to press a button with the left or right hand occurs in the brain up to ten seconds before participants report being consciously aware of making such a decision.

This shows that even our most basic experiences of free will are decided and determined by our brain before we become aware of them. Now there's a thought to keep you awake at night.

Evaluation eXtra

A compromise…?

Typically, an interactionist position may provide us with the best compromise in the free will–determinism debate. Those approaches in psychology that have a cognitive element, such as **social learning theory**, are those which tend to adopt a 'soft determinist' position. For instance, Bandura argued that although environmental factors in learning are key, we are free to choose who or what to attend to and when to perform certain behaviours.

Consider: Bandura suggested 'reciprocal determinism' (discussed in the Year 1 book in the Approaches chapter). Explain how this idea is a compromise in the free will–determinism debate.

Apply it — Concepts: Free will and the law

Determinism is incompatible with our notions of legal responsibility, that criminals are held to be personally and morally accountable for their actions. Very few individuals would represent themselves in court by trying to appeal to a judge and jury that their offence was biologically, environmentally or psychically determined!

Only in extreme circumstances are juries instructed to act with greater leniency – for instance, when the *Law of Diminished Responsibility* is applied. This is comes into play when, for various reasons, a defendant is assumed to have not acted in accordance with their own free will; for example, in cases of *self-defence*, *mental illnesss* and so-called 'crimes of passion' (when a judgement of temporary insanity may be made).

Question

Having said that, there are precedents for the legal defence of biological determinism. Turn to page 329 and read about the cases of Stephen Mobley and Abdelmalek Bayout. What are the implications of these cases for the future of the legal system and our understanding of criminal responsibility?

STUDY TIP

Forensic psychology is one topic area that lends itself particularly well to the free will and determinism debate (however, you may not have studied this). Consider the explanations you have learned about in other topics, e.g. social influence, psychopathology, gender, addiction, etc. Where do they stand on this debate? Are these behaviours determined or acts of free will?

Left or right?
Your brain knows before you do …

Apply it — Concepts: Humanistic psychology and free will

The **humanistic approach** is one of the few to adopt a free will perspective on behaviour. The concept was central to Rogers' **client-centred therapy** in that people are seen as being free to effect change in their lives by choosing to see their situation differently. Having removed the psychological barriers that may be preventing personal growth, people are free to work towards their potential (**self-actualisation**).

Question

Explain why Rogers' approach to therapy illustrates his belief in free will. Refer to humanistic concepts such as **conditions of worth** and **congruence** in your answer.

CHECK IT

1. Briefly outline the free will and determinism debate in psychology. [3 marks]
2. Using an example, explain what is meant by *soft determinism*. [3 marks]
3. Briefly explain the concept of *biological determinism*. [2 marks]
4. Discuss the free will and determinism debate. Refer to **two** topics you have studied in psychology in your answer. [16 marks]

THE NATURE–NURTURE DEBATE

The nature-nurture debate: the relative importance of heredity and environment in determining behaviour; the interactionist approach.

The question of whether characteristics, such as personality, intelligence, abnormality, etc., are caused by innate influences (nature) or are the result of learning/environmental influences (nurture) has a long history in psychology. Recent research, however, has been more concerned with explanations of how nature and nurture interact, i.e. influence each other. Thus, a modern psychologist is more likely to ask: what is the relative contribution of nature and nurture on human behaviour?

KEY TERMS

The nature–nurture debate – Concerned with the extent to which aspects of behaviour are a product of inherited or acquired characteristics.

Heredity – The genetic transmission of mental and physical characteristics from one generation to another.

Environment – Any influence on human behaviour that is non-genetic. This may range from pre-natal influences in the womb through to cultural and historical influences at a societal level.

The interactionist approach – The idea that nature and nurture are linked to such an extent that it does not make sense to separate the two, so researchers instead study how they interact and influence each other.

Of course smoking is bad for you – but could it also be bad for your grandchildren?

Apply it

Concepts: The nature-nurture debate

The continuum from nature to nurture is illustrated on the right.

Question

Match the following approaches with the correct description on the continuum: the behaviourist approach, the cognitive approach, the biological approach, the psychodynamic approach, the humanistic approach.

The nature-nurture debate

The debate

The nature–nurture debate has a long history in psychology.

Nature Early nativists such as René Descartes (1596–1650) argued that human characteristics – and even some aspects of knowledge – are innate: the result of **heredity**. In contrast, **empiricists** including the philosopher John Locke (1632–1704) argued that the mind is a *blank slate* at birth upon which learning and experience writes: the result of the **environment** (a view that was later to become an important feature of the **behaviourist approach**).

The **heritability coefficient** is used to assess heredity. It is a numerical figure ranging from 0 to 1.0 which indicates the extent to which a characteristic has a **genetic** basis (with a value of 1 meaning it is entirely genetically determined). The general figure for heritability in **IQ** is around 0.5 across multiple studies in varying populations (Plomin 1994). This suggests that both genetics and the environment are important factors in intelligence.

Nurture The concept of nurture and environmental influences in psychology requires further clarification as 'the environment' is such a broad and all-encompassing concept. Helpfully, Richard Lerner (1986) has identified different *levels of the environment*. These may be defined in quite narrow pre-natal terms, for instance, the mother's physical and psychological state during pregnancy, or more generally through post-natal experiences such as the social conditions the child grows up in and the cultural and historical context they are a part of.

Relative importance of heredity and environment

In a practical sense, the nature-nurture question is impossible to answer because – as Lerner suggests – environmental influence in a child's life begins as soon as it is born (and perhaps even earlier). Nature and nurture are so closely intertwined that, practically and theoretically, it makes little sense to try to separate the two.

For instance, in twin studies it is often very difficult to tell whether high **concordance rates** are more the result of shared genetics or shared upbringing (see evaluation extra – facing page). As such, the focus of the nature-nurture debate has changed in recent years, and psychologists are now more likely to ask what the relative contribution of each influence is in terms of what we think and what we do.

The interactionist approach In our Year 1 book we have seen how attachment patterns between an infant and its parents are often the result of a 'two-way street' in which the child's innate temperament will influence the way its parents respond to it – and their responses will in turn affect the child's behaviour (Belsky and Rovine 1987). Thus, nature, in a real sense, *creates nurture*; heredity and environment interact.

Diathesis-stress model Models of mental illness which emphasise the interaction of nature and nurture tend to be the most persuasive. The diathesis-stress model suggests that psychopathology is caused by a biological/genetic vulnerability (the diathesis) which is only expressed when coupled with a biological or environmental 'trigger' (the stressor). Pikka Tienari et al. (2004) found that in a group of Finnish adoptees those most likely to develop **schizophrenia** had biological relatives with a history of the disorder (the vulnerability) and had relationships with their adoptive families that were defined as 'dysfunctional' (the trigger).

Epigenetics refers to a change in our genetic activity without changing our genetic code. It is a process that happens throughout life and is caused by interaction with the environment. Aspects of our lifestyle, and the events we encounter – from smoking and diet to pollution and war – leave epigenetic 'marks' on our DNA. These marks – like highlighted text, or bookmarks – tell our bodies which genes to ignore and which to use, and in turn, may go on and influence the genetic codes of our children, as well as their children. Epigenetics therefore introduces a third element into the nature–nurture debate: the life experience of previous generations.

Brian Dias and Kerry Ressler (2014) gave male lab mice electric shocks every time they were exposed to the smell of acetophenone, a chemical used in perfume. As any **behaviourist** would predict, the mice showed a fear reaction as soon as the scent was presented. Surprisingly, the rats' children also feared the smell – even though they had not been exposed to acetophenone before or received any shocks. So did their grandchildren.

Nature		Interactionist		Nurture
The focus is on heredity, hormones and chemicals, though the interaction with the environment is acknowledged.	Basic instinct drives such as sex and aggression drive behaviour but relationship with parents also important.	Innate information processing abilities are constantly refined by experience.	Accepts the influence of basic physiological needs but the focus is on the person's experience of their own environment.	The mind is a blank slate at birth. Behaviour is determined by learning experiences in the environment.

Evaluation

Implications of nativism and empiricism

Nativists suggest that 'anatomy is destiny' in that our inherited genetic make-up determines our characteristics and behaviour, whilst the environment has little input. This extreme **determinist** stance has led to controversy such as that which attempted to link race, genetics and intelligence (see the spread on 'socially sensitive research' page 106) and the application of **eugenics** policies (see 'Race and IQ controversy' on page 107).

In contrast – but also controversially – empiricists would suggest that any behaviour can be changed by altering environmental conditions. **Behaviour shaping**, a behaviourist concept, has had practical application in therapy. Desirable behaviours are selectively reinforced, and undesirable behaviours are punished or ignored. In extreme terms, this may lead one to advocate a model of society that controls and manipulates its citizens using these techniques.

Shared and unshared environments

Research attempting to 'tease out' the influence of the environment is complicated by the fact that even siblings raised within the same family may not have experienced exactly the same upbringing. The idea of *shared and unshared* environments, first introduced by Judy Dunn and Robert Plomin (1990), suggests that individual differences mean that siblings may experience life events differently. For example, age and/or temperament would mean that a life event such as parental divorce would have a different meaning to each sibling.

This would explain the finding that even **MZ** twins reared together do not show perfect concordance rates which supports the view that heredity and the environment cannot be meaningfully separated.

Constructivism

The notion that genes and environment interact is elaborated by **constructivism**. People create their own 'nurture' by actively selecting environments that are appropriate for their 'nature'. Thus, a naturally aggressive child is likely to feel more comfortable around children who show similar behaviours and will 'choose' their environment accordingly. This environment then affects their development.

Robert Plomin (1994) refers to this as *niche-picking* and *niche-building* – further evidence that it is impossible and illogical to try to separate nature and nurture influences on the child's behaviour.

Evaluation eXtra

Genotype–environment interaction

Sandra Scarr and Kathleen McCartney (1983) have put forward a theory of gene–environment interaction that includes three types. *Passive interaction* – the parents' genes influence the way they treat their children (musically gifted parents are likely to play to their children and encourage engagement with music). *Evocative interaction* – the child's genes influence and shape the environment in which they grow up (the musically talented child will be picked for school concerts and given other special opportunities). *Active interaction* – the child creates its own environment through the people and experiences it selects (the child itself chooses similar, musically talented friends and seeks out musical experiences).

Again, this points to a complex and multi-layered relationship between nature and nurture.

Consider: *Which of these types of interaction is most closely connected to Plomin's concepts of niche-picking and niche-building? Explain your answer.*

Relationship to other debates

As hinted at the top of this page, a strong commitment to either a nature *or* nurture position corresponds to a belief in **hard determinism**. The nativist perspective would suggest that 'anatomy is destiny' whilst empiricists would argue that interaction with the environment is all. This equates to **biological determinism** and **environmental determinism** respectively.

Consider: *How could nature–nurture be seen as less determinist? In what ways is constructivism (described above) similar to the idea of 'reciprocal determinism' (page 13)?*

Researchers Norman Nature and Neville Nurture wanted to see whether voting behaviour in a general election was genetically determined. They gathered together a sample of 10 twins. The researchers assumed that all the twins in the sample were identical (monozygotic) because they looked alike.

Each twin was interviewed and the political party they voted for in the 2015 General Election was recorded. It was found that half of the twin pairs in the sample voted for the same political party as their sibling, and the other half did not.

Nature and Nurture concluded that their investigation was strong evidence for the idea that voting behaviour has a genetic basis. The researchers wrote up their findings and submitted the completed article for **peer review**.

Question

Imagine you are the reviewer and the completed report has arrived on your desk. Discuss the methodological limitations of Nature and Nurture's investigation into the genetic basis of voting behaviour. *(8 marks)*

Apply it — **Concepts: 1984 and Walden Two**

George Orwell's novel *1984* (published in 1949) presents a chilling dystopian vision of the future (as it was then!) in which society is an authoritarian state controlled and manipulated by a malevolent force: 'Big Brother'. In 1948, BF Skinner's novel *Walden Two* was published which explores similar themes of social control. However, Skinner presented his society as a 'utopian' ideal in which human beings are reinforced and 'shaped' towards their potential.

Question

Despite their differences, how are both these books based on an **empiricist** approach to the nature-nurture debate?

CHECK IT

1. Explain what is meant by the term *heredity*. **[3 marks]**
2. Briefly outline the nature-nurture debate in psychology. **[3 marks]**
3. Using an example, explain what is meant by an *interactionist approach* in the nature-nurture debate. **[3 marks]**
4. Discuss the nature-nurture debate. Refer to **two** topics you have studied in psychology in your answer. **[16 marks]**

HOLISM AND REDUCTIONISM

Holism and reductionism: levels of explanation in psychology. Biological reductionism and environmental (stimulus-response) reductionism.

In attempting to understand how a car engine works are we best advised to look at the individual parts? Or to see the engine as a whole system – more than the sum of its parts?

The holism and reductionism debate is concerned with the *level* at which it is appropriate to explain human behaviour. Reductionist explanations try to break thought and action down into the smallest, simplest parts, whilst holistic explanations consider the whole person as an indivisible system.

KEY TERMS

Holism – An argument or theory which proposes that it only makes sense to study an indivisible system rather than its constituent parts (which is the reductionist approach).

Reductionism – The belief that human behaviour is best explained by breaking it down into smaller constituent parts.

Biological reductionism – A form of reductionism which attempts to explain social and psychological phenomena at a lower biological level (in terms of the actions of genes, hormones, etc.).

Environmental reductionism – The attempt to explain all behaviour in terms of stimulus-response links that have been learned through experience.

Sociology
Psychology
Biology
Chemistry
Physics

A reductionist hierarchy
Some researchers would suggest that those disciplines towards the top will eventually be replaced by those towards the bottom as our understanding of social and psychological phenomena increases.

Holism and reductionism

A group of German researchers working in the 1920s and 30s – known collectively as Gestalt psychologists – famously declared that 'the whole is greater than the sum of its parts'. This view is the basis of **holism** in psychology: the idea that any attempt to break up behaviour and experience is inappropriate as these can only be understood by analysing the person or behaviour as a whole. This is a view shared by **humanistic** psychologists who saw successful therapy as bringing together all aspects of the 'whole person'.

Reductionism, on the other hand, analyses behaviour by breaking it down into its constituent parts. It is based on the scientific principle of parsimony: that all phenomena should be explained using the most basic (lowest level) principles. This is often the simplest, easiest and most economical level of explanation.

Levels of explanation in psychology

The notion of 'levels of explanation' suggests that there are different ways of viewing the same phenomena in psychology – some more reductionist than others. For instance, **obsessive-compulsive disorder** (OCD) may be understood in a *socio-cultural context* as producing behaviour, such as repetitive hand washing, that most people would regard as odd or irrational; at a *psychological level*, as the experience of having obsessive thoughts; at a *physical level*, as a sequence of movements involved in washing one's hands; at a *physiological level*, as hypersensitivity of the **basal ganglia**; at a *neurochemical level*, as underproduction of **serotonin**. Which of these provides the 'best' explanation of OCD is a matter of debate, but each level is more reductionist than the one before.

Psychology itself can also be placed within a hierarchy of science (below left), with the more precise and 'micro' of these disciplines at the bottom, and the more general and 'macro' of these at the top. Researchers who favour reductionist accounts of behaviour would see psychology as ultimately being replaced by explanations derived from those sciences lower down in the hierarchy.

Biological reductionism

Biological reductionism is based on the premise that we are biological organisms made up of physiological structures and processes. Thus, all behaviour is at some level biological and so can be explained through neurochemical, neurophysiological, evolutionary and **genetic** influences.

This is the assumption of the **biological approach** and has been successfully applied to a number of different topic areas in psychology. For example, the effects of **psychoactive drugs** on the brain have contributed much to our understanding of neural processes and the fact that it might be possible to explain serious mental disorders such as OCD, **depression** and **schizophrenia** at a biochemical level.

Environmental (stimulus-response) reductionism

The **behaviourist approach** is built on **environmental reductionism**. As we saw in Year 1, behaviourists study observable behaviour only, and in doing so, break complex learning up into simple **stimulus-response** links that are measurable within the **laboratory**.

Thus, the key unit of analysis occurs at the *physical level* – the behaviourist approach does not concern itself with mental (**cognitive**) processes of the mind that occur at the *psychological level*. The mind is regarded as a 'black box' – irrelevant to our understanding of behaviour. The process of thought itself was seen by the early behaviourist John Watson as a form of 'sub-vocal' (silent) speech, characterised by physical movement, the same as any other behaviour.

Apply it

Concepts: The nine dot square

Join all nine dots using 4 straight lines without taking your pen off the paper.

Can you solve it? (clue: think outside the box)

Question

Explain why taking a 'holistic approach' to this puzzle is the best option.

Evaluation

The case for holism...

Often, there are aspects of social behaviour that only emerge within a group context and cannot be understood at the level of the individual group members. For instance, the effects of **conformity** to social roles and the **de-individuation** of the prisoners and guards in the Stanford prison experiment could not be understood by studying the participants as individuals, it was the interaction between people and the behaviour of the group that was important.

This shows that holistic/same level explanations provide a more complete and global understanding of behaviour than reductionist approaches.

...and the case against

Holistic explanations in psychology tend not to lend themselves to rigorous scientific testing and can become vague and speculative as they become more complex. For example, humanistic psychology, which takes a holistic approach to behaviour, tends to be criticised for its lack of empirical evidence, and is instead seen by many as a rather loose set of concepts.

Higher level explanations that combine many different perspectives present researchers with a practical dilemma: if we accept that there are many factors that contribute to say, depression, it becomes difficult to establish which is most influential and which one to use, for example, as a basis for therapy.

This suggests, when it comes to finding solutions for real-world problems, lower level explanations may be more appropriate.

The case for reductionism...

A reductionist approach often forms the basis of scientific research. In order to create **operationalised** variables it is necessary to break target behaviours down into constituent parts. This makes it possible to conduct experiments or record observations (**behavioural categories**) in a way that is meaningful and reliable. Also, as we have seen, the behaviourist approach was able to demonstrate how complex learning could be broken down to simple stimulus-response links within the lab.

This gives psychology greater credibility, placing it on equal terms with the natural sciences lower down in the reductionist hierarchy.

...and the case against

Reductionist approaches have been accused of oversimplifying complex phenomena leading to a loss of **validity**. Explanations that operate at the level of the **gene**, **neurotransmitter** or **neuron** do not include an analysis of the social context within which behaviour occurs – and this is where the behaviour in question may derive its meaning. For instance, the physiological processes involved in pointing one's finger will be the same regardless of the context. However, an analysis of these will not tell us *why* the finger is pointed – to draw attention to some object or person, as an act of aggression, as part of a raised hand to answer a question in class, etc.

This means that reductionist explanations can only ever form part of an explanation.

Evaluation eXtra

The interactionist approach

Another alternative to reductionism, which is subtly different to holism, is the **interactionist** stance. Whereas holism is more concerned with higher level explanations of behaviour, such as the behaviour of individuals within a group, interactionism considers how different levels of explanation may combine and interact. An example of the interactionist approach is the **diathesis-stress model** which has been used to explain the onset of mental disorders such as schizophrenia and depression. Such disorders are seen to come about as the result of a predisposition (often genetic) which is 'triggered' by some stressor (often an experience). This model has led to a more multidisciplinary and 'holistic' approach to treatment – combining drugs and family therapy, for instance – and is associated with lower relapse rates (see the study by Tarrier *et al.* on page 213).

Consider: *Describe one study that supports the diathesis-stress model explanation of mental illness.*

Methods: Insight learning – holism in action

Wolfgang Köhler (1925) set hungry chimpanzees a puzzle. A banana and stick were placed outside of a chimpanzee's cage with the stick positioned within reach but the banana was out of reach. Typically the chimpanzee first tried to grasp the banana and failed. There was then a pause in activity and shortly afterwards the chimpanzee, using a seemingly planned and coordinated sequence of actions, grabbed the stick and used it to rake in the banana.

It was as if, in leaving the scene momentarily, the chimpanzee had had a 'eureka' moment in which the solution to the problem had become clear 'in a flash'. There are examples of this in the human world when the solution to a puzzle, problem or issue suddenly appears to us in a flash of inspiration.

Such insight learning can only occur when all the elements of a problem (arm, stick, banana, distance), and the inter-relationship between them, are understood as a meaningful whole.

Questions

1. Explain how the behavioural category 'insight learning' was operationalised in the investigation above. (*2 marks*)
2. Explain why insight learning cannot be explained by behaviourist S-R connections or reinforcement. (*3 marks*)
3. Evaluate the use of **controlled observations** in psychology with reference to Kohler's study above. (*4 marks*)

Monkey puzzle: one of Kohler's chimps has a eureka moment.

Apply it   Concepts: Paralysing the vocal cords

In a bizarre attempt to challenge Watson's idea of thought as 'sub-vocal speech' (see facing page), a Dr Scott Smith (Smith *et al.* 1947) ingested curare (a form of poison) causing all his muscles to become paralysed. If thinking is merely sub-vocal speech, then preventing any speech movements at all, even minute ones, should make it impossible to think. Smith was kept alive using an artificial oxygen supply (as curare prevents breathing) but was still able to recall and solve a series of cognitive puzzles that were presented to him whilst he was in a state of paralysis!

Question

Explain why this contradicts Watson's theory of thought as sub-vocal speech.

CHECK IT

1. Briefly outline the holism–reductionism debate in psychology. *[3 marks]*
2. Using an example, explain what is meant by *levels of explanation* in psychology. *[4 marks]*
3. Using an example of a topic you have studied in psychology, distinguish between *biological reductionism* and *environmental reductionism*. *[5 marks]*
4. Discuss the holism-reductionism debate. Refer to **one** topic you have studied in psychology in your answer. *[16 marks]*

Idiographic and nomothetic approaches to psychological investigation.

Should psychology focus its attention on people in general or the individual? Should the aim of psychological enquiry be to produce *generalities* against which people can be compared and measured? Or should psychology concern itself with what makes people *unique*; the *specific* rather than the general?

These issues are central to the question of whether an idiographic or nomothetic approach should be adopted when investigating human behaviour, and this also has implications for the types of *research method* psychologists use. That said, there is also a sense in which these two approaches *overlap* and both may have their place within a scientific study of the person.

KEY TERMS

Idiographic approach – Derived from the Greek 'idios' meaning 'private or personal'. An approach to research that focuses more on the individual case as a means of understanding behaviour, rather than aiming to formulate general laws of behaviour (the nomothetic approach).

Nomothetic approach – Derived from the Greek 'nomos' meaning 'law'. The nomothetic approach attempts to study human behaviour through the development of general principles and universal laws.

STUDY TIP

As part of this spread, there are several examples of the nomothetic approach and the idiographic approach, as well as examples of topics where both approaches may be used. This does not mean, however, that you cannot discuss your own examples by drawing on the topic areas you have studied.

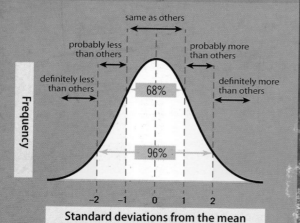

A **normal distribution** or 'bell curve' allows individuals to be plotted along particular dimensions (that measure IQ, extraversion, etc.) to see how they compare with the general population – a key feature of the nomothetic approach in psychology.

Idiographic and nomothetic approaches

The idiographic approach

The **Idiographic approach** in psychology attempts to describe the nature of the individual. People are studied as unique entities, each with their own subjective experiences, motivations and values. There may be no attempt made to compare these to a larger group, standard or norm.

The idiographic approach is generally associated with those methods in psychology that produce **qualitative data**, such as **case studies**, **unstructured interviews** and other **self-report** measures. This reflects one of the central aims of idiographic research: to describe the richness of human experience and gain insight into the person's unique way of viewing the world.

The nomothetic approach

The main aim of the **nomothetic approach** is to produce general laws of human behaviour. These provide a 'benchmark' against which people can be compared, classified and measured, and on the basis of which, likely future behaviour can be predicted and/or controlled.

The nomothetic approach is most closely aligned with those methods that would be regarded as 'scientific' within psychology such as **experiments**. These involve the study of large numbers of people in order to establish ways in which people are *similar* (which will, conversely, also inform us of the ways in which people are *different* from one another).

Examples of the idiographic approach in psychology

Of the approaches you have studied, **humanistic psychology** is probably the best example of the idiographic perspective. Carl Rogers and Abraham Maslow took a *phenomenological approach* to the study of human beings and were interested only in documenting the conscious experience of the individual or 'self'. In describing themselves as 'anti-scientific', humanistic psychologists were more concerned with investigating unique experience 'on its own merits' than producing general laws of behaviour.

The **psychodynamic approach** is often labelled 'idiographic' because of Sigmund Freud's use of the case study method when detailing the lives of his patients. However, Freud also assumed he had identified *universal laws* of behaviour and personality development (which is more akin to a nomothetic approach).

Examples of the nomothetic approach in psychology

The nomothetic approach tends to be a feature of those approaches that are **reductionist**, **determinist** and employ scientific methods of investigation. **Hypotheses** are formulated, tested under controlled conditions and findings generated from large numbers of people (or animals) are analysed for their **statistical significance** (see page 72).

Much of the research conducted by **behaviourist**, **cognitive** and **biological** psychologists would meet the criteria of the nomothetic approach. For example Skinner and the behaviourists studied the responses of hundreds of rats, cats, pigeons, etc., in order to develop the laws of learning; cognitive psychologists have been able to infer the structure and processes of human memory (see Miller's Law – facing page) by measuring the performance of large samples of people in laboratory tests; biological psychologists have conducted **brain scans** on countless human brains (as well as the people who own them!) in order to make generalisations about **localisation** of function (see page 38). In each of these cases, hypotheses are rigorously tested, statistically analysed, and general laws and principles are proposed and developed – all of which are key features of the nomothetic approach.

Apply it · Concepts: Three types of general law

According to John Radford and Richard Kirby (1975) applications of the nomothetic approach in psychology have produced three broad types of general law:

- *Classifying people into groups* – for example, the **Diagnostic Manual of Mental Disorders (DSM-5)** classifies people suffering from psychological disorders.

- *Establishing principles of behaviour* that can be applied to people in general, for example, findings from conformity studies.

- *Establishing dimensions* along which people can be placed and compared, for instance, **IQ** scores.

Question

Look back over your notes from Year 1 and the topics you have studied in Year 2. Can you identify further examples of each of the three types of general law described above?

Evaluation

The case for the idiographic approach...

The idiographic approach, with its in-depth qualitative methods of investigation, provides a complete and global account of the individual. This may complement the nomothetic approach by shedding further light on general laws or indeed by challenging such laws.

For example, a single case may generate hypotheses for further study (see the case of HM – right). It is also true that in the case of brain-damaged individuals, like HM, findings may reveal important insights about normal functioning which may contribute to our overall understanding.

...and the case against

On the other hand, supporters of the idiographic approach must still recognise the narrow and restricted nature of their work.

One of the criticisms levelled at Freud is that many of his key concepts, like the **Oedipus complex**, were largely developed from the detailed study of a single case (Little Hans). Meaningful generalisations cannot be made *without* further examples, as there is no adequate baseline with which to compare behaviour.

Also, methods associated with the idiographic approach, such as case studies, tend to be the least scientific in that conclusions often rely on the subjective interpretation of the researcher and, as such, are open to bias.

The case for the nomothetic approach...

The processes involved in nomothetic research tend to be more scientific, mirroring those employed within the natural sciences – testing under **standardised** conditions, using data sets that provide group averages, statistical analysis, prediction and control, for example in the field of IQ testing.

Such processes have enabled psychologists to establish norms of 'typical' behaviour (such as the average IQ of 100), arguably giving the discipline of psychology greater scientific credibility.

...and the case against

The preoccupation within the nomothetic approach on general laws, prediction and control has been accused of 'losing the whole person' within psychology. Knowing that there is a 1% lifetime risk of developing **schizophrenia** tells us little about what life is like for someone who is suffering from the disorder.

Similarly, in lab studies involving tests of, say, memory, participants are treated as a series of *scores* rather than individual *people* and their subjective experience of the situation is ignored.

This means, in its search for generalities, the nomothetic approach may sometimes overlook the richness of human experience.

Evaluation eXtra

Complementary rather than contradictory

Rather than seeing idiographic and nomothetic approaches as mutually exclusive 'either/or' alternatives, it is possible to consider the same issue or topic from *both* perspectives, depending on the nature of the research question. Thus, in research on gender development, there are attempts to establish general patterns of behaviour (e.g. Sandra Bem's **androgyny** scale, see page 150) sitting alongside case study examples of atypical development (e.g. the case of David Reimer, see page 153).

Contemporary understanding of the two terms, originally introduced by Wilhelm Windelband has converged. The goal of modern psychology is to provide rich, detailed descriptions of human behaviour as well as the explanation of such behaviour within the framework of general laws.

Consider: *Return to the Year 1 topics you studied. Can you find examples of the idiographic and nomothetic approach within* **attachment** *research?*

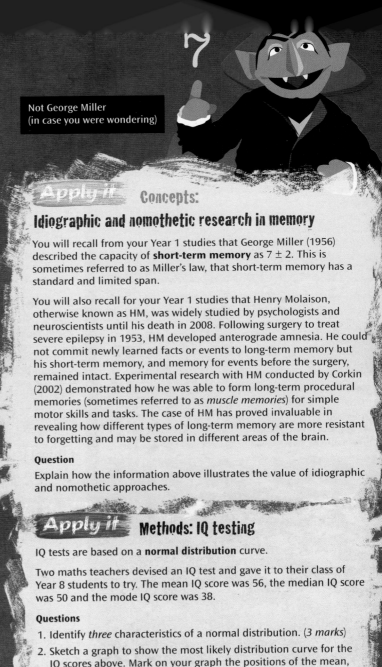

Not George Miller (in case you were wondering)

Apply it — Concepts:
Idiographic and nomothetic research in memory

You will recall from your Year 1 studies that George Miller (1956) described the capacity of **short-term memory** as 7 ± 2. This is sometimes referred to as Miller's law, that short-term memory has a standard and limited span.

You will also recall for your Year 1 studies that Henry Molaison, otherwise known as HM, was widely studied by psychologists and neuroscientists until his death in 2008. Following surgery to treat severe epilepsy in 1953, HM developed anterograde amnesia. He could not commit newly learned facts or events to long-term memory but his short-term memory, and memory for events before the surgery, remained intact. Experimental research with HM conducted by Corkin (2002) demonstrated how he was able to form long-term procedural memories (sometimes referred to as *muscle memories*) for simple motor skills and tasks. The case of HM has proved invaluable in revealing how different types of long-term memory are more resistant to forgetting and may be stored in different areas of the brain.

Question

Explain how the information above illustrates the value of idiographic and nomothetic approaches.

Apply it — Methods: IQ testing

IQ tests are based on a **normal distribution** curve.

Two maths teachers devised an IQ test and gave it to their class of Year 8 students to try. The mean IQ score was 56, the median IQ score was 50 and the mode IQ score was 38.

Questions

1. Identify *three* characteristics of a normal distribution. (*3 marks*)
2. Sketch a graph to show the most likely distribution curve for the IQ scores above. Mark on your graph the positions of the mean, median and mode. (*3 marks*)
3. What sort of distribution does your graph show? (*1 mark*)
4. How might the maths teachers have adjusted their test to produce a more normal distribution of scores? (*3 marks*)
5. Explain how the maths teachers could assess the reliability **and** validity of their IQ test. (*6 marks*)

CHECK IT

1. Using an example, explain what is meant by the *nomothetic approach* in psychology. [3 marks]
2. Using an example, explain what is meant by the *idiographic approach* in psychology. [3 marks]
3. Briefly discuss **one** strength of the nomothetic approach in psychology. [4 marks]
4. Discuss idiographic and nomothetic approaches in psychology. Refer to **two** topics you have studied in your answer. [16 marks]

ETHICAL IMPLICATIONS OF RESEARCH STUDIES AND THEORY

THE SPECIFICATION SAYS...

Ethical implications of research studies and theory, including reference to social sensitivity.

Psychological research does not occur in a vacuum – indeed, it may have a real impact on the lives of those studied and other similar groups that the participants represent. Here, we discuss the wider implications of psychological research – with reference to some cautionary lessons from the past – and consider whether research that may affect 'vulnerable' groups is worthwhile.

KEY TERMS

Ethical implications – The impact that psychological research may have in terms of the rights of other people especially participants. This includes, at a societal level, influencing public policy and/or the way in which certain groups of people are regarded.

Social sensitivity – Sieber and Stanley (1988) define socially sensitive research as, *'studies in which there are potential consequences or implications, either directly for the participants in the research or for the class of individuals represented by the research'*.

How valid was the evidence that led to the 11+ test being introduced?

Ethical implications of research studies and theory

Ethical implications

We have seen how **ethical issues** may arise when there is a conflict between psychology's need to gain **valid** and valuable research findings whilst, at the same time, preserving the rights and dignity of participants. Thus, **ethical guidelines** were established to help protect those involved in research. What may be more difficult to guard against, however, is the social impact of psychological research once it has been conducted.

Although researchers may exercise considerable control over the methods they select and the way they treat participants, they may have relatively little say in terms of how their research findings are represented (or misrepresented) in the media, the impact of their work on public policy, and how it may influence our perception of particular groups in society. This amounts to a concern with the wider **ethical implications** of research.

Socially sensitive research

Clearly, some areas of research are likely to be more controversial, and be subject to greater **social sensitivity**, than others. A study that examines the cognitive processes involved in long-term memory, for instance, is unlikely to have far-reaching consequences for those that take part or for the broader social groups the participants represent. Research investigating the **genetic** basis of criminality on the other hand, might. Studies that tackle socially sensitive 'taboo' topics, such as aspects of race or sexuality, also attract a good deal of attention; not merely from other psychologists but also from the media and the public at large.

However, just because this is the case, it should not lead to psychologists 'shying away' from research that may be socially sensitive. In fact, because of the undoubted importance of such research, psychologists may have a social responsibility to carry it out (Aronson 1999).

Ethical issues in socially sensitive research

Joan Sieber and Liz Stanley (1988) have identified a number of concerns that researchers should be mindful of when conducting socially sensitive research:

- *Implications* – The wider effects of such research should be carefully considered as some studies may be seen as giving 'scientific' credence to prejudice and discrimination, such as studies examining the racial basis of intelligence (see facing page). However, the implications of research may be difficult to predict at the outset.

- *Uses/public policy* – What is the research likely to be used for? And what would happen if it was used for the wrong purpose? This is related to the idea that findings may be adopted by the government for political ends or to shape public policy (see 'Apply it' below).

- *The validity of the research* – Some findings that were presented as objective and value-free in the past have actually turned out to be highly suspect, and in some cases, fraudulent (see Burt's research on **IQ** below). However, many modern **social constructionist** researchers – who may tackle socially sensitive areas of research – are much more up-front about their own biases and preconceptions, and include comment on the **reflexive** nature of their work in their publications (page 65).

Apply it Concepts: Research that influenced public policy: Burt and Bowlby

Cyril Burt was influential in establishing the 11+ examination in the UK, which was used to determine whether children had a secondary modern education or went on to study at grammar school (a decision which arguably had a significant impact on their subsequent life chances). Burt's views were based on the evidence he produced that intelligence was genetic, citing studies of twins that showed a **heritability coefficient** of .77 (Burt 1955).

Discrepancies in his 'data' later revealed that Burt had made much of it up, as well as inventing two research assistants, and he was publically discredited. The 11+ however, and the idea that children should be separated on the basis of their 'natural' intelligence, remained for a good few years afterwards and still lingers.

John Bowlby's research into **attachment** and **maternal deprivation** (see Year 1 book) saw him become an adviser for the World Health Organisation in the early 1950s. Bowlby's argument, that mother love in infancy is as

important for mental health as vitamins are for physical health, influenced the way in which at least a generation of children were raised. It may have also influenced the UK government's decision not to offer free child care places to children under five (despite the fact that this is typical in other European countries). Finally, Bowlby's work could have had an indirect effect on the legal 'norm' that mothers are granted custody of the children in divorce and separation cases (whereas, previously, it was invariably given to fathers).

Questions

1. What were the ethical implications of Burt's work?

2. How does the case of Burt illustrate the importance of the *peer review* process in psychology?

3. Why do you think feminist writers were so critical of Bowlby's work and its wider ethical implications – particularly the view that day care could be damaging for a child?

Evaluation

Benefits of socially sensitive research

Despite the ethical implications associated with research into controversial and 'taboo' topics, Sandra Scarr (1988) argues that studies of underrepresented groups and issues may promote a greater sensitivity and understanding of these. This can help reduce prejudice and encourage acceptance.

Similarly, socially sensitive research has benefitted society – for instance, research into the (un)reliability of **eyewitness testimony** has reduced the risk of miscarriages of justice within the legal system. This suggests that socially sensitive research may play a valuable role in society.

Framing the question

Sieber and Stanley (1988) warn that the way in which research questions are phrased and investigated may influence the way in which findings are interpreted. We saw earlier in the chapter how **cross-cultural research** may be blighted by cultural superiority and **ethnocentrism** on the part of the researchers.

Also, Celia Kitzinger and Adrian Coyle (1995) note how research into so-called 'alternative relationships' has been guilty of a form of 'heterosexual bias' within which homosexual relationships were compared and judged against heterosexual norms.

This suggests that investigators must approach their research with an 'open mind' and be prepared to have their preconceptions challenged if they are to avoid misrepresenting minority groups.

Who gains?

Socially sensitive research has been used by the government and other institutions to shape social policy, despite the sometimes dubious nature of its findings (e.g. Burt's research into IQ) and without full consideration of the moderating effects of the environment on characteristics such as intelligence.

There is other research that may seem harmless but also has socially sensitive consequences. For example, in the 1950s, research into the persuasive effects of *subliminal messages* was used by marketing companies to advertise their products. One study claimed that sales of Coca-Cola and popcorn increased **significantly** when images of these were flashed up on cinema screens too quickly for audiences to be aware of them. It was later revealed that the author of the study, Vance Packard (1957), had made his findings up!

Although there was little damage done in this context, research that seeks to manipulate the public has obvious ethical implications. It also raises the issue of who benefits from such research – which may be particularly difficult to manage once the research is 'out there'.

Evaluation eXtra

Social control

In America in the 1920s and 30s, a large number of US states enacted legislation that led to the compulsory sterilisation of many citizens on the grounds that they were 'feeble-minded' and a drain on society. This included people deemed to be of low intelligence, drug or alcohol addicts and the mentally ill. The rationale, supported by many sections of the scientific and psychological community at the time, was that such feeble-minded people were 'unfit' to breed. The fact that socially sensitive research (such as that conducted by Goddard at the top of the page) has been used to 'prop up' discriminatory practices in the past is an argument against its widespread adoption.

Consider: *How does this tie in with Stephen Gould's idea of scientific racism (see 'Apply-It' above right)?*

Costs and benefits

In Year 1 we saw how research that carries with it possible ethical implications, or is socially sensitive, may be subject to scrutiny by an **Ethics committee** – and it is their job to weigh the potential costs against the possible benefits of the research. However, we have already seen that some of the social consequences of research involving vulnerable groups may be difficult to anticipate. As such, assessments of the 'worth' of such research are invariably subjective, and the real impact of research can only ever be known once it has been made public.

Consider: *Which specific ethical implications of socially sensitive research may be particularly difficult to predict?*

Apply it

Concepts: The race and IQ controversy

Henry Goddard (1917) issued **IQ** tests to immigrants as they arrived in the US and went on to claim that his findings demonstrated how the majority of Russians, Jews, Hungarians and Italians were 'feeble-minded' (though he failed to point out that many of the tests he set required an understanding of English). Fifty years later, William Shockley (1952) sparked controversy by claiming there might be genetic reasons that black people in America tended to score lower on IQ tests than whites. In 1969, Arthur Jensen published a long article with the suggestion that compensatory education for ethnic minorities had failed to that date because of genetic group differences. Finally, the 1994 book *The Bell Curve* by Richard Herrnstein and Charles Murray reignited the debate by claiming that intelligence and race were linked.

In his 1996 book *The Mismeasure of Man* (the second edition of which was published in response to *The Bell Curve*), Stephen Gould criticised research on race and intelligence on account of its **scientific racism**. His argument was that intelligence is not a measurable entity and researchers often fail to acknowledge the in-built **cultural bias** in IQ tests. In addition the attempt to link race and IQ is a form of **biological determinism** that has been used, over the years, to justify social inequality and oppression.

Questions

1. Why might research into race and intelligence be socially sensitive?
2. What ethical implications might there be for the groups studied?

Apply it **Methods: Gender identity disorder**

A psychologist has decided to study a group of teenagers who have been diagnosed with **gender identity disorder** (see page 166). The researcher will conduct **observations** and **interviews** with the teenagers for a year before publishing her findings.

Questions

1. Explain why the proposed research might be considered to be 'socially sensitive'. (*4 marks*)
2. What ethical implications might the research have and how might the psychologist deal with these? (*6 marks*)
3. Evaluate the use of the observational method in psychology. Refer to the study described above in your answer. (*5 marks*)

Could you be manipulated into buying this if the image was 'read' by your unconscious?

If you were, would that be 'ethical'?

CHECK IT

1. Outline **one** ethical implication of psychological research. [*3 marks*]
2. Explain how **one** example of research could be considered *socially sensitive*. [*4 marks*]
3. Discuss ethical implications of research studies and theory, including reference to social sensitivity. [*16 marks*]

PRACTICAL CORNER

THE SPECIFICATION SAYS...

> Knowledge and understanding of ... research methods, practical research skills and maths skills. These should be developed through ... ethical practical research activities.

This means it is important to conduct practical investigations wherever possible. First up, a questionnaire to investigate whether there is a gender difference in students' views on free will and determinism.

Secondly, are students' choices of A level subjects more influenced by their friends or their family? This might lead to some tentative conclusions about whether academic interests are more influenced by nature or nurture.

Ethics check

We suggest strongly that you complete this checklist before starting:

1. Do participants know participation is voluntary?
2. Do participants know what to expect?
3. Do participants know they can withdraw at any time?
4. Are individuals' results anonymous?
5. Have I minimised the risk of distress to participants?
6. Have I avoided asking sensitive questions?
7. Will I avoid bringing my school/teacher/psychology into disrepute?
8. Have I considered all other ethical issues?
9. Has my teacher approved this?

DREAM ON, BUDDY.

PAVLOV'S CAT   VELEY

Leaving aside the debate about whether cats have free will, do males and females think they have?

Practical idea 1: Gender and free will

The aim of this study is to investigate whether there is a gender difference in students' experience of **free will**. Research (e.g. Sherman and McConnell 1995) suggests that females are more likely to have an external locus of control than males, and this may equate to a belief in fatalism (**determinism**) rather than free will.

Will survey data reveal a difference in the judgements between males and females when presented with a number of everyday situations?

The practical bit

The **hypothesis** is that females have a lower control score than males in everyday situations.

To assess this you will need to construct a **questionnaire** that examines how much choice/control people think they have in various situations. In each case, a numerical scale should be included so that respondents are able to indicate their opinion on each of the items they are presented with. Some examples to help you are included below:

Indicate to what extent you think the following are under your own control (free will) or influenced by factors beyond your control.

1 = totally free will; 10 = totally determined by factors you cannot control.

		Rating you give
a	The grades you will get in your A levels.	
b	The career you will pursue.	
c	Whether or not you will get married.	
d	Whether or not you will lose your temper this week.	
e	Whether or not you will be happy.	

Of course you may not want to use these examples, or you may want to include some of them alongside others of your own. You might want to focus on situations, events and behaviours that occur regularly (as in question d above) or situations that are more long term (as in the other four questions above). What you choose to focus on is entirely up to you but you must ensure that your questions/items are clear and unambiguous, are not **leading questions** and are relevant in terms of the debate.

Choosing your sample

You will need to consider a suitable **sampling technique** for this investigation. It is not essential that an equal number of males and females complete the questionnaire if you intend to work out an average score for each gender. However, the age of participants might be something you want to control as views on this issue may vary with age. In terms of the number of respondents, the more the merrier, and this will improve the representative nature of your sample.

Ethical issues

As long as you conduct the investigation appropriately there should be very few **ethical** issues here. It is important to stress the **anonymity** of participants' responses, not least because this may limit the number of **socially desirable** answers they are inclined to give.

Analysing your results

Totalling up the scores for each respondent will allow you to work out the difference in **median** scores between males and females across the whole questionnaire. However, it might also be interesting to analyse the difference within individual items to see in which situations males and females agree – or disagree – most.

Apply it   Methods: The maths bit 1

1. Why is the median the most suitable measure of central tendency when summarising the difference in males' and females' views on free will and **determinism**? (*2 marks*)

2. Investigating whether there is a gender difference in views of free will and determinism is a **quasi-experiment**. Explain why this investigation is a quasi-experiment. (*2 marks*)

3. Which **statistical test** would be most appropriate to calculate the difference in males' and females' views on free will and determinism? Explain *two* reasons for your answer. (*3 marks*) (See page 70)

4. Explain *one* conclusion that can be drawn from the data in the table on the right. (*2 marks*)

5. Explain *two* ways in which the **validity** of the free will and determinism questionnaire could be assessed. (*4 marks*) (See page 68)

	Males	Females
Median	34	32.5
Range	18	16

Table to show the median scores on the free will and determinism questionnaire and the range for males and females.

Practical idea 2: Nature or nurture

The aim of this study is to see whether students' choices of A level subjects are more influenced by their family or their friends.

Is a student's programme of A level subjects more reflective of their family's choices (potentially suggesting an inherited predisposition) or the choice of their friends (suggesting an environmental influence)?

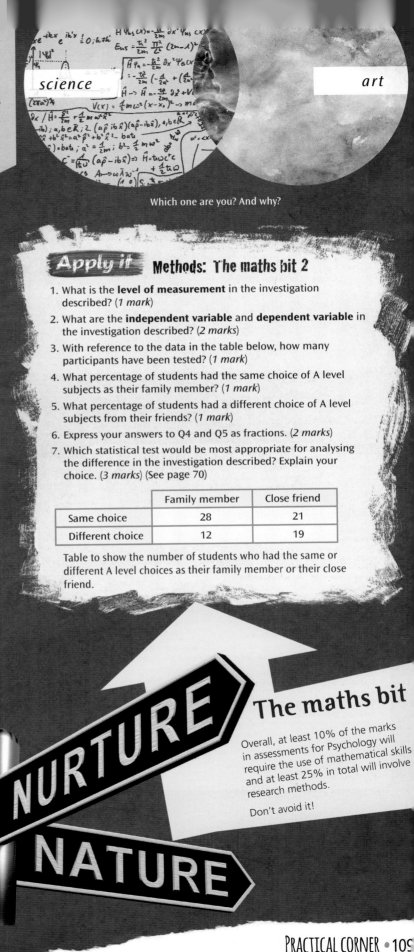

science

art

Which one are you? And why?

The theory bit

Where do our interests and talents come from? Are they genetically determined or a product of our environment? Most researchers in psychology would take an **interactionist** stance on this debate (see page 100), claiming that **nature** and **nurture** influences are so intertwined that they cannot be logically separated. Nevertheless, it might be interesting to see whether students' choices of A level subjects have more in common with their family or their friends. Similarity in A level choices between students and their family members might imply a nature influence, whilst similarity between students and their friends might suggest nurture is the key deciding influence.

Selecting a sample

Some careful thought is required here. Finding students with friends is the easy part! Finding students who have members of their immediate family who have taken A levels at some point might be slightly more difficult. Thus, the first question to ask potential participants is whether they have older siblings or parents who have sat A level exams in the past (just one family member will do). Having recorded the relevant data, you should then move on to the participant's closest friend (and again, you only need to ask one friend to make the process of analysis more straightforward).

Your sample is necessarily an **opportunity sample** based on the outcome of this initial conversation. Once you have found a suitable participant who has both a family member and a friend who has studied A levels, and assuming they are happy to take part, you can proceed with the investigation.

Operationalising subject choice

For ease of recording and analysis, the variable 'A level subject choice' needs to be **operationalised** in as simple a way as possible. How you might want to do this is up to you but the easiest way is to categorise each student in terms of whether they are following an 'arts' or 'sciences' programme. To do this, you will need to draw up a list of A level subjects and divide them using these two categories. Some subjects might be difficult to classify; for instance, psychology used to be classed as an 'arts' subject by some universities, now it's usually thought of as a 'science'. If you are in any doubt you might want to ask other people for their opinion (and perhaps include some teachers in this).

Once you have divided up your list of subjects, you can then categorise each student in terms of whether they are predominantly studying 'arts' or 'sciences'. Those students who are taking an equal number of art and science subjects might be best disregarded! You should repeat this exercise for one of the student's close friends and one of their family members. The crucial question is whether the student's choice of A levels (as 'arts' or 'sciences') is the same or different as their friend and family member's choice.

Problems of interpretation

Whatever the result of this investigation, findings should be treated with caution. Even if it turns out, for instance, that there are significantly more students whose A levels match those of their family member than their friend, this may not necessarily be good evidence for nature over nurture. Can you think why?

Apply it — Methods: The maths bit 2

1. What is the **level of measurement** in the investigation described? (*1 mark*)
2. What are the **independent variable** and **dependent variable** in the investigation described? (*2 marks*)
3. With reference to the data in the table below, how many participants have been tested? (*1 mark*)
4. What percentage of students had the same choice of A level subjects as their family member? (*1 mark*)
5. What percentage of students had a different choice of A level subjects from their friends? (*1 mark*)
6. Express your answers to Q4 and Q5 as fractions. (*2 marks*)
7. Which statistical test would be most appropriate for analysing the difference in the investigation described? Explain your choice. (*3 marks*) (See page 70)

	Family member	Close friend
Same choice	28	21
Different choice	12	19

Table to show the number of students who had the same or different A level choices as their family member or their close friend.

The maths bit

Overall, at least 10% of the marks in assessments for Psychology will require the use of mathematical skills and at least 25% in total will involve research methods.

Don't avoid it!

NURTURE

NATURE

Revision summaries

Gender bias

Predominance of male psychologists has led to biased theories based on a male perspective.

Gender bias

Universality and bias
Bias may be an inevitable part of the research process.

Gender bias: alpha bias
Exaggerates differences between the sexes, e.g. sociobiological theory.

Gender bias: beta bias
Minimises differences between the sexes, e.g. Kohlberg's theory and fight/flight.

Androcentrism
Normal behaviour is judged from the male standard, e.g. female aggression explained by PMS.

Evaluation

Implications of gender bias
May validate stereotypes and discrimination, e.g. research into PMS.

Sexism within the research process
Research questions oriented to male concerns.
Preference for results showing gender differences.
Lab experiment disadvantages women.

Reflexivity
Being 'up-front' about one's biases and preconceptions can reduce gender bias (Dambrin and Lambert).

Essentialism
Gender differences presented as 'fixed' in nature, often politically motivated.

Feminist psychology
Worrell proposes that research should be collaborative and in context.

Cultural bias

Psychology is mainly the study of white American male students.

Cultural bias

Universality and bias (revisited)
Mainstream psychology has generally ignored cultural differences.

Ethnocentrism
When one's own culture is seen as the 'norm' or 'standard', e.g. Ainsworth's ideal attachment type.

Cultural relativism
Berry suggested that psychology has taken an etic approach (e.g. Ainsworth) and should be emic (acknowledging cultural relativism).

Evaluation

Individualism–collectivism
Distinction may be too simple.
May no longer apply; Takano and Osaka found no evidence.

Cultural relativism versus universality
It should not be assumed that all human behaviours are culturally specific, there are some universals – such as aspects of attachment and the facial expression of emotion.

Unfamiliarity with research tradition
Demand characteristics are more likely in an unfamiliar situation.

Operationalisation of variables
Some behaviours may not be expressed in the same way, e.g. displays of aggression may be culturally relative.

Challenging implicit assumptions
Researcher's own cultural views may be challenged. Taken-for-granted assumptions may not be universal.

Free will and determinism

Are we in control of our thoughts and behaviour?

Free will and determinism

Free will
Human beings are self-determining and free to choose their thoughts and actions.

Hard and soft determinism
All behaviour has a cause (the scientific approach) versus some mental control over determined events.

Biological, environmental and psychic determinism
The ANS, genes and hormones cause stress, schizophrenia and aggression.
Skinner and Freud claimed that free will is an illusion.

Scientific emphasis on causal explanations
Knowledge of the causes of events will allow prediction and control.

Evaluation

Determinism – the case for …
Scientific approach is valuable.
No-one would 'choose' to have, say, schizophrenia which casts doubt on the idea of free will.

…and the case against
Not consistent with legal system.
Unfalsifiable: Based on the idea that a cause of an event will always exist even though one may not have been found.

Free will – the case for …
Everyday experience suggests free choice.
Promotes mental wellbeing, internal locus of control (Roberts et al.).

…and the case against
Neurological evidence from Libet and Soon et al. suggests that awareness is pre-determined.

A compromise..?
Best option may be soft determinism, e.g. Bandura's reciprocal determinism.

The nature–nurture debate

Genes and environment interact to produce behaviour.

The nature–nurture debate

Nature
Nativists argue that human characteristics are determined by heredity and the extent of this can be measured using a heritability coefficient.

Nurture
Lerner identified different levels of the pre- and post-natal environment.

Relative importance of heredity and environment
Nature and nurture influences cannot be logically separated.

The interactionist approach
Attachment (temperament and parenting).
Diathesis-stress model to explain schizophrenia (Tienari et al.).
Epigenetics: Interactions between genes and the environment may affect future generations.

Evaluation

Implications of nativism and empiricism
Nativism may indirectly promote eugenicist philosophy.
Behaviour shaping may lead to a 'big brother' society.

Shared and unshared environments
Siblings raised together may have very different experiences and this would explain why MZ twins raised together show different concordance rates.

Constructivism
People create the nurture that fits their nature through niche-picking and niche-building, suggesting it is impossible to separate nature and nurture (Plomin).

Genotype-environment interaction
Gene-environment interaction includes passive, evocative and active forms, pointing to a complex and multi-layered relationship between nature and nurture (Scarr and McCartney).

Relationship to other debates
Nature and nurture approaches are determinist and reductionist – but an interactionist position is an antidote to this.

HOLISM AND REDUCTIONISM

The whole is greater than the sum of it's parts – or not.

HOLISM AND REDUCTIONISM

Holism and reductionism
The Gestalt approach valued holism, reductionism relates to the principle of parsimony.

Levels of explanation in psychology
Socio-cultural, psychological, physical, physiological, neurochemical.

Biological reductionism
Explaining behaviour through physiological processes.
The effect of drugs on the brain has furthered understanding of biochemical processes.

Environmental (stimulus-response) reductionism
Behaviourists are concerned only with learning at a physical level (and ignore cognitive mental processes).

EVALUATION

The case for holism . . .
More complete understanding because it includes social context, e.g. Stanford prison experiment.

. . . and the case against
Vague and speculative, e.g. humanistic psychology.
A combination of different perspectives is difficult to put to practical use, e.g. in therapy.

The case for reductionism . . .
Reductionism means that variables can be broken down (e.g. behavioural categories or behaviourist approach) and studied precisely giving psychology more credibility.

. . . and the case against
Explanations at a genetic level cannot account for meaning within a social context.

The interactionist approach
Combines levels of explanation, e.g. diathesis-stress model, and interactionist approaches to treatment of schizophrenia.

IDIOGRAPHIC AND NOMOTHETIC APPROACHES

In-depth study of unique individuals or formulate general laws.

IDIOGRAPHIC AND NOMOTHETIC APPROACHES

The idiographic approach
People are studied as unique entities, associated with qualitative data.

The nomothetic approach
General laws of behaviour, associated with the scientific approach.

Examples of the idiographic approach in psychology
Humanistic psychology and the psychodynamic approach (Freud's case studies).

Examples of the nomothetic approach in psychology
Behaviourism, biological and cognitive approaches, e.g. animal studies within behaviourism produce general laws of behaviour.

EVALUATION

The case for the idiographic approach . . .
Complete account of the individual.
One case may generate new hypotheses (e.g. HM) within a particular field.

. . . and the case against
The approach may take a narrow and restricted view, e.g. Freud's case studies.
Conclusions drawn from case studies may be subjective.

The case for the nomothetic approach
More scientific – prediction and control, e.g in the field of IQ testing.
Gives psychology greater scientific credibility.

. . . and the case against
Using statistics results in the loss of the 'whole' person.
Subjective experience is ignored.

Complementary rather than contradictory
The same issue can be considered from both perspectives, e.g. gender development.

ETHICAL IMPLICATIONS OF RESEARCH AND THEORY

Research has social and ethical consequences.

ETHICAL IMPLICATIONS OF RESEARCH AND THEORY

Ethical implications
Ethical guidelines protect individuals but research also has an effect on pubic opinion and policy.

Socially sensitive research
Research that has potential consequences for the participants.
Psychologists have a social responsibility to carry this out.

Ethical issues in socially sensitive research
Sieber and Stanley identify concerns: Implications, uses/public policy, the validity of the research.

EVALUATION

Benefits of socially sensitive research
Can benefit society, e.g. reduce prejudice and the effects of unreliable eyewitness testimony.

Framing the question
Phrasing of research questions may influence outcome.
Investigators must keep an open mind so as not to offend minority groups.

Who benefits?
Findings may be misused and/or abused, e.g. research into subliminal messages and manipulation of the public.

Social control
In 1920s USA the feeble-minded were sterilised – based on psychological research on IQ, e.g. Goddard.
Scientific racism (Gould) is the outcome of socially sensitive research.

Costs and benefits
Although socially sensitive research will be subject to scrutiny by an ethics committee, the costs, benefits and wider implications of research may be very difficult to predict.

PRACTICE QUESTIONS, ANSWERS AND FEEDBACK

Question 1 Using examples of psychological research, distinguish between alpha bias and beta bias. (4 marks)

Morticia's answer

Alpha bias is when a theory suggests there are real and enduring differences between men and women. A beta bias is when such differences are ignored or minimised. There are many examples of these approaches in psychology.

As an example of alpha bias we can consider Freud's theory where he described men and women very differently, suggesting that femininity was failed masculinity and that women developed a weaker superego – whereas his observations were based on a society that placed women in a weaker position so they appeared weaker.

Morticia's definitions of the two forms of bias are well written. Her example of alpha bias is also detailed and clear. However, the example of beta bias is absent.

Luke's answer

A theory that is alpha biased is one that exaggerates the differences between men and women, such as sociobiological theory, which portrayed men as sexually promiscuous because it promoted their genes. In contrast, beta bias is kind of the opposite – a theory that minimises or ignores differences which can happen in studies that use males only (such as Kohlberg's research on moral development) and then assumes that women are the same.

Luke's definitions clearly distinguish between the two forms of bias and he cites two relevant examples of each to support the answer.

Vladimir's answer

Alpha and beta bias are two different ways of representing the differences between men and women. In one case the differences are exaggerated (alpha bias) and in the other they are minimised (beta bias). Examples of alpha bias include Freud's theory and sociobiology. Examples of beta bias include Kohlberg's research on morals and fight or flight research.

Vladimir's definitions of alpha and beta bias are brief, though accurate. The examples he identifies are rather 'list-like' and need further description.

Question 2 Briefly outline what is meant by holism in psychological research. (1 mark)

Morticia's answer

Holism is the opposite of reductionism. Reductionism means to break something down into constituent parts whereas holism is looking at the whole thing.

Luke's answer

Studying the whole system.

There is sufficient detail in Morticia's answer for a short question although a reference to 'human behaviour' rather than 'something' might have been more appropriate in the context of psychological research.

Vladimir's answer

A theory or an argument that believes it only makes sense to study the whole system.

The other two answers are too vague. Some contrast with reductionist approaches would have been helpful.

Question 3 Discuss **one** limitation of adopting a holistic approach in psychology. (3 marks)

Morticia's answer

One limitation is that taking the holist approach makes scientific research more difficult because you can't do research as easily. In order to conduct experiments you have to identify and operationalise variables and this requires identifying constituent parts of a behaviour. On the other hand, holists would argue that the end result is not equivalent to the actual behaviour you are studying. The whole is not equivalent to the sum of the parts.

Although the first sentence is not very well expressed, the rest of the response is clear and includes a sophisticated counterargument towards the end.

Luke's answer

A holistic approach prevents people finding solutions to problems such as how to treat depression because you have a whole lot of different influences and can't choose which one to deal with. This means that to find solutions to real-world problems we may need to take a more reductionist approach. That doesn't mean that holist explanations are without value.

The final sentence in Luke's answer is a little redundant without further development, however the rest is clear.

Vladimir's answer

Science is based on reductionism and therefore a holist approach prevents this. It is better to look at the constituent parts of things to build up to a picture of how the whole thing works and see how lower levels contribute to the higher levels.

Vladimir's answer hints at a relevant point though there is no explanation of why science is based on reductionism, or why it is 'better' to focus on constituent parts.

Question 4   Stan Sawdust is being tried for attempted murder. He shot a bank worker during an armed robbery and faces a lengthy prison sentence. Stan claims that there are generations of violent criminals in his family. He also says he had a difficult childhood influenced by criminal role models. Therefore Stan argues that he is not responsible for his actions.

Discuss the free will and determinism debate in psychology. Refer to Stan in your answer. *(16 marks)*

Luke's answer

This debate concerns the argument that an individual's behaviour is controlled by forces outside of an individual's own control or by their own control. It is interesting to consider the debate in the context of criminal behaviour.

From the viewpoint of biological determinism, we could argue that he has inherited particular genes from his family that predispose him to be aggressive or to lose his temper. Genes affect the neurotransmitters and hormones that are produced so it could be that he has high levels of testosterone, which makes him aggressive.

However, research on genetics (such as twin studies) always shows there isn't 100% concordance between parents and their children so Stan's behaviour must be in part due to his environment.

Environmental determinism is the view that conditioning can explain people's behaviour. In Stan's case, the criminal role models would provide vicarious reinforcement for his behaviour to explain why he became a criminal.

However, taking this kind of stance makes it difficult to see how we can expect people in any society to be responsible for their behaviour. It means that anyone can say 'I couldn't help myself, it was in my genes and the environment that made me this way'. This simply is not acceptable because people have to take some responsibility for themselves.

Soft determinism offers a solution, which is to say that within the determinist framework of identifiable causes there is room for manoeuvre. People do have choices about how they behave within the parameters of who they are, and in that sense, people have free will. So Stan may have been predisposed to behave in a particular way but he could also make some choices.

The free will side of the debate argues that people can and do make choices. It says that biological and environmental factors have some influence but we can make choices not just from a limited repertoire. The humanistic approach in psychology emphasises the importance of this sense of responsibility for psychological health.

So this is an advantage of the free will approach and is supported by research such as Roberts et al. who found that people who believe in fatalism were more likely to suffer from depression.

One of the big challenges for the free will approach came from research by Libet who showed that brain activity associated with muscle movement was recorded before a person made a conscious decision to make the movement, suggesting that even the most basic decisions are being made by the physical brain rather than the conscious self.

(414 words)

A good start – Luke clearly sets out the parameters of the debate.

There is descriptive detail in the second paragraph which is clearly and cleverly linked to the stem of the question.

Relevant discussion which is also made relevant to 'Stan'.

Again, good description as well as application.

Paragraph 5 contains relevant discussion, especially in the context of the stem and its links to crime.

Relevant discussion at the end. Luke loses sight of the stem towards the end of the essay which affects the overall quality of the answer but he makes some excellent general points.

Vladimir's answer

The determinist approach says that all behaviour has an identifiable cause; it can be explained in terms of some internal or external factor causing it. The free will approach says that people make choices that are not easily predicted from internal or external factors.

One example of determinism is biological determinism, which is genes, neurotransmitters and hormones, which all can cause behaviours. For example, the hormone adrenaline causes us to prepare for fight or flight. Genes are inherited from parents and can explain lots of behaviours – it's not likely to be just one criminal gene but many genes, but that is still genetic determinism.

Environmental determinism is when someone is conditioned to behave in a certain way, for example if you are rewarded for doing something it makes it more likely that you will repeat this behaviour. You don't behave because of any decision but because our behaviour is shaped by rewards including vicarious reinforcement. Psychic determinism is the outcome of biological drives and instincts, which Freud suggested. Freud also talked about the influence of unconscious conflicts, which make people behave in ways that they have no awareness. In contrast there is the free will approach that is the main idea of humanistic psychologists who also think it is important for healthy psychological living.

The advantage of the determinist approach is that it is the approach taken by science, which assumes all behaviour has a cause. The advantage of the free will approach is that most people have a subjective sense that they can make choices at any time. The view of soft determinism is that those choices are made out of a limited number of determined possibilities. Skinner said that it was just an illusion that we are free. Stan's behaviour might be explained by his family background (biological determinism) and also environmental determinism because the environment he grew up in might have rewarded his behaviour.

(315 words)

Vladimir's answer is mostly descriptive, though the description is generally very good. There is reference to several types of determinism, as well as free will, and each concept is well explained.

Evaluation/discussion points are less in evidence. However, there are a couple of briefly stated discursive points in the penultimate paragraph though these could be explored in much more depth.

Application to the stem is another very weak aspect of this answer. There are only passing references to 'criminal gene' and 'Stan' in the second paragraph and at the end.

Multiple-Choice Questions

Gender bias

1. 'When normal behaviour is judged from a male standard' is a definition of . . .
(a) Androcentrism.
(b) Estrocentrism.
(c) Ethnocentrism.
(d) Egocentrism.

2. Which of the following refers to ignoring or minimising differences between the sexes?
(a) Alpha bias.
(b) Beta bias.
(c) Delta bias.
(d) Theta bias.

3. Who accused Kohlberg of gender bias in his moral development theory?
(a) Finnegan.
(b) Loneghan.
(c) Gilligan.
(d) Mulligan.

4. Presenting gender differences as fixed in nature and inevitable is known as . . .
(a) Fundamentalism.
(b) Solipsism.
(c) Aneurism.
(d) Essentialism.

5. Theories that suggest real and enduring differences between men and women may be displaying . . .
(a) Alpha bias.
(b) Beta bias.
(c) Universality.
(d) Reflexivity.

6. ' Any underlying characteristic of human beings that is capable of being applied to all, despite differences of experience and upbringing' is a description of . . .
(a) Alpha bias.
(b) Beta bias.
(c) Universality.
(d) Reflexivity.

Cultural bias

1. The idea that social norms and values can only be understood within that society is . . .
(a) Cultural optimism.
(b) Cultural relativism.
(c) Cultural reflexivity.
(d) Cultural universalism.

2. Critics have argued that Ainsworth's ideal attachment type is an example of . . .
(a) Imposed etic.
(b) Imposed emic.
(c) Supposed etic.
(d) Supposed emic.

3. A belief in the superiority of one's own cultural group is best described as . . .
(a) Androcentrism.
(b) Egocentrism.
(c) Estrocentrism.
(d) Ethnocentrism.

4. Takano and Osaka (1999) found no evidence of . . .
(a) Universality of human behaviour.
(b) Imposed etic in attachment research.
(c) Methodological issues in cross-cultural studies.
(d) The distinction between collectivism and individualism.

5. The psychologist that drew distinction between emic and etic approaches is called . . .
(a) Barry.
(b) Berry.
(c) Billy.
(d) Burley.

6. Brain fag is an example of a . . .
(a) Culture-based disorder.
(b) Culture-led illness.
(c) Culture-bound syndrome.
(d) Culturally biased creation.

Free will and determinism

1. Which of the following is *not* a form of determinism?
(a) Biological.
(b) Humanistic.
(c) Environmental.
(d) Psychic.

2. Which form of determinism was proposed by William James and underpins the cognitive approach?
(a) Hard determinism.
(b) Soft determinism.
(c) Internal determinism.
(d) External determinism.

3. Which legal principle recognises that perpetrators of crime may not always be acting under their own free will?
(a) Disabled responsibility.
(b) Decreased responsibility.
(c) Deterioration of responsibility.
(d) Diminished responsibility.

4. Free will is a principle at the heart of whose approach to therapy?
(a) Albert Bandura.
(b) Sigmund Freud.
(c) Carl Rogers.
(d) B F Skinner.

5. Which form of determinism is most associated with Sigmund Freud?
(a) Psychic.
(b) Biological.
(c) Environmental.
(d) Soft.

6. An alternative term for determinism is . . .
(a) Free will.
(b) Fatalism.
(c) Favouritism.
(d) Fauvism.

The nature–nurture debate

1. The nature–nurture debate is sometimes referred to as . . .
(a) Holism vs reductionism.
(b) Idiographic vs nomothetic.
(c) Heredity vs environment.
(d) Top-down vs bottom-up.

2. Which of the following would be most closely associated with an nativist approach in the nature–nurture debate?
(a) The cognitive approach.
(b) The behaviourist approach.
(c) The social learning approach.
(d) The biological approach.

3. Which of the following is *not* part of Scarr and McCartney's gene–environment interaction model?
(a) Provocative interaction.
(b) Passive interaction.
(c) Evocative interaction.
(d) Active interaction.

4. The philosopher John Locke was best described as . . .
(a) A nativist.
(b) A geneticist.
(c) A humanist.
(d) An empiricist.

5. An example of an interactionist approach to the nature–nurture debate is . . .
(a) The diagnosis–strain model.
(b) The didactic–strike model.
(c) The diathesis–stress model.
(d) The diagonal–straight model.

6. Which of the following is *not* one of Lerner's levels of the environment?
(a) The child's genetic make-up.
(b) The mother's physical state during pregnancy.
(c) The social conditions of the child's upbringing.
(d) The historical context the child is part of.

Holism and reductionism

1. 'The whole is greater than the sum of its parts' is a quote associated with . . .
(a) Social psychologists.
(b) Skinnerian psychologists.
(c) Gestalt psychologists.
(d) Neo-Freudian psychologists.

2. Stimulus-response learning is a good example of . . .
(a) Environmental reductionism.
(b) Biological reductionism.
(c) Psychic reductionism.
(d) Holism.

3. Which of the following explanations of OCD would illustrate the neurochemical level?
(a) Most people would regard the behaviour as odd or irrational.
(b) The experience of obsessive thoughts.
(c) Overactivity of the basal ganglia.
(d) Underproduction of serotonin.

4. According to the hierarchy of science, which of these is the most reductionist?

(a) Psychology.

(b) Biology.

(c) Chemistry.

(d) Physics.

5. Reductionism is based on the scientific principle of . . .

(a) Hegemony.

(b) Philanthropy.

(c) Theocracy.

(d) Parsimony.

6. Which of the following advocates a holistic view of human behaviour?

(a) The cognitive approach.

(b) The behaviourist approach.

(c) The biological approach.

(d) The humanistic approach.

Idiographic and nomothetic approaches

1. Which of the following would be most closely associated with the nomothetic approach?

(a) Experiments.

(b) Case studies.

(c) Unstructured interviews.

(d) Qualitative data.

2. Which of the following would *not* be associated with the nomothetic approach?

(a) The humanistic approach.

(b) The biological approach.

(c) The behaviourist approach.

(d) The cognitive approach.

3. Which of the following would be associated with the idiographic approach?

(a) Classifying people into groups.

(b) Establishing principles of behaviour in general.

(c) Describing unusual individuals in detail.

(d) Establishing dimensions along which people can be compared.

4. Which of the following is the best example of the idiographic approach?

(a) Miller's law of short-term memory.

(b) Freud's study of Little Hans.

(c) Behaviourist laws of learning.

(d) IQ testing.

5. The idiographic approach is likely to produce . . .

(a) Quantitative data.

(b) Qualitative data.

(c) Numerical data.

(d) Statistical data.

6. Idiographic is derived from the Greek 'idos' which means . . .

(a) Private and personal.

(b) Public and plausible.

(c) General and global.

(d) Separate and specific.

Ethical implications of research studies and theory

1. Which of these is not a concern of socially sensitive research identified by Sieber and Stanley?

(a) Implications.

(b) Public policy.

(c) Validity.

(d) The scale of the research, e.g. sample size.

2. Cyril Burt's research led to the introduction of the . . .

(a) 11+ exam.

(b) 12+ exam.

(c) 7+ exam.

(d) 9+ exam.

3. In the 1920s and 30s, US states enacted legislation to try to control numbers of the . . .

(a) Weak-minded.

(b) Narrow-minded.

(c) Feeble-minded.

(d) Open-minded.

4. Which of the following was not a group deemed to be 'feeble minded' in some US states in the 1920s?

(a) The mentally ill.

(b) Drug addicts.

(c) Alcoholics.

(d) The elderly.

5. In the 1950s, advertising companies tried to influence consumers using . . .

(a) Subconscious codes.

(b) Systematic manipulation.

(c) Subliminal messages.

(d) Selective interpretation.

6. Socially sensitive areas of research are sometimes referred to as . . .

(a) Tattoo topics.

(b) Taboo topics.

(c) Totemic topics.

(d) Total topics.

MCQ answers

Gender bias   1a, 2b, 3c, 4d, 5a, 6c

Cultural bias   1b, 2a, 3d, 4d, 5b, 6c

Free will and determinism   1b, 2b, 3d, 4c, 5a, 6b

The nature-nurture debate   1c, 2d, 3a, 4d, 5c, 6a

Holism and reductionism   1c, 2a, 3d, 4d, 5d, 6d

Idiographic and nomothetic approaches   1a, 2a, 3c, 4b, 5b, 6a

Ethical implications of research studies and theory   1d, 2a, 3c, 4d, 5c, 6b

CHAPTER 5
RELATIONSHIPS

What are the ingredients of a relationship that can keep a couple together for half a century or more?

'The meeting of two personalities is like the contact of two chemical substances: if there is any reaction, both are transformed.'

Carl Gustav Jung, psychologist (1933)

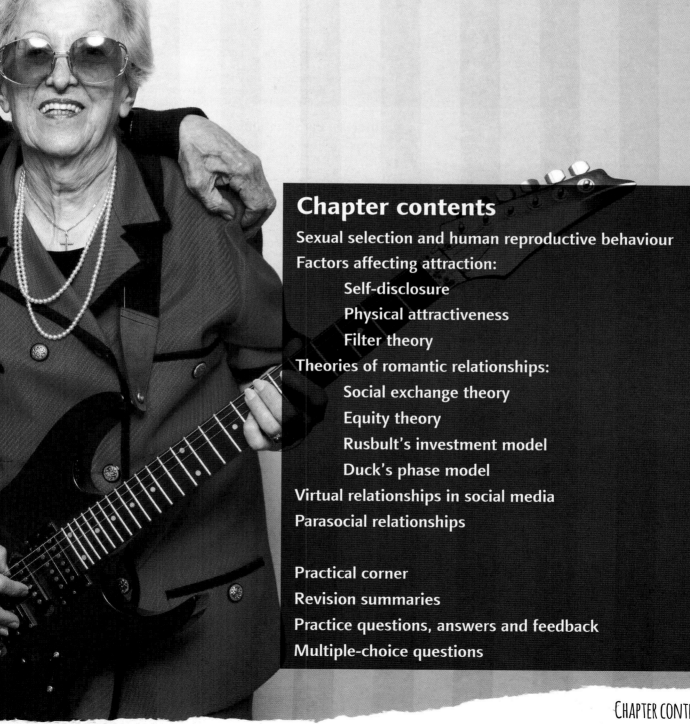

Chapter contents

SEXUAL SELECTION AND HUMAN REPRODUCTIVE BEHAVIOUR

The relationship between sexual selection and human reproductive behaviour.

Charles Darwin noticed that evolution favours the development of some features that are attractive to the opposite sex. These favourable features make it more likely that the possessor will attract a mate and reproduce to pass on their genes. In other words, these features increase the reproductive fitness that is central to evolutionary success.

KEY TERMS

Sexual selection – An evolutionary explanation of partner preference. Attributes or behaviours that increase reproductive success are passed on and may become exaggerated over succeeding generations of offspring.

Human reproductive behaviour – This refers to any behaviours which relate to opportunities to reproduce and thereby increase the survival chances of our genes. It includes the evolutionary mechanisms underlying our partner preferences, such as mate choice and mate competition.

There is famously a 15-year age difference between actors Demi Moore and Ashton Kutcher. They were together for eight years.

Apply it   Concepts: Three relationships

Kaley is an attractive 25-year-old woman who has recently married Ryan, a 60-year-old man who owns five successful businesses. They have no children yet, but are hoping to start a family soon.

Nicole and Keith have been together for just over five years. There is an age gap between them – Keith is 29 and Nicole is 53, but this doesn't seem to make any difference to their relationship or their feelings for each other. Nicole has three children from a previous marriage.

Benedict and Eddie have been in a civil partnership for nearly eight years. They are both in their thirties and looking to adopt a child in the near future.

Question

Use evolutionary explanations of human reproductive behaviour to explain these relationships. Are there any which the evolutionary explanation cannot account for? Explain your answer.

Sexual selection

Sexual selection explains why some characteristics that might appear disadvantageous actually confer an advantage in **human reproductive behaviour** because the characteristics are attractive to potential mates. Either that or they provide an advantage over competitors for reproductive rights (examples in humans include greater height, secondary sexual characteristics, certain facial and bodily features).

Anisogamy

Anisogamy refers to the differences between male and female sex cells (gametes). These are very obvious in humans (and other animals too). Male gametes (sperm) are extremely small, highly mobile, created continuously in vast numbers from puberty to old age, and do not require a great expenditure of energy to produce. In complete contrast, female gametes (eggs or ova) are relatively large, static, produced at intervals for a limited number of fertile years and require a huge investment of energy. A consequence of anisogamy for mate selection is that there is no shortage of fertile males but a fertile woman is a rare 'resource'. Anisogamy is also important in partner preference because it gives rise to two different mating strategies, which in turn means there are two types of sexual selection: inter- and intra-sexual selection. **Inter-sexual selection** is between the sexes – the strategies that males use to select females or females use to select males. **Intra-sexual selection** is within each sex - such as the strategies between males to be the one that is selected.

Inter-sexual selection

This is the preferred strategy of the female – quality over quantity. Ova are rarer than sperm and require greater energy to produce. Also, as Robert Trivers (1972) emphasises, the female makes a greater investment of time, commitment and other resources before, during and after the birth of her offspring. Both sexes are choosy, because both stand to lose if they invest resources in substandard partners. But the consequences of making a wrong choice of partner are much more serious for the female than for the male. So it pays for her to be especially choosy. Therefore, the female's optimum mating strategy is to select a genetically fit partner who is able and willing to provide resources. This leaves the males competing for the opportunity to mate with the fertile female.

It is this female preference for a fit male which determines which features are passed on to the offspring. For example, if height is considered an attractive trait then, over successive generations of females, it would increase in the male population because females would mate with tall males and, over time, produce sons who are taller with each generation and produce daughters who have a greater preference for tall partners. This is known as a *runaway process*, encapsulated by Ronald Fisher (1930) in his *sexy sons hypothesis* – a female mates with a male who has a desirable characteristic, and this 'sexy' trait is inherited by her son. This increases the likelihood that successive generations of females will mate with her offspring.

Intra-sexual selection

This is the preferred strategy of the male – quantity over quality. It refers to the competition between (intra) males to be able to mate with a female. The winner of the competition reproduces and gets to pass on to his offspring the characteristics that contributed to his victory. It is this strategy that has given rise to *dimorphism* in humans, the obvious differences between males and females. For example, in any physical competition between males, size matters. Larger males have an advantage and are therefore more likely to mate. On the other hand, females do not compete for reproductive rights so there is no evolutionary drive towards favouring larger females.

Intra-sexual selection also has behavioural and psychological consequences, although these are more controversial. For example, for males to acquire fertile females and protect them from competing males, they may benefit from behaving aggressively and perhaps even thinking in a certain way.

Anisogamy dictates that the male's optimum reproductive strategy is to mate with as many fertile females as possible. This is because of the minimal energy required to produce enough sperm to theoretically fertilise every woman on earth, and the relative lack of post-coital responsibility the male carries (i.e. it's the woman left 'holding the baby'). A behavioural consequence of this competition for fertile mates is a distinct preference for youth and a sensitivity to the indicators of youth (e.g. certain facial features) as well as fertility (e.g. a certain body shape).

Evaluation

Research support for preferences related to anisogamy

David Buss (1989) carried out a survey of over 10,000 adults in 33 countries. He asked questions relating to age and a variety of attributes that evolutionary theory predicts should be important in partner preference. He found that female respondents placed greater value on resource-related characteristics, such as good financial prospects, ambition and industriousness, than males did. Males valued reproductive capacity in terms of good looks and chastity, and preferred younger mates, more than females did.

These findings reflect sex differences in mate strategies due to anisogamy. They support predictions about partner preference derived from sexual selection theory. Furthermore, the findings can be applied across vastly different cultures, reflecting fundamental human preferences which are not primarily dependent upon cultural influences.

Research support for inter-sexual selection

Russell Clark and Elaine Hatfield (1989) showed that female choosiness is a reality of heterosexual relationships. Male and female psychology students were sent out across a university campus. They approached other students individually with this question: 'I have been noticing you around campus. I find you to be very attractive. Would you go to bed with me tonight?'. Not a single female student agreed to the request, whereas 75% of males did, immediately.

This supports evolutionary theory because it suggests that females are choosier than males when it comes to selecting sexual partners and that males have evolved a different strategy to ensure reproductive success.

Ignores social and cultural influences

Partner preferences over the past century have undoubtedly been influenced by rapidly changing social norms of sexual behaviour. These develop much faster than evolutionary timescales imply and have instead come about due to cultural factors such as availability of contraception.

Women's greater role in the workplace means that they are no longer dependent on men to provide for them (despite the ongoing inequality in earning power). Bereczkei *et al.* (1997) argue that this social change has consequences for women's mate preferences, which may no longer be resource-oriented. Chang *et al.* (2011) compared partner preferences in China over 25 years and found that some had changed but others remained the same, corresponding with the huge social changes in that time.

Mate preferences are therefore the outcome of a combination of evolutionary and cultural influences. Any theory that fails to account for both is a limited explanation.

Evaluation eXtra

Support from waist-hip ratio research

Evolutionary theory makes several predictions about partner preference that can be tested empirically. One is that males will show a preference for a female body shape that signals fertility. Devendra Singh (1993, 2002) studied this in terms of waist-hip ratio (WHR). What matters in male preference is not female body size as such, but the ratio of waist to hip sizes. Up to a point, males generally find any hip and waist sizes are attractive so long as the ratio of one to the other is about 0.7. This combination of wider hips and narrower waist is attractive because it is an 'honest signal' (it is hard to fake) that the woman is fertile but not currently pregnant.

Consider: Why is it adaptive for males to be able to detect female fertility? What does this tell us about males' partner preferences?

Support from lonely hearts research

David Waynforth and Robin Dunbar (1995) studied lonely hearts advertisements in American newspapers. These slightly quaint historical documents were opportunities for men (usually) and women to describe the qualities they desired in a potential partner, whilst cataloguing what they had to offer. The researchers found that women more than men tended to offer physical attractiveness and indicators of youth ('flirty, exciting, curvy, sexy'). Men, on the other hand, offered resources more than women did ('successful, fit, mature, ambitious') and sought relative youth and physical attractiveness.

Consider: Which predictions from sexual selection theory do these findings support?

Voulez-vous coucher avec moi, ce soir? Direct and to the point. But which one is likely to be disappointed?

Apply it Concepts: Young, free, single

Shakira and Gerard are young and single people who seem to have a new partner almost every night. They make no bones about the fact that they are out to have a good time while they're still young.

Question

How do you think society generally would view Shakira's and Gerard's behaviour? Is there an evolutionary explanation for why one of their behaviours might be considered acceptable and the other not? Explain your answer.

Apply it Methods: Replicating Buss

An evolutionary psychologist wanted to replicate the study by Buss (1989) by using an interview method. He carried out face-to-face interviews with 82 participants, 45 of them male and 37 female. He asked various questions about their preferences for certain evolutionarily-important characteristics in a partner. Physical attractiveness was preferred by 40 of the males and 28 of the females. Good financial prospects was an attribute preferred by 25 of the males and 32 of the females.

Questions

1. The study produced a lot of **quantitative data**. Explain what is meant by this term. (*2 marks*)
2. Write a question that could gather quantitative data. (*2 marks*)
3. Explain *two* differences between a **structured** and an **unstructured interview**. (*2 marks + 2 marks*)
4. Explain *one* reason why the psychologist thought interviews might be better than **questionnaires** in this study. (*2 marks*)
5. Calculate the preferences of males and females as percentages (four percentages). (*4 marks*)

CHECK IT

1. Explain what is meant by the term *sexual selection*. [2 marks]
2. Briefly outline **one** evolutionary explanation of partner preference. [4 marks]
3. Describe and evaluate evolutionary explanations of partner preference. [16 marks]
4. Discuss the relationship between sexual selection and human reproductive behaviour. [16 marks]

FACTORS AFFECTING ATTRACTION: SELF-DISCLOSURE

Factors affecting attraction in romantic relationships: self-disclosure.

'The course of true love never did run smooth', Shakespeare tells us in *A Midsummer Night's Dream*. But how can it run smoother? How can it get started at all in the first place?

Psychologists have identified several factors that influence whether or not (and how much) we are attracted to a potential romantic partner. We will be looking at three in total, beginning with *self-disclosure*.

KEY TERM

Self-disclosure – Revealing personal information about yourself. Romantic partners reveal more about their true selves as their relationship develops. These self-disclosures about one's deepest thoughts and feelings can strengthen a romantic bond when used appropriately.

Apply it

Concepts: Hollywood couples still together

The actors Felicity Huffman and William H Macy have been happily married since 1997. When asked the secret of their longevity, Huffman said, 'Once a week we sit down and make sure we get half an hour – each of us gets 15 minutes – just to talk, with no crosstalk. I talk, then you talk. You kind of just deeply check in with the other person.'

Question

Explain how research into self-disclosure confirms Huffman and Macy's experience of a satisfying relationship. What sort of things would you disclose? Why do you think it needs to be a two-way process?

Self-disclosure

In the early days of a relationship, we love to learn as much as we can about our new partner, and the more we learn about them the more we seem to like them. By revealing ourselves to another person, we share our likes and dislikes, our hopes and fears, our interests and attitudes. We share what really matters to us. Our partner understands us better, and we them.

So **self-disclosure** has a vital role in a relationship beyond the initial attraction. But most people are careful about what they disclose, at least to begin with. Used wisely and effectively it really can help the course of true love run smoother.

Social penetration theory

Self-disclosure is a major concept within Irwin Altman and Dalmas Taylor's (1973) *social penetration theory* of how relationships develop. It is the gradual process of revealing your inner self to someone else, of giving away your deepest thoughts and feelings. In romantic relationships, it involves the reciprocal exchange of information between intimate partners. When one partner reveals some personal information they display trust; to go further the other partner must also reveal sensitive information. As they increasingly disclose more and more information to each other, romantic partners 'penetrate' more deeply into each other's lives, and gain a greater understanding of each other.

It is a basic feature of romantic relationships. After all, it's difficult to 'bear one's soul' to a relative stranger. Doing so means that a relationship has reached a certain stage where such self-disclosure will be welcomed and – hopefully – reciprocated.

Breadth and depth of self-disclosure

According to Altman and Taylor, self-disclosure has two elements – breadth and depth. As both of these increase, romantic partners become more committed to each other. The researchers use the metaphor of the many layers of an onion to illustrate this process. We disclose a lot about ourselves at the start of a relationship, but what we reveal is superficial, mostly 'on the surface', like the outer layers of an onion. It is the kind of 'low-risk' information we would reveal to anyone, friends, co-workers, even acquaintances. Breadth of disclosure is narrow because many topics are 'off-limits' in the early stage of a relationship. If we were to reveal too much too soon, we might get the response 'too much information', possibly even threatening the relationship before it's had a chance to get going.

However, as a relationship develops, self-disclosure becomes deeper, progressively removing more and more layers to reveal our true selves and encompassing a wider range of topics, especially concerning those things that matter most to us. Eventually we are prepared to reveal intimate, high-risk information – painful memories and experiences, strongly-held beliefs, powerful feelings, perhaps even secrets (and maybe the odd lie).

Reciprocity of self-disclosure

As Harry Reis and Philip Shaver (1988) point out, for a relationship to develop, as well as an increase in breadth and depth there needs to be a *reciprocal* element to disclosure. Once you have decided to disclose something that reveals your true self, hopefully your partner will respond in a way that is rewarding, with understanding, empathy and also their own intimate thoughts and feelings. So there is a balance of self-disclosure between both partners in a successful romantic relationship, which increases feelings of intimacy and deepens the relationship.

'But soft! What light through yonder window breaks?
It is the east, and Juliet is the sun.
... It is my lady, O, it is my love!
O that she knew she were!'

The most basic self-disclosure in any romantic relationship – telling someone you love them.

Evaluation

Support from research studies

Several predictions about self-disclosure derived from social penetration theory have been supported by research. Sprecher and Hendrick (2004) studied heterosexual dating couples and found strong **correlations** between several measures of satisfaction and self-disclosure (both theirs and their partner's). In short, men and women who used self-disclosure and those who believed their partners did likewise were more satisfied with and committed to their romantic relationship.

Laurenceau *et al.* (2005) used a method that involved writing daily diary entries. They found that self-disclosure and the perception of self-disclosure in a partner were linked to higher levels of intimacy in long-term married couples. The reverse was also true – less intimate couples self-disclosed less often.

Such supportive research findings increase our confidence in the **validity** of the theory that self-disclosure leads to more satisfying relationships.

Real-life applications

Research into self-disclosure can help people who want to improve communication in their relationships. Romantic partners probably use self-disclosure deliberately and skillfully from time to time to increase intimacy and strengthen their bond. Hass and Stafford (1998) found that 57% of gay men and women in their study said that open and honest self-disclosure was the main way they maintained and deepened their committed relationships. If less-skilled partners, for example, those who tend to limit communication to 'small-talk', can learn to use self-disclosure then this could bring several benefits to the relationship in terms of deepening satisfaction and commitment.

Such real-life application demonstrates the value of the psychological insights.

Cultural differences

The prediction that increasing depth and breadth of self-disclosures will lead to a more satisfying and intimate romantic relationship is not true for all cultures. To a large extent it depends on the type of self-disclosure. For example, Tang *et al.* (2013) reviewed the research literature regarding sexual self-disclosure (that is, disclosures related to feelings about specific sexual practices). They concluded that men and women in the USA (an **individualist culture**) self-disclose significantly more sexual thoughts and feelings than men and women in China (a **collectivist culture**). Both these levels of self-disclosure are linked to relationship satisfaction in those cultures.

Self-disclosure theory is therefore a limited explanation of romantic relationships, based on findings from Western (individualist) cultures which are not necessarily generalisable to other cultures.

Evaluation eXtra

Self-disclosure and satisfaction

Social penetration theory claims that romantic relationships become more intimate as self-disclosures deepen and broaden. Using the onion metaphor, relationship breakdown is accompanied by a reduction in self-disclosures, as partners wrap themselves up once again in layers of concealment. However, theories of relationship breakdown (such as Duck's theory on page 132) often recognise how couples discuss and negotiate the state of their deteriorating relationship in an attempt to save it or return to an earlier level of satisfaction. These discussions frequently involve deep self-disclosures of very intimate thoughts and feelings, and yet these may not be enough to rescue the relationship. They may even contribute to its breakdown.

Consider: *Do you think the onion metaphor can account for this behaviour? Does that make it a weakness of the theory? Explain your answer.*

Correlation versus causation

Much self-disclosure research is correlational (e.g. Sprecher and Hendrick's study, above). Although it is usually assumed that greater self-disclosure creates more satisfaction, a correlation does not tell us if this is a valid conclusion to draw.

Consider: *Are there any alternative explanations for this correlation? Briefly describe them, and then explain how they relate to self-disclosure theory. Which are supportive and which contradictory?*

Thinks: *'I like babies too, but we've only been going out with each other for three days'.*

Self-disclosure is a skill. If you reveal too much too early in a relationship, it might not go down too well.

Apply it Concepts: **Public disclosures**

People disclose a lot more in front of strangers in a television studio than we would usually consider publicly acceptable. For example, episodes of *The Jeremy Kyle Show* have included, 'Were you having an affair when you told me you were on holiday?' and 'Was my fiancée lying about being pregnant to avoid a lie detector test?'

Question

Explain some of the pitfalls of excessive and poorly timed self-disclosure. Give some examples of 'too much information!' at the start of a promising romantic relationship.

Apply it Methods: **Tell me what you feel**

Two psychologists recruited 100 married couples for a study of relationship satisfaction. They asked the participants to keep a daily diary of their self-disclosures to their partner over a one-month period. The researchers used **content analysis** to analyse the data from the diaries.

They found that 15% of the self-disclosures related to sex, 10% to experiences in previous relationships, 25% to family matters, 30% to hopes and fears about the future, and 15% to health concerns;. 5% of self-disclosures could not be categorised.

Questions

1. Explain how the psychologists could have carried out their content analysis. (*4 marks*) (See page 64)
2. The study gathered a lot of **qualitative data**. Explain what is meant by qualitative data. (*2 marks*)
3. Outline *one* strength of gathering qualitative data in this study. (*2 marks*)
4. Outline *one* **sampling** method the psychologists could have used to recruit the participants. (*2 marks*)
5. Explain *one* limitation of this method. (*2 marks*)

CHECK IT

1. In relation to factors affecting attraction in romantic relationships, explain what is meant by the term *self-disclosure*. **[2 marks]**
2. Briefly outline self-disclosure as a factor affecting attraction in romantic relationships. **[4 marks]**
3. Describe research into self-disclosure as a factor affecting attraction in romantic relationships. **[6 marks]**
4. Describe and evaluate self-disclosure as a factor affecting attraction in romantic relationships. **[16 marks]**

Factors affecting attraction in romantic relationships: physical attractiveness including the matching hypothesis.

Physical attractiveness is probably the one feature of an individual we notice as soon as we meet them, even before we've spoken or interacted with them in any meaningful way. It is the basis of online dating agencies – the first encounter you have with a potential date is a photograph of their face. On this spread, we look at just how important it really is.

KEY TERMS

Physical attractiveness – An important factor in the formation of romantic relationships. The term usually applies specifically to how appealing we find a person's face. There is general agreement within and across cultures about what is considered physically attractive. There exists an assumption that we seek to form relationships with the most attractive person available.

Matching hypothesis – The belief that we do not select the most attractive person as a prospective partner but, instead, are attracted to people who approximately 'match 'us in physical (i.e. facial) attractiveness. This implies that we take into account our own attractiveness 'value' to others when seeking romantic partners.

Well-matched in the looks department? The matching hypothesis would suggest so. But how true is it?

STUDY TIP

All the explanations in this section focus on the initial stage of a relationship - attraction. Make sure you always focus on this when discussing, for example, physical attractiveness. This is not a theory of relationships, it is an explanation of attraction.

Physical attractiveness

Explaining the importance of physical attractiveness

Psychologists have wondered why **physical attractiveness** seems to be quite so important in forming relationships. One promising explanation draws upon evolutionary theory (see the previous spread). Shackelford and Larsen (1997) found that people with symmetrical faces are rated as more attractive. This is because it may be an honest signal of genetic fitness (it's difficult to fake facial symmetry).

People are also attracted to faces with *neotenous* (baby-face) features such as widely separated and large eyes, a delicate chin, and a small nose – because these trigger a protective or caring instinct, a valuable resource for females wanting to reproduce.

Physical attractiveness is not only important at the start of a relationship. McNulty *et al.* (2008) found evidence that the initial attractiveness that brought the partners together continued to be an important feature of the relationship after marriage, for at least several years.

The halo effect

Physical attractiveness may also matter because we have preconceived ideas about the personality traits attractive people must have, and they are almost universally positive. This is the *physical attractiveness stereotype,* a widely-accepted view of attractive people neatly summed up in a phrase coined by Karen Dion and her colleagues (1972): 'What is beautiful is good'. For example, Dion *et al.* found that physically attractive people are consistently rated as kind, strong, sociable, and successful compared to unattractive people. The belief that good-looking people probably have these characteristics makes them even more attractive to us, so we behave positively towards them – a good example of a *self-fulfilling prophecy.*

Psychologists use the term *halo effect* to describe how one distinguishing feature (physical attractiveness, in this case) tends to have a disproportionate influence on our judgements of a person's other attributes, for example, their personality.

The matching hypothesis

Although we find physical attractiveness desirable (and there is surprising agreement about what is considered attractive), common-sense tells us that we can't all form relationships with the most attractive people. Obviously there just aren't enough of us to go round (see the photos of the authors at the back of the book if you want proof)! Is it possible that our assessment of our own attractiveness may play a role in our choice of romantic partner? The **matching hypothesis** proposed by Elaine Walster and her colleagues (1966) suggests it does.

The hypothesis states that people choose romantic partners who are roughly of similar physical attractiveness to each other. To do this we have to make a realistic judgement about our own 'value' to a potential partner.

In other words, our choice of partner is basically a compromise. We desire the most physically attractive partner possible for all sorts of evolutionary, social, cultural and psychological reasons. But we balance this against the wish to avoid being rejected by someone 'out of our league', that is someone who is very unlikely to consider us physically attractive. Apologies, by the way, if you are highly physically attractive yourself; we're speaking here on behalf of the rest of us. In terms of physical attractiveness at least, there's a difference between what we would like in an ideal partner and what we are prepared to settle for.

Apply it   Concepts: Is my halo slipping?

Rob is generally agreed to be a very good looking chap. In fact, he would by most assessments be described as stunningly handsome. Women – and men – find him physically very attractive and he has received a lot of 'offers' down the years. He has also found that people smile at him everywhere he goes, are very polite and friendly towards him and assume he must be very intelligent as well as handsome (which he is of course, but that's not the point).

Question

Using your knowledge of the halo effect and the physical attractiveness stereotype, explain Rob's experiences. Can you think of any other ways Rob's devastating good looks might prove beneficial? Could there be some drawbacks as well?

Evaluation

Research support for the halo effect

Palmer and Peterson (2012) found that physically attractive people were rated as more politically knowledgeable and competent than unattractive people. This halo effect was so powerful that it persisted even when participants knew that these 'knowledgeable' people had no particular expertise. This has obvious implications for the political process. Perhaps there are dangers for democracy if politicians are judged as suitable for office merely because they are considered physically attractive by enough voters.

The existence of the halo effect has been found to apply in many other areas of everyday life, confirming that physical attractiveness is an important factor in the initial formation of relationships, romantic or otherwise.

Individual differences

Some people just do not seem to attach much importance to physical attractiveness. For example, Towhey (1979) asked male and female participants to rate how much they would like a target individual based on their photograph and some biographical information. The participants also completed a questionnaire – the MACHO scale – designed to measure sexist attitudes and behaviours. Towhey found that the participants who scored highly on the scale were more influenced by the physical attractiveness of the target when making their judgement of likeability. Low scorers were less sensitive to this influence.

This shows that the effects of physical attractiveness can be moderated by other factors, and so challenges the notion that it is a significant consideration in relationship formation for all potential partners.

Research support for the matching hypothesis

Ironically the original research study that attempted to confirm the matching hypothesis failed to do so (Walster *et al.* 1966). However, this may be because the measurement of attractiveness was not reliable. The raters who had to judge the attractiveness of the participants only had a few seconds to do so.

However, it is fair to say that there is some support for the hypothesis in its narrow form as referring to physical attractiveness only. Feingold (1988) carried out a **meta-analysis** of 17 studies and found a significant **correlation** in ratings of attractiveness between romantic partners. This is especially supportive of the matching hypothesis because the studies looked at actual partners, which is a more realistic approach.

Evaluation eXtra

Role of cultural influences

Research shows that what is considered physically attractive is remarkably consistent across cultures. Cunningham *et al.* (1995) found that female features of large eyes, prominent cheekbones, small nose and high eyebrows were rated as highly attractive by white, Hispanic and Asian males. The physical attractiveness stereotype is also culturally pervasive. Wheeler and Kim (1997) found that Korean and American students judged physically attractive people to be more trustworthy, concerned for other people, mature and friendly. It seems that the stereotype is just as strong in **collectivist cultures** as it is in individualist ones.

Consider: *What do you think is the significance of these cross-cultural findings? Do they add support to the view that physical attractiveness is crucial in forming a romantic relationship?*

Research contradicting the matching hypothesis

Taylor *et al.* (2011) studied the activity logs of a popular online dating site. This was a real-life test of the matching hypothesis because it measured actual date choices and not merely preferences. This is in keeping with the original hypothesis which concerned realistic as opposed to fantasy choices. Online daters sought meetings with potential partners who were more physically attractive than them. It seems they did not consider their own level of attractiveness when making decisions about who to date.

Consider: *Can you explain how this finding relates to the matching hypothesis? In what way is it a valid test of the hypothesis?*

Practical activity on page 138

Apply it — Concepts: Celebrity mismatch?

Charlize is very interested in celebrities, and over the years she has noticed that many celebrity couples seem to be very well matched in attractiveness. There's Kanye West and Kim Kardashian, as well as Elton John and David Furnish. But Charlize's friend Sean disagrees: 'What about Catherine Zeta-Jones and Michael Douglas? She's so much more attractive than him.'

Question

Explain how research into the matching hypothesis can help us to decide whether Charlize or Sean is right.

Online dating may have changed forever the way some people form relationships. But it arguably makes physical attractiveness even more important.

Apply it — Methods: Match me up!

A psychologist was interested in testing the matching hypothesis. She recruited 44 female participants by using an **opportunity sampling** method. Each participant was individually introduced to two men. The three of them had a 10-minute discussion about what they found attractive in a partner. One of the men had been rated by independent judges as attractive and the other unattractive. Each female participant was rated in the same way. Each participant then had to choose which of the men she would prefer to go on a date with. The results are shown in Table 1.

Table 1: Number of attractive and unattractive females choosing a date with the attractive or unattractive male

	Attractive male	Unattractive male
Attractive female	17	14
Unattractive female	8	5

Questions

1. Identify and explain the type of **experimental design** used in this study. (*1 mark + 2 marks*)

2. Suggest *one* **extraneous variable** in this study and explain how it might have affected the results. (*3 marks*)

3. Name a suitable **statistical test** to analyse the data in Table 1. (*1 mark*) (See page 70)

4. Explain *two* reasons why you have chosen this test. (*2 marks + 2 marks*)

5. A friend of the researcher disagreed with this result. She has been in many relationships and, in her experience, people always want the best-looking partners. Explain why the friend's personal opinion is no substitute for scientific evidence. (*4 marks*)

CHECK IT

1. In relation to factors affecting attraction in romantic relationships, explain what is meant by the *matching hypothesis*. **[2 marks]**

2. Outline physical attractiveness as a factor affecting attraction in romantic relationships. **[4 marks]**

3. Outline the matching hypothesis as an explanation of factors affecting attraction in romantic relationships. **[4 marks]**

4. Discuss physical attractiveness as a factor affecting attraction in romantic relationships. **[16 marks]**

'So many men, so little time.' Not Shakespeare on this occasion, but old-time Hollywood star Mae West, who knew a thing or two about relationships. Fortunately (or unfortunately) for most of us, the number of men or women available as potential partners is not as huge as it apparently was for Mae West. That's because several factors drastically reduce the size of the 'pond we fish in'. So your partners are likely to come from a surprisingly limited group. At least, that's the claim made by filter theory, our final look at what influences that initial attraction (and beyond).

KEY TERMS

Filter theory – An explanation of relationship formation. It states that a series of different factors progressively limits the range of available romantic partners to a much smaller pool of possibilities. The filters include social demography, similarity in attitudes and complementarity.

Social demography – Demographics are features that describe populations; social demographics include geographical location and social class. Such factors filter out a large number of available partners. This means many relationships are formed between partners who share social demographic characteristics.

Similarity in attitudes – We find partners who share our basic values attractive in the earlier stages of a relationship, so we tend to discount available individuals who differ markedly from us in their attitudes.

Complementarity – Similarity becomes less important as a relationship develops, and is replaced by a need for your partner to balance your traits with opposite ones of their own.

'I go for two kinds of men: those with muscles and those without.' That certainly increased Mae West's field of desirables.

Filter theory

Alan Kerckhoff and Keith Davis (1962) compared the attitudes and personalities of student couples in short-term (defined as less than 18 months) and long-term relationships. They devised a **filter theory** to explain how such romantic relationships form and develop.

In terms of partner choice, we all have a *field of availables*, the entire set of potential romantic partners, all the people we could realistically form a relationship with. But, of course, not everyone who is available to us is desirable. According to Kerckhoff and Davis, there are three main factors that act as filters to narrow down our range of partner choice to a *field of desirables*. Each of these factors assumes greater or lesser importance at different stages of a relationship.

Social demography (1st level of filter)

Social demography refers to a wide range of factors all of which influence the chances of potential partners meeting each other in the first place. They include geographical location (or *proximity*), social class, level of education, ethnic group, religion, and so on. You are much more likely to meet people who are physically close and share several demographic characteristics. Although we might frequently encounter people who live further away, our most meaningful and memorable interactions are with people who are nearby. The key benefit of proximity is *accessibility*. It doesn't require much effort to meet people who live in the same area, go to the same school or university, and so on.

Although there is a vast range and variety of potential partners, the realistic field is much narrower because our choices are constrained by our social circumstances. Effectively, anyone who is too 'different' (too far away, too middle class) is discounted as a potential partner. The outcome of this filtering is *homogamy*, meaning you are more likely to form a relationship with someone who is socially or culturally similar. You will probably have a fair bit in common with someone who shares, for example, your ethnicity, religious beliefs, and educational level and most of us find such shared similarities attractive.

Similarity in attitudes (2nd level of filter)

Partners will often share important beliefs and values, partly because the *field of availables* has already been narrowed by the first filter to those who have significant social and cultural characteristics in common. Kerckhoff and Davis (1962) found that **similarity of attitudes** was important to the development of romantic relationships, but only for the couples who had been together less than 18 months. There is a need for partners in the earlier stages of a relationship to agree over basic values, the things that really matter to them. This encourages greater and deeper communication, and promotes **self-disclosure** (see page 120).

There is considerable evidence that most of us find this similarity attractive, at least to begin with. Donn Byrne (1997) has described the consistent findings that similarity causes attraction as the *law of attraction*. If such similarity does not exist, for example, it turns out the partners have little in common after all, then they may go out together a few times, but the relationship is likely to fizzle out with a 'I'll call you sometime'.

Complementarity (3rd level of filter)

The third filter concerns the ability of romantic partners to meet each other's needs. Two partners complement each other when they have traits that the other lacks. For example, one partner may enjoy making the other laugh, and in turn this partner enjoys being made to laugh. Or perhaps one partner is more dominant in the relationship than the other. Or one likes to nurture and the other to be nurtured. Kerckhoff and Davis found that the need for **complementarity** was more important for the long-term couples. In other words, at a later stage of a relationship, opposites attract. Complementarity is attractive because it gives two romantic partners the feeling that together they form a whole, which adds depth to a relationship and makes it more likely to flourish.

Apply it **Concepts: Still loving after all these years**

Pat and Phil first met when they were both 13 years old, on Pat's paper round. Two years after that they started going out with each other and were madly in love, until they broke up three years later. They lost touch, but 44 years later these childhood sweethearts rediscovered each other and finally got married.

Question

Explain how relationships like the one between Pat and Phil are formed in terms of (a) social demographics, (b) similarity of attitudes, and (c) complementarity.

Evaluation

Support from research evidence

Filter theory assumes that the key factors in a relationship change over time. This makes sense and agrees with most people's experience of romantic relationships, so the theory has **face validity**. More importantly, however, it also benefits from some research support. For example, Peter Winch (1958) found evidence that similarities of personality, interests and attitudes between partners are typical of the earliest stages of a relationship.

This echoes the **matching hypothesis**, but not just in terms of physical attractiveness. Between partners happily married for several years, complementarity of needs is more important than similarity, according to Winch.

Failure to replicate

George Levinger (1974) pointed out that many studies have failed to **replicate** the original findings that formed the basis of filter theory. He put this down to social changes over time and also to the difficulties inherent in defining the depth of a relationship in terms of its length. Kerckhoff and Davis chose an 18-month cut-off point to distinguish between short-term and long-term relationships. They assumed that partners who had been together longer than this were more committed and had a deeper relationship.

This highlights the problems in applying filter theory even to other heterosexual couples in the **individualist** culture, never mind to homosexual partners or relationships in another culture.

Direction of cause and effect

Filter theory suggests that people are initially attracted to each other *because* they are similar (demographically of course, but also attitudinally and in other ways too). But there is evidence that this direction of causality is wrong. Anderson *et al.* (2003) found in a **longitudinal study** that cohabiting partners became more similar in their emotional responses over time, a phenomenon they called *emotional convergence*.

Furthermore, Davis and Rusbult (2001) discovered an *attitude alignment effect* in longer-term relationships. Romantic partners over time bring their attitudes into line with each other's, again suggesting that similarity is an effect of initial attraction and not the cause.

These findings are not predicted by filter theory.

Evaluation eXtra

Lack of temporal validity

The rise of online dating in recent years has changed beyond recognition the process of beginning a romantic relationship. It has reduced the importance of some **social demographic** variables. Technology such as the Internet and mobile apps like Tinder have made meeting potential partners easier than ever, to the extent that we might well pursue a date with someone outside the usual demographic limits (e.g. different culture or social class) than would have applied, say, 30 years ago.

Consider: *Do you think this change in dating patterns has made the filter theory invalid? Explain your answer.*

Similarity or complementarity?

Some research has challenged the claim of filter theory that complementarity becomes more important than similarity later in a relationship. The fact that Anderson *et al.* (2003) found that similarity increases over time suggests that complementarity is not necessarily a common feature of longer-term relationships. Gruber-Baldini *et al.* (1995) carried out a longitudinal study of married couples. They found that the similarities between spouses in terms of intellectual abilities and attitudinal flexibility increased over a 14-year period.

Consider: *What effect does this finding have on the **validity** of the filter theory?*

A variety of men. Different ages, ethnicities, education levels, But filter theory claims we're attracted to those who are similar to us – 'birds of a feather flock together', at least to begin with.

Apply it · Concepts: Growing together

Katie and Peter have been together for 12 years. They had lots in common when they first met. But even after all that time, they still agree with each other over most matters, have similar interests and do a lot of things together.

Question

Do Katie's and Peter's experiences of their relationship support or challenge filter theory? Explain your answer.

Apply it · Methods: You and me, the same!

A psychologist investigated the similarity of attitudes between romantic partners in the early stages of a relationship. He recruited a volunteer sample of ten couples who had been together for less than six months. Each partner completed a questionnaire to measure their attitudes to a variety of issues, each one yielding a score between 1 and 20.

Questions

1. Write a **directional hypothesis** for this study. (*2 marks*)
2. Explain how the psychologist could have checked the **reliability** of the attitude **questionnaire**. (*3 marks*)
3. Explain why a **volunteer sample** was used in this study. (*2 marks*)

The results of the study are given in Table 1 below.

Table 1: Attitude scores for 10 romantic couples

Couple	Partner 1	Partner 2	Couple	Partner 1	Partner 2
1	17	14	6	8	10
2	8	5	7	15	12
3	11	14	8	10	13
4	14	18	9	7	4
5	4	2	10	12	9

4. Identify an appropriate **statistical test** the researcher could use to analyse the data. (*1 mark*) (See page 70)
5. Give *two* reasons why this would be an appropriate test to use. (*2 marks*) (See page 70)

CHECK IT

1. In relation to the filter theory of romantic relationships, explain what is meant by the terms *social demography* and *complementarity*. [2 marks + 2 marks]
2. Outline the filter theory of romantic relationships. [4 marks]
3. Briefly explain **two** limitations of the filter theory of romantic relationships. [2 marks + 2 marks]
4. Describe and evaluate the filter theory of romantic relationships. [16 marks]

THE SPECIFICATION SAYS...

> Theories of romantic relationships: social exchange theory.

Social exchange theory (SET) is one of a number of *economic theories* of relationships, so-called because they are based on the assumption that people in romantic relationships (like all others) both seek *exchange*.

Such theories recognise that people in a relationship both seek to give and receive valuable 'goods' and assume that we act out of self-interest though there is mutual interdependence.

KEY TERM

Social exchange theory – A theory of how relationships form and develop. It assumes that romantic partners act out of self-interest in exchanging rewards and costs. A satisfying and committed relationship is maintained when rewards exceed costs and potential alternatives are less attractive than the current relationship.

Apply it

Concepts: Love is ... never counting the cost?

Anushka and Ranveer are a couple who have been married for over 30 years. Anushka is terminally ill, but Ranveer decided he would care for her at home rather than see her put into a nursing home. He has been looking after Anushka virtually round the clock for several months, and she now has just days to live.

Kareena works in an office with 11 other people. Each year without fail, everyone gives each other a Christmas card. Kareena can remember how embarrassed she was the year she first joined the company, when she accidently left one of her co-workers off her list.

Question

What do you think these scenarios tell us about the rewards and costs involved in relationships? Can they be explained by social exchange theory? Explain why or why not.

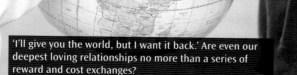

'I'll give you the world, but I want it back.' Are even our deepest loving relationships no more than a series of reward and cost exchanges?

Social exchange theory (SET)

Rewards, costs and profits

John Thibault and Harold Kelley (1959) contend that behaviour in relationships reflects the economic assumptions of exchange. Most importantly, they say we try to minimise losses and maximise gains (the *minimax principle*). We judge our satisfaction with a relationship in terms of the profit it yields, defined as the rewards minus the costs.

Because such rewards and costs are subjective, there exists a very wide range of possible outcomes. What one person considers a significant reward might be viewed by someone else as less valuable. For example, you might consider receiving praise from your partner as a prized reward, but your partner can take it or leave it. Also, the value of rewards and costs might well change over the course of a relationship. What is seen as rewarding or costly in the early stages, for instance, might become less so as time goes on (the converse is also true, of course).

Rewards include such beneficial things as companionship, sex and emotional support. But a romantic relationship is not always 'a bed of roses'. It can involve negative and unpleasant emotions as well as pleasurable ones. In the economic language of Peter Blau (1964) relationships can be 'expensive', so costs include time, stress, energy, compromise, and so on. Also in economic terms, a relationship incurs another kind of cost, an *opportunity cost*. Your investment of time and energy in your current relationship means using resources that you cannot invest elsewhere.

Comparison level (CL)

There are two ways in which we measure the profit in a romantic relationship. The first, the *comparison level* (CL), is essentially the amount of reward that you believe you deserve to get. It develops out of our experiences of previous relationships which feed into our expectations of the current one. It is also influenced by **social norms** that determine what is widely considered, within a culture, to be a reasonable level of reward. This is often reflected in the media, in books, films, and TV programmes such as soap operas. Over time, we get more relationships 'under our belt' and more experience of social norms, so our CL changes as we acquire more 'data' to set it by.

We consider a relationship worth pursuing if our CL is high. There is an obvious link with **self-esteem** here. Someone with low self-esteem will have a low CL and will therefore be satisfied with gaining just a small profit (or even a loss) from a relationship. Someone with higher self-esteem will believe they are worth a lot more.

Comparison level for alternatives (CLalt)

The second measure of profit provides a wider context for our current relationship. Do we believe we could gain greater rewards and fewer costs from another relationship (or from being on our own)? Given that romantic relationships in our culture are usually exclusive, we ask ourselves, 'Could I do better? Is the grass greener elsewhere?'. SET predicts that we will stay in our current relationship only so long as we believe it is more rewarding than the alternatives.

According to relationships researcher Steve Duck (1994), the CLalt we adopt will depend on the state of our current relationship. There are usually 'plenty more fish in the sea', so if the costs of our current relationship outweigh the rewards, then alternatives become more attractive. Being in a satisfying relationship means that you may not even notice that alternatives could be available.

Stages of relationship development

Another feature of Thibault and Kelley's **social exchange theory** concerns the four stages through which relationships (and the social exchanges which underpin them) develop:

- *Sampling stage:* We explore the rewards and costs of social exchange by experimenting with them in our own relationships (not just romantic ones), or by observing others doing so.

- *Bargaining stage:* This marks the beginning of a relationship, when romantic partners start exchanging various rewards and costs, negotiating and identifying what is most profitable.

- *Commitment stage:* As time goes on, the sources of costs and rewards become more predictable and the relationship becomes more stable as rewards increase and costs lessen.

- *Institutionalisation stage:* The partners are now settled down because the norms of the relationship, in terms of rewards and costs, are firmly established.

Evaluation

Research support for preferences related to anisogamy

David Buss (1989) carried out a survey of over 10,000 adults in 33 countries. He asked questions relating to age and a variety of attributes that evolutionary theory predicts should be important in partner preference. He found that female respondents placed greater value on resource-related characteristics, such as good financial prospects, ambition and industriousness, than males did. Males valued reproductive capacity in terms of good looks and chastity, and preferred younger mates, more than females did.

These findings reflect sex differences in mate strategies due to anisogamy. They support predictions about partner preference derived from sexual selection theory. Furthermore, the findings can be applied across vastly different cultures, reflecting fundamental human preferences which are not primarily dependent upon cultural influences.

Research support for inter-sexual selection

Russell Clark and Elaine Hatfield (1989) showed that female choosiness is a reality of heterosexual relationships. Male and female psychology students were sent out across a university campus. They approached other students individually with this question: 'I have been noticing you around campus. I find you to be very attractive. Would you go to bed with me tonight?'. Not a single female student agreed to the request, whereas 75% of males did, immediately.

This supports evolutionary theory because it suggests that females are choosier than males when it comes to selecting sexual partners and that males have evolved a different strategy to ensure reproductive success.

Ignores social and cultural influences

Partner preferences over the past century have undoubtedly been influenced by rapidly changing social norms of sexual behaviour. These develop much faster than evolutionary timescales imply and have instead come about due to cultural factors such as availability of contraception.

Women's greater role in the workplace means that they are no longer dependent on men to provide for them (despite the ongoing inequality in earning power). Bereczkei *et al.* (1997) argue that this social change has consequences for women's mate preferences, which may no longer be resource-oriented. Chang *et al.* (2011) compared partner preferences in China over 25 years and found that some had changed but others remained the same, corresponding with the huge social changes in that time.

Mate preferences are therefore the outcome of a combination of evolutionary and cultural influences. Any theory that fails to account for both is a limited explanation.

Evaluation eXtra

Support from waist-hip ratio research

Evolutionary theory makes several predictions about partner preference that can be tested empirically. One is that males will show a preference for a female body shape that signals fertility. Devendra Singh (1993, 2002) studied this in terms of waist-hip ratio (WHR). What matters in male preference is not female body size as such, but the ratio of waist to hip sizes. Up to a point, males generally find any hip and waist sizes are attractive so long as the ratio of one to the other is about 0.7. This combination of wider hips and narrower waist is attractive because it is an 'honest signal' (it is hard to fake) that the woman is fertile but not currently pregnant.

Consider: Why is it adaptive for males to be able to detect female fertility? What does this tell us about males' partner preferences?

Support from lonely hearts research

David Waynforth and Robin Dunbar (1995) studied lonely hearts advertisements in American newspapers. These slightly quaint historical documents were opportunities for men (usually) and women to describe the qualities they desired in a potential partner, whilst cataloguing what they had to offer. The researchers found that women more than men tended to offer physical attractiveness and indicators of youth ('flirty, exciting, curvy, sexy'). Men, on the other hand, offered resources more than women did ('successful, fit, mature, ambitious') and sought relative youth and physical attractiveness.

Consider: Which predictions from sexual selection theory do these findings support?

Voulez-vous coucher avec moi, ce soir? Direct and to the point. But which one is likely to be disappointed?

Apply it — Concepts: **Young, free, single**

Shakira and Gerard are young and single people who seem to have a new partner almost every night. They make no bones about the fact that they are out to have a good time while they're still young.

Question

How do you think society generally would view Shakira's and Gerard's behaviour? Is there an evolutionary explanation for why one of their behaviours might be considered acceptable and the other not? Explain your answer.

Apply it — Methods: **Replicating Buss**

An evolutionary psychologist wanted to replicate the study by Buss (1989) by using an interview method. He carried out face-to-face interviews with 82 participants, 45 of them male and 37 female. He asked various questions about their preferences for certain evolutionarily-important characteristics in a partner. Physical attractiveness was preferred by 40 of the males and 28 of the females. Good financial prospects was an attribute preferred by 25 of the males and 32 of the females.

Questions

1. The study produced a lot of **quantitative data**. Explain what is meant by this term. (*2 marks*)

2. Write a question that could gather quantitative data. (*2 marks*)

3. Explain *two* differences between a **structured** and an **unstructured interview**. (*2 marks + 2 marks*)

4. Explain *one* reason why the psychologist thought interviews might be better than **questionnaires** in this study. (*2 marks*)

5. Calculate the preferences of males and females as percentages (four percentages). (*4 marks*)

CHECK IT

1. Explain what is meant by the term *sexual selection*. [2 marks]

2. Briefly outline **one** evolutionary explanation of partner preference. [4 marks]

3. Describe and evaluate evolutionary explanations of partner preference. [16 marks]

4. Discuss the relationship between sexual selection and human reproductive behaviour. [16 marks]

Factors affecting attraction in romantic relationships: self-disclosure.

'The course of true love never did run smooth', Shakespeare tells us in *A Midsummer Night's Dream*. But how can it run smoother? How can it get started at all in the first place?

Psychologists have identified several factors that influence whether or not (and how much) we are attracted to a potential romantic partner. We will be looking at three in total, beginning with *self-disclosure*.

KEY TERM

Self-disclosure – Revealing personal information about yourself. Romantic partners reveal more about their true selves as their relationship develops. These self-disclosures about one's deepest thoughts and feelings can strengthen a romantic bond when used appropriately.

Apply it

Concepts: Hollywood couples still together

The actors Felicity Huffman and William H Macy have been happily married since 1997. When asked the secret of their longevity, Huffman said, 'Once a week we sit down and make sure we get half an hour – each of us gets 15 minutes – just to talk, with no crosstalk. I talk, then you talk. You kind of just deeply check in with the other person.'

Question

Explain how research into self-disclosure confirms Huffman and Macy's experience of a satisfying relationship. What sort of things would you disclose? Why do you think it needs to be a two-way process?

Self-disclosure

In the early days of a relationship, we love to learn as much as we can about our new partner, and the more we learn about them the more we seem to like them. By revealing ourselves to another person, we share our likes and dislikes, our hopes and fears, our interests and attitudes. We share what really matters to us. Our partner understands us better, and we them.

So **self-disclosure** has a vital role in a relationship beyond the initial attraction. But most people are careful about what they disclose, at least to begin with. Used wisely and effectively it really can help the course of true love run smoother.

Social penetration theory

Self-disclosure is a major concept within Irwin Altman and Dalmas Taylor's (1973) *social penetration theory* of how relationships develop. It is the gradual process of revealing your inner self to someone else, of giving away your deepest thoughts and feelings. In romantic relationships, it involves the reciprocal exchange of information between intimate partners. When one partner reveals some personal information they display trust; to go further the other partner must also reveal sensitive information. As they increasingly disclose more and more information to each other, romantic partners 'penetrate' more deeply into each other's lives, and gain a greater understanding of each other.

It is a basic feature of romantic relationships. After all, it's difficult to 'bear one's soul' to a relative stranger. Doing so means that a relationship has reached a certain stage where such self-disclosure will be welcomed and – hopefully – reciprocated.

Breadth and depth of self-disclosure

According to Altman and Taylor, self-disclosure has two elements – breadth and depth. As both of these increase, romantic partners become more committed to each other. The researchers use the metaphor of the many layers of an onion to illustrate this process. We disclose a lot about ourselves at the start of a relationship, but what we reveal is superficial, mostly 'on the surface', like the outer layers of an onion. It is the kind of 'low-risk' information we would reveal to anyone, friends, co-workers, even acquaintances. Breadth of disclosure is narrow because many topics are 'off-limits' in the early stage of a relationship. If we were to reveal too much too soon, we might get the response 'too much information', possibly even threatening the relationship before it's had a chance to get going.

However, as a relationship develops, self-disclosure becomes deeper, progressively removing more and more layers to reveal our true selves and encompassing a wider range of topics, especially concerning those things that matter most to us. Eventually we are prepared to reveal intimate, high-risk information – painful memories and experiences, strongly-held beliefs, powerful feelings, perhaps even secrets (and maybe the odd lie).

Reciprocity of self-disclosure

As Harry Reis and Philip Shaver (1988) point out, for a relationship to develop, as well as an increase in breadth and depth there needs to be a *reciprocal* element to disclosure. Once you have decided to disclose something that reveals your true self, hopefully your partner will respond in a way that is rewarding, with understanding, empathy and also their own intimate thoughts and feelings. So there is a balance of self-disclosure between both partners in a successful romantic relationship, which increases feelings of intimacy and deepens the relationship.

'But soft! What light through yonder window breaks?
It is the east, and Juliet is the sun.
… It is my lady, O, it is my love!
O that she knew she were!'

The most basic self-disclosure in any romantic relationship – telling someone you love them.

Evaluation

Inappropriate assumptions underlying SET

Many researchers do not accept the economic metaphor underlying SET. Margaret Clark and Judson Mills (2011) argue that the theory fails to distinguish between two types of relationship. They suggest that *exchange relationships* (for example, between work colleagues) do involve social exchange as SET predicts. But *communal relationships* (such as between romantic partners) are marked by the giving and receiving of rewards without keeping score of who is ahead and who is behind.

SET claims that relationship partners return rewards for rewards, costs for costs, and that these reciprocal activities are monitored. But if we felt this kind of exchange monitoring was going on at the start of a promising relationship, we would probably question what kind of commitment our partner wanted. It is clear from some research that SET is based on faulty assumptions and therefore cannot account for the majority of romantic relationships.

Direction of cause and effect

SET argues that dissatisfaction sets in when we suspect that costs outweigh rewards or that alternatives are more attractive. Michael Argyle (1987) points out that we don't measure costs and rewards in a relationship, nor do we constantly consider the attractiveness of alternatives. That is, not until we are dissatisfied with the relationship.

Research supports this view that dissatisfaction comes first. For example, Rowland Miller (1997) found that people who rated themselves as being in a highly committed relationship spent less time looking at images of attractive people. What's more, less time spent looking was a good predictor of the relationship continuing two months later. So people in committed relationships ignore even the most attractive alternatives. SET cannot account for the direction of causation in this outcome.

SET ignores equity

The central concern of SET is the comparison level, the ratio of perceived rewards and costs. But this focus ignores one crucial factor that may be an overwhelming consideration for romantic partners – fairness or *equity*. The next spread explains how this shortcoming of SET has been addressed by another theory (**equity theory**).

There is much research support for the role of equity in relationships, and the view that this is more important than just the balance of rewards and costs. Neglect of this factor means that SET is a limited explanation which cannot account for a significant proportion of the research findings on relationships.

Evaluation eXtra

Measuring SET concepts

SET deals in concepts that are difficult to quantify. Rewards and costs have been defined superficially (e.g. money) in order to measure them. But psychological rewards and costs are more difficult to define, especially when they vary so much from one person to another. The concept of comparison levels is especially problematic. It is unclear what the values of CL and CLalt must be before dissatisfaction threatens a relationship. How attractive do alternatives need to be, or by how much should costs outweigh rewards?

Consider: *Is it possible to measure rewards and and costs in a valid and reliable way? How does this limit SET?*

Artificial research

The majority of studies supporting SET use artificial tasks in artificial conditions. For example, one common procedure involves two strangers working together on a game-playing scenario in which rewards and costs are distributed. The two 'partners' know nothing about each other and their so-called 'relationship' depends entirely on the task they are performing together. More realistic studies using participants in real relationships have been less supportive of SET, especially noting that **snapshot studies** cannot account for the properties that emerge from a relationship over time, such as trust.

Consider: *How realistic do you think these research 'relationships' are? Can you explain how this limitation of the studies weakens the theory itself?*

Apply it   Concepts: You scratch my back

Eric and Arianna found each other on an online dating site, and have just spent their first day together in the real world. They are both very keen on each other, and both think the other is very attractive. But everywhere they went together, Arianna was totting up how much each of them had spent. It was her idea they split the bill in the restaurant. And every time Eric said something nice to her, she had to do the same to him. But Eric just can't be doing with all that, so now he isn't sure he wants to continue the relationship.

Question

Which of Eric and Arianna is behaving in ways predicted by social exchange theory? Explain which concepts described by SET are particularly important in this scenario and why.

Dodgy first date? Too much exchange monitoring at the start of a relationship and we might wonder if our partner would rather be 'just friends'.

Apply it   Methods: Players of games

A psychologist decides to test the social exchange theory of relationships by using a game-playing scenario. He recruits two groups of romantic partners – some who have been together for less than two months and others for more than two years. One partner in each couple is Player A and the other is Player B. Player A gives £10 to Player B. The experimenter triples this amount and gives it all to Player B. Player B then has to decide how much to give back to player A, from nothing to £30. The psychologist found that in couples who had been together less than two months, the mean amount returned by Player B was £17.50. The corresponding figure for couples who had been together for more than two years was £12.40.

Questions

1. Write a **non-directional hypothesis** for this **experiment**. (*2 marks*)
2. What **experimental design** is used in this study? (*1 mark*)
3. The researcher assigned the roles of Player A and Player B randomly. Explain how he could have done this and why it was necessary. (*2 marks + 2 marks*)
4. Explain why this experiment might be lacking in validity. (*3 marks*)

CHECK IT

1. Explain what is meant by the term *social exchange* in relation to romantic relationships.   [2 marks]
2. Briefly outline the social exchange theory of romantic relationships.   [4 marks]
3. Outline **one** study of social exchange theory.   [4 marks]
4. Describe and evaluate the social exchange theory of romantic relationships.   [16 marks]

THEORIES OF ROMANTIC RELATIONSHIPS: EQUITY THEORY

THE SPECIFICATION SAYS...

Theories of romantic relationships: equity theory.

Do we really think about our closest relationships in terms of the rewards and costs they bring us? Would we leave our current partner if we felt that we could get a better deal elsewhere? We all know lots of couples in which one partner seems to contribute a lot more to the relationship than the other, but both appear to be happy and satisfied.

There's something missing from social exchange theory and that something is equity – the idea that you can put a lot into a relationship and still be happy, as long as there is a perceived sense of fairness.

KEY TERM

Equity theory – An economic theory of how relationships develop. As such, it acknowledges the impact of rewards and costs on relationship satisfaction, but criticises social exchange theory for ignoring the central role of equity – the perception that partners have that the distribution of rewards and costs in the relationship is fair.

Apply it

Concepts: Fair's fair ... or is it?

Since Steph and Dom moved in together two years ago, their relationship has changed drastically. Steph used to make much more of an effort, but now she does very little and seems happy for Dom to do all the running. Apart from doing most of the domestic chores and keeping the house going, it seems he's also responsible for the emotional well-being of the relationship. He's finding it hard work and stressful.

Jess and Justin have been married for 15 years. It took a while, but Jess eventually realised that Justin's depression meant that he couldn't put as much into the relationship as he once did. She's now used to having to keep their relationship going, but she loves her husband and is glad she can do something to help him. And there are times when he feels much better anyway.

Question

Explain Dom's and Jess's experiences of their relationships in terms of equity theory. How are they likely to feel? Why? What do you think they might do to change things?

STUDY TIP

Equity is not the same as equality. Romantic partners do not have to get the same amount of rewards and costs in a relationship. But there needs to be a fair balance between the two.

Equity theory

Equity theory is another economic theory which developed in response to a significant criticism of **social exchange theory** (SET). Maximising rewards and minimising costs are important, but SET fails to take into account the need most people have for equity in a relationship.

The role of equity

The term 'equity' means fairness. According to Elaine Walster and her colleagues (1978), what matters most with equity is that both partners' level of *profit* (rewards minus costs) is roughly the same. This is not the same as equality where levels of costs and rewards have to be the same (i.e., 'equal') for each partner. When there is a lack of equity, then one partner *overbenefits* and the other *underbenefits* from the relationship, and this is a recipe for dissatisfaction and unhappiness.

Both overbenefit and underbenefit are examples of inequity although it is the underbenefitted partner who is likely to feel the greatest dissatisfaction, in the form of anger, hostility, resentment, and humiliation. The overbenefitted partner will likely feel guilt, discomfort, and shame. Thus satisfaction is about perceived fairness.

Equity and equality

According to equity theory, it's not the size or amount of the rewards and costs that matters; it's the ratio of the two to each other. So if one partner puts a lot into the relationship but at the same time gets a lot out of it, then that will seem fair enough.

For example, imagine a relationship in which one partner has a disability that prevents them from carrying out domestic chores or other physical activities. A precisely equal distribution of these tasks would probably not be seen as fair by either partner. The equity in such a relationship may well come from the compensations that the disabled partner could offer in other areas, or from the satisfactions that the more active partner gains from their behaviour. Satisfying relationships are marked by negotiations to ensure equity, that rewards are distributed fairly (not necessarily equally) between the partners. This inevitably involves making trade-offs.

Consequences of inequity

Problems arise when one partner puts a great deal in to the relationship but gets little from it. A partner who is the subject of inequity will become distressed and dissatisfied with the relationship if this state of affairs continues for long enough. The greater the perceived inequity, the greater the dissatisfaction: equity theory predicts a strong **correlation** between the two. This applies to both the overbenefitted and underbenefitted partner to the extent that they both perceive the inequity.

Changes in perceived equity What makes us most dissatisfied is a change in the level of perceived equity as time goes on. For example, at the start of a relationship it may feel perfectly natural to contribute more than you receive. But if the relationship develops in such a way that you continue to put more into the relationship and get less out of it, this will not feel as satisfying as it did in the early days.

Dealing with inequity How do romantic partners react to inequity? The 'put-upon' partner will work hard to make the relationship more equitable as long as they believe it is possible to do so and that the relationship is salvageable. The more unfair the relationship feels, the harder they will work to restore equity (another strong correlation). On the other hand, another possible outcome is a cognitive rather than behavioural one. They will revise their perceptions of rewards and costs so that the relationship feels more equitable to them, even if nothing actually changes. What was once seen as definitely a cost earlier in the relationship (untidiness, thoughtlessness, actual abuse) is now accepted as the norm.

Evaluation

Supporting research evidence

Supporting evidence includes studies of real-life relationships that confirm equity theory as a more **valid** explanation than SET. Mary Utne and her colleagues (1984) carried out a survey of 118 recently-married couples, measuring equity with two **self-report** scales. These husbands and wives were aged between 16 and 45 years, and had been together for more than two years before marrying. The researchers found that couples who considered their relationship equitable were more satisfied than those who saw themselves as overbenefitting or underbenefitting.

This research confirms a central prediction of equity theory, increasing its validity as an explanation of romantic relationships.

Cultural influences

Equity theory assumes that the need for equity is a universal feature of romantic relationships across all cultures, because it's a fundamental feature of human behaviour. However, Katherine Aumer-Ryan *et al.* (2007) found that there are cultural differences in the link between equity and satisfaction. The researchers compared couples in a **collectivist culture** (where the needs of the wider group come first) with those in an **individualist culture** (which prioritises the individual's needs). Couples from an individualist culture considered their relationships to be most satisfying when the relationship was equitable, whereas partners in the collectivist culture were most satisfied when they were overbenefitting. This was true of both men and women.

This suggests that equity theory's claim that equity is a universal need in relationships is unwarranted. So the theory is limited because it cannot account for this cultural difference.

Individual differences

Not all partners in romantic relationships are concerned about achieving equity. Huseman *et al.* (1987) suggest that some people are less sensitive to equity than others. They describe some partners as *benevolents*, who are prepared to contribute more to the relationship than they get out of it. Others are *entitleds* who believe they deserve to be overbenefitted and accept it without feeling distressed or guilty.

This shows that equity is not necessarily a global feature of all romantic relationships and, contrary to the claims of the theory, is certainly not a universal law of social interaction.

Evaluation eXtra

Types of relationship

Margaret Clark and Judson Mills (2011) attempted to make sense of the sometimes confusing body of evidence that equity is an important feature of relationships. Their conclusion is that we should distinguish between different types of relationship. Research studies strongly support the view that equity plays a central role in casual friendships, business/work relationships and acquaintanceships. But the evidence that equity is important in romantic relationships is much more mixed. Many of these studies have questioned the assumptions and predictions of equity theory, such as the link between equity and satisfaction, as they apply to romantic relationships.

Consider: *Do you think there is a greater role for equity in some of your relationships than in others? How does Clark and Mills's point limit equity theory?*

Contradictory research evidence

Some research studies fail to support predictions made by equity theory. For instance the theory claims that satisfying romantic relationships should become more equitable over time. But Daniel Berg and Kristen McQuinn (1986) found that equity did not increase in their **longitudinal study** of dating couples. Equity theory also did not distinguish between those relationships which ended and those which continued, other variables being significantly more important. One of these is **self-disclosure**, which we considered in an earlier spread in this chapter.

Consider: *How significant a criticism of equity theory do you think this is?*

If we perceive inequity in our relationships, rather than doing something concrete about it, we might just settle for adjusting our expectations – a cognitive solution.

CHECK IT

1. Explain what is meant by the term *equity* in relation to romantic relationships. **[2 marks]**

2. Briefly outline the equity theory of romantic relationships. **[4 marks]**

3. Outline **one** study of equity theory. **[4 marks]**

4. Discuss the equity theory of romantic relationships. **[16 marks]**

Theories of romantic relationships: Rusbult's investment model of commitment, satisfaction, comparison with alternatives and investment.

Perhaps there is more to romantic relationships than just the balance of rewards and costs. Perhaps we're not even that bothered about whether the relationship is fair.

The investment model emphasises the central importance of commitment in relationships. Caryl Rusbult devised the model to address the limitations of social exchange theory.

KEY TERMS

Commitment – A romantic partner's intention or desire to continue a relationship, reflecting a belief that the relationship has a viable long-term future.

Satisfaction – The extent to which romantic partners feel the rewards of the relationship exceed the costs.

Comparison with alternatives – A judgement that partners make concerning whether a relationship with a different partner would bring more rewards and fewer costs.

Investment – The resources associated with a romantic relationship which the partners would lose if the relationship were to end.

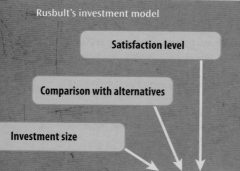

Rusbult's investment model

Satisfaction level

Comparison with alternatives

Investment size

Commitment level

Relationship maintenance mechanisms
Accommodation
Willingness to sacrifice
Forgiveness
Positive illusions
Ridiculing alternatives

Rusbult's investment model

According to Rusbult *et al.* (2011), **commitment** depends on three factors (see diagram, bottom left). Because the investment model is a development of **social exchange theory** (SET), two of these factors – satisfaction and comparison with alternatives – are very similar to elements of that earlier theory discussed on a previous spread.

Satisfaction and comparison with alternatives

Satisfaction is based on the concept of the **comparison level** (**CL**). A satisfying relationship is judged by comparing rewards and costs, and is seen to be profitable if it has many rewards (e.g. support, sex, companionship) and few costs (e.g. conflicts, anxiety). Each partner is generally satisfied if they are getting more out of the relationship than they expect based on previous experience and social norms.

As we've already seen in social exchange theory, a **comparison with alternatives** (CLalt) results in romantic partners asking themselves, 'Could my needs be better met outside my current relationship? Are the alternatives more rewarding and less costly?'. Alternatives include not just relationships with other people, but the possibility of having no romantic relationship at all.

Investment size

Rusbult realised that the CL and CLalt derived from SET are not enough to explain commitment. If they were, then many more relationships would end as soon as either the costs outweighed the rewards (representing a loss) or more attractive alternatives presented themselves. Therefore she introduced a crucial third factor influencing commitment – **investment**.

'Investment' refers to the extent and importance of the resources associated with the relationship. An investment can be understood as anything we would lose if the relationship were to end. Rusbult argues that there are two major types of investment:

- *Intrinsic investments* are any resources we put directly into the relationship. They can be tangible things such as money and possessions. They can also be resources less easy to quantify (intangibles) such as energy, emotion, and **self-disclosures** (see earlier spread).
- *Extrinsic investments* are resources that previously did not feature in the relationship, but are now closely associated with it. Tangibles include possessions bought together (for example, a car), mutual friends acquired since the relationship began and children. A good example of an intangible is shared memories.

So putting these all together: if the partners in a relationship experience high levels of satisfaction (because they are getting many rewards with few costs) and the alternatives are less attractive and the sizes of their investment are increasing, then we can confidently predict that partners will be committed to the relationship.

Satisfaction versus commitment

Rusbult *et al.* (2011) argue that the main psychological factor that causes people to stay in romantic relationships is not satisfaction but commitment. This is an important distinction, because it can help to explain why dissatisfied partners may choose to stay in a relationship – it's because they are committed to their partner. But why are they so committed? That's because they have made an investment that they do not want to see go to waste. Therefore they will work hard to maintain and repair a damaged relationship, especially when it hits a rough patch.

Relationship maintenance mechanisms

Commitment expresses itself in everyday maintenance behaviours. According to the model, enduring partners do not engage in tit-for-tat retaliation but instead act to promote the relationship (accommodation). They will also put their partner's interests first (willingness to sacrifice), and forgive them for any serious transgressions (forgiveness).

There is also a cognitive element to relationship maintenance and repair. Committed partners think about each other and potential alternatives in specific (and predictable) ways. They are unrealistically positive about their partner (positive illusions), and negative about tempting alternatives and other people's relationships (ridiculing alternatives), much more so than less committed partners.

Apply it **Concepts: Should I stay or should I go?**

Christy feels she is trapped in an unhappy relationship. She seems to be the one who always does everything around the house. Her needs always come second. She remembers being treated much better in her previous relationships. On the other hand, at least she has somewhere to live, and she really hates the idea of being on her own. Plus she has put a lot into the relationship. She came into it with a lot of stuff, including the house, and she still remembers the good times she and her partner used to have.

Question

Use the investment model to explain why Christy continues in the relationship. How does the model predict she will behave in the future?

Evaluation

Supporting research evidence

Some of the strongest support for the investment model comes from a **meta-analysis** by Benjamin Le and Christopher Agnew (2003). They reviewed 52 studies from the late 1970s to 1999, studies which together included some 11,000 participants from five countries. They found that satisfaction, comparison with alternatives and investment size all predicted relationship commitment. Relationships in which commitment was greatest were the most stable and lasted longest.

An especially supportive finding was that these outcomes were true for both men and women, across all cultures in the analysis, and for homosexual as well as heterosexual couples.

This suggests there is some **validity** to Rusbult's claim that these factors are universally important features of romantic relationships.

Explains abusive relationships

The investment model is thought to be a particularly valid and useful explanation of relationships involving *intimate partner violence* (IPV, commonly known as 'abusive relationships'). On the face of it, it seems surprising that any rational person subjected to violence by a partner should continue to be committed to the relationship. Why do they not simply leave? The key factor is clearly not satisfaction.

Caryl Rusbult and John Martz (1995) studied 'battered' women at a shelter and found that those most likely to return to an abusive partner (i.e. were most committed) reported making the greatest investment and having the fewest attractive alternatives. The model recognises that a victim of IPV does not have to be satisfied with a relationship to stay in it.

Oversimplifies investment

Wind Goodfriend and Christopher Agnew (2008) point out that there is more to investment than just the resources you have already put into a relationship. After all, in the early stages of a romantic relationship the partners will have made very few actual investments. They may not even live together at this point. Goodfriend and Agnew extended Rusbult's original model by including the investment romantic partners make in their *future plans*. They are motivated to commit to each other because they want to see their cherished plans for the future work out.

The original model is a limited explanation of romantic relationships because it fails to recognise the true complexity of investment, specifically how planning for the future influences commitment.

Evaluation eXtra

Methodological strengths

It is striking that so much of the evidence supporting the investment model relies on **self-report** measures such as **questionnaires** and **interviews**. However, these are appropriate methods because it is not the objective reality of factors such as investment size that matters. What matters is the individual partners' *perceptions* of these factors. It is your *belief* that you have made a big investment in your current relationship, or your belief that you have no attractive alternatives, that will influence your commitment. Whether this belief matches the objective reality of the situation is really neither here nor there.

Consider: *Explain why this is a strength of the model.*

Based on correlational research

Strong **correlations** have been found between all the important factors predicted by the investment model. However, even the strongest correlation is no evidence of causation. Most studies do not allow us to conclude that any of the factors actually *cause* commitment in a relationship. It could be that the more committed you feel towards your partner, the more investment you are willing to make in the relationship, so the direction of causality may be the reverse of that predicted by the model.

Consider: *Explain why this methodological issue is a limitation of the model.*

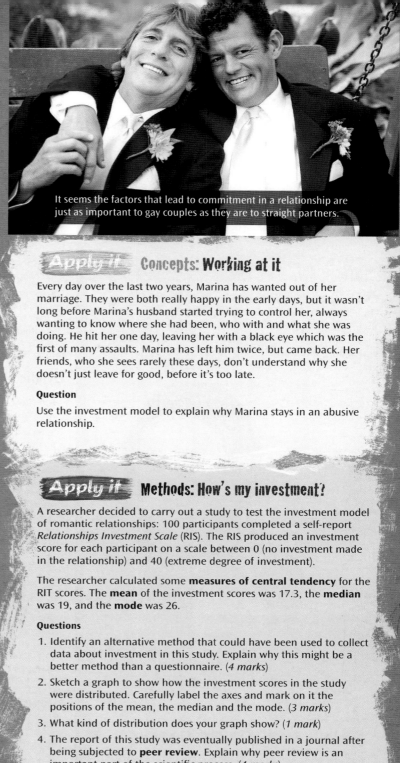

It seems the factors that lead to commitment in a relationship are just as important to gay couples as they are to straight partners.

Apply it Concepts: **Working at it**

Every day over the last two years, Marina has wanted out of her marriage. They were both really happy in the early days, but it wasn't long before Marina's husband started trying to control her, always wanting to know where she had been, who with and what she was doing. He hit her one day, leaving her with a black eye which was the first of many assaults. Marina has left him twice, but came back. Her friends, who she sees rarely these days, don't understand why she doesn't just leave for good, before it's too late.

Question

Use the investment model to explain why Marina stays in an abusive relationship.

Apply it Methods: **How's my investment?**

A researcher decided to carry out a study to test the investment model of romantic relationships: 100 participants completed a self-report *Relationships Investment Scale* (RIS). The RIS produced an investment score for each participant on a scale between 0 (no investment made in the relationship) and 40 (extreme degree of investment).

The researcher calculated some **measures of central tendency** for the RIT scores. The **mean** of the investment scores was 17.3, the **median** was 19, and the **mode** was 26.

Questions

1. Identify an alternative method that could have been used to collect data about investment in this study. Explain why this might be a better method than a questionnaire. (*4 marks*)

2. Sketch a graph to show how the investment scores in the study were distributed. Carefully label the axes and mark on it the positions of the mean, the median and the mode. (*3 marks*)

3. What kind of distribution does your graph show? (*1 mark*)

4. The report of this study was eventually published in a journal after being subjected to **peer review**. Explain why peer review is an important part of the scientific process. (*4 marks*)

CHECK IT

1. In relation to the investment model of romantic relationships, explain what is meant by the terms *investment* and *comparison with alternatives*. [2 marks + 2 marks]

2. Briefly outline Rusbult's investment model of romantic relationships. [4 marks]

3. Distinguish between Rusbult's investment model and social exchange theory. [6 marks]

4. Describe and evaluate Rusbult's investment model of romantic relationships. [16 marks]

Theories of romantic relationships: Duck's phase model of relationship breakdown.

It's a fact of life that even once-strong relationships come to an end, and for all sorts of reasons: lack of communication, disinterest, neglect, betrayal. But can we identify any patterns in the breakdown process? Steve Duck (1997) believes we can and has devised a comprehensive model of relationship breakdown that is widely accepted.

KEY TERM

Phase model of relationship breakdown – An explanation of the stages people go through when their relationship is not working. Once one partner is dissatisfied, there are four phases in the process, each with a different focus: intra-psychic, dyadic, social and grave-dressing.

'Should I stay or should I go?' Couples in the early stage of relationship breakdown spend a lot of time mulling things over in their own minds.

Apply it

Concepts: Breaking up, phase by phase

Karisma and Sanjay had been together for five years before they realised they weren't talking to each other much anymore. And when they did, there were lots of arguments and complaints. Eventually, family and friends became involved and Karisma and Sanjay both found out things they didn't know about each other. Towards the end, they spent a lot of time criticising and blaming each other to their friends.

Question

Identify the phases of Duck's model in the account above. Use the model to explain how Karisma and Sanjay's relationship could have been saved at various points in the breakdown process.

Duck's phase model of relationship breakdown

Duck (2007) proposed a **phase model of relationship breakdown**. He argued that the ending of a relationship is not a one-off event but a process that takes time and goes through four distinct phases. Each phase is marked by one partner (or both) reaching a 'threshold', a point at which their perception of the relationship changes (usually for the worse). The road to break-up begins once a partner realises that they are dissatisfied with the relationship and distressed about the way things are going.

Intra-psychic phase

Threshold: 'I can't stand this anymore', indicating a determination that something has to change.

The focus of this phase is on cognitive processes occurring within the individual. The dissatisfied partner broods on the reasons for his or her dissatisfaction, centring mostly on their partner's shortcomings. The partner mulls their thoughts over privately, and may share them with a trusted friend. They weigh up the pros and cons of the relationship and evaluate these against the alternatives (including being alone). They begin to make plans for the future.

Dyadic phase

Threshold: They eventually come to the conclusion, 'I would be justified in withdrawing'.

The focus here is on interpersonal processes between the two partners. There comes a point when they cannot avoid talking about their relationship any longer. There is a series of confrontations over a period of time, in which the relationship is discussed and dissatisfactions are aired. These are characterised by anxiety, hostility, probably complaints about lack of equity, resentment over imbalanced roles and a rethinking of the commitment that kept the partners together. There are two possible outcomes – a determination to continue breaking up the relationship, or a renewed desire to repair it. But if the rescue attempts fail, another threshold is reached.

Social phase

Threshold: The dissatisfied partner concludes, 'I mean it'.

The focus is now on wider processes involving the couple's social networks. The break-up is made public. Partners will seek support and try to forge pacts. Mutual friends find they are expected to choose a side. Factions are formed. Gossip is traded and encouraged. Some friends will provide reinforcement and reassurance ('I always said you were way too good for him'). Others will be judgemental and place the blame on one partner or the other. Some may hasten the end of the relationship by providing previously secret information ('I didn't want to mention this but . . . '). Still others may pitch in and try to help repair the relationship (perhaps by acting as a go-between). This is usually the point of no return – the break-up takes on a momentum driven by social forces.

Grave-dressing phase

Threshold: 'It's now inevitable'.

The focus of this phase is on the aftermath. Once the relationship is dead, the time comes to bury it, by 'spinning' a favourable story about the breakdown for public consumption. This allows the partners to save face and maintain a positive reputation, usually at the expense of the other partner, showing them in a bad light. Gossip plays an important role in this phase. It is crucial that each partner tries to retain some 'social credit' (La Gaipa 1982) by blaming circumstances, your partner or other people, or everything and everyone but themselves.

Grave-dressing also involves creating a personal story you can live with, which may differ from the public one. This is more to do with tidying up memories of the relationship, in which a certain degree of rewriting of history may be necessary. The traits you found endearing or exciting in your partner at the start of the relationship are now reinterpreted in a much more negative fashion. A 'wild and unpredictable nature' is now seen as an 'irresponsible failure to settle down'. On the other hand, it may be simpler for ex-partners just to agree to let bygones be bygones and admit that they weren't compatible from the beginning.

The dissatisfied partner finally concludes, 'Time to get a new life'.

Evaluation

An incomplete model?

According to Stephanie Rollie and Steve Duck (2006), the original model described on this spread is oversimplified. They modified it to add a fifth phase after grave-dressing, the *resurrection phase*. Ex-partners turn their attention to future relationships using the experiences gained from their recently-ended one.

Rollie and Duck also make it clear that progression from one phase to the next is not inevitable. It is possible to return to an earlier point in the process in any phase. The new model also emphasises the *processes* that occur in relationship breakdown (e.g. the role of gossip in the social phase) rather than linear movement from one phase to the next.

These changes overcome a weakness of the original model, that it is a limited explanation because it does not account for the dynamic nature of break-ups with all their inherent uncertainty and complexity.

Methodological issues

Most of the research relating to Duck's model is retrospective. Participants generally give their experiences of the breakdown process some time after the relationship has ended. This means that what they can recall might not always be accurate or reliable. It's the very early stages of breakdown that understandably tend to be distorted or perhaps even ignored altogether.

To be fair, it is almost impossible to study this phase of the process, the point at which problems first appear. Researchers are very reluctant to study relationships at this early point because their involvement could make things worse, and even hasten the end of a relationship that might otherwise have been rescued. This means that part of Duck's model is based on research that ignores this early part of the process so it is an incomplete description of how relationships end.

Useful real-life applications

A strength of the model is that it not only helps us to identify and understand the stages of relationship breakdown but also suggests various ways of reversing it. The model is especially useful because it recognises that different repair strategies are more effective at particular points in the breakdown than at others. For example, Duck (1994) recommends that people in the intra-psychic phase could be encouraged to focus their brooding on the positive aspects of their partner. Also, as a feature of the dyadic phase is communication, any attempt to improve this and perhaps improve wider social skills could be beneficial in fostering greater stability in the relationship. Neither of these strategies is likely to be of much use in the later phases of the breakdown.

Such insights could be used in relationships counselling, a real-life application.

Evaluation eXtra

Description rather than explanation

Duck's model is less successful as an explanation of *why* breakdowns occur. In contrast, Diane Flemlee's (1995) *fatal attraction hypothesis* argues that the causes of relationship breakdown can be found in the attractive qualities that brought the romantic partners together. Effectively the relationship is threatened by the partners getting too much of what they were looking for. So that 'fantastic sense of humour' that was so dazzling at the start of the relationship may well become 'he can't take anything seriously' later on.

Consider: *Explain how you could use Felmlee's hypothesis to evaluate Duck's model.*

Cultural bias

The model, and most of the research underlying it, are firmly based on the experience of relationships in Western cultures, especially the USA. According to Moghaddam *et al.* (1993), relationships in **individualist cultures** are generally voluntary and frequently come to an end (for example, divorce or separation). Relationships in **collectivist cultures** are more likely to be obligatory, less easy to end, involve the wider family, and in some cases even *arranged* with little involvement of the partners. In fact the whole conception of a romantic relationship differs between cultures. It is therefore very unlikely that the process of relationship breakdown is identical across different cultures.

Consider: *How do these differences between cultures illustrate cultural bias in the research? How does this issue affect the **validity** of Duck's model?*

'Now you're just somebody that I used to know.' Successful negotiation of the grave-dressing phase means moving on to a new life having learned some valuable lessons.

Apply it — Concepts: I will survive

Katie and Tom were both unhappy with their relationship, which just seemed to go from bad to worse. If it had been up to Tom things would have drifted on and on. But Katie decided enough was enough and left.

Question

Some research shows that how ex-partners react to a break-up depends on the role they played in bringing the relationship to an end. Explain how you think Katie and Tom would have felt and behaved.

Apply it — Methods: A case study

A researcher into the psychology of relationships decided to investigate the reasons why romantic relationships break down. She carried out a **case study** of a divorced couple who had been married for 25 years. She used various techniques for collecting data about the process the couple went through before and after their marriage ended.

Questions

1. Describe *one* technique that the researcher could have used to collect data in this case study. (*2 marks*) (See page 64)
2. Explain *one* strength of conducting a case study. (*2 marks*)
3. The researcher wrote up the case study in a report for publication in a scientific journal. What is the purpose of the method section of such a report? (*2 marks*)
4. How could the researcher maintain her participants' **confidentiality** when her report is published? (*3 marks*)
5. Explain why **replication** of the study would be beneficial. (*3 marks*)

CHECK IT

1. Briefly outline Duck's phase model of relationship breakdown. [*4 marks*]
2. Identify and discuss **one** stage in Duck's phase model of relationship breakdown. [*4 marks*]
3. Evaluate Duck's phase model of relationship breakdown. [*6 marks*]
4. Describe and evaluate Duck's phase model of relationship breakdown. [*16 marks*]

VIRTUAL RELATIONSHIPS IN SOCIAL MEDIA

THE SPECIFICATION SAYS...

> Virtual relationships in social media: self-disclosure in virtual relationships; absence of gating on the nature of virtual relationships.

As Internet use has increased, psychologists have become more and more interested in online or virtual relationships and computer-mediated communication (CMC). This term encompasses a wide variety of electronic communication methods by which relationships can be formed and maintained, for example, email, instant messaging, chat rooms, texts, and particularly social networking sites (SNSs) such as Facebook, Twitter and Google+.

KEY TERMS

Self-disclosure – Revealing personal information about yourself. Romantic partners reveal more about their true selves as their relationship develops. These self-disclosures about one's deepest thoughts and feelings can strengthen a romantic bond when used appropriately.

Absence of gating – Face-to-face (FtF) relationships often fail to form because of obstacles such as facial disfigurements that some people might find off-putting. These barriers or 'gates' are absent in computer-mediated communication (CMC) allowing virtual relationships to begin in a way they couldn't in the offline world.

In cyberspace, no-one need know who you are, or what you're doing. Excellent news for some people.

Virtual relationships in social media

Self-disclosure in virtual relationships

Psychologists have long known that **self-disclosure** is a crucial feature of face-to-face (FtF) relationships in the offline world, as we discussed earlier in this chapter. In recent years researchers have turned their attention to its role in relationships rooted in social media. How does self-disclosure operate in CMC relationships? There are two major and contrasting theories.

Reduced cues theory According to Lee Sproull and Sara Kiesler (1986), CMC relationships are less effective than FtF ones because they lack many of the cues we normally depend on in FtF interactions. These include nonverbal cues such as our physical appearance. CMC particularly lacks cues to our emotional state, such as our facial expressions and tone of voice. This leads to **de-individuation** because it reduces people's sense of individual identity, which in turn encourages **disinhibition** in relating to others. Virtual relationships are therefore more likely to involve blunt and even aggressive communication. The upshot of this process is a reluctance to self-disclose. You are unlikely to want to initiate a relationship with someone who is so impersonal, or reveal your innermost feelings to them.

The hyperpersonal model Joseph Walther (1996, 2011) argues that online relationships can be *more* personal and involve *greater* self-disclosure than FtF ones. This is because CMC relationships can develop very quickly as self-disclosure happens earlier, and once established they are more intense and intimate. They can also end more quickly, because the high excitement level of the interaction isn't matched by the level of trust between the relationship partners. Alvin Cooper and Leda Sportolari (1997) called this the *boom and bust phenomenon* of online relationships.

According to the hyperpersonal model, a key feature of self-disclosure in virtual relationships is that the sender of a message has more time to manipulate their online image than they would in an FtF situation. Walther calls this *selective self-presentation*. People online have more control over what to disclose and the cues they send. This means it is much easier to manipulate self-disclosure to promote intimacy in CMC relationships, by self-presenting in a positive and idealised way.

Another aspect of CMC that promotes self-disclosure and makes relationships hyperpersonal is anonymity. John Bargh *et al.* (2002) point out that the outcome of this is rather like the *strangers on a train effect* in FtF relationships. When you're aware that other people do not know your identity, you feel less accountable for your behaviour. So you may well disclose more about yourself to a stranger than to even your most intimate partner.

Absence of gating in virtual relationships

A *gate*, in this context, is any obstacle to the formation of a relationship. FtF interaction is said to be *gated*, in that it involves many features that can interfere with the early development of a relationship. Examples of such gates include physical unattractiveness, a stammer, and social anxiety (shyness, blushing, etc.). Katelyn McKenna and John Bargh (1999) argue that a huge advantage of CMC is the **absence of gating**. This means that a relationship can develop to the point where self-disclosure becomes more frequent and deeper. This absence of gating allows an online relationship to 'get off the ground' in a way that is less likely to happen in an FtF situation.

Absence of gating works by refocusing attention on self-disclosure and away from what may be considered superficial and distracting features. In other words, online I am more interested in what you tell me than in what you look and sound like. This parallels the rationale behind the TV talent show *The Voice*. By performing to the judges' backs, the focus on appearance is removed so that this gate no longer threatens the contestant's chances of making it past the early audition. Absence of gating also means that people are free to create online identities that they could never manage FtF. A man can become a woman, an introvert become an extravert, a plain person the world's most desirable sex symbol. Perhaps the ultimate expression of this ungated existence is *Second Life*, where anyone can create any kind of avatar to represent themselves in a virtual reality.

Apply it Concepts: Second Life

Amy and David met in an Internet chatroom. They soon got together FtF and married two years later. They both had a virtual existence on Second Life – Amy was 'Laura Skye' and David was 'Dave Barmy'. Laura and Dave married soon after Amy and David. Three years later, Laura found out Dave was having avatar sex with 'Modesty McDonnell', a nightclub hostess. Unsurprisingly, Laura and Dave were divorced in Second Life. But so were Amy and David, in their offline lives. As Amy said, 'It may have started online, but it existed entirely in the real world and it hurts just as much.' [NB, based on a true story.]

Question

Explain Amy and David's relationship using the concepts on this spread.

Evaluation

Lack of research support for reduced cues theory

The theory is wrong to suggest that nonverbal cues are entirely missing from CMC. They are different rather than absent. Joseph Walther and Lisa Tidwell (1995) point out that people in online interactions use other cues, such as style and timing of their messages. For instance, taking time to reply to a social network status update is often interpreted as a more intimate act than an immediate response. But not too much time, otherwise that might be thought a snub. Clearly there are nuances here that are just as subtle as they are in FtF relationships. Acrostics (such as LOL), emoticons and, increasingly, emojis, are used as effective substitutes for facial expressions and tone of voice in FtF interactions.

The success of such online communication is difficult for the reduced cues theory to explain, because it shows that CMC interactions can be just as personal as those conducted FtF and that it's possible to express emotional states in virtual relationships.

Research support for the hyperpersonal model

The hyperpersonal model predicts that people are motivated to self-disclose in CMC in ways which are sometimes 'hyperhonest' and sometimes 'hyperdishonest'. Monica Whitty and Adam Joinson (2009) summarise a wealth of evidence that this is the case. For example, questions asked in online discussions tend to be very direct, probing and intimate. This is quite different from FtF conversations, which are often hedged around with 'small talk'. Responses are likewise direct and to the point.

These findings support a central assertion of the model, which is that the way we self-disclose in CMC relationships is designed to present ourselves in an exaggeratedly positive light which aids relationship formation.

Types of CMC

Self-disclosure online is not a blanket phenomenon. Its extent and depth depend very much on the type of CMC being used. In the case of social networking sites (SNSs), people interacting with each other generally have relationships in the offline world. People self-disclose more in their Facebook status updates than they are willing to in completing an online e-commerce webform, when they are quite reluctant to disclose information they consider to be private (Paine *et al.* 2006). An interesting case is online dating, an unusual example of CMC with complete strangers. Self-disclosure is reduced because both communicators anticipate future meetings FtF in the offline world, a consideration that generally doesn't exist in chatrooms and on gaming sites.

Any theory that approaches CMC as a single concept neglects its richness and variety, and is therefore unlikely to be a completely **valid** explanation.

Evaluation eXtra

Relationships are multimodal

Walther (2011) argues that any theory seeking to explain CMC, including the role of self-disclosure, needs to accommodate the fact that our relationships are generally conducted both online and offline through many different media. It is not usually a straightforward matter of 'either/or'. This is in fact probably the central characteristic of many modern relationships. What we choose to disclose in our online relationships will inevitably be influenced by our offline interactions, and vice versa.

Consider: *Do you think the theories on this spread take this into account? Is this a limitation of those theories?*

Support for absence of gating

McKenna and Bargh (2000) looked at CMC use by lonely and socially anxious people. They found that such people were able to express their 'true selves' more than in FtF situations. Of the romantic relationships that initially formed online, 70% survived more than two years. This is a higher proportion than for relationships formed in the offline world.

Consider: *Are you surprised by this finding? Can you explain why it is a strength of the absence of gating explanation?*

A Second Life avatar. For some people, just like real life, only more so.

Apply it — Concepts: A virtual existence

Lucas is a very shy and introverted young man who has great difficulty in making conversation, especially with women he likes. He blushes, stammers and finds it hard to say the right words. But when he posts on social media sites and chatrooms, he's a different person. Other people online seem to like and respect him.

Question

Using the absence of gating theory, explain why Lucas's online and offline lives are so contrasting.

Apply it — Methods: A liking experiment

A psychologist recruited 50 participants to investigate virtual relationships. There were two tasks for the participants to perform. In one, they had to interact with another person online in a 10-minute exchange of messages. In the other task, they interacted with someone face-to-face in a 10-minute discussion. After completing both tasks, the participants had to rate how much they liked the other person on a scale from 0 (didn't like them at all) to 10 (liked them very much).

Questions

1. What were the **operationalised independent** and **dependent variables**? (*1 mark + 1 mark*)
2. The psychologist realised that she would need to use **counterbalancing**. Explain how she could have done so, and why it was necessary. (*4 marks*)
3. Explain how **demand characteristics** might have affected the study. (*2 marks*)
4. Explain how *one* factor in this study might have affected its **external validity**. (*3 marks*)
5. Explain *one or more* **ethical issues** that the psychologists should have taken into account in this study. (*4 marks*)

CHECK IT

1. In relation to virtual relationships, explain what is meant by *self-disclosure*. [2 marks]
2. Explain the effect of absence of gating on virtual relationships. [4 marks]
3. Outline research into self-disclosure in virtual relationships. [4 marks]
4. Describe and evaluate research into virtual relationships in social media. [16 marks]

PARASOCIAL RELATIONSHIPS

Parasocial relationships: levels of parasocial relationships; the absorption-addiction model; the attachment theory explanation.

Psychologists are interested in the attraction of celebrity and have tried to explain parasocial relationships: defined by Donald Horton and Richard Wohl (1956) as those attachments in which the 'fan' knows all about the celebrity, but the celebrity doesn't even know the fan exists. It's not just celebrities that can be the subject of a parasocial involvement. It could be a team, an organisation, a brand or a fictional character. It could even be anyone who stands out in a community enough to make genuine interaction difficult (such as a teacher).

KEY TERMS

Parasocial relationship – The prefix 'para' means 'resembling' so parasocial relationships are those which are similar to 'normal' relationships but lack a key element. They are a one-sided, unreciprocated relationship, usually with a celebrity, on which the 'fan' expends a lot of emotional energy, commitment and time.

Levels of parasocial relationships – A three-step description of one-sided relationships in terms of increasing strength from entertainment-social to intense-personal to borderline pathological.

Absorption-addiction model – Explains parasocial relationships as total pre-occupation in a celebrity's life, plus an addictive striving after a stronger involvement.

Attachment theory – An explanation of how an enduring emotional bond forms between two people that persists over time. Leads to certain behaviours such as clinging and proximity-seeking.

What would Harry do? Is this a question you find yourself asking often?

Parasocial relationships

Levels of parasocial relationships

Lynn McCutcheon and his colleagues (2002) developed the *Celebrity Attitude Scale*, which was used in a large-scale survey by John Maltby *et al.* (2006). They identified three **levels of parasocial relationship**, each level describing the attitudes and behaviours linked to ever more extreme forms of celebrity worship.

- *Entertainment-social:* This is the least intense level of celebrity worship. Celebrities are viewed as sources of entertainment and fuel for social interaction. For example, friends with more than a passing interest in soap operas might enjoy discussing stories in *OK* magazine about actors on *Eastenders* or *Coronation Street*. Giles (2002) found that parasocial relationships were a fruitful source of gossip in offices.
- *Intense-personal:* This is an intermediate level which reflects a greater personal involvement in a parasocial relationship with a celebrity. A fan of Kim Kardashian might have frequent obsessive thoughts and intense feelings about her, perhaps even considering her to be a 'soul mate'.
- *Borderline pathological:* This is the strongest level of celebrity worship, featuring uncontrollable fantasies and extreme behaviours. These might include spending (or planning to spend) a large sum of money on a celebrity-related object, or being willing to perform some illegal act on the celebrity's say-so.

The absorption-addiction model

McCutcheon (2002) explains the tendency to form parasocial relationships in terms of deficiencies people have in their own lives. For example, they may have a weak sense of self-identity and also lack fulfilment in their everyday relationships. They could also be otherwise poorly adjusted psychologically. A parasocial relationship allows them an 'escape from reality', or a way of finding a fulfilment that they can't achieve in their actual relationships. This is linked to the three levels described above. Someone who initially has an entertainment-social orientation to a certain celebrity may be triggered into more intense involvement by some personal crisis or stressful life event. As the name implies, the **absorption-addiction model** has two components:

- *Absorption:* Seeking fulfilment in celebrity worship motivates the individual to focus their attention as far as possible on the celebrity, to become pre-occupied in their existence and identify with them.
- *Addiction:* Just as with an addiction to a psychoactive substance, the individual needs to sustain their commitment to the relationship by feeling a stronger and closer involvement with the celebrity. This may lead to more extreme behaviours and delusional thinking. For example, stalking a celebrity because you believe that he or she really wants to reciprocate your feelings, but someone – their manager perhaps – is stopping them.

The attachment theory explanation

Various psychologists have suggested that there is a tendency to form parasocial relationships in adolescence and adulthood because of attachment difficulties in early childhood. Bowlby's **attachment theory** (which was part of your Year 1 studies) suggested such early difficulties may lead to emotional troubles later in life. Mary Ainsworth (1979) identified two **attachment types** associated with unhealthy emotional development: **insecure-resistant** and **insecure-avoidant**.

Insecure-resistant types are most likely to form parasocial relationships as adults. This is because they need to have unfulfilled needs met, but in a relationship that is not accompanied by the threat of rejection, break-up and disappointment that real-life relationships bring. Insecure-avoidant types, on the other hand, prefer to avoid the pain and rejection of relationships altogether, whether they be social or parasocial.

Apply it **Concepts: A celebrity obsession**

Stuart is 35 years old and a big fan of the Harry Potter books and films. He spends a lot of his spare time reading and watching them. He can't help it, but he frequently fantasises about actually being Harry Potter. He has spent a lot of money on his obsession, and it's fair to say that it is starting to interfere with some areas of his life. He enjoys joining in with online costume play (cosplay) sessions. He's not sure about attending conventions to meet other people face-to-face but he's thinking about it. He's actively trying to get hold of Daniel Radcliffe's mobile phone number.

Question

Explain Stuart's behaviour in terms of the theories on this spread. What do you think are the benefits and risks of his behaviour for Stuart?

Evaluation

Support for the absorption–addiction model

John Maltby and his colleague (2005) investigated the link between celebrity worship and body image in males and females aged 14 to 16 years. Of particular interest were females reporting an intense-personal parasocial relationship with a female celebrity whose body shape they admired. The researchers found that these female adolescents tended to have a poor body image, and speculated that this link may be a precursor to the development of eating disorders such as **anorexia nervosa**.

Other research, by Maltby *et al.* (2003), links the entertainment-social category of celebrity worship with **extraverted** personality traits, the intense-personal category with **neurotic** traits, and the borderline pathological category with **psychotic** personality type.

Both studies support the model because they confirm the prediction of a **correlation** between the level (type and intensity) of celebrity worship and poor psychological functioning.

Problems with attachment theory

Lynn McCutcheon *et al.* (2006) measured attachment types and celebrity-related attitudes in 299 participants. The researchers found that the participants with insecure attachments were no more likely to form parasocial relationships with celebrities than participants with **secure attachments**.

This finding fails to support a central prediction of the attachment theory, raising serious doubts about its validity.

Methodological issues

There are two major issues. Most research studies on parasocial relationships use **self-report** methods to collect data, for example, online **questionnaires**. These are subject to a number of effects that can bias the findings. For instance, participants may respond to quite personal items in a way which they think enhances their social status (**social desirability bias**).

The second issue arises because most studies use **correlational** analysis. Strong correlations are found between celebrity worship and body image, for example. But the conclusion that an intense-personal parasocial relationship *causes* young women to have a poor body image is unwarranted. It could be that young women who already have a poor body image are drawn to an intense-personal worship of an admired celebrity. The issue of cause-and-effect could be addressed by **longitudinal research**, but this is currently lacking in this field.

As the addiction-absorption model is based on such studies, there remain questions about its **validity** as an explanation of parasocial relationships.

Evaluation eXtra

Problems with the absorption–addiction model

The model has been criticised for being a better description of parasocial relationships than it is an explanation. For instance, the model is capable of describing the characteristics of people who are most absorbed by and addicted to celebrity (that is, borderline-pathological). But, unlike attachment theory, it does not explain how such characteristics develop.

Consider: *Do you think this undermines the validity of the model? Explain your answer.*

Cultural influences

Research studies have identified a tendency for some people to form a parasocial relationship with Harry Potter, an entirely fictional character. Developing this, Schmid and Klimmt (2011) report that this tendency is not culturally specific. Using an online questionnaire methodology, they found similar levels of parasocial attachment to Harry Potter in an **individualist culture** (Germany) and a **collectivist culture** (Mexico).

Consider: *What does this finding tell us about the nature of parasocial relationships? Does it support any of the explanations on this spread?*

For some people, a parasocial relationship can offer an escape from the harsh demands of everyday life.

Practical activity on page 139

Apply it Concepts: **Addicted to soap?**

Gloria and her friends enjoy watching soap operas. They all have their preferences but Eastenders features on all their lists. They frequently find themselves talking about the latest developments and the actors who play their favourite characters. Gloria isn't worried that it'll get out of hand because it's all good fun.

Question

What level of parasocial relationship does this describe? Under what circumstances do you think Gloria might develop a greater parasocial involvement?

Apply it Methods: **Men, women and celebs**

A psychologist was interested to see if there is gender difference in the tendency to form parasocial relationships with celebrities. Ten male and ten female participants completed an *Attitudes Towards Celebrities* (ATC) scale. The scale measured the intensity of devotion towards a celebrity, from a score of 0 (no devotion at all) to 20 (extremely intense devotion).

Questions

1. Explain why the research method used in this study is a **quasi-experiment**. (*2 marks*)

2. Explain *one* strength and *one* limitation of this research method. (*2 marks + 2 marks*)

3. Explain how the psychologist could have checked the validity of the ATC scale. (*3 marks*)

4. The psychologist calculated some descriptive statistics, presented in Table 1. With reference to these figures, outline what the findings of the study seem to show. (*2 marks*)

	Male scores	Females scores
Median	9.5	5.5
Range	6	11

CHECK IT

1. Explain what is meant by *levels of parasocial relationships*. [4 marks]

2. Outline the absorption-addiction model of parasocial relationships. [4 marks]

3. Outline the attachment theory explanation of parasocial relationships. [4 marks]

4. Describe and evaluate **one or more** explanations of parasocial relationships [16 marks]

PRACTICAL CORNER

> Knowledge and understanding of ...research methods, practical research skills and maths skills. These should be developed through ... ethical practical research activities.

In both a correlational study and a quasi-experiment, there's no manipulation of variables like you find in a true experiment. Sometimes, ethical or practical reasons mean that we can only measure variables and analyse how they relate to each other. These two investigations give you the opportunity to use questionnaires and participants' ratings.

Ethics check

We suggest strongly that you complete this checklist before starting:

1. Do participants know participation is voluntary?
2. Do participants know what to expect?
3. Do participants know they can withdraw at any time?
4. Are individuals' results anonymous?
5. Have I minimised the risk of distress to participants?
6. Have I avoided asking sensitive questions?
7. Will I avoid bringing my school/teacher/psychology into disrepute?
8. Have I considered all other ethical issues?
9. Has my teacher approved this?

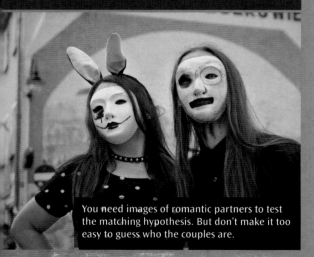

You need images of romantic partners to test the matching hypothesis. But don't make it too easy to guess who the couples are.

Practical idea 1: The matching hypothesis

The **matching hypothesis** is an explanation of relationship formation that puts physical attractiveness very much at the forefront of partner selection. However, in choosing romantic partners we generally don't go for the most attractive person available. We compromise partner choice by taking into account our assessment of our own level of attractiveness.

So the aim of this practical is to test the prediction that most partners in a couple have a similar level of attractiveness to each other. A **correlational** research method is ideally suited to this aim. We expect to find a **significant positive correlation** between ratings of physical attractiveness given for each partner in a couple.

The practical bit

Designing your study

You will need to find images of 10 romantic couples. There are many available on the Internet, but your selection needs to follow some strict criteria. Don't use images of celebrities or any other couples your participants are likely to know. You need to be able to divide the images into separate individuals, in such a way that it's not obvious which ones go together. Ideally, there should be no cues for participants to work out which individuals belong together. For example, one potential **extraneous variable** is image backgrounds.

Because you are aiming to **standardise** your procedure, the images need to be as similar to each other as possible, for example, in terms of size and direction of pose. Images of couples getting married fit most of these criteria so are well worth considering. Limit your selection to heterosexual couples, within a narrow age range and all of same ethnic grouping. This is purely for the sake of standardisation and because you are testing the original matching hypothesis. Once you have prepared the images of individual partners, they are well-suited to being presented to whole classes of students, for instance in a PowerPoint slideshow on an interactive whiteboard. But make sure you present them in a random order.

You should also construct a response sheet on which participants can note their ratings for each individual. Indicate on the sheet the numbers of each individual image. Keep a careful record of which partners belong to which couples. Finally, decide on a rating scale of physical attractiveness, such as 1 to 10 (from 'not at all attractive' to 'extremely attractive'). Include the scale in your **standardised instructions** with a detailed explanation of what the participants need to do.

Ethical issues

Some participants might object to the whole business of rating physical attractiveness as shallow or degrading. You need to make it clear that anyone who does object for this or any other reason has the **right to withdraw** before the procedure begins. You should also obtain **informed consent**, so that participants can make a decision about whether or not to proceed. The ethical matters will be reflected in your standardised instructions and **debriefing** statement.

Selecting your participants

You could, with the co-operation of a teacher, select whole classes **randomly** from the school or college register. But it's more likely that you will use an **opportunity sample** of available classes.

Analysing and presenting your data

You need to calculate a **measure of central tendency** to represent the average attractiveness ratings for each male and female partner (i.e. 20 calculations in all if you have 20 pictures). You can present these in a table, with the figures for the partners in each couple alongside each other. You could then draw a **scattergram**. Each data point represents the average attractiveness ratings for each couple, with the male on one axis and the female on the other (i.e. 10 data points).

For **inferential analysis**, apply a statistical test to assess the relationship between the two sets of attractiveness ratings. Answering the questions in The maths bit 1 will give you some idea of which test you need to use.

Methods:
The maths bit 1

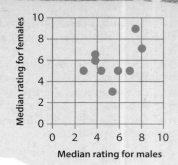

1. What conclusions can you draw based on the **scattergram**? (*3 marks*)
2. Explain why the **median** was used to calculate average attractiveness. (*2 marks*)
3. Which **statistical test** would you use to analyse the significance of the relationship in the scattergram? Give *two* reasons for your choice. (*1 mark + 2 marks*) (See page 70)
4. The appropriate statistical test was calculated and the result was **significant** at p≤0.05. What does this mean? (*2 marks*) (See page 72)

Practical idea 2: Testing the absorption-addiction model

The **absorption-addiction model** has been used to explain how people form parasocial relationships (McCutcheon 2002). These are unreciprocated relationships, often formed with celebrities.

Our aim is to test the prediction that people form parasocial relationships as an escape from the reality of everyday living. To do this, we need to assume that people with stressful lives welcome some escape. Therefore we would expect that the degree of parasocial involvement is linked with how much stress a person experiences in their everyday lives; greater stress is associated with a more intense level of relationship.

Deep parasocial involvement can mean a lot of time spent dressing up as your favourite fictional character. But is this behaviour an attempt to escape from a stressful life?

The practical bit

Designing the study

This practical is a **quasi-experiment**, because the **independent variable** (IV) is pre-existing and not manipulated by you. The IV is the degree of life stress experienced by your participants, low or high. The **dependent variable** (DV) is the level of parasocial involvement: either social-entertainment (lower) or intense-personal (higher). You will need two questionnaires to establish the conditions of the IV and measure the DV.

The questionnaires

Fortunately there are standardised measures readily available on the Internet. These are the *Celebrity Attitude Scale (CAS)* and the *College Student's Stressful Events Checklist (CSSEC)*. You can find both of these using your Internet search engine of choice. However, both of them will need some alterations to make them more useful for this practical.

The *CAS* measures not only the two levels of parasocial involvement we are investigating, but a third called *borderline pathological*. There is a risk that a degree of stress could be caused by asking participants to fill in items relating to this third level. So for ethical reasons, it would be advisable to remove them altogether. Use the scoring key provided with the scale to find out which items these are.

The *CSSEC* has been devised for use with American participants. There's no need to remove any items, but it would be useful to change some of the language to terms that would be more recognisable to UK students (e.g. *course* for *major*, *teacher* for *instructor*, *term* for *semester*). You should also remove any text that indicates how the scale is scored.

Ethical considerations

You will have removed the most risky items on the *CAS*. But you should consider that the questions on the *CSSEC* are somewhat personal and potentially invasive. There is a chance that some participants could experience indignity or embarrassment. On the other hand, this is a standard **questionnaire** which has been used in countless research studies. Nevertheless, think about how you can counteract any potentially negative effects of such personal questioning. For instance, is there any need to collect participants' names? As each participant is going to complete two questionnaires, you need some way of matching them up. But this does not have to involve names. You should certainly think very carefully about how you are going to obtain informed consent and ensure that your participants are aware of their right to withdraw.

Analysing your data

You need to identify 'low stress' and 'high stress' participants on the basis of their *CSSEC* scores. The most straightforward way to do this is to use a cut-off point to divide the set of scores into two groups: high stress participants are those who score 225 or more; low stress is a score of 224 or less. You should have two parasocial involvement scores for each participant, one for *social-entertainment* and one for *intense-personal*. For each participant, take the highest of these two scores to indicate level of parasocial relationship.

Once you have classified each participant into their appropriate stress level group and parasocial level group, you should be able to complete a 2 × 2 contingency table like the one on the right.

The maths bit

Overall, at least 10% of the marks in assessments for Psychology will require the use of mathematical skills and at least a further 15% will be related to research methods.

Don't avoid it!

Apply it **Methods: The maths bit 2**

The table below shows the number of participants in each category based on their *CAS* and *CSSEC* scores.

1. Using the table below, calculate the totals for each row and each column and the overall total. (*5 marks*).

2. Draw a suitable graph to represent the data in the categories. Label the axes carefully and give the graph an appropriate title. (*3 marks*)

3. What type of graph have you drawn? Explain why you made this choice. (*1 mark + 2 marks*)

4. Calculate the frequencies in each cell as a percentage of the total frequency. (*4 marks*)

5. What would you conclude from these figures about the effect of stress on parasocial involvement? (*2 marks*)

6. Name the **statistical test** you think would be appropriate to analyse the data. Give *two* reasons why you have chosen this test. (*1 mark + 2 marks*) (See page 70)

Table: Number of participants in each stress/parasocial involvement category

		Parasocial involvement	
		Social-entertainment	Intense-personal
Stress	Low	18	7
	High	11	14

REVISION SUMMARIES

EVOLUTIONARY EXPLANATION OF PARTNER PREFERENCES

How our preferences for mates have evolved.

SEXUAL SELECTION AND HUMAN REPRODUCTIVE BEHAVIOUR

Anisogamy
Male gametes are produced in large numbers at little cost, in contrast with female gametes. This gives rise to two mating strategies.

Inter-sexual selection
Females prefer quality and are especially choosy. Males compete to be chosen.

Intra-sexual selection
Males prefer quantity but must compete for access to fertile females.

EVALUATION

Research support for preferences related to anisogamy
Buss found that males want fertility and looks; females want resources.

Research support for inter-sexual selection
Clark and Hatfield found that female students are choosier than males.

Ignores social and cultural influences
Social changes occur much faster than evolutionary timescales.

Support from waist-hip ratio research
Singh: Males find a WHR of 0.7 attractive because it's an honest signal of fertility.

Support from lonely hearts research
Waynforth and Dunbar: Women tend to offer attractiveness and youth, men offer resources.

FACTORS AFFECTING ATTRACTION IN ROMANTIC RELATIONSHIPS

SELF-DISCLOSURE

Revealing personal and sensitive information.

SELF-DISCLOSURE

Social penetration theory
Partners penetrate more deeply into each other's lives as they self-disclose (Altman and Taylor).

Breadth and depth of self-disclosure
Layers of on onion metaphor, start with breadth but little depth and then move deeper.

Reciprocity of self-disclosure
Successful relationship needs a balance in self-disclosure (Reis and Shaver).

EVALUATION

Support from research studies
Sprecher and Hendrick found that couples in satisfying relationships disclose more and believe their partners do too.

Real-life applications
Self-disclosure is a communication skill that can be learned and developed.

Cultural differences
Cultural differences in sexual self-disclosure in individualist and collectivist cultures (Tang et al.).

Self-disclosure and satisfaction
Social penetration theory is wrong in predicting that relationship breakdown means less self-disclosure.

Correlation versus causation
More self-disclosure does not necessarily cause satisfaction.

PHYSICAL ATTRACTIVENESS

Physical good looks increase the liking people have for you.

PHYSICAL ATTRACTIVENESS

Explaining the importance of physical attractiveness
Shackelford and Larsen: Symmetrical face is attractive because it's an honest sign of genetic fitness; neotenous female faces trigger caring instinct in males.

The halo effect
We have positive stereotypes of attractive people that influence our judgements of them (Dion et al.).

The matching hypothesis
We choose partners who are of a roughly similar level of physical attractiveness (Walster et al.).

EVALUATION

Research support for the halo effect
Palmer and Peterson found that attractive people rated as more politically competent.

Individual differences
Towhey found that some people are less sensitive to physical attractiveness when making judgements of personality and likeability.

Research support for the matching hypothesis
Feingold: Meta-analysis shows correlation between attractiveness of real-life partners.

Role of cultural influences
Attractive female features and the physical attractiveness stereotype both exist across cultures.

Research contradicting the matching hypothesis
Taylor et al.: Online dating choices tend to be for more physically attractive people.

FILTER THEORY

Because you can't go out with everyone!

FILTER THEORY

Social demography (1st filter)
Kerckhoff and Davis proposed that factors such as proximity and education level reduce the field of availables.

Similarity in attitudes (2nd filter)
Byrne described the law of attraction as being due to similarity, produces a field of desirables.

Complementarity (3rd filter)
Each partner being able to contribute a trait the other lacks becomes more important than similarity later in a relationship.

EVALUATION

Support from research evidence
Winch found similarity in early stages of the most satisfying relationships, and complementarity came later.

Failure to replicate
Times have changed and also original theory wrongly assumed depth was related to duration of the relationship.

Direction of cause and effect
Anderson et al. found that partners in satisfying relationships become more similar as time goes on (emotional convergence).

Lack of temporal validity
Online dating has reduced the importance of the first filter.

Similarity or complementarity?
Similarity in long-term couples may be more important than the third filter.

THEORIES OF ROMANTIC RELATIONSHIPS

SOCIAL EXCHANGE THEORY

The 'give and take' of romance.

SOCIAL EXCHANGE THEORY (SET)

Rewards, costs and profits
Thibault and Kelley's economic theory, predicting that people want a net profit and try to maximise rewards and minimise costs.

Comparison level
Amount of reward you think you deserve from a relationship compared to the costs, informed by social norms.

Comparison level for alternatives
We consider whether we could get more rewards and fewer costs elsewhere.

Stages of relationship development
Sample, bargaining, commitment and institutionalisation stages.

EVALUATION

Inappropriate assumptions underlying SET
Clark and Mills suggest that not all relationships involve exchange of rewards and comparison with costs (e.g. communal relationships).

Direction of cause and effect
Contrary to SET, research shows that dissatisfaction comes before consideration of alternatives (e.g. Miller).

SET ignores equity
Both partners' profits need to be roughly similar; equity theory suggests this is more important than the amount of rewards and costs for each.

Measuring SET concepts
Real-life rewards, costs and comparison levels are difficult to define and measure.

Artificial research
Snapshot studies using game-playing scenarios do not resemble real-life exchange relationships.

EQUITY THEORY

Perceived fairness rather than equal profits.

EQUITY THEORY

The role of equity
Both partners' level of profit needs to be roughly similar, otherwise one overbenefits and the other underbenefits.

Equity and equality
What matters is the ratio of rewards to costs: A high level of costs with a high level of rewards is seen as fair.

Consequences of inequity
Underbenefitted partner is motivated to make the relationship more equitable. The perception of inequality matters.

EVALUATION

Supporting research evidence
Utne *et al.* found that couples in an equitable relationship are more satisfied than those who underbenefit or overbenefit.

Cultural influences
Aumer-Ryan found that in collectivist societies partners are more satisfied when they are overbenefitting, so equity is not universally satisfying.

Individual differences
Not everyone is concerned about equity – benevolents tolerate underbenefit and entitleds believe they deserve overbenefit.

Types of relationship
Clark and Mills: Equity matters more in non-romantic relationships, less important to romantic satisfaction.

Contradictory research evidence
Not all relationships become more equitable over time, other factors are more important.

RUSBULT'S INVESTMENT MODEL

Partners stay because of commitment.

RUSBULT'S INVESTMENT MODEL

Satisfaction and CLalt
A satisfying relationship has many rewards and few costs, and compares well with alternatives.

Investment size
Consider the resources that have been put into a relationship which we would stand to lose if it broke down.

Satisfaction versus commitment
The main psychological factor maintaining relationships is commitment, which explains why dissatisfied partners sometimes do not leave.

Relationship maintenance mechanisms
Committed partners act to promote their relationship through accommodation, willingness to sacrifice, forgiveness, etc.

EVALUATION

Supporting research evidence
Le and Agnew meta-analysis showed all three factors of the model predicted relationship commitment.

Explains abusive relationships
Rusbult and Martz found that abused partners who were committed reported greatest investment and lowest CLalt.

Oversimplifies investment
Goodfriend and Agnew extended the theory to include the importance of future plans as part of investment.

Methodological strengths
Self-report measures are useful because what matters in relationships is perception rather than reality.

Based on correlational research
Many correlations between different parts of the model, but this doesn't mean that satisfaction, comparison or investment cause commitment.

DUCK'S PHASE MODEL

How romantic relationships end.

DUCK'S PHASE MODEL OF RELATIONSHIP BREAKDOWN

Intra-psychic phase
Dissatisfied partner considers the dissatisfactions privately and possibly with close friends.

Dyadic phase
Both partners start talking about the relationship, resulting in arguments, negotiations, recriminations, etc.

Social phase
Partners involve their social networks in an attempt to save the relationship and also muster support.

Grave-dressing phase
The now ex-partners tidy up the loose ends of the relationship by constructing a favourable public and private story.

EVALUATION

An incomplete model?
Rollie and Duck added the resurrection phase, and emphasised the processes within the model.

Methodological issues
Understanding the very early stages of breakdown requires retrospective recall and is also unethical (may hasten end of relationship).

Useful real-life applications
The model identifies strategies for relationship rescue that could be used in relationships counselling at different points in the breakdown process.

Description rather than explanation
Other explanations are better at identifying the factors that create breakdown, e.g. Felmlee's fatal attraction hypothesis.

Cultural bias
Research underlying the model is mostly from individualist Western cultures, relationships in collectivist cultures are different.

VIRTUAL RELATIONSHIPS IN SOCIAL MEDIA

Relationship formation in CMCs compared to FtF.

VIRTUAL RELATIONSHIPS IN SOCIAL MEDIA

Reduced cues theory
CMC relationships lack the cues of FtF interaction so there is greater de-individuation and less self-disclosure.

The hyperpersonal model
CMC presentation gives more control over disclosure and can be manipulated to promote intimacy, so relationships can become more intense than FtF.

Absence of gating in virtual relationships
Certain characteristics act as a barrier to relationship formation when FtF but not in CMCs, e.g. facial disfigurement, social anxiety.

Relationship maintenance mechanisms
Committed partners act to promote their relationship through accommodation, willingness to sacrifice, forgiveness, etc.

EVALUATION

Lack of research support for reduced cues theory
Walther and Tidwell: CMC involves different cues rather than a lack of them (e.g. timing, emojis), so emotional states can be expressed.

Research support for the hyperpersonal model
Whitty and Joinson found that CMC is more direct, blunt, hyperhonest and hyperdishonest than it is FtF, supporting the model.

Types of CMC
Extent of self-disclosure online depends on the type of CMC and nature of the relationship.

Relationships are multimodal
Most of our relationships are conducted both online and offline, and each influences the other.

Support for absence of gating
A higher proportion of relationships formed online than offline survive at least two years.

PARASOCIAL RELATIONSHIPS

One-sided relationships with celebrities or other distant figures.

PARASOCIAL RELATIONSHIPS

Levels of parasocial relationships
Entertainment-social; intense-personal; borderline pathological.

The absorption-addiction model
A fan absorbs themselves in the celebrity's world, then needs to increase their involvement in the same way that addicts do.

The attachment theory explanation
Insecure-resistant individuals have emotional unfulfilled needs; parasocial relationships avoid the threat of rejection.

EVALUATION

Support for the absorption-addiction model
Maltby *et al.* demonstrated correlations between level of celebrity worship and poor psychological functioning (e.g. anorexia).

Problems with attachment theory
McCutcheon *et al.* found no correlation between insecure attachment type and parasocial involvement.

Methodological issues
Most research uses self-report measures and correlational analysis, thus the support for the model lacks validity.

Problems with absorption-addiction model
Model describes characteristics of absorbed/addicted people, but doesn't explain how they form.

Cultural influences
Schmid and Klimmt: Tendency to form parasocial relationships occurs across very different cultures.

Question 1 Kaley is an attractive 25-year-old woman who has recently married Ryan, a 60-year-old man who owns five successful businesses. They have no children yet, but are hoping to start a family soon.

Outline the relationship between sexual selection and human reproductive behaviour. Refer to the information above in your answer. *(4 marks)*

Morticia's answer

Sexual selection is an explanation for our partner choices based on evolutionary theory. The fact that men produce large numbers of sperm means that their reproductive success is best ensured by mating as often as they can and with women who are fertile. Therefore, men like Ryan are programmed to be attracted to young women so his offspring will be strong and more likely to survive.

For women it is different. They do best reproductively if they are choosy about a mate because each pregnancy is costly in terms of the amount of time and energy required. Women are particularly interested in a man who can provide resources because that will protect the survival of each infant. That explains why Kaley may have fallen for a rich businessman.

Morticia's outline for male reproductive behaviour is clear and well informed. The application to the question stem could have been a little clearer.

In the second paragraph, the outline is well written here and again the application – albeit brief – will suffice.

Luke's answer

Kaley and Ryan are examples of sexual selection in action because Kaley went for a man with resources and Ryan went for a young fertile mate.

Anisogamy is a key factor in sexual selection. It is the differences between male and female sex cells, which means that there are plenty of males but a female is a rare resource.

Females go for inter-sexual selection – they choose between available males and go for quality rather than quantity.

Males go for intra-sexual selection – they have to compete with other males to be selected.

Luke's first sentence is a brief acknowledgement of the stem but this is not really linked to appropriate background theory so does not qualify as application.

Although there is material on the differences in sexual selection, it is not really made relevant to the stem described or linked effectively to behavioural strategies.

Vladimir's answer

Human reproduction is basically driven by the same factors as for all mammals. Males produce vast numbers of sperm at little cost whereas women produce only a few eggs. There are two kinds of selection, either selection within one sex or between sexes. For women the better strategy is intra-sexual selection because they choose a man. For men the better strategy is inter-sexual selection because there are lots of them. This doesn't take into account the fact that humans may make conscious decisions and not be driven by their biology, though an example such as Kaley and Ryan might suggest that they are because biology explains why a young woman would go for an older man, because of his resources.

Vladimir's answer is confused, containing some relevant ideas but these are poorly expressed and not appropriately applied. There is attempted application within the final sentence but this is rather weak.

Question 2 Briefly outline the equity theory of romantic relationships. *(4 marks)*

Morticia's answer

Equity theory is an economic explanation for how relationships form and are maintained. It is called 'economic' because it suggests that the key to a relationship is fair trading. Equity theory was developed out of social exchange theory and, in contrast, suggests that relationships are not just about profits and losses but about each partner thinking the inputs and outputs are fair.

One problem with this theory is that it may only apply to individualist cultures who are more concerned with what each person gets whereas collectivist societies are more focused on the needs of others and actually may prefer relationships where their partner overbenefits (Aumer-Ryan et al.).

Morticia's outline of equity theory is accurate and reasonably detailed. The comparison with social exchange theory is useful as a way of demonstrating understanding of equity theory. The rest of the answer is only evaluative. This underlines the importance of understanding the command words within questions – 'outline' is a descriptive term.

Luke's answer

Equity theory, proposed by Walster et al., is concerned with fairness. A partner who is overbenefitted would feel uncomfortable. What is important is the ratio of rewards and costs rather than their size. A lack of equity leads a partner to feel distressed and dissatisfied, the greater the perceived inequity the greater the dissatisfaction. In the early days of a relationship inequity may matter less but, as the relationship progresses the partners in a successful relationship will work at maintaining equity. Actually what may be adjusted is the perception of the rewards and costs rather than the rewards and costs themselves so nothing may change it's just that partners adjust their perceptions.

Luke has focused on a slightly different aspect of the theory than Morticia and demonstrated a thorough understanding.

Vladimir's answer

Equity theory is about equality in a relationship. Partners like to feel a sense of balance in what they have, in the same way a business feels about their partners. It should be fair so that no one is getting more than the other. Partners consider their losses and gains and weigh these up in order to decide whether the relationship is worth pursuing. People dislike being overbenefitted as well as being underbenefitted though this may vary with individual differences – in other words some people prefer one or the other.

Vladimir's answer is less well articulated than Luke's but the understanding is still there. Most of the key aspects of equity theory are explained.

On this spread we look at some typical student answers to questions. The comments provided indicate what is good and bad in each answer. Learning how to produce effective question answers is a SKILL. Read pages 387–397 for guidance.

Question 3   Describe and evaluate Duck's phase model of relationship breakdown. (16 marks)

Luke's answer

Duck's phase model has four phases. In the first phase, which is the intra-psychic phase, the dissatisfied partner considers the dissatisfactions privately and possibly with close friends.

In the second phase, the dyadic phase, both partners start talking about the relationship, resulting in arguments, negotiations, recriminations, etc.

In the social phase, partners involve their social networks in an attempt to save the relationship and also muster support.

And finally in the grave-dressing phase the now ex-partners tidy up the loose ends of the relationship by constructing a favourable public and private story.

At any point the partners may exit and repair the relationship but each phase has a tipping point where things have gone too far and then it is time for the next phase.

Duck himself criticised this phase model saying that it was too simple. He added a fifth phase, the resurrection phase, where partners start thinking ahead to new relationships. In the new model Duck also said that people may return to earlier phases – it's not a simple linear progression. The earlier model lacked the dynamic nature of the newer one.

A good theory should have research support and one of the issues with this theory is that the research is inevitably retrospective – you find couples who have broken up and then ask them to recall what happen. It may be that they don't remember things exactly. In fact their later experiences may affect the way they remember the early phases.

A good theory should also have real-life relevance and this theory offers assistance to relationship counsellors who can see what phase a couple is in and recognise strategies that may help at this time to avoid the tipping point. Duck suggests, for example, that people in the intra-psychic phase could focus on the positive aspects of their partner.

An important criticism is that this theory really is more of a description than an explanation of why breakdown happens. For example, Felmlee's fatal attraction theory explains that the reason relationships breakdown is the thing you found initially attractive becomes very annoying. Such as having a partner who is very outgoing, which you admire initially but then come to dislike. Duck's theory just describes the process of that breakdown and therefore doesn't offer insights into breakdown.

Like many theories, this theory has an individualist bias, describing relationships from the standpoint of one kind of culture. Relationships in collectivist cultures are much more difficult to end because other people are more involved and in fact in such cultures romantic issues wouldn't be important at all. This means the theory has a limited application.

(428 words)

Luke's outline of the phase model is concise but accurate and sufficient for the descriptive content within this question.

This paragraph ('Duck himself criticised . . .') could be read equally as further description or evaluative commentary but, either way, is relevant and well phrased.

The remaining paragraphs all contain good, clear, well-elaborated criticisms of the theory. They all illustrate the skill of sustained commentary.

The most striking thing about this response is that Luke has managed to maintain the appropriate balance between descriptive and evaluative elements for an A level essay.

Vladimir's answer

In this essay I am going to describe and evaluate one of the most important theories of relationship breakdown, Duck's phase model of romantic breakdown – so this shows it is just about the breakdown of romantic relationships though of course there are other relationships too that breakdown, but romantic ones are quite different. Duck described this breakdown in terms of four stages or phases because he could see that there are particular steps in the process, it doesn't all happen at once. The theory was based on research with couples who experienced relationship breakdown and Duck identified thresholds that occur when one partner is dissatisfied. The first threshold is right at the beginning when one partner is distressed about the relationship and feels they can't stand it any more. This starts the intra-psychic phase of thinking about what's wrong in the relationship. The person may discuss their feelings with someone else. The person finally feels they are right to end the relationship. Many people stay in this phase for a very long time. The next phase is the dyadic phase when the two partners start talking to each other. The partners may decide to make things better or that it is time to end. This leads into the social phase where they involve other people in the breakup discussions such as close family and friends. People are likely to take sides and this makes it hard to turn back. Nasty secrets may be revealed. It's really inevitable that the break up will occur. The final phase is grave-dressing where both partners work out their 'story' – their account of what really happened. Such a story is important for future relationships because each partner wants to look 'good'.

Duck's account is culturally biased as it is based in individualist cultures like America and the UK and doesn't relate well to collectivist societies. So we can't generalise it to all people all over the world. It really is for just one group of people. It's also quite determinist because it suggests that this is what will happen to you if your relationship starts to go wrong. It could also be described as reductionist because it reduces a complex relationship to some very simple elements. A more holist approach might look at the whole relationship and that might be better.

Not much research has been done to support the theory because it is quite difficult to ask people about what happens when their relationship breaks down. People don't want to talk about it and they may not tell the truth anyway. Research might involve interviews and these are very subjective anyway and there may be interviewer bias so we can't necessarily trust what people say, though you could check interviewer reliability with test-retest. So it isn't very scientific research. There are other theories that are more explanatory.

(471 words)

An awkward beginning from Vladimir which tends not to go anywhere initially. A clear outline of the theory – a la Luke – would have been preferable.

When Vladimir does begin to tackle the main features of the model, some of the points are a little laboured and there is a lack of conciseness, which will affect the overall balance of the essay.

The cultural point is not well made – why does the theory prioritise Western experience? Determinism and reductionism are 'thrown in' as issues but not really made relevant and there is vague, speculative methodological evaluation at the end.

Overall, Vladimir has focused too much on description rather than evaluation which the question also requires.

MULTIPLE-CHOICE QUESTIONS

Sexual selection and human reproductive behaviour

1. Anisogamy refers to . . .
(a) Female choosiness in mate selection.
(b) Difference between inter-sexual selection and intra-sexual selection.
(c) Indicators of a body shape suggesting fertility.
(d) Differences between male and female gametes.

2. An example of inter-sexual selection is . . .
(a) Male competition for reproductive rights.
(b) Female choosiness.
(c) Male protection of fertile females.
(d) Sensitivity to indicators of fertility and youth.

3. Dimorphism is mostly the outcome of . . .
(a) Intra-sexual selection.
(b) Inter-sexual selection.
(c) The female's greater investment in offspring.
(d) Female competition for fit males.

4. Sexual selection as an explanation of partner preference is supported by . . .
(a) Changing norms of sexual behaviour.
(b) Buss's research into mate selection.
(c) Women's greater role in the workplace.
(d) Widespread availability of contraception.

Factors affecting attraction: Self-disclosure

1. Self-disclosure is a central concept of which theory?
(a) Intimacy theory.
(b) Reciprocity theory.
(c) Social penetration theory.
(d) Commitment theory.

2. Over time, self-disclosure should increase in . . .
(a) Depth only.
(b) Breadth only.
(c) Both breadth and depth.
(d) Breadth or depth.

3. A feature of self-disclosure in satisfying relationships is . . .
(a) It is used rarely.
(b) It is reciprocated.
(c) It is needed less and less over time.
(d) It just comes naturally and does not need to be used deliberately.

4. What metaphor do Altman and Taylor use to explain self-disclosure?
(a) Peeling an orange.
(b) Coring an apple.
(c) Digging a tunnel.
(d) Layers of an onion.

Factors affecting attraction: Physical attractiveness

1. 'People who are physically attractive are assumed to have other attractive traits' is a description of the . . .
(a) Matching hypothesis.
(b) Social desirability effect.
(c) Halo effect.
(d) Effects of facial symmetry.

2. A feature of faces we seem to find especially attractive is . . .
(a) Symmetry.
(b) Signs of ageing.
(c) Averageness.
(d) Individuality.

3. The matching hypothesis suggests that . . .
(a) We all prefer the most physically attractive person available.
(b) Physical attractiveness plays only a small role in relationship formation.
(c) The halo effect is unimportant.
(d) We take account of our own level of physical attractiveness.

4. Cross-cultural research shows . . .
(a) That 'beauty is in the eye of the beholder'.
(b) Surprising agreement about what is physically attractive.
(c) A significant effect of cultural influences on attractiveness.
(d) That the matching hypothesis is wrong.

Factors affecting attraction: Filter theory

1. An example of a social demography filter is . . .
(a) Attitudinal similarity.
(b) Complementarity.
(c) Ethnic group.
(d) Physical attractiveness.

2. Filters narrow our choice of partner . . .
(a) From a field of desirables to a field of availables.
(b) To people who are different from us.
(c) To people who are more physically attractive than us.
(d) From a field of availables to a field of desirables.

3. Complementarity of partners is most important . . .
(a) At the start of a relationship.
(b) Before the relationships begins.
(c) Later on in a relationship.
(d) Throughout a relationship.

4. Partners becoming more similar to each other over time is illustrated by . . .
(a) Reciprocity.
(b) Attitude alignment.
(c) Complementarity.
(d) Social demography.

Theories of romantic relationships: Social exchange theory

1. According to SET, an individual will find a relationship satisfying when . . .
(a) Their partner's profit is greater than their own.
(b) Their comparison level is high.
(c) Their self-esteem is high.
(d) There is fairness.

2. The comparison level for alternatives states . . .
(a) We consider the costs and rewards we could get elsewhere.
(b) Similarity is an important feature of successful relationships.
(c) Any relationship is better than being on our own.
(d) Alternatives become more attractive the longer partners are together.

3. The correct order of Thibault and Kelley's stages of relationship development is . . .
(a) Bargaining, Sampling, Commitment, Institutionalisation.
(b) Sampling, Bargaining, Commitment, Institutionalisation.
(c) Sampling, Commitment, Bargaining, Institutionalisation.
(d) Commitment, Sampling, Bargaining, Institutionalisation.

4. Economic assumptions underlying SET do not apply to . . .
(a) Exchange relationships.
(b) Any relationships.
(c) Romantic relationships.
(d) Communal relationships.

Theories of romantic relationships: Equity theory

1. Equity is . . .
(a) An equal distribution of costs and rewards between each partner.
(b) A disparity between partners.
(c) A similar ratio of costs and rewards for each partner.
(d) Rewards minus costs.

2. Overbenefitted partners . . .
(a) May experience some guilt and shame because of inequity.
(b) May be angry and resentful at their poor treatment.
(c) Are likely to be dissatisfied with the relationship.
(d) Always work hard to increase equity.

3. A cognitive consequence of inequity is . . .
(a) We might end the relationship.
(b) We will act to make the relationship fair.
(c) We might adjust our expectations of the relationship.
(d) Feeling depressed because the relationship is unfair.

4. Benevolents are people who . . .
(a) Overbenefit from a relationship.
(b) Tolerate inequity.
(c) Think they deserve more rewards than they get.
(d) Work hard to make the relationship equitable.

Theories of romantic relationships: Rusbult's investment model

1. A committed relationship is one in which . . .
(a) There is no dissatisfaction.
(b) Each partner's costs are about the same as their rewards.
(c) Alternatives are attractive.
(d) Both partners make an increasing investment.

2. Rusbult defines an investment as . . .
(a) Anything the partners stand to lose if the relationship ends.
(b) Something you have to be able to put a price on.
(c) A fair balance of rewards and costs.
(d) A cause of satisfaction.

3. The main psychological factor in romantic relationships is . . .
(a) Satisfaction.
(b) Reciprocity.
(c) Commitment.
(d) Investment.

4. An important strength of the investment model is . . .
(a) It is supported by correlational research.
(b) Its understanding of investment.
(c) It can explain relationships involving intimate partner violence.
(d) It views satisfaction as necessary for commitment.

Theories of romantic relationships: Duck's phase model

1. Creating a 'story' of the relationship is most associated with the . . .
(a) Social phase.
(b) Intra-psychic phase.
(c) Grave-dressing phase.
(d) Dyadic phase.

2. The model was extended to include . . .
(a) The Resurrection phase.
(b) Simpler links between each phase.
(c) Cultural differences.
(d) Breakdown thresholds.

3. The correct order of the model's phases is . . .
(a) Dyadic, Social, Intra-psychic, Grave-dressing.
(b) Social, Intra-psychic, Dyadic, Grave-dressing.
(c) Intra-psychic, Dyadic, Social, Grave-dressing.
(d) Intra-psychic, Social, Dyadic, Grave-dressing.

4. A useful application of the model is that it . . .
(a) Can explain relationship breakdown in most cultures.
(b) Identifies when and how relationships can be repaired.
(c) Is based on research into the very earliest steps in relationship breakdown.
(d) Shows that one phase inevitably leads to another.

Virtual relationships

1. According to reduced cues theory . . .
(a) Tone of voice is unimportant.
(b) CMC promotes de-individuation.
(c) There is a high level of self-disclosure in CMC.
(d) Emoticons are good substitutes for facial expressions in CMC.

2. The *boom and bust phenomenon* is associated with the . . .
(a) Hyperpersonal model.
(b) Reduced cues theory.
(c) Absence of gating.
(d) De-individuation.

3. An ungated online relationship is one in which . . .
(a) Your appearance really matters.
(b) Self-disclosure is poor.
(c) Shy people are at a disadvantage.
(d) You can manipulate your identify.

4. The widespread use of emoticons and emojis in CMC is a limitation of . . .
(a) Reduced cues theory.
(b) The hyperpersonal model.
(c) CMC in general.
(d) Selective self-presentation.

Parasocial relationships

1. Contemplating doing something illegal to impress a celebrity is a feature of which level of parasocial relationship?
(a) Borderline pathological.
(b) Intense-personal.
(c) Entertainment-social.
(d) All of these levels.

2. Having a weak sense of identify is a feature of . . .
(a) Attachment theory.
(b) All parasocial relationships.
(c) The absorption-addiction model
(d) The entertainment-social level.

3. According to attachment theory, parasocial relationships are more likely to be formed by people who are . . .
(a) Insecure-avoidant.
(b) Insecure-resistant.
(c) Securely attached.
(d) Borderline pathological.

4. A serious weakness of much research in this field is . . .
(a) It's mostly correlational.
(b) It lacks ecological validity.
(c) It hasn't tested predictions derived from the main theories.
(d) It doesn't explain cultural differences.

MCQ answers

Sexual selection and human reproductive behaviour   1d, 2b, 3a, 4b
Factors affecting attraction: Self-disclosure   1c, 2c, 3b, 4d
Factors affecting attraction: Physical attractiveness   1c, 2a, 3d, 4b
Factors affecting attraction: Filter theory   1c, 2d, 3c, 4b
Theories of romantic relationships: Social exchange theory   1b, 2a, 3b, 4d
Theories of romantic relationships: Equity theory   1c, 2a, 3c, 4b
Theories of romantic relationships: Rusbult's investment model   1d, 2a, 3c, 4c
Theories of romantic relationships: Duck's phase model   1c, 2a, 3c, 4b
Virtual relationships   1b, 2a, 3d, 4a
Parasocial relationships   1a, 1c, 3b, 4a

The female and male brains featured on these pages are based on popular stereotypes. Do any of these stereotypes represent 'real' differences between the sexes? Or are they popular myths? If there are differences in thought and behaviour between males and females, what are they? And where do they come from? Are they biologically determined or caused by culture/society? Or something else?

And what about people in society who do not conform to typically 'masculine' or 'feminine' behaviour and adopt a different gender identity? How might this be explained?

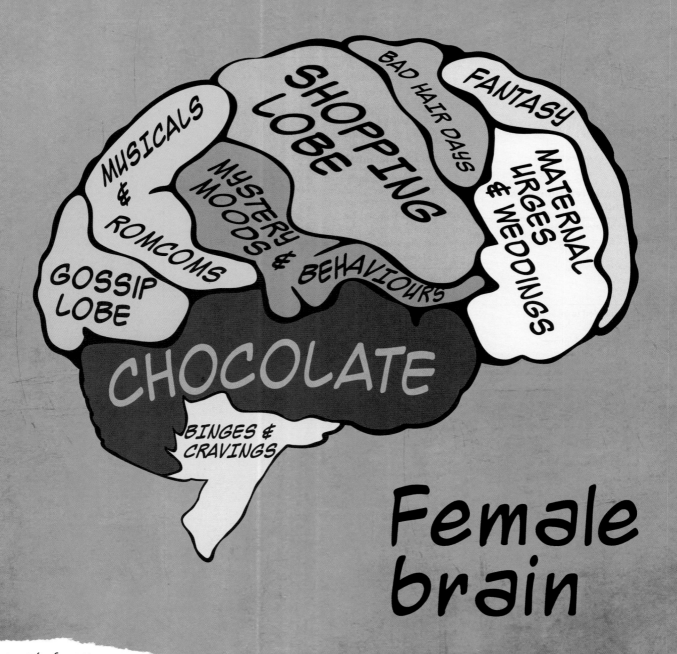

Female brain

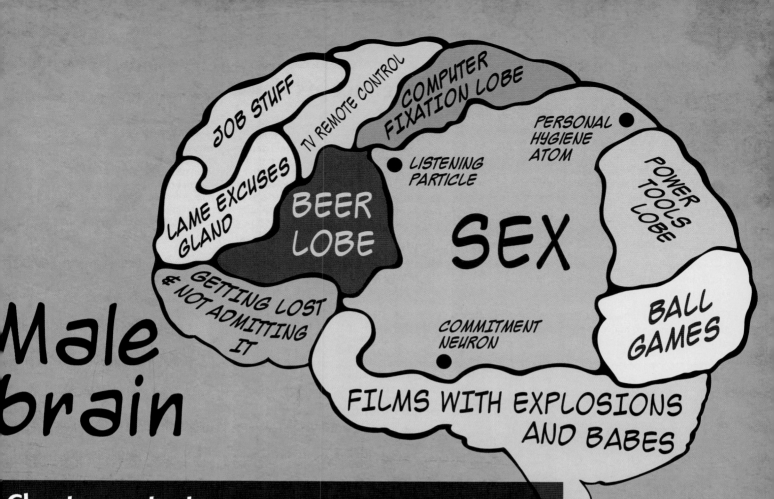

Male brain

JOB STUFF

TV REMOTE CONTROL

COMPUTER FIXATION LOBE

LAME EXCUSES GLAND

BEER LOBE

LISTENING PARTICLE

PERSONAL HYGIENE ATOM

SEX

POWER TOOLS LOBE

GETTING LOST & NOT ADMITTING IT

COMMITMENT NEURON

BALL GAMES

FILMS WITH EXPLOSIONS AND BABES

Chapter contents

Sex and Gender

Practical activity on pages 168 and 169

Sex and gender. Sex-role stereotypes.

Sex and gender are different things. This spread explains the distinction that researchers have drawn between the two concepts and how our social and cultural understanding of what it means to be 'male' or 'female' gives rise to sex-role stereotypes.

KEY TERMS

Sex – The biological differences between males and females including chromosomes, hormones and anatomy.

Gender – The psychological and cultural differences between males and females including attitudes, behaviours and social roles.

Sex-role stereotype – A set of beliefs and preconceived ideas about what is expected or appropriate for males and females in a given society.

Key concepts

SEX

OK, now I've got your attention, let's begin . . .

In everyday life, the terms **sex** and **gender** are often used interchangeably suggesting they are one and the same. Job application forms, for instance, may equally ask someone to specify their 'sex' or their 'gender' when trying to establish whether the applicant is male or female. Most psychologists, however, recognise sex and gender as distinct and separate concepts. Sex refers to a person's biological status as either male or female. This is determined by different **chromosomes** in the first instance, which then influence **hormonal** differences as well as differences in anatomy, such as reproductive organs, body shape, hair growth, etc.

Gender

By contrast, gender refers to a person's psychosocial status as either masculine or feminine. This includes all the attitudes, roles and behaviours that we associate with 'being male' or 'being female' and these are heavily influenced by social norms and cultural expectations. To put it another way, sex is **innate** and the result of **nature** whilst gender is at least partly environmentally determined and therefore also due to **nurture**.

It follows then, that if an individual's sex is innate (i.e. **genetic**), it is a biological fact and cannot be changed. People who undergo so-called 'sex change' operations do not actually change their sex as this is fixed from birth (hence, the more modern and technically accurate term is *gender reassignment surgery*). It may be that gender, however, as a learned concept, is more fluid and open to change. A person may become 'more masculine' or 'more feminine' depending on the social context they are in, and the norms and expectations associated with it.

Gender identity disorder

For most people, their biological sex and gender identity correspond. In other words, the majority of biological males tend to 'feel' masculine and readily identify themselves as such, whilst most biological females would likewise perceive themselves as feminine. Some people, however, experience **gender identity disorder** when their biologically prescribed sex does not reflect the way they feel inside and the gender they identify themselves as being. Such individuals may choose to have gender reassignment surgery in order to bring their sexual identity in line with their gender identity. (On pages 166–167 there is a further spread on atypical gender development.)

Apply it — Concepts:

Is it as simple as male or female?

Some children are exposed (not purposely) to hormonal imbalances in the womb which mean that their genitals appear neither obviously male nor female at birth. Such children are known as '**intersex**' and their parents are often encouraged to opt for surgery to make the child's sex clear so they can be classified as a boy or a girl.

In 2013, Germany became the first European country to introduce a third gender category ('X') on birth certificates to prevent parents having to make choices about their child's sex before the child itself can decide.

Questions

1. What are the potential issues and benefits of a third gender category?
2. Do you think this is something that should be introduced in this country? Explain your answer.

Apply it — Concepts: Can a person change their gender?

The unusual case of the Batista boys

Julianne Imperato-McGinley *et al.* (1974) studied a unique family who lived in the Dominican Republic. Four of the children within the family were identified as girls at birth and raised as such until puberty, when they 'changed' into males – each of the children's vaginas closed over, testicles appeared and they grew normal-sized penises.

The four girls (now boys) were all affected by a very rare genetic disorder, which meant their male genitalia were not external at birth but were concealed inside (they were normal XY males). During prenatal development, a crucial chemical step (the introduction of *dihydrotestosterone*) was missed, which would normally externalise the male genitalia. As such, although their biological sex was male (unbeknown to their family), they had the external appearance of girls at birth. Because of this the four boys were raised as girls and adopted a female gender identity until the change at puberty.

Due to the onset of hormonal changes at puberty, the dihydrotestosterone that was absent in the womb was produced and the boys' true biological sex was revealed.

The interesting thing that the researchers found was that, in each case, the boys abandoned their female gender identity with very few problems of adjustment, and quickly adapted to their new roles as boys and men – suggesting that gender identity may be flexible rather than fixed.

Question

Although this study would appear to support the idea that gender identity can change, critics have suggested that these findings should be interpreted with caution. The Dominican Republic was a highly patriarchal society when the boys grew up. Males were valued over women to the extent that the Batista boys were described as 'little miracles' by members of the local community. How might this have helped them adjust to their newly-acquired gender role?

Sex-role stereotypes

Consider a typical heterosexual couple – whose job is it to take out the bins, put up shelves and fix the car? Likewise, who is usually responsible for remembering birthdays and sending greetings cards, preparing food and getting the children ready for school?

There is no obvious biological reason as to why these tasks should exclusively apply to either sex, but you might well have identified the first set of jobs as appropriate for the male in a relationship and the second set of jobs as appropriate for the female.

Sex-role stereotypes are a set of shared expectations that people within a society or culture hold about what is acceptable or usual behaviour for males and females. These expectations are somehow communicated or transmitted throughout society and may be reinforced by parents, peers, the media, as well as other institutions such as schools. Although some sex-role stereotypes may contain a 'grain of truth' (see right), many do not, and may lead to sexist assumptions being formed, such as the idea that a woman will not have the capacity to cope with a position of high responsibility in the workplace, as she may become 'over-emotional'.

There are a number of studies of sex-role stereotyping within this chapter (see, for example, Smith and Lloyd on page 167 and Furnham and Farragher on page 164). These studies can be used to support the **social learning theory** of gender (see page 164) that various *agents of socialisation*, such as parents or the media, support and sustain the stereotypical expectations we have of men and women in society.

(see, for example, Smith and Lloyd on page 167 and Furnham and Farragher on page 164)

(see page 164)

Concepts: Sex-role stereotyping I

Question

Which of the following sex-role stereotypes traditionally apply to men and which to women in our society?

- *Settle arguments with their fists*
- *The breadwinner in a family*
- *Poor drivers*
- *Commitment phobic*
- *Leaves the toilet seat up*
- *Loves shopping*
- *Settle arguments with the 'silent treatment'*
- *The child carer in a family*
- *Spend hours getting ready in a morning*
- *Cries at a sad film*
- *Obsessed with sex*
- *Hates shopping*

Although some of the more popular sex-role stereotypes above may have little basis in fact, others do. The widely-held belief that women are better at multi-tasking than men has been supported in a recent study of the differences in neurological (brain) activity between men and women.

Madhura Ingalhalikar *et al.* (2014) scanned the brains of 949 young men and women in the biggest investigation of its kind to date. Using hi-tech diffusion **MRI** imaging, they mapped the connections between the different parts of the brain.

The researchers discovered that women's brains (top pictures) have far better connections between the left and right sides of the brain, while men's brains (pictured bottom) display more intense activity within the brain's individual parts, especially the **cerebellum** which controls motor skills.

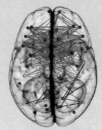
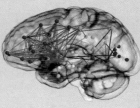
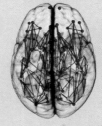
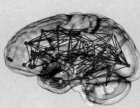

The conclusion from this is that the female brain is hard-wired to cope better with several tasks at once whereas the male brain prefers to focus on a single complex task.

Concepts: We raised our baby gender-neutral

Beck Laxton and her partner Kieran Cooper took the decision not to reveal their baby Sasha's gender to the world so he would not be influenced by society's prejudices and stereotypes. They referred to their child as 'the Infant' and only allowed him to play with gender-neutral toys in their television-free home. For the first five years of his life Sasha alternated between girls' and boys' outfits, leaving friends, playmates and relatives guessing. The couple finally decided to reveal his sex in 2012 after Sasha started primary school.

Miss Laxton, describing gender stereotyping as 'fundamentally stupid' said: 'I wanted to avoid all that stereotyping. Why would you want to slot people into boxes? Gender affects what children wear and what they can play with, and that shapes the kind of person they become.'

Questions

1. What might be the benefits and potential issues of raising a child as gender-neutral?

2. To what extent do you agree with the idea that a child's gender 'shapes the kind of person they become'?

Source: http://www.telegraph.co.uk/news/9028479/Couple-raise-child-as-gender-neutral-to-avoid-stereotyping.html

---

Concepts: Sex-role stereotyping II

David was playing football in the garden when his sister Judith began to join in. 'When I grow up I want to be a footballer', said Judith. 'Don't be silly', David replied, 'girls can't play football'.

Question

Define the term sex-role stereotype. Refer to David and Judith's conversation in your answer.

CHECK IT

1. Using an example, explain the term *sex-role stereotype*. [3 marks]

2. Distinguish between sex and gender. [3 marks]

3. Describe **one** study that has investigated sex-role stereotypes. [4 marks]

4. Describe **one** study that illustrates the difference between sex and gender. [4 marks]

ANDROGYNY AND THE BSRI

Androgyny and measuring androgyny including the Bem Sex Role Inventory.

Many researchers have suggested that, in recent decades, there has been a blurring of the distinction between traditional ideas of masculinity and femininity in Western culture. It is claimed that young people in particular are becoming increasingly androgynous in their behaviour and attitudes.

In this spread, we explore the concept of androgyny as well as Sandra Bem's attempt to measure it.

KEY TERMS

Androgyny – Displaying a balance of masculine and feminine characteristics in one's personality.

Bem Sex Role Inventory – The first systematic attempt to measure androgyny using a rating scale of 60 traits (20 masculine, 20 feminine and 20 neutral) to produce scores across two dimensions: masculinity-femininity and androgynous-undifferentiated.

David Beckham may score highly on an androgyny scale because he is competitive and aggressive on the football field as well as a caring and sensitive father.

Apply it

Methods: Androgyny and parental influence

Psychologists were interested to know whether children who were raised by same-sex parents were more likely to be androgynous than children raised by mixed-sex parents. A total of 40 children (20 raised by same-sex parents and 20 raised by mixed-sex parents) completed the BSRI and it was found that there was no **significant** difference in androgyny scores between the two groups.

Questions

1. What is the **IV** and the **DV** in the investigation above? *(2 marks)*

2. What type of **experiment** is the investigation above? Explain your answer. *(3 marks)*

3. Which **statistical test** should the psychologists have used to compare the androgyny scores between the two groups? Justify your answer. *(3 marks)* (See page 70)

Androgyny and the BSRI

Defining androgyny

The term **androgyny**, like the terms **sex** and **gender**, is useful in illustrating the difference between common-sense understanding and the way a concept has come to be used in psychological research. In everyday language, to be 'androgynous' is to have the appearance of someone who cannot be clearly identified as male or female, and this 'look' may often be seen as an asset in the fashion or music industry, for example.

Within psychology, androgyny refers to a personality type that is characterised by a mixture – or, more accurately, a *balance* – of masculine and feminine traits, attitudes or behaviours. This could include a man, or woman, who is competitive and aggressive at work, but a caring and sensitive parent. Sandra Bem developed a method for measuring androgyny (see below) and suggested that high androgyny is associated with psychological well-being. Individuals who are – psychologically at least – both masculine and feminine in roughly equal measure, are better equipped to adapt to a range of situations and contexts that other non-androgynous people would find difficult.

As suggested, it is important to recognise that both males and females can be androgynous. However, it is worth noting that an over-representation of opposite-sex characteristics does not qualify as androgyny – a female who is very masculine or a male who is very feminine, would not exhibit the necessary balance of male and female traits.

Measuring androgyny: The Bem Sex Role Inventory (BSRI)

Bem's 1974 scale presents 20 characteristics that would be commonly identified as 'masculine' (such as competitive and aggressive), and 20 that would be typically judged as 'feminine' (including tender and gentle). A further 20 'neutral' traits are also included in the scale.

Respondents are required to rate themselves on a seven-point **rating scale** for each item (where 1 is 'never true of me' and 7 is 'always true of me'). Scores are then classified on the basis of two dimensions – masculinity-femininity and androgynous-undifferentiated – as follows:

Score	Classification
High masculine, low feminine	Masculine
High feminine, low masculine	Feminine
High masculine, high feminine	Androgynous
Low feminine, low masculine	Undifferentiated

Items on the Masculinity, Femininity and Social desirability scale of the BRSI

Masculine items	Feminine items	Neutral items
49. Acts as leader	11. Affectionate	51. Adaptable
46. Aggressive	5. Cheerful	36. Conceited
58. Ambitious	50. Childlike	9. Concientious
22. Analytical	32. Compassionate	60. Conventional
13. Assertive	53. Does not use harsh language	45. Friendly
10. Athletic	35. Eager to soothe hurt feelings	15. Happy
55. Competitive	20. Feminine	3. Helpful
4. Defends own beliefs	14. Flatterable	48. Inefficient
37. Dominant	59. Gentle	24. Jealous
19. Forceful	47. Gullible	39. Likeable
25. Has leadership abilities	56. Loves children	6. Moody
7. Independent	17. Loyal	21. Reliable
52. Individualistic	26. Sensitive to the needs of others	30. Secretive
31. Makes decisions easily	8. Shy	33. Sincere
40. Masculine	38. Softly spoken	42. Solemn
1. Self-reliant	23. Sympathetic	57. Tactful
34. Self-sufficient	44. Tender	12. Theatrical
16. Strong personality	29. Understanding	27. Truthful
43. Willing to take a stand	41. Warm	18. Unpredictable
28. Willing to take risks	2. Yielding	54. Unsystematic

The number preceding each item relects the position of each adjective as it actually appears on the inventory.

Evaluation

The scale would appear to be valid and reliable

The BSRI was developed by asking 50 male and 50 female judges to rate 200 traits in terms of how desirable they were for men and women. The traits that were the highest scorers in each category became the 20 masculine and 20 feminine traits on the scale. The BSRI was then piloted with over 1000 students and the results broadly corresponded with the participants' own description of their gender identity. This suggests the BSRI has a degree of **validity**.

A follow-up study involving a smaller sample of the same students revealed similar scores when the students were tested a month later. This suggests that the scale has high **test-retest reliability** (for a more detailed discussion of these issues see pags 66–69).

Association between androgyny and psychological well-being

Within her research, Bem placed great emphasis on the idea that androgynous individuals are more psychologically healthy as they are best placed to deal with situations that demand a masculine, feminine or androgynous response. This assumption has since been challenged. Some researchers have argued that people who display a greater proportion of masculine traits are better adjusted as these are more highly valued in Western society (e.g. Adams and Sherer 1985).

This suggests that Bem's research may not have taken adequate account of the social and cultural context in which it was developed.

Oversimplifies a complex concept

It has been suggested that gender identity is too complex to be reduced to a single score. Alternatives to the BSRI have been developed; for instance, the *Personal Attribute Questionnaire* (PAQ), which replaces Bem's masculinity-femininity dimension with one which measures *instrumentality* and *expressivity*. However, like the BSRI, the PAQ is still based on the idea that gender identity can be quantified.

Susan Golombok and Robyn Fivush (1994) have claimed that gender identity is a much more global concept than is suggested by these scales. In order to understand gender identity more fully, the broader issues should be considered, such as the person's interests and perception of their own abilities.

The 'ladette': the subject of many an outraged tabloid front page in the 1990s.

Evaluation eXtra

Cultural and historical bias

The BSRI was developed over 40 years ago and behaviours that are regarded as 'typical' and 'acceptable' – particularly in relation to gender – have changed significantly since then. Bem's scale is made up of stereotypical ideas of masculinity and femininity that may be outdated and lacking in **temporal validity**.

In addition, the scale was devised using a panel of judges who were all from the United States. Western notions of 'maleness' and 'femaleness' may not be shared across all cultures and societies.

Consider: *Explain one way in which cultural norms of masculinity and femininity in our society have changed in recent decades.*

Measuring gender identity using questionnaires

Asking people to rate themselves on a **questionnaire** relies on an understanding of their personality and behaviour that they may not necessarily have. Gender is a hypothetical construct which is much more open to interpretation than, say, sex – which is a biological fact. Furthermore, the questionnaire's scoring system is subjective and people's interpretation of the meaning of each end of the 7-point scale may differ.

Consider: *As well as this, questionnaires often suffer from two particular forms of bias. Use these forms of bias to further criticise the BSRI.*

Apply it Concepts:

Metrosexuals and ladettes – the changing face of masculinity and femininity in Western society

One criticism of the BSRI (see facing page) is that it relies on stereotypical and outdated notions of masculinity and femininity. The argument put forward by many commentators is that the traditional dividing line between what is considered typical male and female behaviour has become increasingly blurred in recent years. This can be illustrated by two terms, both of which became new entries into the Oxford English Dictionary in the 1990s: the *metrosexual* and the *ladette*.

Metrosexual is derived from *metropolitan* and *heterosexual* and is a word first coined in 1994. It refers to a man who is especially preoccupied with his grooming and appearance, typically spending a significant amount of time and money on shopping as part of this (which would be traditionally recognised as a feminine pursuit).

Meanwhile the mid-90s also saw the birth of the *ladette* as more and more young women embraced lager-drinking culture, football and loutishness (traditionally the exclusive domain of males). The increasingly ubiquitous ladette – 'a woman who behaves in a boisterously assertive or crude manner and engages in heavy drinking sessions' (Oxford English Dictionary) – gave rise to a number of outraged tabloid headlines (see above) and even a TV show (*Ladette to Lady*) that aimed to transform the new caricature into its more feminine counterpart.

Question

Explain why ladettes and metrosexuals would not be classified as androgynous using Bem's criteria.

CHECK IT

1. Using an example, define the term *androgyny*. [3 marks]
2. Outline **one** way of measuring androgyny. [3 marks]
3. Explain **two** criticisms of the BSRI. [6 marks]
4. Discuss the Bem Sex Role Inventory. Refer to evidence in your answer. [16 marks]

The role of chromosomes and hormones in sex and gender

THE SPECIFICATION SAYS...

The role of chromosomes and hormones (testosterone, oestrogen and oxytocin) in sex and gender.

Earlier in this chapter we stated that sex and gender are distinct concepts. However, from the biological perspective, sex and gender are one and the same. Behavioural, psychological and social differences between the sexes are seen to be the result of anatomical, chromosomal and hormonal differences within the body.

From this perspective, 'anatomy is destiny' in the sense that our biological sex *determines* our gender identity and development. In this spread, we examine the extent to which this claim is true.

KEY TERMS

Chromosomes – Found in the nucleus of living cells carrying information in the form of genes; the 23rd pair of chromosomes determines biological sex.

Hormone – A chemical substance circulated in the blood that controls and regulates the activity of certain cells or organs.

Testosterone – A hormone from the androgen group that is produced mainly in the male testes (and in smaller amounts in the female ovaries). Associated with aggressiveness.

Oestrogen – The primary female hormone, playing an important role in the menstrual cycle and reproductive system.

Oxytocin – A hormone which causes contraction of the uterus during labour and stimulates lactation.

The role of chromosomes and hormones in sex and gender

The role of chromosomes

Chromosomes are made from DNA (which stands for *deoxyribonucleic acid* – you knew that). Genes are short sections of DNA that determine the characteristics of a living thing. There are 46 chromosomes in the human body arranged into 23 pairs – with the last of these, the 23rd pair, determining biological sex. The chromosomal structure for females is XX, and for males XY – so named because this is how they appear when viewed under a microscope.

All normal egg cells produced by a human ovary have an X chromosome. Half the sperm carry an X chromosome, and half a Y. The baby's sex is determined by the sperm that fertilises the egg cell. The baby will be a girl if the fertilising sperm carries an X chromosome, the baby will be a boy if the sperm carries a Y chromosome. The Y chromosome carries a gene called the 'sex-determining region Y', or SRY for short. The SRY gene causes testes to develop in an XY embryo. These produce **androgens**: male sex hormones. Androgens cause the embryo to become a male; without them, the embryo develops into a female. (Not all babies follow the same basic pattern, however, which is discussed on the next spread.)

The role of hormones

Chromosomes initially determine a person's sex but most gender development actually comes about through the influence of **hormones**. Prenatally in the womb, hormones act upon brain development and cause development of the reproductive organs. At puberty, during adolescence, a burst of hormonal activity triggers the development of secondary sexual characteristics such as pubic hair. Males and females produce many of the same hormones but in different concentrations. Of primary importance in male development are a number of hormones called **androgens**, the most widely known of which is **testosterone**.

Testosterone

Testosterone is a male hormone which controls the development of male sex organs, which begins to be produced at around eight weeks of foetal development. Much research has focused on the behavioural effects of testosterone, most notably in terms of its link to aggression. Human (see below) and animal studies have demonstrated the influence of increased testosterone on aggressive behaviour, for instance, Nanne Van de Poll *et al.* (1988) showed that female rats who had been injected with testosterone became more physically and sexually aggressive.

Oestrogen

Oestrogen is a female hormone that determines female sexual characteristics and menstruation. Alongside the physical changes, oestrogen causes some women to experience heightened emotionality and irritability during their menstrual cycle. This is referred to as *pre-menstrual tension* (PMT) or *pre-menstrual syndrome* (PMS) when these effects become a diagnosable disorder. In extreme cases, PMS has been used (successfully) as a defence in cases of shoplifting and even murder! That said, some researchers dispute the existence of PMS as a viable medical category (see evaluation on facing page).

Oxytocin

Women typically produce **oxytocin** in much larger amounts than men, particularly as a result of giving birth. The hormone stimulates lactation, making it possible for mothers to breastfeed their children. It also reduces the stress hormone **cortisol** and facilitates bonding, for this reason it has been referred to as the 'love hormone'. Oxytocin is released in massive quantities during labour and after childbirth and makes new mothers feel 'in love' with their baby. The fact that men produce less of this hormone has, in the past, fuelled the popular stereotype that men are less interested in intimacy and closeness within a relationship. However, evidence suggests that both sexes produce oxytocin in roughly equal amounts during amorous activities such as kissing and sexual intercourse.

The hormone oxytocin is thought to reduce stress and promote feelings of love and intimacy between couples (such as these two lovebirds).

Apply it

Methods: Congenital adrenal hyperplasia (CAH)

CAH is a rare genetic disorder that causes high prenatal levels of male hormones such as testosterone. The condition can affect males or females. However, it can be more easily identified in newborn baby girls who may have ambiguous genitals due to the masculinising effect of the male hormones.

A study by Sheri Berenbaum and Michael Bailey (2003) found females with CAH are often described by their family and friends as tomboys, exhibit higher levels of aggression than other girls and show a preference for 'male' toys.

Question

This would appear to be sound evidence for the powerful influence of male sex hormones on gender behaviour. However, why might we be cautious when generalising findings from these cases? *(3 marks)*

Evaluation

Evidence supports the role of chromosomes and hormones

The determining influence of chromosomes on gender identity is supported by the case of David Reimer (see Apply it – right). In relation to sex hormones, James Dabbs et al. (1995) found, in a prison population, that offenders with the highest levels of testosterone were more likely to have committed violent or sexually motivated crimes.

Stephanie Van Goozen et al. (1995) studied **transgender** individuals who were undergoing hormone treatment and being injected with hormones of the opposite sex. Transgender women (male-to-female) showed decreases in aggression and visuo-spatial skills whilst transgender men (female-to-male) showed the opposite. This research seems to suggest that sex hormones do exert some influence on gender-related behaviours.

Contradictory evidence

Despite the above, other evidence is rather less convincing. In a **double-blind** study conducted by Ray Tricker et al. (1996), 43 males were given either a weekly injection of testosterone or a **placebo**. No significant differences in aggression were found after the ten-week period between the two groups. Similarly, Ditte Slabbekoorn et al. (1999) demonstrated that sex hormones had no consistent effect on gender-related behaviour.

It is also the case that many studies of biological factors in gender involve small samples of unusual people (for example, the study by Van Goozen, above), or are conducted on animals, limiting the extent to which meaningful generalisations can be made.

Objections to pre-menstrual syndrome

Many commentators have questioned the effects of oestrogen levels on a woman's mood and object to the medical category *pre-menstrual syndrome* on the grounds that it stereotypes female experience and emotion. Feminist critiques (e.g. Rodin 1992) claim that PMS is a **social construction** – not a biological 'fact' but a way of privileging certain groups over others (in this case men over women). Feminists have pointed to the medicalisation of women's lives and the dismissal of women's emotions, especially anger, by explaining them in biological terms.

Evaluation eXtra

Overemphasis on nature

If gender identity is purely down to biology then we would expect to find many more differences in male and female behaviour than there actually are. In a major review of research in this area, Eleanor Maccoby and Carol Jacklin (1974) found **significantly** more differences in behaviour *within* the sexes than *between* them. Alternative explanations such as **social learning theory** (see page 162) would point to the importance of social context in the learning of our gender identity and gender role. The influence of social norms would explain cross-cultural differences in gender-role behaviour, and the fact that, in Western society at least, males and females are gradually becoming more **androgynous** in their behaviour.

Consider: *Why would an explanation based on biological factors alone have difficulty explaining cross-cultural differences in gender, and changes in gender role over time?*

Oversimplifies a complex concept

Biological accounts that reduce gender to the level of chromosomes and hormones have been accused of ignoring alternative explanations for gender development. The **cognitive approach** would draw attention to the changing thought processes that underpin gender development. Even though these may come about through maturation of the developing brain, they are not adequately explained by the biological model.

In addition, although the biological approach would acknowledge the importance of innate factors in gender development, the **psychodynamic approach** would also point to the importance of childhood experiences such as interaction within the family.

Consider: *Explain how the biological model takes a **reductionist** approach when explaining gender development. Why is this a problem?*

Apply it   Concepts: The case of David Reimer

Twin boys Bruce and Brian Reimer were born in Canada in 1965. Following a horrifically botched circumcision operation at six months of age, one of the twins – Bruce – was left without a penis.

Shortly after, Bruce's traumatised parents were made aware of the pioneering work of John Money, an up-and-coming psychologist who was developing his theory of 'gender neutrality' – that biological sex is less important than environmental influence in establishing gender identity. In other words, a biological male or female could be encouraged to develop the gender identity of the opposite sex if they were brought up in such a way, and this is what Money instructed the Reimers to do with their son. Bruce was raised in a stereotypically feminine way, dressed in girls' clothes and given dolls to play with. As he grew up, Bruce's progress was monitored by Money though he never advised Bruce of the truth of his gender re-assignment.

By the time Bruce (or Brenda as she was now known) was in her teens, Money had written extensively of the success of the case – dramatic proof of his theory of neutrality. Unfortunately for Brenda, the reality was somewhat different. Brenda had never adjusted to life as a female and was suffering from severe psychological and emotional problems. When she was eventually told the truth about her childhood by her parents, she immediately went back to living as a man ('David'). Sadly there is no happy ending here, David committed suicide in 2004.

Question

Explain why the distressing case of David Reimer is evidence that chromosomal influence is more powerful than environment in gender development.

Apply it   Concepts: Caster Semenya

Caster Semenya, a South African 800m runner, stormed to victory in the 2009 World Championships in Berlin at just 18 years of age. Her victory was somewhat tarnished, however, in the weeks that followed. An Australian newspaper publically outed her as having an **intersex** condition and therefore she was accused of having 'cheated' because she was not truly female. Semenya, it was revealed,  had external female genitalia but no uterus or ovaries and had undescended testes. The newspaper left the impression that extra testosterone had assisted Semenya's performance and that she should be stripped of her gold medal (even though, often, in intersex cases, the body fails to make use of the increased testosterone).

After a lengthy enquiry, athletics' governing body, the IAAF, declared Semenya 'eligible to compete' and she achieved a silver in the 2012 Olympic games.

Question

Explain how the Australian newspapers adopted a '**determinist**' approach in explaining Semenya's athletic performance.

CHECK IT

1. Identify the chromosomal structure of:
   (i) males; (ii) females.   *[2 marks]*
2. Outline the role of testosterone and oxytocin in gender development.   *[4 marks]*
3. Describe **one** study that investigated the role of hormones in sex and gender.   *[3 marks]*
4. Discuss the role of chromosomes and hormones in sex and gender. Refer to evidence in your answer.
                                                               [16 marks]

ATYPICAL SEX CHROMOSOME PATTERNS

Atypical sex chromosome patterns: Klinefelter's syndrome and Turner's syndrome.

Not all individuals conform to the typical XX or XY chromosome pattern. Two examples of atypical sex chromosome combinations are Klinefelter's and Turner's syndrome.

On this spread we explore the physical and psychological differences that are characteristic of these conditions. We also consider how atypical sex chromosome patterns can contribute to our understanding of the nature-nurture debate in gender development.

KEY TERMS

Atypical sex chromosome patterns – Any sex chromosome pattern that deviates from the usual XX/XY formation and which tends to be associated with a distinct pattern of physical and psychological symptoms.

Klinefelter's syndrome – A syndrome affecting males in which an individual's genotype has an extra X chromosome (in addition to the normal XY), characterised by a tall thin physique, small infertile testes, and enlarged breasts.

Turner's syndrome – A chromosomal disorder in which affected women have only one X chromosome, causing developmental abnormalities and infertility.

STUDY TIP

Don't confuse the physical and psychological characteristics. Although both are relevant, the latter are more interesting to researchers trying to establish whether gender behaviour is biological or environmental.

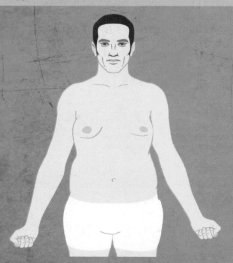

The additional breast tissue and soft body contours associated with a man who has Klinefelter's syndrome.

Atypical sex chromosome patterns

Klinefelter's syndrome

Klinefelter's syndrome is an example of an **atypical chromosome pattern**. It affects between 1 in 500 and in 1 in 1000 people. Individuals who have this condition are biological males – with the anatomical appearance of a male – and have an additional X **chromosome**. As such, their sex chromosome structure is XXY. Although 10% of cases are identified by prenatal diagnosis, it is thought that around two-thirds of people who have Klinefelter's syndrome are not aware of it. Diagnosis often comes about accidentally via a medical examination for some unrelated condition.

Physical characteristics One of the effects of the additional X chromosome is reduced body hair when compared to a 'normal' male. There may be some breast development at puberty (*gynecomastia*) and a 'softening' or 'rounding' of body contours. Individuals with the syndrome tend to have long gangly limbs, underdeveloped genitals and may have problems with co-ordination and general clumsiness. XXY men are also susceptible to health problems that are usually more commonly found in females, such as breast cancer.

Psychological characteristics In terms of psychological and behavioural characteristics, Klinefelter's syndrome is often linked to poorly developed language skills and reading ability. Sufferers tend to be passive, shy and lack interest in sexual activity. Many tend not to respond well to stressful situations and may often exhibit problems with 'executive functions', such as memory and problem solving.

Turner's syndrome

Approximately 1 in 5000 biological females have **Turner's syndrome**, caused by an absence of one of the two allotted X chromosomes – this it is referred to as X0. This means that affected individuals have 45 chromosomes rather than the usual 46.

Physical characteristics Individuals with Turner's syndrome do not have a menstrual cycle (*amenorrhoea*), their ovaries fail to develop and thus they are sterile. They do not develop breasts at puberty and instead have a broad 'shield' chest. Turner's syndrome is also associated with low set ears and a 'webbed' neck (an area of folded skin that runs along the neck to the shoulders). There is high waist-to-hip ratio in that the hips are not much bigger than the waist. Generally, adults with Turner's syndrome are physically immature and tend to retain the appearance of pre-pubescent girls.

Psychological characteristics In contrast to Klinefelter's syndrome, a feature of Turner's is higher than average reading ability. However, performance on spatial, visual memory and mathematical tasks is lower than normal. As well as their immature appearance, people with Turner's syndrome tend to be socially immature, have trouble relating to their peers and experience difficulty 'fitting in'.

Apply it — Methods: Comparing the language skills of Klinefelter's individuals and chromosome-typical males

Ten chromosome-typical males and ten males with Klinefelter's syndrome were given a verbal fluency task that involved coming up with as many synonyms for the word 'big' as they could in two minutes.

The **mean** number of words for the chromosome-typical group was 14.4 and the mean number of words for the Klinefelter's group was 8.1.

Questions

1. Identify the type of **experimental design** used in the investigation described above. Explain your answer. *(2 marks)*

2. Explain *one* limitation of the experimental design you identified in Q1 in the context of the investigation above. *(3 marks)*

3. What is the most suitable graphical display to represent the mean values in the investigation above? Justify your choice. *(2 marks)*

4. What conclusion can be drawn from the mean values in the investigation above? *(2 marks)*

5. The **standard deviation** for the chromosome-typical group was 0.6 and the standard deviation for the Klinefelter's group was 3.2. What do the standard deviations tell us about the scores in each group? *(2 marks)*

Evaluation

Contribution to the nature-nurture debate

Studies of people with atypical sex chromosome patterns are useful as they contribute to our understanding of the **nature-nurture debate** in gender development. By comparing people who have these conditions with chromosome-typical individuals it becomes possible to see psychological and behavioural differences between the two groups (such as the finding that people with Turner's syndrome tend to have higher verbal ability and tend to talk more than 'typical' girls). It might be logically inferred that these differences have a biological basis and are a direct result of the abnormal chromosomal structure.

This would suggest that innate 'nature' influences have a powerful effect on psychology and behaviour.

Environment explanations

However, there may be issues in leaping to the above conclusion. The relationship between the chromosomal abnormalities associated with Kllinefelter's and Turner's syndrome and the differences in behaviour seen in these individuals is not *causal*. It may actually be that environmental and social influences are more responsible for the behavioural differences seen in these individuals. For instance, social immaturity observed in females with Turner's syndrome may arise from the fact that they are treated 'immaturely' by the people around them. Parents, teachers and others may react to the pre-pubescent appearance of people with Turner's in a way that encourages immaturity and this may have an indirect impact upon their performance at school (hence the specific learning and developmental problems identified).

This shows that it is wrong to assume that observed psychological and behavioural differences are due to nature.

Practical application

Continued research into atypical sex chromosome patterns is likely to lead to earlier and more accurate diagnoses of Turner's and Klinefelter's syndromes as well as more positive outcomes in the future. An Australian study of 87 individuals with Klinefelter's syndrome showed that those who had been identified and treated from a very young age had significant benefits compared to those who had been diagnosed in adulthood (Herlihy *et al*. 2011).

This suggests that increased awareness of these conditions may have practical application.

Evaluation eXtra

Unusual sample

Caution should always be exercised when drawing conclusions from such an unusual and unrepresentative sample of people. The main issue is the lack of **generalisability** from atypical individuals to the wider population. It is also the case that individuals who look different (because of their unusual chromosomes), are unlikely to be treated in the same way as their peers. This may muddy the waters when trying to assess the relative contribution of nature and nurture in terms of behavioural and psychological differences.

Consider: *Only around a third of people with Klinefelter's are aware that they have the condition, and significantly fewer of those will have been the subject of psychological research. Why does this further limit the extent to which generalisation can be made?*

The idea of typical vs atypical

The presumed contribution of Turner's and Klinefelter's syndromes to the nature-nurture debate is based on the idea that there are 'typical' gender behaviours associated with males and females. For instance, the idea that Turner's individuals are socially immature is based on the idea that there is a typical level of social maturity for the vast majority of females. However, this may be based on stereotypical assumptions of what constitutes 'average' or 'normal' behaviour for males and females rather than fact.

Consider: *Explain how the Maccoby and Jacklin study on page 153 supports the idea that there may not be a typical standard for male and female behaviour.*

page 153

Apply it — Concepts: Treating Klinefelter's and Turner's syndrome

Testosterone replacement therapy can help people with Klinefelter's syndrome increase their **hormone** levels towards a normal range. This can produce bigger muscles, deepen the voice, and stimulate facial and body hair growth. Some XXY males can also benefit from fertility treatment to help them father children.

Growth hormone injections are beneficial for some individuals with Turner's syndrome. Injections often begin in early childhood and may increase final adult height by a few inches. **Oestrogen** replacement therapy is usually started at the time of normal puberty to start breast development. Oestrogen and progesterone are given a little later to begin a monthly menstrual period, which is necessary to keep the womb healthy.

Question

Hormone replacement therapy may address some of the phsyical differences that Klinefelter's and Turner's patients may have. Outline the psychological effects of Klinefelter's syndrome and Turner's syndrome.

A person with Turner's syndrome may have a wide 'webbed' neck, a broad 'shield' chest and low set ears.

Apply it — Concepts: Howard

Howard is 14 and has been diagnosed with Klinefelter's syndrome. He is quite tall for his age and long-limbed. Howard is often described by others as a clumsy boy and although he has some close friends, he tends to be quite shy and passive at school.

Questions

1. Identify how Howard's sex chromosome pattern differs from that of most boys.

2. Explain how studying people like Howard can contribute to our understanding of gender.

CHECK IT

1. Identify the atypical sex chromosome pattern for Turner's syndrome. *[1 mark]*

2. Identify **two** physical effects of Klinefelter's syndrome. *[2 marks]*

3. Explain **one** problem of studying people with atypical sex chromosomes. *[3 marks]*

4. Discuss atypical sex chromosome patterns and what they tell us about gender development. *[16 marks]*

Cognitive explanations of gender development, Kohlberg's theory, gender identity, gender stability and gender constancy.

There are several explanations of gender development, which we will examine over the next four spreads. Two are cognitive explanations, specifically *cognitive-developmental* because they share the view that a child's mental concept of gender becomes more sophisticated with age.

The first cognitive-developmental explanation was proposed by Lawrence Kohlberg who suggested that a child's understanding of gender develops in three stages.

KEY TERMS

Gender identity – Acquired around age 2. The child recognises that they are a boy or a girl and possesses the ability to label others as such.

Gender stability – Happens around age 4. The child understands that their own gender is fixed and they will be male or female when they are older.

Gender constancy – Usually reached by age 6 or 7. The child realises that gender is consistent over time and situations; they begin to identify with people of their own gender and start to behave in gender-appropriate ways.

Apply it — Methods:
Questioning children at different ages

In his research, Kohlberg interviewed children about their understanding of gender using a **structured interview** technique.

Questions

1. Outline what is meant by a structured interview. *(2 marks)*

2. Explain *one* methodological limitation of interviewing children about their understanding of gender. *(3 marks)*

3. Interviews often produce **qualitative data**. Explain *one* strength and *one* limitation of qualitative data. Refer to Kohlberg's interviews with children in your answer. *(6 marks)*

STUDY TIP

Students often have difficulty distinguishing between gender stability and gender constancy. During stability, the child understands their own sex is permanent but cannot apply this to the people around them until they reach gender constancy; then, the 'sex is fixed' idea is transferred to everybody.

Kohlberg's theory

Stages in development

Kohlberg's cognitive-developmental theory of gender (1966) is based on the idea that a child's understanding of gender (including what counts as appropriate gender-roles, behaviours and attitudes) becomes more sophisticated with age.

Understanding of gender runs parallel to intellectual development as the child matures biologically (see the work of Piaget on facing page). Gender development is thought to progress through three stages. The ages suggested by Kohlberg are approximate and reflect the fact that the transition from stage to stage is gradual rather than sudden.

Stage 1: Gender identity

Around the age of 2, children are able to correctly identify themselves as a boy or a girl. This is **gender identity**. At 3, most children are able to identify other people as male or female, and can correctly respond to questions such as, 'Which one of these is like you?' if they are shown a picture of a man or a woman. Their *understanding* of gender tends not to stretch much beyond simple labelling, however. Often, children of this age group are not aware that sex is permanent; for instance, a two and a half-year-old boy may be heard to say 'when I grow up I will be a mummy'.

Stage 2: Gender stability

At age 4, children acquire **gender stability**. With this comes the realisation that they will always stay the same gender and that this is an aspect of themselves that remains consistent over *time*. That said, children of this age cannot apply this logic to other people in other situations. They are often confused by external changes in appearance – they may describe a man who has long hair as a woman and they also believe that people change sex if they engage in activities that are more often associated with the opposite gender (such as a female builder or a male nurse).

Stage 3: Gender constancy

Gender constancy appears in the final stage of development. Around the age of 6, children recognise that gender remains constant and consistent across time and situations, and this understanding is applied to other people's gender as well as their own. As a consequence, they are no longer fooled by changes in outward appearance. Although they may regard a man wearing a dress as strange or unusual, the child is able to acknowledge that he is still a man 'underneath'.

Imitation of role models

Gender constancy is also significant in that children of this age begin to seek out gender-appropriate role models to identify with and imitate. As we shall see, this connects closely with ideas in **social learning theory** (though social learning theorists, in contrast, argue that these processes can occur at any age rather than only after the age of 6). For Kohlberg, once the child has a fully developed and internalised concept of gender at the constancy stage, they embark upon an active search for evidence which confirms that concept.

Apply it

Concepts: Questioning children at different ages

Place a tick or cross in the appropriate box based on whether a boy of that age could answer the question correctly.

Question	Age 3	Age 5	Age 7
Are you a boy or a girl?			
Which one of the two pictures on the right is like you?			
When you were a baby, were you a boy or a girl?			
When you grow up, will you be a mummy or a daddy?			
Could you ever be a mummy?			
If you wore a dress, would you be a girl?			

Evaluation

Evidence supports the sequence of stages

In a study by Ronald Slaby and Karin Frey (1975) children were presented with split-screen images of males and females performing the same tasks. Younger children spent roughly the same amount of time watching both sexes. Children in the gender constancy stage, however, spent longer looking at the model who was the same sex as them. This would suggest Kohlberg was correct in his assumption that children who have acquired constancy will actively seek gender-appropriate models.

Further to this, Robert Munroe *et al.* (1984) found cross-cultural evidence of Kohlberg's theory in countries as far afield as Kenya, Samoa and Nepal. This suggests that the sequence of stages Kohlberg put forward may well be universal.

Constancy not supported

Despite the above, Kohlberg's theory is undermined by the observation that many children begin to demonstrate gender-appropriate behaviour *before* gender constancy is achieved. Kay Bussey and Albert Bandura (1992) found that children as young as 4 reported 'feeling good' about playing with gender-appropriate toys and 'bad' about doing the opposite.

This contradicts what Kohlberg would predict, but may support **gender schema theory** (see next spread), which suggests that children begin to absorb gender-appropriate information as soon as they identify themselves as either male or female.

Methodological issues

Kohlberg's theory was developed using **interviews** with children who were, in some cases, as young as two or three. Although the questions asked were tailored towards the particular age group he was dealing with, Kohlberg may not have acknowledged that very young children lack the vocabulary required to express their understanding. Such children may have relatively complex ideas about gender but do not possess the verbal ability to articulate these. Therefore, what they express does not truly represent their understanding.

Evaluation eXtra

Comparison with social learning theory

Social learning theorists would take issue with the notion that gender development occurs as a consequence of natural processes of maturation. Social learning theory places much more emphasis on external influences on the child's development, such as the role of socialisation, than Kohlberg does.

Evidence suggests that boys have a much less flexible concept of gender role than females, and boys show greater resistance to opposite-sex activities than girls. These differences are likely to be social/cultural in origin and are difficult to explain from the perspective of cognitive-developmental theory.

Consider: *Explain why these differences are difficult to explain from the perspective of Kohlberg's theory.*

Comparison with the biological approach

The argument that changes in a child's understanding of gender are maturational would gain support from the biological approach which sees gender development as genetically determined. Kohlberg's explanation is in line with a biological viewpoint, suggesting that gender development is genetically governed. Kohlberg's stages are heavily influenced by changes in the developing child's brain and increased cognitive and intellectual capacity with age.

The biological basis of the theory is supported by Munroe *et al.* (see above) who found cross-cultural evidence of Kohlberg's stages. This suggests that the sequence of stages Kohlberg put forward may well be universal.

Consider: *Why does the apparent 'universality' of Kohlberg's stage theory support its biological basis?*

Concepts: Piaget, egocentrism and conservation

Kohlberg's stage theory was heavily influenced by the cognitive-developmental theory of Jean Piaget (1926) (see page 180). Piaget described all children as **egocentric** until the age of around 6 or 7. In other words, they assume everyone sees the world in the same way as they do. When they **decentre**, children begin to appreciate that other people's views and feelings may not always match their own.

Piaget also introduced the notion of **conservation**. Older children acquire the understanding that the properties of an object (the object's 'essence') remain the same even when its outward appearance changes. This also occurs around age 6 or 7. For instance, the same amount of liquid may 'look' different when placed in a different sized glass but the volume of liquid (provided none is spilt or drank!) remains the same.

Questions

1. How can Piaget's concept of egocentrism be used to explain the errors children make in the gender stability stage?
2. How can Piaget's concept of conservation be used to explain the mental leap forward that children make at the gender constancy stage?

When playing hide and seek, a young child will often be found covering their eyes ...they assume that if they cannot see you, you cannot see them!

Piaget would describe this as egocentric behaviour, which may offer an explanation for gender stability.

Concepts: Bryan and Ryan

Bryan is 3 years old. When his nursery school teacher asks him what he will be when he grows up, Bryan replies, 'I will be a mummy'.

Ryan is 5. When his mum tells him that daddy has a new job as a nurse, Ryan is shocked. 'Does that mean daddy is a lady now?' asks Ryan.

Questions

1. What is meant by *gender stability*? Refer to the comment made by Bryan as part of your answer.
2. What is *gender constancy*? Refer to Ryan's question as part of your answer.

CHECK IT

1. Using an example, explain what is meant by *gender constancy*. **[3 marks]**
2. Describe **one** study that has investigated Kohlberg's theory of gender development. **[3 marks]**
3. Explain **one** methodological issue with Kohlberg's research into gender development. **[3 marks]**
4. Outline and evaluate Kohlberg's theory of gender development. As part of your evaluation, refer to **two** other explanations of gender development. **[16 marks]**

Cognitive explanations: Gender schema theory

Cognitive explanations of gender development, gender schema theory.

On the previous spread we looked at Kohlberg's cognitive-developmental explanation of gender development. A second cognitive-developmental theory of gender is Carol Martin and Charles Halverson's gender schema theory. As would be expected of an explanation within the same approach, there are a number of similarities between gender schema theory and the theory advanced by Kohlberg but also some important differences.

KEY TERM

Gender schema – An organised set of beliefs and expectations related to gender that are derived from experience. Such schema guide a person's understanding of their own gender and gender-appropriate behaviour in general.

Gender schema theory

Like Kohlberg's theory, Martin and Halverson's account is a cognitive-developmental theory which argues that children's understanding of gender increases with age. Also, **gender schema** theory shares Kohlberg's view that children develop their understanding of gender by *actively* structuring their own learning, rather than by *passively* observing and imitating role models (the view proposed by **social learning theory**, described on page 162).

Gender schema acquired with gender identity

Schema is a concept that was introduced as part of the cognitive approach. Schema are mental constructs that develop via experience (though some are present at birth in a basic form) and are used by our cognitive system to organise knowledge around particular topics. Thus, a gender schema is a generalised representation of everything we know in relation to gender and gender-appropriate behaviour.

According to Martin and Halverson, once a child has established **gender identity** around the age of 2–3 years he or she will begin to search the environment for information that encourages development of gender schema. This contrasts with Kohlberg's view that this process only begins *after* they have progressed through all three stages, around age 7 with **gender constancy**.

Schema direct behaviour and self-understanding

Schema expand to include a wide range of behaviours and personality traits. For young children, schema are likely to be formed around stereotypes, such as boys play with trucks and girls play with dolls, and these provide a framework that directs experience as well as the child's understanding of itself ('I am a boy so I play with trucks'). By 6 years of age, the child has a rather fixed and stereotypical idea about what is appropriate for its gender.

For this reason, children are likely to misremember or disregard information that does not fit with their existing schema (see Martin and Halverson's study – facing page).

Ingroups and outgroups

Children tend to have a much better understanding of the schemas that are appropriate to their own gender (the **ingroup**). This is consistent with the idea that children pay more attention to information relevant to their gender identity, rather than that of the opposite sex (the **outgroup**). It is not until children are a little older (around 8) that they develop elaborate schemas for *both* genders, as opposed to just their own. Ingroup identity also serves to bolster the child's level of **self-esteem**.

Apply it

Concepts: Jessica's plans

Jessica is 6 years old and is talking to her mum about what she wants to do when she grows up.

'I want to be a doctor because doctors are caring and kind', says Jessica.

'That's nice', says her mum, 'and will you get married?'

'Yes I will', replies Jessica, 'and I'll wear a beautiful pink wedding dress with a bow in my hair and carry flowers'.

'Lovely', says her mum, 'and what will your husband wear?'

Jessica thinks for a minute and finally replies, 'I don't really know what boys wear at weddings'.

Question

Use your knowledge of gender schema theory to explain the conversation between Jessica and her mum.

Apply it   Methods:

Recall of gender-consistent and gender-inconsistent images

A study investigated whether six-year-old children were more likely to recall gender-consistent or gender-inconsistent images. Twenty children were shown ten photographs of adults performing gender-consistent activities (such as a woman washing the dishes) and a further ten photographs of adults performing gender-inconsistent activities (such as a man bottle-feeding a baby).

A week later, the children were tested on their recall of all the photographs they had seen.

Questions

1. Write a **directional hypothesis** for the investigation above. *(2 marks)*
2. Explain how **counterbalancing** could have been used in the investigation above. *(2 marks)*
3. Of the 20 children tested, 15 of them recalled more of the gender-consistent photographs than the gender-inconsistent photographs. What percentage of the total number of children recalled more of the gender-consistent photographs when tested a week later? Show your calculations. *(2 marks)*
4. The investigation above used a **repeated measures design**. Explain how the investigation could be redesigned using a **matched pairs design**. *(3 marks)*

Evaluation

Evidence supports gender schema theory

Martin and Halverson's (1983) own study found that children under the age of six were more likely to remember photographs of gender-consistent behaviour than photographs of gender-inconsistent behaviour when tested a week later. Children tended to change the sex of the person carrying out the gender-inconsistent activity in the photographs when asked to recall them. This supports the idea that memory may be distorted to fit with existing gender schemas.

Further, Carol Martin and Jane Little (1990) found that children under the age of four, who showed no signs of gender stability or constancy, nevertheless demonstrated strongly sex-typed behaviours and attitudes. This contradicts Kohlberg's theory but is consistent with the predictions of gender schema theory.

Rigidity of gender beliefs

This theory can account for the fact that young children tend to hold very fixed and rigid gender attitudes. Information that conflicts with existing schema, such as the idea of a woman working on a building site, would be discounted or ignored in favour of information that confirms ingroup schema, such as a woman working as a secretary.

Similarly, children display a strong *in-group bias* in terms of how they process information (the examples above would be more relevant to a girl than a boy) and this is explained by the fact that children pay more attention to information that is relevant to their own experience.

Thus, Martin and Halverson's theory can explain many aspects of young children's thinking about gender.

Complements Kohlberg's theory

Although many critics have drawn attention to the contradiction that lies at the heart of the two cognitive theories, Charles Stangor and Diane Ruble (1989) have suggested that gender schema and gender constancy may actually describe two different processes. Gender schema is concerned with how organisation of information affects memory, and this explains why gender-inconsistent information is misremembered or forgotten. Gender constancy, on the other hand, is more appropriately linked to motivation. Once children have a firmly established concept of what it means to be a boy or a girl – at gender constancy stage – they are motivated to find out more about this role and engage in gender-appropriate activities.

Evaluation eXtra

Overemphasis on the role of the individual in gender development

It is likely that the importance of schemas and other cognitive factors in determining behaviour are exaggerated within the theory. As with Kohlberg's theory, there may not be sufficient attention paid to the role of social factors such as parental influence and the role of rewards and punishments the child receives for their gendered behaviour. For this reason, the theory does not really explain *why* gender schemas develop and take the form they do.

Consider: *What role might rewards and punishments play in the development of gender role behaviour?*

Key assumptions of the theory are not supported

It is assumed within gender schema theory that it should be possible to change children's behaviour by changing their schemas or stereotypes. In fact it is very difficult to change behaviour even if certain beliefs are held. This is reflected in the fact that many married couples have strong views related to equality of the sexes and equal division of labour in the home, but research suggests that this rarely has much effect on their behaviour (Kane and Sanchez 1994).

Consider: *Explain why this finding represents a challenge to gender schema theory.*

Apply it — Concepts:

Representation of gender – Disney at the movies

If children require confirmation of their gender schemas then they need look no further than Disney animations. There are stark differences in the way in which male and female characters have traditionally been portrayed in Disney films. Male leads are typically characterised as independent, assertive, intelligent, athletic, important, competent, responsible and stronger than female characters. For example, Tarzan, Prince Charming and Hercules all conform to the alpha-male stereotype.

In contrast, female characters have often been portrayed as weaker, more controlled by others, emotional, warmer, romantic, affectionate, sensitive, passive, complaining, domestic and more troublesome than male characters. Step forward Snow White, Sleeping Beauty, *et al.*

Question

Which other Disney characters would tend to confirm children's gender schemas/stereotypes and why?

A woman engaged in gender-inconsistent behaviour.

In the Martin and Halverson study (above left), children's recall of photos such as these tended to be poorer and/or distorted.

STUDY TIP

You can use studies, such as the Martin and Halverson study, when writing essays either as part of description or as evaluation. If you do use them as part of evaluation then you should keep your description of these to a minimum. The main focus should be on how the study supports (or challenges) the theory. A useful phrase is 'This suggests that…'.

In this case, the Martin and Halverson study supports gender schema theory as it demonstrates how children will disregard or misremember information that is not consistent with their existing gender schema.

This is the important bit to emphasise in evaluation – rather than a detailed description of the study's procedure and findings.

CHECK IT

1. Using an example, explain what is meant by *gender schema*. [3 marks]
2. Describe **one** study that has investigated gender schema theory. [3 marks]
3. Briefly evaluate gender schema theory [6 marks]
4. Describe and evaluate gender schema theory. Refer to Kohlberg's theory of gender development in your evaluation. [16 marks]

PSYCHODYNAMIC EXPLANATION OF GENDER DEVELOPMENT

THE SPECIFICATION SAYS...

Psychodynamic explanation of gender development, Freud's psychoanalytic theory, Oedipus complex; Electra complex; identification and internalisation.

You are already familiar with Sigmund Freud's psychodynamic approach from your study of psychological approaches in Year 1. His concepts and ideas, often considered controversial and unusual, have been applied to many topic areas including the development of gender.

KEY TERMS

Oedipus complex – Freud's explanation of how a boy resolves his love for his mother and feelings of rivalry towards his father by identifying with his father.

Electra complex – A term proposed by the neo-Freudian Carl Jung which refers to a process similar to the Oedipus complex. In girls, an attraction to and envy of their father is resolved through identification with their mother.

Identification – A desire to be associated with a particular person or group often because they possess certain desirable characteristics.

Internalisation – An individual adopts the attitudes and/or behaviour of another.

Freud's psychoanalytic theory

Pre-phallic children

Freud's general developmental theory sees children pass through five **psychosexual stages** that begin with the **oral stage** and end with the **genital stage** around the time of puberty. The third of these stages – the **phallic stage** – is when gender development occurs. Prior to reaching the phallic stage, which occurs between the ages of 3 and 6, children have no concept of **gender identity**. Freud described pre-phallic children as *bisexual* in the sense that they are neither masculine nor feminine. In the phallic stage, the focus of pleasure for the child switches to the genitals, and it is within this stage that children experience the **Oedipus complex** (boys) or the **Electra complex** (girls). These stages are crucial in the formation of gender identity.

Oedipus complex

In the phallic stage, boys develop incestuous feelings towards their mother. They harbour a jealous and murderous hatred for their father who stands in the way of the boy possessing his mother. However, the boy also recognises that his father is more powerful than he is and fears he may be castrated by his father for his feelings towards his mother (**castration anxiety**). To resolve the conflict, the boy gives up his love for his mother and begins to identify with his father (**identification** with the aggressor).

Electra complex

At the same age, girls experience **penis envy**, seeing themselves and their mother as being in competition for their father's love. Girls develop a double-resentment towards their mother. Firstly, the mother is a love rival standing in the way of the father, and secondly, girls blame the mother for their lack of penis (believing the mother castrated her daughter's when the mother castrated her own). Freud (1909) was much less clear on the process in girls and there is no record of him actually using the term Electra complex in his writings. The concept came from Carl Jung who suggested that girls, over time, come to accept that they will never have a penis and substitute penis envy for the desire to have children, identifying with their mothers as a result.

Identification and internalisation

The crux of Freud's theory is that children of both sexes identify (**identification**) with the same-sex parent as a means of resolving their respective complexes. Boys adopt the attitudes and values of their father, and girls adopt those of their mother. This involves children taking on board the gender identity of the same-sex parent, a process Freud referred to as **internalisation**. Essentially then, both boys and girls receive a 'second-hand' gender identity *all at once* at the end of the phallic stage.

Little Hans

Freud's evidence for the existence of the Oedipus complex was limited but he did present the case of Little Hans to illustrate the concept. Hans was a 5-year-old boy with a morbid fear of being bitten by a horse. Hans' fear appeared to have stemmed from an incident when he had seen a horse collapse and die in the street. However, Freud's interpretation was that Hans' fear of being bitten represented his fear of castration (by his father because of Hans' love for his mother). Freud suggested that Hans had transferred his fear of his father onto horses via the unconscious defence mechanism of **displacement**.

Daddy's boy. To resolve the Oedipus and Electra complexes, children identify with the same-sex parent and internalise their gender identity.

Apply it · Methods: Little Hans

The case of Little Hans is described above. Much of the analysis of Hans' phobia was conducted by his father – Max Graf – who explained the development of his son's condition to Freud through a series of letters.

Questions

1. Explain how the case of Little Hans supports the existence of the Oedipus complex. *(2 marks)*

2. Discuss the strengths and limitations of the **case study** approach in psychology. Refer to the case of Little Hans in your answer. *(8 marks)*

3. Explain how Freud's case study of Little Hans is an example of the use of **secondary data**. *(2 marks)*

4. Evaluate the use of secondary data in psychological research. Refer to the case of Little Hans in your answer. *(4 marks)*

Evaluation

Research does not support the Oedipus complex

Many commentators have criticised Freud's concept of the Oedipus complex (see Horney below) and the use of the Little Hans case study particularly as support for the idea. As well as this, Freud's theory implies that sons of very punitive and harsh fathers should go on to develop a more robust sense of gender identity than other boys because higher levels of anxiety should produce stronger identification with the aggressor.

However, this is not supported by evidence and in fact the reverse would seem to be true: that boys with more liberal fathers tend to be more secure in their masculine identity (Blakemore and Hill 2008).

Inadequate account of female development

Although Freud wrote extensively about the Oedipus complex, much of the theorising on girls' parallel development was undertaken by Carl Jung, one of Freud's contemporaries. Freud admitted that women were a mystery to him and his notion of penis envy has been criticised as reflecting the patriarchal Victorian era within which he lived and worked.

Indeed, the feminist psychoanalyst Karen Horney argues that a more powerful emotion than penis envy is the male experience of 'womb envy' – a reaction to women's ability to nurture and sustain life. Horney argued that penis envy (like womb envy) was a cultural concept, rather than an innate trait, and challenged the idea that female gender development was founded on a desire to want to be like men – an **androcentric** assumption (see page 94).

What about non-nuclear families?

Freud's theory relies on the child having two parents of different genders so they are able to manage the Oedipus or Electra complex effectively. It is logical to assume from the conclusions Freud drew that being raised in a **non-nuclear family** would have an adverse effect on a child's gender development. Evidence does not support this assumption, though. For example, Susan Golombok et al. (1983) demonstrated how children from single-parent families went on to develop normal gender identities. Similarly, Richard Green (1978) studied a sample of 37 children who were raised by gay or transgender parents, and discovered that only one had a gender identity that was described as 'non-typical'.

Evaluation eXtra

Lack of scientific rigour

Freud has often been criticised for the lack of rigour in his methods and the fact that many of the concepts he refers to in his account of gender development, because of their **unconscious** nature, are untestable. This contrasts sharply with other explanations of gender that are based on objective, verifiable evidence derived from controlled lab studies, for example, the biological approach. According to the philosopher of science Karl Popper (1959), this makes Freud's theory **pseudoscientific** (not genuine science) as his key ideas cannot be **falsified**, i.e. proved wrong through scientific testing.

Consider: *Which aspects of the psychoanalytic theory of gender development would be particularly difficult to test?*

Disagreement over gender identity

Freud argued that gender identity is formed at the end of the phallic stage (age 6), when the child identifies with the same sex parent. Prior to this the child is described as bisexual, neither male nor female. Freud also sees no further development of the child's gender identity beyond the resolution of the Oedipus or Electra complex. This is in contrast to other explanations of gender development, such as Kohlberg's theory which suggests that the child's concept of gender develops gradually - across a sequence of stages which coincide with an increase in the child's cognitive capacity.

Consider: *Explain how Freud's account compares and contrasts with other explanations.*

Mummy's boy. Young boys are possessive and protective of their mothers. Towards the end of the phallic stage, however, their attentions switch to their fathers.

Apply it

Concepts: Is my son behaving normally?

The following letter appeared in the agony aunt column of a newspaper.

Dear Deirdre,

I am currently experiencing some issues with my five-year-old son. He used to be a very loving little boy who always enjoyed cuddles and kisses from me. Our relationship was so close that he would often upset his father by refusing to go to him when he was frightened or upset.

More recently, however, my son has become more rejecting of my affections, and prefers to spend time with his father. On the one hand, I am pleased that they have suddenly become much closer (and my husband is delighted). However, I cannot hide my upset at how my little boy now seems to push me away.

Is this normal? Do all mums experience this?

Question

Write a reply to the mother's letter from the point of view of psychoanalytic theory.

Apply it   Concepts:

The gender difference in Freudian gender identity

According to Freud, because the threat of castration is not present for girls in the phallic stage, they are not under the same pressure as boys to identify with the same-sex parent. This means that girls develop a weaker gender identity than boys.

Although this is debatable, it does seem to be the case that boys are more reluctant than girls to engage in counter-stereotype behaviour that might be construed as 'sissy' or 'feminine'. This would imply that boys develop a strong masculine identity at a relatively early age, suggesting Freud may have been right.

Question

What alternative explanations may be given for boys' unwillingness to engage in feminine behaviour?

CHECK IT

1. Distinguish between *identification* and *internalisation* in Freud's psychoanalytic theory of gender. **[3 marks]**
2. Describe **one** study that investigated Freud's psychoanalytic theory of gender. **[4 marks]**
3. Briefly evaluate the Oedipus complex in Freud's psychoanalytic theory of gender development. **[6 marks]**
4. Discuss Freud's psychoanalytic theory of gender development. **[16 marks]**

SOCIAL LEARNING EXPLANATION OF GENDER DEVELOPMENT

Social learning theory as applied to gender development.

In the Year 1 course social learning theory (SLT) was introduced as one of two learning approaches (the other being behaviourism). Social learning theory has been applied to a number of different topic areas including gender development.

Children are seen to acquire their gender identity – and associated gender-appropriate behaviour – through key social learning concepts of vicarious reinforcement, identification and modelling.

KEY TERM

Social learning theory (SLT) – A way of explaining behaviour that includes both direct and indirect reinforcement, combining learning theory with the role of cognitive factors.

Apply it

Concepts: Mediational processes

Five-year-old Mary watched intently as her mum applied her make-up. She paid careful attention to the way her mum added the lipstick and darkened her eyelashes with a brush. Mary also noticed how her father described her mother as 'beautiful' when he entered the room.

When left alone, Mary sneaked back into her mum's room and proceeded to give herself a makeover. Unfortunately, she ended up getting mascara in her eye and lipstick all over her face.

Question

Use the four mediational processes of social learning theory (see right) to explain Mary's experiences.

Social learning theory applied to gender development

Social learning theory acknowledges the role that the social context plays in development and states that all behaviour (including gender) is learned from observing others. As such, it draws attention to the influence of the environment (**nurture**) in shaping gender development. This includes significant others that the child comes into contact with – parents, peers and teachers amongst others – as well as the wider influence of culture and the **media** (see next spread).

Direct reinforcement Children are more likely to be reinforced (praised, encouraged) for demonstrating behaviour that is gender-appropriate. For instance, boys may be encouraged to be active, assertive and engage in rough and tumble play. In contrast, boys are likely to be punished for being passive, gentle and staying close to their parent. The way in which boys and girls are encouraged to show distinct gender-appropriate behaviour is called **differential reinforcement**. It is through this differential reinforcement that a child learns their gender identity (I am a boy).

Behaviours that are reinforced are then imitated. A child is more likely to imitate behaviour that has been reinforced (rewarded). This reinforcement may be direct or indirect.

Indirect (vicarious) reinforcement If the consequences of another person's behaviour are favourable, that behaviour is more likely to be imitated by a child. For instance, if a little girl sees her mother receive a compliment when she wears make-up and a pretty dress, the girl may try and replicate this behaviour when she is able.

If the consequences of behaviour are seen to be unfavourable, i.e. punished, behaviour is less likely to be imitated. If a little boy sees a male classmate teased for displaying feminine or 'cissy' behaviour, such behaviour is unlikely to be copied.

Identification and modelling

Identification refers to the process whereby a child attaches himself or herself to a person who is seen to be 'like me' or because a person is like someone 'I want to be'. In short, the person possesses qualities that the child sees as rewarding. These people are known as **role models** and may be part of the child's immediate environment (parents, teachers, siblings, etc.) or may be present within the media, such as pop stars or sports stars. Role models tend to be attractive, high status, and are usually (and crucially) the same sex as the child.

From the role model's perspective, **modelling** is the precise demonstration of a behaviour that may be imitated by an observer. A mother may model stereotypically feminine behaviour when tidying the house or preparing dinner. The same term is also used to explain learning from the observer's perspective. When a little girl copies her mother setting the table, or attempts to 'feed' her doll using a toy bottle, she is modelling the behaviour she has witnessed.

Mediational processes

Social learning theorists have also suggested four mediational (cognitive) processes that are central to the learning of gender behaviour:

- *Attention:* for instance, a little boy might want to emulate his favourite Premier League footballer by paying close *attention* to what he does.
- *Retention:* remembering the skills he showed on the pitch and trying to reproduce these in the playground with his friends.
- The *motivation* for the little boy comes from wanting to be like his hero (identification).
- *Motor reproduction:* be physically capable of doing it.

Apply it — Concepts: Geronimo!

Using the key social learning theory concepts described above, explain the gender differences in children's play in the picture on the left.

Question

In your answer, make sure you make some reference to each of the following:

- Imitation
- Reinforcement (direct and vicarious)
- Identification
- Modelling.

Evaluation

Supporting evidence

A classic study by Caroline Smith and Barbara Lloyd (1978) involved 4–6-month-old babies who (irrespective of their actual sex) were dressed half the time in boys' clothes and half the time in girls' clothes. When observed interacting with adults, babies assumed to be 'boys' were given a hammer-shaped rattle and encouraged to be adventurous and active. When the same babies were dressed as girls they were handed a cuddly doll, frequently told they were 'pretty' and were reinforced for being passive.

This suggests that gender-appropriate behaviour is stamped in at an early age through differential reinforcement and supports social learning theory.

Explains changing gender roles in Western society

We noted earlier, when explaining **androgyny,** that there exists less of a clear-cut distinction between what people regard as stereotypically masculine and feminine behaviour in our society today than there was in, say, the 1950s. This can be explained by a shift in social expectations and cultural norms over the years that has meant new forms of acceptable gender behaviour have been reinforced. As there has been no corresponding change in people's basic biology within the same period, such a shift is much better explained by social learning theory than the biological approach.

Not a developmental theory

Critics have argued that social learning theory does not provide an adequate explanation of how learning processes change with age. There are some age limitations, for example, *motor reproduction* as a **mediational process** suggests that children may struggle to perform behaviours if they are not physically or intellectually capable. However, the general implication is that modelling of gender-appropriate behaviour can occur at any age, i.e. from birth onwards. This may not be the case, however. Andrew Dubin (1992) suggests that, although the child may take note of the behaviour of same-sex role models at an early age, selection and imitation of gender-role behaviour does not come until later. This is consistent with Lawrence Kohlberg's theory that children do not become active in their gender development until they reach gender constancy.

The influence of age and maturation (i.e. *development*) on learning gender concepts is not a factor considered by social learning theory and this may be a limitation of the explanation.

Evaluation eXtra

Comparison with the biological approach

Social learning theory places very little emphasis on the influence of **genes** and **chromosomes** and only considers the role of the environment in gender development. We have seen how, in the case of David Reimer, it was not possible to raise a biological male as a female and override chromosomal influence. Modern researchers are more likely to accept the **biosocial theory** of gender: that there are innate biological differences between boys and girls that are reinforced through social interaction and cultural expectations.

Consider: *Explain how the Smith and Lloyd study (above) could be reinterpreted as supporting the biosocial theory.*

Comparison with the psychodynamic approach

Freud, in agreement with social learning theory, would accept the key influence of the same-sex parent on the child's gender identity. However, the social learning view of **identification** is much more all-encompassing than psychoanalytic theory and would include a whole host of gender-appropriate role models. Freud would also point to the importance of *unconscious forces* in determining gender development as well as being critical of what he would see as social learning theory's over-reliance on *conscious* mediational processes.

Consider: *How does the influence of unconscious forces on gender development challenge social learning theory?*

Two birthday cards for an 8-year-old, but which one is for a girl and which for a boy?

Apply it — Methods: Fruity behaviour

Psychologists conducted a **laboratory experiment** to see whether children were more likely to select a particular fruit if they had seen a same-sex role model choose the same fruit earlier (based on Perry and Bussey 1979). In the experiment 20 girls and 20 boys aged between 8 and 10 were shown a short film of a male and female adult selecting fruit from a bowl. The male adult chose an orange and the female adult chose a banana.

The children were then presented with a fruit bowl which contained a selection of fruits (including an orange and a banana) and their chosen fruit was recorded.

Questions

1. Outline *one* strength of a laboratory experiment. Refer to the investigation above in your answer. *(3 marks)*
2. Identify *one* possible **extraneous variable** in the experiment above. Explain *why* it could be controlled and *how* it could be controlled. *(3 marks)*
3. Write a set of **standardised instructions** that could be read out to the participants in the experiment above. *(4 marks)*

STUDY TIP

If you write about the social learning theory of gender development you must apply the theory to gender development rather than producing a general essay on social learning theory. The best way to do this is to use examples that relate to gender to illustrate the key features of social learning theory.

Apply it — Concepts: Lily and Millie

Lily and Millie are two 6-year-old girls. Lily is very feminine and loves to wear pink frilly dresses and play with dolls. She is calm and softly spoken. Millie, on the other hand, is loud and boisterous. She enjoys running around, playing football and is often described as a 'tomboy' by other members of her family.

Questions

1. How would biological explanations of gender account for the differences in behaviour of Lily and Millie?
2. How would social learning theory account for the differences in behaviour of Lily and Millie?

CHECK IT

1. Describe **one** study in which the social learning theory of gender was investigated. In your answer include what the researchers did and what was found. *[3 marks]*
2. Outline the social learning theory as applied to gender development. *[5 marks]*
3. Briefly evaluate social learning theory as applied to gender development. *[6 marks]*
4. Outline and evaluate the social learning theory of gender development. As part of your evaluation make some reference to Kohlberg's theory of gender development. *[16 marks]*

THE INFLUENCE OF CULTURE AND MEDIA ON GENDER ROLES

The influence of culture and media on gender roles.

Social learning theorists (previous spread) see gender-role behaviour as largely determined by the environment and socialisation. Two key areas through which social norms are transmitted and communicated are culture and the media.

Indeed, these may be linked in the sense that the media (TV, film, etc.) may reflect, confirm and occasionally challenge dominant cultural norms of gender roles.

KEY TERMS

Gender roles – A set of behaviours and attitudes that are considered appropriate for one gender and inappropriate for the other.

Culture – The ideas, customs and social behaviour of a particular group of people or society.

Media – Communication channels, such as TV, film and books, through which news, entertainment, education and data are made available.

Apply it   **Concepts: Third gender**

In several cultures, the term 'third gender' is variously applied to individuals who fall outside of the strict classification 'male' or 'female'.

The five million *hijras* (picture below) of Pakistan, India and Bangladesh live as **transgender** and are now recognised as having legal identities on passports (as E for *eunuch* alongside the traditional M and F).

The *fa'afafine* of Samoa are biological males who adopt the female gender role and are known for their hard work in a domestic context and dedication to the family. Although fa'afafine may have sexual relations with non-fa'afafine men, they are not considered 'gay' as no such label exists in Samoa.

Question

Why might the fa'afafine role be considered different from Western notions of androgyny?

Culture and gender roles

Cross-cultural research is noted for its valuable contribution to the **nature-nurture debate** in gender. For instance, if a particular **gender-role** behaviour appears to be *consistent* across different **cultures**, we might conclude that this represents an **innate**, biological difference between males and females. Conversely, if we find that some gender-role behaviours are *culturally specific* we might assume that the influence of shared norms and socialisation is decisive (as suggested by **social learning theory**).

Cultural differences

One of the earliest cross-cultural studies of gender roles was carried out by Margaret Mead (1935) of tribal groups on the island of New Guinea:

- The Arapesh were gentle and responsive (similar to the Western stereotype of femininity).
- The Mundugumor were aggressive and hostile (similar to the Western stereotype of masculinity).
- The Tchambuli women were dominant and they organised village life; men were passive and considered to be 'decorative' (the reverse of the Western stereotype).

This suggests that there may not be a direct biological relationship between sex and gender, and that gender roles may be culturally determined. In her later work, Mead conceded that she had underestimated the universal nature of many gender-typical behaviours. However, she went on to argue that the extent to which innate behaviours are expressed is largely the result of cultural norms.

Cultural similarities

It is also the case that there are many cross-cultural similarities in gender roles. For example, David Buss (1995) found consistent patterns in mate preference (a kind of gender role behaviour) in 37 countries across all continents. In all cultures, women sought men who could offer wealth and resources, whilst men looked for youth and physical attractiveness in a potential partner.

Also, a study by Robert Munroe and Ruth Munroe (1975) revealed that in most societies, division of labour is organised along gender lines (with males typically the 'breadwinners' and females often the 'nurturers').

Media and gender roles

The **media** provide **role models** with whom children may **identify** and want to **imitate**. As we have seen on the previous spread, children are likely to select **role models** who are the same sex as they are and who engage in gender-appropriate behaviour (as this is more likely to be **reinforced**).

Rigid stereotypes

There is evidence that the media do provide very clear **gender stereotypes** that are quite rigid: men are independent, ambitious 'advice-givers', whereas women are depicted as dependent, unambitious 'advice seekers' (Bussey and Bandura 1999). Similarly, a study of TV adverts by Adrian Furnham and Elena Farragher (2000) found that men were more likely to be shown in autonomous roles within professional contexts whereas women were often seen occupying familial roles within domestic settings. This suggests that the media may play a role in reinforcing widespread social stereotypes concerning male and female behaviour.

Information giving

There is also evidence that children who have more exposure to popular forms of media tend to display more gender-stereotypical views in their behaviour and attitudes (McGhee and Frueh 1980).

The media does more than confirm gender-typical behaviour, it may also give information to males and females in terms of the likely success, or otherwise, of adopting these behaviours. Seeing other people perform gender-appropriate behaviours increases the child's belief that they are capable of carrying out such behaviours in the future (what Bandura referred to as **self-efficacy**).

Evaluation

Criticisms of Mead's research

Mead's research has been criticised for not separating her own opinions from her description of Samoan life (**observer bias**) and for making sweeping generalisations based on a relatively short period of study.

Derek Freeman (1983) was highly critical of Mead's conclusions and conducted a follow-up study of the Samoan people decades after Mead's original investigation. He argued that Mead's findings were flawed as she had been misled by some of her participants, and that her preconceptions of what she would find had influenced her reading of events. However, Freeman's account has also been challenged as supporting his own theoretical viewpoint (Shankman 1996).

Imposed etic

Cross-cultural research is typically undertaken by Western researchers who take indigenous populations to be their object of study. There is a danger that researchers, armed with theories and methods that have been developed in the West, impose their own cultural interests and understanding upon the people they are studying. John Berry *et al*. (2002) refers to **imposed etic** – the idea that Western ways of doing research that are assumed to be universal, may be largely meaningless when transferred to other cultures. Berry advocates the inclusion of at least one member of the local population within the research team, as a way of guarding against this possibility (which is what Buss did in his research).

Nature or nurture

Although cross-cultural research can provide insight into the different cultural practices that impact upon gender-role behaviour, such research does not *solve* the nature-nurture debate. In reality, it is practically and theoretically impossible to separate the two influences on the development of gender roles. As soon as children are born, their socialisation into a particular society starts, along with all the gender-role expectations that come with it. Therefore it becomes very difficult to determine where nature (biology) stops and nurture (social influence) begins. It is likely that there is a complex and constant interaction between both influences, and that each influences the other in the development of gender role (as Mead was hinting at in her later work).

Evaluation

Correlation not causation

Although it is generally concluded that the media has considerable influence on the formation and maintenance of children's gender role stereotypes, it is difficult to establish cause and effect within these studies. It may be that media output *reflects* prevailing social norms about males and females. Alternatively, it may be the case that media, to a large degree, is the *cause* of such norms by depicting men and women in particular ways. The vast majority of children are exposed to the media on a regular basis and therefore **control groups** of children who are beyond the media's influence are not available for comparison. Such a comparison would make the direction of the media's effect easier to establish. The Notel study (above right) is different in this respect and provides good support for media influences.

Counter-stereotypes

Most research in this area has focused upon how, in terms of gender stereotypes, the general effect of the media has been to reinforce the status quo. However, in recent years there have been many examples of counter-stereotypes in the media (such as the Disney movie *Brave*) which challenge traditional notions of masculinity and femininity. Caution should be exercised though. Suzanne Pingree (1978) found that gender stereotyping was reduced when children were shown TV adverts featuring women in non-stereotypical roles. However, it was also found that pre-adolescent boys' stereotypes became stronger following exposure to the non-traditional models. Such a 'backlash' may be explained by the boys' desire to maintain a view that ran counter to the adult view.

Evaluation eXtra

Research support for the effects of culture and media

Research into the effects of culture and the media on gender roles provides support for the social learning theory explanation of gender.

Consider: *Explain why this is the case.*

Apply it

Methods: Notel, unitel and multitel

In the early 1960s a unique experiment was conducted in a town in British Colombia (Canada) that was about to receive a TV signal for the first time. Nicknamed 'Notel' by Tannis Williams and her team of researchers (1986), the town offered a rare opportunity to examine the effect of new media on the townsfolk.

The researchers carried out extensive surveys around the town to assess the behaviour and attitudes of the population prior to the introduction of television. They also collected similar data from two other neighbouring towns, 'Unitel' (that had access to one TV channel) and 'Multitel' (that had access to several). After a two-year-period, all three towns were surveyed again.

Alongside several other measures, Williams *et al*. noted how gender-stereotypical attitudes among the children of the three towns changed over two years. At the beginning of the study, children in Notel and Unitel displayed fewer sex-typed views and less evidence of gender stereotypical behaviour than their Multitel counterparts. At the end of the study, evidence of stereotypes on both of these measures had increased for the children of Notel.

Questions

1. What do the findings from this investigation suggest? *(2 marks)*
2. Outline *one* **sampling method** that could have been used to select participants in the investigation above. *(2 marks)*
3. Explain *one* limitation of the use of this method of sampling in the investigation above. *(3 marks)*
4. Explain *one* strength of the use of survey (**questionnaire**) data in the investigation above. *(3 marks)*

Does the 2012 Disney movie '*Brave*' challenge traditional female stereotypes in children's films?

STUDY TIP

*The point related to **imposed etic** on the left makes reference to some of the methodological difficulties that researchers may face when carrying out cross-cultural research. These are discussed in more detail on page 96. Such issues could be included within an essay on the influence of culture on gender roles as long as the points you make are explicitly linked to this topic.*

CHECK IT

1. Outline **one** study that has investigated the influence of culture on gender roles. *[3 marks]*
2. Briefly evaluate the influence of the media on gender roles. *[5 marks]*
3. Discuss research (theories and/or studies) into the influence of culture **and/or** media on gender roles. *[16 marks]*

ATYPICAL GENDER DEVELOPMENT

Atypical gender development: gender identity disorder; biological and social explanations for gender identity disorder.

Some people experience a feeling of 'being trapped in the wrong body' when the gender they identify themselves as is not the same as their biological sex. This is referred to as gender identity disorder or gender dysphoria. On this spread, we explore the characteristics associated with this condition and the possible causes.

KEY TERM

Gender identity disorder (GID) – Characterised by strong, persistent feelings of identification with the opposite gender and discomfort with one's own assigned sex. People with GID desire to live as members of the opposite sex and often dress and use mannerisms associated with the opposite gender. Also referred to as transgenderism or gender dysphoria.

Apply it Concepts:

The diagnostic criteria for GID

In the fifth edition of the *Diagnostic and Statistical Manual of Mental Disorders* (DSM-5), a person is diagnosed with gender dysphoria (formerly gender identity disorder) if there is a marked difference between the individual's expressed/ experienced gender and the gender others would assign him or her, and this must continue for at least six months. In children, the desire to be of the other gender must be present and verbalised. The condition must cause significant distress or impairment in social, occupational, or other important areas of functioning.

Gender dysphoria is manifested in a variety of ways, including a strong desire to be treated as the other gender or to be rid of one's biological sex characteristics. This may also include a strong conviction that one has feelings and reactions typical of the other gender.

Questions

1. Do you agree that GID (or gender dysphoria) is a psychological disorder?

2. To what extent does it meet the four definitions of abnormality you studied as part of your Year 1 course?

Gender identity disorder (GID)

A small minority of males and females experience a mismatch between their biological sex and the sex they 'feel' that they are (their **gender identity**). Individuals who have **gender identity disorder (GID)** identify much more with the opposite sex than the one they were identified as at birth. For many people who experience this, GID is a source of stress and discomfort and is thus recognised as a psychological disorder in **DSM-5** (see 'Apply it' below). Many individuals with GID will identify themselves as **transgender** and may opt for gender reassignment surgery in order to change their external genitalia to that of the desired sex.

Biological explanations

In its categorisation of GID, DSM-5 specifically excludes **intersex** conditions that have a recognised biological basis, such as **Klinefelter's syndrome** (see page 154) and **CAH** (see page 152). Nevertheless, it is plausible that GID may be subject to some biological influence.

Brain sex theory suggests that GID is caused by specific brain structures that are incompatible with a person's biological sex. Particular attention has been paid to those areas of the brain that are *dimorphic*, in other words, take a different form in males and females. Ning Zhou et al. (1995) studied the *bed nucleus of the stria terminalis* which is assumed to be fully developed at age 5 and around 40% larger in males than females. In **post-mortem studies** of six male-to-female transgender individuals, the BSTc was found to be a similar size to that of a typical female brain.

This was confirmed in a follow-up study by Frank Kruijver et al. (2000) who studied the same brain tissue but focused on the number of neurons in the BSTc rather than the volume. Again, the six transgender individuals showed a sex-reversed identity pattern with an average BSTc neuron number in the female range.

Genetic factors Evidence suggests that GID may have a genetic basis. Frederick Coolidge et al. (2002) assessed 157 twin pairs (96 **MZ** and 61 **DZ**) for evidence of GID using clinical diagnosis of criteria in DSM-4. The prevalence of GID was estimated to be 2.3% with 62% of these cases said to be accounted for by genetic variance. This suggests there is a strong heritable component to GID.

Similarly, Gunter Heylens et al. (2012) compared 23 MZ twins with 21 DZ twins where one of each pair was diagnosed with GID. They found that 9 (39%) of the MZ twins were **concordant** for GID compared to none of the DZs which would indicate a role for genetic factors in the development of GID.

Social-psychological explanations

Social-psychological explanations of GID are based on Freudian theory and insights from cognitive psychology.

Psychoanalytic theory – Lionel Ovesey and Ethel Person (1973) have argued that GID in males is caused by the child experiencing extreme **separation anxiety** before gender identity has been established. The child fantasises of a *symbiotic fusion* with his mother to relieve the anxiety, and the danger of separation is removed. The consequence of this is that the child, in a very real sense, *becomes* the mother and thus adopts a female gender identity. This theory has some support; Robert Stoller (1973) reports that, in interviews with GID males, they were seen to display overly close mother–son relationships that would lead to greater female identification and confused gender identity in the long term.

Cognitive explanation – Lynn Liben and Rebecca Bigler (2002) proposed an extension of **gender schema theory** that emphasises individual differences in gender identity. The theory suggests two pathways of gender development, the *dual pathway* theory. The first pathway acknowledges the development of gender schema which then direct gender-appropriate attitudes and behaviour as part of 'normal development' (in the way that Martin and Halverson suggest – see page 158).

The second *personal* pathway describes how the child's gender attitudes are affected by his or her activity. Here, the individual's personal interests may become more dominant than the gender identity, and these in turn influence the gender schema. For example, a boy who finds himself in a situation where he plays with dolls may come to believe that playing with dolls is for boys as well as for girls. Events such as this lead to the development of non sex-typed schema. In most people this may lead to androgynous behaviour and a more flexible attitude to gender. In a small minority of others, it may lead to the eventual formation of an opposite gender identity (GID).

Evaluation

Contradictory evidence for BSTc

It is claimed that the BSTc is fully formed at age 5 so any hormone treatment that transgender individuals may undergo as part of gender reassignment surgery should not have a bearing on the BSTc. This assumption has been challenged by Hilleke Hulshoff Pol *et al.* (2006) who found that transgender **hormone** therapy *did* affect the size of the BSTc. Therefore observed differences in the BSTc may be due to hormone therapy rather than being a cause of GID.

In addition, Wilson Chung *et al.* (2002) claim that pre-natal hormonal influences (that affect the size of the BSTc) are not triggered until adulthood. So, although the hormonal influences occur before birth, the structural changes in the brain that are a result of these do not occur until much later. This evidence casts doubt on the idea that dimorphic brain differences are present in early childhood.

Twin studies are inconclusive

Although evidence from twin studies suggests that GID may be partly explained by heredity, findings are inconclusive. Aside from the fact that twin studies in this area tend not to yield very high concordance rates (39% for MZ twins in the Heylens *et al.* study), it is very difficult to separate the influence of **nature** and **nurture** within these investigations. Twins (especially MZ twins) may influence each other, and the environmental conditions they are exposed to are likely to be very similar. Also, due to the fact that GID occurs so rarely, sample sizes in twin studies tend to be extremely small, limiting the extent to which effective **generalisations** can be made.

Biological explanations oversimplify a complex concept

Biological explanations are often criticised for their tendency to reduce complex conditions and behaviours to a simpler genetic, neuroanatomical and/or hormonal level. The danger here is that other contributory factors occurring at a 'higher' psychological or social level may be obscured or ignored (although these explanations have their own problems too – see below).

An **interactionist** combination of several different levels of explanation may be especially relevant in the case of GID, a complex condition that is unlikely to be explained by a single influence.

Evaluation eXtra

Issues with psychoanalytic theory

Ovesey and Person's explanation does not provide an adequate account of GID in females as the theory only applies to male transgender individuals. In any case, research by George Rekers (1986) suggests that gender disturbance in boys is more likely to be associated with the absence of the father than fear of separation from the mother. Furthermore, the assumption that GID is caused by separation anxiety in childhood is very difficult to test. The fantasies which trigger GID and centre on the mother, are thought to occur at an unconscious level. This means that even those individuals who were subject to these fantasies may not be aware of them!

Consider: *Explain why the lack of testability of unconscious concepts is a general problem for psychoanalytic theory.*

Issues with cognitive theory

In common with other cognitive explanations of gender, Liben and Bigler's theory is descriptive rather than explanatory. There is very little explanation of why a child may become interested in activities that are not consistent with its own sex, or how such activities bring about the development of non sex-typed schema. Cognitive theories are guilty of simply describing the effects of gender identity disorder without providing information on its possible causes.

Consider: *Explain why the other (non-cognitive) approaches on this spread provide much better explanations of the cause of GID.*

Apply it — Concepts: Zach Avery

Zach Avery is a little boy who has insisted on wearing girls' clothes since the age of three. As their son became increasingly upset at being referred to as a boy, Zach's parents decided to seek the guidance of experts.

After months of consultations, doctors diagnosed Zach with gender identity disorder, making him one of the youngest children in Britain to have the belief that they were born the wrong sex.

Zach became unrecognisable from the little boy he was a couple of years earlier, though his parents acknowledged that Zachy, as he became known at 5-years-old, is happier than he ever was.

His primary school has supported the family, informing other pupils that Zach felt he was a girl trapped in a boy's body and even converting some lavatories to gender-neutral unisex.

Question

Explain why the case of Zach Avery contradicts the arguments of Hulshoff *et al.* and Chung (above left).

Apply it — Methods: BSTc study

Researchers compared the size of the BSTc in 15 gender-typical individuals and 15 individuals with GID. A significant difference was found between the two sets of data at the 0.01 level.

Questions

1. Which **statistical test** should the researchers have used to compare the difference in BSTc size in the investigation above? Justify your answer with reference to **levels of measurement**. *(3 marks)* (See page 71)

2. With reference to the investigation above, explain what is meant by 'a significant difference was found at the 0.01 level'. *(3 marks)* (See page 72)

CHECK IT

1. Explain what is meant by *gender identity disorder*. **[3 marks]**

2. Briefly evaluate **one** social explanation for gender identity disorder. **[4 marks]**

3. Describe **one** study in which gender identity disorder was investigated. In your answer, explain what the researcher(s) did and what was found. **[3 marks]**

4. Discuss biological **and/or** social explanations for gender identity disorder. Refer to evidence in your answer **[16 marks]**

PRACTICAL CORNER

Knowledge and understanding of … research methods, practical research skills and maths skills. These should be developed through … ethical practical research activities.

This means that you should conduct practical investigations wherever possible. On this spread there are two ideas for practical activities you might like to conduct, this time based on gender development research – a quasi-experiment to investigate whether there is a difference in males' and females' ability to multitask and an opportunity to practise your observation skills by carrying out a content analysis of TV adverts to see if there is a difference in the way in which men and women are represented.

Ethics check

We suggest strongly that you complete this checklist before starting:

1. Do participants know participation is voluntary?
2. Do participants know what to expect?
3. Do participants know they can withdraw at any time?
4. Are individuals' results anonymous?
5. Have I minimised the risk of distress to participants?
6. Have I avoided asking sensitive questions?
7. Will I avoid bringing my school/teacher/psychology into disrepute?
8. Have I considered all other ethical issues?
9. Has my teacher approved this?

How much could you remember?

	Males	Females
Median	6.5	9
Range	4.5	3

Table to show the median accuracy for recall of both passages and the range for males and females.

Practical idea 1: Gender and multitasking

The aim of this study is to investigate whether there is a gender difference in multitasking, thus this is a **quasi-experiment** with an IV of gender.

In particular, we are interested to know whether male or female participants perform better in an experiment that tests *dichotic listening*. Dichotic listening (processing two different messages at once) may be a good indicator of whether someone is able to multitask – so let's see how males and females fair on such a task.

The practical bit

There are many ways to define *multitasking* but one of these is the ability to attend to two or more messages at once – otherwise known as **dichotic listening**. There have been many experimental studies that have investigated peoples' ability to process simultaneous messages. These have generally concluded that – when listening to two pieces of information at the same time – our attentional system must 'filter out' one and prioritise the other. Although it is not possible to 'hear' both messages at the same time, it *is* possible to constantly switch our attention between the two so we can pick up some sense of what is going on; but who can do this most effectively – males or females?

The task

You'll need a mate to carry out this investigation with – your co-researcher. Before you begin to recruit participants you will need to prepare two passages of information, both similar in length. These need to be long enough so they each cover 30–40 seconds worth of reading time (you might want to time yourself reading each passage to make sure it is the right length). The content of the two passages doesn't really matter, though you should avoid too many complicated words or technical terms. Your task is to read one of the passages into one of the participant's ears whilst your co-researcher reads their passage into the participant's other ear at the same time. The participant's task is to recall as much detail as they can from *both* passages by switching their attention between the two.

Measuring multitasking

Before they attempt the experimental task, participants should be told that they are being tested on their ability to switch attention between the two passages so they should try to recall as much information as they can from *both*. After hearing the passages read simultaneously, participants should divide a piece of paper into two halves and write down as much as they can remember from each passage on either side of the paper.

You then have the slightly laborious task of counting the number of words they successfully recall from each of the passages (the DV).

Pilot study

Before the full investigation begins you might want to practise a couple of times to make sure you and your co-researcher are reading at a similar level. As you have different voices, it will be impossible to match the tone and pitch of your voices exactly, but you should at least try to ensure that you are reading at the same steady pace and at a similar volume.

Choosing your sample

You will need to consider a suitable **sampling technique** for this investigation. If you're using students from your school or college, you might want select participants from the same year group (as age might be a **confounding variable** within this experiment).

Apply it   Methods: The maths bit 1

1. Why are **measures of dispersion** calculated alongside **measures of central tendency** when analysing data? Refer to the table on the left in your answer. (*3 marks*)
2. Explain why the **median** is the most suitable measure of central tendency in this investigation. (*2 marks*)
3. Which graphical display would be most appropriate to represent the difference in median accuracy of recall between males and females? Explain your answer. (*2 marks*)
4. Which **inferential test** would be most appropriate when calculating the difference in median accuracy of recall between males and females? Give *two* reasons for your answer. (*3 marks*) (See page 70)

Practical idea 2: Gender stereotyping in TV ads

The aim of this study is to see if there is evidence of gender stereotyping in TV advertisements. This practical is based on the study by Furnham and Farragher (page 164) who investigated whether there are differences in the way males and females are portrayed in TV ads. Are these differences based on popular social stereotypes?

Mr Muscle – a male product user in a domestic location; but is that the norm in today's TV adverts?

"Loves the jobs you hate."

The practical bit

There is a considerable body of research that has investigated whether gender stereotyping is a feature of the **media**. Do TV programmes, books, films, magazines or adverts represent men and women in typically masculine and feminine ways? Or are such rigid **gender stereotypes** a thing of the past? Has today's society 'moved on' in this respect? Your task is to undertake a **content analysis** of TV adverts to investigate the **hypotheses** that males and females will be represented as occupying different roles, will advertise different products, and will be seen to have 'authority' in different contexts. You can either carry out this investigation with a friend (to increase the **reliability** of observations) or on your own.

Coding and categories

The processes involved in content analysis are discussed on page 64. As an observational technique, content analysis is flexible enough to produce both **qualitative** and **quantitative** data. However, it will probably make the data you collect more **objective** if the observations you make are **coded** using specific **behavioural categories**. But which categories should you use? The following are merely suggestions, you might want to incorporate these within your analysis or develop your own (though the first one, given the aim of the investigation, is probably essential!)

- The sex of the character.
- Whether the character is a 'product user' or 'product authority' (that is, an 'expert' giving information about the product/service).
- The character's 'role' (as a central or peripheral figure).
- The context (domestic, e.g. home/family environment or professional, e.g. at work).

It is predicted that men will be depicted in more central roles as product authorities in a professional context. Women, on the other hand, will be presented as product users in peripheral roles within domestic contexts.

Sampling adverts

How many adverts you sample is up to you but it might be an idea to spread your analysis across different times of the day. It is likely, for instance, that daytime adverts during the week may be 'targeted' more towards users of domestic products in the home. For this reason, a more representative sample will be gained from analysing at the weekend as well as during the week. Those researchers amongst you who are fortunate enough to have the ability to 'pause live TV' might be at an advantage as some adverts are quite complex and might require a second look!

Ethical issues

One of the great benefits of content analysis is that the usual **ethical issues** tend not to apply. As the adverts you are analysing are already in the public domain there is no need to ask for **informed consent** – you don't need permission to watch the telly! **Protection from harm**, **confidentiality** and **right to withdraw** can also be disregarded as there is no direct contact with the 'participants' (if we can call them that!) in your investigation.

Analysing data

Once you have collected your data don't forget to summarise it using appropriate graphs and charts.

Apply it — Methods: The maths bit 2

1. Explain how two researchers could have improved the **reliability** of their observation of TV ads. *(3 marks)*
2. Explain *one* strength and *one* limitation of **content analysis**. Refer to this investigation in your answer. *(6 marks)*
3. What percentage of 'product users' were female in the table below? *(2 marks)*
4. What fraction of characters represented in 'domestic' roles were male? *(2 marks)*
5. Explain *one* conclusion that can be drawn for the data in the table. *(2 marks)*

Table 1 Show the number of males and females in each behavioural category in TV adverts.

Sex of character	Product user	Product authority	Central	Peripheral	Domestic	Professional
Male	16	7	22	16	14	17
Female	31	8	24	17	26	9

AS SEEN ON TV

The maths bit

Overall, at least 10% of the marks in assessments for Psychology will require the use of mathematical skills.

Revision summaries

Sex and gender

In psychology, sex and gender are different things.

Key concepts

Sex
Biological status as male or female.

Gender
Psychosocial differences between males and females.

Gender identity disorder
When the way someone 'feels' does not match their biological sex.

Sex-role stereotyping
Expected behaviour of males and females in a given society.

Androgyny and the BSRI

Young people are becoming increasingly androgynous in their behaviour and attitudes.

Androgyny and the BSRI

Defining androgyny
Possessing a balance of masculine and feminine traits.

Measuring androgyny: The BSRI
Respondents rate themselves for 60 masculine, feminine and neutral traits on a seven-point scale.
Classified as masculine, feminine, androgynous or undifferentiated.

Evaluation

Valid and reliable
Student results corresponded with self-descriptions and good test-retest.

Androgyny and wellbeing
High masculinity may be a better indicator of psychological health (Adams and Sherer).

Oversimplistic
Gender identity may not be reducible to a single score.

Cultural and historical bias
US scale and over 40 years old, lacking temporal and cultural validity.

Use of questionnaires
People may not be able to identify their true characteristics, socially desirable answers, subjective rating.

The role of chromosomes and hormones

Biologists see sex and gender as one and the same.

The role of chromosomes and hormones in sex and gender

The role of chromosomes
XX for females, XY for males.
Y chromosome triggers development of male genitalia.

Testosterone
Associated with increased aggression in males.

Oestrogen
Associated with reproduction and emotionality in women.

Oxytocin
The 'love hormone', released in large quantities during labour.
Reduces level of cortisol.

Evaluation

Supporting evidence
Case study of David Reimer.
Dabbs *et al.* studied prison population.
Van Goozen *et al.* studied transgender individuals.

Contradictory evidence
Tricker *et al.* found no difference with testosterone or placebo.

Pre-menstrual syndrome
Feminists claim this stereotypes female emotion.

Overemphasis on nature
There are more differences within males and females than between (Maccoby and Jacklin).

Oversimplifies a complex concept
Cognitive approach considers how thought processes influence gender.
Psychodynamic approach: Role of childhood experiences.

Atypical sex chromosome patterns

Not everyone conforms to the XX XY chromosomal pattern.

Atypical sex chromosome patterns

Klinefelter's syndrome
XXY chromosomal structure (biological males).

Physical effects
Reduced body hair, rounded body contours, clumsiness.

Psychological effects
Poor language development, shyness and passivity.

Turner's syndrome
X0 chromosomal structure (biological females).

Physical effects
Webbed neck, shield chest, ovaries fail to develop.

Psychological effects
High reading ability, reduced spatial memory, social immaturity.

Evaluation

Contribution to the nature-nurture debate
Behavioural differences may indicate biological basis for gender.

Environmental explanations
Biological differences may cause people to treat them differently.

Practical application
Knowledge of Turner's and Klinefelter's likely to lead to earlier identification and more accurate prognosis, e.g. Herlihy.

Unusual sample
There is an issue of generalisation of findings to the wider population when dealing with atypical groups of people.

The idea of typical vs atypical
The contribution of Turner's and Klinefelter's patients to the nature-nurture debate is based on the idea that there are 'typical' gender behaviours associated with males and females but this may not be the case.

Cognitive explanations of gender development

Kohlberg's theory

Maturation underlies the appearance of three stages.

Kohlberg's theory

Stages in development
Driven by maturation, similar to Piaget's stages of cognitive development.

Gender identity
Child can label own gender correctly.

Gender stability
Child understands that they will always stay the same sex.

Gender constancy
Child understands that sex stays the same regardless of appearance and context.

Imitation of role models
Children who have achieved gender constancy seek out appropriate role models.

Evaluation

Evidence supports sequence of stages
e.g. Slaby and Frey: Children only attend to same-sex models in gender constancy stage.

Constancy not supported
Evidence of gender-appropriate behaviour before gender constancy (Bussey and Bandura).

Methodological issues
Young children lack the vocabulary for interviews.

Social learning theory
Kohlberg underestimated, social factors.

Biological approach
Maturational changes in child's thinking would gain support from biological approach.
Monroe *et al.* gave cross-cultural evidence for role of biology.

Gender schema theory

Schema generate expectations about gender behaviour.

Gender schema theory

The basics
A cognitive-developmental theory, children actively structure their experience.

Gender schema developed with gender identity
A generalised representation of everything we know in relation to gender, starts around the age of 2–3 years.

Schema direct behaviour and self-understanding
Schema provide a framework to direct behaviour. Information inconsistent with the dominant schema is misremembered.

Ingroups and outgroups
Children have a much better understanding of schemas for their own gender.

Evaluation

Evidence supports gender schema
Martin and Halverson: Memory worse for gender-inconsistent pictures.

Rigidity of gender beliefs
Theory can explain why children display in-group bias and discount contradictory information.

Complements Kohlberg's theory
Schema theory about memory, Kohlberg about motivation (Stangor and Ruble).

Overemphasis on the role of the individual in gender development
Not enough attention paid to the role of social factors and rewards and punishments in gender development.

Key assumptions of the theory are not supported
Changing gender schema does not necessarily lead to changes in behaviour which is resistant to change.

Social learning explanation of gender development

Children acquire gender concepts through differential reinforcement.

Social learning theory (SLT)

Social learning theory
Gender behaviours are learned within a social context.

Direct reinforcement
Children repeat gender behaviours that are rewarded and avoid those that are punished = differential reinforcement.

Indirect (vicarious) reinforcement
Children learn the consequences of behaviour by observing others and imitate behaviours that have favourable consequences for the model.

Identification and modelling
The child attaches to role models and imitates modelled behaviour, especially same-sex models.

Mediational processes
Learning of gender-role behaviour is influenced by attention, retention, motor reproduction and motivation.

Evaluation

Supporting evidence
Smith and Lloyd: Differential reinforcement of gender role occurs at an early age.

Explains changing gender roles
Change in cultural expectations and norms of gender behaviour are best explained by social learning theory.

Not a developmental theory
The influence of age on gender development is not considered by social learning theory.

Biological approach
Modern research accepts the biosocial theory, that nature and nurture interact.

Psychodynamic theory
The influence of unconscious processes is a challenge to the SLT concept of identification.

Psychodynamic explanation of gender development: Freud's theory

Developments in the phallic stage.

Freud's theory

Pre-phallic children
Are bisexual: Neither male nor female.

Oedipus complex
In the phallic stage, desire for mother leads to castration anxiety, this drives eventual identification with the aggressor.

Electra complexes
Girls reject mother because of penis envy, the desire to have children drives identification with the mother.

Identification and internalisation
Gender identity is received second-hand from the same-sex parent.

Little Hans
Freud's evidence for the Oedipus complex. Hans' fear of horses was a displaced fear of castration.

Evaluation

Evidence does not support Oedipus complex
Boys with more liberal fathers have stronger gender identity (contradicts Freudian theory) (Blakemore).

Inadequate account of female development
Penis envy is based on an androcentric assumption and male 'womb envy' is more powerful (Horney).

Non-nuclear families
Evidence (e.g. Golombok et al.) shows gender identity develops normally in one parent families.

Lack of scientific rigour
Many of the key concepts in Freud's account of gender development are not open to testing and cannot be falsified.

Disagreement over gender identity
Gender identity formed at the end of the phallic stage (age 6) and that is the end of gender development, in contrast with Kohlberg who placed identity earlier and saw a developmental sequence.

The influence of culture and media on gender roles

Two key ways in which social norms of gender are communicated.

Culture and gender roles

The influence of culture
Provides gendered role models with whom children identify.

Cultural differences
Mead studies in Papua New Guinea, gender roles may be culturally rather than biologically determined.

Cultural similarities
Buss: Consistencies in mate preference and division of labour across cultures.

Evaluation

Criticisms of Mead's research
Freeman accused Mead of observer bias and of being misled by the Samoan people.

Imposed etic
Western methods may be meaningless in other cultural settings, should include indigenous researchers.

Nature or nurture
As soon as children are born their gender socialisation begins so it's impossible to separate the two influences.

Media and gender roles

Rigid stereotypes
Males are autonomous, females are unambitious (Bussey and Bandura, Furnham and Farragher).

Information giving
Children who watch more TV have more gender stereotypes (McGhee and Frueh). Exposure increases children's self-efficacy to perform the same behaviour.

Evaluation

Correlation not causation
Research lacks control groups of children who do not use media, except for study of Notel.

Counter-stereotypes
Media promote counter-stereotypes, though this may create a 'backlash' (Pingree).

Atypical gender development

Some people feel 'trapped in the wrong body' in terms of their gender.

Gender identity disorder (GID)

Gender identity disorder
A mismatch between biological sex and the gender the person identifies with.

Biological explanations: Brain sex theory
GID caused by size of BSTc – a dimorphic area of the brain (Zhou et al.).

Biological explanations: Genetic influences
Twin studies indicate 62% of GID cases accounted for by genetic variance (Coolidge et al.).

Social-psychological explanations: Psychoanalytic theory
GID in males is caused by extreme separation anxiety (Ovesey and Person).

Social-psychological explanations: Cognitive explanation
Dual pathway theory suggests the development of non sex-typed schema causes GID (Liben and Bigler).

Evaluation

Contradictory evidence for BSTc
Hulshoff Pol et al.: BSTc affected by transgender hormone therapy, brain area is not fixed in childhood.

Twin studies are inconclusive
Low concordance rates and small sample sizes, difficult to separate nature and nurture.

Biological explanations oversimplify a complex concept
Alternative higher level explanations are not addressed.

Issues with psychoanalytic theory
Only applies to males, and more likely to be related to absence of father (Rekers); concept difficult to test.

Issues with cognitive theory
There is very little explanation of how a child may become interested in activities that are not gender-typical.

PRACTICE QUESTIONS, ANSWERS AND FEEDBACK

Question 1   Using an example, define the term androgyny. *(2 marks)*

Morticia's answer

Androgyny refers to when a person is both male and female, for example, Bem's idea about androgyny.

Luke's answer

Bem suggested that it was healthy to have a mixture of male and female characteristics, for example, be assertive and affectionate.

Vladimir's answer

Male and female behaviour mixed together rather than having to be just one or the other. An example would be someone who has both male and female characteristics.

Nothing of value here – the key idea of a 'balance' between male and female traits is not conveyed and the example is vague.

Luke's answer contains both elements and is clear (full credit) whereas Vladimir's example is not really an example and reads more like a definition.

Question 2   Outline **one** way in which androgyny might be measured. *(2 marks)*

Morticia's answer

It can be measured using Bem's scale. This consists of a list of male and female characteristics and you tick the ones that apply to you.

Luke's answer

The BSRI is used to measure androgyny by getting people to rate 60 characteristics on a scale of 1 to 7. You then add the scores up to see whether you are more feminine than masculine.

Vladimir's answer

Bem selected a list of 20 feminine and 20 masculine characteristics and then asked people to rate how much each was like them.

Interesting to see three very different answers here. Morticia's represents the 'bare minimum' for this answer but she has identified an appropriate scale and provided a (limited) outline. Luke's answer is the most sophisticated, and Vladimir has also provided a sufficiently thorough answer.

Bryan is 3 years old. When his nursery teacher asks him what he will be when he grows up, Bryan replies, 'I will be a mummy'.
Ryan is 5. When his mum tells him that daddy has a new job as a nurse, Ryan is shocked. 'Does that mean daddy is a lady now?' asks Ryan.

Question 3 (a)   What is meant by gender stability? Refer to the comment made by Bryan as part of your answer. *(2 marks)*
Question 3 (b)   What is meant by gender constancy? Refer to the comment made by Ryan as part of your answer. *(2 marks)*

Morticia's answer

(a) Bryan is an example of gender stability because he thinks his gender will change when he gets older.

(b) Ryan is in a stage of gender constancy because he doesn't think a man can change to a woman.

Unfortunately no credit for Morticia. She has not provided an outline for either term and, because of this, her attempted application points are not adequate. In the first part, she has not recognised that Bryan has not yet reached stability given his answer.

Luke's answer

(a) Gender stability is the second stage around the age of 4 so we would expect Bryan to be at that stage. At the stage of stability a child should recognise that gender is consistent over time but Bryan clearly doesn't recognise this because he thinks he may change gender when he's older.

(b) Gender constancy is when a child recognises gender is stable over time and situations, which is usually achieved by age 7. Ryan has not achieved this yet because he thinks that his father will change gender because of having a different job.

The first sentence in (a) is inaccurate (Bryan is 3) but the rest of the answer is strong which compensates for the inaccuracy.

Part (b) is also very good – there is a clear definition of the term followed by appropriate application.

Vladimir's answer

(a) Kohlberg said there were three stages of development. Gender identity is first and that's the stage Bryan is in because he is just 3. When he gets to the next stage, gender stability, he will realise that gender can't change like this but he still thinks it's changeable.

(b) Ryan is 5 so he is probably in the gender stability stage, when he reaches gender constancy he will realise gender can't change at all. It isn't just about appearance. At the moment he thinks that nursing is just for women and his father would have to become a woman to be a nurse.

Most of Vladimir's answer is focused on gender identity but there is a brief outline of stability in the last sentence.

The opposite problem this time: Vladimir's application to the stem is OK but the outline of constancy that precedes it is weak.

On this spread we look at some typical student answers to questions. The comments provided indicate what is good and bad in each answer. Learning how to produce effective question answers is a SKILL. Read pages 387–397 for guidance.

Question 4 Discuss Freud's psychoanalytic theory of gender development. (*16 marks*)

Luke's answer

Sigmund Freud wrote one of the most important theories in psychology, his theory of personality called psychoanalysis. This is the basis of the psychodynamic approach in psychology. This approach believes that we are driven by unconscious thoughts that have been repressed there because of conflicts. One of those conflicts comes from early gender development. In his theory of psychoanalysis, Freud explained how a little boy or girl comes to think of their gender. He called this the Oedipus and Electra complexes. In the Oedipus complex, a little boy starts off by falling in love with his mother. (The word Oedipus is named after a Greek myth of a man who married his mother without realising it.) When the boy starts to love his mother he resents his father because his father is a rival. In fact he starts to wish his father was dead. This makes him feel guilty and scared because he thinks his father may castrate him because he is a bad boy. Eventually the boy comes to resolve his feelings by identifying with his father and through this identification the boy learns about being a boy and man. Freud supported this theory with his case study of Little Hans who went through just these experiences. He loved his mother and wished his father was dead but eventually identified with his father. However, one case study like this is not really enough to support a theory. The case study was also subjective and biased and we can't generalise from a case study that may be unique. There isn't any other research to support it.

Freud described a similar process in girls but it was less strong. A girl resents her mother because she hasn't got a penis and she envies the fact that her father has one (penis envy). Eventually she realises she can have babies instead and comes to identify with her mother. There is even less evidence to support this and some people say that Freud was confused between penis envy and really an envy of male power. So his theory is gender-biased because he doesn't really represent women very well.

Freud's ideas rely on the fact that children have two parents but many children don't grow up with both a mother and father so how does their gender develop? There is evidence that they develop perfectly well so gender development can't be related to identification with one parent. It is a very biased theory because it ignores one parent families or homosexual parents. In Freud's defence he did write the theory a long time ago and things were very different.

(433 words)

Luke's answer demonstrates a common flaw in essay answers on this topic – there is very little focus on gender *development*. As a generic description of the Oedipus complex this is accurate, though much too detailed. Unfortunately though, Luke fails to link the key concepts he presents to the development of gender.

The evaluation of Freud's case study method lacks similar focus. It is only in the last paragraph that Luke begins to include reference to gender.

A disappointing answer that does not address the central issue.

Vladimir's answer

Freud identified five stages of psychosexual development. The third stage is the phallic stage. Before this stage (before the age of about 4) children have no gender identity but around the age of 4 they become interested in their genitals and experience the Oedipus or Electra complex. Little boys develop a desire for their mother and a hatred for their father who stands in their way. The boy fears that his father may find out and experiences castration anxiety. To resolve the conflict, the boy gives up his love for his mother and begins to identify with his father.

Little girls at the same age, experience penis envy, seeing themselves and their mother as being in competition for their father's love. Girls eventually accept that they will never have a penis and substitute penis envy for the desire to have children, identifying with their mothers as a result.

Central to this account are the concepts of identification and internalisation. Gender identity is achieved when a child identifies with the same sex parent and then begins to internalise the parents' gender concepts.

There is very little evidence to support either account of gender development. One of the only things is the case study of Little Hans who experienced the Oedipus complex but this is quite subjective and only one individual so we can't really generalise this. It also occurred a long time ago and may not apply today.

Freud's account doesn't make good sense because it suggests that boys who have an especially harsh father should develop a very strong gender identity because they identify more strongly. In fact Blakemore found that the opposite was true – that boys with more liberal fathers identified more strongly.

Freud's theory also doesn't make sense in the way that gender development occurs all at once when identification is achieved, rather than through a series of gradual changes as described by theories such as gender schema.

People are even more critical about Freud's description of female gender development. For example, Karen Horney argued that men might equally experience womb envy and that in fact both womb envy and penis envy are cultural concepts, which therefore may not apply beyond the European 19th century where Freud lived. Freud's views were androcentric as he viewed development from a male perspective, suggesting the female development was inferior.

Freud's views cannot explain more modern families where often there may not be two parents. Freud suggested that such non-nuclear families would have an adverse effect on gender development but this is not supported by research. For example, Golombok et al. found that children from one parent families developed quite normal gender identities and the same has been found in research by Green on children raised by gay or transgender couples.

In general, Freud has been accused of producing pseudoscientific theories because his concepts were basically untestable and in this sense his theory isn't really a theory at all because it cannot be falsified.

(484 words)

Compare Luke's description of the theory to Vladimir's here. This is a much more concise account that is clearly focused on gender *development* throughout. Oedipus and Electra complexes are well-used here, rather than being long and rambling.

Perhaps the case study of Little Hans could have been more clearly linked to gender development but is still relevant.

In paragraph 5 evidence is used effectively as counterargument. This is followed by a good contrast with an alternative theory and then a sophisticated analysis using Horney's critique of Freud.

A well-constructed and well-informed critical point in the penultimate paragraph the same point as Luke made is much better elaborated and includes relevant evidence.

MULTIPLE-CHOICE QUESTIONS

Sex and gender

1. The term 'sex' refers to a person's . . .
(a) Psychological status as male or female.
(b) Cultural status as male or female.
(c) Biological status as male or female.
(d) Marital status as male or female.

2. A 'sex-role stereotype' is . . .
(a) A set of beliefs and preconceived ideas about what is expected or appropriate for males and females.
(b) A person's psychosocial status as male or female.
(c) A person's biological status as male or female.
(d) A person who has a balance of masculine and feminine traits.

3. In the Batista family study the boys chromosomal sex was . . .
(a) XY.
(b) XX.
(c) XXY.
(d) XYY.

4. Which of the following was the first European country to introduce a third gender category?
(a) UK.
(b) France.
(c) Germany.
(d) Japan.

Androgyny and the BSRI

1. Which of the following is the definition of androgyny?
(a) A person who is gender-neutral.
(b) A person who has ambiguous genitalia at birth.
(c) A person who is neither male or female.
(d) A person who has a balance of masculine and feminine traits.

2. What does BSRI stand for?
(a) The Bem Sex-Role Inventory.
(b) The Bem Sex-Rating Index.
(c) The Bem Social Role Items.
(d) The Bem Sausage Roll Incident.

3. High levels of androgyny are associated with . . .
(a) Psychological well-being.
(b) Psychological abnormality.
(c) Psychological trauma.
(d) Psychological boredom.

4. Gender identity is difficult to measure using questionnaires as it is a . . .
(a) Hybrid contrast.
(b) Hypothetical conflict.
(c) Hyperactive concept.
(d) Hypothetical construct.

The role of chromosomes and hormones in sex and gender

1. Which hormone is *not* associated with sex and gender?
(a) Adrenaline.
(b) Oxytocin.
(c) Testosterone.
(d) Oestrogen.

2. Sex is determined by which pair of chromosomes?
(a) 21st.
(b) 22nd.
(c) 23rd.
(d) 24th.

3. Maccoby and Jacklin . . .
(a) Found more differences between the sexes than within the sexes.
(b) Found more differences within the sexes than between the sexes.
(c) Found no differences within or between the sexes.
(d) Did not investigate sex differences.

4. Which is the correct chromosomal structure for males and females?
(a) XY YX
(b) XY YY
(c) XX YY
(d) XY XX

Atypical sex chromosome patterns

1. Which *one* of the following is *not* associated with Turner's syndrome?
(a) XO chromosomal structure.
(b) Webbed neck.
(c) Clumsiness.
(d) Lower than average visual memory.

2. Which one of the following is *not* associated with Klinefelter's syndrome?
(a) XYY chromosomal structure.
(b) Reduced body hair.
(c) Rounding of body contours.
(d) Poor reading ability.

3. Approximately how many females have Turner's syndrome?
(a) 1 in 50
(b) 1 in 500
(c) 1 in 5000
(d) 1 in 50000

4. Which of the following might individuals with Klinefelter's benefit from?
(a) Testosterone injections.
(b) Oestrogen injections.
(c) Progesterone injections.
(d) There is no known treatment for Klinefelter's.

Cognitive explanations of gender: Kohlberg's theory

1. Which is the odd one out?
(a) Gender identity.
(b) Gender schema.
(c) Gender stability.
(d) Gender constancy.

2. Children in the gender identity stage . . .
(a) Understand that they will stay the same sex for the rest of their life.
(b) Understand that other people will stay the same sex for the rest of their life.
(c) Can label themselves as male or female.
(d) Understand that sex stays the same irrespective of appearance or context.

3. According to Piaget, children in gender constancy are no longer . . .
(a) Egotistic.
(b) Ego idealistic.
(c) Egocentric.
(d) Egomaniacal.

4. At which stage do children begin to seek out gender-appropriate role models to imitate?
(a) Gender schema.
(b) Gender stability.
(c) Gender constancy.
(d) Gender identity.

Cognitive explanations of gender: Gender schema theory

1. The concept of schema comes from which approach?
(a) Cognitive.
(b) Behaviourist.
(c) Biological.
(d) Social learning.

2. Which *two* of the following are correct in relation to the Martin and Halverson study?
(a) Children recalled information that was inconsistent with their gender schema.
(b) Children struggled to recall information that was inconsistent with their gender schema.
(c) Children recalled information that was consistent with their gender schema.
(d) The children did not recall any information.

3. At what age are children thought to develop elaborate schemas for both genders?
(a) 2.
(b) 4.
(c) 6.
(d) 8.

4. Stangor and Ruble linked gender schema and gender constancy to which two processes?
(a) Memory and motivation.
(b) Attention and emotion.
(c) Perception and performance.
(d) Assimilation and adaptation.

Psychodynamic explanation of gender development

1. At which stage is the acquisition of gender identity thought to occur?

(a) Oral.

(b) Anal.

(c) Phallic.

(d) Genital.

2. Which other explanation of gender uses the term *identification*?

(a) Biological.

(b) Social learning theory.

(c) Cognitive schema.

(d) Humanistic.

3. What do girls experience during the Electra complex?

(a) Penis envy.

(b) Parent envy.

(c) Womb envy.

(d) Castration anxiety.

4. What evidence did Freud use to illustrate the Oedipus complex?

(a) Little Anne.

(b) Little Hans.

(c) Little Heinz.

(d) Little Horse.

Social learning theory as applied to gender development

1. Seeing someone else being rewarded for gender-appropriate behaviour is known as?

(a) Direct reinforcement.

(b) Virtual reinforcement.

(c) Differential reinforcement.

(d) Vicarious reinforcement.

2. 'The process whereby a child attaches himself or herself to a person who is seen to possess qualities that the child regards as rewarding' is ...

(a) Identification.

(b) Imitation.

(c) Internalisation.

(d) Modelling.

3. Which of the following is a strength of social learning theory?

(a) It offers a stage theory of gender development.

(b) It places no emphasis on the role of genes and hormones on behaviour.

(c) It acknowledges the role of the unconscious in gender development.

(d) It can explain the changing nature of gender roles in Western society.

4. Which of the following would *not* be a characteristic associated with a role model?

(a) Attractive.

(b) High status.

(c) Different sex to the child.

(d) Same sex as the child.

The influence of culture and media on gender roles

1. Cultural differences in gender behaviour would best support?

(a) Social learning theory.

(b) Biological theory.

(c) Psychoanalytic theory.

(d) Cognitive theory.

2. Which of these was *not* a South Pacific tribe studied by Mead?

(a) Arapesh.

(b) Mundugumor.

(c) Hijra.

(d) Tchambuli.

3. In Bussey and Bandura's study women were often seen to be ...

(a) Independent, ambitious advice-givers.

(b) Dependent, unambitious advice-seekers.

(c) Insensitive, aggressive advice-takers.

(d) Sensitive, non-aggressive advice-offerers.

4. Which of the following was *not* a town in the Williams' media study?

(a) Motel.

(b) Notel.

(c) Unitel.

(d) Multitel.

Gender identity disorder

1. Gender identity disorder is also referred to as ...

(a) Gender dysphoria.

(b) Gender dyskinesia.

(c) Gender dyslexia.

(d) Gender euphoria.

2. The part of the brain known as the BSTc is normally ...

(a) Larger in males.

(b) Larger in females.

(c) The same size in males and females.

(d) Not present in males or females.

3. Heylens *et al.* found what percentage of MZ twins were concordant for GID?

(a) 29%.

(b) 39%.

(c) 49%.

(d) 59%.

4. Liben and Bigler's extension of gender schema theory is called ...

(a) The double pathway theory.

(b) The dual parallel theory.

(c) The double parallel theory.

(d) The dual pathway theory.

MCQ answers

Sex and gender   1c, 2a, 3a, 4c

Androgyny and the BSRI   1d, 2a, 3a, 4d

The role of chromosomes and hormones in sex and gender   1a, 2c, 3b, 4d

Atypical sex chromosome patterns   1c, 2a, 3c, 4a

Cognitive explanations of gender: Kohlberg's theory   1b, 2c 3c, 4c

Cognitive explanations of gender: Gender schema theory   1a, 2b&c, 3d, 4a

Psychodynamic explanation of gender development   1c, 2b, 3a, 4b

Social learning theory as applied to gender development   1d, 2a, 3,d 4c

The influence of culture and media on gender roles   1a, 2c, 3b, 4a

Gender identity disorder   1a, 2a, 3b, 4d

CHAPTER 7
COGNITION AND DEVELOPMENT

Mine is the difficult slow task to blaze
A road of Facts, through labyrinths of dreams
To tear down Maybe and establish IS:
And substitute I Know for I Believe.
I follow closely where the Seers have led:
But that intangible dim path of theirs,
Which may be trodden but by other Seers,
I seek to render solid for the feet
Of all mankind. With reverent hands I lift
The mask from Mystery: and show the face
Of Reason, smiling bravely on the world.

Extract from the poem *Science*, by Ella Wheeler Wilcox

Chapter contents

PIAGET'S THEORY OF COGNITIVE DEVELOPMENT

THE SPECIFICATION SAYS...

Piaget's theory of cognitive development: schemas, assimilation, accommodation, equilibration.

This spread is concerned with Jean Piaget's approach to understanding the processes of learning. Piaget was concerned with both what *motivates* us to learn and *how* our knowledge of the world develops.

KEY TERMS

Cognitive development – A general term describing the development of all mental processes, in particular thinking, reasoning and our understanding of the world. Cognitive development continues throughout the lifespan but psychologists have been particularly concerned with how thinking and reasoning develops through childhood.

Schemas – Contain our understanding of an object, person or idea. Schemas become increasingly complex during development as we acquire more information about each object or idea. A mental framework of beliefs and expectations that influence cognitive processing. They are developed from experience.

Assimilation – A form of learning that takes place when we acquire new information or a more advanced understanding of an object, person or idea. When new information does not radically change our understanding of the topic we can incorporate (assimilate) it into an existing schema.

Accommodation – A form of learning that takes place when we acquire new information that changes our understanding of a topic to the extent that we need to form one or more new schemas and/or radically change existing schemas in order to deal with the new understanding.

Equilibration – Takes place when we have encountered new information and built it into our understanding of a topic, either by assimilating it into an existing schema or accommodating it by forming a new one. Everything is again balanced and we have escaped the unpleasant experience of a lack of balance – disequilibrium.

Piaget's theory of cognitive development

Writing from the 1930s until the 1970s, Swiss biologist and psychologist Jean Piaget produced an influential theory of **cognitive development**. Piaget's great contribution was to realise that children do not simply know less than adults do. Instead Piaget realised that children think in entirely different ways from grown-ups.

Based on this understanding, Piaget divided childhood into stages, each of which represents the development of new ways of reasoning. Piaget *also* looked at children's learning, in particular at two aspects: the role of *motivation* in development and the question of *how* knowledge develops. We will look at Piaget's stages on the next spread but begin with a more general overview of the theory.

Schemas: units of knowledge

The world is represented in the mind – that is where knowledge is stored. As children develop they construct more and more detailed and complex mental representations of the world. These representations are stored in the form of **schemas**. A schema is a mental structure containing all the information we have about one aspect of the world.

As adults we have schemas for people (including ourselves), for objects, physical actions and also for more abstract ideas like justice and morality. According to Piaget, children are born with a small number of schemas, just enough to allow them to interact with other people. In infancy we construct new schemas. One of these is the 'me-schema' in which all the child's knowledge about themselves is stored.

The *motivation* to learn: Disequilibrium and equilibration

A key element of Piaget's theory is the motivation to learn. According to Piaget, we are motivated to learn when our existing schemas do not allow us to make sense of something new. This leads to the unpleasant sensation of *disequilibrium*. To escape disequilibrium we have to adapt to the new situation by exploring and learning what we need to know. By doing this we achieve **equilibration**, the preferred mental state.

How learning takes place: Assimilation and accommodation

Piaget saw the process of learning as adapting to the new situation so that we understand it. He identified two processes by which this adaptation takes place. **Assimilation** takes place when we understand a new experience and equilibrate by adding new information to our existing schemas. For example, a child in a family with dogs can adapt to the existence of different dog breeds by assimilating them into their dog schema.

Accommodation takes place in response to dramatically new experiences. The child has to adjust to these by either radically changing current schemas or forming new ones. So a child with a pet dog may at first think of cats as dogs (because they have four legs, fur and a tail) but then accommodate to the existence of a separate species called cats. This will involve altering the animal/pet schemas to include cats and forming a new 'cat-schema'.

COGNITIVE DEVELOPMENT

The term 'cognitive' refers to our mental processes. These include perception, language, memory and thinking, so the term cognitive development refers to the ways in which all these processes change and develop throughout the human lifespan. Much of the research in cognitive development has concerned the development of thinking and reasoning in children. In this chapter we are particularly interested in the development of children's reasoning and their understanding of social situations and what is happening in the minds of others.

A child may initially try to assimilate their cat into an existing 'dog schema' but will eventually form a new 'cat schema' to accommodate the existence of cats.

Apply it

Concepts: Schemas at the zoo

At the age of four years Paige is visiting the zoo for the first time. She has enjoyed feeding ducks and pigeons in her local park before but this is the first time she has learned about the existence of parrots and bats.

Question

Referring to Piaget's theory, explain the processes of learning Paige might go through when she sees parrots and bats and asks questions about them in order to understand what they are.

Evaluation

Children form individual mental representations by discovery

Piaget believed that children learn by forming their own mental representations of the world. This suggests that even children who have had similar learning experiences will form quite individual mental representations. This hypothesis has been tested in a series of studies by Christine Howe. In one study, Howe *et al.* (1992) put children aged between 9 and 12 years in groups of four to study and discuss movement of objects down a slope. Their understanding of the topic was assessed before and after this discussion.

Following their experience of working together and discussing the topic the children were found to have increased their level of knowledge and understanding. However, critically, the children had *not* come to the same conclusions or picked up the same facts about movement down a slope. This supports Piaget's idea that children learn by forming their own personal mental representations.

Applications in education

Piaget's idea that children learn by actively exploring their environment and forming their own mental representation of the world has revolutionised classroom teaching. Since Piaget's ideas became popular in the 1960s, the old-fashioned classroom, in which children sat silently in rows copying from the board, has been replaced by activity-oriented classrooms in which children actively engage in tasks that allow them to construct their own understandings of the curriculum.

Learning by discovery can take different forms. In the Early Years classroom children may, for example, investigate the physical properties of sand and water. By the time you are studying for A levels, discovery may take the form of 'flipped' lessons where students read up on the material independently before lessons so that lesson time can be focused on higher level evaluation skills and practising exam questions.

Piaget may have underplayed the role of other people in learning

Piaget did not believe children learn best on their own. He saw other people – both adults and peers – as important sources of information during discovery learning and, of course, the adults that set up situations in which discovery learning can take place. However, other people were not the main focus of Piaget's theory, and he saw learning in terms of what happens in the mind of the individual.

However, other theories of learning and cognitive development and a range of research findings suggest that other people are absolutely central to the processes of learning. In particular Lev Vygotsky proposed that learning is essentially a social process, and that children are capable of much more advanced learning if this is supported by peers or an expert adult. Vygotsky's ideas and supporting research are explored in detail on pages 182–183.

Evaluation eXtra

Piaget may have overplayed the importance of equilibration

Piaget saw learning as very much a motivated process in which children learn in order to equilibrate because disequilibrium is such an unpleasant experience. Actually children vary greatly in their intellectual curiosity. It may be that Piaget over-estimated just how motivated children are to learn – the children he studied were mainly from the nursery attached to his university and this was a biased sample of clever middle-class children.

Consider: *If Piaget over-estimated how motivated children are to learn, what does this suggest about his theory?*

Piaget may have underplayed the importance of language

The development of language is an important aspect of cognitive development. To Piaget, language was just a cognitive ability that developed in line with other developing abilities. However, other theorists have placed a lot more importance on language development.

Consider: *How important might language be in a child's learning and cognitive development? Suggest examples of where language might be particularly important and use those examples to evaluate Piaget's theory.*

Science practicals are an example of discovery learning. Equilibration takes place when children find the answers through experiments.

Apply it — Concepts: Equilibration and Masterchef

Gurpal is six years old. Recently she has seen her parents watching *Masterchef* and she begun to show an interest in food preparation. At first Gurpal has very little understanding of how the raw meat and vegetables she sees her parents unpacking become the food she sees at meals. She is frustrated and unhappy about this. After watching a couple of *Masterchef* episodes, however, Gurpal begins to grasp the idea of cooking. Once she gets this she is happier and more relaxed.

Questions

1. Outline what is meant by the term 'equilibration.'
2. Explain what has happened to Gurpal. Refer to the concept of equilibration in your answer.

Apply it — Methods: Keen kids

A psychologist is interested in the role of equilibration in learning. She asks a Year 1 teacher and a Year 9 teacher to rate each of 30 children in a class on a scale of 1–10 (where 10 is very keen) for their keenness to learn new things. For the Year 1 class the **mean**, **median** and **mode** were all 7 and the **standard deviation** was 1.5.

Questions

1. Sketch out the **distribution** of these scores. (*3 marks*)
2. What sort of distribution does your graph show? (*1 mark*)
3. Explain *one* strength and *one* weakness of using a teacher rating as a measure of intellectual curiosity. (*2 marks + 2 marks*)
4. For the Year 9 class the mean was 4 and the standard deviation 2. What could you conclude about the differences between the two sets of scores from Year 1 and 9? (*3 marks*)

CHECK IT

1. Outline what Piaget meant by the word *schema*. [*3 marks*]
2. Distinguish between *assimilation* and *accommodation*. [*4 marks*]
3. Outline and discuss Piaget's idea of equilibration. [*8 marks*]
4. Describe and evaluate Piaget's theory of cognitive development. [*16 marks*]

PIAGET'S STAGES OF INTELLECTUAL DEVELOPMENT

THE SPECIFICATION SAYS...

Piaget's theory of cognitive development: Stages of intellectual development. Characteristics of these stages, including object permanence, conservation, egocentrism and class inclusion.

Jean Piaget's approach to understanding cognitive/intellectual development involves the identification of a series of stages, each of which is characterised by a set of particular mental abilities.

KEY TERMS

Stages of intellectual development – Piaget identified four stages of intellectual development. Each stage is characterised by a different level of reasoning ability. Although the exact ages vary from child to child, all children develop through the same sequence of stages.

Object permanence – The ability to realise that an object still exists when it passes out of the visual field. Piaget believed that this ability appears at around eight months of age. Prior to this, children lose interest in an object once they can't see it and presumably are no longer aware of its existence.

Conservation – The ability to realise that quantity remains the same even when the appearance of an object or group of objects changes. For example, the volume of liquid stays the same when poured between vessels of different shapes.

Egocentrism – The child's tendency to only be able to see the world from their own point of view. This applies to both physical objects – demonstrated in the three mountains task – and arguments in which a child can only appreciate their own perspective.

Class inclusion – An advanced classification skill in which we recognise that classes of objects have subsets and are themselves subsets of larger classes. Pre-operational children usually struggle to place things in more than one class.

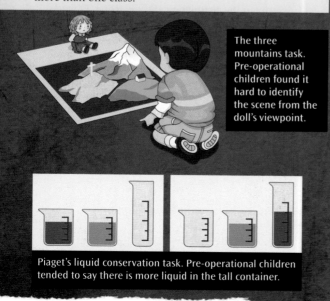

The three mountains task. Pre-operational children found it hard to identify the scene from the doll's viewpoint.

Piaget's liquid conservation task. Pre-operational children tended to say there is more liquid in the tall container.

Piaget's stages of intellectual development

Sensorimotor stage (approximately 0–2 years)

According to Piaget, a baby's early focus is on physical sensations and on developing some basic physical co-ordination. Children learn by trial and error that they can deliberately move their body in particular ways, and eventually that they can move other objects. The baby also develops an understanding during the first two years that other people are separate objects and acquires some basic language.

By around eight months the child is capable of understanding **object permanence**. This is the understanding that objects still exist when they are out of sight. Piaget observed babies looking at objects as they were removed from sight throughout the first year. He noted that before eight months, children immediately switched their attention away from the object once it was out of sight. However, from around eight months they would continue look for it. This led Piaget to believe that it was from this age that children understood that objects continue to exist when removed from view.

Pre-operational stage (approximately 2–7 years)

By the age of two a toddler is mobile and can use language but still lacks reasoning ability. This means that they display some characteristic errors in reasoning.

Conservation is the basic mathematical understanding that quantity remains constant even when the appearance of objects changes. Piaget demonstrated this in a number of situations. In his number conservation experiments Piaget placed two identical rows of counters side by side. Even young children correctly reasoned that each row of counters had the same number. However, when the counters in one of the rows were pushed closer together, pre-operational children struggled to conserve and usually said there were fewer counters.

In his liquid conservation procedure (see illustration below) Piaget found that when two containers are placed side by side with the contents at the same height, most children spotted that they contain the same volume. However, if the liquid is poured into a taller, thinner vessel, younger children typically believed there is more liquid in the taller vessel.

Egocentrism means to see the world only from one's own point of view. Piaget and Inhelder (1956) described how egocentrism was demonstrated in the **three mountains task**, in which children were shown three model mountains, each with a different feature: a cross, a house or snow (see illustration on left). A doll was placed at the side of the model so that it faced the scene from a different angle to the child. The child was asked to choose what the doll would 'see' from a range of pictures. Pre-operational children tended to find this difficult and often chose the picture that matched the scene from their own point of view.

Class inclusion Early in the pre-operational stage children begin to understand classification – the idea that objects fall into categories. So, most pre-operational children can classify pugs, bull terriers and retrievers as dogs. However, Piaget and Inhelder (1964) found that children under the age of seven struggle with the more advanced skill of class inclusion, the idea that classifications have subsets. So when they showed 7–8-year-old children pictures of five dogs and two cats and asked 'are there more dogs or animals?' children tended to respond that there were more dogs. He interpreted this as meaning that younger children cannot simultaneously see a dog as a member of the dog class *and* the animal class.

Stage of concrete operations (approximately 7–11 years)

Piaget found that from the age of around seven most children can conserve and perform much better on tasks of egocentrism and class inclusion. However, although children now have better reasoning abilities – what Piaget called **operations** – these are strictly concrete operations, i.e. they can be applied only to physical objects in the child's presence. They still struggle to reason about abstract ideas and to imagine objects or situations they cannot see. Those more advanced abilities appear in the final stage of formal operations.

Stage of formal operations (11+)

Piaget believed that from about 11 years of age, children became capable of formal reasoning. This means that children become able to focus on the *form* of an argument and not be distracted by its content.

Formal reasoning can be tested by means of syllogisms. For example: 'All yellow cats have two heads. I have a yellow cat called Charlie. How many heads does Charlie have?' The correct answer is 'two' (Smith *et al.* 1998). Piaget found that younger children became distracted by the content and answered that cats do not really have two heads. Piaget believed that once children can reason formally they are capable of scientific reasoning and become able to appreciate abstract ideas.

Evaluation

Practical activity on page 192

Piaget's questioning when studying conservation was dubious

It has been suggested that children taking part in Piaget's conservation experiments were influenced by seeing the experimenter change the appearance of the counters or liquid. In other words they believed that they were *meant* to think the quantity had changed; otherwise why would the experimenter change the appearance then ask them if it was the same?

James McGarrigle and Margaret Donaldson (1974) set up a number conservation experiment in which the counters appeared to be moved by accident. In a **control condition** they **replicated** the standard Piaget task with 4–6-year-olds and, like Piaget, they found that most children answered incorrectly. However, when a 'naughty teddy' appeared and knocked the counters closer together 72% correctly said there were the same number as before. This suggests that children aged 4–6 could conserve, as long as they were not put off by the way they were questioned. This in turn suggests that Piaget was wrong about conservation in the pre-operational stage.

Piaget's conclusions on class inclusion may be dubious

Piaget concluded from his studies of class inclusion that pre-operational children were simply unable to understand that an object can be a member of two classes at the same time, e.g. that a pug can be both a dog and an animal. The observation that children struggle with this type of question has been replicated by Robert Siegler and Matija Svetina (2006). However, this study also provided evidence that children were in fact capable of understanding class inclusion.

Siegler and Svetina tested 100 5-year-olds from Slovenia, who each undertook three sessions of ten class-inclusion tasks, receiving an explanation of the task after each session. In one condition they received feedback that there must be more animals than dogs because there were nine animals but only six dogs. A different group received feedback that there must be more animals as dogs were a subset of animals (a true explanation of class inclusion). The scores across the three sessions improved more for the latter group, suggesting that they had acquired a real understanding of class inclusion. This is contrary to what Piaget believed – that children under seven could not understand class inclusion.

Children's ability to decentre

Piaget believed that younger children were only able to see the world from their own, personal perspective, and that the ability to decentre or see the world from multiple viewpoints increased gradually with age. However, some later research has challenged Piaget's conclusions. Martin Hughes (1975) tested the ability of children to see a situation from two people's viewpoints using a model with two intersecting walls and three dolls, a boy and two police officers (similar to the three mountains task). Once familiarised with the task, children as young as 3½ years were able to position the boy doll where one police officer could not 'see' him 90% of the time, and four-year-olds could do this 90% of the time when there were two police officers to hide from. Studies like this pose a problem for Piaget because they suggest that he underestimated younger children's ability to decentre.

Evaluation eXtra

Abilities both under- and overestimated

Piaget may have underestimated younger children and overestimated the abilities of adolescents. Modern studies have shown that, at least with the right kind of adult help, pre-operational children have or are capable of developing a good understanding of conservation and class inclusion. Later studies of egocentrism that have located scenes in contexts familiar to children have found pre-operational children to be less egocentric than is suggested by the three mountains study.

Consider: *Putting these two sets of findings together, what might we conclude about the extent to which children's reasoning ability changes throughout childhood and into adolescence? What is the implication of this for Piaget's stage theory?*

Domain-general and domain-specific development

Piaget believed that intellectual development is a single process and that all aspects of cognition develop together. So language, reasoning and egocentrism all develop pretty much in tandem. However, research with children with learning difficulties such as **autistic spectrum disorder** (ASD) suggests that actually these abilities may develop separately. Children with **Asperger syndrome** are very egocentric but develop normal reasoning and language. Children with other types of ASD typically have problems with language and egocentrism.

Consider: *What does ASD research suggest about Piaget's belief that cognitive development is domain-general? What does this suggest about his theory?*

Baillargeon challenged Piaget's ideas about object permanence – you can read about her research on pages 184–185.

Apply it — Concepts: iPhone permanence

Since Roissin was a tiny baby she has been fascinated by the shiny case and bright screen of her mother's iPhone. For the last few months her mother has discouraged this interest by simply moving the phone out of her line of sight. However, Roissin is now eight months old and is no longer satisfied by this. She continues to reach for the phone after her mother has hidden it.

Question

Explain why Roissin's behaviour has changed at eight months of age. Refer to Piaget's concept of object permanence in your answer.

Apply it — Concepts: Stealing sweets

Tom and Bob are brothers aged eight and five years old respectively. Their parents always give them an equal number of sweets, but Tom thinks, as the older child, he should have more. One day he puts a cunning plan into operation to get extra sweets. He places two rows of sweets side by side. In one row are there are ten sweets and in the other row eight. The row with eight sweets is longer because the sweets are slightly more spread out. He suggests to Bob that he might like the longer row.

Question

Explain Tom's reasoning. Make reference in your answer to the pre-operational stage, the stage of concrete operations and conservation.

Apply it — Methods: Longitudinal research

Studies have not supported the idea that most people develop formal thinking skills in early adolescence. Bradmetz (1999) followed up the development of 62 children from seven to 15 years, regularly testing them with a range of formal thinking tasks. At age 15 only one participant could reliably carry out the tasks. This is an example of a **longitudinal study**.

Questions

1. What is meant by a longitudinal study? (*2 marks*)
2. Outline *one* strength and *one* limitation of doing this as a longitudinal study. (*2 marks + 2 marks*)
3. Explain *one* reason why Bradmetz gave participants a range of formal reasoning tasks rather than just one. (*3 marks*)
4. Giving children formal reasoning tasks can be regarded as a more **valid** research technique than asking parents to rate their children for formal reasoning ability. Explain what is meant by this statement. (*3 marks*)

CHECK IT

1. Identify **one** of Piaget's stages of intellectual development and outline the features at this stage. [4 marks]
2. Explain what Piaget meant by the term *conservation*. Use an example in your explanation. [4 marks]
3. Outline **one** study that Piaget conducted to demonstrate the stages of intellectual development. [3 marks]
4. Describe and evaluate Piaget's stages of intellectual development. [16 marks]

This spread is concerned with a second theory of cognitive development, that of Lev Vygotsky. The key difference between the two theories is that Vygotsky placed more emphasis on the role of other people in learning and cognitive development.

KEY TERMS

Zone of proximal development (ZPD) – The gap between a child's current level of development, defined by the cognitive tasks they can perform unaided, and what they can potentially do with the right help from a more expert other, who may be an adult or a more advanced child.

Scaffolding – The process of helping a learner cross the zone of proximal development and advance as much as they can, given their stage of development. Typically the level of help given in scaffolding declines as the learner crosses the zone of proximal development (ZPD).

Apply it   Concepts: The ZPD

Tarquin and Mark-Francis are identical twins. Anxious not to disadvantage them socially by sending them to the same school, their parents send them to different schools. Tarquin's school has a strong emphasis on personal responsibility in learning and so he spends a lot of time engaged in individual discovery learning. Mark-Francis on the other hand attends a school where the emphasis is very much on group work and adult help. The twins' parents are puzzled to find that Mark-Francis learns to read and do basic arithmetic much faster than Tarquin.

Question

Suggest a reason why Mark-Francis seems to be developing more quickly than Tarquin. Refer to Vygotsky's theory of cognitive development in your answer.

Both adults and more experienced children are important in scaffolding learning.

Vygotsky's theory of cognitive development

Vygotsky was a Russian psychologist writing in the 1920s and 1930s, who was influenced by Piaget's work. They agreed on many of the basics of **cognitive development**. Most importantly they agreed that children's reasoning abilities develop in a particular sequence, and that such abilities are qualitatively different at different ages, with a child typically capable of particular logic at particular ages.

The major difference is that Vygotsky saw cognitive development as a social process of learning from more experienced others (referred to as 'experts'). Knowledge is first *intermental*, between the more and less expert individual, then *intramental*, within the mind of the less expert individual. Vygotsky also saw language as a much more important part of cognitive development than did Piaget.

Cultural differences in cognitive abilities

If reasoning abilities are acquired from the more experienced individuals with whom a child has contact, it follows that the child will acquire the reasoning abilities of those particular people. This means that there may be cultural differences in cognitive development, with children picking up the mental 'tools' that are most important for life within their physical, social and work environments. These mental tools can be anything from the hand–eye co-ordination needed to hunt with a bow and arrow to the evaluation skills needed to succeed in Psychology A level.

The zone of proximal development (ZPD)

Vygotsky put tremendous emphasis on the role of learning through interaction with others. He identified a gap between a child's current level of development, i.e. what they can understand and do alone, and what they can potentially understand after interaction with more expert others. This gap is known as the **zone of proximal development** (or ZPD).

Expert assistance allows a child to cross the ZPD and understand as much of a subject or situation as they are capable – children are still to some extent limited by their developmental stage. Vygotsky believed that children develop a more advanced understanding of a situation and hence the more advanced reasoning abilities needed to deal with it by learning from others, as opposed to through individual exploration of the world.

Critically, Vygotsky was not just saying that children can learn more facts during social interaction, but also that they acquire more advanced reasoning abilities. In fact he believed that higher mental functions, such as formal reasoning, could *only* be acquired through interaction with more advanced others.

Scaffolding

Scaffolding is the next logical step in understanding the ZPD. The term 'scaffolding' refers to all the kinds of help adults and more advanced peers give a child to help them to cross the zone of proximal development. Actually Vygotsky did not focus much on this process in his writing, and so most of what we know about scaffolding is from psychologists influenced by his theory, such as Jerome Bruner and colleagues, so this approach is sometimes called 'the Vygotsky-Bruner model'.

David Wood, Jerome Bruner and Gail Ross (1976) identified five aspects to scaffolding which are general ways in which an adult can help a child better understand and perform a task:

- *Recruitment*: engaging the child's interest in the task.
- *Reduction of degrees of freedom*: focusing the child on the task and where to start with solving it.
- *Direction maintenance*: encouraging the child in order help them to stay motivated and continue trying to complete the task.
- *Marking critical features*: highlighting the most important parts of the task.
- *Demonstration*: showing the child how to do aspects of the task.

Wood *et al.* also noted the particular strategies that experts use when scaffolding (as shown below). In general, as a learner crosses the zone of proximal development, the level of help given in scaffolding declines from level 5 most help to level 1 least help. An adult is more likely to use high level of help strategies when first helping, then to gradually withdraw the level of help as the child grasps the task.

An example of scaffolding: helping a child draw		
Level of help	**Nature of prompt**	**Example**
5	Demonstration	Mother draws an object with crayons.
4	Preparation for child	Mother helps child grasp a crayon.
3	Indication of materials	Mother points to crayons.
2	Specific verbal instructions	Mother says 'How about the green crayon?'
1	General prompts	Mother says 'Now draw something else'.

Evaluation

Support for the zone of proximal development

There is clear evidence to show that there is indeed a gap between the level of reasoning a child can achieve on their own and what they can achieve with help from a more expert other. An example of such a study comes from Roazzi and Bryant (1998).

Antonio Roazzi and Peter Bryant gave 4–5-year-old children the task of estimating the number of sweets in a box. In one condition the children worked alone and in another they worked with the help of an older child. Most children working alone failed to give a good estimate. In the expert help condition the older (expert) children were observed to offer prompts, pointing the younger children in the right direction to work out how to arrive at their estimate. Most 4–5-year-olds receiving this kind of help successfully mastered the task.

Studies like that by Roazzi and Bryant support Vygotsky's idea that children can develop additional reasoning abilities when working with a more expert individual. This in turn suggests that the zone of proximal development is a valid concept.

Support for the idea of scaffolding

It has been observed in many studies – such as that of Roazzi and Bryant above – that adults and older children provide support for younger children learning to master new tasks. This in itself does not tell us anything about what happens during that support though. Better evidence for the idea of scaffolding comes from research showing that the level of help given by the expert partner declines during the process of learning.

An example of such a study comes from David Conner and David Cross (2003). In a longitudinal procedure they followed up 45 children, observing them engaged in problem-solving tasks with the help of their mothers at 16, 26, 44 and 54 months. Distinctive changes in help were observed over time; mothers used less and less direct intervention and more hints and prompts as children gained experience. They also increasingly offered help when it was needed rather than constantly.

Applications in education

Vygotsky's ideas have been highly influential in education in the last decade. The idea that children can learn more and faster with appropriate scaffolding has raised expectations of what they should be able to achieve. Social interaction in learning, through group work, **peer tutoring** and individual adult assistance from teachers and teaching assistants, has been used to scaffold children though their zones of proximal development.

There is evidence to suggest that these strategies are effective. For example Hilde Van Keer and Jean Pierre Verhaeghe (2005) found that 7-year-olds tutored by 10-year-olds, in addition to their whole-class teaching, progressed further in reading than controls who just had standard whole-class teaching. A review of the usefulness of teaching assistants (Alborz *et al.* 2009) concluded that teaching assistants are very effective at improving the rate of learning in children provided they have received appropriate training.

Evaluation eXtra

What children learn from interactions is surprisingly individual

There is plenty of evidence to support the idea that, as Vygotsky said, interaction can enhance learning. However, if Vygotsky was right about the process of interactive learning, we would expect all children learning together to pick up very similar skills and a very similar mental representation of material. However, recall the work of Christine Howe discussed on page 179. Howe found that what children learn actually varies considerably between individuals, even in group learning situations.

Consider: *What does this suggest about Vygotsky's theory as opposed to Piaget's?*

The role of individual differences

Like Piaget, Vygotsky assumed that the processes of learning are largely the same in all children. This does not take account of individual differences. Some children learn best during social interaction but this may not be true for everyone. Personality and style of information processing may have powerful effects on what sort of activities and what sort of help works for different children.

Consider: *What does this say about the practical value of Vygotsky's theory in education?*

STUDY TIP

The concepts of the zone of proximal development and scaffolding are closely related. Be clear on what each means, and if asked about one or the other, make sure you explain that thoroughly. It is, however, fine to mention ZPD and scaffolding in an explanation of either.

Teaching assistants have an important role in guiding children through their zones of proximal development.

Apply it Concepts:
Scaffolding homework

Seven-year-old Abigail now has maths homework. Mum Lisa helps Abigail with her homework every weekend. At the start of the year Abigail is anxious and unsure where to begin each piece of homework. By the end of the year though she is in a good routine. Lisa finds that the kind of help she gives Abigail changes during the year.

Question

Suggest how the kind of help Lisa gives Abigail will change during the course of the year. Refer to the concept of scaffolding in your answer.

Apply it
Methods: Van Keer and Verhaeghe study

The study by Van Keer and Verhaeghe (2005) compared classes that were taught using whole-class teaching plus peer tutoring with classes just taught by whole-class teaching. Existing classes were allocated to each condition as opposed to individual children. This study can therefore be described as a **natural experiment**.

Questions

1. Outline the key features of a natural experiment. (*2 marks*)

2. Explain *one* strength and *one* limitation of natural experiments as compared to **lab experiments**. Refer to this study in your answer (*3 marks + 3 marks*)

3. This study used standard measures of reading to judge progress in each condition. Briefly explain *one* strength of using standard measures in this study. (*2 marks*)

4. In the Van Keer and Verhaeghe study, the group that had the benefit of peer tutoring maintained their superior reading when followed up a few months later. Explain *one* strength of studies that follow up initial findings like this. (*2 marks*)

CHECK IT

1. Outline what Vygotsky meant by the *zone of proximal development*. [4 marks]
2. Explain the role of *scaffolding* in cognitive development. [4 marks]
3. Evaluate the concept of scaffolding. [4 marks]
4. Describe and evaluate Vygotsky's theory of cognitive development. [16 marks]

VYGOTSKY'S THEORY OF COGNITIVE DEVELOPMENT • 183

Baillargeon's explanation of early infant abilities including knowledge of the physical world; violation of expectation research.

This spread is concerned with an extensive range of research from Renee Baillargeon into understanding exactly how well developed cognitive abilities are in infancy. Baillargeon has challenged Piaget's ideas about the sensorimotor stage, proposing that even very young babies have a fairly well-developed understanding of the physical world, including object permanence.

KEY TERMS

Knowledge of the physical world – Refers to the extent to which we understand how the physical world works. An example of this knowledge is object permanence, the understanding that objects continue to exist when they leave the visual field. There is a debate concerning the ages at which children develop this kind of knowledge.

Violation of expectation research – An approach to investigating infant knowledge of the world. The idea is that if children understand how the physical world operates then they will expect certain things to happen in particular situations. If these do not occur and children react accordingly, this suggests that they have an intact knowledge of that aspect of the world.

Familiarisation events

Short rabbit event   Tall rabbit event

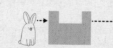

Test events

Possible event   Impossible event

Children looked for longer at the impossible event in which the tall rabbit did not appear at the window.

Apply it

Concepts: Violation of expectation

Gwyneth has two daughters, Storm, aged five years and Skye, four months. For Storm's birthday party Gwyneth books a magician. Gwyneth does not expect Skye to enjoy the magician but she is surprised to see that Skye stares with great attention whenever the magician appears to make an object appear or disappear.

Question

Explain why Skye might be so fascinated by the magic show. Refer to violation of expectations and Baillargeon's explanation for infant abilities in your answer.

Baillargeon's explanation of infant abilities

Early research on knowledge of the physical world

Recall Piaget's ideas about the **sensorimotor stage**. Piaget believed that babies less than 8–9 months of age have a very primitive understanding of the nature of the physical world. For example, he claimed they are not aware that objects continue to exist after they leave the visual field. Piaget's reasoning was based on his research showing that from this age babies would reach for an object removed from their view but prior to this they would immediately lose interest once the object was out of sight.

However, some later psychologists were critical of Piaget's research in this area. It is possible, for example, that younger babies do not pursue a hidden object simply because they do not have the motor skills. Alternatively they may lose interest because their abilities of selective attention are not well enough developed to stop themselves becoming distracted.

Renee Baillargeon working in the 1980s pointed out that alternative research methods have suggested that younger babies may have a better-developed understanding of the physical world than was previously thought. She developed the **violation of expectation** (VOE) method to investigate infant understanding of the physical world.

Violation of expectation (VOE) research

Baillargeon (2004) explains VOE as follows: 'In a typical experiment, infants see two test events: an expected event, which is consistent with the expectation examined in the experiment, and an unexpected event, which violates this expectation' (2004, page 392). So if the VOE method is used to test object permanence, infants will typically see two or more conditions in which objects pass in and out of sight. In a **control condition** the object behaves as a person with object permanence would expect. For example, a tall object will appear in a window as it passes behind a screen but a short object will not because it passes below the window.

Procedure In an early VOE experiment Baillargeon and Graber (1987) showed 24 infants, aged 5–6 months, a tall and a short rabbit pass behind a screen with a window. In the possible condition the tall rabbit can be seen passing the window but the short one cannot. In the impossible condition neither rabbit appeared at the window (see picture on left).

Findings The infants looked for an average of 33.07 seconds at the impossible event as compared to 25.11 seconds in the possible condition. The researchers interpreted this as meaning that the infants were surprised at the impossible condition. For them to be surprised it follows that they must have known that the tall rabbit should have re-appeared at the window. This demonstrates an understanding of object permanence.

Other studies The Baillargeon and Graber study described above is an example of an *occlusion* study, in which one object occludes another, i.e. it is in front of it. VOE experiments have also been used to test infant understanding of *containment* and *support*. 'Containment' is the idea that when an object is seen to enter a container it should still be there when the container is opened. 'Support' is the idea that an object should fall when unsupported but not when it is on a horizontal surface. In all these cases infants have shown that they pay more attention to 'impossible' events and so appear to have an understanding of the physical world (Hespos and Baillargeon 2008).

Baillargeon's theory of infant physical reasoning

Baillargeon *et al.* (2012) propose that humans are born with a *physical reasoning system* (or PRS). In other words we are born hard-wired with both a basic understanding of the physical world and the ability to learn more details easily. Initially we have a primitive awareness of the physical properties of the world and this becomes more sophisticated as we learn from experience. One aspect of the world of which we have a crude understanding from birth is *object persistence*. This is roughly the same idea as Piaget's object permanence; the idea that an object remains in existence and does not spontaneously alter in structure.

In the first few weeks of life infants begin to identify event categories. Each event category corresponds to one way in which objects interact. For example, occlusion events take place when one object blocks the view of another. Because a child is born with a basic understanding of object persistence and quickly learns that one object can block their view of another, by the time they are tested in tasks like Baillargeon and Graber's VOE with tall and short rabbits, children actually have a good understanding that the tall rabbit should appear at the window. The 'impossible' event captures infants' attention because the nature of their PRS means they are predisposed to attend to new events that might allow them to develop their understanding of the physical world.

Evaluation

A better test of infant understanding than Piaget's

There were always problems with Piaget's methods for studying children's **knowledge of the physical world**. Piaget assumed that when a baby shifted attention away from an out-of-sight object this meant that the child no longer knew it existed. However, the child might have shifted attention simply because they lost interest. The VOE method is probably a better method for investigating whether a child has some understanding of the permanent nature of objects because it eliminates this **confounding variable**. Simply losing interest in an object would not explain findings that children look for longer at impossible events. This means that the VOE method has better **validity** than some alternatives.

It is hard to judge what an infant understands

Baillargeon's research clearly shows that infants look for significantly longer at some scenes than others. It appears that they look longer at scenes where objects appear to violate physical laws like object permanence. However, what VOE experiments really show is that babies behave as *we might expect them to* if they understood the physical world. There are two logical problems with this:

1. We are guessing and can never know how a baby might actually behave in response to a violation of expectations. They might not actually look at impossible events for longer than possible events.

2. Although infants look for different lengths of time at different events, this merely means that they see them as different. There may be any number of reasons why they find one scene more interesting than another.

These problems mean that the VOE method may not be an entirely valid way of investigating infant understanding of the physical world.

The PRS explains why physical understanding is universal

Susan Hespos and Kristy van Marle (2012) point out that without learning and regardless of experience we all have a very good understanding of the basic properties of physical objects. They give the example of dangling keys. We all know that if we let go of a key ring it will fall to the floor. According to Hespos and van Marle this understanding requires a physical reasoning system (PRS).

The fact that this understanding is universal (to be found anywhere) strongly suggests that this system (which we can call the physical reasoning system) is **innate** – otherwise we would expect cultural differences for which there is a lack of evidence.

This is a strength of Baillargeon's idea of the PRS because its universal nature suggests that it is innate, as Baillargeon believed.

Evaluation eXtra

Behavioural response is not the same as understanding

This is a more advanced idea to get your head around so read carefully. Gavin Bremner (2013) reminds us that Piaget distinguished between acting in accordance with a principle and understanding that principle. Even if we accept that the infant behaviour of maintaining attention for longer on an impossible scene is a response to its impossibility, this is very different from the kind of conscious understanding we can use to reason about the physical world.

Consider: *To what extent can we be said to understand object permanence if we respond to an impossible event but do not consciously reason about it?*

The PRS is consistent with what we know of other infant abilities

It is very difficult to directly test Baillargeon's idea that there is an innate physical reasoning system that contains some basic understanding from birth but which becomes more sophisticated with age. However, the PRS is consistent with other research into infant cognitive abilities. For example, research shows that infants can use crude patterns to judge distance from an early age but that experience is required to make use of more subtle texture differences (Pei *et al.* 2007). Distance perception therefore appears to be an innate system that becomes more sophisticated with age.

Consider: *In the absence of direct evidence, how valuable is this kind of consistency as evaluation of the PRS?*

The understanding that dropped keys will fall to the floor is universal and does not appear to require learning, supporting Baillargeon's idea of the PRS.

Apply it — Concepts:
Children understanding physical properties

Baillargeon suggested that even very young infants have a crude awareness of the physical properties of objects. Nursery nurse Tina is surprised at the reaction when she drops her keys behind a desk one day. The keys land silently in an open drawer rather than jingling noisily on the floor. Tina finds the children that saw the keys fall looking intently. She wonders about this.

Question

How could you explain to Tina why the children might have been so interested by this event. Refer to Baillargeon's theory in your answer.

Apply it
Methods: Staring at the impossible

In the Baillargeon and Graber (1987) study (facing page) infants looked for an average of 33.07 seconds at an impossible condition as opposed to 25.11 seconds at a possible condition.

Questions

1. The **mean** was used as the measure of average. Explain why the mean was the most appropriate average to use in this study. (*2 marks*)

2. Plot the means on a **bar chart**. Pay attention to the scale on your y-axis and to following the conventions of bar charts. (*4 marks*)

3. Time in seconds can be described as **interval data**. Explain what this means. (*2 marks*)

4. What would be the most appropriate **statistical test** to use to assess the significance of the results in this study. Explain your choice. (*3 marks*)

CHECK IT

1. Explain what is meant by *violation of expectation* (VOE). **[4 marks]**

2. Outline Baillargeon's explanation of early infant abilities, including knowledge of the physical world. **[6 marks]**

3. Describe **one** study conducted by Baillargeon. Include details of what she did and what she found. **[4 marks]**

4. Describe and evaluate Baillargeon's explanation of early infant abilities. **[16 marks]**

SOCIAL COGNITION: SELMAN'S LEVELS OF PERSPECTIVE-TAKING

This is the first of three spreads dealing with social cognition, the mental processes that underlie human social interaction. In particular we deal here with the work of Robert Selman, who studied the role of perspective-taking in children's development of pro-social reasoning.

KEY TERMS

Social cognition – Describes the mental processes we make use of when engaged in social interaction. For example, we make decisions on how to behave based on our understanding of a social situation. Both the understanding and the decision making are cognitive processes.

Perspective-taking – Our ability to appreciate a social situation from the perspective (point of view) of other people. This cognitive ability underlies much of our normal social interaction.

Whether to risk upsetting a worried parent by rescuing a kitten is a complex social decision that involves taking the perspective of everyone involved.

Apply it

Concepts: Spenny and Lauren's computer time

Selma and Emma are working to limit the time their children, Spenny (aged 11) and Lauren (aged 5), spend playing computer games. Spenny seems able to appreciate his mother's point of view although it is not convenient for him. Lauren, however, is very resistant to alternative activities. She can see that her mother is worried by this but cannot see why.

Question

Referring to Selman's stages, explain why Spenny's and Lauren's responses are so different.

Selman's work on perspective-taking

Recall Piaget's idea of **egocentrism** and in particular the **three mountains task** (page 180). This is an example of physical perspective-taking – physically understanding what someone else can see. There is also social **perspective-taking** which is more about understanding what someone else is feeling or thinking, i.e. **social cognition**.

Piaget believed in domain-general cognitive development, so he believed that physical and social perspective-taking would occur hand-in hand. Robert Selman (1971, 1976) proposed that the development of social perspective-taking is a separate process. This is a domain-specific approach to explaining cognitive development.

Perspective-taking research

Selman (1971) looked at changes that occurred with age in children's responses to scenarios in which they were asked to take the role of different people in a social situation.

Procedure 30 boys and 30 girls took part in the study, 20 aged four, 20 aged five and 20 aged six years. All were individually given a task designed to measure role-taking ability. This involved asking them how each person felt in various scenarios. One scenario featured a child called Holly who has promised her father she will no longer climb trees, but who then comes across her friend whose kitten is stuck up a tree. The task was to describe and explain how each person would feel if Holly did or did not climb the tree to rescue the kitten.

Findings A number of distinct levels of role-taking were identified (see below). Selman found that the level of role-taking correlated with age, suggesting a clear developmental sequence.

Selman's stages of development

Based on children's typical responses to perspective-taking scenarios at different ages, Selman (1976) proposed five stages of social cognitive development:

- Stage 0 (3–6 years) *Socially egocentric*: The child in this stage cannot reliably distinguish between their own emotions and those of others. They can generally identify emotional states in others but do not understand what social behaviour might have caused them.

- Stage 1 (6–8 years) *Social information role-taking*: The child can now tell the difference between their own point of view and that of others, but they can usually focus on only one of these perspectives.

- Stage 2 (8–10 years) *Self-reflective role-taking*: At this stage the child can put themselves in the position of another person and fully appreciate their perspective. They can, however, only take on board one point of view at a time.

- Stage 3 (10–12 years) *Mutual role-taking*: Children are now able to look at a situation from their own and another's point of view at the same time.

- Stage 4 (12 years +) *Social and conventional system role-taking*: Young people become able to see that sometimes understanding others' viewpoints is not enough to allow people to reach agreement. This is why social conventions are needed to keep order.

Selman believed that development through these stages is based on both maturity and experience.

Later developments to Selman's theory

Selman has recognised that the above descriptions of cognitive reasoning do not fully explain social development. Schultz, Selman and La Russo (2003) have identified three aspects to social development:

1. *Interpersonal understanding*: This is what Selman measured in his earlier role-taking research. If we can take different roles then this shows we can understand social situations.

2. *Interpersonal negotiation strategies*: As well as understanding what others think in social situations we also have to develop skills in how to respond to them. We therefore develop social skills such as asserting our position and managing conflict.

3. *Awareness of personal meaning of relationships*: As well as understanding social situations and how to manage them, social development also requires the ability to reflect on social behaviour in the context of life history and the full range of relationships. Thus a violent gang-member may have an advanced social understanding and good social skills, but choose a simple approach to conflict (violence) because of their role in the gang.

Evaluation

Evidence that perspective-taking gets better with age

Selman provided solid evidence that perspective-taking ability improves with age in line with his theory. In one study Selman (1971) gave perspective-taking tasks to 60 children, half boys and half girls, aged 4–6 years. **Significant positive correlations** were found between age and ability to take different perspectives in scenarios like that of Holly and the kitten (on facing page).

Longitudinal follow-up studies (e.g. Gurucharri and Selman 1982) have shown that perspective-taking develops with age in each individual child. This shows that his earlier **cross-sectional** research (Selman 1971) was not simply the result of individual differences in social-cognitive ability in children in different groups.

This is a strength because Selman's ideas are both based on solid research and supported by a range of studies.

Mixed evidence for the importance of perspective-taking

There is strong evidence to support Selman's idea that children's ability to take on the perspectives of others develops throughout childhood. However, evidence is much more mixed as to just how important the cognitive ability to take alternative perspectives is in understanding children's social development. In an **observation** of child–parent interaction in toyshops and supermarkets Moniek Buijzen and Patti Valkenburg (2008) found a **negative correlation** between age, perspective-taking and coercive behaviour, i.e. trying to force parents to buy them things. This suggests that perspective-taking is important in developing **prosocial behaviour**, i.e. alternatives to coercion.

However, Luciano Gasser and Monika Keller (2009) found that bullies displayed no difficulties in perspective-taking. This is a problem for Selman's approach as it suggests perspective-taking may not be an important factor in the development of socially desirable behaviour.

Applications in understanding atypical development

The development of the cognitive ability to take a range of perspectives appears to be important in atypical development. Research has shown that children with **ADHD** and those on the **autistic spectrum** have problems with perspective-taking. In one study Marton et al. (2009) compared 50 8–12-year-old children with a diagnosis of ADHD with a **control group** on performance on perspective-taking tasks like those used by Selman. Those with ADHD did worse on understanding the scenarios, identifying the feelings of each person involved and evaluating the consequences of different actions.

This is a strength of Selman's work because it shows it is helpful in understanding atypical development.

Children who struggle to take on board others' perspectives also struggle socially. This is a feature of ADHD and autistic spectrum disorder.

Evaluation eXtra

Overly cognitive

A limitation of Selman's approach is that it is entirely based on an understanding of cognition. Perspective-taking is a cognitive ability but there is more to children's social development than their developing cognitive abilities. Selman's approach does not take into account a range of other factors that impact on a child's social development. Internal factors include the development of empathy and emotional self-regulation, whilst external factors include family climate and opportunities to learn from peer interaction.

Consider: *Should a theory or a line of research in psychology aim to explain everything about a topic or is it okay for it to explain one aspect of a complex situation well?*

Cultural differences in perspective-taking

Selman's methods have allowed us to compare different groups of people on their perspective-taking ability. In one study, for example, Shali Wu and Boaz Keysar (2007) found that young adult Chinese participants did significantly better in perspective-taking than matched Americans. This shows that there is more to the development of perspective-taking than just cognitive maturity because the differences must be due to different cultural inputs.

Consider: *To what extent do cultural differences in perspective-taking ability pose a problem for Selman's approach? Remember that Selman believed that both maturity and experience contribute to the development of perspective-taking.*

Apply it **Concepts: Anders**

Anders is ten years old. In a recent shopping trip he had a tantrum when he asked for an expensive computer game and his mother tried to explain that they could not afford it for the moment. It appeared that he could not appreciate his mother's perspective on the matter.

Question

What could you tell Anders's mother about his development of perspective-taking. Refer to Selman's stages in your answer.

Apply it **Methods: Different designs**

Selman used both **cross-sectional** and **longitudinal designs** in his research into the development of perspective-taking. For example, Selman (1971) compared groups of four-, five- and six-year-olds on their perspective-taking abilities, whilst Gurucharri and Selman (1982) followed up children, testing whether their perspective-taking abilities changed with age.

Questions

1. Explain what is meant by a cross-sectional design. *(2 marks)*

2. Explain what is meant by a longitudinal design. *(2 marks)*

3. Outline *one* strength of using a longitudinal design in the study by Gurucharri and Selman. *(2 marks)*

4. Outline *two* strengths of using a cross-sectional design in the study by Selman. *(4 marks)*

CHECK IT

1. Explain what is meant by *social cognition*. [4 marks]

2. Outline Selman's levels of perspective-taking. [6 marks]

3. Describe **one** study that has investigated levels of perspective-taking. [4 marks]

4. Describe and evaluate Selman's work on perspective taking. [16 marks]

SOCIAL COGNITION: THEORY OF MIND (TOM)

THE SPECIFICATION SAYS...

The development of social cognition: theory of mind, including theory of mind as an explanation for autism; the Sally-Anne study.

This is the second spread dealing with social cognition, the mental processes that underlie human social interaction. In particular we deal here with theory of mind, our understanding of what is going on in the mind of another person. Theory of mind, or rather a lack of it, has been proposed as an explanation for autism (more correctly called autistic spectrum disorder, ASD). The Sally-Anne study is an example of a false belief task, used to study theory of mind.

KEY TERMS

Theory of mind – Our personal understanding (a 'theory') of what other people are thinking and feeling. It is sometimes called 'mind-reading'.

Autism – (more correctly called autistic spectrum disorder, ASD) is an umbrella term for a wide range of symptoms. All disorders on the spectrum share impairments to three main areas: empathy, social communication and social imagination.

Sally–Anne study – Uses the Sally–Anne task to assess theory of mind. To understand the story participants have to identify that Sally will look for a marble in the wrong place because she does not know that Anne has moved it. Very young children and children with autism spectrum disorder (ASD) find this difficult.

The Sally–Anne task

Sally puts the marble in her basket

While Sally is away Anne moves the marble to her box

When Sally returns, where will she look for her marble?

An example of an item from the Eyes Task.

Theory of mind (ToM)

You could be forgiven for thinking '**theory of mind**' is a psychological theory. It isn't! It refers to the ability that each of us has to 'mind-read' or to have a personal theory of what other people know or are feeling or thinking. Each of us has a theory of mind when we have a belief (i.e. a theory) about what is in someone else's mind.

Different methods are used to study ToM at different points in development. The emergence of simple ToM can be seen in toddlers by means of intentional reasoning research. A more sophisticated level of ToM can be assessed in 3–4-year-olds using false belief tasks. In older children and adults advanced ToM has been tested with the **Eyes Task** (see below), in which participants judge complex emotions with minimal information about facial expression.

Intentional reasoning in toddlers

In one study Andrew Meltzoff (1988) provided convincing evidence to show that toddlers (aged about 18 months) have an understanding of adult intentions when carrying out simple actions. Children of 18 months observed adults place beads into a jar. In the **experimental condition** the adults appeared to struggle with this and dropped the beads. In the **control condition** the adults placed the beads successfully in the jar. In both conditions the toddlers placed the beads in the jar; they dropped no more beads in the experimental condition. This suggests they were imitating what the adult *intended* to do. This kind of research shows that very young children have a simple ToM.

False belief tasks

False belief tasks were developed in order to test whether children can understand that people can believe something that is not true. The first was developed by Heinz Wimmer and Josef Perner (1983). They told 3–4-year-olds a story in which Maxi left his chocolate in a *blue* cupboard in the kitchen and then went to the playground. Later, Maxi's mother used some of the chocolate in her cooking and placed the remainder in the *green* cupboard. Children were asked where Maxi would look for his chocolate when he comes back from the playground. Most 3-year-olds incorrectly said that he would look in the *green* cupboard because Maxi doesn't know his mother moved it. However, most 4-year-olds correctly identified the *blue* cupboard. This suggests that ToM undergoes a shift and becomes more advanced at around four years.

Sally–Anne studies

Simon Baron-Cohen *et al.* (1985) used a similar false belief task called the **Sally-Anne task** (see left). Children were told a story involving two dolls, Sally and Anne. Sally places a marble in her basket, but when Sally is not looking Anne moves the marble to her box. The task is to work out where Sally will look for her marble. Understanding that Sally does not know that Anne has moved the marble requires an understanding of Sally's false belief about where it is.

Baron-Cohen and colleagues have explored the links between ToM deficits and **ASD** using false belief tasks. Much of the research has made use of the Sally–Anne task, for example, the following study by Baron-Cohen *et al.* (1985).

Procedure 20 high-functioning children diagnosed as being ASD and **control groups** of 14 children with **Down's syndrome** and 27 without a diagnosis were individually administered the Sally-Anne test.

Findings 85% of children in the control groups correctly identified where Sally would look for her marble. However, only four of the children in the ASD group (20%) were able to answer this. This dramatic difference demonstrated that ASD involves a ToM deficit. Baron-Cohen and his colleagues suggested that deficits in ToM might in fact be a complete explanation for ASD.

Testing older children and adults

Asperger syndrome (AS) is a type of ASD characterised by problems with empathy, social communication and imagination but normal language development. Studies of older children and adults with AS, showed that this group succeeded easily on false belief tasks. This was a blow to the idea that ASD can be explained by ToM deficits.

However, Baron-Cohen and colleagues developed a more challenging task to assess ToM in adolescents and adults. The Eyes Task involves reading complex emotions in pictures of faces just showing a small area around the eyes. Baron-Cohen *et al.* (1997) found that adults with AS and those with a diagnosis of high-functioning ASD struggled with the Eyes Task. This supports the idea that ToM deficits might be the cause of ASD.

Evaluation

Practical activity on page 193

Low validity of false belief tasks

The mainstay of ToM research has been the false belief task. Hundreds of studies have made use of the Sally–Anne task and variations on it. However, some psychologists have been sharply critical of the false belief approach. Bloom and German (2000) suggest two reasons why false belief tasks lack **validity**. First, success on a false belief task requires other cognitive abilities apart from ToM, for example, memory. Although the Sally–Anne story is slightly shorter and simpler than the original Maxi story, it is still quite a bit for a 3-year-old to remember. Some studies have given ASD children visual aids to help them remember the false belief stories and have found that younger ASD children quite often succeed.

Bloom and German's second criticism is that a child can have a well-developed ToM and still struggle with false belief tasks. Thus children who cannot perform well on false belief tasks still enjoy pretend-play, which requires a ToM.

Both these criticisms challenge the validity of false belief tasks. This is a huge problem for ToM research because it has been dominated by false belief research.

Hard to distinguish ToM from perspective-taking

Recall Robert Selman's work on perspective-taking (previous spread). This is the cognitive ability to view social situations from another person's point of view. ToM, the ability to understand mental states in others, and perspective-taking appear to be closely related cognitive abilities. The problem is that many of the methods that have been used to study ToM could simply be measures of perspective-taking. For example responses to the Sally–Anne task could be explained in terms of children's ability to take Sally's perspective. Similarly, although performance on ToM tasks distinguishes between children on the autistic spectrum and others, the same is true of perspective-taking tasks (Rehfeldt *et al.* 2007).

The possibility that much of the research into ToM may simply be measuring perspective-taking is a further challenge to the validity of ToM research.

A partial explanation for ASD

One of the major applications of ToM research is in understanding ASD. It is widely agreed that people on the autistic spectrum have more difficulty than others on age-appropriate ToM tests. ToM research has been extremely useful in helping us understand the differing experiences of those on the autistic spectrum and those who are 'neurotypical' (the term used by people on the autistic spectrum to describe the rest of the population).

What is more controversial is the idea that ASD is the direct *result* of ToM deficits, as suggested by Baron-Cohen. Helen Tager-Flusberg (2007) suggests that more recent research has questioned the assumption that ToM problems are specific to ASD and that all those on the autistic spectrum suffer ToM problems. ASD and ToM may therefore not be as closely linked as was once believed.

Also, ASD has many other characteristics including cognitive strengths such as superior visual attention and highly systematic reasoning. ToM cannot easily explain these characteristics.

Evaluation eXtra

No clear understanding of how ToM develops

There are a number of theories around to account for how we develop our ToM. Perner *et al.* (2002) adopt a Piagetian approach and see ToM as simply developing in line with all cognitive abilities, i.e. it is based on an **innate** ability which matures with age and experience. Janet Wilde Astington (1998) takes a more Vygotskian line and suggests that we internalise our ToM during early interactions with adults. There is no clear evidence to suggest which explanation is correct.

Consider: *How important is it to understand the origins of theory of mind? Should our lack of knowledge about this stop us using the idea?*

Critique of the Eyes Task

Much of the criticism of ToM research has been leveled against false belief tasks. However, the Eyes Task may also lack validity because the experience of looking at a static pair of eyes in isolation is so different from real life where we usually have access to much additional information.

Consider: *If both false belief tasks and the Eyes Task have validity problems, what does this suggest about the field of theory of mind research?*

Sheldon Cooper is a much loved character from the TV show *The Big Bang Theory*. Sheldon's lack of social skills can be explained by a theory of mind deficit.

Apply it Concepts: Sheldon Cooper

It has been suggested by many viewers, including those with Asperger syndrome, that Sheldon Cooper, the much-loved character from *The Big Bang Theory*, is a classic example of Asperger syndrome. Sheldon struggles to read facial expressions, finds it hard to change his routine in response to the wishes of others and he does not 'get' sarcasm. He finds social interaction in general difficult.

Question

Explain Sheldon's characteristics with regard to theory of mind and its possible role in autistic spectrum disorder.

Apply it Methods: ToM tasks

Baron-Cohen *et al.*'s Sally–Anne study (facing page) compared performance of three groups, 20 children on the autistic spectrum and 41 children either without any diagnosis or with Down's syndrome on the Sally–Anne task; 85% of children in the Down's and no-diagnosis groups got the answer right whereas only 20% of those in the autism group did so.

Questions

1. Explain why an **independent groups design** was used in this study. (*2 marks*)
2. Present these findings on a suitable graph. (*4 marks*)
3. Present the numbers of children getting the Sally–Anne task right in the experimental and control conditions as fractions of the total. (*2 marks*)

Apply it Concepts: Andy's homework

Andy is in infant school and has just misplaced his first piece of homework. His teacher does not believe Andy when he tells him that he completed the work. Andy finds this response very difficult to understand and gets extremely confused and upset.

Question

Explain Andy's response to the situation using the concept of theory of mind. You might refer to the Sally–Anne study in your answer.

CHECK IT

1. Outline **one** Sally–Anne study. [6 marks]
2. Explain what is meant by *theory of mind*. [3 marks]
3. Evaluate theory of mind as an explanation for autism. [4 marks]
4. Describe and evaluate research into theory of mind. Include evidence in your answer. [16 marks]

SOCIAL COGNITION: THE MIRROR NEURON SYSTEM

This is the final spread dealing with social cognition, the cognitive processes that underlie human social interaction. In particular we deal here with the likely role of a particular class of brain cell, the mirror neuron. It seems likely that mirror neurons are involved in the social-cognitive processes of empathy, understanding intention, perspective-taking and theory of mind.

KEY TERM

The mirror neuron system consists of special brain cells called mirror neurons distributed in several areas of the brain. Mirror neurons are unique because they fire both in response to personal action and in response to action on the part of others. These special neurons may be involved in social cognition, allowing us to interpret intention and emotion in others.

STUDY TIP

This is quite a current area of research so it may pay to do some extra reading so you are well informed. Use Google Scholar to find out about recent research on mirror neurons.

According to Ramachandran the ability to share the emotions of those around us is due to mirror neurons and this ability has shaped the development of human society.

The role of mirror neurons

The discovery of mirror neurons

Like many great scientific discoveries, researchers came across mirror neurons quite by accident. Giacomo Rizzolatti *et al.* (2002) were studying electrical activity in a monkey's **motor cortex** (the part of the brain controlling movement) when one of the researchers reached for his lunch in view of the monkey. This monkey's motor cortex became activated in exactly the same way as it did when the animal itself reached for food. Further investigation revealed that it was in fact the same brain cells that fired when the monkey reached itself or watched some else reach. The researchers called these cells **mirror neurons** because they mirror motor activity in another individual.

Mirror neurons and intention

Understanding mirror neurons has given us a whole new way of thinking about the way we understand each other's intentions – this is central to social cognition. Vittorio Gallese and Alvin Goldman (1998) suggested that mirror neurons respond not just to observed actions but to intentions behind behaviour. Rather than the common-sense view that we interpret people's actions with reference to our memory, Gallese and Goldman suggested that we simulate other's actions in our motor system and experience their intentions using our mirror neurons.

Mirror neurons and perspective-taking

It has also been suggested that mirror neurons are important in other social-cognitive functions, for example, theory of mind and the ability to take others' perspectives. If mirror neurons fire in response to others' actions and intentions this may give us a neural mechanism for experiencing, and hence understanding, other people's perspectives and emotional states. Just as we can simulate intention by making judgements based on our own reflected motor responses, this same information may allow us to interpret what others are thinking and feeling.

Mirror neurons and human evolution

Vilayanur Ramachandran (2011) has suggested that mirror neurons are so important that they have effectively shaped human evolution. The uniquely complex social interactions we have as humans require a brain system that facilitates an understanding of intention, emotion and perspective. Without these cognitive abilities we could not live in the large groups with the complex social roles and rules than characterise human culture. Ramachandran suggests that mirror neurons are absolutely key to understanding the way humans have developed as a social species.

Mirror neurons and autistic spectrum disorder

A major source of evidence concerning mirror neurons and perspective-taking comes from the study of mirror neurons in children suffering from **autistic spectrum disorders** (ASD). ASD is associated with problems with all these social-cognitive abilities. If children on the autistic spectrum can be shown to have a poor mirror neuron system then this may go a long way to explaining ASD.

Ramachandran and Oberman (2006) have proposed the 'broken mirror' theory of ASD. This is the idea that neurological deficits including dysfunction in the mirror neuron system prevent a developing child imitating and understanding social behaviour in others. This manifests itself in infancy when children later diagnosed with ASD typically mimic adult behaviour less than others. Later, problems with the mirror neuron system lead to difficulties in social communication as children fail to develop the usual abilities to read intention and emotion in others.

Apply it   **Concepts: Andy Murray wins Wimbledon**

In 2013 Andy Murray won the prestigious Wimbledon Tennis Tournament. This was watched by a record 17 million people. Millions of people shared Murray's joy at finally winning the competition after trying unsuccessfully for several years.

Question

Explain how the public response to Murray's struggle and eventual win might have involved their mirror neurons.

Evaluation

Evidence for the role of mirror neurons

There is evidence to support an important role for mirror neurons in human social cognition. Helene Haker et al. (2012) demonstrated that an area of the brain believed to be rich in mirror neurons is involved in contagious yawning, which is widely seen as a simple example of human empathy, the ability to perceive mental states in others. A **brain scanning** technique called **functional magnetic resonance imaging** (fMRI) was used to assess brain activity in participants while they were stimulated to yawn by showing them film of others yawning. When they yawned in response, participants showed considerable activity in *Brodmann's area*, an area in the right **frontal lobe** believed to be rich in mirror neurons.

Another region of the brain believed to be rich in mirror neurons is the *pars opercularis*. Mouras *et al.* (2008) provided evidence to suggest that the pars opercularis is involved in perspective-taking. Male participants watched either a fishing documentary, Mr Bean or heterosexual pornography. Brain activity was again measured by fMRI and arousal by a pressure sensitive penis ring. Pars opercularis activity was seen immediately before sexual arousal, consistent with the idea that mirror neurons produced the perspective-taking that made the pornography arousing.

Both of these studies support the importance of mirror neurons in social cognition because they show that regions of the brain believed to be rich in mirror neurons activate when empathy or perspective-taking takes place.

Difficulty studying mirror neuron activity in humans

Note that, in the above point, evidence for mirror neuron activity comes from brain scanning, which identifies activity levels in regions of the brain. Scanning does not allow us to measure activity in individual brain cells. For ethical reasons it is not possible to insert electrodes into the human brain to measure activity on a cellular level.

This is a weakness of mirror neuron research because researchers are generally measuring activity in a part of the brain and inferring that this means activity in mirror neurons. There is a lack of direct evidence for mirror neuron activity from studies like this.

Mixed evidence for abnormal mirror neuron function in ASD

Nouchine Hadjikhani (2007) has reviewed evidence for the link between ASD and a deficit in mirror neuron function and found some support. Structural brain scans have shown a smaller average thickness for the pars opercularis in participants on the autistic spectrum. Similarly, studies using functional scans have shown lower activity in brain areas associated with mirror neurons in participants with ASD. However, not all such findings have been replicated consistently and evidence linking ASD to mirror neurons is mixed.

This is a problem for the broken mirror theory of ASD. The theory is credible because of the close link between the signs of ASD and the likely role of mirror neurons in social cognition. However, there is a lack of reliable direct evidence to support the theory.

Evaluation eXtra

Questions over the existence of mirror neurons

Gregory Hickok (2009) has questioned the most basic assumption in mirror neuron research – that mirror neurons exist all. Hickok proposed that we only know mirror neurons by what they do and that we cannot actually identify individual cells and point to their differences from other neurons. This is controversial – other researchers (e.g. Mukamel *et al.*, 2010) do believe there are isolated mirror neurons.

Consider: *How big a problem is this challenge for mirror neuron research? Bear in mind that the functions of mirror neurons may still be carried out by brain cells, just not by special ones.*

Questions over the precise role of mirror neurons

Hickok also suggests that whilst it is likely that mirror neurons do exist and play a role in social cognition, it may not be quite what has been suggested by mirror neuron enthusiasts. For example, mirror neuron activity may have more to do with using others' behaviour to plan our own rather than understanding the cognitions behind it.

Consider: *How big a problem is this for mirror neuron research?*

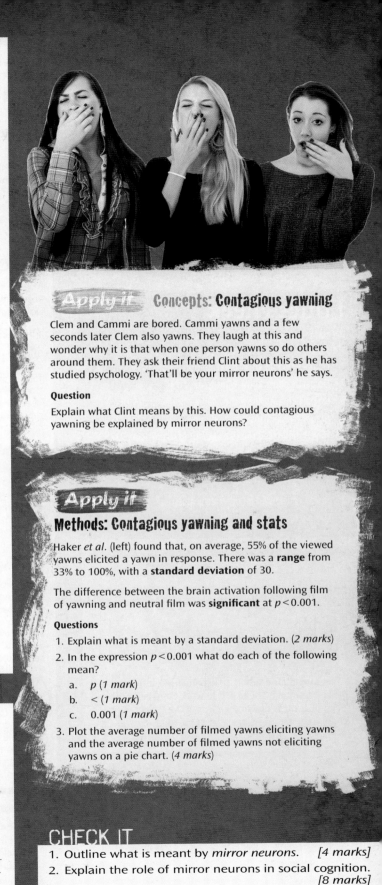

Apply it · Concepts: Contagious yawning

Clem and Cammi are bored. Cammi yawns and a few seconds later Clem also yawns. They laugh at this and wonder why it is that when one person yawns so do others around them. They ask their friend Clint about this as he has studied psychology. 'That'll be your mirror neurons' he says.

Question

Explain what Clint means by this. How could contagious yawning be explained by mirror neurons?

Apply it · Methods: Contagious yawning and stats

Haker *et al.* (left) found that, on average, 55% of the viewed yawns elicited a yawn in response. There was a **range** from 33% to 100%, with a **standard deviation** of 30.

The difference between the brain activation following film of yawning and neutral film was **significant** at $p < 0.001$.

Questions

1. Explain what is meant by a standard deviation. (*2 marks*)
2. In the expression $p < 0.001$ what do each of the following mean?
   a. p (*1 mark*)
   b. $<$ (*1 mark*)
   c. 0.001 (*1 mark*)
3. Plot the average number of filmed yawns eliciting yawns and the average number of filmed yawns not eliciting yawns on a pie chart. (*4 marks*)

CHECK IT

1. Outline what is meant by *mirror neurons*. [*4 marks*]
2. Explain the role of mirror neurons in social cognition. [*8 marks*]
3. Evaluate research into mirror neurons. [*8 marks*]
4. Outline and evaluate the role of mirror neurons in social cognition. [*16 marks*]

PRACTICAL CORNER

Knowledge and understanding of ...research methods, practical research skills and maths skills. These should be developed through ... ethical practical research activities.

This means that you should conduct practical investigations wherever possible. For both practical and ethical reasons we don't recommend you carry out practical work with young children, but there are relevant things you can do using your peers as participants as suggested here. One practical uses a questionnaire technique, the other involves carrying out a quasi-experiment online.

Ethics check

We suggest strongly that you complete this checklist before starting:

1. Do participants know participation is voluntary?
2. Do participants know what to expect?
3. Do participants know they can withdraw at any time?
4. Are individuals' results anonymous?
5. Have I minimised the risk of distress to participants?
6. Have I avoided asking sensitive questions?
7. Will I avoid bringing my school/teacher/psychology into disrepute?
8. Have I considered all other ethical issues?
9. Has my teacher approved this?

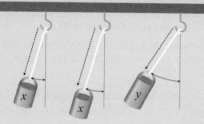

Piaget's pendulum task is an example of a test for formal reasoning. The task is to work out whether the speed of swing is due to the mass of the weight, string length or height of swing.

Practical idea 1: Formal reasoning in teenagers

Much of the research in this chapter has been carried out on young children but there are some topics where teenagers make suitable participants. Rather than go through all the faffing and ethical safeguards needed to work with children we suggest you focus on the kind of practical work that can be done with 16–19-year-olds. The first of these concerns Piaget's idea of formal reasoning.

The **aim** of this study is to test Piaget's idea that most teenagers can carry out formal reasoning tasks. Remember that, although Piaget believed this, most later researchers have concluded that he was extremely optimistic. This is important as it means you shouldn't feel bad if you find the task hard. You will be using a **questionnaire** method.

The practical bit

You are testing the idea that 16–19-year-old students can successfully carry out formal reasoning tasks. This is not an **experiment** – you are not controlling an **independent variable** here, just testing a simple idea on a single group of participants.

Choosing your participants

The representativeness of your **sample** is quite important for this study. Remember you are testing Piaget's idea that most teenagers can do formal thinking tasks. If your sample is not fairly representative of teenagers then you won't really be testing that idea. Your sample population will probably be your peers in your own college or school 6th form. You will need to decide on a sampling procedure. A **random** method is likely to produce a fairly representative sample but you may decide to prioritise sample size and ask all available students to participate.

Formal thinking tasks

We have identified syllogisms as one type of formal thinking task (page 180). You can find more here: www.simplypsychology.org/formal-operational.html. An important decision you will have to make concerns how many tasks you give your participants. If you just use one task it will be nice and quick for participants, meaning you should get plenty of people willing to volunteer. However, a single task might be too easy or hard and therefore not fairly represent formal reasoning. Using several tasks may be a more **valid** assessment but you risk a lower response rate. Think carefully about this and come to a reasoned decision.

Ethical issues

You will almost certainly find that some of your participants will not be able to do all the tasks you set them. This raises issues of **confidentiality**; you cannot reveal to anyone which participants failed the tasks. Anonymise data before sharing it. You also need to be quite sure participants have given **informed consent** and are fully aware of their **right to withdraw**. You will need a **debrief** handy that makes it very clear that research has found that most teenagers struggle with formal reasoning tasks. You must not destroy anyone's **self-esteem** by letting them leave the study thinking they are stupid.

Analysing your data

This should be extremely straightforward because you are not comparing two conditions or looking for a relationship between variables. You will need a table and graph to summarise your findings. Their precise nature will depend on how many tasks you gave people. At its simplest, with a single formal reasoning task, you just need a table of numbers correct and incorrect, and a **bar chart** with a column for number of people getting it correct and a column for number getting it incorrect. You may also wish to use a statistical test (see question 2 below).

Table showing correct and incorrect answers for three tests of formal reasoning

Task	Number correct	Number incorrect
Syllogism	18	7
Pendulum	5	20
Extra eye task	16	9

Apply it **Methods: The maths bit 1**

1. (a) In the table on the left, express the numbers correct and incorrect for syllogisms as fractions. (*2 marks*)
   (b) Express them as ratios. (2 marks)

2. What **statistical test** would you use to analyse the **significance** of the results on each of the three tasks? Explain your answer. (*3 marks*) (See page 70)

3. The significance for the pendulum task is $p < 0.05$. Explain what this means. (*3 marks*)

4. Draw a **bar chart** to represent the data in the table on the left. (*4 marks*)

5. What conclusion would you reach based on the table? (*1 mark*)

Practical idea 2: Sex differences in advanced theory of mind

Recall the idea of **theory of mind** (page 188). The **Eyes Task**, developed by Baron-Cohen *et al.* (1997) tests advanced theory of mind. In the original study it was found that in the neurotypical group female participants scored a mean of 21.8 correct out of 25 whereas males averaged 18.8 correct.

The aim of this study is to **replicate** Baron-Cohen's study, just using male and female neurotypical participants. This is a **quasi-experiment** because you will be comparing boys and girls. The independent variable is gender and the **dependent variable** is advanced theory of mind as measured by the number of items correct on the Eyes Test.

(c) REFLECTIVE vs. Unreflective.

(d) SYMPATHETIC vs. Unsympathetic.

Baron-Cohen and colleagues found that girls typically did slightly better than boys on the Eyes Task.

The practical bit

It is important to ensure that, as far as possible, you have control over your variables. You can arrange for all participants to take the Eyes Task online but you need to ensure that conditions are comparable. The same would apply if doing a pen-and-pencil version of the test.

Choosing your participants

If your aim is to compare Eyes Task performance in boys and girls you will need a comparable group of boys and girls. You may wish to use a **matched pairs design** and need to draw up a list of characteristics you might use for matching.

Administering the Eyes Task

We recommend running the test online (see right). This will take care of a lot of **extraneous variables** for you and ensure your participants have a highly standardised experience. It will also help avoid the kind of mistakes I (Matt) tend to make in experiments like dropping piles of paper on the floor and getting them muddled up!

You can, if you wish, print the test out and administer it that way but must ensure standardised procedures.

Ethical issues

There are important ethical issues. Remember that you are not competent to research on participants with any learning disability or mental health issue. You should not therefore actively involve participants who are on the **autistic spectrum**. Neither, however, should you offend a student with **ASD** by deliberately excluding them if they wish to participate. Refer any volunteer with ASD to your teacher who will need to make a judgement.

If anyone does have low scores, do not suggest that they might have ASD (although if someone is anxious about their low score refer them to your teacher). As always take care to preserve the **anonymity** of your participants and don't identify low-scorers.

Presenting your data

This is a straightforward gender comparison so your tables and graphs should be designed to compare two conditions. You will need a **measure of central tendency** for the number of items boys and girls get right. Consider as well an appropriate **measure of dispersion**. You may also wish to use a statistical test (see question 2 below).

The Eyes Test

There are two versions of the Eyes Test available. The original version has 25 items and the updated version has 37. Either should be fine for your practical. You can run the Eyes Test online at the following websites:

www.questionwritertracker.com/quiz/61/Z4MK3TKB.html

http://kgajos.eecs.harvard.edu/mite/

Or you can download paper versions at these sites:

www.autismresearchcentre.com/arc_tests

www.resourcd.com/@psychexchange/file/show/7693

The maths bit

Overall, at least 10% of the marks in assessments for Psychology will require the use of mathematical skills and at least a further 15% will be related to research methods.

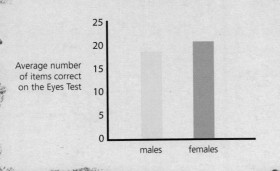

Apply it · Methods: The maths bit 2

1. The graph on the left represents the findings of Baron-Cohen *et al.* (1997). What does this graph tell us about the average male and female performance on the Eyes Task? (2 marks)

2. Create a set of data that could produce the bar chart on the left. (4 marks)

3. What statistical test could you use with this data? Explain your answer. (3 marks) (See page 70)

4. Explain why the data shown on this graph can be described as **quantitative data**. (3 marks)

REVISION SUMMARIES

PIAGET'S THEORY OF COGNITIVE DEVELOPMENT

The process of acquiring knowledge.

GENERAL APPROACH

Schemas: units of knowledge
Each schema contains information about one thing.

Motivation to learn
Not understanding something causes disequilibrium.
This is unpleasant so child is motivated to escape it by learning.

Assimilation and accommodation
Either add new information to existing schemas.
Or accommodate to radically new experiences by forming new schemas.

EVALUATION

Children form individual representations by discovery
Children form their own conclusions from group work (Howe *et al.*).

Applications in education
Discovery learning has led to e.g. activity-based classrooms and flipped learning.

Piaget underplayed the role of others in learning
Vygotsky proposed that children learn largely from other people.
This is not emphasised in Piaget's theory.

Piaget may have overplayed the importance of equilibration
Equilibration not as important as Piaget believed. Other factors include help from others and the role of language in helping understanding.

Piaget may have underplayed the importance of language
Some theorists believe language contributes to cognitive development but Piaget thought it just developed along with everything else.

PIAGET'S STAGES OF INTELLECTUAL DEVELOPMENT

Each stage characterised by particular mental abilities.

STAGES OF DEVELOPMENT

Sensorimotor stage (0–2 years)
Babies acquire basic physical co-ordination, object permanence (8 months) and basic language.
Object permanence, child fails to understand that objects continue to exist when no longer visible.

Pre-operational stage (2–7 years)
Child lacks logic so is egocentric and fails tests of conservation and class inclusion.
- Egocentricity – child fails to see another's perspective, tested by three mountains task.
- Conservation – child fails to to understand quantities cannot change, tested with e.g. liquid in glasses.
- Class inclusion – child fails to recognise subsets within larger classes, tested with questions e.g. about dogs and animals.

Stage of concrete operations (7–11 years)
Child has basic logic so can perform tasks of decentring, conservation and class inclusion.
However, logical operations require physical objects.

Stage of formal operations (11+ years)
Children become capable of full adult reasoning, including about abstract ideas and scientific reasoning.

EVALUATION

Piaget's questioning was dubious
Piaget may have confused young children with his questioning, making them appear less advanced than they really were.

Piaget's conclusions on class inclusion may be dubious
Siegler and Svetina clarified information in class inclusion tasks and found good inclusion abilities in younger children.

Children's ability to decentre
Hughes found children of 3½ could decentre (task more realistic with dolls representing two boys and a policeman).

Piaget may have underestimated younger children and overestimated adolescents
Siegler and Svetina: Young children were capable of class inclusion while Bradmetz found most teenagers could not do formal reasoning tasks.

Domain-general and domain-specific
Piaget's theory is domain-general. However, this cannot explain autism, in which some abilities develop better than others.

VYGOTSKY'S THEORY OF COGNITIVE DEVELOPMENT

Emphasises the role of other people.

VYGOTSKY'S THEORY OF COGNITIVE DEVELOPMENT

Cultural differences in cognitive abilities
Because cognitive abilities are acquired in social interaction they reflect the abilities of local adults and therefore may vary according to culture.

The zone of proximal development
This is the difference between what a child can learn on their own and with an expert helper.

Scaffolding
The help given by an expert to guide children through the zone of proximal development.
Stages are:
- Recruitment.
- Reduction of degrees of freedom.
- Direction maintenance.
- Marking critical features.
- Demonstration.

EVALUATION

Support for the zone of proximal development
Roazzi and Bryant found that 4–5-year-olds performed better with prompts.

Support for scaffolding
Connor and Cross observed decreased intervention in help given by mothers as their children got older.

Applications in education
Peer tutoring and the use of teaching assistants. Effectiveness shown by Van Keer and Verhaeghe, and Alborz *et al.* respectively.

What children learn is individual
Children's learning during interaction is surprisingly individual if Vygotsky is right that knowledge is cultural.

The role of individual differences
Vygotsky did not take much account of individual differences in children's learning.

Baillargeon's explanation of infant abilities

Very young babies have a well-developed understanding of the physical world.

Baillargeon's explanation

Early research
Piaget proposed children understood object permanence from around 8 months.
The violation of expectation method was developed as a more valid procedure.

VOE research
Infant attention to physically possible and impossible events is compared.
E.g. Baillargeon and Graber showed short and tall rabbit passing behind a window.

Baillargeon's theory
Infants born with a physical reasoning system (PRS), which becomes more sophisticated with experience.

Evaluation

A better test of understanding than Piaget's
Lack of object permanence may be because infant has lost interest, VOE eliminates this confounding variable.

Hard to judge infant understanding
Cannot directly tell what an infant understands but have to infer it from their behaviour. The fact that infants attend for longer to impossible events does not prove they understand the events are impossible.

PRS explains why physical understanding is universal
Children all appear to have some understanding of the physical world regardless of their experiences, which makes sense if this understanding is the product of an innate system.

Behavioural response not the same as understanding
A behaviour like sustained attention may be a response to an impossible event without there being any conscious understanding of its impossibility.

PRS is consistent with what we know of other infant abilities
Pei *et al.*: There is some innate distance perception but this increases in sophistication with age.

Social cognition

Selman's levels of perspective-taking

Mental processes underlying social interaction.

Selman's levels of perspective-taking

Perspective-taking research
Selman used scenarios to test role-taking abilities.
Procedure: 60 children of various ages asked to imagine how different people feel in a situation.
Findings: Clear developmental sequence.

Selman's stages of development
· Socially egocentric.
· Social information role-taking.
· Self-reflective role-taking.
· Mutual role-taking.
· Social system role-taking.

Later developments
Selman added two further dimensions:
1. Interpersonal negotiation, i.e. strategies for managing complex social situations.
2. Awareness of personal meaning to relationships, i.e. awareness of how situations can have different personal significance according to the relationships with others involved.

Evaluation

Evidence that perspective-taking gets better with age
Both cross-sectional (Selman) and longitudinal (Gurucharri and Selman) studies support Selman's idea that perspective-taking gets more advanced with age.

Mixed evidence for the importance of perspective-taking
Buijzen and Valkenburg found a negative correlation between age, perspective-taking and coercive behaviour (supporting Selman) but Gasser and Keller didn't.

Applications in atypical development
Selman's theory has proved helpful in understanding the development of children with ADHD and those on the autistic spectrum.

Overly cognitive
Selman's theory may be overly cognitive, failing to include higher level explanations, e.g. development of empathy and emotional self-regulation.

Cultural difference in perspective-taking
Wu and Keysar: Chinese outperformed age-matched Americans on perspective-taking, suggesting that it must be due to more than cognitive maturity.

Theory of mind

Understanding of what is going on in the mind of another person.

Theory of mind (ToM)

Intentional reasoning in toddlers
Meltzoff demonstrated that even children of 18 months have some understanding of intention, i.e. basic ToM.

False belief tasks
Wimmer and Perner: From around age 4 children can cope with tasks requiring an understanding of false beliefs.

Sally-Anne studies
A false belief task requiring an understanding that Sally will look in the wrong place for a marble because she does not know that Anne has moved it.
Baron-Cohen *et al.* found ToM rare in ASD children.

Testing older children and adults
Baron-Cohen *et al.* used the Eyes Task to demonstrate that adults also had ToM deficits.

Evaluation

Low validity of false belief tasks
False belief tasks may test memory as well as ToM.
Bloom and German found that children with ToM can struggle with false belief tasks.

Hard to distinguish ToM from perspective-taking
Most of the research into ToM could equally be measuring perspective-taking.

Partial explanation for ASD
Although ASD is associated with ToM problems, it may not be the cause of ASD. There are additional aspects of ASD not explicable by ToM deficit.

No clear understanding of how ToM develops
Perner suggests it is the result of individual construction of understanding, whereas Astington suggests it develops through social interaction.

Critique of the Eyes Task
The Eyes Task lacks validity because we never look at static eyes in real-life situations.

The mirror neuron system

Brain cells underlying empathy, understanding intention and perspective-taking.

The role of mirror neurons

Mirror neurons and intention
Mirror neurons in the motor cortex may allow us to simulate actions of others and so help us understand their intentions.

Mirror neurons and perspective-taking
The same ability to simulate others' actions may help us to take their perspective.

Mirror neurons and human evolution
Ramachandran suggests that mirror neurons have shaped the direction of human evolution by allowing us to live in large complex groups with roles and rules.

Mirror neurons and ASD
It has been suggested that ASD is the result of a poor mirror neuron system.

Evaluation

Evidence for the role of mirror neurons
Studies show that areas of the brain believed to be rich in mirror neurons activate in tasks of social cognition.

Difficulty in studying mirror neurons in humans
Current techniques for studying brain activity do not measure activity at the cellular level so we cannot see individual mirror neurons in action.

Mixed evidence for mirror neurons and ASD
Some evidence for abnormal brain structure and function people with ASD (e.g. Hadjikhani), but findings have not been replicated consistently.

Questions over the existence of mirror neurons
Can't identify individual cells, mirror neurons may just be ordinary motor neurons (Hickok).

Questions over the precise role of mirror neurons
Even if motor neurons exist, their precise role may not be to help with social cognition (Hickok).

PRACTICE QUESTIONS, ANSWERS AND FEEDBACK

Question 1 A psychologist who was interested in the work of Piaget selected two groups of children, aged 5 and aged 10, for an experiment. Each child was presented individually with two identical balls of clay. The psychologist then rolled one of the balls into a sausage shape. Each child was asked to say whether the amount of clay in each piece was 'the same' or whether 'one had more'.

Which cognitive ability is being tested in the experiment above? *(1 mark)*

Morticia's answer This is an example of a conservation experiment where children are tested to see if they realise the quantity doesn't change despite its appearance changing.	A good, clear answer which actually doesn't require the definition Morticia supplies.
Luke's answer The ability to conserve.	Straight to the point and accurate from Luke!
Vladimir's answer The children's cognitive ability is being tested here to see what children can do at different ages. Older children become capable of more abstract thinking and don't get confused by the shape of the clay objects. They understand the logical principles.	Vladimir has misunderstood the nature of the study in the stem here and has therefore not answered the question.

Question 2 The psychologist found that there was a difference in the cognitive ability of the 5-year-olds and the 10-year-olds in the experiment described above.

Identify and explain one other difference in cognitive ability between 5-year-olds and 10-year-olds that Piaget identified. *(3 marks)*

Morticia's answer Piaget also looked at egocentricity. This is the fact that young children see the world from their own point of view.	Morticia has identified the difference but only done a little bit more as she has not explained how older children see the world differently.
Luke's answer Egocentricity changes with age, as in the three mountains study. Children were asked to identify the view of three mountains from the perspective of a doll. Young children selected a view that was actually what they saw, but older children could imagine how it would be from a different position – therefore they were no longer egocentric.	Although not required by the question, Luke has used evidence effectively to illustrate the difference between the age groups.
Vladimir's answer Children who are older can understand conservation. This is a difference in cognitive ability. They can keep quantities constant and know that they wouldn't change	Unfortunately, this is the cognitive ability Vladimir should have focused on in question 1. Even allowing for that his explanation of conservation is weak.

Question 3 Outline Vygotsky's theory of cognitive development. *(4 marks)*

Morticia's answer Vygotsky wrote a theory about cognitive development about the same time as Piaget but because they lived in different countries they didn't know about each other. The central point in Vygotsky's theory was that thinking develops because of social influences. It is the input from other people especially experts that helps children to develop their thinking. An expert is just anyone who knows more so it could be peers as well as parents and teachers.	The first part of Morticia's answer does not really reveal anything about Vygotsky's theory. The rest of the response focuses on just one key aspect – social influences.
Luke's answer One of Vygotsky's key concepts was the zone of proximal development (ZPD). At any time there is a gap between a child's current level of development, i.e. what they can understand and do alone, and what they can potentially understand after interaction with more expert others. The assistance of experts enables a child to cross the ZPD. Experts do this using scaffolding. They provide assistance such as engaging interest, focusing a child on task, highlighting key things to pay attention to and demonstrating what to do. In this way a child is assisted in doing things that are challenging and cognitive development takes place.	Luke provides an accurate and detailed summary of Vygotsky's theory which includes appropriate terminology.
Vladimir's answer Vygotsky's theory was about helping learners to do things they couldn't do. Piaget was much more focused on the individual learning for themselves whereas Vygotsky saw the child being taught by others especially through the process of scaffolding. Scaffolding is a process like giving someone a scaffold to climb on, it gives them some structure to help them do things that are quite hard. Vygotsky's theory was influenced by the fact that he was Russian and believed in communism so he this meant that he saw the value of people all working together to develop. His work has led to lots of educational applications such as peer tutoring.	Vladimir's response is not quite as articulate and well-expressed as Luke's – though there is lots of good content and understanding. Unlike Luke, Vladimir does not identify the ZPD but does understand the concept and has accurately described scaffolding and peer tutoring.

On this spread we look at some typical student answers to questions. The comments provided indicate what is good and bad in each answer. Learning how to produce effective question answers is a SKILL. Read pages 387–397 for guidance.

Question 4 Describe and evaluate research into theory of mind. *(16 marks)*

Luke's answer

Theory of mind refers to the idea that each of us can form a theory of what is in other people's minds. This is an important part of social development. Meltzoff demonstrated that even children of 18 months have some understanding of intention, which is basic ToM. Wimmer and Perner used the story of Maxi to test children and found that, from around age 4 children can cope with tasks requiring an understanding of false beliefs.

Baron-Cohen et al. proposed that a lack of ToM might explain autism and used the Sally-Anne task to show that ToM is rare in children on the autistic spectrum. Baron-Cohen et al. further developed the Eyes Task to demonstrate that adults also had ToM deficits. The Eyes Task was used because the Sally-Anne test was too easy for adults but the Eyes Task shows that adults continue to have difficulties.

The tests used to assess ToM and false beliefs have been criticised so we may not be able to rely on these findings. First of all Bloom and German suggest that the reason children fail the false belief tasks is not because they lack ToM but because the tasks require a lot to be remembered, so it may be memory rather than ToM that explains successful performance.

Bloom and German also suggest that children with ToM may still struggle with false belief tasks so that this way of assessing ToM may be flawed. This is a big problem for the research because that's the main way that ToM is tested so research may not be assessing ToM at all.

The Eyes Task has also been accused of lacking validity because it involves the use of static eyes but people don't read emotions from motionless eyes in real life situations. So the Eyes Task is really not testing anything meaningful.

A further issue is that it is difficult to distinguish ToM from perspective-taking. Perspective-taking is a lower level ability where you are simply seeing the world as if standing where someone else is and this is not the same as understanding thoughts and emotions, it could be that the tests of ToM are simply assessing perspective-taking.

The assumption that a lack of ToM might explain autism is not justified as the research, at best, just shows that the two may be associated. It is quite different to suggest that lack of ToM is the cause. It could be an effect.

(400 words)

The first sentence of Luke's answer is rather like common sense but the rest of the paragraph is well informed and includes some concise use of evidence (though it may have been helpful to explain the concept of 'false belief').

In paragraph 2 there are again references to relevant evidence but precious little detail in terms of procedure and findings. The Sally-Anne task and the Eyes Task could be described in more depth.

A relevant evaluation point in this paragraph that is well expanded.

Again, relevant critique.

Good point again here.

In these essays the term 'research' can equally refer to the theory or relevant studies so this is good commentary.

An unusual essay insofar as the evaluation/discussion is better than the description. The response would have been improved with more basic detail on the theory and associated studies. Some explanation of what theory of mind is would be helpful.

Vladimir's answer

Theory of mind has been used to study autistic behaviour. These are people who find social relationships difficult and it might be because they lack a theory of mind. The Sally-Anne test is used to test this ability. You have two dolls called Sally and Anne. Sally has a ball that she puts in her basket and then she leaves the room. While she is gone, Anne moves the ball to a box. So the child who is watching knows the ball is really in the box and not the basket. The question is, when Sally returns where will she look? If she has a theory of mind she should look in the basket but a child without a theory of mind will say in the box because they think everyone will know what they know. When autistic children are tested, they generally fail the test. This might explain why they find social relationships difficult – because they can't understand what people are thinking and this makes it hard for them to interact. I know a child who is autistic and this is similar to his behaviour. He finds it difficult to talk to other people or understand.

Another study tested theory of mind using pictures of eyes. People had to say what emotion was being expressed by the eyes. This requires a kind of mind reading. Again autistic children found this difficult. The test was also used with autistic adults who didn't do well either.

This research is useful because it tells us about what might be causing autism. It could help people with autism because maybe this is a skill they could practise. They could be taught to understand what people were thinking. If they could learn to have a theory of mind maybe they would find social relationships easier.

The problems with this research are that it is difficult to test children with autism because they don't understand what they are being asked to do. Another problem is that it might not be ethical to test children with disabilities. It might upset them. The theory is reductionist because it reduces autism to one thing whereas it is more complex than that.

Theory of mind is also studied in normal children using similar tests and other tests as well. They usually develop theory of mind around the age of 2 or 3. That helps their social development because they can understand others.

(399 words)

Almost the opposite problem to Luke's answer here: Vladimir has overdone the description of the Sally-Anne study. More focus on the details of the theory would have been a better strategy.

The study is used effectively with the link to social difficulties but the anecdotal reference does not add anything to the answer.

This point is a somewhat vague and would benefit from some reference to evidence.

Paragraph 3 is reasonably well-explained though the link to the theory could have been made more explicit.

Again, a rather vague paragraph. The final point related to 'reductionism' is speculative and suggests Vladimir has run out of things to say!

Overall, this response focuses slightly too much on description rather than evaluation.

MULTIPLE-CHOICE QUESTIONS

Piaget's theory of cognitive development

1. The major force underlying learning in Piaget's theory is . . .
(a) Disequilibrium.
(b) Reinforcement.
(c) Modelling.
(d) Culture.

2. A schema is best described as . . .
(a) A stage of development.
(b) A way to overcome disequilibrium.
(c) A unit of knowledge.
(d) An area of the brain.

3. Which of the following educational strategies is a direct result of Piaget's theory?
(a) Emphasis on language and literacy.
(b) Discovery learning.
(c) Co-operative group work.
(d) Use of the cane.

4. Which of the following terms best describes learning that involves radical change to schemas?
(a) Assimilation.
(b) Disequilibrium.
(c) Equilibration.
(d) Accommodation.

5. Which of the following is a valid criticism of Piaget's theory?
(a) It has no practical applications.
(b) It does not take full account of the role of other people.
(c) There is no evidence for discovery learning.
(d) There is no evidence for the formation of individual mental representations.

Piaget's stages of intellectual development

1. At what approximate age did Piaget believe children acquired object permanence?
(a) 3 months.
(b) 8 months.
(c) 18 months.
(d) 24 months.

2. Which of the following refers to the child's tendency to see the world only from their own perspective?
(a) Egocentrism.
(b) Conservation.
(c) Class inclusion.
(d) Object permanence.

3. Which of the following refers to the child's developing ability to understand quantity?
(a) Egocentrism.
(b) Conservation.
(c) Class inclusion.
(d) Object permanence.

4. Which of the following only becomes true at Piaget's stage of formal operations?
(a) Children become capable of conservation for the first time.
(b) Egocentrism begins to decline.
(c) Children become capable of scientific reasoning.
(d) Children become capable of class inclusion.

5. Which of the following is *not* a valid criticism of Piaget's theory?
(a) There is no evidence for the development of formal reasoning in adolescence.
(b) Piaget's questioning techniques, for example in assessing conservation, have been criticised.
(c) Piaget underestimated the abilities of younger children and overestimated those of adolescents.
(d) Piaget's conclusions about class inclusion have been questioned.

Vygotsky's theory of cognitive development

1. Vygotsky emphasised the role of which of the following in development?
(a) Disequilibrium.
(b) Maturation.
(c) Interaction.
(d) Punishment.

2. According to Vygotsky mental tools are . . .
(a) Present at birth.
(b) Acquired through the medium of culture.
(c) Learned through imitation.
(d) Acquired through discovery play.

3. What term best describes the process in which adults help a child's learning?
(a) Scaffolding.
(b) Laddering.
(c) Zoning.
(d) Bricking.

4. Which of the following educational techniques is closely linked to Vygotsky's theory?
(a) Discovery learning.
(b) Peer tutoring.
(c) Use of the cane.
(d) Coursework.

5. Which of the following examples of scaffolding represents the highest level (greatest amount) of help?
(a) General prompts.
(b) Indication of materials.
(c) Demonstration.
(d) Specific instructions.

Baillargeon's explanation of infant abilities

1. Which of Piaget's major ideas did Baillargeon particularly challenge?
(a) Egocentrism.
(b) Object permanence.
(c) Class inclusion.
(d) Formal reasoning.

2. Baillargeon's physical reasoning system is best described as . . .
(a) Fully developed at birth.
(b) Non-existent at birth and learned through experience.
(c) Present at birth but refined through experience.
(d) Not present at birth but acquired through maturation.

3. In Baillargeon's VOE research . . .
(a) Infants looked for longer at possible events.
(b) Infants looked for an equal time at possible and impossible events.
(c) Infants looked for longer at impossible events.
(d) Infants did not look at all at impossible events.

4. Which of the following is an example of violation of expectation?
(a) A short object passing behind a screen does not appear at a window.
(b) A tall object passing behind a screen does not appear at a window.
(c) An unsupported object falls to the floor.
(d) An object is placed in a container and is there when it is opened.

5. Which of the following is a valid criticism of Baillargeon's theory?
(a) It is hard to judge what young children are thinking.
(b) Baillargeon cannot explain why physical understanding is universal.
(c) Baillargeon's tests for infant reasoning are less valid than Piaget's.
(d) The PRS is not consistent with what we know about other infant abilities.

Social cognition: Selman's levels of perspective-taking

1. Perspective-taking is most closely related to which of Piaget's research topics?
(a) Conservation.
(b) Egocentrism.
(c) Object permanence.
(d) Class inclusion.

2. At which of Selman's stages do children first take the perspective of another?
(a) Socially egocentric.
(b) Social information role-taking.
(c) Self-reflective role-taking.
(d) Mutual role-taking.

3. Which of the following is *not* a Selman dimension of psychosocial maturity?
(a) Social reasoning.
(b) Interpersonal negotiation.
(c) Awareness of personal meanings.
(d) Theory of mind.

4. A legitimate criticism of Selman's theory is . . .
(a) Overly cognitive.
(b) Lack of evidence for developing perspective-taking.
(c) Lack of reliability in the VOE method.
(d) Lack of practical applications.

5. Which of the following children are likely to have problems with perspective-taking?
(a) Children with a diagnosis of ADHD.
(b) Children on the autistic spectrum.
(c) Children under the age of six years.
(d) All of the above.

Social cognition: Theory of mind

1. A research technique used to study theory of mind in children aged 18 months is . . .
(a) False belief tasks.
(b) Intentional reasoning tasks.
(c) The Eyes Task.
(d) The three mountains task.

2. At what age did Wimmer and Perner find most children could succeed in their false belief task?
(a) 2 years.
(b) 3 years.
(c) 4 years.
(d) 5 years.

3. What percentage of children in the autistic group succeeded in Baron-Cohen *et al.*'s Sally–Anne task?
(a) 20%
(b) 50%
(c) 80%
(d) 85%

4. In which of the following abilities do people on the autistic spectrum outperform neurotypicals?
(a) Theory of mind.
(b) Perspective-taking.
(c) Social imagination.
(d) Visual attention.

5. At the end of the Sally–Anne task . . .
(a) Only Sally knows where the marble is.
(b) Only Anne knows where the marble is.
(c) They both know where the marble is.
(d) Neither of them know where the marble is.

Social cognition: The mirror neuron system

1. Mirror neurons are believed to be what type of cell?
(a) Glial cells.
(b) Motor neurons.
(c) Sensory neurons.
(d) Interneurons.

2. Which symptoms of autism might be explained by a 'faulty' mirror neuron system?
(a) Weak theory of mind.
(b) Highly developed systematic reasoning.
(c) Superior visual attention.
(d) Reliance on routine.

3. Which of the following do mirror neurons appear to be involved in?
(a) Imitation.
(b) Judging intentions.
(c) Perspective-taking.
(d) All of the above.

4. What method did Haker *et al.* use to study mirror neuron activity?
(a) Autopsy.
(b) EEG.
(c) fMRI.
(d) Deep brain stimulation.

5. Mirror neurons have been used to explain . . .
(a) Well-coordinated motor skills.
(b) Contagious yawning.
(c) Artistic abilities.
(d) Sneezing.

MCQ answers

Piaget's theory of cognitive development 1a, 2c, 3b, 4d, 5b
Piaget's stages of intellectual development 1b, 2a, 3b, 4c, 5a
Vygotsky's theory of cognitive development 1c, 2b, 3a, 4b, 5c
Baillargeon's explanation of infant learning 1b, 2c, 3c, 4b, 5a
Social cognition: Selman's levels of perspective taking 1b, 2b, 3d, 4a, 5d
Social cognition: Theory of mind 1b, 2c, 3a, 4d, 5b
Social cognition: The mirror neuron system 1b, 2a, 3d, 4c, 5b

CHAPTER 8
SCHIZOPHRENIA

Chapter contents

From *The Voice*, by Sarah Teasdale

The living thoughts in me
Spring from dead men and women,
Forgotten time out of mind
And many as bubbles of foam.

Here for a moment's space
Into the light out of darkness,
I come and they come with me
Finding words with my breath.

Schizophrenia

Classification of schizophrenia. Positive symptoms of schizophrenia, including hallucinations and delusions. Negative symptoms of schizophrenia, including speech poverty and avolition.

Reliability and validity in diagnosis and classification of schizophrenia, including reference to co-morbidity, culture and gender bias and symptom overlap.

This spread is concerned with the symptoms and diagnosis of schizophrenia. There are many issues surrounding the diagnosis of schizophrenia, including its reliability and validity.

KEY TERMS

Schizophrenia – A severe mental illness where contact with reality and insight are impaired, an example of psychosis.

Classification of mental disorder – The process of organising symptoms into categories based on which symptoms cluster together in sufferers.

Positive symptoms of schizophrenia – Atypical symptoms experienced *in addition* to normal experiences. They include hallucinations and delusions.

Hallucinations – A positive symptom of schizophrenia. They are sensory experiences of stimuli that have either no basis in reality or are distorted perceptions of things that are there.

Delusions – A positive symptom of schizophrenia. They involve beliefs that have no basis in reality, for example, that the sufferer is someone else or that they are the victim of a conspiracy.

Negative symptoms of schizophrenia – Atypical experiences that represent the *loss* of a usual experience such as clear thinking or 'normal' levels of motivation.

Speech poverty – A negative symptom of schizophrenia. It involves reduced frequency and quality of speech.

Avolition – A negative symptom of schizophrenia. It involves loss of motivation to carry out tasks and results in lowered activity levels.

Co-morbidity – The occurrence of two illnesses or conditions together, for example a person has both schizophrenia and a personality disorder. Where two conditions are frequently diagnosed together it calls into question the validity of classifying the two disorders separately.

Symptom overlap – Occurs when two or more conditions share symptoms. Where conditions share many symptoms this calls into question the validity of classifying the two disorders separately.

Auditory hallucinations can be distracting and make it difficult to focus on other tasks requiring an auditory channel like speaking on a phone.

Diagnosis and classification of schizophrenia

Schizophrenia is a serious mental disorder suffered by about 1% of the world population. It is more commonly diagnosed in men than women, more commonly diagnosed in cities than the countryside and in working-class rather than middle-class people. The symptoms of schizophrenia can interfere severely with everyday tasks, so that many sufferers end up homeless or hospitalised.

Classification of schizophrenia

Schizophrenia does not have a single defining characteristic. It is a cluster of symptoms some of which appear to be unrelated. The two major systems for the **classification of mental disorder**, are the World Health Organisation's *International Classification of Disease* edition 10 (**ICD-10**) and the American Psychiatric Association's *Diagnostic and Statistical Manual* edition 5 (**DSM-5**, sometimes written as DSM-V). These differ slightly in their classification of schizophrenia. For example, in the DSM-5 system one of the so-called **positive symptoms** – **delusions**, **hallucinations** or speech disorganisation – must be present for diagnosis whereas two or more **negative symptoms** are sufficient under ICD.

ICD-10 recognises a range of subtypes of schizophrenia. *Paranoid schizophrenia* is characterised by powerful delusions and hallucinations but relatively few other symptoms. *Hebephrenic schizophrenia,* on the other hand, involves primarily negative symptoms. The defining characteristic of *catatonic schizophrenia* is disturbance to movement, leaving the sufferer immobile or alternatively overactive. Previous editions of the DSM system also recognised subtypes of schizophrenia but this has been dropped in DSM-5.

Positive symptoms

Positive symptoms of schizophrenia are additional experiences beyond those of ordinary existence. They include hallucinations and delusions.

Hallucinations These are unusual sensory experiences. Some hallucinations are related to events in the environment whereas others bear no relationship to what the senses are picking up from the environment, for example, voices heard either talking to or commenting on the sufferer, often criticising them. Hallucinations can be experienced in relation to any sense. The sufferer may, for example, see distorted facial expressions or occasionally people or animals that are not there.

Delusions Also known as paranoia, delusions are irrational beliefs. These can take a range of forms. Common delusions involve being an important historical, political or religious figure, such as Jesus or Napoleon. Delusions also commonly involve being persecuted, perhaps by government or aliens or of having superpowers. Another class of delusions concerns the body. Sufferers may believe that they or part of them is under external control. Delusions can make a sufferer of schizophrenia behave in ways that make sense to them but seem bizarre to others. Although the vast majority of sufferers are not aggressive and are in fact more likely to be victims than perpetrators of violence, some delusions can lead to aggression.

Negative symptoms

Negative symptoms of schizophrenia involve the loss of usual abilities and experiences. Examples include **avolition** and **speech poverty**.

Avolition Sometimes called 'apathy', can be described as finding it difficult to begin or keep up with goal-directed activity, i.e. actions performed in order to achieve a result. Sufferers of schizophrenia often have sharply reduced motivation to carry out a range of activities. Andreason (1982) identified three identifying signs of avolition; poor hygiene and grooming, lack of persistence in work or education and lack of energy.

Speech poverty Schizophrenia is characterised by changes in patterns of speech. The ICD-10 recognises speech poverty as a negative symptom. This is because the emphasis is on reduction in the amount and quality of speech in schizophrenia. This is sometimes accompanied by a delay in the sufferer's verbal responses during conversation.

Nowadays, however, the DSM system places its emphasis on speech *disorganisation* in which speech becomes incoherent or the speaker changes topic mid-sentence. This is classified in DSM-5 as a positive symptom of schizophrenia, whilst speech poverty remains as a negative symptom.

Evaluation

Reliability

Reliability means consistency. An important measure of reliability is **inter-rater reliability**, the extent to which different assessors agree on their assessments. In the case of diagnosis this means the extent to which two or more mental health professionals arrive at the same diagnosis for the same patients. Elie Cheniaux *et al.* (2009) had two psychiatrists independently diagnose 100 patients using both DSM and ICD criteria. Inter-rater reliability was poor, with one psychiatrist diagnosing 26 with schizophrenia according to DSM and 44 according to ICD, and the other diagnosing 13 according to DSM and 24 according to ICD. This poor reliability is a weakness of diagnosis of schizophrenia.

Validity

Validity is the extent to which we are measuring what we are intending to measure. In the case of a mental disorder like schizophrenia there are a number of validity issues to consider. One standard way to assess validity of a diagnosis is **criterion validity**; do different assessment systems arrive at the same diagnosis for the same patient? Looking at the figures in the Cheniaux *et al.* study above we can see that schizophrenia is much more likely to be diagnosed using ICD than DSM. This suggests that schizophrenia is either over-diagnosed in ICD or under-diagnosed in DSM. Either way, this is poor validity – a weakness of diagnosis.

Co-morbidity

'Morbidity' refers to a medical condition or how common it is (hence we talk about morbidity rates). **Co-morbidity** is the phenomenon that two or more conditions occur together – hence we speak of co-morbidity rates. If conditions occur together a lot of the time then this calls into question the validity of their diagnosis and classification because they might actually be a single condition. Schizophrenia is commonly diagnosed with other conditions. In one review Peter Buckley *et al.* (2009) concluded that around half of patients with a diagnosis of schizophrenia also have a diagnosis of **depression** (50%) or substance abuse (47%). **Post-traumatic stress disorder** also occurred in 29% of cases and OCD in 23%. This poses a challenge for both classification and diagnosis of schizophrenia. In terms of diagnosis, if half the schizophrenia patients are also diagnosed with depression, maybe we are just quite bad at telling the difference between the two conditions. In terms of classification, it may be that, if very severe depression looks a lot like schizophrenia and vice versa, then they might be better seen as a single condition. This confusing picture is a weakness of diagnosis and classification.

Symptom overlap

There is considerable **overlap** between the **symptoms** of schizophrenia and other conditions. For example, both schizophrenia and **bipolar disorder** involve positive symptoms like delusions and negative symptoms like avolition. This again calls into question the validity of both the classification and diagnosis of schizophrenia.

Under ICD a patient might be diagnosed as a schizophrenic; however, many of the same patients would receive a diagnosis of bipolar disorder according to DSM criteria. This is unsurprising given the overlap of symptoms. It even suggests that schizophrenia and bipolar disorder may not be two different conditions but one.

Evaluation eXtra

Gender bias in diagnosis

Julia Longenecker *et al.* (2010) reviewed studies of the prevalence of schizophrenia and concluded that since the 1980s men have been diagnosed with schizophrenia rather more often than women (prior to this there appears to have been no difference).

This may simply be because men are more **genetically** vulnerable to developing schizophrenia than women. However, another possible explanation is **gender bias** in the diagnosis of schizophrenia. It appears that female patients typically function better than men, being more likely to work and have good family relationships (Cotton *et al.* 2009). This high functioning may explain why some women have not been diagnosed with schizophrenia where men with similar symptoms might have been; their better interpersonal functioning may bias practitioners to under-diagnose schizophrenia, either because symptoms are masked altogether by good interpersonal functioning, or because the quality of interpersonal functioning makes the case seem too mild to warrant a diagnosis.

Consider: *What does possible under-diagnosis of schizophrenia in women suggest about the validity of the diagnosis?*

Cultural bias in diagnosis

African Americans and English people of Afro-Caribbean origin are several times more likely than white people to be diagnosed with schizophrenia. Given that rates in Africa and the West Indies are not particularly high, this is almost certainly *not* due to genetic vulnerability. Instead diagnosis seems to be beset with issues of **culture bias**.

There may be several factors at work here. One issue is that positive symptoms such as hearing voices may be more acceptable in African cultures because of cultural beliefs in communication with ancestors, and thus people are more ready to acknowledge such experiences. When reported to a psychiatrist from a different cultural tradition these experiences are likely to be seen as bizarre and irrational. In addition, Javier Escobar (2012) has pointed out that (overwhelmingly white) psychiatrists may tend to over-interpret symptoms and distrust the honesty of black people during diagnosis.

Consider: *What does the over-diagnosis of schizophrenia in Black British and Americans suggest about the validity of the diagnosis?*

Practical activity on page 214

Apply it
Concepts: Agwe's story

Jamaican-born Agwe has been referred to a psychiatrist because he has told people that he has recently heard his dead grandfather talking to him.

Questions

1. With reference to the terms 'positive symptoms' and 'hallucinations' explain why Agwe might receive a diagnosis of schizophrenia.
2. How might issues of culture bias affect this potential diagnosis?

Artist Louis Wain reportedly captured the visual distortions of his descent into schizophrenia in these pictures of a cat.

Apply it
Methods: Buckley *et al.*

According to Buckley *et al.*, 50% of patients with a diagnosis of schizophrenia also have depression, whilst 47% have one of substance abuse. For PTSD the figure is 29% and for OCD it is 23%.

Questions

1. Estimate how many people from a sample of 1637 patients with a diagnosis of schizophrenia also have OCD. *(1 mark)*
2. What is the ratio of patients with co-morbid OCD to those with co-morbid substance abuse? *(2 marks)*

CHECK IT

1. Explain what is meant by the *positive symptoms of schizophrenia*. [4 marks]
2. Explain the term *avolition*. [2 marks]
3. Explain the issues of culture bias and gender bias in the diagnosis of schizophrenia. [8 marks]
4. Describe and evaluate the classification and diagnosis of schizophrenia. [16 marks]

> Biological explanations for schizophrenia: genetics, the dopamine hypothesis and neural correlates

Most modern mental health professionals believe that schizophrenia is at least partly biological in origin. This spread is concerned with genetic vulnerability to schizophrenia, the possible role of the neurotransmitter dopamine and the neural correlates of schizophrenia. These three explanations are inter-related because, if schizophrenic is genetic, then those genes lead to biological differences such as abnormal levels of dopamine and/or abnormal structure of the brain (neural correlates).

KEY TERMS

Genetics – Genes consist of DNA strands. DNA produces 'instructions' for general physical features of an organism (such as eye colour, height) and also specific physical features (such as neurotransmitter levels and size of brain structures). These may impact on psychological features (such as intelligence and mental disorder). Genes are transmitted from parents to offspring, i.e. inherited.

Dopamine – A neurotransmitter that generally has an excitatory effect and is associated with the sensation of pleasure. Unusually high levels are associated with schizophrenia and unusually low levels are associated with Parkinson's disease.

Neural correlates – Patterns of structure or activity in the brain that occur in conjunction with an experience and may be implicated in the origins of that experience.

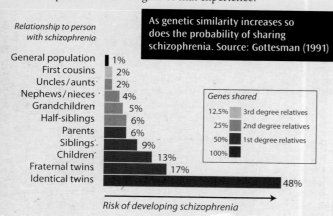

Relationship to person with schizophrenia

As genetic similarity increases so does the probability of sharing schizophrenia. Source: Gottesman (1991)

Relationship	Risk
General population	1%
First cousins	2%
Uncles/aunts	2%
Nephews/nieces	4%
Grandchildren	5%
Half-siblings	6%
Parents	6%
Siblings	9%
Children	13%
Fraternal twins	17%
Identical twins	48%

Risk of developing schizophrenia

Genes shared	
12.5%	3rd degree relatives
25%	2nd degree relatives
50%	1st degree relatives
100%	

Apply it — Concepts: Gene's genes

Gene and his partner Kary are considering having children. However, Gene is concerned that, as his own father has suffered severely with schizophrenia for many years, he may pass on 'the gene' for schizophrenia to his own children. Gene and Kary attend genetic counselling in order to learn about the risks of their children developing schizophrenia.

Questions

1. What is the probability of Gene and Kary's child developing schizophrenia?

2. What might the genetic counsellor tell them about their understanding of 'the gene' for schizophrenia?

Biological explanations

The genetic basis of schizophrenia

Schizophrenia runs in families It has been noted for many years that **schizophrenia** runs in families. This is quite weak evidence in itself for a **genetic** link because family members tend to share aspects of their environment as well as many of their genes. However, there have been systematic investigations of the extent to which greater genetic similarity between family members is associated with the likelihood of both developing schizophrenia. For example, we share 100% of our genes with an identical twin, 50% with a sibling or parent and so on. There is a strong relationship between the degree of genetic similarity and shared risk of schizophrenia. This is shown in the graph below left, which presents the findings from Irving Gottesman's (1991) large-scale family study.

Candidate genes Individual genes are believed to be associated with risk of inheritance. Because a number of genes each appear to confer a small increased risk of schizophrenia it appears that schizophrenia is polygenic, i.e. it requires a number of factors to work in combination. Because different studies have identified different candidate genes it also appears that schizophrenia is aetiologically heterogeneous, i.e. *different* combinations of factors can lead to the condition. Stephen Ripke *et al.* (2014) carried out a huge study combining all previous data from **genome**-wide studies (i.e. those looking at the whole human genome as opposed to particular genes) of schizophrenia. The genetic make-up of 37,000 patients was compared to that of 113,000 controls; 108 separate genetic variations were associated with increased risk of schizophrenia. Genes associated with increased risk included those coding for the functioning of a number of **neurotransmitters** including **dopamine**.

The dopamine hypothesis

Neurotransmitters The brain's chemical messengers appear to work differently in the brain of a patient with schizophrenia. In particular dopamine (or DA) is widely believed to be involved. Dopamine is important in the functioning of several brain systems that may be implicated in the symptoms of schizophrenia.

Hyperdopaminergia in the subcortex The original version of the dopamine hypothesis focused on the possible role of high levels or activity of dopamine (*hyper*dopaminergia) in the **subcortex**, i.e. the central areas of the brain. For example, an excess of dopamine receptors in **Broca's area** (which is responsible for speech production) may be associated with poverty of speech and/or the experience of auditory hallucinations.

Hypodopaminergia in the cortex More recent versions of the dopamine hypothesis have focused instead on abnormal dopamine systems in the brain's **cortex**. Goldman-Rakic *et al.* (2004) have identified a role for low levels of dopamine (*hypo*dopaminergia) in the **prefrontal cortex** (responsible for thinking and decision making) in the negative symptoms of schizophrenia.

It may be that both hyper- and hypodopaminergia are correct explanations – both high and low levels of dopamine in different brain regions are involved in schizophrenia.

Neural correlates of schizophrenia

Neural correlates are measurements of the structure or function of the brain that correlate with an experience, in this case schizophrenia. Both **positive** and **negative symptoms** have neural correlates.

Neural correlates of negative symptoms One negative symptom **avolition** involves the loss of motivation. Motivation involves the anticipation of a reward, and certain regions of the brain, for example, the **ventral striatum**, are believed to be particularly involved in this anticipation. It therefore follows that abnormality of areas like the ventral striatum may be involved in the development of avolition. Juckel *et al.* (2006) have measured activity levels in the ventral striatum in schizophrenia and found lower levels of activity than those observed in controls. Moreover, they observed a **negative correlation** between activity levels in the ventral striatum and the severity of overall negative symptoms. Thus activity in the ventral striatum is a neural correlate of negative symptoms of schizophrenia.

Neural correlates of positive symptoms Positive symptoms also have neural correlates. Allen *et al.* (2007) scanned the brains of patients experiencing auditory **hallucinations** and compared them to a **control group** whilst they identified pre-recorded speech as theirs or others. Lower activation levels in the **superior temporal gyrus** and **anterior cingulate gyrus** were found in the hallucination group, who also made more errors than the control group. We can thus say that reduced activity in these two areas of the brain is a neural correlate of auditory hallucination.

Evaluation

Multiple sources of evidence for genetic susceptibility

There is now very strong evidence for genetic vulnerability to schizophrenia from a variety of sources. The Gottesman (1991) study (facing page) clearly shows how genetic similarity and shared risk of schizophrenia are closely related. **Adoption studies** such as that by Pekka Tienari *et al.* (2004), discussed on page 210, clearly show that children of schizophrenia sufferers are still at heightened risk of schizophrenia if adopted into families with no history of schizophrenia. There is also evidence from studies conducted at the molecular level showing that particular genetic variations significantly increase the risk of schizophrenia (Ripke *et al.* 2014, facing page).

There is thus overwhelming evidence for the idea that genetic factors make some people much more vulnerable to developing schizophrenia than others. This does not of course mean that schizophrenia is entirely genetic. There are a number of factors in the environment associated with risk of schizophrenia, but the available evidence suggests that genetic susceptibility is very important.

Mixed evidence for the dopamine hypothesis

There is support from a number of sources for abnormal dopamine functioning in schizophrenia. Dopamine **agonists** like amphetamines that increase the levels of dopamine make schizophrenia worse and can produce schizophrenia-like symptoms in non-sufferers (Curran *et al.* 2004). **Antipsychotic drugs**, on the other hand, work by reducing dopamine activity (Tauscher *et al.* 2014). Both kinds of drug study suggest an important role for dopamine in schizophrenia. Radioactive labelling studies such as that by Lindstroem *et al.* (1999) have found that chemicals needed to produce dopamine are taken up faster in the brains of schizophrenia sufferers than controls, suggesting that they produce more dopamine.

There is also evidence to suggest that dopamine does not provide a complete explanation for schizophrenia. Some of the genes identified in the Ripke *et al.* study code for the production of other neurotransmitters, so it appears that although dopamine is likely to be one important factor in schizophrenia, so are other neurotransmitters. Much of the attention in current research has shifted to the role of a neurotransmitter called **glutamate** (Moghaddam and Javitt 2012). Evidence for the dopamine hypothesis can perhaps be best described as mixed.

The correlation-causation problem

There are a number of neural correlates of schizophrenia symptoms, including both positive and negative symptoms. Although studies like those on the facing page are useful in flagging up particular brain systems that may not be working normally, this kind of evidence leaves some important questions unanswered. Most importantly, does the unusual activity in a region of the brain *cause* the symptom? Logically there are other possible explanations for the correlation.

Take, for example, the correlation between levels of activity in the ventral striatum and negative symptoms of schizophrenia. It may be that something wrong in the striatum is causing negative symptoms. However, it is just as possible that the negative symptoms themselves mean that less information passes through the striatum, resulting in the reduced activity. A third possibility is that another factor influences both the negative symptoms and the ventral striatum activity. The existence of neural correlates in schizophrenia therefore tells us relatively little in itself.

Evaluation eXtra

The role of mutation

Schizophrenia can take place in the absence of a family history of the disorder. One explanation for this is **mutation** in parental DNA, for example, in paternal sperm cells. This can be caused by radiation, poison or viral infection. Evidence for the role of mutation comes from a study showing a **positive correlation** between paternal age (associated with increased risk of sperm mutation) and risk of schizophrenia, increasing from around 0.7% with fathers under 25 to over 2% in fathers over 50 (Brown *et al.* 2002).

Consider: *Does this link between mutations in paternal sperm and risk of schizophrenia support the importance of genetic factors in the development of schizophrenia? Explain your answer.*

The role of the psychological environment is important but unclear

The evidence supporting the role of biological factors in schizophrenia is overwhelming. However, there is also evidence to suggest an important role for environmental factors, including psychological ones such as family functioning during childhood. After all, the probability of developing schizophrenia even if your identical twin has it is less than 50%. Psychological explanations are further explored on page 206.

Consider: *To what extent should we see schizophrenia as a biological condition?*

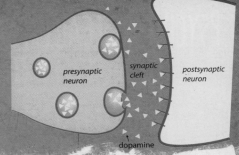

The action of dopamine at a synapse. This appears to be disrupted in schizophrenia.

presynaptic neuron — *synaptic cleft* — *postsynaptic neuron* — dopamine

Apply it — Concepts:

Parkinson's and the dopamine hypothesis

Parkinson's disease is a degenerative condition in which cells in a region of the brain called the *substantia nigra* die, resulting in a reduction in dopamine levels. This in turn affects the brain's ability to control movement. Parkinson's is treated with drugs that help the brain produce more dopamine. However, these drugs worsen the symptoms of schizophrenia.

Questions

1. What does this suggest about the dopamine hypothesis as an explanation for schizophrenia?

2. Now imagine that a new drug for treating Parkinson's also worked by raising dopamine levels only in the cortex, and that this *reduced* the symptoms of schizophrenia. What would this suggest about the dopamine hypothesis?

Apply it — Methods: A correlation

The following graph shows the correlation between avolition and activity in the brain's reward system in schizophrenia (from Simon *et al.* 2015).

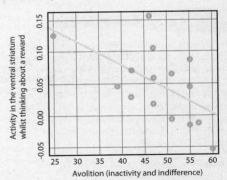

Questions

1. Estimate the **correlation coefficient** shown in the picture. (*2 marks*) (See page 63)

2. Explain what this graph shows. (*2 marks*)

3. What **statistical test** would you use to test the significance of these results? Explain the reasons for your choice. (*3 marks*) (See page 70)

CHECK IT

1. Explain the role of genetics in the development of schizophrenia. [4 marks]

2. Evaluate the role of genetics in the development of schizophrenia. [8 marks]

3. What is meant by *neural correlates*? [2 marks]

4. Outline the dopamine hypothesis. [4 marks]

5. Describe and evaluate biological explanations for schizophrenia. [16 marks]

PSYCHOLOGICAL EXPLANATIONS FOR SCHIZOPHRENIA

Psychological explanations for schizophrenia: family dysfunction and cognitive explanations, including dysfunctional thought processing.

Although there is little doubt that biological processes are important in both the origins and symptoms of schizophrenia, this does not mean that psychological processes are not also important. This spread is concerned with the role of family dysfunction and cognitive explanations in schizophrenia.

KEY TERMS

Family dysfunction – Abnormal processes within a family such as poor family communication, cold parenting and high levels of expressed emotion. These may be risk factors for both the development and maintenance of schizophrenia.

Cognitive explanations – Explanations that focus on mental processes such as thinking, language and attention.

Dysfunctional thought processing – A general term meaning information processing that is not functioning normally and produces undesirable consequences.

Apply it   Concepts: Raj

Raj, a patient with schizophrenia, and his mother are planning for Raj's release from a psychiatric hospital with Raj's psychiatrist. Raj's mother says that she fears that he will not cope living on his own but also that his living with her will require sacrifices on her part. She points to Raj's record of coping without her in the past. The psychiatrist notes that Raj's family functioning appears to be dysfunctional.

Question

In what ways does this interaction suggest that Raj's family functioning is dysfunctional?

The schizophrenogenic mother is cold and rejecting.

Psychological explanations

There are a range of psychological explanations for **schizophrenia**. Some of these have focused on the psychological environment, in particular the family, and its role in making individuals particularly vulnerable to schizophrenia. Others have focused more on the mind of the sufferer and emphasising the role of abnormal cognition in the experience of schizophrenia.

Family dysfunction

Psychologists have attempted to link schizophrenia to childhood and adult experiences of living in a dysfunctional family (**family dysfunction**).

The schizophrenogenic mother Frieda Fromm-Reichmann (1948) proposed a psychodynamic explanation for schizophrenia based on the accounts she heard from her patients about their childhoods. Fromm-Reichm an noted that many of her patients spoke of a particular type of parent, which she called the **schizophrenogenic mother**. 'Schizophrenogenic' literally means 'schizophrenia-causing'. According to Fromm-Reichmann the schizophrenogenic mother is cold, rejecting and controlling, and tends to create a family climate characterised by tension and secrecy. This leads to distrust that later develops into paranoid delusions (i.e. the belief that one is being persecuted by another person), and ultimately schizophrenia.

Double-bind theory Gregory Bateson et al. (1972) agreed that family climate is important in the development of schizophrenia but emphasised the role of communication style within a family. The developing child regularly finds themselves trapped in situations where they fear doing the wrong thing, but receive mixed messages about what this is, and feel unable to comment on the unfairness of this situation or seek clarification. When they 'get it wrong' (which is often) the child is punished by withdrawal of love. This leaves them with an understanding of the world as confusing and dangerous, and this is reflected in symptoms like disorganised thinking and paranoid delusions. Bateson was clear that this was neither the main type of communication in the family of schizophrenia-sufferers nor the only factor in developing schizophrenia, just a risk factor.

Expressed emotion and schizophrenia Expressed emotion (or EE) is the level of emotion, in particular negative emotion, expressed towards a patient by their carers. EE contains several elements:

- Verbal criticism of the patient, occasionally accompanied by violence.
- Hostility towards the patient, including anger and rejection.
- Emotional over-involvement in the life of the patient, including needless self-sacrifice.

These high levels of expressed emotion in carers directed towards the patient are a serious source of stress for the patient. This is primarily an explanation for relapse in patients with schizophrenia. However, it has also been suggested that it may be a source of stress that can trigger the onset of schizophrenia in a person who is already vulnerable, for example, due to their genetic make-up (the **diathesis-stress model** discussed fully on page 212).

Cognitive explanations

A **cognitive explanation** for any phenomenon is one which focuses on the role of mental processes. Schizophrenia is associated with several types of abnormal information processing, and these can provide possible explanations for schizophrenia as a whole.

Schizophrenia is characterised by disruption to normal thought processing. We can see this in many of its symptoms. We have already seen that reduced processing in the **ventral striatum** is associated with negative symptoms, whilst reduced processing of information in the **temporal** and **cingulate gyri** are associated with **hallucinations** (see page 202). This lower than usual level of information processing suggests that cognition is likely to be impaired.

Christopher Frith et al. (1992) identified two kinds of **dysfunctional thought processing** that could underlie some symptoms:

- *Metarepresentation* is the cognitive ability to reflect on thoughts and behaviour. This allows us insight into our own intentions and goals. It also allows us to interpret the actions of others. Dysfunction in metarepresentation would disrupt our ability to recognise our own actions and thoughts as being carried out by ourselves rather than someone else. This would explain hallucinations of voices and delusions like thought insertion (the experience of having thoughts projected into the mind by others).

- *Central control* is the cognitive ability to suppress automatic responses while we perform deliberate actions instead. Disorganised speech and thought disorder could result from the inability to suppress automatic thoughts and speech triggered by other thoughts. For example, sufferers with schizophrenia tend to experience derailment of thoughts and spoken sentences because each word triggers associations, and the patient cannot suppress automatic responses to these.

Evaluation

Practical activity on page 215

Support for family dysfunction as a risk factor

There is evidence to suggest that difficult family relationships in childhood are associated with increased risk of schizophrenia in adulthood. For example, Read *et al.* (2005) reviewed 46 studies of child abuse and schizophrenia and concluded that 69% of adult women in-patients with a diagnosis of schizophrenia had a history of physical abuse, sexual abuse or both in childhood. For men the figure was 59%. Adults with **insecure attachments** to their primary carer are also more likely to have schizophrenia (Berry *et al.* 2008).

There is thus a large body of evidence linking family dysfunction to schizophrenia. However, most of this evidence shares a weakness. Information about childhood experiences was gathered after the development of symptoms, and the schizophrenia may have distorted patients' recall of childhood experiences. This creates a serious problem of **validity**. A much smaller number of studies (e.g. Tienari *et al.*, see page 213) have been carried out prospectively, i.e. they followed up children following childhood experiences to see if the childhood experience predicted any adult characteristics. There *is* prospective evidence linking family dysfunction to schizophrenia but not a huge amount and results have been inconsistent.

Weak evidence for family-based explanations

Although there is plenty of evidence supporting the broad principle that poor childhood experiences in the family are associated with adult schizophrenia, there is almost none to support the importance of the schizophrenogenic mother or double bind. Both these theories are based on clinical observation of patients, and early evidence involved assessing the personality of the mothers of patients for 'crazy-making characteristics' – an approach that makes many modern psychiatrists wince (Harrington 2012).

Another problem with dysfunctional family explanations for schizophrenia is that they have led historically to parent-blaming. Parents, who have already suffered at seeing their child's descent into schizophrenia and who are likely to bear lifelong responsibility for their care, underwent further trauma by receiving the blame for the condition. This is literally adding insult to injury. In fact the shift in the 1980s from hospital to community care, often involving parental care, may be one of the factors leading to the decline of the schizophrenogenic mother and double bind theories – parents no longer tolerated them.

Strong evidence for dysfunctional information processing

There is strong support for the idea that information is processed differently in the mind of the schizophrenia sufferer. In one study Stirling *et al.* (2006) compared 30 patients with a diagnosis of schizophrenia with 18 non-patient **controls** on a range of cognitive tasks including the Stroop Test (see right), in which participants have to name the ink colours of colour words, suppressing the impulse to read the words in order to do this task. In line with Frith's theory of central control dysfunction, patients took over twice as long to name the ink colours as the control group.

Although there is a mass of evidence like this to show that information processing is different in the mind of schizophrenia sufferer, there is a problem with cognitive explanations for schizophrenia. Links between symptoms and faulty cognition are clear; however, this does not tell us anything about the *origins* of those cognitions or of schizophrenia. Cognitive theories can explain the proximal causes of schizophrenia, i.e. what causes current symptoms but not the distal causes, i.e. the origins of the condition.

Evaluation eXtra

Evidence for biological factors is not adequately considered

In their pure forms at least, psychological explanations (particularly family dysfunction) for schizophrenia can be hard to reconcile with the biological explanations we looked at on the previous spread. It could be that both biological and psychological factors can separately produce the same symptoms, which raises the question of whether both outcomes are really schizophrenia. Alternatively, we can view this in terms of the diathesis-stress model where the diathesis may be biological (as discussed on the previous spread) or psychological (as discussed on this spread).

Consider: *Given the strength of evidence for biological factors in schizophrenia, what is the place of psychological explanations?*

Direction of causality

We have a mass of information concerning abnormal cognitions as well as a mass of information about abnormal biology in schizophrenia. However, it remains unclear what causes what, including whether cognitive factors are a cause or are a result of the neural correlates and abnormal neurotransmitter levels seen in schizophrenia.

Consider: *What does this mean for the validity of psychological and biological explanations for schizophrenia?*

Apply it

Concepts: A case of speech poverty

Melanie is having a psychiatric assessment after reporting to her GP that she is hearing voices and believes that someone else is projecting thoughts into her mind. During the interview Melanie finds it hard to keep her attention on what she is saying and frequently her conversation goes off 'on a tangent'. The psychiatrist notes this as 'derailment'.

Question

How might the psychiatrist explain each of these symptoms using the idea of dysfunctional thought processing?

Apply it **Methods: Stirling et al.**

Stirling *et al.* (2006) studied the performance of people with schizophrenia and non-patient groups on the Stroop test. The results were as follows:

Time (s)	Mean	Standard deviation
schizophrenia	123.20	65.52
controls	58.12	11.26

Questions

1. What is meant by **standard deviation**? (*2 marks*)
2. What do the standard deviations in this table of results show? (*2 marks*)
3. Taken together with the **mean**, what do the results tell us? (*2 marks*)
4. Explain *one* strength of using the standard deviation over other **measures of dispersion**. (*2 marks*)

Sufferers of schizophrenia typically struggle with the Stroop task where you are required to name the colour that the word is written in (see text), suggesting difficulty in suppressing automatic processing.

RED	YELLOW	**GREEN**
ORANGE	BLUE	**GREEN**
YELLOW	BLUE	**RED**
ORANGE	**RED**	GREEN
RED	YELLOW	**GREEN**
ORANGE	BLUE	**GREEN**
YELLOW	BLUE	**RED**
ORANGE	**RED**	GREEN

CHECK IT

1. Outline what is meant by *dysfunctional thought processing*. Use examples in your answer. **[3 marks]**
2. Evaluate family dysfunction as an explanation for schizophrenia. **[8 marks]**
3. Explain **one** limitation of family dysfunction as an explanation of schizophrenia. **[4 marks]**
4. Describe and evaluate psychological theories of schizophrenia. **[16 marks]**

BIOLOGICAL THERAPIES FOR SCHIZOPHRENIA: DRUG THERAPY

Drug therapy: typical and atypical antipsychotics

This spread is concerned with antipsychotic medication. This is the most commonly used treatment for schizophrenia. Antipsychotic drugs can be split into older typical antipsychotics and newer atypical antipsychotics.

KEY TERMS

Antipsychotics – Drugs used to reduce the intensity of symptoms, in particular the positive symptoms, of psychotic conditions like schizophrenia.

Typical antipsychotics – The first generation of antipsychotic drugs, having been used since the 1950s. They work as dopamine antagonists and include *Chlorpromazine*.

Atypical antipsychotics – Drugs for schizophrenia (a psychotic disorder) developed after typical antipsychotics. They typically target a range of neurotransmitters such as dopamine and serotonin. Examples include *Clozapine* and *Risperidone*.

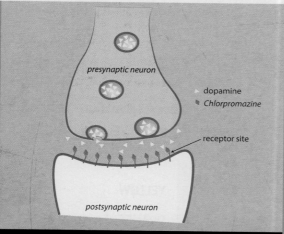

presynaptic neuron

▷ dopamine
■ *Chlorpromazine*

receptor site

postsynaptic neuron

Chlorpromazine acts as a dopamine antagonist, i.e. it acts against dopamine, in this case by blocking dopamine receptors at the postsynaptic neuron.

Apply it Concepts:

Explaining it to Brendan

Brendan has recently been diagnosed with schizophrenia with accompanying depression and suicidal thoughts. Brendan is a scientist and is curious about how antipsychotics work. He is also curious about his psychiatrist's choice of *Clozapine* as his antipsychotic.

Questions

1. How might Brendan's psychiatrist explain the effects of antipsychotics. Refer to the dopamine hypothesis in your answer.
2. Why might Brendan's psychiatrist have prescribed *Clozapine*?

Drug therapies

The most common treatment for **schizophrenia** involves the use of **antipsychotic drugs**. Antipsychotics can be taken as tablets or in the form of syrup. For those particularly at risk of failing to take their medication regularly some antipsychotics are available as injections given every 2–4 weeks.

Antipsychotics may be required in the short or long term. Some patients can take a short course of antipsychotics then stop their use without the return of symptoms. Other patients may require antipsychotics for life or face the likelihood of a recurrence of schizophrenia. Antipsychotics can be divided into **typical** (traditional) and newer **atypical** or second-generation drugs.

Typical antipsychotics

These have been around since the 1950s and include *Chlorpromazine*. *Chlorpromazine* can be taken as tablets, syrup or by injection. If taken orally it is administered daily up to a maximum of 1000mg, although initially doses are much smaller and for most patients the dosage is gradually increased to a maximum of 400 to 800mg. Typical prescribed doses have declined over the last 50 years (Liu and de Haan 2009).

There is a strong association between the use of typical antipsychotics like *Chlorpromazine* and the **dopamine hypothesis**. Typical antipsychotics like *Chlorpromazine* work by acting as **antagonists** in the dopamine system. Antagonists are chemicals which reduce the action of a **neurotransmitter**. Dopamine antagonists work by blocking dopamine receptors in the synapses of the brain, reducing the action of dopamine. Initially when a patient begins taking *Chlorpromazine* dopamine levels build up, but then its production is reduced. According to the dopamine hypothesis of schizophrenia this dopamine-antagonist effect normalises neurotransmission in key areas of the brain, reducing symptoms like **hallucinations**.

As well as having antipsychotic properties *Chlorpromazine* is also an effective sedative. This is believed to be related to its effect on histamine receptors but it is not fully understood how this leads to sedation. *Chlorpromazine* is often used to calm patients not only with schizophrenia but also with other conditions. This has often been done when patients are first admitted to hospitals and are very anxious. Syrup is absorbed faster than tablets so it tends to be used when *Chlorpromazine* is used for its sedative properties.

Atypical antipsychotics

These drugs have been used since the 1970s. The aim in developing newer antipsychotics was to maintain or improve upon the effectiveness of drugs in suppressing the symptoms of psychosis and also minimise the side effects. There are a range of atypical antipsychotics and they do not all work in the same way. In fact we do not know how some of them work.

Clozapine *Clozapine* was developed in the 1960s and first trialled in the early 1970s. It was withdrawn for a while in the 1970s following the deaths of some patients from a blood condition called *agranulocytosis*. However, in the 1980s when it was discovered to be more effective than typical antipsychotics *Clozapine* was remarketed as a treatment for schizophrenia to be used when other treatments failed. It is still used in this way today, and people taking it have regular blood tests to ensure they are not developing agranulocytosis. Because of its potentially fatal side effects *Clozapine* is not available as an injection. Daily dosage is a little lower than for *Chlorpromazine*, typically 300 to 450mg a day.

Clozapine binds to dopamine receptors in the same way that *Chlorpromazine* does, but in addition it acts on **serotonin** and **glutamate** receptors. It is believed that this action helps improve mood and reduce **depression** and anxiety in patients, and that it may improve cognitive functioning. The mood-enhancing effects of *Clozapine* mean that it is sometimes prescribed when a patient is considered at high risk of suicide. This is important as 30 to 50% of people suffering from schizophrenia attempt suicide at some point.

Risperidone *Risperidone* is a more recently developed atypical antipsychotic, having been around since the 1990s. It was developed in an attempt to produce a drug as effective as *Clozapine* but without its serious side effects. Like *Chlorpromazine*, *Risperidone* can be taken in the form of tablets, syrup or an injection that lasts for around two weeks. In common with other antipsychotics a small dose is initially given and this is built up to a typical daily dose of 4–8mg and a maximum of 12mg.

Like *Clozapine*, *Risperidone* is believed to bind to dopamine and serotonin receptors. *Risperidone* binds more strongly to dopamine receptors than *Clozapine* and is therefore effective in much smaller doses than most antipsychotics. There is some evidence to suggest that this leads to fewer side effects than is typical for antipsychotics.

Evaluation

Evidence for effectiveness

There is a large body of evidence to support the idea that both typical and atypical antipsychotics are at least moderately effective in tackling the symptoms of schizophrenia. Ben Thornley *et al.* (2003) reviewed studies comparing the effects of *Chlorpromazine* to control conditions in which patients received a **placebo** so their experiences were identical except for the presence of *Chlorpromazine* in their medication. Data from 13 trials with a total of 1121 participants showed that *Chlorpromazine* was associated with better overall functioning and reduced symptom severity. Data from three trials with a total of 512 participants showed that relapse rate was also lower when *Chlorpromazine* was taken.

In addition there is support for the benefits of atypical antipsychotics. In a review Herbert Meltzer (2012) concluded that *Clozapine* is more effective than typical antipsychotics and other atypical psychotics, and that it is effective in 30–50% of treatment-resistant cases where typical antipsychotics have failed. A number of studies have compared the effectiveness of *Clozapine* and other atypical antipsychotics like *Risperidone* but results have been inconclusive, perhaps because some patients respond better to one drug or the other. It does seem though that antipsychotics in general are reasonably effective, and this is a strength.

Serious side effects

A problem with antipsychotic drugs is the likelihood of side effects, ranging from the mild to the serious and even fatal. Typical antipsychotics are associated with a range of side effects including dizziness, agitation, sleepiness, stiff jaw, weight gain and itchy skin. Long-term use can result in *tardive dyskinesia*, which is caused by dopamine supersensitivity and manifests as involuntary facial movements such as grimacing, blinking and lip smacking.

The most serious side effect of typical antipsychotics is *neuroleptic malignant syndrome* (NMS). This is believed to be caused because the drug blocks dopamine action in the **hypothalamus**, an area of the brain associated with the regulation of a number of body systems. NMS results in high temperature, delirium and coma, and can be fatal. As typical doses of antipsychotics have declined NMS has become rarer. Estimates of its frequency range from less than 0.1% to just over 2%.

Atypical antipsychotics were developed to reduce the frequency of side effects and generally this has succeeded (Meltzer 2012). However, side effects still exist and patients taking *Clozapine* have to have regular blood tests to alert doctors to early signs of *agranulocytosis*. Side effects are thus still a significant weakness of antipsychotic drugs.

Use of antipsychotics depends on the dopamine hypothesis

This is more a theoretical issue than a practical one. Our understanding of the mechanism of antipsychotic drugs is strongly tied up with the dopamine hypothesis in its original form. Remember this is the idea that there are higher than usual levels of dopamine activity in the **subcortex** of the brain. There is, however, quite a bit of evidence to show that this original dopamine hypothesis is not a complete explanation for schizophrenia, and that in fact dopamine levels in parts of the brain other than the subcortex are too low rather than too high. If this is true then it is not clear how antipsychotics, which are dopamine antagonists, can help with schizophrenia when they reduce dopamine activity. In fact our modern understanding of the relationship between dopamine and psychosis suggests that antipsychotics *shouldn't* work. This has undermined the faith of some people that antipsychotics do in fact work.

Evaluation eXtra

Problems with the evidence for effectiveness

Although there is an impressive mass of evidence to support the effectiveness of antipsychotics, there have been some vigorous challenges to their usefulness. David Healy (2012) has suggested that some successful trials have had their data published multiple times, exaggerating the evidence for positive effects. Healy also suggests that because antipsychotics have powerful calming effects, it is easy to demonstrate that they have some positive effect on patients. This is not the same as saying they really reduce the severity of psychosis. To make matters worse, most published studies assess short-term benefits rather than long-term benefits and compare patients who keep taking antipsychotics with those suffering withdrawal having just stopped taking them.

Consider: *What do these issues suggest about the effectiveness of antipsychotics?*

The chemical cosh argument

It is widely believed that antipsychotics have been used in hospital situations to calm patients and make them easier for staff to work with, rather than for the benefits to the patients themselves. Although short-term use of antipsychotics to calm agitated patients is recommended by the National Institute for Health and Clinical Excellence (NICE), this practice is seen by some as a human rights abuse (Moncrieff 2013).

Consider: *How serious are the ethical issues associated with the use of antipsychotics to calm agitated patients?*

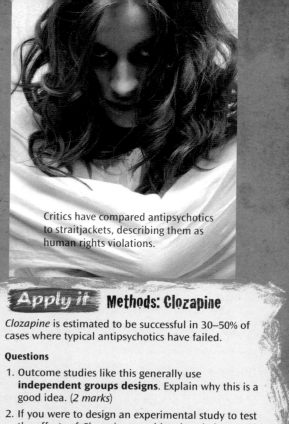

Critics have compared antipsychotics to straitjackets, describing them as human rights violations.

Apply it — **Methods: Clozapine**

Clozapine is estimated to be successful in 30–50% of cases where typical antipsychotics have failed.

Questions

1. Outcome studies like this generally use **independent groups designs**. Explain why this is a good idea. (*2 marks*)

2. If you were to design an experimental study to test the effects of *Clozapine* on schizophrenia how could you control for **confounding variables**? (*3 marks*)

3. (a) Explain what is meant by the term **demand characteristics**. (*2 marks*)
(b) How could you eliminate the effect of demand characteristics in this study? (*2 marks*)

Apply it

Concepts: Questioning antipsychotics

You are a mental health professional and a family friend of Cally. Cally has been prescribed antipsychotics, but is refusing to take them because she has heard that they have serious side effects and that they do not work.

Question

Cally's family ask your advice. What might you tell them about Cally's concerns?

STUDY TIP

Don't shy away from using technical terms and concepts as they really contribute to the quality of your answers. You may wish to reread the spread on synaptic transmission in our Year 1 book to fully understand the processes discussed on this spread.

CHECK IT

1. Explain what is meant by an *atypical antipsychotic* drug. **[2 marks]**
2. Outline the use of typical antipsychotics. **[6 marks]**
3. Evaluate the use of antipsychotic drugs to treat schizophrenia. **[10 marks]**
4. Describe and evaluate antipsychotics as a treatment for schizophrenia. **[16 marks]**

Cognitive behaviour therapy and family therapy as used in the treatment of schizophrenia. Token economies as used in the management of schizophrenia.

This spread is concerned with psychological approaches to treating schizophrenia. The conventional wisdom has been that these should be used alongside antipsychotic drugs.

KEY TERMS

Cognitive behaviour therapy (CBT) – A method for treating mental disorders based on both cognitive and behavioural techniques. From the cognitive viewpoint the therapy aims to deal with thinking, such as challenging negative thoughts. The therapy also includes behavioural techniques.

Family therapy – A psychological therapy carried out with all or some members of a family with the aim of improving their communication and reducing the stress of living as a family.

Token economies – A form of behavioural therapy, where desirable behaviours are encouraged by the use of selective reinforcement. For example, patients are given rewards (tokens) as secondary reinforcers when they engage in correct/socially desirable behaviours. The tokens can then be exchanged for primary reinforcers – favourite foods or privileges.

Family therapy aims to reduce stress and expression of negative emotion in families.

Apply it   Concepts: Bronwyn

Bronwyn has been an in-patient in her local psychiatric hospital for the last year. She was admitted with a diagnosis of schizophrenia after developing a strong belief that she was being controlled by the government. After a year of medication and a course of CBT her symptoms are now under control. However, Bronwyn has become institutionalised in the hospital setting and she no longer takes good care of her appearance as she used to.

Questions

1. How might CBT have been used to help Bronwyn with her belief that she was being controlled by the government?

2. How might a token economy be used to improve Bronwyn's grooming behaviour?

Psychological therapies

Cognitive behaviour therapy (CBT)

Cognitive behaviour therapy is now commonly used to treat patients with schizophrenia. It usually takes place for between five and twenty sessions, either in groups or on an individual basis. The aim of CBT in general involves helping patients identify **irrational thoughts** and trying to change them. This may involve argument or a discussion of how likely the patient's beliefs are to be true, and a consideration of other less threatening possibilities – see case example below. This will not get rid of the symptoms of schizophrenia but it can make patients better able to cope with them.

How CBT helps Patients can be helped to make sense of how their **delusions** and **hallucinations** impact on their feelings and behaviour. Just understanding where symptoms come from can be hugely helpful for some patients. If, for example, a patient hears voices and believes the voices are demons, they will naturally be very afraid. Offering psychological explanations for the existence of hallucinations and delusions can help reduce this anxiety. Delusions can also be challenged so that a patient can come to learn that their beliefs are not based on reality.

A case example Turkington et al. (2004) describe an example of CBT used to challenge where a paranoid patient's delusions come from:
Paranoid patient: The Mafia are observing me to decide how to kill me.
Therapist: You are obviously very frightened . . . there must be a good reason for this.
Paranoid patient: Do you think it's the Mafia?
Therapist: It's a possibility, but there could be other explanations. How do you know that it's the Mafia?

Family therapy

Family therapy takes place with families rather than individual patients, aiming to improve the quality of communication and interaction between family members. There is a range of approaches to family therapy for schizophrenia. In keeping with psychological therapies like the **double bind** and the **schizophrenogenic mother**, some therapists see the family as the root cause of the condition. Nowadays though, most family therapists are more concerned with reducing stress within the family that might contribute to a patient's risk of relapse. In particular, family therapy aims to reduce levels of **expressed emotion** (EE).

How family therapy helps Fiona Pharoah et al. (2010) identify a range of strategies by which family therapists aim to improve the functioning of a family with a member suffering from schizophrenia:

* Forming a therapeutic alliance with all family members.
* Reducing the stress of caring for a relative with schizophrenia.
* Improving the ability of the family to anticipate and solve problems.
* Reduction of anger and guilt in family members.
* Helping family members achieve a balance between caring for the individual with schizophrenia and maintaining their own lives.
* Improving families' beliefs about and behaviour towards schizophrenia.

Pharoah et al. suggest that these strategies work by reducing levels of stress and expressed emotion, whilst increasing the chances of patients' complying with medication. This combination of benefits tends to result in a reduced likelihood of relapse and re-admission to hospital.

Token economies

Token economies are reward systems used to manage the behaviour of patients with schizophrenia, in particular those who have developed patterns of maladaptive behaviour through spending long periods in psychiatric hospitals (referred to as 'institutionalised'). Under these circumstances it is common for patients to develop bad hygiene or perhaps to remain in pyjamas all day. Modifying these bad habits does not cure schizophrenia but it improves the patient's quality of life and makes it more likely that they can live outside a hospital setting.

Tokens The idea is that tokens – for example, in the form of coloured discs – are given immediately to patients when they have carried out a desirable behaviour that has been targeted for **reinforcement**. This may be getting dressed in the morning, making a bed, etc., according to the patient's individual behaviour issues. This immediacy of reward is important because it prevents 'delay discounting', the reduced effect of a delayed reward.

Rewards Although the tokens have no value in themselves they can be swapped later for more tangible rewards. Token economies are a kind of behavioural therapy based on **operant conditioning**. Tokens are **secondary reinforcers** because they only have value once the patient has learned that they can be used to obtain rewards. These rewards might be in the form of materials such as sweets, cigarettes or magazines or rather in the form of services such as having a room cleaned or privileges such as a walk outside the hospital.

Evaluation

Evidence for effectiveness

There is some support for the benefits of psychological treatment for schizophrenia. Sameer Jauhar *et al.* (2014) reviewed the results of 34 studies of CBT for schizophrenia. They concluded that CBT has a significant but fairly small effect on both positive and negative symptoms.

Pharoah *et al.* reviewed the evidence for the effectiveness of family therapy for families of schizophrenia sufferers. They concluded that there is moderate evidence to show that family therapy significantly reduces hospital readmission over the course of a year and improves quality of life for patients and their families. However, they also noted that results of different studies were inconsistent and that there were problems with the quality of some evidence. Overall then the evidence base for family therapy is fairly weak.

A review of the evidence for token economies (McMonagle and Sultana 2009) found only three studies where patients had been **randomly allocated** to conditions, with a total of only 110 patients. Random allocation is important in matching patients to treatment and **control groups**. Only one of the three studies showed improvement in symptoms and none yielded useful information about behaviour change.

Overall there is only modest support for the effectiveness of psychological treatments and schizophrenia remains one of the harder mental health problems to treat. This is a limitation of psychological treatments.

Treatments improve quality of life but do not cure

All the psychological treatments for schizophrenia discussed here aim to make schizophrenia more manageable and in some way improve patients' quality of life. CBT helps by allowing patients to make sense of and in some cases challenge some of their symptoms. Family therapy helps by reducing the stress of living with schizophrenia in a family, both for the patient themselves and other family members. Token economies help by making patients' behaviour more socially acceptable so that they can better re-integrate into society. These things are all worth doing, but should not be confused with *curing* schizophrenia. Of course biological treatments do not cure schizophrenia either but they do reduce the severity of some symptoms.

This failure to cure schizophrenia is a weakness of psychological treatments.

Ethical issues

Although psychological treatments for schizophrenia do not have the serious side effects or medical risks of drug treatments, they can raise ethical issues. In particular token economy systems have proved controversial. The major issue is that privileges, services, etc., become more available to patients with mild symptoms and less so for those with more severe symptoms of schizophrenia that prevent them complying with desirable behaviours. This means that the most severely ill patients suffer discrimination in addition to other symptoms, and some families of patients have challenged the legality of this. This has in turn reduced the use of token economies in the psychiatric system.

Other psychological therapies can raise additional issues. CBT may involve, for example, challenging a person's paranoia, but at what point does this interfere with an individual's freedom of thought? If, for example, CBT challenged a patient's beliefs in a highly controlling government, this can easily stray into modifying their politics.

Ethical issues like this are a weakness of psychological treatments for schizophrenia.

Evaluation eXtra

Quality of the evidence for effectiveness

Many small-scale studies in which mental health professionals have compared patients before and after psychological treatments have found more positive results than those described above. However, these studies have problems; there is often a lack of a control group, or, if there is one then patients are not randomly allocated to treatment and control conditions. Where these studies are included in reviews, conclusions are generally more optimistic than those that strictly control which studies are included. The other way of looking at this of course is that reviews with tight controls on what studies are included may be too pessimistic in their conclusions.

Consider: *What does this disparity in conclusions suggest about the effectiveness of psychological treatments?*

Alternative psychological treatments

There are other psychological therapies that can be helpful for some people with schizophrenia that are less well-known and less likely to be available to patients. For example, the National Institute for Health and Clinical Excellence (NICE) recommends art therapy, provided a qualified art therapist with experience of working with schizophrenia sufferers is available.

Consider: *Is there a case for making a wider variety of psychological treatments available for sufferers of schizophrenia? Quality of the evidence for effectiveness*

Token economies raise ethical issues.

Apply it — **Concepts: A case of high EE**

Randolph has just come out of hospital after an episode of schizophrenia. His symptoms are under control as long as he takes his medication and he has returned to live with his mother and two sisters. Randolph's psychiatrist is concerned, however, by the high levels of expressed emotion in Randolph's family. She recommends family therapy for Randolph's family.

Questions

1. What might be the benefits of family therapy for Randolph and his family?

2. If Randolph's family ask his psychiatrist about the effectiveness of family therapy what might she tell them?

Apply it — **Methods: Meta-analysis**

Jauhar *et al.* (2014) carried out a meta-analysis on the results of 34 studies assessing the effectiveness of CBT in the treatment of schizophrenia. They concluded that patients in CBT were better off for both positive and negative symptoms than controls (p<0.001).

Questions

1. Explain what p<0.001 means. (*2 marks*)

2. Typically we say that a difference between conditions is significant when p<0.05. How significant is p<0.001 compared to p<0.05? (*2 marks*)

STUDY TIP

All three therapies on this spread are named in the specification, which means you need to be able to describe each of them separately and offer some evaluation. We don't have space here for every possible question but you should be prepared for all possibilities.

CHECK IT

1. Explain how cognitive behaviour therapy is used in the treatment of schizophrenia. [*3 marks*]

2. Outline the use of family therapy to treat schizophrenia. [*6 marks*]

3. Evaluate the use of cognitive behaviour therapy to treat schizophrenia. [*6 marks*]

4. 'Cognitive behaviour therapy, family therapy and token economies are all used in the treatment and management of schizophrenia.' Discuss the use of these methods. Include comparisons with drug therapies in your answer. [*16 marks*]

THE INTERACTIONIST APPROACH TO SCHIZOPHRENIA

The importance of an interactionist approach in explaining and treating schizophrenia: the diathesis-stress model.

This spread is concerned with the interactionist approach to schizophrenia. This involves taking account of both biological and psychological factors in the development of schizophrenia. Treatment involves combining medication with psychological therapies.

KEY TERMS

The interactionist approach – A broad approach to explaining schizophrenia, which acknowledges that a range of factors, including biological and psychological factors, are involved in the development of schizophrenia.

The diathesis-stress model – An interactionist approach to explaining behaviour. For example schizophrenia is explained as the result of both an underlying vulnerability (diathesis) and a trigger, both of which are necessary for the onset of schizophrenia. In early versions of the model, vulnerability was genetic and triggers were psychological. Nowadays both genes and trauma are seen as diatheses, and stress can be psychological or biological in nature.

High doses of cannabis can trigger schizophrenia in people with a pre-existing vulnerability.

Apply it   Concepts: Alison

Alison has a family history of schizophrenia and has spent time in foster care following childhood abuse. At the age of 17 she has recently been in a serious accident and is considering smoking cannabis for pain relief and to help her relax.

Questions

Referring to the diathesis-stress model of schizophrenia, how could you explain to Alison that she would be unwise to smoke cannabis?

The interactionist approach

Put simply the **interactionist approach** (also sometimes called the 'biosocial approach') is an approach that acknowledges that there are biological, psychological and societal factors in the development of **schizophrenia**. Biological factors include genetic vulnerability and neurochemical and neurological abnormality. Psychological factors include stress, for example, resulting from **life events** and **daily hassles**, including poor quality interactions in the family.

Explaining the interactionist approach: The diathesis-stress model

Diathesis means vulnerability. In this context *stress* simply means a negative psychological experience. The **diathesis-stress model** says that both a vulnerability to schizophrenia and a stress-trigger are necessary in order to develop the condition. One or more underlying factors make a person particularly vulnerable to developing schizophrenia but the onset of the condition is triggered by stress.

Meehl's model In the original diathesis-stress model (Meehl 1962) diathesis (vulnerability) was entirely **genetic**, the result of a single 'schizogene'. This led to the development of a biologically based *schizotypic personality*, one characteristic of which is sensitivity to stress. According to Paul Meehl, if a person does not have the schizogene then no amount of stress would lead to schizophrenia. However, in carriers of the gene, chronic stress through childhood and adolescence, in particular the presence of a **schizophrenogenic mother** (see page 208), could result in the development of the condition.

The modern understanding of diathesis One way in which our understanding of diathesis has changed is that it is now clear that many genes each appear to increase genetic vulnerability slightly; there is no single 'schizogene' (Ripke *et al.* 2014). Modern views of diathesis also include a range of factors beyond the genetic, including psychological trauma (Ingram and Luxton 2005) – so trauma becomes the diathesis rather than the stressor. Read *et al.* (2001) proposed a neurodevelopmental model in which early trauma alters the developing brain. Early and severe enough trauma, such as child abuse, can seriously affect many aspects of brain development. For example the **hypothalamic-pituitary-adrenal** (HPA) system can become over-active, making the person much more vulnerable to later stress.

The modern understanding of stress In the original diathesis-stress model of schizophrenia, stress was seen as psychological in nature, in particular related to parenting. Although psychological stress, including that resulting from parenting may still be considered important, a modern definition of stress (in relation to the diathesis-stress model) includes anything that risks triggering schizophrenia (Houston *et al.* 2008). Much of the recent research into factors triggering an episode of schizophrenia has concerned cannabis use. In terms of the diathesis-stress model cannabis is a stressor because it increases the risk of schizophrenia by up to seven times according to dose. This is probably because cannabis interferes with the **dopamine** system. However, most people do not develop schizophrenia after smoking cannabis so it seems there must also be one or more vulnerability factors.

Treatment according to the interactionist model

The interactionist model of schizophrenia acknowledges both biological and psychological factors in schizophrenia and is therefore compatible with both biological and psychological treatments. In particular the model is associated with combining **antipsychotic** medication and psychological therapies, most commonly **CBT**.

Douglas Turkington *et al.* (2006) point out that it is perfectly possible to believe in biological causes of schizophrenia and still practise CBT to relieve psychological symptoms. However, this requires adopting an interactionist model; it is not possible to adopt a purely biological approach and tell patients that their condition is purely biological and that there is no psychological significance to symptoms, and to simultaneously treat them with CBT.

In Britain it is increasingly standard practice to treat patients with a combination of antipsychotic drugs and CBT. In the USA there is more of a history of conflict between psychological and biological models of schizophrenia and this may have led to slower adoption of an interactionist approach. Thus medication without an accompanying psychological treatment is more common than in the UK.

It is unusual to treat schizophrenia using psychological therapies alone. CBT, family therapy and the use of token economies with sufferers of schizophrenia are usually carried out with patients taking antipsychotics.

Evaluation

Evidence for the role of vulnerability and triggers

There is evidence to support the dual role of vulnerability and stress in the development of schizophrenia. Pekka Tienari *et al.* (2004) investigated the combination of genetic vulnerability and parenting style (the trigger). Children adopted from 19,000 Finnish mothers with schizophrenia between 1960 and 1979 were followed up. Their adoptive parents were assessed for child-rearing style, and the rates of schizophrenia were compared to those in a **control group** of adoptees without any genetic risk. A child-rearing style characterised by high levels of criticism and conflict and low levels of empathy was implicated in the development of schizophrenia but only for the children with high genetic risk but not in the control group. This suggests that both genetic vulnerability and family-related stress are important in the development of schizophrenia – genetically vulnerable children are more sensitive to parenting behaviour.

This is very strong direct support for the importance of adopting an interactionist approach to schizophrenia, including hanging on to the idea that poor parenting is a possible source of stress.

The original diathesis–stress model is over-simple

The classic model of a single schizogene and schizophrenic parenting style as the major source of stress is now known to be very over-simple. Multiple genes increase vulnerability to schizophrenia, each having a small effect on its own; there is no single schizogene. Also stress can come in many forms, including but not limited to dysfunctional parenting. Therefore vulnerability and stress do not have one single source.

In fact it is now believed that vulnerability can be the result of early trauma as well as genetic make-up, and that stress can come in many forms including biological. In one recent study by James Houston *et al.* (2008) childhood sexual trauma emerged as a vulnerability factor whilst cannabis use was a trigger. This shows that the old idea of diathesis as biological and stress as psychological has turned out to be overly simple.

This is a problem for the old idea of diathesis-stress but not for newer models.

Support for the effectiveness of combinations of treatments

There is support for the usefulness of adopting an interactionist approach from studies comparing the effectiveness of combinations of biological and psychological treatments for schizophrenia versus biological treatments alone. As Turkington *et al.* (2006) point out it is not really possible to use combination treatments without adopting an interactionist approach.

Studies show an advantage to using combinations of treatments for schizophrenia. For example, in one study by Nicholas Tarrier *et al.* (2004) 315 patients were **randomly allocated** to a medication + CBT group, medication + supportive counselling or a control group. Patients in the two combination groups showed lower symptom levels than those in the control group (medication only) although there was no difference in rates of hospital readmission.

Studies like this show that there is a clear practical advantage to adopting an interactionist approach in the form of superior treatment outcomes, and therefore highlight the importance of taking an interactionist approach.

Evaluation eXtra

We don't know exactly how diathesis and stress work

There is strong evidence to suggest that some sort of underlying vulnerability coupled with stress can lead to schizophrenia. We also have well-informed suggestions for how vulnerabilities and stress might lead to symptoms. However, we do not yet fully understand the mechanisms by which the symptoms of schizophrenia appear and how both vulnerability and stress produce them.

Consider: *How does this incomplete understanding affect our evaluation of the diathesis-stress model?*

The treatment-causation fallacy

Turkington *et al.* argue that there is a good logical fit between the interactionist approach and using combination treatments. However, the fact that combined biological and psychological treatments are more effective than either on their own does not necessarily mean the interactionist approach to schizophrenia is correct. Similarly the fact that drugs help does not mean that schizophrenia is biological in origin. This error of logic is called the treatment-causation fallacy.

Consider: *Why does this matter? How does it affect our evaluation of the interactionist approach to explaining schizophrenia?*

A combination of genetic vulnerability and growing up in a dysfunctional family increases the risk of schizophrenia. Each on their own may not be problematic but they interact in such a way to produce mental health problems.

Apply it

Concepts: The interactionist approach

Whitney is in hospital having recently been diagnosed with schizophrenia. Her family are confused at the doctor's explanation that schizophrenia is an illness and his recommendation that she be treated by both antipsychotics and CBT.

Questions

Referring to the interactionist approach to schizophrenia, explain why Whitney's psychiatrist takes this view and recommends both medication and a psychological treatment.

Apply it

Methods: A survey of diathesis-stress

In the Houston *et al.* (2008) study 5877 participants responded to a survey; 543 reported a childhood sexual trauma and 643 reported using cannabis before the age of 16.

Questions

1. Is the data above **quantitative** or **qualitative data**? Explain your answer. (*2 marks*)
2. Surveys can involve **questionnaires** or **interviews**. Explain *one* advantage of using a questionnaire to gather this data. (*2 marks*)
3. (*a*) What is a **closed question**? (1 mark)
   (*b*) Why might closed questions be used here? (2 marks)
4. Explain *one* **ethical issue** with this study. (*2 marks*)

CHECK IT

1. Explain the importance of adopting an interactionist approach to schizophrenia. **[4 marks]**
2. Outline the diathesis-stress model of schizophrenia. **[6 marks]**
3. Evaluate the diathesis-stress model of schizophrenia. **[10 marks]**
4. Describe and evaluate the interactionist approach to both explaining and treating schizophrenia. **[16 marks]**

PRACTICAL CORNER

> Knowledge and understanding of . . . research methods, practical research skills and maths skills. These should be developed through . . . ethical practical research activities.

This means that you should conduct practical investigations wherever possible. Because you cannot carry out research on participants with mental health problems you are limited here to research using a non-clinical population. We suggest a survey to investigate how good the layperson's understanding is of schizophrenia and an experiment to show how distracting it is to have experience of voices.

Ethics check

We suggest strongly that you complete this checklist before starting:

1. Do participants know participation is voluntary?
2. Do participants know what to expect?
3. Do participants know they can withdraw at any time?
4. Are individuals' results anonymous?
5. Have I minimised the risk of distress to participants?
6. Have I avoided asking sensitive questions?
7. Will I avoid bringing my school/teacher/psychology into disrepute?
8. Have I considered all other ethical issues?
9. Has my teacher approved this?

It is likely that the layperson will think of schizophrenia as 'split personality'?

Practical idea 1: Survey on knowledge of schizophrenia

Studies of **media** portrayal of serious mental disorders like **schizophrenia** have shown highly stereotyped representations. It appears that people who have not studied psychology or related subjects like medicine do not have a good understanding of schizophrenia. The aim of this study is to explore how well the public understands the nature of schizophrenia.

More specifically we are interested in whether there is a difference between psychology students and non-psychology students in their response to statements concerning schizophrenia.

This is an **experiment** because studying psychology is the **independent variable**. A **questionnaire** is used to collect data.

The practical bit

This is a study of knowledge of schizophrenia. As such data can only be collected using a **self-report** method, i.e. a questionnaire or an **interview** study. We recommend a questionnaire. You will need to construct a questionnaire and use it to collect data from students.

Designing your questionnaire

There are various ways to assess public understanding of schizophrenia. We recommend you test whether people endorse beliefs about schizophrenia. The simplest way to do this is by having participants respond to a set of true-or-false questions. Alternatively you could ask people to respond to statements using a **Likert scale** (strongly agree to strongly disagree).

We suggest that you base some of your statements on false stereotypes about schizophrenia, for example, that schizophrenia involves a 'split personality' and that only sufferers experience hallucinations and delusions. Other statements could concern correct information, such as the incidence of schizophrenia in the population. Try to use between five and ten statements.

It is important to record information about participants that will determine what they might know about schizophrenia. For the independent variable you will need a question asking whether the respondent has studied psychology or not, and whether their studies included schizophrenia. You might also wish to record any other ways the respondent might know about schizophrenia, for example, having a family member with the condition.

Ethical issues

Because people may see schizophrenia as a sensitive topic it is critical that participants are fully aware that participation is voluntary, that they know exactly what will take place in the study and that they are aware that they have the **right to withdraw** at any time. Make sure that when you approach participants they are informed straight away what the study is about.

Choosing your sample

You will need to consider a suitable **sampling technique** for this study. As always there is a trade-off between sampling techniques that allow you to get a large number of participants quickly and those that allow you to obtain participants who are more representative of their **population**. You also need to think about what is an appropriate sample size for this study.

Analysing your data

You will need to present your results in the form of tables and graphs. You will want to be able to show your results so that someone will instantly be able to see whether there is indeed a difference in understanding of schizophrenia between those who have studied psychology and those who have not.

You may wish to carry out a statistical test on your data (see question 4 below).

Median number of statements correct	
Psychology student (n=15)	Lay person (n=18)
8	5

Table 1

Apply it — Methods: The maths bit 1

1. In Table 1 $n = 18$. What does this mean? (*1 mark*)
2. Express the numbers in the table as fractions and percentages. (*4 marks*)
3. At what level is the data shown in this table? (*1 mark*)
4. What **statistical test** would you carry out to assess the significance of the difference between the two groups? Explain your answer. (*3 marks*)
5. What conclusion would you reach about public understanding of schizophrenia based on the results shown in this table? (*2 marks*)

Practical idea 2: The distracting effect of voices

One common symptom of schizophrenia is hearing voices. As well as the distress caused by the things the voices are heard to say, the sufferer has to cope with carrying out day-to-day tasks whilst being distracted by voices. It is possible to simulate the experience of having to perform everyday tasks whilst listening to voices by means of playing participants a recording as they complete cognitive tasks.

The **aim** of this study is to test the effect of voices on performance of an everyday cognitive task.

This is a **laboratory experiment**, with the independent variable being the presence of simulated voices and the **dependent variable** being performance on a cognitive task.

You should find that voice distraction has a negative effect on cognitive performance.

The practical bit

Designing your experiment

You will need a design that allows you to compare performance on a task under two **conditions**. In the **experimental condition** participants will listen to voices while they carry out the task, whereas in a **control condition** they will carry out an identical task without the voices. To make sure that all participants have as similar experience as possible they should listen to the same recorded voices at the same volume and use headphones so as to minimise the effect of other sounds in the room. You will need to make a decision about whether to use a **repeated measures** design or an **independent groups** design. A repeated measures design might be better in terms of eliminating the effects of **participant variables** but if you opt for this make sure you can control for order effects by **counterbalancing**.

The voices

You can obtain recordings designed to simulate the voices heard in schizophrenia on *YouTube*, but these tend to be distressing because of their aggressive content. For ethical reasons you might be better off recording your own voices or something like the news headlines and making sure the content is unlikely to cause distress. The recording will need to be long enough for the task. Check how long it takes to perform your task when you have chosen it.

The cognitive task

In a professional piece of research you would probably give participants more than one task but one should be okay for an A level practical. You can design your own task but in order to ensure all participants have as similar an experience as possible you might be better off using an online procedure. A suitable example is the Stroop Test, in which you are required to name ink colours on colour words (see table above right for web links). Other suitable tests include reaction time tests and short-term memory tests such as memorising number or letter sequences.

Ethical issues

This experiment should be acceptable as long as you remember you are simply testing the effect of voice-distraction on cognitive performance. Although this is relevant to understanding the experience of schizophrenia, remember that you are not meant to be experimenting on schizophrenia itself. Make sure that your teacher checks that it is appropriate for each individual to take part.

Analysing your data

You will need to present your results in the form of tables and graphs. You will want to be able to show your results so that someone will instantly be able to see whether there is indeed a difference between cognitive performance with and without voice-distraction.

You may wish to carry out a statistical test on your data (see question 4 on right).

Examples of online cognitive tasks

Stroop Test	www.onlinestrooptest.com/stroop_effect_test.php
Digit span (short-term memory)	http://cognitivefun.net/test/7
Reaction time	http://getyourwebsitehere.com/jswb/rttest01.html

The maths bit

Overall, at least 10% of the marks in assessments for Psychology will require the use of mathematical skills and at least 25% in total will involve research methods.

Don't avoid it!

Number of items remembered in a short-term memory test		
Participant number	With voices	Without voices
1	6	8
2	4	7
3	7	8
4	6	9
5	6	7
6	4	7
7	5	5
8	6	8
9	5	6
10	4	7

Apply it **Methods: The maths bit 2**

1. From the table on the left, calculate the **mean** and **median** number of items remembered with and without voice-distraction. (*4 marks*)
2. Calculate the **range** for each condition. (*2 marks*)
3. What would you conclude from these figures about the effect of voice-distraction on cognitive performance? (*2 marks*)
4. What **statistical test** would you use to analyse the significance of the difference between the scores in the two conditions? Explain your answer. (*3 marks*)
5. These data are **quantitative**. Explain *one* strength of quantitative data. (*2 marks*)

REVISION SUMMARIES

SCHIZOPHRENIA

The nature of schizophrenia.

CLASSIFICATION OF SCHIZOPHRENIA

Classification of schizophrenia
More common in men and working-class people.

Positive symptoms
Additional symptoms beyond normal experience, including:
- Hallucinations – sensory experiences with no basis in reality.
- Delusions – beliefs not based in reality.

Negative symptoms
Deficits in normal experience, including:
- Avolition – loss of motivation.
- Speech poverty – affects frequency and quality.

EVALUATION

Reliability
Cheniaux *et al.*: Inter-rater reliability is poor;
two psychiatrists rated 100 patients with DSM and ICD.

Validity
Different diagnostic systems do not agree on who has schizophrenia, therefore criterion validity is poor.

Co-morbidity
Buckley *et al.*: Around half of patients also have another diagnosis, e.g. depression, substance abuse.

Symptom overlap
There is major overlap between the symptoms of schizophrenia and bipolar disorder, and different diagnosis with ICD and DSM.

Gender bias
Longenecker: Since the 1980s more men than women have received a diagnosis of schizophrenia, suggests there is bias in diagnosis, with women being underdiagnosed due to good interpersonal functioning.

Culture bias
Differential diagnosis may be a bias because cultural norms in black communities are misinterpreted or perhaps because of distrust of black patients by white clinicians.

BIOLOGICAL EXPLANATIONS FOR SCHIZOPHRENIA

Genetic, neurochemical and neurological explanations.

BIOLOGICAL EXPLANATIONS

The genetic basis of schizophrenia
Gottesman *et al.*: Relationship between the degree of genetic similarity and shared risk of schizophrenia.
Ripke *et al.*: There are 108 genetic variations that increase the risk of schizophrenia.

The dopamine hypothesis
High levels dopamine in the subcortex (hyperdopaminergia) and low levels in the cortex (hypodopaminergia) have been linked to the symptoms of schizophrenia.

Neural correlates of schizophrenia
Avolition linked to ventral striatum (Junckel *et al.*).
Hallucinations linked to superior temporal gyrus and anterior cingulate gyrus (Allen *et al.*).

EVALUATION

Multiple sources of evidence for genetic vulnerability
Adoption, family and genetic linkage studies all point to a role of genetic make-up in vulnerability to schizophrenia (e.g. Tienari *et al.*).

Mixed evidence for the dopamine hypothesis
Support: As predicted, some dopamine agonists make symptoms worse and antipsychotic drugs are dopamine antagonists.
However, some genes associated with vulnerability to schizophrenia code for unrelated chemicals, e.g. glutamate (Moghaddam and Javitt).

The correlation-causation problem
Neural correlates of schizophrenia are just correlates; we do not know whether they cause schizophrenia, e.g. negative symptoms may be caused by low activity in ventral striatum or low activity observed in the ventral striatum is the result of reduced information processing due to some other factor.

The role of mutation
Positive correlation between paternal age and risk of schizophrenia (Brown *et al.*), supporting the existence of a genetic basis.

The role of psychological environment is important but unclear
Appears to be an important role for the psychological environment, e.g. stressful upbringing, suggests that biological explanations for schizophrenia alone are not complete.

PSYCHOLOGICAL EXPLANATIONS FOR SCHIZOPHRENIA

Social and cognitive explanations.

PSYCHOLOGICAL EXPLANATIONS

Family dysfunction
Fromm-Reichmann: Schizophrenogenic mother leads to distrust and paranoid delusions.
Bateson *et al.*: Double bind theory, confusing communications a factor in schizophrenia.
Expressed emotion (EE): Families with high levels of expressed negative emotion create a stressful environment that may cause schizophrenia or at least its relapse.

Cognitive explanations
Cognitive dysfunction (Firth *et al.*):
Poor metarepresentation leading to hallucinations.
Poor central control leading to negative symptoms.

EVALUATION

Support for family dysfunction as a risk factor
A large proportion of patients report childhood sexual abuse (Read *et al.*) or insecure attachment (Berry *et al.*). This supports link between upbringing and schizophrenia.
However, most evidence is retrospective so lacks validity.

Weak evidence for family-based explanations
Little or no direct evidence for the schizophrenogenic mother or double bind theory.
An additional problem is that family-based explanations may encourage blaming of parents whose children develop schizophrenia.

Strong evidence for dysfunctional thought processing
Stirling *et al.*: Patients with schizophrenia took longer to complete the Stroop task, showing impairment to cognition.
However, a limitation of cognitive explanations is that they do not tell us about the origins of symptoms.

Evidence for biological factors is not adequately considered
Strong support for biological explanations challenge value of psychological explanations.
However, it does seem likely that schizophrenia has important psychological and biological factors so we cannot eliminate psychological explanations.

Direction of causality
There is no clear evidence for the direction of causality between cognitive and biological factors.

Biological Therapies for Schizophrenia: Drug Therapy

Most common treatment for schizophrenia.

Drug Therapies

Typical antipsychotics
Dopamine antagonists, e.g. *Chlorpromazine*, block dopamine receptors, normalising transmission.
Also a sedative.

Atypical antipsychotics
Aim to reduce symptoms without the side effects of typical antipsychotics.
Clozapine: Acts on glutamate and serotonin receptors as well as dopamine receptors. It enhances mood as well as reducing symptoms.
Risperidone: Also binds to serotonin receptors but can be used in much smaller doses, leading to fewer side effects.

Evaluation

Evidence for effectiveness
Thornley *et al.*: Review, *Chlorpromazine* is more effective than a placebo in reducing symptom severity.
Meltzer review: *Clozapine* is more effective than typical antipsychotics.

Serious side effects
Antipsychotics, particularly typical ones, associated with a range of side effects including dizziness, agitation, sleepiness, and the life threatening neuroleptic malignant syndrome.

Depends on the dopamine hypothesis
Use of antipsychotics tied up with the dopamine hypothesis for which there is mixed support. If we do not accept the dopamine hypothesis there is no rationale for antipsychotics.

Problems with evidence for effectiveness
Healy: Some data sets with positive findings published more than once, exaggerating positive findings.
Behaviour change in patients may simply be response to sedative properties of drugs.

The chemical cosh argument
Some people believe that antipsychotics are popular because they make patients easier for staff to deal with rather than because they help patients.
Human rights abuse (Moncrieff).

Psychological Therapies for Schizophrenia

Used alongside antipsychotic drugs.

Psychological Therapies

CBT
Aims to challenge irrational thoughts and teach patients to cope better with symptoms, e.g. hallucinations and delusions. Reduces anxiety.

Family therapy
Works with the patient and their family to improve communication (double bind) within the family and reduce expressed emotion.
Pharaoh *et al.* identified various aims, e.g. form therapeutic alliance, reduce stress of caring.

Token economies
A system of rewards designed to reinforce socially normal behaviour and so help the patient re-integrate into society. Tokens given immediately, exchanged for rewards.

Evaluation

Evidence for effectiveness
Studies of CBT (Jauhar *et al.*) and family therapy (Pharoah *et al.*) and token economy (McMonagle and Sultana) have shown modest evidence for benefits of psychological therapies.

Therapies improve quality of life but do not cure
A limitation of all psychological therapies is that they do not cure schizophrenia, although they are likely to help the patient by enabling them to cope and to avoid relapse. Each achieves this in a different way, but none makes the condition go away.

Ethical issues
Token economies deprive the most severely affected people from small pleasures, making their quality of life worse in the short term.
CBT also raises ethical issues because it challenges patient beliefs that might be part of their core identity.

Quality of evidence for effectiveness
Many published studies do not use standard protocols like having a randomly allocated control group. This is not therefore the best quality evidence.

Alternative psychological treatments
Given the small body and poor quality of some evidence for psychological treatments it may be that other psychological therapies are just as effective, e.g. NICE recommends art therapy.

The Interactionist Approach to Schizophrenia

Biological, psychological and societal factors.

The Interactionist Approach

The diathesis-stress approach
Meehl: Schizophrenia is the result of a schizogene and a schizophrenogenic mother.
Modern diathesis-stress approach suggests a range of vulnerability factors including multiple genes, early trauma, and stress, which may be psychological (e.g. family dynamics) or biological (e.g. cannabis).

Treatment according to the interactionist model
Combination treatments including both biological and psychological therapies are based on an interactionist understanding of schizophrenia.
For example, antipsychotics might be combined with CBT or family therapy.

Evaluation

Evidence for the role of vulnerability and triggers
Tienari *et al.*: Schizophrenia more likely in children with genetic vulnerability and parents with child-rearing style high in criticisms/low in empathy. Shows how genetic vulnerability and parenting style interact.

Original diathesis-stress model is over-simple
We used to see vulnerability as purely biological and stress as psychological. However, recent evidence suggests that early trauma causes vulnerability and that biological events like cannabis smoking can be environmental stressors.

Support for the effectiveness of combination therapies
Tarrier *et al.*: Greater effectiveness for combined medication plus CBT over medication plus supportive counselling, or medication alone.

We don't know exactly how diathesis or stress work
May be that both particular genetics and early trauma make the developing brain less resilient to later stress but the precise mechanisms by which this might take place are unclear.

The treatment-causation fallacy
Just because combination treatments are effective, this does not necessarily mean that the interactionist model is correct.

PRACTICE QUESTIONS, ANSWERS AND FEEDBACK

Question 1   Outline **one** treatment for schizophrenia. *(2 marks)*

Morticia's answer

One treatment is family therapy where a therapist works with the patient and their family to improve communication (double bind) within the family and reduce expressed emotion.

A clear, concise answer from Morticia.

Luke's answer

Both typical and atypical antipsychotic drugs are used in the treatment of schizophrenia. Typical antipsychotics are dopamine antagonists that block dopamine receptors, normalising transmission.

Atypical antipsychotics such as Clozapine act on glutamate and serotonin receptors as well as dopamine receptors. This enhances mood as well as reducing symptoms.

A sophisticated response from Luke which makes good use of relevant terminology.

Vladimir's answer

Drugs are often used to treat schizophrenia, called antipsychotics that reduce levels of dopamine.

There are also psychological therapies such as family systems or CBT. These work well in combination with drug therapies.

Vladimir has misread the question and offers numerous therapies (although the material on drug therapy is the strongest). His answer would be better if he expanded the first point.

Question 2   Outline **one** study in which the treatment you have outlined in Q1 was investigated. *(2 marks)*

Morticia's answer

Pharoah et al. looked at the effectiveness of family therapy in a review of studies and found moderate evidence that it reduces hospital readmission and improves quality of life for patients and their families. However, the data from different studies was not always in agreement.

Morticia's answer lacks procedural detail but makes up for this by providing detailed findings.

Luke's answer

Drug studies tend to show that drugs are more effective than placebos such as a review by Thornley et al. This involved looking at the results of a number of different studies.

Despite the named researcher, Luke's answer is too generic. He should have selected a more detailed study (assuming he knows one!)

Vladimir's answer

Drug studies tend to show that drugs are more effective than placebos such as a review by Thornley et al. This involved looking at the results of a number of different studies.

Vladimir has not provided a discernible study.

Question 3   Briefly discuss reliability and/or validity in the diagnosis of schizophrenia. *(4 marks)*

Morticia's answer

Reliability means consistency so we are looking at whether two diagnosticians produce the same diagnosis for the same patient/symptoms.

In one study, 100 patients were diagnosed by two people and inter-rater reliability was very poor. They used both DSM and ICD (the two main classification systems). There was low agreement on both of them.

Validity concerns whether we are measuring what was intended and one of the issues is co-morbidity, that is the symptoms may not always lead to a diagnosis of schizophrenia, they may also lead to a diagnosis of another disorder.

The definition of reliability is well expressed as it is explicitly linked to diagnosis of schizophrenia. The study is plausible though additional detail would have been helpful.

The issue of co-morbidity is relevant to the validity of diagnosis. Evidence to illustrate this could have been provided.

Luke's answer

Cheniaux et al. found that inter-rater reliability for schizophrenia was poor using both DSM and ICD. Low reliability affects validity.

Different diagnostic systems do not agree on who has schizophrenia, therefore criterion validity is poor.

Two brief points from Luke, both of which could have been expanded.

Vladimir's answer

Reliability and validity are both key concepts in making diagnosis meaningful. A diagnosis should be the same every time (reliable) and it also must be valid. You can't say someone has schizophrenia when they don't so we need valid ways of assessing the disorder in the same way that physical illnesses are assessed.

A fairly unfocused 'ramble' from Vladimir here. The brief reference to reliability is the most convincing part but is not quite detailed enough.

On this spread we look at some typical student answers to questions. The comments provided indicate what is good and bad in each answer. Learning how to produce effective question answers is a SKILL. Read pages 387–397 for guidance.

Question 4 Joel and Joey are identical twins in their mid-20s. The twins' mother suffered with schizophrenia. Joel has a good job, is married and has never shown any symptoms of schizophrenia. Joey, however, has recently been diagnosed with schizophrenia. He was made redundant recently and has been having relationship problems with his girlfriend.

Discuss the importance of an interactionist approach in explaining and/or treating schizophrenia. Refer to Joel and Joey in your answer. *(16 marks)*

Morticia's answer

The interactionist approach suggests that we should draw on both biological and psychological explanations when trying to account for the development of schizophrenia. Such an approach can explain the twins described above because it would combine the genetic influence – both twins would inherit the same genes from their mother, as they are identical. So we presume they both inherited a gene for schizophrenia. However, this gene has only been expressed in one of the twins, which can be explained in terms of life experiences. The diathesis-stress model expresses this relationship. A diathesis is the biological/genetic factor and `stress' is the trigger caused by life experiences. In Joey that would appear to be his redundancy at work and relationship problems, which have acted as a trigger to an existing biological vulnerability.

There is plenty of evidence that genetics do play a role in the development of schizophrenia. Family and twin studies showing an increasing concordance the closer two people are genetically – so concordance is highest for identical twins and lower in non-identical twins, siblings, cousins and so on. However, concordance is never 100%, which means that genes can't be the whole story. There must be other factors involved. There is also evidence that supports psychological explanations, such as a large number of patients report childhood sexual abuse or insecure attachment that would act as stressors. In the case of Joey the stressors are literally stressful experiences in life. The diathesis-stress model makes sense in terms of our understanding of epigenetics and nature versus nurture in general because we now know that neither nature nor nurture exist alone. Epigenetics is the understanding that genes are switched on and off during development by things such as stressful experiences.

This integrationist understanding has important implications for therapy as it suggests that combined therapies may be best. A genetic cause would lead to abnormal levels of neurotransmitters and therefore drug therapy may be useful to treat this aspect of the disorder. At the same time psychological therapies such as CBT may help to deal with issues such as child abuse or depression from redundancy/relationship breakdown. There is research support for this kind of interactionist view. However, just because such approaches are successful doesn't mean the interactionist model does explain schizophrenia.

The twins may also think about their own children and the fact that they may also have vulnerabilities for the disorder. However, understanding how genes works means they shouldn't worry too much because they are only one of many influences.

(415 words)

Morticia's outline of the diathesis-stress model is clear and accurate, whilst the application to the stem is very well explained.

In paragraph 2 a specific study might have been better here, though the point made is relevant.

In this paragraph there is another good link to the stem and sophisticated material linking the model to the emerging field of epigenetics.

Paragraph 3 contains relevant material and the question does allow for discussion of therapy as well as theory.

One issue with this essay is the rather vague references to evidence. Although this is not a requirement of the question, specific examples of research would have helped.

Vladimir's answer

The diathesis–stress model is an interactionist approach. According to this model, both twins would have inherited genes that cause schizophrenia. These create a vulnerability to develop the disorder (a diathesis) which is only expressed if something triggers the conditions such as the stressful life events that Joey has recently experienced.

In fact, a more modern understanding of diathesis is that it isn't just genes but anything can act as a vulnerability, for example, abuse in early childhood. For example, Read et al. proposed a neurodevelopmental model in which early trauma alters the developing brain. So it might be that that the twins have other diatheses which have made them vulnerable. It might not be genetic at all. Along with a more modern understanding of diathesis is a more modern understanding of `stress', which is really anything that triggers schizophrenia. In fact, one of the currently `popular' stressors is cannabis use. It is thought that cannabis interferes with dopamine. Therefore this is a stressor which is in fact biological.

Research supports the importance of genetic factors in schizophrenia. For example, a study by Gottesman et al. showed that risk of developing schizophrenia increased as genetic similarity increased: 2% of first cousins developed schizophrenia compared with 17% of non-identical twins and 48% of identical twins. Clearly this evidence also shows there is a large component not accounted for by the genes. In a very large-scale study Tienari et al. illustrated the interactionist model. They followed 19,000 adopted children in Finland whose mothers had schizophrenia. The child-rearing styles of the adopted parents were observed. Those children who were brought up in families with a lot of conflict and low empathy were much more likely to develop schizophrenia when compared to a control group of adopted children who did not have any genetic vulnerability.

Using an interactionist model has implications for therapies that address biological elements such as dopamine levels as well as providing psychological support such as CBT. Tarrier et al. found that patients given combined therapies of medication + CBT/counselling had lower symptom levels than a control group with just one treatment; a medication + CBT group, medication + supportive counselling or a control group. However, the success of such approaches does not mean that the explanation is correct. This is called the treat-causation fallacy. Another issue is that the exact mechanism of diathesis-stress is not clear. Without such an explanation, we cannot be sure that there is an interaction going on rather than some other process involving one or the other element.

(421 words)

A much more concise opening from Vladimir but the description and application is still effective.

Good use of evidence here (something the previous answer lacked) to support an impressive discussion on the nature of 'diathesis' and 'stress'.

In paragraph 3 there is specific detail of relevant evidence and it's used effectively to support the argument. The classic study by Tienari is explained clearly and made relevant to the debate.

The contrast between this and the previous essay is clear in the final paragraph. Here there is excellent use of evidence to illustrate points and support discussion. However, the essay lacks application.

MULTIPLE-CHOICE QUESTIONS

Schizophrenia

1. What percentage of the population are diagnosed with schizophrenia?

(a) 1%

(b) 2%

(c) 5%

(d) 10%

2. Which of the following is a positive symptom of schizophrenia?

(a) Avolition.

(b) Hallucinations.

(c) Speech poverty.

(d) Emotional flatness.

3. How many people with schizophrenia also suffer substance abuse?

(a) 5%

(b) 29%

(c) 47%

(d) 81%

4. With which of the following does schizophrenia have the most symptom overlap?

(a) OCD.

(b) Bipolar disorder.

(c) Depression.

(d) Phobia of dogs.

5. Which of the following is true of the diagnosis of schizophrenia?

(a) Women have always been more likely to be diagnosed than men.

(b) White Americans are more likely than African Americans to receive a diagnosis.

(c) Since the 1980s women are more likely to receive a diagnosis.

(d) Since the 1980s men are more likely to be diagnosed than women.

6. Which of the following is a negative symptom of schizophrenia?

(a) Hallucinations.

(b) Avolition.

(c) Delusions.

(d) Speech disorganisation.

Biological explanations for schizophrenia

1. Approximately how many candidate genes are believed to be associated with schizophrenia?

(a) 1

(b) 25

(c) 100

(d) 2000

2. What is the risk of developing schizophrenia for someone who has a sibling with the condition?

(a) 1%

(b) 9%

(c) 25%

(d) 50%

3. Which of the following is a neural correlate of schizophrenia?

(a) Low levels of activity in the ventral striatum.

(b) High activity levels in the superior temporal gyrus.

(c) High activity levels in the anterior cingulate gyrus.

(d) All the above.

4. Which description best matches the evidence for the dopamine hypothesis?

(a) None.

(b) Strong.

(c) Weak.

(d) Mixed.

5. Which of the following is a true statement about dopamine and schizophrenia?

(a) Schizophrenia is associated with low levels of dopamine in the subcortex.

(b) A high number of dopamine receptors in Broca's area may be associated with auditory hallucinations.

(c) Schizophrenia is associated with high levels of dopamine in the cortex.

(d) Dopamine appears to be the only neurotransmitter associated with schizophrenia.

6. Which of the following is *not* true of dopamine?

(a) It is associated with the sensation of pleasure.

(b) High levels are associated with Parkinson's.

(c) High levels are associated with schizophrenia.

(d) High levels are associated with excitation.

Psychological explanations for schizophrenia

1. Parenting characterised by mixed messages is the main feature of which explanation?

(a) The double bind theory.

(b) The schizophrenogenic mother.

(c) Expressed emotion.

(d) Dysfunctional thought processing.

2. According to Fromm-Reichmann, who is mostly involved in causing schizophrenia?

(a) The father.

(b) Siblings.

(c) The whole family.

(d) The mother.

3. What kind of dysfunctional thought processing might lead to hallucinations?

(a) Central control problems.

(b) Double-binds.

(c) Metarepresentation difficulty.

(d) Thought insertion.

4. Which of the following is *not* a weakness of family-based explanations for schizophrenia?

(a) Most studies are conducted retrospectively.

(b) There is little direct evidence for the schizophrenogenic mother.

(c) Family-based explanations can end up blaming parents of sufferers.

(d) There is no evidence for the role of family dysfunction.

5. Which of the following is a component of high expressed emotion?

(a) Verbal criticism of the patient, occasionally with violence.

(b) Parenting characterised by double binds.

(c) Cold, harsh and rejecting mothering.

(d) Dysfunctional thought processing.

6. Which of the following best describes the weakness of the evidence for dysfunctional information processing in schizophrenia?

(a) There is no evidence for dysfunctional information processing in schizophrenia.

(b) Evidence for dysfunctional information processing in schizophrenia is mixed.

(c) Evidence for dysfunctional information processing in schizophrenia only explains its proximal causes.

(d) Evidence for dysfunctional information processing in schizophrenia only explains its distal causes.

Biological therapies for schizophrenia

1. What explanation for schizophrenia are antipsychotics most strongly linked to?
(a) The subcortical hyperdopaminergic theory.
(b) The cortical hypodopaminergic theory.
(c) Neural correlates.
(d) The genetic basis of schizophrenia.

2. Which of the following distinguishes atypical psychotics from typical?
(a) They are all more effective.
(b) They have fewer side effects.
(c) They are taken in higher doses.
(d) They act on just the dopamine system.

3. Generally antipsychotics act on which neurotransmitter system?
(a) Serotonin.
(b) Glutamate.
(c) Dopamine.
(d) Cortisol.

4. A symptom of neuroleptic malignant syndrome is . . .
(a) Weight gain.
(b) Facial twitching.
(c) Dizziness.
(d) Delirium.

5. Which of the following best describes the effectiveness of antipsychotics?
(a) There is no evidence for their effectiveness.
(b) Antipsychotics are associated with symptom reduction.
(c) Antipsychotics are associated with improved overall functioning.
(d) Antipsychotics are associated with improved function and symptom reduction.

6. What is the problem with evidence for the effectiveness of antipsychotics?
(a) Some data has been published several times.
(b) Antipsychotics may make patients simply appear better because they have a calming effect.
(c) Most trials look at short term effects not long term effects.
(d) All of the above.

Psychological therapies for schizophrenia

1. CBT for schizophrenia involves which of the following?
(a) Reviewing the patient's early family life.
(b) Using tokens to reward appropriate behaviour.
(c) Challenging delusional beliefs.
(d) Reducing expressed anger in family members.

2. Which of the following is an aim of family therapy?
(a) Reducing the stress of caring for a relative with schizophrenia.
(b) Reducing anger in the family.
(c) Improving beliefs about and behaviour towards the person with schizophrenia.
(d) All the above.

3. Which of the following is true of token economies?
(a) Tokens are given a few hours after good behaviours.
(b) Tokens are valuable in themselves.
(c) Rewards include privileges and services.
(d) Tokens are primary reinforcers

4. Which of the following is a limitation of psychological treatments for schizophrenia?
(a) Psychological treatments do not cure schizophrenia.
(b) There is no evidence for the effectiveness of psychological treatments.
(c) Psychological treatments are generally considered unethical.
(d) Treatments do not improve quality of life for patients.

5. Which of the following is an ethical issue associated with token economies?
(a) Token economies have serious side effects.
(b) Token economies lead to discrimination against the most severely ill patients.
(c) Token economies can make symptoms worse.
(d) There is no evidence for the effectiveness of token economies.

6. Which of the following is an ethical issue associated with CBT?
(a) CBT has serious side effects.
(b) CBT discriminates against the most severely ill patients.
(c) Challenging paranoia may lead to modifying political beliefs.
(d) There is no evidence for the effectiveness of CBT.

The interactionist approach to schizophrenia

1. The interactionist approach is also known as the . . .
(a) Psychological model.
(b) Biosocial model.
(c) Biological model.
(d) Social-psychological model.

2. The term 'diathesis' means . . .
(a) Biological.
(b) Genetic.
(c) Vulnerability.
(d) Early trauma.

3. Meehl's model of schizophrenia includes which of the following elements?
(a) A schizogene.
(b) A schizophrenogenic mother.
(c) A schizotypic personality.
(d) All the above.

4. Treatment according to the interactionist model is most likely to combine . . .
(a) Typical and atypical antipsychotics.
(b) Antipsychotics and CBT.
(c) CBT and family therapy.
(d) Antipsychotics and nursing support.

5. Which best describes a modern understanding of schizophrenia diathesis?
(a) A schizogene and later trauma.
(b) Multiple candidate genes.
(c) Cannabis use and early trauma.
(d) Multiple candidate genes and early trauma.

6. Which of the following statements best describes the findings of the Tarrier *et al.* study of treatment combinations?
(a) Patients in the counselling + medication group did best overall.
(b) Patients in both combination groups showed fewer symptoms and had fewer readmissions than the control group.
(c) Patients in both combination groups showed fewer symptoms than the control group.
(d) Patients in both combination groups had fewer readmissions than the control group.

MCQ answers
Schizophrenia   1a, 2b, 3c, 4b, 5d, 6b
Biological explanations   1c, 2b, 3a, 4d, 5b, 6b
Psychological explanations   1a, 2d, 3c, 4d, 5a, 6c
Biological therapies   1a, 2b, 3c, 4d, 5d, 6d
Psychological therapies   1c, 2d, 3c, 4a, 5b, 6c
Interactionist approach   1b, 2c, 3d, 4b, 5d, 6c

CHAPTER 9
Eating Behaviour

Not green stuff again!

Children definitely dislike certain foods.
Which ones, and why?

THE SPECIFICATION SAYS...

Explanations for food preferences: the evolutionary explanation, including reference to neophobia and taste aversion.

There are two survival requirements that have to be balanced by evolutionary forces. One is the need for a varied diet high in energy and rich in essential nutrients such as fats and salt. The other is the need to avoid potentially toxic foods that threaten our survival and thus our chances of reproducing. Therefore humans and other animals have developed food preferences based on tastes that indicate energy, and aversions to tastes that indicate toxins.

KEY TERMS

Food preferences – A desire for particular foods created because ancestral animals preferred to eat foods that were high in energy in order to increase their survival and reproductive chances.

Neophobia – An innate predisposition to avoid anything new. An adaptive behaviour which reduces the risks of unfamiliar objects, experiences and activities until we learn they are safe.

Taste aversion – An innate predisposition to learn to avoid potentially toxic foods, as signalled by a bitter or sour taste.

Just what the doctor (or dentist) didn't order. Children have strong evolutionarily determined food preferences. Here's one of them.

Evolutionary explanations for food preferences

Preference for sweetness

Food preferences are linked to sweet taste as it is a reliable signal of high-energy food. Jacob Steiner (1977) placed sugar on the tongues of newborn humans and observed positive facial expressions (such as upturned mouth corners). Newborns can even distinguish between different sugars. Fructose is especially sweet and babies will consume large amounts of it if allowed. This makes a lot of sense in evolutionary terms. Fructose is a 'fast-acting' sugar providing energy quickly, and is present in ripe fruit, which would have been a favoured food for our distant ancestors.

Preference for salt

Salts are essential for many cell functions in animals. A preference for salt taste appears in humans at around four months of age. Gillian Harris *et al.* (1990) found that infants between the ages of 16 and 25 weeks who had been breastfed preferred salted rather than unsalted cereal. Breast milk is low in salt, so this finding suggests that they had not learned a salt preference and that it is innate, even though it only appears months after birth.

Preference for fat

High-calorie foods, such as fat, were often not readily available to our evolutionary ancestors. So quickly learning to prefer foods which are high in calories would have carried a definite advantage because calories provide energy important for survival. As fat contains twice as many calories as the equivalent amount of protein or carbohydrate, a taste preference for fat is therefore the most efficient route to energy consumption. But this is not the only advantage of fat. It also contributes to *palatability* (making food taste pleasant) and appeals to our other senses, especially smell.

Neophobia

Like most omnivores, humans have an innate unwillingness to eat new or unfamiliar foods. This food **neophobia** appears to be most pronounced in childhood, between the ages of about two and six years. Leann Birch (1999) suggests that it appears at a time when children begin to explore their environments and may encounter foods independently of their parents' guidance as to what is safe to eat and what isn't. Therefore, because untried foods are potentially dangerous to health, neophobia is adaptive because it means we are less likely to consume substances that could cause us illness or even prove fatal. Neophobia diminishes once we learn that specific foods will not poison us or cause us to become ill. Once it has served its purpose it is no longer needed and gives way to a different evolutionary mechanism that encourages consumption of a more varied diet, giving us greater access to important nutrients.

Taste aversion

According to Martin Seligman's (1971) theory of **biological preparedness**, we acquire certain **taste aversions** or fears more quickly than others. These are generally to objects or situations that posed the greatest threats to our distant ancestors' survival. Humans and other animals are therefore **genetically** hardwired to learn taste aversions that make us less likely to eat food that has gone bad or is otherwise toxic.

An example of this was provided by John Garcia and Robert Koelling (1966) who **classically conditioned** rats to acquire a taste aversion to sweetened water after pairing it with a poison, but they were much less successful when they paired the water with electric shocks. On the other hand, an aversion to light and clicking sounds was easily conditioned in another group of rats when these were paired with electric shocks, but not when paired with a poison. The researchers explained these findings in terms of preparedness, an evolutionary mechanism. A taste aversion is much more likely to be the outcome of eating poisoned food than it is of encountering a light or a clicking sound. It is an adaptive response that aids survival.

Bitter compounds in food are usually a reliable warning sign of toxins or that the food has gone off, so it is beneficial to survival to be able to detect these compounds quickly. In his research with newborn humans, Jacob Steiner (1977) found evidence of negative facial expressions (such as downturn of the corners of the mouth) in response to bitter tastes. This occurred before any learning of taste preference had taken place, strongly suggesting an innate mechanism at work.

Apply it

Concepts: The 'picky' eater

Oscar is a two-year-old boy and a 'fussy' eater. Obviously, he hates most vegetables, and often pulls a disgusted face when he is given something to try for the first time. On the other hand, there are some foods Oscar likes to eat over and over again. He loves sweet and fatty foods, and his parents are worried that he is going to become obese when he grows up.

Question

How would you explain Oscar's eating habits to his parents? Refer in your explanation to the concepts of (1) food preferences and (2) neophobia.

Evaluation

Practical activity on page 244

Research support

The evolutionary explanation for food preferences is supported by research into the link between stress and eating behaviour. Susan Torres *et al.* (2008) reviewed relevant studies and concluded that humans have a marked tendency to prefer high-fat foods during periods of stress. These findings suggest that a preference for fat may have provided energy to fuel a more effective **fight or flight response** in stressful times.

This preference was adaptive because it would have given our ancestors a survival advantage over those who did not have it.

Explaining the evolution of food preferences

Joel Alcock *et al.* (2014) propose a different evolutionary explanation for food preferences – evolved as an adaptive response to gut microbes. The researchers describe gut microbes as influencing their host's behaviour in order to increase their own survival chances via a number of routes.

For example, Caroline de Weerth *et al.* (2013) found a link between infant colic and changes in gut microbiota. The pain of colic causes the baby to cry in distress, which leads parents to increase feeding. This means more nutrients are delivered to the baby's gut, to the benefit of the microbes. Therefore the creation of colic by microbes is adaptive. The microrobes may even manipulate taste preferences by altering the activity of receptors on the tongue, at least in rats.

This suggests that our distant ancestors' food preferences were not for their benefit but to enhance the survival chances of the microbes that colonised their guts.

Individual differences in taste aversion

Adam Drewnowski *et al.* (2001) found that people differ in their ability to detect the bitter-tasting chemical 6-n-propylthiouracil (PROP). Some people cannot taste it whereas others are very sensitive to it and they avoid foods containing similar bitter compounds. PROP insensitivity seems to be an inherited trait. It is difficult for an evolutionary theory to explain this inability to detect bitterness when it was apparently so important for our ancestors' survival.

Unless, of course, this inability was linked with another trait that offered a different survival benefit. Remarkably, research shows that some bitter compounds in foods such as soy products, green tea, red wine and grapefruit juice (flavonoids, polyphenols, etc.) may be protective against cancer. Those individuals who could not detect bitterness would therefore have access to foods with anti-carcinogenic properties. A preference for them would therefore have been an adaptive trait.

Evaluation eXtra

Neophobia is maladaptive

Neophobia is a good example of an adaptation that was beneficial to our ancestors' survival chances in our evolutionary history, but is now frequently maladaptive. Most of the food we consume is bought from retailers of one sort or another, so it is safer and more plentiful than it has ever been. In our modern food environment, neophobia merely restricts the variety of children's diet by limiting what they eat.

Consider: *Can you see any flaws in this argument? Are there any benefits of neophobia in the modern world in terms of greater food safety?*

The role of culture

Evolutionary explanations ignore cultural influences of food preferences. According to Elizabeth Cashdan (1998), culture plays a major role in determining which foods are accepted and rejected, and also a role in ethnic identity. She gives the example of someone brought up in a Jewish Kosher household, who would probably be repulsed by the idea of eating a prawn cocktail with a non-Jewish neighbour. Food preferences seem to be a lot more difficult to change than other elements of a culture, such as style of dress.

Consider: *Is there any part of this argument which supports the evolutionary explanation? Explain your answer.*

Apply it

Concepts: Eat up your veggies? No thanks.

Lena is 15 years old and finds the tastes of certain foods very unpleasant. In fact, her whole family shares her distaste of grapefruit juice, soy sauce, green vegetables, and plenty of other foods which make them all feel sick. Lena has often wondered what these foods have in common and why everyone in her family hates them.

Questions

1. What do you think these foods have in common?

2. How does the concept of taste aversion help us to understand Lena's family's eating behaviour?

Fat, salt, sugar, energy – all the food preferences of our evolutionary ancestors. But are they now slowly killing us?

Apply it

Methods: Babies' loves (and hates)

A psychologist intended to conduct an **observational study** of the food likes and dislikes of young babies (aged between 16 and 24 weeks). She decided to carry out a **pilot study** of five babies' behaviours when they were given a sweet-tasting liquid and a bitter-tasting liquid. Two independent observers were used to identify these behaviours.

Questions

1. Suggest *three* **operationalised behavioural categories** the observers could use to identify taste-related behaviours. (*3 marks*)

2. Write an appropriate **directional hypothesis** for this study. (*2 marks*)

3. The observers recorded each taste-related behaviour as it occurred. Identify the **level of measurement** used and explain your answer. (*2 marks*)

4. What is a pilot study and why might one be useful in this research? (*3 marks*)

5. **Inter-observer reliability** was low in this pilot study. Explain what the researcher could do to improve it before carrying out the main observational study. (*3 marks*) (See page 67)

CHECK IT

1. In relation to food preferences, explain what is meant by the terms *neophobia* and *taste aversion*
   [2 marks + 2 marks]

2. Outline the evolutionary explanation for food preferences. *[6 marks]*

3. Describe **one** study related to the evolutionary explanation for food preferences. *[3 marks]*

4. Describe and evaluate the evolutionary explanation for food preferences. *[16 marks]*

Explanations for food preferences: The role of learning

We saw in the previous spread how we are born with innate food preferences and aversions, which may be evolutionarily and genetically determined. However, it would be a waste of valuable resources to have any fixed innate tendency to like or dislike many foods. This means that most of our preferences have to be acquired through experience, and there are several ways in which they can be learned.

KEY TERMS

Social influences – Behaviour related to social factors, such as family influences, peers and media advertising, and through processes of modelling and imitation (social learning theory).

Cultural influences – 'Culture' refers to the norms and values that exist within any group of people.

Daddy draws the short straw . . . again. Providing role models for children can be a labour of love.

Apply it

Concepts: A poor diet

Ellen and Portia think their children have picked up some bad eating habits at school. The children complain about the healthy food they get given at home. When they go to the supermarket, the kids always try to use their 'pester power' at the checkout. Ellen wonders if it's her fault because she eats crisps and sweets around the children.

Question

Identify the features of this scenario that highlight the following social influences: (1) family, (2) peers and (3) the media. For each, explain one way in which Ellen and Portia could help their children learn to make healthy food choices.

The role of learning in food preference

The process of learning: Classical and operant conditioning

One common form of **classical conditioning** is *flavour–flavour learning*. We develop a preference for a new food because of its association with a flavour we already like. Because of our innate preference for sweetness, we learn to prefer many new foods by sweetening them. For example, porridge and yoghurt both become immediately more acceptable after sugar is added to them. According to flavour-flavour learning principles, this association eventually leads to liking of the new food on its own.

In terms of **operant conditioning**, children are often directly **reinforced** for their food preferences, mainly by parents and older siblings. They provide the child with rewards for eating certain foods, in the form of encouragement, praise and punishment ('if you don't eat your meat you can't have any pudding'). However, it is still notoriously difficult to establish a preference (e.g. for green vegetables) in children using rewards, which is why classical conditioning is probably the more powerful form of food preference learning.

Social influences

Social learning theory (SLT) explains **social influences** in terms of **modelling** and imitation. Children will readily acquire the food preferences of **role models** they observe eating certain foods. This is especially so if the model appears to be rewarded (by showing obvious enjoyment or being praised by others), and if they are someone the child identifies with (e.g. a parent or teacher). This has an adaptive function because it ensures that children eat foods that are obviously safe because others are eating them without harmful effects. This is important because without this modelling toddlers can and do attempt to eat potentially dangerous foods (Shutts *et al.* 2013).

Family influences Social influences on the learning of food preferences are most obvious within the family and in childhood. Parents' food preferences have powerful effects on those of children, not least because parents are 'gatekeepers' of their children's eating.

Peer influences Leann Birch (1980) arranged for participant children to be placed at school lunchtimes next to three or four other children who had different vegetable preferences from them. After four days, the participant children had changed their preferences more than the non-participant children (they switched from carrots to peas, or vice versa) in response to observing the other children. This change was still evident after several weeks.

Media influences As children get older and more independent of their parents' food choices, other models outside the family become more important. An obvious example of this is television advertising. Young people who watch even a moderate amount of television encounter a significant number of adverts for foods generally considered 'unhealthy' (high in salt, sugar and fat). These adverts are often marked by 'fun'-related themes and the products themselves promoted by characters younger and older children identify with.

Cultural influences

According to Paul Rozin (1984) **cultural influences** are the single most reliable predictor of food preference, especially family eating patterns. According to Mette Vabø and Hårvard Hansen (2014), we learn around the family table when, what and how much to eat. We learn the cultural 'rules' of preference early and these are powerful enough to overcome innate aversions. Culture determines to a large extent the foods we put on the table, and our children are exposed to, in the first place.

Cultural norms One powerful cultural influence on food preferences is ideals or norms. An example of this is attitudes towards what constitutes a 'proper meal'. For many of an older generation it has to include 'meat and two veg'. The 'rule' that the main Sunday meal has to be a roast dinner is a common ideal in British households.

Meat-eating Many culturally determined food preferences centre around meat. There is a cultural tradition in Britain and France (and elsewhere) to eat every part of an animal, which is why offal (kidneys, liver, heart, etc.) is a common preference in those countries. But this is much less the case in the USA. Most Americans consume a lot of meat in the form of steaks and the like, but they have a strong aversion to offal.

Culture and learning Culture influences which foods parents present to their children. Learning processes such as flavour-flavour learning and **vicarious reinforcement** then establish these culturally validated preferences. We associate many of the foods we eat and enjoy as adults with feelings of security and happy experiences growing up. They may be linked in memory to enjoyable special occasions spent with friends and family, which are nearly always marked by culturally specific food choices ('feasts').

Evaluation

Limited role of classical conditioning

Flavour-flavour learning can theoretically explain both food preferences and aversions. If an untried food is paired with sweetness, it will be accepted. But if it is paired with an aversive taste, then it will be rejected. However, the evidence is much stronger for the rejection scenario than it is for the acceptance one. For instance, Frank Baeyens et al. (1996) found that pairing an untried food with a soapy-flavoured chemical called *Tween* led to a long-lasting aversion to the food. It appears that this type of learning is much more efficient in forming food aversions than preferences.

Flavour-flavour learning may be less crucial in food preferences than other learning mechanisms. For instance, there is substantial evidence that repeatedly feeding a child a new food will eventually lead to a preference for that food, without the need to sweeten it first (the *mere exposure* effect). Of course, this example just reinforces the general point that experience is central to the development of food preferences, regardless of the specific learning processes involved.

Short-term versus long-term effects of SLT

Family influences on food preferences can last essentially a lifetime. However, the social learning effects of television (programmes and advertisements) are much less persistent. Helle Hare-Bruun et al. (2011) studied a group of eight- to ten-year-old Danish boys and girls over a six-year period. The researchers found that the children who watched the most TV also had the most unhealthy food preferences. However, this link was much weaker in the researchers' six-year follow-up, and had disappeared altogether for girls.

They concluded that the effects on food preferences from television are mostly short-term. It seems that, as children get older, close friends rather than television are more powerful social influences on children's longer-term food preferences.

Multiple influences

Chilli is one of the most widespread food spices in the world. It causes a characteristic 'burn' that is aversive in all cultures. Innately people dislike chilli, yet still eat it. In the cultures where chilli is traditionally used in cooking, children are carefully, gradually and repeatedly exposed to it until, as Paul Rozin (2006) puts it, 'almost everyone . . . is converted from a chilli hater to a chilli liker by the age of six years . . .'.

This is a classic demonstration of how family and cultural influences can switch an innate food aversion into a preference via learning and experience.

Evaluation eXtra

Research support for SLT

Anita Jansen and Nienke Tenney (2001) gave children either an energy-dense or energy-dilute yoghurt drink they had never tasted before. The most preferred taste was the energy-dense drink taken at the same time as a teacher who praised it and showed clear signs of enjoyment.

Consider: *In what ways does this study illustrate the importance of social learning in food preferences? Does it support any other theory? Explain your answer.*

Support for cultural influences

One of the biggest cultural changes in Western societies has been the increasing availability of food outside the home, accompanied by a decline in family mealtimes and cooking. Some 46% of spending on food in the USA goes on food eaten in places other than the home. American adolescents eat up to 30% of their meals outside the home, half of them in fast-food restaurants.

Consider: *Explain how these findings provide support for the argument that culture influences food preferences.*

Apply it **Concepts: A matter of tastes**

Sophie and Sahal are comparing what they had for breakfast. Sophie had apricot jam on toast, something she has had for as long as she can remember. Sahal had canjeero, a bread that looks a bit like a pancake, with a goat stew. He explains how he used to have it with camel meat when he was growing up in Somalia.

Question

Explain at least *two* ways in which culture influences Sophie's and Sahal's breakfast preferences.

The family that eats together . . . we learn many of our food likes and dislikes around the meal table. But how long before this scene becomes a rarity?

STUDY TIP

Social learning theory features a lot in this book as an explanation for different behaviours. It is easy to write a general description of SLT, but you absolutely must avoid this. If you are writing about the role of learning in food preferences, you have to apply SLT concepts to this specific behaviour. Always **THINK LINK** *(see page 360 for an explanation): how do modelling, vicarious reinforcement and media influences explain food preferences?*

Apply it **Methods: Questioning preferences**

A team of health psychologists carry out **interviews** to help them understand how children learn food preferences. They recruit 20 children between the ages of eight and ten years. Each child is given a 20-minute interview, in which they are asked a mixture of **closed** and **open questions** about their food likes and dislikes.

Questions

1. Explain *two* differences between a **structured** and an **unstructured interview**. (2 marks + 2 marks)
2. Write *one* example of an open question and *one* example of a closed question suitable for this study. (2 marks + 2 marks)
3. Identify *one* sampling technique the psychologists could use to recruit the children, and explain how they could do so. (1 mark + 2 marks)
4. Explain *one* reason why the psychologists thought interviews might be better than **questionnaires** in this study. (2 marks)
5. Explain *one* **ethical issue** that could arise in this study and how the psychologists could deal with it. (2 marks + 2 marks)

CHECK IT

1. Outline social **and/or** cultural influences on the learning of food preferences. [6 marks]
2. Outline research into the role of learning in food preferences. [6 marks]
3. Describe **one** study of social influences on the learning of food preferences. [4 marks]
4. Describe and evaluate the role of learning in food preferences. [16 marks]

NEURAL AND HORMONAL MECHANISMS IN THE CONTROL OF EATING BEHAVIOUR

Neural and hormonal mechanisms involved in the control of eating behaviour, including the role of the hypothalamus, ghrelin and leptin.

Eating is such a central feature of human behaviour. It is bound up with all sorts of cultural traditions, psychological motives and social activities but perhaps most of all it provides the body with energy and the means for survival. Therefore it is not surprising that the controlling mechanisms of this behaviour should be deeply rooted in our biology.

KEY TERMS

Hypothalamus – A small subcortical brain structure made up of two centres: the lateral hypothalamus (LH) and the ventro-medial hypothalamus (VMH).

Ghrelin – A hormone produced by cells in the stomach wall which acts as a powerful appetite stimulant, contributing to the 'on switch' of eating behaviour.

Leptin – A hormone produced by adipose (fat) cells which acts as a powerful appetite suppressant, contributing to the 'off switch' of eating behaviour.

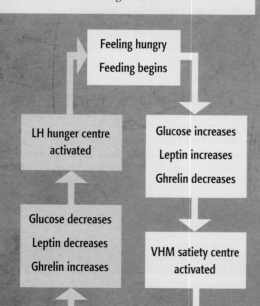

Neural and hormonal mechanisms

The role of the hypothalamus

The **hypothalamus**, a pea-sized structure of the brain, has a crucial role in integrating the **nervous** and **endocrine systems**. It is also involved in maintaining **homeostasis**, the balancing of bodily processes within certain limits. This biological mechanism regulates the level of glucose in the blood. Glucose is the most basic of sugars and the body's main source of energy. Fluctuations in blood glucose concentration are first of all detected by glucose-sensing neurons in the hypothalamus. The hypothalamus can then regulate glucose levels by influencing the output of insulin and anti-insulin hormones, e.g. glucagon (Chan and Sherwin, 2012). Both insulin and glucagon are secreted from the pancreas, and play a key role in maintaining blood glucose homeostasis within a very narrow range of values.

The dual-centre model of eating

According to the *dual-centre model* of eating behaviour, two structures of the hypothalamus provide the homeostatic control.

Lateral hypothalamus (LH) Often described as the 'feeding centre' or 'on switch' of the hypothalamus, the LH contains cells that detect levels of glucose in the liver. The LH is activated when glucose levels fall below a certain level. This causes the individual to become hungry, and triggers the motivation to eat, along with all its accompanying behaviours such as searching for and preparing food.

A further neural mechanism associated with LH activity is the secretion of a hypothalamic **neurotransmitter** called *neuropeptide Y* (NPY), which is closely associated with hunger and a reduction in physical activity. NPY is a powerful stimulant of hunger. Rats injected with NPY directly into the hypothalamus will eat excessively, and eventually become obese as the injections continue.

Ventro-medial hypothalamus (VMH) This part of the hypothalamus is the 'satiety centre', the 'off switch' of eating behaviour. Eating food provides the body with glucose, so the levels of glucose circulating in the bloodstream and stored in the liver (as glycogen) rise once again. These levels are detected by cells in the VMH. Activity in the VMH is then triggered once they increase past a set point. LH activity is inhibited at the same time. The individual becomes satiated; they feel full and stop eating.

Damage to the VMH is linked with continued eating past the point of satiety. Alexander Reeves and Fred Plum (1969) reported the case of a woman whose weight more than doubled in a two-year period. A **post-mortem** investigation revealed that she had a tumour on her VMH, which caused its normal 'stop eating' function to fail.

The role of ghrelin

Ghrelin is a hormone secreted by the stomach. It is a **hormonal** marker of how long since we have last eaten because the amount produced is closely related to how empty our stomach is – more ghrelin is released the longer we go without food. Ghrelin levels are detected by receptors in a part of the hypothalamus called the *arcuate nucleus*. When levels rise above a set point, the arcuate nucleus sends signals to the lateral hypothalamus to secrete neuropeptide Y (see above).

Ghrelin is now known to be an appetite stimulant in humans. Alison Wren *et al.* (2001) found that given intravenously, ghrelin caused a short-term increase in the amount of food eaten. The amount of ghrelin circulating in the bloodstream doubles just before a meal, decreasing very quickly afterwards, and is closely correlated with subjective feelings of hunger.

The role of leptin

Leptin is a hormone produced by adipose (fat) cells. Levels of leptin in the blood increase along with fat levels, and these are detected in the brain by the VMH. As leptin is an appetite suppressant, it contributes to the VMH satiety mechanism outlined above. Once levels increase beyond a certain point, the individual feels full and stops eating. Julio Licinio *et al.* (2004) studied an extremely rare **genetic** condition in which individuals are unable to produce leptin naturally. This condition is associated with severe obesity. Treatment involves leptin-replacement therapy, and over an 18-month period the researchers found that this led to an average weight loss of more than 40% and a reduction in food intake initially of 49%.

Apply it **Concepts: The dual-centre model**

Mauricio Russek (1971) starved rats before giving them an opportunity to feed. Injecting glucose directly into their livers stopped them feeding. Philip Teitelbaum (1955) created lesions in the hypothalamuses of rats and found that this caused them to overeat.

Question

Which study demonstrates the role of:
(1) The lateral hypothalamus?
(2) The ventro-medial hypothalamus?

Explain your answer.

Evaluation

Research support

Research support for the dual-centre model comes mainly from *lesion studies* with rats – creating surgical wounds in various strategic brain areas confirms their roles in controlling eating behaviour. For example, Albert Hetherington and Stephen Ranson (1942) showed that lesioning the VMH of rats caused these animals to become *hyperphagic* (overeat) and eventually severely obese. When Bal Anand and John Brobeck (1951) lesioned the LH of rats, the outcome was *aphagia* (a cessation of all eating behaviour). This illustrates the homeostatic nature of the mechanism.

However, experimental lesions are often not limited to one small part of the brain; other areas are frequently damaged too. Richard Gold (1973) found that lesions that really are limited to the VMH do not produce hyperphagia. This only occurred when another part of the hypothalamus, the *paraventricular nucleus* (PVN), was also damaged. Nevertheless, this finding is disputed because it has not been **replicated**, and the overwhelming consensus is that VMH lesions do cause overeating, as predicted by the model.

An oversimplified explanation

Elana Valassi *et al.* (2008) point out that research continues to reveal more neural and hormonal influences on eating behaviour. Even putting social, psychological and cultural factors to one side (see below), the biological contributions are numerous. To take just one example, a hormone called *cholecystokinin* (CCK) is produced in the duodenum (upper intestine). It activates the nerve that sends signals from the gastro-intestinal tract to the hypothalamus. These signals indicate satiety and contribute to the 'stop eating' mechanism. CCK may be an even more powerful appetite suppressant than leptin.

Several other chemicals appear to be involved in eating behaviour, including the neurotransmitters **serotonin** and **dopamine**. To add further to the complexity of the picture, these biochemicals interact to either enhance or inhibit each other's activities. So the dual-centre model presents a relatively straightforward homeostatic account which does not accurately reflect the true complexity of how eating behaviour is controlled.

Roles of social and cultural factors

Research by Stephen Woods (2004) suggests that the glucostatic view that the LH feeding centre always detects falls in blood glucose levels and stimulates hunger is outdated. In fact, this only occurs in 'emergency' conditions of severe energy deprivation. Normal meal onset is much less under neurochemical control and is usually initiated by social and cultural factors that are related to lifestyle (such as traditional times of day considered appropriate for eating). A purely biological approach to understanding eating behaviour tends to ignore potentially important non-biological factors that may be more influential.

Evaluation eXtra

Non-human animal research

Much of what we understand about the neural and hormonal control of eating behaviour comes from research with non-human animals, especially rats (e.g. lesion studies). As usual, it is important to be cautious about extrapolating such findings to humans without considering the differences between species that may make such **generalisations** invalid.

Consider: *Explain why it is and is not **valid** to generalise findings about control of eating behaviour in this way.*

Practical applications

A better understanding of the neural and hormonal mechanisms controlling eating behaviour offers great therapeutic possibilities. As the complex interactions between the nervous system and the many hormones involved in regulating eating become clearer, treatments for both **obesity** and **anorexia** become more realistic. The research by Licinio *et al.* (see facing page) into treatment of leptin deficiency is a good example of this.

Consider: *Explain what the potential benefits of this research could be. Do you see any possible drawbacks?*

Apply it — Concepts: Jed's struggle

Jed has always struggled with his weight and has been diagnosed as diabetic. As dieting has never worked, Jed's doctor has recommended he consider having a gastric band fitted, which would limit the amount of food he could eat and change his biochemistry so he feels less hungry. But Jed is not convinced that his problem is biological and would like to know more.

Question

Use your knowledge of eating behaviour to outline why Jed might be right.

Do I look big in this? Zucker rats are bred to be obese for research into diabetes and the effects of ghrelin, leptin and other biological mechanisms.

Apply it — Methods: Fat rats

A researcher was interested in how the eating behaviour of rats is controlled by hormones. He allowed two groups of rats to feed freely, and measured the quantity of food eaten. One group of the rats had been selectively bred to be deficient in leptin. The other rats had normal leptin functioning. The researcher found that in a single feeding session, the leptin-deficient rats ate **significantly** more than the other group.

Questions

1. Identify the **operationalised IV** and **DV**. *(1 mark + 1 mark)*
2. Identify and explain the type of **experimental design** used in this study. *(1 mark + 2 marks)*
3. Explain *one* strength and *one* weakness of this design in the context of this study. *(2 marks + 2 marks)*
4. Explain what is meant by the term validity. *(2 marks)*
5. Explain why this experiment might be lacking in validity. *(3 marks)*

STUDY TIP

Neural and hormonal mechanisms are both biological concepts and are easy to mix up. Remember that 'neural' refers to the involvement of the brain and nervous system, so includes the hypothalamus. 'Hormonal' is about chemical messengers and includes the roles of ghrelin and leptin.

CHECK IT

1. Outline the role of the hypothalamus in the control of eating behaviour. *[6 marks]*
2. Outline the roles of ghrelin and leptin in the control of eating behaviour. *[6 marks]*
3. Describe neural **and/or** hormonal mechanisms involved in the control of eating behaviour. *[6 marks]*
4. Discuss some of the neural and hormonal mechanisms involved in the control of eating behaviour. *[16 marks]*

BIOLOGICAL EXPLANATIONS FOR ANOREXIA NERVOSA

Biological explanations for anorexia nervosa including genetic and neural explanations.

Anorexia nervosa (AN) is a devastating and life-threatening eating disorder that is estimated to affect between 0.3% and 1.2% of the population at any one time, with a female to male ratio of about nine to one. AN is defined by many symptoms, including: a refusal to eat, intense dieting, a pathological fear of gaining weight, a distorted body image, self-disgust and food-related anxiety.

It is this bewildering range of symptoms that makes AN so difficult to explain from just one perspective. We begin our four-spread exploration of AN by considering two prominent biological explanations.

KEY TERMS

Genetic explanation – Genes consist of DNA strands. DNA produces 'instructions' for general physical features of an organism (such as eye colour, height) and also specific physical features (such as neurotransmitter levels and size of brain structures). These may impact on psychological features (such as intelligence and mental disorder). Genes are transmitted from parents to offspring, i.e. inherited.

Neural explanation – Any explanation of behaviour (and its disorders) in terms of (dys)functions of the brain and nervous system. This includes the activity of brain structures such as the hypothalamus, and neurotransmitters such as serotonin and dopamine.

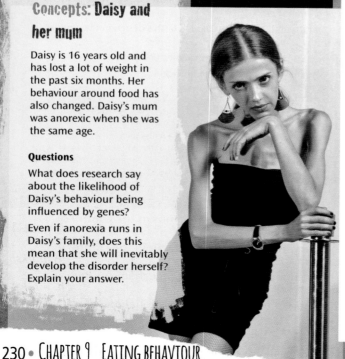

What makes someone starve themselves to such an extent that it threatens their health and even their life?

Apply it

Concepts: Daisy and her mum

Daisy is 16 years old and has lost a lot of weight in the past six months. Her behaviour around food has also changed. Daisy's mum was anorexic when she was the same age.

Questions

What does research say about the likelihood of Daisy's behaviour being influenced by genes?

Even if anorexia runs in Daisy's family, does this mean that she will inevitably develop the disorder herself? Explain your answer.

Genetic explanations for anorexia nervosa

Anorexia runs in families

Evidence for the **genetic explanation** of **anorexia nervosa** (AN) comes from **twin studies** of **MZ** and **DZ twins**. The **concordance rate** indicates the proportion of twin pairs in which both individuals have AN, relative to pairs in which only one individual has it. As MZ twins share 100% of their genes but DZ twins only 50% (on average), a higher concordance rate for MZs is strong evidence of a genetic component to AN.

Anthony Holland et al. (1988) studied 45 pairs of female twins (and one set of triplets). They found a concordance rate of 56% for MZ twins but only 5% for DZs. This study was **replicated** several years later by Janet Treasure and Anthony Holland (1995) with less dramatic findings – an MZ concordance rate of 65%, with 32% for DZs. This is still strong evidence for the role of genes.

Candidate genes

Researchers are hunting for genes that may be involved in causing anorexia, and there are many candidates. Ashley Scott-Van Zeeland et al. (2014) carried out a *candidate-gene association study* (CGAS). They compared 1205 AN patients and 1948 control participants by sequencing 152 candidate genes suspected to be linked with features of AN. They discovered that only one gene was **significantly** associated with AN: *epoxide hydrolase 2 (Ephx2)*. It codes for an enzyme involved in cholesterol metabolism. Surprisingly, it so happens that many people in the acute phase of AN, when symptoms are particularly severe, do have abnormally high levels of cholesterol.

Genome-wide association studies (GWAS)

These offer a different approach because they do not make assumptions about which genes *might* be involved in anorexia. They look at the entire collection of human genes rather than just individual ones. GWASs of anorexia are rare. Vesna Boraska et al. (2014) conducted one with 5551 AN patients and 21080 **matched controls** – 72 separate genetic variations were identified, but none of them were significantly related to AN. However, the researchers argued that this was not because genetic influences on AN are non-existent. Rather, it was because their study was not sensitive enough to detect them.

Neural explanations for anorexia nervosa

The most direct and well-evidenced **neural explanation** of AN is in terms of **neurotransmitters**, especially **serotonin** and **dopamine**.

Serotonin

Research has established the involvement of serotonin in many behaviours that are features of AN (such as appetite reduction and obsessiveness). In a review article, Ursula Bailer and Walter Kaye (2011) present evidence of low levels of serotonin breakdown byproducts (**metabolites** such as 5-HIAA) in people with AN. These levels return to normal after short-term weight recovery, and increase beyond normal levels after long-term recovery. Evelyn Attia et al. (2014) studied AN patients who had not returned to their pre-illness weight. These individuals responded less well to drugs that stimulate serotonin activity (serotonin agonists) than AN patients who had restored a healthy weight.

The pattern of results from these studies clearly indicates underactivity of the serotonin system in AN.

Dopamine

Findings have been inconsistent but some research shows that decreased dopamine levels are associated with AN. Attention has focused on *homovanillic acid* (HVA), a metabolite of dopamine, which is decreased in AN patients. Research by Walter Kaye et al. (1991) shows that HVA levels are also lower in recovered AN patients compared with control participants. A study by Ursula Bailer et al. (2012) suggests how dopamine may operate in AN. They administered amphetamine to their participants to increase the release of dopamine. Healthy participants experienced euphoria (pleasure), but the AN patients experienced anxiety. As eating increases dopamine release, it may be that AN patients restrict their food intake as a means of reducing their anxiety levels.

Evaluation

Limitation of twin studies

The **validity** of twin studies of AN depends on the *equal environments assumption*. To compare concordance rates, we have to assume that MZ and DZ twins are treated with equal degrees of similarity. Only if this is true can we conclude that differences in AN concordance rates are due to genetic factors. Views differ, but many psychologists continue to question the equal environments assumption (e.g. Joseph 2002). The argument is that MZ twins are treated more similarly than DZs in many ways – primarily by their parents, but also by other family members, friends, teachers and even passing acquaintances. They spend more time together and may even have a closer bond than DZ twins. This greater environmental similarity means that **heritability** estimates are artificially inflated and genetic influences on anorexia may not be as great as twin studies suggest.

Limitations of gene studies

Many candidate genes have been put forward only to 'fall by the wayside' in later research. These studies (e.g. Pineiro *et al.* 2010) show that the search for a single gene is futile. It is widely accepted that no one gene can be responsible for the wide variety of physical and psychological symptoms that characterise AN, such as appetite loss, body image distortions and fear of weight gain. Instead, anorexia is **polygenic** – many genes make important but modest contributions to the disorder. In addition other factors are important too (see **diathesis-stress explanation** below).

Evaluation

Supporting evidence

Research by Walter Kaye *et al.* (1999) showed that levels of the dopamine metabolite HVA were lower in recovered AN patients compared with control participants. The recovered participants were of normal weight and not restricting their diets. This is an important strength of the study because most studies measure HVA levels in people *currently experiencing* the symptoms of AN. The problem with this is that the weight loss and malnutrition of AN may account for the lower levels of HVA/dopamine. Kaye *et al.*'s study avoids these **confounding variables**. Because lower HVA levels persist after recovery, the researchers conclude that their findings are evidence that disturbance of dopamine metabolism may be a causal factor in anorexia.

Interactions with other neurotransmitters

Ken Nunn *et al.* (2012) argue that serotonin (under)activity on its own does not distinguish between people who have AN and those who do not. In their view, serotonin accounts for some features of AN but not for others. AN can be better explained by considering the interaction between serotonin and another neurotransmitter – **noradrenaline**. According to these researchers, serotonin and dopamine are both secondary to the activity of noradrenaline in AN. They claim that other neurotransmitters, such as **GABA**, are also involved. This is a useful reminder that neurotransmitter systems do not operate in isolation, but in complex interactions. However, the explanation is recent and remains to be fully tested.

Evaluation eXtra

Diathesis-stress explanation

Suzanne Abraham (2008) makes the widely-accepted point that AN can only be fully understood by considering the interaction between genetic and non-genetic factors. For example, genes may create a vulnerability (a diathesis) to AN that only expresses itself when an individual tries to lose weight (a stressor), which she (or he) may do for many social, cultural or psychological reasons. Other non-biological risk factors also play a triggering role, as do many 'perpetuating factors' that maintain disordered eating behaviours.

Consider: *Do you think this argument completely undermines the **validity** of biological explanations of AN? Explain your answer.*

Genetic and neural theories can explain some aspects of anorexia, but can they explain symptoms such as having a distorted body image?

Apply it — Concepts: **Male anorexia?**

Jackson is getting thinner and thinner and may have an eating disorder. His parents have noticed that he is much more anxious these days. His appetite is non-existent and he is becoming more and more obsessive.

Questions

1. Referring to (1) serotonin and (2) dopamine, what features of Jackson's behaviour might indicate problems of neural functioning?
2. Some **antidepressant** drugs work by boosting levels of serotonin and dopamine. Explain how they might help Jackson.

Apply it — Methods: **A study of twins**

A psychologist decided to conduct a study into eating behaviours. She recruited a **volunteer sample** of 10 pairs of identical twins. Each participant completed the *Restrained Eating Questionnaire* (REQ), made up of ten questions (for example, 'Do you feel guilty after overeating'), each with a four point scale (going from 1 to 4 where 1 represented 'never' and 4 represented 'always'). Each participant provided an overall score between 10 and 40, with a higher score indicating more restrained eating. The psychologist was interested in the degree of relationship between the twins in their scores.

The results of the study are given in Table 1 below.

Table 1: Restrained eating scores for 10 twin pairs

Pair	Twin 1	Twin 2	Pair	Twin 1	Twin 2
1	32	38	6	29	31
2	26	20	7	10	14
3	37	29	8	30	26
4	18	12	9	15	17
5	14	34	10	18	15

1. Sketch a **scattergram** of the data in Table 1. Give it an appropriate title and label the axes carefully. (*3 marks*)
2. Discuss what the table of results and the graph you have sketched show about the relationship of the twin pairs' eating behaviours. (*3 marks*)
3. Identify an appropriate **statistical test** the researcher could use to analyse the data. (*1 mark*) (See page 70)
4. Give *two* reasons why this would be an appropriate test to use. (*2 marks*)

CHECK IT

1. Outline research into the genetic explanation for anorexia nervosa. [6 marks]
2. Outline the neural explanation for anorexia nervosa. [6 marks]
3. Evaluate the genetic explanation for anorexia nervosa. [10 marks]
4. Describe and evaluate **one or more** biological explanations for anorexia nervosa. [16 marks]

PSYCHOLOGICAL EXPLANATIONS FOR ANOREXIA NERVOSA: FAMILY SYSTEMS THEORY

Psychological explanations for anorexia nervosa: family systems theory including enmeshment, autonomy and control.

Salvador Minuchin and his colleagues (1978) developed a psychodynamic theory of anorexia which focuses on the role of the family as a complex social system, the most pervasive system influencing development and behaviour. According to the family systems theory (FST) of eating disorders, interactions between family members become tightly structured around the AN sufferer's symptoms. This is adaptive for family members, because it distracts attention away from their many interpersonal conflicts. Minuchin labelled such dysfunctional families as *psychosomatic*. The effect on an adolescent child in such a family is to produce any one of a range of possible disorders, including anorexia.

KEY TERMS

Family systems theory – A psychodynamic explanation that views dysfunctional family interaction as a major factor in the development and maintenance of anorexia nervosa (AN).

Enmeshment – Members of an anorexic family are over-involved and over-protective. Their self-identities are bound up with each other. Roles are poorly defined and there is little privacy.

Autonomy – Our experience of freedom in deciding how we should behave, and degree of independence from others.

Control (in anorexia) – The experience of being in charge of one's own self and behaviour. People with AN are thought to struggle against family dependence for control, as they also do for autonomy.

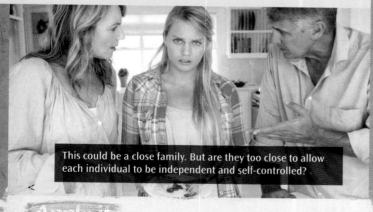

This could be a close family. But are they too close to allow each individual to be independent and self-controlled?

Apply it

Concepts: Applying the theory to therapy

Ruby has recently been diagnosed with anorexia. She is 19 years old but weighs just 40 kilos and has a body mass index of 13.5. Her weight has now been stabilised and she is seeing a therapist. The therapist suspects that Ruby's family relationships may be involved in her anorexia and wants to find out more.

Question

Write some questions the therapist could ask Ruby to find out if her anorexia is linked to the following: (i) enmeshment; (ii) overprotectiveness; (iii) rigidity; (iv) conflict avoidance; (v) lack of autonomy; (vi) lack of control.

Family systems theory (FST)

Minuchin *et al.* (1978) identified four main features of what they called a typical *anorexic family*. Because **anorexia nervosa** (AN) overwhelmingly affects females more than males, **family systems theory** focuses on the relationship between daughter and mother when being used to explain AN.

1. Enmeshment

Members of anorexic families are overly involved with each other. This comes about because boundaries within the family are 'fuzzy', the result of poorly defined roles and a lack of leadership. Family members spend a lot of time together, to the exclusion of others; they constantly impinge upon each other's privacy; they speak for each other on the assumption that they know what each other is thinking and what their views are. Families become **enmeshed** because the self-identities of each member are all tied up with one another. An adolescent daughter in an anorexic family faces the challenge of asserting her independence and differentiating her identity from everyone else's, especially her mother's. But the enmeshed family is structured in a way that prevents this, so one way for the adolescent to assert her independence is by refusing to eat.

2. Overprotectiveness

Family members are constantly involved in protecting each other from external threats. They nurture each other obsessively, in a way that reinforces family loyalty and leaves no room for independence. Mara Palazzoli (1974) described how the mother of a daughter with anorexia in an enmeshed family consistently understood her role as a personal sacrifice. That is, all the decisions she made she felt were for the benefit of her daughter and not for herself. This may sound admirable, but of course it makes it much easier to blame the anorexic daughter when things go wrong.

3. Rigidity

Interactions within the anorexic family are extremely inflexible. Members deny the need for change and work hard to maintain things as they are. In most situations rigidity is not dysfunctional because the family 'coasts' along as it always has done. But problems arise when circumstances change, due to some internal pressure or external threat. The family is too rigid to adapt and is thrown into a crisis. For example, an adolescent daughter seeking greater independence cannot be accommodated. The rest of the family – particularly the mother – moves to quash this attempt at self-differentiation, giving the daughter no room for manoeuvre. The predictable outcome is dysfunctional behaviour of some kind, often an eating disorder.

4. Conflict avoidance

The foremost priority of the anorexic family is to avoid conflict, and members will take whatever steps are necessary to prevent it or to suppress it if it occurs. For instance, there can be no discussion of any issues where a difference of opinion might arise. As these issues are often problems of one kind or another, this means that they are not resolved and continue to fester until a crisis develops. So the anorexic daughter continues to refuse to eat, and starves herself, as the family refuses to accept there is anything to discuss.

Autonomy and control

Minuchin *et al.* argued that families exhibiting the features outlined above (i.e. they are over-involved, over-protective, inflexible and conflict-avoidant) are actively preventing its members exercising **autonomy** and **control**.

This argument was extended by the psychoanalyst Hilde Bruch (1978). She suggested that anorexia is caused by the adolescent daughter's struggle to achieve the autonomy and control she craves. Although the father is involved in the dysfunctional family dynamic, it is the mother in particular who is domineering, intrusive, discourages separation and does not accept her daughter's need for independence. One outcome of this is confusion in the daughter, which expresses itself in three major symptoms of AN: a distorted body image, an inability to identify internal body states such as hunger, and an overwhelming feeling of a loss of control. The self-starvation that is central to anorexia is, according to Bruch, a desperate attempt by the daughter to control her self-identity as someone independent of the family. She controls her destiny by controlling her body, and weight loss is the visible measure of her success – the thinner she gets, the greater her degree of control. She also gains autonomy, by disrupting her dependent relationship with her mother.

Evaluation

Supportive research

Timo Brockmeyer et al. (2013) studied 112 female AN patients and healthy control participants. They found that the AN patients showed a **significantly** greater desire to be autonomous. This corresponds with the results of an earlier study by Jaine Strauss and Richard Ryan (1987) which found that female AN patients demonstrated greater disturbances of autonomy. They had a more controlling style of regulating their own behaviour; they differentiated less clearly between themselves and other family members; and they perceived poorer communication within their families.

Taken together, these findings support FST because they show that the desire for autonomy – especially when it is prevented – may be a risk factor specifically for AN in daughters.

Inconsistent evidence

Massimiliano Aragona et al. (2011) studied the families of 30 female Portuguese patients being treated for eating disorders and found that they were no more enmeshed or rigid than a sample of non-eating disordered families. The researchers suggest that this failure to confirm FST may be because they used a different method of measuring enmeshment and rigidity than other studies (a **self-report** questionnaire as opposed to observer or interviewer ratings). The fact that research studies find different outcomes depending on methodological variations (such as the method of measurement) illustrates a wider problem with a **psychodynamic** explanation of AN: the difficulty in confirming predictions derived from vaguely-defined concepts such as enmeshment and autonomy. Added to this, most research into FST is based on self-reports. So what is being measured is not actual enmeshment, autonomy, overprotection, and so on, but family members' subjective perceptions of these variables, especially in this study.

This is a major limitation of FST, because it means that research has failed to reliably identify the 'typical anorexic family'.

Treatment applications

There is evidence that therapies based on FST have had some success in treating AN. *Behavioural family systems therapy* (BFST) attempts to disentangle family relationships, encourage the AN sufferer to interact more with people outside the family circle, and reduce parental control over eating. Arthur Robin et al. (1995) tested the effectiveness of this therapy on a small sample of 11 female AN patients. The treatment lasted 16 months, at the end of which six patients were considered to have recovered. A further three were found to have recovered after a one-year follow-up period. This compared favourably with the outcome of individual therapy.

However, a serious limitation relates to the assessment of having 'recovered'. This was determined by experienced psychologists who were aware of which patients had undergone which type of therapy (i.e. the study was not **blinded**). This makes the risk of bias too great to draw any firm conclusions.

Evaluation eXtra

Cause or effect (or both)?

Research does not support the view that family dysfunction is a *cause* of anorexia. It is just as likely (perhaps more so) that enmeshment, rigidity, overprotectiveness and conflict avoidance are *consequences* of having a daughter with AN. However, it is worth noting that FST supporters argue that the issue of cause and effect is irrelevant. Their view is that regardless of whether the family is the cause of the illness or not, the symptoms become intimately linked to family interactions anyway. Understanding this link can only help in the search for an effective treatment.

Consider: *Does the issue of cause and effect matter? Does it weaken the* **validity** *of FST? Explain your answer.*

Explanatory power

Despite its evident limitations, FST can explain two important features of AN that other explanations have difficulty with. One is the general tendency for the disorder to first appear in adolescence. The other is its significantly greater incidence in females. It tends to assume that anorexia is a disorder exclusively of females. Unfortunately, this means it is also true that FST has trouble accounting for AN that does not appear in adolescence or its undoubted existence in males.

Consider: *On balance, do you think this is a strength or a limitation of FST?*

Apply it — Concepts: Striving for control

Anoushka's family do lots of things together, which Anoushka enjoyed when she was a child but not now that she's 16. Her parents always want to know what she's doing and where she's been. She wants to wear the clothes that she likes but her mum won't let her. Anoushka has a sign on her bedroom door saying 'authorised personnel only' but that doesn't stop her mum from coming in whenever she feels like it. She seems to know more about Anoushka's friends than Anoushka does.

Question

What aspects of this scenario suggest that Anoushka could be at risk of developing anorexia? Explain how in terms of family systems theory.

Family systems theory (FST) suggests that anorexia may be the result of a mother's attempts to thwart her daughter's desire for autonomy.

Apply it — Methods: A case of anorexia

A psychologist carried out a **case study** into the family of a 17-year-old woman with anorexia nervosa. She used various techniques for collecting data about interpersonal relationships and interactions within the family.

Questions

1. Describe *one* technique that the psychologist could have used to collect data in this case study. (*2 marks*)
2. The study gathered a lot of **qualitative data**. Explain what is meant by qualitative data. (*2 marks*)
3. Outline *one* strength of gathering qualitative data in this study. (*2 marks*)
4. The psychologist wrote up the case study in a report for publication in a scientific journal. What is the purpose of the discussion section of such a report? (*2 marks*)
5. How could the psychologist maintain her participants' **confidentiality** when her report is published? (*3 marks*)

CHECK IT

1. In relation to the family systems theory of anorexia nervosa, explain what is meant by the terms *enmeshment* and *autonomy*. [2 marks + 2 marks]
2. Describe research into the roles of autonomy and control in the family systems theory of anorexia nervosa. [6 marks]
3. Outline the family systems theory of anorexia nervosa. [6 marks]
4. Discuss family systems theory as an explanation for anorexia nervosa. [16 marks]

PSYCHOLOGICAL EXPLANATIONS FOR ANOREXIA NERVOSA: SOCIAL LEARNING THEORY

Psychological explanations for anorexia nervosa: social learning theory including modelling, reinforcement and media.

Our second psychological explanation of anorexia is Albert Bandura's (1978) social learning theory (SLT). Two major learning processes are operating in SLT: observational learning and vicarious reinforcement. A useful feature of this explanation is the role it allows for the media. SLT recognises that in the right circumstances, it is not only people we meet in real life whose behaviour can be imitated but celebrities and even fictional characters as well.

KEY TERMS

Social learning theory – A way of explaining behaviour that includes both direct and indirect reinforcement, combining learning theory with the role of cognitive factors.

Modelling – From the observer's perspective modelling is imitating the behaviour of a role model. From the role model's perspective, modelling is the precise demonstration of a specific behaviour that may be imitated by an observer.

Reinforcement – A consequence of behaviour that increases the likelihood of that behaviour being repeated. Can be positive or negative.

Media – Communication channels, such as TV, film and books, through which news, entertainment, education and data are made available.

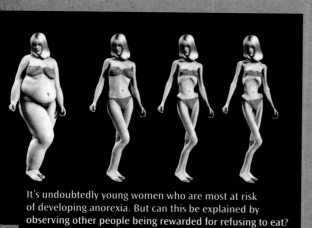

It's undoubtedly young women who are most at risk of developing anorexia. But can this be explained by observing other people being rewarded for refusing to eat?

Social learning theory

Modelling

Anorexia nervosa (AN) can be acquired indirectly, through observation of a model (i.e. **modelling**), an individual who provides a 'template' for behaviour that the observer can imitate. The model can exist in real life, such as a family member; or they can be symbolic, for example a cartoon character. Models are influential because they do not just provide an example of behaviour to follow. They can also modify social norms by establishing what is acceptable or usual behaviour in a situation. For example, a child observing an older sibling constantly restricting her food intake may learn that this behaviour is 'normal'.

Models are especially influential if the child identifies with them. Perhaps the child respects the model or perceives them as successful or glamorous and associates the model's thinness with these desirable characteristics.

Vicarious reinforcement

Social learning theory (SLT) depends not so much on observing behaviour, but on observing the positive or negative consequences of that behaviour. So if the model is rewarded, for example by being praised for losing weight, this makes it more likely that the observer will imitate the model, because they receive **reinforcement** indirectly (or vicariously).

Family members are major sources of vicarious reinforcement. Because they spend a lot of time together, observation of a behaviour is not a one-off occurrence but is repeated frequently over time. If a behaviour such as food restriction is also regularly rewarded, an observing younger child will experience many instances of **vicarious reinforcement** that make imitation much more likely and frequent.

Role of the media

The **media** provides a rich source of symbolic models, and is a powerful transmitter of cultural ideals about body shape and size. Music videos, magazines, websites and (perhaps most importantly) television all communicate images of the ideal body shape for women (and increasingly for men). In recent times, at least in most Western cultures, this ideal has become thinner and thinner, to the point that Size Zero is presented as a body shape for young women to aspire to.

Identification and vicarious reinforcement There is a danger that young women who are aware of media figures may *identify* with the glamour of female celebrities, fashion models, film and TV actors who overwhelmingly conform to this 'thin ideal'. This might motivate them to behave in ways that help them to lose weight and achieve thinness, such as dieting and exercising. This behaviour would be *vicariously reinforced* by the rewarding fame, success, wealth, respect, and satisfaction they observe in female role models in the media.

Key study on SLT and anorexia

Helga Dittmar and her colleagues (2006) studied the influence of one common model of the thin ideal – Barbie. If Barbie was scaled up to adult human size, her waist would be 39% smaller than most AN patients. Estimates suggest that 42% of UK women owned a Barbie when they were children; 99% of three- to ten-year-old US girls own at least one.

Procedure: 162 British girls aged five to eight years were divided into three groups. All were exposed to images (in a storybook) of either Barbie dolls, Emme dolls (more realistic dolls with a bigger body shape), or control images of flowers, balloons, and clothes. Having seen these images, the girls were asked to rate statements about body esteem such as 'I'm pretty happy with the way I look'. Their extent of body shape dissatisfaction was also assessed by them colouring in two body silhouettes: one they thought represented their body shape, and another representing what they wanted to be.

Findings: The girls who saw the Barbie images were significantly more dissatisfied with their body shape and had **significantly** lower body esteem than the girls who saw the Emme or control images. The researchers concluded that the Barbie doll is a powerful 'aspirational role model' for young girls. They identify with Barbie because of the glamour, affluence and success associated with her body shape. As a result they internalise the thin ideal that Barbie's ultrathin proportions represent. This initiates the body dissatisfaction that may ultimately lead to eating disorders such as AN.

Apply it Concepts: Heather's role models?

Heather's mum has always been slim and puts it down to 'natural good genes'. But as Heather has grown older, she's noticed that her mum rarely eats even at mealtimes. Heather's older sister also eats very little. Her sister and her mum often comment on one another's appearance, praising each other for losing weight and offering the latest dieting tips.

Question

Explain how Heather may be at risk of developing anorexia, using the concepts of (1) modelling, (2) identification and (3) vicarious reinforcement.

Evaluation

Research support

Anne Becker *et al.* (2011) carried out a **natural experiment** of the effects of television on eating disorders in Fiji, a Pacific island where television broadcasts only became available in the mid-1990s. The most significant predictor of eating disorders amongst the sample of adolescent female ethnic Fijians was 'social network media exposure'. This was defined as how many friends and schoolmates had access to TV, video or DVD, and was more influential than the number of hours individuals spent watching TV themselves.

These findings are best explained in terms of social learning. An individual girl is more likely to acquire an eating disorder not because she is directly exposed to media influence, but because her friends are. Friends in the girl's social network watch TV (even if she herself does not), and they discuss with each other what they have seen. Broadcast images of thin celebrities may be discussed favourably, for example, and this provides a route to reinforcement of behaviour that seeks thinness, both direct (praise from friends for losing weight) and vicarious (thin celebrities being praised by friends).

SLT explains cultural changes

AN was once considered a **culture-bound syndrome** because it was thought to be found almost exclusively in Western cultures and rarely anywhere else. It is still less common in non-Western cultures but incidence rates are increasing rapidly. SLT can explain this in terms of cultural change. Naomi Chisuwa and Jennifer O'Dea (2010) highlight the increased rates of AN in Japan over the past 40 years as traditional values favouring plumpness as a sign of health have been displaced by the Western cultural thinness ideal. There is evidence that this change has been driven in part by media representations of female body shape aimed especially at adolescents. For example, Natsuki Ozawa *et al.* (2005) found a greater occurrence of AN symptoms in young Japanese women who regularly read magazines promoting the thinness ideal compared with those who did not.

Diathesis–stress explanation

There are many stressors that could trigger anorexia, because young women try to lose weight for a variety of social, psychological and cultural reasons. One of them, as SLT predicts, could be media representations of thinness. But if media influence is a major cause of anorexia then we would expect to see a great many more cases, as most young women are exposed to role models of thinness in the media. The fact that we don't suggests that another factor must be involved. This would explain why some young women develop AN and others do not even when most are exposed to the same media influences. This missing factor could be a *diathesis*, an underlying vulnerability to develop anorexia. This may be **genetic** – as we saw in an earlier spread, there is a wealth of research evidence that points towards a substantial genetic component in the causation of AN. Or it could even be environmental, for example a significant childhood trauma.

So an explanation of anorexia that can accommodate biological and non-biological factors is more valid than one based on social learning processes alone.

Evaluation eXtra

Explains gender differences

As we have seen, the Western cultural ideal for women's body shape is thinness. But for men, increasingly, the ideal body shape is muscular. This has led to recognition of an eating disorder nicknamed *bigorexia*, a drive to develop muscles without gaining fat. According to William Jones and John Morgan (2010) there is mounting evidence that bigorexia is an eating disorder prevalent in men responding to cultural ideals about masculinity transmitted through the media.

Consider: *How do you think social learning theory would explain the influence of the media on 'bigorexia'?*

Treatment applications

Social learning principles are the foundation of many treatment approaches to AN, especially where immediate weight gain is an urgent priority. Various techniques are incorporated into an effective programme including the use of both direct and vicarious reinforcement, and modelling of adaptive eating behaviours.

Consider: *How could social learning concepts be used to treat anorexia? Does this increase the **validity** of the theory?*

Apply it ## Concepts: Celebrity worship

Elysia is a 17-year-old woman who takes a very close interest in what celebrities get up to. She loves reading all the magazines she can get hold of, with headlines like: *Lisa struggles to control her curves! Get your bikini body now! Drop one size! Look great naked!* Elysia thinks she is too fat, although all her friends and family disagree. She's recently started visiting pro-anorexia and 'thinspiration' websites, looking for tips.

Question

Use both biological and psychological approaches to explain why Elysia might be at risk of developing anorexia.

Are media representations of the ideal masculine body responsible for an increase in bigorexia in men?

Apply it ## Methods: Media influences

A clinical psychologist wanted to investigate how the media might influence the acquisition of eating disorders. He carried out face-to-face **interviews** with 20 women between the ages of 16 and 20 years, all of them diagnosed with anorexia. He asked various questions about their use of media such as television and the Internet, and their attitudes towards weight loss and other eating-disorder-related behaviours.

Questions

1. The study produced a lot of **quantitative data**. Explain what is meant by this term. (*2 marks*)

2. Write a question that could gather quantitative data in this study. (*2 marks*)

3. Explain *two* differences between a **structured** and an **unstructured interview**. (*2 marks + 2 marks*)

4. Explain *one* way in which **investigator effects** might have influenced the outcome of this study. (*2 marks*)

5. What is meant by the term **reliability**? Explain *one* way in which reliability could have been an issue in this study. (*1 mark + 2 marks*) (See page 66)

CHECK IT

1. In relation to social learning theory of anorexia nervosa, explain what is meant by the terms *modelling* and *reinforcement*. [2 marks + 2 marks]

2. Outline the social learning theory of anorexia nervosa. [6 marks]

3. Outline **one** study of social learning theory as an explanation for anorexia nervosa. In your answer, include details of what the researcher(s) did and what was found. [4 marks]

4. Describe and evaluate the social learning theory of anorexia nervosa. [16 marks]

PSYCHOLOGICAL EXPLANATIONS FOR ANOREXIA NERVOSA: COGNITIVE THEORY

In Year 1 you studied cognitive theories of depression (Beck and Ellis). Such theories point to maladaptive and faulty thought processes as the origin of mental disorders including anorexia. Indeed, distorted body image is now central to the diagnosis of anorexia in the new diagnostic system, DSM-5 (2012). According to cognitive theory, anorexics filter their experiences of life and their perceptions of the future through their flawed and irrational beliefs about body size. They may even have broader cognitive deficits that are not present in people who do not have anorexia.

KEY TERMS

Cognitive distortions – Faulty, biased and irrational ways of thinking that mean we perceive ourselves, other people and the world inaccurately and usually negatively.

Irrational beliefs – Also called dysfunctional thoughts. In Ellis's model and therapy, these are defined as thoughts that are likely to interfere with a person's happiness. Such dysfunctional thoughts lead to mental disorders such as depression and anorexia.

Apply it

Concepts: The mirror never lies – or does it?

For as long as he can remember, Khalil has always hated his body. He keeps saying that he is fat, even though everybody else disagrees. He can tell they're just being polite. Whenever he looks in the mirror, which is a lot of the time, he can spot areas of excess fat. He thinks he is overweight and out of control of his own body.

Questions

What aspects of this scenario suggest that Khalil might be experiencing cognitive distortions?

How might they cause him to become anorexic?

A distorted body image is a common feature of anorexia. But does it contribute to causing the illness, as cognitive theory suggests?

Cognitive theory

Cognitive distortions

According to the **cognitive** explanation, the core psychopathology of **anorexia nervosa** (AN) is **cognitive distortions** about body shape and weight. In the most significant of these, the AN sufferer has a disturbed perception of their own body image.

Disturbed perceptions Rebecca Murphy *et al.* (2010) argue that all other clinical features of AN stem from these distortions, including preoccupations with thoughts of food, eating, weight, and body shape, and behaviours such as food restriction and checking (e.g. constantly looking in the mirror). People with AN become more and more critical of their own bodies. They misinterpret their emotional states as 'feeling fat', even as they get thinner and thinner.

Several research studies demonstrate that AN sufferers consistently overestimate their body size and weight. Different techniques are used to measure this, such as choosing from silhouettes of increasing size to match one's own body shape. Don Williamson *et al.* (1993) carried out a study using this technique.

Procedure 37 participants diagnosed with anorexia used the *Body Image Assessment* to estimate their current body size and indicate their ideal size. A **control group** of 95 participants who did not having an eating disorder performed the same task.

Findings The participants with AN were **significantly** less accurate in their size estimates than the control participants, with a marked tendency to overestimate their size. The ideal body shape for the AN participants was also significantly thinner than it was for the controls.

Irrational beliefs

Researchers have noted that people with AN often express **irrational beliefs** and attitudes about their disorder that defy logic and rational sense. In Aaron Beck's terms, these irrational beliefs become second nature and give rise to *automatic negative thoughts*. One example is *all-or-nothing thinking*: 'If I'm not thin, I'm fat'; 'If I don't control my weight, I'm worthless'. Another is *catastrophising*, putting the worst possible gloss on even the least important events: 'I ate half a biscuit today; I've got no willpower at all'.

Perfectionism A key irrational belief in AN is perfectionism, the view that the individual has to meet their most demanding standards all the time, and failure to do so is judged severely. This applies to all areas of the AN sufferer's life – academic success, relationships, career aims – but especially to eating, body shape and striving for weight loss. Perfectionism is usually accompanied by intensive record-keeping, to make sure the individual is achieving their harsh goals. It makes some features of AN worse and more resistant to treatment, such as checking behaviours, excessive exercise and food restraint.

Paul Hewitt *et al.* (2003) claim that perfectionism is not satisfied when goals are achieved. In fact, as AN patients reach their exacting targets, they merely raise their standards still higher. So they are forever pursuing an unrealistic goal they can never attain, trapped in a vicious cycle of irrational perfectionism and starvation.

Cognitive inflexibility

Recent research has focused on the possibility that people with AN lack cognitive flexibility. Janet Treasure and Ulrike Schmidt (2013) have proposed a *cognitive interpersonal maintenance model* of anorexia which, among other things, suggests that AN sufferers experience problems with *set-shifting*. That is, they find it difficult to switch fluently from one task to another requiring a different set of cognitive skills. Instead, they tend to apply persistently the same skills in a changed situation where these skills are no longer useful.

This recent research indicates that this may be a significant cognitive deficit leading to the development of anorexia. Once a vulnerable individual gets started on the weight loss process, they rigidly persist with it and continue to perceive themselves as needing to lose weight. They find it hard to switch to a more adaptive way of thinking about their body shape and size. In effect, their weight loss is a solution to a problem that no longer exists, but they are unable to perceive this accurately.

STUDY TIP

You can evaluate one theory by comparing it with another, using their similarities and differences. The SLT and cognitive explanations of anorexia give you an ideal opportunity to do this. Make sure you don't just list the similarities and differences of the explanations for anorexia though. Use them to bring out the strengths and limitations of each other.

Evaluation

Research support for cognitive distortions

Perminder Sachdev et al. (2008) used **fMRI** with AN patients and healthy control participants. As the participants were having their brains scanned, the researchers showed them images of their own and other people's bodies. The same brain areas were activated in both groups when they were shown non-self images. However, the outcome was very different when the participants were shown images of themselves. Compared with the controls, the AN patients showed very little activation in parts of the brain thought to be involved in attention.

This is a very intriguing finding because it suggests that cognitive distortions do exist in AN, but they are limited to the individual's own body image and do not extend to bodies in general.

Research support for perfectionism

Katherine Halmi et al. (2012) studied 728 women over the age of 16 years, all diagnosed with AN. Each participant completed the EATATE *Lifetime Diagnostic Interview*. This measures AN symptoms and indicators of perfectionism in childhood. The researchers found that childhood perfectionism was a significant predictor of the later development of AN. The researchers concluded that perfectionism preceded onset of AN, so is a potential risk factor for development of the disorder.

However, there is a serious limitation to this study which means we have to be cautious in coming to firm conclusions. The method of assessing childhood perfectionism was retrospective. Participants had to think back to their childhoods and recall incidents of perfectionism. Such recall is likely to be distorted. For example, it could be that participants who are currently most perfectionist as adults are more likely to remember being perfectionist as children. This would artificially increase the link between childhood perfectionism and development of AN.

Contradictory research

Piers Cornelissen et al. (2013) compared AN patients with non-AN women on a morphing task – the participants had to adjust a computerised image of themselves until it matched their estimated body size. The researchers found no significant differences between the groups of women in the accuracy of their estimates. As it is not possible to distinguish between the body size estimates of healthy and AN women, this suggests that over-estimation is not pathological. This finding challenges the central role of body image distortion in cognitive theories of AN.

However, in an even more recent review of research over ten years, Rick Gardner and Dana Brown (2014) conclude that body image distortion is a genuine phenomenon characteristic of AN. They attribute conflicting findings in previous research to the different measurement techniques used to assess body size estimates.

Evaluation eXtra

Treatment applications

Different forms of **cognitive behaviour therapy** (CBT) attempt to change the AN patient's distorted cognitions and irrational beliefs about food, eating, weight loss and body shape and size. Riccardo Dalle Grave et al.'s (2014) recent study of enhanced CBT showed a substantial increase in weight and decrease in concerns about body shape amongst 26 hospitalised AN patients, which was maintained after discharge in a one-year follow-up.

Consider: *Explain how these findings strengthen the **validity** of the cognitive theory of AN.*

Issues of causation

Although research shows that distortions and irrational beliefs are features of AN, it is not at all clear that they *cause* the disorder. There is very little research to show that these cognitive factors exist before the onset of AN. For instance, Megan Shott et al. (2012) found that younger AN patients were no worse at set-shifting than non-anorexic controls, but older patients were. This suggests that cognitive inflexibility does not make an individual vulnerable to developing AN, but is instead a consequence of the disorder.

Consider: *How could you establish that cognitive distortions exist before AN develops?*

The anorexic person's struggle to achieve the perfect body size may well begin in childhood attempts to be the best at everything.

THE SPECIFICATION SAYS...

Biological explanations for obesity including genetic and neural explanations.

Obesity is usually defined in terms of body mass index (BMI). This is a common way of classifying people as underweight, normal weight, overweight or obese, and takes into account height. Someone with a BMI of 30 or above is considered obese.

More and more people are dying prematurely or suffering disability due to the often undiagnosed effects of obesity. This is why psychologists believe it is urgent that we understand the causes of obesity. We start our investigation of obesity with the biological approach, looking at genetic and neural explanations.

KEY TERMS

Genetic explanation – Genes consist of DNA strands. DNA produces 'instructions' for general physical features of an organism (such as eye colour, height) and also specific physical features (such as neurotransmitter levels and size of brain structures). These may impact on psychological features (such as intelligence and mental disorder). Genes are transmitted from parents to offspring, i.e. inherited.

Obesity – Having too much body fat, often defined as a BMI (weight divided by the square of the person's height) of more than 30.

Neural explanation – Any explanation of behaviour (and its disorders) in terms of (dys)functions of the brain and nervous system. This includes the activity of brain structures such as the hypothalamus, and neurotransmitters such as serotonin and dopamine.

Is the future fat? There is strong evidence that obesity is substantially genetically inherited. Could this be the reason for the growing obesity crisis?

Genetic explanation for obesity

Obesity runs in families

Genetic explanations often look to family studies for evidence. There are clear family-related patterns to **obesity**, measured in terms of body mass index (BMI). Caution is obviously needed in interpreting findings because of the difficulty of separating shared genetic and environmental influences in any relatives who live together. Even so, **concordance rates** for first-degree relatives are in the region of 20% to 50%, which indicates a moderate rather than substantial degree of heritability (Chaput et al. 2014).

Twin studies have generally suggested a greater **genetic** component. Cassandra Nan et al. (2012) conducted a **meta-analysis** of 12 twin studies involving over 8,000 **MZ** and nearly 10,000 **DZ** twins. Concordance rates ranged from 61% to 80%, which demonstrates a very substantial genetic component to obesity that remained influential from late childhood through adolescence to adulthood.

Polygenic determination

Adam Locke et al. (2015) studied the genomes of more than 300,000 people, and identified 97 genes associated with variations in BMI. This finding very clearly demonstrates that the action of genes on obesity is **polygenic**. That is, genetic inheritance involves multiple genes, their effects interacting with each other. This is made even more complex when you consider there are other ways of measuring obesity (such as waist-to-hip ratio, which focuses on amount of abdominal fat). Different genes may influence different aspects of obesity.

So there is no single genetic cause of obesity; many genes are involved, all with relatively small effects. The researchers discovered that these 97 genes account for only 2.7% of BMI variation, a small fraction of the heritability of obesity. Some researchers suspect that the true figure necessary to explain this 'missing heritability' may be as many as 400 genes (Watson 2009).

Neural explanation for obesity

Neural explanations of obesity focus on monoamine **neurotransmitters** such as **serotonin** and **dopamine**, particularly in terms of their role in the brain's reward systems.

Serotonin

Most research studies of both humans and non-human animals show that obesity is associated with abnormally low levels of serotonin (or its main **metabolite** 5-HIAA). Normal levels of serotonin regulate feeding behaviour by inhibiting the activity of various sites in the **hypothalamus**, including the *ventro-medial hypothalamus* (see page 228). It is serotonin that signals to the hypothalamus that we have eaten to satiety.

Dysfunctions of the serotonin system can occur due to stress or co-morbid disorders such as **depression**. They may even be genetically inherited. In such cases, levels of serotonin are abnormally low, creating inaccurate satiety signals that are sent to the hypothalamus, **disinhibiting** eating behaviour. Low serotonin levels lead to cravings for carbohydrates, energy-dense foods including sugars, causing weight gain through too many calories.

Dopamine

Dopamine has a crucial role in the brain's reward and motivation systems. Normal levels of the neurotransmitter stimulate brain areas such as the hypothalamus, **hippocampus** and **amygdala**, providing rewarding feelings of pleasure and well-being. Dopamine activity is associated with the pleasure we derive from eating and cues associated with eating (such as the smell of food). However, obesity has been linked with a dysfunctional dopamine system in many research studies. Gene-Jack Wang et al. (2001) found that obese individuals had significantly fewer dopamine D2 receptors than normal-weight controls, in a part of the brain called the *striatum*.

Because levels of dopamine are so low in some people, the neurotransmitter cannot perform its usual pleasurable reward function in response to eating, i.e. a person does not feel good after eating. Overeating can therefore be seen as an attempt to activate reward centres in the brain that provide feelings of pleasure, by increasing dopamine levels. This explanation suggests that obesity is the outcome of a food addiction that operates neurochemically in ways similar to other addictions.

Apply it

Concepts: It's in the genes

Harry is a young boy who is quite overweight. He has noticed recently that his mum and dad and most of his family are overweight as well. Harry wonders if obesity might run in families.

Question

Even if obesity runs in Harry's family, does this mean that his weight is only the result of genes? Explain your answer.

Evaluation

Limitation of twin studies

A significant weakness of twin studies is that even MZ twins share more than just their genes. Because they are brought up in the same families, it is difficult to separate environmental and genetic influences on their behaviour. Twin studies attempt to deal with this issue by comparing concordance rates of MZ and DZ twins, because in both cases the children are raised together. However, as we have seen in the case of **anorexia** (see page 231), the **validity** of this approach depends on MZ and DZ twins being treated with equal degrees of similarity (by parents, friends, teachers, etc.). Some researchers argue that this *equal environments assumption* may not be valid, because MZ twins are treated more similarly than DZs.

Therefore twin studies may overestimate the extent of genetic influence. Obesity is not an inevitable outcome of genetic risk because environmental factors play an essential role (as indicated by the **diathesis-stress model**). Nevertheless the contribution of genes to obesity is clear.

Contradictory evidence

Valentina Paracchini *et al.* (2005) carried out a **meta-analysis** of 25 studies that investigated genes thought to be involved in regulating **leptin** (the *LEP* gene) and leptin receptors (the *LEPR* gene). Leptin is an obvious target for speculation about genetic effects, because its activity is known to be central to weight regulation (see page 228). However, the researchers could find no evidence of a link between these genes and obesity. This suggests that whatever the role of leptin may be in obesity, it does not appear to have a solely genetic basis.

This is an important reminder that obesity is a complex phenomenon and that other non-genetic factors are important in its causation and development.

Evaluation

Supporting evidence for serotonin

Sunny Ohia *et al.* (2013) highlight the importance in obesity of one serotonin receptor in particular, the 2C receptor. Studies of 'knockout' mice genetically engineered to have no functioning 2C receptors show that they develop late-onset obesity. This is further evidence of a link between obesity and a dysfunctional serotonin system, albeit in mice.

Supporting evidence for dopamine

Some research shows that there is a genetic basis to dysfunctions of the dopamine reward system. Attention has focused on the *DRD2 gene*, which codes for the D2 receptor that has been implicated in obesity. Terry Ritchie and Ernest Noble (2003) conducted a **PET scan** study and found that people who inherited one version of the DRD2 gene had 30–40% fewer D2 receptors compared to those with other versions.

This finding supports the explanation outlined on the facing page. People with low dopamine levels (due to fewer D2 receptors) experience less dopamine-activated pleasurable reward from eating which makes them more likely to overeat.

Evaluation eXtra

Treatment applications

Biological research is revealing many physiological mechanisms which are plausible causes of obesity, and each one is a candidate for new treatments. Realistic prospects include drug treatments to correct dopamine and serotonin deficiencies, or personalised medicine with drugs tailored to the individual's genetic profile.

Consider: *What are the potential benefits of better treatments? How would this support the **validity** of biological explanations of obesity?*

Apply it — Concepts: A food addiction?

Hadley has tried all sorts of diets to lose weight but none of them have worked. She knows it's not just a matter of willpower because she really has tried hard. She sometimes thinks she must be addicted to food like some people are addicted to cigarettes or alcohol.

Question

Explain what might have gone wrong with Hadley's serotonin and dopamine systems to account for her apparent addiction to food.

A lack of willpower, or something else? Overeating may be a way of compensating for deficiencies in the brain's reward systems.

STUDY TIP

Obesity is one of those topics in which anecdotal evidence is very common. People's personal opinions are important, but they're no substitute for scientific and research evidence. Make sure your answers contain clear psychological content rather than views you can hear from just about anyone.

Apply it — Methods: Obesity and serotonin

A psychologist wanted to investigate the link between neurotransmitters and obesity. He recruited a **volunteer sample** of 20 obese people and 20 lean people. He defined obesity as a body mass index (BMI) of above 30 and lean as a BMI below 19. The psychologist took blood from the participants and measured the levels of serotonin in the blood plasma.

Questions

1. Explain how the **dependent variable** has been operationalised. (*2 marks*)
2. Identify and explain the type of **experimental design** used in this study. (*1 mark*)
3. Explain *one* strength and *one* weakness of this design in this study. (*2 marks + 2 marks*)
4. Write a **non-directional hypothesis** for this study. (*2 marks*)
5. Explain *one* potential **confounding variable** that could arise in this study. (*2 marks*)

CHECK IT

1. Outline research into the genetic explanation for obesity. **[6 marks]**
2. Outline the neural explanation for obesity. **[6 marks]**
3. Evaluate research into the genetic **and/or** neural explanation(s) for obesity. **[10 marks]**
4. Describe and evaluate **one or more** biological explanations for obesity. **[16 marks]**

PSYCHOLOGICAL EXPLANATIONS FOR OBESITY

THE SPECIFICATION SAYS...

Psychological explanations for obesity including restraint theory, disinhibition and the boundary model.

Research by Ancel Keys and his colleagues (1950) conducted during the Second World War suggested a strange possibility. They subjected Americans who did not want to fight (conscientious objectors) to starvation diets. The men found themselves thinking more about food the more they were denied it. So is limiting the amount you eat a risk factor for obesity? In this spread, we look at a psychological explanation that suggests exactly that.

KEY TERMS

Restraint theory – A cognitive explanation which argues that obesity is the paradoxical outcome of attempts to restrain eating (i.e. dieting).

Disinhibition – Normal social constraints against certain behaviours can be weakened by environmental triggers. These behaviours then appear temporarily socially acceptable and therefore more likely.

Boundary model – Explains how restrained eaters are less sensitive to satiety so need more food before feeling full. When they break their self-imposed diet boundary they continue to eat to the satiety boundary, making weight gain more likely.

	Hunger boundary		Satiety boundary	
Aversion hunger		Zone of biological indifference		Aversion satiety

Increasing food intake ⟶

Normal eater

	Hunger boundary	Diet boundary		Satiety boundary	
Aversion hunger		Zone of biological indifference			Aversion satiety

Increasing food intake ⟶

Restrained eater

Herman and Polivy's (1984) boundary model: restrained eaters do not eat according to their biological needs, as normal eaters do.

Apply it   Concepts: Felix gains weight

It all started when Felix lost his job. He noticed that he was getting a bit fatter, so he took action. He decided to cut down on the carbs and eat a bit less. But when Felix next went on the scales, he was astonished to find that he had actually put even more weight on! His BMI is now 26 and it appears he is in danger of becoming officially obese.

Question

How would you use your knowledge of restraint, disinhibition and the boundary model to explain to Felix why he might become obese?

Restraint, disinhibition and the boundary model

Restraint theory

Peter Herman and Janet Polivy (1975) developed a **cognitive** theory of obesity – **restraint theory**. Attempting to lose weight typically involves some form of restrained eating; that is, deliberately limiting the amount of food you eat. Herman and Polivy argued that restrained eating is counterproductive and ultimately self-defeating. They noticed that the vast majority of people who restrain their eating fail to lose any weight. A **significant** proportion of 'restrained eaters' even overeat to the extent that they become obese.

Cognitive control Restrained eaters set strict limits on their food intake. They categorise foods into groups of 'good' and 'bad', and create rules and beliefs about which foods are allowed and which are forbidden, as well as the amounts they believe are consistent with weight loss. A restrained diet is a highly organised way of imposing the control which restrained eaters believe is the way to lose weight. This control is cognitive because the individual has to consciously think about their weight and eating a lot of the time.

Paradoxical outcome However, the result is that the restrained eater becomes *more* preoccupied with food rather than less. By placing limits on what and how much they eat, the restrained eater no longer eats when they are hungry and stops when they are full. Their eating behaviour is no longer under physiological control. In fact, they now actively attempt to ignore physiological indicators that signal hunger and satiety, and this leads to disinhibition of eating behaviour.

Disinhibition

Obesity is not caused by restrained eating alone. It is the result of a dysfunctional cycle of restraint and **disinhibition**. A period of restrained eating is often followed by disinhibited eating in which the individual eats as much as they want. Restrained eaters are vulnerable to internal and external food-related cues such as mood (internal) and smells or **media** images (external). These cues are called *disinhibitors* and lead to a loss of control over restrained eating, unleashing a session of unrestricted eating which may amount to a binge.

The cognitive process that governs disinhibition is a form of distorted thinking such as *all-or-nothing thinking*. Once the restrained eater has been disinhibited by, for instance, a stressful day combined with the sight and smell of their favourite forbidden food, they continue to eat because there's no point in stopping: 'Well I blew it. I might as well eat all of this because I won't be able to tomorrow'.

The boundary model

Herman and Polivy (1984) sought to explain the impact of restrained eating and disinhibition in their **boundary model** of obesity (see diagram, left). Food intake exists on a continuum from hungry to satiated (feeling full). Biological processes are the key determinants of how much we eat at each end of this continuum. So when our energy levels dip below a certain point we feel an aversive state of hunger and are motivated to eat. Eating to fullness creates an aversive state of discomfort, at which point we are motivated to stop eating. In terms of the model, eating begins at the hunger boundary and stops at the satiety boundary. Between these two points is the zone of biological indifference where biological processes have minimal effect. Instead, cognitive and social factors have their greatest influence on food intake, when we are neither particularly hungry nor particularly full.

Restrained eaters (described above) have a lower hunger boundary so are less responsive to feelings of hunger. They also have a higher satiety boundary, so they need more food before they consider themselves full. For restrained eaters, the zone of biological indifference is therefore wider, which means more of their eating behaviour comes under cognitive rather than physiological control. This makes them vulnerable to the effects of disinhibition outlined above.

Restrained eaters have a self-imposed upper boundary, which represents the most they want to eat – 'Two squares of this chocolate bar is the maximum I can let myself eat.' This is some distance below the satiety boundary set by biological processes. When restrained eaters break the diet boundary, they carry on eating up to and beyond the satiety boundary. This is an example of disinhibition which Herman and Polivy call the 'what the hell effect', marked by passivity and resignation: 'What's the point? I might as well eat the lot'.

Evaluation

Supporting research

Jane Wardle and Sally Beales (1988) **randomly allocated** 27 obese women to three groups. The diet group participants followed a restrained-eating diet for seven weeks. The exercise group followed an exercise regime but did not restrain their eating. **Control** participants received no treatment of any kind. The food intake of all participants was assessed in the fouth and sixth weeks. The restrained eaters ate significantly more than the other participants: they consumed the most calories overall. Although they generally tended to eat less throughout the seven-week period, they experienced the occasional disinhibition of their eating when they would binge beyond feeling full. The findings provide support for disinhibition and restraint theory.

Wardle and Beale concluded that this was evidence that restraint is a causal factor in overeating, which inevitably leads to weight gain and obesity.

Disinhibiting effects of the media

Jessica Boyce and Roeline Kuijer (2014) compared the responses of restrained and unrestrained eaters to **media** images. They showed some participants slideshows containing images of thinness (models advertising beauty products). Control participants saw a slideshow of neutral images (e.g. furniture). After viewing the images, the participants' food intake was measured by a ten-minute 'taste test'. They were allowed to eat as much as they liked from four bowls of snack foods such as biscuits. The restrained eaters ate significantly more than unrestrained eaters after being shown media images of thinness. There was no such difference in response to the neutral images.

These images, common in our culture, are therefore disinhibitors which trigger eating in restrained eaters. This provides a potential path to weight gain and obesity, as predicted by the restraint theory.

Contradictory research findings

Jennifer Savage *et al.* (2009) carried out one of the few **longitudinal studies** into restrained eating. They measured dietary restraint and disinhibition in 163 women at the start of the study and every two years afterwards over a six-year period. They also measured changes in the women's weight. They found that increases in restrained eating were linked to decreases in weight (a significant **negative correlation**).

The researchers concluded that restrained eating while dieting leads to weight loss rather than weight gain, at least in the short-term, an outcome the opposite of that predicted by restraint theory.

Evaluation eXtra

Restraint is multifaceted

Restraint is a more complex phenomenon than the boundary model indicates. Researchers have identified at least two different forms: *rigid* restraint, which is an all-or-nothing approach to limiting food intake; and *flexible* restraint, which allows the restrained eater to eat limited amounts of some 'forbidden' foods without necessarily triggering disinhibition. Only one form of restraint – rigid – is likely to lead to obesity. This could explain why Savage *et al.* (above) found that restrained eating can produce weight loss.

Consider: *Explain how this could be considered a strength and a limitation of restraint theory, disinhibition and the boundary model.*

Practical applications

The boundary model predicts that when food intake is consciously limited, the paradoxical outcome can be disinhibition, overeating, weight gain and obesity. Despite this, obesity treatments and advice usually encourage dietary restraint. An alternative, suggested by Modjtaba Zandian *et al.* (2009), is that weight-loss advice should avoid recommending restraint and focus instead on training dieters to eat at a slower rate.

Consider: *Why do you think the boundary model appears to have had so little practical influence on weight-loss advice?*

Apply it — Concepts: Gav and Shona

Gav has tried eating less at times, but is still several kilos overweight. He finds himself thinking about food quite a lot. If he starts eating something he shouldn't, like some chocolate, he'll often eat the whole lot. Shona doesn't really give much thought to food. She just eats when she feels hungry. Her weight is normal and has hardly fluctuated over the years.

Question

Explain which parts of this scenario illustrate: (1) restrained eating, (2) physiological control, (3) cognitive control, (4) diet boundary, (5) disinhibition.

'I might as well eat it all.' A common experience of disinhibition for the restrained eater.

Apply it — Methods: Snack attack!

A psychologist wanted to study restrained eaters, people who limit their food intake because they want to lose a few kilos. Because restrained eaters are poor at estimating how much they have eaten, the psychologist decided to carry out an **observational study**. She recruited 15 restrained eaters and installed cameras in their houses to record their eating behaviour over a one-week period. The footage was then analysed by a research assistant who counted various behaviours.

Questions

1. Outline *one* **sampling method** the psychologist could have used to recruit the participants. (*2 marks*)

2. Explain *one* limitation of this method. (*2 marks*)

3. Explain why the camera footage was analysed by a research assistant rather than by the psychologist. (*2 marks*)

4. Explain *two* **ethical issues** that the psychologist should have taken into account in this study. (*2 marks + 2 marks*)

5. Name *two* **behavioural categories** that might have been used to count behaviours. (*2 marks*)

CHECK IT

1. In relation to psychological explanations of obesity, explain what is meant by the terms *restraint theory* and *disinhibition*. [2 marks + 2 marks]

2. Outline the boundary model of obesity. [6 marks]

3. Outline **one** research study of a psychological explanation for obesity. [3 marks]

4. Describe and evaluate psychological explanations for obesity. [16 marks]

Explanations for the success and failure of dieting.

'Preach not to others what they should eat, but eat as becomes you and be silent.'
(Epictetus, Greek philosopher)

Epictetus's guidance amounts to: 'Eat when you're hungry; don't eat when you're not. And don't go on about it.' If people who want to lose weight followed his advice, that would be the end of the multi-billion-pound dieting industry.

It has been estimated that up to 50% of the adult population take active steps to control or lose weight within a one-year period, with women significantly more likely than men to do so (Melissa Laska *et al.* 2011).

KEY TERM

Dieting – A conscious attempt to lose weight, usually by restricting how much is eaten. Several biological and psychological factors, of the type explored in previous spreads, influence the success or failure of dieting attempts.

Apply it

Concepts: A variety of faddy diets

Shazia has been on many diets over the years to try and lose weight – the Atkins, Cambridge, Slim-Fast, South Beach, New Atkins... she's tried them all. Now she's heard about a new one called the 5:2, so she's thinking of giving that a go. The trouble is, they always start really well. Shazia loses lots of weight in the first couple of weeks, but then it gets harder and harder until it just doesn't seem to work anymore. It doesn't take long before all the weight goes back on again. But she's optimistic that this new diet will be different.

Question

How can the explanations on this spread account for Shazia's 'yo-yo' dieting?

Explanations for the success and failure of dieting

The spiral model

Todd Heatherton and Janet Polivy (1992) proposed a model of **dieting** behaviour in terms of a chain of linked events. Food-restricted dieting often begins in adolescence when individuals (overwhelmingly women) experience body dissatisfaction. Low **self-esteem** may be a risk factor for dieting attempts because it makes the individual more likely to make negative comparisons. Initially, first-time dieters experience some success because they temporarily lose weight. But lasting weight loss is rare, so ultimately weight is regained and the outcome is failure. At this point, some will give up trying to lose weight altogether, but most will attribute the failure to some personal deficiency, for example they didn't try hard enough or they lacked willpower.

Far from radically rethinking their approach to weight loss, dieters 'stick to the plan', only next time they push themselves to make a bigger effort by eating even less. This ever-greater restriction of food intake has physical and psychological effects. The dieter experiences more frustration and emotional distress, which makes them vulnerable to **disinhibited** eating. At the same time, metabolic processes in the body change so that weight loss becomes physically more difficult to achieve. For instance, **ghrelin** levels increase and **leptin** levels decrease after **significant** weight loss. The result is further failure followed by repeated attempts to 'diet harder', and a lowering of self-esteem and increase in **depression** over time. The individual is now trapped in a destructive 'downward spiral' in which weight loss is less and less likely.

Ironic processes theory

We saw in the last spread that when people deliberately restrict their food intake and consider themselves as being 'on a diet', they become more preoccupied with thoughts of food rather than less. An explanation for this was provided by Daniel Wegner (1994) in his *theory of ironic processes*. It stems from his observation in an **experiment** (Wegner *et al.* 1987) that asking people not to think about a white bear almost guaranteed they would think about one, even more often than people specifically asked to think of one. So the paradoxical outcome of trying to suppress a thought is to make it more likely. When dieters label certain foods as 'forbidden', these become more salient (i.e. they stand out). They are more likely to think about these foods precisely because they are trying not to. For example, someone who tells themselves not to think about chocolate finds that images of chocolate bars are easier to retrieve from memory. This leads to disinhibition of eating, a loss of control, excessive food intake and ultimately dieting failure.

There is a further irony to this unfortunate situation. Attempting to distract yourself from thinking about forbidden foods (for example by reading a book) requires mental activity. This leaves you lacking the **cognitive** processing capacity to suppress the thought, which inevitably reappears. This is why 'being on a diet' can be at the same time so all-consuming and yet self-defeating. To be successful at preventing paradoxical thoughts about food that might lead them into disinhibition, the dieter has to spend all their time, energy and undivided attention trying not to think about food.

Restraint, disinhibition and the boundary model

These concepts can be related specifically to dieting success and failure.

Restrained eating The essence of most diets is to place limits on how much food is eaten. However, because dieters are making conscious efforts to restrain their eating, their behaviour is under cognitive control. They now think a great deal more about food-related matters, in ways that are susceptible to cognitive biases and distortions.

Disinhibition Restrained eaters are vulnerable to internal and external food-related cues. These tempt the dieter to break their diets. If they do, their eating may become disinhibited and they could consume a very large amount of calories very quickly. Over time, they lose no more weight than someone who was not dieting, and may even gain some.

Boundary model Dieters do not regulate their eating in response to feelings of hunger or satiety. Instead, they set themselves a limit on how much and what type of food they think they should eat. If they eat past this point they will continue to eat until they are full on the basis of 'What the hell, I might as well'.

That's not going to work. Just the very act of fighting against the fattening food means that you're thinking about the fattening food. How ironic is that?

Evaluation

Practical activity on page 245

Uses of the spiral model

The model proposes several ways in which dieting can become successful, involving 'breaking out' of the spiral at various points. Heatherton and Polivy point out that the key issue is to prevent lowering of self-esteem and avoid the worst consequences of diet failure. For example, people who diet to avoid putting on weight rather than to lose it are less likely to experience disinhibited eating, perhaps because their self-esteem is higher (Lowe and Kleifield 1988). One way to escape the consequences of failure is to give up dieting altogether.

The problem with this option is that it does nothing to address the low self-esteem that created the motivation to diet in the first place. Even worse, Joel Yager et al. (1988) present evidence that disinhibited eaters who give up dieting often turn to substance abuse as a way of reducing their unhappiness. Ultimately, perhaps the only way to dietary success is to promote self-esteem by ending attempts to lose weight and accepting oneself as one is.

Support for ironic processes theory

Marieke Adriaanse et al. (2011) investigated snacking behaviour. Their participants were female students who were trying to cut down on their intake of unhealthy snacks such as chocolate and crisps. They were presented with diet intentions expressed in a negative form (e.g. 'When I am sad, I will not eat chocolate'). The researchers found an ironic rebound effect. Just being exposed to this statement reinforced the association between 'being sad' and 'eating chocolate', making the link between the two more accessible in memory and more likely to be recalled. But the crucial finding was that the ironic effect was not just cognitive, it was also behavioural.

After the participants were exposed to these statements, they kept a snack diary during the following week. The data showed that they ate unhealthy snacks more often and consumed more calories than a **control group**. This study confirms how difficult it is to suppress thoughts of eating once they become accessible in memory. Because ironic cognitive processes generalised to actual snacking behaviour, this demonstrates how thinking of oneself as dieting can lead to the failure of the diet, this supports the **validity** of ironic processes theory as an explanation of dieting failure.

Minimal effects of ironic processes

There is substantial evidence showing the operation of ironic processes in eating behaviour. But it is unclear how far they can account for the success or failure of dieting. Wegner himself accepted that the effects of ironic processes are relatively small. They may be exaggerated in 'snapshot' **laboratory experiments** and less relevant to real-life attempts to lose weight which typically extend over a longer period of time.

The limited effects of these processes mean that other factors are likely to be more important in determining the extent of a diet's success, such as self-esteem, as proposed by the spiral model.

Evaluation eXtra

Increasing dieting success

There is one specific way in which ironic processes theory may offer practical advice to improve the likelihood of dieting success. The theory suggests that overeating is more likely in situations where the dieter has to use cognitive resources on another activity. Therefore, according to Brigitte Boon et al. (2002), dieting is more successful when the dieter pays the fullest possible attention to eating. That rules out eating in front of the television, or reading at mealtimes, or even holding conversations over dinner.

Consider: Can you think of any other examples of practical advice based on the explanations we have covered?

Individual differences

According to Jane Ogden (2010), a challenge for all theories that suggest dieting is counterproductive is to explain why some people succeed in losing weight even when they are preoccupied with food. Such people are in the minority, but they include **anorexics** who lose weight through extremely restricted eating. One explanation is **locus of control.** 'Internals' believe that weight loss is contingent on their own efforts and that they have control over success or failure. Perhaps this accounts for why Katie Hopkins (see above) was able to lose weight relatively easily.

Consider: Explain why this point limits the validity of the explanations Ogden is referring to.

Concepts: Failure into success?

Bradley is very organised and controlling about losing weight. He keeps records of his weight loss and how much exercise he's done. He has apps to help him monitor his progress, and special scales. But in reality Bradley finds it very difficult. He sometimes thinks the more he tries to put food out of his mind, the more it keeps popping back into his head. He's worried that losing weight is taking over his whole life and he can't think about anything else.

Question

Select *one* of the three explanations on the facing page and use it to suggest how you think Bradley could be more successful in his attempts to lose weight.

Right or wrong? Katie Hopkins deliberately gained and then lost 20 kilos, and made a TV programme to demonstrate that losing weight is 'easy'. Not everyone might agree.

Apply it **Methods: Analysing dieting**

A team of researchers recruited a sample of ten dieters to investigate the failure of diets. They collected data from the participants about the reasons why they failed to maintain their initial weight loss. The researchers used **content analysis** to identify two broad categories of reasons: internal (such as, 'I didn't have enough willpower') and external (such as, 'There was too much unhealthy food available').

Questions

1. Explain how the psychologists could have carried out their content analysis. (*4 marks*) (See page 64)
2. Outline how the researchers could have chosen a **volunteer sample** of dieters. (*2 marks*)
3. Explain *one* limitation of this sampling method. (*2 marks*)
4. What is meant by the term **reliability**? (*1 mark*) (See page 66)
5. Explain how the two psychologists could have established the reliability of their content analysis. (*3 marks*)

CHECK IT

1. Outline **one** explanation for the success and failure of dieting. [*6 marks*]
2. Outline **one** study relating to explanations for the success and failure of dieting. [*3 marks*]
3. Discuss **two or more** explanations for the success and failure of dieting. [*16 marks*]

PRACTICAL CORNER

THE SPECIFICATION SAYS...

Knowledge and understanding of . . . research methods, practical research skills and maths skills. These should be developed through . . . ethical practical research activities.

This means you should conduct practical activities wherever possible. The two activities on this spread are both experiments. One of them provides an ideal opportunity to gain an insight into the food preferences of young children. Childhood is the time when our food likes and dislikes are most obvious. The other is a chance to look further into an influential theory of why diets usually do not work – the ironic processes theory

Ethics check

We suggest strongly that you complete this checklist before starting:

1. Do participants know participation is voluntary?
2. Do participants know what to expect?
3. Do participants know they can withdraw at any time?
4. Are individuals' results anonymous?
5. Have I minimised the risk of distress to participants?
6. Have I avoided asking sensitive questions?
7. Will I avoid bringing my school/teacher/psychology into disrepute?
8. Have I considered all other ethical issues?
9. Has my teacher approved this?

The maths bit

Overall, at least 10% of the marks in assessments for Psychology will require the use of mathematical skills and at least 25% in total will involve research methods.

Don't avoid it!

Practical idea 1: Investigating children's taste aversions

Children famously dislike green vegetables such as broccoli and sprouts. Parents have been insisting 'eat your greens' for many generations, so it is certainly not a recent phenomenon. We saw in the first spread in this chapter how this aversion is perhaps evolutionarily adaptive. Green vegetables do harbour bitter tastes, and bitterness is closely associated with toxic compounds in foods. So it makes a lot of survival sense to avoid these until you know for sure that they are safe.

The aim of this practical activity is to find out if children really do have an aversion to green vegetables in particular.

The practical bit

The design

This practical is an **experiment**, in which you compare children's preferences for different foods. So the **independent variable** is food type. The comparison you will make is between green vegetables and other food types – these are the conditions of the IV.

The **dependent variable** is degree of liking, but you will need to give some thought to how best to measure this (see below for more advice).

Your participants

The ideal way to study children's food preferences is to ask them directly. But **ethical** guidelines for A level students are very clear – using children under 16 years of age in your research is inappropriate because they are potentially vulnerable.

The solution is to ask parents about their children's preferences instead. If both of a child's parents are available, it makes sense to select the one most responsible for what the child eats. You could even take steps to control potentially **confounding variables** such as age, by selecting only the parents of, say, seven-year-olds. Recruit as many parents as you can reasonably find, but ten would be a helpful number.

Materials and procedure

Start by putting together a list of different food items, including some green vegetables. Here's a list of examples: broccoli, sprouts, cabbage, lettuce, peas, carrots, tomatoes, mushrooms, fish, chicken, chocolate, ice cream, burgers, crisps, cake, biscuits, etc. It's reasonable to assume that most parents will be aware of the names of everyday food items. If there is any doubt about this you could provide images of each one. To prevent the task becoming boring, don't include too many items. Just a few will do.

As for measuring preferences, you have a couple of options. The most basic is to ask parents whether their child likes or dislikes each item. A more sophisticated method is to get parents to rate their child's liking on a scale, say from one (intensely dislike) to ten (really like).

Analysing your data

You will have a reasonable amount of **quantitative data** at the end of this procedure. Each parent will provide a rating of their child's liking for each food item you choose to include. To begin your analysis, divide the ratings into those for green vegetables and those for 'other foods'. You now need an average rating for each child for both food categories. Think carefully about which **measure of central tendency** is the appropriate one to use. You can then apply a **statistical test** to see if the ratings for green vegetables are **significantly** lower.

Apply it Methods: The maths bit 1

Table 1 Median ratings of liking for two types of food

Parent/child	Green vegetables	Other foods
1	4	6
2	5	8
3	3	8
4	4	9
5	3	6
6	4	10
7	2	7
8	4	5
9	1	10
10	2	7

1. What is the level of measurement of the dependent variable? (*1 mark*)

2. Explain why the **median** is the most suitable measure of central tendency to use to summarise the data. (*2 marks*)

3. State the appropriate statistical test to use to analyse the results and give *three* reasons why you have made this choice. (*1 mark + 3 marks*) (See pages 70–71)

4. Apply the statistical test you identified in your previous answer. What is the **calculated value**? State whether or not this is significant. Explain how you came to this decision. (*1 mark + 1 mark + 3 marks*) (See page 73)

Practical idea 2:
Testing ironic processes theory

Daniel Wegner and his colleagues (1987) found that instructing people not to think of a white bear was counterproductive, because most of his participants couldn't help themselves. Trying to suppress a thought meant that it was paradoxically more likely to be brought to mind. We saw in the previous spread how this helps to explain the failure of dieting.

　　The aim of this activity is essentially to replicate Wegner's study, but using a food-related thought rather than one of a white bear.

The infamous white bear. Admit it: you can't stop thinking about it now, can you?

The practical bit

Following Wegner's procedure, you will be asking your participants to carry out two very straightforward tasks. In one, they will try to suppress thoughts about biscuits (or whatever food-related item you fancy). This is the *suppression task*. In the other task, participants are free to express their thoughts about biscuits (or whatever). This is the *expression task*. All of your participants will need to do both tasks, one after the other. But half of them will carry out the suppression task first, followed by the expression task. For the other half, it's the other way round. The **independent variable** is not the tasks themselves, but the *order* in which they are performed.

　　Your **hypothesis** is that doing the suppression task first will lead to more thoughts of biscuits in the expression task.

Selecting participants

Opportunity sampling is the most convenient method, as usual. You could approach potential participants in communal areas of your school or college. You will then need to find a quiet room with a table and chairs, the more comfortable the better.

Procedure and instructions

Start the procedure by encouraging the participants to relax and get comfortable. You could also reassure them that they will not be doing anything difficult, to put them at ease. You could even consider playing some soothing background music. Because it is crucial that your participants understand what they have to do, you need some clear instructions for each task. Here are some examples:

　　Suppression: *All I want you to do in the next three minutes is to relax. You can close your eyes or keep them open. Please just think about whatever you want with one exception. Please try not to think about biscuits. But if you do think about biscuits, every time you do, please tap on this table.*

　　Expression: *All I want you to do in the next three minutes is to relax. You can close your eyes or keep them open. Please just think about whatever you want, including biscuits. Every time you think about biscuits, please tap on this table.*

You should then ask the participant if they are ready to begin, then time a three-minute period. Repeat this process for the next task. Remember that for half of your participants, you will give the suppression instructions first. For the other half, the expression instructions come first.

　　Your participants will tap on the table every time they become aware of a biscuit-related thought, so you need to keep a careful record of these. You should also time each three-minute session accurately, using a stopwatch or phone app.

Extending the practical

The most relevant way you could extend this activity is to see if there is a difference between dieters and non-dieters. Are you more likely to find an *ironic rebound effect* in people who are currently trying to lose weight? Also, if you wanted to add more scientific rigour, consider **randomly allocating** your participants to the task orders. Decide in advance, and using a random method, which participants will carry out the suppression task first.

Analysing your data

The key measure is the number of taps given in the expression task. This is the **dependent variable**. If ironic processes are at work, we would expect to find more biscuit-related thoughts in the expression task when the suppression task is carried out first. Because these participants have tried to suppress these thoughts, they think about them more when given the opportunity. This is evidence of an ironic rebound effect. You could present your findings in a table like the one on the right, and carry out a statistical test.

Apply it Methods: The maths bit 2

1. Which measure of central tendency would you use to summarise the data? Explain your answer. (*1 mark + 2 marks*)

2. For each column in the table, calculate the statistic you identified in your answer to question 1. (*1 mark + 1 mark*)

3. Which statistical test would you use to analyse the difference between the two sets of data? Give *three* reasons for your choice. (*1 mark + 3 marks*) (See pages 70–71)

4. Use the test you identified in your answer to the previous question to obtain a calculated value for the data below. Is the outcome of the test significant or not? Explain your answer. (*1 mark + 3 marks*) (See page 73)

5. Draw a suitable graph to present the data. Identify the graph you have drawn. (*3 marks + 1 mark*)

Table 2: Number of taps given in the expression task

Suppression task followed by expression task	Expression task followed by suppression task
7	10
12	3
9	13
12	9
10	6
6	7
9	6
14	3
10	5
11	9

EXPLANATIONS FOR FOOD PREFERENCES

EVOLUTIONARY EXPLANATION

Preferred tastes are adaptive.

THE EVOLUTIONARY EXPLANATION

Preference for sweetness
Indicates high-energy food so newborns like fructose present in ripe fruit (Steiner).

Preference for salt
Appears at about 4 months but still innate. Breastfed babies prefer salted cereal (Harris *et al.*).

Preference for fat
Fat is high in calories (energy food) but often unavailable to ancestors. Learning fat preference is an advantage because most efficient way to get energy – a little provides a lot.

Neophobia
Fear of new foods is adaptive because it helps us to avoid foods that might be harmful, especially when we become more independent.

Taste aversion
Biological preparedness (Seligman), being able to quickly learn an aversion to harmful foods (e.g. bitter taste) is adaptive and increases survival chances.

EVALUATION

Research support
Torres and Nowson: We prefer high-fat foods when stressed, to fuel fight or flight response.

Explaining the evolution of food preferences
Alcock *et al.*: Our food preferences are determined by gut microbes which benefit from nutrients we consume.

Individual differences in taste aversion
Drewnowski *et al.*: Some people insensitive to PROP but this may be adaptive because bitter tastes linked to anti-cancer foods.

Neophobia is maladaptive
Food now safer than ever but neophobia persists and limits variety of diet.

The role of culture
Cashdan: Culture plays important role in determining food preferences – ignored by evolutionary theory.

THE ROLE OF LEARNING

We learn to prefer certain foods.

THE ROLE OF LEARNING

Classical conditioning
Preferences for new foods develop because of association with taste we already like – explains why we often sweeten new foods.

Operant conditioning
Parents reinforce food preferences by directly rewarding children when they eat, e.g. vegetables.

Social influences
Social learning theory: Family, peers and later TV all model eating behaviours and give the child direct and indirect reinforcement.

Cultural influences
Culture/ethnicity is most reliable predictor of food preference. We learn cultural norms of preference within the family (e.g. meat eating).

EVALUATION

Limited role of classical conditioning
Little evidence that flavour-flavour learning leads to food preferences. Mere exposure may be more important.

Short-term versus long-term effects of social learning
Hare-Bruun *et al.*: Social learning effects of TV on unhealthy food preferences very weak after six years. Friends became more influential.

Multiple influences
Chilli: Shows how cultural influences can turn an innate food aversion into a learned preference.

Research support for SLT
Jansen and Tenney: Children preferred energy-dense drink when modelled by a teacher.

Support for cultural influences
Eating behaviour in Western cultures has changed dramatically over the last few decades.

THE CONTROL OF EATING BEHAVIOUR

Biological basis of on and off switches.

NEURAL AND HORMONAL MECHANISMS

The role of the hypothalamus
Hypothalamus regulates level of blood glucose within narrow boundaries by adjusting secretion of insulin and anti-insulin hormones.

Lateral hypothalamus (LH)
'Feeding centre': Activated when glucose levels drop. Creates hunger and motivation to eat along with neuropeptide Y (NPY).

Ventro-medial hypothalamus (VMH)
'Satiety centre': Activated when glucose levels rise. Inhibits LH and creates feeling of fullness and end of eating.

The role of ghrelin
An appetite-stimulating hormone secreted by the stomach, detected by the arcuate nucleus of the hypothalamus and closely associated with feelings of hunger.

The role of leptin
An appetite-suppressing hormone secreted by adipose cells. Involved in satiety mechanisms (VMH) and cessation of eating.

EVALUATION

Research support
Hetherington and Ranson: Lesions to VMH in rats caused hyperphagia and obesity. Lesions to LH caused aphagia and starvation.
Gold: PVN involved as well.

An oversimplified explanation
Valassi *et al.*: There are many biological contributors to eating behaviour such as CCK, serotonin and dopamine all interacting.

Roles of social and cultural factors
Woods: Glucostatic mechanism only important in severe energy deprivation, otherwise eating is more socially and culturally influenced.

Non-human animal research
Much research is on rats so need caution in extrapolating to human eating behaviour.

Practical applications
Better treatments are developed as we understand complex interactions between neural and hormonal influences.

EXPLANATIONS FOR OBESITY

PSYCHOLOGICAL EXPLANATIONS

Restricting intake may paradoxically result in obesity.

RESTRAINT, DISINHIBITION AND THE BOUNDARY MODEL

Restraint theory
Herman and Polivy: Restrained eaters become more preoccupied with food and ignore physiological signals of hunger and satiety. This makes them vulnerable to disinhibited overeating.

Disinhibition
Stress, mood and external cues make a restrained eater lose control of their eating, so they overeat because of their 'all-or-nothing' thinking.

The boundary model
Herman and Polivy: Normal eaters start and stop eating at biological boundaries. Restrained eaters set wider boundaries and more eating is under cognitive control, become vulnerable to disinhibition effects.

EVALUATION

Supporting research
Wardle and Beales: Obese women on a restrained-eating diet consumed more calories overall than other participants because of disinhibited eating.

Disinhibiting effects of the media
Boyce and Kuijer: Restrained eaters ate more in a taste test after viewing media images of thinness.

Contradictory research findings
Savage *et al.*: Restrained eating was associated with weight loss over a six-year period.

Restraint is multi-faceted
Restraint is more complex than boundary model says. There are two forms, rigid and flexible, but only rigid leads to obesity.

Practical applications
Most weight loss advice still recommends restrained eating but counterproductive (Zandian *et al.*).

BIOLOGICAL EXPLANATIONS

Obesity has multiple causes.

GENETIC EXPLANATION

Obesity runs in families
Chaput *et al.*: 20% to 50% concordance rates for first-degree relatives.
Nan *et al.*: Up to 80% genetic component to obesity from twin studies.

Polygenic determination
Locke *et al.*: 97 Genes linked with BMI variations but only accounts for 2.7% of variation. Heritability of obesity could involve 400 genes making small but important contributions.

EVALUATION

Limitation of twin studies
MZ twins treated more similarly than DZ twins which confounds findings.
Obesity not inevitable outcome of genes, but genetic influence is clear.

Contradictory evidence
Paracchini *et al.*: Meta-analysis showed genes for leptin and leptin receptors not linked to obesity. Reminder that obesity is complex and other factors involved.

NEURAL EXPLANATION

Serotonin
Kim *et al.*: Serotonin levels abnormally low in obese mice. Sibutramine increases serotonin and leads to weight loss.

Dopamine
Wang *et al.*: Obese people have fewer dopamine D2 receptors so get less reward from eating and overeat to compensate.

EVALUATION

Supporting evidence for serotonin
Ohia *et al.*: 'Knockout' mice with no serotonin 2C receptors become obese.

Supporting evidence for dopamine
Ritchie and Noble: Variation in DRD2 gene linked to lower number of dopamine receptors in obese people.

Treatment applications
Better understanding of physiological mechanisms leads to better treatments such as tackling serotonin deficiency.

Psychological explanations for anorexia nervosa

Family systems theory
Family as a complex social system.

Family systems theory (FST)

Enmeshment
Family members' self-identities are tied up with one another. Poorly defined roles and over-involvement. Refusal to eat is an assertion of independence.

Overprotectiveness
Family members reinforce loyalty and dependence by nurturing one another obsessively and self-sacrificing.

Rigidity
Stress produces a crisis and family cannot adapt. Child's attempts at independence are thwarted.

Conflict avoidance
Family members take all steps to avoid discussion of problems (e.g. eating disorder) until crisis point.

Autonomy and control
Bruch: AN sufferer strives to assert her independence against domineering mother by starving herself.

Evaluation

Supportive research
Brockmeyer et al.: AN patients want to be autonomous. Strauss and Ryan: Disturbances of autonomy.

Inconsistent evidence
Aragona et al.: Research findings depend on how enmeshment is measured, inconsistent because it is vague and difficult to operationalise.

Treatment applications
Robin et al.: BFST effective in recovery of AN patients but small sample and recovery assessment was not 'blinded'.

Cause or effect (or both)?
Family dysfunction may be the result of having an AN sufferer in the family not the cause.

Explanatory power
Can explain AN in females and adolescence. Has trouble explaining it in males and at other ages.

Social learning theory
Indirect and direct reinforcement.

Social learning theory

Modelling
AN can be learned indirectly through observation of real or symbolic models, especially if the observer identifies with the model.

Vicarious reinforcement
An observer is more likely to imitate a model's eating behaviours when the model is rewarded (e.g. with praise).

Role of the media
Various media in Western cultures promote the thin ideal body shape. Young women may identify with thin media figures and gain vicarious reinforcement of their own weight-loss efforts.

Key study on SLT and anorexia
Dittmar et al.
Procedure: Children shown images of Barbie, Emme or flowers.
Findings: Children who saw Barbie images expressed more body dissatisfaction.

Evaluation

Research support
Becker et al.: Best predictor of AN in young Fijian women was how much media their friends used – they then discuss their approval of thin celebrities.

SLT explains cultural changes
Chisuwa and O'Dea: AN in Japan has increased as cultural ideals of body shape are influenced by Western media.

Diathesis-stress explanation
If media depictions of thinness cause AN then more young women would have the disorder. Could be a stressor but needs to interact with a diathesis (genetic, trauma) for fuller explanation.

Explains gender differences
Media and other social influences may be partly responsible for growth of 'bigorexia' in males.

Treatment applications
Therapies based on social learning principles can be very useful when weight gain is urgently needed.

Cognitive theory
Maladaptive and faulty thinking.

Cognitive theory

Cognitive distortions
Disturbed perceptions of body shape.
Williamson et al.: AN patients overestimated their body size and had a thinner ideal shape than non-AN controls.

Irrational beliefs
People with AN hold illogical beliefs about body size and shape and eating behaviour, e.g. all-or-nothing thinking and catastrophising.

Perfectionism
People with AN often have unrealistically high standards of achievement in life generally but especially eating. They raise standards each time they achieve them.

Cognitive inflexibility
Treasure and Schmidt: People with AN have problems with set-shifting because they apply weight loss skills to a changed situation where they are no longer needed.

Evaluation

Research support for cognitive distortions
Sachdev et al.: Brain scans show that AN patients have cognitive distortions of their own bodies not bodies in general.

Research support for perfectionism
Halmi et al.: Childhood perfectionism was reliable predictor of AN. But based on unreliable recall of past events.

Contradictory research
Cornellisen et al.: No difference between AN and non-AN women in estimates of body size. Conflicting findings (Gardner and Brown) due to different measurement methods.

Treatment applications
Grave et al.: CBT with AN patients linked with weight gain after one year.

Issues of causation
Research is unclear whether cognitive factors are causes or effects of AN. Shott et al.: Younger AN patients as good at set-shifting as non-AN so probably symptom not cause.

Biological explanations for anorexia nervosa

Anorexia (AN) has multiple symptoms and causes.

Genetic explanation

Anorexia runs in families
Holland et al.: AN concordance of 56% for MZ and 5% for DZ. Rates lower but strong in other studies.

Candidate genes
Scott-Van Zeeland et al.: EPHX2 only gene of 152 linked with AN; involved in cholesterol metabolism.

Genome-wide association studies
Boraska et al.: No genetic variations linked with AN, but study not sensitive enough to find them.

Evaluation

Limitations of twin studies
Joseph: MZ twins treated more similarly than DZ twins, may explain high concordance.

Limitations of gene studies
Anorexia is polygenic so the search for a single gene is futile as one gene can't explain wide variety of AN symptoms.

Neural explanations

Serotonin
AN linked with underactive serotonin system, e.g. Bailer and Kaye: Low levels of serotonin metabolites.

Dopamine
AN linked with underactive dopamine system, e.g. Kaye et al.: Homovanillic acid levels lower in AN and recovered AN patients.

Evaluation

Supporting evidence
Kaye et al.: Dopamine metabolite HVA lower in recovered anorexics than controls; avoids confounding variables so low dopamine could be causal factor.

Interactions with other neurotransmitters
Nunn et al: Serotonin and dopamine affect AN only by interacting with noradrenaline and possibly GABA.

Diathesis-stress explanation
Abraham: Genes create vulnerability to AN which is triggered by social, cultural and psychological factors.

Explanations for the success and failure of dieting

Failure is more common than success.

Explanations for the success and failure of dieting

The spiral model
Heatherton and Polivy: Body dissatisfaction leads to dieting which usually fails. The dieter eats even less next time and still fails, lowering self-esteem.

Ironic processes theory
Wegner: Dieters label some foods as 'forbidden' but this means they think about them more because they are trying not to, leading to disinhibition.

Restraint, disinhibition and the boundary model
Dieting means eating is subject to cognitive distortions. Disinhibited eating occurs when the dieter breaks their diet limits, so weight may be gained.

Evaluation

Uses of the spiral model
Key to breaking out of 'downward spiral' is to raise self-esteem so that dieting is not seen as necessary.

Support for ironic processes theory
Adraainse et al.: Trying not to think about a snack made thinking about it more likely and led to increased calorie intake.

Minimal effects of ironic processes
Ironic processes in real-life have less effect on dieting than in the lab and are less important than other factors (e.g. self-esteem).

Increasing dieting success
Ironic processes theory suggests paying full attention to eating (e.g. not in front of the TV).

Individual differences
Ogden: Some people lose weight even when preoccupied with food. Perhaps because they have an internal locus of control.

Practice questions, answers and feedback

Question 1 In relation to food preferences, explain what is meant by neophobia and taste aversion. (4 marks)

Morticia's answer

Neophobia is a fear of new foods. Taste aversion is an avoidance of certain tastes such as bitterness because foods with such tastes might be a sign of being bad for you. The same is true for neophobia. Children often overcome such fears and avoidance by following what their parents do.

Morticia has outlined both terms - albeit rather concisely – and there is relevant additional information at the end.

Luke's answer

Neophobia is an innate predisposition to avoid eating new things. This is an adaptive behaviour because it prevents children just putting anything in their mouths that might be poisonous.

Taste aversion is also innate. It is also an innate predisposition to avoid certain tastes such as bitter tastes because toxic foods often taste bitter.

The fact that both of these are hard wired happens because individuals without such innate predispositions are much more likely to die.

A more impressive answer from Luke that makes much more of the fact that these behaviours may be innate tendencies. Both are clearly outlined.

Vladimir's answer

Both neophobia and taste aversion are behaviours that protect the survival of young children because they prevent them trying unknown foods or foods that can be dangerous. Genes for such predispositions are naturally selected because they increase survival. These predispositions explain why children in particular don't like new foods or bitter tastes.

Whereas the previous two answers included clear outlines of the concepts, Vladimir has only talked about both in general terms.

Question 2 Sophie and Sahal are comparing what they had for breakfast. Sophie had apricot jam on toast, something she has had for as long as she can remember. Sahal had canjeero, a bread that looks a bit like a pancake, with a goat stew. He explains how he used to have it with camel meat when he was growing up in Somalia.

Explain two ways in which culture influences Sophie's and Sahal's breakfast preferences. (4 marks)

Morticia's answer

It is obvious from the description that Sophie and Sahal come from two different cultural backgrounds because they are eating foods which are culturally distinct.

It is likely that they learned to like these foods when they were young and these were the foods provided at home. Children model their eating behaviour on their parents, assuming that what they eat is safe.

The first half of Morticia's answer is common-sense and not worthy of credit.

There is a reference to 'modelling' in the second paragraph, but it is easy to become quite anecdotal so candidates need to ensure they use appropriate psychological terms.

Luke's answer

One cultural influence is the norms that we are exposed to. We are surrounded by supermarkets and restaurants and food on TV, which informs us about what is the typical food that people in our culture eat. These media influences are related to culture.

A second cultural influence is what you are given to eat at home. In some homes children might not have meat and this would influence their food preferences because they would continue to feel afraid of this new food. They would grow up to continue to be vegetarian.

Luke's first factor – that of cultural norms – is relevant and there is elaboration but this is not linked to the stem.

The second factor is also relevant and, again, elaborated. Application to the characters in the stem is again absent though.

Vladimir's answer

Culture has a major influence on what we learn to eat. It helps children overcome their fear of new foods and taste aversions.

Sahal would have been served canjeero for breakfast at home and learned to like the taste. He would have modelled what his parents ate, trusting that it was safe. They would have rewarded him for eating up. It would have been the same for Sophie, which explains why they developed such different tastes.

In addition the media show children the norms for their culture and this emphasises what they learn at home.

The first sentence in Vladimir's answer is redundant really as a specific factor is not identified.

The issue of modelling is made clear in paragraph 2 and this is linked to the stem – though the outline lacks detail (just about worth middle range credit).

The influence of the media is not linked to food preference so does not add anything further.

Question 3 Describe and evaluate biological explanations for anorexia nervosa. (16 marks)

Morticia's answer

Anorexia is a severe and potentially fatal disorder that affects as much as 1.2% of the population at any time. Far more females than males are affected, though the number of males is increasing. There are many explanations for anorexia nervosa (AN), some are psychological and some are biological. The main biological explanation is related to genes. This is because research shows that anorexia does run in families. In other words if your mother had anorexia it is more likely that you might develop it than someone who didn't have a mother with anorexia. Or if you are an identical twin who has exactly the same genes as your twin it is more likely that you both have AN than if you are non-identical twins who only share about 50% of their genes.

It may be that there are specific candidate genes for AN and research has identified some but it is unlikely that there is just one gene. It is more likely that it is a number of different genes and these will affect different aspects of behaviour such as obsessiveness or control switches for eating.

The problem with twin studies and genetics is that twins share the same environment so it could equally be their shared environments that is causing the similarity, such as a home environment that is full of conflict. Adoption studies are used to get over this problem and they also show that genetics is important.

There are also neural explanations for AN. One possibility is serotonin, which may have an effect on appetite. It may make people feel less hungry. Another neurotransmitter that may be important is dopamine because people with AN react differently to people without AN.

Of course genetic and neural explanations are linked because the genes would lead to abnormal levels of neurotransmitters such as serotonin and dopamine.

The biological explanations might explain the gender difference in who is affected though that is more likely to be due to a social explanation, i.e. social learning theory. This can explain why AN is common in Western cultures but not others.

In fact the best explanation is always going to be the diathesis–stress model, which suggests that individuals have some kind of innate vulnerability, which might be due to their genetic inheritance but they only develop the disorder if something else happens – some kind of stressor which triggers the disorder. This explains why concordance levels between identical twins are never 100%. There is always some environmental input.

(414 words)

Comments:

The first three sentences are not required – far better to get straight to the explanation.

A rather generic account here without specific evidence.

In paragraph 2 there is a relevant evaluative comment.

Paragraph 3 provides a relevant point but could be more directly applied to anorexia.

The next paragraph contains a weak account of the neural basis of anorexia, particularly the dopamine link.

The remaining points require further analysis and the explanation of diathesis-stress at the end is not made relevant to anorexia.

Overall, this essay contains too many generic and unsubstantiated points.

Luke's answer

There are two main biological explanations: genetic and neural. The genetic explanation proposes that certain genes actually cause anorexia. Van Zeeland et al. (2014) looked at 152 candidate genes suspected to be linked with features of anorexia and found only one with a significant association. This codes for an enzyme involved in cholesterol metabolism which is something that is abnormally high in people who have very bad cases of anorexia.

An alternative approach is to focus more widely instead of on specific genes. A very recent study by Boraska et al. didn't find any patterns that were significantly related to anorexia but argued that this was because their study was not sensitive enough to detect them.

Twin studies have been used as support for genetic explanations but there are criticisms of such studies because they assume that both identical and non-identical twins share identical environments. However, there is reason to believe that identical twins are treated much more the same because they look at behaviour much more the same, and therefore higher concordance rates may be due to this.

Research focused on identifying candidate genes has been criticised because the cause is likely to be polygenic and affect many different behaviours. To look for one root cause and a biological basis for this is to oversimplify anorexia.

The second biological explanation relates to neurotransmitters. Serotonin is implicated in anorexia in appetite reduction and obsessiveness. Bailer and Kaye reviewed a number of studies and concluded that there appear to be low levels of serotonin metabolites in anorexics. Similarly, research has also looked at dopamine (e.g. Kaye et al.) and found low levels of dopamine metabolites. These results suggest low levels of both serotonin and dopamine in people with anorexia.

Kaye et al. produced strong supporting evidence that controlled for confounding variables because ex anorexics with normal weight and not restricted food intake were studied – both factors that may affect dopamine levels. The ex-anorexics still had lower HVA levels.

One issue for neural explanations is that it is probably unrealistic to think that neurotransmitters act on their own. It is probably better to explain anorexia in terms of an interaction between dopamine, serotonin and also GABA.

A further danger is to consider that biological explanations may be functioning on their own. The diathesis-stress model proposes that biological factors merely act as a vulnerability which on their own won't lead to anorexia. It takes psychological factors such as stressors to act as a trigger for the disorder.

(414 words)

Comments:

Luke begins with some clear and precisely presented evidence which was all but absent in Morticia's account.

In paragraph 2 there is good use of evidence plus counterargument.

In paragraph 3 a specific twin study may have been useful so the point looks a little generic.

Paragraphs 4 and 5 provide a well-made point followed by a much more sophisticated account than was provided earlier including relevant evidence.

In paragraph 6 a good methodological evaluation is provided, finally followed by a conclusion based on diathesis-stress (which is a little more applied than Morticia's).

Explanations for food preferences: Evolutionary explanation

1. Humans have a preference for sweet-tasting foods because they . . .
(a) Provide salt for crucial cell functions.
(b) Are an important source of protein.
(c) Are a fast-acting source of energy.
(d) Are always safe to eat.

2. Neophobia is adaptive because . . .
(a) It means we eat a varied diet.
(b) We don't eat potentially toxic foods until we learn they are safe.
(c) We learn quickly to avoid certain foods.
(d) It forces us to eat a wide range of nutrients.

3. The development of taste aversions is mainly due to . . .
(a) Neophobia.
(b) A preference for bitter tastes.
(c) Biological preparedness.
(d) Cultural influences.

4. Insensitivity to bitter compounds is . . .
(a) An example of neophobia.
(b) A learned characteristic.
(c) Always maladaptive.
(d) Beneficial because bitter foods may be anti-carcinogenic.

Explanations for food preferences: The role of learning

1. Liking a new food because we associate it with a preferred taste is an example of . . .
(a) Social learning.
(b) Flavour-flavour learning.
(c) Cultural influences.
(d) Imitation.

2. An adaptive function of modelling in children is to . . .
(a) Learn from parents which foods are safe.
(b) Prevent them eating too many high-calorie foods.
(c) Learn to dislike vegetables because they taste bitter.
(d) Learn which foods to eat from media advertising.

3. Culture influences children's food preferences by . . .
(a) Causing them to dislike bitter-tasting foods.
(b) Influencing neophobia.
(c) Determining the preference for energy-giving foods.
(d) Determining what parents choose to feed them.

4. According to Hare-Bruun et al., the social learning effects of TV advertising are mainly . . .
(a) On girls' preferences.
(b) Short-term.
(c) Permanent.
(d) More important than family influences.

Neural and hormonal mechanisms in the control of eating behaviour

1. The ventromedial hypothalamus is . . .
(a) A feeding centre.
(b) Involved in stimulating appetite.
(c) Activated when glucose levels rise above a set point.
(d) Associated with neuropeptide Y.

2. Ghrelin . . .
(a) Is produced by adipose cells.
(b) Triggers hunger when it rises above a certain level.
(c) Suppresses appetite.
(d) Is a neurotransmitter.

3. Leptin . . .
(a) Increases in the bloodstream just before a meal.
(b) Is detected by receptors in the ventro-medial hypothalamus.
(c) Is associated with feelings of hunger.
(d) Is secreted by the stomach.

4. The dual-centre hypothesis is limited because it . . .
(a) Fails to recognise the true complexity of control of eating behaviour.
(b) Ignores the role of glucose levels.
(c) Argues that cultural influences on eating are more important than biological ones.
(d) Fails to account for the role of the VMH.

Biological explanations for anorexia nervosa

1. A gene identified by Scott-Van Zeeland et al. is . . .
(a) Involved in serotonin metabolism.
(b) Known as GWAS.
(c) Involved in cholesterol metabolism.
(d) The only cause of anorexia.

2. Serotonin is implicated in AN because . . .
(a) Levels of homovanillic acid are lower in AN patients.
(b) Research shows levels of 5-HIAA are lower in AN patients.
(c) There is overactivity of the serotonin system.
(d) Amphetamines cause anxiety in AN patients.

3. A problem with gene studies of AN is . . .
(a) There are at least two different types of study: CGAS and GWAS.
(b) One gene cannot explain all the symptoms of anorexia.
(c) They cannot be replicated.
(d) Anorexia does not have a genetic basis.

4. According to Nunn et al. . . .
(a) Serotonin interacts with noradrenaline in AN.
(b) Dopamine activity is the central feature of AN.
(c) Serotonin levels can explain all features of AN.
(d) GABA is the most important neurotransmitter in AN.

Psychological explanations for anorexia nervosa: Family systems theory

1. FST focuses mainly on . . .
(a) The father–daughter relationship.
(b) Individuals with anorexia.
(c) The mother–daughter relationship.
(d) The role of culture.

2. A lack of individual self-identity within the family is an example of . . .
(a) Rigidity.
(b) Over-protectiveness.
(c) Enmeshment.
(d) Conflict avoidance.

3. According to Bruch, a lack of autonomy can lead to . . .
(a) Distorted body image.
(b) Over-sensitivity to feelings of hunger.
(c) Avoidance of conflict within the family.
(d) A feeling of being independent.

4. It is difficult to test family systems theory because . . .
(a) Concepts such as enmeshment are vague.
(b) There are not enough AN patients available to study.
(c) There is only one type of family.
(d) Researchers all use the same measurement methods.

Psychological explanations for anorexia nervosa: Social learning theory

1. Models are most likely to be imitated when . . .
(a) Their eating behaviour is frowned upon by others.
(b) They have the same status as the observer.
(c) The observer identifies with them.
(d) The observer is praised for losing weight.

2. Dittmar et al. found that . . .
(a) Girls who saw Barbie images had lower body esteem.
(b) The control images had the greatest effect.
(c) Girls who saw Emme images had more body dissatisfaction.
(d) Exposure to Barbie dolls caused anorexia.

3. Magazines aimed at young women influence AN because . . .
(a) They include a lot of articles about anorexia.
(b) They reflect the full variety of body shapes in society.
(c) Most young women are very impressionable.
(d) They promote cultural ideals about a thin body shape.

4. The diathesis-stress model suggests that anorexia is . . .
(a) Not explained by social learning factors alone.
(b) Purely a genetic disorder.
(c) Caused mainly by cultural factors.
(d) A disorder of adolescence.

Psychological explanations for anorexia nervosa: Cognitive theory

1. Evidence that people with AN show cognitive distortions is that they . . .

(a) Only think of food when they are hungry.

(b) Take little interest in their appearance.

(c) Never try hard to succeed.

(d) Consistently overestimate their body size.

2. Perfectionism is an example of . . .

(a) Misinterpreting body size and shape.

(b) A failure of set-shifting.

(c) Automatic negative thinking.

(d) An irrational belief.

3. People with AN have difficulty in 'set-shifting'. This means . . .

(a) They are cognitively very flexible.

(b) They are perfectionists.

(c) They carry on applying old skills to new situations.

(d) They misinterpret their emotional states.

4. Studies of perfectionism in AN may be unreliable because . . .

(a) Perfectionism is the result of anorexia and not the cause.

(b) They depend on recall of childhood events.

(c) AN is not linked to perfectionism.

(d) Some AN sufferers are more perfectionist than others.

Biological explanations for obesity

1. The contribution of genes to obesity suggested by twin studies is . . .

(a) Substantial.

(b) Moderate to substantial.

(c) Weak to moderate.

(d) No more than 50%.

2. In terms of neurotransmitters, obesity seems to be linked with . . .

(a) Abnormally high levels of dopamine.

(b) Low serotonin levels combined with high dopamine levels.

(c) Abnormally low levels of serotonin.

(d) Higher numbers of dopamine receptors in the brain.

3. The most likely genetic influence on obesity is . . .

(a) A single gene as the primary cause.

(b) Many genes interacting to make small but significant effects.

(c) A few genes, some with greater effects than others.

(d) A problem with the gene that determines leptin activity.

4. Evidence for dopamine's role in obesity is . . .

(a) Dopamine activity is determined by 5-HT2C receptors.

(b) Higher levels of 5-HIAA in obese people.

(c) Fewer D2 receptors in the brains of obese people.

(d) The amygdala is overstimulated in obese people.

Psychological explanations for obesity: Restraint theory, disinhibition and the boundary model

1. Restrained eaters often fail to lose weight because they . . .

(a) Are sensitive to physiological signals of hunger.

(b) Become preoccupied with food.

(c) Have no willpower.

(d) Have low self-esteem.

2. According to the boundary model, restrained eaters . . .

(a) Stop eating if they break their diet boundary.

(b) Have a lower hunger boundary than normal eaters.

(c) Notice when they are full more quickly than normal eaters.

(d) Have a narrower 'zone of biological indifference'.

3. Dieters consume more calories than normal eaters because they . . .

(a) Are constantly eating more food.

(b) Only eat high-calorie food.

(c) Have occasional periods of disinhibited eating.

(d) Don't think about what they eat.

4. Media images of thinness can contribute to obesity because . . .

(a) They act as disinhibitors of eating behaviour.

(b) Obese people do not have as much willpower as celebrities.

(c) They reinforce the obese person's desire to be thin.

(d) Most people find such images inspiring.

Explanations for the success and failure of dieting

1. The spiral model argues that . . .

(a) Most dieters will stop dieting when they see it doesn't work.

(b) The more someone diets, the easier it gets to lose weight.

(c) Dieters who fail to lose weight usually blame themselves.

(d) The more a dieter tries not to think about food, the more they do so.

2. According to ironic processes theory, one way to lose weight is . . .

(a) Monitor your food intake more carefully.

(b) Join a slimming programme such as Weightwatchers.

(c) Raise self-esteem.

(d) Distract yourself by thinking of something other than food.

3. Adriaanse *et al.* found that people who tried to avoid unhealthy snacks . . .

(a) Thought about unhealthy snacks but didn't eat more.

(b) Switched to healthier snacks instead.

(c) Had low self-esteem.

(d) Ate more unhealthy snacks.

4. Ironic processes in dieting . . .

(a) Are more important than self-esteem.

(b) Are easier to find in real life than they are in lab studies.

(c) Are more obvious in long-term dieting attempts.

(d) Have a fairly limited influence.

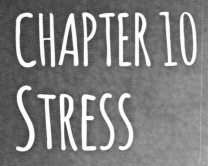

CHAPTER 10
STRESS

'TO ACHIEVE GREAT
THINGS, TWO THINGS ARE
NEEDED: A PLAN AND NOT
QUITE ENOUGH TIME.'

MILLARD DALE BAUGHMAN,
TEACHER (1958).

CAN STRESS BE
GOOD FOR US?

Chapter contents

Stress has at least three different meanings in psychology. It can be something that happens to us, i.e. some demand our environment makes upon us. Psychologists prefer the word *stressor* to describe these causes of stress. Secondly, stress can be seen as a *transaction* between a person and their environment. You experience stress when the perceived demands of your environment are greater than your perceived ability to cope with them. So you find exams a real threat; every time you think about them you feel sick. And you believe you haven't done enough revision. It's a recipe for high stress levels.

On this spread, we start with the third meaning of stress: how the body physically responds to a stressor.

Key Terms

Sympathomedullary pathway (SAM) – This controls how the body initially responds to an acute stressor. The sympathetic nervous system triggers the fight or flight response including the hormones adrenaline and noradrenaline which communicate with target organs in the body such as the heart.

Hypothalamic-pituitary-adrenal system (HPA) – This controls how the body responds to a chronic stressor. The hypothalamus triggers the pituitary gland to release the hormone ACTH which, in turn, stimulates release of cortisol.

Cortisol – An important hormone produced by the adrenal cortex. It helps the body to cope with stressors by controlling how the body uses energy. Cortisol suppresses immune system activity.

General Adaptation Syndrome – Selye's explanation of how the body responds in the same way to any stressor. The response goes through three stages: alarm reaction, resistance and exhaustion.

The physiology of the stress response – the sympathomedullary pathway (left) and the hypothalamic-pituitary-adrenal system (right).

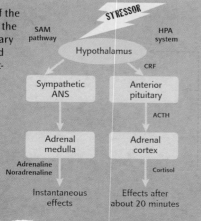

The General Adaptation Syndrome (GAS)

Hans Selye (1936) was the first to use the term *stress* in a psychological context. He viewed the response as an attempt by the body to *adapt* to a stressor. This is an effective protective response, in the short term, to an acute stressor. If the stressor is prolonged (i.e. it is chronic) serious damage can occur, including stress-related illnesses. Selye believed that the process of adapting to a stressor goes through three stages, which he called the **General Adaptation Syndrome**:

Alarm reaction Once a stressor is perceived, the physiological responses of the body are activated (as described below in terms of acute and chronic stress) in preparation for fight or flight.

Resistance This is the point at which the body attempts to adapt to the stressful environmental demands by resisting the stressor. Physiological activity is greater than normal and uses a lot of energy. The individual appears to be coping but the body's resources are being consumed at a potentially harmful rate. For instance, stress hormones are produced in huge quantities and it is only a matter of time before they cause damage to the heart and blood vessels. So the **parasympathetic nervous system** is activated to conserve energy for the longer term, because the stressor is becoming chronic.

Exhaustion Adaptation to a chronic stressor is now failing. The resources needed to resist have become drained. The individual begins to re-experience the symptoms of sympathetic arousal that first appeared in the alarm stage (for example, sweating, raised heart rate and blood pressure, and so on). The adrenal glands may become damaged and the **immune system** compromised. Stress-related illnesses or *diseases of adaptation* (as Selye called them) are now likely, such as raised blood pressure, coronary heart disease and depression.

The physiological response

Acute stress

You learned about the body's immediate response to an acute stressor as part of biopsychology – this is the **sympathomedullary pathway** (SAM), also called the **fight or flight response** (see page 35).

Sympathetic arousal When an individual perceives a stressor as threatening, the **sympathetic branch** of the **autonomic nervous system** (ANS) is activated by the **hypothalamus**. Sympathetic nerves connect the brain with many organs of the body, such as the heart and various glands including the two **adrenal glands**.

Adrenal medulla The adrenal glands sit on top of the kidneys, and are made up of two main components: the **adrenal medulla** is the central part of the gland, and the **adrenal cortex** surrounds the medulla. Sympathetic arousal stimulates the adrenal medulla to release the **hormones adrenaline** and **noradrenaline** into the bloodstream.

Adrenaline and noradrenaline cause the heart to beat faster, muscles to tense and the liver to convert stored glycogen into glucose which is released into the bloodstream to provide energy to fuel the fight or flight response.

End of response The ANS is divided into two branches that have generally opposing effects, the **sympathetic nervous system** and parasympathetic system. Once a stressor is no longer a threat, the parasympathetic system is activated and the physiological arousal associated with the fight or flight response decreases. The priority now is for energy conservation rather than expenditure, which is why this pattern of activity is sometimes called the *rest and digest response*.

Chronic stress

The body's response to long-term (chronic) stress is activated by the **hypothalamic-pituitary-adrenal system** (HPA). The HPA takes longer than the SAM to activate by a stressor but can persist for several hours, or longer. When the hypothalamus is activated because of a stressor it sends a signal to activate the sympathetic nervous system but also produces a hormone called *corticotropin releasing factor* (CRF). CRF is detected by the anterior lobe of the **pituitary gland** causing the release of *adrenocorticotropin hormone* (ACTH) into the bloodstream. ACTH levels are detected by the adrenal cortex which secretes the hormone **cortisol** in response.

Cortisol is often called *the* stress hormone because it has a central role to play in the body's stress response. Some of its functions help the body to cope with a stressor. For instance, cortisol is a *glucocorticoid* because it affects glucose metabolism by mobilising and restoring energy supplies to power the stress response. But it has other effects that are damaging to the body. For instance, cortisol suppresses the immune system (which we will explore on the next spread).

Negative feedback loop The HPA is self-regulating via a *negative feedback loop*. Levels of cortisol circulating in the bloodstream are monitored back at the pituitary and the hypothalamus. High levels of cortisol trigger a reduction in both CRF and ACTH, resulting in a corresponding reduction in cortisol.

Evaluation of the GAS

Research evidence for the GAS

Selye (1936) supported his model with research. He initially experimented with rats, subjecting them to various stressors including extreme cold, excessive muscular exercise and surgical injury. He found that the same typical collection of responses occurred (a syndrome) regardless of the stressor. This was a general response of the body that could not be attributed to any specific injury, a bodily reaction to damage that appeared after six to 48 hours. Selye was then able to track the rats' response to a continuing stressor through the resistance and exhaustion stages, providing the first evidence for the GAS.

This shows that the body's general response to a stressor is a physiological reality, at least in rats.

Is the GAS really general?

Key to the GAS is the idea that the stress response is non-specific, that it is always the same regardless of the stressor. However, John Mason (1971) replicated Selye's procedures using seven stressors in studies of monkeys rather than rats. He measured the monkeys' levels of urinary cortisol and found varied effects depending on the stressor. For instance, extreme cold increased cortisol levels, extreme heat reduced them, and excessive exercise produced no changes (this is also discussed on page 94).

These findings reach to the very heart of the **validity** of the GAS. They challenge a central concept of Selye's theory by showing that specific stressors can produce specific patterns of responses.

Evaluation of the physiological response

Male bias in biological research

There were dangers for our evolutionary female ancestors in a stress response geared towards fight or flight. If a female responds with fight or flight this creates a risk for her children because it leaves them vulnerable (if their mother runs away, they are left defenseless). Therefore, some psychologists (e.g. Taylor 2006) argue that the stress response explained on these pages is characteristic of males only. More adaptive in females is the '**tend and befriend**' response, in which a threat is met with tending of offspring and befriending of other females to provide social support (this is also discussed on page 94).

The assumption that fight or flight is a valid explanation of the stress response in all humans is a reflection of bias towards male physiology.

Psychological factors are ignored

Perhaps because much research is conducted on non-human animals such as rats, physiological accounts of the stress response ignore psychological factors such as **cognitive appraisal**. Richard Lazarus (1999) argues that we make appraisals of a stressor by actively working out if it is a threat (primary appraisal) and whether we have the resources to cope with it (secondary appraisal).

Speisman et al. (1964) asked students to watch a primitive (and gruesome) medical procedure on film while their heart rates were measured. Changes to heart rate depended on how the students interpreted what was happening in the film. If they believed the procedure to be traumatic, their heart rates increased. But if they interpreted the procedure to be part of a voluntary and joyful rite of passage, their heart rates actually decreased.

It is difficult for purely physiological explanations to account for this finding. It shows that humans are not as passive in the face of stressors as physiological theories assume.

Evaluation eXtra

Real-life benefits

Addison's disease is a rare disorder of the adrenal glands, in which sufferers cannot produce cortisol. This leaves the body lacking the crucial hormone cortisol to deal with stress, which can trigger a life-threatening Addisonian crisis. Symptoms include mental confusion, abnormal heart rhythm and a catastrophic drop in blood pressure. This requires immediate medical treatment. Once diagnosed, it can be treated with self-administered cortisol replacement therapy. Patients can lead relatively normal lives, although they do need to be aware of the dangers of stressful situations when medication needs to be increased.

Consider: Can you think of any other benefits there could be to improving our understanding of the physiology of stress?

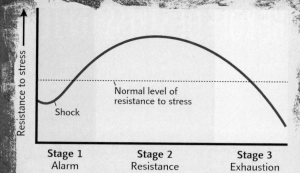

The GAS explains how the stress response develops over time through three stages.

Apply it

Concepts: A stressful near miss

Imagine you are sawing a piece of wood when the saw slips and narrowly misses your finger. You realise that you have been lucky and very nearly caused yourself a serious injury. Your heart starts to race and you get a sick feeling in the pit of your stomach. Your mouth goes dry and you start to sweat. But after a few minutes, these symptoms disappear and you start to feel better.

Question

Use your knowledge of the physiology of stress to explain why these changes came about. Make sure you refer to the changes that occurred immediately and to those changes that occur later.

Apply it

Concepts: The stress of caring

Jianping's mother suffered damage to her spinal cord and is no longer able to look after herself. Jianping is her main carer and has to look after all her physical needs. She has been doing this for two years with hardly any time off. She loves her mother so she doesn't complain, but it is a very stressful situation and it shows no sign of getting any better. Because she felt ill recently, Jianping went to see her doctor who found that her blood pressure is much too high so now she has to take medication. Not surprisingly, she also feels very down a lot of the time and doesn't know how she's going to cope.

Question

What kind of stressor is Jianping experiencing? Explain the physiological processes taking place in her body that might account for her high blood pressure.

CHECK IT

1. Outline the main features of the sympathomedullary pathway. [4 marks]
2. Outline the hypothalamic-pituitary-adrenal system. [6 marks]
3. Explain the role of cortisol in the physiology of stress. [4 marks]
4. Discuss the General Adaptation Syndrome. [10 marks]
5. Discuss the physiology of stress. [16 marks]

The role of stress in illness including reference to immunosuppression and cardiovascular disorders.

The immune system is our defensive barrier against invading germs and other foreign bodies (*antigens*).

One line of defence is innate, such as white blood cells (*leucocytes*) and *natural killer (NK)* cells. The second line of defence is *acquired immunity* which is specific to the invading antigen in question because it has been encountered before. This acquired response involves *lymphocytes* that destroy specific antigens including *B cells* that produce *antibodies* to destroy antigens. There are also several types of *T cells*, such as *memory T cells* which recognise antigens, and *killer T cells* which destroy cells infected with antigens.

KEY TERMS

Immunosuppression – Stress can cause illness by preventing the immune system from working efficiently and carrying out its usual task of identifying and destroying pathogens.

Cardiovascular disorders – Any disorder of the heart (cardio) or blood vessels (vascular) including those of the brain (e.g. stroke).

A very familiar scenario indeed. Stressful for most students, but can exams damage your health?

The role of stress in illness

Immunosuppression

Stress can suppress the **immune system** directly. For example, **cortisol** produced by the **hypothalamic-pituitary-adrenal** stress response inhibits production of *lymphocytes*. There are some indirect **immunosuppressive** effects too. Stress can influence lifestyle behaviours (smoking, drinking, sleep patterns) that in turn have a detrimental effect on immune functioning. There is evidence that this happens in many different stress experiences.

Chronic stress and the immune system Janice Kiecolt-Glaser has investigated the effect of two chronic (long-term) stressors: preparing for exams and looking after relatives who are ill.

Study 1: Procedure Kiecolt-Glaser *et al.* (1984) investigated the effects of exams: 75 medical students gave blood samples twice, one month before an exam period (low-stress) and on the day of the first exam (high-stress). They also completed questionnaires measuring sources of stress and self-reported psychological symptoms.

Findings The researchers found that the activity of NK and killer T cells decreased between the first and second samples, evidence of an immune response being suppressed by a common stressor. This decline was most apparent in students who reported feeling most lonely and in those experiencing other sources of stress such as significant events in their lives.

Study 2: Procedure Kiecolt-Glaser et al. (1991) carried out another **longitudinal study** in which they compared the health and immune functioning of two groups of people – caregivers looking after a relative with Alzheimer's disease, and a matched group of non-caregivers.

Findings Over a period of 13 months, the caregivers showed an increase in antibodies to the Epstein-Barr Virus (EBV), a herpes virus. There was no such increase in the **control** participants. This finding is a clear indicator of a weaker cell-based immune response. The caregivers also had infectious illnesses on significantly more days, and higher levels of depression with 32% of the caregivers meeting the criteria for clinical depression (only 6% in the control group).

Cardiovascular disorders (CVDs)

There is evidence that stress may contribute to the development of various **cardiovascular disorders** such as heart disease and strokes. We return to this in a later spread when we look at the role of personality in CVDs (page 266). It appears that stress can have both immediate (acute) and longer-term (chronic) effects on CVDs.

Acute stress: Procedure A good example of an event which can be considered an acute (short-term) stressor is sudden emotional arousal, for example, of the type some people experience when watching a sporting performance. Ute Wilbert-Lampen *et al.* (2008) looked at incidences of heart attacks during football matches played in Germany during the 1996 World Cup.

Findings On the days when Germany played, cardiac emergencies increased by 2.66 times compared with a control period. It appears that the acute emotional stress of watching your favourite football team can more than double your risk of suffering a cardiovascular event.

Chronic stress: Procedure Salim Yusuf *et al.* (2004) examined chronic stressors in the INTERHEART study. This was an investigation involving 52 countries, seeking to identify major risk factors for CVDs that exist across different cultures. They compared 15000 people who had had a heart attack (*myocardial infarction* or MI) with a similar number of people who had not.

Findings They found several chronic stressors with a strong link to MI, including **workplace stress** and stressful **life events**. In fact, the contribution of stress was greater than obesity and third only to smoking and cholesterol levels. It seems that stress not only contributes to the development of CVDs in the first place, it also makes existing disorders worse.

Apply it Concepts: Stress and healing

Janice and Roxanne are in the same rugby team and a week ago played in their first match together. They both ended up with the usual bruises and grazes, but each of them also had quite bad cuts. Janice's cut appears to be healing nicely, but Roxanne's is taking a lot longer and she has to change the dressing on it frequently. Roxanne has important A level exams coming up at college, but Janice is a year younger and doesn't have any exams.

Question

Use your knowledge of the relationship between stress and illness to explain why Roxanne's wound is taking so much longer to heal than Janice's.

Evaluation

Stress can benefit immunity

The fundamental assumption underlying research into stress and illness is that stress suppresses the immune system. But some studies show that stress can actually have *immunoenhancing* effects. Firdaus Dharbhar (2008) subjected rats to mild stressors and found that this was enough to stimulate a substantial immune response. Immune cells such as lymphocytes flooded into the bloodstream and onwards into body tissues in preparation for physical damage.

Chronic stressors are dangerous because of their immunosuppressive effects, but this research shows that acute stressors do not act on the immune system in the same way. Instead, they stimulate it and give some protection against short-term stress. Clearly then, the relationship between stress, the immune system and illnesses is complex and not yet fully understood.

Immunosuppression and cancer

There is support for the immunosuppressive effects of stress from studies of illnesses other than CVDs. The development of certain cancers (such as cervical cancers) is known to be affected by immune functioning. José Pereira *et al.* (2003) studied women who were HIV-positive. Women who experienced many stressful events in their lives were more likely, one year later, to develop pre-cancerous lesions of the cervix than those who experienced fewer stressful events.

This study demonstrates that the effects of stress on the immune system may have wider and more direct consequences on health and illness than research into CVDs has indicated.

Direct versus indirect effects

We have seen that stress can have both direct and indirect effects on CVDs. However, the evidence for stress as an indirect precipitating factor in CVDs is much stronger than the evidence that it directly causes CVDs. For example, stress can increase the risk of a heart attack in people who already have CVDs. Kristina Orth-Gomer *et al.* (2000) have shown in women with CVDs that marital conflict created stress that tripled the risk of a heart attack. This is a different proposition to demonstrating that stress causes CVDs to develop in the first place. Especially when you consider that most people who experience stressors do not develop illnesses at all.

So stress increases a person's risk or vulnerability to developing CVDs, mostly through indirect effects such as lifestyle and behavioural changes or activation of the immune system. But the evidence that stress directly causes CVDs is mixed at best.

Evaluation eXtra

Real-life applications

Research into the effects of stress on illness has many potential real-life benefits. For example, Dharbhar's research (above) may eventually lead to patients being given low doses of stress hormones before surgery to improve their chances of making a full and fast recovery afterwards. Kiecolt-Glaser and Glaser (1992) found that students who took a relaxation training programme seriously had better immune functioning during an exam period than those who didn't bother with it.

Consider: Why are real-life applications considered to be a strength of research?

Limitations of research studies

Researchers have conducted many laboratory-based studies of stress to assess the relationship between stress and the immune system and illness. These studies use certain types of stressor (short-term acute ones such as mild electric shocks or unfair distribution of money) that can easily be manipulated in lab conditions.

Other research conclusions about stress come from studies of the effects of stressors on non-human animals.

Consider: Do you see any difficulties in using such studies to gain a better understanding of the links between stress and illness in humans? Explain your answer.

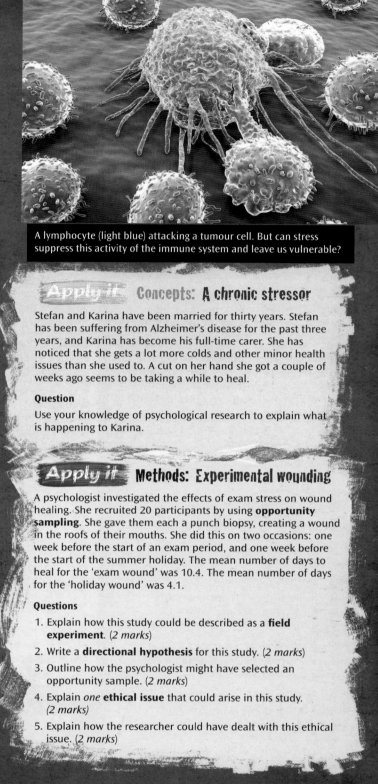

A lymphocyte (light blue) attacking a tumour cell. But can stress suppress this activity of the immune system and leave us vulnerable?

Apply it Concepts: **A chronic stressor**

Stefan and Karina have been married for thirty years. Stefan has been suffering from Alzheimer's disease for the past three years, and Karina has become his full-time carer. She has noticed that she gets a lot more colds and other minor health issues than she used to. A cut on her hand she got a couple of weeks ago seems to be taking a while to heal.

Question

Use your knowledge of psychological research to explain what is happening to Karina.

Apply it Methods: **Experimental wounding**

A psychologist investigated the effects of exam stress on wound healing. She recruited 20 participants by using **opportunity sampling**. She gave them each a punch biopsy, creating a wound in the roofs of their mouths. She did this on two occasions: one week before the start of an exam period, and one week before the start of the summer holiday. The mean number of days to heal for the 'exam wound' was 10.4. The mean number of days for the 'holiday wound' was 4.1.

Questions

1. Explain how this study could be described as a **field experiment**. (*2 marks*)

2. Write a **directional hypothesis** for this study. (*2 marks*)

3. Outline how the psychologist might have selected an opportunity sample. (*2 marks*)

4. Explain *one* **ethical issue** that could arise in this study. (*2 marks*)

5. Explain how the researcher could have dealt with this ethical issue. (*2 marks*)

CHECK IT

1. In relation to the role of stress in illness, explain what is meant by *immunosuppression*. [2 marks]

2. With reference to immunosuppression and cardiovascular disorders, briefly outline the role of stress in illness. [6 marks]

3. Outline **one** study into the role of stress in illness. [6 marks]

4. Describe and evaluate research into the role of stress in illness. [16 marks]

SOURCES OF STRESS: LIFE CHANGES

THE SPECIFICATION SAYS...

Sources of stress: life changes.

This spread and the next two focus on *stressors* that arise from various sources in people's lives. On this spread we concentrate on experiences to do with family, relationships, money and personal issues. How stressful these experiences are depends on how we perceive or interpret them, and on whether we believe we can handle them or not. This is the transactional model of stress.

KEY TERMS

Sources of stress – Any feature of the environment that causes stress, including factors associated with work, everyday minor hassles and major changes in our lives.

Life changes – Significant and relatively infrequent events in people's lives that cause stress. They are stressful because we have to expend psychological energy coping with changed circumstances.

Apply it

Concepts: Relationship stress

Erika and Eduardo have been happily going out with each other for two years. Last month they finally decided to move in together. They thought they would carry on being just as happy, but much to their surprise they now have many more arguments than before. Also, Erika's granddad died two weeks after she moved in with Eduardo, and now she has noticed that she isn't sleeping, and gets a lot more headaches than she used to.

Question

Use your knowledge of psychology to explain Erika's experiences. Refer to some psychological research in your explanation.

The life changes approach assumes that happy events can be just as stressful as unpleasant and threatening ones, but is this true?

Life changes as a source of stress

What are life changes?

Common **sources of stress** for most people are the big events that take place in our lives, the really important things that happen to us from time to time: you get married, or divorced, a close relative dies, your financial state changes for better or worse, a new family member arrives. These **life changes** are not everyday events, and they are often major stressors. They are stressful because you have to make a significant psychological adjustment to adapt to changed circumstances. The bigger the change, the greater the adjustment and the associated stress. The effects of life changes are also cumulative – they add together to create more stress because, jointly, they require even more change to adapt. This applies as much to positive or pleasant life changes as it does to negative ones.

Life changes and illness

Life changes are thought to be linked to the onset of illness. Research has attempted to establish which physical and psychological illnesses are especially likely to be preceded by stressful life changes.

To do this, researchers have developed ways of measuring life changes. One of the most commonly used methods is Thomas Holmes and Richard Rahe's (1967) *Social Readjustment Rating Scale* (SRRS), which you can read more about on page 264. It measures stress by assigning a certain number of **life change units** (**LCU**s) to each item on a list. The higher the LCU value, the more adjustment the life change needs, making it more stressful. For example, divorce has 73 LCUs associated with it, marriage has 50, and death of a close friend 37.

Early research using the SRRS was retrospective. Participants ticked off all the life changes they could recall over the previous 12 months. The LCUs for these changes were added up to produce a total score, and this would be correlated with a measure of the illnesses the participants had experienced over the same period. Rahe (1972) suggested that people scoring under 150 LCUs in a given year were likely to experience reasonable health in the following year. Of people who scored between 150 and 300 LCUs, about 50% experienced illness the next year. Of people who scored over 300 LCUs, almost 80% reported illnesses within the next year.

Research into life changes

A classic study by Rahe *et al.* (1970) used the SRRS in a prospective study which aimed to measure life changes and then see who eventually became ill.

Procedure They studied US Navy personnel assigned to three ships (aircraft carriers). The participants completed a version of a scale called the *Schedule of Recent Experiences* (the forerunner to the SRRS). This covered the six months before their deployment on a tour of duty. A total LCU score was calculated for each participant for this retrospective six-month period.

Once on board ship for the tour of duty, every illness, no matter how trivial, had to be reported to the medical unit. After the ships returned from their missions, an independent researcher reviewed all the medical records and calculated an illness score for each participant. Neither the participants nor the on-board medical staff were aware of the purpose of the study or what the data were being used for.

Findings The researchers found a **significant positive correlation** (of .118) between the LCU scores for the six months before departure and the scores for illnesses aboard ship. In other words, those who experienced the most stressful life changes in the final six months before leaving on active service, also had the most (or most severe) illnesses in the following six months aboard ship. Rahe *et al.* concluded that life changes were a reasonably robust predictor of later illness.

Evaluation

Practical activity on page 280

Supporting research

Decades of research supports the view that life changes are linked to illness. For example, Raija Lietzén *et al.* (2011) used data from the Health and Social Support (HeSSup) study in Finland to follow over 160,000 adults who did not have asthma at the start of the study. They found that a high level of life change stress was a reliable predictor of asthma onset. This link was not explained by other known risk factors such as having a cat or dog at home or smoking. Study after study has found a moderate but robust and significant correlation between the stress of life changes and illnesses.

Some of this research has been **prospective**, which is methodologically more powerful because it attempts to predict illness in the future based on past life changes (e.g. Rahe *et al.* 1970).

Individual differences

The same life changes do not affect everyone in the same ways. To take just two examples: if a woman gets pregnant her sense of stress depends at least partly on whether the pregnancy is planned or unexpected; and the stress associated with moving house depends on the reasons why the move is necessary (being worse off or better off financially, for instance). Donald Byrne and Henry Whyte (1980) tried to predict who would experience a myocardial infarction (heart attack) on the basis of life change scores. The researchers found that this only worked when they took into account the subjective interpretations each participant gave life changes on the SRRS.

The classic life changes approach fails to consider the impact of individual differences in how life changes are perceived, reducing its **validity** as an explanation of stress.

Positive and negative life changes

Because the SRRS is based on the assumption that all change is stressful, it muddles together several different types of life changes, including positive and negative ones. Many psychologists now believe that positive and negative life changes have different effects. For example, Jay Turner and Blair Wheaton (1995) asked their participants to rate the desirability of the life changes they selected on the SRRS. They found that undesirable or negative life events caused most of the stress measured by the scale, and not life changes as such. They propose that this might be due to the frustration associated with negative life changes that are not associated with positive events.

This challenges the validity of the life changes approach, suggesting that a global measure of life changes should be abandoned in favour of looking at the effects of specific life stressors.

Evaluation eXtra

Life changes versus daily hassles

Richard Lazarus and his colleagues argue that **daily hassles** are more important sources of stress than life changes, especially when it comes to effects on our health. This is because the accumulative force of many minor everyday stressors is greater than that of a few relatively rare major events. For example, Anita DeLongis and her colleagues (1988) studied the effects of hassles in 75 married couples over a six-month period. They found that the more hassles their participants experienced, the more likely they were to suffer consequent health problems such as headaches and flu. But there was no such relationship between life changes and illnesses in her study.

Consider: *What effect does this have on the validity of the life changes concept?*

Correlation not causation

Most life changes research is **correlational**. As ever with this kind of research, it is very difficult to know what is the exact nature of the relationship between life changes and illness. Because we are not justified in drawing conclusions about cause and effect based on correlational analysis, we cannot claim that the stress of life changes *causes* illness. It is possible that some other causal factor (for example, having less money) could explain the relationship. The effects could also be indirect, as suggested on the facing page.

Consider: *Can you think of another causal factor? Explain how this limits research into life changes.*

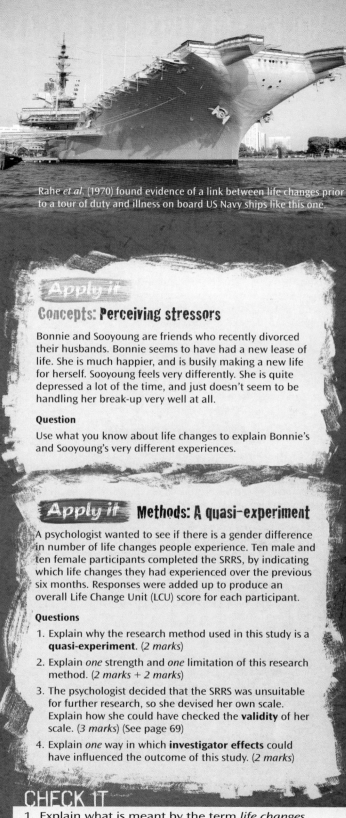

Rahe *et al.* (1970) found evidence of a link between life changes prior to a tour of duty and illness on board US Navy ships like this one.

Apply it

Concepts: Perceiving stressors

Bonnie and Sooyoung are friends who recently divorced their husbands. Bonnie seems to have had a new lease of life. She is much happier, and is busily making a new life for herself. Sooyoung feels very differently. She is quite depressed a lot of the time, and just doesn't seem to be handling her break-up very well at all.

Question

Use what you know about life changes to explain Bonnie's and Sooyoung's very different experiences.

Apply it

Methods: A quasi-experiment

A psychologist wanted to see if there is a gender difference in number of life changes people experience. Ten male and ten female participants completed the SRRS, by indicating which life changes they had experienced over the previous six months. Responses were added up to produce an overall Life Change Unit (LCU) score for each participant.

Questions

1. Explain why the research method used in this study is a **quasi-experiment**. (*2 marks*)
2. Explain *one* strength and *one* limitation of this research method. (*2 marks + 2 marks*)
3. The psychologist decided that the SRRS was unsuitable for further research, so she devised her own scale. Explain how she could have checked the **validity** of her scale. (*3 marks*) (See page 69)
4. Explain *one* way in which **investigator effects** could have influenced the outcome of this study. (*2 marks*)

CHECK IT

1. Explain what is meant by the term *life changes*. [2 marks]
2. Explain what research has shown about life changes as a source of stress. [6 marks]
3. Evaluate research into life changes as a source of stress. [6 marks]
4. Describe and evaluate research into life changes as a source of stress. [16 marks]

Sources of stress: Daily hassles

Sources of stress: daily hassles.

We saw on the last spread that life can present very significant challenges that cause us a lot of stress when they happen. But ordinary day-to-day life has its own ways of tripping us up with unremarkable trifling events that we don't even consider 'proper' stressors. Psychologists have wondered whether such trifling events may be more significant than life changes in explaining how stress affects our health.

KEY TERM

Daily hassles – The relatively minor but frequent aggravations and annoyances of everyday life that combine to cause us stress, such as forgetting where you have put things and niggling squabbles with other people.

Apply it

Concepts: Anita's everyday hassles

Anita had always been a healthy person, becoming ill only very rarely. But six months ago she started getting a lot more colds and niggling headaches and muscle pains than usual. She went to see her doctor, who said that her blood pressure was too high and she would need to start taking medication. Anita wondered why she was feeling so run down, so she started keeping a diary. She noticed that her symptoms often coincided with times when she seemed to be losing things a lot, getting frustrated in traffic, and just generally having too much to do.

Question

How would you explain what is happing to Anita? Use at least one psychological research study to support your explanation.

Daily hassles as a source of stress

What are daily hassles?

Richard Lazarus and his colleagues (1980) questioned whether stress is best characterised by the big **life changes** that by definition happen to us only infrequently and often unpredictably. They suggested that looking at **daily hassles** instead could give us a better understanding of how stress can make us ill.

Daily hassles are those frequent and everyday irritations and frustrations that seem to get on top of us sometimes. They range from minor and even trivial inconveniences to greater pressures and difficulties, although not approaching the significance of a major life change. We can't find our keys, we've just got too much to do and not enough time, we're worried about that argument we had with a friend, and somehow we have to fit in the shopping because it's our turn to cook the tea. Oh, and the washing machine's broken. Nothing major happened, but the added effects of all those hassles leave us feeling stressed.

Primary and secondary appraisal

Lazarus argued that when we experience a hassle we engage in *primary appraisal*. We work out subjectively how threatening it is to our psychological health. If we deem it threatening we then engage in *secondary appraisal*, we subjectively consider how well equipped we are to cope with the hassle. So the theory of daily hassles has built into it the importance of psychological appraisal or interpretation of the meaning of hassles to individuals.

Life changes, daily hassles and illness

Life changes exert their effects on well-being through daily hassles. Major changes such as a serious illness severely disrupt the normal everyday routines that we are used to. Having been ill, it can be a struggle to get back to the usual ways of doing things. Everything is more difficult, and the little things that you used to take for granted and would cause you no problem are now, literally, hassles. So life changes have indirect effects – they are *distal* sources of stress. But daily hassles are *proximal* sources of stress because their effects are direct and immediate.

Research into daily hassles

Allen Kanner *et al.* (1981) researched the question of whether daily hassles were a better predictor of psychological ill-health than life changes.

Procedure They constructed a Hassles Scale which 100 participants (aged 45 to 64 years) completed every month for nine consecutive months, along with a measure of life changes. There is more detail about this scale on page 264. It uses a checklist to measure 117 hassles in terms of how often they occur, and how severe they are.

The participants also twice completed a scale to measure life changes (this was not the SRRS, although it did closely resemble it). The first occasion was one month before the study began, and the second was during the tenth month. This meant the researchers had two measures of life changes: one for the ten months of the study, and another for the two and a half years prior to the start of the study.

Finally, the participants completed the *Hopkins Symptom Checklist*, a scale to measure psychological symptoms of anxiety and depression, such as feeling lonely and worthless and crying for no reason.

Findings Kanner *et al.* found **significant positive correlations** between hassle frequency and psychological symptoms at the start and the end of the study, for both men and women. So the more hassles the participants experienced, the more severe were their psychological symptoms of depression and anxiety. Most importantly, again for both men and women, hassles were a stronger predictor of psychological symptoms than life changes. This was true regardless of whether life changes were measured over the two and a half years before the study or the ten months during it.

'There may be trouble ahead.' Losing things – just one of the many everyday hassles that can cause us a great deal of stress.

Even when you're not required to, it's always helpful to use examples for illustration. There are lots of possibilities for daily hassles so make sure you're familiar with a few of them and use them to elaborate on a definition or to clarify an explanation. You can even contrast hassles with life changes. But make sure you focus clearly on hassles and don't get distracted by life changes.

Evaluation

Supportive research evidence

Research described on the facing page suggests that daily hassles and life events both have effects on health, but daily hassles are more significant. This is supported by John Ivancevich (1986). The participants in this study completed the Hassles and Uplifts Scale plus the SRE (*Schedule of Recent Experiences*, a version of the SRRS). Assessments of general health, performance and absenteeism were also taken. Ivancevich found that daily hassles were superior predictors of poor health, poor job performance and absenteeism from work compared with life changes. So in terms of these organisational measures it seems to be the day-in day-out stressors that matter more than the significant life changes we experience only rarely.

There exists now a significant body of research to suggest that daily hassles are a more valid explanation of stress than life changes.

Retrospective research

Most research into daily hassles is retrospective. Participants complete checklists by recalling the hassles they have experienced over a particular time period, such as the past month. The usefulness of any data that relies on retrospective recall depends on how accurate the participants' memories are. But this is a particularly problematic issue for research into daily hassles such as losing keys, filling out an annoying form, or being fed-up with the weather. This is because such hassles are by definition minor (and even trivial) happenings and so may very easily be forgotten.

So the **validity** of hassles research may be doubtful because the chances are that people underestimate the number of daily hassles they experience. Ironically, however, this could mean that daily hassles are even more important stressors which suggests that the final conclusion *is* valid.

Daily hassles and life changes

There is evidence that daily hassles exert their influence over our health by interacting with life changes. The *amplification hypothesis* suggests that daily hassles might contribute to ill-health at times when we are experiencing significant life changes. The chronic stress of a major life change could make relatively minor daily stressors seem much worse than they otherwise would. For instance, for someone moving house (a life change), losing an everyday item such as a key or a CD (a hassle) might take on much greater significance than normal. According to Luo Li (1991) the hassle becomes a 'last straw' that nudges us over the edge into psychological symptoms or physical illness. But it is the life change that is the real culprit, and the daily hassle is just the immediate precipitating factor.

The claim that daily hassles operate through life changes is a mirror-image of the argument on the facing page. Perhaps there is a two-way relationship, and a more valid approach would be for research to look more closely at how both sources of stress interact, rather than considering them in isolation.

Evaluation eXtra

Gender differences

Not everyone agrees about what constitutes a hassle, and there may be systematic differences between males and females in what they are considered to be. Heather Helms *et al.* (2010) argue that because men and women have different roles within most families, they experience the same everyday events differently. Feminist researchers have been keen to point out that a domestic chore performed rarely may be bearable, enjoyable even. But it becomes a hassle for whoever has to carry it out regularly.

Consider: *Why do you think such differences cast doubt on the validity of hassles research?*

Correlation not causation

Hassles research suffers from the same problems of drawing cause and effect conclusions as we saw in the case of life changes. Despite the consistent and significant **correlations** found between hassles and illness, we are not justified in claiming that hassles *cause* illness. This is because, once again, another factor (e.g. being depressed) may be causing both a tendency to report daily hassles and illnesses.

Consider: *Explain why this is a weakness of hassles research.*

□ **YES**
□ **NO**
□ **MAYBE**

A real problem for research. Sometimes it can be quite difficult to remember accurately which hassles we've experienced, even at the end of the same day.

Apply it — Concepts: Hassles and life changes

Avron and Heidi were waiting for a bus when they got to talking about their lives. Avron explained how he was quite lonely because he doesn't see many people, and his kids live too far away. Heidi said she had recently got divorced just a couple of months after she retired.

Question

Use Avron and Heidi's experiences to explain some of the differences between daily hassles and life changes.

Apply it — Methods: Hassles and illness

A researcher wanted to see whether daily hassles or life changes were the better predictors of ill health: 50 volunteer participants downloaded a mobile app. This prompted them every few days over a one-month period to complete the Hassles and Uplifts Scale and the Social Readjustment Rating Scale. They also rated the severity of illnesses experienced each time. **Median** scores for hassles, life changes and illness severity were calculated.

Questions

1. How might the researcher choose a **volunteer sample** for this study? (*2 marks*)
2. Explain why the researcher calculated medians for hassles, life changes and illness severity. (*2 marks*)
3. Explain how **demand characteristics** could have affected the outcome of this study. (*2 marks*)
4. The researcher was concerned that the assessment of illness severity was not reliable. Explain *one* way in which this could be true, and *one* way in which **reliability** could have been improved. (*2 marks + 2 marks*) (See page 66)
5. The researcher gained **primary data** from this study. Briefly outline *one* difference between primary and **secondary data**. (*2 marks*)

CHECK IT

1. Explain what is meant by the term *daily hassles*. [2 marks]
2. Explain what research has shown about daily hassles as a source of stress. [4 marks]
3. Describe **one** study that has investigated daily hassles as a source of stress. [6 marks]
4. Discuss research into daily hassles as a source of stress. [16 marks]

SOURCES OF STRESS: WORKPLACE STRESS

Sources of stress: workplace stress including the effects of workload and control.

A Health and Safety Executive (HSE) report (2004) revealed that half a million people in the UK suffer workplace stress to a degree that they believe is making them ill. Millions more work in jobs that they rate as 'very' or 'extremely' stressful. The costs to individuals and to society are enormous. The HSE (2013) calculate that work-related stress costs the UK economy £3.6 billion every year.

Because of these high human and financial costs, psychologists are urgently trying to answer the question of what causes stress in the workplace.

KEY TERMS

Workplace stress – Sources of stress that people experience at work.

Workload – The amount of work someone has to do. Can refer to underload as well as overload, but is usually taken to mean the latter.

Control – The degree of freedom a worker has to perform their job how they wish. Often defined in terms of the autonomy they have to make decisions.

Having too much work to do is one of the biggest workplace stressors for most people in most cultures.

Research into workplace stress

Researchers have identified several factors in the workplace that create stress and may contribute to physical, psychological and behavioural symptoms of illness. Two factors which have attracted a great deal of research attention are **workload** and **control**.

Job demands-control model

These two major stressors are linked by Robert Karasek's (1979) *job demands-control model* of **workplace stress**. The model states that the stressful demands of a job, such as work overload, can lead to poor health, dissatisfaction, and absenteeism. But, crucially, this relationship can be modified by the amount of control the employee has over their work. So when two people have equally demanding jobs (because the workload is too great, perhaps), only one of them becomes ill, the one who lacks control over their work. Having job control acts as a *buffer* against the negative effects of job demands.

Research supporting the effects of control

Sir Michael Marmot led the Whitehall I and II Studies. These were major investigations into the jobs and health of thousands of civil servants working in Whitehall, London. For example, Bosma *et al.* (1997) carried out a **prospective** study of over 10,000 civil servants in a wide range of job grades.

Procedure The study used a detailed **questionnaire** to measure various aspects of workload and job control. Participants were also examined for symptoms of coronary heart disease (CHD), and followed up after five years.

Findings The researchers found no **correlation** between workload and illness, so job demands appeared not to be a significant workplace stressor.

As for control, the study painted a very different picture. Those employees who reported having a low degree of control at the start of the study were more likely to have CHD five years later, even when other risk factors (lifestyle, smoking, diet) were statistically accounted for. This was true across all job grades. So the status and the support given to higher grade civil servants did not offset the risk of developing CHD, if their jobs lacked control. A later analysis (Bosma *et al.* 1998) confirmed that this relationship was not affected by individual differences in personality (such as anger and competitiveness), or by coping skills.

Research supporting the effects of workload and control

Procedure Gunn Johansson *et al.* (1978) carried out a **natural experiment** comparing two very different groups of workers in a Swedish sawmill. One group consisted of 14 wood 'finishers', whose job was to prepare the timber that came out of the sawmill. The job was repetitive and the finishers were cut off from the other workers. Because it was dictated by machine these employees had little control over their work. Yet the job was demanding because it was complex, skilled and carried a lot of responsibility. The wages of everyone else on the production line depended on the finishers' productivity. The second group consisted of cleaners, who had a very different role. They had more control, greater flexibility, more contact with other workers, and much less responsibility.

The researchers measured levels of employee illness and absenteeism from personnel records. They also measured levels of the stress hormones **adrenaline** and **noradrenaline** in the workers' urine, once before leaving home in the morning and then at work three times a day.

Findings They found a higher level of stress hormones in the finishers group overall. The first samples of each day showed the finishers already had higher hormone levels than the cleaners, even before they got to work. Also, the finishers' hormone levels increased over the day, but the cleaners' levels decreased. Finally, there were more stress-related illnesses among the finishers, and absenteeism was higher.

As the job demands-control model indicates, these findings show that both demands (overload) and lack of control create chronic physiological arousal (even when resting). This in turn leads to the production of stress hormones and the development of stress-related illnesses.

Apply it Concepts: Stress at work

Priti and Cary were talking about their jobs recently. Priti explained how her company had been through a big restructuring. Several people left and weren't replaced, but everyone else was still expected to get the work done. There are now some parts of her job she can't do until other people have done their bit, and her pay depends on how well they all do. Priti has been off work ill twice in the past month, and she is worried about her health. Cary feels sorry for her, because nothing has changed in his job and he hasn't had a day off ill for years.

Question

Use your knowledge of workplace stress to explain how Priti has been affected by the restructuring. Refer to at least two stressors, and to psychological research.

Evaluation

Job demands-control model is simplistic

Lack of control and workload are indeed significant stressors for many workers, at least in some cultures, but they are not the only ones. How much stress a worker experiences is the outcome of a complex interaction between such factors as the kind of work they do and how well they use coping mechanisms. Furthermore, there is very likely a difference between, for example, the *objective* amount of control or support or workload an employee has, and their *perception* of how much they have.

The job demands-control model ignores these factors and lacks **validity** because of its simplistic focus on just two major job-related sources of stress.

Cultural differences

Christina Györkös *et al.* (2012) reviewed cross-cultural studies and found that lack of job control was seen as stressful in **individualist cultures** such as the UK and USA. But in **collectivist cultures**, such as China and many other Asian countries, control was considered less desirable. The very concept of job control may be a Western notion reflecting individualist ideals of equity and personal rights. It may not generalise to non-Western cultures which prioritise the good of the wider group, community and society.

Cong Liu *et al.* (2007) found no significant cultural differences in terms of workload. It was rated as the third most stressful workplace stressor in both individualist and collectivist cultures. It would appear that workload *is* a culturally generalisable concept and understood as stressful wherever in the world work is done.

Is having control more stressful?

It is almost taken for granted (at least in individualist cultures) that a lack of job control is stressful. However, some research shows that *too much* control can also be a source of workplace stress. Whether it is or not depends on **self-efficacy**, the degree to which you *believe* you have the capability to perform tasks successfully. It makes sense that someone who believes they aren't 'up to the job' is going to find having a lot control over that job a stressful experience. Laurenz Meier *et al.* (2008) used a detailed **questionnaire** to measure feelings of stress (job strain). Employees with a low sense of self-efficacy reported feeling more strain in jobs that gave them more control. The reverse was true for employees with high self-efficacy beliefs – low control was more stressful.

People with low self-efficacy are not capable of taking advantage of the opportunities that control over their jobs gives them, for example in the choices they have, the greater scope to make decisions, etc. So, for them, control is stressful.

Evaluation eXtra

The Whitehall Studies

The focus of the Whitehall II studies was job demands (workload) and control in order to test the control-demands model. So other potentially vital sources of stress were ignored, such as pay and conditions, and job security. To complicate matters further, these factors are confounded with employment grade. Civil servants in senior positions have greater job security and workload, more control, better pay and conditions, in contrast with those in lower grades.

Consider: *Why is this a problem for the validity of these studies?*

The sawmill study

This was a natural experiment because the finishers and cleaners were jobs assigned to groups of workers but not by the researchers. The researchers were not able to **randomly allocate** the workers to the two groups, for obvious practical reasons. This meant that the finishers and the cleaners could have differed systematically in ways that had an effect on the outcome.

Consider: *Explain in what other ways they might have systematically varied and how this might affect the validity of Johansson et al.'s findings.*

Out of control? A lack of control over the job is stressful for many people, but not for all.

Apply it — Concepts: Reducing stress

Peggy runs her own business and employs ten people. She thinks of herself as an enlightened employer and wants to keep her workers happy and as stress-free as possible. She is prepared to make any changes necessary to her employees' jobs, within reason.

Question

Imagine Peggy is a friend of yours who knows that you have been studying workplace stressors. What advice would you give her, based on psychological research?

Apply it — Methods: A stress diary

Two psychologists recruited 100 employees for a study of workplace stressors. They asked their participants to keep a daily diary of their stressful experiences at work over a one-month period. The researchers used **content analysis** to analyse the data from the diaries.

They found that 35% of the entries related to a lack of control over the job, 10% to problems with colleagues, 25% to having too much work to do, 15% to poor environmental conditions such as noise, 10% to not understanding their role clearly and 5% of entries could not be categorised.

Questions

1. Explain how the psychologists could have carried out their content analysis. (*4 marks*) (See page 64)
2. The study gathered a lot of **qualitative data**. Explain what is meant by qualitative data. (*2 marks*)
3. Outline *one* strength of gathering qualitative data in this study. (*2 marks*)
4. What is meant by the term **reliability**? (*1 mark*) (See page 66)
5. Explain how the two psychologists could have established the reliability of their content analysis. (*3 marks*)

CHECK IT

1. In relation to workplace stress, explain what is meant by the terms *workload* and *control*.
[2 marks + 2 marks]
2. Outline research into workplace stress. [6 marks]
3. Briefly outline the effects of control **and** workload on workplace stress. [3 marks + 3 marks]
4. Discuss research into the effects of **two** sources of stress on workplace stress. [16 marks]

> Measuring stress: self-report scales (Social Readjustment Rating Scale and Hassles and Uplifts Scale) and physiological measures including skin conductance response.

Psychologists are very keen to understand the ways in which stress can make us ill. There are very significant real-life benefits to be had from understanding this relationship. But before psychologists can get to this point, they need reliable and valid ways of measuring stress. Two broad categories of measurement have been developed: self-report and physiological methods.

KEY TERMS

Social Readjustment Rating Scale (SRRS) – A self-report checklist measure of the stress associated with 43 life changes. Each one is linked with a number of Life Change Units (LCUs) reflecting the degree of readjustment needed to cope with the change (e.g. 'Divorce' is 73 LCUs).

Hassles and Uplifts Scale – A self-report measure of the stress associated with everyday irritations (hassles) and of the small pleasures of daily life that are thought to partly offset the negative effects of hassles (uplifts).

Skin conductance response (SCR) – A physiological measure of the degree of sweating associated with arousal of the autonomic nervous system. ANS arousal activates the body's fight or flight response when a stressor occurs. Small increases in sweating can be detected as greater electrical conductance across the skin.

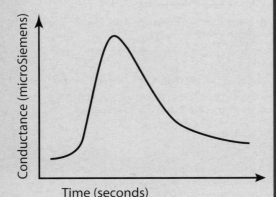

A typical skin conductance response (SCR), a slope at the start indicating the onset of the response, which then takes time to rise, reaches a peak and then decays in a long 'tail' on the trace, all within a few seconds.

Self-report measures of stress

Social Readjustment Rating Scale (SRRS)

The **Social Readjustment Rating Scale** is a very well-established **self-report** method of measuring **life changes**, developed by Thomas Holmes and Richard Rahe (1967). They studied the medical records of thousands of hospital patients, identifying the events in the patients' lives that happened not long before they became ill. The SRRS presents a list of 43 of these life changes.

However, it was obvious that not all of the events were equally stressful, because they didn't require the same degree of adjustment to adapt to them. Therefore Holmes and Rahe knew they would need to attach a value to each life change to reflect the degree of adjustment needed. So they asked several hundred participants to rate each item in these terms: 'How much readjustment do you think would be needed to adapt to each of these life changes on a scale of 1 to 1000 units?' As a guide, the raters had to imagine that marriage was an arbitrary 500 units of life change.

The researchers calculated **means** for each item and further divided these figures by ten. This created a **life change unit** (**LCU**) score for each change. The changes were then put in rank order from highest LCU score to lowest (see examples on right).

The SRRS is used by asking participants to indicate which life changes on the scale they have experienced over a period of time, typically 12 months. The LCUs for these items are then added to give an overall score.

Examples from the SRRS of some life events and their LCUs

Rank Position	Life event	LCUs
1	Death of spouse	100
2	Divorce	73
7	Marriage	50
10	Retirement	45
12	Pregnancy	40
17	Death of friend	37
25	Outstanding personal achievement	28
30	Trouble with boss	23
33	Change in school	20
42	Christmas	12

Hassles and Uplifts Scale

Allen Kanner *et al.* (1981) proposed that the combined effects of daily hassles and uplifts would be more useful indicators of stress, and developed the **Hassles and Uplifts Scale** to measure them. The Hassles Scale consists of 117 items selected by the researchers from seven categories: work, health, family, friends, environment, practical considerations and chance occurrences. Examples of hassles include troublesome neighbours, too much responsibility, disliking work colleagues and planning meals. The scale measures the severity of each hassle on a three-point scale: somewhat, moderately or extremely severe. The severity measure reflects the fact that the psychological meaning of each hassle to the individual is more important than how often it happens.

The Uplifts Scale was constructed by a similar process: 135 items were produced from the same content areas as the Hassles Scale. Examples of uplifts include getting enough sleep, liking fellow workers, relating well with friends and meeting responsibilities. The individual identifies all of the uplifts that apply and then indicates how often they have experienced them over a specified time period (for example, that day). After several years of research with the Hassles and Uplifts Scale some limitations were identified, so it was updated by Anita DeLongis *et al.* (1988) and became the Hassles and Uplifts Questionnaire.

Physiological measures of stress: Skin conductance response (SCR)

The rationale behind using skin conductance is based on the **fight or flight response**. When we experience stress, the **autonomic nervous system** is aroused and one of the consequences is that we sweat more, and the most sensitive (and practical) part of the body where this can be detected is the hand. To detect sweating, electrodes are attached to the index and middle fingers of one hand. A tiny current, so weak it can't be felt, is applied to the electrodes to measure how much electricity is being conducted. Human skin is a good conductor of electricity, so the more we sweat, the more conductance there is. This can be measured, in microSiemens, the signal amplified and displayed on a screen.

There are two types of skin conductance. *Tonic conductance* is skin conductance when we are not experiencing a stimulus (it is sometimes called the *skin conductance level* or *SCL*). It is used as a baseline measure against which to compare *phasic conductance*. This type occurs when something happens, for example, you are shown an image or someone asks you a question. The response is called a **skin conductance response** (**SCR**) and it follows a typical pattern (see diagram on left). The whole response can take four or five seconds. Along with heart rate, respiration and blood pressure, the SCR makes up a *polygraph*, more commonly known (especially on the *Jeremy Kyle Show*) as the 'lie detector test'.

Evaluation

Validity issues

Many items on self-report stress measures are more like general categories than individual events. This means that they are open to varying interpretations by different participants in research studies. This was illustrated in a study by Bruce Dohrenwend *et al.* (1990) in which participants were asked what they thought the items meant. To take just two examples: 'serious illness and injury' was interpreted in a huge variety of ways from 'flu' and 'sprained arm' to 'a life-threatening heart attack'; 'Death of a close friend' was understood by some participants to refer to childhood friends they had not been in touch with for years. Dohrenwend (2006) points out that people experiencing the greatest degree of stress when they complete a self-report scale place the most negative interpretations on the items (and vice versa).

This problem of intracategory variability reduces the **validity** of self-report measures and makes it difficult to assess the true relationship between stress, life events, hassles and illness.

The contamination effect

The SRRS and Hassles Scale are intended to be used as predictors of stress-related illness. But many items on both scales overlap with symptoms of physical and psychological disorders. Examples of such items include 'personal injury or illness' on the SRRS and 'hospitalisation' on the Hassles Scale. So rather than *predicting* illness, these scales *reflect* it. Stress and illness are confounded with hassles and life changes, when they should be separate.

Some researchers believe that self-report measures of life changes and hassles are so compromised by methodological problems like the contamination effect that they should be abandoned and replaced by direct observations of behaviour by independent observers.

Individual differences in SCRs

SCR measurement takes account of the fact that different people have different patterns of skin conductance, which is why a baseline measure (*tonic conductance*) is always taken before any stimulus is presented in a research study. However, issues of individual differences go way beyond this. Some people are said to be *stabiles* – their SCRs vary little when they are at rest, and are not much influenced by internal thoughts or external events. *Labiles*, on the other hand, produce a lot of SCRs even when they are at rest.

Therefore SCR measurement is not a straightforward matter of comparing baseline SCRs against stimulated SCRs. Failure to take into account these differences between participants threatens the validity of research studies using SCRs to measure stress.

Evaluation eXtra

Global versus specific

The SRRS and the Hassles and Uplifts Scale are *global* measures of stress. That is, they provide one score which combines many different aspects of the stressors they measure. The assumption is that a single measure of stress can be used to predict any kind of illness. It makes more sense to assume that there are *specific* types of life changes (or hassles) within these scales that may predict particular illnesses. For example, there are several items on the SRRS which relate to losses of one kind or another (death of a close family member, fired at work, retirement). Perhaps loss is a specific form of stressful life change that predicts some illnesses rather than others.

Consider: *Explain how this issue may reduce the validity of these self-report scales.*

Controllable versus uncontrollable

Some life changes and hassles are controllable and some are not. Participants in a study by Gary Stern *et al.* (1982) completed the SRRS in the usual checklist fashion. But they were also asked to indicate which items they believed were controllable life changes and which were uncontrollable. The uncontrollable life changes were reasonably reliable predictors of later physical illness whereas the controllable changes were not.

Consider: *What effect does this have on the validity of self-report measures of stress?*

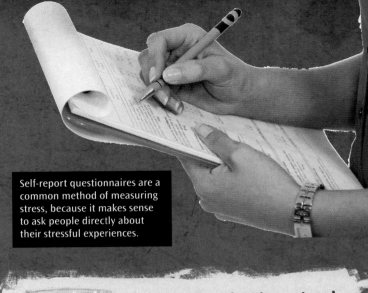

Self-report questionnaires are a common method of measuring stress, because it makes sense to ask people directly about their stressful experiences.

Apply it Concepts: **Measuring stress at work**

As part of her efforts to keep her workforce as stress-free as possible, Peggy has asked you to measure her employees' stress levels. However, she's not sure how this is done, although she has heard that there are different methods available.

Question

Imagine you have to explain stress measurement methods to Peggy. Give a brief explanation of each one, and indicate what limitations they might have for her measurement needs.

Apply it Methods: **Measuring SCRs**

A researcher wanted to measure the stress caused by watching a video of students taking an exam. He chose a physiological indicator of stress – the skin conductance response (SCR). He recruited 10 participants from a local sixth-form college. He measured each participant's total number of SCRs in a five-minute period, once when at rest (tonic), and again when they were watching the video (phasic).

Questions

1. The psychologist realised that he would need to use **counterbalancing**. Explain how he could have done so and why it was necessary. (*2 marks + 2 marks*)

2. The psychologist wanted to calculate a **measure of central tendency**. Identify the appropriate one to use and explain why. (*1 mark + 2 marks*)

3. The psychologist decided to analyse the difference between the number of SCRs measured at rest and when watching the video. Which **statistical test** would be appropriate to use? Give *two* reasons for your answer. (*1 mark + 2 marks*) (See pages 70–71)

4. The result of the test turned out to be **significant**. Explain what this means. (*2 marks*)

CHECK IT

1. In relation to measuring stress, explain what is meant by skin *conductance response*. **[2 marks]**

2. Briefly outline any **one** self-report scale used to measure stress. **[4 marks]**

3. Explain **one** limitation of the Social Readjustment Rating Scale. **[3 marks]**

4. Describe and evaluate methods of measuring stress. **[16 marks]**

Individual differences in stress: personality types A, B and C and associated behaviours.

Psychologists have been interested to discover if there are any links between personality and the experience of stress. They have asked, 'Can your personality influence whether or not you become ill as a result of stress?' In slightly more technical terms, is personality a *moderator* of the effects of stress on illness?

Several aspects of personality have been proposed as important moderators of the stress-illness relationship. But a significant focus of research has been on the personality types called Type A, Type B and Type C. Of these, Type A has attracted the most interest, at least until recently.

KEY TERMS

Type A personality – Describes someone who is competitive, time-urgent (e.g. impatient) and hostile in most situations. Research has linked this personality type to coronary heart disease (CHD).

Type B personality – Describes someone who is laid-back, relaxed and tolerant of others in most situations (i.e. the opposite of Type A).

Type C personality – Describes someone who is compliant, avoids conflict and suppresses their emotions, especially anger, in most situations. Some research has linked Type C with cancer.

People who always try to avoid conflict might do so by suppressing their own emotions, with negative consequences for their health.

Apply it

Concepts: Footballing personalities

Meyer, Helen and Ted are three friends who play for the same football team on Sunday mornings. Meyer has always been competitive and gets very impatient when he thinks the others aren't putting in the effort. He also gets irritated and angry when the team doesn't win. Helen is completely different – she enjoys playing, but she doesn't take it too seriously and likes to have a laugh more than anything else. But this attitude annoys Meyer and when he and Helen argue, Ted has to step in and be the peacemaker. Ted goes out of his way to please everyone, because he hates conflict. He just wishes everyone would agree with each other.

Question

What personality types are Meyer, Helen and Ted. Explain how each one is likely to respond in stressful situations.

Stress and personality

Type A Personality

The scientific interest in the links between personality, stress and illness began in the 1950s with two cardiologists, Meyer Friedman and Ray Rosenman – Friedman, M. and Rosenman, R. H. (1959). They suspected that their patients – who mostly had **coronary heart disease** (CHD) – shared some common personality characteristics. Their **hypothesis** was that CHD was associated with a certain pattern of behaviour which they called **Type A** Personality. Friedman (1996) later described Type A in terms of three major groups of behaviours. He suggested that people with a Type A personality demonstrated high levels of:

- *Competitiveness:* They are driven, achievement-motivated, ambitious, aware of their own and other people's status, and view life in terms of challenges, goals and targets.
- *Time urgency:* Type As are fast-talking, impatient, determinedly proactive, see creative pursuits as a waste of time, and have a distinct preference for multi-tasking.
- *Hostility:* They are aggressive, intolerant, inflexible, and quick to anger.

Type B Personality

Friedman and Rosenman also identified the characteristics of **Type B** personalities. Basically, these contrast in every way with the features of Type A. People who are Type B are more relaxed, tolerant, reflective, 'laid back', and less competitive than Type As.

Research into Types A and B

The Western Collaborative Group Study (WCGS) was Friedman and Rosenman's **prospective** study of over 3000 males living in California.

Procedure The men were all medically assessed as free of CHD at the start of the study. They were also assessed for personality type, by being asked 25 questions in a **structured interview**. The questions concerned their responses to everyday irritations, such as having to wait in queues. The interviews were conducted in a way designed to incite Type A-related behaviour in the participants. For example, the interviewer would be aggressive and frequently interrupt. Behaviour (such as speed of talking) was observed and measured, and this enabled the researchers to classify participants as Type A or Type B.

Findings Eight and a half years later (Friedman and Rosenman 1974), 257 men had developed CHD; 70% of these individuals had been assessed at the start of the study as Type A. This was almost twice as many as the Type Bs who developed CHD, even when known CHD risk factors were accounted for. Type As had higher levels of the stress hormones **adrenaline** and **noradrenaline** and higher blood pressure and cholesterol levels. This suggests that Type A people, because of their personality, are vulnerable to stressors. Their impatience and hostility causes a raised physiological stress response, which in turn makes them prone to CHD.

Type C Personality

It seemed unlikely that just two personality types could account for the whole range of stress-related responses to illness. A third personality type, **Type C**, was proposed to be linked with cancer by Lydia Temoshok (1987). Type C people have memorably been described as manifesting *pathological niceness*. Because they are 'people pleasers', they strive to be compliant, patient beyond all reason, passive and self-sacrificing. Sounds fine, but there is a serious downside. Because they wish above all else to avoid conflict, Type Cs frequently achieve this by **repressing** their emotions, including anger. It is this behaviour that is thought to be especially relevant to cancer-proneness.

Research into Type C

Procedure Patrick Dattore *et al.* (1980) studied 200 veterans of the Vietnam War; 75 of them were cancer patients and the rest formed a **control group** of people with non-cancer diagnoses. They had all completed scales to measure repression of emotions and symptoms of depression several years before they were diagnosed. So this was a prospective study.

Findings The researchers found that the cancer patients reported **significantly** greater emotional repression and *fewer* depression symptoms than the non-cancer controls. The finding related to depression may appear surprising, but it supports the view that people who repress their emotions (especially negative ones) are unlikely to acknowledge they are depressed. This is evidence of a link between Type C and cancer-proneness.

Evaluation

Support from research studies

José Edigo *et al.* (2012) studied 150 Spanish men and women, under 65 years old, who had had a stroke, and compared them with a **matched control group**. The researchers found that the stroke sufferers were significantly more likely to have Type A personalities. This was true of men and women and could not be explained by traditional lifestyle-associated risk factors (such as smoking and diet).

The fact that recent research continues to support the view that Type A personality plays a role in cardiovascular diseases suggests that the concept of Type A has some **validity**.

Contradictory evidence

Some research shows that Type B personality is associated with a greater, not lesser, risk of CHD than Type A. David Ragland and Richard Brand (1988) followed-up men from the original WCGS who survived a heart attack. They confirmed Friedman and Rosenman's finding that there were more Type As in this group. But after a further follow-up period, the researchers found that survivors who were Type B were more likely to die than Type As. This is difficult to explain in terms of Type A coronary-proneness.

It may be that Types As are more motivated to make positive lifestyle and behavioural changes after a first heart attack than Type Bs, reducing further risk. The finding demonstrates that the relationship between Type A/B personality and illness is a complex one and not yet fully understood.

Problems with Type A concept

Psychologists quickly realised that Type A as a global personality construct is much too broad and encompasses too many different traits. Researchers subsequently focused on the *hostility* component of Type A as linking with stress and CHD. Hostile people are cynical, selfish, manipulative, mistrusting and openly contemptuous. Theodore Dembroski *et al.* (1989) reanalysed the data from the WCGS and found that ratings of hostility significantly predicted later incidence of CHD. An analysis of 27-year follow-up data from the same study by Dorit Carmelli *et al.* (1991) confirmed this by finding exceptionally high CHD death rates in a subgroup of men with high hostility scores.

This certainly casts doubt on the validity of the global conception of Type A, but it also supports the view that *some* aspect of Type A personality is involved in CHD.

Evaluation eXtra

Modification of Type A and Type B

The Type A/B classification was modified by Friedman *et al.* (1985) because research produced many inconsistent and even contradictory findings. They argued that 'Type A' is not the same as 'coronary-proneness'. Some Type As can be described as confident and active, and these people are unlikely to develop CHD. On the other hand, some Type Bs are quiet and unaggressive because they are suppressing their ambition and hostility (characteristics usually associated with Type A). These people may well develop CHD, despite being assessed as Type B.

Consider: *Do you think that 'tweaking' Type A and B in this way supports the validity of these concepts? Explain your answer.*

Contradictory Type C evidence

Steven Greer and Tina Morris (1975) found a link between the emotional suppression typical of Type C, and breast cancer, but only in women under the age of 50. Research into the links between Type C and cancer is plagued by inconsistent findings and failures to replicate apparently significant results (e.g. McKenna *et al.* 1999). If Type C is associated with cancer-proneness, it appears that the relationship is not straightforward and is probably moderated by age and other factors.

Consider: *Explain how this casts doubt on the validity of the Type C concept.*

Relaxed, chilled, patient, tolerant, not interested in rushing around and getting ten things done at once? That'll be Type B, then.

⚡ Apply it — Concepts: Changing Type A

Molly was told recently that she is a Type A kind of person. She is now worried that she might be vulnerable to developing heart disease because she read that there could be a link between the illness and Type A personality. She wants to know how she could change her behaviour to reduce her risk.

Question

What advice would you give Molly? How is she likely to behave at the moment and what does she need to do to change?

Apply it — Methods: Observing Type A

Eveline Bleiker *et al.*'s (1996) participants were more than 9,000 women who completed a detailed **questionnaire** at the start of the study to assess various personality characteristics. These included one closely associated with Type C: anti-emotionality, which involves an absence of emotional expression. Of these women, 131 were diagnosed with breast cancer during the following five-year period. The study also included a matched control group of women without cancer.

The researchers found that anti-emotionality was the only personality characteristic that differed significantly between the two groups, with the women diagnosed with breast cancer scoring significantly higher on average.

Questions

1. Explain why this study could be described as **longitudinal**. (*2 marks*)
2. Explain *one* possible **confounding variable** in this study. (*2 marks*)
3. Briefly outline *one* difference between a **population** and a **sample**. (*2 marks*)
4. Outline *one* method the researchers could have used to recruit participants for this study. (*2 marks*)
5. Explain *one* strength and *one* limitation of using a questionnaire in this study. (*2 marks + 2 marks*)

CHECK IT

1. In relation to individual differences in stress, explain what is meant by *Type C personality*. [2 marks]
2. Outline research into personality types as individual differences in stress. [4 marks]
3. Describe **one** study that has investigated Type A personality. Refer in your answer to what the researchers did and what they found. [6 marks]
4. Discuss research into personality types as individual differences in stress. [16 marks]

INDIVIDUAL DIFFERENCES IN STRESS: HARDINESS

THE SPECIFICATION SAYS...

Individual differences in stress: hardiness including commitment, challenge and control.

Hardiness has been proposed as another difference between individuals in how they respond to stressors. Faced with the same stressful circumstances, some people become physically or psychologically ill (or both), but others not only seem protected against the ill-effects of stress but actually thrive.

KEY TERMS

Hardiness – A personality factor used to explain why some people seem able to thrive in stressful circumstances. It consists of three elements, nicknamed the Three Cs.

Commitment – Hardy people throw themselves fully into all life has to offer them rather than standing on the sidelines.

Challenge – Hardy people view stressful situations as opportunities for self-development rather than threats to their self-esteem.

Control – Hardy people believe that stressful situations can be overcome through their own efforts.

Apply it

Concepts: Developing hardiness

Stella works in a big organisation where there has been a lot of change in recent months. The job she used to do has changed beyond recognition and she is struggling to cope. Stella feels stressed all the time, and finds it increasingly difficult to relax at home. She is ill more often than she used to be and has taken more days off work in the last two months than in the whole of the previous five years.

Question

How could Stella change her behaviour to become more hardy and therefore better able to resist stressors? Give examples referring to each of the Three Cs.

STUDY TIP

There are two important research studies covered in detail on this spread. You might have to describe the procedures of a study, or the findings, or both. Your description of a study will be much clearer if you keep procedures and findings separate from each other rather than mixing them up together.

In an essay you can use such studies as a part of a description of hardiness, or you could use them as evaluation – but then the procedures are not relevant.

Hardiness

Suzanne Kobasa (1979) proposed that **hardiness** is an aspect of personality, a set of characteristics that some people have but others don't. According to her co-worker, Salvatore Maddi (1986), hardiness gives us *existential courage*, the will or determination to keep going despite all the setbacks life throws at us and the uncertainties we have about what the future might bring. Early research identified three dimensions to hardiness, collectively known as *the Three Cs*:

Commitment Hardy people are deeply involved in their relationships, their activities, and their selves. This means they throw themselves wholeheartedly into what life has to offer them, optimistic that they will get something valuable out of the experience. This is always better than withdrawing and becoming isolated. Essentially their attitude is, 'If something's worth doing, it's worth doing fully, even if it's stressful.'

Challenge Hardy people respond to change in a distinctive way. They are resilient and welcome change as an opportunity or a challenge rather than as a threat. They recognise that life is unpredictable, but see this as exciting and stimulating. Stressful situations can help us to learn, and this is ultimately more fulfilling than retreating into comfort and an easy life.

Control Hardy people have a strong belief that they are in charge of events, that it is they who make things happen, rather than things happening to them. Even if those events are stressful, they actively strive to influence their environments rather than becoming powerless and passive observers of life passing them by.

Research into hardiness

Both Kobasa and Maddi have conducted research into hardiness.

Procedure Kobasa (1979) measured the life changes of 670 male American middle and senior managers aged between 40 and 49 years. She used the *Schedule of Recent Experiences* (the forerunner of the SRRS) to identify those who had experienced high levels of stress over the previous three years. When she came to look at their absenteeism records and levels of illness (measured by the *Seriousness of Illness Survey*), she found some wide variations.

Findings The managers didn't all respond to the same degree of stress in the same way. Some of them appeared to be more resilient because they could tolerate high levels of stress without becoming ill or taking time off work. Kobasa interpreted this finding as confirming the role of hardiness. Sure enough, when they were assessed, this subset of resilient managers scored highly on the Three Cs of challenge, commitment and control.

Procedure Maddi (1987) spent several years studying 400 managers and supervisors at the Bell Telephone company in the US. During this time, the company underwent one of the biggest reorganisations in American corporate history. Thousands of people lost their jobs and it was an extremely stressful experience for the employees who stayed with the company.

Findings There were significant declines in performance and health in about two-thirds of the study participants, with outcomes including heart attacks, strokes, depression and drug abuse. But the rest of the managers (about one-third) were not affected in this way. Instead, they flourished: their health did not deteriorate, they felt happier and more fulfilled at work than ever and seemed to be rejuvenated by the whole stressful experience. Just as Kobasa had done, Maddi found that these resilient managers scored highly on measures of the Three Cs. They basically welcomed the reorganisation as a challenge over which they could exercise control, and threw themselves into making it 'work for them'.

Hardy people welcome challenges – they find them invigorating rather than threatening.

Evaluation

Measurement problems

There has been much controversy over how hardiness should be measured. Steven Funk (1992) pointed out that the most popular scales measure hardiness by asking questions about negative traits such as powerlessness and alienation. A hardy individual will get low scores on these items, so a *lack* of these negative traits is taken to indicate hardiness. Therefore these scales may be measuring a lack of **neuroticism** rather than hardiness as such because neuroticism is characterised by anxiety, fear, moodiness and worry.

This means that a substantial amount of research into the relationship between hardiness, stress and illness is based on measures of hardiness that lack **validity**.

However, on the positive side, more recent scales such as the *Dispositional Resilience Scale* (Bartone 2000) have been developed to avoid the **confounding** of hardiness with neuroticism, providing a more valid measure.

Roles of all three Cs

Serious doubts have been raised about the relative contributions of the Three Cs to hardiness. It is not clear how truly independent they are and whether they overlap. For instance, it seems plausible that there is an element of control at the heart of commitment and challenge. There is also a wealth of psychological research showing how important a sense of personal control is to well-being in all sorts of contexts. So it is likely that control is the overwhelmingly crucial factor determining a hardy response to stressors.

Research now tends to consider the components of hardiness separately. Jay Hull *et al.* (1987) recommended that research focuses on control and commitment only and abandons the challenge component altogether.

Indirect effects of hardiness

There is some debate about whether the effects of hardiness on health and illness are direct or indirect. For example, Richard Contrada (1989) found that hardy people had lower blood pressure, but he was not able to choose between two explanations of this finding. One possibility is that being a hardy person could reduce the physiological effects of stressors on the body. The alternative explanation is that hardy people might be better at engaging in healthy behaviours, such as taking regular exercise and not smoking, and this indirectly reduces their risk of becoming ill. The evidence is inconclusive on this issue. But in a practical sense, it matters little. If research shows that hardiness has any beneficial effects on health, then it makes sense to assume that hardy characteristics are desirable and should be developed through training and education.

Evaluation eXtra

Supporting research

The role of hardiness in relation to illness has been confirmed in a variety of research studies. For example, Contrada (1989) studied male students' responses to a stressful **laboratory** task. He found that those students who scored highest on a measure of hardiness had lower levels of blood pressure in response to the stressor. Interestingly, the lowest blood pressure levels were found in students who were not only hardy but also had Type B personalities.

Consider: *Explain how supportive research is a strength of the hardiness concept.*

Real-life applications

Paul Bartone *et al.* (2008) measured hardiness in a sample of candidates applying for positions within the US Army Special Forces. This is a particularly stressful role within the US military, so candidates have to endure a tough selection procedure including a four-week assessment course. The researchers found that those who passed the course were significantly hardier than those who did not. Thanks to this and other research showing that hardiness is linked to resilience in the face of combat stress (Bartone 1999), the elite units of the US military now routinely assess candidates for high levels of hardiness, with training programmes frequently used to increase them yet further.

Consider: *Why are such applications a strength of the hardiness concept?*

Hardy people are committed and resilient. They don't let impossible odds hold them back and are quick to bounce back.

Apply it Concepts: **Exam hardiness**

Salvatore and Suzanne are friends doing A levels at a sixth-form college. They both have exams coming up and Salvatore is worried. He knows from past experience that he goes to pieces at exam time. He just doesn't seem to cope very well with the stress. Suzanne, on the other hand, has always had no problem. It's almost as if she enjoys exams and has a really positive attitude towards them.

Question

Use your knowledge of psychological hardiness to explain how Salvatore and Suzanne respond to the stress of exams.

Apply it Methods: **Workplace hardiness**

A researcher decided to investigate the link between hardiness and illness. He recruited ten people from a local company and asked them to complete a *How Hardy Am I?* **questionnaire**. This produced a hardiness score for each participant on a scale between 0 (not hardy at all) and 20 (maximum degree of hardiness). The researcher also found out from their managers how many days of illness each participant had taken off in the past year. The researchers found a **significant negative correlation** between hardiness and illness.

Questions

1. The questionnaire consisted of **closed questions**. What is meant by this term? (*1 mark*)

2. Outline how the researcher could have selected a **systematic sample** of participants from the local company. (*2 marks*)

3. The researcher was concerned that the hardiness questionnaire lacked validity. Briefly outline *two* ways in which he could improve its **validity**. (*2 marks + 2 marks*)

4. Explain what is meant by the phrase 'a significant negative correlation between hardiness and illness'. (*3 marks*) (See page 63)

5. The researcher wrote up his study in a paper for publication in a journal. It eventually featured in a **meta-analysis** into the link between hardiness and illness. Explain what is meant by a meta-analysis. (*2 marks*)

CHECK IT

1. In relation to individual differences in stress, explain what is meant by the term *hardiness*. [2 marks]

2. In relation to hardiness, briefly explain what is meant by the terms *commitment* and *challenge*. [2 marks + 2 marks]

3. Outline research into hardiness as an individual difference in stress. [6 marks]

4. Describe and evaluate hardiness as an individual difference in stress. [16 marks]

MANAGING AND COPING WITH STRESS: DRUG THERAPY

Managing and coping with stress: drug therapy (benzodiazepines and beta blockers).

Stress appears to be an inevitable part of everyday life, and it occasionally threatens to become overwhelming. So one of the most beneficial things psychologists can do is to help people manage the stress we all experience so it doesn't become too much to bear.

On this spread, we look at a physiological method of stress management – drug therapy. This method directly targets the physiological systems that control the stress response, such as sympathomedullary and hypothalamic-pituitary-adrenal responses (see page 254).

KEY TERM

Drug therapy – Treatment involving drugs, i.e. chemicals that have a particular effect on the functioning of the brain or some other body system. In the case of psychological disorders such drugs usually affect neurotransmitter levels.

1. Empty GABA receptor site on the postsynaptic neuron

Receptor is inactive and chloride channel is closed.

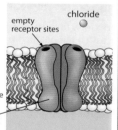

2. GABA binding with receptor

GABA binds with the receptor, operating the channel and allowing chloride into the cell.

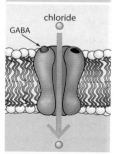

3. Both GABA and benzodiazepine binding with receptor

Benzodiazepine enhances binding of GABA, opening the channel for longer and allowing more chloride through.

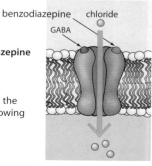

Drug therapy

The psychological symptom of stress we find most disturbing is the feeling of anxiety. This is accompanied by several unpleasant physiological symptoms, all characteristic of the **fight or flight response**. **Drug therapies** can offer some effective relief from stress-related anxiety. Two broad categories of drugs are recommended for the management of stress.

Benzodiazepines (BZs)

Benzodiazepines such as diazepam (*Valium*) and alprazolam (*Xanax*) are very commonly-prescribed drugs in the Western world. They lessen the anxiety associated with stress by quickly reducing physiological arousal in the **central nervous system**. The drugs do this by tapping into one way in which the body naturally combats anxiety.

Mode of action Gamma-aminobutyric acid (or just **GABA**) is the most important **neurotransmitter** for inhibiting the activity of **neurons** in most areas of the brain. During the process of **synaptic transmission** (see page 37), GABA combines with GABA-A receptors on the **postsynaptic neuron**. Because GABA inhibits neurons, this reduces activity in the post-synaptic neuron making it less likely that signals will be passed on from one neuron to the next. BZs work by enhancing this natural inhibition, so there is even less neuronal activity in the brain.

BZ drug molecules combine with GABA receptors so that the channels are opened, but without blocking them. Instead, channels are opened more often for *chloride ions* to enter the neuron. This makes the neuron more responsive to the inhibitory effects of GABA and less responsive to other neurotransmitters. The outcome is inhibition of activity throughout the central nervous system and an associated reduction of anxiety (see diagram below left).

Beta blockers

Beta-adrenergic blockers (or **beta blockers**) act on the **sympathetic nervous system** to reduce sympathetic arousal, a key part of stress-related anxiety. This is a different mode of action to BZs, which act more directly on the brain itself. Beta blockers include atenolol and propranolol and are commonly prescribed to reduce blood pressure and treat various heart problems.

Mode of action **Adrenaline** and **noradrenaline** are **hormones** that are produced as part of the **sympathomedullary pathway**. They circulate in the bloodstream when this pathway is triggered in response to a stressor. The hormones combine with beta-adrenergic receptors located throughout the cardiovascular system, principally receptors in the heart and blood vessels. This accounts for the increased heart rate and blood pressure associated with stress.

Beta blockers work by blocking beta-adrenergic receptors. The drug stops the receptors being stimulated by adrenaline and noradrenaline. This slows heart rate, reduces blood pressure and causes the heart to pump less intensely, which reduces its need for oxygen. There are different types of beta blockers. For instance, some act on the beta-adrenergic receptors of the heart only. Some have wider effects on the receptors of the heart, blood vessels and even the lungs.

Beta blockers reduce anxiety without altering consciousness because they don't operate directly on the brain. They are therefore ideal for people who want to eliminate the physical and psychological symptoms of stress but remain alert (for example, stage performers, musicians, surgeons). It's because of their performance-enhancing effects in sports that require hand-eye co-ordination (e.g. archery, shooting) that they're banned by the International Olympic Committee.

Apply it   Concepts: Do I need drugs?

Larry suffers badly from the effects of stress. When things get too much for him he experiences physical symptoms and even becomes ill. He has heard that there are drugs available that might be able to help him.

Question

Imagine you are Larry's friend, and he has approached you for information. Using your knowledge of managing stress, how would you explain to Larry how drugs work in very simple terms?

Evaluation

Effectiveness of BZs

The gold standard of drug testing is the **double-blind placebo**-controlled trial. A placebo is an inactive version of the drug you want to study. It looks identical, but it has no pharmacological effects on the body. Half of the participants in a drug trial take the placebo, because just knowing that you are meant to be taking a drug can have some beneficial effects (the placebo effect). The drug trial is said to be double-blind because neither the participants nor the researchers know who is taking the placebo.

A recent **review** of studies by David Baldwin *et al.* (2013) concluded that there is good evidence that BZs are **significantly** more effective than placebo in treating acute anxiety, but that some BZ drugs are more effective than others. Given the risk of dependency (see below) and the fact that other classes of drugs have proven effectiveness against anxiety, BZs may not be the first choice of drug therapy for many people.

Effectiveness of beta blockers

A review of research by Desmond Kelly (1980) concluded that beta blockers were effective for treating everyday anxieties associated with public speaking, exam nerves, and even the civil disturbances of living in Northern Ireland in the 1970s. Beta blockers can be useful for people with social anxiety disorder, in which fear of speaking in public is a major stressor. Sufferers in these situations are acutely aware of their physiological responses (such as racing heartbeat), and this makes them even more anxious. Because beta blockers reduce this arousal, they can prevent further anxiety developing.

Research studies have consistently demonstrated that beta blockers are an effective treatment for the physical symptoms of stress but may be even more useful in combination with other drugs such as BZs (Hayes and Schulz 1987).

Side effects

Well-known side effects of BZs are drowsiness, weight gain, respiration problems in some cases, and according to Raghu Gaind and Robin Jacoby (1978), *paradoxical reactions*. These are the opposite outcomes to the ones you expect from treatment by the drug. They include criminal behaviour such as shoplifting, other impulsive behaviours, and uncontrollable emotional responses like weeping.

Beta blockers can reduce heart rate and blood pressure too much in some patients, and they are not considered suitable for people with diabetes or severe depression. When side effects occur there is a danger that the patient will stop taking the drug and the symptoms of anxiety will return.

So side effects need to be carefully weighed up against the benefits of the drug, and also against alternatives including psychological therapies such as **stress inoculation therapy** (see page 272).

Evaluation eXtra

Symptoms not causes

Drugs like BZs and beta blockers focus on anxiety reduction. Rather like our own physiological stress response, they are effective in dealing with the symptoms of acute stress. This gives the patient short-term relief, but is not an appropriate treatment for chronic stressors. Coupled with the risk of dependency, there comes a point where the treatment for chronic stress may do more harm than good, in which case a psychological therapy might be more appropriate.

Consider: *Apart from dependency, what is the main danger of using drugs to treat long-term stressors?*

Dependency

People become dependent on BZs for two main reasons: they need more of the drug over time to get the original effects and they experience withdrawal symptoms when they stop taking it. The main symptoms are anxiety, depressed mood, sleep disturbances, headaches and muscular aches. Heather Ashton (2005) argues it is possible to manage the withdrawal syndrome if done carefully with appropriate psychological support. She also points out that, to avoid such a situation arising in the first place, BZs should be prescribed for just two to four weeks. But some doctors are still prescribing them for months or even years. Dependency can create greater problems for the users of drug therapy than the stress that it is intended to manage.

Consider: *This suggests there are both advantages and disadvantages to using BZs to treat the effects of stress. In your view, where does the balance lie?*

Apply it Concepts: **Treating exam stress**

Moira is an A level student who panics when she thinks about exams and this makes it difficult for her to revise. She has heard that drugs called beta blockers are taken by people who experience performance stress, and she wonders if they might help her.

Question

If you were her doctor, what advice would you give Moira? Explain both the benefits and limitations of beta blockers, and consider whether there are any alternatives that might be more suitable.

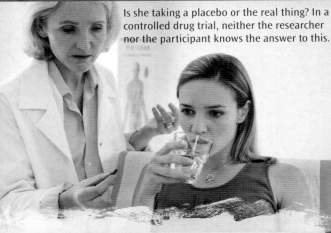

Is she taking a placebo or the real thing? In a controlled drug trial, neither the researcher nor the participant knows the answer to this.

Apply it Methods: **A drug therapy trial**

Two researchers conducted a double-blind placebo trial to test the effectiveness of a drug in treating the effects of stress: 100 participants completed the *Feelings of Stress* **questionnaire**, providing a score from 0 (feeling no stress at all) to 20 (feeling extreme stress). They were then **randomly allocated** to one of two groups. Participants in the **experimental group** were given a two-week course of the drug, but those in the placebo group were given an inactive version. At the end of two weeks, all the participants completed the questionnaire again.

Questions

1. Write a **non-directional hypothesis** for this experiment. (*2 marks*)
2. What **experimental design** is used in this study? (*1 mark*)
3. Explain *one* strength and *one* weakness of this design. (*2 marks + 2 marks*)
4. Explain how the participants could have been randomly allocated to the two groups. (*2 marks*)
5. Explain what is meant by **double-blind** procedure and how it could have been carried out. (*2 marks + 2 marks*)

CHECK IT

1. In relation to managing and coping with stress, explain what is meant by *drug therapy*. [2 marks]
2. Outline drug therapy as a method of managing stress. [6 marks]
3. Identify and discuss **one** type of drug therapy used to manage and cope with stress. [6 marks]
4. Discuss drug therapy as a method of stress management. [16 marks]

Managing and coping with stress: stress inoculation therapy.

In contrast with physiological methods of dealing with stress discussed on the previous spread there are also *psychological methods*. These focus on the cognitive and/or behavioural aspects of coping, by helping people to think about stressors more adaptively, and learning techniques that can combat the effects of stress.

Preparation is key in stress inoculation therapy. We can strengthen our ability to cope *before* we experience stressors. Rather like in the case of a vaccination against an infectious disease, we experience a weak 'dose' of a stressor to give us some immunity to more intense stressors when they arrive.

KEY TERM

Stress inoculation therapy (SIT) – A psychological method of stress management which helps individuals develop coping skills and then exposes the individual to moderate amounts of anxiety to enable practice of coping.

A violist who is stressed is likely to experience some tension in their arms and hands – the strings on a violin are quite sensitive to this tension. Therefore some violinists seek cognitive behaviour therapies like SIT to help them.

Apply it Concepts: A case of stage fright

Teri is a very talented singer and musician. She plays guitar in a band and sings in choirs and groups. But recently she has been having a crisis of confidence. One performance did not go as well as she hoped, and since then Teri has started to think that she is nowhere near as good as the other people she plays and sings with. She now goes on stage expecting to perform badly, and her singing does seem to be suffering as a result.

Question

Use your knowledge of stress management to explain how Teri might benefit from stress inoculation therapy. Refer in your explanation to Teri's specific situation and to all three phases of SIT.

Stress inoculation therapy (SIT)

The rationale behind any psychological method of stress management is that it is often not possible for us to change a stressful situation. We can't eliminate or even reduce many of the stressors we face because we have no control over them. So the alternative is to change the one thing we do have control over – ourselves. **Stress inoculation therapy** (SIT) is a cognitive behaviour approach to stress management, it advocates that we change the ways we *thin k* about stress.

Don Meichenbaum and Roy Cameron (1973) identified three phases of SIT. Each phase focuses on the practical steps needed to help the client. The phases are not completely distinct, they overlap and there may be some working backwards to an earlier phase to refresh before moving on.

Conceptualisation phase

SIT begins with the client and therapist working together to identify and understand the stressors the client faces. This therapeutic relationship is crucial to the success of SIT. According to Meichenbaum (2007) there should be a warm and collaborative rapport. The therapist is supportive and has a facilitating role, but the client retains responsibility for their progress. It is the client who is the expert on his or her own stress experiences, not the therapist.

The client is educated about the nature of stress and its effects on the individual. For example, they learn that anxiety has many causes, including their own thought processes. So there is a focus in SIT on the client's **cognitive appraisal** of stressors and their own ability to cope with them. The main aim of this phase is for the client to understand that stressors can be overcome, by viewing them not as the end of the world but as challenges. The client is also educated to tell the difference between the aspects of a stressful situation that can be changed and those that can't. They should come to realise that they need to work on the things they can change, and accept the things they can't.

Skills acquisition and rehearsal phase

The client is helped to learn the skills they need to cope with stress. There are several such skills but the use of them should be tailored to the client's specific needs. Examples include relaxation, social skills, communication, and cognitive restructuring, where the client thinks about stressful situations more optimistically. A major element of skills acquisition is learning to monitor and use self-talk effectively. The client uses *coping self-statements* (such as 'You can do this!', or 'Stick to the plan!') to replace negative and anxious internal dialogue with more positive thoughts. In this phase, the client plans in advance how to cope when stress occurs – how they can overcome it through the skills they learn and the resources they can bring to bear on the stressful situation.

Real-life application and follow-through phase

The therapist creates opportunities for the client to try out their skills in a safe environment. Various techniques are used to increase the realism of stressful situations. These include role playing, visualisation, even virtual reality and mobile apps. There is also a gradual transfer of these skills to the real world. The therapist sets homework tasks for the client to use in everyday life by deliberately seeking out moderately stressful situations and using their coping skills. They later feed back to the therapist for discussion and further work if necessary. Meichenbaum calls these *personal experiments*. The therapist's involvement lessens as the client gains greater control over their anxiety.

Another important feature of this phase is *relapse prevention*. The therapist helps prepare the client to cope with setbacks. The likelihood of reversals is accepted and built into SIT. The client learns to cognitively restructure setbacks as temporary learning opportunities and not permanent catastrophic failures. This is all part of inoculation, to identify potential problems in advance and plan how to deal with them. Part of this involves the therapist preparing the client to attribute success to their own skills and not to luck or chance or some other external agent (internal versus external **locus of control**).

Duration of therapy

The duration of therapy varies from one client to another but typically it will be between nine and twelve sessions of an hour to an hour-and-a-half each. There could be one session a week for two to three months or they might be spread out over a longer period. At least one or two sessions are reserved for follow-up after several months.

Evaluation

Flexibility

SIT is impressively flexible in a number of ways. It can incorporate a wide variety of stress management techniques in the skills acquisition phase including, if appropriate, physiological ones. It can be used with individuals, couples, groups large and small, families, and in a variety of settings. Duration of training can be from 20 minutes to 40 or more hours over several months. Techniques can be tailored to specific needs; for example, some skills might be especially suitable for elderly people, or people with learning difficulties. It has even been adapted for use online (Litz *et al.* 2004).

SIT is so flexible, according to Martin Spiegler (2012), that it has the potential to be an effective method of managing any form of stress, including in situations where people face racism and homophobia. This is a distinct advantage of this therapy.

A demanding therapy

SIT is quite demanding of clients, who have to make big commitments of time and effort. They also have to be highly motivated for SIT to be most effective. The training can be lengthy, and involves a lot of self-reflection and learning of new skills. The third phase of applying SIT techniques to real life is especially challenging. For example, some people are less able than others to use coping self-statements when they are experiencing the anxiety of a stressful situation. The almost inevitable failures clients face at this point would test the motivation of most people.

Such demands and the sense of failure mean that some people don't continue the treatment, making it unsuccessful. However, SIT does take this potential to quit into account and aims to help the client prepare for setbacks and explore ways of overcoming them.

Overcomplicated

SIT is a *multidimensional* approach to stress management, meaning that it uses lots of different techniques to target a variety of stressors and symptoms. It is unlikely that every aspect of such a wide-ranging approach is equally effective. Is there one feature all effective elements of SIT have in common that might explain its success in managing stress? Control has been mooted as the key factor. As the client's coping skills develop, he or she gradually gains a growing feeling of control over stressful situations.

This view is supported by evidence that SIT is not effective for some disorders and groups of people. For example, Dorothea Hensel-Dittman *et al.* (2011) used SIT with asylum seekers who were suffering from post-traumatic stress disorder caused by torture. The researchers found that SIT was relatively ineffective in these clients. They speculated that this could be because they were in a state of 'continuous trauma' in constant fear of being deported. Perhaps transfer of skills to everyday life does not work when the client feels they cannot gain control over their situation.

Evaluation eXtra

Research support

Teri Saunders *et al.* (1996) conducted a **meta-analysis** of 37 studies into SIT effectiveness. They concluded that SIT is effective for reducing anxiety in performance situations (e.g. in exams or public speaking) and for enhancing performance under stress (e.g. doing better in exams). They also found that SIT was as effective for people experiencing extreme anxiety as it was for those with moderate or normal levels. Surprisingly, the effectiveness of SIT did not depend on how experienced the therapist was.

Consider: *What do you think these findings tell us about the usefulness of SIT?*

Prevention

A strength of SIT is that it is 'future oriented' because it centres on inoculation. Clients are confronted with minor stressors so they can gain the skills and experience to face greater stress in the real world. It encourages clients to plan for what could happen, to be psychologically prepared not just for success but for potential failure too. It is very far from being a 'quick fix', a criticism often levelled against physiological methods of stress management such as **drug therapy**.

Consider: *Explain why not being a quick fix is seen as a strength.*

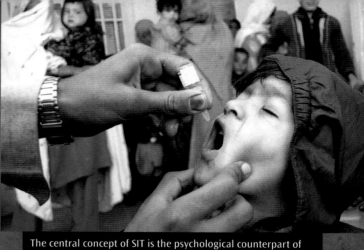

The central concept of SIT is the psychological counterpart of vaccination against physical diseases such as polio.

Apply it Concepts: **Drugs or SIT?**

Don has been suffering a great deal from stress of all kinds recently, and has decided that he could do with some help. He knows that drugs and SIT are two commonly-used methods of managing stress, but he is finding it hard to choose between them because they both have certain strengths and limitations.

Question

If Don asked you for advice, what would you tell him?

Apply it Methods: **Assessing SIT**

A researcher carried out a study into the effectiveness of stress inoculation therapy. She recruited forty participants and **randomly allocated** them to one of two groups. Twenty participants underwent a course of six SIT sessions, one per week. The other twenty took part in a discussion group for six sessions, but no specific SIT techniques were used. Levels of perceived stress were assessed by **questionnaire** before and after the six-week period. The scale used went from 0 (no stress at all) to 50 (extreme stress). The SIT group's **median** score improved by 16 points, but for the discussion group the corresponding figure decreased by 7.

Questions

1. What was the **operationalised dependent variable** for this study? (*2 marks*)

2. Explain why twenty of the participants took part in a discussion group. (*2 marks*)

3. Outline *one* way in which the researcher should take care to follow the British Psychological Society's *Code of Ethics*. (*2 marks*)

4. Explain *one* reason why the median was used as a measure of central tendency in this study. (*2 marks*)

5. Briefly explain how research such as this can benefit the economy. (*2 marks*)

CHECK IT

1. Explain what is meant by *stress inoculation therapy*.
   [3 marks]

2. Outline stress inoculation therapy as a method of coping with stress.
   [6 marks]

3. Explain **one** limitation of stress inoculation therapy as a method of coping with stress.
   [4 marks]

4. Describe and evaluate stress inoculation therapy as a method of coping with stress.
   [16 marks]

MANAGING AND COPING WITH STRESS: BIOFEEDBACK

Managing and coping with stress: biofeedback.

Many of our muscles can be stretched or contracted voluntarily, in order to reach out and pick something up, for example. But some muscular activity is involuntary, like the contractions of the gut involved in digestion. Other involuntary processes include several linked to the stress response, such as heart rate, blood pressure and sweating. Biofeedback was developed to gain conscious control over physiological processes that are involved in the stress response.

KEY TERM

Biofeedback – A method of stress management that turns physiological processes such as heart rate into signals that a client then learns to control. Clients do this by applying the techniques they have learned, such as relaxation and cognitive restructuring.

STUDY TIP

When describing biofeedback, it's good to include the concepts behind it such as its basis in conditioning. But central to any description should be the steps of the training procedure itself. What does the client practically have to do? How is the technology actually used? What are the phases involved in biofeedback? Become familiar with the process so you can describe each element in detail.

Apply it

Concepts: Using biofeedback

Jeff has heard that there are many methods that might be able to help him cope better with stress. He doesn't want to use drugs because he is worried about the side effects, and he thinks that SIT would be too much of a commitment. He has heard that biofeedback could be suitable, so he is keen to learn more about it before he goes to see his doctor.

Question

How would you explain to Jeff the processes involved in biofeedback? Refer to the different phases of the procedure and what he will be expected to do. Address his concerns about the other two methods in your explanation.

Biofeedback

The aim of **biofeedback** is to enable people to have control over involuntary physiological processes. The reason we can't normally control these internal processes is because we have no feedback from them. So biofeedback aims to provide that information using technology that allows us to see or hear our physiological functioning.

The biofeedback concept

The client is connected to a machine which converts physiological activity into a visual or auditory signal. A physiological activity (such as heart rate) is monitored, the signal is amplified and fed back immediately to the client via a display on a monitor or the sound of a tone through earphones.

For example, muscular tension can be measured using an **electromyogram** (EMG), with electrical activity of the muscles converted into a tone of varying pitch. An **electroencephalogram** (EEG) measures brain activity, which can be shown on a screen. The same goes for **skin conductance responses** (see page 264) that indicate sweating activity. Heart rate monitors are widely available these days, even as mobile apps. These machines give visual or auditory feedback providing a meaningful representation of the physiological process being monitored.

The training procedure

Clients are trained to use this feedback to become aware of their physiological functioning. They learn how to make adjustments (for example, to their breathing) to make the signal change in the desired direction, for example, by lowering the pitch of a tone, or moving the line of a graph on a display. Biofeedback with children (and increasingly with adults) uses a game-based interface where the client has to adjust their physiological response to successfully complete an on-screen maze.

The client makes these changes by applying stress management techniques they have learned, for example, relaxation training (learning to tighten and relax specific muscle groups). With practice, as the client relaxes his or her muscles (or slows their heartbeat), this eventually triggers biofeedback from the machine. This, and perhaps praise from the therapist, is rewarding and **reinforces** the client's behaviour, making further success more likely (i.e. **operant conditioning**).

Thomas Budzynski (1973) has identified three main phases to biofeedback training:

1. The client learns to become aware of their physiological response and how it can be adjusted in a desired direction (for example, reducing heart rate or muscle activity).
2. The client learns how to use various techniques to control the response.
3. Control of the response has to be transferred to everyday life, so the client practises in stressful situations rather than in the safety and comfort of a therapy room.

Research into biofeedback

Henry Davis (1986) used EMG biofeedback with breast cancer patients.

Procedure There were thirteen 45-minute sessions held over an eight-week period, during which the patients learnt deep-breathing and relaxation techniques.

Findings After eight months, levels of urinary **cortisol** and self-reported anxiety were **significantly** lower in these patients than they had been at the start of the study. In a group of control participants, who had no form of therapy, cortisol levels increased. The researchers concluded that this was evidence of significant stabilisation of the **hypothalamic-pituitary-adrenal system** by biofeedback.

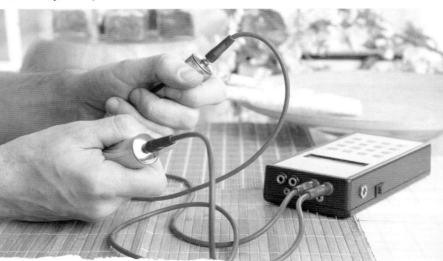

Biofeedback devices these days are smaller, more portable and less expensive than they used to be.

Evaluation

Research support

Jane Lemaire et al. (2011) used medical doctors as their participants and trained them to use a biofeedback device. They used it three times a day over a 28-day period, and also completed a **questionnaire** measuring their perception of how stressed they were. The **mean** stress score for the biofeedback users fell significantly over the course of the study. The corresponding score for a **control group** also fell, but by a much smaller amount.

This suggests that biofeedback has benefits in helping to improve the psychological state of someone who is experiencing stress.

Outcome measures

Lemaire et al. (2011) also took measurements of heart rate, blood pressure and cortisol levels on each occasion biofeedback was used over the 28-day duration of the study. There were no significant changes in these physiological measurements between the start and end of this period, suggesting that biofeedback had very little effect on objective, physiological indicators of the stress response. Janette Greenhalgh et al. (2009) reviewed 36 studies (with 1660 patients) of biofeedback treatment for hypertension (persistent high blood pressure), a physiological outcome. They concluded that biofeedback was no more effective than other treatments such as drugs for treating hypertension, **cognitive behaviour therapy** and self-monitoring. It was also no more effective than **placebo** or even no treatment at all.

It appears that the effectiveness of biofeedback depends on the outcome measure, what it is you actually aim to 'treat'. It may help to make the individual 'feel better' or 'less stressed' (which is not to be disregarded). But biofeedback's effects on stress-related physiological risk factors for CVD are much less apparent.

Are both biofeedback and relaxation necessary?

In biofeedback-assisted relaxation treatment (BART), clients use biofeedback to help them learn to relax more deeply. Gennaro Bussone et al. (1998) treated children suffering from tension headaches with either relaxation on its own or with BART (relaxation plus biofeedback). Headache frequency reduced in both groups by 55% three months after treatment. However, improvements were greater in the BART group after one year and three years.

This finding suggests that well-established relaxation techniques such as meditation and progressive muscle relaxation are effective, but can be improved with the addition of machine-based biofeedback. The benefits of biofeedback may therefore come from its use as an aid to relaxation rather than as a stress management technique in itself.

Evaluation eXtra

Convenience

The use of biofeedback these days is much more convenient and inexpensive than it once was. Recent devices are about the size of a mobile phone, and work by representing the targeted physiological function (e.g. heart rate) with colours. The client tries to change the colour of the device by controlling his or her breathing to reduce heart rate. Further developments in 'wearable technology' (e.g. smartwatches) should make it even cheaper and easier to use biofeedback in stressful everyday situations.

Consider: *Is this convenience unique to this method? Do you think a technological method of managing stress is a good or bad thing?*

Individual differences

Biofeedback as a stress management method does not suit everyone. The client needs to be able to understand the relationship between their physiological functioning and the visual/auditory signals they are receiving. They need to be very motivated to apply the skills they learn to altering these signals. Motivation can be improved by introducing a gaming element to the proceedings. But the client also has to be highly motivated to practise the skills they have learned in the real world outside the safety of the clinic.

Consider: *Explain why this is a limitation of biofeedback.*

Do the benefits of biofeedback come from relaxation techniques taught alongside it? If so, then meditation might be just as effective.

Apply it — Concepts: Which is best?

Two students are having a discussion about stress management techniques. Harry is a biology student and his argument is that physiological methods are superior. But Adrianne – a psychology student – thinks that psychological methods are better.

Question

How would you use your knowledge of stress management to settle this argument? What would your position be?

Apply it — Methods: Did it work for you?

Biofeedback is a controversial method of stress management. There is much debate about its effectiveness, and it seems to work for some people but not for others. A psychologist decided to address this issue by investigating people's experiences of biofeedback. She carried out face-to-face interviews with 85 participants, 38 of them male and 47 female. She asked questions about their perceptions of whether biofeedback had helped them cope better with stress, and the reasons why or why not.

Questions

1. Outline *one* strength of gathering **qualitative data** in this study. (*2 marks*)

2. Explain *two* differences between a **structured** and an **unstructured interview**. (*2 marks + 2 marks*)

3. Identify an alternative method that could have been used to collect data about biofeedback experiences in this study. Explain why this might be a better method than an interview. (*4 marks*)

4. Calculate the proportions of males and females as percentages of the total number of participants (*two* percentages). (*4 marks*)

5. The psychologist wanted to calculate the average length of time participants used biofeedback. Which **measure of central tendency** would you advise her to use, and why? (*1 mark + 2 marks*)

CHECK IT

1. In relation to managing and coping with stress, explain what is meant by *biofeedback*. [3 marks]

2. Outline biofeedback as a method of managing stress. [6 marks]

3. Explain **one** limitation of biofeedback as a method of stress management. [4 marks]

4. Discuss biofeedback as a method of managing stress. [16 marks]

THE SPECIFICATION SAYS...

Gender differences in coping with stress.

It has often been noted that women tend to live longer than men in most cultures. Psychologists have wondered if this gender difference might be linked to stress, and have suggested three possibilities. It could be that different physiological responses to stress have evolved in males and females. On the other hand, perhaps women behave differently in terms of stress-related matters such as lifestyle. Or maybe women have more constructive ways of coping with stress.

KEY TERMS

Gender differences – The ways in which men and women differ behaviourally and psychologically, and which may be due to biological differences and/or due to socially defined expectations of male and female behaviour.

Apply it

Concepts: Roland's coping method...

Like a lot of students, Roland gets pretty stressed in the run-up to exams. He has always tried to cope with them in the same way: by thinking carefully how he will plan his time to avoid as much stress as possible.

Question

What method of stress management is Roland using? Based on your understanding of gender, what else is he likely to do to cope?

Stereotype or reality? Is it true that men take a more problem-solving approach in times of stress than women?

Gender differences in coping with stress

It is all too easy to stereotype male and female responses to stress (men bottle things up, women talk openly to their friends). But psychological research has supported such differences and found that men and women generally do employ different strategies to cope with stress.

Gender-related coping methods

Some researchers have suggested that men have a tendency to use problem-focused methods of coping with stress, but women generally use emotion-focused methods.

This broad distinction between problem- and emotion-focused coping was first made by Richard Lazarus and Susan Folkman (1984). Problem-focused methods reduce stress by tackling its root causes in a direct, practical and rational way. This typically involves taking control to remove or escape from the stress, and learning new skills such as time management or relaxation techniques. Emotion-focused methods reduce stress indirectly by tackling the anxiety associated with a stressor. Ways of doing this include various forms of avoidance, such as distraction and keeping busy. It is also possible to use **cognitive appraisal** to think about the stressor more positively.

Research into gender and different coping methods Although most people use some combination of both methods, some research supports the hypothesis that men are more likely to use problem-focused techniques but women tend to be more emotion-focused. Brennan Peterson *et al.* (2006) assessed the coping strategies of men and women who had been diagnosed as infertile. They used several measures including the *Ways of Coping* **questionnaire** (Folkman *et al.* 1986). Men and women used a variety of strategies, but a key **gender difference** emerged. Women were more likely to accept blame and use various avoidance tactics, both of which are thought to be characteristic of an emotion-focused approach. Men were more likely to use planful problem-solving, a feature of a problem-focused approach.

Tend and befriend

There is some evidence men and women have different physiological responses to stressors. The typical response to an acute stressor, in humans and other animals, is **fight or flight** (see page 254). But Shelley Taylor and her colleagues (2000) point out that most research into this response has been conducted with male participants. So 'fight or flight' does not best describe the stress response of women. From an evolutionary perspective, fight or flight is disadvantageous for a female because confronting or fleeing from a predator would make it difficult for her to protect her offspring.

Therefore what has evolved in females is a very different response to stressors, which Taylor *et al.* (2000) call **tend and befriend**. Tending is protecting, calming and nurturing offspring and blending in with the environment rather than confronting a threat. Befriending involves seeking support from social networks at times of stress in order to cope.

Research into tend and befriend Luckow *et al.* (1998) reviewed 26 studies of gender differences in 'seeking and using social support' as a way of coping with stress. Women were much more likely to use this method in 25 of these studies. So it seems that women very strongly favour befriending in stressful situations, much more so than men.

But this befriending is selective – it tends to be with other women. Lewis and Linder (2000) found that most of their female participants, when confronted with a stressful experience, preferred to wait for female support rather than seek it from a man. This may in part have evolved as a mechanism for protecting females and their offspring against threatening males, even close family members.

Oxytocin

Biochemically, the tend and befriend stress response is driven by **oxytocin**, a **hormone** produced by males and females. Oxytocin promotes feelings of goodwill and affiliation with others, and has a role in the formation of the mother-infant attachment bond. It also helps the body recover more quickly from the physiological effects of a stressor.

Taylor *et al.* (2002) found that higher levels of oxytocin were linked with lower **cortisol** levels in their female participants only. There was also a quicker recovery of the HPA system (see page 254) after exposure to a stressful task. It appears that the female sex hormone **oestrogen** increases the effects of oxytocin, but male hormones (**androgens**) reduce them. Thus oxytocin effects are stronger in women, generally creating a reduced stress response.

Evaluation

Explaining gender differences

Role constraint theory argues that differences in how men and women cope with stress are mostly due to the different stressors they face. Coping strategies are highly situation-specific. For example, work stressors lend themselves to problem-focused coping. But for relationship stressors, emotion-focused strategies are more suitable. Pilar Matud (2004) found that women and men experienced similar numbers of stressful life changes, but of different types. Women reported more family-related stressors and men more work-related ones. Women also perceived their stressors as more negative and less controllable, and their coping style was more emotion-focused than that of men.

This shows that gender differences in coping strategies could be due to men and women experiencing different stressors, rather than reflecting something fundamental about being a man or a woman, as role constraint theory predicts.

Are emotion and problem-focused strategies different?

Brennan Peterson *et al*. (2006) studied infertility stress in men and women referred for IVF. They found some gender differences, but importantly they discovered that men and women used coping methods that did not fit the classic distinction between emotion-focused and problem-focused. For example, is seeking social support an emotion-focused or problem-focused method? In fact, it can be either or both. Women used it extensively, sometimes to seek information (problem-focused) and sometimes for emotional support (emotion-focused).

This highlights the difficulty in making a clear distinction between the two methods, and therefore the difficulty in concluding that women use one type and men another. The truth is that men and women use both methods depending on the nature of the stressor.

Research support for tend and befriend

Lisa Tamres *et al*. (2002) carried out a **meta-analysis** of 26 studies comparing the coping strategies of men and women. Women were significantly more likely than men to seek social support, a coping method that is a central part of the befriending response to stressful situations. There is also some research support for the tending element of the stress response. Ruth Feldman *et al*. (2007) measured oxytocin in women during pregnancy and soon after they had given birth. They found that women with the highest oxytocin levels formed stronger bonds with their newborn babies.

This illustrates the growing body of research evidence to suggest that several predictions derived from the tend and befriend theory are **valid**, including those relating to differences between men and women in coping responses to stress.

Evaluation eXtra

Evidence against gender differences

Laura Porter and Arthur Stone (1995) measured coping behaviour daily throughout their study. Women reported more relationship-related stressors and men more work-related ones, as other research has shown. But when this variation in stressors was accounted for, there were no gender differences in coping methods. The choice of coping style does not depend on gender but on the nature of the stressful situation.

Consider: *Does this mean there are no gender differences in coping at all?*

Retrospective research

Many studies are retrospective – participants think back to stressful occasions and recall the methods they used to cope. Denise De Ridder (2000) found that women reported using emotion-focused coping more than men, but only when recalling retrospectively. This difference disappeared when participants used *ecological momentary assessment* (EMA), a method of reporting coping strategies at regular intervals during the day.

Consider: *Why do you think the difference exists when people have to remember the coping methods they used? How does this affect the validity of research?*

Practical activity on page 281

Keeping busy is an emotion-focused method of coping with stress because it distracts us from our feelings. Some research suggests this method may be used more often by women.

Apply it — Methods: Assessing coping methods

A researcher was interested in investigating gender differences in coping with stress. He selected twenty men and twenty women, all of them carers for a spouse with Alzheimer's disease. They filled in a questionnaire to assess the methods they used to cope with stress. Based on their responses, each participant was classified as either emotion-focused or problem-focused in their stress management approach.

Questions

1. Explain *one* strength and *one* limitation of using a questionnaire in this study (2 *marks*)
2. Write a **directional hypothesis** for this study. (2 *marks*)
3. Outline how the researcher might have selected a **volunteer sample** of suitable participants. (2 *marks*)
4. A friend of the researcher disagreed with this result. He knows lots of men who are emotion-focused and women who are problem-focused in managing stress. Explain why the friend's personal opinion is no substitute for scientific evidence. (4 *marks*)

Apply it — Concepts: … And Shelley's too

Shelley is Roland's twin sister (see facing page). Her approach to dealing with stress has always been very different from her brother's. She prefers to keep herself as busy as possible so she doesn't have to think too much about her upcoming exams and get anxious.

Questions

1. What method of stress management is Shelley using? How does it differ from Roland's preferred approach?
2. Explain why Shelley is more likely than Roland to seek out her friends at exam time.

CHECK IT

1. Describe **one** gender difference in stress. [3 *marks*]
2. Outline research into gender differences in stress. [6 *marks*]
3. Briefly describe **one** research study into gender differences in stress. Refer to what the researcher(s) did and what they found. [4 *marks*]
4. Describe and evaluate research into gender differences in stress. [16 *marks*]

THE ROLE OF SOCIAL SUPPORT IN COPING WITH STRESS

THE SPECIFICATION SAYS...

The role of social support in coping with stress; types of social support including instrumental, emotional and esteem support.

'Many relationships may be better for the having of them than the using of them' (Taylor 2011).

It may be just as valuable to know you have friends you can call on for support as actually having to call on them. There is always the danger that actively calling upon support from a social network leaves you open to rejection, making the situation worse. Just believing that you could get help if you needed it avoids having to test this possibility.

KEY TERMS

Social support – People cope with stressful situations by seeking help from their friends, family and acquaintances.

Instrumental support – Practical help such as lending money, cooking a meal, providing information.

Emotional support – Giving someone a 'shoulder to cry on' to help them feel better.

Esteem support – Helping someone to attach greater value to themselves so they view their abilities with greater confidence.

STUDY TIP

Be careful when explaining different types of social support. If you have to explain one type (e.g. esteem support) then limit yourself to that one and don't be tempted to stray. On the other hand, if you need to explain social support in general, then you should aim to include something about all three types.

Social support comes in many forms, from the purely practical to helping someone cope with the emotions associated with stress.

The role of social support

Types of social support

Social networks vary in their size and the strength of the support they offer. It's possible that someone with a relatively small social network can get a great deal of support from few people. The converse is also true – just because someone has a large and widespread social network does not mean they will get much support from it. Therefore another factor is important: how integrated into their social networks someone is. Being very closely involved in a small network of close friends, relatives and work colleagues is likely to provide greater support than if you spread yourself too thinly.

Mark Schaefer *et al.* (1981) identified at least three distinct forms of **social support**:

1. **Instrumental support:** This is best understood as practical and tangible support, which could be in the form of physically doing something to help (such as giving someone a lift to the hospital) or providing information (telling someone what you know about stress).
2. **Emotional support:** This is summed up in what we mean when we say things like 'I really feel for you', or 'I'm sorry you're going through such a tough time'. It expresses warmth, concern, affection, empathy and love. Emotional support isn't intended to offer any kind of practical help, but rather to make the stressed person feel better, to lift their mood.
3. **Esteem support:** This is when we try to reinforce someone's faith in themselves, their belief in their ability to tackle a stressful situation. We might express our confidence in them, increasing their confidence in themselves and reducing their feelings of stress.

Clearly there is a lot of overlap between these types of support. For example, being a 'shoulder to cry on' could conceivably involve all three. Even old-fashioned matter-of-fact instrumental support can help emotionally because of what it means to the individual who receives it – it is a sign of caring.

All three types have something in common: they can be provided without physical presence. Emotional and esteem support are just the kinds of support given every minute of every day over online social networks such as Facebook and Twitter. Or a cheque sent with a card or letter through the post offers instrumental support without anyone meeting face-to-face.

Research into social support

Social support (especially emotional) can be expressed through physical touch. Sheldon Cohen *et al.* (2015) wondered if hugs offered protection against stress-related infections.

Procedure They telephoned 404 healthy adult participants every evening for 14 consecutive days to measure the number of hugs they received each day. The participants also completed a **questionnaire** to assess perceived social support. Stress was measured in terms of daily interpersonal conflicts. The researchers then placed the participants in quarantine, exposed them to a common cold virus, and monitored them for signs of illness (remember that stress acts as an immunosuppressant therefore we expect people who are more stressed to become ill).

Findings The participants who experienced the most interpersonal conflict (i.e. stress) were most likely to become ill. But those who perceived they had greater social support had a significantly reduced risk of illness. Hugs accounted for up to one-third of the protective effect of social support. Participants who had the most frequent hugs were less likely to become infected and, for those who did, the symptoms were less severe than for those who had fewer hugs. Perceived social support acts as a buffer against stress, and hugs are a behavioural sign of actual emotional support.

Apply it Concepts: Helping hands

Danuta suffers the negative effects of stress a great deal. She finds it difficult to function normally because of this. But fortunately she has a lot of friends who try their best to help. Some give Danuta lifts in their cars to her various medical appointments. Others spend time with her, talking and listening to her sympathetically. Yet others reassure her that she is a worthwhile person with a lot to offer.

Question

Identify the types of social support being shown to Danuta. How do the various forms of support help Danuta in her attempts to cope? Refer to psychological research in your explanation.

Evaluation

Supportive research studies

There is a wealth of research linking various forms of social support with well-being, and absence of support with illness. Fawzy Fawzy et al. (1993) **randomly allocated** patients with malignant melanoma to a support group for just six weeks, one session a week. The group provided an opportunity for patients to express their feelings (emotional support) but also to get information and advice about their illness (instrumental support). Six years later, the support group patients had better *NK cell* functioning (a type of white blood cell, see page 256), and were more likely to be alive and free of cancer than patients in a control group.

This shows that the beneficial effects of social support can be substantial and long-lasting. The validity of these findings is greater because the study was well-controlled and prospective (i.e. social support could predict outcomes several years later).

Gender differences

One of the most consistent findings in the whole of stress research is that men and women use social support differently. Men appear to have larger social networks than women, but the size of network is not the crucial factor influencing the effectiveness of social support. In times of stress, on virtually every measure one cares to name, women are more likely to seek out and use social support as well as provide it.

Luckow et al. (1998) reviewed 26 studies that investigated gender differences in social support coping. One of the studies showed no difference, but 25 found that women used social support as a means of coping with stress more than men did. This difference was especially pronounced in the case of emotional support.

Negative effects of social support

Social support is not universally beneficial, but can backfire and have negative effects. What matters is who provides the support and what type they give. Emotional support is usually welcomed from friends and relatives, and we appreciate them 'being there for us'. But instrumental support in the form of information is more valued when it comes from medical professionals, for example. Also there are times when emotional support from a close relative or friend is not helpful. For instance, if they insist on coming with us to a hospital appointment, we might end up feeling more anxious than if we went alone.

This might explain why online support from people we have never met face-to-face can sometimes help us to cope better. Perhaps support is more beneficial when it is sought by the recipient than when it is imposed by the supporter.

Support isn't always welcome. It can backfire if the supporter insists on offering it, making us more stressed than ever.

Apply it — Concepts: Online social support

Colleen collects friends on Facebook. She never defriends anyone so now has a network of hundreds of people and spends a lot of time exchanging posts with many of them. She feels they are a real source of support even though she knows very few of them in the offline world. Dylan has only a handful of friends on Facebook, but is very close to all of them and they spend a lot of time together offline.

Question

Which of Colleen and Dylan is likely to get the best support from their social networks? Explain your answer, referring to types of support and any other relevant issues.

Apply it — Methods: A stress case study

A researcher into the psychology of stress decided to investigate the reasons why people seek social support. He carried out a **case study** of a woman who was going through a very stressful period in her life. He used various techniques for collecting data about the types of social support she was receiving and her reasons for seeking it.

Questions

1. Describe *one* technique that the researcher could have used to collect data in this case study. (*2 marks*)

2. Explain *one* strength and *one* limitation of conducting a case study. (*2 marks + 2 marks*)

The researcher wrote up the case study in a report for publication in a scientific journal.

3. What is the purpose of the discussion section of such a report? (*2 marks*) (See page 81)

4. How could the researcher maintain his participant's **confidentiality** when his report is published? (*3 marks*)

5. Explain *one* other **ethical issue** that could arise in this case study and how the researcher could deal with it. (*2 marks + 2 marks*)

Evaluation eXtra

Cultural influences

Some studies show that the effectiveness of social support is influenced by cultural factors. Taylor et al. (2004) compared Americans of European and Asian origins. They found that Asian-Americans were much less likely to seek and use social support networks in times of stress. They were concerned not to disrupt the harmony of their communities by bringing their own problems to everybody's attention. European-Americans viewed relationships as resources to draw upon to help cope with stressful situations.

Consider: *Do you think Asian-Americans in this study would welcome social support? Is it universally beneficial?*

Explaining the benefits

According to the *buffering hypothesis* (Cohen and Wills 1985), social support is beneficial because it protects us against the negative effects of stressors by creating a psychological distance. But the **hypothesis** also argues that social support provides few benefits when stress is absent. Support acts as a reserve that dampens the impact of stressors and allows us to cope better.

Consider: *Do you think this is a complete explanation? Can social support be beneficial when we are not stressed? Explain your answer.*

CHECK IT

1. In relation to coping with stress, explain what is meant by *instrumental support* and *esteem support*.
   [2 marks + 2 marks]

2. Describe **one** study supporting the role of social support in coping with stress.
   [6 marks]

3. Outline the role of social support in coping with stress.
   [6 marks]

4. Discuss the role of social support in coping with stress.
   [16 marks]

PRACTICAL CORNER

THE SPECIFICATION SAYS...

> Knowledge and understanding of ... research methods, practical research skills and maths skills. These should be developed through ... ethical practical research activities.

This means you should conduct practical activities wherever possible. On this spread, you will find a correlational study looking at the possible links between daily hassles and illness. There is also a quasi-experiment that uses a questionnaire to collect data. There is some flexibility to this practical, though, as you can easily turn it into an interview and content analysis.

Ethics check

We suggest strongly that you complete this checklist before starting:

1. Do participants know participation is voluntary?
2. Do participants know what to expect?
3. Do participants know they can withdraw at any time?
4. Are individuals' results anonymous?
5. Have I minimised the risk of distress to participants?
6. Have I avoided asking sensitive questions?
7. Will I avoid bringing my school/teacher/psychology into disrepute?
8. Have I considered all other ethical issues?
9. Has my teacher approved this?

Sometimes the hassles of everyday life just make us want to go back to bed.

Apply it

Methods: The maths bit 1

Practical idea 1: Daily hassles and illness – is there a link?

The relationship between everyday sources of stress and illness has been much investigated. Findings are mixed, but many psychologists argue that **daily hassles** are more strongly associated with illness than major **life changes**.

The main aim of this practical is to find out if there is a link between hassles and illness in a sample of students. This is also an opportunity for you to construct your own scale to measure an important source of stress.

The practical bit

Designing your scale

You could use any freely-available scale to measure daily hassles, but there are two problems with this approach. Scales such as Kanner *et al.*'s (1981) original Hassles Scale are very lengthy and quite likely to test the patience of your participants. Also not all are applicable to students (though there are some). So a better solution is to produce your own tailor-made scale.

You will need to think up some daily happenings that fit the definition of a hassle, a relatively minor but frequent occurrence that causes annoyance or irritation. They should be ones likely to be experienced by your **target population** of students. Decide on a maximum number of hassles; probably no more than 20, and of different types. If you get short of ideas, you could refer to Kanner *et al.*'s original for inspiration. You should be able to find this with the aid of your favourite Internet search engine.

Another decision you have to take relates to the measurement scale you are going to use. The original scale measured the severity of each hassle with three points (somewhat, moderately, extremely). You might want to use a different wording or even a different size scale. Think carefully about how you will word **standardised instructions** and include them with the scale. Make sure you indicate the period of time over which you want participants to recall the hassles they have experienced (e.g. one month).

Ethical issues

Hassles are relatively minor so they are unlikely to provoke distress or be interpreted as personal or an invasion of privacy. Even so, you should keep these issues in mind when constructing your scale and writing your standardised instructions. You should also, as ever, pay attention to **informed consent** and how to obtain it, and make your participants' **right to withdraw** clear.

Selecting your participants

An **opportunity sample** of students is perfectly acceptable for this practical. Your school or college canteen is the most obvious place to recruit individuals, although distributing questionnaires to whole classes is straightforward as long as you get permission. If you approach individuals, you need to make sure there is somewhere relatively quiet available to fill out the scale for a few minutes.

Using the scale

You could look at the relationship between daily hassles and self-reported illness or absenteeism from school or college. For absenteeism, you might ask your participants to simply estimate how many days off they have had over a specified period. If illness is what you wish to measure, then construct a brief scale asking participants to indicate how many times they have been ill in the specified period and to rate the severity of each one, again on a scale of your choosing.

Analysing and presenting your data

You could **correlate** overall hassles score with illness severity score. This is a good chance to draw a **scattergram** to visualise the relationship between the two variables. You could also calculate appropriate measures of central tendency for each variable and place them in a table. Finally, apply a suitable **statistical test** to establish the statistical significance of the correlation you have found (see pages 78–79).

Participant	Hassles score	Illness severity score
1	44	9
2	32	6
3	13	4
4	24	5
5	17	4
6	35	6
7	29	8
8	54	7
9	26	5
10	40	7

1. What is the **level of measurement** of the two variables? Explain your answer *(1 mark + 1 mark)*
2. Calculate a suitable **measure of central tendency** for the two variables. *(1 mark + 1 mark)*
3. Calculate a suitable **measure of dispersion** for the two variables. *(1 mark + 1 mark)*
4. What is meant by the terms **Type I error** and **Type II error**? *(1 mark + 1 mark)* (See page 73)
5. Draw a suitable graph to represent the data in the table. *(4 marks)*

Practical idea 2: Do men and women cope differently?

Lazarus and Folkman (1984) distinguished between two major ways of coping with stressors – emotion-focused and problem-focused. Although we all use both of these when we need to, there is some evidence that men and women have distinct preferences.

The aim of this practical is to test the claim that women tend to use emotion-focused methods and men use problem-focused methods.

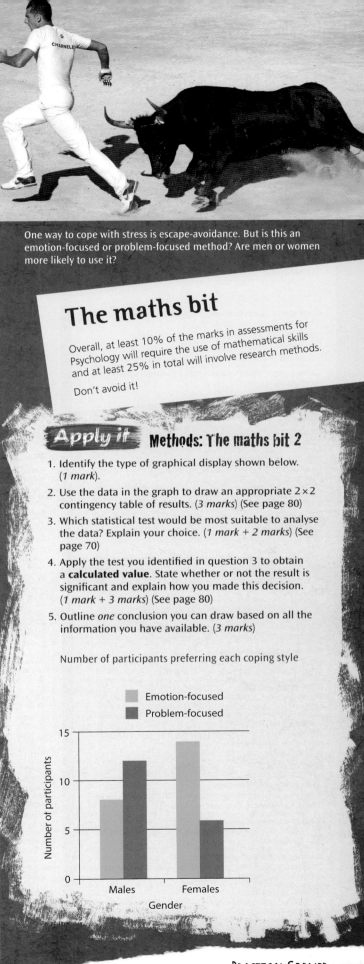

One way to cope with stress is escape-avoidance. But is this an emotion-focused or problem-focused method? Are men or women more likely to use it?

The practical bit

Designing the study

This study is a quasi-experiment because the **independent variable** is gender. The **dependent variable** is method of coping with stress, emotion-focused or problem-focused. You can construct your own questionnaire to measure coping styles.

The questionnaire

First, think about different coping methods that fall into the categories of emotion-focused or problem-focused. Once you have done that, you can devise some questions that assess each method. An ideal way to do this is to be guided by Folkman *et al.*'s (1986) *Ways of Coping* questionnaire, which is widely available via any Internet search engine.

Don't just reproduce the same items, but use them to make your own, ones that are more suitable for your target population (that is probably students, but it doesn't have to be – see below). Limit the number of items you create, but make sure you have equal numbers related to emotion-focused and problem-focused methods (perhaps ten of each). Decide on a scale of measurement, perhaps from 'never use that method' to 'use that method a lot' with one or two points (no more) in between. Produce some standardised instructions and make sure they are clear and easy to follow without any further clarification.

There is an alternative to asking closed questions, and that is to give your participants the chance to tell you about their coping methods in their own words. You could devise some open questions and leave space for responses, or even consider using a **semi-structured interview** method instead. The downside is that it becomes more difficult to analyse the data you collect. But it would be a good opportunity to apply content analysis techniques to test the **hypothesis** about a gender difference.

Sampling method

Opportunity sampling is, as always, a very convenient way of recruiting participants, especially students. However, for a bit of variety, and to make your sample slightly more representative, you could extend your target population a little by including people who are not students. But you should stick to people you know (family, friends) rather than approach people on the street.

Ethical considerations

If you use the *Ways of Coping* questionnaire to help you, think carefully about the ethical implications of some of the items. Most of them are likely to be acceptable to everyone, but some are fairly intrusive and perhaps sensitive. These are best avoided altogether. Asking people about stress always carries ethical risks, so you need to minimise these as much as possible. Gaining informed consent and offering the right to withdraw are very important protections for participants and should never be neglected.

Analysing your data

If you have taken the open question or semi-structured interview routes, then think about the **coding system** you will use to categorise your participants' responses into the two coping styles. Identify all the separate statements each participant has made. Decide whether they are more indicative of an emotion-focused or problem-focused style. Watch out for repetitive and duplicate statements (i.e. when a participant just says the same thing in a slightly different way). Categorise each participant according to whichever style is associated with the most comments.

Once you have 'scored' the questionnaire responses, you will know how many males and females prefer which style. You can then draw up a 2 × 2 **contingency table** with these figures in the four cells, calculating the row and column totals, as well as overall total. An appropriate statistical test could tell you whether there are significant differences in coping style between males and females.

The maths bit

Overall, at least 10% of the marks in assessments for Psychology will require the use of mathematical skills and at least 25% in total will involve research methods.

Don't avoid it!

Apply it Methods: The maths bit 2

1. Identify the type of graphical display shown below. (*1 mark*).
2. Use the data in the graph to draw an appropriate 2 × 2 contingency table of results. (*3 marks*) (See page 80)
3. Which statistical test would be most suitable to analyse the data? Explain your choice. (*1 mark + 2 marks*) (See page 70)
4. Apply the test you identified in question 3 to obtain a **calculated value**. State whether or not the result is significant and explain how you made this decision. (*1 mark + 3 marks*) (See page 80)
5. Outline *one* conclusion you can draw based on all the information you have available. (*3 marks*)

Number of participants preferring each coping style

Revision summaries

The physiology of stress

How the body responds to stressors.

The General Adaptation Syndrome (GAS)

- Alarm reaction
- Resistance: Body tries to adapt.
- Exhaustion: Resources depleted.

Evaluation

Research evidence
Selye's research with rats established three stages as a general response to any stressor.

Is the GAS really general?
Mason replicated Selye's research with monkeys; specific responses occurred to specific stressors.

The physiological response

Acute stress: Sympathomedullary pathway (SAM)
Hypothalamus activates sympathetic ANS.
Adrenal medulla produces adrenaline and noradrenaline.
Liver releases glucose.
Stressor ends; parasympathetic branch initiates rest and digest.

Chronic stress: Hypothalamic-pituitary-adrenal system (HPA)
Hypothalamus releases CRF.
Anterior pituitary releases ACTH.
Adrenal cortex releases cortisol (for energy).
Hypothalamus detects cortisol and inhibits response.

Evaluation

Male bias in biological research
Taylor: Females respond to stressors with tend and befriend, promotes survival of offspring.

Psychological factors are ignored
Speisman *et al.*: Cognitive appraisal affected stress response to gruesome film.

Real-life benefits
Understanding of the physiology of stress has led to cortisol replacement therapy.

The role of stress in illness

Cortisol reduces immune system activity.

The role of stress in illness

Immunosuppression
Kiecolt-Glaser *et al.*: Stressful experiences (exams and long-term caring) suppress the immune system directly (e.g. T cell activity).

Acute stress and CVDs
Wilbert-Lampen *et al.*: Acute stress of watching football match doubled risk of cardiac event.

Chronic stress and CVDs
INTERHEART study: Workplace stressors and life change stress both linked to MIs (heart attacks) more than obesity.

Evaluation

Stress can benefit immunity
Acute stress stimulates immune response without physical damage. Links between stress and immune system complex.

Immunosuppression and cancer
Pereira *et al.*: HIV+ women with stressors more likely to develop cancerous lesions later.

Direct versus indirect effects
Orth-Gomer *et al.*: Marital stress tripled risk of heart attack in women who already had one (indirect effect).

Real-life applications
Pre-operation doses of stress hormones (Dharbhar) and relaxation training (Kiecolt-Glaser and Glaser).

Strengths and weaknesses of research studies
Lab-based studies and artificial stressors; research with animals.

Sources of stress

Life changes

Major changes in our lives can be stressful.

Life changes as a source of stress

What are life changes?
Major events in our lives that happen infrequently but require adjustment to cope with.

Life changes and illness
Holmes and Rahe: LCUs (measured by SRRS) positively related to illness.

Research into life changes
Rahe *et al.*: US Navy personnel, +.118 correlation between LCUs and illness.

Evaluation

Supporting research
Lietzen *et al.*: Life changes were reliable predictor of asthma.

Individual differences
Approach does not consider how individuals perceive life changes differently.

Positive and negative life changes
Turner and Wheaton: Most stress measured by SRRS caused by negative events only.

Life changes versus daily hassles
Lazarus: Daily hassles more important than life changes because their effects accumulate.

Correlation not causation
Effects could be indirect because there are other causes.

Daily hassles

It's the little things that cause us stress.

Daily hassles as a source of stress

What are daily hassles?
Small but frequent occurrences build up until we have trouble coping with them.

Primary and secondary appraisal
Primary: Working out if hassle is threatening.
Secondary: Working out if we can cope.

Life changes, daily hassles and illness
Life changes disrupt usual routines, create more hassles which may cause illness.

Research into daily hassles
Kanner *et al.*: Hassles better predictor of psychological symptoms than life changes.

Evaluation

Supportive research evidence
Ivancevich: Hassles better predictors of work-related stress than life changes.

Retrospective research
Hassles may be forgotten, so research is an underestimate of the effect.

Daily hassles and life changes
Amplification hypothesis: Hassles might make life changes seem worse, so illness more likely.

Gender differences
Helms et al: Men and women different roles in family so different interpretations of hassles.

Correlation not causation
Hassles do not necessarily cause illness or may indirectly affect illness.

Individual differences in stress

Personality type

People with different personalities respond to stress in different ways.

Stress and personality

Type A personality
Friedman and Rosenman: Type A competitive, time-urgent and hostile.

Type B personality
Relaxed, tolerant, not in a hurry, one thing at a time.

Research into types A and B
Western Collaborative Group Study: Prospective, 70% of Type A men developed CHD over nearly 9 years.

Type C personality
Avoid conflict, excessively nice and suppress emotions.

Research into type C
Dattore *et al.*: Repression of emotions predicted later development of cancer.

Evaluation

Support from research studies
Edigo *et al.*: Stroke sufferers more likely to be Type A – not explained by traditional risk factors.

Contradictory evidence
Ragland and Brand: Type Bs more prone to second heart attack, Type As motivated to change behaviour after first one.

Problems with Type A concept
Type A is a broad personality construct, hostility is a more specific factor (Dembroski *et al.*).

Modification of Type A and Type B
Friedman *et al.*: Type A not coronary proneness, Type B suppresses hostility.

Contradictory Type C evidence
McKenna *et al.*: Many inconsistent results and replication failures.

Hardiness

Hardy people are better at dealing with stress.

Hardiness

Hardiness
Commitment: Throw oneself into activities with gusto.
Challenge: Welcome stressful changes.
Control: Make things happen rather than behave passively.

Research into hardiness
Kobasa: Managers who coped with stress were less ill and scored highly on commitment, challenge and control.

Research into hardiness
Maddi *et al.*: One-third of managers flourished during a major company re-organisation.

Evaluation

Measurement problems
Funk: Hardiness often measured as lack of negative traits (e.g. powerlessness). Recent studies overcome this.

Role of the Three Cs
Control is most important. Hull: Drop challenge altogether.

Indirect effects of hardiness
Contrada: Hardy people have lower blood pressure; better at making lifestyle changes to reduce risk.

Supporting research
Contrada: Hardy males had lower blood pressure after a stressful lab task.

Real-life applications
US military screens applicants for hardiness and provides training (Bartone).

MANAGING AND COPING WITH STRESS

DRUG THERAPY

Drugs aim to treat the physiological symptoms of stress.

BIOFEEDBACK

Benzodiazepines (BZs)
Reduce physiological arousal in the central nervous system.

Mode of action
BZs combine with GABA-A receptors to open chloride channels, inhibiting activity of post-synaptic neuron more than usual.

Beta blockers
Inhibit arousal of the sympathetic nervous system.

Mode of action
Block beta-adrenergic receptors in heart and blood vessels, preventing adrenaline and noradrenaline stimulating receptors.

EVALUATION

Effectiveness of BZs
Baldwin *et al.* review: Not all BZs are effective in treating of anxiety.

Effectiveness of beta blockers
Kelly: Review showed beta blockers treat everyday anxieties such as exam stress.

Side effects
Both drugs have potentially serious side effects; patients might stop taking them.

Symptoms not causes
Drugs treat symptoms of acute anxiety, may do more harm than good.

Dependency
BZs often prescribed for longer than 4 weeks, creates dependency and withdrawal symptoms.

STRESS INOCULATION THERAPY

A cognitive therapy that aims to change how we think about stress.

STRESS INOCULATION THERAPY (SIT)

Conceptualisation phase
Client and therapist identify stressors client faces. Client encouraged to think differently.

Skills acquisition and rehearsal phase
Client learns coping skills, e.g. relaxation, cognitive restructuring, coping self-statements.

Real-life application and follow-through phase
Client applies skills in real life, therapist helps client prepare for setbacks.

EVALUATION

Flexibility
Can be used with variety of clients, individually or in groups, to treat just about any form of stress.

A demanding therapy
Needs commitment; some people drop out; planning to cope with setbacks is built in.

Overcomplicated
Lots of techniques but not all equally useful, control may be key factor.

Research support
Saunders *et al.* meta-analysis: SIT effective in lots of situations with different stressors; did not depend on therapist experience.

Prevention
Useful because it focuses on inoculation against future stressors.

BIOFEEDBACK

Learning to control your ANS.

BIOFEEDBACK

The biofeedback concept
Client connected to machine giving read-out of involuntary physiological responses.

The training procedure
Slowing e.g. heartbeat shown on the read-out and reinforces their behaviour.

Research into biofeedback
Davis: Breast cancer patients using biofeedback had lower cortisol and anxiety levels after eight weeks.

EVALUATION

Research support
Lemaire: Doctors using biofeedback had lower levels of perceived stress than controls.

Outcome measures
Lemaire: But no lasting effect of biofeedback. Success depends on what is measured.

Is feedback necessary?
BART: Biofeedback a useful aid in improving effectiveness of relaxation to treat stress.

Convenience
Biofeedback devices are much more widely available and cheaper.

Individual differences
Not suitable for everyone because the client has to be highly motivated and willing to practise.

GENDER DIFFERENCES IN COPING WITH STRESS

Women might be more emotion-focused.

GENDER DIFFERENCES

Gender-related coping methods
Men use problem-focused methods, e.g. learning practical skills.
Women use emotion-focused methods, e.g. avoidance and distraction.

Research into gender and coping methods
Peterson *et al.*: Infertility stress – men cope by planning, women by accepting blame.

Tend and befriend
Men: Fight or flight. Women: Tend and befriend; offered evolutionary benefits in raising offspring (Luckow).

Oxytocin
Oxytocin linked with lower cortisol levels in females. Effects of oxytocin inhibited by male sex hormones (Taylor *et al.*).

EVALUATION

Explaining gender differences
Role constraint theory: Men and women face different stressors and thus need different ways of coping.

Are emotion and problem-focused strategies different?
Seeking social support can be both. Men and women use both methods depending on the stressor.

Research support for tend and befriend
Tamres: Meta-analysis showed women more likely to seek social support as predicted by tend and befriend.

Evidence against gender differences
Porter and Stone: Gender difference in coping methods disappeared when differences in family- and work-related stressors accounted for.

Retrospective research
De Ridder: Gender differences only exist when participants have to recall coping methods they used.

SOURCES OF STRESS: WORKPLACE STRESS

Overload and control are the issues.

RESEARCH INTO WORKPLACE STRESS

Job-demands control model
Karasek: High workload can make us ill, but risk reduced if we control our work.

Research supporting effects of control
Marmot: Workload did not predict heart disease, but lack of job control did.

Research supporting workload and control
Johansson *et al.*: Sawmill workers with low control and high workload had higher stress hormone levels, illness and absenteeism.

EVALUATION

Job demands-control model is simplistic
Model ignores other work-related stressors and workers' perceptions.

Cultural differences
Job control does not generalise to non-Western collectivist cultures.

Is control always stressful?
Having too much control stressful, if employee has low self-efficacy (Meier *et al.*).

The Whitehall Studies
Pay and conditions confounded with job grade.

The sawmill study
Finishers and cleaners were not randomly allocated to jobs.

MEASURING STRESS

How do we know when someone is stressed?

SELF-REPORT MEASURES OF STRESS

Social Readjustment Rating Scale (SRRS)
Measures adjustment to 43 life changes in terms of LCUs.

Hassles and Uplifts Scale
117 daily hassles: Seven categories rated in terms of severity.
135 daily uplifts: Pleasurable events rated in terms of frequency.

Physiological measures of stress: Skin conductance response (SCR)
ANS arousal creates tiny increases in electrical conductance of the skin caused by sweating.

EVALUATION

Validity issues
Dohrenwend: People interpret items on self-report scales very differently.

Contamination effect
Some items on self-report scales reflect illness rather than predicting it.

Individual differences in SCRs
Stabiles and labiles: Different resting SCRs; respond differently to stimulus.

Global versus specific
Specific types of stressor linked to specific illnesses.

Controllable versus uncontrollable
Stern *et al.*: Only controllable life changes predicted later illness.

THE ROLE OF SOCIAL SUPPORT IN COPING WITH STRESS

Hugs can reduce stress.

THE ROLE OF SOCIAL SUPPORT

Types of social support
Instrumental support: Practical and concrete (e.g. giving money).
Emotional support: A 'shoulder to cry on'.
Esteem support: Helps the person value themselves more highly.

Research into social support
Cohen *et al.*: People with greater perceived social support were less likely to be infected by a cold virus when stressed.

EVALUATION

Supportive research studies
Fawzy *et al.*: Social support predicted improved immune functioning and survival in a group of malignant melanoma patients after six years.

Gender differences
Luckow *et al.* meta-analysis showed women more likely to use social support to cope with stress.

Negative effects of social support
Social support can backfire if imposed by supporter or if type of support inappropriate to relationship.

Cultural influences
Taylor *et al.*: Support in some cultures seen as self-indulgent and imposition on others.

Explaining the benefits
Cohen and Wills, buffering hypothesis – social support blunts effects of stressors, but unhelpful at other times.

Question 1 Outline findings of research into the role of stress and illness. *(4 marks)*

Morticia's answer

The classic study on stress and illness was conducted by Rahe et al. who looked at the relationship between stress and illness in thousands of men in the navy. They filled in the SRRS before they went on a tour of duty and during their 6-month tour of duty kept a record of any visits to the sick bay. This produced a small but significant correlation between life changes and health.

Other research has looked at daily hassles and illness. For example, Kanner et al. used the hassles scale and also the SRRS over a period of 9 months and found positive correlations with psychological problems. This was much stronger for hassles than life changes.

Much of Morticia's account of the Rahe *et al.* study in the first paragraph is focused on *procedure* when the question asks for 'findings'. The correlation point is the only discernible finding.

Morticia only provides a similarly brief reference to the findings.

Luke's answer

Kiecolt-Glaser has conducted research on the relationship between immune functioning and stress. Stress leads to immunosuppression, i.e. stops the immune systems functioning as well. In one study on students they found that during a period of high stress (during exams) the students had lower levels of NK and killer T cells (components of the immune system) than when the students were less stressed (before exams). Lower levels of immune activity mean a person is more likely to be ill.

Research has also looked at stress and cardiovascular disorders. Acute emotional distress was shown to be linked to heart attacks in a study of audience reaction during the World Cup. Incidences of heart attacks in Germany increased by 2.6 times when Germany was playing!

Much more of a clear emphasis on findings in Luke's answer and the description is impressively detailed and accurate too.

Vladimir's answer

There is a lot of research on the relationship between stress and illness which is all correlational. For example, stress has been shown to suppress the immune system, though some research shows it may actually be immunoenhancing, i.e. being stressed may cause the immune system to function better. This seems to be the case for acute stressors rather than long-term ones. For example, in the case of injury, lymphocytes flood into injury sites.

The main issue in Vladimir's answer is a lack of specific studies. The findings presented are quite general whereas particular details might have been better.

Question 2 Janet is considering leaving her teaching job as her anxiety means she often cannot sleep the night before a school day. She is reluctant to take drug treatment but has heard that stress inoculation therapy may help.

Outline and briefly evaluate a stress inoculation therapy that may help reduce Janet's anxiety about teaching. *(4 marks)*

Morticia's answer

There are three steps in stress inoculation therapy (SIT). In the first step Janet would discuss her anxieties with the therapist so they can conceptualise what it is that is causing stress. In the second step Janet would be taught skills that might help her cope with the stress and in the third step she would practise these skills over a longer period. The aim is to provide her with long-term tools that would help her cope in future situations. This contrasts with drug treatments which are only helpful as long as you take them – though it might be good if she could reduce her anxiety for a while because she might gain her confidence back.

The outline of SIT in Morticia's answer is just about sufficiently clear and detailed. The final evaluative/contrasting point is relevant too.

Luke's answer

The aspects of stress inoculation that would help Janet reduce her anxiety would first be to try to understand what aspects of teaching are creating anxiety. The therapist educates the client about the nature of stress and tries to convince the client that the solution lies in reconceptualising the problem as one that they can cope with.

The therapist would then help Janet by selecting skills that would be of particular use for her. For example, learning relaxation skills might help her the night before school so she can sleep better. She could also learn coping self-statements to reduce her anxiety when in difficult situations.

The therapist would offer continued support over time to stop Janet relapsing and going back to old habits. The therapist would consider what problems might crop up and work out solutions in advance.

Luke's description of SIT is very clear and, in fact, rather more than is necessary here.

Unfortunately, Luke seems to have overlooked the second requirement of the question – to 'briefly evaluate'. Thus, his excellent explanation does not count as a high-level answer overall.

Vladimir's answer

Janet may be feeling worried about taking on stress inoculation therapy because it takes a lot of time and effort and she would prefer the quick fix that drugs offer her. Especially because she might just want to sleep better if that is all that is causing her problems. The therapist might reassure her that the time and effort are worth it because she would learn a new way of coping in general, which she could then apply in the future when new stressors occur. Drugs are really only a temporary solution but this would offer long-term help.

The opposite problem for Vladimir. This answer is wholly evaluative. Although well informed there isn't any descriptive content that would satisfy the requirement of the first part of the question.

On this spread we look at some typical student answers to questions. The comments provided indicate what is good and bad in each answer. Learning how to produce effective question answers is a SKILL. Read pages 387–397 for guidance.

Question 3 Describe and evaluate **two** methods of measuring stress. *(16 marks)*

Morticia's answer

There are two main ways of measuring stress. One is to use self-report techniques where people are asked to describe their own stress and the other is to make direct physiological measurements.

There are two well-known self-report scales. One of them is the SRRS (Social Readjustment Rating Scale) devised by medical doctors Holmes and Rahe. They listed 43 important life changes such as divorce, birth of a child and Christmas. Each of these events requires readjustment and that creates stress. To measure how much stress a person is feeling Holmes and Rahe asked people to assign a value to each event using marriage as an arbitrary 500. They then worked out life change units for each event. To calculate stress a person is asked to indicate how many events have been experienced in the last 6 months or year and then a total can be calculated.

The other self-report measure is the Hassles and Uplifts Scale (HSUP) devised by Kanner et al. This lists 117 hassles and 135 uplifts. A person rates each one on a scale of 1 to 3 to indicate severity or frequency. Again a total score is calculated by setting hassles against uplifts.

The main physiological measure is the skin conductance response. When you are stressed by something the sympathetic nervous system is aroused, which results in sweating amongst other symptoms. This sweating enhances how much electricity can be conducted on the skin. To detect this, electrodes are placed on the skin. This is done when a person is not stressed (tonic conductance) or as a kind of baseline and then again when feeling stressed (phasic conductance). This way you can tell when someone is feeling stressed.

Of course, this assumes that a person does sweat when stressed because there are individual differences. Some people are stabiles who do not show much change when they feel stressed and other people are labiles who produce a lot of sweat even at rest.

There have been quite a few criticisms of the self-report scales that mean they may lack validity. For example, one issue is that they don't distinguish between controllable and uncontrollable events/hassles. It may be the uncontrollable events, in particular, that create a feeling of stress for obvious reasons. In other words both self-report measures are global measures – they put altogether lots of different kinds of stressor whereas it may be that particular stressors are associated with particular illnesses so this may not be desirable, such as Type C behaviours being linked to cancer.

(415 words)

A good, clear beginning.

There is precise and detailed description of the first method throughout this second paragraph.

As Morticia introduced these methods using the umbrella term, 'self-report methods' then any number of these are relevant.

In paragraph 4 a physiological measure is described – again, detailed and accurate – but Morticia needs to move on to evaluation soon if this essay is to have some balance.

The final two paragraphs are evaluative. The final paragraph contains sustained, informed commentary but there is not enough of this overall.

It would have been better to replace the material on the HSUP with evaluation in order to improve this extended response.

Vladimir's answer

I am going to focus on two of the main methods used to measure stress, both of which are self-report measures. Most stress research uses the SRRS (Social Readjustment Rating Scale or the HSUP (Hassles and Uplifts Scale) which was developed after the SRRS because the researchers felt that life events are much rarer and don't apply to all people. Also stress is created on a daily basis. Research by Kanner does suggest that hassles are a better predictor of illness.

The SRRS is a checklist of 43 life events or life changes. These events were identified by Holmes and Rahe from studying the medical records of thousands of hospital patients and identifying the events in the patient's lives that happened not long before they became ill. Each event was not equivalent in terms of how stressful it was, for example, death of a spouse is more stressful than being fired at work. They worked out the stressfulness of each event by asking several hundred participants to rate each item in terms of how much readjustment would be needed to adapt to each of these life. As a guide, the raters had to imagine that marriage was an arbitrary 500 units of life change. The scale is then used by asking a person to tick which events they have experienced over a period of usually one year and then the life change units for these vents can be added up.

One problem is that each event may have a different meaning. For example, the death of a spouse may be a much bigger stressor in a happy marriage or a young couple than in an unhappy marriage or older couple, yet it is always given the same score. Another issue is about the relevance of the scale. Younger people without children may not have experienced any of the events on the scale but may have experienced other stressful events.

The HSUP scale was developed by Kanner. He asked colleagues to identify things that were daily hassles from seven categories such as work, health, family and friends and selected over 100 items. To rate stress a person is asked to rate each item in terms of how severe it is using a scale of 1–3. To balance hassles people were also asked about uplifts, which are also rated.

Similar criticisms have been made about this scale as for the SRRS because the items are not relevant to all people. Also there is a contamination effect because some of the items relate to ill health such as 'hospitalisation'. If this is a hassle then it is not surprising that score on this scale correlates positively with illness.

Many other scales have been developed from these two original ones to address some of the issues raised.

(420 words)

A different approach adopted by Vladimir to focus on two self-report methods, but just as legitimate as Morticia's.

A very detailed account is given of SRRS. Given the description-evaluation balance a more concise descriptive summary would have been more appropriate, and like Morticia's answer above, may upset the balance of the answer.

Paragraph 3 does contain two clear evaluation points that are accurate and relevant.

A more focused description of the HSUP scale (perhaps because Vladimir is running out of time) but possibly better for it.

Again, relevant evaluation at the end but this answer – like the one before it – relies too heavily on description when a little more evaluation would have been ideal.

Multiple-Choice Questions

The physiology of stress

1. A feature of the resistance stage of the GAS is . . .
- (a) Detection of a stressor by the hypothalamus.
- (b) Diseases of adaptation.
- (c) Depletion of the body's energy resources.
- (d) Activation of the fight or flight response.

2. The sympathomedullary pathway involves . . .
- (a) Stimulation of the anterior pituitary.
- (b) Release of ACTH.
- (c) Release of CRF.
- (d) Release of adrenaline.

3. The hypothalamic-pituitary-adrenal system . . .
- (a) Involves release of cortisol.
- (b) Is involved in acute stress.
- (c) Releases adrenaline into the bloodstream.
- (d) Involves activation of the ANS by the hypothalamus.

4. The General Adaptation Syndrome may *not* be a general response because . . .
- (a) The alarm reaction is always followed by resistance.
- (b) The resistance stage uses a lot of the body's energy.
- (c) It takes into account psychological factors.
- (d) The body responds in specific ways to specific stressors.

The role of stress in illness

1. An example of a direct effect of stress on the immune system is . . .
- (a) People smoke and drink more.
- (b) Cortisol suppresses lymphocyte production.
- (c) We exercise less.
- (d) Sleep patterns are disturbed.

2. Kiecolt-Glaser *et al.* (1984) found that exam stress . . .
- (a) Decreased activity of NK cells.
- (b) Was less damaging in students experiencing other stressors.
- (c) Had an indirect effect on the immune system.
- (d) Had less effect on students who were lonely.

3. The best example of an acute stressor linked to cardiovascular disorder is . . .
- (a) Having too much to do at work.
- (b) Changes in your relationships.
- (c) Caring for an ill person.
- (d) Sudden emotional arousal.

4. Darbhar's (2008) study showed that stress can have immunoenhancing effects because . . .

- (a) Severe stress is not as damaging as once thought.
- (b) Lymphocytes do not respond to mild stressors.
- (c) Acute and chronic stressors have similar effects.
- (d) A mild stressor activates the immune system without causing damage.

Sources of stress: Life changes

1. A life change is . . .
- (a) One of those little things that just makes you stressed.
- (b) Something that effects everyone in the same way.
- (c) A relatively infrequent event.
- (d) Generally good for your health.

2. Most research has found that . . .
- (a) Life changes are strong predictors of illnesses.
- (b) A high life change unit score is associated with illness.
- (c) Positive life changes are just as stressful as negative ones.
- (d) Controllable life changes are more stressful.

3. Rahe *et al.* (1970) found . . .
- (a) A negative correlation between LCU and illness scores.
- (b) Only negative life changes were associated with illness.
- (c) A weak but significant correlation between LCU and illness scores.
- (d) LCUs are not useful predictors of illness.

4. The life changes approach does *not* take into account that . . .
- (a) Some life changes require more adjustment than others.
- (b) Positive and negative life changes are both stressful.
- (c) Most people are capable of coping with life changes.
- (d) People perceive stressors differently.

Sources of stress: Daily hassles

1. Daily hassles are stressful because their effects are . . .
- (a) Unpredictable.
- (b) Cumulative.
- (c) Similar to life changes.
- (d) Controllable.

2. Subjectively assessing the potential threat to our health of a hassle is an example of . . .
- (a) Primary appraisal.
- (b) Secondary appraisal.
- (c) A distal source of stress.
- (d) The interaction between life changes and daily hassles.

3. The amplification hypothesis states that . . .
- (a) Daily hassles are more likely to make us ill when there are a lot of them at the same time.
- (b) Stress occurs when we believe we cannot cope with hassles.
- (c) Life changes make the effects of daily hassles seem worse.
- (d) A hassle can be the 'last straw' that pushes us over the edge.

4. The main problem with retrospective research is . . .
- (a) People overestimate how many hassles they experience.
- (b) It relies on remembering the hassles from the past.
- (c) It is time-consuming and costly.
- (d) Many people drop out early.

Sources of stress: Workplace stress

1. The most accurate statement of the job demands-control model is . . .
- (a) Lack of job control is stressful.
- (b) Having too much control in a job is worse than having none.
- (c) Having job control buffers against the effects of workload.
- (d) The stress of having too much work causes illness.

2. In the Whitehall Studies . . .
- (a) Workload was a significant predictor of illness.
- (b) Top grade civil servants were less likely to become ill.
- (c) Lack of job control was correlated with illness.
- (d) Competitive civil servants were more likely to become ill.

3. The Swedish sawmill study found that . . .
- (a) Cleaners had higher hormone levels than finishers before they got to work.
- (b) Both lack of control and high workload were associated with illness and absenteeism.
- (c) The finishers' stress hormone levels were higher than the cleaners' at the start of the day but gradually decreased.
- (d) Finishers and cleaners had similar levels of illness.

4. Collectivist and individualist cultures differ because . . .
- (a) Workload is viewed as less stressful in collectivist cultures.
- (b) Collectivist cultures emphasise personal rights.
- (c) Job control is seen as desirable in individualist cultures.
- (d) Workplace stress is not considered important in collectivist cultures.

Measuring stress

1. A life change unit measures . . .
- (a) How much stress is caused by the little annoyances of the day.
- (b) The small pleasures of everyday life.
- (c) Control over stressful events.
- (d) How much adjustment is needed to adapt to change.

2. The Hassles Scale measures . . .
- (a) The frequency of life events.
- (b) The severity of daily hassles.
- (c) How much control we have over daily hassles.
- (d) Our physiological responses to daily hassles.

3. The two types of skin conductance response are . . .
- (a) Resting and active.
- (b) Tonic and phasic.
- (c) Resting and phasic.
- (d) Active and phasic.

4. The problem of people interpreting life events and hassles differently is known as . . .
- (a) The contamination effect.
- (b) Stabiles versus labiles.
- (c) Intracategory variability.
- (d) The conductance effect.

Individual differences in stress: Personality type

1. A common trait of Type A people is . . .
- (a) Tolerance.
- (b) Ambition.
- (c) Conflict avoidance.
- (d) Patience.

2. A finding of the Western Collaborative Group Study was . . .
- (a) There were twice as many Type B people with CHD as Type A.
- (b) 70% of CHD sufferers were Type A.
- (c) Type A personality was not a risk factor for CHD.
- (d) Type B people had higher levels of adrenaline.

3. Type C may be linked with cancer because . . .
- (a) Type C people suppress their emotions.
- (b) Cancer is more common in people who are impatient.
- (c) Type C people are less likely to change lifestyle to avoid illness.
- (d) Type C people are hostile.

4. The component of Type A most associated with CHD is . . .
- (a) Competitiveness.
- (b) Time-urgency.
- (c) Hostility.
- (d) Emotional suppression.

Individual differences in stress: Hardiness

1. Commitment is best described as . . .

(a) Welcoming change as an opportunity not a threat.

(b) Actively influencing your environment.

(c) Getting involved with life and squeezing every drop out of it.

(d) Learning something new from stressful situations.

2. Kobasa found that hardy managers . . .

(a) Scored lower on the three Cs.

(b) Were under less pressure than other managers.

(c) Took less time off work ill.

(d) Weren't bothered about losing their jobs.

3. According to some researchers, which component(s) of hardiness should be abandoned?

(a) Commitment.

(b) Challenge and control.

(c) Commitment and control.

(d) Challenge.

4. Hardiness could benefit health indirectly because . . .

(a) It increases physiological stress on the body.

(b) Hardy people are more likely to look after themselves.

(c) Hardy people avoid stressful situations.

(d) Being hardy makes you better at ignoring stressors.

Managing and coping with stress: Drug therapy

1. Benzodiazepines reduce anxiety by . . .

(a) Enhancing the activity of GABA.

(b) Shutting down GABA-A receptors in the CNS.

(c) Inhibiting the effects of adrenaline and noradrenaline.

(d) Blocking chloride ions at the synapses.

2. Beta blockers help people with anxiety because they . . .

(a) Act directly on the brain and cause sedation.

(b) Help them perceive stressors in a different way.

(c) Reduce physiological symptoms like racing heartbeat.

(d) Increase their resistance to stressors.

3. Benzodiazepines are beneficial in reducing anxiety because they . . .

(a) Have no side effects.

(b) Are more convenient than beta blockers.

(c) Do not create dependency.

(d) Are better than placebos.

4. Side effects are a problem of drug therapy because . . .

(a) If they get too bad, patients stop taking their medication.

(b) People can become dependent on their drugs.

(c) It means the drugs aren't very effective at treating anxiety.

(d) They are usually completely unpredictable.

Managing and coping with stress: Stress inoculation therapy

1. The three phases of stress inoculation therapy are . . .

(a) Conceptualisation, relaxation, follow-up.

(b) Conceptualisation, practice, transfer.

(c) Conceptualisation, skills acquisition, real-life application.

(d) Conceptualisation, learning, restructuring.

2. A feature of the conceptualisation phase of SIT is . . .

(a) Client learns techniques for coping with stress.

(b) Client learns to overcome stressors by thinking about them differently.

(c) Therapist gives the client opportunities to practise their coping skills.

(d) Client prepares to accept setbacks.

3. SIT is useful in managing stress because . . .

(a) We just have to take control of stressful situations.

(b) Sometimes the only thing we can change is ourselves.

(c) We want an easy solution.

(d) The therapist tells us what to do.

4. SIT is flexible because . . .

(a) It can be adapted to suit individuals.

(b) It even uses drugs to reduce stress.

(c) The client doesn't have to put a lot of effort into it to get results.

(d) Everybody benefits from it.

Managing and coping with stress: Biofeedback

1. Biofeedback works by . . .

(a) Reducing the amount of stress people experience.

(b) Changing the way that people think about stressors.

(c) Providing information about involuntary functions.

(d) Helping us avoid stressful situations.

2. An important step in biofeedback training is to . . .

(a) Accept stressors as challenges rather than threats.

(b) Transfer control over bodily responses to everyday life.

(c) Collaborate with the therapist to identify stressful situations.

(d) Become aware of how you think about stress.

3. The effectiveness of biofeedback depends on . . .

(a) The gender of the therapist.

(b) The patient's reaction to side effects.

(c) How you measure the outcome of treatment.

(d) The cost of the equipment.

4. Biofeedback is . . .

(a) More effective than any other method of managing stress.

(b) More convenient than other physical methods.

(c) Not effective in improving someone's psychological state.

(d) A useful way to improve the effectiveness of relaxation.

Gender differences in coping with stress

1. The best example of problem-focused coping is . . .

(a) Throwing yourself into work to distract yourself.

(b) Telling yourself everything's going to be OK.

(c) Telling a friend all your troubles.

(d) Checking websites to find out how to handle stress better.

2. An example of tending and befriending is . . .

(a) Ringing a friend for a chat.

(b) Having an argument.

(c) Drowning your sorrows.

(d) Running away very fast.

3. Oxytocin . . .

(a) Reduces the stress response in males more than in females.

(b) Is inhibited by female sex hormones.

(c) Promotes social bonding.

(d) Increases levels of cortisol in the bloodstream.

4. Women generally . . .

(a) Are more likely to seek social support than men.

(b) Use problem-focused coping more than men.

(c) Have a stronger physiological response than men.

(d) Are not as good at coping with stress than men.

The role of social support in coping with stress

1. An example of esteem support is . . .

(a) Answering the phone when a friend calls you at 3 a.m.

(b) Telling someone they're really good at something.

(c) Insisting your friend goes out to a party with you.

(d) Paying for your friend to go on holiday with you.

2. What do the three types of social support have in common?

(a) They all cost money.

(b) They can all be given without the supporter being present.

(c) They involve strong emotions.

(d) They all involve practical help.

3. One study showed that a good way of communicating social support is through . . .

(a) Saying 'pull your socks up'.

(b) Hugs.

(c) Kisses.

(d) Spending a lot of money.

4. Social support can backfire because . . .

(a) People don't know what's good for them.

(b) Most of us don't mind others asking personal questions.

(c) It isn't always welcome.

(d) Experts don't always know best.

MCQ answers

The physiology of stress   1c, 2d, 3a, 4d
The role of stress in illness   1b, 2a, 3d, 4d
Sources of stress: Life changes   1c, 2b, 3c, 4d
Sources of stress: Daily hassles   1b, 2a, 3c, 4b
Sources of stress: Workplace stress   1c, 2c, 3b, 4c
Measuring stress   1d, 2b, 4c
Individual differences in stress: Personality type   1b, 2b, 3a, 4c
Individual differences in stress: Hardiness   1c, 2c, 3d, 4b
Managing and coping with stress: Drug therapy   1a, 2c, 3d, 4a
Managing and coping with stress: Stress inoculation therapy   1c, 1b, 3b, 4a
Managing and coping with stress: Biofeedback   1c, 2b, 3c, 4d
Gender differences in coping with stress   1d, 2a, 3c, 4a
The role of social support in coping with stress   1b, 2b, 3b, 4c

CHAPTER 11
AGGRESSION

Cold-blooded and hot-blooded aggression.
What are the differences?
How can we explain them?

Chapter contents

NEURAL AND HORMONAL MECHANISMS IN AGGRESSION

Neural and hormonal mechanisms in aggression, including the roles of the limbic system, serotonin and testosterone.

Aggression is one of the most critical social problems facing the world today, and psychologists are keen to understand its causes. But what do we mean by aggression? This question has created endless controversy, but one way of understanding it is in terms of two types of behaviour. What psychologists call *proactive aggression* is 'cold-blooded', a planned method of getting what you want. *Reactive aggression* is commonly understood as 'hot-blooded'; it is angry and impulsive, and accompanied by physiological arousal. It is this type of aggression that psychologists have been most interested in, because it is probably responsible for a greater proportion of social problems. The spreads in this chapter range across a wide selection of explanations. On this one, we begin to consider the biological underpinnings of such behaviour.

KEY TERMS

Limbic system – Subcortical structures in the brain (including the hypothalamus and amygdala) thought to be closely involved in regulating emotional behaviour including aggression.

Serotonin – A neurotransmitter with widespread inhibitory effects throughout the brain. It has a key role in aggressive behaviour.

Testosterone – A hormone from the androgen group that is produced mainly in the male testes (and in smaller amounts in the female ovaries). Associated with aggressiveness.

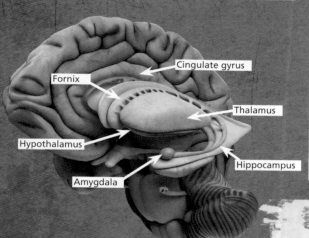

The limbic system is made up of several subcortical structures, of which the amygdala is most closely associated with aggression.

Neural mechanisms in aggression

The limbic system

Buried deep inside the brain is a network of structures collectively labelled the **limbic system**. The first attempt to link limbic structures to emotional behaviours such as aggression was by James Papez (1937), and later revised by Paul Maclean (1952). They identified the limbic system as comprising the cingulate gyrus, septal area, **hypothalamus**, fornix, **amygdala** and parts of the **hippocampus** and the **thalamus** (see diagram below). The most important structure by far is the amygdala. This has a key role in humans and nonhuman animals in how an organism assesses and responds to environmental threats and challenges. The reactivity of the amygdala in humans has proven to be an important predictor of aggressive behaviour.

Katarina Gospic *et al.* (2011) used a well-established laboratory method of assessing aggressive behaviour called the *Ultimatum Game*. This features two players. The Proposer offers to split money in a certain way with the Responder. If the Responder accepts, the money is split as proposed. But if the Responder rejects the offer, both receive nothing. Participants in this study played as Responders while having their brains scanned by **fMRI**, which highlights activity in different areas of the brain. The researchers found that when Responders rejected unfair offers (an aggressive reaction to a social provocation), scans revealed a fast and heightened response by the amygdala. They also found that a **benzodiazepine** drug (which reduces arousal of the **autonomic nervous system**) taken before the game had two effects on responses to unfair offers. It halved the number of rejections (i.e. reduced aggression) and decreased the activity of the amygdala. This is strong evidence of an association between reactive aggression and amygdala activity.

Serotonin

Serotonin is a **neurotransmitter** involved in communication of impulses between **neurons**. It has widespread inhibitory effects on the brain; it slows down and dampens neuronal activity. Normal levels of serotonin in the *orbitofrontal cortex* are linked with reduced firing of neurons, and this is associated with a greater degree of behavioural self-control. Decreased serotonin may well disturb this mechanism, reducing self-control and leading to an increase in impulsive behaviour including aggression (Denson *et al.* 2012).

Matti Virkkunen *et al.* (1994) compared levels of a serotonin breakdown product (a **metabolite** called 5-HIAA) in the cerebrospinal fluid of violent impulsive and violent non-impulsive offenders. The levels were **significantly** lower in the impulsive offenders, and they also suffered from more sleep irregularities. This is significant because serotonin regulates sleep patterns. Disturbance of this pattern strongly implies some disruption of serotonin functioning, further supporting the role of serotonin in reactive aggression.

Hormonal mechanisms in aggression

Testosterone

It is a reliable observation that males are generally more aggressive than females. Attention has therefore focused on the male sex hormone **testosterone**, an androgen responsible for the development of masculine features. It also has a role in regulating social behaviour via its influence on certain areas of the brain implicated in aggression. Animal studies (e.g. Giammanco *et al.* 2005) have demonstrated **experimental** increases in testosterone are related to greater aggressive behaviour in several species (and the converse is true, with decreases leading to reductions in aggression in castration studies).

Some evidence for a similar association in humans comes from studies of prison populations, for example violent offenders. Mairead Dolan *et al.* (2001) found a **positive correlation** between testosterone levels and aggressive behaviours in a sample of 60 male offenders in UK maximum security hospitals. These men mostly suffered from personality disorders (such as **psychopathy**) and had histories of impulsively violent behaviour.

Apply it   Concepts: Flora the bully

Flora is an eight-year-old girl whose parents have been called in to her primary school once again to see the headteacher. On previous occasions it was because Flora had been bullying other children, usually verbally but sometimes physically as well. This time she is in trouble because she has been biting other children, one so badly she had to have hospital treatment. Flora doesn't seem to be able to control herself; even when she's not being aggressive she sometimes behaves in dangerous ways. Only last week she tried to climb onto the school roof.

Question

Explain Flora's aggressive behaviour in terms of neural mechanisms involving the limbic system and serotonin.

Evaluation

Role of other brain structures

Recent studies indicate that the amygdala does not operate in isolation in determining aggression. It appears to function in tandem with the orbitofrontal cortex (OFC), which is not part of the limbic system. The OFC is thought to be involved in self-control, impulse regulation and inhibition of aggressive behaviour. According to Emil Coccaro *et al.* (2007), in patients with psychiatric disorders that prominently feature aggression, activity in the OFC is reduced, disrupting its impulsive-control function and thus leading to increased aggression.

Combined with the findings of Gospic *et al.* (2011) outlined on the facing page, this indicates that the regulation of aggression is highly complex and involves at least three neural structures in the brain: the amygdala, the OFC and the connection between the two.

Effects of drugs on serotonin

Drugs that increase serotonin activity also reduce levels of aggressive behaviour. Mitchell Berman *et al.* (2009) gave their participants either a **placebo** or a dose of *paroxetine*, a drug which enhances serotonin activity. Participants then took part in a **laboratory**-based game in which electric shocks of varying intensity were given and received in response to provocation. The *paroxetine* participants consistently gave fewer and less intense shocks than those in the placebo group. However, this was only true of the participants who had a prior history of aggressive behaviour.

Nevertheless this study is useful evidence of a link between serotonin function and aggression that goes far beyond the usual correlational findings.

Evaluation

Explaining the role of testosterone

Allan Mazur (1985) formulated the *biosocial model of status* (BMoS) to explain the link between testosterone and aggression in humans. Testosterone levels change rapidly during the course of the day, especially in response to social interactions related to status (e.g. competition). A change in testosterone levels following a loss of status, for example, should affect post-competition aggression.

Pranjal Mehta and Robert Josephs (2006) measured changes in their male participants' testosterone levels before and after a competitive game (which they all lost). Once the second sample was taken, the participants were given a choice. They could either challenge their victorious opponent to another competition (aggressive) or complete an unrelated task (non-aggressive). Of the losers whose testosterone levels rose after their loss, 73% rechallenged. But of the losers whose testosterone dropped, only 22% rechallenged. Therefore, after a loss of status, individuals behaved aggressively (choosing to rechallenge) only after an increase in testosterone levels. These findings confirm Mazur's BMoS, increasing its **validity** as a plausible explanation of how testosterone may exert its effects on aggression.

Other hormones

Evidence of the link between testosterone and aggression in humans is mixed. Justin Carre and Pranjal Mehta's (2011) *dual-hormone hypothesis* attempts to explain why. They claim that high levels of testosterone lead to aggressive behaviour only when levels of **cortisol** are low. When cortisol is high, testosterone's influence on aggression is blocked. Cortisol is a glucocorticoid hormone that plays a central role in the stress response. A study by Arne Popma *et al.* (2007) of adolescent males confirmed this hypothesis in relation to direct physical aggression. The combined activity of testosterone and cortisol may be a better predictor of human aggression than either hormone alone.

Evaluation eXtra

Issues of cause and effect

Most research into both neural and hormonal influences on aggression is **correlational**. There are good **ethical** reasons for this, because opportunities to experimentally manipulate brain structures and **hormones** are very limited. But when two variables are correlated, it is impossible to establish which one is the cause of the other, or if a third variable is involved.

Consider: *Explain how this issue could affect our understanding of the links between (a) limbic activity and aggression and (b) hormone levels and aggression.*

Physical bullying as a form of aggression could well be caused by the activity of serotonin in the brain.

Apply it — Concepts: Angry young man

Benedict is a young man of 16 who has been involved in antisocial behaviour since he was at primary school. He seems to be getting worse. He easily gets into fights, even with men who are much bigger than him. He reacts very angrily when he thinks people are looking at him or talking about him. His parents are at their wits' end because he has finally been arrested by the police for seriously assaulting an elderly man.

Question

Use what you know about the role of testosterone in aggression to explain Benedict's behaviour.

Apply it — Methods: Testing testosterone

A team of psychologists wanted to investigate hormonal factors that might influence aggressive behaviour. They decided to compare testosterone levels in two groups of prisoners. One group consisted of men who had committed crimes involving direct physical assault. The other group was made up of men who had committed fraud. The psychologists measured testosterone levels of each prisoner by taking saliva samples.

Questions

1. Identify the operationalised **independent variable** and **dependent variable**. (*1 mark + 1 mark*)
2. Name the **experimental design** used in this study. (*1 mark*)
3. Explain *one* strength and *one* weakness of this design. (*2 marks + 2 marks*)
4. Explain what is meant by the term **validity**. (*2 marks*) (See page 68)
5. Explain why this experiment might be lacking in validity. (*3 marks*)

CHECK IT

1. Outline the roles of the limbic system **and** serotonin in aggression. [6 marks]
2. Outline **one** research study into the role of neural **or** hormonal mechanisms in aggression. [6 marks]
3. Discuss the role of neural **and/or** hormonal mechanisms in aggression. [16 marks]

THE SPECIFICATION SAYS...

Genetic factors in aggression, including the MAOA gene.

To understand the role of genetic factors in aggression, we have to try and disentangle these influences from those of the environment. Psychologists have several methods for doing this. These include twin studies, adoption studies and techniques for investigating the important role of one particular gene, the MAOA gene.

KEY TERMS

Genetic factors – Genes consist of DNA strands. DNA produces 'instructions' for general physical features of an organism (such as eye colour, height) and also specific physical features (such as neurotransmitter levels and size of brain structures). These may impact on psychological features (such as intelligence and mental disorder). Genes are transmitted from parents to offspring, i.e. inherited.

MAOA gene – The gene responsible for the activity of the enzyme monoamine oxidase in the brain. The low-activity variant of the gene is closely associated with aggressive behaviour.

Identical twins – perfect for studying the contributions of genetic and environmental factors to aggressive behaviour.

STUDY TIP

Biological-related topics like this one are challenging for most students. Getting your head around the specialist technical terms like monoamine oxidase A gene can be a struggle, but it's worth it. So by all means use initials (e.g. MAOA or 5-HIAA from the previous spread). Remember that these terms are just words for you to learn, like lots of other words in all A level subjects. The glossary of terms in the back of this book should help you hugely in this.

Genetic factors in aggression

Twin studies

Several **twin studies** have suggested that heritability (i.e. **genetic factors**) accounts for about 50% of the variance in aggressive behaviour. For example, Emil Coccaro *et al.* (1997) studied adult male **monozygotic** (MZ) and **dizygotic** (DZ) twins. Because MZ twins share 100% of their genes but DZ twins share only 50% (on average), we would expect to find greater similarities in aggressive behaviour between MZ twins if aggression is mostly influenced by genetic factors. This is because both MZ and DZ twins are raised together in the same environment, but MZ twins have a greater degree of genetic similarity than DZs. For aggressive behaviour defined as direct physical assault, the researchers found **concordance rates** of 50% for MZ twins and 19% for DZs. The corresponding figures for verbal aggression were 28% (MZs) and 7% (DZs).

Adoption studies

Similarities in aggressive behaviour between an adopted child and their biological parents suggest that genetic influences are operating. Similarities with the adopted parents suggest that environmental influences are operating.

Soo Rhee and Irwin Waldman (2002) carried out a **meta-analysis** of **adoption studies** of direct aggression and antisocial behaviour, a prominent feature of which is aggressive behaviour. They found that genetic influences accounted for 41% of the variance in aggression, more or less in line with findings from twin studies.

The MAOA gene

Monoamine oxidase A (MAOA) is an enzyme. Its role is to 'mop up' **neurotransmitters** in the brain after a nerve impulse has been transmitted from one neuron to another. It does this by breaking down the neurotransmitter – especially **serotonin** – into constituent chemicals to be recycled or excreted (a process called catabolism). The production of this enzyme is determined by the **MAOA gene**. A dysfunction in the operation of this gene may lead to abnormal activity of the MAOA enzyme, which in turn affects levels of serotonin in the brain.

One variant of the MAOA gene (nicknamed the 'warrior gene') leads to low MAOA activity in areas of the brain, and has been associated with various forms of aggressive behaviour. For example, Han Brunner *et al.* (1993) studied 28 male members of a large Dutch family who were repeatedly involved in impulsively aggressive violent criminal behaviours such as rape, attempted murder and physical assault. The researchers found that these men had abnormally low levels of MAOA in their brains and the low-activity version of the MAOA gene.

Gregory Stuart *et al.* (2014) studied 97 men who, because they had been involved in inflicting intimate partner violence (IPV), were part of a batterer treatment programme. Men with the low-activity MAOA gene were found to be the most violent perpetrators of IPV. They engaged in the highest levels of physical and psychological aggression and inflicted the worst injuries on their partners.

Gene-environment (GxE) interactions

Genes are crucial influences on aggressive behaviour but they do not function in isolation. It appears to be the case that low MAOA gene activity is only related to adult aggression when combined with early traumatic life events.

For example, Giovanni Frazzetto *et al.* (2007) found an association between higher levels of antisocial aggression and the low-activity MAOA gene variant in adult males, as expected. But this was only the case in those who had experienced significant trauma (such as sexual or physical abuse) during the first 15 years of life. Those who had not experienced such childhood trauma did not have particularly high levels of aggression as adults, even if they possessed the low-activity MAOA variant. This is strong evidence of a gene-environment interaction (sometimes described as **diathesis-stress**).

Apply it   Concepts: Barney's aggressive kids

Barney has three children in their teens, and all of them seem to behave quite aggressively. They have all been in trouble at school for getting into fights. They take after their mother, who even has a criminal record for assault. Barney's father was also a very aggressive person who even spent some time in prison for seriously assaulting a teacher. Barney's worried that aggression runs in families and is concerned how his grandchildren – if he ever has any – will turn out.

Question

Using your knowledge of genetic factors in aggression, explain how Barney is right to be concerned.

Evaluation

Isolating genetic factors

It has proven remarkably challenging to establish how influential genes are in aggressive behaviour. One major reason for this is the difficulty researchers have in separating genetic and environmental factors, as we saw when we looked at GxE interactions (on the facing page). An individual may possess a gene associated with aggression, but that behaviour is only expressed if the environmental conditions are favourable. For example, Rose McDermott *et al.* (2009) showed that participants with the low-activity MAOA gene behaved aggressively in a **laboratory**-based money-allocation game, but only when they were provoked. Otherwise, they were no more or less aggressive than other participants.

Multiple genetic influences

The sizes of genetic effects are statistically significant but they are also small. This means there are probably other genes involved in aggression. In the study by Stuart *et al.* (see facing page), intimate partner violence (IPV) in men was associated not just with the low-activity form of the MAOA gene but also with the **serotonin** transporter gene (5-HTT), another gene that influences serotonin activity in the brain. It was the combination of the two genes that was most closely linked with IPV.

The hunt for other genes is currently a very active research area. Evangelos Vassos *et al.* (2014), in a **meta-analysis**, could find no evidence of an association between any single gene and aggression. Their explanation for this surprising result is that even several genes are unlikely to fully explain a behaviour as multifaceted as aggression. In fact, they calculate that hundreds or thousands of genes interact in complex ways to determine aggressive behaviour, casting doubt over any search for single candidate genes.

Measuring aggression

Methods of measuring aggression differ significantly between studies, and include **self-reports**, parent and teacher reports, and direct **observations**. In Rhee and Waldman's (see facing page) meta-analysis of 51 twin and adoption studies, genetic factors had a greater influence on aggression in studies using self-reports rather than parent or teacher reports.

If research findings vary depending upon how aggression is measured, then it becomes very difficult to draw valid conclusions about the role of genetic factors (or other factors for that matter).

Evaluation eXtra

Research support for role of MAOA gene

If the low-activity variant of the MAOA gene is associated with greater aggression, is the converse also true? Are people with the high-activity variant more prosocial and less aggressive? Vanessa Mertins *et al.* (2011) studied participants with low-activity and high-activity variants of the MAOA gene in a money-distributing game. Participants had to make decisions about whether or not to contribute money for the good of the group. The researchers found that males with the high-activity variant were more co-operative and made fewer aggressive moves than the low-activity participants.

Consider: *What does this tell us about the role of the MAOA gene in aggression? Does it increase the validity of the genetic explanation? Explain your answer.*

Non-human animal studies

The **hypothesis** that the MAOA gene might play a role in human aggression originated in research with mice. Genetic deletion techniques allow researchers to 'knockout' single genes, an experimental manipulation that lets them observe subsequent effects on aggression. For example, Sean Godar *et al.* (2014) showed that MAOA knockout mice have **significantly** increased brain serotonin levels and are hyperaggressive. Furthermore, when serotonin was blocked by the drug *fluoxetine*, the mice reverted to their non-aggressive behaviour.

Consider: *What do you think is the significance of the drug-related finding in this study?*

Aggression is more likely to develop when a genetic predisposition interacts with 'suitable' conditions, such as a traumatic family environment

Apply it

Concepts: Ashley and her twin

Ashley and Marina are identical twins in their late teens. They grew up doing everything together. They had the same friends, went to the same places, wore similar clothes. Even their parents sometimes had trouble telling them apart. Everyone who met them commented on how polite, friendly and happy they both were. But a few of years ago, Marina was involved in a serious car accident. The physical scars are healing, but she seems like a different person. She is much more irritable, and quite aggressive, even sometimes physically so. She's very different from her twin sister these days.

Question

Use your knowledge of the role of genetic factors and GxE interactions to explain why Marina's behaviour has changed.

Apply it

Methods: Ultimatum time

A researcher investigating the genetics of aggression divided a sample of participants into two groups: those with the low-activity variant of the MAOA gene, and those with the high-activity variant. Each participant played as the Responder in the *Ultimatum Game*, in which a Proposer suggested how £20 should be split between them. Half of the high-activity and half of the low-activity participants were made a fair offer (£10 each) and the other half were made an unfair offer (only £5 for them). The Responders could reject or accept the offer. The researcher defined an unfair offer as a provocation, and defined a rejection as an aggressive act. The results of the study are shown below.

	Low-activity gene	High-activity gene
Fair offer (unprovoked)	9	12
Unfair offer (provoked)	16	7

Questions

1. With reference to these figures, outline what the findings of the study seem to show. (*2 marks*)
2. Identify an appropriate **statistical test** the researcher could use to analyse the data. (*1 mark*) (See page 70)
3. Give *two* reasons why this would be an appropriate test to use. (*2 marks*)
4. Draw a suitable graph to represent these data. Identify the type of graph you have drawn. (*3 marks + 1 mark*)

CHECK IT

1. Outline the role of genetic factors in aggression. *[6 marks]*
2. Outline **one** research study into genetic factors in aggression. Include details of what the researcher(s) did and what they found. *[4 marks]*
3. Explain the role of the MAOA gene as a genetic factor in aggression. *[4 marks]*
4. Discuss the role of genetic factors in aggression. *[16 marks]*

The ethological explanation of aggression

> The ethological explanation of aggression, including reference to innate releasing mechanisms and fixed action patterns.

Ethology is the study of animal behaviour in natural settings. Konrad Lorenz (1966), the founder of ethology, defined aggression as '... *the fighting instinct in beast and man which is directed against members of the same species*'. This definition reveals two key elements of the ethological approach:

Aggression is an instinct. It occurs in all members of a species without the need for learning; it is innate and mostly genetically determined.

Ethologists study aggression in non-human animals and extrapolate their findings to humans because we are all subject to the same forces of natural selection (Darwin, 1859).

KEY TERMS

Ethological explanation – An explanation that seeks to understand the innate behaviour of animals (including humans) by studying them in their natural environments.

Innate releasing mechanism (IRM) – A biological structure or process (e.g. in the brain) which is activated by an external stimulus that in turn triggers a fixed action pattern.

Fixed action pattern – A sequence of stereotyped pre-programmed behaviours triggered by an innate releasing mechanism.

Tinbergen's stickleback models. A realistically shaped model (top) did not provoke aggressive behaviour because it lacked a red underbelly. All the other models did, despite their unstickleback-like shapes.

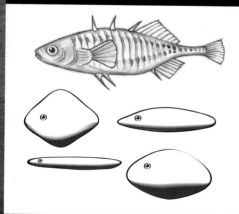

The ethological explanation of aggression

Adaptive functions of aggression

Ethological explanations suggest that the main function of aggression is **adaptive**. That is, aggression is beneficial to survival because a 'defeated' animal is rarely killed (see below), but rather is forced to establish territory elsewhere. This means that members of a species spread out over a wider area and have to discover resources in a different place, which reduces competition pressure and the possibility of starvation.

Another adaptive function of aggression is to establish dominance hierarchies. Male chimpanzees use aggression to climb their troop's social hierarchy. Their dominance gives them special status (for example, mating rights over females). This happens in humans too. Gregory Pettit *et al.* (1988) studied play groups of young human children and observed how aggression played an important role in the development of some children's dominance over others. This would be adaptive (and thus **naturally selected**) because dominance over others brings benefits such as the power to get your own way and access to resources.

Ritualistic aggression

A ritual is a series of behaviours carried out in a set order. One of Lorenz's intriguing early observations of fights between animals of the same species was how little actual physical damage was done. Most aggressive encounters consisted mainly of a period of ritualistic signalling (e.g. displaying claws and teeth, facial expressions of threat) and rarely reached the point of becoming physical.

Furthermore, Lorenz pointed out that intra-species aggressive confrontations end with ritual appeasement displays. These indicate acceptance of defeat and inhibit aggressive behaviour in the victor, preventing any damage to the loser. For instance, at the end of an aggressive confrontation a wolf will expose its neck to the victor, deliberately making itself vulnerable to a single bite to its jugular vein. This is adaptive because if every aggressive encounter ended with the death of one of the combatants, that could threaten the existence of the species.

Innate releasing mechanisms and fixed action patterns

An **innate releasing mechanism** (IRM) is a built-in physiological process or structure, for instance a network of **neurons** (a circuit) in the brain. An environmental stimulus (such as a certain facial expression) triggers the IRM which then 'releases' a specific sequence of behaviours. This behavioural sequence is called a **fixed action pattern** (FAP). According to Stephen Lea (1984), FAPs have six main features. They are:

- Stereotyped, or relatively unchanging sequences of behaviours.
- Universal, because the same behaviour is found in every individual of a species.
- Unaffected by learning, the same for every individual regardless of experience.
- 'Ballistic', once the behaviour is triggered it follows an inevitable course and cannot be altered before it is completed.
- Single-purpose, the behaviour only occurs in a specific situation and not in any other.
- A response to an identifiable specific sign stimulus (or, if it involves communication between members of the same species, it is known as a *releaser*).

Key study: Research into IRMs and FAPs

Procedures Male sticklebacks are highly territorial during the spring mating season, when they also develop a red spot on their underbelly. If another male enters their territory, a sequence of highly-stereotyped aggressive behaviours is initiated (a FAP). The sign stimulus that triggers the innate releasing mechanism is the sight of the red spot. Niko Tinbergen (1951) presented sticklebacks with a series of wooden models of different shapes.

Findings Regardless of shape, if the model had a red spot the stickleback would aggressively display and even attack it. But if there was no red spot, there was no aggression, even if the model looked realistically like a stickleback. Tinbergen also found that these aggressive FAPs were unchanging from one encounter to another. Once triggered, the FAP always ran its course to completion without any further stimulus.

Apply it   Concepts: Lars, Elvis and Bungee

Lars has two pet dogs called Elvis and Bungee. They have lived together for a while now and get on well, but in the early days they used to fight a lot. Elvis always seemed to be the most aggressive. He would bare his teeth and growl at Bungee, who would half-heartedly respond by waving a paw in Elvis's general direction, before rolling over and showing his belly. Funnily enough, they never seemed to really go for it badly enough to hurt each other.

Question

Use your knowledge of the ethology of aggression to explain Elvis's and Bungee's behaviour.

Evaluation

Practical activity on page 310

Supporting research

In the previous spread we considered research by Han Brunner *et al.* (1993) showing that the low-activity variant of the **MAOA gene** is closely associated with aggressive behaviour in humans, suggesting an innate basis. The first spread in this chapter also presented evidence for the existence of innate releasing mechanisms for aggression in the brain – activity in the **limbic system** has been shown to trigger aggressive behaviour in humans and other animals. As the ethological explanation argues that aggression is genetically determined and heritable, its **validity** is supported by evidence that demonstrates the genetic and physiological basis of aggression.

Cultural differences in aggression

There is evidence that aggressive behaviour is more common in some human cultures than in others. For example, Richard Nisbett (1993) found there was a north-south divide in the United States for homicide rates. Killings are much more common amongst white males in the southern states than in the northern states. Because this was only true for reactive aggression triggered by arguments, Nisbett concluded that the difference in homicide rates was caused by a 'culture of honour', in other words the response to impulsive aggression was a learned social norm. This was supported in a lab study by Richard Nisbett and his colleagues (1996) who found that when white males from the south were insulted in a research situation, they were more likely than northern white males to become aggressive.

It is difficult for ethological theory, with its view of aggression as instinctive, to explain how culture can override innate influences.

Evidence against ritualistic aggression

The view that aggression has evolved into a self-limiting and relatively physically harmless ritual has been challenged by observations made by Jane Goodall (2010) of chimpanzees at the Gombe Stream National Park in Tanzania. During what she called the 'four-year war', male chimps from one community set about systematically slaughtering all the members of another group. They did this in a co-ordinated and premeditated fashion. On some occasions, a victim was held down by some rival chimpanzees while others hit and bit it in an attack lasting up to 20 minutes. The violence continued like this despite the fact that the victims were offering signals of appeasement and defencelessness. These signals did not inhibit the aggressive behaviour of the attacking chimps as predicted by the ethological explanation.

Evaluation eXtra

FAPs are not that fixed

Morton Hunt (1973) points out that sequences of behaviours that appear to be fixed and unchanging are in fact greatly influenced by environmental factors and learning experiences. So fixed action patterns are more flexible than implied by the term 'fixed' (many ethologists now prefer the term *modal action pattern* to reflect this). For instance, a FAP is typically made up of several aggressive behaviours in a series. The duration of each behaviour varies from one individual animal to another, and even in the same animal from one encounter to another.

Consider: *Does the flexibility of FAPs reduce the validity of the ethological explanation aggression? Explain your answer.*

Unjustified generalisation to humans

Lorenz did not study higher mammals such as primates, and Tinbergen chose not to study the kind of extreme destructive violence that is an all-too-frequent feature of human aggression. However, they both made generalisations about aggressive behaviour in humans, including warfare. Lorenz also extrapolated from the behaviour of individual animals to the behaviour of entire countries and states. But as the anthropologist Robin Fox (2000) points out, war is a '...*collective undertaking that cannot be explained by any individual impulse*'.

Consider: *Explain why it may not be valid to make such generalisations to human aggression and how this undermines the validity of the ethological explanation.*

Apply it **Concepts: Robin rage**

Asif often sees different species of bird in his garden, including robins. One day, he noticed two robins appearing to square up to each other. One in particular was making a lot of noise, flapping its wings, sticking its chest out, and making head-down charging gestures at the other.

Question

Using your knowledge of ethology, explain the robin's aggressive behaviour. How could Asif investigate it further? Refer to innate releasing mechanisms, fixed action patterns and some research in your explanation.

Lorenz's famous example of a wolf displaying its jugular vein is not a form of appeasement. Rudolph Schenkel (1967) argued it is a challenge that leads to further fighting.

Apply it **Methods: Observing aggression**

A psychologist wanted to carry out an **observational** study of children's aggressive play behaviour. She conducted a pilot study of a play group of five children. She identified several categories of aggressive behaviour and two independent observers recorded instances of each behaviour to see how a child might use aggression to establish dominance over the others in the group.

Questions

1. Suggest *three* **operationalised behavioural categories** the observers could use to identify aggressive behaviours. (*3 marks*)
2. Explain how **time sampling** and **event sampling** could be used in this study. (*2 marks + 2 marks*)
3. The observers recorded each aggressive behaviour as it occurred. Identify the **level of measurement** used and explain your answer. (*2 marks*)
4. What is a **pilot study** and why might one be useful in this research? (*3 marks*)
5. **Inter-observer reliability** was low in this pilot study. Explain what the researcher could do to improve it before carrying out the main observational study. (*3 marks*) (See page 66)

CHECK IT

1. In relation to the ethological explanation of aggression, explain what is meant by the terms *innate releasing mechanisms* and *fixed action patterns*.   [2 marks + 2 marks]
2. Outline the ethological explanation of aggression.   [6 marks]
3. Describe and evaluate the ethological explanation of aggression.   [16 marks]

Evolutionary explanations of human aggression.

Aggression is usually seen as a wholly destructive behaviour, and of course its consequences often are. But does it bring any benefits to those who use it? For evolutionary explanations, the answer has to be 'yes'.

David Buss and Joshua Duntley (2006) have identified several adaptive functions of aggression, including acquiring resources and increasing status. But two highly researched functions are defeating sexual rivals and retaining mates.

KEY TERM

Evolutionary explanation – An account of the changes in species over millions of years; characteristics that enhance survival and reproduction are naturally selected.

Apply it   Concepts: **Getting out**

Shula has finally accepted that she is in an abusive relationship. For years she had to put up with her partner keeping a close eye on her every move. Every time she went out he wanted to know where she'd been and who she'd seen. She suspected he was checking her phone for messages and calls. Sometimes he had to go away for work, and he was even worse when he got back. Recently his behaviour has taken a turn for the worse, and on a couple of occasions he has hit her. Shula is now making plans to leave as soon as possible.

Question

How does evolutionary theory explain the behaviour of Shula's partner?

How far would a man go to keep his partner from straying? Violence would not be out of the question, according to evolutionary theory.

Evolutionary explanations of human aggression

Evolutionary explanation of sexual jealousy

Sexual jealousy is a major motivator of aggressive behaviour in males which can be given an **evolutionary explanation**. This is because, unlike women, men can never be totally sure about whether or not they have truly fathered a child. This *paternity uncertainty* is a result of the very real threat for the male of *cuckoldry*, or having to raise offspring that are not his own. Any investment in offspring that do not share the male's genes is a waste of his resources. It contributes to survival of a rival's **genes** and leaves the 'father' with fewer resources to invest in his own future offspring.

Men in our evolutionary past who could avoid cuckoldry were more reproductively successful. So psychological mechanisms have evolved to increase anti-cuckoldry behaviours in males. For instance, sexual jealousy is more strongly experienced in males than in females. This drives the often aggressive strategies men employ to retain their partners and prevent them from 'straying', strategies that were **adaptive** in our evolutionary history.

Mate retention strategies Margo Wilson and Martin Daly (1996) identify several mate retention strategies which involve aggression and even physical violence, including:

- *Direct guarding* involves male vigilance over a partner's behaviour, for example checking who they've been seeing, coming home early, keeping tabs on their whereabouts, installing tracking apps on their mobiles, etc.
- *Negative inducements,* such as issuing threats of dire consequences for infidelity ('I'll kill myself if you leave me').

Such behaviours are clearly linked to violence. For example, Margo Wilson *et al.* (1995) found that women who reported mate retention strategies in their partners (they agreed with statements like 'He insists on knowing who you are with and where you are at all times'), were twice as likely to have suffered physical violence at the hands of their partners. Of these women, 73% required medical attention and 53% said they feared for their lives.

Intimate partner violence Todd Shackelford *et al.* (2005) studied intimate partner violence (IPV) in heterosexual couples:

Procedure Men and women in 107 married couples completed different **questionnaires**. All of the participants had been married less than one year. The men completed the *Mate Retention Inventory*, which assessed mate retention behaviours in various categories (such as direct guarding). The women completed the *Spouse Influence Report*, which measured the extent of their partner's violence in their relationship.

Findings There was a strong **positive correlation** between men's reports of their mate retention behaviours and women's reports of their partners' physical violence. So men who used guarding (e.g. coming home early) or negative inducements (e.g. threats to kill) were more likely to use physical violence against their partners. According to the researchers, these retention behaviours reliably predicted husbands' use of violence against their wives.

Evolutionary explanation of bullying

Bullying occurs because of a power imbalance: a more powerful individual uses aggression deliberately and repeatedly against a weaker person. Researchers have traditionally viewed bullying as a maladaptive behaviour, for example the result of poor social skills or childhood abuse. However, our evolutionary ancestors may have used bullying as an adaptive strategy to increase their chances of survival by promoting their own health and creating opportunities for reproduction.

Tony Volk *et al.* (2012) argue that the characteristics associated with bullying behaviour are attractive to the opposite sex. In males, it suggests dominance, acquisition of resources, and strength. It also has the benefit of warding off potential rivals. Bullying-associated characteristics therefore deliver the ideal combination of access to more females and minimal threat from competing males. Therefore such behaviour would be naturally selected because these males would have greater reproductive success.

Female bullying more often takes place within a relationship and is a method of controlling a partner. Women use bullying behaviour to secure their partner's fidelity, which means they continue to provide resources for future offspring. Again such behaviour would be **naturally selected** because of enhanced reproductive success.

STUDY TIP

It is vital that you link evolutionary explanations to aggressive behaviour as this topic is not just about evolutionary explanations – it is evolutionary explanations of human aggression.

Evaluation

Practical activity on page 311

Research support for aggression and sexual jealousy

Many research studies demonstrate that mate retention strategies are associated with sexual jealousy and aggression. The study by Shackelford *et al.* (2005) on the facing page is a particularly dramatic example. Strategies such as direct guarding and negative inducements are overwhelmingly used by males, against both females and other males.

This indicates a clear link between the greater risk of infidelity and cuckoldry, and aggression. This supports predictions derived from the evolutionary explanation concerning the adaptive value of aggression.

Evolutionary explanations account for gender differences

It is a common observation that males engage more often than females in most aggressive acts, especially *physical* aggression, i.e. there are gender differences. Evolutionary theory can explain this. For example, Anne Campbell (1999) argues that a female with offspring is motivated to be less aggressive because such behaviour would put not only her own survival at risk but also that of her child. So a more adaptive strategy for females is to use *verbal* aggression as a means of retaining a partner who provides resources, and to avoid becoming involved in life-threatening situations involving physical aggression (Buss and Shackelford 1997). This would also explain why women are more likely than men to use non-aggressive methods of resolving disputes.

This ability to explain gender differences is a strength of evolutionary theory.

Real-life applications

An evolutionary understanding of bullying as an adaptive behaviour can help us to devise more effective anti-bullying interventions. Ken Rigby (2010) reviewed several established interventions based on the assumption that bullying is a maladaptive behaviour that can be eradicated by addressing the bully's perceived deficiencies. Despite the availability of these strategies, bullying is still prevalent.

The evolutionary approach acknowledges that bullies bully because they stand to gain advantages for themselves. So it would make no sense for them to voluntarily give up the power they have over others without some form of compensation. Volk *et al.* (see facing page) argue that anti-bullying interventions therefore need to increase the costs of bullying and the rewards of prosocial alternatives. One method could be to encourage bullies to compete aggressively but fairly in sporting activities. This would give them the opportunity to display prowess, strength and other attractive qualities, including some not available to them through bullying.

Evaluation eXtra

Cultural differences

The !Kung San people of the Kalahari have very negative attitudes towards the use of aggression. Aggressive behaviour is discouraged from childhood and is therefore rare. Those who do use it find that their status and reputation within the community are diminished. The Yanomamo of Venezuela and Brazil have been described as 'the fierce people'. There is some dispute about the issue, but it appears that aggression is an accepted and required behaviour in order to gain status in their highly structured society.

Consider: *How does the existence of such wide cultural differences in aggression affect the **validity** of the evolutionary explanation?*

Methodological issues

It is extremely difficult to test **hypotheses** about the evolution of behaviours to solve problems of adaptation in our evolutionary past. Most research is therefore **correlational**, for example finding associations between mate retention behaviours and aggression. This method does not allow us to draw cause-and-effect conclusions.

Consider: *Explain how this methodological weakness undermines the validity of the evolutionary explanation.*

Bullying persists because it brings the bully certain benefits he or she does not want to give up.

Apply it

Concepts: Bullies never prosper – or do they?

Fred is being bullied at school. His bully is making his life a misery, but Fred is too scared to tell anyone in case it makes the situation worse. What he can't understand is why his bully seems to be so popular. Fred can't tell if it's because people genuinely like him or if it's because they're just frightened of him.

Question

Knowing what you do about the evolutionary explanation of bullying, how would you explain to Fred why his bully behaves the way he does?

Apply it   Methods: Questions of aggression

A psychologist recruited 60 married couples for a study into the relationship between male sexual jealousy and aggression.

The 60 males completed a questionnaire measuring jealousy in terms of mate retention behaviours: 17 males indicated they monitored their partner closely, and 26 issued aggressive threats. The 60 females completed a different questionnaire indicating how much aggression they had experienced at the hands of their partner. 5 of the female participants said they had experienced serious verbal aggression, and 12 had experienced physical aggression.

Questions

1. For either questionnaire, write *one* question that could gather **quantitative data** and *one* that could gather **qualitative data**. (*2 marks*)

2. Explain *one* reason why the psychologist thought questionnaires might be better than **interviews** in this study. (*2 marks*)

3. Calculate the responses of males and females as percentages (*four percentages*). (*4 marks*)

4. Draw a **bar chart** to represent the findings of the study. Make sure you label the axes carefully. (*3 marks*)

5. Explain *one* **ethical issue** that the researcher should have considered, and how she could have dealt with it. (*2 marks + 2 marks*)

CHECK IT

1. Outline evolutionary explanations of human aggression. [6 marks]

2. Explain **one** limitation of evolutionary explanations of human aggression. [3 marks]

3. Describe and evaluate evolutionary explanations of human aggression. [16 marks]

SOCIAL PSYCHOLOGICAL EXPLANATIONS OF AGGRESSION: FRUSTRATION - AGGRESSION HYPOTHESIS

THE SPECIFICATION SAYS...

Social psychological explanations of aggression, including the frustration-aggression hypothesis.

Biological explanations don't really get to the heart of most people's experience of aggression. If you were to ask people about how they understand their own aggressive behaviour, they might talk about how they felt, or what they were thinking, or what events triggered them to be aggressive. Social psychological explanations address these better.

KEY TERMS

Social psychological explanations of aggression – Any theory that argues aggression is the result of an interaction between an individual's characteristics and features of the situations in which behaviour occurs.

Frustration-aggression hypothesis – A social psychological theory that argues that anger, hostility and even violence are always the outcome when we are prevented from achieving our goals (i.e. frustration).

Gaming isn't always fun. It can be frustrating too, especially when you lose. But does this frustration always translate into aggression?

Apply it

Concepts: Jacinta's frustrating day

Jacinta is a sixth-form student who decided to look for a part-time job. Eventually she went for an **interview** at a new pizza place opening up in town. Despite preparing really thoroughly, she didn't get the job. On her way out of the interview, which was two miles from her house, she found that she'd lost the £10 note for her bus fare, and she'd forgotten to bring her phone with her, so she had to walk home. All the way back Jacinta thought long and hard about how unfair it all was, so by the time she arrived home she was fuming. The first thing she did was shout at her little sister.

Question

Explain how the frustration-aggression hypothesis accounts for Jacinta's behaviour.

The frustration-aggression hypothesis

John Dollard and his colleagues (1939) first formulated the **frustration-aggression hypothesis**. According to them, frustration always leads to aggression, and aggression is always the result of frustration. This hypothesis is based on the **psychodynamic** concept of *catharsis*, and views aggression as a psychological drive akin to biological drives such as hunger. If our attempt to achieve a goal is blocked by some external factor, we experience frustration. This creates an aggressive drive, which leads to aggressive behaviour, such as a violent fantasy, a verbal outburst or perhaps even physical violence. This is cathartic because the aggression created by the frustration is satisfied, thereby reducing the drive and making further aggression less likely. We feel better for having gotten it 'off our chest'.

The hypothesis recognises that aggression is not always expressed directly against the source of frustration, for three reasons:

- The cause of our frustration may be abstract, such as the economic situation, the government, or the music industry.
- The cause may be too powerful and we risk **punishment** by aggressing against it, for example the teacher who gave you a lower grade than you expected.
- The cause may just be unavailable at the time, for example perhaps the teacher left before you realised what grade you got.

So our aggression is deflected (or *displaced*) onto an alternative – one that is not abstract, is weaker and is available (an inanimate object, perhaps, or a pet, or a younger sibling).

Research into frustration-aggression

Russell Geen (1968) carried out a study to investigate the effects of frustration on aggression.

Procedure Male university students were given the task of completing a jigsaw puzzle. Their level of frustration was experimentally manipulated in one of three ways. For some participants, the puzzle was impossible to solve. For others, they ran out of time because another student in the room (a **confederate** of the researcher) kept interfering. For a third group, the confederate took to insulting the participant as they failed to solve the puzzle. The next part of the study involved the participant giving electric shocks to the confederate when they made a mistake on another task.

Findings The insulted participants gave the strongest shocks on average, followed by the interfered group, then the impossible task participants. All three groups selected more intense shocks than a (non-frustrated) **control group**.

The role of environmental cues

Even if we become angry, we still might not behave aggressively. According to Leonard Berkowitz (1989), frustration merely creates a readiness for aggression. But the presence of aggressive cues in the environment make acting upon this much more likely. Therefore cues are an additional element of the frustration-aggression hypothesis. Leonard Berkowitz and Anthony LePage (1967) demonstrated this in a famous study.

Procedure They arranged for student participants to be given electric shocks in a **laboratory** situation, creating anger and frustration. The individual who gave the shocks was a confederate of the researchers. The participants then had the opportunity to turn the tables and give electric shocks to the confederate.

Findings The number of shocks given depended on the presence or absence of weapons in the lab. In one condition, two guns were present on a table next to the shock machine. The average number of shocks given in this condition was 6.07. When no guns were present, the average number of shocks was significantly fewer, at 4.67.

This so-called **weapons effect** supports Berkowitz's contention that the presence of aggressive environmental cues stimulates aggression. ('The finger pulls the trigger, but the trigger may also be pulling the finger', as he put it.)

Evaluation

Research support

Amy Marcus-Newhall *et al.* (2000) conducted a **meta-analysis** of 49 studies of displaced aggression, a key concept in the frustration-aggression hypothesis. These studies investigated situations in which aggressive behaviour had to be directed against a target other than the one that caused frustration.

The researchers concluded that displaced aggression is a reliable phenomenon. Participants who were provoked but unable to retaliate directly against the source of their frustration were **significantly** more likely to aggress against an innocent party than people who were not provoked. This is exactly the outcome predicted by the frustration-aggression hypothesis.

Is aggression cathartic?

Brad Bushman (2002) found that participants who vented their anger by repeatedly hitting a punchbag actually became more angry and aggressive rather than less. In fact, doing nothing was more effective at reducing aggression than venting anger. Bushman argues that using venting to reduce anger is like using petrol to put out a fire. But this is exactly the advice many therapists and counsellors give to their clients.

The outcome of this study is very different from that predicted by the frustration-aggression hypothesis. This casts doubt on the **validity** of a central assumption of the hypothesis.

Berkowitz's reformulation: negative affect theory

It became clear from research that frustration does not always lead to aggression, and that aggression can occur without frustration. So the hypothesis was reformulated by Leonard Berkowitz (1989) who argued that frustration is just one of many aversive stimuli that create negative feelings; others include jealousy, pain, and loneliness. So aggressive behaviour is triggered by negative feelings generally (such as anger) rather than by frustration specifically. Furthermore, the outcome of frustration can be a range of responses, only one of which is aggression. For example, the frustration someone experiences at getting a low grade for an essay might not necessarily lead to aggression but to despair, anxiety, helplessness or determination.

Berkowitz's *negative affect theory* arose because the original frustration-aggression hypothesis was inadequate, as it could only explain how aggression arises in some situations but not in others.

Evaluation eXtra

Justified and unjustified frustration

Joy Dill and Craig Anderson (1995) showed that different *kinds* of frustration have different effects. An experimenter showed participants how to perform a paper-folding task (origami). The experimenter made the demonstration difficult to follow by going too quickly. In the unjustified condition he said he had to hurry because his girlfriend was waiting for him, in the justified condition he said his boss had told him to finish quickly.

The unjustified frustration produced the most aggression (measured in terms of negative judgements of the experimenter). But, more importantly, justified frustration produced more aggression than the control condition (absence of frustration).

Consider: *Is this finding predicted by the frustration-aggression hypothesis? Explain how this affects the validity of the hypothesis.*

Real-life application

Berkowitz's argument that 'the trigger can pull the finger' has featured in the gun control debate in the United States. Some states allow 'open carry', where a gun does not have to be concealed. There is concern, bolstered by many research studies, that the open presence of a weapon can act as a cue to aggression, making its use more likely.

Consider: *Do you think it's important that psychological theories and studies should contribute to addressing social issues? Explain your answer.*

Apply it — Concepts: A pain in the neck

Ethan was working very hard trying to finish an essay that he had to hand in the next morning. Unfortunately, his little sister had other ideas and kept pestering him, wanting to play, insisting on talking to him, fiddling around with his pens and just generally getting in the way. Ethan eventually became very anxious, because he could see that he was never going to get his essay done.

Question

Use your knowledge of the frustration-aggression hypothesis to explain why Ethan responded in the way he did rather than becoming angry and aggressive.

The American way? Openly carrying a gun, as in some states of the USA, may stimulate violence as well as enable it.

Apply it — Methods: Winding them up

A researcher arranged for his participants to play a video game against a skilled opponent. This individual was a confederate of the researcher. She was told to 'trash talk' half of the participants by being sarcastic, disparaging and dismissive during the game. She was friendly towards the other half of the participants. She was also instructed to win all her games, which she did.

After their game, each participant had to rate the confederate's skill on a scale from 0 (no skill at all, just lucky) to 10 (extremely skilled). This was the researcher's measure of aggression.

Questions

1. What are the **operationalised independent variable** and **dependent variable** in this study? (*1 mark + 1 mark*)
2. Write a **non-directional hypothesis** for this experiment. (*2 marks*)
3. The researcher assigned the participants **randomly** to the two conditions. Explain how he could have done this and why it was necessary. (*2 marks + 2 marks*)
4. Explain why this **experiment** might be lacking in validity. (*3 marks*)
5. The researcher wanted to calculate a **measure of central tendency** to summarise the aggression scores. Identify a suitable measure and give *one* reason why it would be appropriate. (*1 mark + 1 mark*)

CHECK IT

1. Outline the frustration-aggression hypothesis as an explanation of aggression. [6 marks]
2. Describe **one** research study related to the frustration-aggression hypothesis. Refer to what the researcher(s) did and what was found. [4 marks]
3. Describe and evaluate research into the frustration-aggression hypothesis as an explanation of aggression. [16 marks]

Social psychological explanations of aggression ...including social learning theory as applied to human aggression.

According to Albert Bandura (1973), aggression is behaviour learned in social contexts. Social learning theory (SLT) does not deny that biological factors play a role in how we acquire aggressive behaviours. But everything that really matters about aggression is learned.

KEY TERM

Social learning theory – A way of explaining behaviour that includes both direct and indirect reinforcement, combining learning theory with the role of cognitive factors.

Apply it

Concepts: The imitation game

Willie has a three-year-old daughter called Marina and a pet dog called Brutus. One day, while she was playing with Brutus, Marina suddenly tapped him firmly on the nose and said 'very naughty dog'. Willie was surprised because it was the first time he had seen his daughter do this. Then he realised that this was exactly what he himself had done to the dog the day before.

Question

How would you explain Marina's aggressive behaviour in terms of social learning?

Some of the children in Bandura et al.'s 'Bobo doll' study imitated adult behaviour incredibly closely.

Social learning theory applied to human aggression

Direct and indirect learning

Albert Bandura acknowledged that aggression can be learned directly, through mechanisms of **operant conditioning** involving **positive** and **negative reinforcement** and **punishment**. So a child who angrily snatches a toy off another child, for example, is likely to learn that aggressive behaviour brings results. This direct reinforcement makes it more likely that the child will do this again in a similar situation. However, Bandura also realised that aggressive behaviour often cannot be explained by such direct forms of learning, especially in humans. So he argued that an indirect mechanism – **observational learning** – accounts for **social learning** of most aggressive behaviours.

Observational learning and vicarious reinforcement

Children (and adults to an extent) acquire specific aggressive behaviours through observing aggressive models, such as siblings, parents, peers, and characters in the media. In this way, the child works out how an aggressive behaviour is performed, but this does not mean that they will behave aggressively themselves. As well as observing the behaviour of models, children also observe the *consequences* of their behaviour. If the model's aggressive behaviour is rewarded (or at least not punished), then the child learns that aggression can be effective in getting what they want. This is known as **vicarious reinforcement**, and it makes it more likely that the observing child will imitate the model's aggressive behaviour.

There is a parallel form of indirect learning called *vicarious punishment*. If a model's use of aggression to achieve a goal is punished, an observing child is less likely to imitate that specific behaviour.

Cognitive control of aggressive behaviour

Bandura points out that four **cognitive** conditions are needed for observational learning to take place:

- *Attention*: a basic cognitive requirement is that the observer must pay attention to the model's aggressive actions.
- *Retention*: the observer also needs to be able to remember the model's aggressive actions, to form a symbolic mental representation of how the behaviour is performed.
- *Reproduction*: the individual must be able to transform the mental representation of the aggressive behaviour into actual physical action. This involves the individual mentally appraising his or her ability to do this.
- *Motivation*: the individual needs a reason to imitate the behaviour, which will depend on his or her expectations that behaving aggressively in a specific way in a specific situation will be rewarding.

Self-efficacy

Self-efficacy is the extent to which we believe our actions will achieve a desired goal. A child's confidence in their ability to be aggressive grows as they learn that aggression can bring rewards. For example, consider a child who regularly hits other children to get hold of a toy. They learn that they have the motor skills necessary to force another child to hand over the toy, and that this ability comes easily to them. The child's sense of self-efficacy develops with each successful outcome. He or she is confident that because their aggression has been effective in the past it will continue to be so in the future. In others words, they learn that aggression works and they are good at it.

Research into social learning of aggression

Bandura *et al*.'s (1961) famous Bobo doll study illustrates many of the features of SLT discussed on this spread.

Procedure Young children individually observed an adult model assaulting an inflatable plastic toy called a 'Bobo doll'. The aggressive behaviours included throwing, kicking, hitting with a mallet, and were accompanied by verbal outbursts such as 'Sock him in the nose!' There followed a short period during which the children were not allowed to play with some attractive toys, which created a degree of frustration. They were then taken to another room where there was a Bobo doll, plus some other toys including ones the adult model had used.

Findings Without being instructed to do so, many of these children imitated the behaviour they had seen performed by the model, physically and verbally. The closeness of the imitation was remarkable in some cases, virtually a direct copy of what the children had observed, including the use of specific objects and verbal phrases. There was also another group of children who had observed an adult interacting non-aggressively with the doll. Aggressive behaviour towards the Bobo doll by these children was almost non-existent.

Evaluation

Supporting research

François Poulin and Michel Boivin (2000) applied a social learning analysis to aggressive behaviour in boys aged between nine and twelve years. They found that most aggressive boys formed friendships with other aggressive boys. The researchers describe such cliques as 'training grounds' for antisocial behaviour. These friendships were lasting, stable, and mutually reinforcing of aggression. The boys used their alliances with each other to gain resources through aggressive behaviour, usually successfully. This means that they were exposed frequently to models of physical aggression (i.e. each other) and to the positive consequences of it. They also gained reinforcement from the rewarding approval of the rest of the 'gang'. These are precisely the conditions under which social learning theory predicts that aggressive behaviour would occur.

Cannot explain all aggression

As we have noted before, there are two broad categories of aggression recognised by researchers: reactive ('hot-blooded', angry) and proactive ('cold-blooded', calculated). Children who are experienced in using proactive aggression have high levels of self-efficacy – they are confident that their aggressive behaviour will bring benefits. They use aggression as a way of achieving their goals (i.e. instrumentally). This type of behaviour is well-explained by social learning theory.

However, reactively aggressive children habitually use aggression to retaliate in the heat of the moment. They tend to be hostile, suspicious of others, and do not use aggression to achieve anything except retribution. This behaviour is less explicable from a social learning perspective, and may be better explained by Leonard Berkowitz's *negative affect theory* (see page 299).

The benefits of non-aggressive models

There are practical applications of SLT. The theory argues that people are not passive recipients of reinforcement, whether direct or vicarious, but active influencers of their own environments. People shape their own aggressive behaviour by selecting and creating their surroundings (**reciprocal determinism**).

There is a practical benefit to understanding this aspect of SLT. One way to reduce aggression is to break this cycle in which individuals become yet more aggressive by choosing situations which reward their behaviour. Encouraging aggressive children to form friendships with children (and adults) who do not habitually behave aggressively gives them more opportunities to model non-aggressive behaviour.

Evaluation eXtra

Real-life applications

Rowell Huesmann and Leonard Eron (2013) argue that **media** portrayals of aggressive behaviour can be powerful influences on a child's acquisition of aggression. This is especially true if a character (in, for example, a soap opera) is rewarded for being aggressive, and if the child is able to identify with the character in some way (for instance, he or she has appealing traits, such as a sense of humour). Under these conditions, vicarious reinforcement experienced by children observing violent behaviour by media characters may be just as influential in encouraging imitation as it is in real life.

Consider: *Does this increase or decrease the **validity** of the social learning theory of aggression? Explain your answer.*

Cultural differences

Different cultures have different norms about which behaviours should be reinforced. In some cultures, such as the !Kung San of the Kalahari desert, direct reinforcement of children's aggression is unlikely because social norms do not encourage it, and parents tend not to use it to discipline children. This also means that models of aggression are unavailable for children to observe, and certainly vicarious reinforcement is a rare experience. Nevertheless they display aggressive behaviour.

Consider: *Does this support social learning theory or not? Explain your answer.*

According to Francois Poulin and Michel Boivin's 'training ground' hypothesis, aggressive teenagers who hang out together get lots of opportunities to reinforce each other's behaviour.

Apply it

Concepts: Cycle of violence

Russell grew up in a family where physical aggression was a feature of everyday life. This sometimes took the form of actual physical violence. He even witnessed his dad hitting his mum on several occasions. Now that he is 15, Russell has a reputation as an aggressive bully who is always prepared to use physical means to get what he wants. He is attracted to situations in which violence is likely to 'kick off', and has made friends with other boys who are just as aggressive as him.

Questions

1. Use your knowledge of social learning theory to explain Russell's behaviour.

2. What other explanation could acccount for his behaviour?

Apply it

Methods: Observing observational learning

Two researchers carried out an **observational study** of aggressive behaviour. Children between the ages of five and seven years individually observed an adult behaving aggressively towards an inflatable plastic figure. The children were then given the opportunity to play with the figure and with some other toys as well. The researchers devised some **behavioural categories** which they used to record the incidence of several aggressive behaviours.

Questions

1. Explain *one* strength and *one* limitation of using an observational method in this study. (*2 marks + 2 marks*)

2. Explain how this observational study could be conducted to make it **controlled**, **covert** and **non-participant**. (*3 marks*)

3. Explain *one* **sampling technique** the researchers could use to recruit children for this study. (*2 marks*)

4. Evaluate the technique you have identified in your previous answer. (*4 marks*)

5. Explain *one* **ethical issue** that the researchers should have considered before conducting the study and how they could have dealt with it. (*2 marks + 2 marks*)

CHECK IT

1. Outline the social learning theory of human aggression. [*6 marks*]

2. Describe **one** study in which the social learning theory of human aggression was investigated. Include details of what the psychologist(s) did and what was found. [*4 marks*]

3. Discuss the social learning theory of human aggression. [*16 marks*]

SOCIAL PSYCHOLOGICAL EXPLANATIONS OF AGGRESSION: DE-INDIVIDUATION

THE SPECIFICATION SAYS...

Social psychological explanations of aggression, including ...de-individuation.

Aggression often happens in groups, but this context has mostly been overlooked by the explanations we have explored so far. But the de-individuation explanation argues that by immersing our personal identity in a group, we are all capable of behaving in aggressive and even violent ways that we never would on our own.

KEY TERM

De-individuation – A psychological state in which an individual loses their personal identity and takes on the identity of the social group when, for example, in a crowd or wearing a uniform. The result may be to free the individual from the constraints of social norms.

STUDY TIP

De-individuation is one of several theories/explanations of aggression in this chapter. For all of them, it's tempting to describe them as explanations of behaviour in general. However, you must always make sure your description is closely linked to aggression. Whenever you write such a description, read through it and ask yourself whether you can clearly tell that it's about aggression. If you can't, then it's a weak answer.

Just one face in a crowd of many. But does knowing that make it more likely that this woman will behave aggressively?

De-individuation

Crowd behaviour

De-individuation is a concept originally used by Gustave Le Bon (1895) to explain the behaviour of individuals in crowds. Usually, because we are easily identified by others, our behaviour is constrained by social norms, and we live in a society where most forms of aggressive behaviour are discouraged. But when we become part of a crowd, we lose restraint and have the freedom to behave in ways we wouldn't otherwise contemplate. We lose our senses of both individual self-identity and responsibility for our behaviour, and we have a greater disregard for norms and even laws. Responsibility becomes shared throughout the crowd, so we experience less personal guilt at harmful aggression directed at others.

How does de-individuation lead to aggression?

Philip Zimbardo (1969) distinguished between individuated and de-individuated behaviour. In an individuated state, our behaviour is generally rational and normative (i.e. it conforms to social norms). But de-individuated behaviours are emotional, impulsive and irrational; most importantly, they are anti-normative and disinhibited. So when we are in a de-individuated state, we lose self-awareness, we stop monitoring and regulating our own behaviour, we ignore social norms and 'live for the moment', failing to form longer-term plans.

The conditions of de-individuation which promote aggressive behaviour include darkness, drugs, alcohol, uniforms, masks and disguises. A major factor is anonymity; according to John Dixon and Kesi Mahendran (2012), *'anonymity shapes crowd behaviour'*. We have less fear of retribution because we are a small and unidentifiable part of a faceless crowd; the bigger the crowd, the more anonymous we are. Crucially, anonymity provides fewer opportunities for others to judge us negatively.

The role of self-awareness

The experience of de-individuation as part of a faceless crowd creates a greater likelihood of aggression. But according to Steven Prentice-Dunn and Ronald Rogers (1982), this is not due to anonymity directly, but to the *consequences* of anonymity. They explain this process in terms of two types of self-awareness:

- *Private self-awareness* concerns how we pay attention to our own feelings and behaviour. This is reduced when we are part of a crowd. Our attention becomes focused outwardly to the events around us, so we pay less attention to our own beliefs and feelings. We are less self-critical, less thoughtful and less evaluative, all of which foster a de-individuated state.
- *Public self-awareness* refers to how much we care about what other people think of our behaviour, and this is also reduced in crowds. We realise that we are just one individual amongst many; we are anonymous and our behaviour is less likely to be judged by others. We no longer care how others see us, so we become less accountable for our aggressive and destructive actions.

Research into de-individuation

David Dodd (1985) was a psychology teacher who developed a classroom exercise to illustrate de-individuation.

Procedure He asked 229 undergraduate psychology students in 13 classes this question: 'If you could do anything humanly possible with complete assurance that you would not be detected or held responsible, what would you do?' The students were aware that their responses were completely anonymous. Three independent raters who did not know the **hypothesis** decided which categories of antisocial behaviour (see below) the responses belonged to.

Findings Dodd found that 36% of the responses involved some form of antisocial behaviour; 26% were actual criminal acts, the most common of which was 'rob a bank'. A few students opted for murder, rape and assassination of a political figure. Only 9% of responses were prosocial behaviours (such as helping people). In terms of how people *imagine* they would behave, this study demonstrates a link between anonymity, de-individuation and aggressive behaviour.

Apply it **Concepts: Mum knows best**

On 28 April 2015 a funeral in Baltimore USA of a young man who died in police custody became a violent riot. Michael Graham was one of many who put on a balaclava, picked up a makeshift weapon, and joined the rioters burning down buildings and assaulting police officers. Michael's mother Toya recognised him on live TV coverage, and went onto the streets to forcibly march him back home. When she ripped off his balaclava in front of the cameras, Michael became a lot more co-operative. (*Based on a real event.*)

Question

How does de-individuation theory explain Michael's behaviour?

Evaluation

Research support for de-individuation

Karen Douglas and Craig McGarty (2001) looked at aggressive online behaviour in chatrooms and uses of instant messaging. They found a strong **correlation** between anonymity and 'flaming', that is sending or posting threatening and/or hostile messages. The most aggressive messages were sent by those who chose to hide their real identities.

This suggests the existence of a link between anonymity, de-individuation and aggressive behaviour in a context that has even greater relevance today. This is because of the explosion in social **media** use, the activities of online 'trolls', and the exit from Twitter of several high-profile media celebrities.

Lack of support

Some research studies show that de-individuation does not always lead to aggression. In their 'deviance in the dark' study, Gergen *et al.* (1973) selected groups of eight participants, who were all strangers to each other. They were placed in a completely darkened room for one hour, and told to do just whatever they wanted to, with no rules to stop them. It was impossible for the participants to identify one another, and they were given a guarantee that they would never encounter each other again. It did not take long for them to stop talking and start kissing and touching each other intimately. The study was repeated, but this time the participants were told they would come face-to-face with each other after the 'hour of darkness'. Unsurprisingly, the amount of touching and kissing declined dramatically. Of all the behaviours that de-individuation could have given rise to in this study, aggression was not one of them.

De-individuation and prosocial behaviour

Robert Johnson and Leslie Downing (1979) conducted a study where female participants had to give (fake) electric shocks to a **confederate**. In one condition, the participants were dressed in a Ku Klux Klan-type outfit, with masks hiding their faces. Participants in another condition dressed as nurses, and a third group (control) wore their own clothes. Compared with the **control group**, the KKK-dressed participants gave more (and more intense) electric shocks, and the 'nurses' gave fewer at lower levels. The researchers also noted that the nurses were more compassionate towards their 'victim', in line with the prosocial role associated with a nurse's uniform.

It seems that both aggression and prosocial behaviour are potential outcomes of de-individuation (not just aggression), and normative cues in the situation determine which is most likely to occur.

Evaluation eXtra

Real-life applications

De-individuation theory can help us to understand aggressive behaviour in online gaming services such as Xbox Live. These services have many features that promote a psychological state of de-individuation. There is a reduction of personal identity, with players using 'handles' to identify themselves; game-playing in such an environment is arousing and immersive; and there is the presence of a 'crowd' in the form of a (potentially worldwide) audience.

Consider: *What sort of aggressive behaviours are encountered online? Do you think they can really be explained by de-individuation?*

Explaining de-individuation

Russell Spears and Martin Lea (1992) applied **social identity theory** (SIT) to de-individuation in their *Social Identity model of De-individuation Effects* (the SIDE model). They noted that de-individuation does not inevitably lead to aggression or any other anti-normative behaviour. Anonymity and reduced self-awareness specifically do not have the wider effects predicted by the de-individuation explanation. Instead, they lead to behaviour that conforms to local group norms, which could be antisocial or prosocial. This happens because anonymity shifts the individual's attention from his or her personal identity to their social identify as a member of a group.

Consider: *Is this a major challenge to the de-individuation explanation of aggression, or a development of it? Explain your answer.*

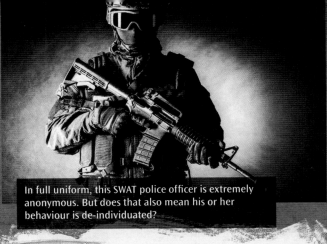

In full uniform, this SWAT police officer is extremely anonymous. But does that also mean his or her behaviour is de-individuated?

Apply it Concepts: **Help not harm**

Carmen is a physiotherapist who one weekend took part in a protest against cuts to the NHS. She travelled to the protest on her own but soon joined in with thousands of other people – nurses, doctors and many other healthcare workers. They were all chanting and carrying placards about 'care not cuts'. Carmen saw a police officer collapse in the road, apparently having had a heart attack. She rushed over, and was soon followed by quite a few others all expressing concern for the officer and doing their utmost to help him.

Questions

1. Explain how de-individuation can account for this prosocial behaviour.

2. How would this make de-individuation an invalid explanation of aggression?

Apply it Methods: **Uniform anonymity**

A psychologist conducted an **experiment** to investigate the effect of anonymity on behaviour. Twenty volunteers were recruited to take part in a reaction-time game against a confederate of the experimenter. Every time the confederate lost the game, the participant was allowed to punish him with a loud noise delivered through headphones. The volume of this noise was selected by the participant and measured in decibels (dB). In one condition of the experiment, the participants all wore a soldier's uniform, complete with face camouflage, dark glasses and helmet. In the other condition they all wore their own clothes.

Questions

1. Write a **directional hypothesis** for this study. (*2 marks*)

2. Name the **experimental design** used in this study. (*1 mark*)

3. The psychologist realised that he would need to use **counterbalancing**. Explain how he could have done so, and why it was necessary. (*4 marks*)

4. Explain how **demand characteristics** might have affected the study. (*2 marks*)

5. Explain how *one* factor in this study might have affected its **external validity**. (*3 marks*) (See page 68)

CHECK IT

1. Explain what is meant by the term *de-individuation* in relation to aggression. [*2 marks*]

2. Outline **one** study of de-individuation as an explanation of aggression. [*6 marks*]

3. Describe and evaluate de-individuation as an explanation of aggression. [*16 marks*]

INSTITUTIONAL AGGRESSION IN THE CONTEXT OF PRISONS

Institutional aggression in the context of prisons: dispositional and situational explanations.

Psychologists have been very interested in how institutions such as prisons might cultivate aggressive and violent behaviour. Two major theoretical stances have arisen to account for institutional aggression.

Dispositional explanations locate the causes of aggressive behaviour within the individual, in terms of factors that make one person different from another. Situational explanations, on the other hand, attribute responsibility for aggression to factors within the prison environment, and emphasise the importance of social context.

KEY TERMS

Institutional aggression – Aggressive or violent behaviour that takes place within the social context of a prison or other formal organised settings.

Dispositional explanations – Any explanation of behaviour that highlights the importance of the individual's personality (i.e. their disposition). Such explanations are often contrasted with situational explanations.

Situational explanations – Any explanation that identifies the causes of behaviour as existing within the environment, which may include other people. Such explanations are contrasted with dispositional explanations.

Some people respond to imprisonment with despair rather than aggression. Either way, psychologists want to know how influential the prison environment is.

Dispositional explanations

The importation model

The most influential **dispositional explanation** of how aggression develops within prisons is the importation model of John Irwin and Donald Cressey (1962). It argues that prisons are not completely insulated from the happenings of everyday life outside in the 'real world'. After all, it is the real world from which prison inmates come and they bring with them a subculture typical of **criminality**. This includes beliefs, values, norms, attitudes, and a history of learning experiences as well as other personal characteristics such as gender, race and class.

The willingness of inmates to use violence inside prison to settle disputes reflects their lives before they were imprisoned. As Jim Thomas and Patrick McManimon (2005) put it: '... *people who prey on others on the streets also prey on others in the prison*'. Inmates import such behaviours as a means of negotiating their way through the unfamiliar and frightening prison environment in which existing inmates use aggression to establish power, status, influence and access to resources (the 'convict subculture').

Therefore, aggression is the product of individual characteristics of inmates and not of the prison environment. So it follows that inmates predisposed to using violence would be likely to do so in any setting, and were experienced in doing so outside prison.

Research into the importation model

Procedure Matt DeLisi and his colleagues (2011) studied 813 juvenile delinquents confined in institutions in California. These were inmates who brought into confinement several negative dispositional features such as experiences of childhood trauma, high levels of anger and irritability, a history of substance abuse, and a history of violent behaviour.

Findings These inmates were more likely to engage in suicidal activity and sexual misconduct, and committed more acts of physical violence that were brought to the attention of the parole board (compared with a **control group** of inmates with fewer negative dispositional features).

Situational explanations

The deprivation model

Donald Clemmer's (1958) deprivation model places the causes of **institutional aggression** within the prison environment itself, i.e. a **situational explanation**. Harsh prison conditions are stressful for inmates, who have to cope by resorting to aggressive and often violent behaviour. These conditions include being deprived of freedom, independence, goods and services, safety, and heterosexual intimacy. Deprivation of material goods is especially important because it increases competition amongst inmates to acquire them, and is accompanied by a corresponding increase in aggression.

Aggression is also influenced by the nature of the prison regime. If it is unpredictable and regularly uses 'lock ups' to control behaviour, then this creates frustration, reduces stimulation by barring other more interesting activities, and reduces even further access to 'goods' (such as television). This is a recipe for violence, which becomes an adaptive solution to the problem of deprivation.

Research into the deprivation model

Procedure Benjamin Steiner (2009) investigated the factors that predicted inmate aggression in 512 prisons in the United States.

Findings He found that inmate-on-inmate violence was more common in prisons where there were higher proportions of female staff, African-American inmates, Hispanic inmates, and inmates in protective custody for their own safety. These are all prison-level factors because they are independent of the individual characteristics of prisoners. In this study the factors reliably predicted aggressive behaviour in line with the deprivation model.

Apply it Concepts: Marilyn

Marilyn has been an inmate of a tough prison for just two months. She is still finding it quite hard to cope and a week ago she was involved in a riot organised by two of the longer-term inmates. They set fire to their bedding, and barricaded themselves in the recreation room using whatever objects they could get their hands on. Five prison officers were hurt, one of them seriously. Marilyn had prepared for the riot by making herself a couple of 'shivs' (makeshift knives) in the prison workshop. She didn't use them, but she would have if necessary.

Question

Use your knowledge of situational factors to explain Marilyn's behaviour.

Evaluation

Support from research

Scott Camp and Gerald Gaes (2005) studied 561 male inmates with similar criminal histories and predispositions to aggression. Half were placed in low-security Californian prisons and the other half in the second-highest category of prisons: 33% of prisoners in the low security prisons and 36% in the higher category prisons were involved in aggressive misconduct within two years, a difference that was not statistically **significant**. The researchers concluded that features of the prison environment are significantly less important predictors of aggressive behaviour than characteristics of inmates.

This is strong evidence because the study is a **field experiment** with **random allocation** of inmates to prisons of different security levels, allowing more valid conclusions than **correlational studies** or **natural experiments**.

Alternative explanation

John Dilulio (1991) claims that the importation model is an inadequate explanation of aggressive behaviour because it ignores the roles of prison officials and factors relating to the running of prisons. He proposes an *administrative control model* (ACM) which states that poorly managed prisons are more likely to experience the most serious forms of inmate violence, including homicides and rioting. Poor management is characterised by several factors including weak and indecisive leadership, a thriving culture of informal and unofficial rules, staff who remain distant from inmates, and few opportunities for education. According to the ACM, these factors are more influential in determining aggression than inmate characteristics.

Evaluation

Supporting evidence

Individual-level factors are reliable predictors of aggression independent of the prison environment (see above), but research shows that some situational variables are also influential. Mark Cunningham *et al.* (2010) analysed 35 inmate homicides in Texas prisons and found that motivations for the behaviours were linked to some of the deprivations identified by Clemmer. Particularly important were arguments over drugs, homosexual relationships and personal possessions.

As these are factors predicted by the model to make aggression more likely, these findings support its **validity**.

Contradictory research

The deprivation model predicts that a lack of freedom and heterosexual contact should lead to high levels of aggressive behaviour in prisons. However, the available evidence does not support this. For example, Christopher Hensley *et al.* (2002) studied 256 male and female inmates of two prisons in Mississippi, a state of the USA which allows conjugal visits (that is, visits from partners specifically to have sex). There was no link between involvement in these visits and reduced aggressive behaviour.

This shows that situational factors do not affect prison violence.

Evaluation eXtra

Interactionist model

We have seen that the importation and deprivation models are both supported and challenged by research evidence. Perhaps both models are valid. For instance, Shanhe Jiang and Marianne Fisher-Giorlando (2002) suggest that the importation model is a better explanation of violence between inmates, but the deprivation model is more useful in understanding innate aggression against prison staff. Rhonda Dobbs and Courtney Waid (2004) argue in favour of an interactionist model. Inmates entering prison for the first time will suffer deprivation. But deprivation does not necessarily lead to violence unless or until it combines with the individual characteristics imported into the prison by inmates, and which influence the prison's culture.

Consider: *Explain why an interactionist model might be more valid than the importation and deprivation models on their own.*

Apply it Concepts: **One bad apple?**

Sergio is serving a five-year prison sentence for serious violence which put a police officer in hospital. He has a history of bullying during his time at school, and in the six months since he started his sentence he has been involved in several fights. He is now in trouble for assaulting a prison officer. If he carries on like this, Sergio's aggressive behaviour will definitely one day affect his chances of being released on parole.

Question

How would a dispositional explanation account for Sergio's behaviour?

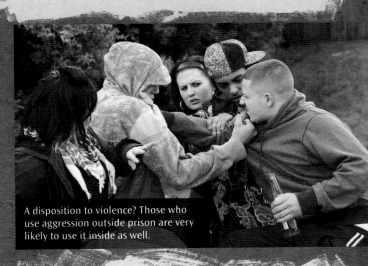

A disposition to violence? Those who use aggression outside prison are very likely to use it inside as well.

Apply it Methods: Three prisons

A psychologist wanted to find out if situational factors in prisons were responsible for aggressive behaviour. She identified three prisons with different regimes. In Prison A, inmates are frequently locked in their cells (lock-ups) with few educational opportunities. Prison B never uses lock-ups and there are many classes for inmates to choose from. Prison C is judged to be somewhere between Prisons A and B. The proportions of inmates committing acts of violence in the previous 12 months were: 37% in Prison A, 12% in Prison B, and 19% in Prison C.

Questions

1. Explain why the research method used in this study is a natural experiment. (*2 marks*)

2. Explain *one* strength and *one* limitation of this research method. (*2 marks + 2 marks*)

3. Sketch a graph of the results. Give it an appropriate title and label the axes carefully. (*3 marks*)

4. Identify the type of graph you have drawn. (*1 mark*)

5. Explain *one or more* **ethical issues** that the psychologists should have taken into account. (*4 marks*)

CHECK IT

1. Outline **one** dispositional and **one** situational explanation of institutional aggression.
   [3 marks + 3 marks]

2. Outline research into institutional aggression in the context of prisons. *[6 marks]*

3. Discuss explanations of institutional aggression in the context of prisons. *[16 marks]*

Media influences on aggression, including the effects of computer games.

It is certainly true that images of aggression and violence frequently appear in all sorts of media, from children's cartoons to the latest Hollywood blockbuster. But does it necessarily follow that they can make us behave more aggressively?

We address this question on the next two spreads, starting with a look at the research.

KEY TERMS

Media – Communication channels, such as TV, film and books, through which news, entertainment, education and data are made available.

Computer games – A game generally played onscreen using a keyboard, mouse or other controller. Types include simulations, first-person shooters, adventures, sports, and role-playing games, often conducted using an online service.

STUDY TIP

Be careful when you include criticisms of methodology as evaluation. What makes them effective criticisms is how you use them. Link them explicitly to the context being discussed, in this case the effect of computer games on aggression. For instance, if correlational studies cannot let us draw conclusions about cause and effect, why is this a problem in this context? It's because we cannot conclude that playing violent computer games causes aggressive behaviour on the basis of these studies.

Concern about the effects of aggressive media is particularly acute when it comes to children's viewing habits.

The effects of computer games on aggression

Whichever form of **media** psychologists study, they do so using three basic methodologies: **experimental** studies, which are usually lab-based and look at short-term effects; **correlational studies**, which can investigate real-life variables and may be short-term or may be **longitudinal studies**. A fourth methodology – **meta-analysis** – brings together these three types to give an overall judgement of the size of the effect of violent media on aggressive behaviour.

Experimental studies

In a lab-based study by Bruce Bartholow and Craig Anderson (2002), students played either a violent **computer game** (*Mortal Kombat*) or a nonviolent game (*PGA Tournament Golf*) for ten minutes. They all then carried out the *Taylor Competitive Reaction Time Task* (TCRTT), a standard **laboratory** measure of aggression in which the students delivered blasts of white noise at chosen volumes to punish a (non-existent) opponent.

Those who played the violent game selected **significantly** higher noise levels compared with the nonviolent players (means of 5.97 and 4.60 decibels respectively).

Correlational studies

Matt DeLisi *et al.* (2013) studied 227 juvenile offenders, all with histories of serious aggressive behaviours such as hitting a teacher or parent, or gang fighting. Using **structured interviews**, they gathered data on several measures of aggression and violent computer game-playing. They found that the offenders' aggressive behaviour was significantly correlated with how often they played violent computer games and how much they enjoyed them.

The researchers argued that the link is so well-established that aggression should be considered a public health issue, like HIV/AIDS, and computer game violence a significant risk factor, like condom non-use.

Longitudinal studies

Lindsay Robertson *et al.* (2013) wanted to see if there was a link between what they called 'excessive' television viewing in childhood and aggressive behaviour in adulthood. They studied 1037 people born in New Zealand in 1972 and 1973, and measured their TV viewing hours at regular intervals up to the age of 26 years.

They found that time spent watching TV was a reliable predictor of aggressive behaviour in adulthood, measured in terms of convictions for aggressive and violent **crimes**. Those who watched the most TV were also more likely to be diagnosed with **antisocial personality disorder** and to have aggressive personality traits. It appears that the most important media-related factor in influencing aggressive behaviour may be the amount of TV watched rather than whether it has violent content or not.

Meta-analyses

Craig Anderson *et al.* (2010) performed a meta-analysis of 136 studies which included all three types of methodology outlined above. They found that exposure to violent computer games was associated with increases in aggressive behaviours, thoughts, and feelings. This finding was true for both males and females and across **collectivist** and **individualist cultures**. Furthermore, the higher quality studies in the analysis showed an even greater significant effect. To put the outcome into perspective, the researchers claim that the effect of violent game-playing on aggressive behaviour is greater than the effect of second-hand smoke on cancer. Importantly, the analysis also showed no indication that publication bias influenced the results (see facing page).

Apply it   Concepts: Playing games again

Olga and Jimmy are good friends, who both go to the local sixth-form college. Jimmy would like them to hang out together a bit more, but is getting a bit fed up of asking Olga for dates and getting knocked back. It turns out she would rather stay in and play computer games into the early hours. When Olga explains how aggressive and violent the games are, Jimmy doesn't like the sound of it and is concerned that it might affect her. Olga insists that it's all a laugh and there's nothing to worry about.

Question

Who is right? Use your knowledge of psychological research studies to justify your response.

Evaluation

Experimental studies

The single greatest strength of experimental studies is that they allow us to establish a causal link between media aggression and aggressive behaviour. However, a weakness of these studies is that measures of aggression in lab situations are often accused of being artificial and unrealistic, such as the *Taylor Competitive Reaction Time Task* which measures how much loud noise is selected. Of course, it would be unethical to allow realistic forms of aggression in an experiment, for example by letting people hit each other. So researchers have no choice but to be creative in devising ways of measuring aggression.

There is another reason why aggression measures in lab situations are unrealistic – they do not involve any fear of retaliation. Unlike in the real world, the experimenter gives the participant implied permission to be 'safely' aggressive.

Correlational studies

These studies allow us to investigate realistic forms of aggression, including violent crime. However, a major limitation is the inability to draw cause-and-effect conclusions. No variables are manipulated or controlled, and there is no **random allocation** of participants to violent or nonviolent media conditions.

To indicate how serious a problem this is, consider a **positive correlation** between viewing or playing of violent media and aggressive behaviour. This outcome does not help us choose between two competing hypotheses of media effects. One is the *socialisation hypothesis*, which states that aggressive media causes people to become more aggressive. The other is the *selection hypothesis*, which claims that people who are already aggressive select aggressive media. The direction of causality cannot be settled by correlational studies.

Longitudinal studies

Researchers use this methodology to investigate changes in aggressive behaviour over time. So the dynamic nature of media influences in the long term can be studied. This approach also views people as active consumers rather than as passive recipients, which is a much more realistic view of how people interact with media.

However, studying change over time leaves longitudinal studies vulnerable to the effects of **confounding variables**. Many other sources of aggression interact with media influences over a period of time, such as role models in the form of friends and family members. It becomes difficult to separate them all and assess their contributions to aggressive behaviour.

Evaluation eXtra

Non-equivalence problem

Experimental studies compare participants who play a violent computer game with those who play a nonviolent one. It is difficult to be certain that the two games are equivalent apart from the presence or absence of violence. For instance, Andrew Przybylski *et al.* (2014) looked at two often-used games. *Marathon 2* is a violent first-person shooter set in a complex three-dimensional environment and which requires players to use the computer mouse as well as 20 keys. *Glider Pro 4*, on the other hand, is a two-dimensional game in which the player uses just two keys to fly a paper airplane.

Consider: *Explain how this might affect the **validity** of competing theories about media influences on aggression.*

Publication bias

There is a well-known tendency in scientific research towards publishing only findings that are statistically significant (sometimes called the **file drawer problem** because nonsignificant results get left in the filing cabinet). This is a problem for meta-analyses, because they generally only include published studies.

Consider: *How could this bias influence the conclusions of research?*

It certainly isn't 'game over' for the debates about aggressive behaviour and computer games; explanations continue to be developed and disagreements continue to flourish.

Apply it — Concepts: **Getting critical**

Two students are arguing in the college canteen about whether or not aggressive media can affect people's behaviour. As they are not psychology students, they are sadly not very well informed, so the argument is mostly based on personal opinion. They both realise that some scientific evidence would probably help, so they decide to look at the research together. Unfortunately, their sources of information are not very evaluative, so they turn to you for help.

Question

Select *three* key points you would tell the two students about the strengths and weaknesses of the research evidence.

Apply it — Methods: **An aggressive correlation**

A psychologist wanted to investigate the correlation between exposure to aggressive media and aggressive behaviour. She used **opportunity sampling** to recruit teenagers from a local college. They kept a diary of their TV viewing for a one-month period. **Content analysis** was used to derive an aggressive viewing score for each participant. This was correlated with teachers' rating of the participant's aggressive behaviour over the same period, on a scale from 0 (no aggression) to 10 (extreme aggression).

Questions

1. Explain how the psychologist could have carried out her content analysis. (*4 marks*) (See page 64)

2. The study gathered a lot of **qualitative data**. Explain what is meant by qualitative data. (*2 marks*)

3. Outline *one* strength of gathering qualitative data in this study. (*2 marks*)

4. The psychologist wanted to calculate the average teacher rating of aggressive behaviour. Which **measure of central tendency** would you advise her to use, and why? (*1 mark + 2 marks*)

5. The psychologist decided to analyse her results using a **statistical test**. Identify the appropriate test for her to use and give *two* reasons for your choice. (*1 mark + 2 marks*) (See page 70)

CHECK IT

1. In relation to aggression, explain what is meant by *media influences.* [2 marks]

2. Outline **one** study related to media influences on aggression. Include details of what the researcher(s) did and what they found. [6 marks]

3. Describe and evaluate research into the effects of computer games on aggression. [16 marks]

MEDIA INFLUENCES ON AGGRESSION: DESENSITISATION, DISINHIBITION AND COGNITIVE PRIMING

THE SPECIFICATION SAYS...

> Media influences on aggression: The roles of desensitisation, disinhibition and cognitive priming.

Psychologists have formulated several explanations of how media aggression might influence aggressive behaviour. We look here at the roles of three factors which may account for the research that we explored in the previous spread. To put them into context, according to Nathan DeWall and Craig Anderson's (2011) *general aggression model*, no single factor on its own can explain all of the research. Therefore, desensitisation, disinhibition and cognitive priming all operate together – along with other influences – to explain the long-term effects on behaviour of habitual use of violent media.

KEY TERMS

Desensitisation – Repeated exposure to violence reduces normal levels of physiological and psychological arousal associated with anxiety, making aggressive behaviour more likely.

Disinhibition – Normal social constraints against certain behaviours can be weakened by environmental triggers. These behaviours then appear temporarily socially acceptable and therefore more likely.

Cognitive priming – Violent images provide us with ready-made scripts about aggression which are stored in memory and triggered when we perceive aggressive cues in a situation.

Even if media violence does influence behaviour, it's only one of many sources of aggression. Here's another.

Roles of desensitisation, disinhibition and cognitive priming

Desensitisation

Normally when we witness violent actions we experience physiological arousal associated with the **sympathetic nervous system**, such as increased heart rate, higher blood pressure, greater sweat activity, and so on. But when children in particular repeatedly view aggression on TV or play violent computer games, they become habituated to its effects. So a stimulus that is usually aversive has a diminishing impact, resulting in a reduction of anxiety and physiological arousal on repeated viewing or playing.

This **desensitisation** is psychological as well as physiological. Repeated exposure to violent **media** promotes a belief that using aggression as a method of resolving conflict is socially acceptable. Negative attitudes towards violence weaken, less empathy is felt for victims, and their injuries are minimised and dismissed (Funk *et al.* 2004).

A **laboratory** study which highlighted these desensitisation effects was conducted by Monica Weisz and Christopher Earls (1995). They showed their participants the feature film *Straw Dogs*, which contains a prolonged and graphic scene of rape. Participants then watched a re-enactment of a rape trial. Compared with those who watched a non-sexually violent film, male viewers of *Straw Dogs* showed greater acceptance of rape myths and sexual aggression. They also expressed less sympathy towards the rape victim in the trial, and were less likely to find the defendant guilty. There was no such effect of film type on female participants.

Disinhibition

Most people generally hold the view that violence and aggression are antisocial and harmful. Consequently, there are powerful social and psychological inhibitions against using aggression to resolve interpersonal conflicts. These are learned, directly and indirectly, by processes explained by **social learning theory** (SLT, see page 300). According to the **disinhibition** explanation, these usual restraints are loosened after exposure to violent media. Aggressive behaviour is often made to appear normative and socially sanctioned in such media, especially if portrayals minimise the effects of violence on its victims and suggest that it is justified. It is not unusual for video games to show violence being rewarded at the same time as its consequences are minimised or ignored. This creates new social norms in the viewer.

Cognitive priming

Repeated viewing of aggressive media, especially game playing, can provide us with a 'script' about how violent situations may 'play out'. According to Rowell Huesmann (1998), this script is stored in memory, and so we become 'ready' or primed to be aggressive. The process is mostly automatic; it can direct our behaviour without us even being aware of it. The script is triggered when we encounter cues in a situation that we perceive as aggressive.

A study that illustrates the priming of aggressive scripts in memory was carried out by Peter Fischer and Tobias Greitemeyer (2006). They looked at the priming of aggressive scripts in memory by investigating a neglected form of media violence – song lyrics. Male participants listened to songs featuring aggressively derogatory lyrics about women. Compared with when they listened to neutral lyrics, participants subsequently recalled more negative qualities about women and behaved more aggressively towards a female **confederate**. This procedure was **replicated** with female participants, using 'men-hating' song lyrics, with similar results.

Apply it — Concepts: Selina gets educated

Selina is very concerned about her son's viewing habits. Arthur seems to spend a lot of his time downloading and watching the most explicitly gruesome films, videos and programmes he can find. Selina is sure that she has noticed a change in Arthur's behaviour recently. He seems to be a lot more touchy, irritable and even angry on occasion. She is really worried that the things he watches are having a bad effect on him. They argue a lot about it, but Selina would like to know more.

Question

Selina is a friend of yours, and knows you are doing A level psychology. She comes to you for advice, the kind of advice that will help her win the argument. You're happy to oblige. How could you use your knowledge of psychology to provide Selina with the ammunition she needs?

Evaluation

Research support for desensitisation

Barbara Krahé et al. (2011) showed participants violent (and nonviolent) film clips while measuring physiological arousal using skin conductance (see page 264). Participants who were habitual viewers of violent media showed lower levels of arousal as they watched the violent film clips. They also reported higher levels of pleasant arousal and lower levels of anxious arousal. Lower arousal was **correlated** with unprovoked (proactive) aggression in a 'noise blast' task.

These findings confirm hypotheses based on desensitisation. The lower arousal in violent media users reflects desensitisation to the effects of violence, and a greater willingness to be aggressive.

Research support for disinhibition

Leonard Berkowitz and Joseph Alioto (1973) found that participants who saw a film depicting aggression as vengeance gave more (fake) electric shocks of longer duration to a confederate. This suggests that media violence may disinhibit aggressive behaviour when it is presented as justified. This is because vengeance is a powerful justification for violence, and justified violence is more likely to be seen as socially acceptable.

This adds **validity** to the disinhibition concept because it demonstrates the link between removal of social constraints and subsequent aggressive behaviour, at least in the case of justified aggression.

Practical application of cognitive priming

There are potentially life-saving benefits in understanding how **cognitive priming** influences aggression in real-life situations. Whether such situations break out into violence often depends on how the participants interpret environmental cues. This in turn depends on the cognitive scripts they have stored in memory.

According to Brad Bushman and Craig Anderson (2002), someone who habitually watches violent media accesses stored aggressive scripts more readily. This means they are more likely to interpret cues as aggressive, resort to a violent solution and fail to consider the alternatives.

This explanation provides a possible means by which violent media could trigger aggressive behaviour through the priming of cognitive scripts. Effective interventions could potentially reduce aggressive behaviour by challenging hostile cognitive biases and encouraging habitual violent media users to consider alternatives to aggression, such as humour or negotiation.

Evaluation eXtra

Alternative explanation for desensitsation

The study by Krahé et al. (above) failed to find a link between media viewing, lower arousal and provoked (reactive) aggression. This suggests that desensitisation may not explain the impact of violent media exposure on all forms of aggressive behaviour.

A more valid explanation might be **catharsis**, the psychodynamic theory that viewing violent media acts as a safety valve mechanism, allowing people to release aggressive impulses without the need to behave violently.

Consider: *Does this alternative explanation increase or decrease the validity of the desensitisation concept? Explain your answer.*

Explaining cartoon violence

According to SLT, aggression carried out by media models is partly influential because it suggests to the observer that it is socially normative, especially when it goes unpunished. This disinhibits the use of aggression in the observer in a general rather than specific way. Stephen Kirsh (2006) argues that this can help explain aggressive responses to cartoon violence. Children do not learn specific behaviours from cartoon models (it is not possible to punch someone so their head spins round 360 degrees).

Consider: *So if children do not learn specific aggressive behaviours from cartoon models, what do they learn?*

The disinhibiting effects of the media are not always what you might expect.

Apply it — Concepts: Arthur's turn

Arthur gets home from college one day and is extremely surprised when his mum starts presenting him with all the arguments for why he should stop watching his beloved films. She certainly seems to have the facts at her fingertips, that's for sure. Unfortunately, he doesn't have any arguments he can use to come back at her with … but he knows someone who has.

Question

As it happens, Arthur is also a good friend of yours. Funnily enough, he comes to you for some advice as well. Not wanting to appear unfriendly, you outline some arguments to support his point of view. Explain the psychological knowledge you would pass on to Arthur.

Apply it — Methods: Experimental violence

A researcher recruited participants for a study investigating the effects of playing violent computer games on aggressive behaviour. Half of the participants were regular players of violent computer games. The other half did not play violent computer games on a regular basis. All the participants were shown a violent film clip while having their levels of physiological arousal measured using the **skin conductance response**. Statistical testing showed that arousal was significantly lower in the participants who were regular game players.

Questions

1. Write an appropriate **aim** for this study. (*2 marks*)

2. Identify *one* potential **confounding variable** and explain how it could have influenced the outcome of the study. (*1 mark + 2 marks*)

3. Explain how **investigator effects** might have influenced the study. (*2 marks*)

4. Identify and explain a **sampling method** the researchers could have used to recruit participants for this study. (*1 mark + 2 marks*)

CHECK IT

1. In relation to media influences on aggression, explain what is meant by the terms *desensitisation*, *disinhibition* and *cognitive priming*.
   [2 marks + 2 marks + 2 marks]

2. Outline research into the role of desensitisation in media influences on aggression. *[4 marks]*

3. Outline research into the role of cognitive priming in media influences on aggression. *[4 marks]*

4. Discuss media influences on aggression. Refer to desensitisation, disinhibition and cognitive priming in your answer. *[16 marks]*

> Knowledge and understanding of ...research methods, practical research skills and maths skills. These should be developed through ...ethical practical research activities.

This means you should conduct practical activities wherever possible. But there are serious ethical risks involved in investigating any aspect of aggressive behaviour. Even asking people to consider how aggressive they are or have been raises issues of privacy and protection from harm. The two activities on this spread will give you a chance to develop your practical skills further while thinking carefully about the ethical context in which research is conducted.

Ethics check

We suggest strongly that you complete this checklist before starting:

1. Do participants know participation is voluntary?
2. Do participants know what to expect?
3. Do participants know they can withdraw at any time?
4. Are individuals' results anonymous?
5. Have I minimised the risk of distress to participants?
6. Have I avoided asking sensitive questions?
7. Will I avoid bringing my school/teacher/psychology into disrepute?
8. Have I considered all other ethical issues?
9. Has my teacher approved this?

Is this man's yawn a sign of tiredness, or is he trying to communicate a more aggressive and hostile message to his colleagues? Will they respond in kind? And are you feeling the urge to yawn?

Practical idea 1: Observing fixed action patterns (FAPs)

A widespread FAP in humans is yawning. Various theories have been proposed to explain why we yawn, but there is no scientific agreement as to its function. One possibility is that yawning in humans is a passive-aggressive way of displaying hostility or rejection. Yawning is certainly considered antisocial in most cultures, which is why it's usually polite to hide it from view.

Given that yawning could be viewed as an aggressive behaviour, the aim of this study is to investigate it from an **ethological** perspective by observing how contagious it is.

The practical bit

There are two ways you could provoke a yawn in your participants. You could use a **confederate**, someone able to produce a convincing yawn. Alternatively, your participants could watch a video clip of someone yawning. There are plenty of possibilities available on the Internet, or you could produce your own. The benefit of the video option is that you know for sure that your participants have noticed the yawn. This isn't guaranteed in a 'live' situation, and risks introducing **confounding variables** such as having to yawn more than once or more loudly. Whichever method you choose, you should simply keep a record of whether or not each participant yawns in response to the confederate/video.

As it stands, this activity is just an **observation** with little scientific rigour. To turn it into a true **experiment**, you will need a comparable **control condition** using different participants. Perhaps a confederate (or video clip of someone) who merely opens their mouth without actually yawning would be suitable (a kind of '**placebo**' yawn').

Variations

Think about what conditions you could vary to test the **hypothesis** that a yawn is an aggressive act. For instance, does the likelihood of the participant yawning depend on the number of people present? You could alter the number of confederates who yawn one at a time. What about gender differences? Is the situation with a male yawner and a male participant the one most likely to produce a yawn? How does this compare with other combinations? A FAP is a behaviour that is always seen through to completion, so a yawn requires a huge effort to stop once it has begun. You could assess how difficult participants find it to stifle a yawn, perhaps by measuring its extent. Is it accompanied by stretching (technically called *pandiculation*) or an audible noise? How long does it last?

Demand characteristics

Demand characteristics are potentially very influential in this study ('Why am I watching someone yawning?'). You don't want to give the game away, so you will need a pretext ('cover story') to recruit your participants. If you are too vague about what you want them to do ('Take part in a psychology study'), your participants will probably just ask you for more details anyway. Once you have used your cover story and recruited a participant, you would take them to a room to wait for the 'study' to begin. This room should contain either another person (your confederate) or a means of showing a video clip (laptop, tablet, etc.). You should make sure you are in a position to observe the participants' behaviour.

Ethical issues

Clearly, a small degree of **deception** is necessary for this procedure to work. This has implications for consent and **debriefing**. It is your responsibility to make sure that the consequences of the deception are harmless (e.g. your cover story should be as close to the truth as possible). Consider how you could get **prior general consent** before the study begins (be honest with your participants about what you can and cannot tell them). What will you tell them in the debriefing?

Analysing your data

If you have followed the basic procedure, then you should have figures for the numbers of participants who did or did not yawn, in both conditions. You could calculate each as a percentage of the overall number of participants. You can analyse your findings for **significance**.

Apply it   Methods: The maths bit 1

	Yawn	No Yawn
Yawn video	9	6
'Placebo' yawn	5	10

Table 1: Contingency table of the numbers of participants who yawned and did not yawn

1. In the table on the left, what is the **level of measurement** of the variable indicating whether participants yawned or did not yawn? Explain your answer (*1 mark + 1 mark*) (See page 71)

2. Identify the appropriate **statistical test** to use to analyse the data. Explain your choice. (*1 mark + 3 marks*) (See page 70)

3. Calculate the statistical test you have identified to obtain a **calculated value**. State whether or not the outcome is significant and explain how you made this decision. (*1 mark + 3 marks*)

4. What is meant by the terms **Type I error** and **Type II error** in the context of this study? (*4 marks*) (See page 73)

Practical idea 2: Male sensitivity to cuckoldry

Because of the **ethical** difficulties inherent in studying aggression, this activity focuses on a closely linked evolutionary concept – fear of cuckoldry. A woman who gives birth can be 100% sure the baby is hers (obviously). But men do not have this degree of certainty. The possibility that a man might raise a child who does not share his **genes** is a powerful motivator of sexual jealousy and ultimately male aggression against female partners and potential male rivals.

The aim of this activity is to test the prediction that males are sensitive to the possibility of cuckoldry.

Can you see any resemblance between this father and his son? If males are better at spotting these similarities, does that show they are sensitive to the possibility of being cuckolded?

The practical bit

'Awww, doesn't he look like his dad? He's the spitting image, he's got his nose and everything.' These are the sort of comments often heard upon the arrival of a new baby, intended to reassure the father of his paternity. If it is **adaptive** for males to recognise the signs of cuckoldry, are they better at spotting facial similarities between fathers and their offspring? We could test this by seeing if males are more accurate than females at matching images of fathers and their children.

Devising materials

This is by far the most challenging part of this activity. You will need a number of pictures of a father with son. The pictures should be similar in terms of the way each individual presents themselves (see below) and also you will need to cut the pictures up so you just have the father and the son as two separate pictures (so they can't be hugging).

There are many such images available on the Internet. But a major problem with many of them is that we cannot guarantee that the man and the child are genetically related (e.g. in advertising or publicity images). There is a better solution which requires a lot more effort but is worth it. You could either borrow such images from friends and family, or take your own pictures. Ten should be enough for this practical.

Designing the study

As you are comparing male and female responses, this is a **quasi-experiment** with gender as the **independent variable**. The **dependent variable** is the number of correct matches. There are several ways you should control potentially confounding variables.

Try your best to make sure it's not possible to tell (e.g. from backgrounds, or size of picture) which child goes with which father. Also, on this occasion, use images of fathers and sons rather than daughters. It also helps if all the individuals are the same ethnicity and roughly the same age. You may also be able to think of other factors – apart from gender – that make some participants better at this task (such as experience). The more effort you make to **control** these variables, the more **valid** the activity becomes (and your findings and conclusions).

Ethical considerations

If you collect images from family or friends, or produce your own, you should be extremely sensitive to issues of **privacy** and **confidentiality**. This is also true in relation to your participants. You are investigating a hypothesis with serious implications, which include the possibility that some fathers and sons are not biologically related after all. In this situation, it is absolutely vital that you obtain fully **informed consent** from whoever provides you with photos and take every possible step to reduce the possibility of distress, embarrassment, and invasion of privacy.

Analysing your data

Your data will be the number of correct matches for each participant. You could then calculate various **descriptive statistics** for males and females separately: percentage correct matches, a **measure of central tendency** to find the average for each gender, and a suitable measure of dispersion (see Maths bit 2). You should also consider the most appropriate graphical representation. Finally, a suitable **statistical test** will tell you whether or not males are significantly more accurate than females in correctly matching fathers and sons.

The maths bit

Overall, at least 10% of the marks in assessments for Psychology will require the use of mathematical skills and at least 25% in total will involve research methods.

Don't avoid it!

Apply it — Methods: The maths bit 2

1. State a suitable **hypothesis** for this study. (*2 marks*)
2. Which is the appropriate measure of central tendency to use to summarise the data below? Give *one* reason for your choice. (*1 mark + 1 mark*)
3. Which is the appropriate **measure of dispersion** to use? Give *one* reason for your choice. (*1 mark + 1 mark*)
4. Calculate the descriptive statistics you identified in questions 1 and 2 for males and females separately. Draw up a table to present these statistics. (*4 marks + 3 marks*)
5. Which statistical test is the most suitable to analyse the results? Give *three* reasons for your choice. (*1 mark + 3 marks*) (See pages 70–71)
6. Apply the test you identified in question 5 to obtain a **calculated value**. Is the result significant or not? Explain your answer. (*1 mark + 3 marks*)

Table 2: Number of correct matches made by male and female participants

Participant	Gender	Correct matches
1	M	6
2	M	4
3	M	7
4	M	6
5	M	5
6	F	3
7	F	5
8	F	2
9	F	1
10	F	4

Revision summaries

Neural and hormonal mechanisms in aggression

How our biology contributes to aggressive behaviour.

Neural mechanisms

The limbic system
Most important limbic structure is the amygdala. Strong link between amygdala activity and reactive aggression.

Serotonin
Denson *et al.*: Decreased levels of serotonin associated with more impulsive aggression.

Evaluation

Role of other brain structures
Brain regulation of aggression is complex and involves at least amygdala, OFC and connection between them.

Effects of drugs on serotonin
Berman *et al.*: Drug to enhance serotonin reduced aggression in lab-based game, compared with placebo.

Hormonal mechanism

Testosterone
Animal studies: Increased testosterone linked with aggression (and vice versa in castration studies).

Evaluation

Explaining the role of testosterone
Josephs and Mehta: Losers of a challenge game more likely to rechallenge if their testosterone levels rose. Supports biosocial model of status.

Other hormones
Carre and Mehta: High testosterone only leads to aggression when cortisol is low – dual hormone hypothesis.

Issues of cause and effect
Much research is correlational so unclear if neural and hormonal factors are causes or effects of aggression.

Genetic factors in aggression

Are we born to behave aggressively?

Genetic factors

Twin studies
Coccaro *et al.*: Concordance rates for physical assault – 50% for MZs and 19% for DZs.

Adoption studies
Rhee and Waldman: Meta-analysis also shows 41% genetic factors.

The MAOA gene
Brunner *et al.*: Low-activity variant of this gene associated with aggressive behaviour in criminally violent males.

Gene-environment (GxE) interactions
The low-activity variant of MAOA gene only associated with aggression in people who experienced childhood trauma (Frazzetto *et al.*).

Evaluation

Isolating genetic factors
Difficult because genes interact with environment (e.g. abusive experience, provocation).

Multiple genetic influences
Stuart *et al.*: Serotonin transporter gene also important.
Vassos *et al.*: Thousands of genes make small contributions.

Measuring aggression
Studies differ in how aggression measured so hard to draw valid conclusions about genetics.

Research support for role of MAOA gene
Mertens *et al.*: People with high-activity variant of MAOA gene more co-operative and less aggressive in lab-based game.

Non-human animal studies
Godar *et al.*: Mice with MAOA gene knocked out are hyperaggressive and have high serotonin levels.

Social psychological explanations of aggression

Frustration–aggression hypothesis

How we learn to be aggressive directly and indirectly.

Frustration and aggression always go together.

Frustration–aggression hypothesis

The original hypothesis
Dollard *et al.*: If a goal is blocked this creates frustration, which is relieved by aggression – a cathartic experience.

Research into frustration-aggression
Procedure: Geen created frustration in students trying to complete jigsaw puzzle.
Findings: Most frustrated students gave strongest electric shocks.

The role of environmental cues
Procedure: Berkowitz and LePage: Students given electric shocks to create frustration.
Findings: Students gave stronger shocks to victim when guns were present in room.

Evaluation

Research support
Marcus-Newhall *et al.*: Meta-analysis shows that aggression is reliably displaced onto innocent parties when the source of frustration is unavailable.

Is aggression cathartic?
Bushman: Participants 'venting' their anger made them more aggressive not less.

Negative affect theory
Berkowitz: Many things cause negative feelings, not just frustration. These feelings might lead to aggressive behaviours, but they might not.

Justified and unjustified frustration
Dill and Anderson: Aggression is less likely to be produced by justified frustration, challenging Dollard because aggression is not inevitable.

Real-life application
Research into the role of aggressive cues has fed into the gun control debate in the USA.

Social learning theory

How we learn to be aggressive directly and indirectly.

Social learning theory

Direct and indirect learning
Aggression can be explained in terms of operant conditioning (direct) and observational learning (indirect).

Observational learning and vicarious reinforcement
Children learn that aggression is effective when they observe models being rewarded for behaving aggressively.

Cognitive control of aggressive behaviour
Cognitive requirements are: Attention, retention, reproduction and motivation.

Self-efficacy
Aggressive children have successfully used aggression in the past and expect it to continue to be rewarding.

Research into social learning of aggression
Procedure: Bandura *et al.* got children to observe adult model assault Bobo doll.
Findings: Very close imitation of model's aggression.

Evaluation

Supporting research
Poulin and Boivin: Aggressive boys formed friendships with each other in 'training grounds for antisocial behaviour', rewarding each other for aggression.

Cannot explain all aggression
SLT is weak at explaining reactive, 'hot-blooded' aggression in which rewards are less obvious.

The benefits of non-aggressive models
People shape aggressive behaviour by selecting aggressive environments; providing non-aggressive models can break this cycle.

Real-life applications
Huesmann and Eron: Vicarious reinforcement through media characters just as powerful as in real life.

Cultural differences
!Kung San children display aggression even though they have no aggressive models and aggression is not reinforced.

De-individuation

We become aggressive when in a crowd.

De-individuation

Crowd behaviour
Le Bon: Loss of self-identity and responsibility in crowd, ignoring social prohibitions against aggression.

How does de-individuation lead to aggression?
Zimbardo: Individuated versus de-individuated state where we monitor our behaviour less and this is more likely to happen when we feel anonymous.

The role of self-awareness
Prentice-Dunn and Rogers: Private versus public self-awareness where we pay less attention to our own behaviour and care less about what others think of us.

Research into de-individuation
Procedure: Dodd asked students to list what they would do if they could never be found out.
Findings: 36% responses were antisocial behaviour, 26% criminal acts.

Evaluation

Research support for de-individuation
Douglas and McGarty: Strong correlation between online anonymity and flaming – link between aggression and de-individuation.

Lack of support
Gergen *et al.*: Deviance in the dark study: De-individuation led to intimate and sexual behaviour but not aggression.

De-individuation and prosocial behaviour
Johnson and Downing: Participants dressed as nurses were less aggressive than those dressed in KKK outfits. Outcome of de-individuation depends on situational cues.

Real-life applications
Helps us to understand aggressive behaviour in online gaming services.

Explaining de-individuation
Spears and Lea SIDE model: De-individuation leads to behaviour that could be prosocial or antisocial depending on local group norms.

The ethological explanation of aggression

The aggressive instinct in humans and other animals.

The ethological explanation

Adaptive functions of aggression
Aggression forces animals into different territories reducing pressure on resources. Also establishes dominance in social groups.

Ritualistic aggression
Appeasement displays by loser inhibit physical damage from victor.

IRMs and FAPs
IRM: Built-in physiological structure/process that triggers a FAP (e.g. facial expression).
FAP: Specific stereotyped and unchanging sequence of behaviours (e.g. aggressive attack).

Key study: Research into IRMs and FAPs
Procedures: Tinbergen showed male sticklebacks models of different shapes.
Findings: Males were aggressive if model had red spot even if not stickleback-shaped.

Evaluation

Supporting research
Research into MAOA gene (Brunner *et al.*) and neural brain mechanisms (limbic system) show that aggression is genetically determined.

Cultural differences in aggression
Nisbett: Southern US males show more impulsive aggression than northern males. Can't be explained in terms of innate instincts.

Evidence against ritualistic aggression
Goodall: Appeasement displays in Gombe chimpanzees did not inhibit aggression.

FAPs are not that fixed
Hunt: FAPs are relatively flexible because they change from one individual or aggressive encounter to another.

Unjustified generalisations to humans
Fox: Lorenz and Tinbergen wrong to explain human warfare between countries in terms of instincts in non-human animals.

Evolutionary explanations of human aggression

Aggression as a way of enhancing reproductive success.

Evolutionary explanations

Evolutionary explanation of sexual jealousy
Sexual jealousy is greater in males because it has evolved as a defence against cuckoldry and drives aggressive strategies for retaining mates.

Mate retention strategies
Wilson and Day: Direct guarding and negative inducements, linked to physical violence towards partners (Wilson *et al.*).

Key study: Shackleford
Procedure: Couples completed questionnaires about mate retention strategies and male violence.
Findings: Men using aggressive retention strategies were more likely to be violent.

Evolutionary explanation of bullying
Volk *et al.*: Male bullying is adaptive because it signals desirable characteristics for females, e.g. dominance.

Evaluation

Research support
Shackelford *et al.*: Evidence that males use aggressive mate retention strategies; shows link with cuckoldry.

Can account for gender differences
Campbell: Females avoid risk of physical aggression because threatens safety of offspring, so more likely to use verbal aggression.

Real-life applications
Evolutionary approach can lead to better anti-bullying interventions by 'compensating' bullies with rewards for turning to non-aggressive ways of getting what they want.

Cultural differences
Some cultures (e.g. !Kung San) strongly disapprove of aggression, but others (e.g. Yanomamo) encourage it.

Methodological issues
Cannot conclude that evolutionary factors cause aggression because research is mostly correlational.

Institutional aggression in the context of prisons

Prisons – aggressive person or aggressive situation?

Dispositional explanations

The importation model
Irwin and Cressy: Prisoners bring their criminal attitudes and aggressive behaviours into the prison. They would be aggressive in any situation.

Research into the importation model
Procedure: DeLisi *et al.* studied imprisoned juveniles with negative dispositional traits.
Findings: These prisoners more likely to behave aggressively.

Situational explanations

The deprivation model
Clemmer: Prison is a situation of deprivation which leads to aggression especially if prison regime is unpredictable.

Research into the deprivation model
Procedure: Steiner studied 512 US prisons.
Findings: Several situation-level factors reliably predicted aggression in prison (e.g. use of protective custody).

Evaluation

Support from research
Camp and Gaes: Offenders randomly allocated to different types of prison equally likely to be aggressive inside, so disposition is key.

Alternative explanation
Dilulio: Administrative control model, factors relating to how prisons are run (e.g. indecisive leadership) are better predictors of aggression than prisoner dispositions.

Supporting evidence
Cunningham: 35 prison homicides mostly linked to deprivation (e.g. arguments over drugs).

Contradictory research
Hensley *et al.*: No link between opportunities for conjugal visits and level of aggression in prison, so deprivation not a factor.

Interactionist model
Both factors are important ,e.g. situational factors only lead to aggression if they interact with the aggressive disposition of the prisoner.

Media influences on aggression

Effects of computer games

Can using violent media make us more aggressive?

Effects of computer games

Experimental studies
Bartholow and Anderson: Players of a violent game chose higher volumes of white noise than players of a non-violent game.

Correlational studies
DeLisi *et al.*: Aggression significantly correlated with violent game-playing in sample of juvenile offenders.

Longitudinal studies
Robertson *et al.*: Time spent watching TV in childhood was reliable predictor of aggressive crimes as adults.

Meta-analyses
Andersen *et al.*: Playing violent games linked with aggressive behaviour across different types of study for males and females.

Evaluation

Experimental studies
Measures of aggression are artificial (e.g. no fear of retaliation) but ethical reasons prevent realistic measures.

Correlational studies
Uses realistic measures of aggression but no cause-and-effect conclusions so cannot choose between competing hypotheses (e.g. socialisation versus selection).

Longitudinal studies
Studies dynamic changes in media influences on aggression and is more realistic, but vulnerable to confounding variables (e.g. influence of family role models).

Non-equivalence problem
Violent and non-violent games are often very different in more ways than just presence or absence of violence – major confounding variable.

Publication bias
Most meta-analyses only include published studies, so usually exclude non-significant results.

Desensitisation, disinhibition and cognitive priming

Reduced sensitivity, reduced inhibitions, mental triggers.

Desensitisation, disinhibition and cognitive priming

Desensitisation
Repeatedly viewing or playing violent media leads to reduced arousal and greater acceptance of aggression as a problem-solving method.

Disinhibition
Normal learned social inhibitions against using aggression are loosened by repeated exposure to violent media, creating new social norms.

Cognitive priming
Exposure to violent media provides a 'script' about aggression which is stored in memory and readies us to behave aggressively in situations where we perceive aggressive cues.

Evaluation

Research support for desensitisation
Krahé *et al.*: Regular violent media viewers showed lower arousal and more proactive aggression in response to watching violent film clips.

Research support for disinhibition
Berkowitz and Alioto: More electric shocks given after viewing film featuring aggression as vengeance, because justified.

Practical application of cognitive priming
Watching violent media makes it easier to access aggressive cognitive scripts and resort to violent behaviour in real-life situations.

Alternative explanation for desensitisation
No link with reactive aggression in Krahé *et al.*, so catharsis may be a better explanation.

Explaining cartoon violence
Kirsh: Cartoon violence disinhibits already-learned aggressive behaviours in a general rather than specific way.

PRACTICE QUESTIONS, ANSWERS AND FEEDBACK

Question 1   Outline the roles of the limbic system and serotonin in aggression. *(4 marks)*

Morticia's answer

The limbic system and serotonin are both aspects of aggression that are related to brain activity. The limbic system is in the brain and is a group of structures such as the amygdala.

Serotonin affects the synapses in neurons in the brain. Low levels of serotonin are associated with aggressive behaviour. It is related to self-control so some people lack self-control.

The reference to the amygdala in the first half of Morticia's answer is relevant but the point is not explicitly linked to aggression. The material on serotonin is better with the reference to self-control – overall a weak response.

Luke's answer

The limbic system contains the amygdala and there is a strong link between amygdala activity and reactive aggression.

Denson et al. found that decreased levels of serotonin are associated with more impulsive aggression.

A much better use of the amygdala link here from Luke and the Denson study is relevant. The answer lacks sufficient detail.

Vladimir's answer

Both of these play a role in aggression. The limbic system is a subcortical set of structures in the brain, including the hypothalamus. It is regarded as one of the main areas of the brain controlling aggressive behaviour.

The role of serotonin is generally to dampen down activity in the brain so low levels mean that there is less control.

Another good but not strong answer from Vladimir. Again, additional detail related to aggression for either point would have been useful but the answer is informed and accurate.

Question 2   Asif often sees different species of bird in his garden, including robins. One day, he noticed two robins appearing to square up to each other. One in particular was making a lot of noise, flapping its wings, sticking its chest out, and making head-down charging gestures at the other.

Using your knowledge of ethological explanations of aggression, explain the behaviour of the robins. *(4 marks)*

Morticia's answer

This aggressive behaviour by the robins must have some adaptive value, that's what ethologists would argue. They said that the main function of aggression was to enhance survival. It is not intended to kill another animal but to encourage the other animal to move away and thus disperse the species.

Alternatively, aggression helps create dominance hierarchies, which is also adaptive because of the benefits an individual gets by being dominant.

Morticia's answer includes knowledge and understanding of ethological explanations (reference to adaptive value and dominance hierarchies in particular) but the reference to the stem is limited. The description is relevant but there is no application.

Luke's answer

Both of the robins are obviously engaging in some ritualistic behaviour and are using it to signal aggression. But neither of them are actually doing any attacking. They are displaying their intentions. This is good for survival and therefore is adaptive.

Ethologists explain this kind of behaviour as a confrontation, which avoids causing damage because overall that is better for both individuals. Even the animal that wins a contest may be damaged if they start attacking each other so rituals evolve where one animal can display its superiority such as sticking out his chest which shows his size.

One of the robins will back down, recognising that the other is more powerful.

Not all research supports the fact that encounters like this do not result in harm.

Luke presents the necessary knowledge and understanding in his reference to adaptive value and ritualistic behaviour. In comparison with Morticia, Luke has demonstrated a much more thorough engagement with the scenario in the stem. His knowledge is successfully and effectively linked to the robins' behaviour.

Vladimir's answer

This could be an innate releasing mechanism. Such mechanisms are a built-in physiological process or structure.

An environmental stimulus (such as a certain facial expression) triggers the IRM which then 'releases' a specific sequence of behaviours. This behavioural sequence is called a fixed action pattern (FAP). So we could be seeing a fixed action pattern here. Such patterns are stereotyped, universal, unaffected by learning, ballistic, single purpose and a response to a releaser. It is a form of adaptive behaviour.

In many ways, this is a similar answer to the one offered by Morticia. If anything, the knowledge of ethological explanations is more impressive here – a highly sophisticated account of the processes involved in innate releasing mechanisms. Again though, the application is very limited – the phrase 'we could be seeing a fixed action pattern here' is not enough for a strong answer.

On this spread we look at some typical student answers to questions. The comments provided indicate what is good and bad in each answer. Learning how to produce effective question answers is a SKILL. Read pages 387–397 for guidance.

Question 3   Describe and evaluate **two** social psychological explanations of aggression. *(16 marks)*

Morticia's answer

The two social psychological explanations I am going to describe are frustration–aggression hypothesis and social learning theory, and I will evaluate each of them.

Frustration–aggression theory (Dollard) proposes that frustration always leads to aggression, and aggression is always the result of frustration. This theory was developed from the psychodynamic idea of catharsis – that if a person experiences a drive that is blocked (i.e. they are frustrated) then they have to express the drive and this produces aggression.

There is research support for this explanation. For example, one meta-analysis of almost 50 studies of displaced aggression. They all found that people did displace their aggressive feelings on to something other than the original target which supports frustration–aggression. In contrast other research suggests that people actually don't get a sense of relief when they displace their aggression. Bushman found that when people repeatedly were hitting a punchbag they actually got even more angry rather than less angry. Another issue for frustration–aggression hypothesis is that different kinds of frustration have different effects. Dill and Anderson did a study where an experimenter showed participants how to perform a paper-folding task. The experimenter frustrated the participants by going too quickly so they couldn't follow him. In the unjustified condition he said he had to hurry because his girlfriend was waiting for him, in the justified condition he said his boss had told him to finish quickly. Afterwards the participants were asked to judge the experimenter and they found that the unjustified frustration produced the most negative comments (i.e. produced more aggression). So frustration only produces aggression in some situations.

The second theory I am going to describe is social learning theory (Bandura). This theory suggests that people behave aggressively because they have observed others behaving like this and being rewarded for it (vicarious reinforcement). This leads people to imitate such behaviour, especially behaviour they have seen on TV or in films.

This theory clearly explains many examples of aggression and there is research support, such as Bandura's Bobo doll study where young children imitated specific actions they had observed by a role model and also just behave more aggressively than children who didn't observe the model. In a real-life analysis by Poulin and Boivin they observed friendship groups of young boys who reinforced aggressive behaviour in each other. However, this explanation doesn't explain all kinds of aggression – it is less good for the kind of reactive, in the heat of the moment aggression which may actually be better explained by frustration-aggression. Social learning theory can be applied to explaining why watching violent videos is bad.

(431 words)

The introduction could be dispensed with and start the essay with the good summary in paragraph 1 – clear and concise.

The meta-analysis described in paragraph 3 is a genuine study but the details are somewhat lacking. Later in this paragraph there is good use of evidence as counterargument here (in contrast . . .) and finally a lengthy description of another study (Dill and Anderson). In contrast with the first study, the second study will add to the value of the description, and it's used well.

The second explanation covered is SLT – a rather short summary. One or two concrete examples might have brought the explanation 'to life' a bit more.

The answer ends with a very popular study to cite (the Bobo doll) – but relevant.

Some pertinent critical points to finish – the last one particularly could have been developed. A well-organised account, with slightly better evaluation than description.

Luke's answer

Social learning theory was proposed by Albert Bandura in the 1960s. He did a study with a Bobo doll where very young children watched an adult who hit the Bobo doll and said things like 'Pow'. Later the children were observed while they played with some toys including a Bobo doll. The children who had observed the aggressive model behaved more aggressively in general and also imitated specific things they saw or heard. This shows that aggression can be learned by watching someone else behave aggressively.

The trouble with this study is that it was in a lab and it was just a doll that they were hitting so the study lacks ecological validity because it was very artificial and not like everyday life. We can't really generalise the results because of this.

Another thing was that children were involved in this study and they are more impressionable than adults so it may explain their learning aggression but adults may not be as impressionable. So it may just be an explanation that applies to children and in fact the children in Bandura's study were very young. Older people may have more free will and can make decisions about whether to imitate behaviour.

There are real-life applications of this theory because it suggests that children shouldn't be exposed to aggressive role models in cartoons and films because they might imitate such behaviour, especially when they see someone they admire behaving in this way. Some people say that cartoon violence doesn't have any effect but I don't think this is true.

Another real-life application is using the idea to reduce aggressiveness by exposing people to non-violent role models, especially showing this on TV programmes that young children watch. You could have people being kind to each other or examples of how someone responded to an aggressive situation by being non-aggressive and then children might imitate this.

This research may be gender and culture biased because it is conducted in America where people are more violent. In fact quite a few studies have found that the aggressive role models in the media don't have such a big effect in some other cultures where there are no norms for behaving aggressively. So it means that just seeing aggressive role models is not enough.

There are other social theories of aggression such as frustration aggression. This suggests that people are aggressive when they feel frustrated. In fact in the Bobo doll study they frustrated the children before showing them the toys so this study supports the frustration-aggression hypothesis.

(422 words)

A common failing is shown here in Luke's answer – launching straight into the evidence when the explanation is the focus of the question.

This is followed by a fairly generic methodological evaluation that doesn't really add to a discussion of the theory.

In paragraph 3 there is an attempt to broaden this point out and make it a little more theoretical, which just about stands up.

In paragraph 4 there is a good evaluation point that is well-expanded but spoilt slightly by the anecdotal reference at the end. This is followed by another rather anecdotal critical point – a specific study to illustrate the point would be better.

Some speculative evaluation in the penultimate paragraph and finally the introduction of a second explanation but this is only a very brief reference.

A flawed essay. Lacking thorough discussion of a second explanation, some weak evaluation and very little description of social learning theory.

Neural and hormonal mechanisms in aggression

1. The most important part of the limbic system involved in aggression is the ...
(a) Hypothalamus.
(b) Hippocampus.
(c) Amygdala.
(d) Thalamus.

2. Decreased levels of serotonin are linked with aggression because ...
(a) Self-control is increased.
(b) Impulsive behaviours generally are increased.
(c) Serotonin speeds up neuronal activity.
(d) Levels of 5-HIAA in cerebrospinal fluid are high.

3. Research with violent offenders by Dolan *et al.* found a positive correlation between aggression and ...
(a) Serotonin levels.
(b) Amygdala activity.
(c) Testosterone levels.
(d) 5-HIAA levels.

4. The dual hormone hypothesis suggests the involvement in aggression of ...
(a) Testosterone and adrenaline.
(b) Testosterone and noradrenaline.
(c) Testosterone and cortisol.
(d) Adrenaline and cortisol.

Genetic factors in aggression

1. The proportion of aggressive behaviour accounted for by genetics seems to be ...
(a) Significantly more than 50%.
(b) About 50%.
(c) 27%.
(d) Very unclear.

2. The MAOA gene ...
(a) Controls the production of the monoamine oxidase enzyme.
(b) Determines the amount of testosterone in the body.
(c) Operates identically in every individual.
(d) Determines the activity of the amygdala.

3. It is difficult to establish the role of genetics in aggression because ...
(a) There is little research into this issue.
(b) Most of the research is experimental.
(c) It is hard to separate genetic and environmental influences.
(d) Environmental factors are clearly much more important.

4. Research into genetic factors lacks validity because ...
(a) Studies use different ways of measuring aggression.
(b) Different variants of the MAOA gene have similar effects.
(c) Genetic research cannot easily be generalised from animals to humans.

(d) Genes and environment have separate effects.

The ethological explanation of aggression

1. An important adaptive function of aggression is to ...
(a) Kill potential competitors.
(b) Make sure every animal has a similar status within the group.
(c) To reduce pressure on resources such as food.
(d) Distribute access to fertile females equally.

2. An innate releasing mechanism is ...
(a) A collection of stereotyped aggressive behaviours.
(b) An environmental stimulus that triggers a fixed action pattern.
(c) A response that is learned through experience.
(d) A biological structure or process.

3. One feature of a fixed action pattern is that it ...
(a) Can be found in the brain.
(b) Responds directly to an environmental stimulus.
(c) Follows a predictable sequence that is always completed.
(d) Occurs in many different situations.

4. The ethological explanation of aggression is supported by research that shows ...
(a) Aggression is mostly influenced by cultural factors.
(b) Genetic and neural mechanisms are major influences on aggression.
(c) Non-human animals frequently use aggression to kill.
(d) Fixed action patterns are fairly flexible.

Evolutionary explanations of human aggression

1. Sexual jealousy is stronger in males because ...
(a) Females are more likely to be unfaithful.
(b) Females make a greater investment in offspring.
(c) They face the possibility of cuckoldry.
(d) They can always be sure of their paternity.

2. An aggressive mate retention strategy commonly used by males is ...
(a) Direct guarding.
(b) Romantic gestures.
(c) Sexual favours.
(d) Providing resources.

3. Bullying is adaptive for a male mainly because ...
(a) It ensures his partner continues to provide resources.
(b) It increases the possibility of cuckoldry.
(c) Females are more sexually jealous than males.
(d) It gives him more mating opportunities.

4. Females are generally less aggressive than males because ...
(a) Aggression is a more adaptive behaviour for females.

(b) Men are physically stronger than women.
(c) Males invest more resources in offspring then females.
(d) Female involvement in physical aggression is risky for their offspring.

Social psychological explanations of aggression: The frustration-aggression hypothesis

1. Aggression is cathartic because ...
(a) It is always the result of frustration.
(b) Behaving aggressively reduces the drive to be aggressive.
(c) It is not always expressed against the true source of frustration.
(d) Violent fantasies make us even more angry and aggressive.

2. Berkowitz and LePage found that ...
(a) Aggressive cues in the situation make aggression inevitable.
(b) There was no significant difference between their participant groups.
(c) Frustration always makes us behave aggressively.
(d) The presence of weapons can make aggression more likely.

3. We displace aggression onto innocent targets when ...
(a) The true source of our frustration is weaker than us.
(b) The true source of our frustration is unavailable.
(c) We are particularly frustrated.
(d) Our frustration is justified.

4. According to negative affect theory ...
(a) Frustration always produces aggression.
(b) Negative feelings always lead to aggression.
(c) Frustration can lead to negative feelings.
(d) We all perceive frustrations in the same ways.

Social psychological explanations of aggression: Social learning theory

1. An example of vicarious reinforcement is ...
(a) Watching an adult being shouted at for kicking someone.
(b) Watching an adult being praised for punching someone.
(c) A child being told off for biting another child.
(d) A child being allowed out of their room after apologising for hitting another child.

2. Forming a mental image of how to perform an aggressive act is an example of ...
(a) Cognitive control of aggression.
(b) Positive reinforcement.
(c) Negative reinforcement.
(d) Vicarious punishment.

3. Self-efficacy in this context refers to ...
(a) Expecting that using aggression in future interactions will be just as successful as in the past.

(b) Lacking confidence in your ability to get what you want.

(c) Believing that aggression never pays.

(d) Having a good reason to be aggressive.

4. Reciprocal determinism in relation to SLT means . . .

(a) Aggressive people are attracted to aggressive situations.

(b) Being with aggressive people makes you more aggressive.

(c) Aggressive people and aggressive environments influence each other.

(d) Being rewarded for behaving in aggressive ways.

Social psychological explanations of aggression: de-individuation

1. Which is the best example of de-individuated behaviour?

(a) Driving at 25mph in a 30mph zone.

(b) Waiting patiently in the queue for lunch.

(c) Using your real name on internet forums.

(d) Throwing a brick through the window of a bank during a protest.

2. Public self-awareness is . . .

(a) Increased when we are part of a crowd.

(b) How much we care about what other people think of us.

(c) Monitoring your own behaviours when with others.

(d) Becoming less self-critical when part of a crowd.

3. In the 'deviance in the dark' study, the participants . . .

(a) Became argumentative and aggressive with each other.

(b) Behaved no differently to when the lights were on.

(c) Sat in silence throughout the procedure.

(d) Became quite intimate when the lights went out.

4. The SIDE model predicts that . . .

(a) Anonymity always leads to aggressive behaviour.

(b) People conform to group norms when they are anonymous.

(c) Reduced self-awareness encourages anti-normative behaviour.

(d) When people are anonymous, they focus more on their own thoughts and feelings.

Institutional aggression in the context of prisons

1. According to the importation model . . .

(a) Prisons reflect criminal subcultures in the real world.

(b) Prison aggression is caused mostly by situational factors.

(c) Most prisoners are more likely to use aggression in prison than in the outside world.

(d) Prisoners are aggressive because they have lost their freedom.

2. Deprivation leads to aggression in prisons because . . .

(a) It creates competition amongst inmates for material goods.

(b) Some prisoners are just more aggressive than others.

(c) Many prisoners have a history of violent behaviour.

(d) Dispositional factors are more important than situational ones.

3. Camp and Gaes's conclusions are especially valid because . . .

(a) They found a significant positive correlation between prison category and aggression.

(b) They selected a representative sample of prison inmates.

(c) The inmates in their study were randomly allocated to prisons.

(d) It was a laboratory experiment.

4. The deprivation model is contradicted by research into . . .

(a) Conflict in prisons over drugs.

(b) Conjugal visits.

(c) Weak prison leadership.

(d) Loss of material goods in prisons.

Media influences on aggression

1. DeLisi *et al.* (2013) argued that . . .

(a) Computer game violence causes aggressive behaviour.

(b) Aggression is a serious public health issue.

(c) Viewing media violence has long-term effects on behaviour.

(d) Structured interviews are not valid for measuring aggression.

2. In the meta-analysis by Anderson *et al.*, particularly significant results were found in . . .

(a) Studies of individualist cultures.

(b) Longitudinal studies.

(c) High quality studies.

(d) Unpublished studies.

3. The main problem with experimental studies of media influences on aggression is . . .

(a) They do not investigate short-term effects of media.

(b) We cannot draw cause-and-effect conclusions.

(c) The measures of aggression are quite unrealistic.

(d) They are always lab-based.

4. Longitudinal studies are limited because . . .

(a) They assume that people are passive recipients of media.

(b) They only focus on short-term effects of media.

(c) They cannot be used to predict how media influences aggressive behaviour.

(d) Confounding variables can interfere over time.

Media influences on aggression: desensitisation, disinhibition and cognitive priming

1. One feature of desensitisation to violent media is . . .

(a) Storage of aggressive 'scripts' in memory.

(b) We no longer respond to media aggression with arousal.

(c) Realisation that aggression is an unacceptable form of conflict resolution.

(d) Greater empathy for victims of aggression.

2. Cognitive priming occurs when . . .

(a) We perceive cues in a situation as aggressive when they are neutral.

(b) We no longer respond to media aggression with arousal.

(c) Social norms discourage the use of aggression.

(d) We realise there are alternatives to aggression.

3. 'Loosening social constraints against aggressive behaviour' is an example of . . .

(a) Desensitisation.

(b) Inhibition.

(c) Disinhibition.

(d) Cognitive priming.

4. A problem with desensitisation is that it . . .

(a) Suggests that aggression is a safety valve.

(b) Is based only on lab experiments.

(c) Cannot explain media influence on reactive aggression.

(d) Has no research support.

MCQ answers

Neural and hormonal mechanisms in aggression   1c, 2b, 3c, 4c
Genetic factors in aggression   1b, 2a, 3c, 4a
The ethological explanation of aggression   1c, 2d, 3c, 4b
Evolutionary explanations of human aggression   1c, 2a, 3d, 4d
Social psychological explanations of aggression: The frustration-aggression hypothesis   1b, 2d, 3b, 4c
Social psychological explanations of aggression: Social learning theory   1b, 2a, 3a, 4c
Social psychological explanations of aggression: De-individuation   1d, 2b, 3d, 4b
Institutional aggression in the context of prisons   1a, 2a, 3c, 4b
Media influences on aggression   1b, 2c, 3c, 4d
Media influences on aggression: Desensitisation, disinhibition and cognitive priming   1b, 2a, 3c, 4c

CHAPTER 12
FORENSIC PSYCHOLOGY

Chapter contents

In order to study forensic psychology, we first need to understand what crime is. So, to begin with, a light-hearted look at a serious subject . . .

Which of the following UK and US laws are genuine and which are made up?

1. It is illegal to die in the Houses of Parliament.
2. In Liverpool, it is illegal for a woman to be topless except as a clerk in a tropical fish store.
3. In the UK a pregnant woman can legally relieve herself anywhere she wants, including in a policeman's helmet.
4. The head of any dead whale found on the British coast automatically becomes the property of the King, and the tail belongs to the Queen.
5. In the city of York it is legal to murder a Scotsman within the ancient city walls, but only if he is carrying a bow and arrow.
6. In Ohio, it is illegal to get a fish drunk.
7. In Utah, it is illegal to walk down the street carrying a paper bag.
8. In Alabama, it is illegal to be blindfolded while driving a vehicle.
9. In Florida, unmarried women who parachute on a Sunday could be jailed.
10. In Vermont, women must obtain written permission from their husbands to wear false teeth.

(Answers on page 353)

Problems in defining crime. Ways of measuring crime, including official statistics, victim surveys and offender surveys.

'Crime' is a slippery concept which may be culturally and historically specific. This raises problems when trying to define it. We shall consider these issues here.

Once we have settled on a definition of crime, we are also concerned with the *extent* of crime. Recorded data based on the incidence of crime is of use to the government. It means policies and initiatives can be developed by the police and resources directed to areas where crime is most prevalent.

KEY TERMS

Crime – An act committed in violation of the law where the consequence of conviction by a court is punishment, especially where the punishment is a serious one such as imprisonment.

Official statistics – Figures based on the numbers of crimes that are reported and recorded by the police which are often used by the government to inform crime prevention strategies.

Victim survey (or victimisation survey) – A questionnaire that asks a sample of people which crimes have been committed against them over a fixed period of time and whether or not they have been reported to the police.

Offender survey – A self-report measure that requires people to record the number and types of crime they have committed over a specified period.

Apply it

Methods: Measuring crime

A team of researchers developed a form of victim survey to investigate levels of crime around the country. They called it the *National Crime Questionnaire* (NCQ) and conducted a **pilot study** involving 50 respondents who were **randomly selected**.

Questions

1. Outline *one* reason why researchers conduct pilot studies. Refer to the NCQ in your answer. (*2 marks*)

2. Explain *one* way in which the **reliability** of the NCQ could be assessed. (*3 marks*) (See page 66)

3. Explain *one* way in which the **validity** of the NCQ could be assessed. (*3 marks*) (See page 68)

4. The respondents involved in the pilot study were randomly selected. Explain how this could have been achieved. (*3 marks*)

5. Briefly evaluate the use of **questionnaires** – like the NCQ – when measuring crime. (*6 marks*)

Problems in defining crime

Crime might be defined as any act that breaks the law and therefore warrants some form of punishment. However, this *legalistic* definition is complicated by the fact that laws are often subject to change and that not all acts that break the law are punished. Researchers have pointed out that what counts as a crime varies from culture to culture as well as over time.

Cultural issues in defining crime

What is considered a crime in one culture may not be judged as such in another. One example of this is laws on marriage. In the UK having more than one wife is the crime of bigamy. However, it is not a crime in cultures where polygamy is practised (having multiple partners). In 2014, forced marriage was made illegal in the UK, yet this is still practised in some cultures.

Historical issues in defining crime

Definitions of crime change over time. A parent's right to smack their child was outlawed in 2004 with the introduction of the Children's Act. Homosexuality was considered a crime in this country until 1967. The latter is an example of how some behaviours judged to be criminal may be historically *and* culturally specific. There are many African and Asian countries where homosexuality is still classed as illegal.

Ways of measuring crime

Three methods are used to measure crime rates: official statistics, victim surveys and offender surveys.

Official statistics

Official statistics are government records of the total number of crimes *reported* to police and *recorded* in the official figures. These are published by the Home Office on an annual basis and are a useful 'snapshot' of the number of crimes occurring across the country and in specific regions. This allows the government to develop crime prevention strategies and policing initiatives, as well as direct resources to those areas most in need.

Victim surveys

Victim surveys record people's experience of crime over a specific period. The *Crime Survey for England and Wales* (formerly the *British Crime Survey*) asks people to document the crimes they have been a victim of in the past year. In order to compile the figures, 50,000 households are **randomly** selected to take part in the survey and this has enabled the *Office for National Statistics* to produce crime figures based on victim surveys since 1982. In 2009, a separate survey was introduced to record the experiences of younger people aged 10–15, and the complete results (from both surveys) are published on an annual basis.

Offender surveys

Offender surveys involve individuals volunteering details of the number and types of crimes they have committed. These tend to target groups of *likely* offenders based on 'risk' factors such as previous convictions, age range, social background, etc. *The Offender Crime and Justice Survey*, which ran from 2003–2006, was the first national **self-report** survey of its kind in England and Wales. As well as measuring self-reported offending, the OCJS looked at indicators of repeat offending, trends in the prevalence of offending, drug and alcohol use, the role of co-offenders and the relationship between perpetrators and victims.

Headlines such as these may mask the fact that official crime rate statistics are often unreliable.

B4 | HOME | MONDAY, SEPTEMBER 23, 2013 | THE STRAITS TIMES

Crime rate at a 29-year-low

Experts cite better policing focused on the community, a wiser public

Evaluation

Official statistics

Official statistics have been criticised as unreliable in that they **significantly** underestimate the true extent of crime. Some commentators suggest that so many crimes go unreported by victims or unrecorded by police that only around 25% of offences are included in the official figures. The other 75% make up what criminologists refer to as the 'dark figure' of crime. Crimes may not appear in the official statistics for many reasons (see study tip on right) but one of these is police recording rules. One study found that police in the county of Nottinghamshire were more likely than other regions to record thefts of under £10 and this explained an apparent 'spike' of thefts in this area (Farrington and Dowds 1985). This suggests that policing priorities may distort official figures.

Victim surveys

Victim surveys are more likely to include details of crimes that were not reported to the police and so are thought to have a greater degree of accuracy than official statistics (and, as such, are less likely to conceal the 'dark figure'). As evidence of this, 2006/7 official statistics suggested a 2% decrease in crime from the previous year whereas the *British Crime Survey* showed a 3% *increase*. That said, victim surveys rely on respondents having accurate recall of the crimes they have been a victim of. 'Telescoping' may occur where a victim may misremember an event as happening in the past year when it did not (perhaps because the trauma is fresh in the mind it seems to have been that recent) and this may distort the figures.

Offender surveys

The main strength of offender surveys over alternative methods is that they provide insight into *how many* people are responsible for certain offences (as a small group of people, or single individual, may have committed many crimes). Although confidentiality in offender surveys is assured, responses may be unreliable. Offenders may want to conceal some of the more serious crimes they have committed, or even exaggerate the number for reasons of bravado. Finally, the targeted nature of the survey means that certain types of crime (such as burglary) are overrepresented, whereas 'middle-class' offences such as corporate crime and fraud are unlikely to be included.

Evaluation eXtra

The politics of measuring crime

Political parties have a vested interest in using some measures rather than others when discussing rates of crime across the country. The political party in opposition will typically focus on measures that make the government look bad by suggesting that crime is increasing, whereas the party in power will emphasise measures that show crime is falling (see the difference between official statistics and the *British Crime Survey* for 2006–07 above). Even though crime statistics in the UK are compiled by an independent body free from political interference (the Office for National Statistics), questions are frequently raised as to their **validity**, usually by those with political motives.

Consider: *Why do you think the government are more likely to quote official statistics than alternative methods (such as the Crime Survey) when explaining their own record on combatting crime?*

A multidisciplinary approach

Each of the methods presented here has particular issues in terms of the **reliability** and validity of the data they produce. This means that all crime figures should be carefully scrutinised and interpreted with caution. Researchers advocate a multidisciplinary approach when measuring crime: a combination of all available methods provides the best insight into the true extent of offending.

Consider: *What would be gained from a combined approach that could not be understood by analysing data from one method alone?*

The main explanation for the dark figure of crime, described in text left, is the fact that crime may be under-reported by victims and under-recorded by the police. Reasons for crime not being reported may include mistrust of the police or the victim fears reprisal (revenge). Reasons for crime not being recorded include variations in police recording rules. Try to come up with your own list of reasons why certain offences maybe go unreported or unrecorded so you can use these as examples in your essays.

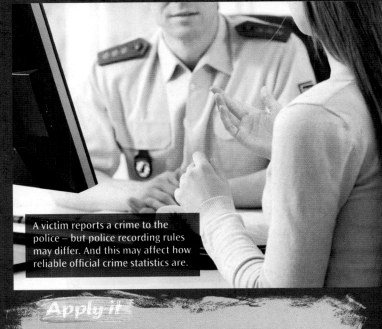

A victim reports a crime to the police – but police recording rules may differ. And this may affect how reliable official crime statistics are.

Apply it

Concepts: Official statistics and cases of rape

An alarming fall in the number of rape convictions has led the Director of Public Prosecutions to express concern that victims are not having their cases dealt with properly. Recent figures revealed that 129 fewer rape suspects were convicted in 2013 than the year before, and the number of rape cases referred to prosecutors for charging has fallen by a third since 2011. This is despite a rise in offences recorded by police.

In an interview with the *Independent*, Alison Saunders, the Director of Public Prosecutions, said there were worrying variations in the way rape cases are dealt with across the country. 'We have certainly seen some indication that cases which we thought should have gone through (to charge) didn't', she said.

She added, 'There is best practice out there. It's just that not everyone is doing it'.

Question

How does the information above illustrate some of the problems with official statistics as a way of measuring crime?

Source: *The Independent* 2 May 2015

CHECK IT

1. Outline **two** problems with official statistics as a way of measuring crime. [4 marks]
2. Explain **two** problems in defining crime. [6 marks]
3. Outline and briefly evaluate **one** way of measuring crime. [5 marks]
4. Describe and evaluate ways of measuring crime. Refer to evidence and/or published examples in your answer. [16 marks]

Offender profiling is based on the idea that the characteristics of an offender can be deduced from the characteristics of the offence and the particulars of the crime scene. The work of offender profilers has often been the subject of TV dramatisations (such as *Cracker* in the 1990s, and more recently, *Criminal Minds*) as well as depicted on film (*Silence of the Lambs*).

We shall consider three approaches to profiling: the top-down approach (on this spread) and two examples of the bottom-up approach on the next spread.

KEY TERMS

Offender profiling – Also known as 'criminal profiling', a behavioural and analytical tool that is intended to help investigators accurately predict and profile the characteristics of unknown criminals.

The top-down approach – Profilers start with a pre-established typology and work down in order to assign offenders to one of two categories based on witness accounts and evidence from the crime scene.

Organised offender – An offender who shows evidence of planning, targets the victim and tends to be socially and sexually competent with higher than average intelligence.

Disorganised offender – An offender who shows little evidence of planning, leaves clues and tends to be socially and sexually incompetent with lower than average intelligence.

Bundy's victims – like the woman in the picture left – wore their hair long and parted in the middle.

The top-down approach

Offender profiling

Offender profiling is an investigative tool employed by the police when solving **crimes**, the main aim of which is to narrow the field of enquiry and the list of likely suspects. Professional profilers will often be called upon to work alongside the police especially during high profile murder cases. Methods vary, but the compiling of a profile will usually involve careful scrutiny of the crime scene and analysis of the evidence (including witness reports) in order to generate **hypotheses** about the probable characteristics of the offender (their age, background, occupation, etc.).

The American approach

The top-down approach to profiling originated in the United States as a result of work carried out by the FBI in the 1970s. More specifically, the FBI's Behavioural Science Unit drew upon data gathered from in-depth **interviews** with 36 sexually motivated serial killers including Ted Bundy (see below) and Charles Manson.

Also known as the typology approach, offender profilers who use this method will match what is known about the crime and the offender to a pre-existing template that the FBI developed. Murderers or rapists are classified in one of two categories (organised or disorganised) on the basis of the evidence, and this classification informs the subsequent police investigation.

Organised and disorganised types of offender

The organised and disorganised distinction is based on the idea that serious offenders have certain signature 'ways of working' (often referred to as their *modus operandi*) and these generally **correlate** with a particular set of social and psychological characteristics that relate to the individual.

Organised offenders show evidence of having planned the crime in advance; the victim is deliberately targeted and will often reflect the fact that the killer or rapist has a 'type'. They maintain a high degree of control during the crime and may operate with almost detached surgical precision. There is little evidence or clues left behind at the scene. They tend to be of above-average intelligence, in a skilled, professional occupation and are socially and sexually competent. They are usually married and may even have children.

In contrast, **disorganised offenders** show little evidence of planning, suggesting the offence may have been a spontaneous, spur of the moment act. The crime scene tends to reflect the impulsive nature of the attack – the body is usually still at the scene and there appears to have been very little control on the part of the offender. They tend to have a lower than average IQ, be in unskilled work or unemployed, and often have a history of sexual dysfunction and failed relationships. They tend to live alone and often relatively close to where the offence took place.

Constructing an FBI profile

There are four main stages in the construction of an FBI profile:

- Data assimilation – the profiler reviews the evidence (crime scene photographs, pathology reports, etc.).
- Crime scene classification – as either organised or disorganised.
- Crime reconstruction – hypotheses in terms of sequence of events, behaviour of the victim, etc.
- Profile generation – hypotheses related to the likely offender, e.g. of demographic background, physical characteristics, behaviour, etc.

Apply it Concepts: Ted Bundy – the classic 'organised' killer?

Theodore Robert 'Ted' Bundy is one of the United States' most notorious serial killers. During the 1970s, Bundy is known to have raped, tortured and brutally murdered over 30 women (though the actual figure may be much higher) across seven US states.

Handsome, charming and highly intelligent – traits he used to win the trust of his victims – Bundy attended the University of Washington and later, law school, where he excelled. While a student, Bundy fell in love with a wealthy young woman from California. Devastated by their subsequent breakup, many of Bundy's victims resembled his college girlfriend, they were attractive students with long, dark hair parted in the middle. His killings usually followed a gruesome pattern. He often raped his victims before beating them to death.

After escaping police custody twice, Bundy was executed by electric chair in 1989.

Question

To what extent does Bundy fit the profile of the organised offender?

Evaluation

Only applies to particular crimes

Top-down profiling is best suited to crime scenes that reveal important details about the suspect, such as rape, arson and cult killings, as well as crimes that involve such macabre practices as sadistic torture, dissection of the body and acting out fantasies. More common offences such as burglary and destruction of property (or even murder or assault during the course of committing these) do not lend themselves to profiling because the resulting crime scene reveals very little about the offender. This means that, at best, it is a limited approach to identifying a criminal.

Based on outdated models of personality

The typology classification system is based on the assumption that offenders have patterns of behaviour and motivations that remain consistent across situations and contexts. Several critics (e.g. Alison *et al.* 2002) have suggested that this approach is naïve and is informed by old-fashioned models of personality that see behaviour as being driven by stable dispositional traits rather than external factors that may be constantly changing.

This means the top-down approach, which is based on 'static' models of personality, is likely to have poor **validity** when it comes to identifying possible suspects and/or trying to predict their next move.

Evidence does not support the 'disorganised offender'

David Canter *et al.* (2004), using a technique called *smallest space analysis*, analysed data from 100 murders in the USA. The details of each case were examined with reference to 39 characteristics thought to be typical of organised and disorganised killers. Although the findings did indeed suggest evidence of a distinct *organised* type, this was not the case for *disorganised* which seems to undermine the classification system as a whole.

Nevertheless, the organised/disorganised distinction is still used as a model for professional profilers in the US and has widespread support.

Evaluation eXtra

Classification is too simplistic

The behaviours that describe each of the organised and disorganised types are not mutually exclusive; a variety of combinations could occur in any given murder scene. For instance, Grover Godwin (2002) asks how police investigators would classify a killer with high intelligence and sexual competence who commits a spontaneous murder in which the victim's body is left at the crime scene. This has prompted other researchers to propose more detailed typological models. For instance, Ronald Holmes (1989) suggests there are four types of serial killer: visionary, mission, hedonistic and power/control, whilst Robert Keppel and Richard Walter (1999) focus more on the different motivations killers might have rather than trying to determine specific 'types'.

Consider: *Explain why this represents a challenge to the typology approach.*

Original sample

As mentioned, the typology approach was developed using interviews with 36 killers in the US – 25 of which were serial killers, the other 11 being single or double murderers. Critics have pointed out that this is too small and unrepresentative a sample upon which to base a typology system that may have a significant influence on the nature of the police investigation. Canter has also argued that it is not sensible to rely on **self-report** data with convicted killers when constructing a classification system.

Consider: *Why do you think such self-report methods may be a problem for the classification?*

Apply it

Concepts: Organised or disorganised?

Case One
A teenage victim was attacked in the morning on a secluded path that is very rarely used. She was seized from behind, dragged into some bushes, gagged and bound with duct tape, and sexually assaulted. The path cannot be seen from nearby roads, and can only be accessed from an estate on one side. The victim had unexpectedly spent the night at a friend's house and had not used the path before.

Case Two
Between 1986 and 1988, seven attacks on elderly women took place in tower blocks in Birmingham. Women in their 70s and 80s, often infirm, were followed into the lifts by a stocky young man who took them to the top floor of the tower block. He would rape the women and then flee. Consistent patterns seemed to suggest the same man was responsible. In his interactions with the women he appeared confident and at ease. He made no attempt to disguise himself and forensic evidence was found on each occasion. Police eventually arrested Adrian Babb, an attendant at the local swimming pool, to which all of Babb's victims were regular visitors.

Questions

1. Would you classify Case One as organised or disorganised? Explain your answer.

2. Would you classify Case Two as organised or disorganised? Explain your answer.

3. How do both of these cases illustrate some of the problems with the top-down approach to offender profiling?

Apply it

Methods: Analysis of police records

A team of researchers analysed historical police records of 100 solved murder cases and found no **significant correlation** between details of the crime scene and the characteristics of the offender.

Questions

1. Outline what is meant by **secondary data**. Refer to the investigation above in your answer. (*2 marks*)

2. Evaluate the use of secondary data in psychological research. (*4 marks*)

3. Identify the **co-variables** in this correlation. (*2 marks*)

4. Evaluate the use of correlational analysis in psychological research. (*6 marks*) (See page 63)

CHECK IT

1. Define what is meant by *offender profiling*. [3 marks]

2. Outline **one** investigation of the top-down approach to offender profiling. In your answer, include what the psychologist(s) did and what was found. [3 marks]

3. Distinguish between organised and disorganised types of offender. [4 marks]

4. Discuss the top-down approach to offender profiling. Refer to evidence in your answer. [16 marks]

The bottom-up approach to offender profiling, unlike its American counterpart, was largely developed in this country and is most closely associated with the work of David Canter. Canter's work is wide-ranging and Canter has contributed much to the field of offender profiling in moving it into a more scientific and empirical domain. Here, we consider two examples of the bottom-up approach: investigative psychology and geographical profiling.

KEY TERMS

The bottom-up approach – Profilers work up from evidence collected from the crime scene to develop hypotheses about the likely characteristics, motivations and social background of the offender.

Investigative psychology – A form of bottom-up profiling that matches details from the crime scene with statistical analysis of typical offender behaviour patterns based on psychological theory.

Geographical profiling – A form of bottom-up profiling based on the principle of spatial consistency: that an offender's operational base and possible future offences are revealed by the geographical location of their previous crimes.

Apply it

Concepts: The Railway Rapist

David Canter came to prominence after he assisted police in the capture of John Duffy (the 'Railway Rapist') in the 1980s. John Duffy carried out 24 sexual attacks and 3 murders on women near railway stations in North London. Canter analysed geographical information from the crime scenes and combined this with details of similar attacks in the past supplied by police. In doing so, Canter was able to draw up a profile of Duffy (below) which was surprisingly accurate and led to his eventual arrest and conviction.

Question

How does this case support both versions of the bottom-up approach described on this page?

Canter's profile	True facts about Duffy
Lives in Kilburn	Lived in Kilburn
Marriage problems	Separated
Physically small, unattractive	5ft 4in with acne
Martial artist	Member of martial arts club
Need to dominate women	Violent – attacked wife
Fantasies of rape, bondage	Tied up his wife before sex

The bottom-up approach

The aim of the **bottom-up approach** is to generate a picture of the offender – their likely characteristics, routine behaviour and social background – through systematic analysis of evidence at the **crime** scene. Unlike the US **top-down approach**, the British bottom-up model does not begin with fixed typologies. Instead, the profile is 'data-driven' and emerges as the investigator engages in deeper and more rigorous scrutiny of the details of the offence. Bottom-up profiling is also much more grounded in psychological theory than the top-down approach, as we shall see.

Investigative psychology

The discipline of **investigative psychology** is an attempt to apply statistical procedures, alongside psychological theory, to the analysis of crime scene evidence. The aim, in relation to offender profiling, is to establish patterns of behaviour that are likely to occur – or co-exist – across crime scenes. This is in order to develop a statistical 'database' which then acts as a baseline for comparison. Specific details of an offence, or related offences, can then be matched against this database to reveal important details about the offender, their personal history, family background, etc. This may also determine whether a series of offences are linked in that they are likely to have been committed by the same person.

Central to the approach is the concept of *interpersonal coherence* – that the way an offender behaves at the scene, including how they 'interact' with the victim, may reflect their behaviour in more everyday situations. For instance, whilst some rapists want to maintain maximum control and humiliate their victims, others are more apologetic (Dwyer, 2001). This might tell police something about how the offender relates to women more generally.

The *significance of time and place* is also a key variable and, as in geographical profiling below, may indicate where the offender is living.

Finally, *forensic awareness* describes those individuals who have been the subject of police interrogation before; their behaviour may denote how mindful they are of 'covering their tracks'.

Geographical profiling

This is a technique first described by Kim Rossmo in 1997. **Geographical profiling** uses information to do with the location of linked crime scenes to make inferences about the likely home or operational base of an offender – known as *crime mapping*. It can also be used in conjunction with psychological theory (such as that informed by investigative psychology above) to create hypotheses about how the offender is thinking as well as their *modus operandi*. The assumption is that serial offenders will restrict their 'work' to geographical areas they are familiar with, and so understanding the spatial pattern of their behaviour provides investigators with a 'centre of gravity' which is likely to include the offender's base (often in the middle of the spatial pattern). It may also help investigators make educated guesses about where the offender is likely to strike next – called the 'jeopardy surface'.

Canter's circle theory (Canter and Larkin 1993) proposed two models of offender behaviour:

- The marauder – who operates in close proximity to their home base.
- The commuter – who is likely to have travelled a distance away from their usual residence.

Crucially, though, the pattern of offending is likely to form a circle around their usual residence, and this becomes more apparent the more offences there are. Such spatial decision making can offer the investigative team important insight into the nature of the offence, i.e. whether it was planned or opportunistic, as well as revealing other important factors about the offender, such as their 'mental maps', mode of transport, employment status, approximate age, etc.

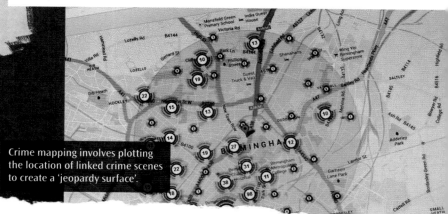

Crime mapping involves plotting the location of linked crime scenes to create a 'jeopardy surface'.

Evaluation

Evidence supports investigative psychology

David Canter and Rupert Heritage (1990) conducted a **content analysis** of 66 sexual assault cases. The data was examined using the statistical technique *smallest space analysis* – a computer program that identifies **correlations** across patterns of behaviour. Several characteristics were identified as common in most cases, such as the use of impersonal language and lack of reaction to the victim. These characteristics will occur in different patterns in different individuals. This can lead to an understanding of how an offender's behaviour may change over a series of offences, or in establishing whether two or more offences were committed by the same person. This supports the usefulness of investigative psychology because it shows how statistical techniques can be applied.

Evidence supports geographical profiling

Samantha Lundrigan and David Canter (2001) collated information from 120 murder cases involving serial killers in the USA. Smallest space analysis revealed spatial consistency in the behaviour of the killers. The location of each body disposal site was in a different direction from the previous sites, creating a 'centre of gravity'; the offender's base was invariably located in the centre of the pattern. The effect was more noticeable for offenders who travelled short distances (marauders).

This supports Canter's claim that spatial information is a key factor in determining the base of an offender.

Scientific basis

Canter's argument is that bottom-up profiling is more objective and scientific than the top-down approach as it is more grounded in evidence and psychological theory, and less driven by speculation and hunches. With the aid of advanced artificial intelligence, investigators are able to manipulate geographical, biographical and psychological data quickly to produce insights and results that assist in the investigation. Similarly, the field of investigative psychology has recently expanded to include such areas as suspect interviewing and examination of material presented in court, which supports its utility in all aspects of the judicial process.

Evaluation eXtra

Wider application

Another advantage the bottom-up approach has over its US rival is that it can be applied to a wide range of offences. Techniques such as smallest space analysis and the principle of spatial consistency can be used in the investigation of crimes such as burglary and theft as well as more serious offences such as murder and rape.

Consider: *In contrast, the top-down approach is best suited to explaining a limited number of crimes. Which crimes?*

Mixed results for profiling

Despite the many successes that the bottom-up approach to profiling has produced, there have been some significant failures (see the case of Rachel Nickell, above right) and studies examining the effectiveness of offender profiling have produced mixed results. For example, Gary Copson (1995) surveyed 48 police forces and found that the advice provided by the profiler was judged to be 'useful' in 83% of cases, but in only 3% did it lead to accurate identification of the offender. Richard Kocsis *et al.* (2002) found that chemistry students produced a more accurate offender profile on a solved murder case than experienced senior detectives!

Consider: *Using the information on this spread and the previous spread, briefly summarise the case for and against offender profiling.*

Metropolitan Police were heavily criticised as a result of the Rachel Nickell enquiry.

Apply it   **Concepts: The case of Rachel Nickell**

In 1992, 21-year-old Rachel Nickell was stabbed 47 times and sexually assaulted in a frenzied attack on Wimbledon Common. Her 2-year-old son was the only witness. Police launched a massive manhunt and enlisted criminal profiler Paul Britton to help with the enquiry. The investigation quickly targeted Colin Stagg, a local man who often walked his dog on the common and fitted the offender profile Britton had drawn up. Under Britton's direction the Metropolitan Police instigated a 'honey trap'. Over the course of 5 months, an undercover policewoman pursued Stagg feigning a romantic interest in him and tried to get him to confess to Rachel's murder. When the case eventually came to court, the judge threw it out – the only link between Stagg and Rachel's death was Britton's profile and the expensive undercover police operation.

In 2008, following examination of new forensic evidence, Robert Napper was convicted of Rachel's murder. It turned out that Napper had been ruled out of the Rachel Nickell enquiry at an early stage because he was several inches taller than the profile.

Question

How does this case illustrate some of the problems with offender profiling?

Apply it   **Methods: Comparing profiles**

Ten professional profilers in the UK (using the bottom-up approach) and ten professional profilers in the USA (using the top-down approach) were given details of a solved murder case that they had never seen before. All were asked to write a profile of the killer based on the information they were presented with. The accuracy of the profiles was rated by two independent judges and the difference in accuracy between the UK and US profiles was analysed.

Questions

1. What type of **experimental design** was used in the investigation above? Justify your answer. (*2 marks*)

2. Explain *one* limitation of this experimental design in the investigation above. (*3 marks*)

3. Explain *one* way in which the independent judges could have assessed the **reliability** of their ratings. (*3 marks*)

4. Which **statistical test** should be used to analyse the difference in the accuracy of the profiles? Give *two* reasons for your answer. (*3 marks*) (See page 70)

CHECK IT

1. In the context of offender profiling, explain what is meant by the *bottom-up approach*.   [3 marks]

2. Explain **one** strength and **one** limitation of investigative psychology.   [6 marks]

3. Explain **one** strength and **one** limitation of geographical profiling.   [6 marks]

4. Discuss investigative psychology and/or geographical profiling. Refer to evidence in your answer.   [16 marks]

Biological explanations of offending behaviour: an historical approach (atavistic form).

The question of whether criminals are born or made is one that has puzzled scientists and philosophers for centuries. Biological explanations of offending share the assumption that crime is an innate tendency which may be genetically determined or the result of abnormalities in brain structure or function.

An early biological explanation of offending was advanced by Cesare Lombroso – the atavistic form. By today's standards, many of Lombroso's methods and conclusions would be regarded as laughable, even though – as we shall see – he was one of the first researchers to establish a more scientific basis for the study of crime.

KEY TERM

Atavistic form – A biological approach to offending that attributes criminal activity to the fact that offenders are genetic throwbacks or a primitive sub-species ill-suited to conforming to the rules of modern society. Such individuals are distinguishable by particular facial and cranial characteristics.

Above: images of criminal subjects from Lombroso's research who would be classified as possessing atavistic characteristics.

STUDY TIP

Remember, Lombroso's theory has a genetic basis and so can be discussed as part of an essay on 'biological explanations of offending', unless of course, 'early biological explanations' are specifically ruled out in the question.

Atavistic form

An historical approach to offending

In 1876, Cesare Lombroso, an Italian physician, wrote a book *called L'Huomo Delinquente* within which he suggested that criminals were '**genetic** throwbacks' – a primitive sub-species who were biologically different from non-criminals. By today's standards, Lombroso's theory of the **atavistic form** would be best described as speculative and naïve, though he is credited as moving criminology into a more rigorous and scientific realm, and his ideas may well have laid the foundation for the modern **offender profiling** techniques that were to follow.

Offenders were seen by Lombroso as lacking evolutionary development, their savage and untamed nature meant that they would find it impossible to adjust to the demands of civilised society and would inevitably turn to **crime**. As such, Lombroso saw criminal behaviour as a natural tendency, rooted in the genealogy of those who engage in it.

Atavistic characteristics

What's more, Lombroso argued, the criminal sub-type could be identified as being in possession of particular physiological 'markers' that were linked to particular types of crime. These are biologically determined 'atavistic' characteristics, mainly features of the face and head (though can include other features), that make criminals physically different from the rest of us.

In terms of cranial characteristics, the atavistic form included a narrow, sloping brow, a strong prominent jaw, high cheekbones and facial asymmetry. Other physical markers included dark skin and the existence of extra toes, nipples or fingers.

Lombroso went on to categorise particular types of criminal in terms of their physical and facial characteristics. Murderers were described as having bloodshot eyes, curly hair and long ears; sexual deviants – glinting eyes, swollen, fleshy lips and projecting ears, whilst the lips of fraudsters were thin and 'reedy'.

Besides physical traits, Lombroso suggested there were other aspects of the born criminal including insensitivity to pain, use of criminal slang, tattoos and unemployment.

Lombroso's research

Lombroso meticulously examined the facial and cranial features of hundreds of Italian convicts, both living and dead, and proposed that the atavistic form was associated with a number of physical anomalies which were key indicators of criminality.

In all, Lombroso examined the skulls of 383 dead criminals and 3839 living ones, and concluded that 40% of criminal acts could be accounted for by atavistic characteristics.

Apply it

Concepts: Serial killers and the atavistic form

Lombroso's theory suggests it should be possible to identify offenders from their unusual facial and physical features. Below is a list of six high profile serial killers (who were convicted in UK or the US) within recent decades:

- Fred West
- Peter Sutcliffe (the Yorkshire Ripper)
- Ian Brady
- Myra Hindley
- Jeffrey Dahmer
- John Wayne Gacy

Question

Find some images of these individuals on the Internet. Do they have any of the facial or physical features that Lombroso was talking about? Does this support or challenge Lombroso's explanation?

Evaluation

Contribution to criminology

Lombroso has been hailed as the 'father of modern criminology' (Hollin 1989). He is credited as shifting the emphasis in crime research away from a moralistic discourse (within which offenders were judged as being wicked and weak-minded) towards a more scientific and credible realm (that of evolutionary influences and genetics). Also, in trying to describe how particular types of people are likely to commit particular types of crime, Lombroso's theory, in many ways, heralded the beginning of criminal profiling. In this way he made a major contribution to the science of criminology.

Scientific racism

Several critics, including Matt DeLisi (2012), have drawn attention to the distinct racial undertones within Lombroso's work. Many of the features that Lombroso identified as criminal and atavistic, such as curly hair and dark skin, are most likely to be found among people of African descent. Similarly, his description of the atavistic being as 'uncivilised, primitive, savage' would lend support to many of the **eugenic** philosophies of the time (see Apply it, right).

Whether Lombroso intended this to be the case or not is a matter of debate; though there is little doubt it is an uncomfortable and controversial aspect of his legacy which continues to overshadow criminology.

Contradictory evidence

Charles Goring (1913), like Lombroso, set out to establish whether there were any physical or mental abnormalities among the criminal classes. After conducting a comparison between 3000 criminals and 3000 non-criminals he concluded that there was no evidence that offenders are a distinct group with unusual facial and cranial characteristics (though he did suggest that many people who commit crime have lower than average intelligence).

Whilst the point about intelligence does offer some limited support to Lombroso's argument that criminals are a 'sub-species', it does question the key element of his theory that criminals are different in terms of their appearance.

Evaluation eXtra

Poor control in Lombroso's research

Unlike Goring, Lombroso did not compare his criminal sample with a non-criminal **control group**. It is possible that, had he done so, the **significant** differences in atavistic form that Lombroso reported may have disappeared. Lombroso also failed to account for other important variables within his research. Many of the criminals he studied had suffered from a history of psychological disorders which may have confounded the findings.

Consider: *Explain why these factors would have confounded the findings.*

Causation is an issue

Even if there are criminals who have some of the atavistic elements in their facial appearance that Lombroso suggested, this does not necessarily mean this is the *cause* of their offending. Facial and cranial differences may be influenced by other factors, such as poverty or poor diet, rather than being an indication of delayed evolutionary development. In his later work, Lombroso took a less extreme stance – acknowledging that criminals could be made as well as born due to a range of environmental factors.

Consider: *Identify as many environmental influences on criminal behaviour that you can think of.*

Practical activity on page 347

Francis Galton, author of *Hereditary Genius* which established the Eugenics Movement, often described as 'the peak of scientific racism'.

Apply it · Concepts: The Eugenics movement

The work of Francis Galton in the 1880s is generally cited as the beginning of the Eugenics Movement. Galton was heavily influenced by his first cousin, Charles Darwin, whose concept of 'survival of the fittest' became the cornerstone of eugenics philosophy.

Galton's basic argument was that not all people in society are born equal. Desirable human traits, such as intelligence, morality and civility, are inherited and found in some social and cultural groups (the genetically 'fit') more than others (the genetically 'unfit'). Those groups with a genetic advantage should be allowed to breed for the good of society, whilst those without should be eliminated.

Question

Explain how Lombroso's theory might be read as supporting the eugenics philosophy and its practices.

Apply it · Methods: Lombroso's study

As we have seen, the methodology Lombroso used to find support for his atavistic form theory has been heavily criticised. In part this can be excused as, at the time Lombroso was writing, the scientific study of criminology was in its infancy and experimental research of this type was still undergoing development.

Question

If you were to re-investigate Lombroso's hypothesis – that criminals are physiologically different from non-criminals – what changes would you make to Lombroso's study in order to improve it?

In particular you should consider the following:

- The **sample** you will include and an appropriate method of selection.
- A suitable comparison/**control group**.
- The **experimental design**.
- The **IV** and **DV** and the **hypothesis**.
- Control of possible **confounding variables**.
- How you will analyse the data (**descriptive** and **inferential** **statistics**). (See page 70)

CHECK IT

1. Outline how the atavistic form can explain offending behaviour. [3 marks]
2. Outline **one** study in which the atavistic form was investigated. Include details of what the psychologist(s) did and what was found. [3 marks]
3. Briefly discuss **two** contributions the atavistic form theory made to our modern understanding of crime. [4 marks]
4. Discuss **one** historical approach to offending behaviour. Refer to evidence in your answer. [16 marks]

THE SPECIFICATION SAYS...

Biological explanations of offending behaviour: genetics and neural explanations.

Though Lombroso's early explanation of offending has been largely discredited, his suggestion that criminality may be an inherited characteristic (i.e. genetic) continues to be investigated.

Biological psychologists also claim to have established important neural (brain) differences between criminals and non-criminals. The genetic and neural explanations for criminality are not unconnected. It may be that some underlying genetic abnormality is causing structural and functional differences in the criminal brain.

KEY TERMS

Genetics – Genes consist of DNA strands. DNA produces 'instructions' for general physical features of an organism (such as eye colour, height) and also specific physical features (such as neurotransmitter levels and size of brain structures). These may impact on psychological features (such as intelligence and mental disorder). Genes are transmitted from parents to offspring, i.e. inherited.

Neural explanation – Any explanation of behaviour (and its disorders) in terms of (dys)functions of the brain and nervous system. This includes the activity of brain structures such as the hypothalamus, and neurotransmitters such as serotonin and dopamine.

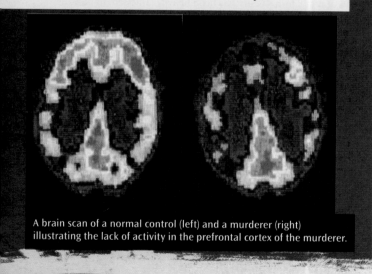

A brain scan of a normal control (left) and a murderer (right) illustrating the lack of activity in the prefrontal cortex of the murderer.

Genetic and neural explanations

Genetic explanations

Genetic explanations for **crime** suggest that would-be offenders inherit a gene, or combination of genes, that predispose them to commit crime.

Twin studies The importance of genes is illustrated by twin studies. The first criminal twin study was conducted by Johannes Lange (1930) who investigated 13 identical (**MZ**) and 17 non-identical (**DZ**) twins where one of the twins in each pair had served time in prison. Lange found that 10 of the MZ twins but only 2 of the DZ twins had a co-twin who was also in prison. Lange concluded that genetic factors must play a predominant part in offending behaviour.

More recent research by Karl Christiansen (1977) studied 87 MZ and 147 DZ pairs and found a **concordance** of 33% for MZs and 12% for DZs which supports the view that offending may have a genetic component.

Candidate genes A genetic analysis of almost 900 offenders by Jari Tiihonen *et al.* (2014) revealed abnormalities on two genes that may be associated with violent crime – the **MAOA** gene (which controls **dopamine** and **serotonin** in the brain and has been linked to aggressive behaviour) and CDH13 (that has been linked to substance abuse and **attention deficit disorder**). Within the Finnish sample, individuals with this high risk combination were 13 times more likely to have a history of violent behaviour. However, it must be emphasised that this research is in its infancy and has, so far, not been **replicated**.

Diathesis-stress model If genetics do have some influence on offending, it seems likely that this is at least partly moderated by the effects of the environment. Elsewhere, we have seen how the diathesis-stress model has been applied to **schizophrenia** (see page 212). A tendency towards criminal behaviour may come about through the combination of genetic predisposition and biological or psychological trigger – for example, being raised in a dysfunctional environment or having criminal role models.

Neural explanations

Evidence suggests there may be **neural** differences in the brains of criminals and non-criminals. Much of the evidence in this area has investigated individuals diagnosed with **antisocial personality disorder** (formerly referred to as *psychopathy*). **APD** is associated with reduced emotional responses, a lack of empathy for the feelings of others, and is a condition that characterises many convicted criminals.

Prefrontal cortex Adrian Raine has conducted many studies of the APD brain, reporting that there are several dozen brain-imaging studies demonstrating that individuals with antisocial personalities have reduced activity in the **prefrontal cortex**, the part of the brain that regulates emotional behaviour. Alongside this, Raine and his colleagues (2000) found an 11% reduction in the volume of grey matter in the prefrontal cortex of people with APD compared to controls.

Mirror neurons Recent research suggests that criminals with APD *can* experience empathy but they do so more sporadically than the rest of us. Christian Keysers *et al.* (2011) found that only when criminals were *asked* to empathise (with a person depicted on film experiencing pain) did their empathy reaction (controlled by **mirror neurons** in the brain) activate. This suggests that APD individuals are not totally without empathy, but may have a neural 'switch' that can be turned on and off, unlike the 'normal' brain which has the empathy switch permanently on. (Mirror neurons are also discussed on pages 190–191.)

Apply it — Methods: Comparing brain volume

Researchers conducted a study in which they compared the total brain volume of violent criminals with non-criminals using an MRI scan. An **unrelated t-test** revealed that there was a difference in total brain volume between the two groups and that this difference was **significant** at the 0.05 level.

Questions

1. Write a suitable **non-directional hypothesis** for the investigation. (*2 marks*)

2. Explain what is meant by **interval data**. Refer to the investigation in your answer. (*3 marks*) (See page 71)

3. Apart from the use of interval data, explain *two* reasons why researchers chose to analyse the data using an unrelated *t*-test. (*4 marks*) (See page 76)

4. Explain what is meant by the phrase 'significant at the 0.05 level'. (*2 marks*) (See page 72)

5. Distinguish between a **Type I** and a **Type II** error in psychological research. Refer to the investigation in your answer. (*4 marks*) (See page 73)

Evaluation

Problems with twin studies

Early twin studies of criminality, such as Lange's research (see facing page), were poorly controlled and judgements related to zygosity (that is, whether twin pairs were MZ or DZ) were based on appearance rather than DNA testing. As a result they may lack validity.

Also, twin studies typically involve small sample sizes; and furthermore twins are an unusual sample in themselves and may not represent the rest of the population. Finally, the fact that most twins are reared in the same environment is a major **confounding variable** as concordance rates may be due to shared learning experiences rather than genetics.

Support for the diathesis–stress model of crime

A major study of over 13,000 Danish adoptees was conducted by Sarnoff Mednick et al. (1984). The researchers defined criminal behaviour as being in possession of at least one court conviction and this was checked against Danish police records for each of the adoptees. When neither the biological nor adoptive parents had convictions, the percentage of adoptees that did was 13.5%. This figure rose to 20% when either of the biological parents had convictions, and 24.5% when both adoptive and biological parents had convictions.

This data suggests that although genetic inheritance plays an important role in offending, environmental influence cannot be disregarded – support for the diathesis-stress model of crime.

Problems with adoption studies

The presumed separation of genetic and environmental influences in adoption studies is complicated by the fact that many children experience late adoption, which means that much of their infancy and childhood may have been spent with their biological parents anyway. Similarly, lots of adoptees maintain regular contact with their biological parents following their adoption.

Both of these points make it difficult to assess, from adoption studies, the environmental impact the biological parents might have had. As well as this, in the Mednick et al. study (above) the figures quoted only applied to petty offences, such as burglary, and not violent crime. This means that any conclusions drawn may not apply to more serious forms of crime.

Evaluation eXtra

Biological reductionism

Criminality is complex; explanations that reduce offending behaviour to a genetic or neural level may be inappropriate and overly simplistic. Crime does appear to run in families, but so does emotional instability, mental illness, social deprivation and poverty (Katz et al. 2007). This makes it difficult to disentangle the effects of genes and neural influences from other possible factors. It is also the case that, whilst there is often a difference in concordance rates between MZ and DZ twins, MZ pairs do not show 100% concordance.

Consider: What do the relatively low concordance rates in genetic studies suggest?

Biological determinism

In the field of criminality, the notion of a 'criminal gene' presents something of a dilemma. Our legal system is based on the premise that criminals have personal and moral responsibility for their crimes, and only in extreme cases, such as a diagnosis of mental illness, can someone claim they were not acting under their own **free will** (see 'The Mobley defence' top right). This raises **ethical** questions about what society does with people who are suspected of carrying criminal genes, and what implications this may have for sentencing.

Consider: Why does the (potential) discovery of a criminal gene present society with an **ethical** dilemma?

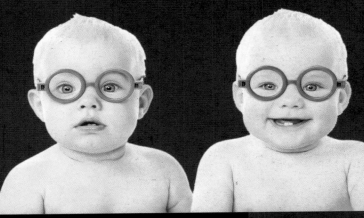

Double trouble ... but why might the findings from twin studies related to crime be difficult to interpret?

CHECK IT

1. Outline the neural explanation of offending. **[3 marks]**
2. Outline the genetic explanation of offending. **[3 marks]**
3. Outline **one** study that has investigated a neural explanation of offending. **[3 marks]**
4. Discuss genetic and/or neural explanations of offending. Refer to evidence in your answer. **[16 marks]**

Psychological explanations of offending shift the focus away from biological causes of crime towards social and psychological influences. These include the influence of dysfunctional learning environments and the influence of the family, cognitive factors and personality.

Hans Eysenck's theory is something of a 'halfway house' in this respect. Even though his theory of the criminal personality would be properly classed as psychological – he does argue that all personality types have a biological basis.

KEY TERM

The criminal personality – An individual who scores highly on measures of extraversion, neuroticism and psychoticism and cannot easily be conditioned, is cold and unfeeling, and is likely to engage in offending behaviour.

Make sure you're aware that Eysenck's theory can serve a dual purpose. As it appears under the heading of psychological explanations in the specification, it can obviously be used as part of a discussion of these. However, because Eysenck made links between personality type, genetic influences and the nervous system, there is a clear biological element here, too. As long as you make this clear, the theory might also be used as a biological explanation if made relevant.

Eysenck's theory of the criminal personality

General personality theory

Hans Eysenck was an important figure in personality and intelligence research during the 1950s and 60s. Eysenck (1947) proposed that behaviour could be represented along two dimensions: **introversion/extraversion** (E) and **neuroticism/stability** (N). The two dimensions combine to form a variety of personality characteristics or traits. Eysenck later added a third dimension – **psychoticism** (P).

Biological basis

According to Eysenck, our personality traits are biological in origin and come about through the type of nervous system we inherit. Thus, all personality types – including the **criminal personality** type – have an innate, biological basis. **Extraverts** have an underactive nervous system which means they constantly seek excitement, stimulation and are likely to engage in risk-taking behaviours. They also tend not to condition easily and do not learn from their mistakes. **Neurotic** individuals tend to be nervous, jumpy and over-anxious, and their general instability means their behaviour is often difficult to predict.

The criminal personality

The criminal personality type is neurotic-extravert – a combination of all the characteristics and behaviours described above for both neuroticism and extraversion. In addition, Eysenck suggested that the typical offender will also score highly on measures of psychoticism – a personality type that is characterised as cold, unemotional and prone to aggression.

The role of socialisation

In Eysenck's theory, personality is linked to criminal behaviour via socialisation processes. Eysenck saw criminal behaviour as developmentally immature in that it is selfish and concerned with immediate gratification – they are impatient and cannot wait for things. The process of socialisation is one in which children are taught to become more able to delay gratification and more socially oriented. Eysenck believed that people with high E and N scores had nervous systems that made them difficult to condition. As a result, they would not learn easily to respond to antisocial impulses with anxiety. Consequently, they would be more likely to act antisocially in situations where the opportunity presented itself.

Measuring the criminal personality

The notion that personality can be measured is one that is central to Eysenck's theory. He developed the *Eysenck Personality Inventory* (**EPI**), a form of psychological test which locates respondents along the E and N dimensions to determine their personality type. A later scale was introduced that is used to measure psychoticism.

Apply it   Concepts: Three offenders

Margaret Tibbs is a company accountant for a small firm and has been stealing small amounts of money from petty cash for years. Since joining the firm 18 years ago, Margaret has stolen several thousands of pounds. She is quiet, unassuming and does not have a great many friends at work.

Vince Douglas is a family man with a highly-paid job. His many friends would describe him as a 'steady bloke' who is well-adjusted. Vince is also a serial killer. He has murdered dozens of women over the years, leaves no evidence at the scene and disposes of the bodies without a trace. Vince tells his wife of 25 years that he often stays behind at the office and she has no reason to disbelieve him.

Barry Phillips is 19 and a self-confessed 'boy racer'. Since passing his test two years ago, Barry has been convicted of stealing cars and writing them off and has spent time in a young offender's institute. Barry has also been given a six-month suspended sentence for burglary and has since had to wear an electronic tag. Barry also has drug and alcohol problems and sees a counsellor regularly to help him with his **depression**.

Questions

1. Which of the three cases above most clearly fits Eysenck's description of the criminal personality? Explain your answer.

2. How could the other two cases be seen as criticisms of Eysenck's theory?

Evaluation

Evidence supporting Eysenck's theory

Sybil Eysenck and Hans Eysenck (1977) compared 2070 male prisoners' scores on the EPI with 2422 male controls. Groups were subdivided into age groups, ranging from 16 to 69 years. On measures of psychoticism, extraversion and neuroticism – across all age groups – prisoners recorded higher scores than **controls** which accords with the predictions of the theory.

However, David Farrington *et al.* (1982) reviewed several studies and reported that offenders tended to score high on P measures, but not for E and N. There is also very little evidence of consistent differences in **EEG** measures (used to measure cortical arousal) between extraverts and introverts, which casts doubt on the physiological basis of Eysenck's theory.

The idea of a single criminal type

The idea that *all* offending behaviour can be explained by a single personality type has been heavily criticised. For instance, Terrie Moffitt (1993) proposed several distinct types of adult male offender based on the timing of the first offence, and how long offending persists. Further, Eysenck's criminal type is out-of-step with modern personality theories. For example, John Digman's (1990) *Five Factor Model* of personality suggests that alongside E and N, there are additional dimensions of *openness, agreeableness* and *conscientiousness*. From this perspective, multiple combinations are available and therefore a high E and N score does not mean offending is inevitable.

Cultural bias

Curt Bartol and Howard Holanchock (1979) looked into cultural differences. They studied Hispanic and African-American offenders in a maximum security prison in New York and divided these into six groups based on their criminal history and the nature of their offence. It was revealed that all six groups were found to be less extravert than a non-criminal control group.

Bartol *et al.* suggested that this was because their sample was a very different cultural group than that investigated by Eysenck, which questions the **generalisability** of the criminal personality.

Evaluation eXtra

The (mis)measurement of personality

Eysenck's theory is built on the premise that it is possible to measure personality through the use of a psychological test. Critics have suggested that personality type may not be reducible to a 'score' in this way; indeed, many argue there is no such thing as personality – in the sense of a *stable entity*, the like of which Eysenck was talking about. On a daily basis, we play many different parts and our personality may change depending who we are with and the situation we are involved in (Mischel 1988). There may be no fixed and unchangeable 'true self' directing our behaviour, criminal or otherwise.

Consider: As well as this, what are the specific problems with using psychological tests to measure personality?

Biological basis

Eysenck's theory recognises that personality may have a genetic basis and thus fits well with other biological explanations. There is also some overlap with research into **APD** and the suggestion that offenders are cold, uncaring and incapable of empathy (though, unlike Raine who explained APD through differences in brain structure and function, Eysenck attributes this to the activity of the nervous system). Because of its biological basis, Eysenck's theory does suffer from some of the same limitations as genetic and neural explanations.

Consider: *Why is Eysenck guilty of a form of biological determinism and why is this problematic when it comes to explaining crime?*

---

on page 346

Concepts: The criminal personality on film

Few characters in movie history fit the profile of the archetypal baddie quite as much as the Joker in Christopher Nolan's 2008 film *The Dark Knight*. Both fascinating and terrifying in equal measure, the arch enemy of Christian Bale's Batman ticks every box with respect to Eysenck's criminal personality. Possessed of a warped, wisecracking humour, as well as being unpredictable and hugely unstable, the Joker is the very epitome of the extravert-neurotic. Add to this, his chilling, murderous tendencies and a high score on the psychoticism scale would seem to be assured!

Question

Apart from the Joker, can you think of any other screen villains who would match Eysenck's description of the criminal personality? Explain your choices in each case.

The Joker. Probably a fair bet that he would score pretty high for extraversion, neuroticism and psychoticism on the EPI.

Apply it — **Methods: Comparing E and N scores in offenders and non-offenders**

A researcher wanted to investigate whether there is a difference in personality type between criminals and non-criminals. She administered the EPI to a group of young offenders and a group of students. It was found that the group of young offenders scored **significantly** higher than the students on measures of extraversion and neuroticism.

Question

1. What type of **experiment** is the investigation above? Explain your answer. (*3 marks*)

2. Explain *one* limitation of the type of experiment you have identified in Q1. Refer to the investigation above in your answer. (*3 marks*)

3. Explain how the **dependent variable** has been **operationalised** in the investigation above. (*2 marks*)

4. Identify which type of data would be produced in the investigation above. (*1 mark*)

5. Explain *one* strength and *one* limitation of the type of data you identified in Q4. Refer to the investigation above in your answer. (*6 marks*)

CHECK IT

1. Briefly explain Eysenck's theory of the criminal personality. [*4 marks*]

2. Outline **one** study in which Eysenck's criminal personality was investigated. [*3 marks*]

3. Identify and explain **two** criticisms of Eysenck's theory of the criminal personality. [*4 marks*]

4. Discuss Eysenck's theory of the criminal personality. Refer to evidence in your answer. [*16 marks*]

THE SPECIFICATION SAYS...

Psychological explanations of offending behaviour: cognitive explanations – level of moral reasoning and cognitive distortions, including hostile attribution bias and minimalisation.

There is often talk in the media about whether it is possible to delve into and better understand the criminal mind, which suggests that criminal activity might have a cognitive basis.

Here we explore two examples of cognitive explanations for offending. First, a theory that builds on the work of Lawrence Kohlberg which claims that crimes may be committed by individuals who have a lower level of moral reasoning than non-criminals. Second, the idea that criminal behaviour is the result of faulty information processing in the minds of offenders, so-called cognitive distortions.

KEY TERMS

Level of moral reasoning – Moral reasoning refers to the process by which an individual draws upon their own value system to determine whether an action is right or wrong. Kohlberg attempted to objectify this process by identifying different levels of reasoning based on people's answers to moral dilemmas.

Cognitive distortions – Faulty, biased and irrational ways of thinking that mean we perceive ourselves, other people and the world inaccurately and usually negatively.

Hostile attribution bias – The tendency to judge ambiguous situations, or the actions of others, as aggressive and/or threatening when in reality they may not be.

Minimalisation (or minimisation) – A type of deception that involves downplaying the significance of an event or emotion. A common strategy when dealing with feelings of guilt.

Someone with a hostile attribution bias might interpret this facial expression as threatening or confrontational.

Cognitive explanations

Level of moral reasoning

Lawrence Kohlberg was the first researcher to apply the concept of moral reasoning to **criminal** behaviour. Kohlberg proposed that people's decisions and judgements on issues of right and wrong can be summarised in a stage theory of moral development (see facing page) – the higher the stage, the more sophisticated the reasoning. Kohlberg based his theory on people's responses to a series of moral dilemmas, such as the *Heinz dilemma* (also on facing page).

Many studies have suggested that criminals tend to show a lower **level of moral reasoning** than non-criminals. Kohlberg *et al.* (1973), using his moral dilemma technique (see facing page), found that a group of violent youths were significantly lower in their moral development than non-violent youths – even after controlling for social background.

Kohlberg's model and criminality

Criminal offenders are more likely to be classified at the *pre-conventional level* of Kohlberg's model (stages 1 and 2), whereas non-criminals have generally progressed to the *conventional level* and beyond. The pre-conventional level is characterised by a need to avoid punishment and gain rewards, and is associated with less mature, childlike reasoning. Thus, adults and adolescents who reason at this level may commit **crime** if they can get away with it or gain rewards in the form of money, increased respect, etc.

This assumption is supported by studies which suggest that offenders are often more egocentric (self-centred) and display poorer social perspective-taking skills than non-offender peers (e.g. Chandler 1973). Individuals who reason at higher levels tend to sympathise more with the rights of others and exhibit more conventional behaviours such as honesty, generosity and non-violence.

Cognitive distortions

Cognitive distortions are errors or biases in people's information processing system characterised by faulty thinking. We all occasionally show evidence of faulty thinking when explaining our own behaviour (especially if the behaviour was unexpected or out of character) but research has linked this to the way in which criminals interpret other people's behaviour and justify their own actions.

Two examples of cognitive distortions are:

Hostile attribution bias Evidence suggests that a propensity for violence is often associated with a tendency to misinterpret the actions of other people – in other words, to assume others are being confrontational when they are not. Offenders may misread non-aggressive cues (such as being 'looked at') and this may trigger a disproportionate, often violent, response. Michael Schönenberg and Aiste Justye (2014) presented 55 violent offenders with images of emotionally ambiguous facial expressions. When compared with a non-aggressive matched **control group**, the violent offenders were significantly more likely to perceive the images as angry and hostile.

The roots of this behaviour may lie in childhood. Kenneth Dodge and Cynthia Frame (1982) showed children a video clip of an 'ambiguous provocation' (where the intention was neither clearly hostile nor clearly accidental). Children who had been identified as 'aggressive' and 'rejected' prior to the study interpreted the situation as more hostile than those classed as 'non-aggressive' and 'accepted'.

Minimalisation is an attempt to deny or downplay the seriousness of an offence and has elsewhere been referred to as the application of a 'euphemistic label' for behaviour (Bandura 1973). For instance, burglars may describe themselves as 'doing a job' or 'supporting my family' as a way of minimising the seriousness of their offences. Studies suggest that individuals who commit sexual offences are particularly prone to minimalisation. Howard Barbaree (1991) found among 26 incarcerated rapists, 54% denied they had committed an offence at all and a further 40% minimised the harm they had caused to the victim. Similarly, Nathan Pollock and Judith Hashmall (1991) reported that 35% of a sample of child molesters argued that the crime they had committed was non-sexual (they were 'just being affectionate') and 36% stated that the victim had consented.

Evaluation

Level of moral reasoning evidence

Emma Palmer and Clive Hollin (1998) compared moral reasoning between 210 female non-offenders, 122 male non-offenders, and 126 convicted offenders using the *Socio-Moral Reflection Measure-Short Form (SRM-SF)*, which contains 11 moral dilemma-related questions such as not taking things that belong to others and keeping a promise to a friend. The delinquent group showed less mature moral reasoning than the non-delinquent group which is consistent with Kohlberg's predictions. Ronald Blackburn (1993) suggests that delinquents may show poor moral development due to a lack of role playing opportunities in childhood. Such opportunities to develop moral reasoning should therefore be provided.

Alternative theories of moral reasoning

John Gibbs (1979) proposed a revised version of Kohlberg's theory comprising two levels of reasoning: *mature* and *immature*. In the first level, moral decisions are guided by avoidance of punishment and personal gain; in the second level, by empathy, social justice and one's own conscience. These stages are equivalent to Kohlberg's pre-conventional and conventional levels. Gibbs argued that Kohlberg's post-conventional level should be abandoned because it was culturally biased (towards Western culture) and did not represent a 'natural' maturational stage of cognitive development (see Piaget's theory of cognitive development on page 178).

Gibbs' view is supported by Jean Piaget's theory of moral development, which suggests that child-like (criminal) reasoning is self-centred and egocentric which gives way to empathy and a concern for the needs of others as children get older.

Application of research

Understanding the nature of cognitive distortions has proven beneficial in the treatment of criminal behaviour. The dominant approach in the rehabilitation of sex offenders is **cognitive behaviour therapy** which encourages offenders to 'face up' to what they have done and establish a less distorted view of their actions. Studies suggest that reduced incidence of denial and minimalisation in therapy is highly **correlated** with a reduced risk of reoffending (as 'acceptance' of one's crimes is thought to be an important aspect of rehabilitation) and this is a key feature of **anger management** (see page 348).

Evaluation eXtra

Individual differences

The level of moral reasoning may depend on the type of offence. David Thornton and R. L. Reid (1982) found that individuals who committed crimes for financial gain, such as robbery, were more likely to show pre-conventional moral reasoning than those convicted of impulsive crimes such as assault where reasoning of any kind tended not to be evident. Pre-conventional moral reasoning tends to be associated with crimes in which offenders believe they have a good chance of evading punishment.

Also, Peter Langdon *et al.* (2010) have suggested that intelligence may be a better predictor of criminality than moral reasoning. This would explain the finding that groups of people with very low intelligence are actually less likely to commit crime (despite the fact they show lower levels of moral reasoning).

Consider: *How does this finding challenge Kohlberg's theory?*

Descriptive not explanatory

One key failing with the cognitive approach is that, whilst it is good at *describing* the criminal mind, it is rather less successful when it comes to *explaining* it. Cognitive explanations are essentially 'after the fact' theories and, although they may be useful when predicting reoffending, they tend not to give us much insight into why the offender committed crime in the first place.

Consider: *Which of the other explanations we have studied are much more concerned with identifying the cause of criminal behaviour?*

Apply it Concepts: The Heinz dilemma

This is one of the moral dilemmas Kohlberg used in his research:

In Europe, a woman was near death from a special kind of cancer. There was one drug that the doctors thought might save her. It was a form of radium that a druggist in the same town had recently discovered. The drug was expensive to make, but the druggist was charging ten times what the drug cost him to make. He paid $400 for the radium and charged $4000 for a small dose of the drug. The sick woman's husband, Heinz, went to everyone he knew to borrow the money, but he could only get together about $2000, which was half of what the drug cost. He told the druggist that his wife was dying and asked him to sell it cheaper or let him pay later. But the druggist said, 'No, I discovered the drug and I'm going to make money from it'. So Heinz got desperate and considered breaking into the man's store to steal the drug for his wife.

Participants were then asked various questions, including: Should Heinz steal the drug? Why (or why not)? Does the druggist have the right to charge what he likes for the drug? What if the dying person were a stranger, should he steal the drug?

Question

Answer the questions above yourself. Based on your answers, where would you place yourself in Kohlberg's model below?

Level I Preconventional morality	Stage 1 Punishment orientation *Rules are obeyed to avoid punishment*
	Stage 2 Instrumental orientation or personal gain *Rules are obeyed for personal gain*
Level II Conventional morality	Stage 3 'Good boy' or 'Good girl' orientation *Rules are obeyed for approval*
	Stage 4 Maintenance of the social order *Rules are obeyed to maintain the social order*
Level III Postconventional morality	Stage 5 Morality of contract and individual rights *Rules are obeyed if they are impartial; democratic rules are challenged if they infringe on the rights of others*
	Stage 6 Morality of conscience *The individual establishes his or her own rules in accordance with a personal set of ethical principles*

Apply it Methods: Kohlberg's methods

Kohlberg interviewed his participants using the Heinz dilemma (top of page) and other stories like it. Based on their responses he would allocate them to one of six stages of moral reasoning (above).

Questions

1. What are the problems/difficulties with categorising responses in this way? (*4 marks*)

2. Describe *one* way in which Kohlberg could have improved the **reliability** of his categorisation system. (*3 marks*) (See page 67)

3. Outline what is meant by a **structured interview**. (*2 marks*)

4. Briefly evaluate the use of structured interviews in psychological research. Refer to Kohlberg's research in your answer. (*6 marks*)

CHECK IT

1. Outline **one** cognitive explanation of offending. [*4 marks*]

2. Outline **one** study in which a cognitive explanation for offending was investigated. [*3 marks*]

3. Using an example, explain what is meant by *cognitive distortion*. [*3 marks*]

4. Describe and discuss cognitive explanations of offending. Refer to **at least one** other explanation of offending in your answer. [*16 marks*]

THE SPECIFICATION SAYS...

Psychological explanations of offending behaviour: differential association theory.

Differential association is a social learning theory of crime which has stood the test of time, first proposed by sociologist Edwin Sutherland in 1939. The theory suggests that offending is learned in the same way as any other behaviour – through the relationships and associations we form with the people around us.

At the time it was written, Sutherland's theory represented a departure from previous accounts which tended to assume crime was genetically determined or due to some kind of weakness of character. Differential association has remained an influential theory ever since.

KEY TERM

Differential association theory – An explanation for offending which proposes that, through interaction with others, individuals learn the values, attitudes, techniques and motives for criminal behaviour.

Apply it — Concepts: Gary

Growing up, Gary was generally considered to be a good boy. He came from a stable background with supportive parents and always performed well at school.

Since turning 15, Gary has started to hang around with a new group of friends. Locally, the group has a reputation for being 'the wrong crowd'. Despite being told to stay away from these lads by his parents and his former friends, Gary continues to associate with them. Last week, he was arrested for trying to steal a car – his first offence.

Question

With reference to Gary, outline the main principles of differential association theory.

Through differential association offenders learn specific techniques that enable them to commit crime.

Differential association theory

The theory proposes that individuals learn the values, attitudes, techniques and motives for **criminal** behaviour through association and interaction with different people (hence, **differential association**).

Scientific basis

Edwin Sutherland set himself the task of developing a set of scientific principles that could explain all types of offending – that is, 'the conditions which are said to cause crime should be present when crime is present, and they should be absent when crime is absent' (Sutherland 1924). His theory is designed to discriminate between individuals who become criminals and those who do not, whatever their race, class or ethnic background.

Crime as a learned behaviour

Offending behaviour may be acquired in the same way as any other behaviour through the processes of learning. This learning occurs most often through interactions with significant others that the child associates with, such as the family and peer group. Criminality arises from two factors: *learned attitudes towards crime*, and the *learning of specific criminal acts*.

Pro-criminal attitudes

When a person is socialised into a group they will be exposed to values and attitudes towards the law. Some of these values will be pro-crime, some of these will be anti-crime. Sutherland argues that if the number of pro-criminal attitudes the person comes to acquire outweighs the number of anti-criminal attitudes, they will go on to offend. The learning process is the same whether a person is learning criminality or conformity to the law (or anything else for that matter).

Differential association suggests that it should be possible to mathematically predict how likely it is that an individual will commit crime if we have knowledge of the frequency, intensity and duration of which they have been exposed to deviant and non-deviant norms and values.

Learning criminal acts

In addition to being exposed to pro-criminal attitudes, the would-be offender may also learn particular techniques for committing crime. These might include how to break into someone's house through a locked window or how to disable a car stereo before stealing it.

As well as offering an account of how crime may 'breed' amongst specific social groups and in communities, Sutherland's theory can also account for why so many convicts released from prison go on to reoffend. It is reasonable to assume that whilst inside prison inmates will learn specific techniques of offending from other, more experienced criminals that they may be eager to put into practice upon their release. This learning may occur through observational learning and imitation or direct tuition from criminal peers.

Apply it — Concepts: Farrington et al. (2006)

The *Cambridge Study in Delinquent Development* was a prospective **longitudinal** survey of the development of offending and antisocial behaviour in 411 males. The study began when the children were aged 8 in 1961 and all living in a working-class, deprived, inner-city area of South London. The findings describe their criminal careers up to age 50, looking at both officially recorded convictions and self-reported offending.

Of the males sampled, 41% were convicted of at least one offence between age 10 and age 50. The average conviction career lasted from age 19 to 28 and included five convictions. The most important childhood 'risk factors' at age 8–10 for later offending were measures of family criminality, daring or risk-taking, low school attainment, poverty and poor parenting.

A small proportion of participants (7%) were defined as 'chronic offenders' because they accounted for about half of all officially recorded offences in this study.

Question

How do the findings of this study and the key 'risk factors' identified support differential association theory?

Evaluation

Explanatory power

One of the great strengths of differential association theory is its ability to account for crime within all sectors of society. Whilst Sutherland recognised that some types of crime, such as burglary, may be clustered within certain inner-city, working-class communities, it is also the case that some crimes are more prevalent amongst more affluent groups in society. Sutherland was particularly interested in so-called 'white-collar' or corporate crime (indeed he coined the term *white-collar crime* himself) and how this may be a feature of middle-class social groups who share deviant norms and values.

Shift of focus

Sutherland was successful in moving the emphasis away from early biological accounts of crime, such as Lombroso's **atavistic theory** (page 326), as well as away from those that explained offending as being the product of individual weakness or immorality. Differential association theory draws attention to the fact that dysfunctional social circumstances and environments may be more to blame for criminality than dysfunctional people.

This approach is more desirable because it offers a more realistic solution to the problem of crime instead of **eugenics** (the biological solution) or punishment (the morality solution).

Difficulty of testing

Despite Sutherland's promise to provide a scientific, mathematical framework within which future offending behaviour could be predicted, differential association theory suffers from being rather difficult to test. It is hard to see how, for instance, the number of pro-criminal attitudes a person has, or has been exposed to, could be measured. Similarly, the theory is built on the assumption that offending behaviour will occur when pro-criminal values outnumber anti-criminal ones.

However, without being able to measure these, it is difficult to know at what point the urge to offend is realised and the criminal career triggered. The theory does not provide a satisfactory solution to these issues, undermining its scientific credibility.

Evaluation eXtra

Alternative explanations

Sutherland suggested that the response of the family is crucial in determining whether the individual is likely to engage in offending. If the family is seen to support criminal activity, making it seem legitimate and reasonable, then this becomes a major influence on the child's value system. This is supported by the fact that offending behaviour often seems to run in families, and certainly in the Farrington *et al.* study (facing page), such *intergenerational* crime was a key feature of the findings. It was also the case in the study by Mednick *et al.* (1984, see page 329) that boys who had criminal adoptive parents and non-criminal biological parents were more likely to go on to offend than boys whose biological and adoptive parents were non-criminal (14.7% compared to 13.5%) illustrating the importance of family influence.

Consider: *However, how might the fact that offending runs in families support: (i) genetic explanations, (ii) psychodynamic explanations (covered on the next spread)?*

Individual differences

Not everyone who is exposed to criminal influences goes on to commit crime. Even though Sutherland took great care to point out that crime should be considered on an individual case-by-case basis, there is a danger within differential association theory of stereotyping individuals who come from impoverished, crime-ridden backgrounds as 'unavoidably criminal'. The theory tends to suggest that exposure to pro-criminal values is sufficient to produce offending in those who are exposed and ignores the fact that people may *choose* not to offend despite such influences.

Consider: *Differential association theory represents which form of determinism and why?*

Apply it

Methods: Farrington *et al.* – you do the maths

With reference to the Farrington *et al.* study (facing page).

Questions

1. 41% of the sample of 411 participants went on to commit crime. How many participants is this? (*1 mark*)

2. What is the ratio of participants who went on to commit crime compared to those who did not commit crime? (*1 mark*)

3. 7% of the sample of 411 were defined as 'chronic offenders'. How many participants is this? (*1 mark*)

4. Express 7% of 411 as a fraction and as a decimal. (*2 marks*)

5. What would be the most suitable graphical display to represent the percentage of participants who went on to commit crime and those who did not? Justify your answer. (*2 marks*)

Sutherland first used the term 'white-collar crime' in 1938 to describe financially motivated nonviolent crime committed by business and government professionals.

STUDY TIP

*One important skill that you must develop at A level is the skill of **comparison**. One way of evaluating the worth of a particular theory or explanation is by examining how it compares with alternatives. Effective comparison does more than just **list** similarities and differences. Instead, it **uses** the key features of one theory, approach or treatment to point out the strengths and/or shortcomings of another.*

Compare differential association with the other biological and psychological explanations of offending. What are the similarities and differences with each approach? Which do you consider to be the most valid in accounting for the emergence of criminal behaviour?

Remember, you must present evidence to support your judgements rather than just relying on your own opinion.

CHECK IT

1. Outline the differential association theory of offending. [4 marks]

2. Outline **one** study in which the differential association theory of offending was investigated. [3 marks]

3. Briefly evaluate the differential association theory of offending. [6 marks]

4. Discuss the differential association theory of offending. Refer to **at least one** other explanation of offending in your answer. [16 marks]

Psychological explanations of offending behaviour: psychodynamic explanations.

All psychodynamic explanations originate from the work of Sigmund Freud. Although Freud did not address the issue of criminal behaviour himself, other researchers have attempted to apply some of his key concepts to offending.

Here, we focus on two psychodynamic explanations: Ronald Blackburn's idea of the inadequate superego and John Bowlby's maternal deprivation theory (which you studied in Year 1). Both of these explanations abide by the Freudian principle that the roots of (criminal) behaviour are formed in childhood.

KEY TERM

Psychodynamic explanations – A group of theories influenced by the work of Sigmund Freud which share the belief that unconscious conflicts, rooted in early childhood and determined by interactions with parents, drive future – and in this case criminal – behaviour.

STUDY TIP

Remember how Freud says the superego comes about? Children in the phallic stage – that's 3 to 6 years old – experience the Oedipus or Electra complex. They resolve this by identifying with the same-sex parent and wanting to be like them. This leads to internalisation of the same-sex parent's superego, that is, children take on board the values and moral beliefs of the same-sex parent. Thus, the superego the child gets arrives second-hand and becomes their internal parent (or conscience) from then on.

Did this man experience maternal deprivation as an infant?

Psychodynamic explanations of offending

The inadequate superego

You may recall that the **superego**, alongside the **id** and the **ego**, make up the tripartite structure of personality. The superego is formed at the end of the **phallic stage** of development when children resolve the **Oedipus complex** (sometimes referred to as the **Electra complex** in girls – both complexes are described on page 160). The superego works on the *morality principle* and exerts its influence by punishing the ego through guilt for wrongdoing, whilst rewarding it with pride for moral behaviour.

Ronald Blackburn (1993) argued that if the superego is somehow deficient or inadequate then criminal behaviour is inevitable because the id is given 'free rein' and not properly controlled. Three types of inadequate superego have been proposed:

- *The weak superego* – If the same-sex parent is absent during the phallic stage, the child cannot **internalise** a fully-formed superego as there is no opportunity for **identification**. This would make immoral or criminal behaviour more likely.
- *The deviant superego* – If the superego that the child internalises has immoral or deviant values this would lead to offending behaviour. For instance, a boy that is raised by a criminal father is not likely to associate guilt with wrongdoing.
- *The over-harsh superego* – A healthy superego is like a kind but firm internal parent: it has rules, but it is also forgiving of transgressions. In contrast, an excessively punitive or overly harsh superego means the individual is crippled by guilt and anxiety. This may (unconsciously) drive the individual to perform criminal acts in order to satisfy the superego's overwhelming need for punishment.

The maternal deprivation theory

John Bowlby (1944) argued that the ability to form meaningful relationships in adulthood was dependent upon the child forming a warm, continuous relationship with a mother-figure. The maternal bond was seen by Bowlby as unique, superior to any other, and vital to the child's well-being and development. Failure to establish such a bond during the first few years of life means the child will experience a number of damaging and irreversible consequences in later life. One of these is the development of a particular personality type, known as **affectionless psychopathy**, characterised by a lack of guilt, empathy and feeling for others. Such maternally deprived individuals are likely to engage in acts of delinquency and cannot develop close relationships with others, as they lack the necessary early experience to do so.

44 juvenile thieves John Bowlby (1944) supported his claims with his own investigation of 44 juvenile thieves. He found, through **interviews** with the thieves and their families, that 14 of the sample he studied showed personality and behavioural characteristics that could be classified as 'affectionless psychopathy'. Of this 14, 12 had experienced prolonged separation from their mothers during infancy (in particular, the first two years of their lives). In a non-criminal group, only two had experienced similar early separation. Bowlby concluded that the effects of **maternal deprivation** had caused affectionless and delinquent behaviour among the juvenile thieves.

Apply it — Concepts: Harry, Barry and Gary

Barry has never met his dad, he left Barry's mother before he was born.

Harry does live with his dad but Harry's dad makes his 'living' as a burglar.

Gary's parents are extremely strict, yet he is always in trouble with the local police. It is almost as if Gary enjoys being in trouble.

Barry, Harry and Gary are all serving prison sentences.

Question

How would a psychodynamic psychologist explain this?

Evaluation

Gender bias

An implicit assumption within Freudian theory is the idea that girls develop a weaker superego than boys. Having not experienced **castration anxiety**, girls are under less pressure to identify with their mothers (than boys are with their fathers), so their superego – and consequently their sense of morality – is less fully realised. The implication of this is that females should be more prone to criminal behaviour than males.

This is simply not supported by evidence – not least, statistics of the male–female ratio of inmates in prison. In a study where children were required to resist temptation, Martin Hoffman (1975) found hardly any evidence of gender differences, and when there was, little girls tended to be more moral than little boys.

Contradictory evidence

There is very little evidence that children raised without a same-sex parent are less law-abiding as adults (or fail to develop a conscience). This contradicts Blackburn's weak superego argument.

Similarly, if children who are raised by deviant parents go on to commit **crime** themselves, this could be due to the influence of **genetics** or socialisation, rather than the formation of a deviant superego. Finally, the idea that criminal behaviour reflects an unconscious desire for punishment seems implausible, as most offenders go to great lengths to conceal their crimes which suggests they want to avoid punishment at all costs.

Unconscious concepts

Psychodynamic explanations in general suffer from a lack of **falsifiability**. The many unconscious concepts within Freudian theory mean that applications to crime, such as those considered here, are not open to empirical testing. In the absence of supporting evidence, arguments such as the inadequate superego can only be judged on their face value rather than their scientific worth. For this reason, psychodynamic explanations are regarded as **pseudoscientific** ('fake' science) and may contribute little to our understanding of crime, or how to prevent it.

To be fair Bowlby did provide evidence to support his assertions – though his 44 thieves study has been criticised on methodological grounds (see below).

Evaluation eXtra

Methodological issues with Bowlby's research

Bowlby's 44 thieves study has been heavily criticised. He has been accused of researcher bias insofar as his preconceptions of what he expected to find may have influenced the responses of his interviewees. Bowlby also failed to draw a distinction between **deprivation** and **privation** within his research. Many of the thieves he studied had experienced privation, which many commenters consider to be more damaging than deprivation.

Consider: *Based on your studies in Year One, explain the difference between deprivation and privation.*

Correlation not causation

Hilda Lewis (1954) analysed data drawn from interviews with 500 young people and found that maternal deprivation was a poor predictor of future offending and the ability to form close relationships in adolescence. Even if there is a link between children who have experienced frequent or prolonged separation from their mothers and committing crime in later life, this does not necessarily indicate a causal link between deprivation and delinquency. There are countless other reasons for this apparent link such as genetic factors (see page 328) and the influence of other people – see differential association theory on the previous spread. Maternal deprivation may be one of these reasons, but it may not be the only reason, or the most decisive.

Consider: *Explain what is meant by the **third variable problem** in this context and how this may influence the relationship between maternal deprivation and crime.*

Apply it **Concepts: The case of Jim**

Jim spent the first five years of his life in a children's home as his alcoholic parents were judged not fit to take care of him.

Jim is 15 and has very few close friends. His most recent school report described him as 'lacking empathy' and his progress grades are among the lowest in the class. In the last few weeks, Jim has also started to get in trouble with the police. He has a criminal record for vandalism after damaging a bus shelter and has started stealing from the local shop.

Questions

1. How would Blackburn's inadequate superego theory explain Jim's recent criminal behaviour?

2. How would Bowlby's maternal deprivation theory explain Jim's recent criminal behaviour?

3. Briefly evaluate *one* of the explanations given above. Refer to Jim's behaviour in your answer.

The feminist writer Germaine Greer has been an outspoken critic of Bowlby over the years. She has suggested it is not just the woman's responsibility to look after a child but the whole community – and that maternal deprivation does not inevitably lead to criminal behaviour.

Apply it **Methods: The case of Jim (revisited)**

Jim has recently been referred to a psychologist who has conducted a **case study** of Jim's life. The psychologist has conducted interviews and **naturalistic observations** with Jim as well as talking to his teachers and care workers at the children's home. He has concluded that Jim's criminal behaviour is a result of his early childhood experiences.

Questions

1. Outline what is meant by a case study. Refer to Jim and his psychologist in your answer. (*3 marks*) (See page 64)

2. Briefly evaluate the use of case studies in psychological research. Refer to Jim and his psychologist in your answer. (*6 marks*)

3. Outline the main features of a naturalistic observation. (*2 marks*)

4. Explain *one* strength and *one* limitation of the use of naturalistic observations as applied to this study. (*2 marks + 2 marks*)

CHECK IT

1. Outline **one** psychodynamic explanation of offending. [*4 marks*]

2. Outline **one** study in which a psychodynamic explanation of offending was investigated. [*3 marks*]

3. Briefly evaluate **one** psychodynamic explanation of offending. [*6 marks*]

4. Discuss **two or more** psychodynamic explanations of offending. Refer to evidence in your answer. [*16 marks*]

THE SPECIFICATION SAYS...

Dealing with offending behaviour: the aims of custodial sentencing and the psychological effects of custodial sentencing. Recidivism.

There are a number of ways in which different societies deal with offending behaviour but the most common form of punishment is custodial sentencing (prison). Surveys in this country suggest that the majority of the public would like to see harsher conditions in prison and tougher sentences – but does prison work?

Here, we address this question by considering the aims of prison (what it is designed to achieve), its effectiveness, (with reference to rates of recidivism) and the psychological effects of the prison system.

KEY TERMS

Custodial sentencing – A judicial sentence determined by a court, where the offender is punished by serving time in prison (incarceration) or in some other closed therapeutic and/or educational institution, such as a psychiatric hospital.

Recidivism – Reoffending, a tendency to relapse into a previous condition or mode of behaviour; in the context of crime, a convicted criminal who reoffends, usually repeatedly.

Apply it

Concepts: Aims of custodial sentencing

The following excerpt is taken from a prosecution lawyer's closing statement in court:

'I think you'll agree, ladies and gentlemen of the jury, that Keith Catflap – the notorious serial burglar who stands accused of yet another crime – should be sent to prison for a very long time. As we have seen, he has caused immense suffering to families over the years – now it's his turn to pay with the loss of his liberty. At least then the public will be safe and he might eventually mend his ways. It might also send a message to others that crimes of this nature do not pay.'

Questions

Outline *four* aims of custodial sentencing. Refer to the closing statement above in your answer.

Custodial sentencing

The aims of custodial sentencing

Custodial sentencing involves a convicted offender spending time in prison or another closed institution such as a young offender's institute or psychiatric hospital. There are four main reasons for doing this:

1. Deterrence The unpleasant prison experience is designed to put off the individual (or society at large) from engaging in offending behaviour. Deterrence works on two levels: *general deterrence* aims to send a broad message to members of a given society that **crime** will not be tolerated. *Individual deterrence* should prevent the individual from repeating the same crime in light of their experience. In other words, this view is based on the behaviourist idea of conditioning through **punishment**.

2. Incapacitation The offender is taken out of society to prevent them reoffending as a means of protecting the public. The need for incapacitation is likely to depend upon the severity of the offence and the nature of the offender. For instance, individuals in society will require more protection from a serial murderer or rapist than an elderly person who refuses to pay their council tax.

3. Retribution Society is enacting revenge for the crime by making the offender suffer, and the level of suffering should be proportionate to the seriousness of the crime. This is based on the biblical notion of an 'eye for an eye', that the offender should in some way pay for their actions. Many people see prison as the best possible option in this sense and alternatives to prison are often criticised as soft options.

4. Rehabilitation In contrast to the above, many commentators would see the main objective of prison as not being purely to punish, but to reform. Upon release, offenders should leave prison better adjusted and ready to take their place back in society. Prison should provide opportunities to develop skills and training or to access treatment programmes for drug addiction, as well as give the offender the chance to reflect on their crime.

The psychological effects of custodial sentencing

Research has revealed several psychological effects associated with serving time in prison:

- **Stress** and **depression** Suicide rates are considerably higher in prison than in the general population, as are incidents of self-mutilation and self-harm. The stress of the prison experience also increases the risk of psychological disturbance following release.

- **Institutionalisation** Having adapted to the norms and routines of prison life, inmates may become so accustomed to these that they are no longer able to function on the outside.

- **Prisonisation** Refers to the way in which prisoners are socialised into adopting an 'inmate code'. Behaviour that may be considered unacceptable in the outside world may be encouraged and rewarded inside the walls of the institution.

The problem of recidivism

Recidivism refers to reoffending. Statistics produced by the Ministry of Justice in 2013 suggest that 57% of UK offenders will reoffend within a year of release. In 2007, 14 prisons in England and Wales recorded reoffending rates of over 70%.

Although statistics vary according to the type of offence committed, the UK – alongside the US – has some of the highest rates of recidivism in the world. This is in stark contrast to Norway where reoffending rates are the lowest in Europe and less than half of those in the UK. Norwegian prisons are very different to the system that operates in this country. Penal institutions are much more 'open' in Norway and there is much greater emphasis placed on rehabilitation and skills development than there is in the UK. However, many commentators are very critical of the Norwegian model labelling it a 'soft option' that does not sufficiently punish its inmates.

Life behind bars. But is custodial sentencing the best way to deal with offending behaviour?

STUDY TIP

You may be asked to discuss the aims of custodial sentencing, or discuss the psychological effects of custodial sentencing. In either case, the discussion points on the right may be helpful.

Evaluation

Evidence supports psychological effects

Curt Bartol (1995) has suggested that, for many offenders, imprisonment can be 'brutal, demeaning and generally devastating'. In the last twenty years, suicide rates among offenders have tended to be around fifteen times higher than those in the general population. Most at risk are young single men during the first 24 hours of confinement. A recent study conducted by the Prison Reform Trust (2014) found that 25% of women and 15% of men in prison reported symptoms indicative of psychosis. It would seem that the oppressive prison regime may trigger psychological disorders in those that are vulnerable.

This suggests that custodial sentencing is not effective in rehabilitating the individual, particularly those who are psychologically vulnerable.

Individual differences

Although time in prison may be psychologically challenging for many, it cannot be assumed that all offenders will react in the same way. Different prisons have different regimes, so there are likely to be wide variations in experience. In addition, the length of sentence, the reason for incarceration and previous experience of prison may all be important mitigating factors. Finally, many of those convicted may have had pre-existing psychological and emotional difficulties at the time they were convicted (and this may explain their offending behaviour in the first place).

Therefore, it is difficult to make general conclusions that apply to every prisoner and every prison.

Opportunities for training and treatment

The rehabilitation model is based on the argument that offenders may become better people during their time in prison, and their improved character means they are able to lead a crime-free life when back in society. Many prisoners access education and training whilst in prison increasing the possibility they will find employment upon release. Also, treatment programmes such as **anger management schemes** (see page 342) and social skills training may give offenders insight into their behaviour, reducing the likelihood of recidivism.

This suggests prison may be a worthwhile experience assuming offenders are able to access these programmes. That said, many prisons may lack the resources to provide these programmes and, even when they can, evidence to support the long-term benefits of such schemes is not conclusive – as you will see on the next few spreads.

Evaluation eXtra

Universities for crime

Alongside the legitimate skills that offenders may acquire during their time in prison, they may also undergo a more dubious 'education' as part of their sentence. Incarceration with hardened criminals may give younger inmates in particular the opportunity to learn the 'tricks of the trade' from more experienced offenders. This may undermine attempts to rehabilitate prisoners, making reoffending more likely.

Consider: *The idea that younger criminals may learn from more experienced criminal* **role models** *supports which psychological approach and why?*

Alternatives to custodial sentencing

Judge Geoffrey Davies and co-author K M Raymond (2000), in a review of custodial sentencing, concluded that government ministers often exaggerate the benefits of prison in a bid to appear tough on crime. The review suggested that, in reality, prison does little to deter others or rehabilitate offenders. Alternatives to custodial sentencing, such as community service and restorative justice, have been proposed which mean family contacts and perhaps employment can be maintained.

Consider: *Read through the spread on restorative justice (see pages 344–345). How does this scheme compare with custodial sentencing? What are the benefits/shortcomings of each?*

The prison system has been likened to a 'revolving door' because of high rates of recidivism.

Apply it — **Methods: Comparing recidivism rates**

The inmates at Badchaps Prison receive compulsory education, training and anger management as part of their prison sentence. By contrast, Nortilads Prison, in the neighbouring town has funding problems, is overcrowded and does not provide any such opportunities for its inmates.

Out of 150 prisoners released from Badchaps in 2012, 48 had reoffended within three years. Out of 150 released from Nortilads in the same year, 87 were back 'inside' within three years.

Questions

1. What percentage of the prisoners released from Badchaps had reoffended within three years? Show your calculations. (*2 marks*)
2. What percentage of the prisoners released from Nortilads had reoffended within three years? Show your calculations. (*2 marks*)
3. Sketch an appropriate graphical display to show the percentage of prisoners released from Badchaps and Nortilads who reoffended over the three-year period. (*4 marks*)
4. Identify and explain *one* sampling technique that could have been used to select offenders in the investigation above. (*3 marks*)
5. Evaluate the sampling technique you identified in Q4 with reference to the investigation above. (*4 marks*)

Apply it

Concepts: The Stanford Prison experiment

The classic illustration of the psychological effects of the prison environment is Zimbardo's Stanford Prison experiment (1973). The study demonstrated how quickly 'prisoners' conformed to the role they had been assigned, becoming helpless and apathetic in the process. Prisoners (and prison guards) experienced **de-individuation** – a loss of identity and self-awareness as the experimental role overtook them.

Question

1. How does the Zimbardo study illustrate the possible psychological effects of prison?
2. How might the criticisms of Zimbardo's research (artificiality, **validity**, etc.) undermine its contribution to a discussion of the psychological effects of prison?

CHECK IT

1. What is recidivism? Briefly discuss recidivism in relation to **two** of the aims of custodial sentencing. [5 marks]
2. Outline **one or more** aims of custodial sentencing. [6 marks]
3. Outline **two** psychological effects of custodial sentencing. [4 marks]
4. Discuss the psychological effects of custodial sentencing. Refer to evidence in your answer. [16 marks]

Dealing with offending behaviour: Behaviour modification in custody.

Behaviour modification is one of several schemes that may form part of the custodial sentence – another is anger management, which we will turn to shortly. The aim of these programmes is to effectively manage and monitor offenders during their sentence, as well as reduce the likelihood that they will reoffend after they are released.

Behaviour modification – or as it is more commonly called in its applied form, token economy – uses systems of reward and punishment to encourage obedience and avoidance of conflict in prison inmates.

KEY TERMS

Behaviour modification – An application of the behaviourist approach to treatment (such as the management of offenders in penal institutions). It is based on the principles of operant conditioning. The general aim is to replace undesirable behaviours with more desirable ones through the selective use of positive and/or negative reinforcement.

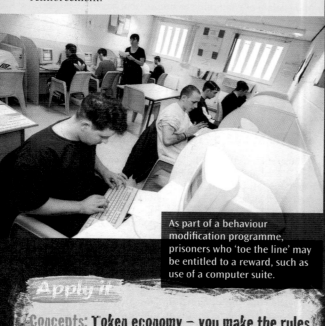

As part of a behaviour modification programme, prisoners who 'toe the line' may be entitled to a reward, such as use of a computer suite.

Apply it

Concepts: Token economy – you make the rules

Imagine you are a prison superintendent with responsibility for the effective management of offenders.

Questions

1. Make a list of all the behaviours you would consider to be good or desirable and would be positively reinforced within your token economy system.

2. Which of the behaviours you have listed do you think would be most resistant to change? Why?

Behaviour modification in custody

Behaviourist principles

If we accept the argument put forward by the **behaviourist approach** – that all human behaviour is learned – then it should be possible to encourage the *unlearning* of behaviour by applying the same principles that brought it about in the first place. **Behaviour modification** programmes are designed with the aim of reinforcing obedient behaviour in offenders, whilst punishing disobedience, in the hope that the former continues and the latter dies out (becomes extinct). This is made possible in prison through the use of a **token economy system**, which can be managed and co-ordinated by prison staff, and is something that all inmates within an institution would be required to adhere to.

Token economy

Based on **operant conditioning**, token economy involves reinforcing desirable behaviour with a token that can then be exchanged for some kind of reward. Within the walls of the prison, desirable behaviour may take many forms but is likely to include avoiding conflict, following prison rules, keeping one's cell orderly, and so on. Prisoners are given a token each time they perform a desirable behaviour. Tokens are **secondary reinforcers** because they derive their value from their association with a reward.

The subsequent reward will also vary according to the institution, but may include exchanging tokens for a phone call to a loved one, time in the gym or exercise yard, extra cigarettes or food.

Each of these behaviours and rewards would be made clear to the prisoners before the programme is implemented. It would also be emphasised that non-compliance, or disobedience, may result in the tokens, and the associated privileges, being withheld or removed (a form of **punishment**).

Changing behaviour

As with all behaviour modification programmes, the desirable behaviour is identified (let's say, avoiding confrontation), broken down into small steps (called increments) and a baseline measure is established. The behaviours to be reinforced are decided upon, and all those who come into contact with offenders must follow the same regime of **selective reinforcement**. So, the prison officers may reinforce a particular prisoner for working positively in a group, 'turning the other cheek' when provoked, etc.

The whole programme can be overseen by prison officials who are able to monitor the programme's effectiveness on the management of the prison as a whole, as well as on the behaviour of individual offenders.

Research example

Tom Hobbs and Michael Holt (1976) introduced a token economy programme with groups of young delinquents across three behavioural units (and a fourth unit acted as a 'control'). They observed a **significant** difference in positive behaviour compared to the non-token economy group. A similar effect was found with offenders in an adult prison (Allyon *et al.* 1979).

Apply it

Concepts: Long-term effects

Although it seems to be the case that behaviour modification may produce an increase in compliant behaviour within institutions, its long-term effectiveness is less certain. Cohen and Filipczak (1971) demonstrated how a token economy group showed more desirable behaviour than a **control group** within an adult prison. Even though the researchers noted that those offenders who took part in the programme were less likely to have reoffended two years later – after three years, rates of recidivism went back to reflecting national statistics.

This suggests that whilst behaviour modification may *delay* recidivism, it has little overall impact in the longer term.

Question

Using the evaluation points (facing page), explain why the benefits of behaviour modification may not generalise beyond the prison setting.

Evaluation

Easy to implement

The appeal of behaviour modification rests largely upon the ease with which it can be administered. There is no need for expertise or specialist professionals as there would be for other forms of treatment such as **anger management**. Rather, token economy systems can be implemented by virtually anyone in any institution. They are also cost-effective and easy to follow once workable methods of reinforcement have been established.

However, the use of such systems does depend on a consistent approach from prison staff; John Bassett and Edward Blanchard (1977) found any benefits were lost after staff applied the techniques inconsistently due to factors such as lack of appropriate training of staff or high staff turnover.

Little rehabilitative value

In the words of Ronald Blackburn (1993), behaviour modification has 'little rehabilitative value' and any positive changes in behaviour that may occur whilst the offender is in prison may quickly be lost when they are released. The token economy system is at its best when establishing appropriate conduct within prison with respect to a very specific set of behaviours but progress is unlikely to extend beyond the custodial setting.

This may be because law-abiding behaviour is not always reinforced on the outside, or the rewards the offender receives from breaking the law, such as group status, may be more powerful.

Ethical issues

The terms and conditions of behaviour modification are regarded as manipulative and dehumanising by several commentators (e.g. Moya and Achtenburg 1974). In an institution using the token economy system, participation in the scheme is obligatory for all offenders rather than optional. Although ultimately the offender can decide whether to comply with the scheme or break the rules, critics have suggested that a programme, which may involve withdrawal of 'privileges' such as exercise and contact with loved ones (in the form of withdrawal of tokens), is **ethically** questionable.

Evaluation eXtra

Passive token learning

Behaviour modification deals with surface behaviour only and encourages a passive form of rather superficial learning. Other treatments, such as anger management (see next spread), are much more active in their approach – the individual is required to reflect on the cause of their offending and is given greater responsibility for their own rehabilitation. Offenders are also likely to play along with the token economy system in order to access the rewards, but this produces little change in their overall character. This may explain why, once the treatment is discontinued, the individual will quickly regress back to their former behaviour.

Consider: *Many commentators advocate an eclectic approach in the treatment of offenders. Explain what this means and why it may have more of a long-term effect on behaviour.*

Individually tailored programmes are most effective

Clinton Field *et al.* (2004) examined a token economy programme used with young people with behavioural problems. The programme was generally effective, although there were still a number of young people who did not respond. Later these youths were placed on a special programme where the rewards were more immediate and more frequent and the results were positive. This suggests that for maximum effectiveness the programme should be designed so that the rewards, and frequency of rewards, suit each individual.

Consider: *Explain how individually tailored programmes might be difficult to achieve in a typical prison.*

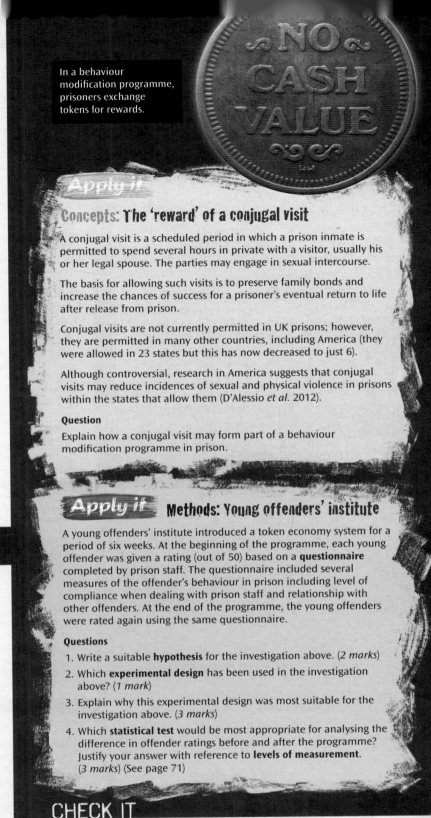

In a behaviour modification programme, prisoners exchange tokens for rewards.

Apply it
Concepts: The 'reward' of a conjugal visit

A conjugal visit is a scheduled period in which a prison inmate is permitted to spend several hours in private with a visitor, usually his or her legal spouse. The parties may engage in sexual intercourse.

The basis for allowing such visits is to preserve family bonds and increase the chances of success for a prisoner's eventual return to life after release from prison.

Conjugal visits are not currently permitted in UK prisons; however, they are permitted in many other countries, including America (they were allowed in 23 states but this has now decreased to just 6).

Although controversial, research in America suggests that conjugal visits may reduce incidences of sexual and physical violence in prisons within the states that allow them (D'Alessio *et al.* 2012).

Question

Explain how a conjugal visit may form part of a behaviour modification programme in prison.

Apply it
Methods: Young offenders' institute

A young offenders' institute introduced a token economy system for a period of six weeks. At the beginning of the programme, each young offender was given a rating (out of 50) based on a **questionnaire** completed by prison staff. The questionnaire included several measures of the offender's behaviour in prison including level of compliance when dealing with prison staff and relationship with other offenders. At the end of the programme, the young offenders were rated again using the same questionnaire.

Questions

1. Write a suitable **hypothesis** for the investigation above. (*2 marks*)
2. Which **experimental design** has been used in the investigation above? (*1 mark*)
3. Explain why this experimental design was most suitable for the investigation above. (*3 marks*)
4. Which **statistical test** would be most appropriate for analysing the difference in offender ratings before and after the programme? Justify your answer with reference to **levels of measurement**. (*3 marks*) (See page 71)

CHECK IT

1. Outline the principles of behaviour modification. **[4 marks]**
2. Outline **one** study in which behaviour modification was investigated. **[3 marks]**
3. Explain **one** strength and **one** limitation of behaviour modification for offenders. **[6 marks]**
4. Discuss behaviour modification in custody. Refer to the issue of recidivism in your answer. **[16 marks]**

Dealing with offending behaviour: Anger management.

Unlike behaviour modification, anger management has the advantage that treatment can be administered outside of the institutional setting as well as inside. The focus of anger management is different too – it concentrates more on the cognitive factors that may influence offending behaviour.

Here, we consider the stages involved in the delivery of anger management, evidence for and against its effectiveness, as well as general commentary.

KEY TERM

Anger management – A therapeutic programme that involves identifying the signs that trigger anger as well as learning techniques to calm down and deal with the situation in a positive way. The aim of anger management is not to prevent anger but to recognise it and manage it. Anger management can be offered in prison to encourage self-awareness and facilitate rehabilitation.

STUDY TIP

Students often have difficulty remembering the names of the three stages in anger management:

Cognitive Preparation; Skills Acquisition; Application Practice.

This mnemonic may help:

Calm People Should Avoid Angry People

Perhaps he ordered a blue phone... a possible candidate for anger management.

Anger management

Cognitive behaviour treatment

Raymond Novaco (1975) suggests that **cognitive** factors trigger the emotional arousal which generally precedes aggressive acts. His argument is that, in some people, anger is often quick to surface especially in situations that are perceived to be anxiety-inducing or threatening.

In **behaviourist** terms, becoming angry is **reinforced** by the individual's feeling of control in that situation. As such, **anger management** programmes are a form of **cognitive behaviour therapy** (CBT) – the individual is taught how to recognise when they are losing control, and then encouraged to develop techniques which bring about conflict-resolution without the need for violence.

Three stages

1. **Cognitive preparation** This phase requires the offender to reflect on past experience and consider the typical pattern of their anger. The offender learns to identify those situations which act as triggers to anger and, if the way in which the offender interprets the event is irrational, the therapist's role is to make this clear. For instance, the offender may view someone looking at them or their partner as an act of confrontation. In redefining the situation as non-threatening, the therapist is attempting to break what may well be an automatic response for the offender.

2. **Skill acquisition** In this stage offenders are introduced to a range of techniques and skills to help them deal with anger-provoking situations more rationally and effectively. Techniques may be *cognitive*: positive self-talk to encourage calmness; *behavioural*: assertiveness training in how to communicate more effectively, and *physiological*: methods of relaxation and/or meditation. The latter particularly promotes the idea that it is possible for the offender to be in control of their emotions rather than ruled by them.

3. **Application practice** In the final phase, offenders are given the opportunity to practise their skills within a carefully monitored environment. Such **role play** is likely to involve the offender and the therapist re-enacting scenarios that may have escalated feelings of anger and acts of violence in the past. This requires a certain amount of commitment from the offender – they must see each scenario as real. It also requires a certain amount of bravery from the therapist whose job it is to 'wind up' the offender in order to assess their progress! Successful negotiation of the role play would be met with **positive reinforcement** from the therapist.

An example

Julia Keen *et al.* (2000) has studied the progress made with young offenders aged between 17 and 21 who took part in a nationally recognised anger management programme. First devised in 1992 and updated in 1995, the *National Anger Management Package* was developed by the England and Wales Prison Service. The course comprises eight two-hour sessions, the first seven over a three-week period with the last session a month afterwards, and the content broadly accords with that which is described above. Although there were initial issues in terms of offenders not taking the course seriously, and individuals forgetting routines such as the requirement to bring their diary, the final outcomes were generally positive. Offenders reported increased awareness of their anger management difficulties and an increased capacity to exercise self-control.

Apply it · Concepts: Anger management – does it work?

In another study, Jane Ireland (2004) compared the progress of two groups of offenders: one of which took part in an anger management programme (adapted from the package above) and the other, a non-treatment **control**. After the treatment group had completed 12 sessions, outcomes were assessed using three measures: an **interview**, a **behaviour checklist** completed by prison officers and a **self-report questionnaire**: 92% of the experimental group showed an improvement on at least one measure, 48% showed an improvement on the checklist and the self-report. There were no such improvements within the control group.

Question

In terms of the effectiveness of anger management programmes, what do these two studies suggest?

Practical idea 2:
Investigating the atavistic form

The aim of this study is to see if people associate particular facial features with offending.

Following Cesare Lombroso (page 326), will an individual with an **atavistic** face be seen by participants as more likely to have committed crime than a person with a 'neutral' face?

The practical bit

Your task here is to conduct an **experiment** based on Lombroso's theory of the atavistic form. You will need to gather a sufficient number of participants to create two **independent groups**. Each group will be shown a different picture of a face – one face has a number of features that Lombroso identified as atavistic; the other, a more 'neutral' face should not include any of these characteristics. All participants will then have to rate the person they see in the picture in terms of how likely they are to have a criminal record (see below).

Making a face

There are a number of options here – the more sophisticated of which might rely on how much access to technology you have. The simplest way of creating two faces is to trawl the images section of any search engine on the Internet. Typing in atavistic or Lombroso should produce a number of pictures of faces that fit the criminal criteria that Lombroso was talking about. You then need to find a more neutral picture of a face to present to the other group. In deciding on this face, you should avoid images, as far as is possible, that include those features listed on page 326 such as low brow, prominent jaw, high cheekbones and facial asymmetry. Both faces should be similar in all key respects such as gender, hair line, age, etc., to control for **confounding variables**.

The slightly more ambitious amongst you might want to create your own pictures. This method has the advantage that you can include as many of Lombroso's atavistic features as you like, rather than relying on images taken from the Internet. There are a number of face creator apps and websites that you might want to try such as *flash face free*, which is free to download.

Standardised procedures

Once you are happy that your faces are suitably 'atavistic' and 'neutral' it's time to carry out the investigation. You will need to approach your potential participants with a briefing statement. This should be written and read out so everyone receives the same information. You should introduce yourself and the aim of the investigation (without giving the game away) and make sure you observe all relevant **ethical issues** (see facing page). Half the participants should be given the atavistic face and the other half the neutral image. Participants should then be asked to rate the person in the picture (let's say, out of 10) in terms of how likely they are to have a criminal record. The following statement would do the job:

> *Study the person on the picture you have been presented with. How likely, on a scale of 1 to 10, would you say it is that the person in the picture has a criminal record? A rating of 1 suggests you think they definitely do not have a criminal record; a rating of 10 suggests you definitely think they do.*

Once you have recorded their rating, you must **debrief** each participant using a standard statement. Remember, again, to ensure that all ethical issues have been properly addressed.

Analysing data

Once you have collected your data, don't forget to summarise it using appropriate graphs and tables (example on right). Although there may be a difference in terms of median ratings, you might want to examine whether the difference is **significant** by employing the correct **statistical test**. Remember, when comparing your calculated value with the **critical value** you need to know whether the test is **one-tailed** or **two-tailed** as well as the appropriate **level of significance**.

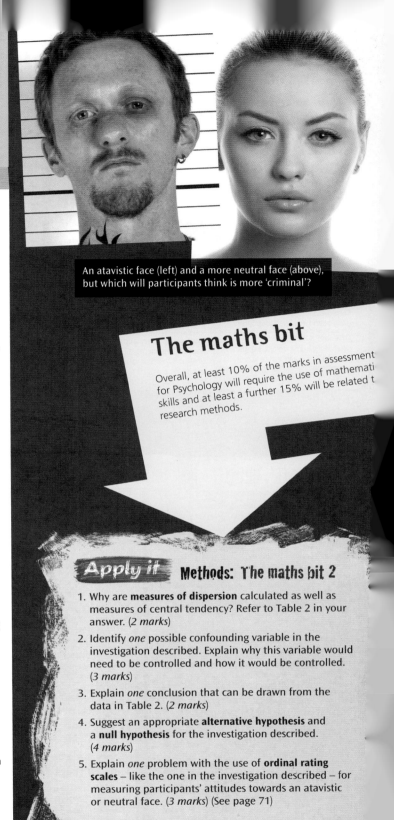

An atavistic face (left) and a more neutral face (above), but which will participants think is more 'criminal'?

The maths bit

Overall, at least 10% of the marks in assessment for Psychology will require the use of mathemati[cal] skills and at least a further 15% will be related t[o] research methods.

Apply it — **Methods: The maths bit 2**

1. Why are **measures of dispersion** calculated as well as measures of central tendency? Refer to Table 2 in your answer. (*2 marks*)

2. Identify *one* possible confounding variable in the investigation described. Explain why this variable would need to be controlled and how it would be controlled. (*3 marks*)

3. Explain *one* conclusion that can be drawn from the data in Table 2. (*2 marks*)

4. Suggest an appropriate **alternative hypothesis** and a **null hypothesis** for the investigation described. (*4 marks*)

5. Explain *one* problem with the use of **ordinal rating scales** – like the one in the investigation described – for measuring participants' attitudes towards an atavistic or neutral face. (*3 marks*) (See page 71)

Table 2 **Median** and **range** values for ratings for atavistic and neutral face

	Atavistic face	Neutral face
Median rating	7	2.5
Range	2	3

REVISION SUMMARIES

DEFINING AND MEASURING CRIME

We need to know what crime is and the extent of it.

PROBLEMS IN DEFINING CRIME

Cultural issues
What is considered a crime in one culture may not be in another, e.g. laws on marriage.

Historical issues
Definitions of crime change over time, e.g. laws on homosexuality.

WAYS OF MEASURING CRIME

Official statistics
Records of reported and recorded crimes published by Home Office.

Victim surveys
Record experience of crime over a given period, e.g. the Crime Survey.

Offender surveys
Offenders disclose details, e.g. the Offender Crime and Justice Survey.

EVALUATION

Official statistics
Underestimate 'dark figure'.
Farrington and Dowds: Differences in police recording rules.

Victim surveys
More likely to include unreported and unrecorded crime.
Problems of telescoping.

Offender surveys
Insight into numbers of criminals responsible for certain crimes.
Some crimes over- or under-represented.

The politics of measuring crime
Government ministers will use those statistics that make their record on crime look most favourable.

Multidisciplinary approach
Each of these methods has problems of reliability and/or validity so a combination of all is preferred.

OFFENDER PROFILING

THE TOP-DOWN APPROACH

US model of profiling.

THE TOP-DOWN APPROACH

Offender profiling
To narrow down the list of suspects and generate hypotheses about the likely offender.

The top-down approach
A match is made between what is known about the crime and a pre-existing template developed by the FBI.

Organised offenders
Show evidence of planning, control and deliberate targeting of their victim. Professional with high IQ.

Disorganised offenders
Little planning, spontaneous, lower than average IQ and in low-paid work.

EVALUATION

Only applies to particular crimes
Rape, arson and cult killings.

Outdated model of personality
Personality is situation-specific so static models of personality are unlikely to help identify an offender.

Evidence not supportive
Canter *et al.*: No evidence for disorganised type.

Classification is too simplistic
Other sub-types, e.g. four types of serial killer (Holmes). Motive more important than type (Keppel and Walter).

Original sample
Small and unrepresentative. Also convicted killers are deceptive so self-report evidence is not sensible.

THE BOTTOM-UP APPROACH

UK approaches to profiling.

THE BOTTOM-UP APPROACH

The bottom-up approach
Profile emerges from analysis of the crime scene.

Investigative psychology
Interpersonal coherence: Behaviour at scene reflect everyday behaviour.
Time and place: May suggest dwelling place.
Forensic awareness: Suggests previous crimes.

Geographical profiling
Crime mapping may reveal the offender's 'centre of gravity' and whether a marauder or commuter.

EVALUATION

Evidence for investigative psychology
Canter and Heritage identified features of a 'typical' rape that may be of use to investigators.

Evidence for geographical profiling
Lundrigan and Canter: Spatial information was key in determining the base of an offender.

Scientific basis
Grounded in evidence and psychological theory.

Wider application
Principle of spatial consistency can be used in the investigation of any crime.

Mixed results for profiling
Many successes, but significant failures, e.g. successful capture in only 3% of cases (Copson).

PSYCHOLOGICAL EXPLANATIONS OF OFFENDING BEHAVIOUR

EYSENCK'S THEORY

A 'halfway house' between biological and psychological explanations.

EYSENCK'S THEORY

General personality theory
Behaviour can be understood along two dimensions: Introversion–extraversion; neuroticism–stability.

Biological basis
Activity of the nervous system determines personality type: Extraverts have an underactive N/S, neurotics are nervous and jumpy.

The criminal personality
Scores high on extraversion, neuroticism, psychoticism.

The role of socialisation
Criminal behaviour is developmentally immature and criminal personalities are difficult to condition.

Measuring the criminal personality
The Eysenck Personality Inventory locates respondents on E and N dimensions (a separate scale for psychoticism).

EVALUATION

Mixed evidence
Eysenck and Eysenck: Higher E, N and P scores in offenders, not supported by Farrington *et al.*

The idea of a single criminal type
Too simplistic: Moffitt proposed several types of male offender; Digman proposed the five factor model.

Cultural bias
Bartol *et al.*: Cultural differences in levels of E with Hispanic and African-American offenders.

(Mis)measurement of personality
Personality may not be reducible to a single score and not a stable entity (Mischel).

Biological basis
Some overlap with APD research (offenders are cold and uncaring), may just be activity of nervous system.

COGNITIVE

What goes on in the criminal mind?

COGNITIVE EXPLANATIONS

Level of moral reasoning
Criminals reason at a less sophisticated level than the rest of the population.

Kohlberg's model and criminality
Offenders at pre-conventional level, egocentric, childlike reasoning.

Cognitive distortions
Errors or biases in the way we explain our own and others' behaviour.

Hostile attribution bias
Tendency to see other people's behaviour as confrontational and threatening.

Minimalisation
Downplaying the seriousness of an offence.

EVALUATION

Level of moral reasoning evidence
Hollins and Palmer support Kohlberg's predictions that delinquents are premoral.

Alternative theories of reasoning
Gibbs: Mature–immature reasoning better, no cultural bias.

Application of research
CBT encourages offenders to develop a less distorted view of their actions.

Individual differences
Reasoning may vary due to type of offence and level of intelligence.

Descriptive not explanatory
Cognitive theories are 'after the fact', no insight into oorigins of criminality.

DIFFERENTIAL ASSOCIATION THEORY

A social learning theory of offending.

DIFFERENTIAL ASSOCIATION THEORY

Scientific basis
Sutherland: Set of principles to explain all types of offending.

Crime as a learned behaviour
Acquired from significant others.

Pro-criminal attitudes
If pro-criminal attitudes exceed anti-criminal, the person will offend.

Learning criminal acts
Offender learns techniques of offending through imitation or direct tuition.

EVALUATION

Explanatory power
Can account for crime within all sectors of society including 'white collar crime'.

Shift of focus
Draws attention to dysfunctional environments as a cause of crime.

Difficulty of testing
Hard to measure exposure to pro-criminal attitudes.

Alternative explanations
Crime in families supports genetics or psychodynamic theory.

Individual differences
May lead to stereotyping of people from poorer backgrounds.

PSYCHODYNAMIC

Early parental influences.

PSYCHODYNAMIC EXPLANATIONS

The inadequate superego
Blackburn identified three types: Weak, deviant and over-harsh.

The maternal deprivation hypothesis
Bowlby: Lack of a continuous relationship with mother figure leads to delinquency.

44 juvenile thieves
Of the 14 thieves classified as affectionless psychopaths, 12 had maternal deprivation.

EVALUATION

Gender bias
Evidence doesn't show males more moral; little girls better at resisting temptation (Hoffman).

Contradictory evidence
Lack of evidence to support any of the forms of superego that Blackburn suggested.

Unconscious concepts
These are not open to testing, so their application to explaining crime is unfalsifiable.

Methodological issues
Bowlby didn't distinguish between deprivation and privation. Also possible investigor issues.

Correlation not causation
Lewis found that maternal deprivation was a poor predictor of criminality.

BIOLOGICAL APPROACHES OF OFFENDING BEHAVIOUR

ATAVISTIC FORM

A historical approach to offending.

ATAVISTIC FORM

A historical approach to offending
Lombroso in 1876: Criminals are genetic throwbacks who cannot cope with the demands of civilised society (and so commit crime).

Atavistic characteristics
E.g. strong jaw, high cheekbones, asymmetric face. Also dark skin, extra toes.

Lombroso's research
Examined over 4000 convicts, 40% of criminal acts related to atavistic form.

EVALUATION

Contribution to criminality
Lombroso brought the study of criminology into science, theory was forerunner to offender profiling.

Scientific racism
Many of the facial features he identified were associated with people of Black African origin.

Contradictory evidence
Goring compared 3000 criminals and non-criminals and found no significant differences in atavistic form.

Poor control in Lombroso's research
No comparison with non-criminal sample and important confounding variables, e.g. psychological disorders.

Causation is an issue
Other factors, such as poverty or poor diet, may cause physical differences among criminals.

GENETIC AND NEURAL EXPLANATIONS

Modern-day biological theories.

GENETIC EXPLANATIONS

Twin studies
Christianson: 33% concordance rates for criminality in MZ and 12% DZ twins.

Candidate genes
MAOA and CDH13 have been implicated as the genetic basis of criminality in a study in Finland (Tihonen et al.).

Diathesis-stress model
A genetic predisposition to crime is triggered by a social or psychological stressor, e.g. dysfunctional environment.

NEURAL EXPLANATIONS

Prefrontal cortex
Raine et al.: 11% less grey matter in the prefrontal cortex of criminals.

Mirror neurons
Keyser et al.: Found that only when criminals were asked to empathise did their empathy reaction (controlled by mirror neurons) activate.

EVALUATION

Problems with twin studies
Early studies were poorly controlled, twin studies include small samples; shared environments may produce high concordance.

Support for diathesis-stress model of crime
Mednick et al.: 20% if biological parents were criminals and 24.5% if both biological and adoptive parents.

Problems with adoption studies
Late adoption and contact with biological parents are confounding factors.

Biological reductionism
Explanations that reduce offending to a genetic or neural level may be overly simplistic, complex interactions (Katz et al.).

Biological determinism
The discovery of a criminal gene presents an ethical dilemma: What to do with people who have it.

DEALING WITH OFFENDING BEHAVIOUR

CUSTODIAL SENTENCING

What is prison for and does it work?

CUSTODIAL SENTENCING

The aims of custodial sentencing
Deterrence: Put others off.
Incapacitation: Protect the public.
Retribution: Revenge for the act.
Rehabilitation: Reform the offender.

Psychological effects of custodial sentencing
Include stress, depression, institutionalisation and prisonisation (adoption of the 'inmate code').

Recidivism
UK figures = 57%, higher than Norway with more skill-based system.

EVALUATION

Evidence supports psychological effects
High rates of suicide and psychosis suggest that prison is brutal, demeaning (Bartol).

Individual differences
Length of sentence, previous experience and pre-existing disorders affect offender's reaction to prison.

Opportunities for training and treatment
Access to education and therapy, e.g. anger management, supports the rehabilitation model.

Universities for crime
Young offenders learning from the more experienced may explain high rates of recidivism.

Alternatives to custodial sentencing
Community service and restorative justice mean family contacts and employment can be maintained.

ANGER MANAGEMENT

Cognitive factors that may influence offending.

ANGER MANAGEMENT

Cognitive behaviour therapy
Novaco: Cognitive factors trigger arousal. Clients learn how to recognise loss of control and reinforced for managing conflict.

Three stages
Cognitive preparation: Recognising triggers.
Skills acquisition: Learning behavioural techniques.
Application practice: Role plays to assess progress.

An example
Keen reported positive outcomes from the National Anger Management Package.

EVALUATION

Eclectic approach
Includes cognitive, behavioural and social elements – a multidisciplinary approach.

Comparison with behaviour modification
Tackles root cause and may self-discover insight through therapy, unlike behaviour modification (promotes superficial and passive learning).

Limited long-term effectiveness
Little evidence that it reduces recidivism. Role play may not reflect real-life triggers to anger.

Anger may not cause offending
May provide offenders with an excuse rather than being the reason individuals offend (Loza and Loza-Fanous).

Expensive and requires commitment
Prisoners may be uncooperative and apathetic and may not engage fully with the process.

BEHAVIOUR MODIFICATION IN CUSTODY

Systems of reward and punishment to encourage compliance.

BEHAVIOUR MODIFICATION IN CUSTODY

Behaviourist principles
Maladaptive behaviour can be unlearned by positively reinforcing obedient behaviours.

Token economy
Tokens (secondary reinforcers) are associated with reward, e.g. following prison rules.

Changing behaviour
The desired behaviour is broken down into increments and each step is successively reinforced.

Evidence
Hobbs and Holt: Groups of young delinquents responded positively to a token economy system.

EVALUATION

Easy to implement
No specialist professionals required so the procedure can be cheaply administered, but techniques applied inconsistently (Bassett and Blanchard).

Little rehabilitative value
Studies show a short-term effect but progress may not be maintained after release.

Ethical issues
Behaviour modification may involve withdrawal of privileges which is manipulative and ethically questionable.

Passive token learning
Prisoners gain no insight into causes of offending unlike cognitive treatments such as anger management.

Individually tailored programmes are most effective
Field et al.: For maximum effectiveness programmes should be designed to meet the individual's needs.

RESTORATIVE JUSTICE

Making amends directly to the victim.

RESTORATIVE JUSTICE

Changing the emphasis
Restorative justice focuses on the needs of the individual victim rather than the needs of the state to punish.

The restorative justice process
Based on the principles of healing and empowerment through a supervised meeting between offender and survivor.

Key features of the process
Focus on positive change and active involvement beyond the courtroom.

Variations of the process
Could be financial or repairing property, can function as an 'add on' to community service or alongside prison.

The Restorative Justice Council
An independent body which establishes standards for professionals in the field.

EVALUATION

Diversity of programmes
General conclusions may be difficult to draw as there is a wide range of possible applications.

Relies on offender showing remorse
Offender may not regret crimes and may become involved because of the promise of a reduced sentence.

Expensive
Saves money for criminal system but requires a trained mediator and there is a risk of high dropout rates which increases costs.

Feminist critique
Not suitable in domestic violence cases due to the power imbalance between the abuser and the abused.

Soft option
Lack of public support for alternatives to prison and among politicians who want to appear 'tough on crime'.

Question 1   Outline **two** problems in defining crime. *(4 marks)*

Morticia's answer

A crime is a violation of the law where a person will be convicted by a court. One problem with this definition is that many crimes go undetected so you can't just define crime in terms of whether it has been detected.

Another problem with defining crime is that people don't always agree about what is wrong especially in different countries.

The actual definition of crime is not a requirement of the question here and Morticia's first 'problem' is muddled and contributes nothing.

The second paragraph is poorly expressed but does convey the idea of cultural difference.

Luke's answer

There are two key problems with defining crime. One is a cultural issue because people in different cultures have different views about right and wrong, for example laws on marriage.

Another issue is changes in crime over time, e.g. laws on homosexuality.

Luke has clearly outlined two problems. His examples are merely identified, however, and further elaboration would be required.

Vladimir's answer

Crime is very difficult to define. There are two main reasons for this. One is related to culture and the other is related to history.

From a cultural viewpoint, the issue is that things which are regarded as immoral in one culture are acceptable in another.

For example, in some cultures, it is acceptable to have more than one wife and it isn't a crime whereas it is a crime in the UK. The same is true in terms of a historical perspective.

Things that are at one time in history seen as a crime, such as homosexuality, change and are no longer crimes.

This means that definitions of crime are not absolute.

In contrast, there is a much more thorough answer from Vladimir, which is nicely and logically explained. If one were being picky, the point about homosexuality could still be slightly clearer but there is sufficient information here.

Question 2   When questioned by police, Max claimed he punched the man in the bar because 'he looked at me funny'. In court – defending his actions – Max told the judge that the man he punched 'wasn't even hurt that bad' and 'what was I supposed to do? I was just taking care of business'.

With reference to Max above, explain what is meant by cognitive distortions. *(4 marks)*

Morticia's answer

A cognitive distortion is when the way you think is biased or changed in some way, in other words distorted. This can be used to explain why some people are criminals. For example, the hostile attribution bias is when someone sees someone else shouting and interprets this in a negative way and then gives an aggressive response.

There is evidence that some criminal people have this problem of seeing other people's behaviour in a bad light and in the end they behave criminally because they got very angry.

A muddled answer from Morticia. The definition of cognitive distortions is weak and not effectively linked to offending behaviour. The example of hostile attribution bias conveys some minimal understanding of the concept. There is no application to the stem here.

Luke's answer

There are two main types of cognitive distortions – hostile attribution bias and minimalisation, and both can be seen in Max's behaviour. Max shows the negative attribution bias when he says he hit him because he looked at him funny. So the problem was the Max interpreted what was probably a perfectly innocent behaviour as being aggressive so he responded aggressively.

Max shows minimalisation when he says `he wasn't even hurt that bad', in other words he is downplaying the damage caused by his behaviour which means he can do bad things and then excuse it.

Luke's answer is a good one. His definition of hostile attribution bias comes at the end of the first paragraph and is clearly linked to 'Max'.

Similarly minimalisation is clearly defined and linked to the appropriate part of the stem.

Vladimir's answer

In the example of Max he punched someone else because the other person looked at him funny. That is quite common in criminals that they get angry at the littlest thing and think it is OK as Max says in the quote, that he was just taking care of business.

So to Max his behaviour seems totally reasonable and normal and this is a cognitive distortion. This is a psychological explanation for criminal behaviour.

Vladimir's first paragraph amounts to little more than a repeat of the stem. The attempted definition of cognitive distortion is also not strong.

Question 3 A recent review of evidence in a forensic psychology journal concluded that offender profiling is 'a waste of time'. Discuss the view that offender profiling is 'a waste of time'. Refer to **two** methods of offender profiling in your answer. *(16 marks)*

Morticia's answer

Many people see offender profiling as a waste of time because it doesn't actually result in catching criminals. On the other hand, there is evidence that in fact it is useful. In this essay, I will first of all briefly explain offender profiling and then look at arguments for and against it.

There are in fact two kinds of offender profiling – bottom-up and top-down. The aim is to use a method in order to narrow down the list of suspects and generate hypotheses about the likely offender. The top-down approach originated in America especially with the FBI. A match is made between what is known about the crime and a pre-existing template developed by the FBI. Organised crimes show evidence of planning, control and deliberate targeting of their victim. The offender is professional with high IQ whereas disorganised crimes are the opposite. In the bottom-up approach, which is a UK system, the profile emerges from analysis of the crime scene. Investigators look at such things as time and place and forensic awareness.

On the negative side one of the problems with the top-down approach is that it applies to crimes where the crime scene contains important details about the criminal such as rape or arson. Crimes such as burglary don't often involve information left about the criminal. So this is a significant limitation. Perhaps a bigger issue is that the personality profile is really based on outdated and rather simplistic ideas about what criminals are like. The evidence for the model isn't very good especially for the disorganised type of criminal. On the positive side, the top-down approach continues to be used in America so it must have some value and it is based on research evidence that looked at 36 killers.

The bottom-up approach also has criticisms though there is probably more evidence in its favour. For example, Canter has done a number of studies that show that this approach is quite objective and scientific, and has a wide number of applications. So this is a strength of the approach and it makes it much more useful than the top-down approach. On the other hand there have been some notable failures for this approach such as the Rachel Nickell case.

So on balance I would probably agree with the review in the forensic journal that the disadvantages outweigh the successes and it is a waste of time especially the top-down approach.

(399 words)

Morticia's preamble is not really necessary here nor is it well informed.

The next paragraph is better. The descriptive account of the top-down approach is the superior one here, the bottom-up approach lacks detail. The definition of profiling would have made a better beginning.

This is followed by a reasonable evaluative paragraph. Each point is relevant but rather 'list-like' in presentation. Fewer points explored in more depth would be preferable.

A similar theme in the next paragraph. The points made lack sufficient evidence and depth to be convincing.

At least there is reflection on the question at the end. This answer would have benefitted from more evidence and greater depth of discussion.

Luke's answer

There are two methods of offender profiling. The American top-down system originated in the United States as a result of work carried out by the FBI in the 1970s. The FBI gathered data on 36 serial killers and used this to create a type of offender, classing them as organised or disorganised. The FBI uses this classification system to make predictions about criminals. They examine a crime scene and classify it as organised or disorganised and this coupled together with aspects of the crime (such as sequence of events and type of victim) enables them to predict features of the criminal such as demographic background and physical characteristics.

The evidence is not very good for this approach so it is easy to see why it would be regarded as a waste of time. First, the type of crime it is relevant to is very limited to killers or rapists. Secondly, it assumes a model of personality that is really very outmoded – the model assumes that people belong to fixed typologies which are consistent across situations and contexts. In fact altogether the classification system is too simplistic and subsequent researchers such as Holmes have suggested four types rather than the basic two. The original sample was only 36 killers of a certain type, so the concept might be salvageable if more criminals were studied and the typology extended.

The UK bottom-down system does not begin with fixed typologies but is more data-driven, i.e. the investigator first looks at the details generated at the crime scene and applies statistical procedures to analyse this data. Details from past crime scenes are stored and act as a base for making comparisons. This means that current offences can be matched with past ones and generate expectations about the criminals' personal history, family background, etc.

The bottom-up approach is more grounded in evidence than the US system in that the whole system is based on a database of previous cases. An example of the kind of statistical techniques that are used is one developed by Canter and Heritage who use the statistical technique smallest space analysis to identify patterns of behaviour in over 60 sexual assault cases. This supports the usefulness of investigative psychology because it shows how statistical techniques can be applied.

A particular strategy developed by Canter was the geographical profile that an offender's operational base and possible future offences are revealed by the geographical location of their previous crimes. In Canter's circle theory, he identified the 'marauder' who works within a small radius of where he lives and the 'commuter' who will travel to the crime location.

This also has supportive research evidence, for example Lundrigan and Canter put together information from 120 murder cases involving serial killers in the USA. Smallest space analysis revealed spatial consistency in the behaviour of the killers. This supports Canter's claim that spatial information is a key factor in determining the base of an offender.

(483 words)

A clear contrast here in Luke's answer which provides detailed, well-focused description.

In paragraph 2 there is a clear 'nod' to the essay stem at the beginning of this paragraph which is good. Note the higher level of discussion here compared to the previous answer from Morticia.

'Bottom-down' is an unfortunate error but this does not detract from the quality of the description.

The first criticism is well-illustrated using relevant evidence. The last two paragraphs are good too.

The limitation to this answer is that Luke should have made time to reflect on the essay stem at the end. Though this is still a strong answer, he should have considered whether the British approach is also a 'waste of time'.

Defining and measuring crime

1. Which of the following is *not* a method of measuring crime?
   (a) Official statistics.
   (b) Self-interest survey.
   (c) Victim survey.
   (d) Offender survey.

2. An estimated 75% of crimes are unreported or unrecorded. This is known as . . .
   (a) The dark shadow.
   (b) The dark alley.
   (c) The dark figure.
   (d) The dark night.

3. Assuming a crime was committed more recently than it actually was is known as . . .
   (a) Telescoping.
   (b) Microscoping.
   (c) Transporting.
   (d) Moonlighting.

4. In the Farrington and Dowds study which police authority recorded theft under 10 pounds?
   (a) Nottinghamshire.
   (b) Leicestershire.
   (c) Derbyshire.
   (d) Ayrshire.

Offender profiling: The top-down approach

1. The top-down approach is *most* associated with the . . .
   (a) FBI.   (c) MI5.
   (b) MFI.   (d) CIA.

2. Which of the following is *most* associated with an organised offender?
   (a) Married.
   (b) Low IQ.
   (c) Lack of sexual problems.
   (d) Irrational and stressed during the incident.

3. Which of the following is *most* associated with a disorganised offender?
   (a) Leaves few clues.
   (b) Carefully planned.
   (c) In skilled work.
   (d) Lives alone.

4. Which of the following is *least* likely to be investigated using a top-down approach?
   (a) Rape.
   (b) Arson.
   (c) Cult killings.
   (d) Burglary.

Offender profiling: The bottom-up approach

1. Which of the following is *not* associated with the bottom-up approach?
   (a) Data-driven.
   (b) Profile emerges from analysis of crime scene.
   (c) Use of typologies.
   (d) Investigative psychology.

2. Which of the following is *most* associated with the geographical approach?
   (a) Interpersonal coherence.
   (b) The significance of the time of the incident.
   (c) Spatial consistency.
   (d) Forensic awareness.

3. An offender who operates close to their operational base is known as a . . .
   (a) Marauder.
   (b) Commuter.
   (c) Navigator.
   (d) Promoter.

4. Which of the following is *not* an advantage the bottom-up approach has over the top-down approach?
   (a) It can be applied to a greater range of crimes.
   (b) It is based on scientific techniques.
   (c) It is grounded in psychological theory.
   (d) It was developed through interviews with real serial killers.

Biological approaches to offending: atavistic form

1. Lombroso thought criminals were genetic . . .
   (a) Throwbacks.
   (b) Slingbacks.
   (c) Drawbacks.
   (d) Setbacks.

2. Which of the following is *not* a physical feature associated with murderers?
   (a) Short fingers.
   (b) Bloodshot eyes.
   (c) Curly hair.
   (d) Long ears.

3. In Lombroso's study what percentage of crimes did he claim could be accounted for by the atavistic form?
   (a) 25%   (c) 66%
   (b) 40%   (d) 80%

4. Goring's study was an improvement on Lombroso's because it included . . .
   (a) Double-blind procedures.
   (b) Real criminals.
   (c) A control group.
   (d) Analysis of cranial features.

Genetic and neural explanations

1. The degree of similarity between twin pairs and family members on a specific characteristic is known as . . .
   (a) Concurrence.
   (b) Accordance.
   (c) Occurrence.
   (d) Concordance.

2. Individuals with antisocial personality disorder may have reduced activity in . . .
   (a) The prefrontal cortex.
   (b) The parietal cortex.
   (c) The peripheral cortex.
   (d) The presynaptic cortex.

3. In the Mednick study, when both biological and adoptive parents had convictions, the percentage of adoptees that did was . . .
   (a) 2%   (b) 24.5%
   (c) 44.5%   (d) 71%

4. The MAOA gene which has been linked to aggressive behaviour is thought to regulate which two chemicals in the brain?
   (a) Adrenaline and noradrenaline.
   (b) Acetylcholine and insulin.
   (c) Testosterone and oestrogen.
   (d) Dopamine and serotonin.

Eysenck's theory of the criminal personality

1. Eysenck suggested that the criminal type would score highly on measures of extraversion, neuroticism and which other characteristic?
   (a) Introversion.
   (b) Stability.
   (c) Psychoticism.
   (d) Barbarism.

2. Which of the following is *not* associated with extraverts?
   (a) An underactive nervous system.
   (b) Seek excitement and stimulation.
   (c) Engage in risk-taking behaviour.
   (d) Easy to condition.

3. Farrington *et al.* (1982) found that offenders scored . . .
   (a) High on E measures but not for P or N.
   (b) High on N measures but not for E or P.
   (c) High on P measures but not for E or N.
   (d) High on E, N and P measures.

4. Which of the following is *not* part of Digman's five-factor model?
   (a) Openness.
   (b) Calmness.
   (c) Agreeableness.
   (d) Conscientiousness.

Cognitive explanations

1. Which of the following is *not* part of Kohlberg's model?
   (a) Multi-conventional reasoning.
   (b) Pre-conventional reasoning.
   (c) Conventional reasoning.
   (d) Post-conventional reasoning.

2. 'A tendency to interpret the behaviour of others as threatening or confrontational' describes . . .
   (a) Minimalisation.
   (b) Euphemistic label.
   (c) Hostile attribution bias.
   (d) Moral reasoning.

3. Studies suggest that which group are particularly prone to minimalisation?
   (a) Burglars.
   (b) Sex offenders.
   (c) Serial killers.
   (d) Arsonists.

4. Gibbs proposed a revised version of Kohlberg's model with two levels ...

(a) Antimoral and promoral.

(b) Law abiding and law infringing.

(c) Mature and immature.

(d) Primary and secondary.

Differential association theory

1. Sutherland argues that people will commit crime when ...

(a) Number of pro-criminal attitudes outnumber anti-criminal.

(b) Number of anti-criminal attitudes outnumber the pro-criminal.

(c) Number of pro-criminal attitudes is the same as the number of anti-criminal.

(d) They have neither pro- or anti-criminal attitudes.

2. What percentage of participants in the Cambridge Study in Delinquent Development were defined as 'chronic offenders'?

(a) 7% (c) 70%

(b) 41% (d) Zero

3. Sutherland coined which term?

(a) Blue-collar crime.

(b) Blue-shirt crime.

(c) White-shirt crime.

(d) White-collar crime.

4. Which of the following is *not* a strength of Sutherland's theory?

(a) Can account for crimes in different sectors of society.

(b) Shifted focus away from individual accounts of crime.

(c) Drew attention to the importance of dysfunctional environments.

(d) Exposure to pro- and anti-criminal attitudes is easy to measure.

Psychodynamic explanations

1. Which of the following is *not* a form of inadequate superego identified by Blackburn?

(a) Weak superego.

(b) Infantile superego.

(c) Deviant superego.

(d) Over harsh superego.

2. The superego is based on the ...

(a) Reality principle.

(b) Morality principle.

(c) Ethical principle.

(d) Gratification principle.

3. Which of the following is a long-term effect of maternal deprivation?

(a) Delinquent behaviour.

(b) Affectionate behaviour.

(c) Empathy.

(d) Guilt.

4. How many of Bowlby's affectionless psychopaths had experienced prolonged separation from their mother?

(a) 14 (c) 44

(b) 12 (d) 0

Custodial sentencing

1. Which of the following is 'society enacting revenge by making the offender suffer'?

(a) Rehabilitation.

(b) Deterrence.

(c) Incarceration.

(d) Retribution.

2. Which of the following is *not* a psychological effect of custodial sentencing?

(a) Prisonisation.

(b) Recidivism.

(c) Institutionalisation.

(d) Depression.

3. Young single men are most at risk of suicide in the first ... of prison.

(a) Fortnight.

(b) Week.

(c) 24 hours.

(d) Hour.

4. In 2013, the rate of reoffending within a year of being released from prison was?

(a) Nearly 50%.

(b) Nearly 60%.

(c) Nearly 70%.

(d) Nearly 80%.

Behaviour modification in custody

1. The token economy system is based on what form of learning?

(a) Vicarious conditioning.

(b) Classical conditioning.

(c) Operant conditioning.

(d) Observational learning.

2. The breaking of behaviour up into small steps is called?

(a) Incidents.

(b) Inclement.

(c) Incessant.

(d) Increments.

3. Who found that behaviour modification delayed recidivism but did not eradicate it?

(a) Bassett and Blanchard.

(b) Hobbs and Holt.

(c) Cohen and Filipczak.

(d) Allyon and Milan.

4. Removing tokens to encourage compliant behaviour is a form of ...

(a) Positive reinforcement.

(b) Primary reinforcement.

(c) Punishment.

(d) Vicarious reinforcement.

Anger management

1. Which of the following is *not* one of the phases of anger management?

(a) Mental restructuring.

(b) Cognitive preparation.

(c) Skills acquisition.

(d) Application practice.

2. Which of these would *not* be part of 'skills acquisition'?

(a) Learning positive self-talk.

(b) Assertiveness training.

(c) Exercises on how to communicate more effectively.

(d) Exchanging tokens for rewards.

3. Keen (2000) studied young offenders who had participated in the ...

(a) National Anger Management Package.

(b) Offender's Anger Management Programme.

(c) British Anger Management Strategy.

(d) Anger Management Reduction Scheme.

4. Which of the following approaches is *not* really part of anger management?

(a) Behavioural.

(b) Cognitive.

(c) Psychodynamic.

(d) Social.

Restorative justice

1. An offender seeing the hurt their actions caused is an important part of what process?

(a) Rehabilitation.

(b) Recidivism.

(c) Retribution.

(d) Prisonisation.

2. Which of the following would *not* be a function of restorative justice?

(a) As an alternative to prison.

(b) As an addition to community service.

(c) As an incentive to reduce an existing sentence.

(d) As a form of reward in a token economy scheme.

3. How many studies of restorative justice did Sherman and Strang review in their meta-analysis?

(a) 3 (c) 36

(b) 6 (d) 63

4. Shapland concluded that every £1 spent on restorative justice would save the criminal justice system ...

(a) £2 (c) £6

(b) £4 (d) £8

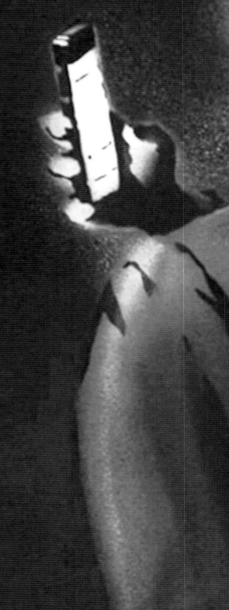

CHAPTER 13 ADDICTION

Chapter contents

Heroin, gambling, sex, cocaine, cigarettes, booze, pies, chocolate, caffeine, danger, your phone.

What is addiction?

Is it possible to become addicted to these things?

How would you know if you were addicted to your phone?

DESCRIBING ADDICTION

> Describing addiction: physical and psychological dependence, tolerance and withdrawal syndrome.

Addiction is a term included in the Diagnostic and Statistical Manual of Mental Disorders (DSM-5). It is an official diagnostic label, albeit only since 2013. Some psychologists are concerned that this creates a new stigma for addiction, being labelled as a mental illness. Such negative connotations may explain why so many addicts are put off seeking treatment. On this page we look at what is involved in addiction.

KEY TERMS

Addiction – A disorder in which an individual takes a substance or engages in a behaviour that is pleasurable but eventually becomes compulsive with harmful consequences. Marked by physiological and/or psychological dependence, tolerance and withdrawal.

Physical dependence – A state of the body due to habitual drug use and which results in a withdrawal syndrome when use of the drug is reduced or stopped.

Psychological dependence – A compulsion to continue taking a drug because its use is rewarding.

Tolerance – A reduction in response to a drug, so that the addicted individual needs more to get the same effect.

Withdrawal syndrome – A set of symptoms that develop when the addicted person abstains from or reduces their drug use.

Determined to stop smoking. A good move, but withdrawal symptoms won't be far behind.

Apply it   Concepts: Harriet and smoking

Harriet is a long-term smoker who has always found having a cigarette relaxing – it calms her nerves and helps her to cope with stress. But she has found over the months that her daily intake has gradually crept up, and she doesn't quite get the same pleasure from smoking as she once did. But she still gets cravings for a cigarette when she has to go a couple of hours without one.

Question

Explain what is happening to Harriet using the concepts of drug dependence and tolerance.

What is addiction?

Addiction is more than simply doing something a lot. Key features are dependence, tolerance and withdrawal symptoms.

Physical and psychological dependence

Physical dependence is defined in terms of withdrawal. It's only possible to establish for certain that someone is physically dependent on a substance when they abstain from it. Physical dependence is said to have occurred when a **withdrawal syndrome** is produced by stopping the drug (see below).

Psychological dependence refers to the compulsion to experience the effects of a drug, usually in terms of an increase in pleasure or a lessening of discomfort. Either way, taking the drug is reliably followed by a reward. A consequence of psychological dependence is that the person will continually take the drug (or engage in a behaviour) until it becomes a habit, despite the harmful consequences.

Tolerance

Tolerance occurs when an individual's response to a given amount of a drug is reduced. This means they need ever greater doses to produce the same effect on behaviour. So tolerance is caused by repeated previous exposure to the effects of a drug.

One type of tolerance is behavioural tolerance which happens when the individual learns through experience to adjust their behaviour to compensate for the effects of a drug. For instance, people addicted to alcohol learn to walk more slowly when they are drunk to avoid falling over.

A special instance of tolerance is cross-tolerance, whereby developing tolerance to one type of drug (alcohol, for example) can reduce sensitivity to another type (**benzodiazepines**). This is a classic issue in surgery. People who have developed a tolerance to the sleep-inducing effects of alcohol need higher doses of anaesthetics. Cross-tolerance can be used therapeutically by giving benzodiazepines to people withdrawing from alcohol to reduce the withdrawal syndrome.

Withdrawal syndrome

A withdrawal syndrome is a collection of symptoms associated with abstaining from a drug or reducing its use. The symptoms are almost always the opposite of the ones created by the drug, and indicate that a physical dependence has developed. For example, effects of withdrawal from nicotine include irritability, anxiety, restlessness, increased appetite and weight gain.

Once a physical dependence develops, the addicted person experiences some symptoms of withdrawal whenever they cannot get the drug. This happens relatively often so they become familiar with these symptoms. Their motivation for continuing to take the drug is partly to avoid the withdrawal symptoms, a secondary form of psychological dependence.

Apply it   Concepts: Mick and gambling

Mick spends a lot of money playing online fruit machines for several hours most days. Although he's a bit worried he might be addicted, he loves the thrill and excitement of playing, and it takes his mind off the stresses of his everyday life when he can feel his anxieties drop away. But there are times when Mick can't get online, so he starts to feel irritable, anxious and jittery, just constantly thinking about fruit machines.

Question

Explain Mick's behaviour using the concept of withdrawal syndrome.

CHECK IT

1. In relation to addiction, what is meant by the terms *physical dependence* and *psychological dependence*?
   [2 marks + 2 marks]

2. What is meant by *tolerance* in relation to addiction?
   [2 marks]

3. Explain how withdrawal might occur in someone who is addicted to nicotine. In your answer, give **two** examples of the effects of withdrawal. [4 marks]

Practical activity on page 379

Risk factors in the development of addiction including genetic vulnerability, stress, personality, family influences and peers.

A risk factor is anything that increases the chances that someone will use a drug of addiction (or engage in an addictive behaviour) or increase their current level of use. Research has focused on five particularly important risk factors. We start, on this page, with genetic vulnerability.

KEY TERMS

Genetic vulnerability – Any inherited predisposition that increases the risk of a disorder or condition.

Risk factors – Any internal or external influence that increases the likelihood someone will start using drugs or engage in addictive behaviours.

Apply it — Concepts: Richie and drinking

Richie likes a drink every now and again but he is very careful to monitor his intake. Both his father and his grandmother were addicted to alcohol. He is concerned that addiction runs in his family and that he is bound to become dependent on alcohol as well. Every time he has a drink he is worried that he is turning into his father.

Question

What is Richie's risk of becoming addicted to alcohol? Is it inevitable? Referring to some research, use your understanding of genetic vulnerability to explain your answer.

If an addiction runs in families, is this evidence of a genetic vulnerability, a family influence, or both?

Risk factors in the development of addiction

Genetic vulnerability

What is inherited is not an addiction itself, but a predisposition or vulnerability to drug dependence. **Genes** are not inevitable causes of addiction on their own. After all, an individual will never become addicted to a drug if they never take it, and whether or not they take it depends mostly on psychosocial factors (see next spread). But once someone is exposed to a drug, **genetic vulnerability** can help explain why some become dependent and others do not. Or it may help to explain the progression from occasional use of a drug to outright dependence on it.

Genetic mechanisms

There are two plausible direct genetic mechanisms involved in addiction:

- The way that the **neurotransmitter dopamine** communicates in the brain depends on the presence of receptors for dopamine molecules on the surfaces of **neurons**. There are different types of dopamine receptor. One of these is the D2 receptor, abnormally low numbers of which are thought to be involved in addiction. The proportion of all receptors in the brains of individuals is determined genetically.

- Some individuals are more able to metabolise (i.e. break down) certain substances and this is linked to addiction. For example, Michael Pianezza et al. (1998) found that some people lack a fully functioning enzyme (CYP2A6) which is mainly responsible for metabolising nicotine. They also smoke significantly less than those smokers with the fully functioning version. Because expression of the CYP2A6 enzyme is genetically determined, individuals with the fully functioning enzyme are at greater genetic risk of nicotine addiction.

Evaluation

Research support

Kenneth Kendler et al. (2012) used data from the *National Swedish Adoption Study*. They looked especially at adults who had been adopted away, as children, from biological families in which at least one parent had an addiction. These people had a **significantly** greater risk of developing an addiction themselves (8.6%), compared with adopted away individuals with no addicted parent in their biological families (4.2%). This is strong evidence for the role of genetic vulnerability as an important **risk factor**, and it is supported by other research.

Indirect effects

Genetic factors may play an indirect role in increasing risk by determining certain addiction-related behavioural characteristics. For example, self-control and the ability to regulate emotions may well be at least partly genetically determined. A young person who is less able to control their behaviour might have difficulty in concentrating on the kinds of tasks that are typical of schoolwork. If an individual does not function well in school, they could become caught up in a self-fulfilling downward spiral of negative attitudes, disruptive behaviour, poor reputation and low achievement. They may gravitate towards friends who share such characteristics, leading ultimately to involvement with drugs. Genetic vulnerability is therefore a significant risk factor, as it might influence addiction risk more than it appears because some of its effects are indirect.

CHECK IT

1. In relation to risk factors for addiction, explain what is meant by *genetic vulnerability*. [2 marks]
2. Discuss genetic vulnerability as a risk factor in the development of addiction. [6 marks]

Risk factors in the development of addiction including genetic vulnerability, stress, personality, family influences and peers.

We look on this spread at the remaining four major risk factors for addiction (genetic vulnerability was covered on the previous spread). One of them – personality – is an internal factor that may increase the likelihood of some people developing an addiction. The others – stress, family influences and peers – are external environmental or context factors.

KEY TERMS

Stress – A physiological and psychological state of arousal that arises when we believe we do not have the ability to cope with a perceived threat (stressor).

Personality – Patterns of thinking, feeling and behaving that differ between individuals. These are relatively consistent from one situation to another, and over time.

Family influences – The effects that other members of our families have on our thoughts, feelings and behaviours over the course of our development.

Peers – People who share our interests and are of similar age, social status and background to ourselves. Peers become more influential in adolescence, when we spend more time with them and less with family.

Addiction – everyone's got an opinion about it haven't they? Parents, politicians, celebrities, us, probably you as well. But when you're writing about risk factors for addiction, opinion doesn't get you very far. We all have stories about why some people take drugs or gamble. But this sort of anecdotal evidence is no substitute for scientific research. Anything you say must be backed up by psychological research.

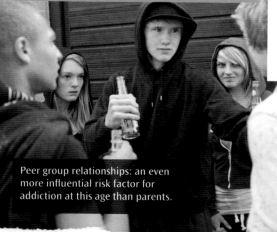

Peer group relationships: an even more influential risk factor for addiction at this age than parents.

Risk factors in the development of addiction

Stress

Increased risk is linked with periods of chronic, long-lasting **stress** and traumatic life events in childhood. Jeffrey Epstein *et al.* (1998) looked at data from the *National Women's Study*. They found a strong **correlation** between incidence of childhood rape and adult alcohol addiction, but only for those women who were diagnosed with **post-traumatic stress disorder** (PTSD). So it appears that there is not an inevitable relationship between a traumatic childhood event and later **addiction**. In other words a child will only have an addiction problem if they have a vulnerability (e.g. early abuse) and a later stressful situation (e.g. PTSD).

Susan Andersen and Martin Teicher (2008) suggest that early experiences of severe stress have damaging effects on the brain in a sensitive period of development. This creates a vulnerability to addiction by adolescence or young adulthood.

Personality

Psychologists generally agree that there is no such thing as an overarching 'addictive **personality**'. However, that does not mean that individual personality traits such as hostility and neuroticism are not linked with addiction (Butler and Montgomery 2004). The strongest correlation has been found between addiction-related behaviour and **antisocial personality disorder** (APD). APD begins in early adolescence and incorporates many personality-related risk factors, but the key one is *impulsivity*. This is marked by a lack of planning, a high degree of risk-taking, a preference for immediate gratification of desires, and a chaotic lifestyle. In a review of relevant research, Ivanov *et al.* (2008) concluded that many studies strongly support the link between impulsivity and addiction. The researchers speculated that this could be because they share a neurological basis, or even a common genetic component.

Family influences

Of all the ways in which **family influences** can create vulnerability to addiction, perceived parental approval is perhaps the most consistently reliable risk factor. This is the extent to which an adolescent believes that his or her parents have positive attitudes towards a particular drug, or drugs in general, or potentially addictive behaviours such as gambling. For example, Livingston *et al.* (2010) found that final-year high-school students who were allowed by their parents to drink alcohol at home were **significantly** more likely to drink excessively the following year at college.

The key determinant here is the at-risk individual's *perception* of approval. On what basis is this formed? Adolescents who believe that their parents have little or no interest in monitoring their behaviour (e.g. Internet use, peer relationships) are **significantly** more likely to develop an addiction.

Another factor is exposure; for example adolescents are more likely to start using alcohol in families where it is an everyday feature of family life or where there is a history of alcohol addiction.

Peers

Amongst older children, **peer** relationships become the most important psychosocial risk factor, outstripping even family influences. This is true even in cases where peers have not used drugs themselves. Mary O'Connell *et al.* (2009) suggest that there are three major elements to peer influence as a risk factor for alcohol addiction:

- An at-risk adolescent's attitudes and norms about drinking are influenced by associating with peers who use alcohol.
- These experienced peers provide more opportunities for the at-risk individual to use alcohol.
- The individual over-estimates how much their peers are drinking, which means they drink more to keep up with the perceived norm.

Peer attitudes that ultimately influence drug use do not have to specifically concern drugs. What is influential is the creation of a group norm that favours rule-breaking generally, and drug use is just one instance of this.

Apply it

Concepts: Gabrielle at risk

Gabrielle is 15 years old and has just started hanging around with a group of girls at school. They spend time drinking vodka around the local shopping centre. Gabrielle has joined in a couple of times. Everyone else in her family drinks so she reckons they obviously don't have a problem with it.

Question

Using your knowledge of addiction, explain *two* risk factors that could contribute to Gabrielle's drinking. Refer to some relevant research in your explanation.

Evaluation

Interactions between all risk factors

No one risk factor is causal in addiction; combinations of risk matter more than single factors. Linda Mayes and Nancy Suchman (2006) point out that different combinations of risk factors partly determine the nature and severity of an addiction. Furthermore, the factors that we have described so far as 'risky' can also be *protective* – some personality traits, **genetic** characteristics, family and peer influences make addiction less likely (for example greater parental monitoring, lower levels of impulsivity).

Therefore, there are many 'pathways' to addiction. This is a much more complex, interesting and realistic picture of addiction vulnerability than the simplistic suggestion that one risk factor is hugely more important than any other.

Cause and effect

Research into risk factors is often correlational, which raises serious issues of cause and effect. For example, many studies have shown there is a strong correlation between stressful experiences and addiction-related behaviours. However, many addictions can create greater levels of stress because of their generally negative effects on lifestyle, relationships, financial affairs, and so on.

Because risk factors and addiction co-relate in these ways, it is difficult to separate out the effects of one upon the other. In the case of peer influences, adolescents who are already vulnerable to drug use (because of other risk factors such as family influences), are attracted to a peer group which enjoys rule-breaking. As Michael Vaughn (2013) points out, 'Risk factors are not in and of themselves causes but are instead correlates unless tested...as such' (for example in longitudinal studies).

Proximate and ultimate risk factors

Some risk factors may be partly genetically determined. For instance, Lara Ray and her colleagues (2009) have shown that novelty-seeking (in which the individual continually craves new experiences) may be associated with genetic markers for the D4 **dopamine** receptor. This research also shows that novelty-seekers are more likely to become problematic alcohol users. Perhaps this is because they are more sensitive to the rewarding effects of dopamine activation brought about by drug use.

This suggests that some risk factors for addiction may not be all they seem. The personality trait of novelty-seeking is a *proximate* risk factor, because it is the immediate influence on addiction. But, to fully understand the role of risk factors, and to use this understanding to help people who are addicted, we have to look further back in the chain of influences to the *ultimate* risk factor – in many cases it is genetic. This is another reason why genetic vulnerability may well be the most significant risk factor in addiction, because it has the ultimate influence on all the others.

Evaluation eXtra

Real-life applications

Researchers such as David Hawkins *et al.* (1992) believe that a focus on risk factors is a highly promising strategy for preventing and treating addictions. If we can understand what the risk factors are, and more importantly how they interact, then we have an opportunity to identify those in the population who are most at risk. For example, Nancy Tobler *et al.* (2000) created a peer-pressure resistance training programme to help prevent young people taking up smoking.

Consider: *What do you think are the benefits of identifying risk factors for addiction? In what way is this a strength of the approach?*

Methodological issues

Research into the risk factors associated with addictions has been very productive. But a significant methodological problem is the retrospective nature of many studies. Assessing some of the major risk factors requires participants to recall incidents of stress, trauma, and family behaviours from the past, sometimes from years previously. Some such incidents may be especially difficult to recall accurately because of the related stress or trauma.

Consider: *How serious a limitation do you think this is? How does it affect the **validity** of research into risk factors?*

Apply it Concepts: Will Gavin smoke?

Gavin is 14 years old and has always done things on the spur of the moment. He often doesn't think things through and this usually gets him into a lot of trouble. He's behind at school, finds it difficult to concentrate and everyone sees him as a bit of a troublemaker. What most people don't realise is that this situation is quite stressful for him, especially with mock exams coming up. A couple of days ago, he took a couple of his dad's cigarettes and is seriously considering smoking them.

Question

Referring to relevant research, explain *two* risk factors that could lead to Gavin becoming addicted to nicotine.

Impulsive and risk-taking personality traits developing in childhood could lead to addiction in adolescence.

Apply it Methods: A case of addiction?

A psychologist decided to carry out a **case study** of a young man experiencing several risk factors for addiction. She asked the participant to keep a daily diary of incidents involving four major risk factors, and any experiences involving alcohol. She used **content analysis** to analyse the data from the diaries. She found that 20% of the diary entries related to stressful events, 25% to family influences, 10% to the participant's personality, and 35% to the participant's peer group; 10% of the entries could not be classified.

Questions

1. Explain how the psychologist could have carried out her content analysis. (*4 marks*) (See page 64)
2. The study gathered a lot of **qualitative data**. Explain what is meant by qualitative data. (*2 marks*)
3. Outline *one* weakness of gathering qualitative data in this study. (*2 marks*)
4. Explain *one* strength of conducting a case study. (*2 marks*) (See page 64)
5. Explain *one* **ethical issue** that could arise in this case study and how the psychologist could have dealt with it. (*2 marks + 2 marks*)

CHECK IT

1. Explain the roles of any **two** risk factors in the development of addiction. [6 marks]
2. Discuss how family influences may be a risk factor in addiction. [4 marks]
3. Describe and evaluate risk factors in the development of addiction. [16 marks]

Explanations for nicotine addiction: brain neurochemistry including the role of dopamine.

Addictions to drugs such as heroin, cocaine and LSD attract a great deal of media attention. But they are nowhere near as prevalent and dangerous as addiction to a drug used every day by millions of people, perhaps up to one-third of the global adult population – nicotine, the psychoactive component of tobacco.

We look in this spread at the neurochemistry of nicotine addiction, in which the neurotransmitter dopamine is thought to have a central role.

KEY TERMS

Neurochemistry – Relating to chemicals in the brain that regulate psychological functioning.

Dopamine – A neurotransmitter that generally has an excitatory effect and is associated with the sensation of pleasure. Unusually high levels are associated with schizophrenia and unusually low levels are associated with Parkinson's disease.

The desensitisation hypothesis: Nicotine stimulates nicotinic receptors primarily located in the ventral tegmental area (VTA) of the brain. This causes dopamine to be transmitted along the mesolimbic and mesocortical pathways to the nucleus accumbens and the frontal cortex (yellow lines). Dopamine is then released into the frontal cortex (blue arrows) creating rewarding effects.

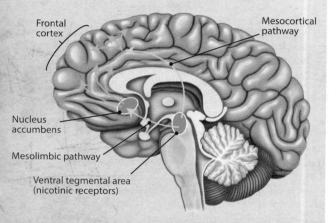

Frontal cortex
Mesocortical pathway
Nucleus accumbens
Mesolimbic pathway
Ventral tegmental area (nicotinic receptors)

What's the Number One route to evaluating a theory or explanation? The answer is – THINK LINK. You'll notice that the evaluation pages of each spread in this book are chock full of research studies. They are usually there to support or contradict an explanation. But you need to make sure you use them effectively. THINK LINK – how does the evidence relate to the explanation? What does McEvoy et al.'s study tell us about the neurochemistry of nicotine addiction? Don't get sidetracked into describing the evidence at length. Instead, THINK LINK – explain how it supports the explanation. That's effective evaluation.

Nicotine addiction and brain neurochemistry

The desensitisation hypothesis

John Dani and Steve Heinemann's (1996) desensitisation hypothesis focuses on brain **neurochemistry** – specifically on the **neurons** in the brain that produce the **neurotransmitter** dopamine.

Acetylcholine receptors Like many neurons in the central nervous system, dopamine-producing neurons have on their surfaces receptors that bind with another neurotransmitter – **acetylcholine** (ACh). Binding allows communication across **synapses** to take place. In neurotransmission, when enough ACh molecules bind with receptors, an electrical impulse (action potential) is able to continue from one neuron (the **presynaptic** neuron) to another (the **postsynaptic** neuron).

One subtype of ACh receptor is called the *nicotinic acetylcholine receptor* (nAChR). This can bind with both ACh and nicotine. When nicotine molecules bind with nAChRs the neuron becomes stimulated and transmits dopamine (see 'dopamine transmission' below). But immediately after this (a matter of just milliseconds), the nicotinic receptor shuts down and temporarily cannot respond to neurotransmitters. The neuron is said to be *desensitised* and this leads to *downregulation*, a reduction in the number of active neurons because fewer of them are available.

Dopamine transmission nAChRs are concentrated in the *ventral tegmental area* (VTA) of the brain. When nAChRs in the VTA are stimulated by nicotine, the neurotransmitter dopamine is transmitted along the **mesolimbic pathway** to the **nucleus accumbens** (NA). This triggers the release of dopamine from the NA in to the *frontal cortex*. Dopamine is also transmitted along the *mesocortical pathway* to be released in the frontal cortex.

The mesolimbic and mesocortical pathways are part of the brain's reward and pleasure centre, so nicotine powerfully activates this system and results in pleasurable effects, such as mild euphoria, increased alertness and reduction of anxiety. This mechanism is thought to be very similar to that involved in addictions to classic drugs of abuse such as cocaine, heroin and amphetamines.

The nicotine regulation model

As long as the individual is smoking, nicotinic receptors are desensitised and cravings and withdrawal symptoms held off. But when smokers go without nicotine for a prolonged period (e.g. when they are asleep at night) nicotine disappears from the body. This allows more nicotinic receptors to become functional, so dopamine neurons resensitise and more become available (upregulation).

Withdrawal More nAChRs are available but are not stimulated, so the smoker experiences an acute **withdrawal syndrome** with symptoms including anxiety and agitation. At this point, after a period of abstinence, nAChRs are at their most sensitive. This is why smokers often describe the first cigarette of the day as the most enjoyable – it re-activates the dopamine reward system (as outlined above).

Dependence and tolerance According to the model, this explains how nicotine *dependence* is maintained. The smoker is motivated to avoid unpleasureable physiological and psychological withdrawal states by having another cigarette. But repetition of the cycle of daytime downregulation and night-time upregulation creates chronic desensitisation of nAChRs. So continuous exposure of nAChRs to nicotine causes permanent changes to brain neurochemistry – a *decrease* in the number of active receptors. *Tolerance* develops as the smoker has to smoke more to get the same effects.

Concepts: Kiki's craving

Kiki is a heavy smoker. Although she wouldn't describe herself as an addict, she knows she would find it almost impossible to give up smoking. She currently smokes about 40 cigarettes a day, including late at night. She often wakes up in the morning with a massive craving to smoke a cigarette, and has noticed how the first one of the day is usually the best.

Question

How would you explain Kiki's behaviour in terms of what is going on with her brain neurochemistry?

Evaluation

Supporting research evidence

There is indirect support for the role of neurochemistry in nicotine addiction from research with humans. For example, Joseph McEvoy *et al.* (1995) studied smoking behaviour in patients with **schizophrenia**. *Haloperidol* is a dopamine **antagonist** which blocks dopamine receptors in the brain (and is used as drug treatment for **schizophrenia** for this reason). *Haloperidol* treatment increased smoking in this sample of participants. It appears that this was a form of self-medication, an attempt to achieve the nicotine 'hit' by increasing dopamine release.

There is also more direct evidence for the importance of the dopamine reward system in the mesolimbic pathway from brain imaging studies (Ray *et al.* 2008).

Real-life applications

A greater understanding of neurochemistry can lead to development of new treatments for nicotine addiction, such as nicotine replacement therapy (NRT) in the form of patches and inhalers (see page 368). Research is even raising the possibility of nicotine immunisation.

But the potential practical benefits of greater understanding go beyond nicotine addiction. This is because some diseases have high **co-morbidity** with nicotine use; that is they occur together frequently. Examples include schizophrenia, **depression** and alcoholism, all of which are strongly associated with continued smoking.

So further research which offers more effective treatments for nicotine addiction also holds out the prospect of greater advances in treatments for these co-morbid disorders.

Limited explanation

Any explanation of nicotine addiction which considers only the role of dopamine is limited because research increasingly shows that there are many other neurochemical mechanisms involved. The current research picture is one of a vastly complex interaction of several neurochemical systems, including neurotransmitter pathways such as **GABA** and **serotonin** (5-HT), plus other systems such as endogenous opioids (endorphins, the brain's natural painkillers).

However, as Fernando Berrendero *et al.* (2010) point out, the dopamine system is nevertheless central to the neurochemistry of nicotine addiction and these other systems all interact with it to have their effects.

The first cigarette of the day – almost invariably the nicest, especially with a cup of coffee.

Evaluation eXtra

A reductionist explanation

Neurochemical explanations are **reductionist** accounts of why people become addicted to nicotine. They explain addiction at the most fundamental level of the activity of neurotransmitter molecules, rather than at 'higher' levels (e.g. social and psychological influences). At most, only 50% of people who experiment with cigarette smoking become dependent on nicotine. Won Choi *et al.* (2003) found that adolescents who were most likely to become dependent were not committed to abstaining, had friends who smoked, and perceived themselves to be underachieving at school – all of these are psychological factors.

Consider: *Why is reductionism a problem for neurochemical theories? Can you think of any ways in which it could be a strength?*

Individual differences

Saul Shiffman *et al.* (1995) studied 'chippers', people who regularly smoke even for decades, but do not become dependent on nicotine. Those who smoked an average of five cigarettes a day showed no signs of a withdrawal syndrome when they abstained. They also performed better on **cognitive** tasks (such as mental arithmetic) than dependent smokers. It appears that there must be non-chemical factors that protect some smokers from addiction, although it is currently unclear what these factors are. One possibility the researchers suggest is that some people smoke because they have learned to do so through **modelling**. So their motivation has nothing to do with nicotine at all.

Consider: *Can this be explained by neurochemical theories? Is this a limitation of such theories? Explain your answer.*

Concepts: The never-ending habit

Nick has smoked cigarettes for nearly two decades and has noticed that he is smoking more and more per day as the years have gone by. Despite this, he feels he doesn't get the same feeling from smoking that he used to and is worried that this means he'll just keep on increasing his intake more and more.

Question

Using your knowledge of the neurochemistry of addiction, explain why this is happening to Nick.

Methods: A smoking correlation

As we saw in Evaluation extra, Shiffman *et al.* (1995) investigated several differences between 26 'chippers' and a **matched** group of 25 regular smokers. All participants smoked normally for two days and were deprived of nicotine for two days. These two-day periods were separated by a week. The order in which participants completed these periods was **counterbalanced**. Chippers suffered no apparent withdrawal effects. But regular smokers experienced more cravings, poorer mood, and sleep disturbances. They also performed more slowly on cognitive tasks.

Questions

1. Write an appropriate **aim** for this study. (*2 marks*)
2. What does it mean to say that the two groups were 'matched'? (*2 marks*)
3. What does it mean to say that the 'order in which participants completed these periods was counterbalanced'? (*2 marks*)
4. Identify *one* **dependent variable** in this study and explain how you would **operationalise** it. (*1 mark + 2 marks*)
5. Explain how the researchers could have obtained their samples of chippers and regular smokers. Identify the **sampling method** you have chosen. (*2 marks + 1 mark*)

CHECK IT

1. Outline the role of dopamine in nicotine addiction. *[4 marks]*
2. Outline the brain neurochemistry explanation of nicotine addiction. *[6 marks]*
3. Describe and evaluate **one or more** neurochemical explanations of nicotine addiction. *[16 marks]*

When habitual smokers smoke cigarettes that contain no nicotine, they report almost identical levels of enjoyment to when they smoke the real thing. Non-nicotine cigarettes can even reduce the withdrawal symptoms that occur when a smoker kicks their habit (Rose and Corrigall 1997). This strongly implies that there is more to nicotine addiction than brain neurochemistry.

KEY TERMS

Learning theory – A behaviourist explanation based on the mechanisms of classical and operant conditioning, such as positive and negative reinforcement.

Cue reactivity – Cravings and arousal can be triggered in, for example, nicotine addicts when they encounter cues related to the pleasurable effects of smoking, such as the social situations in which they have smoked previously.

Apply it

Concepts: No going back?

Simon is a 40-year-old man who recently gave up smoking after several years, mainly because he was concerned about his health and how he couldn't play squash as well as he used to.

But he is finding it very hard to stay away from cigarettes for several reasons. He is friends with the same group of people who carry on smoking, he still likes to go out with them to pubs and clubs, and he carries his favourite lighter round with him as a kind of souvenir.

Question

Do you think Simon is at risk of relapsing back into smoking? Use your knowledge of learning theory to explain why.

Learning theory of smoking behaviour

Psychologists, naturally, have explored possible psychological causes of **addiction** – one plausible explanation is that it is a learned behaviour which can be explained in terms of **learning theory** – either operant or classical conditioning.

Operant conditioning

Positive reinforcement

Nicotine addiction can be partly explained by the concept of **positive reinforcement**. If the consequence of a behaviour is rewarding to the individual (for example, a feeling of pleasure), then that behaviour is more likely to occur again. Nicotine is a powerful reinforcer because of its physiological effects on the **dopamine** reward system of the **mesolimbic pathway**, as we saw on the previous spread. The drug stimulates release of dopamine in the **nucleus accumbens**, producing a feeling of mild euphoria, which the smoker finds rewarding and so this positively reinforces their smoking behaviour.

According to Koob and Le Moal (2008), positive reinforcement can therefore explain both the early stages of smoking addiction, or how people take up smoking in the first place.

Negative reinforcement

However, a smoker's continuing dependence on nicotine is better explained by **negative reinforcement**. Cessation of nicotine use leads to the appearance of an acute withdrawal syndrome, with all its accompanying unpleasant symptoms. These include: behavioural effects such as disturbed sleep patterns and agitation; **cognitive** effects such as poor concentration; and mood disturbances such as anxiety and depression. Such wide-ranging withdrawal symptoms make it very difficult for the smoker to abstain for very long, so the smoker seeks to reduce and eliminate these effects by smoking again.

Therefore, smoking another cigarette is negatively reinforcing because it stops an unpleasant stimulus. In fact, smokers become quite skilled at anticipating the symptoms of withdrawal and avoiding them altogether by regulating their nicotine intake (see *nicotine regulation model* on the previous spread).

Classical conditioning – the role of cue reactivity

The pleasurable effect of smoking is known as a **primary reinforcer**. This is because it is intrinsically rewarding (i.e. not learned) because of its effects on the brain's dopamine reward system. So the individual is more likely to smoke again. Any other stimuli that are present at the same time (or just before) become associated with this pleasurable effect. These other stimuli are called **secondary reinforcers** because they take on the properties of the primary reinforcer and therefore become rewarding in their own right.

Cigarette smoking often occurs in certain environments (pubs, smoking areas in colleges) and with certain people (friends). Over time and with repeated associations these become secondary reinforcers, and there are plenty of others too: a favourite lighter, the ritual elements of lighting up, the boxy feel of a cigarette packet, the tobacco smell, and so on. Smokers even come to enjoy the harsh feeling of the smoke hitting the back of the throat, because they associate it with the pleasurable effects of nicotine.

These stimuli also act as cues, because their presence produces a similar physiological and psychological response to nicotine itself. The term **cue reactivity** refers to this response, which has three main elements. There is the self-reported subjective desire or craving for a cigarette. There are also physiological signs of reactivity, including autonomic responses such as heart rate and skin temperature. Finally, there are objective behavioural indicators such as how many 'draws' are taken on a cigarette and how strongly.

Friends, food, drink, happy times. Exactly the sort of enjoyable situation that provides countless cues to entice people back into smoking.

Evaluation

Support from non-human animal studies

A substantial body of research with non-human animals confirms the role of conditioning in nicotine addiction. For example, Edward Levin *et al.* (2010) gave rats the choice of self-administering doses of a nicotine or water by licking one of two water spots (one with nicotine). The rats licked the nicotine waterspout significantly more often.

This suggests that the effects of nicotine positively reinforce nicotine self-administration in rats, pointing towards the operation of a similar mechanism in humans.

Research support for cue reactivity

Brian Carter and Stephen Tiffany (1999) conducted a **meta-analysis** of studies into the effects of cue reactivity. They included 41 studies that investigated a range of substance addictions. Typically, such studies present dependent and non-dependent smokers (and non-smokers) with images of smoking-related cues, such as lighters, ashtrays and cigarette packets. Self-reported desire or craving is measured, along with several physiological indicators of arousal (heart rate, etc.). Carter and Tiffany found that dependent smokers reacted strongly to cues presented to them, reporting high levels of craving and increased physiological arousal. The findings were consistent with predictions derived from cue reactivity theory.

Secondary conditioning operates so that addicts have a powerful tendency to experience the arousing effects of nicotine in response to cues associated with smoking, even when no nicotine is present.

Real-life applications

There exist several treatment programmes based on conditioning principles, which we explore in more detail on page 370. One such is **aversion therapy** which **counterconditions** nicotine addiction by associating the pleasurable effects of smoking with an aversive stimulus such as a painful electric shock. Some research studies have found this to be an effective treatment. For instance, James Smith's (1988) participants gave themselves aversive electric shocks whenever they engaged in any smoking-related behaviours. After one year, 52% of the participants were still abstaining, a much higher proportion than the 20–25% of people who continue not to smoke after deciding to give up.

Such effective applications of learning theory have measurable and significant practical benefits in terms of reducing NHS spending, improving health and ultimately saving lives.

Why do addicted smokers persist in their behaviour? Operant and classical conditioning together may offer an explanation.

Evaluation eXtra

Gender differences

It has often been observed that women are generally less successful at giving up smoking than men. Even cessation programmes based on conditioning principles are less effective for women. Matthew Carpenter *et al.* (2014) suggest that young women are more sensitive to smoking-related cues, which makes it more difficult for them to stop smoking and to prevent relapse after a period of abstention. This could be explained by the concept of **self-efficacy**. It may be that female smokers have less confidence in their ability to give up smoking, which undermines their attempts to do so.

Consider: *Does this mean that learning theory can explain gender differences. Is this a strength of the theory? Explain your answer.*

Limited explanation

Despite the apparently overwhelming power of positive reinforcers to initiate nicotine addiction, the fact remains that no more than half of people who experiment with smoking in adolescence go on to become dependent. Many adolescents smoke cigarettes occasionally, even daily, but few are dependent to the extent that they experience withdrawal symptoms when they don't smoke. This is a difficulty for any theory that seeks to explain addiction in terms of a limited number of factors or processes. There are likely to be several other causes of smoking behaviour.

Consider: *What do you think these other factors might be? Does their existence weaken the learning theory of nicotine addiction?*

Apply it — **Concepts: Can't stop, won't stop**

Roxanne is a 15-year-old who started smoking against her better judgement just over a year ago, mainly because her friends were all into it. She is now desperate to give up but finds it really hard. Although she knows smoking is damaging her health, there is a lot about it that she enjoys.

Question

Outline some of the pleasurable effects that Roxanne gets from smoking, and explain in terms of learning theory why she finds it so hard to stop.

Apply it — **Methods: Cues to addiction**

A psychologist investigated the effects of cues on smoking behaviour. She selected a **volunteer sample** of smokers and non-smokers. The participants were asked to imagine in their own minds how they would go about smoking a cigarette, from unwrapping the packet to lighting up. They then had to rate how much they would like to smoke a cigarette at that moment, on a scale of 0 (not at all) to 10 (desperately).

Questions

1. Explain why the research method used in this study is a **quasi-experiment**. (*2 marks*)
2. Explain *one* strength and *one* limitation of this research method. (*2 marks + 2 marks*)
3. What is the **independent variable** in this study and how could you **operationally** define it? (*1 mark + 1 mark*)
4. The researchers conducted a **pilot study**. What is a pilot study and why might the researchers have thought one would be useful? (*2 marks*)
5. Explain how **demand characteristics** might have affected the study. (*2 marks*)

CHECK IT

1. In relation to nicotine addiction, explain what is meant by the term *cue reactivity*. [2 marks]
2. Outline the learning theory explanation of nicotine addiction. [6 marks]
3. Describe and evaluate the learning theory explanation of nicotine addiction. [16 marks]

THE SPECIFICATION SAYS

Explanations for gambling addiction: learning theory as applied to gambling including reference to partial and variable reinforcement.

The DSM-5 (2013) reclassified problem gambling as an addictive disorder because it shares many of the characteristics of substance addictions. It is currently the only addiction in the special category of behavioural addictions in DSM-5.

KEY TERMS

Reinforcement – A consequence of behaviour that increases the likelihood of that behaviour being repeated. Can be positive or negative.

Partial reinforcement – When a behaviour is reinforced only some of the time it occurs (e.g. every tenth time or at variable intervals).

Variable reinforcement – A type of partial reinforcement in which a behaviour is reinforced after an unpredictable period of time or number of responses.

The glamour surrounding some forms of gambling can act as a cue, triggering feelings of arousal and making relapse more likely.

STUDY TIP

Students sometimes find that similar concepts can be confusing. For example, on this spread there are several concepts related to learning theory and they have quite a bit in common, including the same terminology – at least five different types of reinforcement! It's really important you're sure in your own mind about the differences between them – your answers will be a lot clearer. It's worth finding a way of distinguishing between concepts that works for you, even if that means using bizarre mental images of each one (how would you picture vicarious reinforcement?).

Learning theory of gambling addiction

Vicarious reinforcement

One way in which many people begin gambling is through **vicarious reinforcement**. That is, the experience of seeing others being rewarded for their gambling, their pleasure and enjoyment as well as the occasional financial returns. This doesn't have to be direct observation of other people's behaviour – newspapers, magazines and other media report positively on big lottery winners, or broadcast the glamour and excitement of horse-racing, for example. This may be enough to trigger a desire for the same reinforcement in someone who hasn't gambled before.

Direct positive and negative reinforcement

Gambling can provide two sources of direct **positive reinforcement**. Winning money is an obvious reinforcer of continued betting or wagering, and the 'buzz' that accompanies a gamble is also reinforcing because it is exciting.

Gambling can also be an escape for many, albeit a temporary one. This is **negative reinforcement** to the extent that it offers a distraction from aversive stimuli such as the anxieties of everyday life.

Partial reinforcement

B F Skinner's research with rats (see page 10) and pigeons demonstrated that a continuous reinforcement schedule, which rewards every desired response from the animal, does not lead to the most persistent behaviour. Under this schedule, once the rewards stop, the desired behaviour quickly disappears (a process known as **extinction**). A **partial reinforcement** schedule, on the other hand, does create the kind of persistent behaviour that is seen in gambling. In some types of partial reinforcement (such as **variable reinforcement** below) only some bets are rewarded, so there is an unpredictability about which gambles will pay off, which is enough to keep the gambling going even when rewards are hard to come by.

Variable reinforcement

Of all the ways in which behaviour can be reinforced only intermittently, the variable schedule produces the most persistent learning. Variable reinforcement is provided after an always changing proportion of wagers are placed. For example, a slot machine might pay out after an average of 25 spins, but not on every 25th spin. So the first payout might come after the 11th spin, the second after the 21st, the third after the 38th, and so on.

This is a highly unpredictable pattern of reinforcement. It takes longer for learning to be established but once it is established, it is much more resistant to extinction. It is possible to go for many spins with no payout at all, but the gambler continues to place wagers for a long time even when their behaviour is no longer reinforced. This helps to explain why some people continue to gamble despite experiencing big losses. The gambler learns that they will not win with every gamble, but they will eventually win if they persist.

Cue reactivity

Just as in the case of nicotine **addiction** (see page 362), **cue reactivity** can explain how a behavioural addiction like gambling can be maintained and reinstated after relapse. In the course of their gambling experiences, the individual will encounter many **secondary reinforcers**, stimuli that become reinforcing because of their associations with the exciting arousal experienced by gamblers.

Such reinforcers include the atmosphere of a betting shop, the colourful look of lottery scratchcards, a TV horse-racing channel, or the razzamatazz of Internet betting sites. Their presence can cue the arousal that the gambler craves, even before they think about placing a bet, or playing a slot machine, or whatever it might be.

Given that these cues saturate the social and media environment, they are difficult for the abstaining gambler to avoid. They offer continuous low-level reminders of the pleasures of gambling, and make relapse a fairly predictable outcome for many.

Apply it   Concepts: Horace and the horses

Horace's gambling addiction almost ruined his life, until he joined Gambler's Anonymous. He used to spend most of his income betting on horses, but he hasn't placed a bet for more than six months now. Unfortunately, his walk to work every morning takes him past a betting shop. He hasn't been inside it, but he has noticed that every time he goes past, he feels a little bit of the 'buzz' he used to get when he gambled.

Question

Explain how learning theory would account for Horace's experience.

Evaluation

Support from research evidence

Mark Dickerson (1979) observed the behaviour of gamblers in real-life gambling environments, two betting offices in Birmingham. He found that the gamblers who placed the most bets on horse races (high-frequency gamblers) were consistently more likely than low-frequency gamblers to place their bets in the last two minutes before the start of the race (the 'off'). Low frequency gamblers who waited until this point tended to place their bets on the *next* race. The high-frequency gamblers may have delayed betting to prolong the rewarding excitement they felt, for example at the tension built by the radio commentary broadcast in the betting shop.

This is evidence for the role of positive reinforcement on gambling behaviour in those who gamble most often, in a more 'real-life' setting than a psychology lab.

Lack of explanatory power

Learning theories are better at explaining some types of gambling than others. Gambling games vary in the balance of skill and chance they involve. Success with fruit machines and lottery scratchcards is due entirely to chance, with no opportunity for the gambler to influence the outcome. But there are many other games, such as poker, in which the gambler's skill plays an important role. Also, some games (fruit machines again) are *temporally contiguous*. That is, there is almost no delay between placing the bet and knowing the outcome. The two events occur very close together, as required for conditioning to take place.

Addiction to games requiring skill, especially those in which there is a significant delay between bet and outcome, is more difficult to explain in terms of conditioning. Therefore, learning theories lack explanatory power because they do not provide a general explanation of all gambling addiction.

Individual differences

Mark Griffiths and Paul Delfabbro (2001) argue that conditioning processes do not occur in everyone in the same ways. Responses to identical stimuli can differ from one person to another. Motivations also differ – some people gamble to relax, some to be aroused. Some people stop gambling and never relapse, despite being subjected to the same cues as other lapsed abstainers. These well-established observations of gambling behaviour are difficult for learning theory to explain without invoking some cognitive features of addiction which are shared by some individuals but not others, such as distortions of thinking.

Evaluation eXtra

Limited explanation

Gambling addiction is not a single phenomenon but has many facets. Psychologists have tried to understand how the cycle of gambling addiction develops, from initiation, through maintenance to cessation and – in most cases – relapse. Conditioning processes such as reinforcement are less important at some points. For example, Brown (1987) suggests that reinforcement schedules can explain the remarkable persistence (and escalation) of gambling behaviour, but not how it begins.

Consider: *Do you think gambling addiction is a single phenomenon, or are there many aspects to it? If learning theory can't explain them all, in what way is this a weakness?*

Explains failure to stop gambling

Gambling addiction develops and is maintained through conditioning processes that do not require the individual to make any active decisions, or even to be aware that learning is taking place. Gambling addiction – like all addictions – is explained by the same process of reinforcement that allowed us to survive and reproduce in our evolutionary history. Thus learning theory is an effective explanation of a common phenomenon – how gamblers persistently fail to stop gambling whilst at the same time being absolutely determined to do so. Their conscious desire to give up conflicts with the motivational forces that drive them to continue gambling.

Consider: *Do you think this is a significant strength of learning theory?*

High speed, high stakes betting machines provide even more attractive rewards to reinforce gambling behaviour. Liverpool was the first city in the UK to ban them.

Apply it — **Concepts: Aisha's gamble**

Aisha is beginning to get worried. She spends large sums of money which she can't afford on online fruit machines. She thinks that if it wasn't for gambling her life would be dull, boring and depressing. She spends so much time online that she hasn't seen her friends for weeks. But it's like she can't help herself. Every time she says she's going to give up, she finds herself back online.

Question

Use your knowledge of learning theory to explain why Aisha continues to gamble.

Apply it — **Methods: Place your bets**

Two researchers carried out an **observational** study of gambling behaviour in a betting shop. They observed customers choosing runners and riders in horse races, placing bets, and following the progress of the race on TV. They were interested in whether there was any link between the number of bets placed by the customers and their level of excitement during races.

Questions

1. Suggest *three* **operationalised behavioural categories** the observers could use to measure level of excitement. (*3 marks*)
2. Explain what is meant by **time sampling** and **event sampling** in relation to this study. (*2 marks + 2 marks*)
3. The researchers had to choose one betting shop in which to conduct their study. Explain *one* factor that they should have taken into account in making their choice. (*2 marks*)
4. The researchers conducted a **pilot study**. What is a pilot study and why might the researchers have thought one would be useful? (*3 marks*)
5. The researchers found that **inter-observer reliability** was low in the pilot study. Explain what the researchers could have done to improve it before carrying out the main observational study. (*3 marks*)

CHECK IT

1. In relation to learning theory of gambling addiction explain what is meant by *partial reinforcement* and *variable reinforcement*. [2 marks + 2 marks]
2. Outline learning theory of gambling addiction. [6 marks]
3. Outline the roles of partial and variable reinforcement in gambling addiction. [6 marks]
4. Discuss the learning theory explanation of gambling addiction. [16 marks]

Explanations for gambling addiction: cognitive theory as applied to gambling including reference to cognitive bias.

Psychologists have often wondered why it is that people become addicted to some things rather than to others – nicotine rather than to cocaine, alcohol or heroin. Perhaps there are genetic factors at play, or maybe it all depends entirely on the individual's reinforcement history.

One possibility is that we all differ in how we perceive, interpret or think about various addictive substances. So if someone lacks confidence, they might believe that alcohol is more likely than heroin to make them interesting. There is evidence that cognitive factors play an important role in initiating and maintaining addiction, especially behavioural addictions such as gambling.

KEY TERM

Cognitive bias – A distortion of attention, memory and thinking. It arises because of how we process information about the world, especially when we do it quickly. For instance, we recall memories that confirm our existing views and ignore others. This can sometimes lead to irrational judgements and poor decision-making.

Frequent gamblers often think of slot machines as if they have personalities – is this irrational?

Cognitive theory of gambling addiction

Expectancy theory

Expectancies are at the heart of the **cognitive** explanation of gambling. Gamblers have expectations (as we all do, in fact) about the future benefits and costs of their behaviour. If they expect the benefits of gambling to outweigh the costs, then **addiction** becomes more likely. This sounds like a conscious process that the gambler goes through in order to come to a rational decision about whether or not to gamble, but it is not. This is because memory and attention processes do not operate in a rational and logical manner.

Cognitive biases

The cause of gambling addiction lies in the common beliefs that addicts have about gambling that are **cognitive biases**, and the thinking, attention and memory processes linked to those beliefs. Gambling addiction develops and is maintained because the addict pays more attention to gambling-related information and remembers it selectively. Debra Rickwood and her colleagues (2010) classify these cognitive biases and distortions into four categories:

- *Skill and judgement*: Gambling addicts have an illusion of control which means they overestimate their ability to influence a random event (e.g. being especially skilled at choosing lottery numbers).
- *Personal traits/ritual behaviours*: Gambling addicts believe that they have a greater **probability** of winning because they are especially lucky or they engaged in some superstitious behaviour (e.g. touching a certain item of clothing before placing a bet).
- *Selective recall*: Gamblers can remember the details of their wins but they forget, ignore or otherwise discount their losses, which are often interpreted as completely unexplainable mysteries.
- *Faulty perceptions*: Addicted gamblers have distorted views about the operation of chance, exemplified in the so-called **gambler's fallacy**, the belief that a losing streak cannot last and is always about to be ended by a win.

Research into cognitive biases

Mark Griffiths (1994) investigated cognitive biases in gamblers.

Procedure He used the 'thinking aloud' method (a form of **introspection**) to see if there were any differences in the cognitive processes of regular slot machine gamblers compared with people who used the machines only occasionally. The participants had to verbalise any thoughts that passed through their minds as they played the machine. A **content analysis** classified these utterances into rational ('Wow, I won ten pence') or irrational ('This machine likes me'). A **semi-structured interview** method was also used to seek the participants' opinions about the degree of skill required to win on slot machines. Various objective behavioural measures were also recorded using **observation** (for example, the number of plays in a session, the total winnings, and so on).

Findings Griffiths found that there were no differences between regular and occasional gamblers in objective behavioural measures. For instance, the regulars did not win more money. But regular gamblers did make almost six times as many irrational verbalisations than the occasionals (14% compared with 2.5%). They were particularly prone to an *illusion of control* ('I'm going to bluff this machine'). Finally, regular gamblers both overestimated the amount of skill required to win on slot machines, and considered themselves to be especially skillful at doing so, at least above average, compared with the occasional gamblers.

Self-efficacy

Self-efficacy refers to our expectations that we have the ability to behave in a way that achieves a desired outcome. It can explain why some people relapse into gambling after abstaining. An individual takes up gambling again because they simply do not believe they are capable of giving it up permanently. This sets up a *self-fulfilling prophecy*, in which the individual behaves in a way that confirms this expectation (i.e. they gamble: 'You see, I told you I couldn't do it'), which is in turn **reinforced**.

Apply it   Concepts: No chance of winning

Sukarita plays the national lottery every day. She never selects a lucky dip but very carefully chooses the numbers. She always gets a very strong feeling that this time she will win the jackpot, right up to the moment the lottery balls are drawn.

Sukarita also spends a lot of money on scratchcards. Every time she buys one she is convinced that by revealing the numbers in a certain order, she is bound to win.

Question

Explain Sukarita's gambling behaviour in terms of cognitive biases and distortions.

Evaluation

Practical activity on page 378

Research support

Rosanna Michalczuk *et al.* (2011) studied 30 addicted gamblers attending the National Problem Gambling Clinic in the UK, and compared them with 30 non-gambling control participants. The addicted gamblers showed significantly higher levels of gambling-related cognitive distortions of all types (e.g. illusions of control). They were also more impulsive ('Sometimes when I feel bad, I can't stop what I'm doing even though it is making me feel worse'), and were more likely to prefer immediate rewards even when they were smaller than rewards they could gain if they waited.

These findings support the view that there is a strong cognitive component to gambling addiction. Because addicted gamblers make gambling decisions impulsively, they have a powerful tendency towards distorted thinking during play.

Explains automatic behaviour

Research shows that frequent gamblers seem to be able to place their bets automatically, as predicted by cognitive theory. For example, George McCusker and Briege Gettings (1997) used a modified **Stroop** procedure. Participants had to identify as quickly as possible the ink colour in which words were printed. To do this, it is necessary to pay attention to one thing (ink colour) while ignoring another (word meanings). Gamblers took longer to perform this task than **controls** when the words related to gambling. They were unable to prevent the word meanings from automatically interfering with the intended task.

This is evidence that gamblers have an automatic cognitive bias to pay attention to gambling-related information, a bias that does not exist in non-gamblers. This supports the view of the cognitive explanation that many cognitive biases influence addiction and operate without us even being aware we have them.

Individual differences

Several individual differences may determine the manner in which gamblers perceive and interpret their gambles. For example, Jerry Burger and Norris Smith (1985) investigated one personality factor, degree of control motivation. People differ in their motivation to achieve control over their lives: those who have a high level of 'control motivation' are more likely to believe they can influence chance-determined situations. It may be that they are therefore attracted to certain types of gamble where they (wrongly) believe their 'skill' can make a difference to the outcome, such as choosing lottery numbers.

Such individual differences mean that cognitive biases alone cannot explain gambling.

Evaluation eXtra

Real-life applications

The suggestion that addicted gamblers may have systematically different ways of thinking from non-gamblers has valuable implications for effective treatment (and prevention). Cognitive treatments, such as **cognitive behaviour therapy** (CBT), directly address the distorted thinking of the gambler's fallacy, or the great significance gamblers attribute to the near miss. Luke Clark (2010) points out that cognitive distortions probably have an underlying cause in brain **neurochemistry**. So cognitive theories are stimulating research into biological treatments as well as psychological ones.

Consider: *Do you think that this kind of treatment is an effective way of treating gambling addiction? Why might this be a strength of the cognitive theory?*

Methodological issues

Many research studies into cognitive distortions in gambling access the thinking processes of gamblers using **self-report** methods such as the thinking aloud technique. According to Mark Dickerson and John O'Connor (2006), a problem with this method is that the things people say in gambling situations do not necessarily represent what they really think. Frivolous or off-the-cuff remarks during a slot machine session might not reflect the addict's deeply-held beliefs about the roles of chance and skill in their behaviour.

Consider: *Is this a serious problem of the research? Does it also pose a problem for the theory the research is based on?*

Apply it **Concepts: Lucky Lewis?**

Lewis spends a lot of time feeding coins into slot machines. He gets the occasional payout, but is spending a lot more money than he wins. He can go for dozens of 'spins' without any success at all, but he knows that lady luck has a way of balancing things out. One day, he will get a big win, he thinks.

Question

Use your knowledge of cognitive theory to explain Lewis's attitude to gambling.

Can you control the numbers? Some addicted gamblers demonstrate the kind of distorted thinking which suggests they can.

Apply it **Methods: Word play**

A psychologist carried out a **laboratory experiment** with frequent gamblers. She wanted to see if they were better at recalling words that were gambling-related or non-gambling-related. The participants learned two lists of words – one contained words such as 'bets', 'odds', and 'races'. The other contained more neutral words such as 'desk' and 'apple'. For each list, they had to recall as many words as they could remember.

Questions

1. Name the **experimental design** used in this study. (*1 mark*)
2. The psychologist realised that she would need to use **counterbalancing**. Explain how she could have done so, and why it was necessary. (*4 marks*)
3. Explain how *one* factor in this study might have affected its **external validity**. (*3 marks*)
4. Identify an appropriate **statistical test** the researcher could use to analyse the data. (*1 mark*) (See page 70)
5. Give *two* reasons why this would be an appropriate test to use. (*2 marks*)

CHECK IT

1. In relation to cognitive theory of gambling addiction, explain what is meant by the term *cognitive bias*. [2 marks]
2. Outline the cognitive theory of gambling addiction. [6 marks]
3. Describe and evaluate the cognitive theory of gambling addiction. Refer to evidence in your answer. [16 marks]

REDUCING ADDICTION: DRUG THERAPY

Reducing addiction: drug therapy.

Beginning with this spread, we now look at ways in which addictions to substances and behaviours can be treated. The view that addictions can best be explained in terms of neurochemical factors within the brain, or by genetic influences, has naturally led to the development of a biological treatment that tackles these physical causes. Drug therapy has been used for decades, with varying degrees of success.

KEY TERM

Drug therapy – Treatment involving drugs, i.e. chemicals that have a particular effect on the functioning of the brain or some other body system. In the case of psychological disorders such drugs usually affect neurotransmitter levels.

STUDY TIP

Here are two pieces of advice to consider when writing about drug therapy.

Firstly, it's very tempting to 'set the scene' by explaining the biology of addiction (e.g. the neurochemistry of nicotine addiction). But remember that your focus must be on <u>*treating*</u> *addiction, not on how it develops in the first place.*

Secondly, there has to be some biological content in your answer. The more you can explain the neurochemistry of drug therapy, the better your answer will be (and that ideally means using the right technical terms as well).

Transdermal nicotine patches are an increasingly popular method of giving up smoking, and evidence suggests they are effective.

Drug therapy for addiction

Three types of drug therapy

Aversives The main effect of aversives is to produce unpleasant consequences such as vomiting. For example, *disulfiram* is a **drug therapy** used to treat alcoholism by creating hypersensitivity to alcohol. The effects of a severe hangover (especially nausea) are felt just five or ten minutes after an alcoholic drink is taken.

Agonists are effectively drug substitutes. They bind to **neuron** receptors and activate them, providing a similar effect to the addictive drug. Agonists such as *methadone*, used to treat heroin **addiction**, satisfy the addict's craving for a state of euphoria. But they have fewer harmful side effects and are 'cleaner' because they are administered medically rather than dealt on the streets. Agonists stabilise the addict because they are used to control the **withdrawal syndrome**, allowing a gradual reduction in dose and symptoms.

Antagonists treat addiction by binding to receptor sites and blocking them so that the drug of **dependence** cannot have its usual effects, especially the feeling of euphoria that addicts crave. *Naltrexone* is an opiate antagonist used to treat the physiological dependence of heroin addiction. However, other interventions (such as **counselling**) should be used alongside the drug to tackle the psychosocial causes of the addiction.

Drug therapy for nicotine addiction

Nicotine replacement therapy (NRT) uses gum, inhalers or patches to deliver the psychoactive substance in tobacco smoke but in a less harmful fashion. Nicotine is the major addictive chemical in tobacco, but it is not the most harmful to health.

NRT provides the user with a clean, controlled dose of nicotine which operates neurochemically by binding to nicotinic **acetylcholine** receptors in the **mesolimbic pathway** of the brain stimulating release of **dopamine** in the **nucleus accumbens**, just as it does in cigarette smoking. Using NRT means that the amount of nicotine can be reduced over time by using smaller and smaller patches, for example. So the withdrawal syndrome can be managed over a period of two or three months, reducing the aversiveness of withdrawal symptoms.

Drug therapy for gambling addiction

There are no drugs currently officially approved for use in treating gambling addiction. However, there is ongoing research into several candidates, the most promising being opioid antagonists such as *naltrexone* which is conventionally used to treat heroin addiction. This has come about because of the similarities between gambling and substance addiction that are now recognised in DSM-5.

The neurochemical explanation of gambling addiction is that it taps into the same dopamine reward system as heroin, nicotine and other drugs. Opioid antagonists have a round-about effect on gambling behaviour. They reduce the release of dopamine in the nucleus accumbens by enhancing the release of another **neurotransmitter**, **GABA**, in other parts of the mesolimbic pathway. The outcome of all this neurochemical activity is a dampening down of the cravings associated with gambling addiction. This has been linked in some research (e.g. Kim *et al.* 2001) with subsequent reductions in gambling behaviour.

However, even if *naltrexone* was prescribed for addiction, people probably wouldn't use it because of the unpleasant side effects.

Opioid antagonist treatment is still considered highly promising, so the search is on for other drugs that are just as effective but without the limiting side effects.

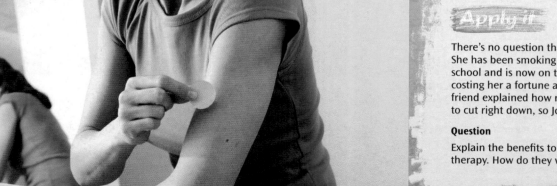

Apply it Concepts: **Patch it up**

There's no question that Joni is addicted to cigarettes. She has been smoking since her first year of secondary school and is now on to at least two packs a day. It's costing her a fortune and her health is suffering. A friend explained how nicotine patches have helped her to cut right down, so Joni has decided to give them a go.

Question

Explain the benefits to Joni of nicotine replacement therapy. How do they work? Are there any drawbacks?

Evaluation

Research support

Lindsay Stead *et al.* (2012) reviewed 150 high-quality research studies into the effectiveness of nicotine replacement therapy (NRT). They concluded that all forms of NRT are significantly more effective in helping smokers quit than both **placebo** and no treatment at all. Nasal spray was the most effective method of nicotine delivery. NRT users were up to 70% more likely to still be abstaining from smoking six months after quitting. Research also indicates two added benefits of NRT: it is safer than cigarette smoking because it eliminates the harmful elements of tobacco smoke; and it does not appear to foster dependence.

Apart from providing an effective treatment, this shows that there is **validity** in the neurochemical explanation of nicotine addiction which may yet lead to further life-saving drug therapies.

Side effects

Common side effects of NRT are sleep disturbances, gastro-intestinal problems, dizziness and headaches. In comparison the side effects are a serious concern in drug treatment of gambling addiction. The dose required for *naltrexone* to have an effect on gambling behaviour is generally much higher than when it is used conventionally to treat opiate addiction, so the side effects are correspondingly worse. Even when such negative effects are expected, there is a risk that the patient will discontinue the therapy, especially when those negative effects are experienced without the counterbalancing benefits of the drug of dependence, such as a state of euphoria ('all pain, no gain').

The risk of side effects should be carefully weighed up against both the benefits of the drug therapy and alternative psychological therapies such as **covert sensitisation** (see next spread).

Limited treatment

An advantage of drug therapy is often said to be the convenience of simply taking a tablet every day rather than, for instance, having to make wholesale changes to one's thought processes. But this strength breaks down in the case of most substance and behavioural addictions. For example, people addicted to heroin who spend most of their time searching for their next fix are too disorganised and undermotivated to take daily medication.

This means, paradoxically, that drug therapy is not effective for everyone despite its perceived convenience. It is probably best suited to a relatively small subset of addicts who are extremely highly motivated and not leading chaotic lifestyles.

Evaluation eXtra

Removal of stigma

One under-appreciated benefit of continuing research into drug treatment is that it encourages a growing perception that drug addiction is a medical problem. Research is rapidly revealing the neurochemical, genetic and physiological basis of addiction. This is gradually eroding the view, implicitly held by many people, that addiction is a form of moral failure or psychological weakness. Addiction therefore becomes less and less stigmatised as more people accept that a neurochemical imbalance (for instance) can hardly be considered the addict's 'fault'.

Consider: *Do you think this is a good thing? How might it improve treatment of addiction?*

Individual differences

Drugs do not work in the same way in everyone. Small **genetic** variations between individuals have a **significant** impact on the outcomes of drug treatment. For instance, the effectiveness of *naltrexone* as a treatment for alcohol addiction depends on a variation in a single **gene**. Alcoholics with one variant respond much more readily to treatment than those with the other version. Tammy Chung *et al.* (2012) therefore suggest drug treatments need to become more tailored to individual genetic profiles before they are likely to be consistently effective.

Consider: *Do you think this is a limitation of drug therapy as a treatment? Explain your answer.*

Apply it — Concepts: Taking a punt on drugs

Saul has finally recognised that his addiction to online poker has ruined his life. He has decided to get help, and has heard that there may be a drug he can take to reduce his gambling and the cravings he has for it. However, he is a bit concerned that there might be side effects and wants to know how useful the treatment will be.

Question

Explain how drug therapy could help reduce Saul's gambling addiction. As part of your explanation, consider both the advantages and disadvantages of such treatment.

A drug to reduce gambling addiction? It seems unlikely, but research is promising. But is it more effective than the alternatives?

Apply it — Methods: Gambling case study

A researcher was interested in the effectiveness of a drug to treat gambling addiction. She conducted a **case study** of a man with a gambling addiction who was receiving treatment with the opioid antagonist *naltrexone*. She used various techniques to assess whether or not the treatment was effective for this individual.

Questions

1. Describe *one* technique that the researcher could have used to collect data in this case study. (*2 marks*)
2. Explain *one* strength and *one* weakness of conducting a case study. (*2 marks + 2 marks*)
3. Identify *two* variables that the researcher could measure to establish the effectiveness of the drug. (*2 marks*)

The researcher wrote up the case study in a report for publication in a scientific journal.

4. What is the purpose of the discussion section of such a report? (*2 marks*)

A friend of the researcher thought the research was pointless. He believes that people become addicted because they are weak and giving them drugs will just make things worse.

5. Explain why the friend's personal opinion is no substitute for scientific evidence. (*4 marks*)

CHECK IT

1. Outline drug therapy as a way of reducing addiction.
   [6 marks]
2. Explain **one** limitation of using drug therapy to treat addiction.
   [4 marks]
3. Discuss drug therapy as a way of reducing addiction.
   [16 marks]

Reducing addiction: behavioural interventions including aversion therapy and covert sensitisation.

People who are addicted to a substance or behaviour experience many seriously negative consequences of their addiction, including health problems, relationship breakdown, job loss, trouble with the law, and many more besides. None of these negative consequences are enough to prevent most people continuing with their addictive behaviour. One reason is that these consequences usually happen a long time after the addictive behaviour has taken place.

On this spread, we look at two behavioural interventions for reducing addiction. They operate by reducing the time lag between the desired effects of a drug and its negative consequences so that they occur more-or-less together.

KEY TERMS

Behavioural interventions – Any treatment based on behaviourist principles of learning such as classical and operant conditioning.

Aversion therapy – A behavioural treatment based on classical conditioning. A maladaptive behaviour is paired with an unpleasant stimulus such as a painful electric shock. Eventually, the behaviour is associated with pain without the shock being used.

Covert sensitisation – A form of aversion therapy also based on classical conditioning. Instead of experiencing an unpleasant stimulus, the patient imagines (*in vitro*) how it would feel.

The indignity of induced vomiting is one of the ethical issues raised by aversion therapy.

Behavioural interventions for addiction

Aversion therapy

Aversion therapy is a **behavioural intervention** for addiction based on **classical conditioning**. It exploits the *principle of contiguity*, which states that two stimuli will become associated if they frequently occur together. According to **learning theory**, an addiction can develop through repeated associations between a drug and the pleasurable state of arousal caused by it. Therefore it follows that the **addiction** can be reduced by exploiting the same conditioning process, but by associating the drug with an unpleasant state (**counterconditioning**).

Aversion therapy for alcohol addiction Aversion therapy has been extensively used in treating alcoholism. The client is given an aversive drug (an emetic) which causes vomiting. They experience severe nausea and, five or ten minutes later, they vomit. But before this point is reached, the client is given an alcoholic drink, usually whisky because it is has a particularly strong alcoholic taste and smell. Vomiting (emesis) begins almost immediately after this. Treatment continues with several repetitions of this process, using higher doses of the aversive drug and often other types of alcoholic drink.

An alternative aversive treatment is a drug such as *disulfiram* (e.g. Antabuse). This interferes with the normal bodily process of metabolising alcohol into harmless chemicals. Someone drinking alcohol while taking the drug experiences severe nausea and vomiting – effectively an instant hangover. Conditioning operates so that the client associates alcohol with these unpleasant symptoms. The fear of experiencing the symptoms may be enough to prevent the client drinking alcohol. However, the client could end up vomiting in social situations where alcohol is available. This potentially serious loss of dignity – and the risk of harm – raises **ethical** issues and has led to a reduction in the use of this form of aversion therapy in recent years.

Aversion therapy for gambling addiction Electric shocks have also been used in place of drugs in some aversion treatments, especially for behavioural addictions such as gambling, and for people whose medical conditions (such as high blood pressure) might be worsened by frequent vomiting. The shocks used do not cause permanent damage, but because they are meant to be aversive, they are painful. The addicted gambler thinks of phrases that relate to his or her gambling behaviour and writes them down on cards. Some non-gambling behaviours are also included (such as 'Went straight home'). The participant reads out each card, and when they get to a gambling-related phrase they are given a two-second electric shock. The intensity of the shock is pre-selected by the participant themselves, following instructions that it should be painful but not distressing.

Covert sensitisation

Traditional aversion therapy was a popular treatment for drug addictions in the 1960s and 1970s. It is used much less these days and has been superseded by other treatments such as **covert sensitisation**. This is a type of aversion therapy but occurs *in vitro*. That is, rather than actually experiencing the unpleasant stimulus of an electric shock or vomiting, the individual is instructed to *imagine* how it would feel.

Covert sensitisation for nicotine addiction The client is first of all encouraged to relax. The therapist then reads from a script instructing the client to imagine an aversive situation. The client conjures up an image of themselves smoking a cigarette, followed by the most unpleasant consequences, such as the feeling of nausea and the experience of vomiting. The more vivid this imaginary scene the better, which is why the therapist goes into graphic detail about the elements of the imagery including the sights, smells, sounds and physical movements involved.

One very unpleasant technique is to get the client to imagine being forced to smoke cigarettes covered in faeces. Sometimes, for added unpleasantness, the therapy will incorporate aversive stimuli chosen by the client. For example, Mary McMurran (1994) reports a habitual user of slot machines who had a phobia of snakes. The imaginative scenario involved him picturing a slot machine paying out its winnings not in cash but in writhing snakes. Towards the end of a session, the client then imagines a scene in which they 'turn their back' on cigarettes and experience the resulting feelings of relief.

Apply it — Concepts: **Aversion advice**

Cyril is a long-term heavy smoker. He has tried all sorts of treatments including nicotine patches, gum, and inhalers but nothing has worked. He is smoking more than ever and is now desperate. He has heard of a treatment where you're given a drug that makes you throw up. Cyril doesn't much like the sound of it, but is so desperate he's prepared to give it a go.

Question

Imagine Cyril is a friend of yours who asks you for some advice. Based on your knowledge of aversion therapy, explain why you would or would not recommend that he tries this treatment.

Evaluation

Methodological problems with studies of aversion therapy

Peter Hajek and Lindsay Stead (2001) reviewed 25 studies of aversion therapies used to treat nicotine addiction. They found that it was impossible to judge the effectiveness of these therapies because all but one of the reviewed studies suffered from 'glaring' methodological problems.

Perhaps the most damaging of these was a failure to 'blind' the procedures, so the researchers who evaluated the outcomes of the studies knew which participants received therapy or **placebo**. Such inbuilt biases usually make therapy appear more effective than it actually is. Tellingly, most research studies into the effectiveness of aversion therapy are quite dated. This reflects the current reality that aversion therapy has fallen out of favour and been generally replaced by covert sensitisation.

Treatment adherence issues

By its very nature, aversion therapy uses stimuli that are unpleasant, disturbing and even traumatising. Induced vomiting or the pain caused by electric shocks are experiences that most people normally wish to avoid. It is no surprise therefore that many patients or research participants do exactly this and drop out of treatment before it is completed. This lack of treatment adherence makes it difficult for researchers to assess the effectiveness of aversion therapy.

This is a particular problem because there may be a systematic pattern to which patients or participants drop out. Those less likely to respond to treatment are the ones who leave early. If this is the case then research is probably overoptimistic about the efficacy of aversion therapy. However, this issue does highlight yet another advantage of covert sensitisation – it is a much less traumatic therapy than aversion therapy.

Research support for covert sensitisation

Nathaniel McConaghy *et al.* (1983) directly compared conventional electric shock aversion therapy with covert sensitisation in treating gambling addiction. At a one-year follow-up, those who had received covert sensitisation were **significantly** more likely to have reduced their gambling activities (90% of covert sensitisation participants compared with just 30% undergoing aversion). They also reported experiencing fewer and less intense gambling cravings than the aversion-treated participants.

This is one of many studies suggesting that covert sensitisation is a highly promising behavioural intervention for a range of addictions, including to alcohol, nicotine and gambling.

Evaluation eXtra

Short-term versus long-term effectiveness

The benefits of aversion therapy seem to be mostly short-term. McConaghy *et al.* (above) found that aversion therapy was much more effective in reducing gambling behaviour and cravings after one month than after one year. In a long-term follow-up (McConaghy *et al.* 1991), after between two and nine years, aversion therapy was no more effective than placebo (covert sensitisation was more beneficial).

Consider: *Do you think that this means aversion therapy should be abandoned? Explain your answer.*

Ethical issues

The popularity of aversion therapy was severely dented both by research which questioned its efficacy and by concerns over the ethics of its use. Inflicting extreme nausea, pain and loss of dignity came to be seen as ethically questionable. Allowing patients to select their own level of painful shock was little more than a token attempt to address these objections. This was one reason for the gradual rise in preference for covert sensitisation, which does not use shock or induced vomiting and poses fewer medical risks. It also allows patients to retain their dignity and is less challenging to their self-esteem.

Consider: *Explain why these ethical issues are a limitation of aversion therapy and a strength of covert sensitisation.*

Covert sensitisation is a much less traumatic experience than aversion therapy, with the client only imagining throwing up rather than actually doing so.

Apply it — Concepts: **Gambling on a cure**

Tamara gambles a lot on all sorts of different games, including the lottery, scratchcards, horse racing, poker, and slot machines. She enjoys the thrill and isn't all that bothered about winning, although she worries her hobby is becoming an addiction and wonders if she should do something about it.

Question

Choose one of these forms of gambling and explain how covert sensitisation could be used to help Tamara.

Apply it — Methods: **Reducing the urge**

A psychologist interviewed 65 gambling addicts one month after they underwent covert desensitisation treatment. On the basis of questions related to gambling urges and cravings, she assessed their severity of gambling urges in the preceding month and placed each participant into one of four categories: urges absent (19 participants), urges markedly reduced (25), urges slightly reduced (13), urges unchanged (8).

Questions

1. Explain *two* differences between a **structured** and an **unstructured interview**. (*2 marks + 2 marks*)

2. Explain *one* reason why the psychologist thought interviews might be better than **questionnaires** in this study. (*2 marks*)

3. Write *one* example of an **open question** that the psychologist could have asked. (*2 marks*)

4. Calculate the proportions of participants in each outcome category as percentages (*four* percentages). (*4 marks*)

5. Identify *one* issue of **reliability** in this study and explain how the psychologist could have improved it. (*1 mark + 2 marks*)

CHECK IT

1. Explain what is meant by the term *behavioural interventions* in relation to reducing addiction. [2 marks]

2. Outline covert sensitisation as a behavioural intervention for reducing addiction. [4 marks]

3. Outline aversion therapy as a behavioural intervention for reducing addiction. [4 marks]

4. Discuss **one or more** behavioural interventions for reducing addiction. [16 marks]

Reducing addiction: cognitive behaviour therapy.

According to the cognitive explanation of addiction (see page 366), people are at high risk of using drugs or becoming addicted to behaviours such as gambling if: (a) they readily form distorted cognitions about the outcomes of drug-related behaviours, and, (b) they lack the effective skills to cope with their problems in any other way. On this spread, we look at how cognitive behaviour therapy addresses both of these concerns.

KEY TERM

Cognitive behaviour therapy (CBT) – A method for treating mental disorders based on both cognitive and behavioural techniques. From the cognitive viewpoint the therapy aims to deal with thinking, such as challenging negative thoughts. The therapy also includes behavioural techniques such as behavioural activation.

Functional analysis in CBT helps the client to understand the reasons why they use drugs or behave in certain ways.

Cognitive behaviour therapy for addiction

Cognitive behaviour therapy (CBT)

Cognitive behaviour therapy aims to change the faulty ways of thinking that lead people to use drugs (or engage in certain behaviours) as maladaptive ways of coping. There are two indispensable elements to a CBT programme. First, CBT identifies and tackles the cognitive distortions that underlie **addictions**, replacing them with more adaptive ways of thinking (*functional analysis*). Secondly, *skills training* helps the client to develop coping *behaviours* to avoid the high-risk situations that usually trigger addiction-related behaviour.

Functional analysis

CBT starts with the client and the therapist together identifying the high-risk situations in which the client is likely to gamble or use a drug such as alcohol or cocaine. The therapist reflects on what the client is thinking before, during and after such a situation. The quality of the client–therapist relationship is therefore critical. It should be warm, collaborative and responsive, but not cosy. This is because the therapist must challenge the client's distorted cognitions and not merely accept them.

The functional analysis isn't just a one-off occurrence; it is ongoing and therefore valuable in two ways. In the early phases of treatment, it helps the client identify the triggers or reasons for their addiction, a necessary starting point. But it is useful later in therapy as well, in helping the client to work out the circumstances in which he or she is still having problems with coping, and what further skills training may be needed.

Skills training

By the time most people seek treatment for an addiction, they usually have a huge range of problems and issues, but only one way of coping with them – their drug of dependence. CBT helps the client to replace this strategy with more constructive ones. The therapist will be able to call upon a wide range of skills training techniques, starting with the basics and moving on to more individually tailored methods such as social skills training.

Cognitive restructuring All CBT programmes include an element of cognitive restructuring to tackle the biases that operate even below the client's level of awareness. So in gambling addiction, training addresses the client's faulty beliefs about probability, randomness, control, gains, and losses. These are confronted and challenged by the therapist. There is an initial educational element, in which the therapist gives the client information about the nature of chance.

Specific skills CBT is a 'broad-spectrum' treatment because it focuses on wider aspects of the client's life that are related to his or her addiction. The functional analysis may reveal that the client lacks specific skills to allow him or her to cope with situations that trigger alcohol use, for example. *Assertiveness training* could be used to help the client confront interpersonal conflicts in a controlled and rational way instead of using avoidance, manipulation or aggression. **Anger management** training can help some clients to cope with the situations that make them angry enough to resort to drinking.

Social skills Most clients can benefit from developing skills that allow them to cope with anxiety in social situations. A recovering alcoholic will almost inevitably find themselves in situations where alcohol is available (e.g. weddings, parties). *Social skills training* (SST) helps clients to learn how to refuse alcohol with minimum fuss in ways that avoid embarrassment, for example by making appropriate eye contact and being firm in refusing an offer of a drink.

Whatever skills training methods are used, the therapist might begin with an explanation of the reasoning behind learning a new skill. Perhaps a lack of that skill was identified in the functional analysis as the reason why the client relapsed during the week. The therapist then explains how the skill is performed, but crucially he or she models the behaviour which the client then imitates in **role play**. The skills training element of CBT is therefore usually highly directive, with constant 'tell and show' by the therapist with the client initially imitating the therapist's performance before eventually using the skill on their own in high-risk situations.

Apply it Concepts: **Give it up!**

Cecilia wants to go on a big holiday next year with her friends and she reckons she could save some money if only she could give up smoking. She has tried on and off over the years, but nothing has worked, not even the nicotine patches that seem to succeed for everyone else. She rang a quit smoking helpline and they suggested that Cecilia goes to see her GP to find out about cognitive behaviour therapy.

Question

Using your knowledge of CBT, describe the sorts of procedures and techniques that Cecilia can expect to experience. Explain how they specifically apply to her smoking addiction.

Evaluation

Research support

Nancy Petry and her colleagues (2006) recruited pathological gamblers through media advertising. They were **randomly allocated** to either a **control group** (Gamblers Anonymous (GA) meetings) or a treatment condition (GA meetings plus an eight-session individual CBT programme). The treatment clients were gambling **significantly** less than the control participants up to 12 months later. An interesting finding was that CBT provided face-to-face by a therapist was more effective than CBT delivered by workbook, which suggests that there is some therapeutic benefit in the client–therapist relationship.

An important feature of this study is that the participants were allocated randomly to the CBT group or the control group, and there were no significant differences in the extent of their gambling at the start. Therefore, the findings are strong evidence that CBT is effective in treating gambling addiction, from a methodologically-sound study.

Short-term versus long-term gains

Unfortunately, the pattern revealed by most research into the efficacy of CBT is not the same as the one above. The picture is one of short-term benefit but long-term disappointment. Sean Cowlishaw *et al.* (2012) reviewed 11 studies comparing CBT for gambling addiction with control conditions. These studies show that CBT has medium to very large beneficial effects in reducing gambling behaviour for periods of up to three months after treatment. But after nine to 12 months, there are no significant differences in outcome between the CBT and control groups. Therefore, CBT is effective in reducing gambling behaviour, but 'the durability of therapeutic gain is unknown' (Cowlishaw *et al.* 2012).

To make matters worse, the researchers also conclude that the studies they reviewed were of such poor methodological quality that they probably overestimate the efficacy of treatment with CBT.

Lack of treatment adherence

Pim Cuijpers *et al.* (2008) indicate that drop-out rates in CBT treatment groups can be up to five times greater than for other forms of therapy. This may be because CBT is a demanding therapy. Even when the most high-risk users continue in treatment, they take it less seriously, completing fewer homework assignments and attending fewer sessions. Clients often seek CBT initially because some life crisis caused by their addiction has driven them into therapy. Once the crisis is resolved, or at least doesn't loom as large in their lives, these clients often give up therapy.

Lack of treatment adherence is a major obstacle to a full understanding of how effective CBT is for reducing addictions

Evaluation eXtra

Relapse prevention

For those clients who do stick with the therapy, CBT appears to be especially effective at preventing relapse. Most people's experience of addictions is one of chronic relapse. A central strength of CBT is that it incorporates the likelihood of relapse into treatment, viewing it as an opportunity for further cognitive restructuring and learning rather than as failure. Relapse may even realistically be seen as an inevitable part of the addict's life, but acceptable as long as his or her psychosocial functioning improves.

Consider: *How would you balance this against the negative view of CBT outlined above? Is CBT beneficial overall?*

What works?

CBT uses a wide variety of techniques to reduce addictions, some of which can be combined with other treatments such as drug therapies. In recent years, there has also been a huge expansion in the ways that CBT is delivered, especially online or with telephone support, without the physical presence of a therapist. This means that treatment can be tailored to individual needs, presumably making it more beneficial. However, this flexibility and variety of use also means that it is difficult for researchers to identify which elements of CBT are most useful in reducing addictions because there is no standard treatment.

Consider: *Is this flexibility a strength or a weakness of CBT? Explain your answer.*

One skill development technique used in CBT is assertiveness training, useful in helping the client to refuse drugs.

Apply it — Concepts: Hugo needs help

Hugo uses alcohol to cope with the pressures of everyday life. He frequently drinks to excess, even during the week, often going to work with a hangover or still drunk. He finally acknowledged he needed help when he woke up lying in a gutter in the street at four in the morning. He knows there are many different treatments available, but he's not sure which one is going to help him the most.

Question

Imagine you are Hugo's friend. You are familiar with how CBT works as a treatment for alcohol addiction. Considering both its strengths and weaknesses, explain the advice you would give to Hugo.

Apply it — Methods: Assessing CBT

A psychologist decided to investigate the effectiveness of cognitive behaviour therapy for cocaine addiction. He selected a group of cocaine users who were following a ten-session CBT programme. and compared their progress with that of a **control group**. He used a **rating scale** from 1 (no progress) to 10 (excellent progress).

Questions

1. Explain what is meant by a control group. (*2 marks*)
2. Identify an appropriate control group for this study and explain why it is suitable. (*2 marks*)
3. Explain *one* **ethical issue** the researcher might have encountered in this study, and *one* way in which he could have dealt with it. (*2 marks + 2 marks*)
4. Identify a suitable **statistical test** to analyse the difference between the CBT and control groups at the end of the study. (*1 mark*) (See page 70)
5. The psychologist used this test to analyse the difference between the CBT and control groups. He found there was a significant difference at p ≤ 0.05. Explain what this statement means. (*2 marks*)

CHECK IT

1. Describe cognitive behaviour therapy as a treatment for reducing addiction. **[6 marks]**
2. Briefly outline how cognitive behaviour therapy (CBT) is used to reduce addiction and explain **one** limitation of using CBT to reduce addiction. **[4 marks]**
3. Describe and evaluate cognitive behaviour therapy as a treatment for reducing addiction. **[16 marks]**

The application of the following theory of behaviour change to addictive behaviour – the theory of planned behaviour.

'Easy is the descent into Hell, for it is paved with good intentions.' (Milton, *Paradise Lost*)

Did you make any New Year's resolutions this year? When we make such resolutions most of us really and truly believe in them, our intentions are completely sincere. But they usually come to nothing.

Psychologists have tried to understand this link (or lack of one) between our intentions and the reality of our actual behaviour. One theory has been applied to attempts to reduce addiction – the theory of planned behaviour.

KEY TERM

Theory of planned behaviour (TPB) – Changes in behaviour can be predicted from our intention to change, which in turn is the outcome of personal attitudes towards the behaviour in question, our beliefs about what others think, and our perceived ability to control our behaviour.

In the text we've illustrated the TPB using gambling as example of an addiction. But of course the theory can also be (and has been) applied to other forms of addiction including nicotine and others not on the specification such as heroin, cocaine, MDMA, etc.

Personal attitudes → Subjective norms → Perceived behavioural control → Behavioural intention → Behaviour

The theory of planned behaviour can be applied to gambling addiction. Intention to stop gambling is central, but does it really determine whether someone actually gives up?

Theory of planned behaviour (TPB)

Formulated by Icek Ajzen (1985; 1991), the **theory of planned behaviour** attempts to explain how we change behaviours over which we can exercise self-control, that is *deliberate* behaviours. Central to the theory is the concept of *intention*. The TPB asserts that behaviour can be predicted from our intention to behave in a certain way. Applied to **addiction**, the TPB tries to link intentions to give up drugs with actual changes in behaviour.

How do people form their intentions to reduce or give up drugs? The theory suggests intentions arise from three key influences: our personal attitudes, our beliefs about what others think and our beliefs about our ability to change our drug-related behaviour.

Personal attitudes

This refers to the entire collection of the addicted person's attitudes towards their addiction. It amounts to whether their opinion of the addiction is favourable or unfavourable. To work this out, addicts would have to take into account the outcomes associated with their addiction.

So, for example, someone addicted to gambling might be able to reel off a long list of favourable attitudes, such as: it gives me a thrill, I occasionally win, it's an escape from my terrible life. They might also hold some unfavourable attitudes: I lose more money than I win, I can't stop, it makes me tense and anxious, it takes up all my time. The addict's overall attitude is formed from weighing up the balance of these positive and negative evaluations.

Subjective norms

Subjective norms are the individual's beliefs about whether the people who matter most to them approve or disapprove of their addictive behaviour. The beliefs are based on what these people believe to be 'normal' behaviour (i.e. norms). The addicted person considers what their friends and family would think if they knew about their addiction. In this case of gambling, for example, this entails thinking about their friends' and family members' own behaviour – do they gamble at all, and how much? And also their attitudes – have they expressed any views about gambling, favourable or unfavourable? The addicted person might conclude: 'Most people who matter to me would be very unhappy with me gambling like this'. This would make them less likely to intend gambling, and therefore less likely to actually gamble.

Notice there is a very subtle but important distinction here. What really matters? It is not other people's approval or disapproval of gambling in general that influences your intentions. It is your *perception* that the people closest to you approve or disapprove of *your* gambling that is influential. Why is this distinction significant? Well, here's an example you might be familiar with. It is not unusual for parents to have favourable attitudes towards something in general (such as getting drunk every now and then), but disapprove of their own children doing so.

Perceived behavioural control

This is about how much control we believe we have over our behaviour, which is called **self-efficacy**. Does the addicted gambler believe that giving up gambling is an easy or difficult thing for them to do? This depends, of course, on their perception of the resources available to them. This perception of resources can be both external (money, time, support) and internal (ability, skill, determination).

According to the TPB, perceived behavioural control has two possible effects. First, it can influence our intentions to behave, so that the more control I believe I have over my ability to stop gambling, the stronger my intention to do so. Secondly, it can also influence behaviour directly, so the greater my perceived control over my gambling, the longer and harder I will try to stop.

In summary, my personal attitudes towards gambling, my perception of what my nearest and dearest think of my gambling, and my beliefs about my ability to quit, all combine to influence my intention to stop gambling, which in turn influences the amount of time and effort I put into actually stopping.

Apply it

Concepts: Why, why, why, Delilah?

After years of her friends and family cajoling her, Delilah has finally decided to stop smoking. Nobody else she knows well smokes, and they're not shy about telling her what they think. Delilah herself has become more and more worried over time about her health and how much money she spends on cigarettes. She thinks she only smokes out of habit these days; she doesn't really enjoy it that much. She feels the time is right, she is ready and reckons this time she can do it.

Question

Based on what you know about the theory of planned behaviour, what do you think Delilah's chances of giving up are? Explain your answer.

Evaluation

Some research support

Martin Hagger et al. (2011) tested the TPB's predictions about alcohol-related behaviours. They found that the three factors of personal attitudes, subjective norms and perceived behavioural control all predicted an intention to limit drinking to the guideline number of units. Intentions were also found to influence the number of units actually consumed after one month and three months. Perceived behavioural control also predicted actual unit consumption directly (and not just intention).

All of these outcomes are exactly as the theory predicts. However, there are two caveats. Firstly, the time periods between intention and behaviour were relatively short. Secondly, the theory was not able to predict behaviour related to all addictions, for example it didn't predict binge drinking behaviour, so the success of the TPB may depend on the addiction that is studied.

Does not explain addiction behaviour

A major limitation of the TPB is that it cannot account for the *intention-behaviour gap*. It cannot adequately explain how actual behaviour arises from intentions. Rohan Miller and Gwyneth Howell (2005) studied the gambling behaviour of underage teenagers. They found strong support for the element of the TPB that predicts intentions from attitudes, norms and perceived control. But the model did not predict the occurrence of actual gambling behaviour. Many psychologists now question whether the TPB is a model of behaviour *change* at all. If the theory cannot predict behaviour change, it becomes very difficult to create drug-related interventions that bridge the gap between intention to reduce addictive behaviours and the actual behaviours themselves.

Short-term versus long-term changes

Rosie McEachan et al. (2011) conducted a **meta-analysis** of 237 studies of health behaviours (including addiction-related ones) and their links with the factors of the TPB. They found that the strength of the **correlation** between intentions and behaviour varied according to the length of time between the two. Intention (to stop drinking, for example) may be a good predictor of actually giving up (or reducing) drinking, but only if the time between intention and behaviour is short (less than about five weeks). The theory is on much weaker ground in trying to predict drug-related behavioural changes in the longer term, or when they come some time after the intention to change has formed.

This may help explain why the research evidence related to the theory is so mixed. But a theory that attracts support for some of its elements but not for others cannot be accepted as an entirely **valid** explanation of drug-related behaviour.

Evaluation eXtra

Methodological issues

The TPB is based on research that uses **self-report** methods of measurement extensively (Ogden 2003). There is an argument that attitudes, norms, perceived control and intentions are subjective variables that are best assessed by asking individuals their views. However, the limitations of self-report methods are substantial and include **social desirability bias**, whereby participants respond to questions in a way that they think will make them 'look good'. Also, correlational studies do not allow us to conclude that drug-related intentions cause drug-related behaviours. The problem is so acute that Sniehotta et al. (2014) conclude, 'We do not need any more correlational studies of the TPB.'

Consider: *Do you agree with this conclusion? Explain how these methodological problems affect the validity of the theory.*

A limited explanation

The TPB is a limited explanation of addiction-related behaviour because it overemphasises rational reasoning in decision-making and choice. It has difficulty in accounting for less rational factors that influence intentions and behaviours involving drugs, such as emotions, cognitive biases, or even past experiences.

Consider: *How rational is the decision to start taking drugs or to give them up? How does this affect the validity of the TPB?*

According to the theory of planned behaviour, our intention to change our behaviour depends partly on what we believe other people think about what we're doing.

Apply it — Methods: Best of intentions?

A researcher decided to investigate whether people's intention to give up smoking is related to who actually gives up. She recruited 100 participants and **interviewed** them to establish their intentions. She asked several questions and derived for each participant an *Intention Score* from 0 (no intention at all to give up smoking) to 15 (strong intention to give up). She then formed two groups from these scores, high intention and low intention. One month later she measured who had given up smoking.

Questions

1. Explain *one* way in which the researcher could use **standardisation** as a method of control in this study. (*2 marks*)
2. The researcher wanted to ensure a balance of genders in her sample of participants. Outline how she could have used **stratified sampling** to achieve this. (*2 marks*)
3. Explain *one* limitation of this sampling method. (*2 marks*)
4. Explain how the researcher could have established the **validity** of the Intention Score. (*2 marks*)
5. Explain how **investigator effects** might have influenced the outcome of this study. (*2 marks*)

Apply it — Concepts: Can I cut down?

Greg doesn't think he is exactly addicted to alcohol, but he is worried about how much he drinks. He has tried in the past to cut down through 'willpower' but it never works. He just wishes he knew what might make a difference if he were to try again.

Question

You are Greg's friend and you're familiar with the theory of planned behaviour. What advice would you give Greg based on this theory?

CHECK IT

1. Outline the theory of planned behaviour in relation to addictive behaviour. [6 marks]
2. Identify **one** form of addictive behaviour and describe how the theory of planned behaviour explains how that addictive behaviour can be changed. [4 marks]
3. Describe and evaluate the theory of planned behaviour in relation to addictive behaviour. [16 marks]

The application of the following theory of behaviour change to addictive behaviour – Prochaska's six-stage model of behaviour change.

James Prochaska and Carlo DiClemente (1983) devised a model of behavioural change that has been used to explain how people overcome addictions. Their model was originally formulated to explain recovery from nicotine addiction, but since then it has developed to the point where it is probably the most widely used model of addiction-related behaviour change.

KEY TERM

Prochaska's six-stage model explains the stages people go through to change their behaviour. It identifies six stages of change (and is sometimes referred to as the 'Stages of change' model), from not considering it at all to making permanent changes. The stages are not necessarily followed in a linear order.

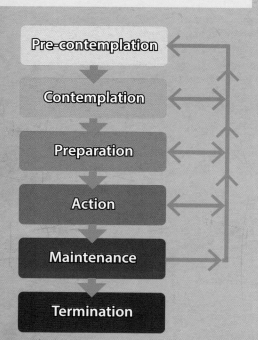

Prochaska's six-stage model of behavioural change.

Students often ask, 'Should I include a diagram in my essay?' Diagrams are great for helping your own understanding, which is why there are some in this book. But they're not so useful in essays as it is likely to simply repeat what you have written – better to focus on a clear and detailed explanation. So, on balance, avoid diagram danger.

Prochaska's six-stage model

Assumptions of the model

Prochaska and DiClemente (1983) noticed that smokers' behaviour changed through a series of stages in their attempts to quit. **Prochaska's six-stage model** recognised that overcoming **addiction** is a complex process that does not happen quickly or in a tidy linear order from first to final stage. It is a cyclical process: there is some orderly progression through stages but also a lot of returning to previous ones, and some stages may even be missed out altogether.

The model is based on two major insights about behavioural change. First, people who are addicted differ in how ready they are to change their behaviour. Some are thinking about it, some are already doing something about it, and yet others have decided not to change at all. Secondly, how useful a treatment intervention is depends on the stage the person has reached. Some interventions will be most effective at an early stage of the recovery process, but less useful later on.

Six stages of behavioural change

Precontemplation (*'Ignorance is bliss'*) People in this stage are not thinking about changing their addiction-related behaviour in the near future, usually defined as the next six months. This may be because of *denial*: the person has never considered changing because they don't believe they have a problem. Or it may be because of *demotivation*: the person may have tried many times to tackle their addiction, without success, so is now demoralised and doesn't currently intend to try again. Intervention at this stage should focus on helping the addicted person to consider the need for change.

Contemplation (*'Sitting on the fence'*) Someone at this stage is thinking about making a change to their behaviour in the next six months. This does not mean they have decided to change; they are ambivalent. They are increasingly aware of the need for change, and they want the benefits of it, but they are also very aware of the costs. Because people can remain in a chronic state of contemplation for a long time, it would not be helpful to introduce a drug treatment intervention at this stage. Much more useful is any attempt to help the person finally see how the pros of overcoming addiction outweigh the cons.

Preparation (*'OK I'm ready for this'*) Now the individual believes that the benefits are greater than the costs, he or she decides to change their addiction-related behaviour, sometime within the next month. However, as they haven't yet decided exactly how and when to change, the most useful form of intervention is support in constructing a plan, or in presenting them with some options such as seeing a drugs counsellor, or calling a helpline, or making a GP appointment.

Action (*'Let's do this'*) People at this stage have done something to change their behaviour in the last six months. For example, this is the point at which the behavioural and cognitive treatment methods outlined on earlier spreads become potentially effective. Or the person will do something less formal but no less meaningful, such as cut up their cigarettes or pour all the alcohol in the house down the sink. The action the addicted person takes must reduce their risk, for example by giving up cigarettes altogether rather than just switching to low tar versions. Effective intervention at this stage focuses on developing the coping skills the client will need to quit and maintain their change of behaviour into the next stage.

Maintenance (*'Stay on track'*) The person has maintained some change of behaviour (stopped gambling perhaps) for more than six months. The focus is on relapse prevention – avoiding situations where cues might trigger reversion to addictive behaviours. This is accompanied by a growing confidence that changes can be continued in the longer term. The change in behaviour is becoming a way of life. Intervention helps the client to apply the coping skills they have learned and use the sources of support available to them.

Termination At this stage, newly acquired behaviours such as abstinence become automatic. The person no longer returns to addictive behaviours to cope with anxiety, stress, loneliness, and so on. This stage may not be possible or realistic for some people to achieve. It may be that the most appropriate goal for many is to prolong maintenance for as long as they can, accepting that relapse is inevitable but providing the person with the skills to work through the earlier stages of the process quickly. No intervention is required.

Jeb has been drinking alcohol to excess for several months and his life is in a mess. His wife has left him, taking the children, and he has recently been sacked from his job for turning up drunk once too often. Although he feels sorry for himself from time to time, he still doesn't really believe he has a problem. He always insists he has his drinking under control and looks astonished and offended when friends suggest he gets help.

Questions

What stage of Prochaska's model is Jeb at? Explain how the model suggests he can best be helped to progress to the next stage of the recovery process. Briefly explain what the model predicts should happen to Jeb next if all goes well.

Evaluation

Dynamic nature of behaviour

More traditional theories have ignored the importance of dynamic process, considering recovery from addiction as a single 'all-or-nothing' event. In contrast the six-stage model emphasises the importance of time, viewing overcoming an addiction such as smoking as a continuing process. This is why the model proposes that behavioural change occurs through six stages of varying duration for each person, and that the stages are recycled backwards and forwards to different degrees. Therefore a strength of this model is that it recognises that changing addictive behaviours is a dynamic process.

Contradictory research evidence

In a major review of the available evidence for the *National Institute for Health and Care Excellence* (NICE), David Taylor *et al.* (2006) concluded that stage-based approaches are no more effective than alternatives in treating nicotine addiction. Despite further research studies being carried out, a later review by Kate Cahill *et al.* (2010) came to precisely the same conclusion. The overall research picture is negative, despite the over-optimistic claims made for the model by some.

Addiction researcher Robert West (2005) is brutal in his assessment of the six-stage model. He concludes that ' . . . the problems with the model are so serious . . . it should be discarded. The model has been little more than a security blanket for researchers and clinicians'.

Arbitrary nature of the stages

The difference between stages is probably too arbitrary. For example, Stephen Sutton (2001) points out that if an individual plans to stop smoking in 30 days' time they are in the preparation stage, but if they plan to give up in 31 days' time, they are in the contemplation stage.

Albert Bandura (1997) claims that the first two stages (precontemplation and contemplation) are not even **qualitatively** different, because the only difference between them is how much (a **quantitative** measure) the individual wants to change.

Pål Kraft *et al.* (1999) argues that the six stages can be reduced to just two useful ones: precontemplation, plus all the others grouped together.

Evaluation eXtra

Attitude to relapse

According to Carlo DiClemente *et al.* (2004), 'relapse is the rule rather than the exception'. The six-stage model does not view relapse as failure, but as an inevitable part of the 'untidy', non-linear, dynamic process of behaviour change. However, as it views relapse as more than just a slip, the model also takes it seriously and does not underestimate its potential to blow change entirely off course. Lots of changes to behaviour require several attempts to get it right, to make it last, or to reach the maintenance or termination stages.

Consider: *How do you think this approach to relapse can help someone trying to recover from addiction? Explain why this is a strength of the model.*

Description versus prediction

Most research applying the six-stage model to addiction describes the stages that people are at in the recovery process and **correlates** this with addiction-related and treatment-seeking behaviours. However, this research has produced mixed findings (see above). This suggests that it is unclear whether or not the model is a good predictor of who is likely to make changes (which is the main aim of a useful model).

Consider: *How **valid** is the model as an explanation of behavioural change if it is unable to predict outcomes?*

Apply it — Concepts: No going back?

Sigourney gave up smoking seven months ago, after taking an online CBT programme. She's quite proud of the fact that she hasn't touched a cigarette in all that time so far. But she isn't complacent and she knows the biggest risk for her now is relapsing back into her old habits.

Question

What stage of Prochaska's model is Sigourney at? What does the model predict could happen to her if she relapses, and how could she be helped?.

Prochaska's six-stage model accepts relapse as an integral part of the addiction recovery process and explains how it can be dealt with.

Apply it — Methods: Ready or not?

A psychologist wanted to see if people who are most ready to give up smoking are more likely to do so. She recruited 20 smokers and gave them a *Readiness to Change* (RtC) questionnaire which included such items as 'How likely are you to give up smoking in the next month?' All the participants then underwent a six-session CBT programme which focused on changing their patterns of thinking about smoking. The participants were all followed up after 12 months. The psychologist found a **correlation coefficient** of −.72 between readiness to change and the average number of cigarettes smoked per day.

Questions

1. Write a **non-directional hypothesis** for this study. (*2 marks*)

2. Identify *one* variable in this study other than those being measured. Explain how it might have affected the results (*3 marks*)

3. Explain how the psychologist could have checked the **validity** of the RtC **questionnaire**. (*3 marks*)

4. Which **measure of central tendency** should the psychologist have used to calculate the average number of cigarettes smoked per day? Explain your answer (*3 marks*)

5. Explain what is meant by the phrase 'a correlation coefficient of −.72 between readiness to change and the average number of cigarettes smoked per day'. (*2 marks*) (See page 63)

CHECK IT

1. Identify **one** addictive behaviour and explain how Prochaska's six-stage model of behaviour change could be used to explain change in addictive behaviour. *[4 marks]*

2. Outline Prochaska's six-stage model of behaviour change as a theory of addictive behaviour. *[6 marks]*

3. Discuss Prochaska's six-stage model of behaviour change as a theory of addictive behaviour. *[16 marks]*

> Knowledge and understanding of ...research methods, practical research skills and maths skills. These should be developed through ... ethical practical research activities.

This means you should conduct practical activities wherever possible. On this spread, there is a quasi-experiment to test a prediction about distorted thinking from the cognitive theory of gambling addiction. You will also find a suggestion for researching the reasons why people smoke using content analysis.

Ethics check

We suggest strongly that you complete this checklist before starting:

1. Do participants know participation is voluntary?
2. Do participants know what to expect?
3. Do participants know they can withdraw at any time?
4. Are individuals' results anonymous?
5. Have I minimised the risk of distress to participants?
6. Have I avoided asking sensitive questions?
7. Will I avoid bringing my school/teacher/psychology into disrepute?
8. Have I considered all other ethical issues?
9. Has my teacher approved this?

Apply it

Methods:
The maths bit 1

Table 1 Number of incorrect answers given by frequent Lottery players and non-players.

Frequent Gamblers	Non-Gamblers
6	1
3	8
8	3
4	4
7	7
4	2
5	6
6	5
7	5
9	4

Practical idea 1: Thinking about probability

The **cognitive** theory of gambling **addiction** emphasises the central role of cognitive biases. These are the many distorted ways of thinking about **probability** and chance that addicted gamblers apparently demonstrate. It would be ethically risky to conduct research with people who are addicted to gambling, but we might expect to find some differences in probability-related thinking between people who gamble regularly and people who do not gamble at all.

The practical bit

Ethical issues

Because gambling (even when it is not an addictive behaviour) is a sensitive subject for most people, it's as well to give **ethical issues** some thought right from the outset. You need to choose a form of gambling that most people would consider 'mild' and doesn't have any real stigma attached to it. It should also be something the majority of people wouldn't mind being asked about. An ideal choice is looking at people who do and do not play the National Lottery.

The questions that you ask must also be carefully written, not just because they could be viewed as an invasion of **privacy** but also because of potential **psychological harm.** Some participants will show evidence of distorted thinking about probability and chance. They could easily assume that this reflects on their intelligence and that their answers must mean they are 'stupid' (or at the very least 'irrational'). Your **debriefing** should provide them with reassurance on this point. Your questions should be phrased very carefully to avoid the impression that you are judging your participants' intelligence.

Assessing cognitive distortions

Bearing in mind these ethical matters, you will need to create your own scale to measure people's views of probability and chance. Produce ten multiple choice and/or 'yes–no' questions which all have objectively correct answers. This will allow you to derive a score out of ten for each participant; the higher the score, the more distorted their thinking about chance. For ethical reasons stick to questions related to the Lottery and general questions about probability. Avoid questions about any other form of gambling.

Your questions should cover a range of cognitive distortions. Here are some suggestions for you to consider. When doing the Lottery, is it best to choose certain numbers such as birthdays? Which of the following set of numbers is more likely to be drawn in the Lottery – 11, 12, 13, 14, 15, 16 or 7, 22, 24, 28, 33, 43? If you toss a coin five times and it comes up heads each time, on the sixth toss is it more likely to come up heads or tails or are both equally likely? Is it better to select your own numbers in the Lottery than choose a 'lucky dip'? If you forgot to do the Lottery one week, how likely is it that your usual numbers would come up?

Selecting your participants

You are going to compare people who play the National Lottery every week and people who never play it. So you need to recruit participants from both categories. The most straightforward way to do this is to use an **opportunity sampling** method. Approach people who may be available to take part, and simply find out from them whether they fit into either of these two groups; aim to find ten participants for each. Try your best to match the participants so that they roughly of similar ages across both groups.

Analysing and presenting your data

Once you have added up the number of incorrect answers for each participant, you will have a 'distorted thinking' score for each one. You can then draw up a table like the one on the left. An appropriate **statistical test** will tell you whether or not the difference in distorted thinking between the two groups is **significant**.

1. What is the **level of measurement** of the **dependent variable** in this study? Explain your answer (*1 mark + 1 mark*)
2. Using the data on the left calculate suitable **measures of central tendency** and **measures of dispersion** for both groups. (*4 marks*)
3. Which **statistical test** would be most suitable to analyse the difference between the two groups? Give *two* reasons for your choice. (*1 mark + 2 marks*) (See page 70)
4. Apply this test to obtain a **calculated value**. State whether or not this value is significant and explain how you reached your conclusion. (*1 mark + 3 marks*)

Practical idea 2: Risk factors for smoking

Research has shown that some people are more likely than others to become smokers. It may be because people differ in their degree of risk or it may be due to a variety of other factors.

This practical is neither an **experiment** nor a **correlational** study, but simply an exploration of the reasons people give for smoking. The aim is to use **content analysis** to find out how important the classic risk factors are in people's decision to start smoking.

It's unusual to see people smoke a pipe. Are the risk factors involved any different from those that lead to cigarette smoking? You could adapt this practical to find out.

The practical bit

Designing the study

You could straightforwardly do this by constructing a **questionnaire** that covers all the potential risk factors. Your participants would simply have to tick some boxes. This would be easy to score and allow you to identify and rank the risk factors in order of importance. But this method doesn't give your participants the opportunity to explain their reasons in the way they might like to. For example, the options you give them may not be the ones they would choose. By using an open-ended approach you can just allow your participants to speak for themselves. Unfortunately, this does mean more work for you, the researcher.

As a minimum, you should give your participants a description of what you would like them to do, which is basically to give as many relevant reasons as they can for why they smoke. You then provide them with the space to write their response. Incidentally, you may have realised by now that you could very easily conduct this whole procedure online, from attracting participants to debriefing them, via email perhaps.

You could opt to add more structure to the procedure by giving an indication of which risk factors you would like your participants to consider (i.e. headings they can give their responses under). For instance, reasons relating to family, peer group, stress; all the factors explained in earlier spreads. But try not to direct your participants too much. Remember that this is their chance to use their own words.

Sampling method

A **volunteer sample** would be appropriate for this practical, although this means you would have to advertise for smokers to come forward to participate. As a further development of the study, you could identify a demographic group that interests you: young people, older people, men, women, etc. Not to compare them but just to get an insight into the risk factors for smoking in a particular group. Aim to recruit between 10 and 20 participants.

Ethical considerations

One advantage of allowing participants to give their accounts in their own words without directing them too much is that they can decide how much information they are prepared to divulge. They are less likely to feel you are invading their privacy. But there is no room for complacency. The ethical dimension involved in asking about smoking behaviour and private matters such as stress and family influences needs to be at the forefront of your mind in designing and carrying out this practical.

Analysing your data

Using content analysis presents us with the challenge of trying to extract **quantitative data** from the information provided by the participants. Read about **content analysis** on page 64 in order to first of all create your categories.

You could start by drawing up a table of the major psychosocial risk factors for smoking: family influences, peer group pressure, stress, personality. Read through your participants' accounts and identify all the reasons they give that match these broad categories. Keep a tally as you go. As you read, consider whether the categories need refining. Do you have enough information to be able to make finer distinctions? For example, can you distinguish between different kinds of family influences, or different types of stress? Is there a case for adding more headings? Be careful though, because you do not want to make the analysis too complex.

You could then calculate the numbers of responses in each category as percentages of the overall responses. You could also put the risk factors in rank order of frequency and draw a suitable graph to represent the data.

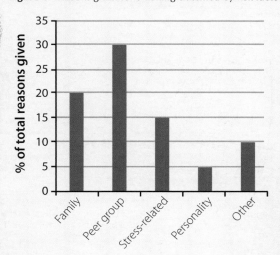

Apply it Methods: The maths bit 2

1. Identify the type of graphical display shown in the graph below. (*1 mark*).
2. Use the data in the graph to draw an appropriate table of results. (*3 marks*)
3. The total number of responses identified in this research was 80. Calculate the figures in each category as a percentage of the total responses. (*4 marks*)
4. Outline *one* conclusion you can draw based on all the information you have available. (*3 marks*)

Figure 1 Reasons given for smoking classified by risk factor.

The maths bit

Overall, at least 10% of the marks in assessments for Psychology will require the use of mathematical skills and at least 25% in total will involve research methods. Don't avoid it!

Revision summaries

Describing addiction

Understanding what addiction is and your chances of becoming addicted.

What is addiction?

Physical and psychological dependence
Physical: Withdrawal occurs when abstaining from a drug.
Psychological: Compulsion to experience effects of a drug.

Tolerance
Because of repeated exposure to a drug, a greater dose is needed to experience the same effects.

Withdrawal syndrome
Symptoms that occur when someone physically dependent on a drug abstains or reduces their use.

Risk factors in the development of addiction

How other factors affect your risk of becoming addicted.

Risk factors

Genetic vulnerability
Some people inherit a vulnerability to drug dependence. Genes determine (1) the proportion of dopamine receptors (D2R) in the brain and (2) functioning of CYP2A6 enzyme which metabolises nicotine.

Stress
Addiction develops only in response to both a vulnerability (e.g. childhood trauma) and later stressful life event (e.g. PTSD). Andersen and Teicher: Early stress causes damage to brain.

Personality
The impulsivity found in antisocial personality disorder increases the risk of addiction, perhaps because APD and addiction share a common genetic element (Ivanov et al.).

Family influences
An adolescent's perception that parents do not care about them or that they approve of drugs (e.g. Livingston et al.).

Peers
O'Connell et al.: Three-step process: (1) norms about drinking influenced by peers; (2) peers provide opportunities to drink; (3) individual overestimates how much peers drink.

Evaluation

Research support
Kendler et al.: Adoption studies: Children adopted away from a family with one addicted member have an increased risk of developing an addiction as adults (8.6% vs 4.2%).

Indirect effects
Genes determine behaviours and characteristics that in turn influence the risk of addiction (e.g. emotional regulation).

Interactions between all risk factors
Many pathways to addiction due to combinations of interacting risks (peers, family, stress, etc.). No single factor responsible.

Cause and effect
A lot of research is correlational, stress may cause addiction but also addiction causes stress.

Proximate and ultimate risk factors
Risk factors may be proximate causes of addiction. They may ultimately be caused by genetics.

Real-life applications
Understanding risk factors and how they interact could lead to improved drug treatment and prevention programmes.

Methodological issues
A lot of studies are retrospective because they involve recalling events from the past (e.g. childhood stressors).

Explanations for nicotine addiction

Brain neurochemistry

A biological explanation.

Brain neurochemistry

The desensitisation hypothesis
Nicotinic receptors (nAChR) in the brain are briefly stimulated by nicotine but then immediately shut down. This stimulates dopamine which has pleasurable effects.

The nicotine regulation model
Going without nicotine (e.g. when asleep) allows nicotinic receptors to sensitise again, triggering an acute withdrawal syndrome and more smoking.

Evaluation

Supporting research evidence
McEvoy et al.: People taking antipsychotic medication are often heavy smokers, possibly because it gives them the dopamine release that their medication inhibits.

Real-life applications
Understanding neurochemistry could lead to better treatments not just for nicotine addiction but for co-morbid disorders (e.g. depression).

Limited explanation
Other neurochemical mechanisms (e.g. serotonin) are involved in nicotine addiction, although dopamine is central.

A reductionist explanation
Neurochemical explanations ignore psychosocial factors (e.g. peer influences) that are at least as important (Choi et al.).

Individual differences
Chippers smoke for decades without developing dependency, which is difficult for neurochemical theories to explain.

Learning theory

A psychological explanation.

Learning theory

Operant conditioning – positive reinforcement
Nicotine is a powerful reinforcer of smoking because of its pleasurable effects on the brain's dopamine reward system.

Operant conditioning – negative reinforcement
People continue to smoke in order to avoid the unpleasant withdrawal effects of stopping, a negative reinforcer.

Classical conditioning – role of cue reactivity
Positive cues (e.g. social occasions) become associated with the pleasurable effects of nicotine (become secondary reinforcers).

Evaluation

Support from non-human animal studies
Levin et al.: Rats self-administer nicotine more frequently when given the opportunity, so nicotine is a positive reinforcer.

Research support for cue reactivity
Carter and Tiffany: Meta-analysis shows that smokers have physiological and psychological responses to smoking cues.

Real-life applications
Aversion therapy to countercondition nicotine addiction. Smith found 52% abstinence.

Gender differences
Women are more sensitive to smoking-related cues, so find it harder to give up. Or they may lack self-efficacy.

Limited explanation
Only about 50% of smokers become dependent on nicotine, suggesting that other factors involved apart from conditioning.

Explanations for gambling addiction

Learning theory

Explaining gambling addiction in terms of conditioning.

Learning theory

Vicarious reinforcement
Observing other people (including media figures) being rewarded for gambling may trigger desire for similar reinforcement.

Positive and negative reinforcement
The 'buzz' of gambling provides positive reinforcement. Escape from anxiety is a negative reinforcer. Both make gambling more likely.

Partial reinforcement
In continuous reinforcement behaviour quickly stops when rewards end. In partial reinforcement gambling persists even when it is not rewarded because uncertain which bets will pay off.

Variable reinforcement
Unpredictable pattern. Gambler is motivated to keep gambling even when rewards are absent.

Cue reactivity
Cues associated with gambling (secondary reinforcers such as the National Lottery programme on TV) can trigger arousal and craving.

Evaluation

Support from research evidence
Dickerson: High-frequency gamblers delay placing their bets until the last moment, to enhance arousal and thrill.

Lack of explanatory power
Learning theories find it harder to explain addiction to games of skill where there is a delay between placing a bet and knowing the outcome.

Individual differences
Griffiths and Delfabbro: Variations in how and why people gamble are difficult for learning theories unless cognitive element included.

Limited explanation
Conditioning processes are relatively less important at some points of the gambling cycle, e.g. how it begins in the first place.

Explains failure to stop gambling
Conditioning does not require active decision making, so can explain why gamblers fail to give up even when consciously motivated to do so.

Cognitive theory

Explaining gambling addiction in terms of distorted thinking.

Cognitive theory

Expectancy theory
Gambling addicts have irrational expectancies that the benefits of their gambling will outweigh the costs.

Cognitive biases
Related to: Skill and judgement (illusion of control), personal traits/ritual behaviours (superstitions), selective recall (forget losses), faulty perceptions (gambler's fallacy).

Research into cognitive biases
Griffiths: Used 'thinking aloud', regular gamblers think in irrational ways while they gamble (e.g. thinking of a slot machine as if it has a personality).

Self-efficacy
Gambling addicts relapse because they don't believe they are capable of abstaining for long.

Evaluation

Research support
Michalczuk et al.: Addicted gamblers show higher levels of distorted thinking and impulsivity, and prefer immediate rewards even if they are small.

Explains automatic behaviour
McCusker and Gettings: Gamblers have an automatic cognitive bias to pay attention to gambling-related information without being aware of it.

Individual differences
Cognitive biases cannot explain all differences in gambling behaviour. Personality plays a role (e.g. control motivation).

Real-life applications
Cognitive biases can be treated with CBT, may also have underlying neurochemistry which can be treated (Clark).

Methodological issues
What gambling addicts say when 'thinking aloud' may not reflect what they really think.

REDUCING ADDICTION

DRUG THERAPY

Drugs are the obvious solution to neurochemical causes.

DRUG THERAPY

Types of drug therapy
Aversives produce unpleasant consequences (e.g. severe hangover). Agonists act like substitute drugs (e.g. methadone). Antagonists block the usual effects of a drug (e.g. *naltrexone*).

Drug therapy for nicotine addiction
Nicotine replacement therapy delivers a nicotine hit without the damaging chemicals in smoke. Dose can be reduced over time to manage withdrawal.

Drug therapy for gambling addiction
No official drugs but *naltrexone* has been used in research studies and is better than placebo in reducing cravings. Opioid antagonist treatment possible.

EVALUATION

Research support
Stead *et al.*: NRT is an effective treatment for nicotine addiction with 70% still abstaining from smoking after six months.

Side effects
Side effects of treatment for gambling addiction are serious because the dose required is very high. NRT has less serious side effects. Could lead to giving up treatment.

Limited treatment
Addicts with chaotic lifestyles are not organised enough to take a drug every day, often dropping out of treatment and research.

Removal of stigma
Explaining drug addiction as a medical or biological condition helps to counter the view that it is somehow the addict's 'fault'.

Individual differences
Small genetic variations between individuals have a big impact on the effectiveness of drug treatments.

BEHAVIOURAL INTERVENTIONS

Therapies based on learning theories.

BEHAVIOURAL INTERVENTIONS

Aversion therapy
Based on classical conditioning and counterconditioning. An unpleasant state is associated with the drug of addiction.

Aversion therapy for alcohol addiction
A drug is given to promote nausea and vomiting, associated with smell and taste of alcoholic drink.
Anatabuse makes individual ill if they drink alcohol.

Aversion therapy for gambling addiction
Painful electric shocks are associated with spoken phrases related to gambling.

Covert sensitisation
A form of aversion therapy but the client imagines experiencing the aversive state rather than actually doing so.

Covert sensitisation in nicotine addiction
The therapist helps the client imagine a scene in which they are smoking and experiencing nausea and vomiting.

EVALUATION

Methodological problems with studies of aversion therapy
Effectiveness studies are poor quality, especially because they are not blinded, so researchers know who gets the therapy and the placebo.

Treatment adherence issues
Shocks and vomiting are very unpleasant and normally avoided, so patients more likely to drop out of treatment. Therefore difficult to assess treatment effectiveness.

Research support for covert sensitisation
McConaghy *et al.* found 90% of gambling addicts were gambling less one year after therapy compared with 30% success for aversion therapy.

Short-term versus long-term effectiveness
McConaghy *et al.*: Aversion therapy has more success over one month than one year.

Ethical issues
Aversion therapy is potentially dangerous and involves serious loss of dignity. Covert sensitisation is less ethically objectionable.

COGNITIVE BEHAVIOUR THERAPY

Therapy based on thinking differently and developing skills.

COGNITIVE BEHAVIOUR THERAPY

Cognitive behaviour therapy (CBT)
Aims to change faulty ways of thinking which are maladaptive.

Functional analysis
A collaborative but challenging therapist helps the client identify high-risk situations and his or her client's thinking processes.

Skills training
Learn skills, e.g. avoid situations which trigger addictive behaviours:
Cognitive correction: Distorted beliefs.
Specific skills, e.g. anger management.
Social skills, e.g. refusal skills.

EVALUATION

Research support
Petry *et al.*: High-quality study found that gamblers who had CBT sessions were gambling less than controls one year later.

Short-term versus long-term gains
Cowlishaw *et al.*: CBT is very effective in the short term but less so after more than a year, studies methodologically poor.

Lack of treatment adherence
Cuijpers *et al.*: Drop-out rates are greater in CBT than in other therapies because it is demanding. Even clients who continue take it less seriously.

Relapse prevention
CBT is good at preventing relapse because it does not see it as failure but as an opportunity for further development.

What works?
CBT uses so many different techniques that it is difficult to understand what works and what doesn't.

APPLYING THE THEORY OF PLANNED BEHAVIOUR TO ADDICTIVE BEHAVIOUR

Explains how we change behaviour we can control.

THEORY OF PLANNED BEHAVIOUR (TPB)

The theory
Ajzen: Central concept is intention.
Giving up drugs or gambling can be predicted from our intention to give them up.

Personal attitudes
The overall evaluation of the favourable and unfavourable attitudes the addicted person has towards their addiction.

Subjective norms
The addicted person's beliefs about whether the people closest to them would approve or disapprove of their addictive behaviour.

Perceived behavioural control
How much control the addicted person believes they have over their addictive behaviour. Do they think it would be easy or hard to give up their addiction?

EVALUATION

Some research support
Hagger *et al.*: Personal attitudes, subjective norms and perceived behavioural control all predicted intentions and actual reduction in drinking.

Does not explain addiction behaviour
Miller and Howell: Theory can explain how intentions are formed, but not the intention-behaviour gap (how intentions lead to behaviour change).

Short-term versus long-term changes
McEachan *et al.* meta-analysis: Change is much less likely when the time between forming the intention and attempting to make the change is longer than about five weeks.

A limited explanation
The TPB overemphasises the role of rational decision making in addiction, ignoring emotion and faulty thinking.

Methodological issues
Most research studies use self-report rather than objective measures and are correlational, preventing causal conclusions.

APPLYING PROCHASKA'S MODEL OF BEHAVIOUR CHANGE TO ADDICTIVE BEHAVIOUR

Related to readiness to change.

PROCHASKA'S SIX-STAGE MODEL

Assumptions of the model
Overcoming addiction occurs through a series of stages in a cyclical rather than linear fashion.

Six stages of behavioural change
- **Precontemplation**: Not thinking about change.
- **Contemplation**: Ready for change but no active plans.
- **Preparation**: Time for change.
- **Action**: Something concrete done in the last six months.
- **Maintenance**: Over at least six months.
- **Termination**: New behaviours now automatic.

EVALUATION

Dynamic nature of behaviour
The model recognises that overcoming an addiction is an active and continuing process, not a single event.

Contradictory research evidence
Taylor *et al.*: The model is no more effective in treating nicotine addiction than any alternative.

Arbitrary nature of stages
The dividing lines between stages are only quantitative and some can be missed.
Kraft *et al.*: Just use precontemplation and one other.

Attitude to relapse
The model takes relapse seriously and incorporates ways to deal with it by working through the stages again quickly.

Description versus prediction
The model can describe the process of overcoming addiction but is poor at predicting the factors that make success likely.

PRACTICE QUESTIONS, ANSWERS AND FEEDBACK

Question 1 Explain aversion therapy as a behavioural intervention for reducing addiction. *(4 marks)*

Morticia's answer

Aversion therapy is used to treat addiction following the principles of classical conditioning. What happens in classical conditioning is that an unconditioned stimulus is paired with an unconditioned response. A neutral stimulus then occurs alongside the unconditioned stimulus and takes on those properties so that it produces the unconditioned response, now called a conditioned response because it is a new stimulus-response link. In aversion therapy a painful stimulus is paired with the addiction so they learn a new stimulus-response to stop them doing the addictive behaviour.

Morticia clearly has a good command of the underlying theory here – the principles of classical conditioning are very well explained. However, the link to addiction is only partial. A clear example linked to a specific addiction would have been useful.

Luke's answer

Alcohol addiction is sometimes treated by giving the addict a drug that causes vomiting (an emetic). Just before they vomit the addict is given an alcoholic drink and then the drinking becomes associated with vomiting instead of pleasure.

Alternatively, the addict is given a drug that makes them vomit every time they have a drink or when taking drugs. This also leads to a new learned association.

Immediately, Luke provides us with the example that Morticia's answer lacked. There is less theoretical information here but much more focus on the question. The two forms of aversion therapy presented are subtly different.

Vladimir's answer

Aversion therapy aims to make an addict avoid their addiction by pairing it with something unpleasant (aversive). So, in the case of gambling, a person might be given electric shocks every time they say a word associated with gambling. Therefore the thoughts of gambling become associated with something unpleasant and when the person thinks of gambling they want to stop.

The basic principle of pairing an aversive stimulus with an addictive behaviour is made clear in Vladimir's answer but this is an odd example to use.

Aversion therapies sometimes use drugs to make someone feel nauseous and this is associated with, for example, alcohol or something else that is addictive such as drugs.

The second paragraph provides an example that is more typical.

There are ethical issues with such aversion therapies because you are causing a person to have a very unpleasant experience and it may not be their choice. Also the unpleasantness may mean they don't really want to continue with the therapy.

The final paragraph is more evaluative than descriptive and is not required by the question.

Question 2 Evaluate **one** explanation of gambling addiction. *(4 marks)*

Morticia's answer

Gambling addiction has been explained in terms of cognitive theory. According to this theory, the reason people gamble is because they have biased beliefs, which make them think they will win, and so they keep going. One criticism of this approach is that it is difficult to do research about what people are actually thinking, you have to rely on what they tell you and they may not be honest. On the other hand, such research is quite systematic and does seem trustworthy. For example, Griffiths uses the 'think aloud method' with gambling addicts and has shown that there are differences in the thoughts of gamblers and non-gamblers when playing on fruit machines.

The initial descriptive detail in Morticia's answer is not asked for in the question and could have been dispensed with. The rest of the answer is relevant, however, and reasonably well-expressed.

Luke's answer

One problem with explanations of gambling is that it isn't one single type of behaviour so no one explanation can explain all gambling. For example, in some types of gambling the reward comes quite a long time after the initial behaviour whereas for conditioning to take place the two things have to happen at almost the same time as in fruit machine wins.

And there are also different aspects of the addiction from when it begins to maintenance and relapse. So initiation might be explained in terms of social learning and role models, maintenance may be due to rewards (operant conditioning) and relapse may be social because your friends have all become addicts.

Luke's is an odd answer that seems more concerned with questioning the premise of the question! If we interpret the answer as an evaluation of the behaviourist explanation of gambling – even though this is not made explicit – then the points he makes are relevant.

Vladimir's answer

One explanation for nicotine addiction is brain neurochemistry. This is a good explanation because there is good supporting evidence. For example, McEvoy looked at patients with schizophrenia who were taking a drug that blocks dopamine receptors in the brain, and found that this was associated with increased smoking. This suggests that the patients were smoking to compensate for the lack of dopamine. And therefore this supports the view that nicotine addiction is related to getting a dopamine reward.

Vladimir's first paragraph is focused on the wrong type of addiction.

On the negative side the research on neurochemistry shows that a dopamine explanation is too simple because lots of neurotransmitters are involved as well as dopamine, such as GABA and serotonin. Though it may be that the dopamine reward system is the most important.

However, the second paragraph (taken on its own) does briefly present some relevant research linking the dopamine reward system to gambling. However this is very brief.

On this spread we look at some typical student answers to questions. The comments provided indicate what is good and bad in each answer. Learning how to produce effective question answers is a SKILL. Read pages 387–397 for guidance.

Question 3 Steph is taking her GCSE exams in a few weeks and is worried as she cannot seem to get around to revising. She has started to spend more and more time with her friends drinking alcohol at the local park. Steph likes her friends as they are generally seen as 'cool' by the other girls at school. Steph's friends like her because she is 'crazy' and does things on the spur of the moment. They also think it's funny that Steph has gone home drunk a couple of times and her parents (who also drink heavily) have not really said anything about it.

Using your knowledge of addiction, describe and evaluate **two or more** risk factors that could contribute to Steph's drinking. *(16 marks)*

Morticia's answer

Reading about Steph you can see that a number of risk factors are described in the scenario. First, there is stress as her exams are coming up. People who are stressed turn to alcohol and drugs for relief. Second, there is the influence of her peers. At her age, peers are one of the strongest influences on behaviour. Peers are important for establishing norms about what behaviour and attitudes are acceptable. Peers also provide opportunities for, e.g. alcohol abuse. Moreover, a particular influence is that young people often overestimate what their peers are doing and therefore they may drink even more to keep up with what they think everyone else is doing. A further risk factor described here is the family. Families also create norms about what is acceptable behaviour. And parental approval is also significant as well as the fact that having parents who drink means you are exposed to it. It may also be that the fact that parents who drink heavily may do so because it is in their genes and then Steph may have inherited these same genes. The genes would be related to dopamine probably, the reward pathway. Of course we must remember about the diathesis-stress model which is that just inheriting genes doesn't mean that you have to become addicted to alcohol or drink a lot. What the genes do is create a vulnerability and all these other factors discussed could act as triggers for a person with vulnerability. Another risk factor is personality. Certain kinds of personality are more likely to develop addiction and this is an example of an indirect genetic effect. For example, genes may predispose someone to have an antisocial personality disorder, which is associated with impulsivity. Having this kind of personality may make someone like Steph more at risk for alcohol problems.

Many explanations are very determinist because they suggest that people can't control their own behaviour. For example, having peers that drink means a person has to drink as well. People have free will. These explanations may also be culturally biased and not apply to non-Western cultures or collectivist ones where the community matters more. The research may lack ecological validity because it is not done with people who actually have addictions. The research is also often correlational so we can't say that such research shows a cause and effect, for example it might not be the peers who are creating the problem but Steph has selected those friends because she drinks.

(414 words)

A very long first paragraph here that manages to link all the information in the stem to relevant risk factors.

There is also reference to the diathesis-stress model in there and there is a hint of evaluation in the way this is used to draw attention to the other factors as possible 'stressors'.

The emphasis is clearly on the side of 'breadth' rather than 'depth' of response but this is a legitimate way to answer the question.

That said, Morticia seems not to have left sufficient space for evaluation. Some of the points, such as that related to culture, are vague and need further explanation. Others (the first and last) are well-explained.

Luke's answer

There are a number of important risk factors for addiction. I will focus on alcohol addiction as that is Steph's problem.

Let's begin with genetic explanations – as she comes from a family of heavy drinkers her drinking may be due to inherited genes. One explanation is that people inherit an inability to metabolise certain substances and this is linked to addiction. However, an important criticism of any genetic explanation is that genes do not inevitably cause addiction they simply create a vulnerability. In fact if a person is never exposed to say alcohol they can't get addicted to it so social factors are important.

Such social factors include family influences. In Steph's case, the fact that her parents do not disapprove of her drinking will increase her risk because she is not being 'punished' for her involvement with alcohol. In fact what may be most significant is the fact that Steph perceives that her parents don't disapprove and this encourages her.

An even stronger influence than parents is peers and we can see that Steph's peers sound like they may have introduced her to drinking. O'Connell suggests that peers may influence an adolescent in three ways: attitudes and norms, opportunities and misperception of how much everyone else is drinking which leads to excessive use to keep up. In addition peer influences may be more generally about rule-breaking rather than being specific to addiction.

A further risk factor described in relation to Steph is the stress of her exams. This could be an important trigger at this time. One issue with stress research and other research is that it is often correlational. For example, many studies have shown there is a strong correlation between stressful experiences and addiction-related behaviours. However, Steph's drinking could equally cause her more stress through feeling guilty or having more trouble with relationships. It is difficult to separate out the effects of one upon the other.

Steph's personality is also mentioned – that she might be a little bit crazy and this may be a further risk factor. Research does not support the idea of an addictive personality but there are personality characteristics that are linked to addiction. Butler and Montgomery suggest that people high in hostility may be more like to become addicted and other research indicates that impulsivity may be a factor, which may actually have a genetic origin. Such understanding is important for real-life applications because if we want to help Steph, we need to look at the risk factors that can be changed, such as peer-pressure resistance training. If she is born with certain vulnerabilities such interventions might be useful.

(436 words)

All three skills are demonstrated by Luke here: description, evaluation and brief application to the stem.

In paragraph 3 there is more detailed application and another relevant explanation.

A further applied explanation is introduced in paragraph 4 and there is evaluative comment and use of evidence.

This is followed by two further excellent paragraphs that follow a similar pattern to those previously: relevant explanation is identified, described, linked to stem and evaluated.

MULTIPLE-CHOICE QUESTIONS

Describing addiction and risk factors in the development of addiction

1. Psychological dependence ...
(a) Rarely leads to habitual use of addictive drugs.
(b) Increases the body's level of arousal.
(c) Is a compulsion to experience the effects of a drug.
(d) Forms even when taking a drug is not followed by a reward.

2. In relation to addiction, tolerance refers to ...
(a) Taking a drug in order to avoid unpleasant withdrawal effects.
(b) Taking more of a drug to get the usual effects.
(c) Symptoms that appear when the addicted person stops taking a drug.
(d) Continuing to take a drug until it becomes a habit.

3. One way in which a genetic vulnerability can be a risk factor for addiction is ...
(a) Friends can provide access to drugs.
(b) Psychosocial factors determine whether someone takes a drug.
(c) Genes determine the number of D2 receptors in the brain.
(d) Some life events are stressful.

4. The best example of an indirect effect of genetic vulnerability on addiction is ...
(a) How much self-control you have over your behaviour.
(b) The amount of stress you are experiencing.
(c) Expression of the CYP2A6 enzyme.
(d) Proportion of dopamine receptors in the brain.

Risk factors in the development of addiction (continued)

1. In terms of personality, the most consistent risk factor for addiction is ...
(a) Hostility.
(b) Extraversion.
(c) Impulsivity.
(d) Neuroticism.

2. The most important family influence on risk of addiction is ...
(a) Lack of communication between parents.
(b) Traumatic childhood experiences.
(c) How much parents are believed to approve of drugs.
(d) Parental monitoring of their child's behaviour.

3. Peers influence an adolescent's risk of addiction mainly because ...
(a) They use threats of violence to enforce antisocial behaviour.
(b) They encourage a rule-breaking attitude towards life in general.
(c) They are often genetically related.
(d) Relationships with friends are a major source of stress.

4. Risk factors generally influence addiction because ...
(a) They cause it.
(b) One factor is nearly always all it takes to trigger addiction.
(c) Addiction is inevitable if enough risk factors are present.
(d) They interact with each other to make addiction more likely.

Explanations for nicotine addiction: Brain neurochemistry

1. The desensitisation hypothesis states that ...
(a) Nicotine has little effect on the dopamine reward system.
(b) Nicotinic receptors shut down temporarily after stimulation.
(c) The neurochemistry of nicotine addiction is completely different from other drug addictions.
(d) Nicotinic receptors are continually being activated.

2. The nicotine regulation model ...
(a) Explains how nicotine addiction is maintained.
(b) Cannot explain why the first cigarette of the day is so pleasurable.
(c) Cannot explain how tolerance to nicotine develops over time.
(d) Claims that withdrawal effects play no role in addiction.

3. Many patients with schizophrenia smoke heavily because ...
(a) It is a symptom of their illness.
(b) Nicotine overcomes the dopamine-blocking effects of their medication.
(c) They always have done.
(d) It reduces the side effects of their medication.

4. Explaining nicotine addiction in terms of dopamine is inadequate because ...
(a) Therapy targeting the dopamine reward system does not work.
(b) Many people with schizophrenia smoke as self-medication.
(c) Research shows dopamine is not that important.
(d) Other neurotransmitters are involved in nicotine addiction.

Explanations for nicotine addiction: Learning theory

1. Smoking to ward off an unpleasant withdrawal syndrome indicates ...
(a) Secondary reinforcement.
(b) Positive reinforcement.
(c) Classical conditioning.
(d) Negative reinforcement.

2. Cue reactivity occurs through a process of ...
(a) Operant conditioning.
(b) Negative reinforcement.
(c) Classical conditioning.
(d) Reward and punishment.

3. When a smoker is presented with images of smoking-related cues ...
(a) They experience an unpleasant aversive reaction.
(b) Physiological arousal increases and they crave a cigarette.
(c) They tend to ignore them.
(d) They take fewer 'drags' on a cigarette.

4. Counterconditioning works by ...
(a) Pairing smoking with a pleasurable stimulus.
(b) Associating smoking with relief from unpleasant cravings.
(c) Associating the effects of nicotine with an electric shock.
(d) Associating smoking-related cues with the effects of nicotine.

Explanations for gambling addiction: Learning theory

1. In a variable reinforcement schedule ...
(a) Reinforcement arrives after an unpredictable number of responses.
(b) Reinforcement arrives after a fixed proportion of responses.
(c) Learning takes place quickly but is persistent.
(d) Learning is extinguished relatively easily.

2. Cue reactivity is a good explanation of how ...
(a) A gambling addiction starts.
(b) Gambling addicts decide to stop gambling.
(c) Addicts relapse into gambling after giving it up.
(d) Males and females differ in their gambling behaviour.

3. Theories based on conditioning find it difficult to explain ...
(a) Addiction to games involving skill.
(b) Addiction to games where the outcome is known soon after a bet is placed.
(c) Addiction to games where the addict has no control.
(d) Why addicts often place their bets at the last moment.

4. Learning theory cannot explain all gambling addiction because ...
(a) Conditioning processes work the same way in everyone.
(b) Gambling cues produce similar cravings in all gambling addicts.
(c) Cue reactivity is not a valid explanation of gambling.
(d) Individuals differ in their responses to identical stimuli.

Explanations for gambling addiction: Cognitive theory

1. The 'gambler's fallacy' refers to ...
(a) Believing you are skilled at games of chance.
(b) Thinking that some numbers are 'lucky'.
(c) Remembering wins but ignoring losses.
(d) Believing that the next gamble will bring a losing streak to an end.

2. Compared with infrequent gamblers, regular gamblers are more likely to ...
(a) Win their bets.
(b) Underestimate their gambling skills.
(c) Think about a slot machine as if it has a personality.
(d) Think about chance-related events in a rational way.

3. Research suggests that gambling addicts differ from occasional gamblers because they ...
(a) Are less impulsive.
(b) Plan gambles carefully and logically whereas occasional gamblers don't.
(c) Prefer smaller immediate rewards.
(d) Can stop placing bets at any time.

4. The cognitive theory of gambling addiction does not take into account ...
(a) The gambler's illusion of control over random events.
(b) Personality factors.
(c) Irrational beliefs about chance.
(d) The gambler's various superstitions about gambling.

Reducing addiction: Drug therapy

1. Antagonists treat addiction by . . .

(a) Mimicking the effects of the drug of dependence.

(b) Pairing the effects of drugs with nausea and vomiting.

(c) Blocking receptors and inhibiting the usual effects.

(d) Creating extreme sensitivity to an addictive drug.

2. A significant advantage of nicotine replacement therapy is . . .

(a) The nicotine operates in the brain in a different way to when the addict smokes.

(b) It can be used for several years with no negative effects.

(c) The nicotine dose can be reduced over time.

(d) Different types of drug therapy are all equally effective.

3. Side effects of drug therapy are a problem because . . .

(a) The patient might give up the therapy to avoid them.

(b) They are usually completely unpredictable.

(c) They affect everyone who goes through drug therapy.

(d) They cause many deaths.

4. Some drug treatments are unsuitable for . . .

(a) People who have been addicted for several years.

(b) Addicts with chaotic and disorganised lifestyles.

(c) Highly motivated addicts, because no effort is needed.

(d) People who want the convenience of taking one dose per day.

Reducing addiction: Behavioural interventions

1. Aversion therapy and covert sensitisation are both based on . . .

(a) Operant conditioning.

(b) Vicarious reinforcement.

(c) Classical conditioning.

(d) Observational learning.

2. In covert sensitisation, the addicted client . . .

(a) Is given electric shocks.

(b) Changes their ways of thinking about their addiction.

(c) Observes someone modelling non-addictive behaviours.

(d) Imagines vomiting after taking their drug of dependence.

3. Many studies of therapy effectiveness are not blinded, which means . . .

(a) The studies' procedures are carefully controlled.

(b) Therapies are more effective than they appear.

(c) The researchers know who is in treatment and placebo groups.

(d) Valid comparisons can be made between different therapies.

4. Treatment adherence is an issue with aversion therapy because . . .

(a) It means the therapy is not challenging enough.

(b) It makes research into effectiveness invalid.

(c) It means studies underestimate the effectiveness of the therapy.

(d) There is no pattern to who drops out and who carries on.

Reducing addiction: Cognitive behaviour therapy

1. Functional analysis in CBT involves the client . . .

(a) Identifying high-risk situations.

(b) Practising anger management techniques.

(c) Observing the therapist modelling a new skill.

(d) 'Thinking aloud' when imagining their addictive behaviour.

2. Skills training in CBT mostly involves . . .

(a) The therapist working out what triggers the client's cravings.

(b) The therapist challenging the client's distorted thinking.

(c) The client learning techniques to cope with high-risk situations.

(d) The client and therapist identifying which skills the client lacks.

3. Effectiveness studies of CBT are especially valid if . . .

(a) Two forms of therapy are compared.

(b) Participants are randomly allocated to the groups.

(c) The researcher is also the therapist.

(d) People with different severities of addiction are compared.

4. Drop-out rates for CBT are high because . . .

(a) The therapy is brief.

(b) The crisis that forced the client into therapy often recedes.

(c) Nearly all clients take homework tasks seriously.

(d) The therapy is not as challenging as clients expect.

Applying the theory of planned behaviour to addictive behaviour

1. The basic assumption of the theory of planned behaviour is . . .

(a) Addiction can be overcome by controlling automatic behaviour.

(b) Intention is the strongest predictor of ending an addiction.

(c) To beat addiction, you have to ignore what other people think.

(d) It doesn't matter what the addict personally thinks about drugs.

2. Addictive behaviour can be directly influenced by . . .

(a) Perceived behavioural control.

(b) Subjective norms.

(c) Personal attitudes.

(d) Automatic thoughts.

3. 'Subjective norms' in the TPB refers to . . .

(a) The addict's beliefs about what people closest to them think about their addiction.

(b) How difficult the addict believes it is for them to abstain.

(c) The balance of the addict's favourable and unfavourable attitudes.

(d) How much effort the addicted person plans to make.

4. The TPB has most difficulty in explaining . . .

(a) How personal attitudes affect intention to change.

(b) Why some people overcome addiction but others don't.

(c) How intentions to change lead to actual changes.

(d) How subjective norms affect intentions to give up drugs.

Applying Prochaska's model of behaviour change to addictive behaviour

1. In the preparation stage of the model, the client is . . .

(a) Thinking seriously about tackling their addiction.

(b) Ready to change their behaviour in the next month.

(c) Working hard to avoid relapsing into addiction.

(d) Developing the skills needed to cope with stress and anxiety.

2. The best way to help someone in the contemplation stage is to . . .

(a) Offer them an eight-session course of CBT.

(b) Praise them for beating their addiction.

(c) Focus on avoiding relapse.

(d) Get them to see how the benefits of overcoming their addiction outweigh the costs.

3. The six-stage model recognises that . . .

(a) People work through the stages of change at the same rate.

(b) Overcoming addiction is a dynamic process over time.

(c) CBT is effective at every stage of the process.

(d) An addict is 'recovered' when they stop taking drugs.

4. According to critics, the stages in the model are . . .

(a) Completed by the addicted person in a strict order one at a time.

(b) All essential for successfully overcoming an addiction.

(c) Divided up arbitrarily.

(d) All qualitatively different from each other.

MCQ answers

Describing addiction and risk factors in the development of addiction 1c, 2b, 3c, 4a

Risk factors in the development of addiction (continued) 1c, 2c, 3b, 4d

Explanations for nicotine addiction: Brain neurochemistry 1b, 2a, 3b, 4d

Explanations for nicotine addiction: Learning theory 1d, 2c, 3b, 4c

Explanations for gambling addiction: Learning theory 1a, 2c, 3a, 4d

Explanations for gambling addiction: Cognitive theory 1d, 2c, 3c, 4b

Reducing addiction: Drug therapy 1c, 2c, 3a, 4b

Reducing addiction: Behavioural interventions 1c, 2d, 3c, 4b

Reducing addiction: Cognitive behaviour therapy 1a, 2c, 3b, 4b

Applying the theory of planned behaviour to addictive behaviour 1b, 2a, 3a, 4c

Applying Prochaska's model of behaviour change to addictive behaviour 1b, 2d, 3b, 4c

REFERENCES

A full set of references are available for download from the Illuminate Publishing website.
Please visit www.illuminatepublishing.com/psychreferences

Chapter 1

Bandura, A. (1977). Self-efficacy: Toward a unifying theory of behavioural change. *Psychological Review, 84,* 191–215. ▶ page **13**

Bandura, A. and Walters, R. H. (1963). *Social Learning and Personality Development*. New York: Holt, Rinehart and Winston. ▶ page **12**

Bandura, A., Ross, D. and Ross, S. (1961). Transmission of aggression through imitation of aggressive role models. *Journal of Abnormal and Social Psychology, 63,* 575–582. ▶ page **12**

Bugelski, B. R. and Alampay, D. A. (1962). The role of frequency in developing perceptual sets. *Canadian Journal of Psychology, 15,* 205–211. ▶ page **15**

Cumberbatch, G., Wood, G. and Littlejohns, V. (2001). *Television: The Public's view 2000*. London: ITC. ▶ page **13**

Skinner, B. F. (1953). *Science and Human Behaviour*. New York: MacMillan. ▶ pages **9, 10**

Stein, C. J. and Test, M. A. (1980) Alternative to mental hospital treatment program and clinical evaluation. *Archives of General Psychology, 37,* 392–397. ▶ page **23**

Watson, J. B. (1913). Psychology as the Behaviourist views it. *Psychological Review, 20,* 158–177. ▶ pages **9, 10**

Wong, D. (2008). *Five creepy ways video games are trying to get you addicted*: http://www.cracked.com/article_18461_5-creepy-ways-video-games-are-trying-to-get-you-addicted.html [Accessed July 2014] ▶ page **11**

Chapter 2

Aschoff, J. and Wever, R. A. (1976). Human circadian rhythms: a multioscillator system. *Federation Proceedings, 35,* 2326–2332. ▶ page **46**

Baraldo, M. (2008). The influence of circadian rhythms on the kinetics of drugs in humans. *Expert Opinion Drug Metabolism and Toxicology, 4,* 175–192 ▶ page **47**

Bezzola, L., Merillat, S. and Jancke, L. (2012). The effect of leisure activity golf practice on motor imagery: and fMRI study in middle adulthood. *Frontiers in Human Neuroscience, 6,* 67. ▶ page **41**

Boivin, D. B., Duffy, J. F., Kronauer, R. E., and Czeisler, C. A. (1996). Dose-response relationships for resetting of human circadian clock by light. *Nature, 379,* 540–542. ▶ page **47**

Campbell, S. S. and Murphy, P. J. (1998). Extraocular circadian phototransduction in humans. *Science, 279,* 396–399. ▶ page **50**

Czeisler, C. A., Duffy, J. F. and Shanahan, T. L. (1999). Stability, precision, and near-24-hour period of the human circadian pacemaker. *Science, 25,* 2177–2181. ▶ page **47**

Damiola, F., Le Minh, N., Preitner, N., Kornmann, B., Fleury-Olelg, F. and Schibler, U. (2000). Restricted feeding uncouples circadian oscillators in peripheral tissues from the central pacemaker in the suprachiasmatic nucleus. *Genes and Development, 14,* 2950–2961. ▶ page **51**

DeCoursey, P. J., Walker, J. K. and Smith, S. A. (2000). A circadian pacemaker in free-living chipmunks: essential for survival? *Journal of Comparative Physiology, 186,* 169–180. ▶ page **50**

Dement, W. and Kleitman, N. (1995). The relation of eye movements during sleep to dream activity: An objective method for the study of dreaming. *Journal of Experimental Psychology, 53,* 339–346. ▶ page **49**

Doidge, N. (2007). *The Brain That Changes Itself: Stories of Personal Triumph from the Frontiers of [...]* New York: Penguin Books. ▶ page **40**

Dougherty, D. D., Baer, L., Cosgrove, G. R., Cassem, E. H., Price, B. H., Nierenberg, A. A., *et al.* (2002). Prospective long-term follow-up of 44 patients who received cingulotomy for treatment-refractory obsessive-compulsive disorder. *American Journal of Psychiatry, 159,* 269–275. ▶ page **39**

Draganski, B., Gaser, C., Kemperman, G., Kuhn, H. G., Winkler, J., Buchel, C. and May, A. (2006). Temporal and spatial dynamics of brain structure changes during extensive training. *The Journal of Neuroscience, 26(23),* 6314–6317. ▶ page **40**

Duffy J. F., Rimmer D. W. and Czeisler C. A. (2001). Association of intrinsic circadian period with morningness–eveningness, usual wake time, and circadian phase. *Behavioural Neuroscience, 115,* 895–899. ▶ page **47**

Eastman, C., Young, M. A., Fogg, L. F. and Liu, L. (a placebo and controlled trial 1998). Bright light treatment of winter depression: a placebo and controlled trial. *Archive of General Psychiatry, 55,* 883–889. ▶ page **49**

Ericsson, A., Krampe, R. and Tesch-Romer, C. (1993). The role of deliberate practice in the acquisition of expert performance. *Psychological Review, 100(3),* 363–406. ▶ page **49**

Folkard, S., Hulme, K. I., Minors, D. S., Waterhouse, J. M. and Watson, F. L. (1985). Independence of the circadian rhythm in alertness from the sleep/wake cycle. *Nature, 313,* 678–679. ▶ page **46**

Folkard, S., Monk, T. H., Badbry, R. and Rosenthall, J. (1977). Time of day effects in school children's immediate and delayed recall of meaningful material. *British Journal of Psychology, 68(1),* 45–50. ▶ page **46**

Gopnik, A., Meltzoff, A. N. and Kuhl, P. K. (1999). *The Scientist in the Crib: Minds, Brains and How Children Learn*. New York: William Morrow and Co. ▶ page **40**

Gupta, S. (1991). Effects of time of day and personality on intelligence test scores. *Personality & Individual Differences, 12 (11),* 1227–1231. ▶ page **46**

Gurton, A. http://anniegurton.com/ ▶ page **41**

Holzel, B. K., Carmody, J., Vangel, M., Congleton, C., Yerramsetti, S. M., Gard, T. and Lazar, S. W. (2011). Mindfulness practice leads to increases in regional grey matter density. *Psychiatry Research, 191,* 36–43. ▶ page **41**

Hubel, D. H. and Wiesel, T. N. (1963). Receptive fields of cells in striate cortex of very young, visually inexperienced kittens. *Journal of Neurophysiology, 26,* 994–1002. ▶ page **41**

Kleitman, N. (1969). Brain rest activity cycle in relation to sleep and wakefulness in Kales, A. *Sleep, Physiology and Pathology*. Philadelphia: Lippincott, 33–38. ▶ page **49**

Knutsson, A. (2003). Health disorders of shiftworkers. *Journal of Occupational Medicine, 53,* 103–108. ▶ page **47**

Lashley, K. S. (1950). In search of the engram. *Society of Experimental Biology Symposium 4,* 454–482. ▶ page **39**

Lazar, S. W., Kerr, C. E., Wasserman, R. H., Gray, J. R., Greve, D. N., Treadway, M. T., McGarvey, M., Quinn, B. T., Dusek, J. A., Benson, H., Rauch, S. L., Moore, C. I. and Fischl, B. (2005). Meditation experience is associated with increased cortical thickness. *Neuroreport, 16,* 1893–1897. ▶ page **41**

Maguire, E. A., Gadian, D. G., Johnsrude, I. S., Good, C. D., Ashburner, J., Frackowiak, R. S. J. and Frith, C. D. (2000). Navigation-related structural change in the hippocampi of taxi drivers. *Proceedings of the National Academy of Sciences, 91(6),* 2016–2020. ▶ page **40**

Manning J. T., Taylor, R. P. and Taylor, B. (2001). Second to fourth digit ratio and male ability in sport: [...]

McClintock, M. K. (1998). Whither synchrony? *Annual Review of S[...]* 77–95. ▶ page **48**

Mechelli, A., Crinion, J. T., Noppen[...] Ashburner, J., Frackowski, R. S.[...] Neurolinguistics: structural plast[...] brain. *Nature, 431,* 757. ▶ page [...]

Medina, K. L., Nagel, B. J., Park, A.[...] and Tapert, S. F. (2007). Depress[...] adolescence: associations with w[...] and marijuana use. *Journal of Ch[...] Psychiatry and Allied Disciplines,* 592–600. ▶ page **41**

Miles, L. E., Raynal, D. M. and Wilson[...] man living in normal society has [...] 24.9 hours. *Science, 198,* 421–42[...]

Petersen, S. E., Fox, P. T., Posner, M. I[...] Raichle, M. E. (1988). Positron em[...] studies of the cortical anatomy of[...] processing. *Nature, 331,* 585–58[...]

Pucetti, R. (1977). Sperry on conscio[...] appreciation. *Journal of Medicine[...]* 127–146. ▶ page **43**

Ralph, M. R., Foster, R. G., Davis, F. C.[...] M. (1990). Transplanted suprachia[...] determines circadian period. *Scien[...]* 975–978. ▶ page **50**

Ramachandran, V. S. and Hirstein, W.[...] of phantom limbs: the D. O. Hebb [...] 1603–1630. ▶ page **41**

Schank, J. C. (2004). Avoiding synchro[...] of female mate choice. *Nonlinear D[...] Psychology, and Life Sciences, 8,* 14[...]

Schneider, E. B., Sur, S. and Stevens, R.[...] Functional recovery after moderate[...] brain injury. *American Journal of Ne[...]* 1636–1642. ▶ page **41**

Sperry, R. W. (1968). Hemisphere deco[...] unity in consciousness. *American Ps[...]* 723–733. ▶ page **42**

Stern, K. and McClintock, M. K. (1998)[...] of ovulation by human pheromones[...] (6672), 177–179. ▶ page **49**

Tang, Y. Y., Lu, Q., Fan, M., Yang, Y., an[...] M. I. (2012). Mechanisms of white m[...] induced by meditation. *Proceedings[...] Academy of Sciences of the United S[...] America, 109,* 1–5. ▶ page **41**

Trevathan, W. R., Burleson, M. H. and G[...] (1993). No evidence for menstrual syn[...] lesbian couples. *Psychoneuroendocri[...]* 425–435. ▶ page **49**

Tulving, E., Kapur, S., Craik, F. I. M., Mosc[...] and Houle, S. (1994). Hemispheric enc[...] retrieval asymmetry in episodic memo[...] emission tomography findings. *Procee[...] National Academy of Sciences of the U[...] America, 91(6),* 2016–2020. ▶ page **39**

Chapter 3

Feyerabend, P. K. (1975). *Against Method.[...] Anarchist Theory of Knowledge*. Londo[...] Books. ▶ page **82**

Furnham, A., and Farragher, E. (2000). A c[...] content analysis of sex-role stereotypin[...] advertisements: A comparison between[...] and New Zealand. *Journal of Broadcast[...] Electronic Media, 44,* 415–436. ▶ page [...]

Kuhn, T. S. (1962). *The Structure of Scientifi[...] Revolutions*. Chicago: University of Chic[...] Press. ▶ page **82**

Matthews, N., Speers, L. and Ball, J. (2012[...] banter: Sex, love, and the bathroom wal[...] *Journal of Human Sexuality, 15.* ▶ page [...]

QUESTION STYLES

At A level you may have multiple-choice, short-answer and/or extended writing/essay questions. How do you know how to answer these? There are clues:

- The command word (see words at bottom right)
- The number of marks
- Extra information in the question

Multiple-choice questions

Questions that require you to select the correct answer. For example:

Which of the statements below best describes the psychodynamic approach?

A All behaviour is learned. ☐

B Unconscious desires influence behaviour. ☐

C Self-concepts are important in motivating behaviour, such as self-actualisation. ☐

Short-answer questions

Such questions may require description, application and/or evaluation. These questions are worth 8 marks or less.

Short answer questions involving description

Explain what is meant by an *exogenous zeitgeber*. (2 marks)

Identify and outline **two** key concepts of the humanistic approach. (4 marks)

Outline Bowlby's theory of attachment. (4 marks)

Describe the role of peer review. (6 marks)

Short answer questions with evaluate

Briefly evaluate the multi-store model of memory. (4 marks)

Explain **one** limitation of adopting a determinist approach in psychology. (3 marks)

Distinguish between alpha bias and beta bias in psychological research. (4 marks)

Discuss **two** limitations of the cognitive approach. (6 marks)

Short answer questions with describe and evaluate

Outline and evaluate gender bias in psychology. (4 marks)

Briefly discuss the benefits of adopting a reductionist approach to the study of human behaviour. (6 marks)

Outline and evaluate split-brain research. (8 marks)

Examples of application questions are shown on page 390.

Longer essay questions

At A level the maximum number of marks for any extended writing question is 16. All A level extended writing/essay questions will have more marks for the evaluation than for the description.

Describe and evaluate the nomothetic approach to explaining behaviour. (10 marks)

Discuss research in which types of long term memory have been investigated. (12 marks)

Describe and evaluate ethical implications of research studies and/or theories. Refer to social sensitivity in your answer. (16 marks)

Discuss research on biological rhythms. (16 marks)

Command words

The following command words are used in questions:

Analyse	Separate information into components and identify their characteristics.
Calculate	Work out the value of something.
Choose	Select from a range of alternatives.
Comment	Present an informed opinion.
Compare	Identify similarities and/or differences.
Complete	Finish a task by adding to given information.
Consider	Review and respond to given information.
Describe	Set out characteristics.
Design	Set out how something will be done.
Discuss	Present key points.
Distinguish	Explain ways in which two things differ. Provide detail of characteristics that enable a person to know the difference between.
Draw	Produce a diagram.
Evaluate	Judge from available evidence.
Explain	Set out purposes or reasons.
Give	Produce an answer from recall or from given information.
Identify	Name or otherwise characterise.
Justify	Provide reasons, reasoned argument to support, possibly provide evidence.
Label	Provide appropriate names on a diagram.
Name	Identify using a recognised technical term.
Outline	Set out main characteristics.
Select	Choose or pick out from alternatives.
State	Express in clear terms.
Suggest	Present a possible case/solution.
What is meant by	Give a definition.
Which is	Select from alternatives.
Write	Provide information in verbatim form.

UNDERSTANDING DESCRIPTION (AO1)

There are three main skills that you need to develop:

- **Description** of psychological knowledge, assessment objective 1 – aka AO1.
- **Application** of psychological knowledge (AO2).
- **Evaluation** of psychological knowledge (AO3).

When we say 'psychological knowledge' we are referring to the concepts, research studies, therapies and theories/explanations used and developed by psychologists.

This spread starts by looking at *description skills*. What is it you have to do when you *describe* something?

Think of describing an orange. You might say – it is round and orange – which is true but that is a rather *limited* description.

A better description would include more *detail* – The skin is a little squishy and pockmarked. The remains of the green stalk are set in a dimple.

To do well you need to grasp this concept of *detail*.

Describing concepts

One of the concepts we have explained in this book is *alpha bias*.

This is what we have written on page 94 in relation to alpha bias:

> Psychological theories that suggest there are real and enduring differences between men and women. These may enhance or undervalue members of either sex, but typically undervalue females.

If you were asked to **outline** this concept you might write:

> *'Alpha bias refers to real and enduring differences.'*

> This is a *basic* answer.

A good answer needs to be accurate, detailed and have clarity and coherence.

> *'Alpha bias occurs when psychological theories suggest there are real and enduring differences between men and women. These typically undervalue females.'*

If you were asked to **explain** this concept you might include an example:

> *'... for example, the sociobiological theory of relationship formation suggests that sexual promiscuity in males is genetically determined whilst females who engage in the same behaviour are regarded as going against their 'nature' - an alpha bias.'*

Describing research studies

Psychology is a science and therefore psychologists seek evidence to support their views. This evidence comes from research studies.

You should be able to describe such studies, for example:

> Outline **one** study in which circadian rhythms have been investigated. In your answer, refer to what the psychologist(s) did and what was found.

It is always wise to provide details of what the researcher(s) did (the procedure) and what was found (the findings).

A good answer should be accurate, detailed and have clarity and coherence.

A special note about research studies

The convention is always to provide the name of the first researcher and the date of the research study. When writing an answer you do not have to include names but it does provide useful detail. It also ensures that the reader knows which study you are describing – otherwise you might not perform so well because your answer does not appear to apply to a specific study.

> Don't worry too much about exact dates.

Another special note about research studies

Research studies may also be used as evaluation – when they are being used in this way you will not be credited for details of the procedure. More about this on page 391.

Timing

On A level exams, there are 96 marks for each paper and 120 minutes.

> This gives you a sense of how much time you should spend on each exam question.

> Don't forget that this timing is not just about writing but you should spend time thinking too.

Key studies

There are some studies in this book which we have called 'key studies' because we feel they are particularly important. For these studies we have included a number of details of what the researcher(s) did (procedures) and what they found.

A useful tip

Description questions use these command words:

Outline

Describe

Explain

Identify

Name

State

Every time you make a point, make sure you also explain it.

Describing theories/ explanations

There is probably more scope for description when asked about theories/ explanations. Such questions look like this:

Explain the process of synaptic transmission. (4 marks)

Describe the cognitive approach in psychology. (6 marks)

In these questions, as with all other questions, there is no *one* answer. A good answer is one that is **accurate**, **detailed** and **has clarity** and **coherence**.

In addition, for longer answer questions **organisation** and **use of specialist terminology** are important.

The mark for any answer is determined by what *descriptors* (in the table below) best represent what a student has written (bearing in mind the amount of time available to write your answer). The appropriate *level* can then be determined.

A student does not have to fulfill *all* the criteria in a particular level – it is the level that best describes the answer.

Once the level is identified, the mark is determined by considering whether the assessor is tempted by the level above or below.

AO1 Mark scheme

In this mark scheme you can see the key descriptors that we identified above.

Level	Marks	Description
3	5–6	Knowledge is accurate and generally well detailed. The answer is clear and coherent. Specialist terminology is used effectively.
2	3–4	Knowledge is evident. There are some inaccuracies. The answer is mostly clear and coherent. There is some appropriate use of specialist terminology.
1	1–2	Knowledge is limited and lacks detail. The answer lacks clarity, accuracy and organisation in places. Specialist terminology is either absent or inappropriately used.
	0	No relevant content.

The mark scheme is presented as an illustration of the AQA mark scheme. Always check the AQA website for the latest version of mark schemes as these may have been amended.

Research

If asked to 'Describe research related to conformity' then you can either describe research studies or concepts or theories.

Concepts and theories are derived from the research process and therefore constitute research.

What do these terms mean?

What is accuracy?

Being correct. You are not *necessarily* penalised for inaccuracy but you should avoid muddled or confused answers. Aim to present material that is correct.

What is detail?

Providing specific pieces of information. This does not always mean writing lots. Instead it means including the small pieces of information that really bring your answer into focus. For example:

Internalisation is when a person changes their opinions in their own mind.

Internalisation is when a person changes their private as well as public opinions.

The second answer is more detailed but not much longer.

What is organisation?

You know what an organised bedroom looks like. No doubt some of you do not have very organised bedrooms and often have to search high and low to find things. Teachers reading student answers often feel like this.

Put the information in your answer so that each point follows the previous one in a systematic way rather than just dumping everything you know onto the page – a teacher can see the mess.

In longer answer questions it is important to have a plan and a structure (see page 396).

What are clarity and coherence?

One of the major issues for people who read what you write is that it doesn't always make sense. Lack of clarity is when you don't quite understand what the person is trying to say.

One useful way to ensure clarity (and coherence) is to always try to explain what you have just written, for example using the phrase 'in other words' to make your meaning clear:

Internalisation is when a person changes their private as well as public opinions. <u>In other words</u> they actually believe the views they are expressing.

What is specialist terminology?

This is linked to 'detail' – using psychologists' specialist terms provides specific information for your answers.

What are these specialist terms? They are the vocabulary used by psychologists for their concepts and theories, such as the term *identification*.

Specialist terms may be words that are used in ordinary English but they have been given a specific meaning in psychology – like *computer model* or *social sensitivity*.

Or they may be terms that are new to you, such as *zeitgeber* or *parametric*. Get used to using these.

UNDERSTANDING APPLICATION (AO2)

We will now move on to the second skill, *application skills*.

The trick of the application questions is that you are required to *apply* what you have learned about psychological concepts, studies and theories – to a **scenario**.

Imagine the following scenario …

> *… it is a dark night, a thin sliver of moon and ink black clouds, the wind is starting to get stronger. You walk home down a street with no lights and suddenly …*

A scenario is a scene – it's context. You now have a chance to put your psychology into action. This kind of question is intended to be something that tests your real understanding of psychology.

You should become brilliant at this because we have supplied lots and lots of practice throughout this book.

Wrong sort of dark night! A different scenario altogether …

 **Concepts**

In Chapter 2 we discuss ways of investigating the brain.

> A team of neuroscientists want to know whether the brain areas that are active when someone is lying can be identified from brain scans. They have been given funding from an American company who are keen to develop technology that could be used as evidence to show whether defendants are, or are not, telling the truth in court cases. The neuroscientists have decided to use fMRI scans as part of their research to see whether lying is localised in the brain.
>
> Explain how fMRI could be used to investigate whether lying is localised in the brain. *(6 marks)*

The description of the event is the 'scenario' (also sometimes referred to as the 'stem'). It provides a context for you to answer the question. When doing this you must include:

1. **CONCEPT** You must describe how fMRI works.

2. **CONTEXT** You must relate your description to the specific issue of how fMRI might be used to identify areas of the brain that could be active when someone is lying.

Some scenarios (and questions) are shorter. For example, in Chapter 13 we discuss addiction.

> Trevor is long-term heavy smoker. Explain how Trevor's nicotine addiction could be treated using aversion therapy. *(4 marks)*

1. **CONTEXT** You must describe how aversion therapy works.

2. **CONCEPT** You must relate your description to the specific issue of how aversion therapy could be used to treat Trevor's addiction to nicotine.

AO2 Mark scheme

These are the levels that may be used when marking an application question. Identify the key descriptors.

Level	Marks	Description
3	5–6	Knowledge related to psychological topic is clear and generally well detailed. Application is mostly clear and effective. The answer is generally coherent with appropriate use of terminology.
2	3–4	Knowledge is evident. There is some effective application. The answer lacks clarity in places. Terminology is used appropriately on occasions.
1	1–2	Knowledge is limited. Application is either absent or inappropriate. The answer as a whole lacks clarity and has inaccuracies. Terminology is either absent or inappropriately used.
	0	No relevant content

 **Methods**

A minimum of 25% of your exam questions will assess skills in relation to research methods. These questions are mainly application questions that begin with a scenario as shown below:

> A psychologist wanted to investigate the memory of older and younger children. He tested memory by giving the children a list of 50 words to memorise.
>
> a) Explain why this study would be considered to be a quasi-experiment. *(2 marks)*
>
> b) Write a suitable hypothesis for this study. *(2 marks)*
>
> c) The research found that the mean score for older children was 20.3 and for younger children was 15.7. What would you conclude from this? *(1 mark)*
>
> d) The mean scores are given to 1 decimal place. Explain what this means. *(1 mark)*

The description of the research study is the scenario. It again provides the context for your answer.

For example, when studying research methods you will learn about quasi-experiments. You now use that knowledge in the context of this research study.

In the case of question a) above this is likely to consist of:

- 1 mark for a correct answer.

- 2 marks for a correct answer with some extra detail, as appropriate.

There are marked examples on pages 88–89.

The mark scheme is presented as an illustration of the AQA mark scheme. Always check the AQA website for the latest version of mark schemes as these may have been amended.

Mathematical content for A level

A minimum of 10% of marks across the whole qualification will involve mathematical content. This 10% is included in the total 25% (or more) for research methods questions.

Some of the mathematical content requires the use of a calculator, which is allowed in the exam. In the specification it states that calculations of the mean, median, mode and range may be required, as well as percentages, fractions and ratios. You may also be asked to apply the Sign Test to a set of data and calculate the statistic.

Other research methods questions

Many research methods questions are application. But not all.

Description

Some research methods questions are just description. For example:

Explain what is meant by a volunteer sample. (2 marks)

If the question said 'Explain how you would collect a volunteer sample in this study' then it would be application.

Evaluation

Some research methods questions are evaluation. For example:

*Give **one** strength of using a volunteer sample. (2 marks)*

If the question said 'Give **one** strength of using a volunteer sample in this study' then it would be application.

Mathematical content

Some research methods questions include mathematical content – see right. All of this content is covered in the Year 1 book as part of the research methods chapter and in Chapter 3 of this book.

Our 'Apply it – methods' questions throughout this book give you further practice. There is a special focus on mathematical content in the questions on each 'Practical Corner' spread.

Remember:

Concept Context

or

Context Concept

	Concepts	Tick here when you are confident you understand this concept
Arithmetic and numerical computation	Recognise and use expressions in decimal and standard form.	
	Use ratios, fractions and percentages.	
	Estimate results.	
Handling data	Use an appropriate number of significant figures.	
	Find arithmetic means.	
	Construct and interpret frequency tables and diagrams, bar charts and histograms.	
	Understand simple probability.	
	Understand the principles of sampling as applied to scientific data.	
	Understand the terms mean, median and mode.	
	Use a scattergram to identify a correlation between two variables.	
	Use a statistical test.	
	Make order of magnitude calculations.	
	Distinguish between levels of measurement.	
	Know the characteristics of normal and skewed distributions.	
	Select an appropriate statistical test.	
	Use statistical tables to determine significance.	
	Understand measures of dispersion, including standard deviation and range.	
	Understand the differences between qualitative and quantitative data.	
	Understand the difference between primary and secondary data.	
Algebra	Understand and use the symbols: $= \ < \ \ll \ \gg \ > \ \propto \ \approx$	
	Substitute numerical values into algebraic equations using appropriate units for physical quantities.	
	Solve simple algebraic equations.	
Graphs	Translate information between graphical, numerical and algebraic forms.	
	Plot two variables from experimental or other data.	

UNDERSTANDING EVALUATION (AO3)

We finally move onto the third skill – *evaluation*.

What is it you have to do when you *evaluate* something?

Think of the orange again (picture on right to help you). How can you evaluate an orange? Most people are puzzled by such a question.

Evaluation means 'consider its value' (eVALUatE). No, the answer is not 30p.

You might say – it is great to take an orange in your bag for lunch because it doesn't get damaged.

That's an advantage/strength of an orange.

You might also say – I don't like oranges because my hands get all sticky.

That's a disadvantage/limitation of an orange.

You could *elaborate* your answer by making a comparison, I don't like oranges because my hands get all sticky whereas they don't get so sticky with a banana.

Understanding elaboration is what it is all about.

AO3 is a bit more than evaluation. It also means to analyse and interpret. To analyse an orange you might consider what it is made of.

Beginner level evaluation: Identify a criticism

There are many different kinds of criticism, as you will discover in this book. For example, research support for a theory is a strength whereas lack of research support is a limitation. High validity is a strength and low validity is a limitation.

To evaluate a concept, study or theory you might say:

This concept is supported by research.
This study has been supported by other studies.
This study was well controlled.
This study had a limited sample.
This theory lacks validity.

You have identified the criticism, which is a beginning! Some students don't ever get much beyond this – and have to rely on their AO1 marks.

It's too easy just to state these rather *generic* criticisms, i.e. criticisms that can be used anywhere. But it is a beginning. So don't feel too bad if that is all you can do for a while.

Intermediate level evaluation: Make it relevant

The next step is to make your criticism relevant to the particular concept/study/theory. You need to say something to make your criticism unique rather than generic.

For example:

- *This concept is supported by research. Elliott* et al. *also found that men were more conformist than women, using a British rather than American sample.*
- *This study had a limited sample. The investigation only involved five people and they were friends of the researcher.*

In the case of the criticism below – it may look good but it is still generic (and therefore not worth much):

This study was well controlled. All important extraneous variables were monitored so that only the independent variable affected the dependent variable.

You can drop that criticism in almost anywhere and it will work.

Higher level evaluation: Explain it well

When you have mastered intermediate level, it is time to move on – but don't do this until you have mastered the intermediate level. Don't run before you can walk.

There are many ways to explain your critical point:

- You can use examples.
- You can elaborate on what you have said already.
- You can end by explaining why your point is a strength or limitation.

Look at any of the critical points in this book. We have tried to ensure that all our critical points follow the same rule:

State the point

Make it relevant

Explain the point

And finally, we have explained why it is a strength or limitation.

Let us know if we haven't

> FOR A LEVEL
> Make sure that your evaluation is 'thorough' – in other words at the higher level.

Some marked examples

Evaluation questions use these command words:

Analyse

Evaluate

Discuss (which may mean describe and evaluate)

There are other command words that also indicate evaluation, such as compare, justify, comment on.

Question: Discuss **one** limitation of adopting a determinist approach to explaining human behaviour. (3 marks)

One limitation is that a determinist approach is not how our legal system works because people in court are seen as responsible for their actions. If determinism can't be applied to everyday life then it is artificial and lacks ecological validity.

Teacher comment: Here you would first be expected to identify the limitation, which has been done here. You should also aim to include additional information about the limitation, including an explanation about why this is a limitation. There has been some attempt to do this (can't apply to real life) but it is very generic so not very effective.

Question: Briefly evaluate Sperry's split-brain research as a way of investigating hemispheric lateralisation. (4 marks)

Sperry's experiments were highly controlled and all the split-brain patients followed the same procedures. For instance, an image or word could be projected to a patient's right eye (processed by the left half of the brain) and the same, or different, image could be projected to the left eye (processed by the right half of the brain). The patients had to describe what they could see.

Teacher comment: If a question just asks for evaluation you can present strengths and/or limitations. There is no requirement for balance and no specific number of criticisms is required. The answer above covers two points of criticism that are both relevant but not very effective – the descriptive content about Sperry's research is not an explanation of the first critical point. In this way the answer has lost focus. The second evaluation point is rather brief and could have been developed further. The explanations are limited and little specialist terminology has been used.

AO3 Mark scheme

The descriptors that may be used to mark a 4-mark AO3 question:

Level	Marks	Description
2	3–4	Evaluation is relevant, well explained and focused, rather than generic criticism. The answer is generally coherent with effective use of specialist terminology.
1	1–2	Evaluation is relevant although there is limited explanation and/or limited focus. Specialist terminology is not always used appropriately. Award one mark for answers consisting of a single point briefly stated or muddled.
	0	No relevant content.

The mark scheme is presented here as an illustration of the AQA mark scheme. Always check the AQA website for the latest version of mark schemes as these may have been amended.

Question: Evaluate the humanistic approach. (6 marks)

A strength is the approach portrays a positive image of the human condition – seeing people as in control of their lives and having the freedom to change. Freud saw human beings as slaves to their past and claimed all of us existed somewhere between 'common unhappiness and absolute despair'. Humanistic psychology offers an optimistic alternative.

A limitation of humanistic psychology is that it includes a number of vague ideas that are abstract and difficult to test, such as 'self-actualisation' and 'congruence'. Rogers did attempt to introduce more rigour into his work by developing the Q-sort – an objective measure of progress in therapy. However, as would be expected of an approach that is 'antiscientific', humanistic psychology is short on empirical evidence.

Teacher comment: In an evaluation question of this length you probably need to present more than one criticism. There is a trade off between writing a few criticisms and having time for great explanation, or writing more criticisms but then less explanation. The two criticisms covered here are both effective, well-explained, focused, organised and there is evidence of specialist terminology.

AO3 Mark scheme

The descriptors that may be used to mark a 6-mark AO3 question:

Level	Marks	Description
3	5–6	Evaluation is clear and effective. The answer is coherent and well organised with effective use of specialist terminology.
2	3–4	Evaluation is mostly effective. The answer is mostly clear and coherent, with some appropriate use of specialist terminology.
1	1–2	Discussion lacks detail/explanation. The answer lacks clarity, accuracy and organisation in places. Specialist terminology is either absent or inappropriately used.
	0	No relevant content.

The mark scheme is presented here as an illustration of the AQA mark scheme. Always check the AQA website for the latest version of mark schemes as these may have been amended.

What do these terms mean?

What is *effective*?

Essentially 'effective' means something that works, such as 'an effective treatment for malaria'.

An effective critical point is therefore one that works – it should not be generic.

What is *generic*?

Essentially the word 'generic' means 'general'. In the context of making criticisms it refers to that nice little list of all-purpose criticisms 'This study lacked validity', 'This theory is culturally biased', etc.

Such all-purpose criticisms can be scattered everywhere and require little understanding. Therefore they are not very useful. Anyone can do that.

Some generic criticisms can be quite lengthy. For example, 'One problem with this research is that it is quite artificial. It was conducted in a laboratory where things are not like they are in everyday life. This makes it difficult to generalise the findings to everyday experience and makes the research worthless.'

Such a comment can be put in many essays with no attempt to make it specifically relevant – and therefore it isn't very effective.

What is *explanation*?

'Explain' means offer some further information to help the reader understand what you are saying. This may include providing more relevant facts, offering an interpretation ('this means that...'), justifying the point you are trying to make, and so on.

Maybe think of the difference between someone asking you to tell them what you did last night and them asking you to *explain* what you did last night. Hmm.

What is *focus*?

If you focus on an image, you concentrate your attention on that one thing. The same is required for good criticism. You need to pay attention just to the study or theory you are criticising rather than making general remarks.

One issue related to focus is that students often describe material (such as describing the procedures of a study) instead of explaining the critical point. They lose focus.

Using research studies as evaluation

On page 388 we noted that you may present information about a research study as part of your descriptive content – but you can also use research studies as evaluation.

If you do this then it is really only the findings/conclusion that can be considered as AO3. Description of procedure is classed more as description (AO1).

ESSAY QUESTIONS

The final kind of question for us to consider is the essay question (AKA extended writing question for the longer ones) – where you are required to include both description (AO1) and evaluation (AO3) and sometimes also application (AO2).

Examples of such questions are shown on the right.

Notice:

- The command words vary.
- Essay questions at A level are likely to be a maximum of 16 marks – on questions worth 16 marks the balance of marks is likely to be skewed towards AO3.
- One of the questions on the right includes some application material.
- One question asks specifically for studies, others concern theories/explanations and there is also one that just mentions research (so a theory or studies would be acceptable).
- Questions sometimes say 'one or more'. This means that you could produce an effective answer if you only discuss one study/theory but you can do more if you wish.

At the end of each chapter in this book are some student answers to practice questions, including answers for essay questions.

- *Briefly outline and evaluate the authoritarian personality as an explanation of obedience to authority.* (4 marks)
- *Discuss* **one or more** *examples of cultural bias in psychology.* (8 marks)
- *Outline and evaluate* **two** *studies of conformity* (10 marks)
- *Describe and evaluate research related to biological rhythms.* (12 marks)
- *Gary is often in trouble at school and has been suspended for bullying his classmates. Both of his older brothers were excluded from school for injuring other children. His teachers have described Gary as 'following in his brothers' footsteps'.*
  Discuss the free will and determinism debate in psychology. Refer to the experiences of Gary in your answer. (16 marks)
- *Describe and evaluate the nature-nurture debate in psychology. Refer to examples from your study of psychology.* (16 marks)
- *Discuss the contribution of Lorenz and Harlow to our understanding of attachment.* (16 marks)

Some useful lead-in phrases for AO3

An application is . . .
This means that . . .
On the other hand . . .
One strength is . . .
One limitation is . . .
This shows that . . .
In contrast . . .
However . . .

Fewer studies/evaluation points.
More time for detail/elaboration.

Essays on research studies

In a question on research studies, just one or two studies may be enough. It's about quality rather than quantity.

Essays with application material

These questions include application in addition to the usual describe and evaluate elements of an essay question.

You are required to make appropriate links between the theory and the scenario (stem) presented. If you do not do this you will not have fully answered the question.

Partial performance

Some questions ask for two things. For example, 'Outline **and** evaluate **two** definitions of abnormality. (16 marks)'

In such an essay if you only describe and evaluate one definition, this is called 'partial performance'. You have only answered half of the question.

What do students do wrong in essays?

- Students give too much description, not enough well-explained evaluation.
- Students fail to make their evaluation effective – use AO3 lead-in phrases (see example above left) to make it clear when you are presenting evaluation.
- Students fail to answer the question – take time to plan your answer to focus on what will be creditworthy. If you just start writing your answer you may forget the focus of the question so it pays to do some planning. It may also help, as you start each new paragraph, to go back to the title to remind yourself what the essay should be about.
- Students do not use paragraphs – which makes the essay very difficult to read. 'Organisation' is one of the criteria by which you are assessed so it will affect the overall impression of the essay.

Discuss idiographic and nomothetic approaches in psychology. *(16 marks)*

Student answer	Teacher comments
The idiographic approach is focused on people as unique individuals. It uses methods that produce qualitative data such as case studies and unstructured interviews, such as Freud's analyses of his patients, and these give a good insight into thoughts and behaviour.	This short opening paragraph contains relevant information but the aims of the idiographic approach are not adequately explained. The student could have gone much further in their description here.
The main aim of the nomothetic approach is to produce general laws of human behaviour. These can then be used as a standard to compare behaviour against and as way of predicting and/or controlling what people might do in the future. The nomothetic approach is most associated with methods that would be classed as 'scientific' in psychology, such as experiments and questionnaires and psychological tests. Using these methods large numbers of people and responses are compared to draw general conclusions, such as in word recall experiments or IQ testing.	In comparison, the material on the nomothetic approach is much more successful. The aims of the nomothetic approach are clearly stated and there are appropriate examples of how this approach has been used in psychological research.
As part of the nomothetic approach, people may be classified into groups such as those suffering from psychological disorders (DSM-5). Principles of behaviour can also be applied to people in general, for example, findings from conformity studies are applied to everyone. Finally, dimensions along which people can be compared can be established e.g. IQ scores.	Instead of a further paragraph on the nomothetic approach, time would have been better spent had the description of the two approaches been a little more balanced.
The idiographic approach is useful for shedding light on unusual cases, challenging accepted theories (if contradictory findings are seen) but it's difficult to generalise findings from unique individuals.	Altogether the description would be described as 'evident', but very close to 'present'.

There are three relevant evaluation points in this fourth paragraph – but only brief statements. At A level, evaluation points must be thoroughly explained and elaborated. |
For instance, HM was studied by psychologists and neuroscientists until his death in 2008. Following surgery to treat severe epilepsy, HM developed anterograde amnesia. He could not commit newly learned facts or events to long-term memory but his short-term memory, and memory for events before the surgery, remained intact. This research has provided useful insights for understanding memory processes.	This is an unfocused paragraph. The student could have made this relevant by using the case of HM as part of an analysis of the evaluation point presented above. On its own though, this does not constitute effective discussion.
Methods associated with the idiographic approach, such as case studies, tend to be the least scientific in that conclusions often rely on the subjective interpretation of the researcher and, as such, are open to bias. This makes generalisation more difficult.	This is a better evaluation point than the material presented above. It's well-explained but needs more elaboration.
The processes involved in nomothetic research tend to be similar to those used in the natural sciences. This includes testing under standardised conditions, using data sets of group averages, statistical analysis and control, for example in the field of IQ testing. This has enabled psychologists to establish norms of 'typical' behaviour (such as the average IQ of 100), which gives psychology greater scientific credibility.	Here, the student uses a well-chosen example – that of IQ testing – to successfully convey the point about the scientific credibility of the nomothetic approach. This is well-argued and thorough.
However, the nomothetic approach has been accused of 'losing the whole person' within psychology. Knowing that there is a 1% lifetime risk of developing schizophrenia tells us little about what life is like for someone who is suffering from the disorder. That would be better coming from a more descriptive idiographic approach. *428 words*	The final criticism is well-explained – using an appropriate example as before and a tentative attempt to compare the two approaches. This could have been developed further, perhaps leading to a general conclusion about how both approaches have their place in psychology. The answer is reasonably balanced (more evaluation than description as required in an A level answer) but the quality of the evaluation is, overall, only partly effective though edging towards 'mostly effective'. The answer is mostly clear and organised. The student's final attainment is calculated by working out the best fit for all these different assessments to see what level best describes the answer. The actual mark will be determined by whether one is drawn to the level above or below.

Mark scheme used for essay questions

In a 16-mark essay where there are 6 marks AO1 and 10 marks AO3.

Level	Marks for A level	Description
4	13–16	*Knowledge is accurate and generally well detailed. Evaluation is thorough and effective. The answer is clear, coherent and focused. Specialist terminology is used effectively. Minor detail and/or expansion of argument is sometimes lacking.*
3	9–12	*Knowledge is evident but lacks focus in places. There are occasional inaccuracies. Evaluation is mostly effective. The answer is mostly clear and organised. Specialist terminology is mostly used appropriately.*
2	5–8	*Knowledge is present. Focus is mainly on description. Any evaluation is only partly effective. The answer lacks clarity, accuracy and organisation in places. Specialist terminology is used inappropriately on occasions.*
1	1–4	*Knowledge is limited. Evaluation is limited, poorly focused or absent. The answer as a whole lacks clarity, has many inaccuracies and is poorly organised. Specialist terminology is either absent or inappropriately used.*
	0	*No relevant content*

To decide on a mark identify the level that best describes the essay, and then consider whether you are more tempted by the level above or below to determine the exact mark to award. Always check the AQA website for the latest version of mark schemes as these may have been amended.

APPLYING PSYCHOLOGY TO SUCCESSFUL STUDYING

There are probably two big challenges ahead for you:
1. Writing essays.
2. Learning all the material in this book.

The suggestions on this spread are informed by psychological research – after all, we are psychologists.

Start by considering the descriptive component of your essay. You are likely to need a maximum of 6 marks' worth of description (AO1). If you identify an appropriate number of key points that will help you structure your answer. We have done this for an essay on locus of control.

Select any essay title in this book, produce an empty frame like the one on the right and fill it in for the description component. You may decide to add a few more rows but don't add much more or you'll end up with too much.

The psychology behind writing frames is called scaffolding. Psychologists use this term to describe the process where a person needs support in the early stages of learning to do something new.

The idea is that, when you are ready, you kick away the scaffold, and – hey presto – you can do it on your own.

Not a good idea if you are standing on a real scaffold.

Writing frame for an essay

AO1 Key point	Description
Unconscious	We are aware of our conscious mind, we can be aware of pre-conscious thinking in dreams and the unconscious is beyond awareness. It stores biological drives and instincts.
Tripartite	The id is the primitive part driven by the pleasure principle. The ego mediates between the id and superego, driven by the reality principle. The superego is driven by the morality principle.
Psychosexual stages	Each stage is marked by a different conflict that the child must resolve to move on to the next stage. Unresolved conflicts lead to fixations.
Fixed sequence	Oral (0–1 years), anal (1–3), phallic (3–5), latency (earlier conflicts repressed), genital (puberty).
Oedipus complex	In the phallic stage, little boys desire their mother and hate their father. Later they identify with the father and take on gender role and morals. Girls experience penis envy.
Defence mechanisms	Unconscious strategies such as repression (distressing memories put in unconscious) and displacement (transferring true feelings).

Now do the same for the evaluation (AO3). To plan your evaluation the organisation of the writing frame is a bit different. On page 392 we explained that good critical points start with the basics, and then you may add further elaboration (intermediate and higher level). The table below will help you plan this.

Always walk before you run:
1. Start with the basics, identify key points. Three may be enough to begin with.
2. Learn how to elaborate these.
3. Extend the number of points you feel you can tackle.

NOTE For an A level essay the maximum is 10 marks of AO3

AO3 Key point	Intermediate level evaluation	High level evaluation
Has explanatory power.	It has been used to explain a wide range of behaviours (moral, mental disorders) and drew attention to the influence of childhood on adult personality.	Alongside behaviourism, it was the dominant approach in psychology for the first half of the twentieth century.
Case study method has limitations.	Freud's ideas were developed using a small number of case studies, e.g. Little Hans, Dora and the Rat Man. Critics have suggested that it is not possible to make universal claims about human nature based on such a limited sample.	Although Freud's observations were detailed and carefully recorded, his interpretations were highly subjective and it is unlikely that any other researcher would have drawn the same conclusions.
There are many untestable concepts.	Karl Popper (philosopher of science) argued that the psychodynamic approach does not meet the scientific criterion of falsification, because many of Freud's concepts, such as the id or the Oedipus complex, occur at an unconscious level making them difficult, if not impossible, to test.	This affords psychodynamic theory the status of pseudoscience ('fake' science) rather than real science.
There are practical applications.	Freud introduced a new form of therapy: psychoanalysis. The therapy is designed to access the unconscious mind using a range of techniques such as hypnosis and dream analysis. It may not be suitable for all people or all disorders.	That said, psychoanalysis is the forerunner to many modern-day psychotherapies and 'talking cures' that have since been established.
The approach is based on psychic determinism.	The psychodynamic approach explains all behaviour as determined by unconscious conflicts that are rooted in childhood. Even something as apparently random as a 'slip of the tongue' is driven by unconscious forces and has deep symbolic meaning.	This is an extreme determinist stance and suggests that free will may have no influence on behaviour.

Some essays also involve some application (AO2) – see an example on page 394. If you are answering an essay like this you must remember to make links to the context (stem) and reduce the number of evaluation points.

Egocentrism The child's tendency to only be able to see the world from their own point of view. This applies to both physical objects – demonstrated in the three mountains task – and arguments in which a child can only appreciate their own perspective. 157, 180–181, 186

Electra complex A term proposed by the neo-Freudian Carl Jung which refers to a process similar to the Oedipus complex. In girls, an attraction to and envy of their father is resolved through identification with their mother. 19, 160, 336

Electroencephalogram (EEG) Electrodes are attached to a person's scalp to record the tiny electrical impulses produced by the brain's activity. By measuring characteristic wave patterns, the EEG can help diagnose certain conditions of the brain. 9, 17, 44–45, 48–49, 274, 331

Electromyogram (EMG) Measures the electrical activity of muscles at rest and during contraction. 274

Emic 96

Emotional support Giving someone a 'shoulder to cry on' to help them feel better. 278

Empirical method Scientific approaches that are based on the gathering of evidence through direct observation and experience. 19, 82, 103

Empiricism A method of gaining knowledge which relies on direct observation or testing. 8, 21, 100–101

Endocrine system One of the body's major information systems that instructs glands to release hormones directly into the bloodstream. These hormones are carried towards target organs in the body. 35, 228

Endogenous pacemakers Internal body clocks that regulate many of our biological rhythms, such as the influence of the suprachiasmatic nucleus (SCN) on the sleep/wake cycle. 46, 48, 50–51

Enmeshment Members of an anorexic family are over-involved and over-protective. Their self-identities are bound up with each other. Roles are poorly defined and there is little privacy. 232–233

Environment Any influence on human behaviour that is non-genetic. This may range from pre-natal influences in the womb through to cultural and historical influences at a societal level. 16, 23, 100–101, 205, 298, 308

Environmental determinism The belief that behaviour is caused by features of the environment (such as systems of reward and punishment) that we cannot control. 11, 98, 101

Environmental reductionism The attempt to explain all behaviour in terms of stimulus-response links that have been learned through experience. 102

Epilepsy 42–45, 47, 105

Episodic memory A long-term memory store for personal events. It includes memories of when the events occurred and of the people, objects, places and behaviours involved. Memories from this store have to be retrieved consciously and with effort. 14, 39

Equilibration Takes place when we have encountered new information and built it into our understanding of a topic, either by assimilating it into an existing schema or accommodating it by forming a new one. Everything is again balanced and we have escaped the unpleasant experience of a lack of balance – disequilibrium. 178–179

Equity theory An economic theory of how relationships develop. As such, it acknowledges the impact of rewards and costs on relationship satisfaction, but criticises social exchange theory for ignoring the central role of equity – the perception that partners have that the distribution of rewards and costs in the relationship is fair. 127–129

Essentialist theory 94–95

Esteem support Helping someone to attach greater value to themselves so they view their abilities with greater confidence. 278

Ethical committee A group of people within a research institution that must approve a study before it begins. Members may be drawn from the wider community. 107

Ethical guidelines A set of principles designed to help professionals behave honestly and with integrity. 106–107

Ethical implications The impact that psychological research may have in terms of the rights of other people especially participants. This includes, at a societal level, influencing public policy and/or the way in which certain groups of people are regarded. 106–107

Ethical issues These arise when a conflict exists between the rights of participants in research studies and the goals of research to produce authentic, valid and worthwhile data. 11, 24–25, 51–52, 65, 84, 106–108, 135, 138–139, 168–169, 192–193, 211, 213–215, 227, 241, 244, 257, 279–281, 291, 297, 301, 305, 310–311, 329, 341, 343, 346–347, 359, 370–371, 373, 378–379

Ethnocentrism Judging other cultures by the standards and values of one's own culture. In its extreme form it is the belief in the superiority of one's own culture which may lead to prejudice and discrimination towards other cultures. 96, 107

Ethological explanation An explanation that seeks to understand the innate behaviour of animals (including humans) by studying them in their natural environments. 294–295

Eugenic A movement which advocated that the human gene pool could be improved by encouraging reproduction in people with desirable traits and preventing reproduction in those with undesirable traits. 101, 327, 335

Event sampling A target behaviour or event is first established then the researcher records this event every time it occurs. 25, 129, 65, 295, 365

Event-related potentials (ERPs) The brain's electrophysiological response to a specific sensory, cognitive, or motor event can be isolated through statistical analysis of EEG data. 44–45

Evolution The changes in inherited characteristics in a biological population over successive generations. 16, 49

Evolutionary explanation An account of the changes in species over millions of years; characteristics that enhance survival and reproduction are naturally selected. 8, 118–119, 224–225, 255, 296–297

Excitation When a neurotransmitter, such as adrenaline, increases the positive charge of the postsynaptic neuron. This increases the likelihood that the neuron will fire and pass on the electrical impulse. 37

Exogenous zeitgebers External cues that may affect or entrain our biological rhythms, such as the influence of light on the sleep/wake cycle. 46, 48, 50–51

Experiment Involves the manipulation of an independent variable (IV) to measure the effect on the dependent variable (DV). Experiments may be laboratory, field, natural or quasi. 9, 23, 52, 65, 67–69, 82–83, 104, 127, 192, 214–215, 242, 244, 290, 299, 303, 306, 310, 331, 347, 379

Experimental condition The condition in a repeated measures design containing the independent variable as distinct from the control condition. 188, 215

Experimental design The different ways in which the testing of participants can be organised in relation to the experimental conditions. 17, 51, 70, 85, 123, 127, 154, 229, 239, 271, 291, 303, 325, 327, 341, 367

Experimental hypothesis The hypothesis in an experiment. 82

Experimental philosophy A field of psychology that uses empirical data as distinct from rational argument. 8

Expressed emotion A measure of the family environment related to the extent that family members express critical, hostile and emotionally over-involved attitudes toward a family member with a disorder. 206, 210

External validity The degree to which a research finding can be generalised to, for example, other settings (ecological validity), other groups of people (population validity) and over time (temporal validity). 15, 65, 68, 135, 303, 367

Extinction In conditioning theory, the disappearance of a learned response when stimuli stop being paired (classical conditioning) or no reinforcement occurs (operant conditioning). 11, 364

Extraneous variable (EV) Any variable, other than the independent variable (IV), that may have an effect on the dependent variable (DV) if it is not controlled. EVs are essentially nuisance variables that do not vary systematically with the IV. 9, 24, 123, 138, 163, 193

Extraversion A personality trait where the individual is outgoing and impulsive. 137, 330–331, 346

Eyes Task A test of how well you can read emotions of others just by looking at their eyes; a test of social intelligence. 188–189, 193

Eyewitness testimony (EWT) The ability of people to remember the details of events, such as accidents and crimes, which they themselves have observed. Accuracy of EWT can be affected by factors such as misleading information, leading questions and anxiety. 14–15, 107

Face validity A basic form of validity in which a measure is scrutinised to determine whether it appears to measure what it is supposed to measure – for instance, does a test of anxiety look like it measures anxiety? 68–69, 99, 125

False belief tasks A method of testing whether a person can hold false beliefs i.e. the ability to recognise that someone else can hold beliefs/thoughts different to one's own. 188–189

Falsification Proving the truth of a research hypothesis by demonstrating that the null version is false. Scientific theories cannot be proved to be true; they can only be subjected to attempts to prove them false. 19, 82, 161, 337

Family dysfunction Abnormal processes within a family such as poor family communication, cold parenting and high levels of expressed emotion. These may be risk factors for both the development and maintenance of schizophrenia. 206–207

Family influences The effects that other members of our families have on our thoughts, feelings and behaviours over the course of our development. 226, 358

Family studies Research where close relatives (parents and their children) are compared on certain traits such as IQ or mental disorder in order to determine whether genetic factors underlie these traits. 17

Family systems theory A psychodynamic explanation that views dysfunctional family interaction as a major factor in the development and maintenance of anorexia nervosa (AN). 232–233

Family therapy A psychological therapy carried out with all or some members of a family with the aim of improving their communication and reducing the stress of living as a family. 23, 103, 210–211

Field experiment An experiment that takes place in a natural setting within which the researcher manipulates the independent variable (IV) and records the effect on the dependent variable (DV). 257, 305

Fight or flight response The way an animal responds when stressed. The body becomes physiologically aroused in readiness to fight an aggressor or, in some cases, flee. 35, 94, 225, 254–255, 264, 270, 276

File drawer problem Bias created because the results of some studies are not published (filed away), for example studies with negative results. 307

Filter theory An explanation of relationship formation. It states that a series of different factors progressively limits the range of available romantic partners to a much smaller pool of possibilities. The filters include social demography, similarity in attitudes and complementarity. 124–125

Fixation In psychoanalytic theory, a focus on a particular stage of psychosexual development because of over- or under-gratification during that stage. 18

Myelin sheath A white fatty substance that protects the neuron and speeds up the transmission of messages along the length of the axon. 25, 36

MZ twins *See* Monozygotic twins

Natural experiment An experiment where the change in the independent variable (IV) is not brought about by the researcher but would have happened even if the researcher had not been there. The researcher records the effect on the dependent variable (DV). 183, 235, 262, 363, 305

Natural selection The major process that explains evolution whereby inherited traits that enhance an animal's reproductive success are passed on to the next generation and thus 'selected', whereas animals without such traits are less successful at reproduction and their traits are not selected. 16, 294, 296

Naturalistic observation Watching and recording behaviour in the setting within which it would normally occur. 25, 337

Nature Those aspects of behaviour that are inherited. The term 'nature' does not simply refer to abilities present at birth but to any ability determined by genes, including those that appear through maturation. 17, 22–23, 100–101, 108–109, 148, 165, 167

Nature–nurture debate The question of whether behaviour is determined more by nature (inherited and genetic factors) or nurture (all influences after conception i.e. experience). 17, 22, 98, 100–101, 109, 155, 164–165

Negative affect theory 299, 301

Negative correlation As one co-variable increases, the other decreases. For example, the following two co-variables: the number of people in a room and amount of personal space are negatively correlated. 53, 63, 187, 204, 241, 269, 346

Negative reinforcement In operant conditioning, a stimulus that increases the probability that a behaviour will be repeated because it leads to escape from an unpleasant situation and is experienced as rewarding. 10, 300, 362, 364

Negative symptoms of schizophrenia Atypical experiences that represent the loss of a usual experience such as clear thinking or 'normal' levels of motivation. 202, 204

Neophobia An innate predisposition to avoid anything new. An adaptive behaviour which reduces the risks of unfamiliar objects, experiences and activities until we learn they are safe. 224–225

Nervous system Consists of the central nervous system and the peripheral nervous system. 16, 24, 34–36, 98, 228, 254, 264, 270, 290, 308, 346

Neural correlates Patterns of structure or activity in the brain that occur in conjunction with an experience and may be implicated in the origins of that experience. 204–205

Neural explanation Any explanation of behaviour (and its disorders) in terms of (dys)functions of the brain and nervous system. This includes the activity of brain structures such as the hypothalamus, and neurotransmitters such as serotonin and dopamine. 230, 238, 328

Neural networks A structure of interconnected neurons, each with multiple connections. 37

Neurochemistry Relating to chemicals in the brain that regulate psychological functioning. 16, 360–362, 367–368

Neurological Related to neurons/nervous system. 14, 39, 44, 98–99, 149, 190, 212

Neuron The basic building blocks of the nervous system, neurons are nerve cells that process and transmit messages through electrical and chemical signals. 22, 34, 36–37, 44–45, 103, 270, 292, 368, 290, 357, 360

Neurorehabilitation 41

Neuroses A personality or mental disturbance characterised by anxiety but where the patient has not lost touch with reality, as distinct from psychosis. 19, 137, 269, 330

Neurosurgery 39

Neurotransmitter Brain chemicals released from synaptic vesicles that relay signals across the synapse from one neuron to another. Neurotransmitters can be broadly divided into those that perform an excitatory function and those that perform an inhibitory function. 17, 37, 103, 204–205, 207–208, 228, 230–231, 238, 270, 290, 292, 357, 360–361, 368

Neutral stimulus (NS) In classical conditioning, the stimulus that initially does not produce the target response, i.e. it is neutral. Through association with the unconditioned stimulus (UCS), the NS acquires the properties of the UCS and becomes a conditioned stimulus (CS) producing a conditioned response (CR). 10

Nicotine addiction 360–363, 368–371

Nicotine replacement therapy (NRT) 368–369

Nodes of Ranvier The gaps in the myelin sheath that protect the axon of a neuron. 36

Nominal data A level of measurement, data that are in separate categories. 71, 80, 85

Nomothetic approach Derived from the Greek 'nomos' meaning 'law'. The nomothetic approach attempts to study human behaviour through the development of general principles and universal laws. 23, 104–105

Non-directional hypothesis A form of hypothesis that states a difference, correlation or association between two variables but does not specify the direction (i.e. does not specify more or less, positive or negative) of such a relationship. 24, 72–76, 127, 239, 271, 299, 328, 377

Non-nuclear family Any family that does not conform to the 'traditional' group of a mother and father and their children e.g. single-parent families or larger extended families. 161

Non-participant observation The researcher remains outside of the group whose behaviour he/she is watching and recording. 301

Noradrenaline A hormone and a neurotransmitter that generally has an excitatory effect, similar to the hormone adrenaline. The hormone is produced by the adrenal gland. 231, 254, 262, 266, 270

Normal distribution A symmetrical spread of frequency data that forms a bell-shaped pattern. The mean, median and mode are all located at the highest peak. 71, 76–77, 85, 104

Nucleus The control centre of a cell containing genetic material. 36, 50–51

Nucleus accumbens A part of the mesolimbic pathway, the reward pathway of the brain. 360, 362, 368

Null hypothesis The statement of no difference, correlation or association between variables being studied. 70, 72–80, 82–83, 347

Nurture Those aspects of behaviour that are acquired through experience, i.e. learned from interactions with the physical and social environment. 17, 22–23, 100–101, 108–109, 148, 162, 165, 167

Obedience A form of social influence in which an individual follows a direct order. The person issuing the order is usually a figure of authority who has the power to punish when obedient behaviour is not forthcoming. 68, 96

Obesity Having too much body fat, often defined as a BMI (weight divided by the square of the person's height) of more than 30. 229, 238–241

Object permanence The ability to realise that an object still exists when it passes out of the visual field. Piaget believed that this ability appears at around eight months of age. Prior to this, children lose interest in an object once they can't see it and presumably are no longer aware of its existence. 180

Objectivity When all sources of personal bias are minimised so as not to distort or influence the research process. 11, 15, 21, 65, 72–83, 169

Observation A research study where only observational techniques are used. 19, 25, 52, 64, 66–69, 83, 107, 129, 187, 225, 241, 265, 293, 295, 301, 310, 365, 366

Observational learning Learning through imitation. 23, 300 *Also see* Social learning theory.

Observational techniques A set of systems to increase the objectivity and validity of data collected when a researcher watches or listens to participants engaging in whatever behaviour is being studied. Observational techniques may be used in an experiment as a method of assessing the dependent variable (DV). 25

Observer bias In observational studies there is a danger that observers' expectations affect what they see or hear. This reduces the validity of the observations. 165

Obsessive-compulsive disorder (OCD) A condition characterised by obsessions and/or compulsive behaviour. 14, 16, 39, 102, 203

Occipital lobe 38–39

OCD *See* Obsessive-compulsive disorder

Oedipus complex Freud's explanation of how a boy resolves his love for his mother and feelings of rivalry towards his father by identifying with his father. 19, 105, 160–161, 336

Oestrogen The primary female hormone, playing an important role in the menstrual cycle and reproductive system. 152–153, 155, 276

Offender profiling Also known as 'criminal profiling', a behavioural and analytical tool that is intended to help investigators accurately predict and profile the characteristics of unknown criminals. 322–326

Offender survey A self-report measure that requires people to record the number and types of crime they have committed over a specified period. 320–321

Official statistics In forensic psychology, figures based on the numbers of crimes that are reported and recorded by the police which are often used by the government to inform crime prevention strategies. 320–321

One-tailed test Form of test used with a directional hypothesis. 73, 75, 77–80, 82, 347

Open question Question for which there is no fixed choice of response and respondents can answer in any way they wish; for example 'why did you take up smoking?' 67, 227, 371

Operant conditioning A form of learning in which behaviour is shaped and maintained by its consequences. Possible consequences of behaviour include positive reinforcement, negative reinforcement or punishment. 10–13, 210, 226, 274, 300, 340, 362–363

Operationalisation Clearly defining variables in terms of how they can be measured. 52, 67, 97, 103, 109, 129, 135, 225, 229, 273, 295, 299, 331, 361, 365

Operations The term used in Piaget's theory of cognitive development for internally consistent, logical mental rules, such as rules of arithmetic. 180

Opportunity sampling A sample of participants produced by selecting people who are most easily available at the time of a study. 109, 123, 138, 237, 245, 257, 280, 307, 378

Optic chiasm 50

Oral stage In psychoanalytic theory, the first stage (0–18 months) of psychosexual development when the organ-focus is on the mouth. 18, 160

Orbitofrontal cortex 290–291

Ordinal A level of measurement. Data is ordered in some way but the intervals between each item are unequal. 71, 74–75, 78, 85, 347

Organised offender An offender who shows evidence of planning, targets the victim and tends to be socially and sexually competent with higher than average intelligence. 322–323

Outgroup Any social group to which you do not belong, as distinct from the ingroup. 158

Oxytocin A hormone which causes contraction of the uterus during labour and stimulates lactation. 152, 276

Paradigm A set of shared assumptions and agreed methods within a scientific discipline. 82

Paradigm shift The result of a scientific revolution: a significant change in the dominant unifying theory within a scientific discipline. 82

Parahippocampal gyrus An area of the cerebral cortex (grey matter) that surrounds the hippocampus. Involved in memory. 14

Parametric test A group of inferential statistics that make certain assumptions about the parameters (characteristics) of the population from which the sample is drawn. 70–71, 79, 85

Parapraxes A Freudian slip, a minor error in action, such as a slip of the tongue. Due to repressed emotions. 18

Parasocial relationship The prefix 'para' means 'resembling' so parasocial relationships are those which are similar to 'normal' relationships but lack a key element. They are a one-sided, unreciprocated relationship, usually with a celebrity, on which the 'fan' expends a lot of emotional energy, commitment and time. 136–137

Parasympathetic nervous system A division of the autonomic nervous system (ANS) which controls the relaxed state (rest and digest), conserving resources and promoting digestion and metabolism. The parasympathetic branch works in opposition to the sympathetic branch of the ANS. One or the other is active at any time. 34–35, 254

Parietal lobe/cortex 38–40

Pars opercularis 191

Partial reinforcement When a behaviour is reinforced only some of the time it occurs (e.g. every tenth time or at variable intervals). 364

Participant reactivity The tendency for participants to react to cues from the researcher or the research environment. 69

Participant variables Characteristics of individual participants (such as age, intelligence, etc.) that might influence the outcome of a study. 215

Pavlov, Ivan 10

Pearson's r A parametric test for correlation when data is at interval level. 70–71, 78–79, 85

Peek, Kim 43

Peer review The assessment of scientific work by others who are specialists in the same field to ensure that any research set for publication is of high quality. 47, 101, 131

Peer tutoring An effective form of learning, recommended by Vygotsky's theory of cognitive development because peers are potential 'experts' (individuals with greater knowledge). 183

Peers People who share our interests and are of similar age, social status and background to ourselves. Peers become more influential in adolescence, when we spend more time with them and less with family. 226, 358–359

Penis envy A girl's recognition of not having a penis, and desire to have one. 19, 68, 94, 160

Perfectionism 236–237

Peripheral nervous system (PNS) Sends information to the central nervous system (CNS) from the outside world, and transmits messages from the CNS to muscles and glands in the body. 34

Personality Patterns of thinking, feeling and behaving that differ between individuals. These are relatively consistent from one situation to another, and over time. 18–19, 67, 266–267, 358

Perspective-taking Our ability to appreciate a social situation from the perspective (point of view) of other people. This cognitive ability underlies much of our normal social interaction. 186–187, 189–191

PET scan Positron emission tomography. A brain-scanning method used to study activity in the brain. Radioactive glucose is ingested and can be detected in the active areas of the brain. 14, 45, 239

Phallic stage In psychoanalytic theory, the third stage of psychosexual development when the organ-focus is on the genitals. 18–19, 94, 160–161, 336

Pharmacokinetics 47

Phase model of relationship breakdown An explanation of the stages people go through when their relationship is not working. Once one partner is dissatisfied, there are four phases in the process, each with a different focus: intra-psychic, dyadic, social and grave-dressing. 132–133

Phenotype The characteristics of an individual determined by both genes and the environment. 16

Phenylketonuria (PKU) An inherited disorder that prevents metabolism of phenylalanine, resulting in a build-up of poisonous substances that cause brain damage. If the disorder is detected at birth, the individual can be given a diet that avoids phenylalanine and thus prevents the potential brain damage. 16–17

Pheromones Chemical substances produced by the body and secreted into the air, whence they are transmitted to other animals of the same species and absorbed into their bloodstream. The pheromones then work like hormones and influence the behaviour of the receiver. 48–49

Phobia An irrational fear of an object or situation. 11, 19, 23, 64

Phototherapy 49

Physical attractiveness An important factor in the formation of romantic relationships. The term usually applies specifically to how appealing we find a person's face. There is general agreement within and across cultures about what is considered physically attractive. There exists an assumption that we seek to form relationships with the most attractive person available. 122–123

Physical dependence A state of the body due to habitual drug use and which results in a withdrawal syndrome when use of the drug is reduced or stopped. 356

Piaget, Jean 157, 178–184, 186

Pilot study A small-scale version of an investigation that takes place before the real investigation is conducted. The aim is to check that procedures, materials, measuring scales, etc., work and to allow the researcher to make changes or modifications if necessary. 25, 47, 66, 129, 168, 225, 295, 320, 365

Pineal gland 50

Pituitary gland Called the master gland of the body's hormone system because it directs much of the hormone activity. 35, 254

PKU See Phenylketonuria.

Placebo A treatment that should have no effect on the behaviour being studied, it contains no active ingredient. Therefore it can be used to separate out the effects of the independent variable (IV) from any effects caused merely by receiving any treatment. 49, 51, 72, 153, 209, 271, 275, 291, 310, 369, 371

Plasticity (Also referred to as neuroplasticity or cortical remapping.) This describes the brain's tendency to change and adapt (functionally and physically) as a result of experience and new learning. 39–41

Pleasure principle In psychoanalytic theory, the drive to do things which produce pleasure or gratification, and to avoid pain. 18

PNS See Peripheral nervous system.

Polygenic A characteristic determined by more than one gene. 231, 238

Popper, Karl 19, 83

Population A group of people who are the focus of the researcher's interest, from which a smaller sample is drawn. 214, 267

Positive correlation As one co-variable increases so does the other. For example, the number of people in a room and noise are positively correlated. 35, 40, 63, 67, 78, 138, 187, 205, 258, 260, 290, 296, 307

Positive reinforcement In operant conditioning, a stimulus that increases the probability that a behaviour will be repeated because it is pleasurable. 10, 300, 342, 362, 364

Positive symptoms of schizophrenia Atypical symptoms experienced in addition to normal experiences. They include hallucinations and delusions. 202, 204

Post-mortem examinations The brain is analysed after death to determine whether certain observed behaviours during the patient's lifetime can be linked to abnormalities in the brain. 44–45, 166, 228

Post-traumatic stress disorder (PTSD) A disabling reaction to stress following a traumatic event. The response does not always appear immediately after the event. The reactions are long-lasting, and include: reliving the event recurrently in flashbacks and dreams, emotional numbness and general anxiety which may result in lack of concentration. 203, 358

Postsynaptic neuron The neuron that is receiving the information at the synapse. 270, 360

Postsynaptic receptor site A receptor on the neuron that is receiving the information at the synapse. A neurotransmitter locks into a specific receptor on the receiving neuron and this triggers an electrical signal in the receiving neuron. 37

Preconscious Consists of information and ideas that could be retrieved easily from memory and brought into consciousness. 18

Prefrontal cortex A region in the frontal lobe which is involved with highest-order cognitive activities, such as working memory. 14, 39, 204, 328

Presynaptic neuron The transmitting neuron, before the synaptic cleft. 360

Presynaptic terminal The end of the transmitting neuron, ending at the synaptic cleft. 37

Primary data Information that has been obtained first hand by the researcher for the purposes of a research project. In psychology, such data is often gathered directly from participants as part of an experiment, self-report or observation. 261

Primary reinforcer Things that are innately reinforcing, such as food or warmth. 362

Prior general consent Prospective participants in a research study are asked if they would take part in certain kinds of research, including ones involving deception. If they say yes they have given their general consent to taking part in such research. 310

Privacy An ethical issue that refers to a zone of inaccessibility of mind or body and the trust that this will not be 'invaded'. Contrasts with confidentiality. Can be dealt with in some situations by providing anonymity. 311, 378

Privation The failure to develop any attachments during early life. This is contrasted with 'deprivation' or 'disruption' where attachment bonds have formed but may be disrupted either through physical or simply emotional separation (the *loss* of attachments). 337

Probability A measure of the likelihood that a particular event will occur where 0 indicates statistical impossibility and 1 statistical certainty. 72–73, 346, 366, 378

Prochaska's six-stage model Explains the stages people go through to change their behaviour. It identifies six stages of change (and is sometimes referred to as the 'Stages of change' model), from not considering it at all to making permanent changes. The stages are not necessarily followed in a linear order. 376–377

Prosocial behaviour Behaviour which is beneficial to others, and may not necessarily benefit the helper. 187

Prospective A longitudinal study that selects participants on the basis of certain characteristics to see how these characteristics affect later behaviours of interest. 207, 259, 262, 266

Protection from harm See Psychological harm

Pseudoscientific A claim, belief, or practice that is presented as scientific but is not following the scientific method. 19, 161, 337

Psychic determinism The belief that behaviour is caused by unconscious conflicts that we cannot control. 19, 23, 98

Psychoactive drugs A chemical substance that alters one's mental processes. 17, 37, 102

Psychoanalysis A form of psychotherapy, originally developed by Sigmund Freud, that is intended to help patients become aware of long-repressed feelings and issues by using techniques such as free association and dream analysis. 8, 19, 21, 23, 166

Psychodynamic approach A perspective that describes the different forces (dynamics), most of which are unconscious, that operate on the mind and direct human behaviour and experience. 8–9, 18–20, 22–23, 104, 153, 160–161, 233, 298, 336–337

Psychological dependence A compulsion to continue taking a drug because its use is rewarding. 356

Psychological harm Participants in psychological research should not experience embarrassment, loss of self-esteem or any other psychological damage – greater than what they might expect to experience in everyday life. 24, 52, 84, 108, 138, 168–169, 192, 214, 244, 310, 346, 378

Psychological test A set of questions or task that assess some aspect of psychological functioning, such as intelligence or personality. 64, 66, 68–69

Psychopathy Lacking a conscience and empathy for others, making it more likely that an individual will commit crimes and have difficulty forming relationships. 290

Psychosexual stages According to Freud, five developmental stages that all children pass through. At most stages there is a specific conflict, the outcome of which determines future development. 18, 22, 160

Psychosis A severe mental disorder where a person has lost touch with reality. The whole person is affected, behaviour is qualitatively different from before and the person lacks insight into their condition (as distinct from a neurosis). 137, 330

Punishment Any procedure that decreases the likelihood that a behaviour will be repeated because the overall experience is unpleasant. 10, 18, 159, 298, 300, 340

Q-sort A person is required to sort 100 statements (e.g. 'I have a great deal of confidence in my abilities') into 9 categories according to how well or poorly the statements describe them (the self sort) and then repeat for how they would like to be (the ideal sort). Well-adjusted people should have more similar sorts. 21

Qualitative data analysis Any means of extracting meaning from data that focuses more on words (i.e. what participants say) than on forms of numerical data. Qualitative analyses interpret the meaning of an experience to the individual(s) concerned. 23, 65, 81

Qualitative data Data that is expressed in words and non-numerical (although qualitative data may be converted to numbers for the purposes of analysis). 64, 69–70, 95, 104, 121, 156, 169, 213, 233, 263, 275, 297, 307, 359, 377

Qualitative methods See Qualitative data analysis

Quantitative data analysis Any means of extracting meaning from data that uses numerical data as the basis for investigation and interpretation (e.g. descriptive or inferential statistics). 65

Quantitative data Data that can be counted, usually given as numbers. 64, 69–71, 119, 169, 193, 213, 215, 235, 244, 297, 377, 379

Quasi-experiment A study that is almost an experiment but lacks key ingredients. The independent variable (IV) has not been determined by anyone (the researcher or any other person) – the 'variables' simply exist, such as being old or young. Strictly speaking this is not an experiment. 17, 25, 108, 137, 139, 168, 193, 237, 259, 311

Questionnaire A set of written questions (sometimes referred to as 'items') used to assess a person's thoughts and/or experiences. 24–25, 49, 52, 64–67, 69, 75, 84, 108, 119, 123, 125, 131, 137–139, 151, 165, 168, 192, 213–214, 227, 244, 262–264, 267, 269, 271, 273, 275–278, 280–281, 296, 310, 320, 341, 346, 371, 377–379

Random allocation An attempt to control for participant variables in an independent groups design which ensures that each participant has the same chance of being in one condition as any other. 51, 211, 213, 241, 245, 263, 271, 273, 279, 305, 307, 343, 373

Random sampling A sample of participants produced by using a random technique such that every member of the target population being tested has an equal chance of being selected. 138, 192, 320

Random technique A method that ensures that each item has an equal chance of being selected i.e. there is no predictable pattern. This can be achieved with random number tables or numbers drawn from a hat. 299

Range A simple calculation of the dispersion in a set of scores which is worked out by subtracting the lowest score from the highest score and usually adding 1 as a mathematical correction. 71, 108, 215, 347

Rating scale A means of assessing attitudes or experiences by asking a respondent to rate statements on a scale of 1 to 3 or 1 to 5, etc. Produces ordinal data. 150, 347, 373

Raw scores Original data that has not been transformed in any way, for example by working out an average. 71, 81

Reality principle In psychoanalytic theory, the drive to accommodate to the demands of the environment in a realistic way. 18

Recidivism Reoffending, a tendency to relapse into a previous condition or mode of behaviour; in the context of crime, a convicted criminal who reoffends, usually repeatedly. 338, 343–345

Reciprocal determinism A person's behaviour both influences and is influenced by personal factors and the social environment. 13, 23, 301

Reduced cues theory 134–135

Reductionism The belief that human behaviour is best explained by breaking it down into smaller constituent parts. 21–23, 102–104, 153, 329

References In a scientific report, a list of sources e.g. journal articles, books or websites, and their full details. 81

Reflexive In qualitative research, a researcher reflects or thinks critically during the research process about the factors that affect the behaviour of both researchers and participants. This reflective process recognises the social dynamics of the research process and how this affects data collected. 65, 95, 106

Reinforcement A consequence of behaviour that increases the likelihood of that behaviour being repeated. Can be positive or negative. 10–12, 22, 98, 162, 164, 210, 226–227, 234, 274, 300–301, 342, 362, 364–366

Related designs See Repeated measures and Matched pairs design

Related t-test A parametric test for difference between two sets of scores. Data must be interval with a related design i.e. repeated measures or matched pairs designs. 70–71, 76–77, 85

Relay neurons These connect the sensory neurons to the motor or other relay neurons. They have short dendrites and short axons. 36

Reliability Refers to how consistent the findings from an investigation or measuring device are. A measuring device is said to be reliable if it produces consistent results every time it is used. 25, 53, 66–68, 83–84, 68, 125, 169, 203, 235, 243, 261, 263, 320–321, 325, 333, 371

REM (rapid eye movement) sleep 48–49

Repeated measures All participants take part in all conditions of the experiment. 24, 70, 75, 77, 85, 158, 215

Replication The opportunity to repeat an investigation under the same conditions in order to test the validity and/or reliability of its findings. 8, 11, 49, 51, 53, 67, 81–82, 83, 97, 119, 125, 133, 181, 193, 229–230, 308, 328

Repression A form of ego defence whereby anxiety-provoking material is kept out of conscious awareness as a means of coping. 18

Research methods The processes by which information or data is collected for the purpose of testing a hypothesis and/or a theory. 62

Restorative justice A system for dealing with criminal behaviour which focuses on the rehabilitation of offenders through reconciliation with victims. This enables the offender to see the impact of their crime and serves to empower victims by giving them a 'voice'. 344–345

Restraint theory A cognitive explanation which argues that obesity is the paradoxical outcome of attempts to restrain eating (i.e. dieting). 240–242

Results In a scientific report, a description of what the researcher(s) found, including descriptive and inferential statistics. 81

Review A consideration of a number of studies that have investigated the same topic in order to reach a general conclusion about a particular hypothesis. 121, 131, 153, 183, 191, 203, 207, 209, 211, 225, 230, 237, 263, 271, 275–277, 279, 297, 331, 339, 369, 371, 373, 377

Right to withdraw An ethical issue; participants should have the right to withdraw from participating in a research study if they are uncomfortable with the study. 24, 52, 84, 108, 138–139, 168–169, 192, 214, 244, 280–281, 346, 378

Risk factors Any internal or external influence that increases the likelihood someone will start using drugs or engage in addictive behaviours. 357–359

Risperidone 208–209

Rogers, Carl 9, 20–21, 23, 99, 104

Role model People who have qualities we would like to have and we identify with, thus we model or imitate their behaviour and attitudes. 12, 23, 156, 162, 164, 226, 234, 339

Role play A technique used in research studies where participants are asked to imagine how they would behave in certain situations, and act out the part. 342, 372

Rule of R 73

Rusbult, Caryl 130–131

Sally–Anne study Uses the Sally–Anne task to assess theory of mind. To understand the story participants have to identify that Sally will look for a marble in the wrong place because she does not know that Anne has moved it. Very young children and children with autism spectrum disorder (ASD) find this difficult. 188–189

Sample A group of people who take part in a research investigation. The sample is drawn from a (target) population and is presumed to be representative of that population, i.e. it stands 'fairly' for the population being studied. 43, 49, 109, 169, 192, 267, 327

Sampling techniques The methods used to select people from the population. 24–25, 81, 108, 121, 123, 165, 168, 214, 241, 301, 309, 346, 361

Satisfaction The extent to which romantic partners feel the rewards of the relationship exceed the costs. 130

Scaffolding The process of helping a learner cross the zone of proximal development and advance as much as they can, given their stage of development. Typically the level of help given in scaffolding declines as the learner crosses the zone of proximal development (ZPD). 182–183

Scanning Used for research purposes and also used to record the structure and action of the brain and body, such as PET scans and MRI scans. This is done for research and also to detect abnormalities such as tumours. 9, 14, 17, 41, 44–45, 104, 191, 290

Scattergram A type of graph that represents the strength and direction of a relationship between co-variables in a correlational analysis. 63, 138, 280

Theory of mind (ToM)   Our personal understanding (a theory) of what other people are thinking and feeling. It is sometimes called 'mind-reading'. 188–189, 193

Theory of planned behaviour (TPB)   Changes in behaviour can be predicted from our intention to change, which in turn is the outcome of personal attitudes towards the behaviour in question, our beliefs about what others think, and our perceived ability to control our behaviour. 374–375

Three mountains task   80, 180, 186, 337

Thyroid gland   A pair of small endocrine glands located in the neck that release hormones important for growth and the activity of cells in the body (metabolism). 35

Thyroxine   One of the main hormones secreted by the thyroid glands, which controls metabolism. 35

Time sampling   A target individual or group is first established then the researcher records their behaviour in a fixed time frame, say, every 60 seconds. 25, 65, 295, 365

Token economies   A form of behavioural therapy, where desirable behaviours are encouraged by the use of selective reinforcement. For example, patients are given rewards (tokens) as secondary reinforcers when they engage in correct/socially desirable behaviours. The tokens can then be exchanged for primary reinforcers – favourite foods or privileges. 11, 210–211, 340–341

Tolerance   A reduction in response to a drug, so that the addicted individual needs more to get the same effect. 356

Top-down approach   In forensic psychology, profilers work with a pre-established typology and work down in order to assign offenders to one of two categories based on witness accounts and evidence from the crime scene. 322–324

Transgender   A person who does not identify with the simple gender binary of being male or female. 148, 153, 161, 164, 166–167

Trauma   18, 40, 64, 207, 212, 235, 359

Triangulation   Comparing the results of two or more studies of the same thing to see if they are in agreement. This demonstrates the validity of the individual results. 69

Turner's syndrome   A chromosomal disorder in which affected women have only one X chromosome, causing developmental abnormalities and infertility. 154–155

Twin studies   Research conducted using twins. Monozygotic (MZ) twins have the same genes whereas dizygotic (DZ) twins are about 50% similar genetically. It is presumed that all twins share a similar environment, so by comparing MZ and DZ twins one can conduct a quasi-experiment, where the independent variable is degree of genetic similarity. This means the influence of genetic factors can be assessed. 16–17, 101, 106, 166–167, 230–231, 238–239, 292, 328

Two-tailed test   Form of test used with a non-directional hypothesis. 73–76, 82, 347

Type A personality   Describes someone who is competitive, time-urgent (e.g. impatient) and hostile in most situations. Research has linked this personality type to coronary heart disease (CHD). 266–267

Type B personality   Describes someone who is laid-back, relaxed and tolerant of others in most situations (i.e. the opposite of Type A). 266–267

Type C personality   Describes someone who is compliant, avoids conflict and suppresses their emotions, especially anger, in most situations. Some research has linked Type C with cancer. 266–267

Type I error   The incorrect rejection of a true null hypothesis (a false positive). 72–73, 280, 310, 328

Type II error   The failure to reject a false null hypothesis (a false negative). 72–73, 280, 310, 328

Typical antipsychotics   The first generation of antipsychotic drugs, having been used since the 1950s. They work as dopamine antagonists and include *Chlorpromazine*. 208–209

Ultradian rhythm   A type of biological rhythm with a frequency of more than one cycle in 24 hours, such as the stages of sleep. 45–46, 48–49

Unconditional positive regard   Providing affection and respect without any conditions attached. 20–21

Unconditioned stimulus (UCS)   A stimulus that produces an innate (unlearned) response – the unconditioned response (UCR). 10

Unconscious   The part of the mind that we are unaware of but which continues to direct much of our behaviour. 18–19, 23, 161, 337

Unfalsifiable   99   *Also see* Falsifiability

Universality   Any underlying characteristic of human beings that is capable of being applied to all, despite differences of experience and upbringing. Gender bias and culture bias threaten the universality of findings in psychology. 94

Unrelated   Two (or more) sets of data are independent. 70, 80

Unrelated *t*-test   A parametric test for difference between two sets of scores. Data must be interval with an unrelated design, i.e. independent groups. 40, 70–71, 76, 85, 328

Unstructured interview   The interview starts out with some general aims and possibly some questions, and lets the interviewee's answers guide subsequent questions. 23, 67, 104, 119, 156, 227, 235, 265, 275, 371

Validity   The extent to which an observed effect is genuine – does it measure what is was supposed to measure, and can it be generalised beyond the research setting within which it was found? 15, 21, 49, 51, 64–65, 68–69, 83–84, 96–97, 103, 106, 108, 121, 125, 129, 131, 133, 135, 137, 151, 181, 185, 189, 192, 203, 207, 229, 231, 233, 235, 237, 239, 243, 255, 259, 261, 263, 265, 267, 269, 277, 291, 295, 297, 301, 305, 307, 309, 311, 320–321, 323, 339, 359, 367, 369, 375, 377

Variable ratio   In operant conditioning when a reward is delivered at intervals that change each time rather than the same interval everytime, for example every 15 seconds. 11

Variable reinforcement   A type of partial reinforcement in which a behaviour is reinforced after an unpredictable period of time or number of responses. 364

Ventral striatum   Major portion of the basal ganglia and functions as part of the reward system. It includes the nucleus accumbens. 204, 206

Vicarious reinforcement   Reinforcement which is not directly experienced but occurs through observing someone else being reinforced for a behaviour. This is a key factor in imitation. 12, 162, 226, 234, 300–301, 364

Video games   *See* Computer games

Video nasties   13

Victim survey (or victimisation survey)   A questionnaire that asks a sample of people which crimes have been committed against them over a fixed period of time and whether or not they have been reported to the police. 320–321

Violation of expectation research   An approach to investigating infant knowledge of the world. The idea is that if children understand how the physical world operates then they will expect certain things to happen in particular situations. If these do not occur and children react accordingly, this suggests that they have an intact knowledge of that aspect of the world. 184

Visual area/cortex   A part of the occipital lobe that receives and processes visual information. 38, 41, 50

Volunteer sample   A sample of participants produced by a sampling technique that relies solely on inviting people to take part. 125, 231, 239, 243, 261, 277, 363, 379

Vygotsky, Lev   182–183

Watson, John B.   9

Weapons effect   The presence of a weapon may act as a cognitive trigger and lead to increased aggressiveness. (Not the same as the weapon focus effect where an eyewitness may focus on a criminal's weapon and therefore not be able to later identify their face.) 298

Wernicke's area   An area of the temporal lobe (encircling the auditory cortex) in the left hemisphere (in most people) responsible for language comprehension. 38–39

Wilcoxon   A test for a significant difference between two sets of scores. Data should be at least ordinal level using a related design (repeated measures). 70, 74–76, 85

Withdrawal syndrome   A set of symptoms that develop when the addicted person abstains from or reduces their drug use. 356, 360, 368

Working memory   An area of memory that deals with information that is being worked on, equivalent to short-term memory. It is divided into separate stores representing different modalities. 14, 45

Workload   The amount of work someone has to do. Can refer to underload as well as overload, but is usually taken to mean the latter. 262–263

Workplace stress   Sources of stress that people experience at work. 256, 262–263

Wundt, Wilhelm   8–9

Yerkes-Dodson Law   Describes the curvilinear relationship between arousal and performance. When arousal is very low or very high, performance is poor. Performance is highest at a medium level of arousal. 24

Zone of proximal development (ZPD)   The gap between a child's current level of development, defined by the cognitive tasks they can perform unaided, and what they can potentially do with the right help from a more expert other, who may be an adult or a more advanced child. 182–183

Acknowledgements

pp188, 193, images from Eyes task reproduced with kind permission; Baron-Cohen, Jolliffe, Mortimore, Robertson, 'Another advanced test of theory of mind: evidence from very high functioning adults with autism or Asperger Syndrome', *J Child Psychol Psychiatry 38*:813–822 (1997); and Baron-Cohen, Wheelwright, Hill, 'The 'Reading the mind in the eyes' test revised version: A study with normal adults, and adults with Asperger Syndrome or High-Functioning autism', *J Child Psychol Psychiatry 42*:241–252 (2001)

p300, film still reproduced with kind permission of Dr Albert Bandura
p101, 1984 Penguin Random House UK; Walden reprinted by permission of Hackett Publishing Co., Inc

© **Julia Trotti**; Front cover image: Model: **Madeline Rae Mason**; Make up: **Chereine Waddell**; Stylist: **Jessie McNaught**

© **Shutterstock:** p5, Photology1971: p6, mary416: p7, Graeme Dawes: p8, AISA – Everett: p11, Mike H: p12, Maxisport: p13, JStone: p13, Callahan: p15, Eric Isselee: p16, Noel Powell: p21, ostill: p23, TijanaM: p25, szefei: p32, Doggygraph 116450380: p34, 3drenderings: p37, BambooK: p38, Nerthuz: p39, Blamb: p41, De Visu: p44, MRI scan _Semnic: p45, landmarkmedia: p47, Siwasan Chiewpimolporn: p49, Voyagerix: p50, Dimj: p51, Ollyy: p52, Monkey Business Images: p52, luminaimages: p53, schankz: p63, Vucicevic Milos: p65, Ammit Jack: p65, jokerpro: p67, Photosiber: p68, Nomad_Soul: p69, FikMik: p70, D. Pimborough: p71, Denis Dryashkin: p72, salajean: p73, CandyBox Images: p77, wavebreakmedia: p82, bahri altay: p83, Tom Prokop: p85, STUDIO GRAND OUEST: p85, Rawpixel.com: p94, Andresr: p96, wavebreakmedia: p97, wavebreakmedia: p98, nikkytok: p99, Silvia Bukovac: p100, Edyta Pawlowska: p106, Stephanus Le Roux: p106, Stephanus Le Roux: p107, NAR studio: p109, Inga Nielsen: p109, Zaksheuskaya: p109, Stuart Miles: p116, tommaso lizzul: p118, vipflash: p119, antoniodiaz: p120, GSerban: p121, Ollyy: p122, freya-photographer: p123, Angela Waye: p125, bikeriderlondon: p126, William Perugini: p127, Belushi: p128, thodonal88: p129, tmcphotos: p131, Lisa F. Young: p132, wavebreakmedia: p133, GoodMood Photo: p134, Tyler Olson: p135, Davi Sales Batista: p136, JStone: p137, bikeriderlondon: p138, Dziurek: p139, Philip Bird LRPS CPAGB: p148, balein: p148, Tribalium: p150, Featureflash: p151, Poznyakov: p152, Joshua Resnick: p156, Alejandro J. de Parga: p156, Nina Buday: p157, TravnikovStudio: p158, infocus: p158, wavebreakmedia: p160, Angela Waye: p163, Igor Zakowski: p163, Igor Zakowski: p164, AJP: p165, Photo Works: p168, Artmim: p176, Riccardo Mayer: p178, VP Photo Studio: p179, Monkey Business Images: p180, Eric Isselee: p182, Iakov Filimonov: p183, racorn: p185, Jetsadaphoto: p186, JetKat: p187, Jenn Huls: p190, dwphotos: p191, marcogarrincha: p202, Aaron Amat: p206, DJTaylor: p209, dgmata: p210, Lisa F. Young: p210, Voronin76: p210, Voronin76: p212, Photographee.eu: p213, SpeedKingz: p214, Twin Design: p215, Vladimir Mucibabic: p223, Angela Waye: p224, rezachka: p225, Lightspring: p226, Elena Vasilchenko: p227, Monkey Business Images: p229, stester: p230, sergo1972: p231, Angela Waye: p232, Monkey Business Images: p233, CREATISTA: p234, Chris Harvey: p235, kiuikson: p236, Mike H: p237, Kiselev Andrey Valerevich: p238, Kletr: p239, Creativa Images: p241, vgstudio: p242, TijanaM: p244, siebenla: p245, Zhiltsov Alexandr: p253, Ollyy: p256, bibiphoto: p257, Juan Gaertner: p258, GlebStock: p259, Christopher Poe: p260, Jozef Sowa: p261, rnl: p262, auremar: p263, Gemenacom: p265, auremar: p266, prudkov: p267, auremar: p268, wanphen chawarung: p269, Brocreative: p270, Image Point Fr: p272, Furtseff: p273, Asianet-Pakistan: p274, Monika Wisniewska: p275, Rawpixel.com: p276, Image Point Fr: p276, CandyBox Images: p277, fototip: p278, wavebreakmedia: p279, Tyler Olson: p280, lenetstan: p281, snowblurred: p289, Cresta Johnson: p290, Sebastian Kaulitzki: p291, Twin Design: p292, mrkornflakes: p293, Ilya Andriyanov: p295, Shaiith: p296, View Apart: p297, pjcross: p298, Diego Cervo: p299, mikeledray: p301, Frenzel: p302, Yiorgos GR: p303, Oleg Zabielin: p304, Fer Gregory: p305, Monkey Business Images: p306, greenland: p307, Frenzel: p308, PathDoc: p309, StockLite: p310, bikeriderlondon: p311, Darren Baker: p318, carl ballou: p321, Kzenon: p322, nakupenda: p323, Tashatuvango: p325, fasphotographic: p326, Everett Historical: p329, Vitalinka: p330, marekuliasz: p331, Toro_the_Bull: p332, Daxiao Productions: p334, deeeepblue: p334, Noel Powell: p335, www.BillionPhotos.com: p336, set: p337, landmarkmedia: p338, nobeastsofierce: p341, tdoes: p342, Peter Gudella: p344, Kheng Guan Toh: p344, Kheng Guan Toh: p346, Noel Powell: p346, Fulop Zsolt: p347, Anton Zabielskyi: p356, Pedro Tavares: p357, Monkey Business Images: p358, Monkey Business Images: p359, Levranii: p360, Alexilusmedical: p361, Fotos593: p362, CandyBox Images: p363, frees: p364, Nata789: p365, Nick_Nick: p366, Kzenon: p367, Icatnews: p368, Image Point Fr: p368, Luis Louro: p368, Luis Louro: p370, Lisa F. Young: p371, wavebreakmedia: p372, Burlingham: p373, Knumina Studios 13263850: p374, sanjagrujic: p377, Kamira: p378, Golubchenko Marina: p379, Ollyy: p387, Stokkete: p388, M.Stasy: p388, FXQuadro: p388, Tim UR: p388, Darren Woolridge: p388, FXQuadro: p388, Carlos A. Oliveras: p388, Carlos A. Oliveras: p389, Helena Ohman: p390, Nejron Photo: p390, Yuriy Vlasenko: p390, Yuriy Vlasenko: p392, BonD80: p394, Gustavo Frazao: p396, Vereshchagin Dmitry: p396, Yuriy Vlasenko: p396, sebra: p396, sebra: p396, sebra: p397, Olga Danylenko: p397, indigolotos

© **Cartoonstock:** p108, Bradford Veley; p344, Chris Slane
© **istockphoto.com:** p40, Photo_Concepts: p44, art2media Kreativagentur
© **Fotolia:** p200, I.M.Redesiuk
© **Alamy:** p64, Johnny Greig / Alamy Stock Photo: p153, Roger Sedres / Alamy Stock Photo: p189, AF archive / Alamy Stock Photo: p324, sjscreens / Alamy Stock Photo: p340, Jeff Morgan 16 / Alamy Stock Photo: p343, Marmaduke St. John / Alamy Stock Photo
© **Rexfeatures:** p243 Katie Hopkins

CC BY-SA
via Flickr; p354, bnksy flickr, dullhunk
via Wikimedia Commons; p44, EEG_cap: p95, Sigmund_Freud: p124, Mae_West_1936: p327, Francis_Galton_1850s

Notes

NOTES

NOTES

THE BACK PAGE

We have now completed our Year 2 book – and that has involved a lot of work from a very skillful team. At the helm is our publisher **Rick Jackman** who is simply a brilliant manager and friend to us all. I know he in turn depends on the great team at Illuminate – **Peter Burton**, **Clare Jackman** and **Saskia Santos**, each of whom works doggedly at all the jobs required behind the scene such as picture research and marketing. A considerable weight falls on the shoulders of designer **Nigel Harriss** who lovingly crafts each and every spread. And last but not least we thank our painstaking editor **Geoff Tuttle** and **Dr Julia Russell** for her detailed and exacting review of the book.

The authors and publisher would also like to thank the team behind the Digital Book Bundle: **Jo Haycock**, **Zoe Johnson**, and **Mark** and **Ruth Jones**. They have all been amazingly creative in producing some excellent support material for this book.

Matt is a Chartered Psychologist and Associate Fellow of the British Psychological Society. He teaches part time, is an editor of *Psychology Review* magazine and works as a freelance trainer and consultant. When not working (which is fairly rare) Matt likes walks in the Lake District, listening to anything by Maynard Keenan and watching anything by Joss Whedon.

Cara has written many books for A level psychology, and she speaks at and organises student conferences as well as being senior editor of the student magazine *Psychology Review*. She has taught for many years and has examining experience. Her spare time (what there is of it) involves her husband and children (all now over 20), travelling and walking. When working she enjoys the beautiful views from her house in the Scottish Highlands.

Rob is an experienced A level psychology teacher and author. Rob's been told often enough (by his wife, mainly) that he's a bit of a geek. It's true that he likes nothing more than to settle down of an evening with a big book of facts. He still buys CDs, and will explain why at great length unless someone stops him. He still hasn't seen Frozen, despite having two grand-daughters.

Dave has been a psychology teacher for 16 years and is Head of Psychology at Oldham Hulme Grammar School. Dave enjoys eating out, eating in, and playing volleyball or making comics with his son. He has an unfortunate – but nevertheless lifelong – commitment to Leeds United Football Club.

About the cover:

Deciding on a book cover is a difficult task and rather than trying to find something especially psychological we wanted something haunting and memorable. The image of a girl with green hair on the cover of the Year 1 book is the same person as you now see with pink hair, the extraordinary **Madeline Rae Mason**. The success of the photographs is of course due to **Julia Trotti**, the photographer. We would also thank the wider creative team – makeup by **Chereine Waddell** and stylist **Jessie McNaught**. We would like to thank them all for allowing us to use the photographs.

AQA Approved

AQA PSYCHOLOGY FOR A LEVEL YEAR 2

CARA FLANAGAN
DAVE BERRY
MATT JARVIS
ROB LIDDLE

Illuminate Publishing

THE END